American Benefits for Seniors

First Edition

by

MATTHEW LESKO

with

Mary Ann Martello

Researchers
Cindy Owens, Jean Neuner, Bev Matson
Jessica Neuner, Chelsea Noble, Dixie St. John

Production
Beth Meserve

Marketing
Kim McCoy

Support
Mercedes Sundeen

Cover & Illustrations
Tom Ford

 Printed in the United States of America. Published by Information USA, Inc., P.O. Box E, Kensington, MD 20895; {www.lesko.com}.

FIRST EDITION

Library of Congress Cataloging-in-Publication date
Lesko, Matthew
Martello, Mary Ann

American Benefits for Seniors

ISBN # 1- 878346-87-3

Other books available from Matthew Lesko:

Free Money To Change Your Life

Free Money To Change Your Life
6-hour instructional audio cassette/CD

Lesko's Info-Power III

Government Giveaways for Entrepreneurs IV

Free Legal Help

Free Health Care

Gobs and Gobs of Free Stuff

Free Stuff For Busy Moms

Free Stuff For Women's Health, Fitness and Nutrition

Free College Money And Training For Women

Free Money And Help For Women Entrepreneurs

Free Money to Change Your Life CD-ROM

Free Money For Your Retirement

How to Write and Get a Grant

Free Money To Pay Your Bills

Free Money for Everybody

For ordering information on any of Matthew Lesko's publications, call 1-800-UNCLE-SAM, or contact his web site at www.lesko.com.

Table of Contents

Free Money (continued)

Legal (continued)

Housing (continued)

Have Fun For the Rest of Your Life (continued)

Have Fun For the Rest of Your Life (continued)

Have Fun For the Rest of Your Life (continued)

Caregivers (continued)

Dedication

Old Isn't Old Any More

Nothing is more fun for me than getting older. I keep thinking of all the stuff that young people worry about that you don't have to anymore, like acne, getting a date for the prom, wondering if you will ever play professional baseball or worrying what other people think of you. It's a liberating experience and a fun journey if you learn how to take advantage of all the wonderful opportunities our country makes available to its senior citizens. Like all sections of life, there are good times and not so good times, and this book will teach you about hundreds of resources that will CREATE MORE GOOD TIMES FOR YOU as well as hundreds of other resources that will help you HANDLE THE NOT SO GOOD TIMES.

Old isn't old anymore. My grandparents all died in their early 60s and I used to think that was really old. I'm 62 and I feel I'm just beginning. Eighty or 90 years sounds pretty easy in today's world. So I may have 30 more years that can be the most fun part of life.

I must be very fortunate, because it was not until my 60s that I realized that I never had more time, less obligations and even more love and wisdom than ever before. For me, it's a liberating time of life, a time to finally get down to the business of enjoying life, and to trying to contribute as much as I can to it. I would not miss this for the world.

American Benefits For Seniors

If you are worried about your retirement, wondering about paying for your senior years, or just want to take advantage of every damn benefit that this great country has to offer for the rest of your life, then this book is for you. This is the most complete collection of little-know benefit programs that are offered to seniors of all incomes, from federal, state and local government sources and nonprofit organizations.

$890 Billion In Benefits For Seniors And Growing

Our country has so much to offer for seniors and the benefits keep growing every year. Out of the total federal budget of approximately $2.6 trillion a year, about $890 billion of this money goes to seniors. That means 35% of everything the federal government spends goes to seniors.

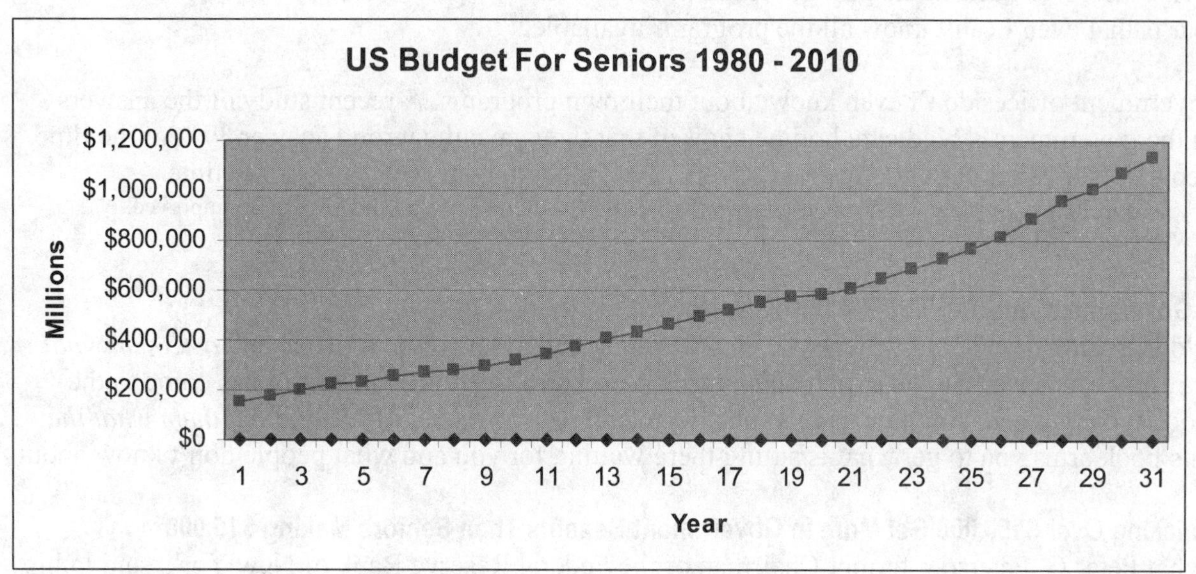

Source: US Budget 2006 http://www.gpoaccess.gov/usbudget/fy06/sheets/hist03z2.xls

No Advertising To Tell You About Benefits

The problem is that most seniors don't know about all the benefits that are due to them. Sure, most seniors may know about the major programs, like Medicare and Social Security, but there are thousands of programs worth billions and the offices giving out the money rarely spend a penny to advertise their availability.

I really believe that I should not be the one telling seniors about what they have already paid for with their tax dollars. The government should be doing this. But I've been doing this for over 25 years and from what I can see it's unlikely I'll have to find something else to do anytime soon. Every year the government keeps getting bigger and the benefits keep increasing, no matter which party is in charge. And people know less and less about what is available.

Over 30 Million Seniors Are Unaware Of Basic Benefits

Government studies show that over 30 million seniors are unaware that they are eligible for even some of the most basic benefit programs, like receiving up to $1,000 from the Department of Health and Human Services or getting their doctor to do free test screenings for cancer, glaucoma, and osteoporosis. A national polling survey conducted by the University of Connecticut and sponsored by Information, USA shows that 81% of Americans believe the government is NOT doing a good job of telling about available benefit programs and 65% of Americans believe they are eligible for benefits that they don't know about.

(Sources: GAO Report, *Medicare Savings Programs*, http://www.gao.gov/new.items/d04363.pdf, GAO Report *Medicare: Most Beneficiaries Receive Some but Not All Recommended Services*, GAP-03-958, http://www.gao.gov/new.items/d03958.pdf), Information USA/ U of Conn survey, http://www.lesko.com/survey.php)

The Government Doesn't Even Know About These Benefits

It would be great if you could call just one government agency and ask about all government programs for seniors. But that is not going to happen. Our country is too big and complex for any one person to know everything. I've been cataloging government programs for over 25 years and what I keep learning every year is that even I can't know all the programs available.

Many government offices don't even know about their own programs. A recent study of the answers given on the government's Medicare hotline showed that they gave the wrong answer 39% of the time. And when a doctor called for an answer they were given the wrong answer 96% of the time.

(Source: U.S. GAO Report, Accuracy of Responses form the 1-800-MEDICARE Help Line Should Be Improved, http://www.gao.gov/new.items/d05130.pdf)

Call The Government And Tell THEM What They Have

Our world is getting to the point where you can no longer call a government office and *ask them what they have*. You can't even call an expert and expect them know what is available. It has come to the point in our society where you now have to be able to call a government office and *tell them what they have.* This book arms you to get what is sitting there waiting for you and what people don't know about.

Seniors Making Over $150,000 Get More In Government Benefits Than Seniors Making $15,000

This is what Peter G. Peterson, former Chairman of the Federal Reserve Bank of New York, said in his book "Running on Empty." He also showed that the government gives out about $1.5 trillion benefits each year and only 12% of this money goes to the poor. And only 25% of the money has an income requirement. This means 75% of all benefit money programs have no income requirement at all. Seniors have to realize that there are benefits for every income category imaginable.

Seniors Who Make Up To $150,000 Are Eligible For These Benefits

A sample list of programs from the book that anyone can use

Free Honorary Diplomas for Veterans…page 262
Produce Your Own TV for Cable TV…page 262
$30,000 To Teach Overseas…page 555
Train to Be a Master Gardner…page 263

Go on a Free Archeological Dig…page 560
Access to Health Info That's Better than Your Doctor…page 93
Free Treatment By Expert Doctors Who Get Government Grants…page 58
60% Discount on Dental Care…page 60
Learn How to Legally Transfer Your Assets to Get the Government to Pay for Long Term Care...page 70
Learn How to Get Medicare to Pay for a Motor Scooter...page 69
$3,000 To Sell Your Products Overseas…page 450
Free Financial Counseling Services…page 22
$10,000 Bonus to Teach If You're A Vet...page 329
Free Computer Classes to Learn to Use The Web...page 266
2 Weeks Free Travel on a Government Weather Ship...page 555
$25,000 For Your Singing Group to Perform Overseas...page 556
Free Rollercoaster Rides...page 558
$25/Day to Be a Park Ranger in Idaho for The Summer…page 536
Get Paid to Be a Teen Counselor In Belize…page 538
Free Passports...page 558
Exempt from Taking SAT Tests for College Admissions...page 260
Spend Your Vacation as a Moose Crossing Guard...page 536
Free Hunting, Fishing and Dog Licenses...page 562
Get Paid to Give a Speech in a Foreign Country...page 566
$1,000,000 At Age 63 to Make High Tech Golf Clubs...page 450
$8,000 To Train for a New Job...page 297
$250,000 To Work on Your Invention...page 530
350 Colleges Where You Can Go For FREE...page 260
50% Discount on Property Taxes...page 365
Money And Help to Start Your Own Nonprofit...page 506
$100,000 Low Interest Loan for a Mobile Home…page 356
Save 50% On Your Fuel Bill…page 400
Get a $100,000 Home For $1 plus Fix-Up Money...page 387
$782,000 Low Interest Loan to Buy a Ranch Or Farm...page 388
$5,000,000 To Buy or Fix up an Apartment Building...page 390
20% Off Your Gas Bill...page 400
25% Discount on Utility Bills Because Of Home Medical Equipment…page 401
0% Interest Loans to Fix up Your Home...page 403
$700 Rebate on Home Insulation…page 404
$150 Rebate on A Dishwasher…page 404
90% Discount On Eyeglasses…page 23

Free Screenings For Breast Cancer, Vaginal Cancer, Colorectal Cancer, Osteoporosis, Prostate Cancer, Glaucoma…page 71
Free Legal Help to Fight The IRS…page 227
$2,000 If You Get Mugged…page 193
Free Copies of Your Credit Report…page 29
$195 A Month Parking Money…page 35
50% Air Line Discount to See Sick Relative…page 36
Free Credit Repair…page 22
Free Help Finding a Lost Loved One…page 41
Free Concert and Theater Tickets…page 566
Get A GED, Degree or PhD For Free …page 260
Free Legal Help To Fight Your Bank Or Credit Card Company…page 24
Free Legal Help to Fight Age Discrimination…page 43
Volunteer for Homeland Security or Police Duty…page 535
Free Or Cheap Flu Shots…page 61
Free Legal Help to Fight Health Care Industry…page 113
Free Health Insurance Counseling…page 94
Free Information Hotlines for Arthritis, Cancer, Diabetes, Tobacco, Parkinson, Disability, Alzheimer, Mental Health, Osteoporosis…page 92

Seniors Who Make Up To $50,000 Are Eligible For These Benefits

These programs are only available to seniors with incomes under the amount stated. If your income is over the amount be sure to investigate the program anyway because all sources of income may not be counted, and some programs allow exceptions.

$3,500 For Emergency Home Repairs….income up to $25,650 per couple … page 395
Free Prescription Drugs…income up to $32,000 per person…page 129
$500 For Caring For A Relative…income up to $50,000 for household…page 605
$120 Off Your Phone Bill…income up to $24,135 per couple…page 23
Personal Emergency Response System …income up to $18,432 per person…page 648
$3,000 To Be a Foster Grandparent...income up to $15,756 per person…page 543
Grants For Alzheimer Caregivers…income up to $67,000 per household…page 606
Free Respite Care For Senior…income up to $30,195 per couple…page 606
55+ Get Paid 20 Hours A Week To Learn A New Skill…income up to $20,112 per couple…page 301
Save 70% On Rent…income up to $30,450 per person…page 344
$7,500 Grant to Fix Up Home…income up to $25,000 per household…page 345
$350 For A New Air Conditioner…income up to $24,120 per couple…page 348
$100 Off Your Phone Bill…income up to $20,600 per person…page 39
$5,000 Grant to Get Rid of Lead Paint in Your Home…income up to $24,135 per couple…page 352
$850 Tax Refund For Seniors In Massachusetts…income up to $55,000...page 365
$2,500 To Pay For New Insulation…income up to $24,135 per couple…page 372
$600 To Pay For Heating Bills…income up to $21,864 per couple…page 376
Free Handyman Services…income up to $34,000 per couple…page 396
Free Night Lights and Door Locks…income up to $34,900 per couple…page 397

$750 For Emergency Rent Money…income up to $31,150 per couple…page 398
$500 To Stop Utility Cut Offs…income up to $22,453 per couple…page 399
Pay No More Than 6% Of Income On Utilities…income up to $24,464 per couple…page 400
Free Wheelchair Ramp For Your Home…income up to $26,750 per couple…page 402
$4,300 Grant From IRS…income up to $35,000 per taxpayer…page 52
Free Health Care When You Have No Insurance (Sliding Scale)…page 59
$100 To Buy Fresh Fruit and Vegetable…income up to $23,737 per couple…page 24
Get An Extra $1,000…income up to $16,872 per couple…page 23
Extra $10,400 For Disability…income up to $9,400 per couple…page 22
Free Meals Delivered to Your Home…determined case by case…page 32
$3 For Every $1 Dollar Your Save…income up to $25,660 per couple…page 33
Discounts at Veterinary Teaching Hospitals….determined case by case…page 33
Free Taxis to the Doctors…determined case by case…page 35
Money For Auto Repairs, Car Insurance, Or A Tank Of Gas…income up to $32,180 per couple…page 34
Free Fans…income determined case by case…page 41
$20,000 Worth of Free Alcohol and Drug Treatment…income up to $45,000 per person…page 60
Free Mammograms and Breast and Cervical Cancer Treatment…income up to $46,000 per family…page 62
$2,000 For Cancer Patient…determined case by case…page 64
$10,000 To Buy A Talking Computer…determined case by case…page 64
$20,000 Forgivable Loans To Fix Up Your Home…income up to $46,680 per couple…page 395
Financial Assistance For Those Needing Heart Surgery…determined case by case basis…page 68
$6,000 To Pay For Groceries…income up to $24,516 per couple…page 23
$2,000 Grant To Pay Rent Or Mortgage…income up to $34,135 per couple…page 22

Benefits Begin At Age 40

That's right, at 40 years of age the government considers you a senior. That's the beginning year for age discrimination. So, you are over 40 and have a job, and they lay you off, but they don't lay off the younger people around you that may be age discrimination. Or if you are looking for a job and you are over 40 and they hire younger people and not you, that, too, may be age discrimination. Laws are complicated. But you don't have to hire a high priced attorney to find out if the employer violated the law. You can call a government office (see page 192) and talk to someone who wrote the law. And if they determine you have a case they will sue the employer for you and get you the money. That's just one of the thousands of benefits you have access to by living in America and being over 40.

Have Fun For The Rest Of Your Life

What is wonderful about the benefits described in this book is that not only can they help you cope with your daily expenses, health care needs, or the needs of the seniors you are caring for, they can also help you live the life you always dreamed of and help you ring out the last bit of life no matter how old you are. As I said in my dedication, "old isn't old anymore." There is so much to life in all of us if we only use it. We all have so much to contribute no matter what our age. The world needs all the skills and love we have while we are here. All we have to do is tap into the benefits that are available in this country to help us do it.

Here are some people who also believe that “old isn’t old”:

- at 72 Jack McKeon was called out of retirement to coach the Florida Marlins to a World Series victory
- at 68 Harry Stonecipher became CEO of Boeing, the world’s leading aerospace company
- at 65 John Reed was named interim chairman and CEO of New York Stock Exchange
- in her 70s Barbara Walters continues to expand her TV work
- at 78 Alan Greenspan still runs the Federal Reserve System
- at 75 Warren Buffet is the world’s most respected investor
- in their 60s and 70s Sophia Loren and Sean Connery are still considered sexy
- at 81 Former President Carter is still very active as a writer and international emissary
- at 77 Joe Paterno signed a 4-year contract extension to coach the Penn State football team
- at near 80 Grandma Moses started painting
- at 65 Groucho Marx launched a new career as a television-show host
- at 94 George Bernard Shaw was at work on a new play
- at 74 Galileo published his masterpiece, “Dialogue Concerning the Two New Sciences”
- at 70 Noah Webster published “An American Dictionary of the English Language”
- at 91 Frank Lloyd Wright designed the Guggenheim Museum in New York
- at 94 conductor Leopold Stokowski signed a 6-year recording contract
- at 72 Mahatma Gandhi completed successful negotiation with Britain for India’s independence
- at 80 B.B. King does 100 concerts a year

(Source: all but the B.B. King story was part of the testimony of Ken Dychtwald, September 20, 2004, “Breaking the Silver Ceiling: A New Generation of Older Americans Redefining the New Rules of the Workplace,” U.S. Senate Committee on Aging http://aging.senate.gov/public/_files/hr131kd.pdf)

Easy Applications: 3-4 pages Of Filling In The Blanks

I hear so many people tell me that what stops them seeking government benefits is the thought of a complicated government application. These statements are usually made by people who have never even seen an application. And they certainly have never seen an application for a benefit that is relevant to them and they wish to apply for. There is an urban myth that all government benefit applications are 20-page complicated messes. And some of them are that way if you are a nonprofit organization wishing to compete for large government grants. But the benefits for individuals are different. 90% of the applications for the benefits listed in this book are simply a few pages of filling in the blanks. And if you have trouble filling out an application, there are government offices that will help you fill out the applications for free.

We Still Don’t Have It All

This book is not intended to be a complete collection of free money programs. The rain forest could not handle it if that were true. This book is intended to give every American an understanding of the major programs available and a number of minor ones that we found to be the most interesting.

It’s not impossible for any one publication, database or anything else really, to be able to collect everything in the universe on a given subject. I know I’m biased, but I certainly believe that we are the best people in the world for collecting information on government money programs. I also know that we cannot possibly get every single program that is available.

One problem is that programs come and go. Our world is changing every second. It is a big complex society we are living in, and people are making decisions throughout the day that make subtle or big changes which affect the contents of this book. Budgets keep changing. Priorities keep changing. People keep changing. Offices keep changing.

A bigger problem is that the world of free money is enormous. Preparing a book for a national audience makes us excellent at identifying national and state programs. But truthfully, it is sometimes beyond our capabilities to completely cover all local, county and nonprofit programs. First of all, if we did collect all of these programs in the country, you would not be able to pick up the book. There are thousands and thousands of local communities in the United States and each of them can have 5 to 50 programs. Fifty times 5,000 would be 250,000 programs. We would never finish researching.

Our goal is to arm you with knowledge. We want to show you the money, but you are going to have to do a little work yourself.

This Book Is Out Of Date

Sorry to disappoint you, but I have to warn you of the truth. In our modern society, it is virtually impossible to expect to include every program possible and have every item completely accurate. The problem is that the world is too big and it is always changing. Every day programs come and go. Every day people change their address, phone number and websites. It is just a fact that these things happen in our modern society.

But remember, if a listing in this book leads you to a non-working number or website, it does not necessarily mean that the program is gone. In all likelihood it is still there, but has changed since we completed our search. Here are some tricks you can try to locate the program:

- call the information operator and ask for the telephone number for the agency listed in the program description
- search the web for the agency name in any of the web search engines like www.dogpile.com or www.google.com
- contact the Federal Information Center at http://www.pueblo.gsa.gov/, or call 1-800-FED-INFO. This is a free service that will help you locate a federal government agency
- go to www.govengine.com on the web for a listing of most federal, state and local government agencies
- contact your federal, state or local elected official. They all have staff people who will help you find what you need at any level of government

It Doesn't Matter If It Sounds Like You Don't Qualify

You are going to find programs that excite you at first and then when you read further it may seem that you will not qualify. Or you will gather more information on a program in this book and you will run into some phrase, or sentence in the description that makes you feel you do not have a chance. You may encounter things like:

A. "all the money is given out by June 30th" and it is already September 1st
B. "the money is only for people who live in the country" and you live in the city
C. "the money goes to nonprofit organizations" and you are not one
D. "you have to come up with 20% of the money for the project" and you don't have any
E. "the money is only for people who live in Minnesota" and you live in New Jersey
F. "the money is for people making less than $60,000/yr" and you make $70,000

Don't look at phrases like these as impassable boulders that stand in your way of getting the money you need. In reality, they can simply be small pebbles in the road that you may not even feel at all. If you don't follow up, you will never know.

Here's what I've seen happen in each of these situations:

1. "all the money is given out by June 30th": The end of the accounting year for most government agencies is September 30th, but the agency can start giving out more money beginning October 1st, and you can be the first in line. I think you can wait another 30 days for your money.

2. "the money is for people who live in the country": That may be so. But it will still pay to get the details of the program to see if there is something in the description that was not obvious to others. A young man in Boston was trying to get money from a program that gave money for teenage entrepreneurs that lived in the country. He lived in Boston. When he got the materials it said that it was for people in the country, but the description also said that it was for people who wanted to start lawn mowing businesses. That is what he wanted to do and he convinced the office that he was qualified. Government officials do not know everything. Get the facts and find out for yourself.

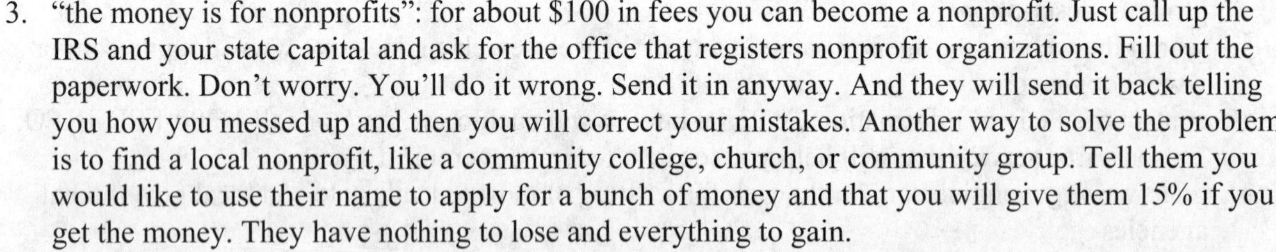

3. "the money is for nonprofits": for about $100 in fees you can become a nonprofit. Just call up the IRS and your state capital and ask for the office that registers nonprofit organizations. Fill out the paperwork. Don't worry. You'll do it wrong. Send it in anyway. And they will send it back telling you how you messed up and then you will correct your mistakes. Another way to solve the problem is to find a local nonprofit, like a community college, church, or community group. Tell them you would like to use their name to apply for a bunch of money and that you will give them 15% if you get the money. They have nothing to lose and everything to gain.

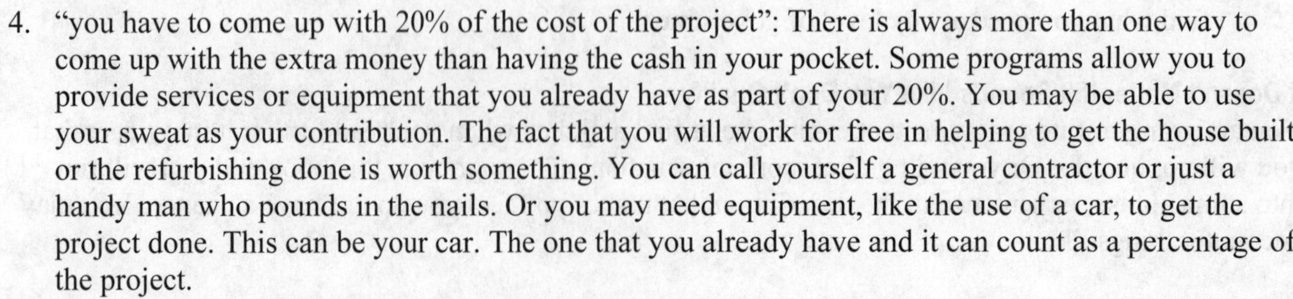

4. "you have to come up with 20% of the cost of the project": There is always more than one way to come up with the extra money than having the cash in your pocket. Some programs allow you to provide services or equipment that you already have as part of your 20%. You may be able to use your sweat as your contribution. The fact that you will work for free in helping to get the house built or the refurbishing done is worth something. You can call yourself a general contractor or just a handy man who pounds in the nails. Or you may need equipment, like the use of a car, to get the project done. This can be your car. The one that you already have and it can count as a percentage of the project.

5. “the money is only for people in Minnesota”: Contact them anyway. It’s likely that if this is a unique program then the program administrators will be aware of similar programs around the country that do the same thing. People doing similar work around the country have a tendency to organize and share information on how they are doing. We are one of the best organized countries in the world. If there are 10 people in the country doing the same thing they will start an association, a newsletter and have annual meetings.

6. “the money is for people making less than $60,000”: We all know that rules are made to be broken and many bureaucrats who hand out money have the power and authority to break the rules. It is especially easier for them to bend a few rules if they like you or they like your project. Or they may be having trouble giving away all their money this year and you are one of the best ideas they have seen. Remember, bureaucrats are human too. They have feelings. Like all of us, unless they are having a bad day, their instinct is to help. Always give them a chance to see if they can help.

Don’t Worry If The Program Is Not Near You

There are some programs in this book that are limited to people in certain geographic areas.. This should not stop you. This does not mean there isn’t a similar program in your area. We were just not good enough to find it yet. You can find it. It just may take a little time and work. Everything worthwhile in life does take effort. Start with your local public library. Ask for the reference librarian. They can give you a good start on where to start looking. You should also contact the local office of your congressman or senator. Your librarian will give you the right number.

So, don’t let us stop you from getting what you need. You can find it yourself.

14 Steps To Getting The Money You Need

Step #1: Review The Book

It is important to go through the entire book. You don’t have to read everything, but you have to at least review the title of every entry. Place a check mark on those entries that you feel MIGHT be of some interest to you. You can also place a post-it on the edge of the page or turn town the corner of the page so you can easily return to it.

Step #2: Assign A Grade To Likely Programs

Two grades can be enough. But it must be at least 2. Read each entry in detail and place either an “A” or “B” next to the entry. Using a “1” or “2” is also good. The higher grade should identify those entries that seem more likely and the lower grade should identify programs that are a little less likely but are “maybes.”

Step #3: Follow Up Immediately

As you probably guessed from reading the step above, you should now go back and contact all your “A” list programs first. Leave your “B” list programs for a later round. You want to tackle the most obvious first. You can start digging deeper later, but you may not have to. I know it sounds like an obvious choice, but some people get overwhelmed with so many places to go to. This prioritizes the process for you.

Step #4: Contact the Agency Directly
This is a must. Do not assume that you know everything about the program just by reading the description in the book. You have to get the details before you make the decision if this is a program for you. You can contact the agency in any of the following ways:

A. by telephone,
B. by email,
C. by website, or
D. in person

You may even want to do a combination. You can go to the website and review their programs and then call and ask for specifics. But remember; even if you get details about a specific program on the web be sure you contact the agency by phone or email to insure you have the complete information. Like printed material in books, a lot of material on the web can also be out of date or even misleading.

Step #5: Be Careful What You Ask For
Your initial contact with an agency should be friendly. Many people are intimidated to contact any government agency. Remember you don't have to know what you are talking about, because most of the bureaucrats don't know what they are talking about either. This is the government, remember. Your best approach is to try to be as inclusive as possible in your initial contact. Try not to say things that can get you a "no" answer right off the bat. For example, don't let the first words out of your mouth be:

"Hi, I want a grant to start a bakery. Will you give me one?"

This can get the door closed on you right away when in fact there may be lots of money sitting there waiting for you. The bureaucrat answering the phone may not be aware of any grant programs because he just started working there a few weeks ago and is really not aware of all the programs. Or he may not be aware of any money that says "bakery" on the label. Or if you are looking for a townhouse he will look down his list for the word "townhouse" and tell you that there is no money available. Or the government may be offering other kinds of money that does not have the name "grant" attached to it but it means the same thing. They may be offering money in the form of "direct payments" or under a program called "loans," but in fact you never have to pay back the money if you live in the house for more than 3 years. That's just as good as a grant.

You can miss a lot by trying to be very specific. The problem is that most people in the government don't even now what is available. By being specific the official can find an easier way to tell you "no" and send you on your way. You'll be happy, because this is what you sort of expected anyway. And the official will be happy because they don't have to do any more work. So it is much better to start with something like:

"Hi. I'm trying to get a description of all the money programs that are available for housing or real estate."

You want the official to stretch her imagination and try to come up with a complete list for you. When you get a complete descriptive listing, review it in close detail and call the office back and tell them all the programs for which you would like to apply.

Step #6: Be Nice To Bureaucrats

When you are calling the government, getting a lot of voice mails or being put on hold, it's hard to remember how important that person is who finally answers the telephone. That's the person who can give you the money. So how well you treat them can determine your success or failure in getting what you need. If you start yelling when the person answers the phone because you've been sitting on hold for the past 10 minutes, you don't sound like you are going to be the highlight of any bureaucrat's day. That bureaucrat gets paid the same amount of money whether they help you for free for 2 weeks or if they hang up on you right after you say hello. What you have to do is try to get that person to want to spend time with you. You want them to enjoy talking with you. The more comfortable they are in talking with you, the more likely they are to share inside information that will increase your chances and make it easier for you to get the money. It is basic common sense that can easily be forgotten, like: a) Don't be nasty when they answer the phone because the first words out of your mouth can set the stage for the entire conversation; b) Don't act like you hate them except for the fact that they are sitting on the money (even though it may be true) because this will come through in your conversation and they will not want to help you; and c) Send "thank you" notes when people are exceptionally nice because it is the best way to ensure that you are remembered the next time you call. I can go on and on, but simply put …. TREAT PEOPLE LIKE YOU WANT TO BE TREATED.

Step #7: Make It Personal

Think of it as being back in school when you would go and brown nose the teacher. The good brown nosers would meet with the teacher after class and not only talk about school, but also talk about their life. They would show the teacher pictures of their dog and talk about how much they like baseball; anything to get the teacher to relate to them not as a student but as a person. Once the teacher sees a student as a person, it's hard to flunk them no matter how bad they are. These bureaucrats have the power to pass or fail you on your money exam. So the more they get to know you as a person, the more likely they are to help you pass the test. So when you are talking to them, don't be afraid to talk about personal stuff along with the professional. They certainly have the power to help, because they are the ones who give out the money.

Step #8: Belly To Belly Is Best

If being good on the phone increases your odds of getting the cash, then face to face will do even more. This may not be practical or even possible all of the time, but it is certainly another way for a bureaucrat to put a face with an application and this will make it that much harder for her to just say "no."

Step #9: Don't Wait

I really mean don't wait until the last minute to apply. Especially with those offices that only give out money at certain times of the year. As deadline time approaches, the bureaucrats can become too busy to provide you with any individualized help. So the best strategy is to call early and to call often.

Step #10: Don't Leave Empty Handed

If after reviewing all of their programs you decide that they have nothing for you, you have one more important thing to do before you move on. Call up one of the program officers and tell them about your search. See if they are aware of any programs that may suit your needs, or if they know of other agencies that have ANY kind of financial assistance for your project. These people are in the business and are likely to attend meetings and conventions with people from other agencies who also hand out money. They are on the front line of government programs and will likely know other people who do this work.

Step #11: Apply, Apply, Apply
Keep going through this process and keep applying to as many programs as possible. Apply even if people tell you that you have a very small chance of getting the money. Apply even if they tell you that you "may" not be qualified. When you hear terms like "may" or "small chance" this still means that you do have a chance, and that is all you need. Don't worry about filling out so many applications. Once you've done the first one the rest are pretty much the same. The whole process is a numbers game. Just like the lottery, you have to play to win.

Step #12: No Application Is A Problem
No matter how easy the application may appear you are likely to encounter some difficulty with at least one question. But this is not a real problem. There is plenty of help.

The best way to handle this is to call the office giving out the money and ask to speak to a "program officer" for the program to which you are applying. They are the people who are directly involved in handing out the money. Be blunt and tell them that you "have no idea what they are talking about in question #6 on the application." You are probably not the first person in the world who had trouble with that question. The office probably realizes it is confusing, but they didn't have money in the budget to reprint the forms.

If for some reason you are not getting help directly from the office giving out the money, you can always contact the office of your elected official. This is your Congressman or Senator at the federal level, your state elected official for state programs and your councilman or mayor at the local level. They all have people on their staff whose job it is to solve problems that taxpayers are having with the government.

Step #13: It's Important To Be A Nag
We all hate to be nags. But it is important because an application can get lost so easily in a mountain of paperwork.

- Call to make sure they sent out your application.
- Call to make sure they received your application.
- Call to make sure you know when you will be notified if you are accepted.
- Call a few days after the notification date if you have not heard anything yet.

It may be uncomfortable at times. But the squeaky wheel does get the grease.

Step #14: Success and Failure are Both Good
If you get the money, call. Make sure you thank them and ask all the stupid questions you think are necessary to know when, where, and how you are going to get your money. If your application is rejected, be sure you call anyway. This is the only way you may learn the truth about why you did not get the money. Ask how soon you can apply again. They may be accepting applications every month

and too many people applied last month. You always have to keep learning how and why organizations give out money and by being an applicant you are in a wonderful position to ask.

Where To Find More Programs

You can't stop if you don't find what you need in this book. As I mentioned earlier, space precludes us from listing the thousands more that are available and publishing deadlines prevent us from having the latest. So, here is where you can turn to continue your work in getting what you need:

1) ***Find More Federal Money Programs***
Look at a book called the *Catalog of Federal Domestic Assistance*. It contains all the federal government programs that give out money. This book is available at your local public library or the U.S. Government Printing Office www.gpo.gov. You can also search the contents of this book, by keyword or government department, for free on the web at www.cfda.gov.

2) ***Find More State Money Programs***
Every state government has dozens of money programs that help people pay their expenses. The problem is that there is never one central place to look. You have to go agency by agency, or department by department and search for what is available. Some good departments to start with are health, agriculture, commerce, and social services. You can find them by dialing 411 and asking for your state capitol operator or by going to the web at www.govengine.com and clicking on your state.

3) ***Find More Local City and County Programs***
Start looking at every local city and county government for programs that might help. If you don't know where to go, you can call 411 and ask for the mayor's office or the office of the county executive. Just tell them you are looking for programs that might provide financial assistance to residents. You can also go to www.govengine.com and under each state there will be a listing of all cities and counties. Click on those of interest and start searching for programs.

4) ***Find More Money From Nonprofit Organizations***
There are two major sources for finding money from these groups:
   - The Foundation Center of New York City maintains a database of all foundations that provide money to nonprofit organizations or individuals. The information is available on the web at http://fdncenter.org or from their participating libraries by contacting 212-620-4230
   - The Guidestar Company in Williamsburg, VA also maintains a database of foundations and they can be reached at 757-229-4631 or at www.guidestar.com. Much of their database is accessible for free on the web.

5) ***Find More Money From Local Nonprofit And Volunteer Organizations***
There are a number of national volunteer organizations around the country that offer grants and other free services to solve problems for people in their community. The Lions Club awarded over $340 million in grants since they started, and the Kiwanis Clubs gives out over $100 million every year.

Catholic Charities USA
1731 King St., #200
Alexandria, VA 22314
703-549-1390

www.catholiccharitiesinfo.org

Over 14,000 local organizations offer a variety of services for many different community problems including child care, elderly services, emergency financial services, rental assistance, and more. To find an office near you go to their main web site and see "Need Assistance? Find A Local Agency?" and put in your state.

Salvation Army National Headquarters
615 Slaters Lane
P.O. Box 269
Alexandria, VA 22313
703-684-5500
www.salvationarmyusa.org/

Families in need can receive a wide range of services, including utility assistance, transitional housing emergency food, clothing, and more. For an office near you contact the headquarters above or http://www.redshield.org/.

6) ***Find A Local Nonprofit With Money And Services***

The United Way is a national organization that raises money for thousands of local nonprofit organizations who offer money and services to people in their community. Your local United Way can identify nonprofits in your area that may offer the resources or services you are looking for. Contact:

United Way of America
701 North Fairfax Street
Alexandria, VA 2314
703-836-7112
www.unitedway.org

To find a local chapter go to the website and enter your zip code under "Find A Local United Way."

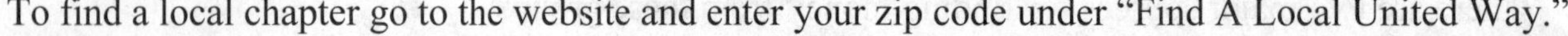

When All Else Fails

Your elected representatives are in the business of seeing how they can help you locate money, services or anything else you need. They can also be handy if you have applied for government money and you can't seem to get a specific government agency to respond to you. Most elected officials have people on their staff whose job it is to do just that for voters. This is why politicians are always getting re-elected. If they do a favor for you, you will vote for them forever, no matter what they do.

- You have 1 congressman and 2 senators at the federal level. You can contact all 3.
- You have more than one elected official in your state capital.
- You also have an elected representative at your city and county level.

Contact them all. They are all getting a government salary to help you and they all have access to different resources. The worst that can happen is that more than one person solves your problem. If you need help finding them go to www.congress.org or your local library.

Use The System Don't Fight It

You might be able to make one contact with an office and get what you want you need, but this is not very likely. What is more likely to happen in today's world is that it may take a dozen contacts to get what you need. And that's not just when dealing with the telephone company, that's true when dealing with anyone: your bank, Microsoft Helpline or your children (at least mine). But even if it takes you a few hours or even days to weeks to get all your health care paid for or a chunk of money to start your own business in retirement, it's worth it. Most of us can't remember what we did in the last few weeks. And these are benefits that can change the rest of your life. So remember, when the going gets a little complicated, you are not here to change the system, you are here to take advantage of it. Changing the system will take a whole heck of a lot longer.

Matthew Lesko,
President
Information USA, Inc.

Free Money

Paying Bills and Other Expenses

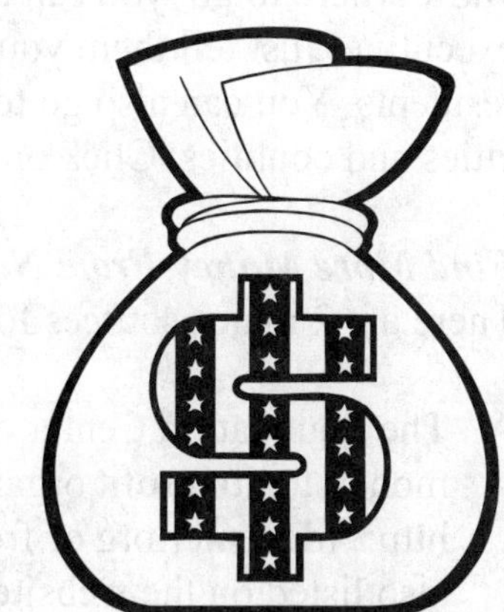

The programs described in this section are mostly for your day-to-day living expenses, like food, telephone or just extra money to pay off anything, like your bills. This section should not preclude you from looking into other sections of the book, because they too can help with expenses, especially expenses for certain situations. For example, prescription drug or doctor bills would be covered under Health and your rent or mortgage would be under Housing.

When you contact a government office for help, please don't just use the word "grant" when asking about available money programs. I know this is the most common term used by people seeking help, but you cut yourself out of a lot of suitable programs. Programs are established using all kinds of names including grants, direct payments, loans you don't have to pay back, assistance payments, vouchers, or even services. So when you are looking for this kind of money try not to use the word "grants" and just use the word "assistance". This way you are more likely to find **all** the possible programs that can help you.

Yes, you are right. There are income requirements for some of these programs. But remember every program has a different requirement. And even if they have an income requirement, it may be different for different parts of the country. And if the program says it is only for people with low income, you may be shocked that what the government considers low income. It can be as much as $35,000 or more for some of the basic programs and I have even seen income requirements going up to $80,000 for some housing programs in the New York area. And remember, by contacting the right bureaucrat there can always be exceptions to the rules.

You can't stop if you don't find what you need in the programs below. Space precludes us from listing the thousands more that are available and publishing deadlines prevent us from having the latest. So here is where you can turn to continue your work in getting what you need.

1. ***Find More Federal Money Programs***
   Look at a book called the *Catalog of Federal Domestic Assistance*. It contains all the federal government programs that give out money. This book is available at your local public library or the U.S. Government Printing Office www.gpo.gov. You can also search the contents of this book, by key word or government department, for free on the web at www.cfda.gov.

2. ***Find More State Money Programs***
   Every state government has dozens of money programs that help people pay their expenses. The problem is that there is never one central place to look. You have to go agency by agency, or department by department and search for what is available. Some good departments to start are

health, agriculture, commerce, and social services. You can find them by dialing 411 and asking for your state capitol operator or by going to the web at www.govengine.com and clicking on your state.

3. ***Find More Local City and County Programs***
Start looking at every local city and county government for programs that might help. If you don't know where to go, you can call 411 and ask for the mayor's office or the office of the county executive. Just tell them you are looking for programs that might provide financial assistance to residents. You can also go to www.govengine.com and under each state there will be a listing of all cities and counties. Click on those of interest and start searching for programs.

4. ***Find More Money From Nonprofit Organizations***
There are 2 major sources for finding money from these groups:

   A. The Foundation Center of New York City maintains a database of all foundations who provide money to nonprofit organizations or individuals. Their information is available on the web at http://fdncenter.org or from their participating libraries by contacting 212-620-4230 (or they are also listed on the website).

   B. The Guidestar Company in Williamsburg, VA also maintains a database of foundations and they can reached at 757-229-4631 or at www.guidestar.com. Much of their database is accessible for free on the web.

5. ***Volunteer Organizations***
There are a number of national volunteer organizations around the country that offer grants and other free services to solve problems for people in their community. The Lions Club awarded over $340 million in grants since they started, and the Kiwanis Clubs give out over $100 million every year.

Find your local club for each of the organizations below and contact them for information on their programs. If they do not have an on going program that specifically suits you, you can ask if you send a letter of request for their consideration. It can't hurt to ask. We've used these clubs in this way to help people in our "Show Me The Money Contest."

These organizations run programs that offer money for:

- day care services
- summer camp
- scholarships
- travel
- free eye glasses
- cataract surgeries
- health problems
- travel
- medical equipment, and
- money for emergencies

- Kiwanis International
  3636 Woodview Trace
  Indianapolis, IN 46268-3196
  317-875-8755
  www.kiwanis.org

  find a local Kiwanis club
  www.kiwanis.org/clubloc/

- United States Junior Chamber
  P.O. Box 7
  Tulsa, OK 74102
  1-800-JAYCEES
  www.usjaycees.org/

find a local Jaycees chapter www.usjaycees.org/chapter_links.htm

- Lions Clubs International
  300 W 22nd Street
  Oak Brook, IL 60523
  630-571-5466 ext 356
  www.lionsclubs.org/

find a local lions club www.lionnet.com/united_states.html

6. ***Find Money For Emergencies***

There are a number of national groups that provide free money and services thru a network of local offices. Check each of the groups below and see what their local offices have to offer.

- Catholic Charities USA
  1731 King St., #200
  Alexandria, VA 22314
  703-549-1390
  www.catholiccharitiesinfo.org

Over 14,000 local organizations offer a variety of services for many different community problems including child care, elderly services, emergency financial services, rental assistance, and more. To find an office near you go to their main web site and see "Need Assistance? Find A Local Agency?" and put in your state.

- Salvation Army National Headquarters
  615 Slaters Lane
  P.O. Box 269
  Alexandria, VA 22313
  703-684-5500
  www.salvationarmyusa.org/

Families in need can receive a wide range of services including utility assistance, transitional housing emergency food, clothing, and more. For an office near you, contact the headquarters above or www.redshield.org/.

7. ***Find a Local Nonprofit With Money and Services***

The United Way is a national organization that raises money for thousands of local nonprofit organizations who offer money and services to people in their community. Your local United Way can identify nonprofits in your area that may offer the resources or services you are looking for. Contact:

- United Way of America
  701 North Fairfax St.
  Alexandria, VA 2314
  703-836-7112
  www.unitedway.org

to find a local chapter go to the web site and enter your zip code under "Find A Local United Way."

8. ***Find Your Local Community Action Agency***

Over 1,000 local nonprofit offices offer free money and help to improve your life in almost any area. Although these agencies do get money from the federal government they also get money from other sources, and as a result, no two of these offices are exactly alike. But most all of them help in the area of employment, bill paying, child care and self employment. The following is a sample of programs you will find when you contact an office near you. Along with the program, we also identify the local agency providing this program. These programs are specific to these areas. Check with your local office to see what they offer.

Get a $3 grant for every $1 you save
Community Action Partnership www.managingmymoney.com/

$10,000 no interest, no payment, forgivable loans for home repairs
CFS Economic Opportunity Corporation www.advant.com/cefs/energy.htm

Buy a home with only $1,000
CEFS Economic Opportunity Corporation
www.advant.com/cefs/homebuy.htm

$3,000 grant to fix your furnace
CEFS Economic Opportunity Corporation
www.advant.com/cefs/ihwap.htm

$25,000 no interest, no payment, forgivable loan for home fix-up
CEFS Economic Opportunity Corporation
www.advant.com/cefs/rehab.htm

$2,000 to pay heating bills
CEFS Economic Opportunity Corporation
www.advant.com/cefs/liheap.htm

Free Cars, if you pay repairs and registration
CAP Agency Shakopee, MI www.capagency.org/pages/service.htm

Free Crisis Nursery, up to 73 hours of overnight care and 10 days day care
CAP Agency Shakopee, MI www.capagency.org/pages/service.htm

Eviction Prevention
TEAM, Inc Derby, CT
www.teamcaa.org/housing.htm

$10,000 to start a business
Community Action Program, Inc of Western Indiana www.capwi.org/new_page_9.htm

$700 for child care
Community and Family Services, Inc. Portland, IN www.comfam.net/pages/childcare.html

$350 for an air conditioner
City of Des Moines, Iowa
www.ci.des-moines.ia.us/departments/CD/Comm%20Serv/L-I%20Assist%20Programs.htm

$1,000 To Repair Furnace
City of Des Moines, Iowa
www.ci.des-moines.ia.us/departments/CD/Comm%20Serv/L-I%20Assist%20Programs.htm

$45/month for pre-school
Mid-Sioux Opportunity, Inc., Remsen, IA
www.mid-siouxopportunity.org/ccr/community_resources/empowerment.html

To find a community action agency near you go to: www.communityactionpartnership.com/about/links/map.asp or contact Community Action Partnership, 1100 17th St NW Suite 500, Washington, DC 20036; 202-265-7546; Fax: 202-265-8850; info@communityactionpartnership.com; www.communityactionpartnership.com.

If your local agency doesn't have what you need, ask for names of other organizations who might be able to help. You live in America and pay taxes. You have a right to know about and use these programs. If you run into a road block, don't let a little negative feedback stop you. Try the next program, and then the next. And then start looking for more. This country has so much to offer, but you have to find it.

9. ***Government Benefits***
GovBenefits.gov helps provide personalized access to government assisted programs. This online program is free and confidential. All you have to do is answer a series of questions about yourself and then GovBenefits.gov will provide you with a list of government programs you may be eligible to receive along with application information. The site will provide both state and federal programs to assist you. Contact: 800-FED-INFO; www.govbenefits.gov.

10. ***BenefitsCheckUp***
BenefitsCheckUp is a service of the National Council on the Aging helping Americans connect with government programs. This online database searches federal, state, some local and public benefits

for adults 55 years old and older. It contains over 1,100 different programs and on average there are 50 to 70 programs available to individuals per state. The online questionnaire is free, confidential and takes about 30 minutes to complete. If you want to find all of the benefits you qualify this is a great place to start. For information contact BenefitsCheckUp, www.benefitscheckup.org.

11. Veterans Pension

Low income veterans who are permanently or totally disabled or 65 years old may be eligible for pension benefits from the US government. The military also offers survivor benefits for surviving spouses and unmarried children of deceased veterans with wartime service. There are some restrictions so you will need to apply to the Veterans Administration. Contact: Veteran Benefits, 810 Vermont Avenue, NW, Washington, DC 20420; 800-827-1000; http://vabenefits.vba.va.gov/vonapp/main.asp.

$2,000 A Month To Pay Your Mortgage While You Are Looking For Work

There are now programs that will make your mortgage payments for you when you get into financial trouble. One of the best ways to find out if there are programs like this in your area is to contact the local HUD approved Housing Counseling agencies. To find your closest agency, contact your state housing office, or the Housing Counseling Center locator at 800-569-4287; www.hud.gov/hsgcoun.html; or Housing Counseling Clearinghouse, P.O. Box 10423, McLean, VA 22102; 800-217-6970.

Free Credit Repair

The Federal Trade Commission has many publications to get you on the road to good credit and can also tell you your rights in dealing with collection agencies. Contact Public Reference, Room 130, Federal Trade Commission, Washington, DC 20580; 877-FTC-HELP; www.ftc.gov. You can also get free counseling at your local County Cooperative Extension Service listed in the government section of your phone book under County Government. Or contact one of the nonprofits that can help with your debt: National Foundation for Credit Counseling, 801 Roeder Rd., Suite 900, Silver Spring, MD 20910; 800-388-2227; www.nfcc.org; or Credit Counseling Center of America, P.O. Box 830489, Richardson, TX 75083; 800-493-2222; www.cccamerica.org. Remember that these nonprofits get money from credit card companies so they are not likely to explain your bankruptcy options to you.

Get Extra $6,000 If You Cannot Work

If you don't qualify for Social Security, or if your benefits are very low, you may qualify for Supplemental Security Income (SSI). This program was established to help poor seniors over 65 and the blind and disabled meet basic living expenses. To find out more about the program contact your local Social Security office or contact the Social Security hotline at 800-772-1213 or online at www.ssa.gov.

$500 In Free Emergency Money

If you need emergency money to pay a bill, or for housing, training, health care, or just additional support, these organizations can be of service and they are likely to have an office near you. Community Action Agencies: nearly 1,000 agencies around the country receive funds from the Community Services Block Grant to offer education, counseling, employment, training, and more. Services vary from agency to agency. To locate an agency serving your area contact National Community Action Partnership, 1100 17th St., NW, Washington, DC 20036; 202-265-7546; www.communityactionpartnership.com.

Extra $1,000 For Seniors and Disabled
Each year over 3 million eligible seniors and people with disabilities fail to apply for a little-known program that will give them over $1,000 extra in their Social Security check. That's how much the government deducts for Medicare Part B payments. The program is called Qualified Medicare Beneficiaries Plan, or Specified Low-Income Medicare Beneficiaries Plan. To learn more contact your local Social Security Office at 800-772-1213. You can also contact the Medicare Hotline and request the publication Guide to Health Insurance for People with Medicare. Contact Medicare Hotline at 800-MEDICARE or online at www.medicare.gov.

50% Discount On Phone Service
Under the Federal Communication Commission's Link-up America and Lifeline programs, low-income households seeking telephone service are given a 50% discount on local connection charges, and may be able to pay installment payments on the remaining charge. To learn more contact your local telephone company.

10% to 100% Off Eyeglasses
Pearle Vision Centers offers 50% off either the lenses or frames when you purchase a complete set of glasses to people 50-59; 60% off to those 60-69; and so on until seniors reach 100 and they are given 100% off either the lenses or frames when they purchase a complete set of glasses. Lens Crafters and Eye Glass Factory also offer discount programs. Now it makes seeing clearly less costly.

$800 for Food
The Food Stamp Program was designed to help low-income families buy the food they need to stay healthy and productive. The amount of Food Stamps you get each month is determined by the number of people in your family and by the household income. Look in the blue pages of your telephone book under "Food Stamps," "Social Services," or "Public Assistance." You can also find more information by contacting U.S. Department of Agriculture, Food and Nutrition Service, 3101 Park Ctr., Dr., Park Office Center Bldg., Alexandria, VA 22302; 703-305-2276; www.fns.usda.gov/fncs.

$2,000 To Pay Your Heating Bills
Storm windows, insulation, and even weatherstripping, can help reduce your fuel bill. Families can receive assistance to weatherize their homes and apartments at no charge if you meet certain income guidelines. States allocate dollars to nonprofit agencies for purchasing and installing energy-related repairs, with the average grant being $2,000 per year. Contact your state Energy Office or the Weatherization Assistance Programs Branch, EE44, U.S. Department of Energy, 1000 Independence Ave., SW, Washington, DC 20585; 202-596-4074; www.eere.energy.gov/weatherization

Make $500 Turning In Annoying Telephone Solicitors
The Federal Communications Commission's Consumer Protection Act says that you can collect $500 or more from telephone solicitors if they call two or more times within a 12 month period after you tell them to stop; they call you with a pre-recorded voice message to your home; they call you at home

before 8am or after 9 pm; and more. For more information contact Federal Communications Commission, Common Carrier Bureau, Consumer Complaints, Mail Stop 1600A2, Washington, DC 20554; 888-CALL-FCC; www.fcc.gov/cgb/consumerfacts/tcpa.html.

$700 Off Your Utility Bills

The legislature in Massachusetts passed a law giving discounts up to $700 on heating bills for families making up to $30,000, along with up to 40% discount on electric bills, $108 off telephone bills, and $100 off oil bills. Contact your state's Public Utilities office to find out about special discounts on your gas, electric, cable or telephone service in your state.

Free Legal Help To Fight Your Credit Card Company

If you are having trouble with your credit card company, remember that they are regulated by a banking institution. Different banks are governed by different agencies, but all take complaints and make efforts to assist customers. Your state Banking Commissioner handles complaints dealing with state chartered banks. For banks with the word "national" or "N.A." in its name contact Comptroller of the Currency, Compliance Management, U.S. Department of the Treasury, 250 E St., SW, Washington, DC 20219; 202-874-4900; 800-613-6743; www.occ.treas.gov. For Savings and Loans contact Office of Thrift Supervision, U.S. Department of the Treasury, 1700 G St., NW, Washington, DC 20552; 202-906-6000; 800-842-6929; www.ots.treas.gov. For FDIC Insured contact Federal Deposit Insurance Corporation, Office of Consumer Affairs, 550 17th St., NW, Room F-130, Washington, DC 20429; 877-ASK-FDIC; www.fdic.gov.

Free Legal Help To Fight The IRS

The Taxpayer Advocate administers the Problem Resolution Program (PRP) that has the authority to cut through red tape. They will keep you informed of your case's progress. PRP can usually help with delayed refunds, unanswered inquiries, and incorrect billing notices. For more information request Publication 1546, The Taxpayer Advocate Service of the IRS. To get in contact the program, call the IRS at 800-829-1040; www.irs.gov.

The Government Owes You Money

You may not know it, but there may be money sitting and waiting for you in government offices. It may be because of an old utility deposit you forgot about or an IRS check that was sent to an old address. Find out if there is hidden money for you at these government offices: National Association of Unclaimed Property Administrators, P.O. Box 7156, Bismarck, ND 58507; www.unclaimed.org; contact the IRS at 800-829-1040; www.irs.gov; U.S. Department of Housing and Urban Development, P.O. Box 23699, Washington, DC 20026; www.hud.gov/refunds/index.cfm; Veterans Affairs at 800-827-1000; www.va.gov; or Social Security at 800-772-1213; www.ssa.gov.

Get $540 To Buy Fresh Fruit

Seniors making up to $22,000/ year can get as much as $540 to buy fresh fruit and vegetables from road side stands. Through the little-known Senior Farmers' Market Nutrition Program, seniors in 40 states can have the government help buy their produce. Find out how much your state can give you to buy food. Contact the USDA Food and Nutrition Service, 3101 Park Center Drive, Room 926, Alexandria, VA 22302; www.fns.usda.gov/fncs. To locate your State office go to www.fns.usda.gov/wic/SeniorFMNP/SFMNPcontacts2004.htm.

Get $25,000 Toward Hotels, Rental Assistance, And Home Repair For Disaster Victims
A victim of disaster and not sure how you are going to pay the mountain of expenses? Through FEMA's Individual Assistance Program, you could be eligible for $25,000 of assistance. FEMA will help pay for hotel stays, apartment rental, home repair or even new construction. Don't miss out on the help you need and deserve. Contact FEMA at 800-621-FEMA (TTY: 800-462-7585) and register. www.fema.gov/rrr/inassist.shtm.

$14,800 in Grant Money For Disaster Victims
Has your family been part of a major disaster? Through FEMA, you can get up to $14,800 in grant money to help get you back on your feet. The money will cover real and personal property, medical and dental bills, as well as many other expenses. To find out more, contact the Department of Homeland Security 245 Murray Drive, S.W. Washington, D.C. 20528; 202-282-8000; http://12.46.245.173/pls/portal30/CATALOG.PROGRAM_TEXT_RPT.SHOW?p_arg_names=prog_nbr&p_arg_values=97.035.

$5,000 Yearly for Certain WWII Vets
If you meet the criteria set by SSI, you could receive over $5,000 a year in benefits. Contact the Social Security Administration, Office of Public Inquiries, Windsor Park Building, 6401 Security Blvd., Baltimore, MD 21235; 800-772-1213; www.ssa.gov/pubs/10157.html. For additional information visit http://12.46.245.173/pls/portal30/CATALOG.PROGRAM_TEXT_RPT.SHOW?p_arg_names=prog_nbr&p_arg_values=96.020.

$2,500 Grants for Everyone
This foundation is dedicated to making a difference in the communities where employees, franchisees, and customers of Jack in the Box restaurants work and live. Its primary charitable partner is Big Brothers Big Sisters, as well as the United Way and local nonprofit organizations in the headquarters city of San Diego in the areas of youth, education, and human services. Hardship grants are made to company employees in need. Giving is on a national basis. Contact Jack in the Box Foundation, c/o Tax Department, 9330 Balboa Avenue, San Diego, CA 92123-1516; www.jackinthe box.com/foundation/.

Tax Free Income, Transportation Expenses, And Free Physicals To Help Seniors
Through the Senior Companion Program, work as a volunteer for the elderly while getting compensated for your time! Benefits include an hourly tax-free wage, transportation expenses, free physicals, and free meal. Make a difference and make money too! For more information, contact the Senior Corps at 800-424-8867 or TTY 800-833-3722; www.seniorcorps.org/joining/scp/.

Over $6,000 Grants for Older Women
This foundation provides grants to economically disadvantaged women over the age of 65. Grants are generally awarded up to $6,000, but could be more. This is a national grant program. Contact Sarah A. W. Devens Trust, c/o Rice, Heard & Bigelow, Inc., 50 Congress St., Ste. 1025, Boston, MA 02109; 617-557-7509; axs@riceheard.com.

Over $11,000 Grants for People in Need
Grants to individuals as well as employee matching gifts are awarded to needy individuals who are economically disadvantaged. Its goals are to prevent homelessness, promote self-sufficiency and to

enhance community services. Giving is on a national basis in areas of company operations. Contact Washington Group Foundation (formerly Morrison Knudsen Corporation Foundation), P.O. Box 73, Boise, ID 83729; 208-386-5201; wwwwgint.com/washington_foundation_how.html; marlene.puckett@wgint.com. Application Address: Washington Group Foundation, 1 Morrison Knudsen Plaza, Boise, ID 83729.

Grants & Other Financial Assistance for Employees
Over $20.0 million is available to disperse as financial assistance for individuals who work or have retired from Abbott Laboratories. Grants, loans, financial education and counseling services are provided due to financial hardships. Assistance is awarded to employees and retirees worldwide. Contact The Clara Abbott Foundation, 200 Abbott Park Rd., D579/AMJ37, Abbott Park, IL 60064-3537; http://clara.abbott.com.

$5,000 for Heroism
This foundation awards medals and monetary awards to civilians within the U.S. and Canada who demonstrated voluntary heroism in saving or attempting to save the lives of others. Maximum award amount is $5,000. Grant monetary assistance, including scholarship aid, is also given to awardees and to the dependents of those who have lost their lives or who have been disabled in such heroic manner. This amount can be up to $3,500. Contact Carnegie Hero Fund Commission, 425 6th Ave., Ste. 1640, Pittsburgh, PA 15219-1823; 412-281-1302 or 800-447-8900; Fax: 412-281-5751; www.carnegiehero.org/; carnegiehero@carnegiehero.org.

Money for Women in Massachusetts
Provides grants to economically disadvantaged elderly Protestant women in Massachusetts. Contact Laura A. Burgess Fund, c/o Fleet Private Clients Group, P.O. Box 6767, Providence, RI 02940-6767. Application Address: Laura A. Burgess Fund, c/o Fleet National Bank, 100 Federal St., Boston, MA 02110; 617-434-4644.

$5,000 for Emergency Situations in Women's Rights
The Urgent Action Fund provides small grants up to $5,000 to support strategic interventions that take advantage of opportunities to advance women's human rights. The Fund supports "urgent actions" that cannot wait for a month or six weeks or six months. Grantmaking categories include: situations of armed conflict, escalating violence or politically volatile environments; precedent-setting legal or legislative action; and protection of women's human rights defenders. Individuals and organizations can apply for this national funding program. Contact Urgent Action Fund for Women's Human Rights, P.O. Box 1287, Boulder, CO 80306-1287; 303-442-2388; Fax: 303-442-2370; www.urgentactionfund.org; urgentact@urgentactionfund.org.

Grants to Aid Victims of Violence
The New England Patriots' R.O.S.E. Award offers a cash award to a female victim of violent crime who is working to overcome her adversities. The award is meant to help her continue in her journey toward regaining her self-esteem and rebuilding her life. Cash awards vary according to funding availability.

Contact The R.O.S.E. Fund, Inc., (formerly Ryka Rose Foundation), 175 Federal St., Ste. 455, Boston, MA 02110; 617-482-5400; Fax: 617-482-3443; www.rosefund.org; rosefund@ici.net.

Achievement Award + Cash Award for Charity
The Heinz Family Foundation R.O.S.E. Achievement Award recognizes a woman survivor of violence for her work and achievements in the area of ending violence against women. The recipient's choice of nonprofit organization receives the cash award. Contact The R.O.S.E. Fund, Inc., (formerly Ryka Rose Foundation), 175 Federal St., Ste. 455, Boston, MA 02110; 617-482-5400; Fax: 617-482-3443; www.rosefund.org; rosefund@ici.net.

Grants up to $7,500 for Social Services and Medical Needs
Grants range from $1,000 to $7,500 for support of social services, higher education, music, museums, and medical needs. This foundation gives on a national basis. Contact The Chazen Foundation, P.O. Box 801, Nyack, NY 10960; www.chazenscholar.com/project.php3; scholarprogram@chazenscholar.com.

Financial Assistance to Victims of Natural Disaster
The fund provides monetary and non-monetary relief to individuals in the U.S. and Canada who are victims of disasters such as hurricanes and earthquakes. Contact Teamster Disaster Relief Fund, 25 Louisiana Ave., N.W., Washington, DC 20001; 202-624-6871; www.teamster.org.

$3,000 Matching Funds for Employees
The Foundation will match active BearingPoint employee and board of director's contributions to eligible nonprofit organizations at 100%, up to a limit of $3,000 total per donor per fiscal year. Full-time & part-time active US & Canadian BearingPoint employees who work 1,000 hours or more in a year and board of director's members are eligible to participate in the matching gift program. Contact BearingPoint, Inc. Corporate Giving Program (formerly KPMG Consulting, Inc. Corporate Giving Program), c/o BearingPoint Charitable Foundation, 106 Allen Road, Liberty Corner, NJ 07938; 908-607-2300; www.bearingpoint.com/about_us/philanthropy/rand_blazer.html; us-kcingivingprogram@kpmg.com; us-becommunitysupp@BearingPoint.net.

Financial Assistance for Employees in Need
Through the Corporate Giving Program, BearingPoint coordinates emotional and financial support for employees impacted by traumatic or catastrophic events, giving employees a place to turn when they are in need. BearingPoint does not accept unsolicited grant proposals from outside organizations. All requests for funding and support are generated by BearingPoint employees. Contact BearingPoint, Inc. Corporate Giving Program (formerly KPMG Consulting, Inc. Corporate Giving Program), c/o BearingPoint Charitable Foundation, 106 Allen Road, Liberty Corner, NJ 07938; 908-607-2300; www.bearingpoint.com/about_us/philanthropy/rand_blazer.html; us-kcingivingprogram@kpmg.com; us-becommunitysupp@BearingPoint.net.

Help for the Elderly and Needy, and for Catholic Organizations
St. Benedict's Charitable Society provides relief assistance to elderly, infirm, and needy people for basic living, medical and funeral expenses; it also provides support for Catholic churches, organizations and scholarship funds. Contact Margaret Kuehmstedt, Treas., St. Benedict's Charitable Society, 1663 Bristol Pike, Bensalem, PA 19020-5702; 215-244-9900.

Employees Volunteer to Get Cash Rewards
WAVE is a volunteer program that helps Fannie Mae and Fannie Mae Foundation employees find volunteer opportunities and provide incentives for employees to participate in volunteer activities. Employees can receive up to 10 hours of paid leave per month to perform community service. The WAVE program also features a grants program called Dollars for Doers which matches employee volunteer hours with cash grants to the organizations for which they volunteer. The Employee Matching Gifts Program is another component of WAVE, which matches personal financial contributions by employees, up to $10,000 per year. Contact Fannie Mae Foundation, 4000 Wisconsin Ave. N.W., N. Tower, Ste. 1, Washington, DC 20016-2804; 202-274-8066 or 202-274-8057 or 202-274-8000; Fax: 202-274-8100; www.fanniemaefoundation.org; grants@fanniemaefoundation.org.

Up to $25,000 for Those in Need
This Foundation offers support for Christian churches, and educational, missionary, and welfare programs and also awards grants to needy individuals. Grants range from $5,000 up to $25,000. Contact Agape Fund, 800 Middlebrook Road, Prescott, AZ 86303; www.communionchapel.org/agape_fund_guidelines.htm.

Money for Italian Americans
The Italian-American Community Services Agency awards grants to Italian-Americans in financial need and indigent individuals, including senior citizens. Contact Italian-American Community Services Agency (formerly Italian Welfare Agency, Inc.), 678 Green St., San Francisco, CA 94133-3896; 415-362-6423; http://Italiancommunityservices.org/index.htm; email: ampierini@italiancommunityservices.org.

Financial Assistance for Daughters of Deceased Railroaders
This foundation provides limited financial assistance to daughters of railroad employees who die (the cause need not be work-related) while in the employ of a railroad in the United States. Funding is provided to encourage each girl to pursue her education. In order to qualify for a grant of financial assistance from the Foundation, the girl must live in the home of the surviving parent or guardian, maintain a good health program, receive satisfactory academic grades and is encouraged to participate in religious services of her faith. Eligibility of the daughter is also dependent upon the parent remaining unmarried. This supplement to family income is to be used in its entirety for the benefit of the girl. The Foundation also provides certain health care benefits to the daughter. Contact The John Edgar Thomson Foundation, c/o The Rittenhouse Claridge, 201 S. 18th Street, Suite 318, Philadelphia, PA 19103; 215-545-6083; www.utu.org/DEPTS/PR-DEPT/ DAUGHTER.HTM.

Free Tax Help For Seniors
The Tax Counseling for the Elderly program was designed to provide free taxpayer assistance to those ages 60 and above. The staff usually consists of retired individuals associated with nonprofit organizations that receive grants from the IRS to perform this service. Often they provide counseling in retirement homes, neighborhood sites or private houses of the homebound. For information on the Tax Counseling for the Elderly program near you, contact your local IRS office, call the hotline at 800-829-1040; www.irs.gov.

Free Copies of Your Credit Report

You can get a free copy of your credit report if:

- you have been denied credit, insurance, or employment within the last 60 days
- you're unemployed and plan to look for a job within 60 days
- you're on welfare, or
- your report is inaccurate because of fraud.

Otherwise they can charge you up to $9 for a copy of your report. For copies of your report, contact the credit reporting agencies listed in the yellow pages of your telephone book, or contact the three major national credit bureaus. You can also get a free copy of your report right now by going to www.ftc.gov/bcp/conline/edcams/freereports/index.html

Equifax
PO Box 740241, Atlanta, GA 30374; 800-685-1111; www.equifax.com

Experian (formerly TRW)
PO Box 949, Allen, TX 75013; 888-397-3742; www.experian.com

Trans Union
P.O. Box 2000, Chester, PA 19022; 800-916-8800; www.transunion.com

If you have trouble getting satisfaction from a credit reporting agency contact: Consumer Response Center, Federal Trade Commission, CRC-240, Washington, DC 20580; 877-FTC-HELP; www.ftc.gov.

$500 Extra for Seniors and Disabled

The state of Pennsylvania offers up to $500 for seniors and people with disabilities who pay property taxes or rent. If you live in Pennsylvania, contact Department of Aging, 555 Walnut St., 5th Floor, Harrisburg, PA 17101; 717-783-1549. If you live elsewhere, contact your state Office on Aging listed in the blue pages of your phone book, or your state Department of Revenue.

Discounts On Your Banking Bills

First Citizens Bank has **Senior Quest Accounts** where customers 60 and over receive unlimited check writing, no per check charge, interest bearing checking, no monthly service charge, free safe deposit box, no ATM fees, free cashier's checks, travelers' checks, and money orders. They even offer special rates on 6 and 12 month CD's, no annual fee credit card, free direct deposit and discount brokerage fees, with some of these services requiring a minimum balance. Other banks offer similar services, with most offering free checks, no minimum balance, and unlimited check writing.

Christian Scientists Get Free Money

The New Horizons Foundation provides financial assistance to residents of Los Angeles County, CA, who are over 65 years of age and active Christian Scientists. Contact New Horizons Foundation, c/o Gifford & Dearing, 700 S. Flower St., Suite 1222, Los Angeles, CA 90017-4160; 213-626-4481.

Grants and camperships are available through the Sunnyside Foundation, Inc. to underprivileged Christian Science children under the age of 20 who regularly attend Sunday School and are Texas residents. Contact Sunnyside Foundation, Inc., 8222 Douglas Ave., Suite 501, Dallas, TX 75225-5936; 214-692-5686.

$1,000 Extra for Seniors

- Monetary assistance is available for living expenses such as food and medicine through the Sarah A.W. Devens Trust to economically disadvantaged women over age 65 residing in MA. Contact Sarah A.W. Devens Trust, c/o Rice, Heard & Bigelow, Inc., 50 Congress St., Suite 1025, Boston, MA 02109; 617-557-7415.
- Supplemental monthly income is available to elderly indigent residents of the Southeastern U.S. through the Alfred I. duPont Foundation. Contact Alfred I. duPont Foundation, 1650 Prudential Drive, Suite 302, Jacksonville, FL 32207; 904-858-3123.

$2,000 For Being Mugged

Millions of people and their families are victimized by crime every year in the U.S. And to better address the growing belief that the law was better at protecting the rights of criminals than those of the victims, Congress enacted a law to establish a Crime Victims Fund to compensate innocent victims of violent crime. Part of the money is given to help compensate victims or their families for costs relating to such crimes as muggings, sexual crimes, and even murder. Part of the money from these funds is given out to victims as direct cash payments to help compensate for costs related to the violent crimes. Contact the office in your state if you find yourself the victim of a violent crime and need money to help pay for such related costs as medical bills, lost wages, and funeral expenses. For more information you may contact:

- Office for Victims of Crime Resource Center, National Criminal Justice Reference Service, P.O. Box 6000, Rockville, MD 20849; 800-851-3420; 301-519-5500 (8:30 am to 7 pm EST); www.ncjrs.org.
- Office for Victims of Crime, U.S. Department of Justice, 950 Pennsylvania Avenue, NW, Washington, DC 20530; 202-514-2601; www.usdoj.gov/crimevictims.htm

Extra Money For Indiana Presbyterians

The Frank L. and Laura L. Smock Foundation offers Presbyterian Indiana residents who are ailing, physically disabled, blind, needy or elderly medical and nursing care assistance. Contact Frank L. and Laura L. Smock Foundation, c/o Wells Fargo Bank Indiana, N.A., P.O. Box 960, Fort Wayne, IN 46801-6632; 219-461-6451.

Extra Money For Pittsburgh-Area Jewish Families in Need

Financial assistance is offered to needy Jewish families residing in the Pittsburgh area through the Jewish Family Assistance Fund for living, personal, food and medical expenses. Contact Jewish Family Assistance Fund, 5743 Bartlett St., Pittsburgh, PA 15217-1515; 412-521-3237.

Free Meals At Adult Day Care

Not only does the government offer free lunches for school children, but your younger children can also receive free meals at day care centers, family day care homes, and adults can receive food as well. Child and Adult Care Food Program (CACFP) provides nutritious meals to 2.6 million children and 74,000 adults who receive day care outside of their home. CACFP reaches even further to provide meals to children residing in homeless shelters, and snacks and suppers to youths participating in eligible afterschool care programs. CACFP reimburses participating centers and day care homes for their meal costs. It is administered at the Federal level by the Food and Nutrition Service (FNS), an agency of the U.S. Department of Agriculture. The State education or health department administers CACFP, in most States. Programs include:

- Child Care Centers
- Adult Day Care Centers
- Family Day Care Homes
- Homeless Shelters
- After School Care Programs

Contact FNS Public Information, 3101 Park Center Drive, Room 926, Alexandria, VA 22302; 703-305-2281; www.fns.usda.gov/cnd/care/cacfp/cacfphome.htm.

$700 Food Money for Women & Children

The Women, Infant and Children (WIC) Program's mission is to safeguard the health of low-income women, infants, and children up to age 5 who are at nutritional risk by providing nutritious foods to supplement diets, information on healthy eating, and referrals to health care. A family of four can make up to $33,485 and still qualify! WIC foods include iron-fortified infant formula and infant cereal, iron-fortified adult cereal, vitamin C-rich fruit and/or vegetable juice, eggs, milk, cheese, peanut butter, dried beans or peas, tuna fish and carrots. In addition to the regular WIC program, a majority of the states have chosen to operate the WIC Farmers' Market Nutrition Program (FMNP), established in 1992, it provides additional coupons to WIC participants that they can use to purchase fresh fruits and vegetables at participating farmers' markets. Contact Supplemental Food Programs Division, Food and Nutrition Service – USDA, 3101 Park Center Drive, Alexandria, VA 22302; 703-305-2746; Fax: 703-305-2196; www.fns.usda.gov/fns/.

Free Food for Seniors

The Nutrition Services Incentive Program (NSIP) is the new name for the United States Department of Agriculture (USDA) cash or commodity program, known as the Nutrition Program for the Elderly (NPE). While there is no means test for participation in this program, services are targeted to older people with the greatest economic or social need, with special attention given to low-income minorities. Since American Indians, Alaskan Natives, and Native Hawaiians tend to have lower life expectancies and higher rates of illness at younger ages, Tribal Organizations are given the option of setting the age at which older people can participate in the program. Contact your state or local Administration on Aging.

National Administration on Aging
Administration on Aging
330 Independence Avenue, SW
Washington, DC 20201
202-619-0724
www.aoa.gov/

Eldercare Locator
800-677-1116
www.eldercare.gov/

USDA Food and Nutrition Service
3101 Park Center Drive
Alexandria, VA 22302

703-305-2060
www.fns.usda.gov/fdd/programs/nsip/

Free Food for Native Americans
The Food Distribution Program on Indian Reservations (FDPIR) is a program that provides commodity foods to low-income households, including the elderly, living on Indian reservations, and to Native American families residing in designated areas near reservations. Participants on many reservations can choose fresh produce instead of canned fruits and vegetables. Contact the office in your area for more information. Contact Food and Nutrition Service – USDA, Food Distribution Division, 3101 Park Center Drive, Alexandria, VA 22302; 703-305-2888; Fax: 703-305-2420; www.fns.usda.gov/fdd/programs/fdpir/fdpirhome.htm.

Free Extra Food
The Commodity Supplemental Food Program (CSFP) works to improve the health of low-income pregnant and breastfeeding women, other new mothers up to one year postpartum, infants, children up to age six, and elderly people at least 60 years of age by supplementing their diets with nutritious USDA commodity foods. Food packages include a variety of foods, such as infant formula and cereal, non-fat dry and evaporated milk, juice, farina, oats, ready-to-eat cereal, rice, pasta, egg mix, peanut butter, dry beans or peas, canned meat or poultry or tuna, cheese, and canned fruits and vegetables. To check eligibility and availability contact Food and Nutrition Service – USDA, Food Distribution Division, 3101 Park Center Drive, Room 504, Alexandria, VA 22302; 703-305-2888; Fax: 703-305-2420; www.fns.usda.gov/fdd/programs/csfp/.

Free Emergency Food
The Emergency Food Assistance Program (TEFAP) is a Federal program that helps supplement the diets of low-income needy people, including elderly people, by providing them with emergency food and nutrition assistance at no cost. States provide the food to local agencies that they have selected, usually food banks, which in turn, distribute the food to soup kitchens and food pantries that directly serve the public. Contact Food and Nutrition Service – USDA, Food Distribution Division, 3101 Park Center Drive, Alexandria, VA 22302; 703-305-2888; Fax: 703-305-2420; www.fns.usda.gov/fdd/programs/tefap/.

$4,008 For You and Your Family
The Earned Income Tax Credit (EITC), also known as the Earned Income Credit (EIC) is a Federal income tax credit for low-income working individuals and families. The EITC reduces the amount of taxes owed. If the credit exceeds the amount of taxes owed, it is possible to get a refund check. The amount of the EITC depends on the size and income of the family. You need publication 596 by calling 800-829-3676; or online at www.irs.gov.

Free Take Out Meals for Seniors
People 60 and over who are homebound because of illness, incapacity, or disability or who are otherwise isolated can receive hot meals delivered to their home. The program is funded in every state by the Older Americans Act. Contact your local area agency on aging or your state Department on Aging to learn who you need to contact in your area. You can also contact the Eldercare Locator hotline at 800-677-1116 for more assistance.

Free Money For Members of Armed Services and Vets to Pay Bills

The American Red Cross helps those in need in a variety of ways. If they have been sent to serve with the U.S. military, then members of the armed services and their families can contact the Red Cross for help in cases of emergency. Services they can provide include communicating with family members, emergency financial assistance, counseling and more. Contact the American Red Cross National Headquarters, 2025 E Street NW, Washington, DC 20006; 202-303-4498; www.redcross.org/services/afes.

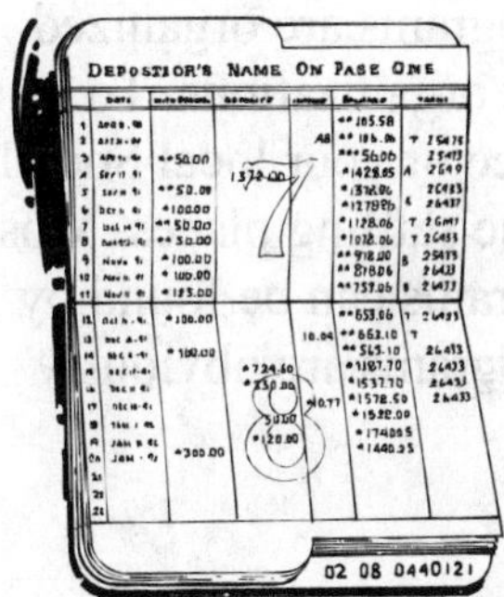

Money To Put In Your Savings Account

Triple your savings by taking advantage of Individual Development Accounts. These accounts are currently available in 350 communities with more in development. Designed to help low-income people save for a down payment, college, or a small business, funds matched with one dollar from the government and one dollar from private funds. A short course on money management is usually required. To learn more about the program or to see what may be available in your community, contact Corporation for Enterprise Development, 777 N. Capitol St., NE, Suite 800, Washington, DC 20002; 202-408-9788; www.idanetwork.org.

372 Sources To Pay Emergency Expenses

Bravekids.org has put together a resource directory that lists over 372 sources for financial and other types of assistance for those with disabled children or adults or low-income families in need of help. It could be anything from paying your utility bill to respite care or medical expenses.
Check out www.bravekids.org.

Services Available From Veterinary Teaching Hospitals

Veterinary teaching hospitals can be an excellent place to take your pet, and most of them will take new patients directly or as referrals from other veterinarians. But as research and teaching institutions, they have access to a lot more resources than your average veterinary hospital. Many but not all of these hospitals provide services like:

- *Free Services and Drugs for People Who Can't Pay*
- *Free Medical Treatment for Strays in Need Brought in by Non-owners*
- *Free Answers to Questions Over the Telephone*
- *Free and Discount Treatment for Companion Animals and Assistance Dogs*
- *Discounts for Seniors*

Call to see what services your local Veterinary Teaching Hospital may offer.

Pay for Taxi Service to Work, School or Day Care

One county in Oregon has a program that picks up you and your child, taking your child to day care and you to work. North Carolina has programs where counties are given vans to transport people back and forth to work, with lower fees charged to those in welfare-to-work programs. Mississippi has a program that will pick you up at your house and take you back and forth to work if you are working to get off welfare. Some communities, like Fairfax County in Virginia, maintain a database that helps locate the necessary transportation for work and day care needs. And Kentucky operates an 800 hotline that tries to solve any work-related transportation need. To start looking for programs like this in your area, contact your local congressman's office or your local social service agency. They won't know about all the programs but can probably give you some starting places. You should also find out about local vanpool and rideshare programs. Your local chamber of commerce or library should have this kind of information for you.

Money for Auto Repairs, Car Insurance, Driver's Ed, or Just a Tank of Gas

There are federal programs as well as state programs to help people with limited incomes keep their vehicles on the road so that they can get back and forth to work, focusing on those trying to get off welfare. Some states will even give you money for driver's education or to pay for a driver's license. The issue, like the programs for free cars, is to help people make it to work. These programs are organized like a patchwork quilt in most areas involving federal, state, county and nonprofit organizations. To start looking for programs like this in your area, contact your local congressman's office or your local Social Services. They won't know about all the programs but can probably give you some starting places. Most branches of the Goodwill Industries have a Wheels to Work program. Other programs can be found by typing in the keywords "Wheels to Work" in an Internet search engine. These programs are obviously only for the those who live in the area.

Here is just a *SAMPLING* of the Wheels to Work programs that we found:

Workforce Transportation Services
Goodwill Industries of Central Arizona
417 North 16th Street
Phoenix, AZ 85006
602-254-2222
Email: dcrews@goodwillaz.org
www.goodwillaz.org/

Good News Garage
Rockingham Community Action
7 Junkins Ave.
Portsmouth, NH 03801
603-431-2911
Client Access: 800-556-9300
Email: w2@rcaction.org
www.reaction.org

Wabash Valley Goodwill Industries, Inc.
2702 South 3rd Street
P.O. Box 2720
Terre Haute, IN 47802
812-235-1827
Fax: 812-235-1397
Email: office@wvgoodwill.org
http://wvgoodwill.org/wtw1.htm

Goodwill Industries of North Carolina
1235 S. Eugene St.
Greensboro, NC 27406-2393
336-275-9801
Fax: 336-274-1352
Email: kcaughron@goodwill-cnc. org;
www.triadgoodwill.org/

New Leaf Services
3696 Greentree Farms Dr.
Decatur, GA 30034
404-289-9293

Citrus Cars
Polk Works
205 Main Street, Suite 107
Bartow, FL 33830
863-519-0100
www.polkworks.org

Wheelz 2 Work
Bucks County Housing Group, Inc.
2324 2nd Street Pike, Suite 17
Wrightstown, PA 18940
866-WLZ-2WRK, ext. 15
(866-959-2975, ext. 15)
www.wheelz2work.org

Wheels to Work
Monticello Area Community Action Agency

1025 Park Street
Charlottesville, VA 22901
434-295-3171
http://avenue.org/macaa/cars.html

Gift of Wheels
The Arc of Find du Lac
500 North Park Avenue
Fond du Lac, WI 54935
920-923-3810
www.geocities.com/arc_of_fdl/index.htm

Free Bus Passes
Detroit's Suburban Mobility Authority for Regional Transportation (SMART) has a program called "Get a Job/Get a Ride" that gives a month's worth of free rides to anyone in the Detroit area who gets a job. The only requirement is that you started a new job within the last 30 days. New Jersey will give a free one-month pass to those on low income that get a job or are going to training. Check with your local Chamber of Commerce, Transit Authority, or your state Department of Transportation.

Free Seminars on Buying a Car
Don't be intimidated by salesmanship. The dealer wants your money, so they don't want you to leave without signing on the bottom line. Many different organizations and groups offer classes on how to buy a car. Contact your county cooperative extension service, your local adult education department, or women's organizations in your area to see what they may have to offer.

Discounts on Buses, Trains and Subways
If you are a senior citizen, you can usually ride most forms of transportation for about half-price. Amtrak and Greyhound offer discounts of 5-15%. Children even get to take advantage of discount programs, with the youngest group often getting a free ride. Check out these websites: www.amtrak.com; www.greyhound.com. Don't forget to ask about a variety of reduced fare programs, including student and military discounts. Often job training programs will compensate you for your travel, so before you begin training, inquire about support services such as transportation and child care.

Get Free Taxi Rides for Grandma to go to the Doctor
The Eldercare Locator provides access to an extensive network of organizations serving older people at state and local community levels. This service can connect you to information sources for a variety of services including transportation. For more information, contact Eldercare Locator, National Association of Area Agencies on Aging, 1112 16th St., NW, Washington, DC 20024; 800-677-1116 between 9 a.m. and 8 p.m. EST; www.aoa.gov.

$195/Mo for Parking Money
Your employer can give you $100 a month to pay for going to work in a bus, van or metro, or give you $195 a month for parking. You get the money tax free, and the employer gets to take a tax deduction. It's called the *Qualified Transportation Fringe Benefit* or *Transit Benefit Program.* Get a copy of IRS Publication 535, *Business Expenses* and show your boss the section entitled "Qualified Transportation Fringe". The publication is available from your local IRS office or from 800-TAX-FORM or from their web site at www.irs.gov.

Cheap Air Fare to See Sick Relatives
When a family member is very ill or has died, families have to make last minute airline reservations. Obviously you lose out on the 21-day advance purchase rates, but almost all airlines offer *bereavement* or *compassion* fares for domestic travel. Generally the fares are available to close family members, and the discount on the full-fare rate varies from airline to airline. Many require that you provide the name of the deceased and the name, address and phone number of the funeral home handling arrangements. In the case of a medical emergency, the name and address of the affected family member and the name, address and phone number of the attending physician or hospital are required. Contact the airline of your choice to learn more about the "Bereavement/Compassion Fares." Full fare rate varies from airline to airline, but you could save up to 50%.

Free Taxi To Take Your Child to a Doctor's Appointment
The Federal Transit Administration provides over $50 million a year to over 1,000 local organizations to provide free non-emergency transportation for people who are elderly or have a disability. But the groups who get this federal money can also provide free transportation services to moms who are in a jam. The regulations state that the vehicles can also be used to "serve the transportation needs of the general public on an incidental basis." You may have to do some educating to get a local group to give you a ride. Tell them to see Circular FTA C9070, 1D, for Section 5310 Program, Chapter V, Program Management, paragraph 3b. It's available from the U.S. Federal Transit Administration or on the web at www.fta.dot.gov/library/policy/circ9070/chapter5.html. To find groups in your area who receive these FTA Section 5310 Grants for Elderly and Persons With Disabilities, contact your state department of transportation or the U.S. Federal Transit Administration, Office of Program Management, Office of Resource Management and State Programs, 400 7th St., SW, Washington, DC 20590; 202-366-4020; www.fta.dot.gov.

$200+ to Use Your Car
You can deduct:

- 34 1/2 cents per mile if you use your car for business (IRS Publication 463, Travel Entertainment, Gift, and Car Expenses)
- 14 cents per mile if you use your car during charity work (IRS Instructions for Schedule A, Itemized Deductions)
- 12 cents per mile if you use your car for medical care (IRS Instructions for Schedule A, Itemized Deductions)
- 12 cents per mile if you use your car to move to a new job (IRS Publication 521, Moving Expenses)

These publications are free from your local IRS office, by calling 1-800-829-3676 or download from www.irs.gov.

Discounts on Car Rentals
You never should pay full-price for car rentals and there are deals aplenty if you keep your eyes opened. AAA and AARP membership will save you a few bucks, as will many other membership programs. Car rental agencies also often offer discounts to senior citizens. Many times, if you book your flight and car rental at the same time, you can get a discount rate, plus get miles added to your frequent flyer program.

The free brochure, *Renting a Car*, outlines some points to consider and questions to ask when you reserve a rental car. You can learn how to choose a rental car company and understand the terms they use for insurance and charges. Contact Public Reference, Room 130, Federal Trade Commission, Washington, DC 20580; 202-326-2222, 877-FTC-HELP; or online at www.ftc.gov.

Free Child Care for AmeriCorp & Vista Workers
Over $10,000,000 a year is paid out to cover child care services for people working with AmeriCorps or VISTA. These programs allow you to tackle community problems on everything from disaster relief to tutoring. National Service jobs also provide a stipend, housing, and even college money; child care is a bonus. Contact Corporation of National Service, 1201 New York Ave., NW, Washington, DC 20525; 202-606-5000; www.nationalservice.org.

Free Child Care When Training or Looking For a Job
Welfare reform, called ***Temporary Assistance for Needy Families (TANF),*** does more to help people not wind up on welfare. The new program includes free training, education, child care, and transportation assistance necessary to help you obtain employment. Child care is an important part of the program. Eligibility requirements vary from state to state, so contact your TANF office nearest you to learn what options are available to you. For more information, contact Office of Family Assistance, Administration for Children and Families, 370 L'Enfant Promenade, SW, Washington, DC 20447; 202-401-9215; www.acf.dhhs.gov/programs/opa/facts/tanf.htm.

Work for Companies That Offer Free/ Discount Child Care
You may be surprised at the number of daycare centers offering services right inside company office buildings. In fact the federal government may be in the lead as they have over 1,000 child care centers that are sponsored by various governmental agencies. Talk to other moms and dads on the playground, call human resources departments, and even check with your local chamber of commerce. All may be able to direct you to companies providing this benefit. A directory of sites is available for $25 from the Work and Family Connection, 5197 Beachside Dr., Minnetonka, MN 55343; 800-487-7898; www.workfamily.com. Another resource is your local Child Care Resource and Referral Agency, who should be aware of programs in their area. To locate your local referral agency, contact Child Care Aware, 1319 F Street, NW, Suite 500, Washington, DC 20004; 800-424-2246, www.childcareaware.org. Besides child care centers, some employers offer a dependent care assistance plan that allows you to pay for child care out of pre-tax dollars. Other employers offer direct subsidies to offset child care costs.

$2,500 to Help Pay for an Adoption
The National Adoption Foundation (NAF) is a national nonprofit organization dedicated to providing financial support, information, and services for adoptive and prospective adoptive families. They recently announced the expansion of its programs to include home equity loans, as well as unsecured loans and grants for adoption expenses. A grant program to cover adoption expenses is also available on a limited basis for prospective adoptive parents.

Other sources of money for adoption include:

- Ask your employer for employee adoption assistance benefits. Approximately 65 percent of Fortune 500 companies now offer some kind of adoption benefit.

- Take advantage of the new adoption expense tax credit in advance by modifying your income tax withholding to reflect your tax savings when you file your return. This frees up cash for adoption expenses due now.

Contact National Adoption Foundation, 100 Mill Plain Rd., Danbury, CT 06811; 203-791-3811; Fax: 203-791-3801; Email: info@nafadopt.org; www.nafadopt.org/default.asp. To download an application: www.nafadopt.org/pdf/adoption.pdf.

Free Credit Repair

Here are some of the free reports you can get from the Federal Trade Commission dealing with free credit repair:

- *Credit Repair: Self-Help May Be The Best*
- *Knee Deep in Debt*
- *How To Dispute Credit Reporting Errors*
- *How To Deal With Credit Problems*
- *Credit Scoring*

For your copies, contact Consumer Response Center, 600 Pennsylvania Ave., NW, H-130, Federal Trade Commission, Washington, DC 20580; 202-326-2222; 877-FTC-HELP; www.ftc.gov.

The following nonprofit and government organizations provide free, or low-fee credit counseling services. You can contact them to find the office nearest you. Some of these offices are financed by the bank and credit card industry, who are biased toward having you pay all your bills without using the bankruptcy option. So be sure that they explain your bankruptcy options.

- ***National Foundation for Credit Counseling***, 801 Roeder Road, Suite 900, Silver Spring, MD 20910; 301-589-5600; www.nfcc.org
- Free internet credit counseling services from the nonprofit organization, ***Credit Counseling Center of America***, P.O. Box 830489, Richardson, TX 75083-0489; 800-493-2222; www.ccamerica.org
- ***County Cooperative Extension Service***: to find your local office, see the blue pages of your phone book.

$100 to Pay Your Heating Bill

The state of Michigan offers a home heating bill tax credit (that means you pay less in taxes) for people who are low income, receiving public assistance or unemployment. Call your state department of taxation to learn about tax credits available to you. Michigan Department of Treasury, Lansing, MI 48956; 800-487-7000; www.michigan.gov/treasury. To download a 2-page form: www.michigan.gov/documents/MI_1040CR7_81085_7.pdf.

Free Voice Mail Services

If you are unemployed and the phone company cut off your phone, how does a potential employer get in touch with you? Free voice mail. You can get set up with your own personalized greeting, as well as get a security code and instructions on how you can retrieve your messages 24 hours a day. The program is available in over 34 cities and is growing. See if you're eligible for your area by contacting Community Technology Institute, P2901 Third Avenue, Suite 100, Seattle, WA 98121; 206-441-7872; Fax: 206-443-3755; www.cvm.org.

Free Directory Assistance
Directory assistance can cost up to 95 cents per request and an additional 50 cents for the connection. To assist persons with visual, hearing, or other disabilities, local telephone companies offer directory and operator assistance exemptions. Simply request and complete a form from the local telephone company and have your physician complete the appropriate section. When you return the form to the phone company, you'll be eligible for the exemptions. Contact the business office of your local telephone company.

$400/wk When You're Out of Work
Mass lay-offs, base closings, trade agreements, and high unemployment in your state, all affect your ability to find and keep a job. If you are out of work, take advantage of unemployment insurance. All states are required to provide benefits up to 26 weeks and some extend them further. If your state has very high unemployment, you may be eligible for 13 additional weeks of compensation. If you lost your job because of an increase in imports, you may qualify to have your benefits extended up to an extra 52 weeks if you are in a job-retraining program. Your weekly benefit amount depends upon your past wages within certain minimum and maximum limits that vary from state to state. Many states also will add additional funds depending upon the number of dependents. If you are denied benefits, learn about the appeal process, as your chances of winning are good. Contact your state Unemployment Insurance office listed in the blue pages of your phone book.

$700 for Your Utility Bills
The legislature in Massachusetts passed a law giving discounts up to $700 on heating bills for families making up to $30,000, along with up to 40% discount on electric bills, $108 off telephone bills, and $100 off oil bills. It's in the Massachusetts Budget for FY 99 (Line Item 4403-2110). Also:

- **Phoenix, Arizona** offers discounts on utility bills, discounts on phone bills and even help paying utility deposits and heating repairs for low-income residents through the Arizona Public Service Energy Support Program, P.O. Box 53999, Phoenix, AZ 85072-3999; 800-253-9406; 602-371-7171; www.aps.com.
- **Ameritech in Illinois** gives a 50% plus $10 discount on connection charges and $6.25 off the monthly bill to low-income residents. To sign up, call Ameritech at 888-256-5378; www.ameritech.com.
- **Ohio** offers reduced or free phone hook up service and possibly $8.00 a month off your phone bill for low-income residents. Contact Public Utilities Commission, 180 E. Broad St., Columbus, OH 43215; 800-686-7826; www.puco.ohio.gov/Consumer/PIC/assistance.html.

Contact your state's utilities office in the blue pages of your phone book to find out about special discounts on your gas, electric, cable or telephone in your state.

Free Private Eye to Find Missing Children
Besides location and investigative services, as well as mediation services for families estranged by parental abduction, you can also get free kidnapping prevention programs and referral and support services. Contact Find-A-Child of America, Inc., P.O. Box 277, New Paltz, NY 12561; 800-I-AM-LOST; 914-255-1848; 800-A-WAY-OUT (for mediation and support); www.childfindofamerica.org.

$1,000 While You Wait For Gov't Money
General Public Assistance or just Public Assistance is a welfare program offered in 42 states. This is a program of last resort for people either waiting to qualify for other government programs such as

disability benefits, or who do not qualify for any programs, yet need money to live. The program eligibility and benefit levels vary within and across state lines. In some states, this benefit is only available in certain areas. There are strict income and asset levels that you must meet to qualify. Contact your local welfare office, your state Department of Social Service, or your state Temporary Assistance to Needy Families office to see what your state offers and the eligibility requirements.

Ca$h for Sharing What You Know

Retired Senior Volunteer Program matches the personal interests and skills of older Americans with opportunities to help solve community problems. RSVP volunteers choose how and where they want to serve - from a few to over 40 hours a week. RSVP makes it easy for older adults to find the types of volunteer service opportunities that appeal to them. RSVP volunteers tutor children in reading and math, help to build houses, help get children immunized, model parenting skills to teen parents, participate in neighborhood watch programs, plan community gardens, deliver meals, offer disaster relief to victims of natural disasters, and help community organizations operate more efficiently. Volunteers receive supplemental insurance while on duty, and receive on-the-job training. Contact National Senior Service Corps, 1201 New York Ave., NW, Washington, DC 20525; 202-606-5000; 800-424-8867; www.seniorcorps.org.

$3,000 While Helping Others

Foster Grandparents devote their volunteer service to one population: children with special or exceptional needs. Across the country, Foster Grandparents are offering emotional support to child victims of abuse and neglect, tutoring children who lag behind in reading, mentoring troubled teenagers and young mothers, and caring for premature infants and children with physical disabilities and severe illnesses. If you meet certain income guidelines and are 60 or older, you may be eligible for this program. You will receive a modest tax free stipend to offset the cost of volunteering, and are reimbursed for transportation, some meals, an annual physical and accident and liability insurance. Contact National Senior Service Corps, 1201 New York Ave., NW, Washington, DC 20525; 800-424-8867; 202-606-5000; www.seniorcorps.org.

Cash for Helping Fellow Seniors

Senior Companions reach out to adults, who need extra assistance to live independently in their own homes or communities. Senior Companions assist their adult clients with in basic but essential ways: they provide companionship and friendship to isolated frail seniors, assist with simple chores, provide transportation, and add richness to their clients' lives. Senior Companions serve frail older adults and their caregivers, adults with disabilities, and those with terminal illnesses. If you meet certain income guidelines and are 60 or older, you may be eligible for this program. You will receive a modest tax free stipend to offset the cost of volunteering, and are reimbursed for transportation, some meals, an annual physical and accident and liability insurance. Contact National Senior Service Corps, 1201 New York Ave., NW, Washington, DC 20525; 800-424-8867; 202-606-5000; www.seniorcorps.org.

Money to Pay Employees At Your Nonprofit

Do you need people to work for your nonprofit, but don't have the budget? There are several agencies within the Federal government which provides staffing for a variety agencies. To register your organization for workers paid by the government, contact the Corporation for National and Community

Service. They have several programs such as AmeriCorps and the Senior Corps that train and pay for volunteers to serve in a variety of public service agencies. In partnership with nonprofit groups, faith-based organizations, schools, and other public agencies, participants in these programs tutor children, build and renovate homes, provide immunizations and health screenings, clean up and preserve the environment, serve on neighborhood crime-prevention patrols, and respond to disasters. Contact Corporation for National and Community Service, 1201 New York Ave., NW, Washington, DC 20525; 202-606-5000; 877-USACORPS; www.nationalservice.org.

Money & Help for Those Who Served

The U.S. Department of Veterans Affairs hotline can provide you with information on such programs as life insurance, comprehensive dental and medical care, nursing homes, home loan programs, burial services, and more. In addition each state offers some additional benefits which could be free license plates, free or reduced hunting and fishing licenses, and more. Contact U.S. Department of Veterans Affairs, 810 Vermont Ave., NW, Washington, DC 20420; 800-827-1000; www.va.gov. For a link to each state's veteran services, check out www.nasdva.com.

Free Fans

Fan Care is a great program sponsored by Virginia Power. If you are a resident of Virginia and 60 or older, you may be eligible for a free fan to help you make it safely through the hot summer. Fans are distributed through the local Area Agencies on Aging. To learn about eligibility requirements, contact Fan Care, Department for the Aging, 1600 Forest Ave., Suite 102, Richmond, VA 23229; 800-552-3402; 804-662-9333. For those outside of Virginia, contact your state Department of Aging or your state utility commission, both listed in the Appendix to see what they have to offer.

Free Help Finding Lost Loved Ones

When a loved one disappears, those left behind struggle and often spend thousands trying to locate their missing person. The Salvation Army received over 35,000 requests for assistance, and was able to trace over 10,000 missing persons. To learn more about the services offered contact the Salvation Army Office near you, or Salvation Army National Headquarters, 615 Slaters Lane, P.O. Box 269, Alexandria, VA 22313; 703-684-5500; www.salvationarmyusa.org.

Pay Your Bills While You Become An Entrepreneur

It is a dream for many people to own their own business, but often money is a concern. There are different programs to help you pay your bills while you start your business or go through microenterprise training. This applies even if you are receiving Temporary Assistance for Needy Families (TANF), as TANF funds can be used to support you while you are being trained or starting your business. Contact your state TANF office to see what programs are available in your area. You can also learn about other microenterprise programs by contacting your state economic development office. For other resources and to locate programs in your area, contact:

- Center for Law and Social Policy, 1015 15th St., NW, Suite 400, Washington, DC 20005; 202-906-8000; www.clasp.org. See Microenterprise Development and Self-Employment for TANF Recipients in the publications section.
- The Aspen Institute, One Dupont Circle, NW, Suite 700, Washington, DC 20036; 202-736-1071; http://fieldus.org/ directory.
- Association for Enterprise Opportunity, 1601 N. Kent St., Suite 101, Arlington, VA 22209; 703-841-7760; www.microenterpriseworks.org.

Money Matters

Money matters never go away, they may even be more crucial as we get older. The Department of Health & Human Services Administration on Aging offers Money Matters, a resource for seniors to sort out their money matters. Contact: Administration on Aging, Washington, DC 20201; 202-619-0724, www.aoa.gov/eldfam/Money_Matters/Money_Matters.asp.

Social Security Manager

If you are having trouble managing your Social Security benefits and need help, you can get a "representative payee" to help. The Social Security Administration can appoint a friend, relative or other third party to serve as your "Representative Payee". Your benefits would be paid directly to the payee and they would help you pay the bills and manage your money. Any money left over after your needs are met would be saved for you by the payee. The payee is appointed to only oversee Social Security funds. Many people use "power of attorney" to handle financial needs. Social Security does not recognize "power of attorney" to handle Social Security funds. Contact: Social Security Administration, Office of Public Inquiry, Windsor Park Building, 6401 Security Boulevard, Baltimore, MD 21235; 800-772-1213; www.ssa.gov/payee/.

Get $250 From A Missing Utility Deposit

Well maybe not a fortune but maybe a forgotten bank account from college. The National Association of Unclaimed Property Administrators helps connect you and your unclaimed property in any of the 50 states or the District of Columbia. The National Association of Unclaimed Property Administrator's web site can link you to your state's unclaimed web site or you can search their database at www.missingmoney.org. All of the searches are free so check it out to see if there is money out there for you or a loved one. Contact: National Association of Unclaimed Property Administrators, www.unclaimed.org.

Help to Fight Your Bank

Finding the right bank, savings and loan, or credit union means figuring out your own needs first. How much money can you keep on deposit and how many checks will you write? Examine your future loans and savings needs, as well as look at the convenience of the financial institution, its service charges, fees, and deposit and loan interest rates. You can contact one of the following offices to learn more. These offices will also help you if you think the bank is messing with your money.

National Banks (banks that have the word "National" in their names or the initials "N.A." after their names)
Comptroller of the Currency
U.S. Department of the Treasury
Customer Assistance group
1301 McKinner St.
Suite 3450
Houston, TX 77010
202-874-4700
800-613-6743
Email: customer.assistance@occ.treas.gov
www.occ.treas.gov/customer.htm

FDIC-Insured Banks
Office of Consumer Affairs
Federal Deposit Insurance Corporation
550 17th St., NW
Washington, DC 20429-9990
202-942-3147
877-275-3342
www.fdic.gov

Savings and Loans
Office of Thrift Suspension
U.S. Department of treasury
1700 G St., NW
Washington, DC 20552
202-906-6237
800-842-6929
www.ots.treas.gov

State Banks
Contact your State Government Banking Commission located in your state capital (look in the blue pages of your phone book or contact your state capital operator).

Help Fighting Age Discrimination

There's no need to take harassment or bullying on the job. Here is your chance to fight back. If you believe you have been discriminated against by an employer, labor union, or employment agency when applying for a job or while on the job because of age, disability, race, color, sex, religion, or national origin, you may file a charge with the Equal Employment Opportunity Commission (EEOC). For more information, contact: Equal Employment Opportunity Commission, 1801 L St., NW, Washington, DC 20507; 202-663-4900; 800-669-4000; www.eeoc.gov.

Fight Lawyers, Accountants, Pharmacists, Doctors, Real Estate Agents and Other Professionals

Lawyer over-charging you? Do you feel you have been mistreated by your doctor? These issues and more are handled by the agency or board that licenses that particular profession. Whether it is your accountant, real estate agent, doctor, dentist, or other professional, you can contact the licensing board directly to file a grievance. These boards will then help you to resolve the problem. To locate the correct board, usually located in your state capital, contact your state operator.

How an Abuser Can Discover Your Internet Activities

The American Bar Association's Commission on Domestic Violence has issued a warning concerning possible threats to you if an abuser has access to your email account and thus may be able to read your incoming and outgoing mail. If you believe your account is secure, make sure you choose a password he or she will not be able to guess. If an abuser sends you threatening or harassing email messages, they may be printed and saved as evidence of this abuse. Additionally, the message may constitute a federal offense. For more information on this issue, contact your local Unite States Attorney's Office. For more information on how to protect yourself, and the efforts of the ABA's Commission on Domestic Violence, please contact: American Bar Association Commission on Domestic Violence, 740 15th St., NW, 9th Floor, Washington, DC, 20005-1022; 202-662-1737/1744; Fax: 202-662-1594; Email: cdv@staff.abanet.org; www.abanet.org/domviol/cdv.html.

Free Help in Writing a Will

Estate planning is not something that people often relish doing, but it is extremely important. It is difficult enough when a loved one dies, but then to have to search through papers trying to find information about insurance or investments is often too much. When children are involved, estate planning is essential. Who will take care of them and how can you secure their financial future? Local Cooperative Extension Services often offer classes or publications on estate planning, living wills, and financial planning. The time to plan ahead is now. Look in the blue pages of your phone book for the nearest Cooperative Extension Office, as they are now in almost every county across the country.

Free Legal Help to Fight Car Dealers and Repair Shops

When you can't get satisfaction from the manager or owner, then it is time to bring in the big guns:

- Your state attorney general's office is set up to handle automobile complaints. Sometimes all you have to do is send a letter to the attorney general with a copy to the business owner.
- Automotive Consumer Action Program (AUTOCAP) is a complaint handling system sponsored by the automobile industry for new or used car purchases from NEW car dealers only. To find a source in your area contact: National Automobile Dealers Association, 8400 Westpark Drive, McLean, VA 22102; 703-821-7000; 800-252-6232; www.nada.org.
- Better Business Bureau (BBB) Auto Line is a FREE, out of court arbitration program paid for by the business community to handle automobile complaints between consumers and most auto manufacturers. Contact your local Better Business Bureau or BBB Auto Line, Dispute Resolution Division, Council of Better Business Bureaus Inc., 4200 Wilson Blvd., Suite 800, Arlington, VA 22202-1838; 703-276-0100; 800-955-5100; Fax: 703-525-8277; www.dr.bbb.org/autoline.

Fight Retailers, Mail Order Companies, Auto Dealers, Contractors, etc.

You go to a store to get the best price on a gift for Uncle George, only to learn that the store is out of stock despite the product being advertised in the paper. Did the salesperson try to get you to buy a higher priced item? You could be a victim of the old bait and switch scam. Is the paint peeling off of the new toy doll you bought your daughter? Problems dealing with your car dealership or car repair shop? (This is the number one complaint heard). What about the contractor that has yet to finish the job? There are ways to deal with all these problems and get them resolved to your satisfaction. You just need to pull in the big guns. The States' Attorney General's Offices have Consumer Protection Offices, and many also have separate offices that handle only car complaints. They will take your complaint and try to help you get the satisfaction you deserve. For other problems contact:

- Defective Products - contact Consumer Product Safety Commission, 4330 East-West Highway, Bethesda, MD 20814-4408; 800-638-2772; 301-504-7923.
- Contractor or Licensed Professional Problems – contact the state Licensing Board for that profession located in your state capital. You can contact the state operator for assistance in finding the office.

- Mail Order Problems – Contact the U.S. Postal Service, Criminal Investigations Service center, Attn: Mail Fraud, 222 S. Riverside Plaza, Suite 1250, Chicago, IL 60606-6100; www.usps.gov/postalinspectors/fraud/welcome.htm.
- Fraud Issues – contact the Federal Trade Commission, Consumer Response Center, 600 Pennsylvania Ave., NW, Washington, DC 20580; 877-FTC-HELP; www.ftc.gov.

Lawyer's Referral Service

The American Bar Association's Lawyer Referral Service is designed to assist you in finding the appropriate service-provider to help you solve your legal problem. There are two steps to this process: first, helping you determine whether you need to see a lawyer, and second, referring you to a lawyer who handles your type of case or to an appropriate community or governmental agency if that will be of more help to you. Lawyer referral can also provide you with information on procedures in the courts and legal system in your community. When you contact Lawyer Referral, be prepared to briefly describe your situation so that the consultant can determine what kind of help you need. Lawyer Referral does not offer legal advice or free legal services. If you are referred to an attorney, you are entitled to a half-hour initial consultation at no charge, or for a nominal fee that goes to fund the Lawyer Referral Service's operation. If additional legal services are required, you may choose to hire the lawyer. It is important to discuss legal fees and costs with the lawyer. We strongly recommend that you and the lawyer sign a written fee agreement, so that there is no question about what services the lawyer will perform, and what those services will cost you. For more information on the Lawyer's Referral Service contact your state Bar Association; The American Bar Association, 321 North Clark Street, Chicago, IL 60610, 312-988-5000; or The American Bar Association, 740 15th St., NW, Washington, DC 20005-1019; 202-662-1000; Email: info@abanet.org; www.abanet,org.

When All Else Fails

People forget that they can turn to their representative or senators for help resolving a complaint. You vote these people into office, and most of them want to stay there. They know that if they can help you, then you and your family will vote for them in each and every election. Their offices have case managers whose job is to cut through red-tape and push your case through quickly. Look in your phone book for their local office or you can contact: U.S. House of Representatives, Washington, DC 20515; 202-224-3121; www.house.gov or U.S. Senate, Washington, DC 20510; 202-224-3121; www.senate.gov.

Up To $10,700/Yr If You Can't Work Because Of A Disability

You must have worked in a job covered by Social Security and have a medical condition covered by Social Security's definition of a disability that can keep you out of work for at least one year. There is no income limitation for this program. You just must be unable to work. To apply 1-800-772-1213 or go to www.ssa.gov/applyfordisability/adult.htm

3.5 Million Families Can Get A Check for Up To $4,300

That's how many people are eligible for this but don't apply. It's called a tax credit, but it is really a grant. It's extra money the IRS will give you that's better than a refund because they will give it to you even if you don't pay any taxes. You just have to have some income, and the less income you have the bigger the check you get. You can make up to $35,458 and still be eligible. Get the free publication called IRS Publication 596, Earned Income Tax Credit by calling 1–800–829–3676 or go to www.irs.gov/pub/irs-pdf/p596.pdf. Free tax services are available for incomes up to $35,000 from a service called Volunteer Income Tax Assistance (VITA). To find your local VITA program contact your local public library or your Congressman's office at www.congress.org. You can also try the IRS hotline at 1-800-TAX-1040; or see www.irs.gov/individuals/article/0,,id=119845,00.html.

Free Help Fighting an Electric Bill or Stopping a Turn Off

The state utility commissions can help you fight high gas or electric bills. Some will even come out and make sure that your meter is not over charging you. They don't have money to pay your bills, but they can negotiate payment arrangements with the company for you or suggest nonprofit organizations to help. For example, Maryland suggests the Fuel Fund for Central Maryland or the Maryland Energy Assistance program. The commission can also force the utility not to cut off your services because of medical emergencies or cold weather. For more information on how the state utility commission can help you, contact your state office from the list below.

State Utility Commission Offices

Alabama
Public Service Commission
PO Box 304260
Montgomery, AL 36130
800-392-8050 (toll free in state)
Fax: 334-242-0727
www.psc.state.al.us

Alaska
Regulatory Commission of Alaska
701 W 8th Ave., Suite 300
Anchorage, AK 99501
907-276-6222
800-390-2782 (toll free in state)
TDD: 907-276-4533
Fax: 907-276-0160
Email: cp_rca@rca.state.ak.us
www.state.ak.us/rca

Arizona
Arizona Corporation Commission
1200 West Washington St.
Phoenix, AZ 85007
602-542-3933
800-222-7000) toll free in state)
TDD: 602-542-2105
Fax: 602-542-5560
Email: mailmaster@cc.state.az.us
www.cc.state.az.us

Arkansas
Public Service Commission
PO Box 400
Little Rock, AR 72203-0400
501-682-2051
800-482-1164 (complaints- toll free in state)
TDD: 800-682-2898
Fax: 501-682-5731
www.state.ar.us/psc

California
Public Utilities Commission
505 Van Ness Ave., Room 5218
San Francisco, CA 94102
415-703-2782
800-649-7570 (Utility Complaints- toll free in state)
TDD: 415-703-2032
Fax: 415-703-1758
www.cpuc.ca.gov

Colorado
Chairman
Public Utilities Commission
1580 Logan St., Office Level 2
Denver, CO 80203
303-894-2070
800-456-0855 (toll free in state)
TDD: 303-894-2512
Fax: 303-894-2065
Email: PUConsumer.Complaints@dora.state.co.us
www.dora.state.co.us/puc/

Connecticut
Department of Public Utility Control
10 Franklin Square
New Britain, CT 06051
860-827-1553
800-382-4586 (toll free in state)
TDD: 860-827-2837
Fax: 860-827-2613
www.state.ct.us/dpuc

Delaware
Commissioner
Public Service Commission
Cannon Bldg. Suite 100
861 Silver Lake Blvd.
Dover, DE 19904
302-739-4247
800-282-8574 (toll free in state)
TDD: 302-739-4333
Fax: 302-739-4849
www.state.de.us/delpsc

District of Columbia
Public Service Commission
1333 H Street, NW
Suite 200, West Tower;
Washington, DC 20005
202-626-5100 (Consumer Services Division)
Fax: 202-393-1389
Email: support@dcpsc.org
www.dcpsc.org

Florida
Chairman
Florida Public Service Commission
2540 Shumard Oak Blvd.
Tallahassee, FL 32399-0850
850-413-6330
800-342-3552 (toll free in state)
TDD/TTY: 800-955-8771
Fax: 800-511-0809
Email: contact@psc.state.fl.us
www.floridapsc.com

Georgia
Chairperson
Public Service Commission
244 Washington Street
Atlanta, GA 30334
404-656-4501
800-282-5813 (toll free in state)
Fax: (404)656-2341
Email: gapsc@psc.state.ga.us
www.psc.state.ga.us

Hawaii
Public Utilities Commission
465 South King St., Room 103
Honolulu, HI 96813
808-586-2020
Fax: 808-586-2066
Email: Hawaii.PUC@hawaii.gov
www.hawaii.gov/budget/puc

Idaho
President
Public Utilities Commission
PO Box 83720
Boise, ID 83720-0074
208-334-0300
800-432-0369 (toll free in state)
Voice/TDD: 800-337-1363
TDD: 800-377-3529
Fax: 208-334-3762
www.puc.state.id.us

Illinois
Chairman
Commerce Commission
527 East Capitol Ave.
P.O. Box 19280
Springfield, IL 62794-9280
217-782-7295
800-524-0795 (toll free in state)
TTY: 800-858-9277
Fax: 217-524-6859
www.icc.state.il.us

Indiana
Utility Regulatory Commission
Consumer Affairs Division
302 West Washington St.
Suite E-306
Indianapolis, IN 46204
317-232-2712
800-851-4268 (toll free in state)
TDD: 317-232-8556
Fax: 317-233-2410
Email: jjohnson@urc.state.in.us
www.IN.gov/iurc

Iowa
Iowa Utilities Board
350 Maple St.
Des Moines, IA 50319-0069
515-281-3839
877-565-4450 (toll free in state)
Fax: 515-281-5329
Email: iubcustomer@iub.state.ia.us
www.state.ia.us/iub

Kansas
Corporation Commission
1500 SW Arrowhead Rd.
Topeka, KS 66604-4027
785-271-3100
800-662-0027 (toll free in state)
TDD: 800-766-3777
Fax: 785-271--3354
Email: public.affairs@kcc.state.ks.us
www.kcc.state.ks.us

Kentucky
Public Service Commission
211 Sower Blvd.
P.O. Box 615
Frankfort, KY 40602
502-564-3940
800-772-4636 (complaints only- toll free in state)
TDD/TTY: 800-648-6056
Fax: 502-564-3460
www.psc.state.ky.us

Louisiana
Public Service Commission
PO Box 91154
Baton Rouge, LA 70821-9154
225-342-4404
800-256-2397 (toll free in state)
Fax: 225-342-2831
www.lpsc.org

Maine
Chairman
Public Utilities Commission
242 State St.
Augusta, ME 04333-0018
207-287-3831
800-452-4699 (toll free in state)
TTY: 800-437-1220
Fax: 207-287-1039
Email: maine.puc@maine.gov
www.state.me.us/mpuc

Maryland
Chairman
Public Service Commission
6 St. Paul St., 16th Floor
Baltimore, MD 21202-6806
410-767-8000
800-492-0474 (toll free in state)
TDD: 800-735-2258
Fax: 410-333-6495
Email: mpsc@psc.state.md.us
www.psc.state.md.us/psc

Massachusetts
Chairman
Dept. of Telecommunications and Energy
1 South Station, 12th Floor
Boston, MA 02110
617-305-3500
800-392-6066 (toll free in state)
TDD: 800-323-6066
Fax: 617-478-2591
www.magnet.state.ma.us/dpu

Michigan
Public Service Commission
6545 Mercantile Way, Suite 7
P.O. Box 30221
Lansing, MI 48909
517-241-6180
800-292-9555 (toll free in state)
Fax: 517-241-6181
Email: mpsc_commissioners@michigan.gov
www.michigan.gov/mpsc

Minnesota
Chairman
Public Utilities Commission
121 7th Place East, Suite 350
St. Paul, MN 55101-2147
651-296-0406
800-657-3782
TDD: 651-297-1200
Fax: 651-297-7073
Email: consumer.puc@state.mn.us
www.puc.state.mn.us

Mississippi
Mississippi Public Service Commission
Woolfolk Building
501 N West St.
Jackson, MS 39201
601-961-5440 (Southern District)
601-961-5430 (Central District)
601-961-5450 (Chairman & Northern District)
800-356-6429 (Southern District)
800-356-6430 (Central District)
800-637-7722 (Chairman & Northern District)
Fax: 601-961-5464 (Chairman & Northern District)
www.psc.state.ms.us

Missouri
Missouri Public Service Commission
P.O. Box 360
Jefferson City, MO 65102
573-751-3234
800-392-4211(toll free in state)
Fax: 573-526-1500
www.psc.mo.gov

Montana
Chairman
Public Service Commission
1701 Prospect Ave.
P.O. Box 202601
Helena, MT 59620-2601
406-444-6199
800-646-6150(toll free in state)
TDD: 406-444-6199

Fax: 406-444-7618
www.psc.state.mt.us

Nebraska
Chairman
Public Service Commission
300 The Atrium, 1200 N St.
P.O. Box 94927 (68508-4927)
Lincoln, NE 68509
402-471-3101
800-526-0017(toll free in state)
TDD: 402-471-0213
Fax: 402-471-0254
Email: celton@mail.state.ne.us
www.psc.state.ne.us

Nevada
Chairman
Public Utilities Commission
1150 East William St.
Carson City, NV 89701
775-687-6001
702-486-2600 (Las Vegas)
775-738-4914 (Elko)
800-992-0900 ext 87-6001 (toll free in state)
Fax: 775-687-6110
www.puc.state.nv.us

New Hampshire
21 South Fruit St, Suite 10
Bldg. No. 1
Concord, NH 03301-2429
603-271-2431
800-735-2964(toll free in state)
Fax: 603-271-3878
Email: www.puc.nh.gov
www.puc.state.nh.us

New Jersey
President
Board of Public Utilities
Two Gateway Center
Newark, NJ 07102
800-624-0241(toll free in state)
www.bpu.state.nj.us

New Mexico
Director
Public Regulation Commission
Consumer Relations Division
P.O. Drawer 1269
Santa Fe, NM 87504-1269
505-827-6940
800-663-9782(toll free in state)
800-947-4722(toll free in state)
TDD: 505-827-6911
Fax: 505-827-6973
Email: BarbaraA.Roel@state.nm.us
www.nmprc.state.nm.us

New York
Director
Public Service Commission
Office of Retail Market Development
3 Empire State Plaza
Albany, NY 12223-1350
518-474-1540
877-342-3377 - Complaints (complaints - gas, electric, telephone)
888-ASK-PSCI (275-7721) - PSC Competition Information
866-GRN-PWR (476-7697) - Green Power Information
Fax: 518-474-1691
Email: ronald_cerniglia@dps.state.ny.us
www.dps.state.ny.us

North Carolina
Consumer Services
4326 Mail Service Center
Raleigh, NC 27699-4326
919-733-9277
Fax: 919-733-4744
Email: consumer.services@ncmail.net
www.ncuc.commerce.state.nc.us

North Dakota
Public Service Commission
600 E. Boulevard Ave., Dept 408
12th Floor
Bismarck, ND 58505-0480
701-328-2400
800-366-6888 (toll free in state)
Fax: 701-328-2410
Email: ndpsc@psc.state.nd.us
www.psc.state.nd.us

Ohio
Public Utilities Commission
180 East Broad St.
Columbus, OH 43215-3793
614-466-3292
800-686-7826 (toll free in state)
TDD: 800-686-1570 (toll free in state)
Fax: 614-752-8351
www.puc.state.oh.us

Oklahoma
Oklahoma Corporation Commission
P.O. Box 52000
Oklahoma City, OK 73152-2000
405-521-2211

800-522-8154 (toll free in state)
TDD: 405-521-3513
Fax: 405-521-2087
www.occeweb.com

Oregon
Consumer Services Division
550 Capitol St., NE, Suite 215
P.O. Box 2148
Salem, OR 97308-2148
503-378-6600
800-522-2404 (consumer services only-toll free in state)
800-553-9600 (toll free in state)
Fax: 503-378-5743
Email: puc.consumer@state.or.us
www.puc.state.or.us

Pennsylvania
Public Utilities Commission
P.O. Box 3265
Harrisburg, PA 17105-3265
717-783-7349
800-782-1110 (toll free in state)
Fax: 717-787-5813
www.puc.state.pa.us

Puerto Rico
Chairman
Public Service Commission
PO Box 190870
San Juan, PR 00919-0817
787-756-1425
Fax: 787-758-3418

Rhode Island
Public Utilities Commission
89 Jefferson Boulevard
Warwick, RI 02888
401-941-4500
TDD: 401-277-3500
Fax: 401-941-4885
www.ripuc.org

South Carolina
Consumer Services Dept.
P.O. Box 11263
Columbia, SC 29211
803-737-5230
800-922-1531 (toll free in state)
TDD: 800-735-2905 (toll free in state)
www.regulatorystaff.sc.gov

South Dakota
Public Utilities Commission
Consumer Affairs
500 East Capitol Ave.
Pierre, SD 57501-5070
605-773-3201
800-332-1782 (consumer affairs only)
Fax: 605-773-3809
www.state.sd.us/puc/puc.htm

Tennessee
Chairman
Tennessee Regulatory Authority
460 James Robertson Pkwy.
Nashville, TN 37243-0505
615-741-8953
800-342-8359
TDD/TTY: 888-276-0677
Fax: 615-741-5015
www.state.tn.us/tra

Texas
Public Utilities Commission
1701 North Congress Ave.
P.O. Box 13326
Austin, TX 78711-3326
512-936-7000
888-PUC-TIPS (toll free)
TDD/TTY: 512-9367136
Fax: 512-936-7003
Email: customer@puc.state.tx.us
www.puc.state.tx.us

Utah
Chairman
Public Service Commission
160 East 300 South
Salt Lake City, UT 84111
801-530-6716
800-874-0904 (toll free in state)
TDD: 801-530-6716
Fax: 801-530-6796
Email: psccal@utah.gov
www.psc.state.ut.us

Vermont
Public Service Board
112 State St., Drawer 20
Montpelier, VT 05620-2701
802-828-2358
800-253-0191 (toll free in state)
Fax: 802-828-3351
Email: clerk@psb.state.vt.us
www.state.vt.us/psb

Virginia
State Corporation Commission
P.O. Box 1197

Richmond, VA 23218
804-371-9967
800-552-7945 (toll free in state)
TDD: 804-371-9206
Fax: 804-371-9211
www.state.va.us/scc

Washington
Utilities and Transportation Commission
1300 S. Evergreen Park Dr., SW
Olympia, WA 98504
360-664-1173
800-562-6150 (toll free in state)
TTY: 360-586-8203
Fax: 360-586-1150
www.wutc.wa.gov

West Virginia
Public Service Commission
201 Brooks St.
Charleston, WV 25301
304-340-0300
800-344-5113 (toll free in state)
Fax: 304-340-0325
www.psc.state.wv.us

Wisconsin
Consumer Affairs Program Director
Public Service Commission
Consumer Affairs Unit
610 North Whitney Way (53705)
P.O. Box 7854
Madison, WI 53707-7854
608-266-2001
800-225-7729
TDD: 608-267-1479
Fax: 608-266-3957
Email: jackie.reynolds@psc.state.wi.us
http://psc.wi.gov

Wyoming
Public Service Commission
2515 Warren Ave., Suite 300
Cheyenne, WY 82002
307-777-7427
888-570-9905 (toll free in state)
TTY: 307-777-7427
Fax: 307-777-5700
http://psc.state.wy.us

Grants From The IRS

The IRS Will Send 3.5 Million Families a Check for Up To $4,300, If They Only Ask*

It's not really a grant, but it looks like a grant, it walks like a grant and it even smells like a grant. They are called tax credits. It's extra money the IRS will give you that's better than a refund because they will give it to you even if you don't pay any taxes. You just have to have some income and the less income you have the bigger the check you get. You can make up to $35,458 and still be eligible.

Free Publications

IRS Publication 596, Earned Income Tax Credit
Call: 1–800–829–3676
Download: http://www.irs.gov/pub/irs-pdf/p596.pdf

This is just one grant from the IRS that millions are missing. The following items will show you more, but don't stop with this book, and don't hire a high priced accountant or lawyer. Use the free tax services listed below or contact your Congressman or Senators' offices to find more free tax services in your area. To locate the offices go to www.govengine.gov or www.congress.org. You can also contact them at U.S. House of Representatives, Washington, DC 20515; 202-224-3121; www.house.gov; Senate, Washington, DC 20510; 202-224-3121; www.senate.gov.

1) ***Free Tax Services***
Don't pay professional tax preparers money when you can have an income up to $35,000 or even more as you can get your taxes prepared for free. No matter what your income, check if the services in your area can help you. The service is called Volunteer Income Tax Assistance (VITA). To find your local VITA program contact your local public library or your Congressman's office at www.congress.org. You can also try the IRS hotline at 1-800-TAX-1040; or see www.irs.gov/individuals/.

2) ***Free Legal Help With Tax Problems***
Families can have incomes up to $50,000, or more even, and get free lawyers to solve their tax problem. There are over 115 Low Income Taxpayer Clinics (LITC) that will help you with legal problems for free. You should check the availability of services in your area no matter what your income is. To find a clinic near you, contact your local public library or your Congressman's office at www.congress.org. You can also try the IRS hotline at 1-800-TAX-1040; or see http://www.irs.gov/advocate/article/0,,id=106991,00.html.

3) ***Free Tax Help For Seniors***
With a grant from the IRS, the AARP organizes over 8,000 "Tax Counseling For The Elderly" sites around the country that specialize in providing free tax help for people 60 and over. They may also

provide free help for others, so it can't hurt to ask. To find a site near you, call the TCE hotline at 1-800-829-1040 or the AARP Tax Aide hotline at 1-888-227-7669 or visit www.irs.gov/pub/irs-utl/pub._4134-04.pdf or www.aarp.org/money/taxaide/. You can also contact your local public library or your Congressman's office at www.congress.org.

4) ***Government Will Fight The IRS For You***
If you have attempted to deal with an IRS problem unsuccessfully, you should contact your Taxpayer Advocate. They will represent your interests and concerns within the IRS by protecting your rights and resolving problems that have not been fixed through normal channels. They can clear-up problems that resulted from previous contacts and ensure that your case is given a complete and impartial review. Call 1-877-777-4778 or www.irs.gov/advocate.

****Sources***
http://www.acorn.org/fileadmin/ACORN_Reports/National_EITC_Report_-_Final_version_01.pdf
http://www.robinhood.org/programs/initiative_details.cfm?initiativeId=5
http://en.wikipedia.org/wiki/Earned_Income_Tax_Credit

More Grants From The IRS

Get a $2,000 Check From Your State

You can claim anywhere from an additional 5% to 50% of what you get from the federal Earned Income Tax Credit from your state government. About 18 states currently offer this credit, as well as a handful of local jurisdictions. Make sure you get this money too. Contact one of the free tax services described above or your state tax office located in your state capital. You can call 411 and ask for this number or go to www.govengine. com and click on your state. You can also contact your local public library or your Congressman's office at www.congress.org; or see: www.cbpp.org/5-14-04sfp.pdf .

$1,000 Check For Each Child

The new federal Child Tax Credit gives working people making up to $110,000 a check for up to $1,000 even if they don't pay taxes. Look into it. Use the free tax sources above or call 1-800-TAX-1040. You can also go to www.irs.gov/publications/p972/ar02.html.

$2,100 Check For Child Care

This federal Child and Dependent Care Tax Credit is for child care for kids under 13 or for caring for dependents mentally or physically incapable of self-support. You can get a tax credit up to $2,100 depending on your income and the amount you pay for care. Unlike the Child Tax Credit and Earned Income Tax Credit, you get this check only if you are paying taxes. Use the free tax sources above or call 1-800-TAX-1040. Or go to: www.irs.gov/newsroom/article/0,,id=106189,00.html.

$2,310 Check From Your State For Child Care

Twenty-seven states offer Child and Dependent Care Tax Credit on your state tax returns. About 14 of these states do not require you to pay any taxes in order to get a check. Contact one of the free tax services described above or your state tax office located in your state capital. You can call 411 and ask for this number or go to www.govengine.com and click on your state. You can also contact your local public library or your Congressman's office at www.congress.org. Also see:
www.nccp.org/policy_long_description_15.html or
www.nwlc.org/pdf/NWLCTaxCreditsOutreachCampaignToolkit2005.pdf.

$1,500 Check For Going To College

You can make up to $100,000 and the government will send you a check under the federal Hope Scholarship Tax Credit if you are at least going to college part-time. It's only for the first two years of college and you have to be paying taxes to get the money. Use the free tax sources above, call 1-800-TAX-1040 or go to www.irs.gov/publications/p972/ar02.html.

$2,000 Check For Taking A Course Or Class

Almost any kind of course that will improve your job skills are eligible under the federal Lifetime Learning Tax Credit. You can make up to $100,000 and still get this credit, but you have to be paying taxes to get the money. Use the free tax sources above, or call 1-800-TAX-1040 or go to www.irs.gov/faqs/faq7-4.html.

$5,000 Check To Pay For Health Insurance

The federal Health Coverage Tax Credit is a bit more complicated, but it will pay 65% of health care insurance for people who lost their job because of imports or are receiving certain retirement benefits. Use the free tax sources above, or call 1-800-TAX-1040 or go to http://www.irs.gov/individuals/article/0,,id=109960,00.html.

$1,125 Check For Seniors Or Disabled

The Tax Credit for Elderly and Disabled is for citizens who are older than 65 or disabled. Your eligibility is based upon your income. Use the free tax sources above, or call 1-800-TAX-1040 or go to www.irs.gov/pub/irs-pdf/p524.pdf

$10,160 Check For Adoptions

As an adoptive parent you may be able to receive a tax credit up to $10,160. The income limits on this go up to $192,390. Use the free tax sources above, or call 1-800-TAX-1040 or go to www.irs.gov/taxtopics/tc607.html.

$30,000 Check From Your State

In addition to the state tax credit programs mentioned above, every state has other tax credits programs that can send you real money for taking advantage of them. Sample programs include:

- $1,160 for renters or homeowners in Wisconsin
  www.uwex.edu/ces/econ/homestead.html
- $300 for buying new appliances in Oregon
  http://egov.oregon.gov/ENERGY/CONS/RES/RETC.shtml
- $1,750 for installing solar panels in Hawaii
  www.hawaii.gov/dbedt/ert/sol_t_hi.html
- $2,000 for seniors who pay property taxes in North Dakota
  www.nd.gov/tax//property/pubs/senior-credit.pdf
- $30,000 to fix-up an old home in North Carolina
  www.hpo.dcr.state.nc.us/tchome.htm

- $250 if you donate to an extracurricular activity at a school in Arizona ww2.chandler.k12.az.us/tax-credit.html

Contact your state Department of Revenue or Taxes to see what is available in your state. You can call 411 and ask for this number or go to www.govengine.com and click on your state. You can also contact your local public library or your Congressman's office at www.congress.org.

Health

How To Get Better Health Services For Free

According to the U.S. Department on Aging Older Americans use more health care than any other group and health care costs are increasing rapidly. Large out of pocket expenditures for health care services has shown to affect health care status, quality of life, and leave insufficient resources for other necessities. Where can seniors turn to get the care they need at the price they can afford? There are thousands of places if you know where to look. The following is a listing of good starting places, ad then specific offices to get the help you need. You need to take care of yourself in order to get the most out of your Golden Years.

Some starting places include:

1) ***Eldercare Locator***
The U.S. Administration on Aging offers this free service to older adult Americans and their caregivers to help them connect with available services. Eldercare Locator links older adults who need assistance with state and local area agencies on aging and community-based organizations. If you need help with any health related problem go to the web site and follow the directions or call a specialist. The web site is available in many different languages. Contact: 800-677-1116, www.eldercare.gov.

2) ***Helpful Health Hotlines***
The National Health Information Center and the National Library of Medicine both offer an online database of health-related organizations operating toll-free telephone services. The databases also include information on services and publications available in Spanish. You can find out whom to call for almost any health issue. Contact: Health Information Resources Database, Referral Specialist, P.O. Box 1133, Washington, DC 20013-1133; 800-336-4797, 301-565-4167; www.health.gov/NHIC/Pubs/tollfree.htm or http://healthhotlines.nlm.nih.gov/.

3) ***National Institute on Aging***
The National Institute on Aging, is the government's leading effort on aging research. In addition to research information and professional training, NIA disseminates health information to the general public. Contact: National Institute on Aging, Building 31, Room 5C27, 31 Center Drive, MSC 2292, Bethesda, MD 20892; 301-496-1752, 800-222-4225, Fax: 301-496-1072; www.nia.n.ih.gov.

4) ***SeniorHealth.gov***
The National Institute of Health offers an on-line information web site for older adults. Their goal is to make age-related health information easily accessible to seniors, family members and friends. The web site is senior friendly including large print, short, easy to read segments and simple navigation. There is even a "talking" feature which reads the text. Information is updated regularly. Contact: http://nihseniorhealth.gov/.

5) Free Care By The Best Doctors In The World

Bob Dole and Sam Donaldson knew where to go to get treatment - The National Institutes of Health (NIH). Each year, close to 75,000 patients receive free medical care by some of the best doctors in the world. To see if your diagnosis is currently being studied, you can contact the Clinical Center, National Institutes of Health, Patient Recruitment; 301-496-2563; 800-411-1222; www.cc.nih.gov; National Institutes of Health, Office of Communications, 9000 Rockville Pike, Bethesda, MD 20892; 301-496-4000; www.nih.gov; or to search a database of research programs, contact CRISP, Office of Reports and Analysis, Office of Extramural Research, 9000 Rockville, Bethesda, MD 20892; 301-435-0656; http://crisp.cit.nih.gov.

6) Free Hospital Care

Don't have money for your gall bladder surgery? What about that hospital visit you had two months ago? You might not have to pay a cent. Call the Hill-Burton Hotline. A copy of the Free Care Brochure can be downloaded at the website listed below. Under this program, certain hospitals and other health care facilities provide free or low-cost medical care to patients who cannot afford to pay. You may qualify even if your income is up to double the Poverty Income Guidelines. That's $36,200 for a family of four! You can apply before or after you receive care, and even after the bill has been sent to a collection agency. Call the Hotline to find out if you meet the eligibility requirements and to request a list of local hospitals who are participating. For more information, contact Hill-Burton Hotline, Health Resources and Services Administration, U.S. Department of Health and Human Services, Parklawn Building, 5600 Fishers Lane, Rockville, MD 20857; 800-638-0742; 800-492-0359 (in MD); www.hrsa.gov/osp/dfcr/about/aboutdiv.htm.

7) Get Health Information Better Than Your Doctor

Want to find out the latest information on your health condition? All you need to do is pick up the phone or go online to get the most up-to-date information from the government's team of health professionals. The latest cures and treatments to any condition are changing every day and it is impossible for people in the medical profession to keep up on the latest developments in any health-related area. There is plenty of free help available from government sponsored and nonprofit organizations who can even tell you what will be in the medical journals next year because they are involved in the research today. So, don't settle for second best when you can get the best. Here is where you can go:

National Health Information Center
P.O. Box 1133
Washington, DC 20013-1133
800-336-4797
301-565-4167
www.health.gov/nhic

National Women's Health Information Center
U.S. Public Health Service
Office of Women's Health
8550 Arlington Boulevard, Suite 300
Fairfax, VA 22031
800-944-WOMAN
www.4woman.gov

National Institutes of Health
Office of Communications
9000 Rockville Pike
Bethesda, MD 20892
301-496-4000
www.nih.gov

Free Health Care When You Have No Insurance Coverage

Over 3,700 government supported healthcare centers around the country offer everything from mental health to dental services near you. Contact the Health Resources and Services Administration at the U.S. Department of Health and Human Services at www.ask.hrsa.gov/Primary.cfm or call 888-275-4772. Another database of over 500 free clinics around the country is available from The Free Clinic Foundation of America, www.medkind.com/FCF/.

$2,000 Worth Of Free Prescription Drugs

Make over $40,000 and get everything except Viagra. Drug companies do not want everybody to know this, but they will give certain people who cannot afford their medications their drugs free of charge. Your doctor needs to write a note to the drug companies stating that you cannot afford the prescriptions. Your doctor will also need to fill out a form, and then the company will ship the medications to your doctor's office. To receive a listing of drug companies, check out the website at www.phrma.org or (www.helpingpatients.org. You can also contact Pharmaceutical Research and Manufacturers of America, 1100 15th St., NW, Washington, DC 20005; 202-835-3400.

Nonprofits Will Pay For Health Expenses

There are thousands of nonprofit organizations that provide help and even financial assistance to individuals and families who are suffering with most any illness or condition you can think of. You can get:

- $1,000 if you are suffering with pancreatic cancer to pay for transportation to treatment, medication or child care from Hirshberg Foundation, 800-813-4673, www.pancreatic.org/html/financial.html
- $3,000 for special expenses related to being a cancer patient from Cancer Care, 800-813-HOPE, www.cancercare.org/FinancialNeeds/ FinancialNeedsList.cfm?c=387
- $750 for people who care for Alzheimer's patients from Alzheimer's Family Relief Programs; 800-437-AHAF; http://198.63.60.19/afrp/guide.htm
- $450 for an eye examination and eye glasses from Vision USA, 800-766-4466; www.aoa.org/visionusa/
- $5,000 to purchase prosthetic limbs from The Barr Foundation, 561-394-6514; www.oandp.com/resources/organizations/barr/ index2.htm

You will have to look at more than just one place to find this kind of help. You can look for relevant organizations by researching National Health Information Center, P.O. Box 1133, Washington, DC 20013, 800-336-4797, www.health.gov/nhic.. Two other resources for finding nonprofits include The Foundation Center, 79 Fifth Ave., New York, NY 10003; 212-620-4230; www.fdncenter.org and Guidestar, 4801 Courthouse St., Suite 220, Williamsburg, VA 23188; 757-229-4631; www.guidestar.org. They both have a database of organizations that you can search.

$10,000 To Help You Out With All Kinds of Trouble

Do you need Meals on Wheels? Are you having trouble paying your bills? Need a new roof on the house? Need extra spending money? Need free legal help for a divorce? Want to know what programs exist for seniors? All these questions and more can be found by contacting the Eldercare Hotline at 800-677-1116. They can connect seniors with all the resources available to them, and all it takes is a phone call. For more info contact the Administration on Aging, Washington, DC 20201; 202 619-0724; www.eldercare.gov.

Emergency Rooms Have To Take You

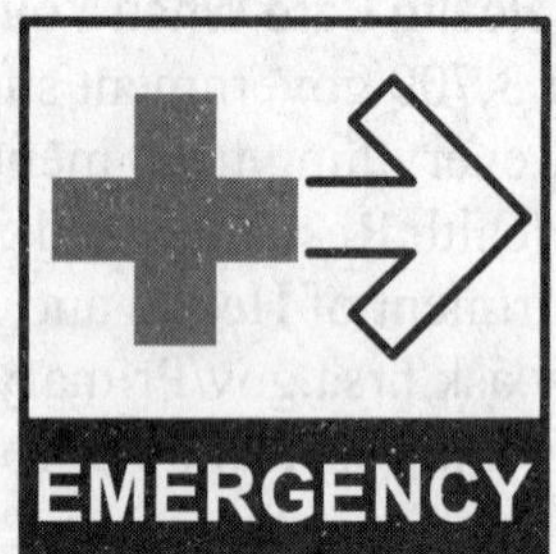

Emergency rooms are now required to provide an initial screening to assess a patient's condition, which is designed to stop the automatic transfer of people unable to pay. Emergency rooms must also treat emergency situations until they are stabilized, then they can refer you to other hospitals or clinics for further treatment. If you feel you have been denied service, contact Centers for Medicare and Medicaid Services, 7500 Security Blvd., Baltimore, MD 21244; 410-786-3000; www.cms.hhs.gov.

Get An Extra $1,000

If you're a senior, check into this because each year over 3 million eligible seniors and people with disabilities fail to apply for a little-known program that will give them over $1,000 extra in their Social Security check. That's how much the government deducts for Medicare Part B payments. The program is called Qualified Medicare Beneficiaries Plan, or Specified Low-Income Medicare Beneficiaries Plan. To learn more contact your local Social Security Office at 800-772-1213. You can also contact the Medicare Hotline and request the publication Guide to Health Insurance for People with Medicare; contact Medicare Hotline at 800-MEDICARE or online at www.medicare.gov.

See If You Qualify For Your State Health Care Programs

Every state has a number of health care programs that are paid for by federal and state government funding. Most of the programs have income requirements, but the income can go up to $40,000 or more for a family. Every state has a number of programs to protect people in financial trouble. There are programs to help pay for food, day care, and medical expenses. www.cbpp.org/1-14-04tanf.htm.

$2,000 To Pay Your Dental Bills

There are close to 60 dental schools in the country that offer quality care at a fraction of the cost of private dentists. I used them for years. An $800 crown can cost you only $200. Sure you get a senior student, but you also get a professor who is better than most private practitioners. Most also offer payment plans. For a school near you go to: www.scholarware.com/dentalschools.htm?source=overture.

$20,000 Of Free Alcohol And Drug Treatment

Georgia provides outpatient counseling services, short-term residential programs, and even school student assistance programs. There are also nonprofit organizations that offer free treatment to people, like the Center for Drug-Free Living in Orlando, Florida. A friend of mine received one- and two-week resident treatments for free in Maryland. So if you need help, keep looking for local free stuff or contact National Drug and Treatment Routing Service, Center for Substance Abuse Treatment, National Institute on Alcohol Abuse and Alcoholism (NIAAA), 5635 Fishers Lane, MSC 9305; Bethesda, MD

20892; 800-662-HELP; www.niaaa.nih.gov; or National Clearinghouse for Alcohol and Drug Information, 11420 Rockville Pike, Suite 200, Rockville, MD 20852; 800-729-6686; www.health.org.

Free Preventive Health Services For Seniors

A report for the U.S. Congress estimates that over 25 million seniors don't take advantage of free preventive health services like flu shots, tetanus shots, pap smear, mammography, vaginal cancer, colorectal cancer - colonoscopy, osteoporosis - bone mass measurement, prostate cancer test, and glaucoma test. They are all covered under the Medicare laws, but most doctors are not aware of this. Tell your senior friends to check it out at: www.medicare.gov or 800-MEDICARE.

Discounts On Dental and Vision Care

If you live near a university that has a dental or optometry school, then you may be in luck. Many of these schools offer reduced fee services for dental care or vision screening. You will receive treatment from students, but they will be supervised by some of the best people in the field. These schools also often conduct research studies, so if you qualify, you may be able to receive treatment for free. To locate schools near you, you can contact American Dental Education Association, 1400 K Street, NW, Suite 1100, Washington, DC 20005: 202-289-7201; Fax: 202-289-7204; www.adea.org. You can also contact American Optometric Association, 243 N. Lindbergh Blvd., St. Louis, MO 63141; 314-991-4100; Fax: 314-991-4101; www.aoa.org.

Free Flu Shots

Who should get flu shots? The U.S. Center for Disease Control recommends it for:

- adults at or over 65 years
- residents of nursing homes
- all children aged 6-23 months
- persons at or over 2 years of age with underlying chronic conditions.
- women in their 2nd or 3rd trimester of pregnancy during flu season
- persons 6 months to 18 years receiving aspirin therapy
- groups, including household members and care givers who can infect high risk persons

Almost anyone can get free or low cost ($10-$15) flu shots from their county health office or other community sources. Some doctors, like Dr. Donald McGee in New Hampshire www.drmcgee.com, offer free shots in their office. Medicare Part B also pays for flu shots. Contact your county office of public health listed in your telephone book or your state Department of Health. If you have trouble finding a local low cost source, or would like more information on the flu vaccine contact the National Immunization Information Hotline at 800-232-2522; www.cdc.gov/nip.

$2,000 Worth Of Dental Care For Seniors and Disabled

The National Foundation of Dentistry for the Handicapped started the Donated Dental Services program to help disabled and elderly persons who are low-income by matching them with volunteer dentists. Mentally compromised people are also helped. Volunteer dentists agree to treat one or two people each year with dental problems, and dental laboratories that make dentures, crowns, and bridges also donate services. The program now serves over 5,000 people each year with each patient receiving an average of $2,000 worth of services. In some areas of the country, Dental House Call projects have been started where dentists will come to homes or centers to provide dental care. To learn where services are located in your area, contact National Foundation of Dentistry for the Handicapped, 1800 15th St., Suite 100, Denver, CO 80202; 303-534-5360, Fax: 303-534-5290; www.nfdh.org.

Grants Assist with Vision Care

The Pearle Vision Foundation offers grants to nonprofit organizations for vision-care assistance. Vision-related services include, eye exam & eyeglass assistance programs, vision-related research, equipment for testing and improving vision, and programs that improve the quality of life for the visually impaired. Contact Pearle Vision Foundation, 2465 Joe Field Road, Dallas, TX 75229; 972-277-6191; www.pearlevision.com.

Sightless Get Free Seeing Eye Dogs, Training, Travel and Air Fare

Pilot Dogs gives its trained animals to the blind at absolutely no charge. They also include four weeks of training in using the dog and will pay for room and board, all equipment, and round trip transportation. Other groups provide similar services:

- Pilot Dogs, Inc., 625 West Town Street, Columbus, OH 43215; 614-221-6367; Fax: 614-221-1577; www.pilotdogs.org.
- Guide Dog Foundation for the Blind, Inc, 371 East Jericho Turnpike., Smithtown, NY 11787-2976; 800-548-4337; 631-930-9000; Fax: 631-361-5192; www.guidedog.org.

Free Wheelchairs

Easter Seals, the American Cancer Society and other helpful organizations provide free wheelchairs and other medical related equipment, like walkers, commodes, bathtub rails, bathtub chairs, crutches, transfer benches, electric wheelchairs and scooters, on a short- or long-term basis. Some programs require deposits that are completely refundable. Check with your local office of Easter Seals and the American Cancer Society. You can also contact your state Department of Health.

- American Cancer Society, Inc., 1599 Clifton Road, NE, Atlanta, GA 30329-4251; 800-ACS-2345; www.cancer.org.
- Easter Seals, 230 West Monroe Street, Suite 1800, Chicago, IL 60606; 800-221-6827; 312-726-6200; Fax: 312-726-1494; TTY: 312-726-4258; www.easterseals.com.

Free Mammograms, Free Tests For Breast and Cervical Cancer

An estimated 2 million American women will be diagnosed with breast or cervical cancer in the next decade, and half a million will lose their lives from these diseases. Screening could prevent up to 20% of these deaths for women over 40. The government's Center for Disease Control will spend about $200 million a year to maintain a state-by-state program to establish greater access to screening and follow-up services. To find the program contact for your state, go to www.cdc.gov/cancer/nbccedp/contacts.htm. Each state runs their program a little differently. Most states have the following requirements:

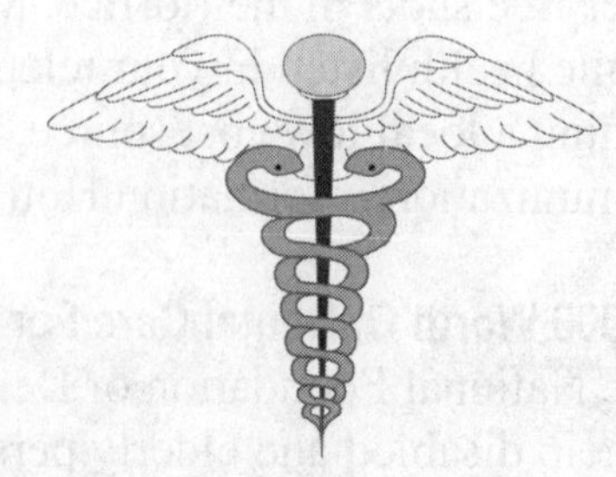

- women starting at 40 or 50 years old,
- are underinsured or have no insurance
- have income below a certain level (usually $46,000 for a family of 4)

Some states can adjust eligibility requirements for special cases. States vary in the array of services covered but they normally include:

- breast and cervical cancer screening
- mammograms
- treatment if diagnosed with cancer
- breast reconstruction or prosthesis

States that don't have direct funds for treatment often make arrangements with other facilities to provide treatment for free. If your screening has been done elsewhere, you can still receive free treatment under this program. Men diagnosed with breast cancer can also receive free treatment. Contact your county office of public health listed in your telephone book or your state Department of Health. You can also contact the main office of this program at Division of Cancer Prevention and Control, National Center for Chronic Disease Prevention and Health Promotion, Center for Disease Control and Prevention, 4770 Buford Highway, NE, MS K-64, Atlanta, GA 30341-3717, 770-488-4751; 888-842-6355; Fax: 770-488-4760; www.cdc.gov/cancer/nbccedp/.

More Free Mammograms

Not all insurance companies pay for mammograms, and not every woman is eligible for the government's program described earlier. The following organizations can help you identify free and low cost mammograms in your area.

1) The ***American Cancer Society***: contact your local office or the national office at 800-ACS-2345; www.cancer.org.
2) ***YWCA's Encore Plus Program***: contact your local office or the national office at 800-95-EPLUS.
3) National Cancer Institute: 800-4-CANCER; www.nci.nih.gov
4) ***State Office of Breast and Cervical Cancer***: contact your state Department of Health
5) October is ***National Breast Cancer Awareness Month***: many mammogram facilities offer their services at special fees during this period. Call and see what kind of deal you can get, or check online at www.nbcam.org/index.cfm.
6) ***Medicare*** coverage of mammograms: call 800-MEDICARE.

Low Cost Immunizations for Travelers

In order to prevent contracting diseases like yellow fever, cholera or Japanese encephalitis when traveling in other countries, the government's Center for Disease Control recommends that certain vaccines would eliminate your risk of infection. Some local Public Health offices offer these vaccines at a fraction of what you would pay at a doctor's office. To find your local county office of health, look in your telephone book or contact your state Department of Health. For more information about disease and vaccines for travel, contact: Center for Disease Control and Prevention, National Center for Infectious Diseases, Division of Global Migration and Quarantine, 1600 Clifton Road, MS E-03, Atlanta, GA 30333; 877-FYI-TRIP; 404-639-3534; www.cdc.gov/travel/.

Fund Helps Foster Independence of Physically Disabled

Individuals with physical disabilities residing in Oregon may be eligible to receive financial assistance through the Blanche Fisher Foundation. The fund assists with the expense of hearing aids, eyeglasses, wheelchairs, ramps, tuition and skills training. Contact Blanche Fisher Foundation, 1511 SW Sunset Blvd., Suite 1-B, Portland, OR 97239; 503-819-8205; Fax: 503-246-4941; www.bff.org.

Free Transportation To Medical Appointments For You

You have to get to a doctor's visit in the middle of the day and no one can take you. Or you have a disability that may cause you to miss an appointment if someone else doesn't drive. You may be able to get free transportation and escort services provided by either your local health office or local office on aging. Some communities even provide very low cost door-to-door services for seniors to go anywhere. If you can't find your local area agency on aging or public health office in your telephone book, contact your state Department of Aging or Health. If that fails, contact the Eldercare Locator Hotline at 1-800-677-1116; www.eldercare.gov/Eldercare/Public/Home.asp. They are available to help anyone identify services for seniors.

Cancer Patients Receive Help with Expenses

Limited financial assistance is available nationwide through Cancer Care, Inc. to cancer patients and their families for home care, child care and transportation expenses. Contact Cancer Care, Inc., 275 7th Ave., 22nd Floor, New York, NY 10001; 800-813-HOPE; 212-712-8080; Fax: 212-712-8495; www.cancercare.org.

Low Cost Home Health Care

Montgomery County in Maryland provides home health care free or on a sliding scale, depending on income, through the local public health office. You don't have to be a senior to qualify. A survey by the Center for Disease Control reports that about half of all local public health agencies provide similar services. To see what is available in your area, contact your county office of health listed in your telephone book or your state Department of Health. If you cannot get satisfaction from these offices, contact your local office of your state or federal elected official. For similar services for seniors, contact your local area agency on aging or your state Department on Aging. If that fails, contact the Eldercare Locator hotline at 1-800-677-1116. They are available to help anyone identify services for seniors.

$$$$$ Money To Buy A Van, A Talking Computer Or Rubber Door Knob Grips

People with disabilities now have a place to turn to learn everything they need to know about how the latest in technology can improve their lives. It can be a specially equipped van, a talking computer, a special kitchen or eating aid. A project funded by the U.S. Department of Education, called Technical Assistance Project has established an office in each state that can provide:

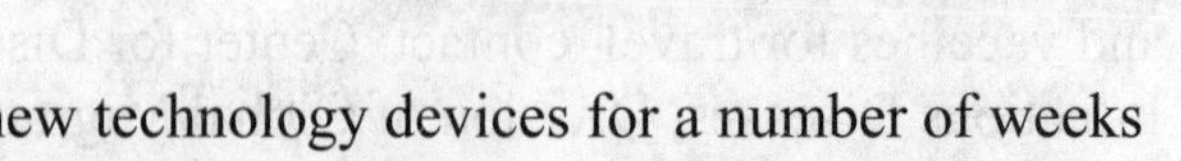

- ***Information Services***: will help you identify the special products that are available to help you cope with your disability.
- ***Equipment Loan Program***: allows people to borrow new technology devices for a number of weeks before they purchase them.
- ***Recycling Program***: matches up people with needs for products with people who want to sell or donate products.
- ***Funding Information***: collects information on the various sources of funding for this equipment from public and private sources.

- *Loans*: many states are offering special loans to help people purchase the necessary equipment; Ohio offers low-interest loans up to $10,000, North Carolina has loans up to $15,000, and California offers loan guarantees up to $35,000.

Contact your state information operator and ask for your state Office of Social Services or Vocational Rehabilitation. They should be aware of your state Assistance Technology Office. If you have trouble locating your state office, you can contact the office that coordinates all state activities: Rehabilitation Engineering and Assistive Technology Society of North America, (RESNA), 1700 North Moore Street, Suite 1540, Arlington, VA 22209-1903; 703-524-6686; Fax: 703-524-6630; TTY: 703-524-6639; www.resna.org.

Free Take Out Taxi For Seniors

People 60 and over who are homebound because of illness, incapacity, or disability, or who are otherwise isolated can receive hot meals delivered to their home. The program is funded in every state by the Older Americans Act. Contact your local area agency on aging or your state Department on Aging. If that fails, contact the Eldercare Locator hotline at 1-800-677-1116; www.eldercare.gov/eldercare/Public/Home.asp. They are available to help anyone identify services for seniors.

Easter Seals in Arizona Offers Free Computers to People With Disabilities

Washington State chapter has a free loan program, and the chapters in Missouri offer computer classes. Contact your local Easter Seals Society to see what they may offer in the way of computers and computer skills for people with disabilities. If you can't find your local office, contact: Easter Seals, 230 West Monroe Street, Suite 1800, Chicago, IL 60606; 800-221-6827; 312-726-6200; Fax: 312-726-1494; TTY: 312-726-4258; www.easterseals.com.

Free & Low Cost Dental Care for Seniors, and Certain Incomes

Many of the local health offices provide dental services to income-eligible adults on a sliding fee scale. Contact your county office of health listed in your telephone book or your state Department of Health. Many states have special free or discount services just for seniors. Contact your local Area Agency on Aging or your state Department on Aging. If that fails, contact the Eldercare Locator Hotline at 1-800-677-1116; www.eldercare.gov/ eldercare/Public/Home.asp.

Service Organizations Provide Free Care

Need help with elderly services or substance abuse treatment? Many large service organizations have local offices that provide all this and more. Services vary depending upon the needs of the community, but before you fight your battles alone, contact these main offices to find out about local programs:

- **Catholic Charities USA**, 1731 King St., Alexandria, VA 23314; 703-549-1390; Fax: 703-549-1656; www.catholiccharitiesusa.org.
- **Salvation Army**, 615 Slaters Lane, P.O. Box 269, Alexandria, VA 22313; 703-684-5500; 800-SAL-ARMY; Fax: 703-684-3478; www.salvationarmyusa.org.
- **United Way of America**, 701 N. Fairfax St., Alexandria, VA 22314; 703-836-7112; www.unitedway.org.

Money For New Hearing Aids

You can get information on different types of hearing loss, lists of hearing professionals, and information on locating financial assistance for assistive hearing devices by calling The Better Hearing Institute, 515 King St., Suite 420, Alexandria, VA 22314, P.O. Box 1840, Washington, DC 20013; 800-EAR-WELL; 703-684-3391; Fax: 703-684-6048; www.betterhearing.org.

Free Eye Care

If you or someone you love needs eye care, but cannot afford it, the following organizations can help:

- For those 65 and older: *Seniors EyeCare Program*, EyeCare America, 655 Beach Street, San Francisco, CA 94109-1336; 800-222-3937; Fax: 415-561-8567; www.eyecareamerica.org/eyecare.
- For low-income families with a working adult, applications are accepted on a first come-first serve basis with treatment following later in the year: *VISION USA*, American Optometric Association, 243 North Lindbergh Blvd., St. Louis, MO 63141; 314-991-4100; 800-766-4466; Fax: 314-991-4101; www.aoanet.org.
- *Lions Clubs International*, 300 West 22nd St., Oak Brook, IL 60523-8842; 630-571-5466; www.lionsclubs.org.
- *EyeCare America – Glaucoma EyeCare Program*, EyeCare America, 655 Beach Street, San Francisco, CA 94109-1336; 415-561-8500; 800-391-EYES; Fax: 415-561-8567; www.eyecareamerica.org/eyecare.
- *Diabetes EyeCare Program*, EyeCare America, 655 Beach Street, San Francisco, CA 94109-1336; 800-272-EYEYS; www.eyecareamerica.org/eyecare.

Free Help For Cancer Families

Local chapters of the American Cancer Society sponsor a wide range of services for cancer patients and their families, including self-help groups, transportation programs, and lodging assistance for those who must travel far for treatment. To find your local chapter or for more information on cancer detection, prevention and treatment, contact American Cancer Society, 1599 Clifton Rd., NE, Atlanta, GA 30329-4251; 800-ACS-2345; www.cancer.org.

Eye Care Helpline

The Eye Care Helpline puts callers in touch with local ophthalmologists who have volunteered to provide medical eye care at no out-of-pocket expense. Individuals must be 65 or older and not have had access to an ophthalmologist within the past three years. The emphasis of this program is to help disadvantaged people. For more information, contact Seniors EyeCare Program, EyeCare America, 655 Beach Street, San Francisco, CA 94109-1336; 415-561-8500; 800-222-3937; Fax: 415-561-8567; www.eyecareamerica.org/eyecare.

Foundation Assists Individuals with Spinal Cord Injuries

The William Heiser Foundation for the Cure of Spinal Cord Injuries, Inc. provides general welfare assistance to individuals with spinal cord injuries residing in the Wantagh, New York area. Contact: William Heiser Foundation for the Cure of Spinal Cord Injuries, 3434 Hawthorne Drive N, Wantagh, NY 11793; 516-826-9747; www.theheiserfoundation.org.

Money To Pay Your Shrink Bills

Many people are suffering needlessly because they think they cannot afford to see a mental health professional. It is estimated that over 38 million people think that they cannot afford the high cost of mental health care. Before all hope is lost, here is a listing of options to pursue:

- **Private Health Insurance**- Most health insurance policies, also cover mental health care cost. Contact your insurance company to see what your plan has to offer.
- **Community Mental Health Centers**- These centers often offer services for free or on a sliding fee scale.
- **Religious Organizations**- Many churches, synagogues, and other religious agencies offer pastoral counseling.

If you have Medicare or Medicaid, mental health services are covered. For more information contact the following organizations:

- *National Mental Health Services*, Knowledge Exchange Network, P.O. Box 42557, Washington, DC 20015; 800-789-2647; TDD: 866-889-2647; www.mentalhealth.org.
- *American Association of Pastoral Counselors*, 9504-A Lee Highway, Fairfax. VA 22031-2303; 703-385-6967; www.aapc.org.
- *American Self-Help Clearinghouse*, Saint Clares Hospital, 100 E. Hanover Ave., Cedar Knolls, NJ 07927; 973-326-6789; www.mentalhelp.net/selfhelp.
- *National Alliance for the Mentally Ill*, Colonial Place Three, 2107 Wilson Blvd., Suite 300, Arlington, VA 22201; 800-950-6264, 703-524-7600; www.nami.org.
- *National Empowerment Center*, 599 Canal St., Lawrence, MA 01840; 800-769-3728, 978-685-1494; www.power2u.org.
- *National Mental Health Consumers Self-Help Clearinghouse*, 1211 Chestnut Street, Suite 1207, Philadelphia, PA 19107; 800-553-4539, 215-751-1810; www.mhselfhelp.org.

Free Health Care For Seniors And The Disabled

Over 16,000 seniors live in centers operated by the Salvation Army, as do 1,600 disabled adults. The Salvation Army also operates hospitals and clinics throughout the world to provide healthcare for those in need. They even provide homes for those recently discharged from the hospital and need more recovery time. To learn more about the services offered contact the Salvation Army Office near you, or Salvation Army National Headquarters, 615 Slaters Lane, P.O. Box 269, Alexandria, VA 22313; 703-684-5500; www.salvationarmy.org.

Free Money To Pay Your Alcohol Rehab Bills

Treatment of alcohol abuse can cost you thousands of dollars. The Salvation Army has 152 homes and centers for the treatment of those suffering from alcoholism, as well as many other drug rehabilitation programs. To learn more about the services offered contact the Salvation Army Office near you, or Salvation Army National Headquarters, 615 Slaters Lane, P.O. Box 269, Alexandria, VA 22313; 703-684-5500; www.salvationarmy.org.

Alcohol and Drug Abuse Counseling & Treatment

Georgia provides outpatient counseling services, short-term residential programs, and even school student assistance programs. Florida provides substance abuse treatment programs through a partnership with 102 public and private not-for-profit community providers. Delaware contracts with private organizations around the state to provide screening, outpatient counseling, and detoxification, as well as short term and long term treatment. Contact your state Department of Health to see what your state has to offer.

There are also nonprofit organizations who, by themselves, offer free treatment to people, like the Center for Drug-Free Living in Orlando, Florida P.O. Box 538350, Orlando, FL 32853-8350; 407-245-0012; Fax: 407-245-0011; www.cfdfl.com. If your state can't help you get the information or treatment you need, one or both of the following hotlines should be able to help:

- National Drug and Treatment Routing Service, Substance Abuse and Mental Health Services Administration's (SAMHSA), National Institute on Alcohol Abuse and Alcoholism (NIAAA), 5635 Fishers Lane, MSC 9304, Bethesda, Maryland 20892-9304; 800-662-HELP; www.niaaa.nih.gov/other/referral.htm.
- The National Clearinghouse for Alcohol and Drug Information, 11420 Rockville Pike, Suite 200, Rockville, MD 20852; 800-729-6686 24 hours a day; 800-487-4889 TDD; www.health.org.

Discount Card And Extra $600 Toward Prescriptions For Seniors

There is finally help for seniors to pay for the ever-growing costs of prescription drugs. Qualifying individuals receive a discount card as well as an additional $600 to help with the purchase of prescriptions. For more information, contact the Centers for Medicare and Medicaid Services, 7500 Security Boulevard, Baltimore, MD 21244-1850; 410-786-3000, 877-267-2323; www.cms.hhs.gov/discountdrugs/overview.asp.

Vouchers for FREE Mammograms

The Actors' Fund's Phyllis Newman Women's Health Initiative (PNWHI) Senior Program provides vouchers for FREE mammograms for members of the entertainment community. Other health-related services are available; mostly support groups and referral services. Contact: The Actors' Fund of America, 729 Seventh Avenue, 10th Floor, New York, NY 10019; 212-221-7300, ext. 119; Fax: 212-764-0238; www.actorsfund.org/human/social/newman.html.

FREE Pharmaceutical Products

This Patient Assistance Program offers needy persons FREE pharmaceutical products on a non-discriminatory basis. Giving is on a national basis. Contact: Janssen Ortho Patient Assistance Foundation, Inc., 1 Johnson & Johnson Plaza, New Brunswick, NJ 08933; 800-652-6227; www.janssen.com/ourproducts/pap.jsp.

$100,000 to Support People with Medical Condition

The National Ataxia Foundation is dedicated to improving the lives of persons affected by ataxia through service, education and research. The foundation also funds research through its three research programs, seed money, young investigator award, and the postdoctoral program. Contact: National Ataxia Foundation, Inc., 2600 Fernbrook Lane, Suite 119, Minneapolis, MN 55447-4752; 763-553-0020; Fax: 763-553-0167; www.ataxia.org/.

Financial Assistance for Those who Need Heart Surgery

The Larry King Cardiac Foundation (LKCF) was established in 1988 to provide funding for life-saving treatment for individuals who, due to limited means or inadequate insurance, would otherwise be unable to receive the treatment and care they so desperately need. The Foundation works in conjunction with hospitals throughout the nation to ensure that such patients receive proper medical attention. Doctors performing these surgeries do so at cost. Hospitals are compensated only for the materials used. Eligible patients must meet the following minimum criteria: US citizens or have a legal right to be in the US; do not have financial resources to pay for the procedures themselves; and be free of any criminal conviction. The Foundation pays for cardiac-related procedures that are: already performed and approved in advance; and that are performed in one of their affiliate care centers with one of their doctors. Funds are sent directly to the hospital for reimbursement, not to the individual. Contact: The Larry King Cardiac Foundation, 15720 Crabbs Branch Way, Suite D, Rockville, MD 20855; 866-302-5523; www.lkcf.org

Prescription Drug and Other Assistance Programs
The Prescription Drug and Other Assistance Programs of Medicare provide information on public and private programs that offer discounted or free medication, programs that assist with costs and Medicare programs and coverage. Contact: Centers for Medicare and Medicaid Services, 7500 Security Boulevard, Baltimore, MD 21244-1850; 800-MEDICARE; www.medicare.gov/AssistancePrograms/home.asp.

Free Diabetes Risk Assessment
If you are looking for information on diabetes prevention, cures, treatments, screenings, support groups or other help this is the place for you. The American Diabetes Association offers all this and more. You can take an online test to determine your risk of diabetes or find a local chapter in your area. For more information, contact the American Diabetes Association, 1701 North Beauregard Street, Alexandria, VA 22311; 800-DIABETES; www.diabetes.org.

Get Free Help To Finally Quit Smoking
Smokefree.gov is the collaboration of the National Cancer Institute, Centers for Disease Control and Prevention Office on Smoking and Health, and American Cancer Society. The mission of Smokefree.gov is to help you or someone you care about quit smoking. You can get assistance in a number of ways: online step-by-step cessation guide, local and state telephone quitlines, national telephone quitline, instant messaging service and a variety of publications. For help quitting, contact Smokefree.gov at 800-QUITNOW; www.smokefree.gov.

One-Time "Welcome to Medicare" Physical Exam
If your Medicare B coverage began on or after January 1, 2005, Medicare will cover a one-time preventative physical exam within the first six months that you are on the plan. The exam will include a thorough review of your health, education and counseling. The exam may include: blood pressure check, Electrocardiogram, vision test, shots and any other test the doctor advices. You pay 20% of the Medicare-approved amount after you meet the yearly Part B deductibles. You can find your state Medical Assistance Office at www.medicare.gov/ContactUs.asp or contact Centers for Medicare & Medicaid Services, 7500 Security Boulevard, Baltimore, MD 21244-1850; 800-MEDICARE; www.medicare.gov/health/physicalexam.asp.

How to Get Medicare To Pay For Your Motor Scooter
A recent study show that when a senior calls the Medicare Hotline they get the wrong answer, or no answer 39% of the time. And when a physician calls they get the wrong answer 96% of the time. If you want to get a power wheelchair and contact Medicare to see if you are eligible, this report says that your answer should be "A physician must prescribe the power wheelchair or determine it to be medically necessary, and a power wheelchair requires a copayment on the part of the Medicare beneficiary. "The study is called U.S. GAO Report Accuracy of Responses from the 1-800-MEDICARE Help Line Should Be Improved, http://www.gao.gov/new.items/d05130.pdf

Co-Payment Assistance

The Patient Advocate Foundation's Patient Assistance Program offers co-payment assistance for pharmaceutical products to insured Americans who qualify medically and financially. They also offer counseling to all patients through the Patient Assistance Program. For additional information, contact PAF Program Assistance Program, 700 Thimble Shoals Boulevard, Suite 201, Newport News, VA 23606; 866-512-3861; www.copays.org.

Free Blood Pressure Monitoring

Free blood pressure monitoring is more available than you may think. Almost every grocery store, discount store and pharmacy has a blood pressure cuff station. It is usually in the pharmacy section and it is free for anyone to use. Most even provide a card to help you keep track of those vital numbers. Take the responsibility for your own health and check your blood pressure as your doctor recommends.

Search for AIDS Clinical Trials

According to aids.org there are currently 60,000 people 50 years old and older affected with AIDS in the U.S. today and that number continues to increase. It may seem strange but seniors must learn about their risks, ways to stay safe, diagnosis and treatment options. To learn current information about AIDS contact either of the following organizations. AIDSinfo, P.O. Box 6303, Rockville, MD 20849-6303; 800-HIV-0440, Fax: 301-519-6616; www.aidsinfo.nih.gov/ or CDC National Prevention Information Network, P.O. Box 6003, Rockville, MD 20849-6003; 800-458-5231, 919-361-4892, Fax: 888-282-7681; www.cdcnpin.org.

$5 For Sexually Transmitted Disease Tests

Seniors may be worried that they have contracted a Sexually Transmitted Disease (STD) or even HIV. If you are worried, you can get tested and even treated for free or for very low cost at one of your local health clinics, or other public and private clinics throughout the country. Contact your county office of health listed in your telephone book or your state Department of Health. If you need more help identifying local help or need further information about STD's or HIV, contact one of the following organizations:

- ***STD and AIDS Hotline*** 800-342-AIDS; www.cdcnpin.org
- ***HIV Testing Resources*** www.hivtest.org/

Protect Your Money

A government report shows that up to 21% of seniors hide their assets to help qualify for Medicaid to pay for long term nursing care (GAO-05-968). Nursing home care can cost up to $70,000 a year, so people can quickly deplete their savings accounts. Medicare only covers 100 days of skilled nursing care. Once all the patient's funds are gone, Medicaid kicks in to cover the bill. There is a certain amount of income that is not counted in qualifying for Medicaid and when a spouse is involved there are even more rules and exemptions. Homes, automobiles, furnishings, and certain income are exempt, but all of this varies from state to state. You are legally allowed to transfer money up to 36 months and up to 60 months for certain irrevocable trusts. That is the time period Medicaid will review your finances to see if you qualify for coverage. It is illegal to hide assets from Medicaid, and to intentionally transfer the assets to qualify for Medicaid. You can do an internet search for "Medicaid Planning" which will turn up several publications and information regarding what the rules are for your state. Some basic rules can be found at http://www.cms.hhs.gov/medicaid/eligibility/assets.asp, although you will need to contact your state directly to find out specifics for your state. You can also locate some specific information at www.elderlawanswers.com which provides rules for each state. Senior Legal hotlines (listed on page 216) can answer your questions and put you in contact with people who can assist you in estate planning.

Become Part of Research

The National Institute of Health operates one of the largest medical research hospitals in the world. The Patient Recruitment and Public Liaison Office has trained nurses that can answer your questions and send you information about the Clinical Center research program and how you may be able to participate. Contact: Patient Recruitment and Public Liaison Office; 800-411-1222, TTY: 866-411-1010, Fax: 301-480-9793; www.cc.nih.gov/ccc/prpl/.

25 Million Seniors and Doctors Are Unaware Of Free Health Services

A government study shows that there are a number of screening and immunizations that are recommended for seniors, but both seniors and doctors are unaware they are covered by Medicare. Nine out of ten seniors visit a doctor once a year but don't know that Medicare will cover immunizations for Influenza, Hepatitis B, and Pneumococcal, as well as screenings for cervical cancer (pap smear), breast cancer (mammography), vaginal cancer (pelvic exam), colorectal cancer (fecal-occult blood test), colorectal cancer (flexible sigmiodoscopy or colonoscopy), osteoporosis (bone mass measurement), prostate cancer (prostate specific antigen test and/or digital rectal examination), and glaucoma.

Free Health Care When You Have No Insurance Coverage

Healthcare centers around the country offer everything from mental health to dental services. Each facility has different requirements, normally on a sliding scale. Contact Health Resources and Services Administration, U.S. Department of Health and Human Services; http://www.ask.hrsa.gov/pc/ Another database, The Free Clinic Foundation of America, 1240 Third Street S.W, Roanoke, VA 24016; 540-344-8242; www.medkind.com/FCF

Free Clinical Trial Search

The National Institute of Diabetes and Digestive and Kidney Disorders will let you search for clinical trials that you may be eligible for to help your health issues. In addition, they can provide you with information on any disease related to diabetes, digestion and kidneys. Contact: National Institute of Diabetes and Digestive and Kidney Diseases, National Institute of Health, Building 31, Room 9A04 Center Drive, MSC 2560, Bethesda, MD 20892-2560; www.niddk.nih.gov.

Free Eye Care

Seniors EyeCare America provides eligible seniors access to medical eye care including an exam and up to one year of treatment with no out of pocket expenses. Participants must be: US citizens, 65 years old and older, not have been to an ophthalmologist in three years and may not belong to an HMO or the VA. If you don't qualify for this program you can still call the free 24 hour a day helpline that will help determine your eligibility for other programs. Contact: 800-222-EYES (3937); www.eyeamerica.org.

Are You Eligible for Free Health Care?

Health insurance can be quite confusing. What exactly do you qualify for? Medicare is a health insurance program, generally for people age 65 or older who are receiving *Social Security* retirement benefits. You can also receive Medicare if you are under 65 and receive Social Security or Railroad Retirement Board disability benefits for 24 months, or if you are a kidney dialysis or kidney transplant patient. Medicaid is a federal program administered by each state, so eligibility and benefits vary from state to state. The program is administered by a state welfare agency, and it provides health insurance to people with low income and limited assets.

To determine your eligibility, contact your state Office of Social Services. For Medicare eligibility, contact Medicare Hotline, Centers for Medicare & Medicaid Services, 7500 Security Blvd., Baltimore, MD 21244-1850; 800-MEDICARE; www.medicare.gov.

Medicaid Hotlines

Alabama
800-362-1504

Alaska
800-478-6065 SeniorCare Senior Office

Arizona
800-523-0231 Out of State
800-962-6690

Arkansas
800-482-8988 Eligibility
800-482-5431

California
Medi-Cal Mental Health Ombudsman Services: 800-896-4042
Medi-Cal Managed Care: 800-430-4263
TTY: 800-896-2512

Colorado
800-221-3943

Connecticut
800-842-1508

Delaware
800-372-2022

District of Columbia
Local: 202-442-5999

Florida
888-419-3456

Georgia
866-322-4260

Hawaii
Oahu: 808-587-3521

Idaho
800-685-3757

Illinois
800-226-0768
TTY: 800-526-5812

Indiana
800-889-9949

Iowa
800-338-8366

Kansas
800-766-9012

Kentucky
800-635-2570

Louisiana
888-342-6207

Maine
800-977-6740

Maryland
800-492-5231

Massachusetts
800-841-2900

Michigan
Beneficiary Help Line: 800-642-3195
Enrollment: 888-367-6557

Minnesota
800-333-2433

Mississippi
800-421-2408

Missouri
800-392-2161

Montana
800-362-8312

Nebraska
800-430-3244

Nevada
800-992-0900
TTY: 800-326-6888

New Hampshire
800-852-3388

New Jersey
800-356-1561

New Mexico
888-997-2583

New York
800-541-2831

North Carolina
800-662-7030
TTY: 877-733-4851

North Dakota
800-755-2604

Ohio
800-324-8680

Oklahoma
800-522-0310

Oregon
800-527-5772

Pennsylvania
800-692-7462

Rhode Island
401-462-5300 (no toll-free number)
TTY: 401-462-3363

South Carolina
888-549-0820

South Dakota
800-452-7691

Tennessee
800-669-1851

Texas
888-834-7406

Utah
800-662-9651

Vermont
800-250-8427

Virginia
800-552-8627

Washington
800-562-3022

West Virginia
304-558-1703

Wisconsin
800-362-3002

Wyoming
307-777-7979

Health Care Close To Home

For more information on services and programs for health care services, contact your state Department of Public Health.

Alabama
Department of Public Health
RSA Tower 201 Monroe Street
Montgomery, AL 36104
MAILING ADDRESS:
RSA Tower
P.O. Box 303017
Montgomery, AL 36130-3017
334-206-5300
http://www.adph.org/aldph.asp

Alaska
Department of Health & Social Services
350 Main Street, Room 404
Juneau, AK 99801
MAILING ADDRESS:
P.O. Box 110610
Juneau, AK 99811-0601
907-465-3030
Fax: 907-586-3068
http://health.hss.state.ak.us

Arizona
Department of Health
Office of Women's & Children's Health
150 North 18th Street
Phoenix, AZ 85007
602-542-1000
Fax: 602-542-0883
http://www.azdhs.gov/

Arkansas
Department of Health
4815 West Markham
Little Rock, AR 72205
501-661-2000
800-235-0002
http://www.healthyarkansas.com/

California
Department of Health Services
Office of Women's Health
MS 0027
P.O. Box 997413
Sacramento CA 95899-7413
916-440-7560
www.dhs.ca.gov

Colorado
Department of Public health and Environment
4300 Cherry Creek Drive South
Denver, CO 80246-1530
303-692-2000
http://www.cdphe.state.co.us/cdphehom.asp

Connecticut
Department of Public Health
410 Capitol Avenue
P.O. Box 340308
Hartford, CT 06134-0308
860-509-8000
TDD: 860-509-7191
http://www.dph.state.ct.us/

Delaware
Division of Public Health
417 Federal Street
Dover, DE 19901
302-744-4700
888-459-2943
Fax: 302-739-3008
http://www.dhss.delaware.gov/dhss/dph/index.html

District of Columbia
Department of Health
825 North Capitol Street, NE
Washington, DC 20002
202-671-5000
http://dchealth.dc.gov/index.asp

Florida
Department of Health
4052 Bald Cypress Way
Bin # A00
Tallahassee, FL 32399-1701
850-245-4321
www.doh.state.fl.us

Georgia
Division of Public Health
Two Peachtree Street, NW
Atlanta, GA 30303-3186
404-657-2700
http://health.state.ga.us/

Hawaii
Department of Health
1250 Punchbowl Street
Honolulu, HI 96813
808-586-4400
Fax: 808-586-4444
www.state.hi.us/health/
Email: pijohnst@health.state.hi.us

Idaho
Department of Health and Welfare
450 W. State St, 10th Floor
Boise, ID 83720-0036
208-334-5500
Fax: 208-334-6558
TDD: 208-334-4921
http://www.healthandwelfare.idaho.gov/

Illinois
Department of Public Health
535 West Jefferson Street
Springfield, IL 62761
217-782-4977
Fax: 217-782-3987
TTY: 800-547-0466
www.idph.state.il.us/

Indiana
Department of Health
2 North Meridian Street
Indianapolis, IN 46204
317-233-1325
http://www.in.gov/isdh/
Email: OPA@isdh.state.in.us

Iowa
Department of Public Health
Lucas Building
321 East 12th Street
Des Moines, IA 50319
517-281-7689
www.idph.state.ia.us

Kansas
Division of Health & Environment
Curtis State Office Building
1000 SW Jackson
Topeka, KS 66612
785-296-1500
Fax: 785-368-6368
www.kdhe.state.ks.us

Kentucky
Cabinet for Health Services
275 East Main Street
Frankfort, KY 40621
502-564-3970
Fax: 502-564-6533
http://chfs.ky.gov/

Louisiana
Department of Health and Hospitals
1201 Capitol Access Road
P.O. Box 629
Baton Rouge, LA 70821-0629
225-342-9500
Fax: 225-342-5568
www.dhh.state.la.us
webadmin@dhh.la.gov

Maine
Department of Human Services
221 State Street
Augusta, ME 04333
207-287-3707
Fax: 207-287-3005
TTY: 207-287-4479
http://www.maine.gov/dhhs/

Maryland
Department of Health & Mental Hygiene
State Office Building Complex
201 West Preston Street
Baltimore, MD 21201
410-767-6860
TTD: 800-735-2258
www.dhmh.state.md.us/index.html

Massachusetts
Department of Public Health
250 Washington Street
Boston, MA 02108-4619
617-624-6000
TTY: 617-624-6001
http://www.mass.gov/dph/dphhome.htm

Michigan
Department of Community Health
Lewis Cass Building-Sixth Floor
320 South Walnut Street
Lansing, MI 48913
517-373-3740
TDD 517-373-3573
http://www.michigan.gov/mdch

Minnesota
Department of Health
717 Delaware Street Southeast
Minneapolis, MN 55440-9441
MAILING ADDRESS:
Minnesota Department of Health
P.O. Box 64975
St. Paul, MN, 55164-0975
651-215-5800
www.health.state.mn.us

Mississippi
State Department of Health
570 East Woodrow Wilson Drive
Post Office Box 1700
Jackson, MS 39215-1700
601-576-7400
Fax: 601-576-7364
www.msdh.state.ms.us/msdhhome.htm
Email: info@msdh.state.ms.us/

Missouri
Department of Health
930 Wildwood
P.O. Box 570
Jefferson, MO 65102-0570
573-751-6400
Fax: 573-751-6041
www.health.state.mo.us
Email: info@dhss.mo.gov

Montana
Department of Public Health & Human Services

111 North Sanders
Helena, MT 59601
MAILING ADDRESS:
P.O. Box 4210
Helena, MT 59604
406-444-2596
Fax: 406-444-1970
www.dphhs.mt.gov

Nebraska
Health & Human Services System
Department of Services
P.O. Box 95044
Lincoln, NE 68509-5044
402-471-2306
www.hhs.state.ne.us/index.htm
Email: system.information@hhss.ne.gov

Nevada
State Health Division
505 East King Street, Room 201
Carson City, NV 89710
775-684-4200
Fax: 775-684-4211
http://health2k.state.nv.us/

New Hampshire
Department of Health & Human Services
6 Hazen Drive
Concord, NH 03301-6505
603-271-4939
http://www.dhhs.state.nh.us/DHHS/DHHS_SITE/default.htm

New Jersey
Department of Health & Senior Services
P.O. Box 360
John Fitch Plaza
Trenton, NJ 08625
609-292-7836
Fax: 609-633-9601
www.state.nj.us/health/

New Mexico
Department of Health
1190 St. Francis Drive
Harold Runnels Building
Santa Fe, NM 87502
505-827-2613
Fax: 505-827-2530
http://www.health.state.nm.us/

New York
Department of Health
Corning Tower Building
Empire State Plaza
Albany, NY 12237
518-486-9002
www.health.state.ny.us

North Carolina
State Center for Health Statistics
Cotton Classing Building
222 Dawson Street
Raleigh, NC 27603-1392
MAILING ADDRESS:
P.O. Box 29358
Raleigh, NC 27626-0538
919-733-4728
Fax: 919-733-8485
http://www.schs.state.nc.us/SCHS/

North Dakota
Department of Health
600 East Boulevard Avenue
Bismarck, ND 58505-0200
701-328-2372
Fax: 701-328-4727
http://www.health.state.nd.us/

Ohio
Department of Health
246 North High Street
P.O. Box 118
Columbus, OH 43215
614-466-3543
www.odh.state.oh.us
Email: OPA@odh.ohio.gov

Oklahoma
State Department of Health
1000 NE 10th Street
Oklahoma City, OK 73117
405-271-5600
800-522-0203
www.health.state.ok.us
Email: webmaster@health.state.ok.us

Oregon
Health Division
800 NE Oregon Street
Portland, OR 97232
503-731-4000
www.ohd.hr.state.or.us
Email: health.webmaster@state.or.us

Pennsylvania
Department of Health
P.O. Box 90
Health & Welfare Building
Harrisburg, PA 17108

800-692-7254
www.health.state.pa.us
Email: webmaster@health.state.pa.us

Rhode Island
Department of Health
3 Capitol Hill
Providence, RI 02908
401-222-2231
Fax: 401-222-6548
TTY: 800-745-5555
www.health.state.ri.us/
Email: library@doh.state.ri.us

South Carolina
Department of Health & Environmental Control
2600 Bull Street
Columbia, SC 29201
803-898-3432
http://www.scdhec.net/

South Dakota
Department of Health
Health Building
600 East Capitol
Pierre, SD 57501-2563
605-773-3361
800-738-2301
Fax: 605-773-5683
http://www.state.sd.us/doh/
Email: DOH.INFO@state.sd.us

Tennessee
Department of Health
425 5th Avenue North
Nashville, TN 37247
1-800-852-2187
www.state.tn.us/health
Email: TN.health@state.tn.us

Texas
Department of Health
1100 West 49th Street
Austin, TX 78756-3199
512-458-7111
www.dshs.state.tx.us

Utah
Department of Health
P.O. Box 141010
Salt Lake City, UT 84114-1010
801-538-6101
http://hlunix.ex.state.ut.us/
Email: pwightma@utah.gov

Vermont
Department of Health
108 Cherry Street
Burlington, VT 05402-0070
800-464-4343
Fax: 802-863-7754
http://www.healthyvermonters.info/

Virginia
Department of Health
P.O. Box 2448
109 Governor Street
Richmond, VA 23219
804-786-5916
Fax: 804-864-7022
www.vdh.state.va.us/

Washington
State Department of Health
101 Israel Road SE
MAILING ADDRESS:
PO Box 47890
Olympia, Washington 98504-7890
800-525-0127
360-236-4501
www.doh.wa.gov/
Email: doh.webmaster@doh.wa.gov

West Virginia
Bureau for Public Health
Room 702, 350 Capitol Street
Charleston, WV 25301-3712
304-558-2971
Fax: 304-558-1035
http://www.wvdhhr.org/bph/

Wisconsin
Department of Health & Family Services
1 West Wilson Street
Madison, WI 53702
608-266-1865
TTY: 608-267-7371
www.dhfs.state.wi.us
Email: webmaster@dhfs.state.wi.us

Wyoming
Department of Health
2300 Capitol Avenue
MAILING ADDRESS:
117 Hathaway Building
Cheyenne, WY 82002
307-777-7657
Fax: 307-777-7439
TTY: 307-777-5648
http://wdh.state.wy.us/main/index.asp
Email: wdh-webmaster@state.wy.us

Health Care For Veterans

The Department of Veterans Affairs provides a Medical Benefits Package to veterans which is a standard health benefits plan. This plan emphasizes preventive and primary care, and offers a full range of outpatient and inpatient services within VA health care system. Enrolled veterans who are traveling or who spend time away from their primary treatment facility may obtain care at any VA health care facility across the country without the worry of having to reapply. All veterans are potentially eligible. Eligibility is based on active military service, and Reservists and National Guard members who are called to active duty are also eligible.

VA's Medical Benefits Package includes:

- Preventive Care Services-immunizations, physicals, health screenings
- Ambulatory Diagnostic and Treatment Services- emergency outpatient care, surgery, mental health, substance abuse
- Hospital Diagnostic and Treatment
- Medications and Supplies

You can apply for care by visiting, calling or writing a VA health care facility, visiting the website www.va.gov/1010EX.htm; or calling toll-free 877-222-VETS (Monday-Friday 7 a.m.-8p.m. EST).

VA Medical Care:
Promote, Preserve and Restore Your Health

In October 1996, Congress passed the Veterans' Health Care Eligibility Reform Act of 1996. This legislation paved the way for the creation of a Medical Benefits Package, a standard health care benefits plan available to all enrolled veterans. Only 15% of eligible veterans take advantage of this service and you must apply to receive benefits. The Medical Benefits Package provides veterans' with hospital care and outpatient care that are needed to promote, preserve, and restore your health. Medical care is provided at a VA health facility. Veterans pay for medical benefits depending on their service-connected level in the military and an assigned Priority Group. You can apply by completing Form 10-10EZ. The form may be obtained by visiting, calling or writing any VA health care facility or veterans' benefits office. You may also receive a form by calling (877) 222-VETS or accessing the form from the internet at www.1010EZ.med.va.gov/sec/vha/1010ez. For more information contact Veterans' Health Administration, 810 Vermont Ave., NW, Washington, DC 20420; 202-273-5400; 877-222-3887; www.va.gov/elig/.

To Copay or not to Copay

There are three outpatient copayment levels for veterans seeking health care. The first level is no copayment. These services are for publicly announced VA health initiatives (i.e.: health fairs) or an outpatient visit consisting solely of preventative screening and immunizations. These may include flu immunization, alcohol or tobacco screenings, breast and cervical cancer screenings and certain blood tests. In the second level, the VHA provides primary care outpatient preventative care, which includes periodic exams, health education, maintenance of drug-use profiles, mental health and substance abuse prevention services. Depending on your Priority group, you may be required to pay a $15 copayment for primary care visits.

The third level is a $50 copay to see a specialist. Many veterans apply for a needs test, which allows them to receive many if not all medical benefits at no cost to them. For additional information contact your local VA health care facility or contact the Veteran's Health Administration. Contact Veterans' Health Administration, 810 Vermont Ave., NW, Washington, DC 20420; 202-273-5400; 877-222-3887; www.va.gov/elig/.

Coverage While You're Lying in the Hospital

Basic care for inpatient services for veterans include: medical, surgical and mental health care, including care for substance abuse. If you are required to remain in the hospital, Congress determined the inpatient copayment should be the current inpatient Medicare deductible rate plus $10 for the first 90 days that you are confined to the hospital. For additional information contact your local VA health care facility or contact the Veteran's Health Administration. Contact Veterans' Health Administration, 810 Vermont Ave., NW, Washington, DC 20420; 202-273-5400; 877-222-3887; www.va.gov/elig/.

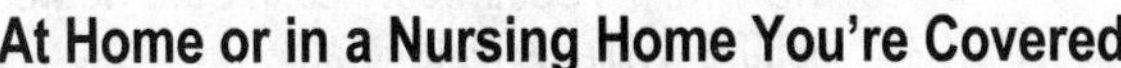

At Home or in a Nursing Home You're Covered

The Veterans' Administration provides coverage for home health care as well as respite, hospice and palliative care. Congress determined the copayment should be the current Medicare deductible rate plus $5.00 for each day. For additional information contact your local VA health care facility or contact the Veteran's Health Administration. Contact Veterans' Health Administration, 810 Vermont Ave., NW, Washington, DC 20420; 202-273-5400; 877-222-3887; www.va.gov/elig/.

Prescriptions for Vets

Prescriptions are available at Veterans' Administration pharmacies. Congress has established the copayment cost to be $7 for a 30 day or less supply of medications provided on an outpatient basis for nonservice-connected condition. Medication copays apply to medications and over-the-counter medications (aspirin, cough syrup, vitamins etc) that are dispensed from a VA pharmacy. For additional information contact your local VA health care facility or contact the Veteran's Health Administration. Contact Veterans' Health Administration, 810 Vermont Ave., NW, Washington, DC 20420; 202-273-5400; 877-222-3887; www.va.gov/elig/.

Help! It's an Emergency

Emergency care is available through VA medical facilities for veterans. If a Federal facility is not feasibly available at the time of the emergency and your emergency is a service-connected disability you may be eligible for reimbursement for treatment at another medical facility. For additional information contact your local VA health care facility or contact the Veteran's Health Administration. Contact Veterans' Health Administration, 810 Vermont Ave., NW, Washington, DC 20420; 202-273-5400; 877-222-3887; www.va.gov/elig/.

Free Medical Care For Veterans

The Veterans Health Administration (VHA) provides a broad spectrum of medical, surgical, and rehabilitative care to Veterans under the Veterans' Health Care Eligibility Reform Act of 1996. This legislation paved the way for the creation of a Medical Benefits Package — a standard enhanced health benefits plan available to all enrolled veterans. Eligible veterans may obtain medical care at facilities throughout the country.

Listed are the Regional and VA Medical Centers. In addition to these facilities, many states also have Outpatient Clinics and Community Outpatient Clinics to serve veterans. Contact the closest VA Medical facility to find an outpatient office near your home or check their web site at www1.va.gov/directory/guide/home.asp. Veterans Health Administration, 800 Vermont Ave., NW, Washington, DC 20420; 202-273-5400; Benefits: 877-222-VETS.

Alabama

Birmingham VA Medical Center
700 S. 19th Street
Birmingham, AL 35233
205-933-8101
Fax: 205-933-4484

Central Alabama Veterans Health Care System
West Campus
215 Perry Hill Road
Montgomery, AL 36109-3798
334-272-4670
Fax: 334-260-4143

Tuscaloosa VA Medical Center
3701 Loop Road, East
Tuscaloosa, AL 35404
205-554-2000
Fax: 205-554-2034

Central Alabama Veterans Health Care System
East Campus
2400 Hospital Road
Tuskegee, AL 36083-5001
334-727-0550
Fax: 334-724-2793

VA Gulf Coast Health Care System
Mobile Outpatient Center
1504 Springhill Ave.
Mobile, AL 36604
251-219-3900

Alaska

VA Healthcare System and Regional Office
2925 DeBarr Road
Anchorage, AK 99508-2989
907-257-4700
Fax: 907-257-6774

Fairbanks VA Medical Clinic
Bassett Army Community Hospital
Building 4065, Gaffney Road, Room 169/176
Fort Wainwright, AK 99703
Toll Free-888-353-5242
907-353-6370
Fax: 907-353-6372

Kenai VA Medical Clinic
BENCO Building
11355 Frontage Road, Suite 130
Kenai, AK 99611
907-283-2231
Fax: 907-283-4236

Arizona

VISN 18: VA Southwest Health Care Network
6950 E. Williams Field Road
Mesa, AZ 85212-6033
602-222-2681
Fax: 602-222-2686
http://www.va.gov/visn18/

Northern Arizona VA Health Care System
500 N. Hwy 89
Prescott, AZ 86313
928-445-4860
Fax: 928-768-6076

Southern Arizona VA Health Care System
3601 South 6th Avenue
Tucson, AZ 85723
520-792-1450
http://www.va.gov/678savahcs/

Carl T. Hayden VA Medical Center
650 E. Indian School Road
Phoenix, AZ 85012
602-277-5551
http://www.phoenix.med.va.gov/

Arkansas

Fayetteville VA Medical Center
1100 N. College Avenue
Fayetteville, AR 72703
479-443-4301

Central Arkansas Veterans Healthcare System
John L. McClellan Memorial Veterans Hospital
4300 West 7th Street
Little Rock, AR 72205-5484
501-257-1000

Eugene J. Towbin Healthcare Center
2200 Fort Roots Drive

North Little Rock, AR 72114-1706
501-257-1000

California
VISN 22: Desert Pacific Healthcare Network
5901 E. 7th Street
Long Beach, CA 90822
562-826-5963
Fax: 562-826-5987
http://www.visn22.med.va.gov/

VISN 21: Sierra Pacific Network
201 Walnut Avenue
Mare Island, CA 94592
707-562-8350
Fax: 707-562-8369
http://www.visn21.med.va.gov/

VA Central California Health Care System
2615 E. Clinton Avenue
Fresno, CA 93703
559-225-6100
Fax: 559-228-6903

Livermore
4951 Arroyo Road
Livermore, CA 94550
925-373-4700

VA Loma Linda Healthcare System
11201 Benton Street
Loma Linda, CA 92357
800-741-8387
Fax: 909-422-3106
FTS: 909-825-7084
FTS Fax: 909-422-3106
http://www.lom.med.va.gov/

VA Long Beach Healthcare System
5901 E. 7th Street
Long Beach, CA 90822
562-826-8000
Fax: 562-826-5972
http://www.long-beach.med.va.gov/

VA Greater Los Angeles Healthcare System (GLA)
11301 Willshire Boulevard
Los Angeles, CA 90073
310-478-3711
Fax: 310-268-3494
http://www.gla.med.va.gov/

Martinez Center for Rehab and Extended Care
150 Muir Rd.
Martinez, CA 94553
925-372-2851

VA Northern California Health Care System
10535 Hospital Way
Mather, CA 95655
916-366-5366
Fax: 916-843-9001

Menlo Park
795 Willow Road
Menlo Park, CA 94025
650-493-5000
http://www.palo-alto.med.va.gov/

VA Palo Alto Health Care System
3801 Miranda Avenue
Palo Alto, CA 94304-1290
650-493-5000
Fax: 650-852-3228
http://www.palo-alto.med.va.gov/

VA San Diego Health Care System
3350 La Jolla Village Drive
San Diego, CA 92161
858-552-8585
http://www.san-diego.med.va.gov/start.htm

San Francisco VA Medical Ctr
4150 Clement Street
San Francisco, CA 94121-1598
415-221-4810
Fax: 415-750-2185
www.sf.med.va.gov

Colorado
VA Health Administration Center
300 S. Jackson St.
Denver, CO 80206
303-331 7500
Fax: 303-331 7800
http://www.va.gov/hac/

VISN 19: Rocky Mountain Network
4100 E. Mississippi Ave., Suite 510
Glendale, CO 80246
303-756-9279
Fax: 303-756-9243

VA Eastern Colorado Health Care System
1055 Clermont Street
Denver, CO 80220
303-399-8020
Fax: 303-393-2861

Grand Junction VA Medical Center
2121 North Avenue
Grand Junction, CO 81501
970-242-0731
Fax: 970-244-1330

Connecticut
VA Connecticut Healthcare System
Newington Campus
555 Willard Avenue
Newington, CT 06111
860-666-6951
Fax: 860-667-6764
http://www.visn1.med.va.gov/vact/

VA Connecticut Healthcare System
West Haven Campus
950 Campbell Avenue
West Haven, CT 06516
203-932-5711
Fax: 203-937-3868
http://www.visn1.med.va.gov/vact/

Delaware
Wilmington VA Medical and Regional Office Center
1601 Kirkwood Highway
Wilmington, DE 19805
302-994-2511
Fax: 302-633-5516

District of Columbia
Washington D.C. VA Medical Center
50 Irving Street, NW
Washington, DC 20422
202-745-8000
Fax: 202-754-8530
http://www.washington.med.va.gov/

Florida
VISN 8: VA Sunshine Healthcare Network
VISN Office: P.O. Box 406
Bay Pines, FL 33744
727-319-1125
Fax: 727-319-1135

North Florida/South Georgia Veterans Health System
Gainesville Division
1601 S.W. Archer Road
Gainesville, FL 32608-1197
352-376-1611
Fax: 352-374-6113
http://www.va.gov/visn8/nfsg

North Florida/South Georgia Veterans Health System
City Division
619 S. Marion Street
Lake City, FL 32025-5898
386-755-3016
Fax: 386-758-3209
http://www.va.gov/north-florida/

Miami VA Medical Center
1201 N.W. 16th Street
Miami, FL 33125
305-575-7000
Fax: 305-575-3266
http://www.va.gov/546miami/

Bay Pines VA Medical Center
10,000 Bay Pines Blvd
St. Petersburg, FL 33708
727-398-6661
Fax: 727-398-9442
www1.va.gov/visn8/baypines

Tampa (James A. Haley-VA Medical Center
13000 Bruce B. Downs Blvd.
Tampa, FL 33612
813-972-2000
Fax: 813-972-7673
www1.va.gov/visn8/Tampa

West Palm Beach VA Medical Center
7305 N. Military Trail
West Palm Beach, FL 33410-6400
561-422-8262
Fax: 561-422-8613
www1.va.gov/visn8/westpalm

Georgia
VISN 7: The Atlanta Network
3700 Crestwood Parkway, NW, Suite 500
Duluth, GA 30096-5585
678-924-5700
Fax: 678-924-5757

Augusta VA Medical Center
1 Freedom Way
Augusta, GA 30904-6285
706-733-0188
Fax: 706-823-3934

Atlanta VA Medical Center
1670 Clairmont Road
Decatur, GA 30033
404-321-6111
Fax: 404-728-7733

Carl Vinson VA Medical Center
1826 Veteran's Boulevard

Dublin, GA 31021
478-272-1210
Fax: 478-277-2717

Guam
Guam Outpatient Clinic
222 Chalan Santo Papast
Reflection Center, Ste. 102
Agana, GU 96910
705-475-7161

Hawaii
VA Pacific Islands Health Care System
459 Patterson Road
Honolulu, HI 96819-1522
808-433-0600
Fax: 808-433-0390
http://www.va.gov/hawaii/

Idaho
Boise VA Medical Center
500 West Fort Street
Boise, ID 83702
208-422-1000
Fax: 208-422-1326

Illinois
VISN 12: Great Lakes Health Care System
P.O. Box 5000
Building 18
Hines, IL 60141-5000
708-202-8400
Fax: 708-202-8424
http://www.vagreatlakes.org/

Jesse Brown VA Medical Center
820 South Damen Avenue
Chicago, IL 60612
312-569-8387
http://www.vagreatlakes.org/

VA Illiana Health Care System
1900 East Main Street
Danville, IL 61832-5198
217-554-3000
Fax: 217-554-4552

Edward Hines Jr. VA Hospital
5th & Roosevelt Rd.
P.O. Box 5000
Hines, IL 60141
708-202-8387
Fax: 708-202-2721
http://www.vagreatlakes.org/

Marion VA Medical Center
2401 West Main Street
Marion, IL 62959
618-997-5311

North Chicago VA Medical Ctr
3001 Green Bay Road
North Chicago, IL 60064
847-688-1900
Fax: 847-578-3806
http://www.n-chicago.med.va.gov/

Springfield Illinois Clinic
326 N 7th Street
Springfield, IL 62769
217-522-4730

Indiana
VA Northern Indiana Health Care System-Fort Wayne Campus
2121 Lake Ave.
Fort Wayne, IN 46805
260-426-5431
Fax: 260-460-1336

Richard L. Roudebush VA Medical Center
1481 W. Tenth Street
Indianapolis, IN 46202
317-554-0000

VA Northern Indiana Health Care System-Marion Campus
1700 East 38th Street
Marion, IN 46953-4589
765-674-3321
Fax: 765-677-3124

Iowa
Des Moines Division- VA Central Iowa Health Care System
3600 30th Street
Des Moines, IA 50310-5774
515-699-5999
Fax: 515-699-5862

Iowa City VA Medical Center
601 Highway 6 West
Iowa City, IA 52246-2208
319-338-0581
Fax: 319-339-7135
http://www.iowa-city.med.va.gov/

Knoxville Division-VA Central Iowa Health Care System
1515-W. Pleasant Street
Knoxville, IA 50138
641-842-3101
Fax: 641-828-5124

Kansas

VA Eastern Kansas Health Care System
Dwight D. Eisenhower VA Medical Center
4101 S. 4th Street
Leavenworth, KS 66048-5055
913-682-2000

VA Eastern Kansas Health Care System
Colmery-O'Neil VA Medical Center
2200 SW Gage Boulevard
Topeka, KS 66622
785-350-3111
Fax: 785-350-4336

Robert J. Dole Department of Veteran Affairs Medical and Regional Office Center
5500 E. Kellogg
Wichita, KS 67218
316-685-2221
Fax: 316-651-3666

Kentucky

Lexington VA Medical Center
1101 Veterans Drive
Lexington, KY 40502-2236
859-233-4511

Louisville VA Medical Center
800 Zorn Avenue
Louisville, KY 40206
502-287-4000
www.va.gov/603Louisville

Louisiana

Alexandria VA Medical Center
P. O. Box 69004
Alexandria, LA 71360
318-473-0010
Fax: 318-483-5029
http://www.alexandria.med.va.gov/

New Orleans VA Medical Center
1601 Perdido Street
New Orleans, LA 70112-1262
504-568-0811
Fax: 504-589-5210

Overton Brooks VA Medical Center
510 E. Stoner Ave.
Shreveport, LA 71101-4295
318-221-8411
Fax: 318-424-6156

Maine

Togus VA Medical/Regional Office Center
1 VA Center
Augusta, ME 04330
207-623-8411
Fax: 207-623-5792
http://www.visn1.med.va.gov/togus/

Maryland

VISN 5: VA Capitol Health Care Network
849 International Dr., Suite 275
Linthicum, MD 21090
410-691-1131
Fax: 410-684-3189
http://www.va.gov/visn5/

Baltimore VA Rehabilitation and Extended Care Center (BRECC)
3900 Loch Raven Boulevard
Baltimore, MD 21218
410-605-7000
Fax: 410-605-7900

Baltimore VAMC-VA Maryland Health Care System
10 North Greene Street
Baltimore, MD 21201
410-605-7000
Fax: 410-605-7901
http://www.vamhcs.med.va.gov/

Perry Point VAMC-VA Maryland Health Care System
Perry Point, MD 21902
410-642-2411
Fax: 410-642-1161
http://www.vamhcs.med.va.gov/

Massachusetts

VISN 1: VA New England Healthcare System
200 Springs Road Building 61
Bedford, MA 01730
781-687-3400
Fax: 781-687-3470
http://www.visn1.med.va.gov/

Edith Nourse Rogers Memorial Veterans Hospital
200 Springs Rd.
Bedford, MA 01730
781-687-2000
Fax: 781-687-2101
http://www.visn1.med.va.gov/bedford/

VA Boston Healthcare System, Brockton Campus
940 Belmont Street
Brockton, MA 02301
508-583-4500
Fax: 700-885-1000
http://www.visn1.med.va.gov/boston/

VA Boston Healthcare System
Jamaica Plain Campus
150 South Huntington Avenue
Jamaica Plain, MA 02130
617-232-9500
Fax: 617-278-4549
http://www.visn1.med.va.gov/boston/

Northampton VA Medical Center
421 North Main Street
Leeds, MA 01053-9764
413-584-4040
Fax: 413-582-3121

VA Boston Healthcare System
West Roxbury Campus
1400 VFW Parkway
West Roxbury, MA 02132
617-323-7700
http://www.visn1.med.va.gov/boston/

Michigan
VISN 11: Veterans In Partnership
P.O. Box 134002
Ann Arbor, MI 48113-4002
734-930-5950
Fax: 734-930-5932

VA Ann Arbor Healthcare System
2215 Fuller Road
Ann Arbor, MI 48105
734-769-7100
Fax: 734-761-7870

Battle Creel VA Medical Center
5500 Armstrong Road
Battle Creek, MI 49015
616-966-5600
Fax: 616-966-5483

John D. Dingell VA Medical Center
4646 John R
Detroit, MI 48201
313-576-1000
Fax: 313-576-1025

Iron Mountain VA Medical Center
325 East H Street
Iron Mountain, MI 49801
906-774-3300
Fax: 906-779-3114
http://www.vagreatlakes.org/

Alesa E. Lutz VA Medical Center
1500 Weiss Street
Saginaw, MI 48602
989-497-2500
Fax: 989-791-2217

Minnesota
VISN 23: Lincoln and Minneapolis Offices
Minneapolis Office
5445 Minnehaha Ave S.
Second Floor
Minneapolis, MN 55417-2300
612-725-1968
Fax :(612)-727-5967
http://www.visn23.med.va.gov/

Minneapolis VA Medical Center
One Veterans Drive
Minneapolis, MN 55417
612-725-2000
Fax: 612-725-2049

St. Cloud VA Medical Center
4801 Veterans Drive
St. Cloud, MN 56303
320-252-1670
Fax: 320-255-6494

Mississippi
VISN 16: South Central VA Healthcare Network
1600 East Woodrow Wilson
3rd Floor, Suite A
Jackson, MS 39216
601-364-7900
Fax: 601-364-7996
http://www.visn16.med.va.gov/

VA Gulf Coast Veterans Health Care System
400 Veterans Avenue
Biloxi, MS 39531
228-523-5000
Fax: 228-523-5719

Jackson VA Medical Center
1500 E. Woodrow Wilson Drive
Jackson, MS 39216
601-362-4471
Fax: 601-364-1359

Missouri
VISN 15: VA Heartland Network
1201 Walnut Street, Suite 800
Kansas City, MO 64106
816-701-3000
Fax: 816-221-3392

Harry S. Truman Memorial
800 Hospital Drive

Columbia, MO 65201-5297
573-814-6000
Fax: 573-814-6600

Kansas City VA Medical Center
4801 Linwood Boulevard
Kansas City, MO 64128
816-861-4700
Fax: 816-922-3303

John J. Pershing VA Medical Center
1500 N. Westwood Blvd.
Poplar Bluff, MO 63901
573-686-4151
Fax: 573-778-4559

St. Louis VA Medical Center
915 North Grand Avenue
St. Louis, MO 63106
314-652-4100
Fax: 314-289-6557
http://www.va.gov/stlouis/

Montana
VA Montana Health Care System
1892 Williams Street
Fort Harrison, MT 59636
406-442-6410
Fax: 406-447-7916

Nebraska
VISN 23: Lincoln and Minneapolis Offices
Lincoln Office, Building 5
600 South 70th Street
Lincoln, NE 68510
402-484-3200
Fax: 402-484-3232
http://www.visn23.med.va.gov/

Grand Island Division VA Nebraska Western Iowa Health Care System
2201 No. Broadwell Avenue
Grand Island, NE 68803-2196
308-382-3660

Omaha Division-VA Nebraska Western Iowa Health Care
4101 Woolworth Avenue
Omaha, NE 68105
402-346-8800
Fax: 402-449-0684

Nevada
VA Southern Nevada Healthcare System (VASNHS)
P.O. Box 360001
North Las Vegas, NV 89036
702-636-3000
Fax: 702-636-4000
www.las-vegas.med.va.gov

VA Sierra Nevada Health Care System
1000 Locust Street
Reno, NV 89502
775-786-7200
Fax: 775-328-1464

New Hampshire
Manchester VA Medical Center
718 Smyth Road
Manchester, NH 03104
603-624-4366
http://www.visn1.med.va.gov/manchester/

New Jersey
East Orange Campus of the VA New Jersey Health Care System
385 Tremont Avenue
East Orange, NJ 07018
973-676-1000
Fax: 973-676-4226
http://www.va.gov/visns/visn03/default.asp

Lyons Campus of the VA New Jersey Health Care System
151 Knollcroft Road
Lyons, NJ 0793
908-647-0180
Fax: 908-647-3452
http://www.va.gov/visns/visn03/default.asp

New Mexico
New Mexico VA Health Care System
1501 San Pedro Drive, SE
Albuquerque, NM 87108-5153
505-265-1711
Fax: 505-256-2855

New York
VISN 2: VA Healthcare Network Upstate New York
P.O. Box 8980
Albany, NY 12208-8980
518-626-7300
Fax: 518-626-7333
http://www.va.gov/visns/visn02/

VISN 3: VA NY/NJ Veterans Healthcare Network
Building 16
130 W. Kingsbridge Road
Bronx, NY 10486
718-741-4110
Fax: 718-741-4141
http://www.va.gov/visns/visn03/default.asp

Albany VA Medical Center: Samuel S. Stratton
113 Holland Avenue
Albany, NY 12208
518-626-5000
Fax: 518-626-5500
http://www.va.gov/visns/visn02/

VA Western New York Healthcare System at Batavia
222 Richmond Avenue
Batavia, NY 14020
716-343-7500
Fax: 716-344-3305
http://www.va.gov/visns/visn02/

Bath VA Medical Center
76 Veterans Avenue
Bath, NY 14810
607-664-4000
Fax: 607-664-4511
http://www.va.gov/visns/visn02/

Bronx VA Medical Center
130 West Kingsbridge Road
Bronx, NY 10468
718-584-9000
Fax: 718-741-4269
http://www.va.gov/visns/visn03/default.asp

Brooklyn Campus of the VA NY Harbor Healthcare System
800 Poly Place
Brooklyn, NY 11209
718-836-6600
http://www.va.gov/visns/visn03/default.asp

VA Western New York Healthcare System at Buffalo
3495 Bailey Avenue
Buffalo, NY 14215
716-834-9200
Fax: 716-862-8759

Canandaigua VA Medical Center
400 Fort Hill Avenue
Canandaigua, NY 14424
585-394-2000
Fax: 585-393-8328
http://www.va.gov/visns/visn02/

Castle Point Campus of the VA Hudson Valley Healthcare System
Castle Point, NY 12511
845-831-2000
Fax: 845-838-5180
http://www.va.gov/visns/visn03/default.asp

Franklin Delano Roosevelt Campus of the VA Hudson Valley Healthcare System
622 Albany Post Rd.
Route 9A
P.O. Box 100
Montrose, NY 10548
914-737-4400 ext. 2400
Fax: 914-788-4244
http://www.va.gov/visns/visn03/default.asp

New York Campus of the NY Harbor Healthcare System
423 East 23rd Street
New York, NY 10010
212-686-7500
Fax: 212-951-3487
http://www.va.gov/visns/visn03/default.asp

Northport VA Medical Center
79 Middleville Road
Northport, NY 11768
631-261-4400
Fax: 631-754-7933
http://www.va.gov/visns/visn03/default.asp

Syracuse VA Medical Center
800 Irving Avenue
Syracuse, NY 13210
315-425-4400
Fax: 315-425-4375
http://www.va.gov/visns/visn02/

North Carolina

VISN 6: The Mid-Atlantic Network
Dept. of Veterans Affairs
300 W. Morgan St., Suite 1402
Durham, NC 27701
919-956-5541
Fax: 919-956-7152

Asheville VA Medical Center
1100 Tunnel Road
Asheville, NC 28805
828-298-7911
Fax: 828-299-2502

Durham VA Medical Center
508 Fulton Street
Durham, NC 27705
919-286-0411
Fax: 919-286-6825

Fayetteville VA Medical Center
2300 Ramsey Street
Fayetteville, NC 28301
910-488-2120
Fax: 910-822-7093

Salisbury-W.G. (Bill-Hefner VA Medical Center)
1601 Brenner Avenue
Salisbury, NC 28144
704-638-9000
Fax: 704-638-3395

North Dakota
Fargo VA Medical/Regional Office Center
2101 Elm Street
Fargo, ND 58102
701-232-3241
Fax: 701-239-3705

Ohio
VISN 10: VA Healthcare System of Ohio
11500 Northlake Drive, Suite 200
Cincinnati, OH 45249
513-247-4621
Fax: 513-247-4620

Chillicothe VA Medical Center
17273 State Route 104
Chillicothe, OH 45601
740-773-1141
Fax: 740-772-7084
www.chillicothe.med.va.gov

Cincinnati VA Medical Center
3200 Vine Street
Cincinnati, OH 45220
513-861-3100
Fax: 513-475-6500
http://www.gcfeb.com/vaweb/

Louis Stokes VA Medical Center
10701 East Boulevard
Cleveland, OH 44106
216-791-3800
Fax: 216-421-3217
http://www.cleveland.med.va.gov/

Dayton VA Medical Center
4100 W. 3rd Street
Dayton, OH 45428
937-268-6511
Fax: 937-262-2179
http://www.dayton.med.va.gov/

Oklahoma
Muskogee VA Medical Center
1011 Honor Heights Drive
Muskogee, OK 74401
918-683-3261
Fax: 918-680-3648

Oklahoma City VA Medical Center
921 N.E. 13th Street
Oklahoma City, OK 73104
405-270-0501
Fax: 405-270-1560

Oregon
VISN 20: Northwest Network
P.O. Box 1035
Portland, OR 97207
360-690-1832
Fax: 360-737-1405
http://www.visn20.med.va.gov/

VA Roseburg Healthcare System
913 NW Garden Valley Blvd.
Roseburg, OR 97470-6513
541-440-1000
Fax: 541-440-1225

Portland VA Medical Center
3710 S. W. US Veterans Hospital Road
PO Box 1034
Portland, OR 97239
503-220-8262
Fax: 503-273-5319
http://www.portland.med.va.gov/

Pennsylvania
VISN 4: VA Stars and Stripes Healthcare Network
c/o VAMC, Delafield Road
Pittsburgh, PA 15240
412-784-3939
Fax: 412-784-3940
http://www.starsandstripes.med.va.gov/visn4/

James E. Van Zandt VA Medical Center-Altoona
2907 Pleasant Valley Boulevard
Altoona, PA 16602-4377
814-943-8164
Fax: 814-940-7898

Butler VA Medical Center
325 New Castle Road
Butler, PA 16001-2480
724-287-4781
Fax: 724-282-4408
http://www.va.gov/butlerva/

Coatesville VA Medical Center
1400 Black Horse Hill Road
Coatesville, PA 19320-2096
610-384-7711
Fax: Not Provided
http://www.coatesville.med.va.gov/

Erie VA Medical Center
135 East 38 Street
Erie, PA 16504
814-868-8661
Fax: 814-860-2135

Lebanon VA Medical Center
1700 South Lincoln Avenue
Lebanon, PA 17042
717-272-6621
Fax: 717-228-6045
http://www.starsandstripes.med.va.gov/visn4/

VA Pittsburgh Healthcare System, Highland Drive Division
7180 Highland Drive
Pittsburgh, PA 15206
866-482-7488
http://www.va.gov/pittsburgh/highland.htm

VA Pittsburgh Healthcare System, University Drive Division
University Drive
Pittsburgh, PA 15240
866-4VAPITT
Fax: 412-688-6121
http://www.va.gov/pittsburgh/

Wilkes-Barre VA Medical Center
1111 East End Blvd.
Wilkes-Barre, PA 18711
570-824-3521
Fax: 570-821-7278
www.va.gov/vamcwb

VA Pittsburgh Healthcare System
H. John Heinz III Progressive Care Center
Delafield Road
Pittsburgh, PA 15260
866-4VAPITT
Fax: 412-784-3724
www.va.gov/pittsburgh/heinz.htm

Puerto Rico
San Juan VA Medical Center
10 Casia Street
San Juan, PR 00921-3201
787-641-7582
Fax: 787-641-4557

Rhode Island
Providence VA Medical Center
830 Chalkstone Avenue
Providence, RI 02908-4799
401-273-7100
Fax: 401-457-3370
http://www.visn1.med.va.gov/providence/

South Carolina
Ralph H. Johnson VA Medical Center
109 Bee Street
Charleston, SC 29401-5799
843-577-5011
Fax: 843-937-6100

Wm. Jennings Bryan Dorn VA Medical Center
6439 Garners Ferry Road
Columbia, SC 29209-1639
803-776-4000
Fax: 803-695-6739

South Dakota
The VA Black Hills Health Care System-Fort Meade Campus
113 Comanche Road
Fort Meade, SD 57741
605-347-2511
Fax: 605-347-7171

The VA Black Hills Health Care System-Hot Springs Campus
500 North 5th Street
Hot Springs, SD 57747
605-745-2000
Fax: 605-745-2091

Sioux Falls VA Medical/Regional Office Center
2501 W. 22nd Street
PO Box 5046
Sioux Falls, SD 57117-5046
605-336-3230
Fax: 605-333-6878

Tennessee
VISN 9: VA Mid South Healthcare Network
1310-24th Avenue South
Nashville, TN 37212-2637
615-340-2380
Fax: 615-340-2398

Mountain Home VA Medical Center
P.O. Box 4000
Johnson City, TN 37684
423-926-1171

Memphis VA Medical Center
1030 Jefferson Avenue
Memphis, TN 38104
901-523-8990

Alvin C. York VA Medical Center
3400 Lebanon Road
Murfreesboro, TN 37129
615-867-6000
Fax: 615-867-5768

Nashville VA Medical Center
1310 24th Avenue, South
Nashville, TN 37212-2637
615-327-4751
Fax: 615-321-6350

Texas

Amarillo VA Health Care System
6010 Amarillo Boulevard, West
Amarillo, TX 79106
806-355-9703
Fax: 806-354-7860

Big Texas VA Health Care System
300 Veterans Blvd.
Big Spring, TX 79720
432-263-7361
Fax: 432-264-4834

El Paso VA Health Care System
5001 North Piedras Street
El Paso, TX 79930-4211
915-564-6100
Fax: 915-564-7920

Central Texas VA Health Care System
1901 Veterans Memorial Drive
Temple, TX 76504
254-778-4811
Fax: 254-771-4588
www.central-texas.med.va.gov

VA North Texas Health Care System:
Sam Rayburn Memorial Veterans Center
1201 E. 9th Street
Bonham, TX 75418
903-583-2111
Fax: 903-583-6688

VA North Texas Health Care System:
Dallas VA Medical Center
4500 South Lancaster Road
Dallas, TX 75216
214-742-8387
Fax: 214-857-1171

Houston VA Medical Center
2002 Holcombe Blvd.
Houston, TX 77030-4298
713-791-1414
Fax: 713-794-7218
http://www.houston.med.va.gov/

Kerrville VA Medical Center
3600 Memorial Blvd
Kerrville, TX 78028
830-896-2020

South Texas Veterans Health Care System
7400 Merton Minter Blvd.
San Antonio, TX 78229
210-617-5300
http://www.vasthcs.med.va.gov/

Central Texas Veterans Health Care System
1901 Veterans Memorial Drive
Temple, TX 76504
254-778-4811
Fax: 254-771-4588
http://www.central-texas.med.va.gov/main/

VISN 17: VA Heart of Texas Health Care Network
2301 East Lamar Boulevard, Suite 650
Arlington, TX 76006
817-652-1111
Fax: 817-385-3700
www.va.gov/visn17

Central Texas Veterans Health Care System-Waco VA Medical Center
4800 Memorial Drive
Waco, TX 76711
254-752-6581
Fax: 254-756-5215
www.central-texas.med.va.gov

Utah

VA Salt Lake City Health Care System
500 Foothill Drive
Salt Lake City, UT 84148
801-582-1565
Fax: 801-584-1289

Vermont

White River Junction VA Medical and Regional Center
215 North Main Street
White River Junction, VT 05009
802-295-9363
Fax: 802-296-6354
www.visn1.med.va.gov/wrj

Virginia

Hampton VA Medical Center
100 Emancipation Drive
Hampton, VA 23667
757-722-9961
Fax: 757-723-6620
www1.va.gov/midatlantic/facilities/hampton

Hunter Holmes McGuire VA Medical Center
1201 Broad Rock Boulevard

Richmond, VA 23249
804-675-5000
Fax: 804-675-5585
www1.va.gov/midatlantic/facilities/richmond

Salem VA Medical Center
1970 Roanoke Boulevard
Salem, VA 24153
540-982-2463
Fax: 540-983-1096
www1.va.gov/midatlantic/facilities/salem

Washington
VA Puget Sound Health Care System
1660 S. Columbian Way
Seattle, WA 98108
800-329-8387
206-762-1010
http://www.puget-sound.med.va.gov/

Spokane VA Medical Center
4815 N. Assembly Street
Spokane, WA 99205-6197
509-434-7000
Fax: 509-434-7119

Jonathon M. Wainwright VA Memorial Center
77 Wainwright Drive
Walla Walla, WA 99362
509-525-5200
Fax: 509-527-3452

West Virginia
Beckley VA Medical Center
200 Veterans Avenue
Beckley, WV 25801
304-255-2121
Fax: 304-255-2431
www1.va.gov/midatlantic/facilities/beckley

Louis A Johnson VA Medical Center
One Medical Center Drive
Clarksburg, WV 26301
304-623-3461
Fax: 304-626-7026

Huntington VA Medical Center
1540-Spring Valley Drive
Huntington, WV 25704
304-429-6741
Fax: 304-429-6713

Martinsburg VA Medical Center
510 Butler Avenue
Martinsburg, WV 25401
304-263-0811
Fax: 304-262-7433

Wisconsin
William S. Middleton Memorial Veterans Hospital
2500 Overlook Terrace
Madison, WI 53705-2286
608-256-1901
Fax: 608-280-7095

Clement J. Zablocki Veterans Affairs Medical Center
5000 West National Avenue
Milwaukee, WI 53295-1000
414-384-2000
Fax: 414-382-5319
http://www.va.gov/milwaukee/

Tomah VA Medical Center
500 E. Veterans Street
Tomah, WI 54660
608-372-3971
http://www.vagreatlakes.org/

Wyoming
Cheyenne VA Medical Center/Regional Office Center
2360 E. Pershing Blvd.
Cheyenne, WY 82001
307-778-7550
Fax: 307-778-7336

Sheridan VA Medical Center
1898 Fort Road
Sheridan, WY 82801
307-672-3473
Fax: 307-672-1900

How to Get the Best Health Information

According to the Aging Initiative, by 2030, the number of older persons is expected to double to over 70 million in the United States. Health is one of the most important aspects of aging. The government is responding to these demographic transformations by providing information and many other services to citizens. If you have any questions or concerns about any health issue, the government most likely can help. There are many specific agencies and places to go for assistance but if you run into dead ends try one of these five agencies that can steer you in the right direction.

1) Eldercare Locator

The U.S. Administration on Aging offers this free service to older adult Americans and their caregivers to help them connect with available services. Eldercare Locator links older adults who need assistance with state and local area agencies on aging and community-based organizations. If you need help with any health related problem go to the web site and follow the directions or call a specialist. The web site is available in many different languages. Contact: 800-677-1116, www.eldercare.gov.

2) Helpful Health Hotlines

The National Health Information Center and the National Library of Medicine both offer an online database of health-related organizations operating toll-free telephone services. The databases also include information on services and publications available in Spanish. You can find out whom to call for almost any health issue. Contact: Health Information Resources Database, Referral Specialist, P.O. Box 1133, Washington, DC 20013-1133; 800-336-4797, 301-565-4167; www.health.gov/NHIC/Pubs/tollfree.htm or http://healthhotlines.nlm.nih.gov/.

3) National Institute on Aging

The National Institute on Aging is the government's leading effort on aging research. In addition to research information and professional training, NIA disseminates health information to the general public. Contact: National Institute on Aging, Building 31, Room 5C27, 31 Center Drive, MSC 2292, Bethesda, MD 20892; 301-496-1752, 800-222-4225, Fax: 301-496-1072; www.nia.n.ih.gov.

4) SeniorHealth.gov

The National Institute of Health offers an on-line information web site for older adults. Their goal is to make age-related health information easily accessible to seniors, family members and friends. The web site is senior friendly including large print, short, easy to read segments and simple navigation. There is even a "talking" feature which reads the text. Information is updated regularly. Contact: http://nihseniorhealth.gov/.

5) ***MedlinePlus***

MedlinePlus offers consumers a wealth of information on health related topics. The information is from the National Library of Medicine and the National Institutes of Health. In addition to the health information the web site also contains lists of hospitals and physicians, a medical encyclopedia, a medical dictionary, prescription information and health information in Spanish. You can even sign up for weekly updates of specific topics that fit your needs. Contact: U.S. National Library of Medicine, 8600 Rockville Pike, Bethesda, MD 20894; http://medlineplus.gov/.

Get Health Information Better Than Your Doctor

Want to find out the latest information on your health condition? All you need to do is pick up the phone or go online to get the most up-to-date information from the government's team of health professionals. The latest cures and treatments to any condition are changing every day and it is impossible for people in the medical profession to keep up on the latest developments in any health-related area. There is plenty of free help available from government sponsored and non-profit organizations who can even tell you what will be in the medical journals next year because they are involved in the research today. So, don't settle for second best when you can get the best. Here is where you can go:

National Health Information Center
P.O. Box 1133
Washington, DC 20013-1133
800-336-4797
301-565-4167
www.health.gov/nhic

National Women's Health Information Center
U.S. Public Health Service
Office of Women's Health
8550 Arlington Boulevard, Suite 300
Fairfax, VA 22031
800-944-WOMAN
www.4woman.gov

National Institutes of Health,
Office of Communications
9000 Rockville Pike
Bethesda, MD 20892
301-496-4000
www.nih.gov

Self-Help Groups Teach You How To Beat The System

They are certainly cheaper than a doctor visit, because they're free, and are probably a lot easier and friendlier. In addition to offering advice on treatment options, they can be a great source for learning the system and how to get the most from it. They can tell you about free services and even money programs that people in the system would never consider. Here are some sources for finding a self-help group near you. They should be able to point you in the right direction.

American Self-Help Clearinghouse
http://mentalhelp.net/selfhelp/

Self-Help Hotlines
http://mentalhelp.net/selfhelp/selfhelp.php?idx=44

Anxiety Disorders Self-Help Groups
Anxiety Disorders Association of America
240-485-1001
www.adaa.org/Public/index.cfm

Free Health Insurance Counseling

Free one-on-one counseling is available to seniors and, in most areas, people with disabilities, to answer questions like:

- How much insurance is too much?
- If something sounds like fraud, where can I go for help?
- What's the best Medigap insurance plan?
- Do I qualify for government health benefits?
- Should I buy long-term care insurance?

The program is called Health Insurance Counseling and Advocacy Program (HICAP) and is sponsored by the Centers for Medicare & Medicaid Services (formerly U.S. Health Care Financing Administration). In most states, it is usually run by the state Department on Aging or the State Insurance Commissioner's office. If that fails, contact the Eldercare Locator hotline at 1-800-677-1116. They can give you the local number.

Free Exercise Book For Seniors

Exercise: A Guide from the National Institute on Aging and *Exercise: Getting Fit for Life* will both get you moving. They describe the benefits of exercise, safety tips, nutritional information and motivational tips, to help you start an exercise program that is right for you. You can see illustrated examples of exercises that you can do at home. There is even a companion video for $7. For your copy, contact the National Institute on Aging, Building 31, Room 5C27, 31 Center Drive, MSC 2292, Bethesda, MD 20892; 800-222-2225; www.niapublications.org/.

Arthritis Information

The Arthritis Foundation's mission is to support research, prevention, and find a cure for 100 forms of arthritis, and to improve the quality of life for people with arthritis. They have chapters nationwide that offer health education programs in local communities, including arthritis self-help courses, aquatic programs, exercise programs, support groups, public forums and more. They have publications, videos and other resources that are available for free or at minimal costs. For additional information, contact Arthritis Foundation, P.O. Box 7669, Atlanta, GA 30357-0669; 800-568-4045; www.arthritis.org.

Hot Flash Hotline

Menopause doesn't have to be the hormonal hurricane women faced in the past. Taking estrogen and progesterone may help relieve the symptoms of menopause, although they may not be without problems of their own. To help clear up these issues, the National Institute on Aging offers the following free publications: *Menopause, Hormones After Menopause* and *Menopause: One Woman's Story, Every Woman's Story*. For these pamphlets and additional information, contact National Institute on Aging Information Center, P.O. Box 8057, Gaithersburg, MD 20898-8057; 800-222-2225; www.nia.nih.gov/.

Healthfinder.gov

This online data base is the gateway to consumer health information from the U.S. government that can lead you to online publications, clearinghouses, databases, web-sites, government agencies, non-profit agencies and support groups. Selected health topics are organized for men and women, by age from kids to seniors, by race and ethnicity and for parents, caregivers, health professionals and others. For additional information, contact Healthfinder, P.O. Box 1133, Washington, DC 20013-1133; www.healthfinder.org.

Free Nutritional Analysis Tools and System (NATS)

This free online tool allows you to analyze the foods you eat for various nutrients. The online tool even helps you calculate how much energy you burn each day. Palm downloads are also available for about $8. The program was developed by the Department of Food Science and Human Nutrition at the University of Illinois. NNATS, 1011 Campus Drive, Mundelein, IL 60060; http://nat.crgq.com/.

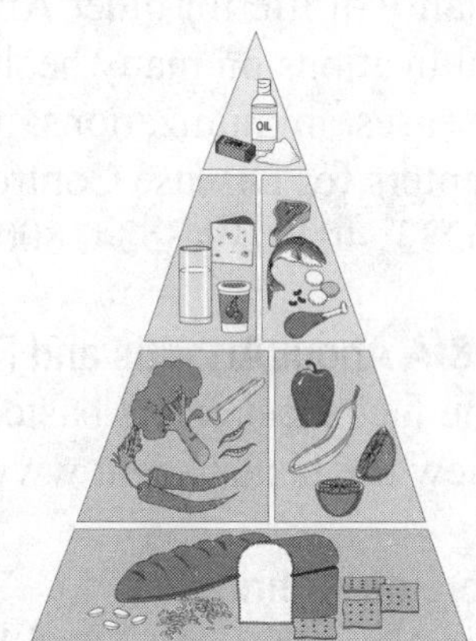

Extended Care Database

Access the *National Directory of Health-Care Service Providers* when you or a loved one has become too frail to live alone but too healthy for hospitalization. It lists over 33,000 acute rehabilitation providers, retirement communities, home health-care agencies and more. You can search by city, state, county, and provider name or provider type. The listings display provider's name, address, telephone number, number of beds and rooms, and the type of care available. It's not an all inclusive list, but it can be a good starting point, especially for those searching from miles away. Contact Extended Care Information Network, 8700 W. Bryn Mawr Avenue, Suite 700N, Chicago, IL 60631; 773-632-1600; www.extendedcare.com/Search/Search.aspx.

Parkinson's Help

The National Parkinson Foundation is a nonprofit organization that provides services and education to patients and their families. The Foundation can provide background information on Parkinson's, exercise materials, a newsletter and more. For additional information, contact National Parkinson Foundation, Inc., 1501 N.W. 9th Avenue/Bob Hope Road, Miami, FL 33136-1494; 800-327-4545, 305-243-6666; www.parkinson.org.

EPA Aging Initiative

The Environmental Protection Agency is committed to all Americans, including seniors. The Aging Initiative's mission is to protect the health of older persons when it comes to environmental hazards. They study the environmental health threats to older adults, examine the effects of the rapidly growing aging population and encourage older persons to volunteer in their communities to reduce hazards and protect the environment. They offer seniors factsheets, reports and other information concerning environmental hazards as it relates to their health. Contact: US Environmental Protection Agency, Aging Initiative, 1200 Pennsylvania Avenue NW, Mail Code 1107A, Room 2512 Ariel Rios North, Washington, DC 20460; 202-564-2188; www.epa.gov/aging/.

Exercise for a Lifetime

Exercise is essential for a long health life, including older adults. The National Institute of Health offers a web site for seniors to learn the benefits of exercise, try new exercises, help chart exercise progress and offers a place to tell your exercise story. Find out more by going to their web site and explore. The web site offers the option of larger text and audio for those that have trouble seeing the text on the screen. Contact: National Institute of Health, 9000 Rockville Pike, Bethesda, MD 20892; 301-496-4000; http://nihseniorhealth.gov/exercise/toc.html.

Healthy Aging

Healthy Aging is a program of The Centers for Disease Control and Prevention. Healthy Aging's mission is to promote health, prevent disease and enhance the quality of life for older Americans. They offer health information and publications on many health topics including: chronic diseases, infectious diseases, immunizations, injuries in older adults, Medicare and more. Contact: Centers for Disease Control and Prevention, 1600 Clifton Road, Atlanta, GA 30333; 404-639-3534, 800-311-3435; www.cdc.gov/aging.

Q & A About Arthritis and Rheumatic Diseases

The fact sheet offers basic answers to frequently asked question about arthritis and rheumatic diseases. View the fact sheet at www.pueblo.gsa.gov/cic_text/health/art-rheu/art-rheu.htm.

More on Arthritis

The National Institute of Arthritis and Musculoskeletal and Skin Diseases provide information on many senior health issues including arthritis. They offer an online A-Z health topics database. You can also order publications free of charge, check out current patient studies and research outreach programs. Contact: National Institute of Arthritis and Musculoskeletal and Skin Diseases, National Institute of Health, Building 31, Room 4C02, 31 Center Drive-MSC 2350, Bethesda, MD 20892-2350; 301-496-8190, Fax: 301-480-2814; www.niams.nih.gov/.

Flu Information

Is it the flu or a cold? Is there a flu vaccine available? What can I do if I get the flu? All of these questions can be answered by the U.S. Department of Health and Human Services Flu Information site. Contact: U.S. Department of Human Services, 200 Independence Avenue, SW, Washington, DC 20201; 202-619-0257, Fax: 877-696-6775; www.hhs.gov/flu/.

Citizen Advocacy

Alliance for Aging Research is a nonprofit organization dedicated to helping improve the lives of older Americans. They sponsor local educational programs, conduct studies and serve as a clearinghouse of aging information. They also offer a variety of free publications on aging and health. Contact: Alliance for Aging Research, 2021 K Street, NW, Suite 305, Washington, DC 20006; 202-293-2856, Fax: 202-785-8574; www.agingresearch.org/.

Mental Health Services Locator

Are you having trouble coping with certain parts of life as you age? Do you need someone to talk to? The Center for Mental Health Services provides a database of mental health services and resources. You can search your state to find the help that you or a loved one needs. Contact: Center for Mental Health

Services, P.O. Box 42557, Washington, DC 20015; 800-789-2647; www.mentalhealth.org/databases/default.asp.

Senior Food Safety

Although Americans enjoy one of the safest food supplies in the world, many things have changed during the life of a senior. Not only is food produced and distributed differently, the way it is prepared and eaten has also changed to some extent. Read the government's publication, *To Your Health! Food Safety for Seniors* and everything you need to know to make your next meal. Contact: Federal Citizens Information Center, 800-FED INFO; www.pueblo.gsa.gov/cic_text/food/fsseniors/page1.htm.

Help When a Loved One Dies

Death is a difficult time in anyone's life. The *Funerals: A Consumers Guide* can help you sort out all of the information that is out there. Most, if not all of your questions can be answered. Contact: Federal Citizens Information Center, 800-FED INFO; www.pueblo.gsa.gov/cic_text/misc/funeral/funeral.htm.

Eat Well, Live Well

Eating well may become a chore as you grow older if you lose a loved one or are faced with an illness. The brochure, *Growing Older, Eating Better* can help you learn the pitfalls that older adults face when it comes to eating well. They also provide guidance in reading those nutritional labels that you find on foods. Contact: Federal Citizens Information Center, 800-FED INFO; www.pueblo.gsa.gov/cic_text/food/grow_old/grow_old.htm.

Up To Date Senior Health Information

What is the latest information on Medicare benefits or current medications? You can stay current with the MedLine Plus topic, *Seniors' Health Issues*. For information to help you stay healthy as you age, check out this website! Contact: MedLine Plus, 8600 Rockville Pike, Bethesda, MD 20894; www.nlm.nih.gov/medlineplus/seniorshealthissues.html.

Dialysis Facility Compare

Dialysis Facility Compare provides detailed information about the dialysis facilities certified by Medicare. The web site offers patients and their families all kinds of details about dialysis facilities including: facility services, quality measures, and other resources. To obtain information about non-Medicare facilities contact your State Survey Agency. Contact: Center for Medicare & Medicaid Services, 7500 Security Boulevard, Baltimore, MD 21244-1850; www.medicare.gov.

Hospice Locator

The National Hospice and Palliative Care Organization is a nonprofit membership organization representing hospice care programs and professionals in the U.S. They offer a search engine to help you find local programs. If you need hospice information or assistance, this may be a good place to start. Contact: National Hospice and Palliative Care Organization, 1700 Diagonal Road, Suite 625, Alexandria, VA 222314; 703-837-1500, Fax: 703-837-1233; www.nhpco.org/custom/directory/.

DisabilityInfo.gov
Where can you go to get comprehensive information if you are disabled? DisabilityInfo.gov may be your answer. With a few clicks of your mouse, you can access information available throughout many government agencies. If you have disability questions concerning employment, education, housing, health, transportation, civil rights, community life, income support or technology go to the web site for a comprehensive online resource. www.disabilityInfo.gov

What Should I Eat?
Dietary guidelines change with the times as new research is published. The *Dietary Guidelines for Americans* is published every five years to help all Americans with their dietary habits. To view the current guidelines and to learn more about eating healthier, get your free copy today. Contact: U.S. Department of Health and Human Services, 200 Independence Avenue, SW, Washington, DC 20201; 202-619-0257, 877-696-6775;
www.healthierus.gov/dietaryguidelines/ or www.nutrition.gov.

Find a Dentist or Doctor
When you need to find a doctor or dentist, don't go to the phone book; check out the online directories for general or specific listings. Medline offers a free database that can help you find a dentist, doctor, specialist, hospital clinic or medical library anywhere in the country. www.nlm.nih.gov/medlineplus/directories.html

Public Health Care Locator
When you need a public health care facility you can find it online. The Bureau of Primary Health Care offers a database that you can search by geographical area, clinic name, program type support received or by type of service. Contact: http://ask.hrsa.gov/pc/.

Bladder Problems
Many men and women have trouble as they get older with incontinence. If you have this problem, you can find out the causes, treatment options and current research conducted by the National Kidney and Urology Information Clearinghouse. They offer free publications, *Urinary Incontinence in Men* and *Urinary Incontinence in Women* to help with understanding this problem. For additional information, contact National Kidney and Urology Diseases Information Clearinghouse, 3 Information Way, Bethesda, MD 20892-3580; 800-891-5390; http://kidney.niddk.nih.gov.

Alzheimer's Information Hotline
Are you concerned with the onset of Alzheimer's disease or does a love one show signs of the disease and you have questions? The Alzheimer's Association offers a toll free 24/7 contact center number to provide information, assistance, caregiver help and referrals. The association offers a database to find local chapters. National programs include: *Coalition of Hope, Safe Return, Memory Walk* and *Maintain You Brain.* For additional information, contact Alzheimer's Association National Office, 225 N. Michigan Avenue, Floor 17, Chicago, IL 60601-7633; 800-272-3900; www.alz.org.

Finding a Doctor In A Haystack
AMA Physician Select offers professional information on virtually every licensed physician in the United States, more than 690,000 doctors. You can search by physician name or medical specialty. For

additional information, contact American Medical Association, 515 N. State Street, Chicago, IL 60610; 800-621-8335; http://dbapps.ama-assn.org/aps/amahg.htm.

Find The Fountain of Youth through Exercise

The President's Challenge has a web site dedicated just for seniors. The web site offers fitness calculators and an activity log to track your progress. As you reach your goals, you can earn patches, ribbons, certificates and medallions as awards for your hard work. For additional information, contact The President's Challenge, 501 N. Morton, Suite 104, Bloomington, IN 47404; 800-258-8146; www.presidentschallenge.org/home_seniors.aspx.

Tool To Help your Heart

The American Heart Association provides many free tools to help you live a heart healthy life. The *Cardiovascular Disease Risk Assessment* can predict your risk of having a heart attack in the next ten years. They also offer a Body Mass Calculator, an Exercise Diary, a Heart Health Tracker and Patient Information Sheets. For additional information, contact American Heart Association National Center, 7272 Greenville Avenue, Dallas, TX 75231; 800-AHA-USA-1; www.americanheart.org.

Free Stroke Magazine

If you or someone you love has had a stroke, you know that there are many struggles that you are faced with on a daily basis. The American Stroke Association offers a free subscription to the *Stroke Connection* which is published six times a year and is full of information. You can receive a variety of free information including: local stroke association finder, 19 fact sheets, online videos, and more. For additional information, contact American Stroke Association National Center, 7272 Greenville Avenue, Dallas, TX 75231; 888-4-STROKE; www.strokeassociation.org.

Free Parkinson Information

The Parkinson's Disease Foundation offers the community a number of programs, all free of charge. Their services include: a newsletter, brochures and pamphlets, videos/DVD's, and fact sheets. For additional information, contact Parkinson's Disease Foundation, 1359 Broadway, Suite 1509, New York, NY 10018; 800-457-6676, 212-923-4700; www.pdf.org.

Free Plastic Surgeon Search

The American Society of Plastic Surgeons offers the Plastic Surgeon Referral Service free of charge. All of the surgeons listed are board certified. You can search by physician name or geographical region. The site also offers information about all kinds of procedures. For additional information, contact American Society of Plastic Surgeons, Plastic Surgery Educational Foundation, 444 E. Algonquin Road, Arlington Heights, IL 60005; 888-4-PLASTIC; www.plasticsurgery.org.

AARP Health Information

AARP assists seniors in many ways and health is no exception. As an organization, they help protect the rights of seniors in the legislature. Their web site has a wealth of information. They can provide you with information on the following: health conditions and treatments, insurance, Medicare, prescription drugs, fitness and staying healthy. If you have any health questions AARP is a good place to start. Contact them at AARP, 601 E. Street NW, Washington, DC 20049; 888-OUR-AARP; www.aarp.org.

Free Fall Prevention Program

A Tool Kit To Prevent Senior Falls is designed to prevent senior falls. Falls present serious health risks to older adults. One of every three adults 65 and older falls each year. Falls are the leading cause of injury death among seniors. To obtain the tool kit contact National Center for Injury Prevention and Control, Mailstop K65, 4770 Buford Highway NE, Atlanta, GA 30341-3724; 770-448-1506; www.cdc.gov/ ncipc/pub-res/toolkit/toolkit.htm.

Prevent Alzheimer's Disease

This new free 28-page booklet *Can Alzheimer's Disease be Prevented?* provides up-to-date information and research on Alzheimer's disease. The Alzheimer's disease Education & Referral Center provides information on every aspect of Alzheimer's from causes to symptoms to treatments. They even provide an online database of current clinical trials. Contact: Alzheimer's disease Education & Referral Center, P.O. Box 8250, Silver Spring, MD 20907-8250; 800-438-4380, Fax: 301-495-3334; www.alzheimers.org.

Free Diabetes Information and Education

The National Diabetes Education Program is federally funded with over 200 state and local partnerships. They offer online information or you can order publications at no cost. Titles include: *More Than 50 Ways to Prevent Diabetes*, *It's Not Too Late to Prevent Diabetes*, *4 Steps to control Your Diabetes for Life*, and *Tips for Helping a Person with Diabetes*. Contact: National Diabetes Education Program, One Diabetes Way, Bethesda, MD 20814-9692; 301-496-3583, 800-438-5383; http://ndep.nih.gov/.

Are You Hearing All You Should Be Hearing?

As we age we sometimes have hearing loss. The National Institute on Deafness and Other Communication Disorders offers information and clinical research trials. You can check their web site and search for currently enrolling trials or order a variety of free publications. Titles include: *Hearing Aids*, *Hearing Loss for Older Adults*, *Ten Ways to Recognize Hearing Loss*, and more. Contact: National Institute on Deafness and Other Communication Disorders, National Institute of Health, 31 Center Drive, MSC 2320, Bethesda, MD 20892-2320; 800-241-1044, 301-496-7243, TTY: 800-241-1055; www.nidcd.nih.gov/.

Free 10-Year Heart Attack Calculator and Body Mass Calculator

You can find out your risk of having a heart attack in the next 10 years by answering a few online questions. You can also determine your body mass index. The National Heart, Lung and Blood Institute should be your first stop if you're looking for ways to stay healthy, learn about potential risks or find treatment options for any disease that has to do with your heart, lungs or blood. They offer free publications and information, assessment tools, healthy recipes and a portion quiz. For all of this and more contact: National Heart, Lung and Blood Institute, P.O. Box 30105, Bethesda, MD 20824-0105; 800-575-WELL, 301-592-8573, TTY: 240-629-3255, Fax: 240-629-3246; www.nhlbi.nih.gov.

Is Your Home and Environment Making You Sick?

The National Institute of Environmental Health Services is a part of the National Institute of Health and works to reduce human illnesses due to environmental causes. They offer free factsheets, pamphlets, research findings, and other publications. Contact: National Institute of Environmental Health Services,

P.O. Box 12233, Research Triangle Park, NC 27709; 919-541-3345, TTY: 919-541-0731; www.niehs.nih.gov/.

Free Daily Bladder Diary

The Bladder Control for Women Campaign is dedicated to informing women about this common problem. You can print out an easy to use daily bladder diary to keep track of liquid intake, urine leaks, bathroom visits and other details so that you can easily report them to your doctor. Other publications are also available. Contact: Bladder Control for Women Campaign, National Kidney and Urology Disease Information, 3 Information Way, Bethesda, MD 20892-3580; 800-891-5390; http://kidney.niddk.nih.gov/kudiseases/pubs/bladdercontrol/.

Free Information Pages

If you are researching information about any disease dealing with neurology, this site will provide you with a wealth of information. Information provided includes: definitions, terms, treatment options, prognosis, other organizations and research currently being studied. Contact: National Institute of Neurological Disorders and Stroke, P.O. Box 5801, Bethesda, MD 20824; 800-352-9424, 301-496-5751, TTY: 301-468-5981; www.ninds.nih.gov.

Help Deciding If Complimentary or Alternative Medicines Are For You

Complimentary and alternative medicine is the use of practices and products that are not currently accepted as conventional medicine in the United States. The National Center for Complimentary and Alternative Medicine is a part of the National Institute of Health and provides information about theses types of alternatives. They have several publications that will help guide your decision. Contact: National Center for Complimentary and Alternative Medicine, P.O. Box 7923, Gaithersburg, MD 20898; 888-644-6226, 301-519-3153, TTY: 866-464-3615, Fax: 866-464-3616; http://nccam.nih.gov/.

Free Link Between You and Current Resources

This National Resource Center provides a link and information to patients and their caregivers on metabolic bone diseases, including osteoporosis, Paget's disease, osteogenesis imperfecta and hyperparathyroidism. They also publish fact sheets, pamphlets, packets and other resources. Contact: National Institute of Osteoporosis and Related Bone Diseases, Resource Center, National Institute of Health, 2 AMS Circle, Bethesda, MD 20892-3676; 800-624-BONE, 202-223-0344, Fax: 202-293-2356, TTY: 202-466-4315; www.osteo.org.

WIN (Weight-Control Information Network)

WIN has initiated the *Sisters Together: Move More, Eat Better* Program. The program encourages Black women to maintain a healthy weight. WIN also provides over 25 publications dealing with weight and weight loss. Contact: The Weight-control Information network, 1 WIN Way, Bethesda, MD 20892-3665; 202-828-1025, 877-946-4627, Fax: 202-828-1028; http://win.niddk.nih.gov.

Free Mental Health Information

The National Institute of Mental Health offers medical information, the latest research findings and clinical trials available on many topics including: anxiety disorder, depression in older adults, eating disorders, panic disorder and more. If you feel like you or someone you love is having difficulties in this area the Institute can provide you with the data you need. Contact: National Institute of Mental Health,

Public Information and Communication Branch, 6001 Executive Boulevard, Room 8184, MSC 9663, Bethesda, MD 20892-9663; 301-443-4513, 866-615-6464, TTY: 301-443-8431, TTY: 866-415-8051, Fax: 301-443-4279; www.nimh.nih.gov/.

Cancer

This word evokes fear in people. The government wants to help alleviate your fears by providing accurate information about the disease. The National Cancer Institute (NCI) the primary agency in the country for cancer research has developed the Cancer Information Service (CIS). The CIS provides patients, their families and health professionals with the latest most accurate cancer information. The information is disseminated through their 15 regional offices throughout the country. They offer personalized, confidential answers to your questions. You can be part of their online live chats available Monday through Friday from 9:00 am to 11:00 pm Eastern Standard Time. They even have a Smoking Quitline 877-44U-QUIT. Contact: National Cancer Institute; 800-4-CANCER; www.cancer.gov; or Cancer Information Service, 800-4-CANCER; http://cis.nci.nih.gov/; or one of the following 15 regional offices.

Cancer Information Service Atlantic Region
Fox Chase Cancer Center
510 Township Line Road
Cheltenham, PA 19012
215-728-3110
Fax: 215-379-1369
Serving: Delaware, New Jersey and Pennsylvania

Cancer Information Service California Region
2201 Walnut Avenue, Suite 300
Fremont, CA 94538
510-608-5000
Fax: 510-745-0394
Serving: California

Cancer Information Service Coastal Region
University of Miami Miller School of Medicine
1550 NW 10th Avenue
Fox Building, Suite 200
Miami, FL 33136
305-243-4821
Fax: 305-243-6678
Serving: Florida, Puerto Rico and U.S. Virgin Islands

Cancer Information Service Heartland Region
University of Kansas Medical Center
3901 Rainbow Boulevard MS 3052
Kansas City, KS 66160
913-588-3729
Fax: 913-588-3779
Serving: Illinois, Kansas, Missouri and Nebraska

Cancer Information Service Mid-Atlantic Region
WVU/MBRCC Cancer Prevention & Control
3040 University Avenue
P.O. Box 6886
Morgantown, WV 26506
304-599-1496
Fax: 304-599-1552
Serving: Washington, DC, Maryland, Virginia and West Virginia

Cancer Information Service Mid-South Region
2365 Harrodsburg Road, Suite A230
Lexington, KY 40504
859-219-9063
Fax: 859-219-2276
Serving: Alabama, Arkansas, Kentucky, Louisiana, Mississippi and Tennessee

Cancer Information Service Mid-West Region
Karmanos Cancer Institute
110 East Warren Avenue
Detroit, MI 48201-1379
313-833-0715 ext 7317
Fax: 313-831-4039
Serving: Indiana, Michigan and Ohio

Cancer Information Service New England Region
Yale Cancer Center
55 Church Street, Suite 400
New Haven, CT 06510
203-865-2655
Fax: 203-865-0163
Serving: Connecticut, Maine, Massachusetts, New Hampshire, Rhode Island and Vermont

Cancer Information Service New York Region
1275 York Avenue

Box 166
New York, NY 10021
212-593-8245
Fax: 212-593-9154
Serving: New York

Cancer Information Service North Central Region
University of Wisconsin
370 WARF Office Building
Madison, WI 53726
608-255-3800
Fax: 608-262-2425
Serving: Iowa, Minnesota, North Dakota, South Dakota and Wisconsin

Cancer Information Service North West Region
1100 Fairview Avenue North
M/S J2-400
Seattle, WA 98109
206-667-4675
Fax: 206-667-7792
Serving: Alaska, Idaho, Nevada, Oregon and Washington State

Cancer Information Service Pacific Region
1236 Lauhala Street, Room 502
Honolulu, HI 96813
808-586-5853
Fax: 808-586-3009
Serving: Hawaii and U.S. Associated Pacific Territories

Cancer Information Service Rocky Mountain Region
Centura Health
Penrose-St. Francis Health Services
P.O. Box 7021
Colorado Springs, CO 80933
719-776-3150
Fax: 719-776-3132
Serving: Arizona, Colorado, Montana, New Mexico, Utah and Wyoming

Cancer Information Service South Central Region
M.D. Anderson Cancer Center
1515 Holcombe Boulevard, Unit 229
Houston, TX 77030
713-792-3363
Fax: 713-794-4418
Serving: Oklahoma and Texas

Cancer Information Service Southeast Region
Duke Comprehensive Cancer Center
Room 6059, Hock Plaza
2424 Erwin Road
Durham, NC 27705
919-286-5837
Fax: 919-286-2558
Serving: Georgia, North Carolina and South Carolina

Access to 67,000 Resources

The National Rehabilitation Information Center (NARIC) offers a free database with over 67,000 resources. NARIC is dedicated to assisting people with their disabilities and rehabilitation issues, questions and concerns. They even have an "Ask Me" time when specialists are available to speak with you over the phone and a live chat time online. Contact: National Rehabilitation Information Center, 4200 Forbes Boulevard, Suite 202, Lanham, MD 20706; 800-346-2742, 301-459-5900, TTY: 301-459-5984; www.naric.com.

Allergies Can Make You Sick

According to the American Academy of Allergy, Asthma and Immunology allergies are the 6th leading cause of chronic diseases in the United States. The National Institute of Allergy and Infectious Diseases can help you decide if you have allergies and how to alleviate your symptoms. They provide many free publications including: *Airborne Allergies: Something in the Air*, *Food Allergy: An Overview*, *How to Create a Dust-Free Bedroom*, *Understanding the Immune System* and more. If you are interested in clinical studies, the Institute maintains a database of current programs. Contact: National Institute of Allergy and Infectious Diseases, 6610 Rockledge Drive, MSC 6612, Bethesda, MD 20892-6612; 301-496-5717, TTY- 800-877-8339, Fax: 301-402-3573; www3.niaid.nih.gov/.

Free Information From the FDA

The Food and Drug Administration overseas many issues that impact consumers. They even provide a variety of pamphlets, brochures, articles and other publications specifically for seniors. Categories include: buying medicines online, food safety, safe use of medicines, and information on health issues. Contact: Food and Drug Administration, 5600 Fishers Lane, Rockville, MD 20857; 888-INFO-FDA (888-463-6332), Fax: 301-827-5308; www.fda.gov/oc/seniors/default.htm.

Food and Nutrition Experts at Your Service

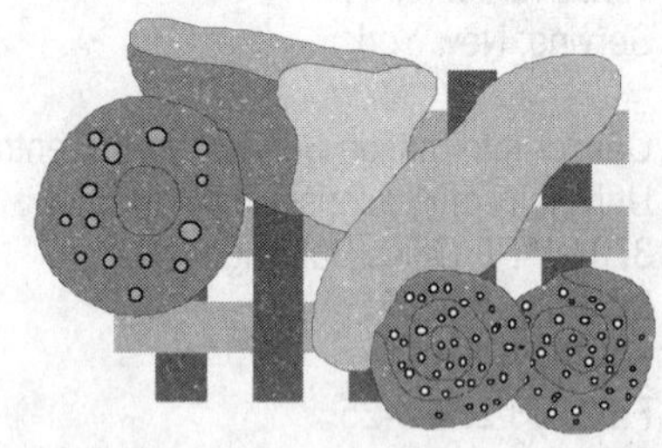

The Food and Nutrition Information Center provides accurate and credible information. They have an A-Z listing of topics, information on dietary supplements, dietary guidelines, food pyramid, consumer information and an aging page. The aging page provides links to articles on nutrition and aging, government programs including Meals on Wheels, and many more interesting topics. Contact: Food and Nutritious Information Center; www.nal.usda.gov/fnic/etext/000002.html.

Help With Your Loss

It is never easy to loose a loved one. Grief is a difficult emotion and you don't have to face it alone. There are many resources available to you. Contact you community aging office for local support groups or your church for guidance. You can view a number of articles online that will help. Here is a short list of what is available:

Loss, Grief and Bereavement (also available in Spanish)
www.cancer.gov/cancertopics/pdq/supportivecare/bereavement/Patient/page2
Coping with Loss-Bereavement and Grief www.nmha.org/infoctr/factsheets/42.cfm
Helping Yourself Through Grief www.americanhospice.org/griefzone/articles/helpingself.htm
Grief http://jama.ama-assn.org/cgi/content/full/293/21/2686
You Know You're Getting Better When... www.americanhospice.org/griefzone/articles/gettingbetter.htm
Seven Choices of Grief www.aarp.org/families/grief_loss/a2004-11-15-sevenchoices.html
Grieving www.acponline.org/public/h_care/10-griev.htm
How to Deal with Grief www.mentalhealth.samhsa.gov/publications/allpubs/ken-01-0104/default.asp

National Institutes of Health Toll-Free Information Lines

AIDS Clinical Trials 800-TRIALSA
AIDS Treatment Information Service 800-HIV-0440
National Institute on Aging Information Center 800-222-2225
Alzheimer's Disease Education and Referral Center 800-438-4380
Cancer Information Service 800-4-CANCER
Patient Recruitment and Public Liaison Office 800-411-1222
NO-National Institute of Child Health and Human Development 800-370-2943
National Diabetes Outreach Program 800-438-5383 http://ndep.nih.gov/
National Institute on Deafness and Other Communication Disorders 800-241-1044
http://www.nidcd.nih.gov/
Different name National Clearinghouse for Alcohol and Drug Information 800-729-6686
http://www.health.org/
EnviroHealth: Information Service of the National Institute of Environmental Health Sciences 800-643-4794 http://www.niehs.nih.gov/
National Heart, Lung, and Blood Institute Information Line 800-575-WELL
http://www.nhlbi.nih.gov/index.htm

National Institute of Diabetes and Digestive and Kidney Diseases ADD- Bladder Control for Women Campaign 800-891-5388 http://kidney.niddk.nih.gov/kudiseases/pubs/bladdercontrol/
National Institute of Mental Health Anxiety 888-8-ANXIETY 888-826-9438 http://www.nimh.nih.gov/healthinformation/anxietymenu.cfm
National Institute of Mental Health Depression 800-421-4211
National Institute of Mental Health Panic 800-64-PANIC
National Network of Libraries of Medicine 800-338-7657 http://nnlm.gov/
National Institute of Neurological Disorders and Stroke Information 800-352-9424 http://www.ninds.nih.gov/
National Center for Complementary and Alternative Medicine 888-NIH-6226 http://nccam.nih.gov/
NO- NIH Ovulation Research 888-644-8891
Osteoporosis and Related Bone Diseases 800-624-BONE http://www.osteo.org/
Weight-Control Information Network 800-WIN-8098 http://win.niddk.nih.gov/index.htm

Free Healthy Helplines

The following government and non-profit organizations are experts in their specific areas and will help you online or on the telephone line with free expertise, publications and referrals.

Women's Health

National Women's Health Information Center, U.S. Public Health Service, Office on Women's Health, 1600 Clifton Rd., NE, Atlanta, GA 30333; 800-944-WOMEN; www.4women.gov.

Any Health Topic

National Health Information Center, P.O. Box 1133, Washington, DC 20013; 800-336-4797; 301-565-4167; Fax: 301-984-4256; nhic-nt.health.org

Adoption

National Adoption Information Clearinghouse, 330 C St, NW, Washington, DC 20447; 703-352-3488; Fax: 703-385-3206; www.calil.com/naic.

National Adoption Center, 1500 Walnut St, #701, Philadelphia, PA 19102; 800-TO-ADOPT; 215-735-9988; Fax: 215-735-9410; www.adopt.org/adopt.

Aging

National Aging Information Center, U.S. Administration on Aging, 330 Independence Ave., NW, Room 4656, Washington, DC 20211; 202-619-7501; Fax: 401-7620; www.aoa.dhhs.gov/naic/.

National Institute on Aging Information Center, Building 31, Room 5C27, 31 Center Drive, MSC 2292, Bethesda, MD 20892; 800-222-2225; 301-496-1752; TDD: 800-222-4225; Fax: 301-589-3041; www.nih.gov/nia.

American Association of Retired Persons (AARP), 601 E St., NW, Washington, DC 20049; 800-424-3410; www.aarp.org.

AIDS

CDC National AIDS Clearinghouse, P.O. Box 6003, Rockville, MD 20849; 800-458-5231; Fax: 301-738-6616; TDD:800-243-7012; AIDS Clinical Trials: 800-874-2572; Fax-Back Service: 800-458-5231; HIV/AIDS Treatment: 800-448-0440; 301-519-0459.

Allergies

National Institute of Allergy and Infectious Diseases, Office of Communications, Building 31, Room 7A50, 900 Rockville Pike, Bethesda, MD 20892; 301-496-5717; www.niaid.nih.gov.

Alternative Medicine

National Center for Complementary and Alternative Medicine Clearinghouse, P.O. Box 8218, Silver Spring, MD 20907; 888-644-6226 (toll-free); 800-531-1794 (Fax-back);nccam.nih.gov/databases.html.

Alzheimer's Disease

Alzheimer's Disease Education and Referral Center, National Institute on Aging, P.O. Box 8250, Silver Spring, MD 20907; 800-438-4380; www.alzheimers.org.

Alzheimer's Association, 919 N. Michigan Ave., Suite 1100, Chicago, IL 60611; 800-272-3900; www.alz.org.

Arthritis

National Arthritis and Musculoskeletal and Skin Diseases Information Clearinghouse, 1 AMS Circle, Bethesda, MD 20892; 301-495-4484; 301-881-2731 (Fax-back service); www.nih.gov/niams.

Arthritis Foundation, P.O. Box 7669, Atlanta, GA 30357; 404-872-7100 ext. 6350; 800-238-7800; www.arthritis.org.

Birth Defects

March of Dimes Birth Defects Foundation, 1275 Mamaroneck Ave., White Plains, NY 10605; 888-MODIMES; 914-428-7100; www.modimes.org.

Cancer

Cancer Information Service, National Cancer Institute; 31 Center Dr., MSC2580; Bldg. 31, Room 10A07; 800-4-CANCER; cis.nci.nih.gov.

Child Abuse

National Clearinghouse on Child Abuse and Neglect Information, 330 C St., SW, Washington, DC 20447; 800-FYI-3366; 703-385-7565; www.calib.com/nccanch.

Child Care

National Child Care Information Center, Administration For Children and Families, 243 Church St., NW, 2nd. Floor, Vienna, VA 22180; 800-616-2242; nccic.org.

Child Health

National Institute on Child Health and Human Development, National Institutes of Health, 31 Center Dr., MSC2425, Room 2A32, Bethesda, MD 20897; 301-496-5133; www.nichd.nih.gov.

Deafness

National Institute on Deafness and Other Communication Disorders Information Clearinghouse, 1 communication Ave., Bethesda, MD 20892; 800-241-1044; 800-241-1055 (TTY); www.nichd.nih.gov/.

Depression

National Mental Health Association, Public Information, 1021 Prince St., Alexandria, VA 22314; 703-684-7722; 800-969-6642; www.nmha.org.

National Institute of Mental Health, National Institutes of Health, 6001 Executive Boulevard, Room 8184, MSC 9663; Bethesda, MD 20892; 301-443-4513; 800-421-4211; 800-64-PANIC (panic disorder hotline); 888-8-ANXIETY (anxiety disorders hotline); www.nimh.nih.gov.

Diabetes

National Diabetes Information Clearinghouse, 1 Information Way, Bethesda, MD 20892; 301-654-3327; www.niddk.nih.gov/health/diabetes/ndic.htm.

American Diabetes Association, 1701 N. Beauregard St., Alexandria, VA 22311; 800-342-2383; www.diabetes.org.

Juvenile Diabetes Foundation International, 120 Wall St., 19th Floor, New York, NY 10005; 212-785-9500; 800-533-2873; www.jdfcure.org.

Digestive Disorders

National Digestive Diseases Information Clearinghouse, 2 Information Way, Bethesda, MD 20892; 301-654-3810; www.niddk.nih.gov.

Disabilities

National Rehabilitation Information Center, National Institute on Disabilities and Rehabilitation Research, 8455 Colesville Rd., Suite 935, Silver Spring, MD 20910; 301-588-9284; 301-495-5626 TTY; 800-346-2742; www.naric.com.

National Information Center for Children and Youth with Disabilities, P.O. Box 1492, Washington, DC 20013; 800-695-0285; www.nichcy.org.

Domestic Violence

National Domestic Violence Hotline, P.O. Box 161810, Austin, TX 78716; 512-453-8117; 800-799-SAFE; www.ndvh.org.

Food and Drug Information

Food and Drug Administration, Office of Consumer Affairs, 5600 Fishers Lane, HFE-88, Rockville, MD 20857; 888-463-6332; www.fda.gov.

Heart Disease

American Heart Association, 7272 Greenville Ave., Dallas, TX 75231; 214-706-1200; 800-242-8721; www.americanheart.org.

National Heart, Lung, and Blood Institute, Information Center, P.O. box 30105; 301-251-1222; 800-575-WELL; www.nhlbi.nih.gov/index.htm.

Immunizations

Centers for Disease Control and Prevention, Mail Stop D25, 1600 Clifton Rd., NE, Atlanta, GA 30333; 800-CDC-SHOT; www.cdc.gov.

Kidney Disease

National Kidney and Urologic Diseases Information Clearinghouse, 3 Information Way, Bethesda, MD 20892; 301-654-4415; www.niddk.nih.gov/health/kidney/ nkudic.htm.

Lead

National Lead Information Center, 8601 Georgia Ave., Suite 503, Silver Spring, MD 20910; 800-424-LEAD (clearinghouse); 800-LEAD-FYI (hotline); www.epa.gov/lead/nlic/htm.

Medicare

Medicare Hotline, Health Care Financing Administration, 6325 Security Blvd, Baltimore, MD 21207; 800-638-6833; www.medicare.gov.

Nutrition

Food and Nutrition Information Center, U.S. Department of Agriculture, 10301 Baltimore Ave., Room 304, Beltsville, MD 20705; 301-504-5719; www.nal.usda.gov/fnic.

American Dietetic Association, 216 W. Jackson Blvd., Suite 800, Chicago, IL 60606; 312-899-0040; 800-366-1655; www.eatright.org.

Weight-Control Information Network, National Institute of Diabetes and Digestive and Kidney Diseases, 1 Win Way, Bethesda, MD 20892; 301-984-7378; 800-WIN-8098; www.niddk.nih.gov/health/nutrit/win.htm.

Oral Health

National Oral Health Information Clearinghouse, 1 NOHIC Way, Bethesda, MD 20892; 301-402-7364; www.aerie.com/nohicweb.

Osteoporosis

Osteoporosis and Related Bone Diseases National Resource Center, 1150 17th St., NW, Suite 500, Washington, DC 20036; 800-624-BONE; 202-223-0344; www.osteo.org.

Pregnancy

International Childbirth Education Association, P.O. Box 20048; Minneapolis, MN 55420; 800-624-4934; www.icea.org.

National Maternal and Child Health Clearinghouse, Health Resources and Services Administration, 2070 Chain Bridge Rd., Suite 450, Vienna, VA 22182; 703-356-1964; www.circsol.com.

Postpartum Support International, 927 North Kellogg Ave., Santa Barbara, CA 93111; 805-967-7636; www.chss.iup.edu/postpart.

La Leche League International, 1400 North Meacham Rd., P.O. Box 4079, Schaumburg, IL 60168; 800-LALECHE; www.lalecheleague.org.

Product Safety

U.S. Consumer Product Safety Hotline, Washington, DC 20207; 800-638-2772; www.cpsc.gov.

Rural Information

Rural Information Center Health Service, National Agricultural Library, Room 304, 10301 Baltimore Blvd., Beltsville, MD 20705; 800-633-7701; www.nal.usda.gov/ric/richs.

Sleep Disorders

National Center on Sleep Disorders Research, 2 Rockledge Center, 6701 Rockledge Dr., MSC 7920, Bethesda, MD 20892; 301-435-0199; www.nhlbi.nih.gov/nhlbi/ sleep/sleep.htm.

Smoking

Office on Smoking and Health, National Center for Chronic Disease Prevention and Health Promotion, Centers For Disease Control and Prevention, Mail Stop K-50, 4770 Buford Hwy, NE, Atlanta, GA 30341; 770-488-5705; 800-CDC-1311; www.cdc.gov/nccdphp/osh.

Substance Abuse

National Clearinghouse for Alcohol and Drug Information, P.O. Box 2345, Rockville, MD 20847; 800-729-6686; www.health.org.

PRIDE, National Parent's Resource Institute for Drug Education, 3610 Dekalb Technology Parkway, Suite 105; Atlanta, GA 30340; 770-458-9900; 800-853-7433; www.prideusa.org.

National Substance Abuse Helplines, 164 W. 74th St., New York, NY 10023; 800-COCAINE; 800-DRUGHELP; 800-RELAPSE; www.drughelp.org.

Ask-An-Expert Websites

The following is a list of websites where you can ask experts in the medical field your health questions. These websites are designed to help educate you on a wide range of health topics. Go ahead and ask them anything. Some questions include: Can I travel by air in my seventh month of pregnancy? What can be done for excessive snoring? Are the herbal medicines sold in health food stores really safe? Can the new cartilage transplant surgery help my arthritic knee?

Allergies: www.allernet.com
Aneurysms: www.westga.edu/~wmaples/doc.html
Arthritis: www.arthritis.org/forms/ask_help.shtml
Asthma: www.asthmacentre.com/ask_the_doctor. html
Attention Deficit Disorder: www.erols.com/ drleeb/
Bipolar Mood Disorder: www.mhsource.com/ bipolar/expert.html
Blood Vessels: www.visi.com/~irm/
Bones and Joints: bunny.lek.net/~fed/
Brain and Nervous System: www.surgery.missouri.edu/
Cancer: www.cancercareinc.org/services/referral2.htm
www.cancerhope.com/ask_a_doctor/question.html

CPR: www.learncpr.org/askdoctor.html
Dentist: www.the-toothfairy.com
Diabetes: www.childrenwithdiabetes.com/dteam/d_0d004.htm
Diet: www.drdiet.com
Eyes: www.visioncare.com
General Health: www.mercyhealthsystem.org/ASKNURSE/askartcl.htm
www.intelihealth.com/IH
www.yahoo.com/health/Ask_the_Nurse
www.harthosp.org/questions/
www.dreamtek.com/doctor.html
www.coloradohealthnet.org/COPD/copd_ask.html
www.bethisraelny.org/interactive/askdoctor.html
Grief: www.death-dying.com/experts/index.html
Heart Disease: www.sacheart.com
Kidneys: www.cnykidney.org
Knee Problems: www.knees.com
Medications: www.wilmington.net/dees/ask.html
Men's Health: methodisthealth.com/Urology/ask.htm
Mental Health: www.mhsource.com/expert.html
Muscles: www.openmri-southtexas.com/askthe.html
Muscular Dystrophy: www.mdausa.org/experts
Neonatology: www.neo.tch.tmc.edu/
Neurology: www.dr-neurosurg.com/index.html
www.bih.harvard.edu/neurology/docbag.htm
Orthodontics: www.bracesrus.com/
Pain: www.pain.com/defaultcon.cfm?direct=dr
Parenting: www.mbnet.mb.ca/crm/granny/granny.html
Pediatric Urology: peds-www.bsd.uchicago.edu/sections/urology/index.html
Pediatrics: www.mindspring.com/~drwarren/wpsl.htm
www.drs4kids.com/index.html
Plastic Surgery: www.ariyan.com/index.html
www.phudson.com/WELCOME/form.html
Pregnancy: www.abilene.com/armc
www.modimes.org/rc/help.htm
Radiology: telescan.nki.nl/SecondOpinion/index.html
Skin Conditions: www.facefacts.com/doctork.htm
Spinal Problems: www.orthospine.com
Sports Medicine: www.kyclinic.com
Surfing Ailments: www.mavsurfer.com/riptide/index.html
Thyroid Disease: www.thyroid.com/index.html
Veterinarian: www.prah.com
www.k9shrink.com/html/askdoc.html
Whiplash: www.whiplash101.com/discussion
Women's Health: www.womenshealth.org
www.healthywomen.com/asknp/index.htm

Note: Obviously, this is not meant to replace seeing a doctor, but to educate you to be a more informed health consumer.

Free Health Insurance Counseling for Seniors

Health care can be very confusing. Programs like Senior Healthcare Insurance Assistant Programs (SHIP) offer volunteers to the elderly to explain how insurance works. This way the seniors can use their benefits more wisely. There is no income eligibility for this program, as it is designed to help all seniors make wise health insurance choices.

Alabama
Alabama Department of Senior Services
770 Washington Avenue
RSA Plaza Suite 470
Montgomery, AL 36130
334-242-5743
877-425-2243
Fax: 334-242-5594
http://www.ageline.net/Default.htm

Alaska
Department of Insurance
240 Main Street, Suite 601
Juneau, AK 99801
907-465-3372
907-465-3165
866-465-3165
Fax: 907-465-1170
http://www.hss.state.ak.us/dsds/

Arkansas
Arkansas Insurance Department
Consumer Services Division
1200 West Third Street
Little Rock, AR 72201-1804
800-852-5494
501-371-2640
http://www.accessarkansas.org/insurance/srinsnetwork/seniorshlth_p1.html

Arizona
Department of Insurance
2910 N. 44th St. Suite 210
Phoenix, AZ 85018-7269
602-912-8400
http://www.id.state.az.us/consumerlifehealth.html#seniorhealth

California
Department of Aging
1600 K Street
Sacramento, CA 95814
916-322-3887
800-735-2929
Fax: 916-324-4989
http://www.aging.ca.gov/

District of Columbia
Office on Aging
441 4th Street, NW, Suite 900S
Washington, DC 20001
202-724-5622
http://dcoa.dc.gov/dcoa/site/default.asp

Florida
Florida Department of Elder Affairs
4040 Esplanade Way
Tallahassee, FL 32399-7000
850-414-2000
Fax: 850-414-2004
http://fcn.state.fl.us/doea/

Georgia
Division of Aging Services
Two Peachtree Street, NW, Suite 9385
Atlanta, GA 30303-3142
404-657-5258
Fax: 404-657-5285
http://aging.dhr.georgia.gov/portal/site

Hawaii
Insurance Division
P.O. Box 3614
Honolulu, HI 96811
808-586-2790
808-586-2799
http://www.hawaii.gov/dcca/areas/ins/

Idaho
Department of Insurance
700 West State Street
P.O. Box 83720
Boise, ID 83720-0043
208-334-4250
http://www.doi.state.id.us/shiba/shibahealth.aspx

Illinois
Illinois Division of Insurance
320 West Washington St.
Springfield, IL 62767-0001
800-548-9034
217-785-9021
Fax: 217-524-4872
www.idfpr.com/DOI/ship/ship_help.asp

Indiana
311 W. Washington St., Suite 300
Indianapolis, IN 46204-2787

800-452-4800
317-232-2385
Fax: 317-232-5251
www.in.gov/idoi/shiip

Iowa
SHIIP
330 Maple St.
Des Moines, IA 50319-0065
800-351-4664
http://www.shiip.state.ia.us/

Kansas
Kansas Department on Aging
New England Building
503 S. Kansas Ave.
Topeka, KS 66603-3404
785-296-4986
1-800-432-3535
Fax: 785-296-0256
http://www.agingkansas.org/shick/shick_index.html

Maine
Bureau of Elder and Adult Services
11 State House Station
442 Civic Center Drive
Augusta, ME 04333
207-287-9200
Fax: 207-287-9229
http://www.maine.gov/dhhs/beas/

Massachusetts
One Ashburton Place
5th floor (The McCormack Building)
Boston, MA 02108
617-727-7750
800-872-0166
http://www.800ageinfo.com/

Minnesota
MN Board on Aging
444 Lafayette Road North
St. Paul, MN 55155-3843
651-296-2770
Fax: 651-297-7855
http://www.mnaging.org/

Montana
Senior And Long Term Care Division
111 North Sanders, Room 210
Helena, MT 59604
406-444-4077
Fax: 406-444-7743
http://www.dphhs.state.mt.us/sltc/index.htm

New York
Department for the Aging
Two Lafayette Street, 16th Floor
New York, NY 10007-1392
212-333-5511
http://hiicap.state.ny.us/home/hiassist.htm

North Carolina
North Carolina Department of Insurance
1201 Mail Service Center
Raleigh, NC 27699-1201
800-443-9354
919-733-0111
http://www.ncshiip.com/Consumer/SHIIP/SHIIP.asp

North Dakota
ND Insurance Department
State Capitol, Fifth Floor
600 East Boulevard Avenue
Bismarck, ND 58505-0320
701-328-2440
Fax: 701-328-4880
http://www.state.nd.us/ndins/

Ohio
Ohio Department of Aging
50 W. Broad St./9th Fl.
Columbus, OH 43215-3363
614-466-5500
http://www.goldenbuckeye.com/oshiip.html

Oklahoma
Oklahoma Department of Insurance
2401 N.W. 23rd
Suite 28
Shepherd Mall
P.O. Box 53408
Oklahoma City, OK 73152-3408
800-763-2828
405-521-6628
http://www.oid.state.ok.us/consumer/shicp.html

Oregon
Oregon Insurance Division
P.O. Box 14480
Salem, OR 97309-0405
503-947-7980
Fax: 503-378-4351
http://www.cbs.state.or.us/external/shiba/

Pennsylvania
Department of Aging
555 Walnut Street, 5th Floor
Harrisburg, PA 17101-1919
717-783-1550

Fax: 717-783-6842
http://www.aging.state.pa.us/

South Dakota
Department of Social Services Adult Services & Aging
700 Governors Drive
Pierre, SD 57501
605-773-3656
866-854-5465
800-536-8197
http://www.state.sd.us/social/ASA/SHIINE/index.htm

Tennessee
Commission on Aging and Disability
500 Deadrick Street, 8th Floor
Nashville, TN 37243-0860
615-741-2056
http://www.state.tn.us/comaging/

Texas
Texas Department of Aging and Disability Services (DADS)
P.O. Box 149030
Austin, TX 78714-9030
512-438-3011
http://www.dads.state.tx.us/services/dads_help/aaa/hicap.html

Washington
Office of Insurance
P.O. Box 40255
Olympia, WA 98504-0255
360-725-7000
http://www.insurance.wa.gov/consumers/SHIBA_HelpLine/dirdefault.asp

West Virginia
WV Bureau of Senior Services
1900 Kanawha Boulevard, East
Holly Grove, Building #10
Charleston, WV 25305-0160
304-558-3317
Fax: 304-558-0004
http://www.wvinsurance.gov/

Wisconsin
Elderly Benefits Specialists
Bureau of Aging & Long Term Care Resources
1 W. Wilson Street
Madison, WI 53702
800-242-1060
http://dhfs.wisconsin.gov/aging/genage/benspecs.htm

Wyoming
Wyoming State Health Insurance Assistance Program (WYSHIIP)
P.O. Box BD
Riverton, WY 82501
800-856-4398
Fax: 307-856-4466
http://www.wyomingseniors.com/WSHIIP.htm

Help Fighting the Health Care System

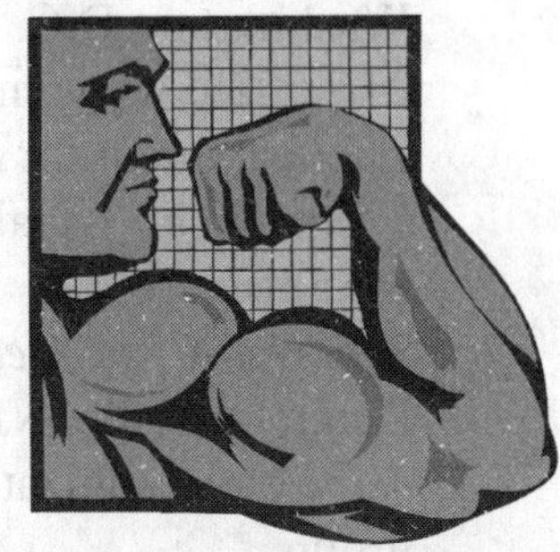

Disputes occur over payments rendered for services or services are denied. You don't have to take this sitting down and you are not alone in your fight. Issues occur with Medicaid, other insurance companies, hospitals, doctors, and more. But don't waste a penny of your money on attorneys when you can get more (and better) help from the government. To get you started we have included some helpful places to begin your battles:

1) ***Eldercare Locator***
The U.S. Administration on Aging offers this free service to older adult Americans and their caregivers to help them connect with available services. Eldercare Locator links older adults who need assistance with state and local area agencies on aging and community-based organizations. If you need help with any health related problem go to the web site and follow the directions or call a specialist. The web site is available in many different languages. Contact: 800-677-1116, www.eldercare.gov.

2) ***SeniorHealth.gov***
The National Institute of Health offers an on-line information web site for older adults. Their goal is to make age-related health information easily accessible to seniors, family members and friends. The web site is senior friendly including large print, short, easy to read segments and simple navigation. There is even a "talking" feature which reads the text. Information is updated regularly. Contact: http://nihseniorhealth.gov/

3) ***Free Help To Fight The Health Care System***
You can call government offices and advocacy groups that will do your fighting for you or give you the needed weapons to do your own fighting. Before you call a lawyer, call these free offices first: Your state Insurance Commissioner will help you learn your legal rights regarding insurance. Your state Medical Board will review your complaint and help resolve disputes. Your state HMO Board will also resolve disputes. You can also contact Patient Advocate Foundation, 700 Thimble Shoals Blvd., Suite 200, Newport News, VA 23606; 800-532-5274; www.patientadvocate.org.

   You can also use the Health Insurance Partnership program at Families USA: www.healthassistancepartnership.org/site/PageServer?pagename=Program_Locator&JServSessionIdr004=h23z93ghj1.app8b.

4) ***How To Fight Your Doctor, Hospital, Or Insurance Company — Call The Marines***
Well, not the actual Marines from the Department of Defense dressed in fatigues and armed with high tech weapons. But you can call other government offices and advocacy groups that will do your fighting for you or give you the needed weapons to do your own fighting. Before you call a lawyer, call these free offices first:
   - ***State Insurance Commissioner***: will help you learn your legal rights regarding insurance.

- ***State Medical Boards***: will review your complaint (including billing issues) and help resolve disputes.
- ***State HMO boards***: will review your complaint (including billing issues) and help resolve disputes.
- ***Center for Medicare Advocacy, Inc***, P.O. Box 350, Willimantic, CT 06226; 860-456-7790; Washington, D.C. office, 1101 Vermont Avenue, NW, Suite 1001, Washington, DC 20005; 202-216-0028; www.medicareadvocacy.org. Attorneys, paralegals, and technical assistants provide free legal help for elderly and disabled who are unfairly denied Medicare coverage in the state of Connecticut. Legal help and other services are also available to residents outside of Connecticut for a fee.
- ***American Self Help Clearinghouse***, Mental Help Net, St. Clares Health Services, 25 Pocono Road, Denville, NJ 07834-2995; 973-326-6789; www.mentalhelp.net/selfhelp: makes referrals to self-help organizations world wide and helps people interested in starting their own self help group.
- ***National Self-Help Clearinghouse***, Graduate School and University Center of the City University of New York, 365 5th Avenue, Suite 3300, New York, NY 10016; 212-817-1822; www.selfhelpweb.org: makes referrals to self-help groups nationwide.
- ***Patient Advocate Foundation***, 700 Thimble Shoals Boulevard, Suite 200, Newport News, VA 23606; 800-532-5274; Fax: 757-873-8999; www.patientadvocate.org: The Foundation specializes in mediation, negotiation and evaluation for patients that experience difficulty with insurance companies in areas of appeals, access to Chemotherapy, access to Pharmaceutical Agents, access to medical devices and more. Publications on dealing with insurance companies are also available.

Hospital Care And Service

If you had to wait three hours in the emergency room with a compound fracture in your leg before you were seen. Or the hospital insisted on discharging you after surgery even though you were still in extreme pain. Or dirty towels and bed sheets were piled in the hallways in the hospital where you stayed. Or the linens on your hospital bed were dirty and the food was cold. Or the nurse who took care of you was rude and impatient when she was explaining how you were supposed to take your medication. . Contact Centers for Medicare and Medicaid Services, 7500 Security Blvd., Baltimore, MD 21244; 410-786-3000; 800-MEDICARE; http://cms.hhs.gov

Hospital Discrimination

If you are denied dialysis because you are HIV positive. Or a hospital refuses to allow your Seeing Eye dog to accompany you during your stay. Or you were denied medical services at a hospital because your physician doesn't have staff privileges. Contact Office for Civil Rights, US. Department of Health and Human Services, 330 Independence Ave., SW, Room 5250, Washington, DC 20201; 800-368-1019; 202-619-0403, www.hhs.go/ocr/

Health Maintenance Organizations

If an HMO won't provide you with care because you're too old. Or the physician at your HMO treats you for the same condition three times in the last month with no improvement, and then he says the pain is all in your head. Or Medicare paid for your gallstone treatment, but the HMO still billed you for it.

Contact Centers for Medicare and Medicaid Services, 7500 Security Blvd., Baltimore, MD 21244; 800-MEDICARE; 410-786-3000, http://cms.hhs.gov

Medical Bills Making You Sick?

If you pay your doctor for a lab test, and he also receives payment for the tests from Medicare, but he won't give you a refund. Or even after repeated calls to your insurance company, they give you the run-around about sending you a refund for doctor's fees that you paid for out-of-pocket. Or you overpaid your doctor for a visit, but you haven't received the refund she promised you months ago. Contact your state capitol operator in your state capitol by calling 1-800-555-1212 and ask for your state's Office of Consumer Protection or go to www.govengine.com and search for Consumer Protection under your state.

Medical Devices

If a piece of your new hearing aid falls off and gets lodged in your ear canal. Or the baby monitor you bought shuts off whenever you use the television remote control. Or your in-home respirator has the annoying habit of switching off after you've fallen asleep. Contact MedWatch, Office of Consumer Affairs, Food and Drug Administration, HFE-88, U.S. Department of Health And Human Services, 5600 Fishers Lane, Rockville, MD 20857; 888-INFO-FDA; 301-443-1240; www.fda.gov/medwatch/

Medicare Fraud And Abuse

If you think your doctor is billing Medicare for procedures that you may not have needed. Or a pharmacist dispenses generic drugs to fill prescriptions and then bills Medicare for more expensive, non-generic drugs. Or the ambulance company you work for is billing Medicare for transporting patients who never existed. Contact: U.S. Department of Health and Human Services, OIG Hotline, 330 Independence Ave, SW, Washington, DC 20201, 800-447-8477, http://oig.hhs.gov

Nursing Homes That Don't Really Care

If the food at your nursing home is often served cold. Or the fees seem to rise every month without notice. Or the staff has treated you abusively. Or you've been unfairly denied admission to a nursing home for reasons that don't make sense to you. Contact your state capitol operator in your state capitol by calling 1-800-555-1212 and ask for your state's office of Nursing Home Ombudsman or go to www.govengine.com and search for Nursing Home Ombudsman under your state.

When Pharmacists Or Pharmacies Make You Sick

If your pharmacist neglects to warn you about taking a certain drug while operating heavy machinery. Or you were charged for 100 pills, but the pharmacist gave you only 75. Or your pharmacist is rude and impatient with you when you ask questions about your prescription. Or your pharmacist dispenses the wrong prescription for you and you have a serious allergic reaction to the drug. Contact your state capitol operator in your state capitol by calling 1-800-555-1212 and ask for your state's Pharmacy Board Office or go to www.govengine.com and search for Pharmacy Board under your state.

Prescription Fraud

If your friend brags to you that his doctor sells her prescriptions for valium under the table. Or your doctor offers to sell you a prescription for codeine. Or even though you've recovered from your depression, your doctor offers to sell you anti-depressants directly whenever you want them at half the normal price. Office of Diversion Control, Drug Enforcement Agency, Washington, DC 20537, 202-307-8010 www.deadiversion.usdoj.gov

Health Fraud

If a medical supply company sells you a miracle cure for cancer that turns out to be aspirin. Or a man, posing as a doctor, promises to cure your arthritis by giving you injections of a new drug that turns out to be sugar water. Or the $1,000 cure for AIDS you bought is actually a bottle of multi-vitamins along with advice to drink a lot of water. Contact your state capitol operator in your state capitol by calling 1-800-555-1212 and ask for your state's office of Consumer Protection or go to www.govengine.com and search for Consumer Protection under your state.

Protect Your Money

A government report shows that up to 21% of seniors hide their assets to help qualify for Medicaid to pay for long term nursing care (GAO-05-968). Nursing home care can cost up to $70,000 a year, so people can quickly deplete their savings accounts. Medicare only covers 100 days of skilled nursing care. Once all the patient's funds are gone, Medicaid kicks in to cover the bill. There is a certain amount of income that is not counted in qualifying for Medicaid and when a spouse is involved there are even more rules and exemptions. Homes, automobiles, furnishings, and certain income are exempt, but all of this varies from state to state. You are legally allowed to transfer money up to 36 months and up to 60 months for certain irrevocable trusts. That is the time period Medicaid will review your finances to see if you qualify for coverage. It is illegal to hide assets from Medicaid, and to intentionally transfer the assets to qualify for Medicaid. You can do an internet search for "Medicaid Planning" which will turn up several publications and information regarding what the rules are for your state. Some basic rules can be found at http://www.cms.hhs.gov/medicaid/eligibility/assets.asp, although you will need to contact your state directly to find out specifics for your state. You can also locate some specific information at www.elderlawanswers.com which provides rules for each state. Senior Legal hotlines (listed on page 216) can answer your questions and put you in contact with people who can assist you in estate planning.

Up to 61% of Appeals Win!

You have the right to appeal any decision about your Medicare services. This is true whether you are in the Original Medicare Plan or a Medicare managed care plan. If Medicare does not pay for an item or service you have been given, or if you are not given an item or service you think you should get, you can appeal. If you file an appeal, ask your doctor or provider for any information related to the bill that might help your case. Your appeal rights are on the back of the Explanation of Medicare Benefits or Medicare Summary Notice that is mailed to you from a company that handles bills for Medicare. The notice will also tell you why your bill was not paid and what appeal steps you can take. If you are in a Medicare managed care plan and you think your health could be seriously harmed by waiting for a decision about a service, ask the plan for a fast decision. The plan must answer you within 72 hours. If the plan does not decide in your favor, the appeal is reviewed by an independent organization that works for Medicare, not for the plan.

To appeal, look at the back of your Benefits Summary Notice, or contact Centers for Medicare & Medicaid Services, 7500 Security Blvd., Baltimore, MD 21244; 800-MEDICARE; www.medicare.gov You can also contact the Quality Improvement Organization (listed on page 117), Senior Legal hotlines (listed on page 216), Center for Medicare Advocacy, P.O. Box 350, Williamantic, CT 06226; 860-456-7790; www.medicareadvocacy.org.

Some Muscle to Fight Medicare Services

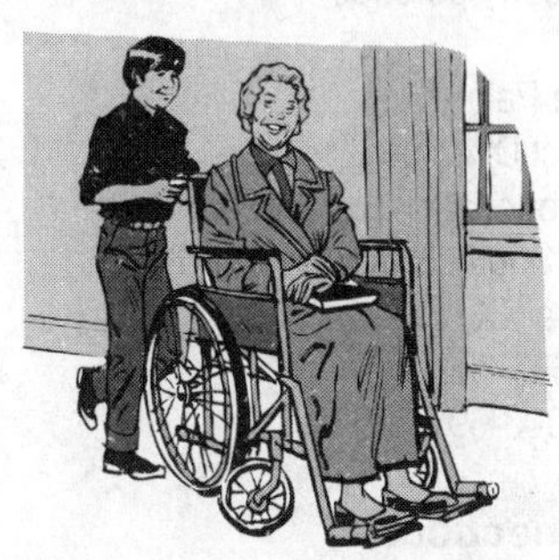

Quality Improvement Organizations (QIOs) monitor the appropriateness and quality of care provided to Medicare beneficiaries. They work to improve the quality of care in nursing homes, hospitals, home health care agencies, and other health care organizations. QIOs work with patients, physicians, hospitals and other care givers to improve care delivery systems to ensure that patients get the proper care at the proper time. The program works to safe guard the integrity of Medicare funds by making sure payment is made only for medically necessary services. They also investigate complaints about quality of care. People covered by Medicare can contact their QIO to request reviews of their medical care if they are concerned about the quality of the care they are receiving or to ask for a review if they feel they are being asked to leave the hospital before they are ready to do so. For more information contact a Quality Improvement Organization located in your state.

Quality Improvement Organizations

Alabama
Robert Sherrill, MD
Interim CEO
AL Quality Assurance Foundation
2 Perimeter Park South
Suite 200 West
Birmingham, AL 35243-2354
205-970-1600
Fax: 205-970-1616

Alaska
Jonathan Sugarman
President/CEO
Qualis Health Alaska Branch Office
721 Sesame Street, Suite 1A
Anchorage, AK 99503
907-562-2252
Fax: 907-562-5659

Arizona
Lawrence Shapiro
President/CEO
Health Services Advisory Group, Inc
301 E. Bethany Home Road
Suite B-157
Phoenix, AZ 85012
602-264-6382
Fax: 602-241-0757

Arkansas
Nancy Archer
HCQIP Director
AR Foundation For Med Care Inc
401 West Capitol
Suite 508
Little Rock, AR 72201
501-375-5700
Fax: 501-375-5705

Russell Brasher, CEO
AR Foundation For Med Care Inc
2201 Brooken Hill Drive
PO Box 180001
Fort Smith, AR 72908
501-649-8501
Fax: 501-649-8180
www.afmc.org

California
Jo Ellen Ross
President/CEO
LUMETRA
1 Sansome Street, Suite 600
San Francisco, CA 94104
415-677-2000
Fax: 415-677-2195
www.cmri-ca.org

Colorado
Marci Cameron
CO Foundation For Medical Care
2851 South Parker Road, #1000
Aurora, CO 80014-2723
303-695-3300
Fax: 303-695-3350

Laura Palmer
Project Director
CO Foundation For Medical Care
2851 South Parker Road, #1000
Aurora, CO 80014-2723
303-695-3300
Fax: 303-695-3350

Connecticut
Marcia Petrillo
Chief Executive Officer
Qualidigm
100 Roscommon DR, Suite 200
Middletown, CT 06457
860-632-2008
Fax: 860-632-5865

Delaware
John Wiesendanger
President/CEO
Quality Insights of Delaware
Baynard Building
3411 Silverside Road, #100
Wilmington, DE 19810
302-475-3600
Fax: 302-475-3873

District of Columbia
Malik Joshi
Chief Executive Officer
Delmarva Foundation For Medical Care
1620 L Street, NW, Suite 1275
Washington, DC 20036-5605
202-293-9650
Fax: 202-293-3253

Florida
Mark Michelman
Interim President
Florida Medical Quality Assurance
4350 W. Cypress Street, Suite 900
Tampa, FL 33607
813-354-9111
Fax: 813-354-0737

Georgia
Dennis White
Interim Chief Executive Officer
Georgia Medical Care Foundation
1455 Lincoln Pkwy., Suite 800
Atlanta, GA 30346
678-527-3404
Fax: 678-527-3504

Hawaii
Dee Dee Nelson, Director
Mountain-Pacific Quality Health Foundation
1360 South Beretania Street, Suite 501
Honolulu, HI 96814
808-545-2550
Fax: 808-440-6030
www.mt.net/~mtwy

Idaho
Marilyn Edmondson
Manager of Medicare Operations
Qualis Health
720 Park Boulevard, Suite 120
Boise, ID 83712-7756
208-343-4617
Fax: 208-343-4705

Illinois
Beth Hackman
Executive Vice President
Illinois Foundation for Quality Health Care
2625 Butterfield Road, Suite 104 S
Oakbrook, IL 60523
630-571-5540
Fax: 630-571-5611

Indiana
Philip Morphew, CEO
Health Care Excel, Incorporated
P.O. Box 3713
2901 Ohio Boulevard, Suite 112
Terre Haute, IN 47803
812-234-1499
Fax: 812-232-3603

Sharon Pygman
President/CEO
Health Care Excel, Inc.
2629 Waterfront Parkway
E. Drive
Indianapolis, IN 46214
317-347-4500
Fax: 317-347-4535

Sharon Smith, O
Health Care Excel, Incorporated
2629 Waterfront Pkwy East Dr.

Suite 200
Indianapolis, IN 46214
317-347-4500
Fax: 317-347-4567

Iowa
Fred Ferree
Executive Vice President
Iowa Foundation For Medical Care
6000 Western Parkway, Suite 350E
West Des Moines, IA 50266-7771
515-223-2900
Fax: 515-222-2407

Kansas
Larry Pitman
President/CEO
Kansas Foundation For Medical Care
2947 S.W. Wanamaker Dr.
Topeka, KS 66614-4193
785-273-2552
Fax: 785-273-5130
www.kfmc.org

Kentucky
Cindy Evinger
Program Director
Health Care Excel of Kentucky, Inc.
9300 Shelbyville Road, Suite 600
Louisville, KY 40222
502-339-7442
Fax: 502-339-8641

Louisiana
Leo Stanley
President/CEO
LA Health Care Review, Inc.
8591 United Plaza Blvd, Suite #270
Baton Rouge, LA 70809
225-926-6353
Fax: 225-293-0957
www.lhcr.org

Maine
Richard LaFleur, President
Northeast Health Care Quality Foundation
15 Old Rollinsford Road, Suite 302
Dover, NH 03820-2830
603-749-1641
Fax: 603-749-1195
(serves Maine)

Maryland
Thomas Schaefer
President/CEO
Delmarva Foundation For Medical Care, Inc.
9240 Centreville Road
Easton, MD 21601
410-822-0697
Fax: 410-822-7971

Massachusetts
Kathleen McCarthy
President/Chief Executive Officer
Mass PRO
235 Wyman Street
Waltham, MA 02451-1231
781-890-0011
Fax: 781-487-0083
www.masspro.org

Michigan
Debra Moss
President & CEO
Michigan Peer Review Organization
22670 Haggerty Road, #100
Farmington Hills, MI 48335-2611
248-465-7400
Fax: 248-465-7428

Minnesota
Patricia Riley, MA
President/CEO Stratis Health
2901 Metro Drive, Suite 400
Bloomington, MN 55425
612-854-3306
Fax: 612-853-8503

Mississippi
Jim McIlwain
President/Principal Clinical Coordinator
Information and Quality Healthcare
385 Highland Colony Parkway
Suite 120
Ridgeland, MS 39157-6035
601-957-1575
Fax: 601-956-1713

Missouri
Richard Royer
Chief Executive Officer
Primaris
200 North Keene Street
Columbia, MO 65201
573-817-8300
Fax: 573-817-8330

Montana
Janice Connors
President/CEO

Mountain-Pacific Quality Health Foundation
3404 Cooney Drive
Helena, MT 59602
406-443-4020
Fax: 406-443-4585
www.mt.net/~mtwy

Nebraska
Fred Ferree
Executive Vice President
The Sunderbruch Corporation/Nebraska
CTU Building
1221 N Street, Suite 402
Lincoln, NE 68508
402-474-7471
Fax: 492-474-7410

Nevada
William Berliner
Medical Director
HealthInsight
500 South Rancho Drive, Suite C-17
Las Vegas, NV 89106
702-385-9933
Fax: 702-385-4586

New Hampshire
Richard LaFleur, President
Northeast Health Care Quality Foundation
(also serves ME and VT)
15 Old Rollinsford Road, Suite 302
Dover, NH 03820-2830
603-749-1641
Fax: 603-749-1195

New Jersey
Martin Margolies
President/CEO
Peer Review Organization of NJ, Inc.
557 Cranbury Road, Suite 21
East Brunswick, NJ 08816-4026
732-238-5570
Fax: 732-432-5647

New Mexico
James Spence, President
New Mexico Medical Review Assn.
Midtown Center
2340 Menaul NE, Suite 300
Albuquerque, NM 87107
505-998-9898
Fax: 505-998-9899

New York
Thomas Sheehy
President IPRO
1979 Marcus Avenue, First Floor
Lake Success, NY 11042
516-326-7767
Fax: 516-326-7791
www.ipro.org

North Carolina
Charles Riddick
Executive Director
Medical Review of North Carolina
5625 Dillard Drive, Suite 203
Cary, NC 27511
919-380-9860
Fax: 919-380-7637
www.carolinaqio.org

North Dakota
David Remillard
Chief Executive Officer
ND Health Care Review, Inc
800 31st Avenue, SW
Minot, ND 58701
701-852-4231
Fax: 701-838-6009

Ohio
Gayle Smith
Chief Executive Officer
Ohio KePRO
Rock Run Center
5700 Lombardo Center Drive
Suite 100
Seven Hills, OH 44131
216-447-9604
Fax: 216-447-7925

Oklahoma
Jim Williams
President/CEO
OK Foundation for Medical Quality, Inc.
14000 Quail Springs Pkwy., Suite 400
Oklahoma City, OK 73134
405-840-2891
Fax: 405-840-1343
www.ofmq.com

Oregon
Jon Mitchell
President and CEO
Oregon Medical Professional Review Org.
2020 SW 4th, Suite 520
Portland, OR 97201-4960
503-279-0100
Fax: 503-279-0190

Pennsylvania
Dan Jones
Chief Executive Officer
Quality Insights of Pennsylvania
2601 Market Place Street, Suite 320
Harrisburg, PA 17110
877-346-6180
Fax: 610-688-5276

Puerto Rico
Jose Robles
Executive Director QIPRO, Inc.
Mercantile Plaza Bldg, Suite 605
Hato Rey, PR 00918
809-641-1240
Fax: 809-641-1248
www.qipro.org

Rhode Island
Jeffrey Newell
RI Quality Partners
235 Promenade Street
Providence, RI 02908
401-528-3200
Fax: 401-528-3210

South Carolina
Blake Williams
Director of Operations
Carolina Medical Review
250 Berryhill Road, Suite 101
Columbia, SC 29210
803-731-8225
Fax: 803-731-8229
www.carolinaqio.org

South Dakota
Mark Hoven
Chief Executive Officer
South Dakota FMC
1323 South Minnesota Avenue
Sioux Falls, SD 57105-0691
605-336-3505
Fax: 605-336-0270

Tennessee
Albert Grobmyer III
CEO/Executive Director
Mid-South Foundation for Medical Care, Inc.
3175 Lenox Park Blvd.
Suite #309
Memphis, TN 38115
901-682-0381
Fax: 901-761-3786

Texas
Phillip Dunne
Chief Executive Officer
Texas Medical Foundation
Barton Oaks Plaza 2, Suite 200
901 South Mopac Express.
Austin, TX 78746-5799
512-329-6610
Fax: 512-327-7159
www.tmf.org

Utah
Marc Bennett, President
HealthInsight
348 E. 4500 S., Suite 300
Salt Lake City, UT 84107
801-892-0155
Fax: 801-892-0160

Vermont
Richard LaFleur, President
Northeast Health Care Quality Foundation
15 Old Rollinsford Road, Suite 302
Dover, NH 03820-2830
603-749-1641
Fax: 603-749-1195
(serves Vermont)

Virginia
Amy Pierce, Ombudsman
LOA-Area Agency on Aging
Long Term Care Ombudsman Program
P.O. Box 14205
Roanoke, VA 24038-4205
540-345-0451
Fax: 540-206-0002
www.loaa.org

Washington
Jonathan Sugarman, MD
President/CEO
Peer Review Organization: Pro-West of Seattle
10700 Meridian Ave., North
Suite 100
Seattle, WA 98133-9075
206-364-9700
Fax: 206-368-2419
www.pro-west.org

West Virginia
John Wiesendanger
Chief Executive Officer
WV Medical Institute, Inc
3001 Chesterfield Place
Charleston, WV 25304

304-346-9864
Fax: 304-346-9863

Wisconsin
Greg Simmons
Chief Executive Officer
MetaStar, Inc.
2909 Landmark Place
Madison, WI 53713
608-274-1940
Fax: 608-274-5008
www.metastar.com

Wyoming
Janice Connors, Executive Director
Mountain-Pacific Quality Health Found.
1950 Bludgrass Circle, Suite 280
Cheyenne, WY 82009
307-778-8404
Fax: 307-778-9161

Medicaid Watchdogs

The mission of a Medicaid Fraud Control Unit is to investigate and prosecute Medicaid provider fraud and incidences of patient abuse and neglect. Medicaid fraud can be committed by doctors, dentists, health care providers and pharmacists. Potentially, anyone who bills Medicaid for services provided to a Medicaid recipient could commit Medicaid fraud. The most common types of Medicaid fraud include billing for services that were never performed; over billing for services provided; billing for tests or services that are medically unnecessary; double billing- billing both the patient and Medicaid; dispensing generic drugs while charging for more expensive brand name drugs; kickbacks-giving or accepting something in return for medical services; and up-coding-billing Medicaid for a more expensive service or procedure that was actually performed or provided. The Medicaid Fraud Control Units also investigate the abuse, neglect and/or exploitation of the residents of long term care facilities that receive Medicaid funding. If you are a victim of Medicaid Fraud or for more information contact Barbara Zelner at The National Association of Medicaid Fraud Control Units, 750 First St., NE, Suite 1100,Washington, DC 20002; 202-326-6220, Fax: 202-326-0884, or contact your state office from the list below.

State Offices of Medicaid Fraud Control Units

Alabama
Bruce Lieberman
Director, MFCU
Medicaid Fraud Control Unit of Alabama
Office of the Attorney General
11 S Union Street
Montgomery, AL 36130
334-242-7327
Fax: 334-353-8796

Alaska
Don Kitchen
Assistant Attorney General
Medicaid Fraud Control Unit of Alaska
Office of the Attorney General
310 K Street
Suite 308
Anchorage, AK 99501-2064
907-269-6279
Fax: 907-269-6202

Arizona
Steven Duplissis
Director, MFCU
Medicaid Fraud Control Unit of Arizona
Office of the Attorney General
1275 W. Washington St.
Phoenix, AZ 85007
602-542-3881
Fax: 602-364-0411

Arkansas
Joe Childers
Director, MFCU
Medicaid Fraud Control Unit of Arkansas
Office of the Attorney General
323 Center Street, Suite 200
Little Rock, AR 72201
501-682-7760
Fax: 501-682-8135

California
Collin Wong
Director, Bureau of Medi-Cal Fraud
Medicaid Fraud Control Unit of California
Office of the Attorney General
1425 River Park Drive
Suite 300
Sacramento, CA 95815
916-274-2994
Fax: 916-263-0864

Colorado
Milton Blakey
Director, MFCU
Medicaid Fraud Control Unit of Colorado
Office of the Attorney General
1525 Sherman Street, 5th Floor
Denver, CO 80203
303-866-5431
Fax: 303-418-1638

Connecticut
John DeMattia
Director, MFCU
Medicaid Fraud Control Unit of Connecticut
Office of the Chief State's Attorney
300 Corporate Place
Rocky Hill, CT 06067-1829
860-258-5986
Fax: 860-258-5848

Delaware
Dan Miller, Director
Medicaid Fraud Control Unit of Delaware
Office of the Attorney General
820 N. French Street, 5th Floor
Wilmington, DE 19801
302-577-8504
Fax: 302-577-3090

Florida
Spencer Levine
Director, MFCU
Medicaid Fraud Control Unit
Office of the Attorney General
The Capitol, PL-01
Tallahassee, FL 32399
850-414-3600
Fax: 850-487-9475

Georgia
Charles Richards
Director, MFCU
Medicaid Fraud Control Unit of Georgia
2100 East Exchange Place
Building One, Suite 200
Tucker, GA 30084
770-414-3655
Fax: 770-414-2718

Guam
Diane Calvo
Chief Division Director
Bureau of Economic Security
PO Box 2816
Hagatna, GU 96932
671-735-7259

Hawaii
Dewey Kim
Director, MFCU
Medicaid Fraud Control Unit of Hawaii
Office of the Attorney General
333 Queen Street, 10th Floor
Honolulu, HI 96813
808-586-1058
Fax: 808-586-1077

Idaho
Mond Warren
Dept of Health & Welfare
Medicaid Fraud and Abuse Unit
450 West State St., 6th Floor
Boise, ID 83720-5450
208-334-0675

Illinois
Gordon Fidler
Master Sergeant, Coordinator
Medicaid Fraud Control Unit of Illinois
Illinois Dept. of State Police
400 Iles Park Place, Suite 302
Springfield, IL 62718
217-785-3322
Fax: 217-524-6405

Indiana
Allen Pope, Director
Medicaid Fraud Control Unit of Indiana
Office of the Attorney General
8005 Castleway Drive
Indianapolis, IN 46250
317-915-5303
Fax: 317-232-6523

Iowa
Bob Galbraith, Director
Medicaid Fraud Control Unit of Iowa
Dept. of Inspections and Appeals
Lucas State Office Building

Des Moines, IA 50319
515-281-6377
Fax: 515-281-4477

Kansas
John Fleenor
Director, Deputy Attorney General
Medicaid Fraud Control Unit of Kansas
Office of the Attorney General
700 SW Jackson Street, Suite 804
Topeka, KS 66603-3758
785-368-6220
Fax: 785-386-6223

Kentucky
Pamela Murphey, Director
Medicaid Fraud Control Unit of Kentucky
Office of the Attorney General
1024 Capitol Center Drive
Frankfort, KY 40601
502-696-5405
Fax: 502-573-8316

Louisiana
Fred Duhy, Jr.
Director, MFCU
Medicaid Fraud Control Unit of Louisiana
Office of the Attorney General
PO Box 94095
Baton Rouge, LA 70804-4095
504-342-7517
Fax: 504-342-5696

Maine
Marci Alexander
Assistant Attorney General
Medicaid Fraud Control Unit of Maine
Office of the Attorney General
6 State House Station
Augusta, ME 04333-0006
207-626-8870
Fax: 207-287-3120

Maryland
David Lunden, Director
Medicaid Fraud Control Unit of Maryland
Office of the Attorney General
200 St. Paul Place, 18th Floor
Baltimore, MD 21202
410-576-6521
Fax: 410-576-6314

Massachusetts
Nicholas Messuri
Director, MFCU
Medicaid Fraud Control Unit of Massachusetts
Office of the Attorney General
200 Portland Street, 4th Floor
Boston, MA 02114-1700
617-727-2200
Fax: 617-727-2008

Michigan
Wallace Hart, Director, MFCU
Medicaid Fraud Control Unit of Michigan
Office of the Attorney General
6520 Mercantile Way
Lansing, MI 48911-6957
517-241-6500
Fax: 517-241-6515

Minnesota
Deborah Peterson
Director, Medicaid Fraud Control Unit
Medicaid Fraud Control Unit of Minnesota
445 Minnesota St.,, Suite 700
St. Paul, MN 55101-2131
651-297-1093
Fax: 651-282-5801

Mississippi
Kenny O'Neal
Assistant Attorney General
Medicaid Fraud Control of Mississippi
Office of the Attorney General
802 N. State Street
PO Box 56
Jackson, MS 39205-0056
601-359-4220
Fax: 601-359-4214

Missouri
Richard Williams
Director, MFCU
Medicaid Fraud Control Unit of Missouri
Office of the Attorney General
P.O. Box 899
Jefferson City, MO 65102-0899
573-751-7192
Fax: 573-751-0207

Montana
Gordon Hauge
Director, MFCU
Medicaid Fraud Control Unit of Montana
Office of the Attorney General
303 N Roberts Street, Room 367
Helena, MT 59601-4543
406-444-3875
Fax: 406-444-2759

Nebraska
Kris Azimi
NE DHHS Finance and Support
PO Box 95026
301 Centennial Mall South
Lincoln, NE 68509
402-471-9365

Nevada
Tim Terry
Director, MFCU
Medicaid Fraud Control Unit of Nevada
Office of the Attorney General
400 W. King Street, #406
Carson City, NV 89703-4204
775-687-4704
Fax: 775-687-5621

New Hampshire
Jeffrey Cahill
Director, MFCU
Medicaid Fraud Control Unit of New Hampshire
Office of the Attorney General
33 Capitol Street
Concord, NH 03301-6397
603-271-1246
Fax: 603-271-2110

New Jersey
John Krayniak
Director, MFCU
Medicaid Fraud Control Unit New Jersey
Division of Criminal Justice
25 Market Street
PO. Box 094
Trenton, NJ 08625-0094
609-896-8772
Fax: 609-896-8696

New Mexico
Katherine Vincent
Director, MFCU
Medicaid Fraud Control Unit of New Mexico
Office of the Attorney General
111 Lomas Boulevard, NW, Suite 300
Albuquerque, NM 87102
505-222-9000
Fax: 505-222-9007

New York
William Comiskey, Director
Medicaid Fraud Control Unit of New York
Office of the Attorney General
120 Broadway 13th Floor
New York, NY 10271
212-417-5250
Fax: 212-417-4284

North Carolina
Christopher Brewer
Assistant Attorney General, MFCU
Medicaid Fraud Control Unit of North Carolina
Office of the Attorney General
P.O. Box 629
Raleigh, NC 27602-0629
919-881-2320
Fax: 919-571-4837

North Dakota
There is no Medicaid Fraud Unit Control office in North Dakota at this time.

Ohio
John Guthrie
Director, MFCU
Medical Fraud Control Unit of Ohio
Office of the Attorney General
150 E. Gay Street, 17th Floor
Columbus, OH 43215-5187
614-466-0722
Fax: 614-644-9973

Oklahoma
Don Brown
Director, MFCU
Medicaid Fraud Control Unit of Oklahoma
Office of the Attorney General
4545 N. Lincoln Boulevard, Suite 260
Oklahoma City, OK 73105-3498
405-528-4274
Fax: 405-528-1867

Oregon
Ellyn Sternfield
Director, Medicaid Fraud Control Unit of Oregon
Department of Justice
1515 SW 5th Avenue, Suite 410
Portland, OR 97204-1818
503-229-5725
Fax: 503-229-5120

Pennsylvania
E. Christopher Abruzzo
Director, MFCU
Medicaid Fraud Control Unit of Pennsylvania
Office of the Attorney General
1601 Strawberry Square
Harrisburg, PA 17120-0048
717-772-2772
Fax: 717-783-5431

Rhode Island
Pamela Woodcock Pfeiffer
Director
Medicaid Fraud Control Unit of Rhode Island
Office of The Attorney General
150 S Main Street
Providence, RI 02903-2994
401-274-4400
Fax: 401-222-3014

South Carolina
Charles Gambrell
Assistant Attorney General, MFCU
Medicaid Fraud Control Unit of South Carolina
Office of The Attorney General
PO Box 11549
Columbia, SC 29211-1549
803-734-3660
Fax: 803-734-8754

South Dakota
Jason Glodt, Director
Medicaid Fraud Control Unit of South Dakota
Office of the Attorney General
110 W. Missouri Street
Pierre, SD 57501-4506
605-773-4102
Fax: 605-773-6471

Tennessee
Bob Schlafly
Special Agent in Charge
Medicaid Fraud Control Unit
TN Bureau of Investigations
901 R.S. Gass Boulevard
Nashville, TN 37216-2639
615-741-2588
Fax: 615-741-2088

Texas
Scott Stephenson
Director, MFCU
Medicaid Fraud Control Unit of Texas
Office of Attorney General
P.O. Box 12307
Austin, TX 78711-2307
512-463-2100
Fax: 512-320-0974
www.oag.state.tx.us

Utah
Wade Farraway
Director, MFCU
Medicaid Fraud Control Unit of Utah
5272 College Drive, Suite 200
Salt Lake City, UT 84123-2772
801-281-1258
Fax: 801-284-6304

Vermont
Linda Purdy
Director, MFCU
Medicaid Fraud Control Unit of Vermont
Office of the Attorney General
103 S Main Street
Waterbury, VT 05671-1401
802-241-4440
Fax: 802-241-4447

Virginia
Randall Clouse
Director, MFCU
Medicaid Fraud Control Unit of Virginia
Office of The Attorney General
900 E Main Street, Suite 600
Richmond, VA 23219-3524
804-786-3510
Fax: 804-225-3064

Washington
David Waterbury
Director, MFCU
Medicaid Fraud Control Unit of Washington
Office of The Attorney General
1019 Pacific Avenue, 3rd Floor
Tacoma, WA 98402
253-593-2154
Fax: 253-593-5135

West Virginia
Sam Cook, Director, MFCU
Medicaid Fraud Control Unit of West Virginia
8 Fletcher Square
Dunbar, WV 25064-3136
304-558-1858
Fax: 304-558-3498

Wisconsin
Amy Smith, Director, MFCU
Medicaid Fraud Control Unit of Wisconsin
Office of The Attorney General
123 West Washington Avenue
PO Box 7857
Madison, WI 53707-7857
608-264-6360
Fax: 608-265-2223

Wyoming
Denise Burke
Director, MFCU

Medicaid Fraud Control Unit of Wyoming
Office of The Attorney General
1807 Capitol Avenue, Suite 108
Cheyenne, WY 82001-4558
307-635-3597
Fax: 307-635-6196

Drugs

Free Drugs From Manufacturers

Leave it to the government to know where you can get free Halcion, AZT, Valium or Motrin but not make any effort to tell you about it. The U.S. Senate's Special Committee on Aging recently published a report on how certain eligible groups, including the elderly and the poor, can actually get their much needed prescription drugs free of charge directly from the companies that manufacture them. Here's what the committee discovered:

Taking prescription medications is often a matter of life and death for millions of Americans, yet many just can't afford the drugs they need simply because they're too expensive. Many are forced to choose between paying for food or their medications, especially the elderly. The relative lack of prescription drug insurance has been compounded by prescription cost increases that can actually surpass the rate of inflation by four times.

Though not widely known, drug companies have programs that offer many prescription drugs free of charge to poor and other vulnerable groups that cannot afford them. However, these free drug programs are being used by only a small number of people that could truly benefit from them. And to add to this, the programs often require long waiting times for qualified patients to receive their free medications from drug manufacturers.

The Pharmaceutical Research and Manufacturer's Association (PMA) has established a Directory of Prescription Drug Patient Assistance Programs, which lists up-to-date information on individual manufacturers' patient programs. Although the directory does not always identify the drugs manufactured, it still should be your first call. Contact: Pharmaceutical Research and Manufacturer's Association, 800-PMA-INFO, www.helpingpatients.org.

The following pages contain an alphabetical list of all drugs currently covered under Prescription Drug Patient Assistance Programs, as well as the manufacturer that supplies them. We have also included some helpful tips and questions you should ask when contacting the programs:

1) If a drug is not listed in the directory, it still may be provided by the company. You should call the manufacturer directly to check.
2) Ask about the eligibility requirements. Some companies require that you have a limited income or no insurance coverage, while others require only that you get a doctor's referral.
3) Ask about the enrollment process. Many drug companies require a phone call or letter from your doctor.
4) If your doctor refuses to call or does not believe the program will work, contact the drug companies yourself and find out about the application process. You will still need a doctor to fill the application, but you can at least get the forms, and then encourage your doctor to complete them. If your doctor still refuses, maybe you can find another doctor who will.

Find out how you will receive the prescription drugs, and how you can get refills. Most companies send the medications directly to your doctor. There have been some problems with delays in receiving the drugs, so check to see what the company's shipping schedule is, and what you or your doctor should do if there is a problem.

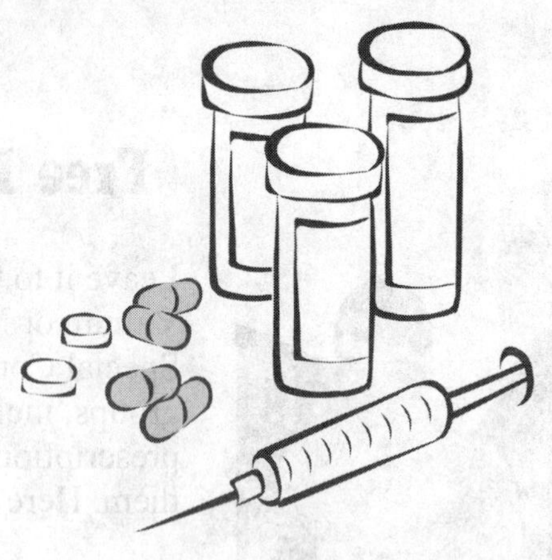

A to Z Drug Listing

In this Section you'll find a comprehensive A to Z listing of all the drugs that are available to certain qualified groups free of charge directly from the manufacturers.

Each company determines the eligibility criteria for its program. Often, determination is based on the patient's income level and lack of insurance.
Unless specified below, manufacturers require a phone call or written statement from your doctor's office requesting the medication.

First, find the drug you need and the corresponding manufacturer. Next, look up the address and telephone number of the appropriate drug manufacturer from the Directory of Pharmaceutical Manufacturers, which follows the A to Z drug listing.

Your doctor will need to contact the drug company to find out about how to receive the drug free of charge. Remember, although they want your doctor to call, if your doctor refuses, make the call yourself. After they enroll you in the program, the drug manufacturer will send the medication directly to your doctor who will pass it along to you.

Important Note: More drugs are constantly being added to this list. If you do not find your drug listed here, contact the manufacturer of the drug to see if your drug is included in this program.

Alphabetical Listing of Drugs and Supplements

Drug	Manufacturer
A —	
8-Mop	Valeant
A/T/S/	Medicis
Abelcet	Enzon, Elan
Abilify	Bristol-Myers
Accolate	AstraZeneca
Accrupril	Pfizer
Accuretic	Pfizer
Accutane	Roche
ACEON	Solvay
ACEON	Solvay
Aciphex	Eisai
Aciphex	Janssen
Aclovate	GlaxoSmithKline
Acthar Gel	Questcor
Acthrel	Ferring
Actiq	Cephalon
Activase	Genentech
Activella	Novo Nordisk
Actonel	Proctor & Gamble
Actos	Takeda
Adalat CC	Bayer
ADEKs	Axcan Scandipharm
Advair Diskus	GlaxoSmithKline
Advera	Abbott
Advicor	Kos
AeroBid	Forest
Aerochamber	Forest
Agenerase	GlaxoSmithKline
Aggrenox	Boehringer
Agrylin	Shire
Alamast	Vistakon
Albenza	GlaxoSmithKline
Aldara	3M
Aldurazyme	Genzyme
Allegra	Aventis Pharmaceuticals
Allegra D	Aventis Pharmaceuticals
Alphagan P .15%	Allergan

Drug	Manufacturer
Amaryl	Aventis Pharmaceuticals
Amerge	GlaxoSmithKline
Amicar	Xanodyne
Amoxil	Glaxo SmithKline
Anadrol	Solvay
Analpram	Ferndale
Anaplex	ECR
Anaprox	Roche
Ancobon	Valeant
Androderm	Watson
Androgel	Solvay
Androgel	Solvay
Antivert	Pfizer
Anzemet	Aventis Oncology
Aralen	Sanofi Synthelabo
Aranesp	Amgen
Arava	Together
Aricept	Eisai and Pfizer
Arimidex	AstraZeneca
Arixtra	Organon
Armour	Forest
Aromasin	Pfizer
Arthrotec	Pfizer
Asacol	Procter & Gamble
Atacand	AstraZeneca
Atrovent	Boehringer
Augmentin	Glaxo SmithKline
Avalide	Bristol-Myers
Avandamet	GlaxoSmithKline
Avandia	GlaxoSmithKline
Avapro	Bristol-Myers
Avelox IV	Bayer
Avelox	Bayer
Aventyl HCL	Eli Lilly
Avodart	GlaxoSmithKline
Avonex	Biogen
Axert	Ortho-McNeil
Azmacort	Kos
Azopt	Alcon
B —	
Bactroban	Glaxo SmithKline
Beconase AQ	Glaxo SmithKline
Benefix	Genetics Institute
Benicar Tablets	Sankyo
Benoquin	Valeant
BenzaClin	Dermik
Benzagel	Dermik
Benzamycin	Dermik
Betagan	Allergan
Betapace	Berlex
Betaseron	Berlex
Betimol	Vistakon

Drug	Manufacturer
Betoptic	Alcon
Bextra	Pfizer
Bexxar	GlaxoSmithKline
Biaxin	Abbott
Bicitra	Ortho-McNeil
BICNU	Bristol-Myers
Biltricide	Bayer
Blenoxance	Bristol-Myers
Bontril	Amarin
Botox	Allergan
Brethine	AAI
Brevoxil	Stiefel
Bumex	Roche
Bupap	ECR
Buphenyl	Ucyclyd
BuSpar	Bristol-Myers
C —	
Caduet	Pfizer
Calcilo XD	Abbott
Calijex	Abbott
Campath	Berlex
Camptosar	Pfizer
Cantil	Aventis
Capital and Codeine	Amarin
Carac	Dermik
Cardene	Roche
Cardura	Pfizer
Carnitor	Sigma-Tau
Carteolol HCl	Alcon
Casodex	AstraZeneca
Catapres	Boehringer
Ceclor	Eli Lilly, Elan
CEENU	Bristol-Myers
Ceftin	Glaxo SmithKline
Cefzil	Bristol-Myers
Celebrex	Pfizer
Celexa	Forest
CellCept	Roche
Celluvisc	Allergan
Cenestin	Duramed
Ceredase	Genzyme
Cerezyme	Genzyme
Cetacaine	Cetylite
Cetrotide	Serono
Cipro	Bayer
Clarinex tablets	Schering-Plough
Climara	Berlex
Clindents	Stiefel
Clorpres	Bertek
Clozapine	Mylan
Clozaril	Novartis, Ivax
Cognex	1st Horizon
Combivent	Boehringer

Drug	Manufacturer
Combivir	GlaxoSmithKline
Compazine	GlaxoSmithKline
Comtan	Novartis
Concerta	McNeil
Copaxone	Teva
Copegus	Roche
Cordarone	Wyeth
Coreg	GlaxoSmithKline
Cortef	Pfizer
Cosmegin	Merck
Cosopt	Merck
Coumadin	Bristol-Myers
Covera HS	Pfizer
Cozaar	Merck
CREON	Solvay
Crestor	Astra
Crinone	Serono
Crixivan	Merck
Cuprimine	Merck
Cutivate	GlaxoSmithKline
Cyclinex	Abbott
Cystadane	Orphan
Cytotec	Pfizer
Cytovene	Roche
Cytoxan	Bristol-Myers
D —	
Danocrine	Sanofi Synthelabo
Dantrium	Proctor & Gamble
Daraprim	GlaxoSmithKline
Darvocet	AAI
Daunoxome	Gilead
DDAVP	Aventis Pharmaceuticals
Declomycin	ESP Pharma
Demadex	Roche
Demser	Merck
Depakene	Abbott
Depakote	Abbott
Depakote ER	Abbott
Depocyt	Chiron
Desferal	Novartis
Desmopressin	Ferring
Desyrel	Bristol-Myers
Detrol	Pfizer
Dexedrine	GlaxoSmithKline
DHE 45	Xcel
Diabeta	Together
Diabinese	Pfizer
Diastat	Xcel
Didronel	Procter & Gamble
Diflucan	Pfizer
Dilantin	Pfizer
Diovan	Novartis
Dipentum	Celltech
Dipivefrin	Alcon
Diprolene	Schering-Plough
Ditropan	Ortho-McNeil
Diurill	Merck
Dolobid	Merck
Domepaste Bandages	Bayer
Dostinex	Pfizer
Dovonex	Bristol-Myers
DOXIL	Ortho Biotech
Drisdol	Sanofi Synthelabo
Droxia	Bristol-Myers
DTIC Dome	Bayer
Duragesic	Janssen
Dyazide	Glaxo SmithKline
Dynacin	Medicis
Dynacirc	Reliant
DynaCirc	Sandoz
E —	
EC Naprosyn	Roche
Effexor	Wyeth
Efudex (Fluorouracil)	Valeant
Eldepryl	Somerset
Eldopaque	Valeant
Eldoquin	Valeant
EleCare	Abbott
Elidel	Novartis
Ellence	Pfizer
Elmiron	Ortho-McNeil
Elocon	Schering-Plough
Elspar	Merck
Emcyt	Pfizer
EMEND	Merck
Emla	Together
Emtriva	Gilead
Enbrel	Amgen
Enlive!	Abbott
Ensure	Abbott
Entocort EC	AstraZeneca
Epivir	GlaxoSmithKline
Epivir-HBV	GlaxoSmithKline
Epogen	Amgen
Esgic	Forest
Eskalith CR	GlaxoSmithKline
Estraderm	Together
Estratest	Solvay
Ethmozine	Shire
Etopophos	Bristol-Myers
Eulexin	Scherling-Plough
Evista	Eli Lilly
Exelon	Novartis

Drug	Manufacturer
F —	
Fabrazyme	Genzyme
Famvir	Novartis
Fareston	Shire
Faslodex	AstraZeneca
Feiba VH	Baxter
Felbatol	Medpointe
Feldene	Pfizer
Femara	Novartis
Ferrlecit	Watson
Flexeril	McNeil
Flomax	Boehringer
Flonase	GlaxoSmithKline
Flovent Rotadisk	GlaxoSmithKline
Flovent	GlaxoSmithKline
Floxin	Ortho-McNeil
Fludara	Berlex
Focalin	Novartis
Foradil Aerolizer	Schering-Plough
Fortaz	GlaxoSmithKline
Forteo	Eli Lilly
Fortovase	Roche
Fosamax	Merck
Foscavir	Astra Zeneca
Fototar	Valeant
Fuzeon	Roche
G —	
Gabitril	Cephalon
Gammagard	Baxter
Gammar-PIV	Aventis Behring
Gantanol	Roche
Gastrocrom	Fisons Celltech
Gengraf	Abbott
Genotropin	Pfizer
Genteal	Novartis
Gleevec	Novartis
Glucagon	Eli Lilly
Glucerna	Abbott
Glucophage	Bristol-Myers
Glucotrol	Pfizer
Glucovance	Bristol-Myers
Glutarex	Abbott
Glyset	Pfizer
Gonal-F	Serono
Grifulvin	Ortho-McNeil
H —	
Haldol	Ortho-McNeil
Hectoral Capsules	Bone Care
Helixate FS	Aventis Behring
Hemofil	Baxter
Hepsera	Gilead
Herceptin	Genentech
Hexalen	MGI Pharma
Hiprex	Aventis
Hivid	Roche
Hominex	Abbott
Humalog	Eli Lilly
Humate-P	Aventis Behring
HUMIRA	Abbott
Humulin	Eli Lilly
Hycamtin	GlaxoSmithKline
Hydrea	Bristol-Myers
Hydrocet	Amarin
Hypotears	Novartis
Hytakerol	Sanofi Synthelabo
Hytone	Dermik
Hyzaar	Merck
I —	
Idamycin	Pfizer
Ifex	Bristol-Myers
Ilentin	Eli Lilly
Imdur tablets	Schering-Plough
Imitrex	GlaxoSmithKline
Imodium	Janssen
IMOGAM Rabies	Aventis Pasteur
IMOVAX Rabies	Aventis Pasteur
Inderal	Wyeth
Inderide	Wyeth
InFed	Watson
Infergen	InterMune
Innohep	Pharmion
Integrilin injection	Millennium
Intron-A	Schering
Invirase	Roche
Iopidine	Alcon
Ismo	ESP Pharma
IsoptoCarbachol	Alcon
IsoptoCarpine	Alcon
I-Valex	Abbott
J —	
Jevity	Abbott
K —	
Kadian	Alpharma, Faulding
Kaletra	Abbott
Kay Ciel	Forest
K-Dur tablets	Schering-Plough
Keflex	Eli Lilly
Kenalog	Bristol-Myers
Keppra	UCB Pharma
Kerlone	Sanofi-Synthelabo
Ketonex	Abbott
Kineret	Amgen
Klaron	Dermik

Drug	Manufacturer
Klonopin	Roche
Klor-Con	Upsher-Smith
Klotrix	Bristol-Myers
K-Lyte	Bristol-Myers
Kytril	Roche
L —	
Lac-Hydrin	Bristol-Myers
Lacrisert	Merck
Lacticare	Stiefel
Lamictal	GlaxoSmithKline
Lamisil	Novartis
Lamprene	Ciba-Geigy
Lanoxicaps	GlaxoSmithKline
Lanoxin	Glaxo SmithKline
Lantus	Aventis
Lescol	Novartis
Leukeran	GlaxoSmithKline
Leukine	Berlex
Leustatin	Ortho-Biotech
Levaquin	Ortho-McNeil
Levobunolol	Alcon
Levothroid	Forest
Lexiva	GlaxoSmithKline
Lidex	Medicis
Lidoderm	Endo
Lipitor	Pfizer
Livostin	Novartis
Locoid	Ferndale
Lodine	Wyeth
Lodosyn	Bristol-Myers
Lodrane	ECR
Lopid	Pfizer
Loprox	Medicis
Lotrel	Together
Lotrisone	Schering-Plough
Lotronex	GlaxoSmithKline
Lovenox	Aventis Pharmaceuticals
Lumigan .03% Q.D	Allergan
Lupron	TAP
Lustra	Medicis
Luxiq	Connetics
Lysodren	Bristol-Myers
M —	
Macrobid	Procter & Gamble
Macrodantin	Procter & Gamble
Mag-Ox	Blaine
Malarone	GlaxoSmithKline
Mandol	Eli Lilly
Marinol	Solvay
Materna	Wyeth
Matulane	SigmaTau

Drug	Manufacturer
Mavik Tablets	Abbott
Maxair Autohaler	3M
Maxalt	Merck
Maxzide	Bertek
Megace	Bristol-Myers
Menomune	Aventis Pasteur
Mephyton	Merck
Mepron	Glaxo SmithKline
Mesnex	Bristol-Myers
Mestinon	Valeant
Metaglip	Bristol-Myers
Metipranolol	Alcon
MetroGel	3M
Mevacor	Merck
Miacalcin	Novartis
Micardis	Boehringer
Midamor	Merck
Migranal	Xcel
Minipress	Pfizer
Minitran	3M
Minizide	Pfizer
Minocin	Wyeth
MiraLax	Braintree
Mirapex	Boehringer
Moban	Endo
Mobic	Boehringer
Moduretic	Merck
Monistat Derm	Ortho-McNeil
Monoclate-P	Aventis Behring
Mononine	Aventis Behring
Monopril	Bristol-Myers
Motofen	Amarin
MS Contin	Purdue
Mustargen	Merck
Mutamycin	Bristol-Myers
Myambutol	Lederle
Mycelex	Ortho McNeil
Mycobutin	Pfizer
Mycostatin	Bristol-Myers
Myfortic	Novartis
Mykrox	Celltech
Myleran	GlaxoSmithKline
Mylocel	MGI Pharma
Mysoline	Xcel
Mytelase	Sanofi Synthelabo
N —	
Naprosyn	Roche
Nasacort AQ Nasal Spray	Aventis Pharmaceuticals
Nasatab	ECR
Nasonex	Schering-Plough
Naturetin	Bristol-Myers

Drug	Manufacturer
Navane	Pfizer
Navelbine	GlaxoSmithKline
NebuPent	Amarin
Neoral	Novartis
Nepro	Abbott
Neulasta	Amgen
Neupogen	Amgen
Neurontin	Pfizer
Neutra-Phos	Ortho-McNeil
Neutra-Phos-K	Ortho-McNeil
Neutrexin	Medimmune
Nexium	AstraZeneca
Niacor	Upsher-Smith
Niaspan	Kos
Nilandron	Aventis Oncology
Nimotop	Bayer
Nitrek	Bertek
Nitro-Dur Patches	Schering-Plough
Nitrogard	Forest
Nitrolingual	First Horizon
Nizoral	Janssen
Nolahist	Amarin
Nolamine	Amarin
Nolvadex	Astra Zeneca
Norflex	3M
Norgesic Forte	3M
Norgesic	3M
Noritate	Dermik
Noroxin	Merck
Norvasc	Pfizer
Norvir	Abbott
Novacet	Medicis
Novantrone	Immunex
Novolin	Novo Nordisk
NovoLog	Novo Nordisk
NutriFocus	Abbott
Nutropin	Genentech
O —	
Ocupress	Novartis
OLUX	Connetics
Omnicef	Together
ONTAK	Ligand
Optimental	Abbott
ORTHOVISC	Ortho Biotech
Oruvail	Wyeth
Osmolite	Abbott
Ovide	Medicis
Ovidrel	Serono
Oxandrin	BTG
Oxepa	Abbott
Oxistat	GlaxoSmithKline, Elan
Oxsoralen	Valeant

Drug	Manufacturer
P —	
Pacerone	Upsher-Smith
Pancrease	Ortho-McNeil
Panoxyl	Stiefel
Panretin	Ligand
Parafon Forte DSC	Together
Paraplatin	Bristol-Myers
Parnate	GlaxoSmithKline
Paxil XR	GlaxoSmithKline
Paxil	GlaxoSmithKline
PediaSure	Abbott
Peg Intron	Schering-Plough
Pegasys	Roche
Penlac	Dermik
Pentasa	Shire
Pentoxil	Upsher-Smith
Pepcid	Merck
Perative	Abbott
Pergonal	Serono
Periostat	CollaGenex
Permax	Athena
Phenergan	Wyeth
Phenex	Abbott
PhisoHex	Sanofi Synthelabo
Phospholine Iodide	Wyeth
Phrenilin	Amarin
Pilopine	Alcon
Plaquenil	Sanofi Synthelabo
Platinol	Bristol-Myers
Plavix	Bristol-Myers
Plendil	Astra Zeneca
Pneumotussin	ECR
Polycitra	Ortho-McNeil
Potaba	Glenwood
Pramosone	Ferndale
Prandin	Novo Nordisk
Pravigard	Bristol-Myers
Pravochol	Bristol-Myers
Precose	Bayer
Premarin	Wyeth
Premphase	Wyeth
Prempro	Wyeth
Prevacid	TAP
Prevalite	Upsher-Smith
Prevpac	Together
Prilosec	Together
Primacor	Sanofi-Synthelabo
Prinivil	Merck
Prinzide	Merck
ProAmatine	Shire
Procardia XL	Pfizer
Procardia	Pfizer
Procrit	Ortho-Biotech
Proleukin	Chiron

Drug	Manufacturer
Prolixin	Bristol-Myers
Promote	Abbott
Pronestyl SR	Bristol-Myers
Pro-Phree	Abbott
Propimex	Abbott
Proscar	Merck
ProSure	Abbott
Protonix	Wyeth
Proventil	Schering
Provigil	Cephalon
ProViMin	Abbott
Prozac	Eli Lilly
Psorcon	Dermik
Pulmicort	AstraZeneca
Pulmocare	Abbott
Pulmozyme	Genentech
Q —	
Quinidine Gluconate	Eli Lilly
Quixin	Vistakon
R —	
RCF	Abbott
RMS	Upsher-Smith
Rabavert	Chiron
Rebetol	Schering-Plough
Rebetron	Schering-Plough
Rebif	Serono
Recombinate	Baxter
Refresh	Allergan
Regranex	Ortho-McNeil
Relafen	Glaxo SmithKline
Relenza	GlaxoSmithKline
Relpax	Pfizer
Remeron SolTab	Organon
Remeron	Organon
Remicade	Centocor
Reminyl	Janssen
Renova	Ortho-McNeil
Reopro	Eli Lilly
Repronex	Ferring
Requip	GlaxoSmithKline
Rescriptor	Pfizer
Rescula	Together
Restasis .15%	Allergan
Retavase	Centocor
Retin-A	Ortho-McNeil
Retrovir	GlaxoSmithKline
Reyataz	Bristol-Myers
Rhinocort	AstraZeneca
Rimactane	Novartis
Risperdal	Janssen
Ritalin LA	Novartis
Rituxan	Genentech
Robinul	First Horizon
Rocaltrol	Roche
Rocephin	Roche
Roferon-A	Roche
Rowasa	Solvay
S —	
Saizen Growth Hormone	Serono
Salagen	MGI Pharma
Salflex	Amarin
Sandimmune	Novartis
Sandostatin	Novartis
Sectral	ESP Pharma
Semprex	Celltech
Septra	Burroughs-Wellcome
Serevent Diskus	GlaxoSmithKline
Seroquel	AstraZeneca
Serostim	Serono
Serzone	Together
Sinemet	Bristol-Myers
Sinequan	Pfizer
Singulair	Merck
Skelid	Sanofi-Synthelabo
Slo-Niacin	Upsher-Smith
Solaquin	Valeant
Somavert	Pfizer
Spectazole	Ortho-McNeil
Spiriva	Boehringer
Sporanox	Janssen
SSKI	Upsher-Smith
Stalevo	Novartis
Starlix	Novartis
Stelazine	GlaxoKlineSmith
Stimate	Aventis Behring
Strattera	Eli Lilly
Stromectol	Merck
Sulfacet	Dermik
Suplena	Abbott
Sustiva	Bristol-Myers
Symmetrel	Endo
Synagis	Medimmune
Synalar	Medicis
Synemol	Medicis
Synthroid	Abbott
Syprine Tablets	Merck
T —	
Tabloid	GlaxoSmithKline
Tagamet	Glaxo SmithKline
Tambocor	3M
Tamiflu	Roche
Targretin	Ligand

Drug	Manufacturer
Tarka	Abbott
Taxol	Bristol-Myers
Taxotere	Aventis Oncology
Tegretol	Novartis
Temodar	Schering-Plough
Temovate	GlaxoSmithKline, Elan
Tenex	ESP Pharma
Tensilon	Valeant
Tequin	Bristol-Myers
Terazol	Ortho-McNeil
Teslac	Bristol-Myers
Tessalon	Forest
Teveten	Biovail
Thalomid	Celgene
Theochron	Forest
Theracys	Aventis Pasteur
Thiola	Mission
Thioplex	Immunex
Thorazine	GlaxoSmithKline
Thyrel	Ferring
Thyrolar	Forest
Tiazac	Forest
Ticlid	Roche
Timentin	GlaxoSmithKline
Timolide	Merck
Timolol Maleate	Alcon
Timoptic	Merck
TNKase	Genentech
TOBI	Chiron
Tolectin	Ortho-McNeil
Topamax	Together
Topicort	Medicis
Toprol XL	AstraZeneca
Toradol	Syntex
Travatan	Alcon
Trecator	Wyeth
Trecator-SC	Wyeth
Trelstar	Pfizer
Trental	Together
Triaz	Medicis
TriCor	Abbott
Trileptal	Novartis
Trisenox	Cell Therapeutics
Trizivir	GlaxoSmithKline
Trusopt opthalmic Solutions	Merck
TwoCal	Abbott
Tylenol	Together
Tylox	Together
Tyrex	Abbott

Drug	Manufacturer
U —	
Ultracet	Ortho-McNeil
Ultram	Ortho-McNeil
Ultravate	Bristol-Myres
Urispas	Ortho-McNeil
Urocit-K	Mission
Uro-Mag	Blaine
Uroxatral	Sanofi-Synthelabo
Urso 250	Axcan Scandipharm
V —	
Vagifem	Novo Nordisk
Valcyte	Roche
Valium	Hoffman-LaRoche
Valtrex	Glaxo SmithKline
Vancocin HCl Pulvules	Eli Lilly
Vasocon-A	Novartis
Vasodilan	Bristol-Myers
VELCADE Injection	Millennium
Venofer	American Regent
Ventolin HFA	GlaxoSmithKline
Ventolin	GlaxoSmithKline
Vepesid	Bristol-Myers
Vermox	Together
Vesanoid	Roche
Viagra	Pfizer
Vibramycin	Pfizer
Videx	Bristol-Myers
Viokase	Axcan-Scandipharm
Vioxx	Merck
Viracept	Pfizer
Viramune	Boehringer
Virazole	Valeant
Viread	Gilead
Vistaril	Pfizer
Vistide	Gilead
Vivelle	Together
Voltaren	Together
Vumon	Bristol-Myers
Vytone Cream	Dermik
Vytorin	Merck/Schering Plough
W —	
Welchol Tablets	Sankyo
Wellbutrin	GlaxoSmithKline
Wellbutrin SR	GlaxoSmithKline
Wellcovorin	Burroughs-Wellcome
X —	
Xalatan	Pfizer
Xanax	Eli Lilly

Drug	Manufacturer
Xeloda	Roche
Xenical	Roche
Z —	
Zaditor	Novartis
Zanaflex	Athena
Zantac	Glaxo SmithKline
Zarontin	Pfizer
Zaroxolyn	Celltech
Zelnorm	Novartis
Zemplar	Abbott
Zerit	Bristol-Myers
Zetia	Merck/ Schering-Plough

Drug	Manufacturer
Ziagen	GlaxoSmithKline
Zinacef	GlaxoSmithKline
Zinecard	Pfizer
Zithromax	Pfizer
Zocor	Merck
Zofran ODT	GlaxoSmithKline
Zofran	GlaxoSmithKline
Zoladex	AstraZeneca
Zoladex	Athena
Zoloft	Pfizer
Zometa	Novartis
Zovirax	Biovail
Zyban	GlaxoSmithKline
Zyprexa	Eli Lilly
Zyrtec	Pfizer

Directory of Pharmaceutical Manufacturer Patient Assistance Programs

NOTE: Most manufacturers require requests for assistance to be initiated by a physician's office.

3m Pharmaceuticals Assistance Program

Patient Assistance Program
Medical Services Department
3M Center Building, 275-6W-13
P.O. Box 33275
St. Paul, MN 55144-1000
800-328-0255
Fax: 651-733-6068
www.3m.com/us/healthcare/pharma/patient_assistance.jhtml

Program Information: Patients whose financial and insurance circumstances prevent them from obtaining 3M Pharmaceuticals drug products considered to be necessary by their physician. Consideration is on a case-by-case basis.

AAI Pharma Inc.

AAI Pharma Assists
P.O. Box 124
Somerville, NJ 08876
866-224-0099
www.aaipharma.com

Abbott Laboratories/Ross Laboratories

Patience Assistance Program
200 Abbott Park Rd.
D31C, J23
Abbott Park, IL 60064-6161
800-222-6885
www.abbott.com

Program Information: Temporary assistance to low income individuals who do not have or qualify for prescription medication benefits through private insurance or government-funded programs.

Virology Patient Assistance Program
800-222-6885
www.abbottvirology.com

Program Information: Provides antiretroviral medications at no cost to eligible patients without any prescription drug coverage on a case-by-case basis.

Ross Medical Nutritional PAP
800-222-6885
www.ross.com

Program Information: Provides adult medical nutritional products to financially disadvantaged individuals.

Ross Metabolic Formula and Elecare PAP
800-222-6885
www.ross.com

Program Information: Provides products to disadvantaged individuals on a case-by-case basis.

HUMIRA Medicare Assistance Program
P.O. Box 789
San Bruno, CA 94066
800-4HUMIRA
www.humira.com

Program Information: The HUMIRA Medicare Assistance Program offers HUMIRA at no cost to eligible Medicare enrollees without any prescription drug coverage until a Medicare drug benefit is enacted.

Alcon Labs

Glaucoma Patient Assistance Program
Humanitarian Services T-7-18
6201 South Freeway
Ft. Worth, TX 76134
800-222-8103 (option 1)
www.alconlabs.com

Program Information: Patients must not be eligible for any other prescription reimbursement insurance, must be indigent and needy.

Allergan

Allergan Patient Assistance Program
PO Box 1003
Wayne, NJ 07474
800-553-6783 (physician request)
Botox Patient Assistance Program
800-530-6680
www.allergan.com

Program Information: The patient must not be eligible for drug coverage by any private or public assistance program. Annual household income limits do apply but each case is reviewed on an individual basis.

Alpharma Pharmaceuticals

Kadian Patient Assistance Program
P.O. Box 66554
St. Louis, MO 63166
866-884-5907
www.alpharma.com

Program Information: Medication is provided at no charge to U.S. citizen needy patients that do not have prescription coverage.

Amarin Pharmaceuticals Inc.

Indigent Patient Program
25 Independence Boulevard
Warren, NJ 07059
908-580-5535
www.amarinpharma.com

Program Information: Patients must be below poverty guidelines and have no prescription coverage.

NebuPent Patient Assistance Program
1101 Perimeter Drive, Suite 300
Schaumberg, IL 60173
847-330-1289

Program Information: Financial and insurance information about the patient must be included in the physician's request.

American Regent Laboratories

Venofer Assistance Program
c/o InTeleCenter
P.O. Box 4280
Gaithersburg, MD 20885-4133
800-282-7712
www.americanregent.com

Program Information: Patients must be a U.S. citizen or legal residence and meet income guidelines. Patients must not be eligible for any prescription coverage.

Amgen, Inc.

Safety Net Program
800-272-9376
www.amgen.com/patient/

Program Information: Amgen's Safety Net Foundation is designed to assist those patients who are medically indigent (patients may be uninsured or underinsured). Eligibility is based on patient's insurance status and income level.

Encourage Foundation
888-436-2735

www.amgen.com/patient

Program Information: For more information on the Encourage Foundation, please contact the program using the information above.

Safety Net Foundation
866-KINERET (546-3738)

Program Information: Amgen's Safety Net Foundation is designed to assist those patients who are medical indigent (patients may be uninsured or underinsured). Eligibility is based on patient's insurance status and income level.

AstraZeneca Foundation

Patient Assistance Program
P.O. Box 15197
Wilmington, DE 19850-5197
800-424-3727
www.astrazeneca-us.com/pap

Program Information: Eligibility is based on income level/assets and absence of outpatient private prescription insurance, third-party coverage, or participation in a public program. Patients should receive their shipment of product within 3-4 weeks.

Athena Neurosciences

Prescription Assistance Program
c/o Athena RX Home Pharmacy
800 Gateway Boulevard
South San Francisco, CA 94080
800-528-4632 x7788

Program Information: Patients must have a net worth of less than $30,000 and have no other third party coverage.

Aventis Behring

Patient Assistance Program
1020 First Avenue
King of Prussia, PA 19406-1310
800-676-4266
www.aventisbehring.com

Aventis Pasteur
Physician requests should be directed to:
NORD - National Organization of Rare Disorders
877-798-8716

Program Information: A Physician must call NORD to fill out application for the patient. The patient must be a US resident, uninsured and ineligible for Medicare or Medicaid.

Aventis Oncology

PACT+ Program
100 Grandview Road
Braintree, MA 02184

800-996-6626
www.aventisoncology.com

Aventis Pharmaceuticals Inc.

Aventis Patient Assistance Program
PO Box 759
Somerville, NJ 08876
800-221-4025

Program Information: Patient cannot have or qualify for any government prescription coverage such as Medicare, Medicaid, Veterans Administration, or any state or local programs. Patient cannot have or qualify for any private coverage such as an MHO or PPO. Patient's total annual household must be below the Aventis Poverty Level.

Lovenox Patient Assistance Program
PO Box 8256
Sommerville, NJ 08876
888-632-8607

Program Information: Aventis will provide Lovenox free of charge under the following qualifications: participants must be U.S. residents, their annual household income must fall below the Aventis Poverty Guidelines, and they must have no insurance coverage for Lovenox. This program is available for outpatients only.

Axcan Scandipharm, Inc

Axcan Scandipharm Care First Program
22 Inverness Center Parkway
Birmingham, AL 35242
800-472-2634
www.axcan.com

Program Information: Patients must be infants under 2 years of age with Cystic Fibrosis.

Axcon Scandipharm Patient Assistance Program
P.O. Box 52150
Phoenix, AZ 85072-2150
866-292-2679

Program Information: Patients must meet income guidelines that are calculated as a percentage of Federal Poverty Limit. Patients must also be U.S. citizens with no prescription coverage.

Comprehensive Care Program for CF
CF Services Inc.
6931 Arlington Road T-200
Bethesda, MD 20814
800-541-4959 x 449

Program Information: Available to any Cystic Fibrosis patient purchasing Ultrase MT products.

Baxter Healthcare

IGIV Services
1582 Barclay Boulevard
Buffalo Grove, IL 60089

888-437-4262 (option 1)
www.baxter.com

Program Information: This is a reimbursement program only. Eligibility is determined on a case-by-case basis.

Baxter Pharmaceutical Products

Factor Plus Program
c/o Intellecenter
P.O. Box 4280
Gaithersburg, MD 20885-4280
800-548-4448 (option 2)

Program Information: Eligibility is based on income and lack of insurance.

Bayer Pharmaceuticals Corporation

Bayer Patient Assistance Program
P.O. Box 29209
Phoenix, AZ 85038-9209
800-998-9180
www.bayerpharma-na.com

Program Information: The Physician must certify that the patient is not eligible for, or covered by, government-funded reimbursement or insurance program for medication; the patient is not covered by private insurance; and the patient's household income is below federal-poverty level guidelines.

Berlex Laboratories

Patient Assistance Program
PO Box 1000, M2/1-5
Montville, NJ 07045-1000
888-237-5394, Option 6, Option 1
www.berlex.com

Program Information: To be accepted into the Program, a patient must meet the following criteria: 1) must be a US citizen; 2) must be ineligible for any public or private health insurance, including Medicare and Medicaid and any other state or private programs and have an annual gross family income of $20,000 or less; or 3) be eligible for Medicare but ineligible for prescription coverage and must have an annual gross family income of $15,000 or less; and 4) must be under the care of a doctor/prescriber who has prescribed Betapace, Betapace AF, or Climara as medically appropriate for the patient applying for assistance.

Berlex Oncology Camcare
800-473-5832

Leukine Reimbursement Hotline
800-321-4669

The Betaseron Foundation
PO Box 221349
Charlotte, NC 28222-1349
800-948-5777

Program Information: Patients must have a confirmed diagnosis of multiple sclerosis and be U.S. residents. Income verification is required.

Bertek Pharmaceuticals, Inc.

Bertek Patient Assistance Program
781 Chestnut Ridge Road
Morgantown, WV 26505
888-823-7835
www.bertek.com

Program Information: Eligible patients cannot have prescription insurance or other program that covers the costs of prescriptions. Income limits: household of 1, under $8,740; household of 2, under $11,060; household of 3, under $13,860; household of 4, under $16,700.

Biogen

Avonex Access Program
MS Active Source
14 Cambridge Center
Cambridge, MA 02142
800-456-2255
www.biogen.com/site/home.html

Program Information: Eligibility is based on patient's insurance status and income level.

Biovail Pharmaceuticals, Inc.

Biovail Patient Assistance Program
P.O. Box 836
Somerville, NJ 08876
866-268-7325
www.biovail.com

Program Information: Patients must be US citizens without prescription coverage and income levels less than 200% of the federal poverty level.

Blaine Company

Blaine Patient Assistance Program
1515 Production Drive
Burlington, KY 41005
800-633-9353
www.blainepharma.com

Program Information: Patient must be under the prescribing care of cardiologist, internist, or a transplant clinic. No co-payment is required by the patient.

Boehringer Ingleheim Pharmaceuticals, Inc.

Boehringer Ingelheim Cares Foundation
c/o ESI/SDS
P.O. Box 66555
St. Louis, MO 63166-6555
800-556-8317
www.boehringer-ingleheim.com

Program Information: The patient must be a U.S. citizen or legal resident ineligible for prescription drug assistance through Medicaid or private insurance. Patient must meet established financial criteria.

Bone Care International, Inc.

Hectoral Patient Assistance Center
Bone Care Center
1600 Aspen Commons
Middleton, WI 53562
888-389-3300
www.hectoral.com

Program Information: Eligible patients must be U.S. citizens that meet financial guidelines with no prescription insurance and be ineligible government assistance.

Braintree Laboratories

Braintree Labs Sample Supply Program
P.O. Box 850929
Braintree, MA 02185-0929
781-843-2202
www.braintreelabs.com

Program Information: For additional information contact the program.

Bristol-Myers Squibb Company

Bristol-Myers Squibb -AmeriCares
Oncology/Virology Access Program
6900 College Boulevard, Suite 1000
Overland Park, KS 66211-1536
800-272-4878
www.bms.com

Program Information: This program is designed to provide assistance to patients with a financial hardship who are not eligible for prescription drug assistance through Medicaid, ADAP, or any other public or private health program.

Patient Assistance Foundation, Inc.
800-736-0003
Fax: 800-736-1611
www.bms.com

Program Information: This program is designed to provide assistance to patients with a financial hardship who are not eligible for prescription drug assistance through Medicaid, ADAP, or any other public or private health program.

BTG Pharmaceuticals

Oxandrin Reimbursement and Patient Assistance Program
P.O. Box 221887
Charlotte, NC 28222-1887
866-692-6374
www.oxandrin.com

Program Information: Patients must be uninsured and meet income guidelines.

Celgene Corporation

Celgene Therapy Assistance Program
6900 College Boulevard, Suite 1000
Overland Park, KS 66211
888-423-5436 option 3
Fax: 800-822-2496
www.celgene.com

Program Information: The patient must have no insurance that covers the drug or has maxed out their insurance benefit; patient must be on a limited income with little or no liquid assets. Supply: 28 cycle as mandated by Federal Law.

Cell Therapeutics Inc

Cell Therapeutics Patient Assistance Program
Suite 400
501 Elliott Avenue West
Seattle, WA 98119
866-261-7730
www.celltherapeutics.com

Program Information: Income guidelines do apply.

Centocor

Remicade Patient Assistance Program
P.O. Box 221709
Charlotte, NC 28222
866-489-5957
Fax: 866-489-5958
www.centocor.com

Program Information: This program provides the product to low-income patients legally residing in the United States when patients meet certain financial need qualifications. When patients qualify, they may be provided with up to six months of the product at a time.

Retavase Solutions
P.O. Box 220807
Charlotte, NC 28222
866-RETAVAS (738-2827)
Fax: 866-279-0712

Program Information: Centocor Solutions Program will replace Retavase used to treat patients who meet specific medical and financial criteria and lack third-party insurance.

Cephalon

Actiq Program
Suite 600
5870 Trinity Parkway
Centreville, VA 20120
877-229-1241
Fax: 800-777-7562
www.cephalon.com

Program Information: Must be diagnosed with cancer and be on adjunct opiate therapy.

Gabitril Patient Assistance Program
P. O. Box 430
Hackettstown, NJ 07840
800-511-2120

Program Information: Eligibility is based on income and insurance coverage.

Provigil Patient Assistance Program
NORD
P.O. Box 1968
Danbury, CT 06813-1968
800-675-8415

Program Information: Prescreening for eligibility is done on initial call, then the application is sent.

Cetylite Industries, Inc.

Cetylite Patient Assistance Program
P.O. Box 90006
Pennsauken, NJ 08110
800-257-7740
www.cetylite.com

Program Information: Eligibility is determined on a case-by-case basis.

Chiron

Chiron Patient Assistance Program
c/o The Lewin Group
San Francisco, CA 94107
800-775-7533
www.chiron.com

Program Information: Patients must not have insurance and not be eligible for government programs.

Tobi Patient Support Program
800-775-7533

Program Information: U.S. residents who have Cystic Fibrosis who meet income guidelines and have no access to health insurance benefits.

CollaGenex Pharmaceuticals, Inc.

CollaGenex Patient Assistance Program
41 University Drive
Newtown, PA 18950
888-339-5678
www.collagenex.com

Program Information: No formal program is available but, the company will assist on a case-by-case basis.

Connetics

Connetics Patient Assistance Program
3290 West Bayshore Road
Palo Alto, CA 94303
888-969-2628

www.connetics.com

Program Information: The patient must be a U.S. resident with no prescription coverage through public or private programs. Income levels must be at or below 200% of the current Federal Poverty Level.

Dermik Laboratories

Dermik Patient Assistance Program
P.O. Box 759
Somerville, NJ 08876
866-267-7326
www.dermik.com

Program Information: Patients must have no prescription coverage and meet income guidelines.

Duramed Pharmaceuticals, Inc.

Cenestin Patient Assistance Program
1878 Arena Drive
Hamilton, NJ 08610
800-425-3122
Fax: 800-685-2577

Program Information: Cenestin will be provided free of charge to patients who have no insurance or other third-party payer prescription drug coverage, including Medicaid coverage or Medicare managed care coverage. Their annual income must fall within a predetermined range. Patients must re-qualify after 90-day initial supply.

Eisai Inc.

Aciphex Patient Assistance Program
P.O. Box 220458
Charlotte, NC 28222-0458
800-523-5870
Fax: 800-526-6651
www.eisai.com

Program Information: U.S. residents who lack access to prescription drug coverage and meet specific financial criteria are eligible. If needed, the patient may reapply after the initial supply.

Aricept Patient Assistance Program
1480 Arthur Avenue, Suite D
Louisville, CO 80027
800-226-2072
Fax: 800-226-2059

Program Information: There are five items that determine a patient's eligibility: Residency – the patient must be a United States resident. Site of care –The Program is for outpatient use only. Income – a patient without dependents must earn less than $25,000 annually. a patient with dependents must earn less than $40,000 annually. Insurance – The patient must have no public or private prescription drug coverage, including Medicaid. Dosage – Daily dosage of Aricept should not exceed 10mg. Should a patient qualify, a 90-day supply of medication will be sent to the physician for distribution.

ECR Pharmaceuticals

ECR Pharmeceuticals
P.O. Box 71600
Richmond, VA 23255
804-527-1950
www.ecrpharma.com

Eli Lilly And Company

Lilly Cares
Program Administrator
P.O. Box 23099
Centreville, VA 20120
800-545-6962

Program Information: Patients must be U.S. residents with an inability to pay and lack of prescription assistance on a case-by-case basis.

LillyAnswers Card
877-RX-LILLY

Program Information: Medicare eligible. Annual income below $18,000 single/$24,000 households. Must not be eligible for public or private insurance coverage.
Patients pay $12 for a 30-day supply.

Humatrope Reimbursement Center
100 Grandview Road, Suite 210
Braintree, MA 02184
800-642-2340
Fax: 800-642-5442
www.lilly.com

Program Information: The program acts as an advocate for the patient and tries to uncover another source for payment. If that fails, the program provides the drug free of charge or with a co-pay, as determined by consideration of patient/household income information.

Endo Pharmaceuticals, Inc.

Endo Patient Assistance Program
100 Painters Drive
Chadds Ford, PA 19317
800-462-3636
www.endo.com

Program Information: Eligibility is based on income and lack of insurance.

Enzon

Financial Assistance Program for Abelcet
750 The City Drive, Suite 210
Orange, CA 92868
908-541-8600
www.enzon.com

Program Information: Patients must have minimal resources and no insurance coverage for Abelcet and unable to afford the drug.

ESP Pharma

ESP Pharma Patient Assistance Program
P.O. Box 430
Hackettstown, NJ 07840
800-319-4031
www.esppharma.com

Program Information: Patient's income must be at or below 200% of the Federal Poverty Level and have no prescription insurance.

Faulding Pharmaceuticals, Inc.

Faulding Patient Assistance Program
5511 Capital Center Drive
Suite 550
Raleigh, NC 27606
919-233-5788

Program Information: Income guidelines apply.

Ferndale Laboratories, Inc.

Ferndale Patient Assistance Program
780 West Eight Mile Road
Ferndale, MI 48220
800-621-6003
www.ferndalelabs.com

Program Information: The patient must be at or below the Federal Poverty Level and a U.S. citizen with no prescription coverage.

Ferring Pharmaceuticals

Ferring Pharmaceuticals Prescription Reimbursement Program
120 White Plains Road, Suite 400
Tarrytown, NY 10591
888-337-7464
www.ferring.com

Program Information: Contact Ferring for additional information.

First Horizon Pharmaceutical Corporation

First Horizon Patient Assistance Program
660 Hembree Parkway, Suite 106
Roswell, GA 30076
800-949-9707 x321
www.firsthorizonpharm.com

Program Information: Patients must be U.S. residents under poverty guidelines (extenuating circumstances considered).

Forest Pharmaceuticals

Forest Pharmaceuticals Indigent Care Program
13600 Shoreline Drive
St. Louis, MO 63045
800-851-0758

www.forestpharm.com
Program Information: Patients must meet income guidelines.

Genentech, Inc.

Genentech Access to Care Foundation
Genentech, Inc.
1 DNA Way MS #13A
P.O. Box 2586
S. San Francisco, CA 94080
800-530-3083
800-879-4747
Fax: 650-225-1366
www.gene.com/gene/products/patient-assist-program.jsp
Program Information: Patients must be ineligible for public or private prescription insurance and must meet income restrictions and medical eligibility.

Genzyme Corporation

The Charitable Access Program
Genzyme Corporation
500 Kendall Square
Cambridge, MA 02142
800-745-4447, ext. 16634
www.genzymetherapeutics.com/cerezyme/support/pap.htm
Program Information: Eligibility is based on financial and medical need.

Gilead Sciences, Inc.

Gilead Reimbursement Support and Assistance Program
333 Lakeside Drive
Foster City, CA 94404
800-226-2056
www.gilead.com
Program Information: Contact Gilead for additional information.

GlaxoSmithKline

Bridges to Access
866-PATIENT (728-4368)
http://bridgestoaccess.gsk.com
Program Information: Patients must be U.S. residents with income less than 250% of Federal Poverty Level and must be ineligible for prescription benefits.

Commitment to Access
8-ONCOLOGY-1 (866-265-6491)
http://commitmenttoaccess.gsk.com
Program Information: Patients must be U.S. residents with income less than 350% of the Federal Poverty Level and must be ineligible for prescription benefits.

Orange Card
888-ORANGE6

www.us.gsk.com/card/

Program Information: Eligible patients must be 65 and older and the disabled enrolled in Medicare. Annual income must be below 300% of the Federal Poverty Level and ineligible for prescription insurance.

Glenwood, LLC

Potaba Patient Assistance Program
19 Empire Boulevard
P.O. Box 1508
South Hackensack, NJ 07606
800-542-0772
www.glenwood-llc.com

Program Information: Income guidelines apply.

Immunex Corporation

Immunex Patient Assistance Program
420 2nd Street, Suite 201
San Francisco, CA 94107
800-321-4669
www.immunex.com

Program Information: Eligible patient must be U.S. citizen that have no prescription insurance and must shoe financial need.

Ivax Pharmaceuticals

Ivax Patient Assistance Program
4400 Biscayne Boulevard
Miami, FL 33137
800-327-4114
www.ivaxpharmaceuticals.com

Program Information: Eligibility is based on financial need and lack of prescription insurance.

Janssen Pharmaceutica

Aciphex Patient Assistance Program
PO Box 220458
Charlotte, NC 28222
800-523-5870
Fax: 800-526-6651
www.aciphex.com

Program Information: Patients must be U.S. residents that are ineligible for prescription coverage and have financial need.

Janssen Patient Assistance Program
P.O. Box 221857
Charlotte, NC 28222
800-652-6227
www.janssen.com/ourproducts/pap.jsp

Program Information: Patients must be U.S. residents who lack prescription coverage and meet financial criteria.

The Risperdal Patient Assistance Program
P.O. Box 222098
Charlotte, N.C. 28222-2098
800-652-6227
Fax: 888-526-5170
www.risperdal.com

Program Information: Patients must be U.S. residents who lack prescription coverage and meet financial criteria.

Senior Patient Assistance Program
P.O. Box 221009
Charlotte, NC 28222-1009
888-294-2400
Fax: 888-770-7266
www.janssen-eldercare.com

Program Information: Eligible patients must be U.S. residents, members of both Medicare and Together Rx, lack access to prescription coverage and meet financial criteria.

Kos Pharmaceuticals

Kos Pharmaceuticals Patient Assistance Program
2200 N. Commerce Parkway, Suite 300
Weston, FL 33326
888-206-7015
www.kospharm.com

Program Information: Patients must be ineligible for government assistance or have prescription insurance.

Ligand Pharmaceuticals, Inc.

Ligand Assistance Program
P.O. Box 222197
Charlotte, NC 28222-2197
877-654-4263
www.ligand.com

Program Information: Financial guidelines apply.

McNeil Consumer & Specialty Pharmaceuticals

Patient Assistance Program
PO Box 1015
San Bruno, CA 94066
866-PAP-4MCN (727-4626)
www.mcneilcampusrecruiting.com

Program Information: Contact McNeil for additional information.

Mead Johnson Nutritionals

Helping Hands Programs
2400 W. Lloyd Expressway
Evansville, IN 47721

800-222-9123
www.meadjohnson.com
Program Information: Specialized infant formulas for children under one year with certain income guidelines.

Medicis

Medicis Patient Assistance Program
4343 E. Camelback Road
Phoenix, AZ 85018
800-533-DERM
http://www.dynacin.com/rebate/instructions.html
Program Information: Rebates are available through the company.

Medimmune, Inc.

Medimmune Oncology Patient Assistance Program
P.O. Box 222197
Charlotte, NC 28222-2197
800-887-2647
www.medimmune.com
Program Information: Income guidelines apply.

Synagis Assistance Program
877-480-8082
Program Information: Income guidelines apply.

MedPointe, Inc.

Felbatol Assistance Program
P.O. Box 1001
Cranbury, NJ 08512
800-678-4657
www.medpointepharma.com
Program Information: Patients must be ineligible for public or private prescription assistance and have annual income of less than $16,000 for individuals and $25,000 for families.

Merck & Co., Inc.

Merck Patient Assistance Program
P.O. Box 690
Horsham, PA 19044-9979
800-994-2111 (physician requests)
800-727-5400
www.merck.com/pap/pap/consumer
Program Information: Eligible patients must be U.S. residents, not be eligible for prescription insurance and have financial need.

ACT Program for EMEND
PO Box 18979
Louisville, KY 40261-0979

866-EMEND (866-363-6379)
Fax: 866-EMEND (866-363-6389)
www.emend.com

Program Information: Assistance is provided to help patients with insurance and reimbursement issues as well as, assistance for those without insurance and financial need.

The Support Program for Crixivan
P.O. Box 222137
Charlotte, NC 28222-2137
800-850-3430
www.crixivan.com

Program Information: Free product is provided to those uninsured patients who qualify, and for who no alternative source of coverage can be identified.

Merck/Schering-Plough Pharmaceuticals

Merck/Schering-Plough
Patient Assistance Program
800-347-7503
www.zetia.com/ezetimibe/zetia/consumer/shared/pap/index.jsp

MGI Pharma Inc.

Patient Assistance Program
PO Box 230538
Centreville, VA 20120
888-743-5711
Fax: 703-310-2534
www.mgi-pharma.com

Program Information: Eligibility determined on financial need and lack of insurance.

Millennium Pharmaceuticals, Inc.

Integrilin Patient Assistance Program
309 Pierce Street
Somerset, NJ 08873
800-232-8723
www.mlnm.com

VELCADE Reimbursement Assistance Program
P.O. Box 986
San Bruno, CA 94066
866-VELCADE (866-835-2233)

Program Information: Qualifying patients may receive VELCADE free of charge.

Mission Pharmacal Company

Mission Pharmaceutical Patient Assistance Program
P.O. Box 786099
San Antonio, TX 78278
800-292-7364

www.missionpharmacal.com
Program Information: Patients must be ineligible for prescription insurance and have income below the Federal Poverty Level.

Mylan Pharmaceuticals

Mylan Clozapine Prescription Access System
P.O. Box 4310
Morgantown. WV 26504
888-823-7835
www.mylan-clozapine.com

Program Information: The patient must be a U.S. resident and the physician feels that the patient is in need of assistance.

Novartis Pharmaceuticals Corporation

Patient Assistance Program
P.O. Box 66556
St. Louis, MO 63166-6556
800-277-2254
www.pharma.us.novartis.com/novartis/pap/pap.jsp

Program Information: This program is for patients that are experiencing financial hardship and have no third-party insurance coverage for their medicines. Patients must meet income eligibility criteria.

Novo Nordisk

Novo Nordisk Diabetes Patient Assistance Program
PO Box 1096
Somerville, NJ 08876
866-310-7549
www.novonordisk-us.com

Program Information: Approved patients will receive a 90-day supply of medication. A new application must be submitted with each request. A maximum of 4 requests will be granted to approved patients.

Hormone Therapy Patient Assistance Program
PO Box 1096
Somerville, NJ 08876
866-668-6336

Program Information: Approved patients will receive a five-month supply of medication sent to the physician's office. A new application must be submitted for a second request. A maximum of 2 requests will be granted to approved patients.

Organon

Organon Patient Assistance Program
Customer Service Department
375 Mount Pleasant Avenue
West Orange, NJ 07052
800-241-8812
www.organoninc.com

The Arixtra Reimbursement Hotline
Quintiles Late Phase
475 Brannan Street, Suite 400
San Francisco, CA 94107
800-ARIXTRA, option 5

Orphan Medical, Inc.

Cystadane Patient Assistance Program
c/o NORD
P.O. Box 1968
Danbury, CT 06813
888-8ORPHAN
www.orphan.com

Program Information: Each case is reviewed individually, but is based on the patient's income and lack of prescription coverage.

Ortho Biotech Inc.

Procritline
P.O. Box 1016
San Bruno, CA 94066
800-553-3851
Fax: 800-987-5572
www.procritline.com

ORTHOVISCline
866-633-VISC (8472)
www.orthoviscline.com

DOXILine
800-609-1083
www.doxiline.com

Program Information: Patient eligibility application forms are available from Ortho Biotech Product Specialists.

Ortho-McNeil

Ortho-McNeil Patient Assistance Program
P.O. Box 969
San Bruno, CA 94066
800-577-3788
Fax: 800-482-1896
www.ortho-mcneil.com/about/patientprogram.html

Program Information: Eligible patients must be ineligible for private or public prescription coverage and fall below 200% of the Federal poverty Level.

Regranex Gel Patient Assistance Program
800-577-3788

Program Information: Patients should not have insurance coverage for prescription medication and not be eligible for other sources of drug coverage. They need to have applied to public sector programs and been denied. Income level should fall below poverty level and retail purchase would cause hardship.

Pfizer Inc

Connection To Care
P.O. Box 66585
St. Louis, MO 63166
800-707-8990
www.pfizer.com/subsites/philanthropy/access/connection.care.index.html

Product Information: Applicants must have an annual gross income of less than $19,000 for individuals and less than $31,000 for families. They must not have prescription drug coverage through any public or private programs such as Medicaid, state sponsored drug assistance programs, employee, military, retirement or pension programs. Patients who have reached their caps or belong to "generics only" plans are ineligible to participate in Connection to Care.

Anti-Infective Patient Assistance Programs
800-869-9979
www.pfizer.com

Program Information: Zithromax is available for MAC prophylactics and treatment only. Patients must not have insurance or other third-party coverage, including Medicaid, and must not be eligible for a state's AIDS drug assistance program. Additionally, patients must have incomes of less than $25,000 (single), or less than $40,000 (family).

Geodon Patient Assistance Program
866-443-6366
www.pfizer.com

Program Information: Eligible patients are at or below 200% of the federal poverty level and have no access to other forms of public or private reimbursement for pharmaceuticals.

Sharing the Care
Pfizer Inc.
235 E. 42nd St., 13th Floor
New York, NY 10017
800-984-1500
www.pfizer.com/susites/philanthropy/access/sharing.care.index.html

Program Information: The program, a joint effort of Pfizer, the National Governors' Association and the National Association of Community Health Centers, works solely through community, migrant and homeless health centers certified by the federal government as meeting criteria of Section 329, 339, or 340 of the Public Health Service Act. Center must have an in-house pharmacy to participate. To be eligible, patient must be a patient of a participating health center and must be uninsured, not eligible for government entitlement programs that cover pharmaceuticals, and at or below federal poverty line.

FirstRESOURCE
877-744-5675

Program Information: Eligible patients be ineligible for prescription coverage and fall below a percentage of the Federal Poverty level.

Pfizer Bridge Program
800-645-1280

Program Information: Eligible patients must be underinsured and meet medical and financial criteria.

Aricept Patient Assistance Program
800-226-2072

Program Information: Eligible patients must be U.S. residents that are ineligible for prescription coverage and meet financial guidelines.

Pharmion Corporation

Pharmion Corporation Patient Assistance Program
2525 28th Street, Suite 200
Boulder, CO 80301
866-742-7646 (option 4)
www.phamion.com

Program Information: The eligible patient must be a U.S. resident that is ineligible for prescription coverage. This company has two programs, one for patient assistance and one for product replacement.

Proctor & Gamble Pharmaceuticals, Inc.

Proctor & Gamble Pharmaceuticals, Inc.
c/o Express Scripts
P.O. Box 66553
St. Louis, MO 63166-6553
800-830-9049
www.pgpharm.com

Program Information: The quantity of product supplied depends on diagnosis and need, but generally a three month supply is provided for a chronic medication. Refills require a new prescription and application from the physician. Applications are reviewed on a case-by-case basis. Patients must meet eligibility requirements.

Questcor Pharmaceuticals, Inc.

Acthar Gel Patient Assistance Program
c/o NORD
P.O. Box 1968
New Fairfield, CT 06812
800-459-7599
www.questcor.com

Program Information: Eligibility is based on income and lack of prescription coverage. Each application is reviewed individually to determine eligibility.

Reliant Pharmaceutical

Rx Support Program
P.O. Box 6842
Somerset, NJ 08875-9878
866-792-2737
www.reliantrx.com

Program Information: Patients must be ineligible for prescription coverage and meet income guidelines.

Roche Laboratories (A Division Of Hoffman-La Roche Inc.)

Roche Laboratories Patient Assistance Program
340 Kingsland St.
Nutley, NJ 07110
877-75-ROCHE
www.roche.com

Program Information: The Roche Laboratories Patient Assistant Program is designed as an interim solution for patients who lack third-party outpatient prescription drug coverage under private insurance, government-funded programs (e.g., Medicaid, Medicare, Veterans Affairs, etc.) or private/community sources and are unable to afford to purchase our products on their own. This program is for individual outpatients who meet the Patient Assistance Program criteria and is offered through licensed practitioners. The program is not intended for clinics, hospitals, and/or other institutions.

CellCept Patient Assistance Program
800-772-5790

Fuzeon Patient Assistance Program
866-487-8591

ONCOLINE Patient Assistance Program
800-443-6676 (option 2)

Pegassist Patient Assistance Program
877-PEGASYS (734-2797)

Roche HIV Therapy Assistance Program
800-282-7780

Sankyo Pharma

Sankyo Pharma Open Care Program
PO Box 8409
Somerville, NJ 08876
866-268-7327
www.sankyopharma.com

Program Information: The Sankyo Pharma Open Care Program is available to qualified patients with demonstrated medical and financial need.

Sanofi-Synthelabo, Inc.

Sanofi-Synthelabo, Inc.
Needy Patient Program
c/o Product Information Department
90 Park Avenue
New York, NY 10016
800-446-6267

Program Information: Each physician is allowed to enroll six patients per year. Each patient can receive a 3-month supply of medication, with an option of one refill for an additional three months supply for a total of six months' medication for one year.

Schering Plough

Commitment to Care
2000 Galloping Hill Road
Kenilworth, NJ 07033-0530
www.sgp.com/schering_plough/corp/commitment_care.jsp

SP Cares
P.O. Box 52122
Phoenix, AZ 85072
800-656-9485
www.sch-plough.com/schering_plough/pc/sp_cares.jsp

Program Information: Patient eligibility is determined on a case-by-case basis based upon economic and insurance criteria.

Serono Laboratories, Inc.

Serono Connections for Growth

MS LifeLines Patient Assistance Program
c/o Assistance Program Administrator
PO Box 5816
Bethesda, MD 20824
877-447-324
www.mslifelines.com

National Organization for Rare Disorders
888-628-6673
Fax: 203-798-2289

Saizen Patient Assistance Program
800-283-8088 x2235
Fax: 781-681-2925

Serono Compassionate Care
888-275-7376
Fax: 781-681-2940

Program Information: Contact Serono Inc. for additional information on all of the available programs.

Shire US, Inc.

Shire US Patient Assistance Program
P.O. Box 698
Somerville, NJ 08876
908-203-0657
www.shire.com

Program Information: Patients must be ineligible for prescription coverage and meet income guidelines. Shire US also has a cost-share program for patients who do not meet guidelines for assistance.

Sigma-Tau Pharmaceuticals

Carnitor Drug Assistance Program Administrator
National Organization for Rare Diseases
P.O. Box 1968
Danbury, CT 06813-1968
800-999-NORD

Program Information: Patients must be US residents and meet medical and financial criteria.

Matulane Patient Assistance Program (same contact for both)
P.O. Box 1968
Danbury, CT 06813-1968
800-999-6673
www.rarediseases.org

Program Information: All applicants must be medically eligible for Matulane by having a diagnosis of Stage III or IV Hodgkin's disease documented by the treating physician, or any other lymphomas where a physician feels a response is possible.

Solvay Pharmaceuticals, Inc.

Patient Assistance Program
Solvay Pharmaceuticals, Inc./
P.O. Box 66550
St. Louis, MD 63168
800-256-8918
www.solvaypharmaceuticals-us.com

Program Information: Eligibility is determined on a case-by-case basis in consultation with each prescribing physician and is based on a patient's inability to pay, lack of insurance, and ineligibility for Medicaid. Patient must be a resident of the U.S.

Somerset Pharmaceuticals, Inc.

Eldepryl Patient Rewards Program
2202 North Westshore Boulevard, Suite 450
Tampa, FL 33607
800-892-8889
www.somersetpharm.com

Program Information: This is a rewards program --after purchase of two months supply of Eldepryl patients may send in receipt and they will send a free month-supply. Patients can use this program indefinitely.

Steifel Laboratories, Inc.

Steifel Laboratories Indigent Care Program
255 Alhambra, Suite 100
Coral Gables, FL 33134
305-443-3800
www.steifel.org/USA

Program Information: Patient must be receiving care at one of Stiefel's authorized clinics. This program is provided through certain residency programs at particular medical schools. A physician with a patient in need should call for the location of an authorized clinic.

Takeda Pharmaceuticals North America, Inc.

Takeda Patient Assistance Program
PO Box 66552
St. Louis, MO 63166
800-830-9159
877-582-5332
Fax: 800-497-0928
www.tpna.com/patasstProgram.asp

TAP Pharmaceuticals

TAP Patient Assistance Drug Program
1700 N. Desert Drive
Temple, AZ 85281
800-830-1015
www.tap.com

Program Information: Patients must be truly financially indigent and with no insurance.

Teva Neuroscience, Inc.

Copaxone Patient Assistance Program
P.O. Box 1968
Danbury, CT 06813
800-887-8100
www.tevaneuroscience.com

Program Information: Each case is reviewed individually, but is based on patient's income and lack of prescription coverage. The patient is given assistance up from 25%-100% for one year.

Together Rx

Together Rx
800-865-7211
www.togetherrx.com

Program Information: Patients must be medicare enrollees with annual income below $28,000 single/$38,000 couple (approximately 310% of poverty) and must not have public or private insurance coverage for prescription medicines. Anticipated savings are approximately 20-40% off retail prices. Each company sets its own level of savings independently with a minimum discount of 15% off its list price to wholesalers.

UCB Pharma, Inc.

UCB Patient Assistance Program
1950 Lake Park Drive
Smyrna, GA 30080
800-477-7877 (option 7)
www.ucbpharma.com

Program Information: Patients must be US residents with no prescription coverage and be ineligible for Medicaid. Income guidelines will apply.

Ucyclyd Pharma, Inc.

Buphenyl and Urea Cycle Treatment Assistance Program
c/o NORD
P.O. Box 1968
Danbury, CT 06813
800-711-0811

Program Information: Each case is reviewed individually, but is based on patient's income and lack of prescription coverage. The patient is given assistance up to 25%-100% for one year.

Upsher-Smith Laboratories, Inc.

Upsher-Smith Patient Assistance Program
14905 23rd Avenue North
Minneapolis, MN 55447
800-654-2299
www.upsher-smith.com

Program Information: This is an informal sample supply program. If a doctor has a patient in need, an Upsher-Smith Representative will contact that doctor and provide samples for the patient to the physician.

Valeant Pharmaceuticals International

Valeant Pharmaceuticals International Patient Assistance Program
3300 Hyland Avenue
Costa Mesa, CA 92626
800-548-5100
www.valeant.com

Program Information: The patient must have applied to Medicaid and been denied.

Vistakon Pharmaceuticals, LLC

Vistakon Pharmaceuticals, LLC Patient Assistance Program
P.O. Box 221857
Charlotte, NC 28222-1857
866-815-6874

Program Information: Patients must be U.S. residents, lack access to prescription drug coverage and meet specific financial criteria.

Watson Laboratories, Inc.

Androderm Compassionate Care Program
1800 Robert Fulton Drive
Reston, VA 20191
800-385-4081
www.watsonpharm.com

Program Information: Income guidelines do apply.

INFeD and Ferrlecit Uninsured Patient Program
360 Mount Kemble Avenue
Morristown, NJ 07962

888-397-4766 (option 3)
www.watsonpharm.com

Program Information: Gross family income must be less than $25,000; patient must be a US citizen and not be eligible for Medicaid, Medicare, private insurance coverage or any other assistance. Patient must be sponsored by licensed pharmacist or physician

Wyeth Pharmaceuticals

Wyeth- Patient Assistance Program
Wyeth Pharmaceutical Assistance Foundation
P.O. Box 1759
Paoli, PA 19301-0859
800-568-9938
www.wyeth.com/contact/contact_patient_assist.asp

Program Information: Patients must be U.S. resident that do not have the ability to pay for their medication, have no government or private insurance to pay for the medication requested, and earn less than 200% of the current HHS Poverty Guidelines.

Xanodyne Pharmacal Inc.

Xanodyne Pharmacal Patient Assistance Program
7300 Turfway Road, #300
Florence, KY 41042
877-926-6396
www.xanodyne.com

Program Information: The patient must be a US resident who meets financial guidelines that are not disclosed.

Xcel Pharmaceuticals

Xcel Patient Assistance Program
6363 Greenwich Drive, Suite 100
San Diego, CA 92122
800-511-2120
www.xcelpharmaceuticals.com

Program Information: Eligibility for this program is based on financial need.

STATE AND LOCAL DISCOUNT PROGRAMS

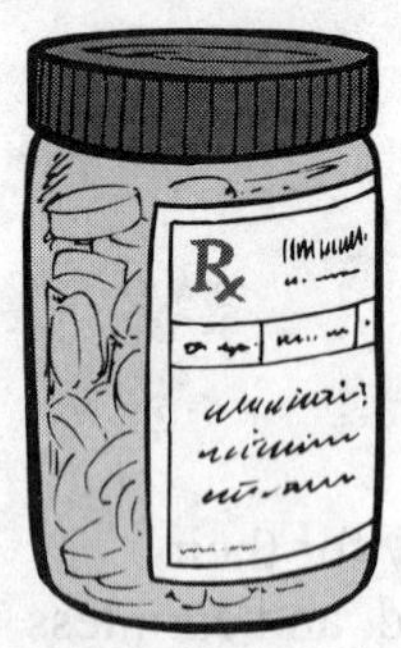

Help can be just a phone call away. Several states have special drug programs that give huge discounts to seniors and others who are ineligible for Medicaid and who don't have private insurance. For example, seniors in New Jersey can get their prescriptions for only $5, and in Vermont they can get them for as little as $1 or $2.

Often all it takes is a phone call and filling out a simple form. You will have to meet income eligibility, but you can make upwards of $23,000 a year and still be eligible in New York, for example. If your state is not listed below, contact your state Department of Aging, but also check out the free drug programs sponsored by the drug manufacturers themselves.

Alabama
Alabama Department of Senior Services
SenioRx
770 Washington Avenue
RSA Plaza Suite 470
Montgomery, AL 36130
334-242-5743
800-AGE-LINE
www.adss.state.al.us/SeniorRx.htm

Eligibility Requirements

- You must be at least 60 years old
- You must have no prescription drug coverage
- You must have a chronic medical condition
- You must be a legal resident of Alabama
- Your annual household income must be less than $18,620 for 1 person and $24,980 for 2 people.

Medication Assistance
Senior Prescription Drug Program
Franklin Primary Health Center
1303 Dr. Martin Luther King Jr. Avenue
Mobile, AL 36603
251-432-4117
www.mobilecounty.org/news/news-seniorprescription.htm
Senior citizens in some areas of Mobile County can participate in the County's Senior Prescription Drug Program. The program provides medication assistance for low-to-moderate income seniors, who are 62 or older and have no prescription drug coverage. Individuals living within the City of Mobile are not eligible for this county program.

Alaska
Chronic and Acute Medical Assistance
Division of Public Assistance
350 Main Street
PO Box 110640
Juneau, AK 99811-0640
800-211-7470
www.hss.state.ak.us/dhcs/CAMA/default.htm
Eligibility Requirements

- be in the age range of 21 years to 64 years
- have a covered medical condition
- have no third party resources to cover treatment of that condition
- have very limited financial resources
- be a US Citizen

Prescription drugs and medical supplies are limited to 3 prescriptions per month and no more than a 30-day supply of any drug.

"SeniorCare Rx" Pharmaceutical Assistance Program
The SeniorCare Senior Information Office
3601 C Street, Suite 310
Anchorage, AK 99503-5984
907-269-3680
800-478-6065 (statewide)
Fax: 907-269-3688
http://health.hss.state.ak.us/dsds/seniorcaresio.htm
Seniors receive a cash benefit of $120 per month to help with basic needs such as food, housing and medication. In a program implemented in April 2004, seniors who qualify for the Senior Assistance Program and who are not receiving comprehensive Medicaid prescription drug coverage will be provided a choice – between the new SeniorCare prescription drug subsidy of $1,600 a year or to continue to receive the Senior Assistance Program cash assistance of $1,440 a year. Together with the $600 Medicare subsidy to begin this spring, these eligible seniors opting for the SeniorCare prescription drug benefit will have a combined drug subsidy of $2,200 a year.

Eligibility:

- Minimum age: 65

- Income: Under $16,815 a year (individual), under $23,419 per year (couple)

Arizona
RxAmerica
c/o Arizona CoppeRx Card Prescription Discount Program
P.O. Box 22690
Salt Lake City, UT 84112-0690
888-227-8315
www.rxamerica.com/az_discount_home.htm?page=mem
Eligibility Requirements

- Be 65 or older
- Be an Arizona resident
- Qualify for SSDI
- Enrollment is free and automatic.

Arizona Drug Discount Program
Plan administrator: Rx America
PBM Facility address:
221 N Charles Lindbergh Dr.
Salt Lake City, UT 84116
888-227-8315
www.rxamerica.com/press_az_discount.html
Savings typically range from 10% to 55% from the overall retail price. Your actual discount may be more or less, depending on the medication and the pharmacy you use.

Eligibility:
Medicare enrollees, 65 and over or disabled. Discounts only. $9.95 enrollment fee.

CoppeRx Card
Plan administrator: Rx America
PBM Facility address:
221 N Charles Lindbergh Dr.
Salt Lake City, UT 84116
888-227-8315
www.rxamerica.com/press_az_discount.html,
www.governor.state.az.us/global/prescription_discounts.htm
Will replace Arizona Drug Discount Program (Rx America) in early 2005. Savings typically range from 10% to 55% from the overall retail price. Your actual discount may be more or less, depending on the medication and the pharmacy you use.

Eligibility:
Medicare enrollees, 65 and over or disabled. No enrollment fee.

Arizona Long Term Care System
Arizona Health Care Cost Containment System
801 E. Jefferson
Phoenix, AZ 85034
800-654-8713
602-417-7000
www.ahcccs.state.az.us/Services/Programs/ALTCS.asp
This program can help income eligible Arizona seniors pay for nursing home care or special care to remain in their homes.

Arkansas
Arkansas Healthcare Access Foundation
PO Box 56248
Little Rock, AR 2215-6248
800-950-8233
http://users.aristotle.net/~ahcaf
Eligibility Requirements

- You must be an Arkansas Resident.
- You must be uninsured.
- Your income level must be within 100% of the Federal Poverty Guidelines.

Patients apply to their County Department of Human Services or Health Unit. After approval, the patient contacts the pharmaceutical company using the toll-free numbers that are supplied. Participating pharmaceuticals are Johnson & Johnson, Glaxo SmithKline, and Pfizer.

Arkansas Department of Human Services
Donaghey Plaza West
Slot S201
P.O. Box 1437
Little Rock, AR 72203-1437
501-682-8650
Pays for two prescriptions per month for qualified individuals.

Eligibility:

- 65 and older. Annual income under $9,310 for any individual covered by the plan, $18,620 for married couple, for 2004 (would provide benefit of 2 prescriptions per month, only after federal approval is received)

California
Discount Prescription Medication Program
Department of Health Services
P.O. Box 997413
Sacramento, CA 95899
916-657-4302
800-434-0222
www.dhs.ca.gov/mcs/mcpd/MBB/contracting/sb393/defualt.htm\
Eligibility Requirements

- Have a Medicare card

Cost

- You can take your Medicare card to any pharmacy that fills Medi-Cal (California's Medicaid) prescriptions. You will be charged the Medi-Cal rate plus a 15 cent processing fee.

Connecticut
Conn PACE
P.O. Box 5011
Hartford, CT 06102
800-423-5026
www.connpace.com
Eligibility Requirements

- You must be 65 years old or older, or 18 and older with a disability.

- You must have lived in Connecticut for six months.
- Your income cannot exceed $20,800 if you are single, and $28,100 if you are married.
- You may not have an insurance plan that pays for all or a portion of each prescription, a deductible insurance plan that includes prescriptions, or Medicaid.

Cost

- You pay a $30 one time registration fee.
- You pay $16.25 for each prescription.
- You must get generic drugs whenever possible, unless you are willing to pay the difference in price.

Citizens Health Card
Citizens for Citizens
99 Black Falcon Ave.
Boston, MA 02210
800-563-5479
508-679-0041
www.citizensenergy.com
Discounts for prescriptions are available to uninsured or underinsured citizens who are not eligible for public programs at participating pharmacies.

Cost

- $12 per year for individuals and $28 per year for families

Delaware
Delaware Prescription Drug Assistance Program
EDS DPAP
P.O. Box 950
New Castle, DE 19720
302-577-4900
800-996-9969, ext. 17
www.state.de.us/dhss/dss/dpap.html
Eligibility Requirements

- You must be resident of Delaware
- You must be at lest 65 years old or qualify for Social Security Disability
- Your income cannot exceed 200% of the Federal Poverty Level

Cost

- You pay $5 or 25% of the cost of the prescription, whichever is greater.

Nemours Senior Pharmaceutical Assistance
1801 Rockland Road
Wilmington, DE 19803
302-651-4403
800-842-1900
www.nemours.org
Eligibility Requirements

- You must be a citizen of Delaware
- You must meet financial qualifications

Cost

- Members pay 20% of the drug's cost for each prescription.

District of Columbia
DC Healthcare Alliance
1025 15th Street, NW
Washington, DC 20005
202-842-5809
www.chartered-health.com/Alliance.htm
Eligibility Requirements

- You must live in the District of Columbia
- You must have no health insurance
- Your income must be at or below 200% of the Federal Poverty Level

Cost

- Membership in the Alliance is free for qualifying D.C. residents. Prescriptions must be from the list of qualifying drugs.

Florida
Silver Saver
1317 Winewood Boulevard
Building 3, 1st Floor
Suite 101
Tallahassee, FL 32399-0700
888-419-3456
www.floridahealthstat.com/silversaver.shtml
With this program, $160 will be put in your Silver Saver account (the balance is held in Medicaid's computer system). Each time you fill a prescription, the amount will automatically be deducted from your account.

Eligibility:

- You must be a Florida resident.
- You must be 65 years or older.
- You must be eligible for Medicare
- Your income must be between $679.01 and $918.00 for an individual, and between $908.01 and $1,232 for a couple.

Costs

- A $2 co-payment is required for generic prescriptions.
- A $5 co-payment is required for brand name drugs that are on Medicaid' Preferred Drug List.
- A $15 co-payment is required for brand name drugs that are not on the list.
- Your doctor must call and request a pre-approval from Medicaid on the prescriptions.

Prescription Discount Program
Agency for Health Care Administration
2727 Mahan Drive
Tallahassee, FL 32308
850-487-4441
888 419-3456

www.floridahealthstat.com/publications/prescripaffordbroch112100.pdf
Drug discount program. Recipients received a nine percent discount on the wholesale price after paying a $4.50 dispensing fee.

Eligibility:
- Any Medicare beneficiary, no age or income limit.

Georgia
Georgia Partnership for Caring Foundation
P.O. Box 450987
Atlanta, GA 31145-0987
678-578-2920
800-982-4723
www.gacares.org
Eligibility Requirements
- You must be a resident of Georgia
- You must be uninsured
- Your family income must be at or below 125% of the Federal Poverty Level

Cost
- Prescription drugs are dispensed by participating pharmacy in the Georgia Partnership for Caring Foundation network at no charge

Savings of up to 20%
Twiggs County
County Commissioner
P.O. Box 202, County Courthouse
Jeffersonville, GA 31044-0202
478-945-3629
https://naco.advancerx.com/advpcsrx_MemberSite/index.jsp
All residents of Twiggs County are eligible to participate in the county's Prescription Drug Discount Program. Twiggs Rx is free and available to all county residents, regardless of age, income or existing health insurance. Simply present the card at a participating pharmacy and save an average of 20% on prescription drugs. Best of all there is no enrollment form or membership fee. Members are also eligible for higher discounts on particular medications, as well as a mail service program which offers an average savings of 50% on a 3-month supply of select medications.

Hawaii
Hawaii Rx Plus Program
P.O. Box 700220
Kapolei, HI 96709-0220
808-692-7999
www.hawaiirxplus.com/
Eligibility Requirements
- You must be a resident of Hawaii
- You do not have all of your drugs paid for by insurance
- Your household income does not exceed 350% of the Federal Poverty Level

Costs
- Consumers can expect to pay 10-15% off of the average wholesale price of a drug

PACE Hawaii
1027 Hala Drive
Honolulu, HI 96817-2198
808-832-6131
Fax: 808-832-1932
www.pacehawaii.org/index.htm
PACE (Program of All Inclusive Care for the Elderly) serves the frail elderly to help them stay in their homes as long as possible. They offer a variety of assistance through their day health centers at Maluhia.

Illinois
Pharmaceutical Assistance Program
Illinois Department of Revenue
P.O. Box 19021
Springfield, IL 62794
800-624-2459
www.revenue.state.il.us/circuitbreaker/
Eligibility Requirements
- You must be 65 years of age or older, or over 16 and totally disabled, or a widow or widower who turned 63 before spouse's death.
- You must be a resident of Illinois.
- Your income must be less than $21,218 for individuals; $28,480 for couples.
- You must file a Circuit Breaker claim form.

Cost
- This program provides grants to help pay for prescriptions. Your grant is figured by a formula using the amount you paid in property tax or mobile home tax and the amount of your total income.
- You must choose the generic brand when available, unless you are willing to pay the difference in price.

Senior Care
Illinois Department on Aging
P.O. Box 19021
Springfield, IL 62794-9021
800-252-8966
www.seniorcareillinois.com
Eligibility Requirements
- You must be a resident of Illinois.
- You must be 65 years or older.

- If you are single, your income must not exceed $18, 620 a year. If you are married, your income must not exceed $24,980 a year.

Costs
- SeniorCare pays up to $1,750 per person per year, with either no co-pays or a low co-pay. After that, you pay 20% of the cost of each prescription plus any co-pays.
- Seniors pay 10% co-payment for each covered prescription drug with a $1,200 maximum per benefit period.

Illinois Rx Buying Club
P.O. Box 94858
Chicago, IL 60690-4858
866-215-3462
http://www.state.il.us/aging/3hot/pharm-assist_irs.htm
The Illinois Rx Buying Club provides discounts of 5 to 50 percent on all prescription drugs approved by the FDA and available through participating pharmacies and a mail-order option.

Eligibility Requirements:
- Senior citizens and disabled. No income limits.

Prescription Savings!!
Sangamon County Department of Public Health
ATTN: Sangamo Scripts
2501 North Dirksen Parkway
Springfield, IL 62702
217-535-3100
www.co.sangamon.il.us/events/SangamoScripts.pdf
Sangamo Scripts, a pharmaceutical discount program is available for any Sangamon County resident over the age of 18 who is not covered by Public Aid though children under 18 can be covered by a parent or guardian under the plan. There is no cost and the average savings per prescription.

Access to Care
2225 Enterprise Drive, Suite 2504
Westchester, IL 60154
708-531-0680
Fax: 708-531-0686
www.accesstocare.org/
Access to Care provides health care to low-income uninsured residents of suburban Cook County and Chicago, west of Pulaski Road and north of North Avenue. There is an enrollment fee and fees are based on family size.

DuPage Physician's Medical Assistance Program
Jack T. Knuepfer Administration Building
Wheaton, IL 60187
800-942-9412
630-407-6500
Fax: 630-407-6501
www.dupageco.org/humanservices/generic.cfm?doc_id=476
The DuPage Physician's Medical Assistance Program assists clients who do not exceed 125% of poverty level, are residents, uninsured and have 90-days of income. Services include prescriptions and other medical supplies and procedures.

Indiana
Hoosier Prescription Drug Program
P.O. Box 6224
Indianapolis, IN 46206
866-267-4679 (toll-free)
www.IN.gov/fssa/hoosierrx
Eligibility Requirements
- You must be 65 years or older
- You must be a permanent resident of Indiana
- You do not have prescription drug insurance
- Your income must be $1,068 or less a month if you are single; and $1,426 per month or less if you are married.
- You can pick up application forms at your local pharmacy, Area Agency on Aging, Social Security office, of Office of Family and Children.

Cost
- Eligible seniors will receive a HoosierRx Drug Card that will give them 75% off the price of their prescriptions.
- For those seniors that also have a Medicare Drug Discount Card, you may use both cards when you purchase prescriptions.

Iowa
Iowa Prescription Drug Corporation
1231 8th Street, Suite 232
West Des Moines, IA 50265
866-282-5817
www.iowapriority.org/default.asp
Eligibility Requirements
- You must be a resident of Iowa.
- You must be eligible for Medicare
- You cannot be receiving Medicaid.

Cost
- There is a $20 annual fee.
- Once you have your card, you will receive a discount on all prescriptions. The discount varies per prescription.

Kansas
Kansas Department of Aging
New England Bldg.
503 S. Kansas
Topeka, KS 66603
785-296-4986
800-432-3535
Senior Pharmacy Assistance Program
www.agingkansas.org/kdoa/programs/pharmassistprog.htm
Eligibility Requirements
- You must be a Kansas resident.
- You must be 65 years of age.

- You must be a current beneficiary of the Medicare Savings Program.
- You must not be covered under a private prescription insurance plan that pays for any part of your prescription costs.
- You must not be eligible for or enrolled in any other local, state, or federal prescription program such as Medicaid or VA prescription assistance;
- You must not have voluntarily canceled a local, state, federal, or private prescription drug program within six months of application to this program.

Costs

- The program will reimburse you for a portion of your prescription costs. They will not exceed 70% of out-of-pocket prescription drug costs. The maximum reimbursement per individual is limited to $1,200 annually.

20% off Prescription Drugs
Sedgwick County Health Department
1900 E. Ninth St.
Wichita, KS 67214
316-660-7300
www.sedgwickcounty.org/healthdept/
Free prescription drug discount cards are available to help Sedgwick County residents save money at participating pharmacies. The cards are designed for people who don't have prescription drug coverage, but they're available to anyone. The cards will offer an average of 20 percent off on commonly prescribed prescriptions and an average of 50 percent off three-month supplies of generics ordered through a mail service. The cards can be used at more than 70 pharmacies in Sedgwick County, and there are no income or age requirements, or claim forms to file.

Save 20 to 50% on Prescription Drugs
Harvey County Department of Health
800 N. Main
P.O. Box 687
Newton, KS 67114
316-284-6806
www.harveycounty.com/
Save money on your prescription purchases by using the free Harvey County Prescription Discount Card. There are no forms to fill out and everyone is eligible. Save an average of 20% off the pharmacies regular price prescribed prescriptions and an average savings of 50% on 3-month supplies of select generics through mail service.

Kentucky
Health Kentucky, Inc.
12700 Shelbyville Road
Louisville, KY 40243
502-254-4214
www.healthkentucky.org
Eligibility Requirements

- You must be a Kentucky resident
- You must be uninsured
- Your income must be at or below 100% of the Federal Poverty Level
- Resource limit of $2,000

Cost

- Participating physicians write prescriptions from the list of available medications. The prescription can be filled at one of 500 participating pharmacies for free.

Louisiana
Louisiana SenioRx Program
P.O. Box 61
Baton Rouge, LA 70821-0061
225-342-7100
www.louisianaseniorx.org
Eligibility Requirements

- You must be 60 years old or older
- You must have an income below $27,930 for a single, $37,470 for a two-person household
- You must have any insurance for prescriptions
- You must have a chronic illness taking prescribed daily medications for the condition
- You have not voluntarily cancelled any prescription drug program in the past 6 months

Costs

- SenioRx is a counseling service for seniors and does not directly supply medications. Their trained staff will help you apply for pharmaceutical company programs. This service is free of charge.

Maine
Elderly Low-Cost Drug Program
Department of Human Services
11 State House Station
Augusta, ME 04333
866-796-2463
207-287-9200
www.state.me.us/dhs/beas/medbook.htm#lcd
Eligibility requirements

- You must be a Maine resident.
- You may not be receiving SSI payments.

- Your income may not exceed $17,232 if you live alone; $23,112 if you are married or have dependents.
- You must be 62 years of age or older; or be at least 19 years of age and disabled.
- If you spend at least 40% of your income on prescriptions, your income limits will be 25% higher.

Cost

- Each drug will cost $2 plus 20% of the price.

Maine Rx Plus
Department of Human Services
11 State House Station
Augusta, ME 04333
800-262-2232
207-287-9200
www.state.me.us/dhs/beas/medbook.htm
Eligibility requirements

- You must be a resident of Maine.
- You must meet the following maximum monthly income guidelines:
- Single: $2,716; Family of 2: $3,643; Family of 3: $4,571; Family of 4: $ $5498.
- You may be eligible if your out-of-pocket expenses are more than 5% of your household income; or if your out-of-pocket medical expenses are more than 15% of your household income.

Costs

- You may get discounts of 15% to 60% off the retail prices. The greatest discounts are for generic drugs.

Rx Cares For ME
877-RxForME
www.rxcaresforme.org/
Rx Care For ME is an online resource to search for patient assistance programs. Patients simply fill out an online form and receive a listing of programs for which they may be qualified.

Maryland
Maryland Pharmacy Assistance Program
P.O. Box 386
Baltimore, MD 21203-0386
410-767-5397
800-226-2142
www.dhmh.state.md.us/mma/mpap
Eligibility requirements

- For anyone in the state who cannot afford their medications. Income requirements vary, so it is best to call. For a single person, income cannot exceed $10,800; for married couples, $12,492.

Cost

- Your co-pay is $2.50 for generic and $7.50 for certain brand names.

Maryland Pharmacy Discount Program
Eligibility Requirements

- You must receive Medicare.
- Your monthly income must be below $1,358 for a single person and below $1,822 for a couple.

Costs

- Eligible recipients pay 65% of the State's reduced cost, plus a $1 processing fee.
- There are no monthly premiums.

MEDBANK of Maryland, Inc.
P.O. Box 42678
Baltimore, MD 21284
410-821-9262
www.medbankmd.org
Eligibility Requirements

- You must be a Maryland resident
- You must have no other prescription coverage
- You must be ineligible for any entitlement programs like Medicaid
- You must meet financial guidelines

Cost

- Participating physicians write prescriptions from the list of available medications. The Medbank representative identifies Patient Assistance Programs, completes required applications.

21% average savings per prescription
ScriptSave
Anne Arundle County Health Department
3 Harry S. Truman Parkway
Annapolis, MD 21401
410-222-7095
ScriptSave
www.scriptsave.com
The Anne Arundel County Health Department offers county residents ScriptSave prescription discount cards. The program is available to all residents regardless of age and there are no enrollment fees. The average discount with the card is about 21% off each prescription.

Savings of up to 20%
Montgomery County Executive
Douglas M. Duncan
Executive Office Building
101 Monroe Street, 2nd Floor
Rockville, MD 20850
240-777-2500
TTY: 240-777-2544
www.montgomerycountymd.gov/mcgtmpl.asp?url=/content/PIO/mont_rx.asp
Montgomery County offers all residents to participate in the county's Prescription Drug Discount Program. Montgomery Rx is free and available to all Montgomery County residents,

regardless of age, income or existing health insurance. Simply present the card at a participating pharmacy and save an average of 20% on prescription drugs. There is no enrollment form or membership fee. Members are also eligible for higher discounts on select medications and inject able drugs, as well as, a mail service program which offers an average savings of 50% on a 3-month supply of select medications.

Senior Prescription Drug Program
CareFirst
BlueCross/Blue Shield
10455 Mill Run Circle
Owings Mills, MD 21117
800-972-4612
www.seniordrugprogram.com
Program lowers the cost of outpatient prescription drugs for those who do not have prescription drug coverage.

Eligibility Requirements:
- Maryland Resident
- Medicare Beneficiary
- No prescription drug coverage
- Your annual income must be below 300% of Federal Poverty Level ($28,710 for single: $38,490 for couple).

Cost
- $10 for generic; $20 for preferred brand-name; $35 for non-preferred brand name.
- $1,100 maximum prescription benefit per 12 month period
- Monthly cost of $10

Massachusetts
Prescription Advantage Plan
P.O. Box 15153
Worchester, MA 01615
800-AGE-INFO
www.800ageinfo.com
Eligibility Requirements
- You must be 65 years or old or have a qualified disability
- You must be a Massachusetts resident

Cost
- Monthly premium for the plan varies for $0-$82 per month depending upon your income. The co-payment also varies for $5-$25 depending upon income.
- After you pay $2,000 or 10% of your gross annual household income (whichever is less) toward your Prescription Advantage deductible and co-payments, the entire cost of your prescription drugs, including the co-payments are covered for the remainder of the year.

Citizens Health Card
Citizens for Citizens
88 Black Falcon Avenue
Center Lobby, Suite 342
Boston, MA 02210
800-563-5479
617-338-6300
www.citizensenergy.com
Discounts for prescriptions are available to uninsured or underinsured citizens who are not eligible for public programs at participating pharmacies.

Cost
- $12 per year for individuals and $28 per year for families

MassMedLine
Massachusetts College of Pharmacy and Health Sciences
19 Foster Street
Worchester, MA 01608-1705
866-633-1617
www.massmedline.com
Massachusetts residents can speak directly to specialists that can answer questions about the medications they take and provide information about programs sponsored by pharmaceutical companies that provide free, low cost or discounted medications.

Michigan
Elder Prescription Insurance Coverage
3850 Second Street, Suite 201
Wayne, MI 48184-1755
866-747-5844
www.miepic.com
Eligibility Requirements
- You must be a Michigan resident for at least 3 months
- You must be age 65 or older
- Your annual income must be at or below 150% of the federal poverty level.
- You may not be receiving prescription drug benefits through any other insurance, except Medicare.

Cost
- Modest co-pay depending upon income, plus a $25 annual fee.

Wayne County Discount Program
Health and Community Services Administrative Office
3850 Second Street
Suite 201
Wayne, MI 48184-1755
866-896-3450
Eligibility Requirements
- You must be a resident of Wayne County.
- You must be at least 60 years old.

Costs
- Discounts vary on generic and brand name prescriptions.

MiRx Prescription Savings Program
Michigan Department of Community Health
Sixth Floor, Lewis Cass Building

320 South Walnut Street
Lansing, MI 48913
866-755-6479
www.michigan.gov/mdch/0,1607,7-132--100833--,00.html
Application:
http://www.michigan.gov/documents/MiRx_brochure_150dpi_103392_7.pdf
Beneficiaries of the MiRx Card program will save as much as 20 percent off the retail prices they would normally pay as a cash customer.

Eligibility:

- No minimum age. Income levels slide depending on family size (1= $27,930 to 8= $94,050). No enrollment fee.

Receive 25% off Prescription Drugs
Washtenaw County Prescription Plan
Jean Higgins
55 Towner, Bldg 1, Room 121
Ypsilanti, MI 48197
734-544-6886
Fax 734-544-6705
www.ewashtenaw.org/government/departments/public_health/ph_wcpp.html
The Washtenaw County Prescription Plan (WCPP) is a discount prescription drug program for County residents of all ages who have limited, exhausted, or no prescription drug coverage. There are no income or age restrictions. WCPP helps County residents to buy prescription drugs at a discount off of the full retail price. Discounts may range from 5-25%. Many pharmacies in Washtenaw County participate.

Medications 20-30% Off
OLHSA Oakland County
196 Cesar E. Chavez Avenue
P.O. Box 430598
Pontiac, MI 48343-0598
517-546-8500
www.olhsa.org/liv_prescriptions.asp
Livingston county residents 60 years of age or older can obtain a discount prescription card. This group discount is offered through the Ingham Health Plan Corporation and applies to most medicines, excluding over-the-counter drugs and has no enrollment costs. The program allows participants to save an average of 20-30% off regular prescription drug prices at participating pharmacies.

Prescription Drug 25% Off Retail Price
Barry-Eaton Discount Prescription
Eaton County
1045 Independence Blvd.
Charlotte, MI 48813
517-541-2614
www.eatoncounty.org/prescription.htm
Any resident of Barry or Eaton counties who does not have other drug coverage can participate in the Barry-Eaton Discount Prescription Plan. The program is a way for people without prescription coverage to purchase prescription drugs at lower prices at their pharmacy. There is no cost for the card and covered with the exception of the over-the-counter drugs and experimental medications.

Discounts as High as 70%
The Jackson County Prescription Discount Plan (JCPDP)
Jackson County Health Department
1697 Lansing Ave.
Jackson, MI 49202
517-788 – 4420
Fax: 517-788 – 4373
www.co.jackson.mi.us/hd/jcpdp.htm
The Jackson County Prescription Discount Plan is a way for people without prescription coverage to purchase prescription drugs at lower prices from their pharmacy. Any resident of Jackson County who does not have drug coverage may participate and there is no cost for the JCPDP card or for enrolling in the program. People who present a JCPDP card at a participating pharmacy can expect to save about 25 percent off the retail price. Saving will typically be between 5 and 25 percent with discounts at times as high as 70%, though not typical.

Minnesota
Minnesota's Prescription Drug Program
Department of Human Services
444 Lafayette Rd., N
St Paul, MN 55155
651-296-8517
800-657-3659
www.dhs.state.mn.us/main/groups/healthcare/documents/pub/dhs_id_006258.hcsp
Eligibility Requirements

- Must be age 65 or older, or disabled and enrolled in Medicaid.
- Must be a Minnesota resident for six months
- Have income at or below 120% of federal poverty guidelines (currently $951 a month for one person and $1,269 a month for a married couple)
- Have liquid assets of $10,000 or less for one; $18,000 or less for married couple
- Be enrolled in either Qualified Medicare Beneficiary (QMB) or Service Limited Medicare Beneficiary (SLMB).

Cost

- The Prescription Drug Program pays for necessary prescription drugs after enrollees pay the first $35 monthly deductible. If no medications are purchased that month, there is no $35 cost. For more information contact your local county human services agency.

Minnesota Health Care Programs
Minnesota Department of Human Services
444 Lafayette Road North

Saint Paul, MN 55155
800-657-3739
651-296-7675
www.dhs.state.mn.us/main/groups/healthcare/documents/pub/dhs_id_006257.hcsp
Low-income adults 21 through 64 may be eligible medical care assistance. Income limits vary by family size and there are limits on the coverage.

Mississippi
Discounts as High as 70%
The Jackson County Prescription Discount Plan (JCPDP)
Jackson County Health Department
1697 Lansing Ave.
Jackson, MI 49202
517-788-4420
Fax: 517-788-4373
www.co.jackson.mi.us/hd/jcpdp.htm
The Jackson County Prescription Discount Plan is a way for people without prescription coverage to purchase prescription drugs at lower prices from their pharmacy. Any resident of Jackson County who does not have other drug coverage may participate and there is no cost for the JCPDP card or for enrolling in the program. People who present a JCPDP card at a participating pharmacy can expect to save about 25 percent off the retail price. Saving will typically be between 5 and 25 percent with discounts at times as high as 70%, though not typical.

Missouri
Senior Rx Program
P.O. Box 208
Troy, MO 63379
800-375-1406
www.dhss.mo.gov/MoSeniorRx/
Eligibility Requirements
- You must be at least 65 years old.
- You must have been a resident of the State for at least 12 months.
- You may not receive Veterans Administration pharmacy benefits or have prescription insurance that is equal to or greater than this program.
- You must not be enrolled in Medicaid.
- An individual must not have an income that is greater than $17,000 and a married household must not have an income above $25,000.

Cost
- Enrollment fee is $25 or $35 per member, depending on household income.
- Deductible of $250 or $500 per member, depending on household income.
- You pay 40% of the cost of eligible prescriptions.
- The maximum annual benefit is $5,000 per member per year.

Montana
Prescription Drug Expansion Program
Department of Public Health and Human Services
111 N Sanders
Room 301/308
PO Box 4210
Helena, MT 59604
800-551-3191
www.dphhs.state.mt.us/
Not yet operational
Offer discounts on prescription drugs for Medicaid members.

Eligibility:
- Minimum age: 62 (disabled 18 and over)
- Maximum annual income of $18,620 for eligible individuals, regardless of spouse's income.

Nebraska
Prescription Drug Savings!!
Dawes County
451 Main Street
County Courthouse
Chadron, NE 69337-2697
308-432-0102
www.co.dawes.ne.us/
Free prescription drug discount cards are available to help Dawes County residents save money at participating pharmacies. The cards are designed for people who don't have prescription drug coverage, but they're available to anyone regardless of income or age. The program offers an average of 20 percent off on commonly prescribed prescriptions and an average of 50 percent off three-month supplies of generics ordered through a mail service. The cards can be used at many participating pharmacies throughout Dawes County and requires no claim forms.

20%-50% Savings on Prescription Drugs
Keith County
511 N Spruce
P.O. Box 149, County Courthouse
Ogallala, NE 69153-0149
308-284-4726
Fax: 308-284-6277
www.co.keith.ne.us/
Keith County wants to help its residents save money on their prescription drugs by offering prescription drug discount cards. The cards are designed for people who don't have prescription drug coverage, but they're available to anyone regardless of

income or age. The program offers an average of 20 percent off on commonly prescribed prescriptions and an average of 50 percent off three-month supplies of generics ordered through a mail service. The cards can be used at many participating pharmacies throughout Keith County and require no claim forms.

Nevada
Senior Rx
1761 E. College Parkway
Building B, Suite 113
Carson City, NV 89706-7954
800-262-7726
www.nevadaseniorrx.com
Eligibility Requirements

- Age 62 and older
- Nevada resident for at least one year
- Not eligible for full Medicaid with prescription benefits
- Household income not over $22,434 for a single person and $29,205 for married couples

Cost

- You pay a co-pay of $10 per generic drug. Senior Rx provides up to $5,000 in benefits per year.

New Hampshire
New Hampshire Prescription Drug Discount Program
New Hampshire Division of Elderly & Adult Services
129 Pleasant Street
Concord, NH 03301-3857
888-580-8902
www.dhhs.state.nh.us/DHHS/BEAS/assist-prescription-drug.htm
This discount card program is for New Hampshire residents age 65 and over who enroll in the program. A discount card is used at participating pharmacies for discounts up to 15% on brand name medications and up to 40% on generic medications. Currently, there are no financial eligibility requirements and no membership fees. Mail order is also available.

New Hampshire Bridge Program
Foundation for Healthy Communities
125 Airport Road
Concord, NH 03301
603-225-0900
www.healthynh.com/fhc/initiatives/access/medicationbridge.php
The goal of the program is to help eligible uninsured and underinsured patients of all ages to receive needed prescription medications from pharmaceutical companies' Patient Assistance Programs. They help residents access medications by helping them find programs.

New Jersey
Pharmaceutical Assistance to the Aged and Disabled (PAAD)
Senior Gold Prescription Discount Program
P.O. Box 725
Trenton, NJ 08625
800-792-9745
609-588-7048
www.state.nj.us/health/seniorbenefits/seniorgolddiscount.htm
Eligibility Requirements

- You must be a New Jersey resident.
- Your income must be less than $20,437 if you are single, or less than $25,058 if you are married. Income can be $10,000 higher and you could qualify for Senior Gold.
- You must be at least 65 years of age, or receiving Social Security Disability.
- Drugs purchased outside the state of New Jersey are not covered, nor any pharmaceutical product whose manufacturer has not agreed to provide rebates to the state of New Jersey.

Cost

- Senior Gold members have a $15 copay plus ½ of the remainder of the cost of the drug.

50% Discount
Camden County Drug Discount Prescription Program
GSPO Provider Service Corp
P.O. Box 4190
Hamilton, NJ 08610
866-792-6226
www.co.camden.nj.us/RX/
If you are a resident of Camden County, New Jersey then you are eligible to participate in the county's Drug Discount Prescription Program. The program is designed to provide Camden County residents with savings of up to 10% to 50% on prescription medications. There are no income requirements, no exclusions for pre-existing condition and no age restrictions. All that is required is a completed application form, proof of residency and a small annual fee of $20 per household ($40 for 3 years). The Camden County Prescription Drug Discount Program is accepted at thousands of participating pharmacies, both local and nationwide.

50% Off Regular Retail Prescription Prices
Cape May County Prescription Savings Program
GSPO Provider Services Corp.
P.O. Box 4190
Hamilton, NJ 08610
800-633-0037
www.co.cape-may.nj.us/FCpdf/PSPBrochure.pdf
Cape May County Prescription Savings Program is available to all Cape May County residents, regardless of your age or income. For an annual fee of $20 per year or $40 for 3 years, you will receive a Cape May County Prescription Savings Card providing up to 10% to 50% off regular retail prescription prices. There are no age requirements, no income requirements and no exclusions for pre-existing conditions.

Save 10% to 50% On Prescription Medications
Atlantic County Resident Prescription Savings Program

GSPO Provider Services Corp.
P.O. Box 4190
Hamilton, NJ 08610
800-633 0037
www.aclink.org/Admin/Main/pres_savings.asp
The Atlantic County Resident Prescription Savings Program provides Atlantic County residents with savings of up to 10% to 50% on prescription medications. All residents of Atlantic County and their dependents living in the same household are eligible, there are no income requirements, and there are no exclusions for pre-existing conditions. For a small annual fee, you will receive an Atlantic County Resident Prescription Savings Card which provides special discounted pricing on prescription medications for all members of your household.

New Mexico
New Mexico SenioRx
866-244-0882
www.nmrhca.state.nm.us/spdp/
Eligibility Requirements

- You must be a resident of New Mexico
- You must be 65 years of age or older

Cost

- There is no enrollment fee required to participate
- You can expect savings of between 13-19% off brand names drugs and 50-55% off of generic drugs. Actual discounts may vary.

20%-50% Savings on Prescription Drugs
San Miguel County
500 West National, County Courthouse
Las Vegas, NM 87701-0000
505-425-9333
Fax: 505-425-7019
www.smcounty.net/
Residents in San Miguel County can save money on their prescription drugs through the county's prescription drug discount program. The discount cards are designed for people who don't have prescription drug coverage, but they're available to anyone regardless of income or age. The program offers an average of 20 percent off on commonly prescribed prescriptions and an average of 50 percent off three-month supplies of generics ordered through a mail service. The cards can be used at many participating pharmacies throughout San Miguel County and require no claim forms.

New York
Elderly Pharmaceutical Insurance Coverage EPIC
P.O. Box 15018
Albany, NY 12212
800-332-3742
518-452-6828
www.health.state.ny.us/nysdoh/epic/faq.htm
Eligibility Requirements

- You must be 65 or older.
- You must reside in New York State.
- Your income must not exceed $35,000 if you are single; or $50,000 if you are married.
- You are not eligible if you receive Medicaid benefits.

Cost

- You pay between $3-$20 per prescription depending upon the prescription cost.
- There are two plans for EPIC. You can pay an annual fee depending upon your income to qualify right away. The annual fee ranges from $8 to over $300, which can be paid in installments. The EPIC Deductible plan is that you pay no fee, but you pay full price for your prescriptions until you spend the deductible amount. The deductible amount also varies by income and starts at $530.

UP to 50% off Medications
RocklandRx
Rockland County Office of the County Executive
11 New Hempstead Rd.
New City, NY 10956
845-638-5122
www.co.rockland.ny.us/
Rockland County of New York provides a prescription discount program with no annual fee to all of its residents regardless of their age or income. The RocklandRx prescription discount card gives an average price cut of 20 percent off and as much as 50 percent off the cost of commonly prescribed medications, including brand name and generic drugs. The card is accepted at 56 Rockland pharmacies and more than 54,000 pharmacies nationwide.

Save Up to 15% on Brand Name and 44% on Generics
The RxChoice Drugstore Savings Club
Monroe County Department of Human and Health Services
111 Westfall Road
Rochester, NY 14620
585-274-6298
Fax: 585-274-6296
www.monroecounty.gov/org30.asp
Monroe County has partnered with The RxChoice Drugstore Savings Club, a prescription drug discount card with 2 million members nationwide. This plan is opened to any senior who is a resident of Monroe County, New York – regardless of income and does not currently have prescription drug coverage. All enrolled seniors receive a Monroe County-RxChoice Card, which can be presented at most retail pharmacies for a discount on all prescription drugs.

50% Prescription Drugs
NassauRx prescription discount card
Office of the Nassau Comptroller
240 Old Country Road
Mineola, NY
516-571-2386
www.co.nassau.ny.us/comptroller/index.html

The new NassauRx prescription discount card is available to Nassau residents free of charge. With the NassauRx card, any family member can get discounts of an average of 20 percent off – and as much as 50 percent off – the cost of commonly prescribed prescription medications. Any county resident, regardless of age, income or existing health insurance, may use the card. Currently, the card is accepted at more than 90 percent of Nassau pharmacies and at more than 54,000 nationwide. There are no claim forms to fill out and no annual fees to pay, simply present your card with your prescription at any participating pharmacy.

Save up to 50% off Your Medications
UlsterRx
5999 South Park Avenue, No. 248
Buffalo NY, 14075
800-780-8738
Fax: 1-800-771-9180
www.ulsterrx.com/
Ulster County residents can participate in a discount drug card program that allows its members access to affordable prescription drugs through a national network of participating pharmacies. Members can expect to save between 10 and 50 percent on their prescriptions, depending on the type of medication you need and where you purchase it. The card can be used at neighborhood pharmacies, through mail order or, for the greatest savings, purchase prescriptions through a Canadian pharmacy. All residents of Ulster County are eligible to enroll and enrollment fees are nominal. The annual cost for a single membership is $15, while the annual cost for a family membership is $26.

Reduced Prescription Drugs Prices
TompkinsRx
Tomkin County Health Department
401 Harris B. Dates Drive, Biggs B
Ithica, NY, 14850
877-321-2652
https://tompkins.advancerx.com/advpcsrx_MemberSite/index.jsp
The TompkinsRx card was endorsed by the Tompkins County Legislature on December 21, 2004 to help uninsured and underinsured residents reduce the cost of prescription drugs. Simply present your card at a participating pharmacy and save an average of 20% on prescription drugs. No enrollment form, no membership fee.

20% off Prescription Drugs
County Executive
22 Market. St.
Poughkeepsie, NY 12601
845-486-2000
Fax 845-486-2021
www.dutchessny.gov/CountyGov/Departments/CountyExecutive/CEIndex.htm
Free prescription drug discount cards are available to help Dutchess County residents save money at participating pharmacies. The cards are designed for people who don't have prescription drug coverage, but they're available to anyone regardless of age or income. The cards will offer an average of 20 percent off on commonly prescribed prescriptions and an average of 50 percent off three-month supplies of generics ordered through a mail service. The cards can be used at many participating pharmacies throughout Dutchess County, and there are no claim forms to file.

North Carolina
Office of the Governor
NC Senior Care Program
P.O. Box 10068
Raleigh, NC 27605-5068
866-226-1388
919-733-4534
www.ncseniorcare.com/index.htm
Eligibility Requirements

- Single applicants must have an annual income of $23,275 or less, and $31,225 or less if married.
- Age 65 and older.

Senior PHARMAssist
123 Market Street
Durham, NC 27701-3221
919-688-4772
www.seniorpharmassist.org/
Eligibility Requirements

- You must be a Durham County resident
- You must be 65 years of age or older

Cost

- Seniors who qualify for financial assistance receive a prescription card to purchase approved medicines. The participant pays $8 per prescription.
- Seniors that do not qualify for financial assistance, can receive information from PHARMAssist about alternative prescription assistance programs and local short-term funding programs.

Ohio
Ohio Department of Aging
50 W. Broad Street, 9th Floor
Columbus, OH 43215-3363
866-311-6446
www.goldenbuckeye.com/buckeye.html
Eligibility Requirements

- You must be an Ohio resident
- You must be 60 years of age or older or 18-59 if Medicare-certified disabled
- You must be ineligible for any other prescription coverage

Cost

- Patient pays a negotiated price for medications

Rx for Ohio
172 East State Street, Suite 410
Columbus, OH 43215
877-RxOhio
www.rxforohio.org
Rx for Ohio is a service for Ohioans that are in need of prescription assistance programs. The web site will help you search for programs that meet your needs.

Ohio's Best Rx
Ohio Department of Job and Family Services
Office of Family Stability
145 South Front Street, 2nd Floor
Columbus, OH 43215
614-466-9783
www.ohiobestrx.com
Eligibility Requirements
- You must be an Ohio resident
- You must be 60 years old or older
- Your income must be 250% of the Federal Poverty Level if you are under the age of 60
- You must be ineligible for prescription coverage

Cost
- There is no cost to participant for the program
- Prescription prices will vary

Prescription Drugs at Reduced Cost
Stark County Prescription Assistance Network
1320 Mercy DR. NW
Mercy Hall
Canton, OH 44708
330-458-4272
Fax: 330-580-4793
www.rxforohio.org/assistance/stark/
The Stark County Prescription Network is funded by 3 non-profit foundations to assist those in the community who fall in to the 200% poverty level. Patients who receive care and prescriptions from private physicians will be assisted through the Network's voucher program; pharmaceutical company patient assistance programs (PAP) and may buy medications through MedShare which offers drugs at reduced cost.

Oregon
Senior Prescription Drug Assistance Program
Oregon Department of Human Services
500 Summer St. NE E25
Salem, OR 97301-1098
503-945-6530
www.dhs.state.or.us/seniors/aging/spdap_info.htm
The Senior Prescription Drug Assistance Program (SPDAP) allows members of the program to purchase prescription drugs from participating pharmacies at the State Medicaid rate. $50 annual fee, provides discount not to exceed state Medicaid prescription rates.

Eligibility:
- Minimum age: 65
- Maximum annual income of $17,223 for individuals.

Pennsylvania
PACE Card
(Pennsylvania Pharmaceutical Assistance Contract For The Elderly)
Pennsylvania Department of Aging
555 Walnut St., 5th Floor
Harrisburg, PA 17101
717-787-7313
800-225-7223
www.aging.state.pa.us/aging/cwp
Eligibility Requirements
- You must be 65 or older.
- Your income cannot exceed $14,500 if you are single; $17,700 for married couples.
- You must also live in the state for at least 90 days.

Cost
- You pay a $6.00 co-payment for each generic prescription. You may not purchase drugs out of state.
- You pay a $9.00 co-payment for each brand name prescription.
- PACE limits drug amounts to no more than a 30-day supply or 100 pills. There are no vacation supplies allowed.

PACENET
Eligibility Requirements
Eligibility is the same as PACE above except for the income limits. A single person's total income can be between $14,500 and $23,500. A couple's combined total income can be between $17,700 and $31,500.

Costs
You must meet a $40 monthly deductible, which is cumulative if it is not met each month. Once you meet the $40 deductible each month, you will pay an $8 co-payment for each generic prescription and a $15 co-payment for each brand name prescription.

Rhode Island
Rhode Island Pharmaceutical Assistance to the Elderly (RIPAE)
Rhode Island Department of Elderly Affairs
35 Howard Ave.
Cranston, RI 02920
800-322-2880
401-462-4000
www.dea.state.ri.us/socialservices.htm
Eligibility Requirements
- You must be a Rhode Island resident.
- You must be 65 years old.
- Your income must not exceed $17,155 if you are single; $21,445 if you are married.

- You can not have any other prescription drug coverage.

Cost
- Members pay 40% of the cost of prescription drugs used to treat certain illnesses.
- For incomes for single $21,535 and married $26,919, you pay 70%. For incomes for single $37,687 and married $43,070, you pay 85%.

Citizens Health Card
Citizens for Citizens
88 Black Falcon Avenue
Suite 342
Boston, MA 02210
800-214-5697
www.citizensenergy.com
Discounts for prescriptions are available to uninsured or underinsured citizens who are not eligible for public programs at participating pharmacies.

Cost
- $12 per year for individuals and $28 per year for families

Rx for Rhode Island
877-743-6779
http://rxforri.org/index.html
Rx4RI is a program that connects qualified, low-income people with discount prescription drugs, direct from the pharmaceutical manufacturer. The web site will help you search for programs that meet your needs.

South Carolina
SILVERRxCARD
1801 Main Street
P.O. Box 100101
Columbia, SC 29202-3101
877-239-5277 (toll-free)
http://southcarolina.fhsc.com/beneficiaries/SILVERxCARD/documents.asp
Eligibility Requirements
- Applications are available at local government offices, pharmacies, libraries, senior centers and Council on Aging offices.
- Must be 65 or older
- Resident of South Carolina for past six months
- Have no other prescription drug coverage
- Have income of $18,620 or less if single or $24,980 or less if married.

Costs
- You must pay $500 deductible before the plan begins to pay benefits
- Once you meet your deductible, you pay $10 co-pay on generic drugs at $15 co-pay on Brand drug.
- You will pay a $21 co-payment for prior authorization drugs.
- You may not be enrolled in both the Medicare Prescription Drug Plan and the SILVERRx Card.

Communicare
P.O. Box 186
Columbia, SC 29202-0186
800-763-0059
803-933-9183
www.commun-i-care.org
Eligibility Requirements
- You must be a South Carolina resident
- You must not be eligible for any prescription coverage
- You must fall within Communicare income guidelines
- You must fall into and document one of the following
- Currently employed
- Currently receiving unemployment compensation
- Currently receiving Social Security Retirement benefits
- Currently receiving Social Security Disability benefits or Workmen's Compensation

Cost
- $20 non-refundable application processing fee
- A patient must have a prescription written by a licensed physician and sent to our Central Fill Pharmacy.

South Dakota
Save 20% on Prescription Drugs
Brookings County Commission
314 6th Avenue
Brookings, SD 57006
605-696-8205
Fax 605-696-8208
www.brookingscountysd.gov
Brookings County Prescription Drug Discount Program offers county residents the opportunity to save an average of 20 percent off the retail price of commonly prescribed prescription drugs. All residents, regardless of age, income or existing coverage, may use the cards as often as people need and with no enrollment form or registration fee. but they may not be used in conjunction with another discount or prescription program. All local pharmacies except Wal-Mart participate in the program.

20%-50% Savings on Prescription Drugs
Davison County
200 East 4th Avenue
County Courthouse
Mitchell, SD 57301-2631
605-995-8608
Fax: 605-995-8618
www.davisoncounty.org/
DavisonCounty helps its residents save money on their prescription drugs by offering prescription drug discount cards. The cards are designed for people who don't have prescription drug coverage, but they're available to anyone regardless of income or age. The program offers an average of 20 percent off on commonly prescribed prescriptions and an average of 50

percent off three-month supplies of generics ordered through a mail service. The cards can be used at many participating pharmacies throughout Davison County and require no claim forms.

Vermont
VScript Program
103 South Main St.
802-241-2880
Waterbury, VT 05676
800-250-8427
Eligibility Requirements
- You must be a resident of Vermont.
- You must be at least 65.
- You may not have income in excess of 175% of the federal poverty guidelines. For singles, $16,292; for couples, $21,857. Vscript Expanded has income requirements of $20,947 for singles and $28,102 for couples. The Vhap Program has income of $13,965 for singles and $18,735 for couples. The Vscript and Vscript Expanded are for maintenance prescriptions only. The Vhap program is for both short-term and long-term prescriptions.
- You may not be in a health insurance plan that pays for all or a portion of the applicant's prescription drugs.

Cost
- There will be a co-payment requirement of $1 or $2 for Vscript and Vhap. Vscript Expanded copay is 50% of the cost of the drug.

The Vermont Medication Bridge Program
c/o RAVNAH
P.O. Box 787
Rutland, VT 05702-0787
866-VTPHARM
www.ravnah.org/vtpharm.htm
The Vermont Bridge Program provides needy patients in Vermont access to necessary prescription medications. The 866 phone number will direct Vermont patients to available programs.

VHAP Pharmacy - Vermont Health Access Program
Office of Vermont Health Access
312 Hurricane Lane

Williston, VT 05495
802 879-5900
800-529-4060 (in state)
800-250-8427 (out of state)
Fax: 802 879-5962
www.dsw.state.vt.us/districts/ovha/ovha8.htm
Covers acute care and maintenance drugs. Discount varies based on income levels.

Eligibility:
- Minimum age: 65
- Maximum annual income of $13,368 for individuals and $17,988 for married couples. Disabled: Recipients of disability benefits through SS or Medicare.

VSCRIPT Expanded
Office of Vermont Health Access
312 Hurricane Lane
Williston, VT 05495
802 879-5900
800-529-4060 (in state)
800-250-8427 (out of state)
Fax: 802 879-5962
www.dsw.state.vt.us/districts/ovha/ovha8.htm
Only covers maintenance drugs. Discount varies, based on income levels.

Eligibility:
- Minimum age: 65
- Maximum annual income of $20,947 for individuals and $28,102 for married couples.

Healthy Vermonters (Plus) Discount Program
Office of Vermont Health Access
312 Hurricane Lane
Williston, VT 05495
802 879-5900
800-529-4060 (in state)
800-250-8427 (out of state)
Fax: 802 879-5962
www.dsw.state.vt.us/districts/ovha/ovha8.htm
Includes a Medicaid waiver with 2% state payment toward cost of drugs. Not operational following adverse, 2002 federal ruling.

Eligibility:
- Minimum age: None.
- Maximum annual income of $37,240 for individuals over 65 and $49,960 for married couples over 65. For all others, $27,930 for individuals and $37,470 for married couples.

Washington
Rx Washington discount plan
Washington Health Care Authority
676 Woodland Square Loop SE
Lacey, WA 98503
http://rx.wa.gov/rx.shtml

800-227-5255
Negotiated discounts between 15% and 25% discounts on all prescription drugs.

Eligibility:

- Minimum age: 50 (disabled over 19)
- Maximum annual income of $27,936 for individuals and $37,470 for married couples.

West Virginia
Gold Mountaineer Discount Card
The West Virginia Bureau of Senior Services
1900 Kanawha Boulevard, East
Holly Grove, Building #10
Charleston, WV 25305-0160
304-558-3317
877-987-3646
www.state.wv.us/seniorservices
Eligibility Requirements

- You must be a West Virginia resident.
- You must be at least 60 years old.

Costs
The card allows a discount for most prescriptions used by seniors. The cost is the Average Wholesale Price minus 13% or the pharmacy's usual and customary price, whichever is lower. For most generic drugs: Maximum Allowable Cost Pricing, which is approximately Average Wholesale Price minus 60%, or the pharmacy's usual & customary price whichever is lower.

Rx for West Virginia
877-WVA-Rx4U
www.rxforwv.org
Rx4WV is a program that connects qualified, low-income people with discount prescription drugs, direct from the pharmaceutical manufacturer. The web site will help you search for programs that meet your needs.

20%-50% Savings on Prescription Drugs
Ohio County
1500 Chapline Street
City County Building
Wheeling, WV 26003-3553
304-234-3628
Fax: 304-234-3827
wvweb.com/cities/wheeling/
Ohio County residents can save money on their prescription drugs by enrolling in the county's prescription drug discount program. The discount cards are designed for people who don't have prescription drug coverage, but they're available to anyone regardless of income or age. The program offers an average of 20 percent off on commonly prescribed prescriptions and an average of 50 percent off three-month supplies of generics ordered through a mail service. The cards can be used at many participating pharmacies throughout Ohio County and require no claim forms.

Wisconsin
SeniorCarex
Department of Health and Family Services
PO Box 6710
Madison, WI 53707-0710
608-266-0554
800-657-2038
www.dhfs.state.wi.us/seniorCare/index.htm
Eligibility Requirements

- You must be a Wisconsin resident.
- You must be 65 years or older.
- You must meet one of the different level income requirements.

Costs

- You pay a $30 annual enrollment fee per person.
- Your co-payment depends on your income level. For the first level, the annual maximum income is $14,896 per individual and $19,984 per couple. With that, there is no deductible and the co-payment is $5 for generic drugs and $15 for brand name drugs. Maximum income amounts for Level 2a are $14,897 to $18,620 per individual and $19,985 to $24,980 per couple. The deductible for that level is $500 and then the same co-payments as above. Level 2b has an $800 deductible and after that is met, the cost is the same co-payment described above. The income levels are $18,621 to $22,344 per individual and $24,981 to $29,976 per couple annually.

Wyoming
Prescription Drug Assistance Program
Department of Health/ Medicaid
Hathaway Bldg., Room 147
2300 Capitol Ave.
Cheyenne, WY 82002
307-777-7531
800-442-2766
http://wyequalitycare.acs-inc.com/
Prescription drug assistance of up to 15 percent off the wholesale price for the elderly. Benefits determined by income level.

Eligibility:

- No age limit.
- Maximum annual income of $9,310 and no more than $1,000 in resource, with home and one vehicle exempt. Enrollees with income under $9,310 are eligible regardless of spouse's income.

THE GOOD AND BAD OF BUYING DRUGS FROM CANADA

Big drug makers say it's risky, and the Food & Drug Administration implies that it may be illegal, yet tens of thousands of Americans are now buying prescription drugs from offshore and Canadian pharmacies, sometimes at savings approaching 80 percent of American prices.

Almost all of the prescriptions being shipped to the United States come from countries which have government-mandated price controls in place. And while the buyer should always beware when making any kind of purchase, it is worth investigating offshore prescriptions when one considers the hundreds or thousands of dollars that can be saved annually.

Sample Savings

Drug	U.S. Price	Canadian Price	Savings
Lipitor	$268	$170	37 percent
Prevacid	$121	$68	44 percent
Zocor	$335	$198	41 percent
Paxil	$82	$70	14 percent
Naxium	$129	$75	42 percent
Plavix	$115	$74	36 percent
Pravachol	$225	$135	40 percent

Prices based on a 30-day supply for a standard dose at drugstore.com and selected, online Canadian pharmacies. Prices may vary.

Like driving To Canada

Officially, the FDA has had a longstanding policy that allows Americans to buy up to a 90-day supply of prescription drugs when they visit a foreign country – hence, the agency has never had problems with bus trips to Canada organized by senior centers, labor unions and other organizations. But the rise of the Internet, opening foreign markets to many more U.S. citizens in recent years, has put the policy in a gray area.

That hasn't been helped by big drug companies, which say they rely on big markups in the U.S. to fund worldwide research efforts. If this is so, then the drug companies are essentially asking American consumers to subsidize drug research around the world and to cover consumers in countries where prices are kept low by law.

In addition to putting pressure on government regulators, the drug companies have implied that drugs shipped from overseas may be unsafe or cheap imitations of the products they sell.

So don't look overseas. Look north, to Canada, which has a government agency that tightly monitors the safety and quality of all drugs sold in that country.

Is it legal?

Officially, the FDA has said that almost any international shipment of prescription medications violates the law. Affordable healthcare advocates, however, argue that there is no difference between someone buying a 90-day supply of prescription medications over the Internet or when they fill a prescription on their trip to Niagara Falls.

And so far, the FDA has made no indications that it will go after the individual consumer. The agency realizes it is on shaky legal ground – not to mention it would face stinging bad publicity if it went after everyday individuals who were simply trying to keep their healthcare costs in check.

The FDA has instead chosen to go after some U.S.-based Internet pharmacies, as well as companies which set up storefront operations that help people place orders with Canadian pharmacies. These companies generally act as middlemen, helping patients and people without access to the Internet place orders. In return, the companies collect a commission generally ranging from five to 15 percent.

The biggest of these companies – Rx Depot – gave up its legal fight on August 20, 2004. A federal judge had ordered it to shut its stores last year, but you may be able to find similar, smaller providers in your local yellow pages.

If not, turn to the Internet. A simple search for "Canadian prescriptions," "Canada pharmacy" or "prescriptions from Canada" will turn up thousands of results. A few of the more reputed Canadian pharmacies offering shipment to the United States include:

- **Canada Pharmacy** (www.canadapharmacy.com, 800-891-0844): The pharmacy's toll free ordering phone number is useful for people who don't have Internet access. Canada Pharmacy offers thousands of name brand and generic drugs, as well as discounted over-the-counter products. Customers who use the promotion code **1067** receive $5 (U.S.) off their first order.
- **Canadian Pharmacy Trust** (www.canadianpharmacytrust.com): Located in Vancouver, the pharmacy offers discounts between 40 and 80 percent when compared to American pharmacies.
- **Canada Drugs** (www.canadadrugs.com): Online orders only, with savings similar to those offered by Canada Pharmacy and Canadian Pharmacy Trust.

All of the legitimate pharmacies will require you to send or fax photocopies of your photo identification card and a copy of your prescription, which must be filled out by a licensed physician. Prescriptions are generally shipped within five to ten business days after the pharmacy receives your documentation.

Safety First

Pills and capsules from Canadian pharmacies may look different than the ones you're currently taking. But the active ingredients will be the same if you deal with a reputed dealer. Manufacturers sometimes opt to use different colors and shapes for pills sold in Canada, even though the pills are often made at the same manufacturing facility.

If you have any concerns about the prescription medications you receive, it is not unreasonable to have the physician who wrote the prescription look them over before you begin taking them. Most doctors we talked to will gladly inspect medications to insure a patient's safety.

(Additionally, we know of some doctors in our area who hand out the free samples they receive from drug companies to their elderly patients. Many of these cash-strapped patients stop into several doctor's office each week to see if the doctor has any samples. It is not the most reliable method in getting your full dosage of necessary medications, but it may help tide you over in between prescription deliveries).

Most importantly, if you have any questions or concerns about a medication, get them answered before taking it! The pharmacies we listed above are reputable and can answer most of the questions you have and provide most of the assurances you need. But if you select a different Canadian pharmacy, be sure you know their physical address, telephone number and licensing information before placing an order.

Other considerations:

- Prescription medications are usually non returnable.
- Like American pharmacies, Canadian and overseas pharmacies will often try to sell generic medications unless you specifically state you want the name brand medication. Generics, however, always contain the same active ingredients and work in the same manner as the name brand medications, and usually offer the consumer even greater savings.
- When ordering drugs from Canada online, make sure the pharmacy displays a seal from CIPARx on its Web site. This is a trade agency which certifies Canadian pharmacies. The red and white logo will say "Certified Canadian International Pharmacy."

More information, including steps consumers should take to safely order drugs from Canada, can be found at http://www.ciparx.ca/consumer_info.html.

THE GOVERNMENT'S NEW DRUG PLAN FOR SENIORS AND PEOPLE WITH DISABILITIES

Leave it to the federal government to make something as simple as saving an average of 10 to 15 percent on prescription medications a big ball of red tape.

Cutting through all of the red tape may be a worthwhile pursuit – a June 2004 study found that Medicare beneficiaries taking medications for nine common health conditions showed savings ranging from 10 to 75 percent. The study by the independent consulting firm CMS also found that beneficiaries did not need to enroll in the program offering the biggest discount to achieve savings between five and 65 percent.

The government began making the cards available in May 2004. Some cards could only be used in certain pharmacies, and the amount of the discount varied from card to card, but generally averaged between 10 and 15 percent. Annual fees were as high as $30 depending on which discount drug card you selected, but in most cases the fees were waived for people below certain income levels.

But one study found savings as high as 75 percent on certain drugs, depending on the geographic area and discount card used:

Sample Savings In The CMS Study

Condition to be treated	Location of Treatment	Prescription Medication	Average National Monthly Price	Best Discount Card Price	Savings
Acid Refluc	Boston	Aciphex, 20mg/day	$135.90	$109.93	19.1%
Congestive Heart Failure	Louisville	Metoprolol, 200mg/day	$24.60	$7/19	70.8%
Diabetes	Cleveland	Metformin, 850mg, twice per day	$38.70	$15.54	59.8%
Hypercholesterolemia	Pittsburgh	Zocor, 40 mg/day	$136.20	$44.80	32.9%
Hypertension	Portland, Ore.	Enalapril, 20mg/day	$24.30	$6.10	74.9%

Prices based on data collected at June 14, 2004.

It's important to note that a drug you take now may not be discounted on all cards. It's also important to know that you do not have to take a card if you do not want one. Not taking a card will have no impact on your Medicare benefits.

All cards have a "Medicare Approved" seal printed on the card. Unfortunately, there are already reports of people selling fake Medicare discount cards. The seal will look like this:

Many Medicare recipients received mailings or saw print and television commercials beginning in April that were designed to alert them to the program. Complete information about the discount cards available in your area can be obtained by calling 800-633-4227 (TTY: 887-486-2408).

Choosing The Right Medicare-Approved Discount Drug Card

Depending on where you live, you may have just a few choices to several different options when it comes time to choose your Medicare-approved discount drug card. First, you need to find out which cards are available for you to use in your area. You can do this by logging on to www.medicare.gov and choosing "Prescription Drug and Other Assistance Programs," or by calling 800-633-4227 (TTY: 887-486-2408).

What follows is a revised work sheet that AARP has made available to its members to assist them in choosing the card that is right for them. Once you know what discount cards you can choose from, answer the following questions about each card:

1. Does this card provide discounts on each prescription drug I take? (Be aware that discount card companies can change what drugs they discount and the amount of the discounts at any time).
2. How much will this card charge me for each of my prescription drugs?
3. Does my pharmacy, or a pharmacy near my home, accept this card?
4. Can I use this card when I travel?
5. Can I use this card for mail-order prescriptions?
6. What is the annual enrollment fee?

All of this information is available directly from Medicare, or by calling the discount drug card company. The company may mail you the information or, if you have Internet access, refer you to its Web site.

Next, narrow the list of discount card providers to three, and use the grid on the next page to help you make your final selection:
(See next page)

What Happens After January 1, 2006

After January 1, 2006, the new plan means you:

- pay an estimated premium of $35 per month or $420 a year
- you have an annual deductible of $250, which means you pay the first $250 a year on your prescriptions
- you then pay only 25% of the next $2,000 worth of drugs, which means you pay $500 and the government pays $1,500

Drugs

Name of Drug *(include strength and amount, i.e. Lipitor, 20 mg, 30 tablets)*	What I pay monthly for the drug *(including current discounts)*	Discount Card #1	Discount Card #2	Discount Card #3
	$	$	$	$
	$	$	$	$
	$	$	$	$
	$	$	$	$
	$	$	$	$
	$	$	$	$
	$	$	$	$
	$	$	$	$
Total Monthly Cost	$	$	$	$
Does this card give discounts for all of my prescriptions?				
Where can I use this card – which pharmacies, mail order, what states?				

Copy this worksheet if you need more space.

- you then pay 100% of the next $2,850 you spend on drugs
- you are now up to spending $3,600 a year on drugs. After that, the government pays for everything except a 5% co pay, or $2 for generic drugs and $5 on brand names, whichever is greater

So is the program right for you? See the next page for a chart of what will happen if you enroll in the program that takes effect January 1, 2006. Congress is still working out the details of the second stage of the plan and how it will work, so the numbers in the chart are subject to change.

	If you spend $500/year on prescription drugs	If you spend $1,000/year on prescription drugs	If you spend $2,000/year on prescription drugs	If you spend $3,000/year on prescription drugs	If you spend $5,000/year on prescription drugs
Estimated fees for year	$420	$420	$420	$420	$420
Cost to you for first $250 spent on prescription drugs	$250	$250	$250	$250	$250
Cost to you for up to the next $2,000 spent on drugs	$62.50	$187.50	$437.50	$500	$500
Cost to you for up to the next $1,350 spent on drugs	N/A	N/A	N/A	$750	$1,350
Cost to you for prescription drugs costs beyond $3,650	N/A	N/A	N/A	N/A	$70 (5% copay)
Total out-of-pocket cost to you	$732.50	$857.50	$1,107.50	$1,920.00	$2,170.00
You save (lose)	**($232.50)**	**$142.50**	**$892.50**	**$1,080.00**	**$2,830.00**

If you choose not to enroll, but later change your mind, their may be a penalty for signing up late. An extra 1% of the national average premium for each month you delay. The enrollment period for incurring no penalty is between November 15, 2005 and May 15, 2006. For those not already on Medicare, you are eligible to join when you sign up for Medicare. If you are already receiving drug coverage, check with your policy to see what changes they may or have done since the Medicare drug program came into effect. You need to decide if your coverage is better or worse with Medicare. You must do the same if you have a Medigap plan that includes prescription drugs. You can change your enrollment during the open enrollment period which is November 15th through December 31 each year. Your Medicare prescription drug plan will begin January 1 of the following year if you enroll them.

Extra $2,100 In Help For People With Limited Income

If your resources are less than $11,500 (single) or $23,000 (married), you may qualify for extra help paying for Medicare Prescription Drug Coverage. You may be able to get help to pay for the premiums, annual deductible, and co-payments related to the new Medicare Prescription Drug Program. If you haven't received an application or information about the extra help you can apply online at https://s044a90.ssa.gov/apps6z/i1020/main.html or by contacting Social Security at 800-772-1213. You are automatically eligible if you receive Supplemental Security Income, if you receive Medicaid with prescription drug coverage; or if your state pays for your Medicare premiums.

Where To Go For Help

There are several places you can go for more information on the Medicare discount drug programs.

- Call Medicare at 800-633-4227 (TTY/TDD 877-486-2048) or visit them on the Web at www.medicare.gov.

- AARP offers a wealth of information on prescription drugs at www.aarp.org/prescriptiondrugs or by calling 888-687-2277 (TTY 877-434-7598).

- The National Council on Aging offers a Web site that will tell you what other benefits are available in your area and how to apply after answering a few simple questions online. Visit their Web site at www.benefitscheckup.org for more information.

- In addition, your State Health Insurance Assistance Program (SHIP), and other local and community-based organizations will also provide you with free health insurance counseling. To locate these services you can contact the Eldercare Locator at 800-677-1116; www.eldercare.gov

Your elected representatives are in the business of seeing how they can help you locate money, services or anything else you need. They all have people on their staff whose job it is to do just that for voters. This is why politicians are always getting re-elected. If they do a favor for you, you will vote for them forever, no matter what they do. You will also tell your friends, your family and most people you meet. This is why over 95% of incumbents who run again get reelected.

- You have 1 congressman and 2 senators at the federal level. You can contact all 3.
- You have more than one elected official in your state capital.
- You also have an elected representative at your city and county level.

Contact them all. They are all getting a government salary to help you and they all have access to different resources. The worst that can happen is that more than one person solves your problem. If you need help finding them go to www.congress.org or your local library.

Your elected officials are also very important people to use when you are having a problem with a government office. They can call the back office of any government office and get your problem resolved immediately. Government officials want to please elected officials because they are the ones that give them money to survive. The Legislative branch, the elected officials, votes every year on how much money each government agency should get. So all government agencies want these elected officials to be happy. And the elected officials want you to be happy because you have a vote that can keep their job.

Legal

Free Legal Services

DID YOU KNOW THAT THE GOVERNMENT WILL FIGHT FOR YOU FOR FREE? Our government offers a great benefit to every consumer that has a problem with any company, organization or professional. Government offices regulate them all and if you find that office, they will investigate your problem and get you justice for free. And the greatest thing about using the government is not that they are free, but they are more powerful than any lawyer you can ever dream of hiring, even Johnny Cochran.

For example, if your insurance company does not pay a claim, you can call the company and they will tell you about some bureaucratic rule about why they won't pay you. So what to you do? Don't hire an attorney to fight that insurance company, because the insurance company's attorneys are better than your attorney at fighting claims, and the insurance company has very little to lose if they fight you. The worst they can lose is your business, which they probably lost already. Or they can lose by having to pay what they owe you anyway. So they are willing to fight you all day while you are being charged big lawyer fees.

But if you contact the government office that regulates insurance companies (your state insurance commissioner's office), they will contact your insurance company for you, even if you are wrong. Now the insurance company has an entirely new problem. The insurance commissioner allows the insurance company to do business in the state, so if they really do something wrong in dealing with the commissioner, they can lose ALL OF THEIR BUSINESS, not just your business. Plus, the insurance company knows it costs a lot of money just to communicate back and forth with a government agency and it could be a lot cheaper just to give you what you want. You now have the power, so use it.

1. ***Help Finding Who Regulates Any Company With Whom You Are Having Trouble***
   Most organizations and professionals are regulated at the state level including: insurance companies, credit card companies, banks, mail order companies, retail companies, contractors, doctors, and even lawyers. To find what office regulates your problem, contact your state capitol operator in your state capitol by calling 1-800-555-1212 and ask for the office that regulates the company that is causing you grief. Or go to www.govengine.com and search under your state. Your state Attorney General's office can always direct you to the appropriate office.

2. ***Your State Agency On Aging***
   The state Area Agencies on Aging will often act on your behalf to help you resolve problems that are special to older people. This could involve calling a nursing home, a bus company, or the Social Security Administration for you. And if the aging agencies can't solve the problems directly, they'll often refer you to the state or federal agency that can. For aging-related problems, the state Agencies on Aging are simply the best starting places. Contact Eldercare Locator at 800-677-1116; www.eldercare.gov.

3. ***To find free legal services***
   If a government office can't help, there are two places to contact when you need a lawyer, but can't afford one. The Legal Services Corporation provides free legal services to those that meet certain income requirements. If you exceed those limits, they may be able to refer you to some place for more help. They have offices throughout the country. Legal Services Corporation, 3333 K St., NW, 3rd Floor, Washington, DC 20009; 202-295-1500; www.lsc.gov. Many lawyers work pro bono depending upon your situation. Contact your state bar association to see if someone there can help. You can contact your state capitol operator by calling 411, or the American Bar Association, 321 N. Clark St., Chicago, IL 60610; 312-988-5000; www.abanet.org/soc/probono/pip.html.

4. ***Help From Your Elected Officials***
   People forget that they can turn to their congressman and senators when they are at a loss for help. Each office has a case manager who can direct you to the appropriate person or office for help in resolving your complaint. You can contact your state representative or senator by contacting your state capitol operator at 411 or online at www.govengine.com. You can contact your representative and senators in Congress by calling U.S. House of Representatives, Washington, DC 20515; 202-224-3121; www.house.gov or U.S. Senate, Washington, DC 20510; 202-224-3121; www.senate.gov.

$2,500 For Being A Victim Of A Crime

When you were mugged, your front teeth were knocked out and you don't have the money to get them fixed. Or a member of your family was killed while your house was being burglarized, and you need help paying for the funeral. Or a family member was raped, but you don't have money for the therapy she needs to help her recover. Contact your state capitol operator in your state capitol by calling 1-800-555-1212 and ask for your state's Crime Victims Compensation Board or go to http://ovc.ncjrs.org/findvictimservices/ to find a local office.

Turning in Counterfeit Products Can Get You a $250,000

If you buy Gucci ice skates only to later discover that Gucci doesn't make ice skates, especially ones made in Peru. Or instead of admiring your new designer jeans, your friend points out that your "Calvin Klein" label reads "Kalvin Cline." Or you discover that your expensive Seiko watch is actually a "Sieko." Or you suspect a business in your community is putting designer labels on low quality goods so that they can sell them at premium prices. Or a business competitor is intentionally undervaluing a product he is importing to avoid paying duty charges. Contact: U.S. Customs Service, Fraud Division, 1300 Pennsylvania Ave., NW, Washington, DC 10119; 800-BE-ALERT or 202-927-1510; www.customs.treas.gov.

Heavy Thumbs At Your Delicatessen

If your local deli sells you a pound of ham that you later discover is only three quarters of a pound. Or your two pounds of sausage you bought at the supermarket turns out to be only a pound and a half. Or the scales in the produce department at your local market are falling apart but used anyway. Contact your state capitol operator in your state capitol by calling 1-800-555-1212 and ask for your state's office of Weights and Measures or go to www.govengine.com and search for Weights and Measures under your state.

Make $500 From Unwanted Faxes

The Telephone Consumer Protection Act of 1991 and the Federal Communications Commission Rules prohibit sending unsolicited advertisements to a fax machine without the recipient's prior express permission or unless the sender has an established business relationship with the recipient. The prohibition applies to fax machines at both businesses and residences. You can recover the actual monetary loss that resulted from the violation or receive up to $500 in damages for each violation, whichever is greater. Contact: Federal Communications Commission, Consumer & Government Affairs Bureau, Consumer Inquiries and Complaints Division, 45 12th st, NW, Washington, DC 20554; 1-888-225-5322; TTY 1-888-835-5322; www.fcc.gov/cgb/consumerfacts/unwantedfaxes.html.

Get $1,000 From Debt Collectors Who Don't Treat You Right

There is little incentive for debt collectors to follow the rules they have to follow. They can't give false information about you to anyone. They cannot threaten you or say you will be arrested, your wages or property will be attached or you will suffer a lawsuit. They cannot call you before 8am or after 9pm and there are ways to stop them from calling. For more information contact the U.S. Federal Trade Commission 1-877-FTC-HELP or go to www.ftc.gov/bcp/conline/pubs/credit/fdc.htm.

Satisfaction From Your Cable Company

As your local cable company gets more competitors it is becoming harder to find your local government regulator. Start by contact your local municipality (city, county, township) and ask for their cable commission. If that does not work, you can contact your state capitol operator in your state capitol by calling 1-800-555-1212 and ask for your state's office of Consumer Protection or go to www.govengine.com and search for Consumer Protection under your state. And if none of these are helpful you can always go direct to the Federal Communications Commission at 1-888-CALL-FCC or at www.fcc.gov/mb/facts/complain.html.

Make $25,000 Turning in a Tax Cheat

You can actually make 15% of what the IRS recovers in back taxes up to $10 million dollars. The law states that this money is to be given to anyone who provides information that leads to the detection and punishment of anyone violating the Internal Revenue laws. Call the IRS Criminal Investigation Division at 1-800-829-0433 or go to www.irs.gov/pub/irs-pdf/p733.pdf.

A Special Fund When Your Lawyer Runs Off With Your Money

It is amazing that there is such a fund set up in every state to repay consumers when lawyers run off with their money. It's called Lawyers' Funds for Client Protection. If your lawyer runs off with your money call your state Bar Association located in your state capital to locate your fund or go to www.abanet.org/cpr/clientpro/cp-dir_fund.pdf.

Don't Let Airlines Lose Your Luggage or Bump You Unfairly

You can seek satisfaction if: you prepaid for a ticket but missed the flight because the airline overbooked it; the airline loses or damages your luggage; the Fight attendant was rude; or a flight delay causes you to miss a connecting flight. Contact: U.S. Department of Transportation, Office of Consumer

Affairs, C-75, Room 4107, Washington, DC 20590; 202-366-2220; http://airconsumer.ost.dot.gov/index.htm.

A Commodity Broker Mishandles Your Pork Belly Investments

If your broker was submitting reports to you that your account was losing money when in fact he was simply taking your money for himself and writing it off as market losses. Or to buy a new house in the Bahamas, your commodity broker skims off larger commissions than you agreed to. Or your broker makes several trades on your account just so he can make more commissions on the sales. Or your brokerage firm makes trades on your account that you didn't authorize. You can get justice by contacting: Commodity Futures Trading Commission, 3 Lafayette Center, 1155 21st St. NW, Washington, DC 20581; 202-418-5525; www.cftc.gov.

Make $250,000 For Squealing On A Drug Runner

If your neighbor in Miami receives late-night shipments on his dock from a boat with Panamanian markings. Or a neighbor farmer uses his fields as an airdrop for low-flying planes coming from the direction of Mexico. Or your neighbor works as a garbage collector but seems to take a lot of trips out of the country and buy expensive cars and boats. For a reward contact: U.S. Customs Service, Fraud Division, 1300 Pennsylvania Ave. NW, Washington, DC 20229; 800-BE-ALERT; 202-923-1510; www.customs.treas.gov.

When There Is Something Fishy About Your Seafood

If a can of tuna you opened has bones in it. Or the processed lobster substitute you bought smells like beef. Or the clam chowder you bought has half an inch of sand on the bottom of the can. Contact: National Marine Fisheries Service, National Oceanic and Atmospheric Administration, U.S. Department of Commerce, 1335 East-West Hwy, Room 6142, Silver Spring, MD 20910; 301-713-2239; www.nmfs.noaa.gov.

Funeral Homes

If a funeral home won't give you the price of their caskets and services over the telephone. Or a mortician tells you that by law your deceased grandmother must be embalmed. Or an undertaker tells you that you must purchase a regular casket for you dearly departed aunt, even though she will be cremated. Contact Federal Trade Commission, Bureau of Consumer Protection, Division of Marketing Practices, Room 238, Washington, DC 20580; 877-FTC-HELP; 202-326-3128; www.ftc.gov. Or contact your state capitol operator in your state capitol by calling 1-800-555-1212 and ask for your state's office that regulates Funeral Homes or go to www.govengine.com and search for Funeral Homes under your state.

When Handicap Access Has Hurdles

If the restroom stalls in the building where you take adult education classes are too narrow to fit your wheelchair. Or there are no special handicap parking spaces at your local Small Business Administration Office. Or the building where you have to apply for Food Stamps doesn't have a wheelchair ramp. Contact: Architectural and Transportation Barriers Complaiance Board, 1331 F St NW, Room 1000, Washington, DC 20004; 800-USA-ABLE; 202-272-5434; TTY 202-272-5499; www.access-board.gov.

Lawyers That Give You The Legal Runaround

If your lawyer bills you for preparing a will that he won't let you see. Or because of a slip-up by your lawyer, you went to jail for a parking ticket. Or after you pay an expensive retainer to your lawyer, and she skips town. Contact your state capitol operator in your state capitol by calling 1-800-555-1212 and ask for your state's Attorney Grievance Office or to go www.govengine.com and search for Attorney Grievance under your state.

Ocean Cruises That Are Rough

If your cruise was canceled, but you weren't compensated. Or a cruise line won't sell you a ticket because of your handicap. Or your cabin was next to the boiler room. Or when you were introduced to the captain, he smelled of gin. Contact Federal Maritime Commission, 800 N Capitol St., Washington, DC 20573; 202-523-5807; www.fmc.gov.

Is Your Boss Messing With Your Pension Money?

If you think you've just been fired so that your boss won't have to pay your pension benefits. Or your boss says you can't join the company pension plan because you're too old. Or you leave your job before retirement age, but your former company won't give you the vested benefits you've accumulated. Or your spouse owes you thousands of dollars in unpaid child support, but his company refuses to allow money from his pension plan to be paid to you to cover what he owes you. Contact: Pension and Welfare Benefits Administration, U.S. Department of Labor, 200 Constitution Ave., Room N5658, Washington, DC 20210; 202-219-8776; www.dol.gov/dol/pwba.

Bad Food Or Service At Restaurants

If there's a fly in your soup. Or you notice that the cook at a restaurant leaves the restroom without washing his hands. Or the cashier who takes your money at a fast food restaurant also handles the food without first washing her hands. Contact your state capitol operator in your state capitol by calling 1-800-555-1212 and ask for your state's Health Department or go to www.govengine.com and search for Health Department under your state.

Telemarketing Scams

If you receive a telephone call congratulating you on winning a yacht. All you have to do is send $200 for shipping and handling charges. But all you receive is an inflatable raft with a leak in it. Or when you received your combination potato peeler/dog leash that you ordered over the phone, you didn't receive your free bonus gift they promised. Or you give the salesman who calls you on the phone your credit card number to reserve the free car you'd just won in a national survey. You never receive the car, and you've been billed for $1,000 on your card. Contact your state capitol operator in your state capitol by calling 1-800-555-1212 and ask for your state's office of Consumer Protection or go to www.govengine.com and search for Consumer Protection under your state.

Free Legal Hotline For Women's Rights

The Equal Rights Advocats' Advice and Counseling Hotline is here to help you understand your legal rights. Free, discreet, individualized advice is available on issues like Family and Medical Leave Laws, Equal Pay, Sexual Harassment and other work place issues buy contacting. The hotline is available on limited hours. Contact: Equal Rights Advocates, 1663 Mission Street, Suite 250, San Francisco, CA 94103; www.equalrights.org (check webstite for hotline hours before you call 1-800-839-4ERA).

Free Legal Help for People with Disabilities

The disability laws not only covers people with disabilities that everyone can see. It's also for children who aren't getting the education they need from the local school, or for the cancer patient who feels discriminated against at work. A free hotline will help you learn about your rights, help you enforce them, and will even handle some high impact legal cases. Contact Disability Rights Education and Defense Fund, Inc., 2212 Sixth Street, Berkeley, CA 94710; 510-644-2555 V/TTY; Fax: 510-841-8645; edf@dredf.org; www.dredf.org.

Free Legal Latino Help

The Mexican American Legal Defense and Educational Fund (MALDEF) is a national nonprofit organization whose mission is to protect and promote the civil rights of the more than 29 million Latinos living in the United States in the areas of education, employment, political access, and more. They take cases to court and provide other legal help for the Latino community. Contact MALDEF, 634 South Spring St., 11th Floor, Los Angeles, CA 90014; 213-629-2512; Fax: 213-629-0266; www.maldef.org.

Free Help with Housing Discrimination

Buying your first home is a very exciting time. But for many, house shopping is more than an eye opening experience. Some people are not shown houses in particular neighborhoods or are denied a home because of their sex, race, or living arrangement. If you feel you have been treated unfairly, contact Office of Fair Housing and Equal Opportunity, U.S. Department of Housing and Urban Development, 451 7th St., SW, Room 5100, Washington, DC 20410; 202-708-4252; 800-669-9777; www.hud.gov.

Discrimination Because You're a Woman, Pregnant, Person of Color, etc.

There's no need to take harassment or bullying on the job. Here is your chance to fight back. If you believe you have been discriminated against by an employer, labor union, or employment agency when applying for a job or while on the job because of race, color, sex, religion, national origin, age, or disability, you may file a charge with the Equal Employment Opportunity Commission (EEOC). For more information, contact Equal Employment Opportunity Commission, 1801 L St., NW, Washington, DC 20507; 202-663-4900; 800-669-4000; www.eeoc.gov.

Free Help in Writing a Will

Estate planning is not something that people often relish doing, but it is extremely important. It is difficult enough when a loved one dies, but then to have to search through papers trying to find information about insurance, or investments is often too much. When children are involved, estate planning is essential. Who will take care of the children and how can you secure their financial future? Your local Cooperative Extension Service often offers classes or publications on estate planning. The time to plan ahead is now. Look in the blue pages of your phone book for the nearest Cooperative Extension office, as they are in almost every county across the country.

Fight Retailers, Mail Order Companies, Auto Dealers, Contractors, etc.

You go to a store to get the best price on the gift for Uncle George, only to learn that the store is out of stock despite the product being advertised in the paper. Did the salesman try to get you to buy a higher priced item? You could be the victim of the old bait and switch scam. Is the paint peeling off of the new toy doll you bought your daughter? Problems dealing with your car dealership or car repair shop? What about the contractor that has yet to finish the job? There are ways to deal with all these problems and get them resolved to your satisfaction. You just need to pull in the big guns. Attorney General's Offices have Consumer Protection Offices, and many also have separate offices that handle only car complaints. They will take your complaint and try to help you get the satisfaction you deserve. For other problems contact:

Defective Products — contact Consumer Product Safety Commission, Washington, DC 20207-0001; 800-638-2772; www.cpsc.gov.

Contractor or Licensed Professional Problems — contact the state Licensing Board for the profession located in your state capitol. You can contact the state operator for assistance in finding the office.

Mail Order Problems — contact the U.S. Postal Service, Public Affairs Branch, 475 L'Enfant Plaza, SW, Room 3140, Washington, DC 202060; 202-268-5400; www.usps.gov.

Fraud Issues — contact Federal Trade Commission, Public Reference, 600 Pennsylvania Ave., Washington, DC 20580; 202-382-4357, 877-FTC-HELP; www.ftc.gov.

Free Help Fighting an Electric Bill or Stopping a Turn Off

The state utility commissions can help you fight high gas or electric bills. Some will even come out and make sure that your meter is not over charging you. They don't have money to pay for your bills, but they can negotiate payment arrangements with the company for you or suggest nonprofit organizations that may have emergency funds to help. For example, Maryland suggests the Fuel Fund for Central Maryland or the Maryland Energy Assistance program. The office can also force the utility not to cut off your service because of medical emergencies or cold weather. Contact your state utility commission listed in the blue pages of your phone book for further assistance.

Free Legal Help to Fight Car Dealers and Repair Shops

When you can't get satisfaction from the manager or owner, then it is time to bring in the big guns:

- Your state attorney general's office is set up to handle automobile complaints. Sometimes all you have to do is send a letter to the attorney general with a copy to the business owner.
- Automotive Consumer Action Program (AUTOCAP) is a complaint handling system sponsored by the automobile industry for new or used car purchases from NEW car dealers only. Contact National Automobile Dealers Association, 8400 Westpark Drive, McLean, VA 22102; 703-821-7000; www.nada.org/
- Better Business Bureau (BBB) Auto Line is a FREE, out-of-court arbitration program, paid for by the business community to handle automobile complaints between consumers and most auto manufacturers. Contact your local Better Business Bureau or BBB Auto Line, Dispute Resolution Division, Council of Better Business Bureaus, Inc., 4200 Wilson Blvd, Suite 800, Arlington, VA 22203-1838; 703-276-0100; www.bbb.org/complaints.asp

Pension Help

The Pension Rights Center is dedicated to helping Americans pension's rights. If you are having trouble with your pension plan contact them for some guidance. Contact: Pension Rights Center, 1350 Connecticut Avenue, NW, Suite 206, Washington, DC 20036; Email: pensionhelp@pensionrights.org; www.pensionrights.org.

Retirement Plans, Benefits & Savings

The Department of Labor offers consumer information to retirement plan participant's information about their rights. They offer general and specific information including rights, plans and compliance issues. Check out the web site for a wealth of information. Contact: U.S. Department of Labor, Frances Perkins Building, 200 Constitution Avenue, NW, Washington, DC 20210; 866-4-USA-DOL; www.dol.gov/dol/topic/retirement/consumerinfpension.htm.

Pension Guaranty Program

What happens if the company you've worked for private-sector pension plan runs out of money before you've gotten your fair share? The Pension Benefit Guaranty Corporation (PBGC) is a federal agency that insures that you will receive your benefit up to the limits of the law. The agency insures defined benefit plans not defined contribution plans. To read more about this program you can view their publication *Your Guaranteed Pension* at the web site below or write for your copy. You can also search the website to see if there is a pension that you are owed. Contact: Pension Benefit Guaranty Corporation, Communications and Public Affairs Department, 1200 K Street NW, Suite 240, Washington, DC 20005-4026; 800-400-7242; www.pbgc.gov/publications/YGPTEXT.HTM#what.

Consumer Information

The Federal Trade Commission provides consumers a wealth of information about money issues. They offer free publications that you can view online or order by contacting the FTC. The publications cover many consumer topics including: scams, identity theft, investments, credit and much more. Federal Trade Commission, 600 Pennsylvania Avenue, NW, Washington, DC 20580; 202-326-2222, 877-FTC-HELP; www.ftc.gov/ftc/consumer.htm.

Lawyers Who Look After You

The mission of the American Bar Association Commission on Law and Aging is to strengthen and secure the legal rights, dignity, autonomy, quality of life, and quality of care of elders. It does this through education, training, advocacy, policy development, research, and technical assistance. The commission is made up of 15 experts in law and aging; including judges, lawyers, health and social services professionals, advocates and academics. They deal with a wide range of elder legal issues such as health and long term care, legal services to older persons, housing needs, court related needs of older persons with disabilities, dispute resolution, professional ethical issues, pain management and end of life care, health care decision making, guardianship, Medicare and Medicaid. They have brochures available online that cover many topics including; Legal Guide for Older Americans, Law and Aging Resource Guide, and Health Care Decision Making. For more information on how they can help you contact the American Bar Association Commission on Law and Aging, 740 15th St., NW, Washington, DC 20005-1019; 202-662-1000; www.abanet.org/aging/home.html.

Need help solving a problem?

If you need help to solve a problem with a consumer good or service, try visiting the Federal Citizen Information Center's Consumer Action Website. It has information on many consumer topics such as general buying tips, shopping from home, telemarketing and Spam, how to protect your identity and privacy, how to resolve a consumer problem, how to write a complaint letter and much, much more. They provide contact information for major corporations, state resources, consumer organizations and the Better Business Bureau. There is also a Consumer Action Handbook that can be viewed online. For more information go to www.consumeraction.gov.

Take The Power Into Your Own Hands

If you feel like you have been ripped off, Take Action! The Free Consumer Action Handbook from the Federal Citizen Information Center can help you with your consumer problems or complaints. The Handbook is an easy to read guide that offers general buying tips and ways to resolve marketplace problems. It has helpful hints on how to complain, and not only tells you how and where to complain, but also explains how to write an effective letter of complaint and includes a sample letter. The Handbook contains lists of federal, state and local government offices that deal with consumer related issues, Better Business Bureaus, corporate consumer affairs offices, trade associations, and national consumer organizations. It also addresses many specific consumer topics such as credit, food and nutrition, investing, internet service providers and many more. You can order your free copy online at www.consumeraction.gov, by calling 888-878-3256, or by sending your name and address to Handbook, Pueblo, CO 81009.

H.E.L.P. for Seniors

Helping People Meet Aging Related Legal and Care Challenges (H.E.L.P.) is a nonprofit, community funded, information resource for Older Americans. They provide planning and problem solving services and information on care related, legal and governmental programs that concern seniors. All of H.E.L.P.'s services are free or low cost. In their community, they offer "Senior Law School" classes and conduct private consultations, but their Resource Center provides Email, telephone and written information as well as referral information to anyone who asks. The H.E.L.P. website contains information and helpful tips for Seniors in various categories such as financial, legal, care, end-of-life, consumer, medical, and general information. Some of the information is California specific, but much of it is useful to Seniors everywhere. All H.E.L.P. publications are available free online at the H.E.L.P. website. H.E.L.P. is HERE is a quarterly mini magazine that provides current information on government programs, legal and care related issues, and valuable services for seniors. Some of their pamphlets include Who will Control My Care?, Your Wishes on Funeral and Burial Arrangements, Checklist: Things to Do When a Person Dies, Power of Attorney for Health Care , Annuities and Older Adults, Help for the Exhausted Care Giver, and Driving and Older Adults. For more information contact H.E.L.P., 1404 Cravens Avenue, Torrance, CA 90501-1996' 310-533-1996, Fax: 310-533-1949; www.help4srs.org.

Government's Consumer Watchdogs

The Federal Trade Commission deals with many consumer protection matters that relate to seniors. Their Consumer Response Center handles a variety of information regarding credit reports, debt collection, buying and working at home, investment fraud, tele-marketing, the internet and e-commerce. They can help you get a free Annual Credit Report, minimize your risk for identity theft or help you report a case of identity theft, and tell you how to get on the National "Do Not Call" Registry. The FTC believes education is an important tool for consumer protection. They have hundreds of publications with advice on avoiding scams and rip-offs as well as informative tips on many other consumer topics such as: Sound Advice on Hearing Aids; Funerals: A Consumer Guide; Living Trust Offers; ID Theft: What's it All About?; Helping Older Consumers Avoid Charity Fraud; No Need to Pay for Information on Free (or low cost) Drugs; Getting Credit When You're Over 62; Aging Parents and Adult Children Together; Generic Drugs: Saving Money at the Pharmacy; and Dialing Up to the Internet: How to Stay Safe Online. All these publications and many more are free to view on their website at www.ftc.gov/ftc/consumer.htm or can be ordered by calling 877-FTC-HELP. For more information on how the Federal Trade Commission can be of assistance to you contact Federal Trade Commission, Consumer response Center, 600 Pennsylvania Ave., NW, H-130, Washington, DC 20580; 877-FTC-HELP, Fax: 703-739-0991; Email: publications@ftc.gov.

Clearinghouse on Abuse

The Clearinghouse on Abuse and Neglect of the Elderly (CANE) is the nation's largest collection of published research, training resources, government documents, and other sources of information on elder abuse. Funded by the National Center on Elder Abuse and located at the University of Delaware, the collection is completely computerized. Documents include such topics as: The Scope of Elder Abuse; Addressing the Needs of Older Battered Women, With Special Emphasis on Intimate Partner Violence; Financial Abuse, Undue Influence, Scams, Frauds, and Protection of Assets; as well as many, many more topics. For more information contact the University of Delaware, Department of Consumer Studies, Alison Hall West, Room 211, Newark, DE 19716; 302-831-3525; Email: CANE-UD@udel.edu.

Elder Abuse Center

The National Center on Elder Abuse is a national resource on Elder Rights for researchers, the public, legal professionals, law enforcement, and public policy leaders. Its mission is to promote action, understanding, and knowledge sharing on elder abuse, neglect and exploitation. The Center provides available news and resources; collaborates on research; provides consultation, education and training; identifies and provides information about promising practices and interventions; answers inquiries and requests for information; operates a listserve forum for professionals; and advises on policy and program development. For more information contact: National Center on Elder Abuse, 1201 15th Street, NW, Suite 350, Washington, DC 20005; 202-898-2586; Fax: 202-898-2583; www.elderabusecenter.org or call the Nationwide toll free Eldercare Locator number 800-677-1116 to get help, support, and resources.

Free Legal Help with Family Law, Grandparent Visitation, Wills and Life Planning, Health Care, and Senior Issues.

Legal Services Corporation is a collection of over 207 government supported local offices that provide free legal services in their area. Over 5000 attorneys and paralegals are available to help seniors with their legal problems. Preference is given to those seniors in social and/or economic need. Legal Services Corporations do not handle criminal issues, personal injury cases, or other cases for money damages. Services vary by location but in general they can help you with Housing, Consumer Issues, Wills and Life Planning, Health Care, Social Security, Nursing Home and Long Term Care, Grandparent Visitation, Family Law, Guardianship, and Elder Abuse. To find an office near you contact Legal Services Corporation, 3333 K Street, NW, 3rd Floor, Washington, DC 20007; 202-295-1500; Fax: 202-337-6797; Email: info@lsc.gov ; www.lsc.gov.

Free Legal Assistance for Domestic Violence Problems

Seven days a week, 24 hours a day, you can call the National Domestic Violence Hotline and not only get access to sources that will solve your immediate problem, but also get information and resources in your area that can explain your legal options and get you through the legal process. For more information contact National Domestic Violence Hotline, P.O. Box 16180, Austin, TX 78716; 800-799-SAFE; TTY: 800-787-3224; Email: ndvh@ndvh.org; www.ndvh.org.

Help for Veterans Fighting for Benefits

Through low cost publications, training courses, and other services, for 25 years the National Veterans Legal Services Program has been helping veterans get their due. Current publications include VA Claims, Agent Orange, Veterans Family Benefits, Veterans Benefits Manual, The Veteran's Advocate, Basic Training Correspondence Course, and other self help guides. Contact: National Veterans Legal Services Program, P.O. Box 753, Waldorf, MD 20604-0753; 301-638-1327; Fax: 301-843-0159; www.nvlsp.org.

Free Lawyers Will Fight for Your Rights

We've all heard of the American Civil Liberties Union (ACLU). If you feel that your civil liberties have been violated, they may take your case. They have over 300 offices around the country and handle around 6,000 cases a year. The ACLU has more than 60 staff attorneys who collaborate with at least 2,000 volunteer attorneys in handling cases. They have appeared before the Supreme Court more than any other organization except the U.S. Department of Justice. The kinds of issues they are most active in include: woman's rights, workplace rights, AIDS, arts censorship, capital punishment, education reform, lesbian and gay rights, national security, privacy and technology, voting rights and prisoners' rights. For more information contact the local ACLU office listed in your telephone directory or contact the main office at: American Civil Liberties Union, 125 Broad Street, 18th Floor, New York, NY 10004-2454; 888-567-ACLU; 212-549-2500 www.aclu.org.

Free Legal Help with Civil Liberties and Religious Freedom

The Rutherford Institute defends people who have been denied civil and human rights without charging them for such services. The issues they cover include civil liberties, religious freedom, parental rights, and sexual harassment. You may remember them from their involvement in the Paula Jones case. If you need legal help contact: The Rutherford Institute, Legal Department, P.O. Box 7482, Charlottesville, VA 22906-7482; 434-978-3888; Fax: 434-989-1789; www.rutherford.org.

Legal Help at a 75% Discount

The only things a paralegal can't do that a lawyer can, is give legal advice and represent you in court. That means they can file uncontested divorce papers, family court petitions, wills and probate, power of attorney, bankruptcy etc. There are states where paralegals can represent clients in cases like those involving evictions or government agencies. And if you are seeking a legal opinion from an attorney, you may want to get a paralegal to research the law for you so that you can make your own decision. Remember 50% of all lawyers lose their cases in court. So why pay $200 or more an hour for a lawyer, when you can get a lot of the same services done for less than $50 an hour. Many paralegal associations also perform pro bono work. For example, the New

Orleans Paralegal Association's Pro Bono Project has an Elderly Advocacy clinic, a Homeless Advocacy clinic, a Succession clinic, and a Divorce clinic. The Rocky Mountain Paralegal Association sponsors a "Wills on Wheels" program where seniors with modest, uncomplicated estates can get a will or living will prepared. Paralegals are listed in the yellow pages, or you can contact the national association for information on a state or local paralegal association near you. Contact: National Federation of Paralegal associations, 2517 Eastlake Avenue E., Suite 200, Seattle, WA 98162; 206-652-4120;fax: 206-652-4122; Email: info@paralegals.org; www.paralegals.org.

Calling Before You Face A Recall

If you have a car where the breaks don't work properly, or the seat belts in your new car lock closed, making you a prisoner in your own car. Or if your airbag in your new car opens when you merely apply the brakes, contact the NHTSA. If they think there's a possibility of a safety-related defect in a car's design, they'll ask the manufacturer for information related to the problem. After analyzing the data, the NHTSA may ask the manufacturer to conduct a voluntary recall. If the manufacturer refuses, the NHTSA may further investigate the problem, and if they determine that a recall is in fact required, they may order the manufacturer to conduct a recall to fix the defect. Contact: Office of Defects Investigation (NEF-10), National Highway Traffic Safety Administration, U.S. Department of Transportation, 400 7th St. SW Room 5319, Washington, DC 20590; 202-366-0123; 800-424-9393; www.nhtfa.dot.gov.

Where To Go When Your Banker Gives You The Run-Around

If you are unhappy with what you see on your monthly credit card bill, or your bank won't give you a car loan because you are divorced even though you have a good credit and a good job. Or the annual percentage rate on your mortgage unexpectedly rises though your mortgage contract says that it should remain the same. Then you have a legitimate complaint and can contact one of the following to get satisfaction. Each of the organizations below regulate a separate institutions. If you contact the wrong office any of them can direct you to where you need to be.

For National Banks contact: Comptroller of the Currency, Compliance Management, U.S. Department of the Treasury, 250 W St., SE, Washington, DC 20219; 202-874-5000; www.occ.treas.gov

For Savings & Loans contact: Office of Thrift Supervision, U.S. Department of the Treasury, 1700 G St., NW, Washington, DC 20552; 202-906-6000; www.ots.treas.gov

For State Regulated Banks contact: Contact your state capitol operator in your state by calling 1-800-555-1212 and ask for your state's Banking Authority or go to www.govengine.com and search for Banking Authority under your state.

For FDIC-Insured Institutions contact:: Federal Deposit Insurance Corporation, Office of Consumer Affairs, 550 17th St., NW, Room F-130, Washington, DC 20429; 800-759-6596; 877-275-3342; www.fdic.gov

Bad Barbers, Hairdressers, And Manicurists:

If you ask your barber for just a trim, and you end up looking like Telly Savalas. Or your new perm curls your hair just the way you like it, but unfortunately also turns your hair green. Or the nail polish remover that your manicurist uses causes the skin on your fingers to peel. There is a special licensing office in your state capitol that allows them to do business in your state and will investigate their misdeeds. Contact your state capitol operator in your state capitol by calling 1-800-555-1212 and ask for your state's Licensing Authority or go to www.govengine.com and search for Licensing Authority under your state.

Dishonest Car Dealers

A new car dealer tries to sell you a rust warranty even though the manufacturer says it's unnecessary. A car dealer won't honor a warranty on your new car, or a dealer insists on charging you for repairs on your new car that you think are covered by your warranty, then contact your state Consumer Protection Office. They are set up to handle car dealer complaints. They get a lot of them. Contact your state capitol operator in your state capitol by calling 1-800-555-1212 and ask for your state's office of Consumer Protection or go to www.govengine.com and search for Consumer Protection under your state.

Annoying Chain Mail

You can get satisfaction if a letter you get tries to recruit you as part of a multi-level marketing plan that will reward you with big money for recruiting others like you. Or you receive a chain letter that includes a prayer, telling you to send it out to others or else you'll die a fiery death. Or you get a letter promising that if you send a dollar to everyone on a list, you'll get back ten times your investment. Contact the U.S. Postal Inspector Service, 475 L'Enfant Plaza, SW, Washington, DC 10160; 202-268-4267; or the Fraud Hotline at 800-654-8896 or your local postmaster. www.usps.gov.

Protecting Your Civil Rights

If someone threatens to harm you if you vote in a local election. Or maybe the mayor of your town won't allow your group to peacefully demonstrate because he doesn't agree with your point of view. Or a bank requires African-American loan applicants to obtain cosigners and then charges borrowers with cosigners higher interest rates. Or an individual isn't allowed to vote because he can't read or write. Contact: U.S. Commission on Civil Rights, 624 9th St. NW, Washington, DC 10425; 202-376-8513; 800-552-6843; www.usccr.gov.

When Cosmetics Are Not So Beautiful

If you lipstick burns your lips, a skin cream gives you a rash, or an eyeliner causes eye irritation, contact Food and Drug Administration, 5600 Fishers Lane, Rockville, MD 20857; 888-463-6332; 301-443-1240; www.fda.gov.

Door To Door Sales People

If a vacuum salesman pressures you into buying a top of the line model, but when you try to cancel the order the next day, he won't let you and threatens to take you to court if you try. Or you buy 5,000 dollars worth of aluminum from a door-to-door salesman, and when three weeks pass without hearing from him, you call the number on his calling card only to discover that it's a pay phone in the bus station. Contact U.S. Federal Trade Commission Enforcement Division, 6th and Pennsylvania Ave., NW Room 4631, Washington, DC 20580; 877-FTC-HELP; 202-326-2996; www.ftc.gov or contact your state capitol operator in your state capitol by calling 1-800-555-1212 and ask for your state's Consumer Protection Office or to go www.govengine.com.

Stop Your Wallet From Being Taken To The Dry Cleaners

If the sweater you dropped off to be dry cleaned comes back the size of a potholder, they charge you more than advertised, or you drop off a wool jacket to be dry cleaned, but the dry cleaner gives you a pair of wool pants instead. Contact your state capitol operator in your state capitol by calling 1-800-555-1212 and ask for your state's Licensing Board office or go to www.govengine.com and search for Licensing Board under your state.

False Advertising & Bait and Switch

If you buy an oven at a going-out-of-business sale only to discover that six months later the store is still in business. Or you go to a store advertising great savings on stereo equipment only to find that store has never sold the items at the non-sale price. Or an ad for low-priced lawn mowers lures you into a store where the salesman tells you they are temporarily out of stock of the lawn mower you want and then tries to sell you a higher priced one that can be delivered immediately. Or a fast food restaurant advertises that their food is wholesome and healthy for you and your kids. Contact: U.S. Federal Trade Commission, Bureau of Consumer Protection, 6th and Pennsylvania Ave., NW Room 466, Washington, DC 20580; 877-FTC-HELP. Or contact your state capitol operator in your state capitol by calling 1-800-555-1212 and ask for your state's office of Consumer Protection or go to www.govengine.com and search for Consumer Protection under your state.

Check If The FBI Has Files On You

If guys in cheap suits and dark sunglasses have been hanging out in your neighborhood ever since you sent the President a letter telling him that his dog is ugly. Or you think the FBI may be developing a file on you because of your environmental activism. Or when you get a copy of your FBI file, you read that it says you are a communist when in fact you are an anarchist. Contact: FBI Headquarters, Freedom of Information Request, 9th and Pennsylvania, Ave., NW, Washington, DC 20535; 202-324-5520; http://foia.fbi.gov.

When A Cord Of Firewood Isn't A Cord

The cord of firewood you buy from your local wood seller seem to noticeably change in size from one purchase to another. Or the wood seller you buy your wood from won't show you how he measures the wood into cords, so you can't tell if he's cheating you out of money. Contact your state capitol operator in your state capitol by calling 1-800-555-1212 and ask for your state's office of Weights and Measures or go to www.govengine.com and search for Weights and Measures under your state.

When Garnishment Of Wages Becomes A Problem

If you can't pay your rent because too much money is being garnished from your paychecks to pay off a bill you owe. Or your boss discovers that you are having your wages garnished and decides to fire you because you are bad for the company's image. Contact: Wage and Hour Division, Fair Labor Standards, U.S. Department of Labor, 200 Constitution Ave., NW, Room S3516, Washington, DC 20210; 866-4USWAGE; 202-693-0051; www.dol.gov/dol/esa .Or contact your state capitol operator in your state capitol by calling 1-800-555-1212 and ask for your state's Department of Labor or go to www.govengine.com and search for Department of Labor under your state.

Health And Safety Hazards At Work

If the repetitious work on the assembly line at work is causing chronic pain in your arms and hands. If you were fired because you pointed out health hazards on the job to your boss. If there is asbestos insulation falling from the ceiling above your desk at work. If your boss continues to make you use power tools with faulty wiring even after you've pointed it out to him. Contact: Office of Field Operations, Occupational Safety and Health Administration, U.S. Department of Labor, 200 Constitution Ave., NW Room N3613, Washington, DC 20210; 202-693-2000; www.osha.gov.

Health Clubs That Flatten Your Wallet

If you pay $500 for a membership to a health club but they close down the very next day. Or you buy a membership to a health club because they claimed they'd have an Olympic size swimming pool built within two months. Six months later, there's still no pool. Or that personal fitness trainer the health club promised you turns out to be the personal trainer for the other 500 members too and has no time for you. Contact your state capitol operator in your state capitol by calling 1-800-555-1212 and ask for your state's office of Consumer Protection or go to www.govengine.com and search for Consumer Protection under your state.

Home Improvement Contractors

If you have your house painted, but it begins to peel again after only two months. Or a contractor makes you put down a 50 percent deposit before he remodels your kitchen but never returns to do the work. Or the new addition you have put on your house has only half the square footage that the contractor said it would. Or ever since the plumber installed your new water heater, all the water in your house has been the color of rust. . Contact your state capitol operator in your state capitol by calling 1-800-555-1212 and ask for your state's Licensing Board or go to www.govengine.com and search for Licensing Board under your state.

Housing Discrimination

If a landlord doesn't rent an apartment to you because he's had bad experiences with other people who are Jewish. Or a landlord refuses to rent to you because he thinks divorced women are too much of a financial risk. Or you call about a house for sale, and the owner says it's still available. When you get there ten minutes later, and she sees that you are African-American she tells you that the house is already sold. Contact: Office of Investigation, U.S. Department of Housing and Urban Development, 451 7th St., SW, Room 5208, Washington, DC 20410; 800-669-9777; 202-708-0836; www.hud.gov/complaints/.

Insurance Companies that Mistreat You

If your insurance company cancels your car insurance without properly notifying you. Or your health insurance premium goes up after one year even though your broker said it would go down. Or an insurance company won't honor your claim for reasons you can't understand. Contact your state capitol operator in your state capitol by calling 1-800-555-1212 and ask for your state's Insurance Commissioner or go to www.govengine.com and search for the Insurance Commissioner under your state.

Did Your Land Purchase Turn Swampy

If you're interested in buying some undeveloped land by mail, but the real estate developer won't give you a property report before you make the purchase. Or within a week after signing a contract to buy some land in another state, you change your mind, but the company that sold you the property won't let you out of the contract. Or you buy some undeveloped land in another state with the understanding that within a year a golf course and marina would be built next to it, but a year later you still have a swamp as a neighbor. Contact Interstate Land Sales Registration Division, U.S. Department of Housing and Urban Development, 451 7th St., SW, Washington, DC 20410; 202-708-0502; www.hud.gov/complaints.

Job Discrimination

If a factory refuses to hire you because you have pre-school-age children, even though there is no such restriction for the male employees. Or the company you work for pays male packers 21 cents an hour more than the female workers because they say that the men can do things that the women can't, such as lifting and stacking cartons and using hand trucks. Or you take a leave of absence from your job because of health reasons but when you return, you are given a temporary position and denied the seniority you've accumulated. Contact: Equal Employment Opportunity Commission, 1400 L St. NW, Washington, DC 20005; 800-669-4000; 202-663-4900; www.eeoc.gov.

Bad Landlords

Your landlord won't return your security deposit and wouldn't give you a good reason why. Or you sign a lease stating that you can move in on the first of the month, but when you arrive, the previous tenants haven't moved out yet, and the landlord says you'll just have to wait a week. Or when you ask your landlord to fix a plumbing leak, he gives you thirty days to move out. Contact your state capitol operator in your state capitol by calling 1-800-555-1212 and ask for your state's Consumer Protection Office or go to www.govengine.com and search for Consumer Protection under your state.

Any Licensed Professionals From Acupuncturists To Veterinarians

If while treating you for back pain, your acupuncturist punctures your eardrum. Or all of the trees that your landscaper planted for you last month have died. Or the private detective you hired to follow your wife ended up having an affair with her and emptying your bank account. Or the mortician who handled your Aunt Zelda's funeral accidentally cremated her and then lost the ashes. Or after a taxidermist stuffed and mounted your dog, all of its hair fell out. Contact your state capitol operator in your state capitol by calling 1-800-555-1212 and ask for your state's Licensing Board or to go www.govengine.com and search for Licensing Board under your state.

Mail Schemes

If you send away $25 for a solar powered clothes dryer advertised in a magazine, but all you receive is 10 feet of rope and two nails. Or you send away $100 for a new cure for arthritis and get a bottle of rubbing alcohol in return. Or the "fine metallic etching" of a U.S. president that you sent $50 away for turns out to be a penny. Or you receive a sweepstakes notice in the mail that says if you send $100 for shipping costs you'll get a brand new car that you've won. You send the money, but no car arrives. Contact Postal Inspection Service,

U.S. Postal Service, 475 L'Enfant Plaza, SW, Washington, DC 20260; 800-654-8896; 202-268-4293; www.usps.gov.

Odometer Tampering

If you take that used car you bought with only 30,000 miles on it into a mechanic, he tells you there's no way the car has less than 90,000 miles on it. Or a car company disconnects the odometers on new cars and allows corporate executives to drive them. The company then reconnects the odometers and sells the cars as new. Or you buy a used car only to find that when you register it at the department of motor vehicles, it has less mileage on it now than it did when the previous owner registered it two years ago. Contact Odometer Fraud Staff, Office of Chief Counsel National Highway Traffic Safety Administration, U.S. Department of Transportation, 400 7th St., SW, Room 5219, Washington, DC 20590, 800-424-9393; 202-366-0123; www.nhtsa.dot.gov.

Political Broadcasting

If a TV station airs an editorial against a political candidate but doesn't offer the candidate an opportunity to respond. Or a radio station invites only pro-life advocates as guests on their talk shows. Or a TV station overcharges candidates for political commercials. Or a newspaper will print letters that support only one point of view concerning a pending piece of legislation on a gun law. Contact Federal Communications Commission, Political Programming, 2025 M St., NW, Room 8202, Washington, DC 20554; 888-CALL-FCC; www.fcc.gov.

Trouble With Your Congressman Or Senator

It you discover that the house of ill-repute that you frequent is run out of one of your U.S. Congressman's homes. Or a U.S. Senator makes huge cash deposits in a corporate account at the bank you work at. Or you discover that a U.S. Senator is paying his wife as a full-time member of his staff, even though she shows up for work only once a month. For Senators contact U.S. Senate Select Committee on Ethics, Hart Senate Office Bldg. Room SH-220, Washington, DC 20510; 202-224-2981; http//ethics.senate.gov. For Congressman (Representatives) contact U.S. House Committee on Standards of Official Conduct, HT2, U.S. Capitol, Washington, DC 20515; 202-225-7103; www.house.gov/ethics/.

Price Fixing

If a store tells you they won't sell you an item because they have an agreement with another store that only they can sell it in your area. Or you notice that the only two stores that sell an item have fixed the price to keep it artificially high. Or you're a furniture store owner, and the wholesale distributor that you buy your chairs from tells you to sell the chairs at a certain price and no lower or else they won't supply you with the chairs anymore. Contact Antitrust Division, U.S. Department of Justice, 10th & Constitution Ave., NW, Room 3103, Washington, DC 20530; 202-514-2401; www.usdoj.gov/atr/.

Unsafe Products

The paint on a toy doll is peeling off, and your kid eats it. You buy a new high chair that has sharp metal screws exposed that scratch your baby's legs. Or your new electric blender falls apart when you puree. Or a Halloween mask interferes with your child's breathing. Or the smoke detector you just bought won't go off even when you set fire to it. Or your son is injured when his all terrain vehicle flips over at a low speed. Contact Consumer Product Safety Commission, 5401 Westbard Ave., Washington, DC 20207; 800-638-8270; TDD 800-638-8270; www.cpsc.gov.

Radio And Television Broadcasts

If the DJ on the morning radio show uses language that you've seen only on the walls in public bathrooms. Or a TV show depicts graphic nudity on a late night broadcast. A local television station "forgets" to bleep out all the obscene language in a movie that they broadcast. Or a TV station airs a program with adult subject matter and language during a time when children are likely to be watching. Contact Federal Communications Commission, Mass Media Bureau, Enforcement Division, Complaints and Investigations Branch, 2025 M St., NW, Room 20554, Washington, DC 20554; 888-CALL-FCC; www.fcc.gov.

Real Estate Agents & Brokers

After buying a house, you discover that your real estate broker neglected to tell you that the house was going to be torn down to make way for the new interstate highway. Or your real estate agent charges you twice what you expected for his commission fee. Or you can't get the money from your escrow account released after the sale of a house falls through. Contact your state capitol operator in your state capitol by calling 1-800-555-1212 and ask for your state's Real Estate Commission's office or go to www.govengine.com and search for Real Estate Commission under your state.

Sexual Harassment At Work

If the men in your office continue to make sexually offensive comments to you, and when you report them to your boss, he says, "Boys will be boys," and tells you to just ignore them. Or your boss tells you that if you don't go along with her sexual advances, you'll lose your job, and when you don't, you do in fact get fired. Or men at the factory where you work hoot and yell sexually explicit comments at the women whenever they walk past them. Contact: Equal Employment Opportunity Commission, 1400 L St., NW, Washington, DC 20005; 800-669-4000; 202-663-4900; www.eeoc.gov.

Stockbrokers

If your stock broker sells you securities at a price far above the current market value. Or your broker skims off a larger commission from the sale of your stocks than what you had agreed to. Or your broker advises you to buy $10,000 in stock for a company that his brother owns, although he knows it is going out of business. Contact: Securities and Exchange Commission, Office of Consumer Affairs and Information Services, 450 5th St., NW, MS 2-6, Washington, DC 20549; 800-SEC-0330; 202-942-8088; www.sec.gov.

Tanning Salons and Devices

If an ad for a tanning lamp promises medical benefits such as reducing blood pressure, treating diabetes, improving your sex life, and promoting vitamin D production.
Or the timing device on a sun lamp in a tanning salon cannot be controlled by the customer. Or the tanning salon does not provide you with protective eye wear because they claim it is perfectly safe without using any. Contact Food and Drug Administration Center for Devices and Radiological Health Office of Compliance and Surveillance, (HSV-312), 1390 Piccard Dr., Rockville, MD 20850; 888-463-6332; 301-827-3009; www.fda.gov/cdrh/.

Taxi Cab Rates

If the cab you take home every day all of sudden starts costing you $1 more even though the rates haven't increased. Or the meter in your cab blinks on and off during your trip, and when you finally arrive, your fare is twice as much as it should be. Contact your state capitol operator in your state capitol by calling 1-800-555-1212 and ask for your state's office of Consumer Protection or office of Weights and Measures or go to www.govengine.com and search for Consumer Protection or Weights and Measures under your state.

Utility Companies: Gas, Electric Phone

If the electric company charged you twice for your hook up. Or your telephone company bills you for twenty calls to Alaska that you didn't make. Or you were without water for an entire week, but the water company still charged you the same monthly flat rate. Or your gas company sent you a notice that it's doubling your rate effective immediately. Contact your state capitol operator in your state capitol by calling 1-800-555-1212 and ask for your state's office of the Utilities Commission or go to www.govengine.com and search for Utilities Commission under your state.

Wages And Overtime Pay

If your boss pays you five cents less per hour than minimum wage because he says you don't work hard enough. Or as a waitress, you average more than minimum wage in tips, but your boss tells you that he'll pay you wages only when your tips fall below the minimum wage rate. Or your boss requires you to work overtime, but refuses to pay you time-and-a-half for the extra hours you put in. Contact: Wage and Hour Division, Fair labor Standards, U.S. Department of Labor, 200 Constitution Ave., NW, Room S3502, Washington, DC 20210; 866-4-US WAGE; 866-487-9243; www.dol.gov/dol/esa/.

Working Conditions

If you're fired for discussing your salary with another employee at the company you worked for. Or you and another employee talk about how unsanitary the bathrooms are where you work. When your boss finds out what you said, he demotes you. Or you and another employee complain to your boss that there's exposed asbestos in your office. The next day both of you are fired for insubordination. Contact: National Labor Relations Board, Division of Information, 1099 14th Street, NW, Washington, DC 20570; 202-273-1991; www.nlrb.gov.

Nursing Home Watchdogs

The State Long Term Care Ombudsman Program is a valuable resource for nursing home residents and their families. It was created to investigate and resolve complaints made on behalf of or by older individuals who are residents of long term care facilities such as nursing homes, assisted living, and board and care facilities. Ombudsmen do not have direct authority to require action by a facility, but they do have the authority to negotiate on a resident's behalf and to work with other state agencies for effective change and enforcement. Ombudsman programs vary by state, but activities and services generally include: information about community groups and activities available to improve life and care for nursing home residents, education on resident's rights, advice on how to select a nursing home, answering questions about long term care facilities, helping people find the services they need in the community instead of entering a nursing home, explanations on how nursing homes are inspected, information on and assistance with family and resident councils, referral to local legal resources if legal assistance is needed, and information regarding current legislative and regulatory efforts in the state. For more information on programs offered in your area contact your state office listed below.

Alabama
Virginia Moore-Bell
State LTC Ombudsman
AL Dept. of Senior Services
770 Washington Avenue
RSA Plaza, Suite 470
Montgomery, AL 36130
334-242-5743
Fax: 334-242-5594
www.ageline.net

Alaska
Robert Dreyer
State LTC Ombudsman
AK Mental Health Trust Auth.
Office of the State LTC Ombudsman
550 West 7th Avenue, Suite 1830
Anchorage, AK 99501
907-334-4480
Fax: 907-334-4486

Arizona
Robert Nixon
State LTC Ombudsman
AZ Aging & Adult Administration
1789 West Jefferson, #950-A
Phoenix, AZ 85007
602-542-6454
Fax: 602-542-6575
www.de.state.az.us/aaa/programs/ombudsman/default.asp

Arkansas
Kathie Gately
State LTC Ombudsman
AR Division of Aging & Adult Services
P.O.B. 1437, Slot S530
Little Rock, AR 72203-1437
501-682-8952
Fax: 501-682-8155

California
Joe Rodrigues
State LTC Ombudsman
CA Department on Aging
1300 National Drive, 2nd Floor
Sacramento, CA 95834
916-419-7510
Fax: 916-928-2503
www.aging.state.ca.us/html/programs/ombudsman.html

Colorado
Pat Tunnell
State LTC Ombudsman
The Legal Center
455 Sherman Street, Suite 130
Denver, CO 80203
800-288-1376
Fax: 303-722-0720
www.thelegalcenter.org/services_older.html

Connecticut
Maggie Ewald
Acting State LTC Ombudsman
CT Department of Social Services
Office of the State LTC Ombudsman
25 Sigourney Street, 12th Floor
Hartford, CT 06106-5033
860-424-5200
Fax: 860-424-4808
www.ltcop.state.ct.us

Delaware
Tim Hoyle
State LTC Ombudsman
Division of Services for Aging & Adults
1901 North Dupont Highway
Main Admin. Bldg. Annex
New Castle, DE 19720
302-255-9390
Fax: 302-255-4445
www.dsaapd.com

Florida
Brian Lee
State LTC Ombudsman
Florida State LTC Ombudsman Council
Department of Elder Affairs
4040 Esplanade Way
Tallahassee, FL 32399
888-831-0404
Fax: 850-414-2377
www.myflorida.com/ombudsman

Georgia
Becky Kurtz
State LTC Ombudsman
Office of the State LTCO
2 Peachtree Street, NW, 9th Floor
Atlanta, GA 30303-3142
888-454-5826
Fax: 404-463-8384
www.georgiaombudsman.org

Guam
Cerina Mariano
State LTC Ombudsman
Division of Senior Citizens
Guam DPHSS
P.O. Box 2816
Hagatna, GU 96932

671-735-7382
Fax: 671-735-7416

Hawaii
John McDermott
State LTC Ombudsman
Executive Office on Aging
250 South Hotel Street, Suite 406
Honolulu, HI 96813-2831
808-586-0100
Fax: 808-586-0185
www2.state.hi.us/eoa

Idaho
Cathy Hart
State LTC Ombudsman
Idaho Commission on Aging
P.O. Box 83720
3380 American Terrace
Suite 120
Boise, ID 83720-0007
208-334-3833
Fax: 208-334-3033
www.idahoaging.com/programs/ps_ombuds.htm

Illinois
Sally Petrone
State LTC Ombudsman
Illinois Department on Aging
421 East Capitol Avenue, Suite 100
Springfield, IL 62701-1789
217-785-3143
Fax: 217-524-9644
www.state.il.us/aging

Indiana
Arlene Franklin
State LTC Ombudsman
Indiana Division Disabilities\Rehab Services
402 W. Washington St., Room W 454
PO Box 7083, MS21
Indianapolis, IN 46207-7083
800-545-7763
Fax: 317-232-7867

Iowa
Jeanne Yordi
State LTC Ombudsman
Iowa Department of Elder Affairs
Clemens Building
200 10th Street, 3rd Floor
Des Moines, IA 50309-3609
515-242-3327
Fax: 515-242-3300

Kansas
Kathy Greenlee
State LTC Ombudsman
Office of the State LTC Ombudsman
900 SW Jackson Street, Suite 1041
Topeka, KS 66612
785-296-3017
Fax: 785-296-3916
http://da.state.ks.us/care

Kentucky
State Ombudsman
State LTC Ombudsman
Cabinet for Health & Family Services
Office of the Ombudsman
275 East Main Street, 1E-B
Frankfort, KY 40621
502-564-5497
Fax: 502-564-9523
http://cfc.ky.gov/agencies/Ombudsman

Louisiana
Linda Sadden
State LTC Ombudsman
Office of Elderly Affairs
412 N. 4th Street, 3rd Floor
P.O. Box 61
Baton Rouge, LA 70821
225-342-6872
Fax: 225-342-7144
www.louisiana.gov/elderlyaffairs/LTC_ombudsman.html

Maine
Brenda Gallant
State LTC Ombudsman
Maine LTC Ombudsman Program
1 Weston Court
P.O. Box 128
Augusta, ME 04332
207-621-1079
Fax: 207-621-0509
www.maineombudsman.org

Maryland
Patricia Bayliss
State LTC Ombudsman
Maryland Department of Aging
301 W. Preston Street, Room 1007
Baltimore, MD 21201
410-767-1091
Fax: 410-333-7943
www.mdoa.state.md.us/Services/Ombudsman.html

Massachusetts
Mary McKenna

State LTC Ombudsman
Massachusetts Exec Office of Elder Affairs
State LTC Ombudsman
1 Ashburton Place, 5th Fioor
Boston, MA 02108-1518
617-727-7750
Fax: 617-727-9368
www.mass.gov/portal/index.jsp?pageID=elderssubtopic&L=3&L0=Home&L1=Servic

Michigan
Sarah Slocum
State LTC Ombudsman
Michigan Office of Services to the Aging
7109 West Saginaw
P.O. Box 30676
Lansing, MI 48909
517-335-0148
Fax: 517-373-4092

Minnesota
Jean Wood
Acting State LTC Ombudsman
Office of Ombudsman for Older Minnesotans
121 East Seventh Place, Suite 410
St. Paul, MN 55101
651-296-0382
Fax: 651-297-5654
www.mnaging.org

Mississippi
Anniece McLemore
State LTC Ombudsman
MS Dept. of Human Services, Div. of Aging
State LTC Ombudsman
750 North State Street
Jackson, MS 39202
601-359-4927
Fax: 601-359-9664
www.mdhs.state.ms.us

Missouri
Carol Scott
State LTC Ombudsman
Department of Health & Senior Services
P.O. Box 570
Jefferson City, MO 65102
800-309-3282
Fax: 573-526-4314
www.dhss.mo.gov/Ombudsman

Montana
Kelly Moorse
State LTC Ombudsman
MT Dept. of Health & Human Services
P.O. Box 4210
111 N. Sanders
Helena, MT 59604-4210
800-551-3191
Fax: 406-444-7743
www.dphhs.state.mt.us/sltc/index.htm

Nebraska
Cindy Kadavy
State LTC Ombudsman
Division of Aging Services
Division of Aging Services
P.O. Box 95044
Lincoln, NE 68509-5044
402-471-2307
Fax: 402-471-4619
www.hhs.state.ne.us/ags/ltcombud.htm

Nevada
Bruce McAnnany
Acting State Ombudsman
Nevada Division for Aging Services
445 Apple Street, #104
Reno, NV 89502
702-486-3545
Fax: 702-486-3572

New Hampshire
Don Rabun
State LTC Ombudsman
NH LTC Ombudsman Program
129 Pleasant Street
Concord, NH 03301-3857
603-271-4704
Fax: 603-271-5574
www.dhhs.state.nh.us/DHHS/BEAS/ltc-ombudsman.htm

New Jersey
William Isele
State LTC Ombudsman
Office of Ombudsman for Institutional Elderly
P.O. Box 807
Trenton, NJ 08625-0807
609-943-4026
Fax: 609-943-3479
www.state.nj.us/health/senior/sa_ombd.htm

New Mexico
Walter Lombardi
State LTC Ombudsman
New Mexico Aging & LTC Services Dept.
1015 Tijeras Avenue, N.W., Suite 200
Albuquerque, NM 87102
505-222-4500
Fax: 505-222-4526

New York
Martha Haase
State LTC Ombudsman
New York State Office for the Aging
2 Empire State Plaza
Agency Building #2
Albany, NY 12223
518-474-7329
Fax: 518-474-7761
www.ombudsman.state.ny.us

North Carolina
Sharon Wilder
State LTC Ombudsman
NC Division of Aging & Adult Services
2101 Mail Service Center
Raleigh, NC 27699-2101
919-733-8395
Fax: 919-715-0868
www.dhhs.state.nc.us/aging/ombud.htm

North Dakota
Helen Funk
State LTC Ombudsman
Aging Services Division
Long Term Care Ombudsman Prog.
600 E. Boulevard Avenue, Dept. 325
Bismarck, ND 58505
800-451-8693
Fax: 701-328-4061
www.state.nd.us/humanservices/services/adultsaging/ombudsman.html

Ohio
Beverley Laubert
State LTC Ombudsman
Ohio Department of Aging
50 W Broad Street, 9th Floor
Columbus, OH 43215-3363
614-466-1221
Fax: 614-644-5201
www.goldenbuckeye.com

Oklahoma
Esther Houser
State LTC Ombudsman
DHS Aging Services Division
Long Term Care Ombudsman Prog.
2401 N.W. 23rd Street, Suite 40
Oklahoma City, OK 73107
405-521-6734
Fax: 405-522-6739

Oregon
Meredith Cote
State LTC Ombudsman
Oregon Office of the LTC Ombudsman
3855 Wolverine NE, Suite 6
Salem, OR 97305-1251
503-378-6533
Fax: 503-373-0852

Pennsylvania
Wilma Gonzalez
State LTC Ombudsman
Pennsylvania Department of Aging
555 Walnut Street, 5th Floor
P.O. Box 1089
Harrisburg, PA 17101
717-783-7247
Fax: 717-772-3382

Puerto Rico
Carmen Matos
State LTC Ombudsman
Puerto Rico Governor's Office of Elder Affair
Call Box 50063
Old San Juan Station
San Juan, PR 00902
787-725-1515
Fax: 787-721-6510

Rhode Island
Roberta Hawkins
State LTC Ombudsman
Alliance for Better Long Term Care
422 Post Road, Suite 204
Warwick, RI 02888
401-785-3340
Fax: 401-785-3391
www.stateomb@alliancebltc.org

South Carolina
Jon Cook
State LTC Ombudsman
SC DHHS, Office on Aging
1301 Gervais Street, Suite 200
Columbia, SC 29201
803-734-9898
Fax: 803-734-9886
www.dhhs.state.sc.us/InsideDHHS/Bureaus/BureauofSeniorServices/service15

South Dakota
Jeff Askew
State LTC Ombudsman
SD Office of Adult Services & Aging
Department of Social Services
700 Governors Drive
Pierre, SD 57501-2291

605-773-3656
Fax: 605-773-6834
www.state.sd.us/social/ASA/services/ombudsman.htm

Tennessee
Adrian Wheeler
State LTC Ombudsman
TN Commission on Aging and Disability
Andrew Jackson Bldg.
500 Deaderick Street, Ste. 825
Nashville, TN 37243
615-741-2056
Fax: 615-741-3309
www.state.tn.us/comaging/ombudsman.html

Texas
John Willis
State LTC Ombudsman
Department of Aging and Disability Services
State Long Term Care Ombudsman Prog.
701 West 51st Street
P.O. Box 149030
Mail Code: 250
Austin, TX 78714-9030
512-438-4356
Fax: 512-438-4374
www.dads.state.tx.us/news_info/volunteer/ombudsman

Utah
Chad McNiven
State LTC Ombudsman
Utah Division of Aging & Adult Services
Department of Human Services
120 North 200 West
Room 325
Salt Lake City, UT 84103
801-538-3910
Fax: 801-538-4395
www.hsdaas.utah.gov/ltco_about.htm

Vermont
Jacqueline Majoros
State LTC Ombudsman
Vermont Legal Aid, Inc.
264 N. Winooski Avenue
P.O. Box 1367
Burlington, VT 05402
802-863-5620
Fax: 802-863-7152
www.dad.state.vt.us/ltcinfo/ombudsman.html

Virginia
Joani Latimer
State LTC Ombudsman
VA Association of Area Agencies on Aging
24 E. Cary Street
Suite 100
Richmond, VA 23219
804-565-1600
Fax: 804-644-5640
www.vaaaa.org

Washington
Kary Hyre
State LTC Ombudsman
Multi-Service Center
1200 South 336th Street
P.O. Box 23699
Federal Way, WA 98093
800-422-1384
Fax: 253-815-8173
www.ltcop.org/index.htm

West Virginia
Larry Medley
State LTC Ombudsman
West Virginia Bureau of Senior Services
1900 Kanawha Boulevard East, Bldg #10
Charleston, WV 25305-0160
304-558-3317
Fax: 304-558-0004
www.state.wv.us/seniorservices

Wisconsin
George Potaracke
State LTC Ombudsman
Wisconsin Board on Aging & Long Term Care
1402 Pankratz Street
Madison, WI 53704-4001
608-246-7014
Fax: 608-246-7001
http://longtermcare.state.wi.us/home/default.htm

Wyoming
Deborah Alden
State LTC Ombudsman
Wyoming Senior Citizens, Inc
756 Gilchrist
P.O. Box 94
Wheatland, WY 82201
307-322-5553
Fax: 307-322-3283

Free Lawyers Just For Seniors

The Senior Legal Hotlines are supported by nonprofit organizations that offer legal advice over the telephone. These organizations are devoted to advancing the legal rights of Seniors and increasing the legal resources available to Seniors. Hotline attorneys can provide callers with free legal advice and counsel, and referrals to organizations that may be able to provide more extensive legal assistance. The hotline is designed to provide advice on issues of importance to the senior community such as AFDC/TANF, Food Stamps, General Assistance, Supplemental Security Income (SSI), Social Security Disability Insurance (SSDI), Medicaid/Medicare, QUEST, temporary restraining orders, evictions, public housing, Section 8 Housing, landlord/tenant conflicts, bankruptcy, debt collection, divorce, custody, visitation, adoption, Grandparent rights, estate planning and wills. The hotline is for telephone counsel and advice only. Full legal representation will not necessarily be provided. Some hotlines may provide additional services such as letter and document preparation, and provision of legal forms. When you place a call to a Legal Hotline, an intake worker will gather basic information such as name, address, phone number, birth date and the general nature of your question or problem. Hotline attorneys use the information collected by the intake workers to return calls. For more information call your state's legal hotline number.

Alabama
Legal Services Corporation of Alabama, Inc
500 Bell Building
207 Montgomery Street
Montgomery, AL 36104
800-844-5342
334-832-5342
www.alabamalegalservices.org

Arkansas
Arkansas Legal Services Programs
303 W. Capital, Suite 200
Little Rock, AR 72201
800-952-9243
501-376-3423
www.arlegalservices.org

Arizona
Arizona Elder Law Hotline
Southern Arizona Legal Aid, Inc
64 E. Broadway Boulevard
Tucson, AZ 85701
520-623-5137
800-231-5441
Callers must be over the age of 60. Calls from relatives or other contacts will not be accepted.

California
Legal Services of Northern California
515 12th Street
Sacramento, CA 95814
800-222-1753
916-551-2140
www.seniorlegalhotline.org

Connecticut
Statewide Legal Services of Connecticut, Inc
426 State Street
New Haven, CT 06112
800-453-3320

Connecticut Legal Services, Inc
872 Main Street
P.O. Box 258
Willimantic, CT 06226
800-296-1467
www.ctelderlaw.org
Hotline deals only with consumer issues.

District of Columbia
Legal Counsel for the Elderly
601 E Street NW
Washington, DC 20049
202-434-2170

Georgia
Georgia Senior Legal Hotline
2 Peachtree Street, Suite 9-398
Atlanta, GA 30303
Toll free: 888-257-9519
404-657-9915

Hawaii
Legal Aid Society of Hawaii
924 Bethel Street
Honolulu, HI 96813-5119
Toll free: 888-536-0011
808-536-0011
www.legalaidhawaii.org

Iowa
Legal Hotline for Older Iowans
1111 9th Street, Suite 230
Des Moines. IA 50314
800-992-8161
515-282-8161

Idaho
Idaho Legal Aid Services
P.O. Box 913
310 North Fifth Street
Boise, ID 83701
Toll free: 866-345-0106
Spanish Speaking: 866-954-2591

Indiana
Legal Services of Indiana Senior Hotline
242 West 7th Street
Bloomington, IN 47404
Toll free: 877-323-6260
www.indianajustice.org

Kansas
Kansas Legal Services
200 N. Broadway, Suite 500
Wichita, KS 67202
Toll free: 888-353-5337
316-265-9681

Kentucky
Legal Helpline for Older Kentuckians
Access to Justice Foundation
400 Old Vine Street, Suite 203
Lexington, KY 40507-1910
800-200-3633
www.seniorlegalhelpline.org

Louisiana
Predatory Lending Project
Southeast Louisiana Legal Services
1919 Common Street
New Orleans, LA 70112
Toll free: 877-521-6242
504-529-1000
www.nolac.org
Hotline deals with predatory lending issues only.

Maine
Legal Services for the Elderly
9 Green Street
P.O. Box 2723
Augusta, ME 04338
800-750-5353
207-623-1797
www.mainelse.org

Maryland
Maryland Senior Legal Hotline
Legal Aid Bureau, Inc
500 East Lexington
Baltimore, MD 21202
800-999-8904
410-539-5340
www.mdlab.org/srhotline.html

Michigan
Legal Hotline for Michigan Seniors
Elder Law of Michigan, Inc
221 N. Pine Street, Suite 720
Lansing, MI 48933
800-347-5297
517-372-5959
www.elderslaw.org

Mississippi
Legal Line for Elder Mississippians
111 Rue Magnolia
P.O. Box 994
Biloxi, MS 39533-0994
Toll free: 888-660-0008
228-374-4168

New Hampshire
Senior Citizens Law Project Advice Line
New Hampshire Legal Assistance
1361 Elm Street
Manchester, NH 03101
Toll free: 888-353-9944
603-624-6000

New Mexico
Lawyer Referral for the Elderly
State Bar of New Mexico Special Projects, Inc
P.O. Box 25883
Albuquerque, NM 87125
800-867-6657
505-797-6005

North Dakota
Senior Legal Hotline
Legal Services of North Dakota
P.O. Box 1666

Minot, ND 58702-1666
Toll free: 866-621-9886
www.legalassist.org

Ohio
Pro Seniors' Legal Hotline
7162 Reading Road, Suite 1150
Cincinnati, OH 45237
800-488-6070
513-345-4160
www.proseniors.org

Pennsylvania
Pennsylvania Senior Law Helpline
100 South Broad Street
Philadelphia, PA 19110
Toll free: 877-727-7529
www.seniorlawcenter.org

Legal Counsel for the Elderly
AARP Foundation
P.O. Box 23180
Pittsburgh, PA 15222
800-262-5297

Puerto Rico
Islandwide Seniors Legal Hotline
Puerto Rico Legal Services
Ponce de Leon 1859
Pda 26, Apartado 9134
San Juan, PR 00908-9134
800-981-9160
800-981-3432
787-728-2323

South Carolina
Serve Our Seniors Telephone Hotline
South Carolina Centers for Equal Justice
1601-K Shop Road
Columbia, SC 29201
Toll Free: 888-346-5592

Tennessee
Tennessee Elder Law Hotline
Southeast Tennessee Legal Services
414 McCallie Ave.
Chattanooga, TN 37402
800-836-0128
423-756-0128
www.setnlegalservices.org

Texas
Legal Hotline for Older Texans
Texas Legal Services Center
815 Brazos, Suite 1100
Austin, TX 78710
800-622-2520 LHOT
888-343-4414 Nursing Home Advocacy Project
www.tlsc.org/hotline.html

Washington
CLEAR*Sr. – Coordinated Legal Education, Advice and Referral for Seniors
Northwest Justice Project
401 Second Avenue South
Suite 407
Seattle, WA 98104
Toll free: 888-387-7111
www.nwjustice.org

West Virginia
West Virginia Senior Legal Aid
1988 Listravia Avenue
Morgantown, WV 26505
800-229-5068
304-291-3900
www.seniorlegalaid.org

Wyoming
Wyoming Legal Services
P.O. Box 1160
Lander, WY 82520
800-442-6710
307-332-6626

Elder Abuse Hotline

The major types of Elder Abuse are: physical abuse, sexual abuse, emotional or psychological abuse, neglect, abandonment, financial or material exploitation, and self neglect. If you suspect some one you care about is being abused or neglected you can help. You do not need absolute proof to report suspected abuse, but you must call the state where the elder lives. If a vulnerable adult is in immediate danger, call 9-1-1 or the police immediately. To report elder abuse or neglect, all you have to do is call the state's Elder Abuse Hotline. All hotlines are anonymous and free for instate calls. Most states have two phone numbers, one for domestic abuse and one for institutional abuse. Some states have toll free lines that allow you to call from anywhere in the country. If the number listed is for instate calls only, call the Eldercare Locator at 800-677-1116 for assistance.

Alabama
Domestic abuse
800-458-7214 (instate only)

Alaska
Domestic abuse
800-478-9996 (instate only)
907-269-3666 (nationwide)
Institutional abuse
800-730-6393 (in-state only)
907-334-4483 (nationwide)

Arizona
Domestic abuse
877-767-2385 (nationwide)
TDD 877-815-8390
Institutional abuse
877-767-2385 (nationwide)
TDD 877-815-8390

Arkansas
Domestic abuse
800-332-4443 (instate only)
Institutional abuse
800-582-4887 (in-state only)
Nationwide calls
800-482-8049

California
Domestic abuse
888-436-3600 (in-state only)
Institutional abuse
800-231-4024 (instate only)

Colorado
Domestic abuse
800-773-1366 (in-state only)
Institutional abuse
800-886-7689 (in-state only)

Connecticut
Domestic abuse
888-385-4225 (in-state only)
Institutional abuse
860-424-5241 (in-state only)

Delaware
Domestic abuse
800-223-9074 (nationwide)
Institutional abuse
800-223-9074 (nationwide)

District of Columbia
Domestic abuse
202-541-3950
Institutional abuse
202-434-2140

Florida
Domestic abuse
800-962-2873 (nationwide)
Institutional abuse
800-962-2873 (nationwide)

Georgia
Domestic abuse
888-774-0152 (nationwide)
404-657-5250 (Metro Atlanta)
Institutional abuse
800-878-6442 (nationwide)
404-657-5728 (Metro Atlanta)

Guam
Domestic abuse
671-646-4455 (weekdays)
671-475-0268 (all other times)
Institutional abuse
671-656-4455 (weekdays)
671-475-0268 (all other times)

Hawaii
Domestic and Institutional abuse
808-832-5115 (Oahu)
808-243-5151 (Maui)
808-241-3432 (Kauai)
808-933-8820 (East Hawaii)
808-327-6280 (West Hawaii)

Idaho
Domestic abuse
877-471-2777 (nationwide)
208-334-3833 (in-state only)
Institutional abuse
877-471-2777 (nationwide)
208-364-1899 (instate only)

Illinois
Domestic abuse
217-524-6911 (nationwide)
800-252-8966 (in-state only)
Institutional abuse
217-785-0321 (nationwide)
800-252-4343 (in-state only)
After hours: 800-279-0400 or 800-677-1116

Indiana
Domestic abuse
800-992-6978 (in-state only)
800-545-7763 ext. 20135 (nationwide)
Institutional abuse

800-992-6978 (in-state only)
800-545-7763 ext 20135 (nationwide)

Iowa
Domestic abuse
800-362-2178 (in-state only)
Institutional abuse
877-686-0027 (nationwide)

Kansas
Domestic abuse
800-922-5330 (in-state only)
785-2966-0044 (nationwide)
Institutional abuse
800-842-0078 (in-state only)

Kentucky
Domestic abuse
800-752-6200 (in-state only)
Institutional abuse
800-752-6200 (in-state only)

Louisiana
Domestic abuse
800-259-4990 (nationwide)
Institutional abuse
800-259-4990 (nationwide)

Maine
Domestic abuse
800-624-8404 (nationwide)
Institutional abuse
800-624-8404 (nationwide)

Maryland
Domestic abuse
800-917-7383 (in-state only)
800-677-1116 (nationwide)
Institutional abuse
800-917-7383 (in-state only)
877-402-8220 (nationwide)

Massachusetts
Domestic abuse
800-922-2275 (in-state only)
Institutional abuse
80-462-5540 (in-state only)

Michigan
Domestic abuse
800-996-6228 (in-state only)
Institutional abuse
800-882-6006 (in-state only)

Minnesota
Domestic abuse
800-333-2433 (nationwide)
Institutional abuse
800-333-2433 (nationwide0

Mississippi
Domestic abuse
800-222-8000 (in-state only)
Institutional abuse
800-227-7308 (nationwide)

Missouri
Domestic abuse
800-392-0210 (nationwide)
Institutional abuse
800-392-0210 (nationwide)

Montana
Domestic abuse
800-551-3191 (in-state only)
406-444-4077 (nationwide)

Nebraska
Domestic abuse
800-652-1999 (in-state only)
Institutional abuse
800-652-1999 (in-state only)

Nevada
Domestic abuse
800-992-5757 (in-state only)
Institutional abuse
800-992-5757 (in-state only)
Reno area: 702-784-8090

New Hampshire
Domestic abuse
800-949-0470 (in-state only)
603-271-4386 (nationwide)
Institutional abuse
800-442-5640 (in-state only)
603-271-4396 (nationwide)

New Jersey
Domestic abuse
800-792-8820 (in-state only)
609-943-4373 (nationwide)
Institutional abuse
800-792-8820 (in-state only)
609-943-4373 (nationwide)

New Mexico
Domestic abuse
800-797-3260 (in-state only)

505-841-6100 (nationwide and Albuquerque)
Institutional abuse
800-797-3260 (in-state only)
505-841-6100 (nationwide and Albuquerque)

New York
Domestic abuse
800-342-9871 (in-state only)
Institutional abuse
Nursing Home Complaint: 888-201-4563
Adult Home Care Complaint: 866-893-6772

North Carolina
Domestic abuse
800-662-7030 (in-state only)
Institutional abuse
800-662-7030 (in-state only)

North Dakota
Domestic abuse
800-451-8693 (nationwide)
Institutional abuse
800-451-8693 (nationwide)

Ohio
Domestic abuse
866-635-3748 (in-state only)
800-677-1116 (nationwide)
Institutional abuse
800-282-1206 (in-state only)
800-677-1116 (nationwide)

Oklahoma
Domestic abuse
800-522-3511 (in-state only)
Institutional abuse
800-522-3511 (in-state only)

Oregon
Domestic abuse
800-232-3020 (in-state only)
Institutional abuse
800-232-3020 (in-state only)

Pennsylvania
Domestic abuse
800-490-8505 (nationwide)
Institutional abuse
800-254-5164 (nationwide)

Puerto Rico
Domestic abuse
787-725-9788
Institutional abuse
787-721-8225

Rhode Island
Domestic abuse
401-462-0550 (in-state only)
401-462-0545 (fax)
Institutional abuse
401-785-3340 (in-state only)
401-785-3391 (fax)

South Carolina
Domestic abuse
800-677-1116 (nationwide)
Institutional abuse
800-677-1116 (nationwide)

South Dakota
Domestic abuse
605-773-3656
Institutional abuse
605-773-3656

Tennessee
Domestic abuse
888-277-8366 (nationwide)
Institutional abuse
888-277-8366 (nationwide)

Texas
Domestic abuse
800-252-5400 (in-state only)
512-834-3784 (nationwide)
Institutional abuse
800-458-9858 (in-state only)
512-834-3784 (nationwide)

Utah
Domestic abuse
801-264-7669 (nationwide)
800-371-7897 (in-state only)
Institutional abuse
801-264-7669 (nationwide)
800-371-7897 (in-state only)

Vermont
Domestic abuse
800-564-1612 (in-state only)
Institutional abuse
800-564-1612 (in-state only)

Virginia
Domestic abuse
888-832-3858 (in-state only)
804-371-0896 (nationwide)
Institutional abuse
888-832-3858 (in-state only)
804-371-0896 (nationwide)

Washington
Domestic abuse
866-363-4276 (nationwide)
Institutional abuse
800-562-6078 (nationwide)

West Virginia
Domestic abuse
800-352-6513 (in-state only)
Institutional abuse
800-352-6513 (in-state only)

Wisconsin
Domestic abuse
608-266-2536 (nationwide)
Institutional abuse
608-246-7013 (nationwide)
800-815-0015 (in-state only)

Wyoming
Domestic abuse
800-457-3659 (in-state only)
307-777-6137 (nationwide)
Institutional abuse
307-777-7123 (nationwide)

Adult Protection

Adult Protective Services provide services to protect vulnerable adults. A vulnerable adult is a person who is being mistreated or is in danger of being mistreated and who, due to age and/or disability, is unable to protect them self. Most Adult Protection Programs help vulnerable adults regardless of age. Some serve only older adults based on their age or incapacity, and a limited number serve adults only, age 18-59, whose disabilities prevent them from protecting themselves. Adult Protective Services are responsible for: receiving reports of elder/vulnerable adult abuse, exploitation and/or neglect; investigation of abuse reports; victim risk assessment; assessment of victim's capacity to understand their risk and ability to give informed consent; case plan development; arrangement of services; service monitoring and evaluation. For more information contact your state office for Adult Protective Services.

Adult Protective Services State Contacts

Alabama
Doris Ball
Program Manager
Office of Adult Services
Family Services Div/Human Resources
50 Ripley Street
Montgomery, AL 36130
Work: 334-242-1355
Fax: 334-242-0939

Alaska
Dwight Becker
Social Services Program Director
Alaska Division of Senior Services
Dept. of Administration
3601 C Street,, #310
Anchorage, AK 99503
907-269-3674
Fax: 907-269-3648

Arizona
Tina Dannenfelser, Operations Manager
Adult Protective Services, Aging & Adult Administration
Dept. of Economic Security
1789 W. Jefferson #950A
Phoenix, AZ 85007
602-542-4446
Fax: 602-542-6575

Arkansas
Raymond Vining
Administrator, Adult Protective Services
P.O. Box 1437
Slot #1412
Little Rock, AR 72203
501-682-8495
Fax: 501-682-6393

California
Vickey Walker
Manager, CA Dept. of Social Services
Adult Programs Branch
8745 Folsom Blvd., #230
Sacramento, CA 95826

916-229-0323
Fax: 916-229-3155

Colorado
Paulette St. James
Administrator
Aging & Adult Services
Dept. of Social Services
1575 Sherman Street
Denver, CO 80203-1714
303-866-2676
Fax: 303-866-2696

Connecticut
Lynn Noyes
Manager, Elder Rights Program
Dept. of Social Services
25 Sigourney Street
Hartford, CT 06106
860-424-5022
Fax: 860-424-4966

Delaware
Vickie Artis
Administrator, Adult Protective Services
Services for Aging & Adults with Disabilities
256 Chapman Road, Suite 200
Newark, DE 19720
302-453-3820
Fax: 302-453-3836

Florida
Chris Shoemaker
Management Analyst
Florida Dept. of Elder Affairs
Director of Volunteer Services
1317 Winewood Boulevard
Tallahassee, FL 32399-0700
850-922-4076
Fax: 850-922-4193

Georgia
Mary Martha Rugg
Program Administrator
Dept. of Human Resources
Division of Aging Services
2 Peachtree Street, NW, 9th Floor
Atlanta, GA 30303
404-657-3421
Fax: 404-657-5340
www.aging.dhr.georgia.gov/portal/site

Guam
Arthur U. San Agustin
Supervisor of Services
Adult Protective Services Unit
P.O. Box 2816
Hagatna, GU 96932
671-475-0263
Fax: 671-477-4779

Hawaii
Patricia Snyder
Program Administrator
Hawaii Department of Human Services
Services and Program Development (ACCS/PD)
P.O. Box 339
Honolulu, HI 96809
808-586-5701
Fax: 808-586-5700

Idaho
Sarah Scott
Program Administrator
Commission on Aging
PO Box 83720
3380 American Terrace
Suite 120
Boise, ID 83720-0007
208-334-3833
Fax: 208-334-3033

Illinois
Lois Moorman
Manager, IL Department on Aging
Bureau of Elder Rights
421 East Capitol Avenue, Suite 100
Springfield, IL 62701-1789
217-785-3386
Fax: 217-524-9644

Indiana
Patrick Calkins
Unit Manager
Indiana Family & Social Services Administration
Advocacy Services Unit
802 W. Washington
P.O. Box 7083, MS-21
Indianapolis, IN 46207-7083
317-232-0135
Fax: 317-232-7867

Iowa
Sandi Koll
Program Manager for Adult Services
Division of Adult Children & Family Services
Dept. of Human Services
1305 E. Walnut
5th Floor, ACFS
Des Moines, IA 50319

515-242-6021
Fax: 515-242-6884

Kansas
Rosalie Sacks
Program Manager
Dept of Social & Rehab Services
Adult Protective Services
915 SW Harrison
DSOB - 681-West
Topeka, KS 66614
785-368-8105
Fax: 785-296-0146

Kentucky
Michelle Sanborn
Director, Div. Protection & Permanency
Adult Protective Services Branch
275 East Main Street, 3E-C
Frankfort, KY 40621
502-564-7043
Fax: 502-564-3096

Louisiana
Robert Seemann
Manager, Louisiana Office of Elderly Affairs
Elderly Protective Services
412 North Fourth Street
Baton Rouge, LA 70802
225-342-9722
Fax: 225-342-7144

Maine
Ricker Hamilton
Director, Maine DHS/Bureau of Elder/Adult Services
Dept of Human Services
161 Marginal Way
Portland, ME 04101
207-822-2150
Fax: 207-822-2162

Maryland
John Kardys
Director of Adult Services
Office of Adult & Family Services/Dept. HR
Community Based Services
311 W. Saratoga Street, #259
Baltimore, MD 21201
410-767-7317
Fax: 410-333-0079

Massachusetts
Gregory Giuliano
Director, Executive Office of Elder Affairs
Protective Services
1 Ashburton Place, 5th Floor
Boston, MA 02108
617-222-7464
Fax: 617-727-9368

Michigan
Cynthia Farrell
Manager, Family Independence Agency
Adult Protective Services
235 S. Grand, Agency Suite 501
Lansing, MI 48909
517-335-6358
Fax: 517-241-7943

Minnesota
Barbara Doherty
Adult Protection Consultant
Aging and Adult Services Division
444 Lafayette Street
St. Paul, MN 55155-3842
651-296-5563
Fax: 651-297-3500

Mississippi
Edna Clark
Program Manager
Adult Protection Services./Family & Child Services
MS. Dept. of Human Services
750 N. State Street
P.O. Box 352
Jackson, MS 39205
601-359-4484
Fax: 601-359-4978

Missouri
Brenda Campbell
Dept. of Health and Senior Services
Division of Senior Services
3418 Knipp Drive, Suite F
Jefferson City, MO 65102
573-751-3626
Fax: 573-751-8687

Montana
Rick Bartos
Chief, Adult Protective Services
Dept. Pub. Health & Human Services
P.O. Box 4210
Helena, MT 59604
406-444-9810
Fax: 406-444-7743

Nebraska
Carol Lieske
Adult Protective Services Coordinator

NE Health & Human Services
Aging and Disabled Division
301 Centennial Mall-So, 5th Floor
P.O. Box 95044
Lincoln, NE 68509-5044
402-471-9190
Fax: 402-471-6352
www.hhs.state.ne.us

Nevada
Gil Johnstone, EPS Chief
Elder Protective Services
Nevada Div. for Aging Services
445 Apple St., #104
Reno, NV 89502
775-688-2964
Fax: 775-688-2969

New Hampshire
Jo Moncher
Director, Bureau of Elderly and Adult Services
Office of the Ombudsman
Brown Building
129 Pleasant Street
Concord, NH 03301-3857
603-271-4681
Fax: 603-271-4643

New Jersey
David Ricci
Program Manager
Office of Area Aging Administration/Senior Affairs
Department of Health & Senior Services
P.O. Box 807
Trenton, NJ 08625-0807
609-943-3473
Fax: 609-943-3343

New Mexico
Shelly Valencia
Adult Section
Protective Services Division
Children Youth & Families Department
Pera Building, #252
P.O. Drawer 5160
Santa Fe, NM 87505-5160
505-827-6393
Fax: 505-827-8480

New York
Susan Somers
Assistant Commissioner
NYS Office of Children & Family Services
Bureau of Adult Services
52 Washington Street, Room 322 North
Rensselaer, NY 12144
518-402-6782
Fax: 518-474-8572

North Carolina
Rosalyn Pettyford
Program Coordinator
APS and Guardianship/Social Services
N.C. Division of Aging & Adult Services
693 Palmer Drive
2101 Mail Service
Raleigh, NC 27699-2101
919-733-3818
Fax: 919-715-0023

North Dakota
Lynne Jacobson
Director, Aging Services Division
Department of Human Services
600 South 2nd Street, #1C
Bismarck, ND 58504-5729
701-328-8910
Fax: 701-328-8989

Ohio
Fran Rembert
Chief, Bureau of Family Services
Dept. of Job & Family Services
255 E. Main Street, 3rd Floor
Columbus, OH 43215-5222
614-466-9274
Fax: 614-466-0164

Oklahoma
Barbara Kidder
Program Administrator
Adult Protective Services/Aging Services
Dept. of Human Services
PO Box 25352
Oklahoma City, OK 73125
405-521-3660
Fax: 405-521-2086

Oregon
Eva Kutas
Administrator, Oregon Department of Human Services
Senior Services Division
P.O. Box 14250
Salem, OR 97309-0740
503-945-9491
Fax: 503-945-9893

Pennsylvania
James Bubb
Chief Council, Department of Aging

Office of Chief Counsel
555 Walnut Street, 5th Floor
Harrisburg, PA 17101-1919
717-783-6207
Fax: 717-783-6842

Puerto Rico
Maria Soldevila-Walsh
Program Director Services to Adults
Department of Social Services
Fernandez Juncos Station
P.O. Box 11398
Santurce, PR 00910
787-723-2127

Rhode Island
Joyce Hall
Director, Department of Elderly Affairs
Adult Protective Services
35 Howard Avenue
Benjamin Rush Bldg. #55
Providence, RI 02920
401-462-0550
Fax: 401-462-0545

South Carolina
Tim Cash
Director, SC Dept. of Social Services
Div. Adult Services & Case Management
P.O. Box 1520
Columbia, SC 29202-1520
803-898-7506
Fax: 803-898-7641

South Dakota
Mike Parker, Executive Director
Office of Adult Services & Aging
700 Governors Drive
Pierre, SD 57501-2291
605-773-3656
Fax: 605-773-6834

Tennessee
Deborah Neill
Director Tennessee Department of Human Services
Adult Protective Services
Citizens Plaza, 14th Floor
400 Deaderick Street
Nashville, TN 37248-9700
615-313-4770
Fax: 615-741-4165

Texas
Bettye Mitchell, Director
Texas Department of Protective & Regulation Services
Adult Protective Services, E-561
P.O. Box 149030
Austin, TX 78714-9030
512-438-3209
Fax: 512-438-4881
www.tdprs.state.tx.us

Utah
C. Ronald Stromberg
Adult Protective Services Director
Utah Division of Aging and Adult Services
Adult Protective Services
120 North - 200 West, Box 45500
Salt Lake City, UT 84103
801-538-4591
Fax: 801-538-4395

Vermont
Veda Lyon
Program Director, Adult Protective Services
Division of Licensing & Protection
Aging & Disabilities Ladd Hall
103 South Main Street
Waterbury, VT 05671-2306
802-241-2345
Fax: 802-241-2358

Virginia
Terry Smith
Adult Protective Services
Adult Services Program
Division of Family Services
730 E. Broad Street, 2nd Floor
Richmond, VA 23219-1849
804-692-1206
Fax: 804-692-2215

Washington
Lori Melchiori
Adult Protective Services Program Manager
Aging and Adult Services Administration
Dept of Social & Health Services
P.O. Box 45600
Mail Stop 45600
Olympia, WA 98504-5600
360-725-2531
Fax: 360-438-8633

West Virginia
Deborah Dodrill
Director, Office of Social Services/Admin & Adult Services
Dept of Health & Human Res.
350 Capitol Street, #691
Charleston, WV 25301-3740
304-558-3076
Fax: 304-558-4563

Wisconsin
Jane Raymond
Advocacy and Protection Systems Developer
Wisconsin Bureau of Aging & LTC Resources
Dept of Health & Family Services
1 West Wilson St., Rm. 450
P.O. Box 7851
Madison, WI 53702
608-266-2568
Fax: 608-267-3203

Wyoming
Jan Stiles
Social Services Division
Programs & Policy Division
Department of Family Services
2300 Capitol Avenue
Hathaway Bldg, 3rd Floor
Cheyenne, WY 82002-0490
307-777-6137
Fax: 307-777-3693

Help Resolving IRS Tax Problems

If you have tried everything to resolve a tax problem with the IRS and you just can't get your problem resolved, the Taxpayer Advocate Service (TAS) may be able to help. TAS helps individuals and business taxpayers resolve their IRS tax problems. This service is designed to help taxpayers who are facing hardships or economic burden that have been unable to resolve their problem through normal channels. For more information contact: Office of the National Taxpayer Advocate, 1111 Constitution Ave., NW, Room 3031, Washington, DC 20224; 202-622-4300; Fax: 202-622-4778; 877-777-4778; www.irs.gov/advocate. Or contact your state office listed below.

Taxpayer Advocate Service State Offices

Alabama
Taxpayer Advocate Service
801 Tom Martin Dr., Room 151-PR
Birmingham, AL 35211
205-912-5631
Fax: 205-912-5156

Alaska
Taxpayer Advocate Service
949 E. 36th Avenue, Stop A-405
Anchorage, AK 99508
907-271-6877
Fax: 907-271-6157

Arizona
Taxpayer Advocate Service
210 E. Earll Dr., Stop 1005 PHX
Phoenix, AZ 85012-2623
602-207-8240
Fax: 602-207-8250

Arkansas
Taxpayer Advocate Service
700 West Capital St., Stop 1005 LIT
Little Rock, AR 72201
501-324-6269
Fax: 501-324-5183

California (Laguna Niguel)
Taxpayer Advocate Service
24000 Avila Rd., Stop 2000
Laguna Niguel, CA 92677
949-389-4804
Fax: 949-389-5038

California (Los Angeles)
Taxpayer Advocate Service
300 N. Los Angeles St., Stop 6710 LA
Los Angeles, CA 90012
213-576-3140
Fax: 213-576-3141

California (Oakland)
Taxpayer Advocate Service
1301 Clay St., Suite 1540S
Oakland, CA 94612
510-637-2703
Fax: 510-637-2715

California (Sacramento)
Taxpayer Advocate Service
4330 Watt Ave., Stop Sa5043
Sacramento, CA 95821
916-974-5007
Fax: 916-974-5902

California (San Jose)
Taxpayer Advocate Service
55 S. Market St., Stop 0004
San Jose, CA 95113
408-817-6850
Fax: 408-817-6851

Colorado
Taxpayer Advocate Service
600 17th St., Stop 1005 DEN
Denver, CO 80202-2490
303-446-1012
Fax: 303-446-1011

Connecticut
Taxpayer Advocate Service
135 High St., Stop 219
Hartford, CT 06103
860-756-4555
Fax: 860-756-4559

Delaware
Taxpayer Advocate Service
409 Silverside Rd.
Wilmington, DE 19809
302-791-4502
Fax: 302-791-5945

District of Columbia (Maryland)
Taxpayer Advocate Service
31 Hopkins Plaza, Room 940
Baltimore, MD 21201
410-962-2082
Fax: 410-9340

Florida (Ft. Lauderdale)
Taxpayer Advocate Service
7850 SW 6th Court, Room 265
Plantation, FL 33324
954-423-7677
Fax: 954-423-7680

Florida (Jacksonville)
Taxpayer Advocate Service
841 Prudential Dr., Suite 100
Jacksonville, FL 32207
904-665-1000
Fax: 904-665-1817

Georgia
Taxpayer Advocate Service
401 W. Peachtree St., NW
Summit Building
Stop 202-D, Room 510
Atlanta, GA 30308-3539
404-338-8099
Fax: 404-338-8096

Hawaii
Taxpayer Advocate Service
300 Ala Moana Blvd., #50089
Stop H-405, Room 1-214
Honolulu, HI 96850
808-539-2870
Fax: 808-539-2859

Idaho
Taxpayer Advocate Service
550 W. Fort St., Box 041
Boise, ID 83724
208-387-2827
Fax: 208-387-2824

Illinois (Chicago)
Taxpayer Advocate Service
230 S. Dearborn St.
Stop 1005-CHI, Room 2855
Chicago, IL 60604
312-566-3800
Fax: 312-566-3803

Illinois (Springfield)
Taxpayer Advocate Service
3101 Constitution Dr., Stop 1005 SPD
Springfield, IL 62704
217-862-6382
Fax: 217-862-6373

Indiana
Taxpayer Advocate Service
575 N. Pennsylvania St.
Room 581, Stop TA770
Indianapolis, IN 46204
317-226-6332
Fax: 317-226-6222

Iowa
Taxpayer Advocate Service
210 Walnut St.
Room 483, Stop 1005DSM
Des Moines, IA 50309-2109
515-284-4780
Fax: 515-284-6645

Kansas
Taxpayer Advocate Service
271 W. 3rd St., North
Stop 1005 WIC
Suite 2000
Wichita, KS 67202

316-352-7506
Fax: 316-352-7212

Kentucky
Taxpayer Advocate Service
600 Dr. Martin Luther King Jr. Place
Room 622
Louisville, KY 40202
502-582-6030
Fax: 502-582-6463

Louisiana
Taxpayer Advocate Service
1555 Poydras St., Suite 220, Stop 2
New Orleans, LA 70112
504-558-3001
Fax: 504-558-3348

Maine
Taxpayer Advocate Service
68 Sewall St., Room 313
Augusta, ME 04330
207-622-8528
Fax: 207-622-8458

Maryland
Taxpayer Advocate Service
31 Hopkins Plaza, Room 940
Baltimore, MD 21201
410-962-2082
Fax: 410-962-9340

Massachusetts
Taxpayer Advocate Service
25 New Sudbury St.
JFK Building, Room 725
Boston, MA 02203
617-316-2690
Fax: 617-316-2700

Michigan
Taxpayer Advocate Service
477 Michigan Ave.
McNamara Federal Bldg., Room 1745, Stop 7
Detroit, MI 48226
313-628-3670
Fax: 313-628-3669

Minnesota
Taxpayer Advocate Service
316 N. Robert St.
Room 383, Stop 1005 STP
St. Paul, MN 55101
651-312-7999
Fax: 651-312-7872

Mississippi
Taxpayer Advocate Service
100 W. Capitol St., Stop JK31
Jackson, MS 39269
601-292-4800
Fax: 601-292-4821

Missouri
Taxpayer Advocate Service
1222 Spruce St.
Stop 1005 STL, Room 10.314
St. Louis, MO 63103
314-612-4610
Fax: 314-612-4628

Montana
Taxpayer Advocate Service
10 West 15th St., Suite 2319
Helena, MT 59626
406-441-1022
Fax: 406-441-1045

Nebraska
Taxpayer Advocate Service
1313 Farnum St.
Room 208, Stop 1005OMA
Omaha, NE 68102-1836
402-221-4181
Fax: 402-221-3051

Nevada
Taxpayer Advocate Service
4750 W. Oakey Blvd.
Stop 1005 LVG
Las Vegas, NV 89102
702-455-1241
Fax: 702-455-1216

New Hampshire
Taxpayer Advocate Service
Thomas J. McIntyre Federal Building
80 Daniel St., Room 403
Portsmouth, NH 03801
603-433-0571
Fax: 603-430-7809

New Jersey
Taxpayer Advocate Service
955 S. Springfield Ave., 1st Floor
Springfield, NJ 07081
973-921-4043
Fax: 973-921-4355

New Mexico
5338 Montgomery Blvd., NE

Stop 1005 ALB
Albuquerque, NM 87109
505-837-5505
Fax: 505-837-5519

New York (Albany)
Taxpayer Advocate Service
Leo O'Brien Federal Bldg., Room 354
1 Clinton Square
Albany, NY 12207
518-427-5413
Fax: 518-427-5494

New York (Brooklyn)
Taxpayer Advocate Service
10 Metro Tech Center
625 Fulton St.
Brooklyn, NY 11201
718-488-2080
Fax: 718-488-3100

New York (Buffalo)
Taxpayer Advocate Service
201 Como Park Blvd.
Buffalo, NY 14227-1416
716-686-4850
Fax: 716-686-4851

New York (Manhattan)
Taxpayer Advocate Service
290 Broadway, 7th Floor
Manhattan, NY 10007
212-436-1011
Fax; 212-436-1900

North Carolina
Taxpayer Advocate Service
320 Federal Pl., Room 125
Greensboro, NC 27401
336-378-2180
Fax: 212-378-2495

North Dakota
Taxpayer Advocate Service
657 Second Ave., North
Stop 1005 FAR, Room 244
Fargo, ND 58102
701-239-5141
Fax: 701-239-5323

Ohio (Cincinnati)
Taxpayer Advocate Service
550 Main St., Room 3530
Cincinnati, OH 45202
513-263-3260
Fax: 513-263-3257

Ohio (Cleveland)
Taxpayer Advocate Service
1240 E. 9th St., Room 423
Cleveland, OH 44199
216-522-7134
Fax: 216-522-2947

Oklahoma
Taxpayer Advocate Service
55 No. Robinson
Room 138, Stop 1005 OKC
Oklahoma City, OK 73102
405-297-4055
Fax: 405-297-4056

Oregon
Taxpayer Advocate Service
1220 SW 3rd Ave.
Stop O-405
Portland, OR 97204
503-326-2333
Fax: 503-326-5453

Pennsylvania (Philadelphia)
Taxpayer Advocate Service
600 Arch St., Room 7426
Philadelphia, PA 19106
215-861-1304
Fax: 215-861-1613

Pennsylvania (Pittsburgh)
Taxpayer Advocate Service
1000 Liberty Ave., Room 1602
Pittsburgh, PA 15222
412-395-5987
Fax: 412-395-4769

Rhode Island
Taxpayer Advocate Service
380 Westminster St.
Providence, RI 02903
401-525-4200
Fax: 401-525-4247

South Carolina
Taxpayer Advocate Service
1835 Assembly St.
Room 466, MDP 03
Columbia, SC 29210
803-253-3029
Fax: 803-253-3910

South Dakota
Taxpayer Advocate Service
115 4th Ave., SE
Room 114, Stop 1005 ABE
Aberdeen, SD 57401
605-226-7248
Fax: 605-226-7246

Tennessee
Taxpayer Advocate Service
801 Broadway, Stop 22
Nashville, TN 37202
615-250-5000
Fax: 615-250-5001

Texas (Austin)
Taxpayer Advocate Service
300 E. 8th St.
Room 136, Stop 1004 AUS
Austin, TX 78701
512-499-5875
Fax: 512-499-5687

Texas (Dallas)
Taxpayer Advocate Service
1114 Commerce St.
Room 1004, MS 1005 DAL
Dallas, TX 75242
214-413-6500
Fax: 214-413-6594

Texas (Houston)
Taxpayer Advocate Service
1919 Smith St.
Room 1650, Stop 1005 HOU
Houston, TX 77002
713-209-3660
Fax: 713-209-3708

Utah
Taxpayer Advocate Service
50 South 200 East, Stop 1005 SLC
Salt Lake City, UT 84111
801-799-6958
Fax: 801-799-6957

Vermont
Taxpayer Advocate Service
Courthouse Plaza
199 Main St.
Burlington, VT 05401-8309
802-860-2089
Fax: 802-860-2006

Virginia
Taxpayer Advocate Service
400 North 8th St.
Room 916
Richmond, VA 23240
804-916-3501
Fax: 804-916-3535

Washington
Taxpayer Advocate Service
915 2nd Ave., Stop W-405
Seattle, WA 98174
206-220-6037
Fax: 206-220-6047

West Virginia
Taxpayer Advocate Service
425 Juliana St., Room 3012
Parkersburg, WV 26101
304-420-6616
Fax: 304-420-4482

Wisconsin
Taxpayer Advocate Service
310 W. Wisconsin Ave.
Suite 1298 West Tower, Stop 1005 MIL
Milwaukee, WI 53203
414-297-3046
Fax: 414-297-3362

Wyoming
Taxpayer Advocate Service
5353 Yellowstone Rd.
Cheyenne, WY 82009
307-633-0800
Fax: 307-633-0918

Speaking Up For Quality Nursing Home Care

Citizen Advocacy Groups are groups of citizens who are concerned about the quality of care available for nursing home residents in their communities. Some of these groups are established organizations with offices and staff, while others may simply be a small association of concerned people who meet to share information and strategize on ways to improve the quality of nursing home care in their community. All of the Citizen Advocacy Groups are committed to finding ways to improve the quality of life and care for nursing home residents. They are a valuable resource for information on the quality of care in particular facilities, the current state of nursing home reform in your state, and other resources that may be available in your area. For more information contact a Citizen's Advocacy Group in your area from the list below, or contact the National Citizen's Coalition for Nursing Home Reform at 1828 L St., NW, Suite 801, Washington, DC 20036; 202-332-2275, Fax: 202-232-2949; www.nccnhr.org

Alabama
Alabama Advocates for Quality Care
3717 Midway Road
Adamsville, AL 35005
205-674-9853

Arkansas
AR Advocates for Nursing Home Residents
961 Paul Drive
Conway, AR 72034
501-327-3152
Fax: 501-884-6728
Email: info@aanhr.org
www.aanhr.org

AR Advocates for Nursing Home Residents
9901 Satterfield Dr
Little Rock, AR 72205
501-225-4082
Fax: 501-884-6728
Email: info@aanhr.org
www.aanhr.org

AR Advocates for Nursing Home Residents
135 Hillview Drive, Apt 112
Fairfield Bay, AR 72088
501-884-6728
Fax: 501-884-6728
Email: info@aanhr.org
www.aanhr.org

California
Foundation Aiding the Elderly
P.O. Box 254849
Sacramento, CA 95865-4849
916-481-8558
916-481-8329
www.4fate.org

CA Advocates for Nursing Home Reform
650 Harrison Street, 2nd Floor
San Francisco, CA 94107-1311
415-974-5171
Fax: 415-777-2904
Email: PatM@canhr.org
www.canhr.org

Connecticut
CT Citizens Coalition for NH Reform
211 State Street
Bridgeport, CT 06604
203-336-3851
Fax: 203-333-4976
Email: skilpatrick@connlegalservices.org

Advocates for Loved Ones in Nursing Homes
28 B Damon Heights Road
Niantic, CT 06357
Email: aflon@hotmail.com

Florida
Fighting Elder Abuse Together (FEAT)
1625 La Maderia Dr., S.W.
Palm Bay, FL 32908
321-984-8883
Fax: 321-956-7606
Email: ahler_friddle@msn.com

Coalition to Protect America's Elders
3699 Plowshare Road
Tallahassee, FL 32309
850-216-2727
Fax: 850-216-1933
Email: coalitiontoprotect@comcast.net
www.protectelders.org

Quality Care Advocates, Inc.
P.O. Box 494224
Port Charlotte, FL 33949
941-743-0987
Email: llpsterling@aol.com

Advocates Committed to Improving Our NH's
4714 W. Euclid Ave.
Tampa, FL 33629
813-837-1714
Email: amspinel@tampabay.rr.com

Georgia
Georgia Council on Aging
2 Peachtree Street, NW
Suite 32-270
Atlanta, GA 30303
404-657-5348
Fax: 404-657-1722
Email: msmcneil@dhr.state.ga.us
www.gcoa.org

Illinois
Nursing Home Monitors
6111 Vollmer Lane
Godfrey, IL 62035
618-466-3410
Fax: 618-466-3410
Email: vkmonitor@earthlink.net
www.nursinghomemonitors.org

Illinois Citizens For Better Care
220 South State Street, Suite 1928
Chicago, IL 60604
312-663-5120
Fax: 312-427-0181
Email: wmicbc@core.com

Tender Loving Care in Long Term Care
620 North Walnut St.
Springfield, IL 62702
217-523-8488
Fax: 217-523-8493
Email: email@tlcinltc.org

Indiana
United Senior Action
324 W. Morris Street, Suite 114
Indianapolis, IN 46225-1491
317-634-0872
Fax: 317-687-3661
Email: robyngrant@comcast.net

Kansas
Kansas Advocates for Better Care
913 Tennessee Street, #2
Lawrence, KS 66044
800-525-1782
Fax: 785-749-0029
Email: info@kabc.org
www.kabc.org

Kentucky
Kentuckians for Nursing Home Reform
1530 Nicholasville Road
Lexington, KY 40503
859-312-5617
Email: kynursinghomereform@yahoo.com
www.kynursinghomereform.org

Louisiana
Citizens Care
1321 8th Street
New Orleans, LA 70118
504-896-8912
Email: citizens@citizenscare.org
www.citizenscare.org

Maryland
Voices for Quality Care (LTC)
PO Box 6555
St. Charles Town Center Mall
Waldorf, MD 20603
888-600-2375
Email: voicesforqualitycare@hotmail.com
www.voicesforqualitycare.org

Massachusetts
MA Advocates for Nursing Home Reform
38 Banks Terrace
Swampscott, MA 01907
781-890-2244
Fax: 781-890-4956
Email: agermain@matrixpartners.com
www.manhr.org

Cape United Elders of Comm. Action Committee
115 Enterprise Road
Hyannis, MA 02601
800-845-1999
Fax: 508-775-7488
Email: susanw@cacci.cc

Michigan
Michigan Campaign for Quality Care
5886 Highgate Avenue
East Lansing, MI 48823
517-324-5754
Fax: 517-333-4339
Email: hirschel@umich.edu
www.campaignforqualitycare.org

Citizens For Better Care
4750 Woodward Avenue, Suite 410
Detroit, MI 48201-1308
313-832-6387
Fax: 313-832-7407
Email: cbcnancyj@yahoo.com
http://cbcmi.org

Minnesota
ElderCare Rights Alliance
2626 East 82nd Street, Suite 230
Bloomington, MN 55425
952-854-7304
Fax: 952-854-8535
Email: thyder@eldercarerights.org

Missouri
Missouri Coalition for Quality Care
P.O. Box 7165
Jefferson City, MO 65102
888-262-5644

Email: mail@mcqc.com
www.mcqc.com

Nebraska
Nebraska Advocates for Nursing Home Residents
10050 Regency Circle
Suite 525
Omaha, NE 68114
402-397-3801
Fax: 402-397-3869
Email: bjseidler@qwest.net

New Mexico
New Mexicans for Quality Long Term Care
P.O. Box 1712
Belen, NM 87002
505-864-7534
Fax: 505-864-7377
Email: jcbeverly@msn.com
www.nmqltc.org

New York
Coalition of Institutionalized, Aged and Disabled
425 East 25th Street
New York, NY 10010
212-481-7572
Fax: 212-481-5149
Email: ciadny@aol.com
www.ciadny.org

Long Term Care Community Coalition
242 West 30th Street, Suite 306
New York, NY 10001
212-385-0355
Fax: 212-239-2801
Email: richard@ltccc.org
www.ltccc.org

FRIA
18 John Street, Suite 905
New York, NY 10038
212-732-5667
Fax: 212-732-6945
Email: apaul@fria.org
www.fria.org

North Carolina
Friends of Residents In Long Term Care
883-C Washington St.
Raleigh, NC 27605
919-782-1530
Fax: 919-782-1558
Email: friends@forltc.org
www.forltc.org

Ohio
Families for Improved Care, Inc.
P.O. Box 21398
Columbus, OH 43221-1355
614-459-8438
Email: fficgroup@aol.com
www.familiesforimprovedcare.org

Oklahoma
Oklahomans for Improvement of NH Care
1423 Oakwood Drive
Norman, OK 73069-4446
405-364-5004
Fax: 405-364-5004
Email: JADCD@aol.com
www.nhadvocates.org/okinch/home.htm

Pennsylvania
CARIE
100 N. 17th Street, Suite 600
Philadelphia, PA 19103
215-545-5728
Fax: 215-546-9963
Email: menio@carie.org
www.carie.org

Rhode Island
Alliance for Better Long Term Care
422 Post Road, Suite 204
Warwick, RI 02888
401-785-3340
Fax: 401-785-3391
Email: rhawkins@alliancebltc.org
www.stateomb@alliancebltc.org

Tennessee
East Tennessee Coalition on Advocacy, Inc.
701 Chateaugay Road
Knoxville, TN 37923
865-531-4638
Fax: 865-531-7216

Texas
Texas Advocates for Nursing Home Residents
500 East Anderson Lane, #234W
Austin, TX 78752
512-719-4757
Fax: 512-719-5057
Email: bethferris@peoplepc.com
www.tanhr.org

Texas Advocates for Nursing Home Residents
1015 Wavecrest Dr.
Houston, TX 77062
281-488-5291

Fax: 281-480-4351
Email: sealbeem@aol.com
www.tanhr.org

Texas Advocates for Nursing Home Residents
634 Green Cove Lane
Dallas, TX 75232
972-572-6330
Fax: 214-376-7707
Email: oreillyl@swbell.net
www.tanhr.org

Texans For The Improvement of Long-Term Care
4545 Cook Road, #303
Houston, TX 77072-1125
281-933-4533
Fax: 281-498-6344
Email: sperlin@aol.com
http://tiltc.virtualave.net

Virginia
Citizens Committee to Protect the Elderly
407 Oakmears Crescent
Virginia Beach, VA 23462
757-518-8500
Fax: 757-518-8501
Email: citizenscommittee@citizenscommittee.org
www.citizenscommittee.org

TLC for Long Term Care
P.O. Box 523323
Springfield, VA 22152
703-338-7333
Fax: 866-487-8470
Email: tlc4ltc@msn.com
www.tlc4ltc.org

Virginia Friends & Relatives of NH Residents
1426 Claremount Avenue
Richmond, VA 23227
804-644-2804
Fax: 804-644-5640
Email: elderights@aol.com

Friends & Relatives of Nursing Home Residents
P.O. Box 551
540-896-2741
Fax: 540-433-2202
Email: asbrls@hotmail.com

Washington
Family Advocates for NH Improvement
10955 W. Villa Monte Drive
Mukilteo, WA 98275
888-647-3367
Fax: 888-647-3367
Email: fanhimg@aol.com

Resident Councils of Washington
220 E. Canyon View Road
Belfair, WA 98528
360-275-8000
Fax: 360-277-0144
Email: rcwexec@residentcouncil.org
www.residentcouncil.org

Wyoming
Concerned Citizens For Quality Nursing Home Care
811 Glenn Road
Casper, WY 82601
307-266-6659
Email: eca@wyoming.com

Fight To Get The Coverage You Deserve

We usually don't think about insurance until we need it. But when we need it we really need to be able to count on it. Insurance can be confusing and is constantly changing. Luckily, there are many organizations that can help! Each state government runs an insurance department and there is even a National Association of Insurance Commissioners (NAIC). Each state offers a variety of assistance including: educational information for consumers, fraud information, complaints, insurance glossary, agent/agency searches, price comparison, consumer alerts and more. Georgia even has an online quiz "Get Smart About Insurance" to help you determine your insurance intellect. Contact the NAIC or your state commissioner.

National
NAIC Executive Headquarters
2301 McGee Street, Suite 800
Kansas City, MO 64108-2662
816-842-3600
Fax: 816-783-8175
www.naic.org/

Alabama
Alabama Department of Insurance
201 Monroe Street, Suite 1700
Montgomery, AL 36104
Mailing Address:
P.O. Box 303351
Montgomery, AL 36130-3351
334-269-3550
Fax: 334-241-4192
www.aldoi.gov

Alaska
Alaska Division of Insurance
9th Floor State Office Building
333 Willoughby Avenue
Juneau, AK 99801
Mailing address:
P.O. Box 99811-0805
907-465-2515
Fax: 907-465-3422
TDD: 907-465-5437
www.dced.state.ak.us/insurance/

Arizona
Arizona Department of Insurance
2910 N. 44th Street, Suite 210
Phoenix, AZ 85018-7269
800-544-9208
602-912-8450
www.id.state.az.us/

Arkansas
Arkansas Insurance Department
1200 West Third Street
Little Rock, AR 72201
501-371-2600
800-282-9134
Fax: 501-371-2618
http://insurance.arkansas.gov/

California
California Department of Insurance
Consumer Communications Bureau
300 South Spring Street, South Tower
Los Angeles, CA 90013
800-927-HELP
213-897-8921
TDD: 800-482-4833
www.insurance.ca.gov/

Colorado
Colorado Division of Insurance
1560 Broadway, Suite 850
Denver, CO 802023
303-894-7499
303-894-7490 Consumer Information
800-930-3745
www.dora.state.co.us/insurance/

Connecticut
Connecticut Insurance Department
153 Market Street, 7th Floor
Hartford, CT 06103
860-297-3800
Fax: 860-566-7410
www.ct.gov/cid/site/default.asp

Delaware
Delaware Insurance Department
841 Silver Lake Boulevard
Dover, DE 19904
302-739-4251
302-739-6775 Consumer Hotline
800-282-8611
www.state.de.us/inscom/default.shtml

District of Columbia
District of Columbia Department of Insurance, Securities and Banking
810 1st Street NE
Suite 701
Washington, DC 20002
202-727-8000
Fax: 202-535-1196
http://disr.washingtondc.gov/disr/site/default.asp

Florida
Florida Department of Financial Services
200 East Gaines Street
Tallahassee, FL 32399-0300
800-342-2762
850-413-3100
www.fldfs.com/

Georgia
Georgia Insurance and Safety Fire Commissioner
Consumer Services Division
2 Martin Luther King Drive, Suite 716
Atlanta, GA 30334
800-656-2298
www.gainsurance.org/

Hawaii
Hawaii Department of Commerce & Consumer Affairs
Insurance Division
King Kalakaua Building
335 Merchant Street, Room 213
Honolulu, HI 96813
Mailing address:
P.O. Box 3614

Honolulu, HI 96811
808-586-2790
808-586-2799
Fax: 808-586-2806
www.hawaii.gov/dcca/areas/ins/

Idaho
Idaho Department of Insurance
700 West State Street
P.O, Box 83720
Boise, ID 83720-0043
208-334-4250
www.doi.state.id.us/

Illinois
Illinois Division of Insurance
Springfield Office
320 W Washington Street
Springfield, IL 62767-0001
217-782-4515
Fax: 217-782-5020

Chicago Office
James R Thompson Center
100 W Randolph Street, Suite 9-301
Chicago, IL 30301-3395
312-814-2420
Fax: 312-814-5416
www.idfpr.com/DOI/Default2.asp

Indiana
Indiana Department of Insurance
311 W Washington Street, Suite 300
Indianapolis, IN 46204-2787
317-232-2385
Fax: 317-232-5251
www.ai.org/idoi/index.html

Iowa
Iowa Insurance Division
330 Maple Street
Des Moines, IA 50319-0065
515-281-5705
877-955-1212
Fax: 515-281-3059
www.iid.state.ia.us/

Kansas
Kansas Insurance Department
420 SW 9th Street
Topeka, KS 66612-1678
785-296-3071
800-432-2484
Fax: 785-296-2283
www.ksinsurance.org/

Kentucky
Kentucky Office of Insurance
215 W Main Street
Frankfort, KY 40601
800-595-6053
TTY: 800-462-2081
http://doi.ppr.ky.gov/kentucky/

Louisiana
Louisiana Department of Insurance
1702 N. 3rd Street
Baton Rouge, LA 70802
Mailing address:
P.O. Box 94214
Baton Rouge, LA 70802
800-259-5300
225-342-5900
www.ldi.la.gov/

Maine
Maine Department of Financial Regulation
Bureau of Insurance
#34 State House Station
Augusta, ME 04333-0034
Mailing address:
124 Northern Avenue
Gardiner, ME 04345
207-624-8475
800-300-5000
TTY: 888-577-6690
Fax: 207-624-8599
www.state.me.us/pfr/ins/ins_index.htm

Maryland
Maryland Insurance Administration
525 St. Paul Place
Baltimore, MD 21202-2272
410-468-2000
800-492-6116
TTY: 800-735-2258
www.mdinsurance.state.md.us/

Massachusetts
Massachusetts Division of Insurance
One South Station, 5th Floor
Boston, MA 02110-2208
617-521-7794
Fax: 617-521-7575
www.mass.gov/doi/

Michigan
Michigan Office of Financial and Insurance Services
P.O. Box 30220
Lansing, MI 48909
517-373-0220

877-999-6442
Fax: 517-335-4978
www.michigan.gov/cis/0,1607,7-154-10555---,00.html

Minnesota
Minnesota Department of Commerce
85 7th Plaza East, Suite 500
St. Paul, MN 55101
651-296-4026
TTY: 651-296-2860
Fax: 651-297-1959
www.state.mn.us/portal/mn/jsp/content.do?subchannel=-536881550&id=-536881350&agency=Commerce

Missouri
Missouri Department of Insurance
301 West High Street, Room 530
Jefferson City, MO 65101
Mailing address: P.O. Box 690
Jefferson City, MO 65102-0690
800-726-7390
573-751-4126
Fax: 573-751-1165
www.insurance.state.mo.us/

Montana
Montana Insurance Division
840 Helena Avenue
Helena, MT 59601
800-332-6148
406-444-2040
TDD: 406-444-3246
www.discoveringmontana.com/sao/insurance/index.html

Nebraska
Nebraska Department of Insurance
Terminal Building
941 "O" Street, Suite 400
Lincoln, NE 68508-3639
402-471-2201
877-564-7323
TD: 800-833-7351
www.doi.ne.gov/

Nevada
Nevada Division of Insurance
Carson City Office:
788 Fairview Drive, Suite 300
Carson City, NV 89701
775-687-4270
Fax: 775-687-3937

Las Vegas Office:
2501 East Sahara Avenue
Suite 302
Las Vegas, NV 89104
702-486-4009
Fax: 702-486-4007
http://doi.state.nv.us/

New Hampshire
New Hampshire Insurance Department
31 South Fruit Street, Suite 14
Concord, NH 03301
800-852-3416
603-271-2261
Fax: 603-271-1406
www.state.nh.us/insurance/

New Jersey
New Jersey Department of Banking and Insurance
P.O. Box 325
Trenton, NJ 08625
800-446-SHOP
609-292-5360
Fax: 609-292-3144
www.state.nj.us/dobi/index.shtml

New Mexico
New Mexico Public Regulatory Commission
Insurance Division
P.E.R.A. Building, 4th Floor
1120 Paseo de Peralta
Santa Fe, NM 87501
Mailing address:
P.O. Box 1269
Santa Fe, NM 87504-1269
800-947-4722
505-827-4601
Fax: 505-827-4734
www.nmprc.state.nm.us/insurance/inshm.htm

New York
New York Insurance Department
State Consumer Services Hotline 800-342-3736
www.ins.state.ny.us/

New York City Office
25 Beaver Street
New York, NY 10004
212-480-6400

Albany Office
One Commerce Plaza
Albany, NY 12257
518-474-6600

Buffalo Office
Walter Mahoney Office Building
65 Court Street

Buffalo, NY 14202
716-847-7618

Long Island Office
163 Mineola Boulevard
Mineola, NY 11501
516-248-5886

Rochester Office
189 N. Water Street
Rochester, NY 14604
585-325-3274- Insurance Fraud

Syracuse Office
620 Erie Boulevard West, Suite 105
Syracuse, NY 13204
315-423-1102- Insurance Fraud

Oneonta Office
Road 4, Box 51E
Oneonta, NY 13820
607-433-3628- Insurance Fraud

North Dakota
North Dakota Insurance Department
State Capitol, Fifth Floor
600 East Boulevard Avenue
Bismarck, ND 58505-0320
701-328-2440
800-247-0560
Fax: 701-328-4880
www.state.nd.us/ndins/

Ohio
Ohio Department of Insurance
2100 Stella Court
Columbus, OH 43215-1067
800-686-1526 Consumer Hotline
614-644-2658
Fax: 614-644-3743
www.ohioinsurance.gov/

Oklahoma
Oklahoma Insurance Department
Oklahoma City Office
2401 N.W. 23rd Street
Suite 28
Oklahoma City, OK 73107
800-522-0071
405-521-2828
Fax: 405-521-6635
www.oid.state.ok.us/

Tulsa Office
3105 E. Skellt Drive, Suite 305
Tulsa, OK 74105-6371
800-728-2906
918-747-7700
Fax: 918-747-7720
Mailing address:
P.O. Box 53408
Oklahoma City, OK 73152-3408
www.oid.state.ok.us/

Oregon
Oregon Department of Consumer & Business Services
Insurance Division
350 Winter Street NE, Room 440
Salem, OR 97309
Mailing address:
P.O. Box 14480
Salem, OR 97309-0405
503-947-7980
Fax: 503-378-4351
www.cbs.state.or.us/external/ins/index.html

Pennsylvania
Pennsylvania Insurance Department
State Consumer Services Hotline 877-881-6388
www.ins.state.pa.us/ins/site/default.asp

Harrisburg Regional Office
1209 Strawberry Square
Harrisburg, PA 17102
717-787-2317
TTY: 717-783-3898
Fax: 717-787-8585

Philadelphia Regional Office
Room 1701, State Office Building
1400 Spring Garden Street
Philadelphia, PA 19130
215-560-2630
TTY: 215-560-2471
Fax: 210-560-2648

Pittsburgh Regional Office
Room 34, State Office Building
300 Liberty Avenue
Pittsburgh, PA 15222
412-565-5020
TTY: 412-564-2376
Fax; 412-565-7648

Rhode Island
Rhode Island Department of Business Regulation
Division of Insurance
233 Richmond Street
Providence, RI 02903
401-222-2246

Fax: 401-222-6098
www.dbr.state.ri.us/insurance.html

South Carolina
South Carolina Department of Insurance
300 Arbor Lake Drive, Suite 1200
Columbia, SC 29223
Mailing address:
P.O. Box 100105
Columbia, SC 29202-3105
803-737-6229
Fax: 803-737-6229
www.doi.state.sc.us/

South Dakota
South Dakota Division of Insurance
445 East Capitol Avenue
Pierre, SD 57501
605-773-3563
Fax: 605-773-5369
www.state.sd.us/drr2/reg/insurance/

Tennessee
Tennessee Department of Commerce & Insurance
500 James Robertson Parkway
Davy Crockett Tower
Nashville, TN 37243-0565
615-741-2241
www.state.tn.us/commerce/insurance/index.html

Texas
Texas Department of Insurance
333 Guadalupe
Austin, TX 78701
Mailing address:
P.O. Box 149104
Austin, TX 78714-9104
800-252-3439 Consumer Helpline
800-578-4677
512-463-6169
www.tdi.state.tx.us/

Utah
Utah Insurance Department
3110 State Office Building
Salt Lake City, UT 84114-6901
801-538-3800
801-538-3800 Consumer Service
800-439-3805
Fax: 801-538-3829
TDD: 801-538-3826
www.insurance.utah.gov/

Vermont
Vermont Department of Banking, Insurance, Securities & Health Care Administration
Insurance Division
89 Main Street, Drawer 20
Montpelier, VT 05620-3101
802-828-3301
Fax: 802-828-3306
www.bishca.state.vt.us/InsurDiv/insur_index.htm

Virginia
Virginia State Corporation Commission
Bureau of Insurance
1300 East Main Street
Richmond, VA 23219
Mailing address:
P.O. Box 1157
Richmond, VA 23218
804-371-9741
877-310-6560 Consumer Hotline
www.scc.virginia.gov/division/boi/index.htm

Washington
Washington Office of the Insurance Commissioner
5000 Capitol Boulevard
Tumwater, WA 98501
Mailing address:
P.O. Box 40255
Olympia, WA 98504-0255
360-725-7000
800-562-6900
TDD: 360-664-3154
Fax: 360-586-3535
www.insurance.wa.gov/

West Virginia
West Virginia Insurance Commission
Consumer Service Division
1124 Smith Street, Room 309
Charleston, WV 25301
Mailing address:
P.O. Box 50540
Charleston, WV 25305-0540
888-TRY-WVIC (888-879-9842)
TTY: 800-435-7381
Fax: 304-558-4965
www.wvinsurance.gov/

Wisconsin
Wisconsin Office of the Commissioner of Insurance
125 South Webster Street
Madison, WI 53702
608-266-3585
800-236-8517
Fax: 608-266-9935
http://oci.wi.gov/oci_home.htm

Wyoming
Wyoming Insurance Department
Herschler Building, 3rd Floor East
122 West 25th Street
Cheyenne, WY 82002
307-777-7401
800-438-5768
Fax: 307-777-5895
http://insurance.state.wy.us/

Your Own Strong Arm

Consumer Protection Offices offer a wide variety of important services to consumers. They may mediate complaints, conduct investigations, prosecute offenders of consumer laws, license and regulate professional service providers, advocate for consumer rights, and provide educational materials. For more information on how to get help with a consumer complaint contact your state consumer protection office listed below.

State Consumer Protection Offices

Alabama
Office of the Attorney General
11 South Union St.
Montgomery, AL 36130
334-242-7335
800-392-5658 (toll free in state)
www.ago.state.al.us

Alaska
Consumer Protection Unit
Office of the Attorney General
1031 West 4th Ave., Suite 200
Anchorage, AK 99501-5903
907-269-5100
Fax: 907-276-8554
www.law.state.ak.us

Arizona
Consumer Protection and Advocacy Section
Office of the Attorney General
1275 West Washington St.
Phoenix, AZ 85007
602-542-3702
602-542-5763 (Consumer Information and Complaints)
800-352-8431 (toll free in state)
TDD: 602-542-5002
Fax: 602-542-4579
www.azag.gov
Consumer Protection
Office of the Attorney General
400 West Congress South Bldg., Suite 315
Tucson, AZ 85701
520-628-6504
800-352-8431 (toll free in state)
Fax: 520-628-6532
www.azag.gov

Arkansas
Consumer Protection Division
Office of the Attorney General
323 Center St., Suite 200
Little Rock, AR 72201
501-682-2007
501-682-2341 (Consumer Hotline)
800-482-8982 (Do Not Call Program)
800-448-3014 (Crime Victims Hotline)
877-866-8225 (In State Do Not Call Program)
TDD: 501-682-6073
Fax: 501-682-8118
Email: consumer@ag.state.ar.us
www.ag.state.ar.us

California
California Department of Consumer Affairs
10240 Systems Parkway
Sacramento, CA 95827
916-255-4300
800-952-5210 (toll free in state)
TDD: 916-322-1700
Fax: 916-255-1369
www.autorepair.ca.gov

California Department of Consumer Affairs
400 R St., Suite 3000 1080
Sacramento, CA 95814
916-445-1254
916-445-4465
916-445-2643 (Correspondence and Complaint Review Unit)
800-952-5210 (toll free in state)
TDD/TTY: 916-322-1700
800-326-2297 (TDD/TTY toll free instate)
Email: dca@dca.ca.gov
www.dca.ca.gov

Office of the Attorney General
Public Inquiry Unit
P.O. Box 944255
Sacramento, CA 94244-2550
916-322-3360
800-952-5225 (toll free in state)
TDD: 916-324-5564
Fax: 916-323-5341
www.caag.state.ca.us

Colorado
Consumer Protection Division
Colorado Attorney General's Office
1525 Sherman St., 5th Floor
Denver, CO 80203-1760
303-866-5079
800-222-4444
Fax: 303-866-5443
ElderWatch
1301 Pennsylvania #280
Denver, CO 80203
1-800-222-4444 option 2

Connecticut
Department of Consumer Protection
165 Capitol Ave.
Hartford, CT 06106
860-713-6050
Fax: 860-713-7243
www.ct.gov/dcp

Delaware
Fraud and Consumer Protection Division
Office of the Attorney General
Carvel State Office Building
820 North French St., 5th Floor
Wilmington, DE 19801
302-577-8600
800-220-5424 (toll free in state)
TTY: 302-577-6499
Fax: 302-577-2496
Email: Attorney.General@State.DE.US
www.state.de.us/attgen/

District of Columbia
Consumer & Trade Protection Section
Office of the Attorney General for the District of Columbia
441 4th St., NW, Suite 450 N
Washington, DC 20001
202-442-9828
Fax: 202-727-6546
Email: consumercomplaint.occ@dc.gov

Florida
Florida Dept. of Agriculture and Consumer Service
2005 Apalachee Parkway
Tallahassee, FL 32399-6500
850-922-2966
800-435-7352 (toll free in state)
Fax: 850-410-3839
www.800helpfla.com

Economic Crimes Division
Office of the Attorney General
PL-01 The Capitol
Tallahassee, FL 32399
850-414-3600
866-966-7226 (toll free in state)
TDD800-955-8771
Fax: 850-488-4483
myfloridalegal.com

Multi-State Litigation and Intergovernmental Affairs
Office of the Attorney General
PL-01 The Capitol
Tallahassee, FL 32399
850-414-3300
866-966-7226 (toll free in state)
Fax: 850-410-2672
myfloridalegal.com

Georgia
Governor's Office of Consumer Affairs
2 Martin Luther King, Jr. Dr., Ste 356
Atlanta, GA 30334
404-656-3790
800-869-1123 (toll free in state, outside of Atlanta)
Fax: 404-651-9018
www2.state.ga.us/gaoca

Hawaii
Office of Consumer Protection
Department of Commerce and Consumer Affairs
345 Kekuanaoa St., Room 12
Hilo, HI 96720
808-933-0910
Fax: 808-933-8845

Office of Consumer Protection
Department of Commerce and Consumer Affairs
235 South Beretania St., Room 801
Honolulu, HI 96813-2419
808-586-2636
Fax: 808-586-2640

Office of Consumer Protection
Dept of Commerce and Consumer Affairs
1063 Lower Main St., Ste C-216
Wailuku, HI 96793
808-984-8244

Fax: 808-243-5807
www.hawaii.gov/dcca/ocp

Idaho
Consumer Protection Unit
Idaho Attorney General's Office
650 West State St.
Boise, ID 83720-0010
208-334-2424
800-432-3545 (toll free in state)
Fax: 208-334-2830
www.state.id.us/ag

Illinois
Consumer Fraud Bureau
1001 East Main St.
Carbondale, IL 62901
618-529-6400
800-243-0607 (toll free in state)
TTY: 618-529-0607
877-675-9339 (TTY toll free in state)
Fax: 618-529-6416
Email: ag_consumer@atg.state.il.us
www.illinoisattorneygeneral.gov

Consumer Fraud Bureau
100 West Randolph, 12th Floor
Chicago, IL 60601
312-814-3580
800-386-5438 (toll free in state)
TDD: 312-814-3374
Fax: 312-814-2549
Email: ag_consumer@atg.state.il.us
www.illinoisattorneygeneral.gov

Governor's Office of Citizens Assistance
222 South College, Room 106
Springfield, IL 62706
217-782-0244
800-642-3112 (toll free in state)
Fax: 217-524-4049
Email: governor@state.il.us

Indiana
Consumer Protection Division
Office of the Attorney General
Indiana Government Center South
402 West Washington St., 5th Floor
Indianapolis, IN 46204
317-232-6201
800-382-5516 (Consumer Hotline- toll free in state)
Fax: 317-232-7979
www.in.gov/attorneygeneral

Iowa
Consumer Protection Division
Office of the Attorney General
1305 East Walnut St., 2nd Floor
Des Moines, IA 50319
515-281-5926
888-777-4590 (toll free in state)
Fax: 515-281-6771
Email: consumer@ag.state.ia.us
www.IowaAttorneyGeneral.org

Kansas
Consumer Protection & Antitrust Division
Office of the Attorney General
120 SW 10th, 2nd Floor
Topeka, KS 66612-1597
785-296-3751
800-432-2310 (toll free in state)
TDD/TTY: 785-291-3767
Fax: 785-291-3699
Email: cprotect@ksag.org
www.ink.org/public/ksag

Kentucky
Consumer Protection Division
Office of the Attorney General
1024 Capital Center Dr.
Frankfort, KY 40601
502-696-5389
888-432-9257 (toll free in state)
Fax: 502-573-8317
Email: consumerprotection@ag.ky.gov
www.ag.ky.gov

Consumer Protection Division
Office of the Attorney General
8911 Shelbyville Rd.
Louisville, KY 40222
502-425-4825
Fax: 502-573-8317

Louisiana
Consumer Protection Section
Office of the Attorney General
P.O. Box 94005
Baton Rouge, LA 70804-9005
800-351-4889
Fax: 225-342-326-6499
www.ag.state.la.us

Maine
Office of Consumer Credit Regulation
35 State House Station
Augusta, ME 04333-0035
207-624-8527

800-332-8529 (toll free in state)
TDD/TTY: 207-624-8563
Fax: 207-582-7699
www.mainecreditreg.org

Consumer Protection Division
Office of the Attorney General
6 State House Station
Augusta, ME 04333
207-626-8800
Fax: 207-626-8812
Email: www.maine.gov

Maryland
Consumer Protection Division
Office of the Attorney General
200 Saint Paul Place, 16th Floor
Baltimore, MD 21202-2021
410-528-8662 (Consumer Complaints)
410-576-6550 (Consumer Information)
410-528-1840 (Health Advocacy unit)
TDD: 410-576-6372 (Maryland only)
Fax: 410-576-7040
Email: consumer@oag.state.md.us
www.oag.state.md.us/consumer

Massachusetts
Executive Office of Consumer Affairs and Business Regulation
10 Park Plaza, Room 5170
Boston, MA 02116
617-973-8700 (General Information)
617-973-8787 (Consumer Hotline)
888-283-3757 (toll free in state)
TDD/TTY: 617-973-8790
Fax: 617-973-8798
Email: consumer@state.ma.us
www.mass.gov/Consumer

Consumer Protection and Antitrust Division
Office of the Attorney General
One Ashburton Place
Boston, MA 02108
617-727-8400 (Consumer Hotline)
Fax: 617-727-3265
www.mass.gov/ago

Southern Massachusetts Division
Office of the Attorney General
105 William Street
New Bedford, MA 02740
508-990-9700
Fax: 508-990-8686

Western Massachusetts Division
Office of the Attorney General
436 Dwight St.
Springfield, MA 01103
413-784-1240
Fax: 413-784-1244
www.ago.state.ma.us

Central Massachusetts Division
Office of the Attorney General
One Exchange Place
Worcester, MA 01608
508-792-7600
Fax: 508-795-1991

Michigan
Consumer Protection Division
Office of Attorney General
PO Box 30213
Lansing, MI 48909
517-373-1140
877-765-8388 (toll free)
Fax: 517-241-3771

Minnesota
Consumer Services Division
Attorney General's Office
1400 NCL Tower
445 Minnesota St.
St. Paul, MN 55101
612-296-3353
800-657-3787
Fax: 612-282-2155
Email: attorney.general@state.mn.us
www.ag.state.mn.us/consumer

Mississippi
Consumer Protection Division
Attorney General's Office
P.O. Box 22947
Jackson, MS 39225-2947
601-359-4230
800-281-4418
Fax: 601-359-4231
www.ago.state.ms.us

Bureau of Regulatory Services
Department of Agriculture and Commerce
121 North Jefferson St.
P.O. Box 1609
Jackson, MS 39201
601-359-1111
Fax: 601-359-1175
www.mdac.state.ms.us

Missouri
Consumer Protection and Trade Offense Division

PO Box 899
1530 Rax Court
Jefferson City, MO 65102
573-751-6887
573-751-3321
800-392-8222
TDD/TTY: 800-729-8668 (toll free in state)
Fax: 573-751-7948
Email: attgenmail@moago.org
www.ago.state.mo.us

Montana
Consumer Protection Office
Department of Administration
1219 8th Ave.
PO Box 200151
Helena, MT 59620-0151
406-444-4500
Fax: 406-444-9680
www.state.mt.us/doa/consumerprotection

Nebraska
Office of the Attorney General
Department of Justice
2115 State Capitol
P.O. Box 98920
Lincoln, NE 68509
402-471-2682
402-471-3891 (Spanish)
800-727-6432 (toll free in state)
800-850-7555 (Spanish toll free in state)
Fax: 402-471-0006
www.nol.org/home/ago

Nevada
Consumer Affairs Division
1850 East Sahara Ave, Suite 101
Las Vegas, NV 89104
702-486-7355
800-326-5202
TDD: 702-486-7901
Fax: 702-486-7371
Email: ncad@fyiconsumer.org
www.fyiconsumer.org

Bureau of Consumer Protection
555 E. Washington Ave., Suite 3900
Las Vegas, NV 89101
702-486-3420

Consumer Affairs Division
4600 Kietzke Lane
Building B, Suite 113
Reno, NV 89502
775-688-1800
800-326-5202 (toll free in state)
TDD: 702-486-7901
Fax: 775-688-1803
Email: renocad@fyiconsumer.org
www.fyiconsumer.org

New Hampshire
Consumer Protection and Antitrust Bureau
Attorney General's Office
33 Capitol St.
Concord, NH 03301
603-271-3641
TDD: 800-735-2964
Fax: 603-271-2110
www.doj.nh.gov/consumer/index.html

New Jersey
Division of Consumer Affairs
Department of Law and Public Safety
124 Halsey St
PO Box 45025
Newark, NJ 07102
973-504-6200
800-242-5846 (toll free in state)
Email: www.state.nj.us/lps/ca/home.htm

New Mexico
Consumer Protection Division
PO Drawer 1508
407 Galisteo
Santa Fe, NM 87504-1508
505-827-6060
800-678-1508 (toll free in state)
Fax: 505-827-6685
www.ago.state.nm.us

New York
Bureau of Consumer Frauds and Protection
Office of the Attorney General
State Capitol
Albany, NY 12224
518-474-5481
800-771-7755 (toll free in state)
TDD/TTY:800-788-9898
Fax: 518-474-3618
www.oag.state.ny.us

New York State Consumer Protection Board
5 Empire State Plaza, Suite 2101
Albany, NY 12223-1556
518-474-8583 (Capitol Region)
800-697-1220
Fax: 518-474-2474
Email: webmaster@state.ny.us
www.nysconsumer.gov

Consumer Frauds and Protection Bureau
Office of the Attorney General
120 Broadway, 3rd FL
New York, NY 10271
212-416-8000
212-416-8345
800-771-7755
800-788-9898 or 212-416-8893
Fax: 212-416-6003

North Carolina
Consumer Protection Division
Office of the Attorney General
9001 Mail Service Center
Raleigh, NC 27699-9001
919-716-6400
877-566-7226 (toll free in state)
Fax: 919-716-6050
www.ncdoj.com

North Dakota
Consumer Protection and Antitrust Division
Office of the Attorney General
4205 State Street
PO Box 1054
Bismarck, ND 58502-1054
701-328-3404
800-472-2600 (toll free in state)
TTY: 800-366-6888
Fax: 701-328-5568
Email: cpat@state.nd.us
www.ag.state.nd.us

Ohio
Consumer Protection Section
Attorney General's Office
30 East Broad St., 14th Floor
Columbus, OH 43215-3428
614-466-8831
800-282-0515 (toll free in state)
TDD: 614-466-1393
Fax: 614-728-7583
Email: consumer@ag.state.oh.us
www.ag.state.oh.us

Ohio Consumers' Counsel
10 W. Broad St. 18th Floor
Columbus, OH 43215
614-466-8574 (outside OH)
877-PICK-OCC (toll free in state)
Email: occ@occ.state.oh.us
wwww.pickoca.org

Oklahoma
Commission on Consumer Credit
4545 North Lincoln Blvd., #104
Oklahoma City, OK 73105
405-521-3653
800-448-4904
Fax: 405-521-6740
Email: dhardin@okdocc.state.ok.us
www.okdocc.state.ok.us

Consumer Protection Unit
Oklahoma Attorney General
4545 N. Lincoln Ave., Suite 260
Oklahoma City, OK 73105
405-521-2029
Fax: 405-528-1867
www.oag.state.ok.us

Oregon
Financial Fraud/Consumer Protection Section
Department of Justice
1162 Court St., NE
Salem, OR 97310
503-947-4333
503-378-4320 (Hotline Salem only)
503-229-5576 (Hotline Portland Only)
877-877-9392 (toll free in state)
TDD/TTY: 503-378-5939
Fax: 503-378-5017
www.doj.state.or.us

Pennsylvania
Bureau of Consumer Protection
Office of Attorney General
14th Floor, Strawberry Square
Harrisburg, PA 17120
717-787-9707
800-441-2555 (toll free in state)
877-888-4877 (Health Care Section- toll free in state))
Fax: 717-787-1190
www.attorneygeneral.gov

Office of the Consumer Advocate
Office of the Attorney General
Forum Place, 5th Floor
Harrisburg, PA 17101-1921
717-783-5048 (Utilities only)
800-684-6560 (toll free in state)
Fax: 717-783-7152
Email: consumer@paoca.org
www.oca.state.pa.us

Puerto Rico
Department of Justice
PO Box 902192
San Juan, PR 00902
787-721-2900
Fax: 787-725-2475

Rhode Island
Consumer Protection Unit
Department of Attorney General
150 South Main St.
Providence, RI 02903
401-274-4400
TDD: 401-453-0410
Fax: 401-222-5110
www.riag.state.ri.us/

South Carolina
South Carolina Department of Consumer Affairs
3600 Forest Drive, Suite 300
PO Box 5757
Columbia, SC 29250
803-734-4200
800-922-1594 (toll free in state)
Fax: 803-734-4286
Email: scdca@dca.state.sc.us
www.scconsumer.gov

Office of the Attorney General
PO Box 11549
Columbia, SC 29211
803-734-3970
Fax: 803-734-4323
Email: info@scattorneygeneral.com
www.scattorneygeneral.org

State Ombudsman
Office of Executive Policy and Program
1205 Pendleton St., Room 308
Columbia, SC 29201
803-734-5049
866-300-9333 (toll free in state)
Fax: 803-734-0799
www.myscgov.com

South Dakota
Consumer Affairs
Office of the Attorney General
State Capitol Building
500 East Capitol
Pierre, SD 57501-5070
605-773-4400
800-300-1986 (toll free in state)
TDD: 605-773-6585
Fax: 605-773-7163
Email: consumerhelp@sate.sd.us
www.state.sd.us/atg

Tennessee
Division of Consumer Affairs
500 James Robertson Pkwy., 5th Floor
Nashville, TN 37243-0600
615-741-4737
800-342-8385 (toll free in state)
Fax: 615-532-4994
Email: consumer.affairs@state.tn.us
www.state.tn.us/consumer

Consumer Advocate and Protection Division
Office of the Attorney General
PO Box 20207
Nashville, TN 37202-02071
615-741-1671
Fax: 615-532-2910
www.attorneygeneral.state.tn.us/cpro/cpro

Texas
Houston Regional Office - Consumer Protection
Office of the Attorney General
808 Travis, Suite 300
Houston, TX 77002
713-223-5886
Fax: 713-223-5821
Email: cac@oag.state.tx.us
www.oag.state.tx.us

Utah
Division of Consumer Protection
Department of Commerce
160 East 300 South
Box 146704
Salt Lake City, UT 84114-6704
801-530-6601
Fax: 801-530-6001
Email: consumerproection@utah.gov
www.consumerprotection.utah.gov

Vermont
Consumer Assistance Program
Office of the Attorney General
104 Morrill Hall, UVM
Burlington, VT 05405
802-656-3183
800-649-2424 (toll free in state)
TTY: 802 828-3665
Fax: 802-656-1423
Email: consumer@uvm.edu
www.atg.state.vt.us

Consumer Assurance Section
Food Safety and Consumer Assurance Division
Agency of Agriculture
116 State St.
Montpelier, VT 05620-2901
802-828-2436
Fax: 802-828-5983

Virgin Islands
Department of Licensing and Consumer Affairs
Golden Rock Shopping Center
Christiansted
St. Croix, VI 00820
340-773-2226
Fax: 340-778-8250
wwww.dlca.gov.vi

Virginia
Antitrust and Consumer Litigation Section
Office of the Attorney General
900 East Main St.
Richmond, VA 23219
804-786-2116
800-451-1525
Fax: 804-786-0122
Email: mail@oag.state.va.us
www.oag.state.va.us

Office of Consumer Affairs
Department of Agriculture and Consumer Services
P.O. Box 1163
Richmond, VA 23218
804-786-2042
800-552-9963 (toll free in state)
TDD: 800-828-1120
Fax: 804-225-2666
www.vdacs.state.va.us

Washington
Office of the Attorney General
Regional Consumer Resource Centers
1125 Washington St. SE
Olympia, WA 98504-0100
800-551-4636
www.atg.wa.gov/

West Virginia
Consumer Protection Division
Office of the Attorney General
812 Quarrier St., 6th Floor
P.O. Box 1789
Charleston, WV 25326-1789
304-558-8986
800-368-8808 (toll free in state)
Fax: 304-558-0184
Email: consumer@wvago.state.wv.us
www.wvs.state.wv.us/wvag

Wisconsin
Department of Agriculture, Trade and Consumer Protection
2811 Agriculture Dr.
PO Box 8911
Madison, WI 53708-8911
608-224-4949
800-422-7128 (toll free in state)
TDD: 608-224-5058
Fax: 608-224-4939
Email: hotline@datcp.state.wi.us
www.datcp.state.wi.us

Wyoming
Consumer Protection Unit
Office of the Attorney General
123 State Capitol Building
Cheyenne, WY 82002
307-777-7874
800-438-5799 (toll free in state)
Fax: 307-777-7956
Email: agwebmaster@state.wy.us
www.attorneygeneral.state.wy.us

Free Lawyers

Every state has a Legal Services Developer who is responsible for the development and enhancement of quality legal and advocate assistance for low income Seniors. These Legal Services Developers often are also involved in elder rights efforts and finding alternative avenues of legal assistance for Seniors. Legal Services Developers do not provide legal help, but they do refer Seniors that are in need of legal assistance to appropriate legal providers. They also help with outreach programs, public education, and design and implement programs to improve the quality and quantity of legal assistance available to Seniors in their individual states. For more information on where to find free or low cost legal assistance for Seniors contact the Legal Services Developer in your state from the list below.

Legal Services Developers

Alabama
Todd Russell
Division Planning/ Legal Services Developer/General Counsel
Alabama Department of Senior Services
770 Washington Ave., RSA Plaza, Suite 470
P.O. Box 301851
Montgomery, AL 36130-1851
334-353-9394
Fax: 334-242-5594
Email: trussell@adss.state.al.us

Alaska
Lisa Morley
Division of Senior and Disability Services
Alaska Department of Health and Social Services
240 Main St., Suite 601
Juneau, AK 99801
907-465-3372
Fax: 907-465-1170

Judith DeMarsh
Staff Attorney
Alaska Legal Services Corporation
P.O. Box 307
Nome, AK 99762
907-443-2230
Fax: 907-443-2239
Email: jndemarsh@yahoo.com

Arizona
Ray De La Rosa
Legal Services Developer
AZ Aging and Adult Administration
Department of Economic Security
1789 W. Jefferson, 950A
Phoenix, AZ 85007
602-542-6440
Fax: 602-542-6575
Email: rdelarosa@azdes.gov

Arkansas
Alice Ahart
Acting Legal Services Developer
AR Department of Human Services
Division of Aging and Adult Services
P.O. Box 1437, Slot S530
Little Rock, AR 72203-1437
501-682-8511
Fax: 501-682-8155
Email: alice.ahart@mail.state.ar.us

California
Chisorom U. Okwuosa
Legal Services Developer
CA Department of Aging
1600 K Street, 4th floor
Sacramento, CA 95814
916-327-6849
Fax: 916-324-1903
Email: cokwuosa@aging.ca.gov

Colorado
Valerie L. Corzine, Esq.
CO State Legal Assistance Developer for the Elderly
The Legal Center
455 Sherman St., Suite 130
Denver, CO 80203-4403
303-722-0300, ext. 220
Fax: 303-722-0720
Email: vcorzine@thelegalcenter.org

Connecticut
Mimi Peck-Llewellyn
Legal Services Developer
CT Department of Social Services
Aging Service Division
25 Sigourney St. 10th Floor
Hartford, CT 06106
860-424-5244
Fax: 860-424-5301
Email: marie.peck.llewellyn@po.state.ct.us

Delaware
Allan Zaback, Director
Division of Services for Aging and Adults with Physical Disabilities
Department of Health and Social Services
1901 N. Dupont Highway
New Castle, DE 19720
302-577-4791
Fax: 302-577-4793
Email: azaback@state.de.us

District of Colombia
Jan Allen May
Legal Services Developer
Legal Counsel for the Elderly/AARP
601 E Street, NW
A Building, 4th Floor
Washington, DC 20049
202-434-2164
Fax: 202-434-6464
Email: jmay@aarp.org

Florida
Sarah Graham, Esq.

Director, Elder Rights Unit
FL Department of Elder Affairs
4040 Esplanade Way
Tallahassee, FL 32399-7000
850-414-2000
Fax: 850-414-2004
Email: Grahamsk@elderaffairs.org

Georgia
Natalie Thomas
Legal Services Developer
GA Division of Aging Services
Department of Human Resources
2 Peachtree St., NW, Suite 9.398
Atlanta, GA 30303-3142
404-657-5328
Fax: 404-657-5285
Email: nkthomas@dhr.state.ga.us

Hawaii
Camille Chun-Hoon
Legal Services Developer
Hawaii Executive Office on Aging
250 South Hotel St., Suite 406
Honolulu, HI 96813
808-586-7309
Fax: 808-586-0185
Email: calchunh@mail.health.state.hi.us

Idaho
Sarah Scott
Adult Protection Coordinator & Legal Services Developer
Manager, Program Operations Unit
Idaho Commission on Aging
P.O. Box 83720
Boise, ID 83720-0007
208-334-3833
Fax: 208-334-3033
Email: sscott@icoa.state.id.us

Illinois
Lee Beneze
Legal Services Developer
Illinois Department on Aging
421 E. Capitol Ave., Suite 100
Springfield, IL 62701-1789
217-524-7945
Fax: 217-524-9644
Email: nlben@aol.com

Indiana
Kate Tewanger
Program Consultant/Legal Services Developer
Bureau of Aging and In-Home Services
Indiana Family and Social Services Administration
402 W. Washington St.
P.O. Box 7083, MS-21
Indianapolis, IN 46207-7083
317-232-7148
Fax: 317-232-7867
Email: ktewanger@fssa.state.in.us

Iowa
Deanna Clingan-Fischer
Legal Services Developer
Iowa Department of Elder Affairs
Clemens Building, 3rd Floor
200 Tenth Street
Des Moines, IA 50309
515-242-3319
Fax: 515-242-3300
Email: Deanna.Clingan@iowa.gov

Kansas
Vern Norwood
Director, Elder Rights/Legal Services Developer
Kansas Department on Aging
New England Building
503 S. Kansas Ave.
Topeka, KS 66603-3403
785-291-3358
Fax: 785-296-0256
Email: VernNorwood@aging.state.ks.us

Kentucky
Gail Lightner, Branch Manager
Acting Legal Services Developer
Kentucky Office of Aging Services
Cabinet for Health Services
275 East Main St., 5-CD
Frankfort, KY 40621
502-564-6930
Fax: 502-564-4595
Email: gail.lightner@mail.state.ky.us

Louisiana
Jane Arieux Thomas
Legal Services Developer
LA Governor's Office of Elderly Affairs
13312 Perkins Road
Baton Rouge, LA 70810
225-767-6225
Fax: 225-767-6292
Email; janethomas@msn.com

Maine
Elizabeth Gattine
Legal Services Developer
Maine Bureau of Elder & Adult Services
442 Civic Center Drive

11 State House Station
Augusta, ME 04333-0011
207-287-9200
Fax: 207-287-9229
Email: Elizabeth.gattine@maine.gov

Maryland
Sue Vaeth
Acting Legal Services Developer
Chief, Client and Community Services
Maryland Department of Aging
301 W. Preston St., Suite 1007
Baltimore, MD 21201
410-767-1108
Fax: 410-333-7943
Email: sjv@mail.ooa.state.md.us

Massachusetts
Peter Antonellis
Assistant General Counsel
Acting Legal Services Developer
Massachusetts Executive Office of Elder Affairs
One Ashburton Place, Fifth Floor
Boston, MA 02108
617-727-7750
Fax: 617-727-9368
Email: peter.antonellis@state.ma.us

Michigan
Lynne Weinstein-McCollum
Legal Services Developer
Michigan Office of Services to the Aging
7109 W. Saginaw, First Floor
P.O. Box 30676
Lansing, MI 48909
517-373-7692
Fax: 517-373-4092
Email: Weinstein@michigan.gov

Minnesota
Krista Boston, Supervisor
Consumer Information, Assistance & Advocacy team
Minnesota Board on Aging
Department of Human Services
444 Lafayette Rd., North
St. Pail, MN 55155-3843
651-296-0378
Fax: 651-297-7855
Email: krista.boston@state.mn.us

Mississippi
George Whitten
Legal Services Developer
Mississippi Division of Aging
P.O. Box 352
Jackson, MS 39205
601-359-4535
Email: gwhitten@mdhs.state.ms.us

Missouri
Vicki Keller
Bureau Chief of Senior Programs
Legal Services Developer
Section for Senior Services
Department of Health and Senior Services
P.O. Box 570
3418 Knipp Drive
Jefferson City, MO 65102-0570
573-526-8601
Fax: 573-751-8687
Email: KelleV@dhss.mo.gov

Montana
John McCrea
Legal Services Developer
Montana Department of Public Health and Human Services
Division of Seniors and Long Term Care
P.O. Box 4210
111 N. Saunders, Room 210
Helena, MT 59604-4210
406-444-7783
Fax; 406-444-7743
Email: jmccrea@state.mt.us

Nebraska
Randy Musselman
Elder Rights Specialist
State Unit on Aging
Nebraska Department of Health and Human Services
301 Centennial Mall South
P.O. Box 95044
Lincoln, NE 68509-5044
402-471-2307
Fax: 402-471-4619
Email: randy.musselman@hhss.ne.gov

Nevada
Sally Crawford Ramm
Elder Rights Attorney
Division for Aging Services, Reno Office
Nevada Department of Human Resources
445 Apple St., #104
Reno, NV 89502
775-688-2964
Fax: 775-688-2969
Email: sramm@aging.state.nv.us

New Hampshire
Mary J. McGuire
Legal Coordinator

Bureau of Elderly and Adult Services
129 Pleasant St.
Concord, NH 03301
603-271-4725
Fax: 603-271-4643
Email: mmcguire@dhhs.state.nh.us

New Jersey
Edward Tetelman
Acting Public Guardian
Department of Health and Senior Services
Office of the Public Guardian
P.O. Box 812
Trenton, NJ 08625
609-943-3519
Fax: 609-943-3444
Email: Edward.Tetelman@doh.state.nj.us

New Mexico
Jack Mack
Legal Services Developer
New Mexico Aging and Long Term Services Department
2550 Cerrillos Rd.
Santa Fe, NM 87501
505-476-4767
Fax: 505-827-7649
Email: jack.mack@state.nm.us

New York
William T. Graham
Assistant Counsel/ Legal Services Developer
New York State Office for the Aging
Two Empire State Plaza
Albany, NY 12223-1251
518-474-0388
Fax: 518-474-0608
Email: Bill.Graham@ofa.state.ny.us

North Carolina
Lynne Berry
Legal Services Developer
North Carolina Division of Aging
Department of Health and Human Services
2101 Mail Service Center
Raleigh, NC 27699-2101
919-733-8395
Fax: 919-715-0868
Email: Lynne.Berry@ncmail.net

North Dakota
Lynne Jacobson
Legal Services Developer/Elder Rights Administrator
Aging Services Division
North Dakota Department of Human Services
600 South Second St., Suite 1C
Bismarck, ND 58504-5729
701-328-8915
Fax: 701-328-8989
Email: sojacl@state.nd.su

Ohio
Jim B. Fultz
Legal Services Developer/Program Administrator
Elder Rights Unit
Ohio Department of Aging
50 W. Broad St., 9th Floor
Columbus, OH 43215-3363
614-466-8598
Fax: 614-466-5741
Email: jfultz@age.state.oh.us

Oklahoma
Richard Ingham
Legal Services Developer
Aging Services Division
Oklahoma Department of Human Services
2401 NW 23rd St., Suite 40
Oklahoma City, OK 73107-2413
405-522-3069
Fax: 405-521-2086
Email: Richard.Ingham@OKDHS.org

Oregon
Janay Haas
Legal Services Developer
Seniors and People with Disabilities Services
Oregon Department of Human Services
500 Summer St., NE, E10
Salem, OR 97301-1076
503-945-8999
Fax: 503-373-7902
Email: Janay.Haas@state.or.us

Pennsylvania
Jim Bubb
Legal Services Developer
Office of the Secretary
Pennsylvania Department on Aging
Forum Place, 5th Floor
555 Walnut St.
Harrisburg, PA 17101-1919
717-783-1550
Fax: 717-772-3382
Email: jbubb@state.pa.us

Puerto Rico
Rossana Lopez-Leon
Director, Governor's Office of Elderly Affairs
P.O. Box 50063
Old San Juan Station

San Juan, PR 00902
787-721-5710
Fax: 787-721-6510

Rhode Island
John Smollins, Jr.
Legal Services Developer
Rhode Island Department of Elderly Affairs
Pastore Center
Benjamin Rush Building
35 Howard Ave.
Cranston, RI 02920
401-462-0537
Fax: 401-462-0503
Email: john@dea.state.ri.us

South Carolina
Dale Watson
Elder Rights Coordinator
Lieutenant Governor's Office on Aging
1301 Gervais St., Suite 200
Columbia, SC 29201
803-734-9900
Fax: 803-734-9886
Email: dwatson@aging.sc.gov

South Dakota
Michael Parker
Legal Services Developer
Office of Adult Services and Aging
South Dakota Department of Social Services
700 Governor's Drive
Pierre, SD 57501-2291
605-773-3656
Fax: 605-773-4855
Email: Mike.Parker@state.sd.us

Tennessee
Lucy E. Utt, Coordinator
Legal Assistance Program
Tennessee Commission on Aging & Disability
Andrew Jackson Building, Suite 825
500 Deaderick St.
Nashville, TN 37243-0860
615-741-3745
Fax: 615-741-3309
Email: lucy.utt@state.tn.us

Texas
Roger Adams
Legal Services Developer, Special Project Coordinator
Texas Department of Aging and Disability Services
701 W. 51st St., Mail Code W 352
Austin, TX 78751
512-438-4205
Fax: 512-438-4374
Email: roger.adams@dads.state.tx.us

Utah
Jilenne Gunther
Legal Services Developer
Utah Division of Aging and Adult Services
Department of Human Services
120 North, 200 West, #325
Salt Lake City, UT 84103
801-538-4263
Fax: 801-538-4395
Email: jgunther@utah.gov

Vermont
Dena Monahan
Legal Services Developer
Vermont Department of Aging & Independent Living
103 South Main
Waterbury, VT 05671
802-241-2401
Fax: 802-241-2325
Email: denam@dad.state.vt.us

Virginia
Janet Dingle Brown
Guardianship Coordinator and Legal Services Developer
Virginia Department for the Aging
1610 Forest Ave., Suite 100
Richmond, VA 23229
804-662-7049
Fax: 804-662-9354
Email: janet.brown@vda.virginia.gov

Washington
Legal Services Developer
Washington Department of Social and Human Services
Aging and Adult Services Administration
State Unit on Aging
640 Woodland Sq., Loop Lacey
P.O. Box 45600
Olympia, WA 98504-5600
360-725-2557
800-422-3263
Fax: 360-438-8633

West Virginia
Linda Calvert
Legal Services Developer
West Virginia Bureau of Senior Services
State Capitol, 1900 Kanawha Blvd., East
Charleston, WV 25305
304-558-3317
Fax: 304-558-0004
Email: lcalvert@boss.state.wv.us

Wisconsin
Glenn Silverberg
Legal Services Developer
Wisconsin Bureau of Aging & Long Term Care Resources
One West Wilson St., Room 450
Madison, WI 53707-7851
Fax: 608-267-3201
Fax: 608-267-3203
Email: silvigj@dhfs.state.wi.us

Wyoming
Karen Matson
Staff Attorney and Legal Services Developer
Wyoming Legal Services
P.O. Box 1160
Lander, WY 82520
307-332-6626
Fax: 307-332-5763
Email: kmatson@wyopminglegalservices.com

10,000 Lawyers that Work for Free

If your income is less than $11,963 or $16,038 for a family of two, it's worth checking out the pro bono legal services that are available in your state. Even if your income is more, it's worth checking out because some of these services have flexible requirements depending on your situation and the problem involved. Every year tens of thousands of lawyers volunteer their services to people who need help with almost any kind of problem. For more information on pro bono organizations in your state contact: American Bar Association, 321 North Clark St., Chicago, IL 60610; 312-988-5000; Email: abaprobono@staff.abanet.org; www.abanet.org/legalservices/probono. You can also contact your state bar association from the list below. Their services vary, but they have a wealth of information for the common man. Just look for the public information section.

State Bar Associations

Alabama
Alabama State Bar
415 Dexter Avenue
Montgomery, AL 36104
334-269-1515
Fax: 334-261-6310
www.alabar.org

Alaska
Alaska Bar Association
PO Box 100279
Anchorage, AK 99510-0279
907-272-7469
Fax: 907-272-2932
www.alaskabar.org

Arizona
State Bar of Arizona
4201 N. 24th St., Ste. 200
Phoenix, AZ 85016-6288
602-252-4804
Fax: 602-271-4930
Email: azbar@azbar.org
www.azbar.org

Arkansas
Arkansas Bar Association
400 W. Markham
Little Rock, AR 72201
501-375-4606
Fax: 501-375-4901
Email: arkbar@ipa.net
www.arkbar.com

California
State Bar of California
180 Howard Street
San Francisco, CA 94105-1639
415-538-2000
Fax: 415-561-8305
www.calbar.ca.gov/state/calbar/calbar_home.jsp

Colorado
Colorado Bar Association
1900 Grant St., #950
Denver, CO 80203
303-860-1115
Fax: 303-894-0821
www.cobar.org

Connecticut
Connecticut Bar Association
30 Bank Street
New Britain, CT 06050
860-223-4400
860-223-4488
www.ctbar.org

Delaware
Delaware State Bar Association
301 N. Market Street
Wilmington, DE 19801
302-658-5279
302-658-5212
www.dsba.org

District of Columbia
District of Columbia Bar
1250 H St., NW
6th Floor
Washington, DC 20005
202-737-4700
Fax: 202-626-3471
www.dcbar.org

Florida
The Florida Bar
650 Apalachee Pkwy.
Tallahassee, FL 32399
850-561-5600
Fax: 850-561-5826
www.floridabar.org/tfb/flabarwe.nsf

Georgia
State Bar of Georgia
104 Marietta Street, NW
Suite 100
Atlanta, GA 30303
800-334-6865
Fax: 404-527-8717
www.gabar.org

Hawaii
Hawaii State Bar Association
Penthouse One
1136 Union Mall
Honolulu, HI 96813
808-537-1868
Fax: 808-521-7936
www.hsba.org

Idaho
Idaho State Bar Association
525 W. Jefferson
Boise, ID 83701
208-334-4500
Fax: 208-334-4515
www.state.id.us/isb

Illinois
Illinois State Bar Association
424 South Second St.
Springfield, IL 62701
217-525-1760
Fax: 217-525-0712
http://www.illinoisbar.org

Indiana
Indiana State Bar Association
One Indiana Square
Suite 530
Indianapolis, IN 46204
317-639-5465
Fax: 317-266-2588
www.inbar.org

Iowa
Iowa State Bar Association
521 E. Locust, 3rd Floor
Des Moines, IA 50309-1939
515-243-3179
Fax: 515-243-2511
www.iowabar.org/main.nsf

Kansas
Kansas Bar Association
1200 Harrison St.
P.O. Box 1037
Topeka, KS 66601-1037
785-234-5696
Fax: 785-234-3813
Email: info@ksbar.org
www.ksbar.org

Kentucky
Kentucky Bar Association
514 W. Main St.
Frankfort, KY 40601-1883
502-564-3795
Fax: 502-564-3225
www.kybar.org

Louisiana
Louisiana State Bar Association
601 St. Charles Avenue
New Orleans, LA 70130
504-566-1600
Fax: 504-566-0930
www.lsba.org/home1

Maine
Maine State Bar Association
124 State St.
P.O. Box 788
Augusta, ME 04332-0788
207-622-7523
Fax: 207-623-0083
www.mainebar.org

Maryland
Maryland State Bar Association
520 W. Fayette St.
Baltimore, MD 21201
410-685-7878
Fax: 410-837-0518
Email: msba@msba.org
www.msba.org

Massachusetts
Massachusetts Bar Association
20 West St.
Boston, MA 02111
617-338-0500
Fax: 617-542-3057
www.massbar.org

Michigan
State Bar of Michigan
306 Townsend St.
Lansing, MI 48933-2083
517-346-6327
Fax: 517-372-2410
www.michbar.org

Minnesota
Minnesota State Bar Association
514 Nicollet Mall
Suite 300
Minneapolis, MN 55402
612-333-1183
Fax: 612-333-4927
www.mnbar.org

Mississippi
Mississippi Bar
643 N. State St.
P.O. Box 2168
Jackson, MS 39225-2168
601-948-4471
Fax: 601-355-8635
www.msbar.org

Missouri
Missouri Bar
326 Monroe
Jefferson City, MO 65101
573-635-4128
Fax: 573-635-2811
www.mobar.org

Montana
State Bar of Montana
7 West Sixth Avenue,
Suite 2B
P.O. Box 577
Helena, MT 59624
406-442-7660
Fax: 406-442-7763
www.montanabar.org

Nebraska
Nebraska State Bar Association
635 S. 14th St.
2nd Floor
Lincoln, NE 68508
402-475-7091
Fax: 402-475-7098
www.nebar.com

Nevada
State Bar of Nevada
600 E. Charleston Blvd.
Las Vegas, NV 89104
702-382-2200
Fax: 702-385-2878
www.nvbar.org

New Hampshire
New Hampshire Bar Association
112 Pleasant St.
Concord, NH 03301
603-224-6942
Fax: 603-224-2910
Email: info@nhbar.org
www.nhbar.org

New Jersey
New Jersey State Bar Association
New Jersey Law Center
One Constitution Center
New Brunswick, NJ 08901-1500
732-249-5000
Fax: 732-249-2815
www.njsba.com

New Mexico
State Bar of New Mexico
5121 Masthead NE
Albuquerque, NM 87109
505-797-6000

Fax: 505-828-3765
Email: sbnm@nmbar.org
www.nmbar.org

New York
New York State Bar Association
One Elk Street
Albany, NY 12207
518-463-3200
Fax: 518-487-5564
www.nysba.org

North Carolina
North Carolina State Bar
P.O. Box 25908
208 Fayetteville Street Mall
Raleigh, NC 27611
919-828-4620
Fax: 919-821-9168
www.ncbar.com/index.asp

North Carolina Bar Association
P.O. Box 3688
Cary, NC 27519
919-677-0561
Fax: 919-677-0761
www.ncbar.org

North Dakota
State Bar Association of North Dakota
P.O. Box 2136
Bismarck, ND 58502-2136
701-255-1404
Fax: 701-224-1621
www.sband.org

Ohio
Ohio State Bar Association
1700 Lake Shore Drive
P.O. Box 16562
Columbus, OH 43216-6562
614-487-2050
Fax: 614-487-1008
www.ohiobar.org

Oklahoma
Oklahoma Bar Association
1901 North Lincoln
Oklahoma City, OK 73105
405-416-7000
Fax: 405-416-7001
www.okbar.org

Oregon
Oregon State Bar
5200 SW Meadows Road
P.O. Box 1689
Lake Oswego, OR 97035-0889
503-620-0222
Fax: 503-684-1366
www.osbar.org

Pennsylvania
Pennsylvania Bar Association
100 South Street
P.O. Box 186
Harrisburg, PA 17108-0186
800-932-0311
Fax: 717-238-1204
www.pabar.org

Rhode Island
Rhode Island Bar Association
115 Cedar St.
Providence, RI 02903
401-421-5720
Fax: 401-421-2703
Email: ribarxxx@councel.com
www.ribar.com

South Carolina
South Carolina Bar
950 Taylor St.
Columbia, SC 29202-0608
803-799-6653
Fax: 803-799-4118
www.scbar.org

South Dakota
State Bar of South Dakota
222 East Capitol Ave.
Pierre, SD 57501-2596
605-224-7554
Fax: 605-224-0282
www.sdbar.org

Tennessee
Tennessee Bar Association
221 4th Avenue N. #400
Nashville, TN 37219-2198
615-383-7421
Fax: 615-297-8058
www.tba.org

Texas
State Bar of Texas
1414 Colorado
Austin, TX 78701
512-463-1463
Fax: 512-473-2295
www.texasbar.com

Utah
Utah State Bar
645 S. 200 East
Suite 310
Salt Lake City, UT 84111-3834
801-531-9077
Fax: 801-531-0660
www.utahbar.org

Vermont
Vermont Bar Association
35-37 Court St.
P.O. Box 100
Montpelier, VT 05601-0100
802-223-2020
Fax: 802-223-1573
www.vtbar.org

Virginia
Virginia State Bar
Suite 1500
707 E. Main St.
Richmond, VA 23219-2803
804-775-0551
Fax: 804-775-0501
www.vsb.org

Virginia Bar Association
701 E. Franklin St.
Suite 1120
Richmond, VA 23219
804-644-0041
Fax: 804-644-0052
Email: vba@vba.org
www.vba.org

Washington
Washington State Bar Association
2101 Fourth Ave.
4th Floor
Seattle, WA 98121-2330
206-727-8244
Fax: 206-727-8320
www.wsba.org

West Virginia
West Virginia State Bar
2006 Kanawha Blvd., E.
Charleston, WV 25311
304-558-7993
Fax: 304-558-2467
www.wvbar.org

West Virginia Bar Association
P.O. Box 2162
Huntington, WV 25722
304-522-2652
Fax: 304-522-2795
www.wvbarassociation.org

Wisconsin
State Bar of Wisconsin
5302 Eastpark Boulevard
P.O. Box 7158
Madison, WI 53707-7158
608-257-3838
Fax: 608-257-5502
www.wisbar.org

Wyoming
Wyoming State Bar Association
P.O. Box 109
Cheyenne, WY 82003-0109
307-632-9061
Fax: 307-632-3737
www.wyomingbar.org

Courses and Degrees

Education: Get A Degree, GED, PhD or Just Learn For Free

Lifelong learning and training is a great way to stay young, alert and active. The opportunities are endless for older Americans when it comes to learning something brand new or staying current with an old interest. The first four listings are all great places to start.

350 Colleges You Can Go To For Free If You're 55+

Believe it or not, more than 350 colleges and universities all across the country have special programs for seniors who are interested in going back to school. This often means auditing courses or taking courses for credit for free or at discounts up to 90% on the list price. They also offer discounts on fees and books, and even special deals on housing. You can audit just one course or get a PhD. Some states call it a Senior Scholar program. Anyone interested should contact the school they wish to attend to find out how to apply for a discount or waiver. Some limitations and restrictions may apply. Contact your local college or university and ask what programs they offer.

$50,000 To Study French Cooking, James Joyce, or Anything

Over $30 billion a year is given out in scholarship money and most of it can not discriminate against the applicant (you) because of age. It's against the law. Also remember that you do not have to be low income to receive a scholarship or grant to attend college. The data show that people making over $100,000 a year get more government money for college than people making less than $100,000 a year. Below in this section you will find a sampling of scholarship programs but there are literally thousands available and no one book can have it all. Here is where to start your research to find them all.

1) <u>Federal Government Grants, Loans and Scholarships</u>
   They are described in a book called the Catalog of Federal Domestic Assistance. This book is available at your local public library or the U.S. Government Printing Office http://bookstore.gpo.gov. You can also search the contents of this book for free on the web at www.cfda.gov.

2) <u>State Government Grants, Loans and Scholarships</u>
   There are close to 400 programs worth almost $3 billion dollars in financial aid available through all 50 states. Did you know that there are state money programs which:
   - Pay for a singing degree?
   - Give you money to study wildlife?
   - Give you $2000 to go to vocational school?
   - Pay for your nursing, teaching or law degree?
   - Give you $7000 to study marine sciences?

Every state has grants and other money available for higher education. Look for the state office of higher education. You can find them by dialing 411 and asking for your state capitol operator or by going to the web at www.govengine.com and clicking on your state.

3) Find All The Non-Government Money Programs
There are dozens of scholarship directories available including this one. Because one directory cannot possibly have everything, it is better to have a collection of scholarship directories, but this can become too expensive. So, you can go to your local library, or you can go into a local large bookstore that has a coffee shop and buy a cup of $3.00 coffee and spend an afternoon looking through all the books. You are only going to get a few scholarships out of any one book. Copy down the info and do your follow up. This way, for the price of a cup of coffee, you have access to hundreds of dollars worth of directories. Most of these book stores have big comfy chairs to encourage you to spend time there using their books. Such a deal.

4) Free Research To Find More Money
This is an information clearinghouse that has free research either on the web or on the phone on any education topic. For example, you can search for information sources on topics such as scholarships or financial aid for graduate students. What do you have to lose? It's FREE. Contact: Education Resources Information Center (ERIC), 800-LET-ERIC (538-3742), www.eric.ed.gov.

Adult Education Classes: French, Web Design, Woodworking, or Estate Planning

Every community in the country offers adult education classes. This is an easy way to learn skills and knowledge in a low pressure environment. If there is a charge is can be as cheap as $25 with seniors getting a 50% discount with waivers and more discounts available for certain incomes or circumstances. Pasadena California offers FREE classes in English as a Second Language, Automotive Technology, Computer Repair, Culinary Arts, Electrician, and Emergency Medical Technician. To get a copy of the Adult Education Classes available in your area contact your local library or contact your state office of Adult Education in your state capitol by calling 411 and asking for your state capitol operator or go to www.govengine.com or www.ed.gov/about/contacts/state/index.html?src=sm. Or contact Office of Vocational and Adult Education, U.S. Department of Education, 400 Maryland Avenue, SW, Washington, DC 20202-7100; 202-245-7700, 800-872-5327, Fax: 202-245-7838; To find a local office go to http://www.ed.gov/about/offices/list/ovae/resource/statelink_txt.html

Free Adult Diploma Program

Check to see if you can get a diploma because of your life experiences. It may require completing a few projects and an interview. But is sure beats going back to high school. Many for these programs are completely free or there may be a small charge for some brush-up courses.

- The Vermont Department of Education has a completely FREE Adult Diploma Program. See http://www.state.vt.us/educ/new/html/pgm_adulted/adp/enroll.html

- Exeter, New Hampshire charges $85/each if you need to take a few courses but also has scholarships available. See http://sau16.org/adulted/diplomaprog.htm or call 603-775-8457.

- Western Connecticut Regional Adult and Continuing Education Adult High School Diploma Program offers classes twice a week for 8 weeks to get a diploma and the cost is FREE. See http://teacherweb.com/CT/NewtownPublicSchools/AdultandContinuingEducation/hf4.stm or call 203-426-1787.

To find a program in your area contact your state office of Adult Education in your state capitol by calling 411 and asking for your state capitol operator or go to www.govengine.com Or contact Office of Vocational and Adult Education, U.S. Department of Education, 400 Maryland Avenue, SW, Washington, DC 20202-7100; 202-245-7700, 800-872-5327, Fax: 202-245-7838; To find a local office go to http://www.ed.gov/about/offices/list/ovae/resource/statelink_txt.html. If you don't get a good answer from these sources contact your elected official: your congressman, senator or state representative.

Vets Get Free Honorary H.S. Diplomas

If you are a Veteran of Vietnam, Korea or WWII you may be eligible to receive an Honorary High School Diploma without homework, tests or anything else. Families of deceased veterans may also be able to receive a diploma in their memory.

- The state of Virginia has a VA State War Veteran Honorary Diploma see http://www.fcps.k12.va.us/DIS/OACE/studentsrvcs.html#senior or call 703-503-6409. Montana calls their program an Honorary High School Diploma Program at http://www.opi.mt.gov/VeteransEd/diploma.html or call 406-444-4438. And the state of Missouri calls their program Operation Recognition and the details are at http://www.dese.state.mo.us/commissioner/pubinfo/FAQs/honorarydiploma.htm or call 866-VET-INFO.

Contact your state office of Adult Education in your state capitol by calling 411 and asking for your state capitol operator or go to www.govengine.com. Or contact Office of Vocational and Adult Education, U.S. Department of Education, 400 Maryland Avenue, SW, Washington, DC 20202-7100; 202-245-7700, 800-872-5327, Fax: 202-245-7838; To find a local office go to http://www.ed.gov/about/offices/list/ovae/resource/statelink_txt.html. If you don't get a good answer from these sources contact your elected official: your congressman, senator or state representative.

Learn Video Production and Produce Your Own TV Show

Every community that has a cable station also has a local nonprofit cable access channel which any member of the community can be trained to use and produce their own TV shows. You will have to pay for one class or a few classes depending on what you want to do. Most classes range from $50 to $200 each. You can train to just be a camera person, or an actor, or a producer. You can have your our sports talk show, foreign affairs show or even comedy hour and the entire cable system can watch it. This can be your first step to Hollywood. Contact your local cable company and ask for the cable access channel. If no one knows what you are talking about call the Mayor's office or County Government Office.

Get Your Degree At Home, For Free

It's no longer necessary to commute to class or even dress for class. Technology allows you to take all your classes sitting at home. The U.S. Distance Learning Association http://www.usdla.org/html/resources/dllp/he.htm states that over the next few years there will be over 2.3 million students taking distance learning courses. It's an ideal lifestyle for busy or lazy, adults and seniors. On the Washington State University website, Katie Paulson of Evans, WA says "You may be thinking that you are too old or that you aren't a good enough student-or that there aren't any scholarships or private grants out there for people who have been out of school 5 or even 50 years. Fortunately you are wrong! I have been able to finance my DDP courses with scholarship money I found by using skills I learned helping high school students research scholarships." So when you are investigating taking courses at a local college, investigate taking distance learning courses from a college far away too.

Free Financial Management Courses At Your County

Your local cooperative extension service offers free or very low fee courses and workshops on all kinds of subjects including personal finance, small business, food and nutrition, plants and gardening, pets and animals, and health care. Contact your local County Cooperative Extension service listed in the blue pages of your telephone directory or you can also find your local office at http://www.csrees.usda.gov/Extension/index.html

Learn To Become A Master Gardner

Master Gardner classes are offered by the USDA County Cooperative Extension Service offices around the country. The program varies throughout the country, but typically, individuals attend at least 30-50 hours of classroom instruction and then contribute a minimum of 30-50 hours of volunteer service. The courses usually have a small cost to cover teaching materials. At lease 20 hours of volunteering is required each subsequent year. Master Gardeners assist with garden lectures, exhibits, demonstrations, school and community gardening, phone diagnostic service, research, and many other projects. Contact your local County Cooperative Extension Service located in the blue pages of your telephone book. The American Horticultural Society keeps database of all programs around the country at http://www.ahs.org/master_gardeners/ or call 800-777-7931.

Free Adult Learning Classes

The National Institute for Literacy is a national resource for adult education and literacy programs that offers a range of educational and instructional classes and tutoring. Not only do they offer free literacy classes, they also have free training for obtaining your GED, offer assistance with learning disabilities, and teach reading, spelling, and math. To find out more, contact National Institute for Literacy, 1775 I Street, NW; Suite 730, Washington, DC 20006-2401; 202-233-2025; www.nifl.gov.

Get Your GED At Age 94

If Cecil Smith of California can get his GED when he was 80 years old after he dropped out of junior high school, anyone can do it. The National Institute for Literacy is a government organization that will find you free help in preparing and taking your High School Equivalency Diploma tests. You can search for help near you online at www.literacydirectory.org, or call them at 1-800-228-8813.

Brighten the Day of a Senior Shut-In

Senior Service America is a nonprofit organization that can help you with training if you are a senior. The Senior AIDES Program offers training and educational opportunities. One program in Ohio trains Senior AIDES to talk to senior shut-ins through daily telephone calls. There are many other programs throughout the country. Contact: Senior Service America, 8403 Colesville Road, Suite 1200, Silver Springs, MD 20910; 301-578-8900; www.seniorserviceamerica.org.

Website To Get You Started

Are you interested in travel, learning about new photography techniques, golf, tennis or cooking? This web site lists thousands of learning and travel programs. Sponsors list their educational programs on this site then; you can search in a variety of ways and find just the right program for you! Contact ShawGuides, Inc., P.O. Box 231295, New York, NY 10023; 212-799-6464; www.shawguides.com.

Wordsmith.Org

This online program is dedicated to words and wordlovers. You can subscribe to word of the day program to explore words with 600,000 fellow wordlovers in 200 countries. Check out www.wordsmith.org.

World Lecture Hall

College courses at your fingertips, that is what World Lecture Hall offers. World Lecture Hall publishes links to curriculum pages created by faculty throughout the world that are using the Web to deliver course materials. All courses listed can be viewed for free on the Internet. There are thousands of listings for any interest from Accounting through Zoology. Take a look at http://web.austin.utexas.edu/wlh.

Learn How Things Work

You can learn how to do almost anything. eHow.com is a privately held company that offers clear instructions for doing thousands of things. If you need help on how to tie a tie, throw a knuckleball, or buy a car, check out the web site for instructions. Contact eHow, Inc., 258 Waverly Street, Palo Alto, CA 943001; www.ehow.com.

Local Classes at Very Low Cost

OASIS is a national nonprofit educational organization designed for mature adults. Membership is free and open to adults 50 or older. They offer classes and workshops in the arts, humanities, wellness, technology and volunteer service. Recent classes included: "Dance for Your Brain Health," "Advanced Adobe Photoshop," "Religion and Politics in The US," and "Create Your Own Greeting Cards". You can take an online course, *Growing Stronger: Strength Training for Older Adults* to help keep you healthy. Below is a listing of the 26 OASIS centers throughout the country. Contact them for programs in your area. Contact The OASIS Institute Headquarters, 7710 Carondelet Avenue, St. Louis, MO 63105; 304-862-2933; www.oasisnet.org.

Akron, OH
OASIS, c/o Kaufmann's
2000 Brittain Road
Akron, OH 44310
330-633-7815
Email: btompkins@oasisnet.org

Albany, NY
OASIS University at Albany
BA 220
Albany, NY 12222
518-442-3913
Fax: 518-442-3939
Email: kgersowitz@uamail.albany.edu

Albuquerque, NM
OASIS c/o Foley's
6600 Menaul NE
Albuquerque, NM 87110
505-889-0927
Fax: 505-872-3865
Email: oasisabq@email.msn.com

Alton, IL
OASIS, Famous-Barr in Alton
100 Alton Square
Alton, IL 62002
618-465-1490
Email: dharris@oasisnet.org

Chicago, IL
OASIS
2336 Northbook Court
Northbrook, IL 60062
847-498-2500, press 1, then ext. 560
Fax: 847-509-1565
Email: lkimball@oasisnet.org

Cleveland, OH
OASIS, c/o Parmatown Kaufmann's
8001 Ridgewood Drive
Parma, OH 44129
440-886-1157
Email: fiordae@ccf.org

Denver, CO
OASIS
303-922-5178
Email: jclover@oasisnet.org.

Escondido, CA
OASIS c/o Robinsons-May at North County Fair
280 East Via Rancho Parkway
Escondido, CA 92025
760-432-0635
Email: dtoasis@cox.net

Eugene, OR
OASIS/Meier & Frank
100 Valley River Center
Eugene, OR 97401
541-342-6611, x2601
Fax: 541-342-5187
Email: bsusman@peacehealth.org

Gaithersburg, MD
OASIS c/o Lord & Taylor at
Lakeforest Mall, second floor
701 Russell Ave
Gaithersburg, MD 20877
301-869-1508
Email: marcy.oasis@verizon.net

Houston, TX
OASIS, c/o Foley's
100 Northwest Mall, 2nd Level
Houston, TX 77092
713-957-2968
Email: mgmatz@sbcglobal.net

Hyattsville, AL
OASIS, c/o Hecht's
3500 East-West Highway
Hyattsville, MD 20782
301-559-6575
Email: hyattsvilleoasis@yahoo.com

Indianapolis, IN
OASIS Washington Square
Headquarters: Second Floor of L.S. Ayres
10202 East Washington Street
Indianapolis, IN 46229
317-895-9976
Email: apellman@netdirect.net

Long Beach/Lakewood, CA
Lower Level, Robinson's May
Lakewood Center Mall
5100 Lakewood Blvd.
Mailing address:
OASIS
P.O. Box 506
Lakewood, CA 90714
562-601-5010
Email: lakewoodoasis@yahoo.com

Los Angeles, CA
OASIS at Robinsons-May Westside Pavilion
10730 West Pico Blvd
Los Angeles, CA 90064
310-475-4911 ext. 2200
oasisla@aol.com

Oklahoma City, OK
OASIS, c/o Foley's
4000 Crossroads Boulevard
Oklahoma City, OK 73149
405-636-0037
Email: oklaoasis@yahoo.com

Phoenix/Scottsdale, AZ
Scottsdale OASIS
OASIS, c/o Robinsons-May
Scottsdale Fashion Square
4500 N Scottsdale Rd

Scottsdale, AZ 85251
480-994-1528
Email: mmorganfield@oasisnet.org

Phoenix OASIS
OASIS, c/o Robinsons-May MetroCenter
9700 N Metro Parkway East
Phoenix, AZ 85051
602-870-8337

Pittsburgh, PA
OASIS, c/o Kaufmann's, Tenth Floor
400 Fifth Avenue
Pittsburgh, PA 15219
412-232-9583
Fax: 412-566-0528
Email: gweisberg@oasisnet.org

Portland, OR
OASIS, c/o Meier & Frank
621 SW Fifth Avenue
Portland, OR 97204
503-241-3059
Fax: 503-241-3068
Email: rcostic@lhs.org

Rochester, NY
OASIS
c/o Monroe Community Hospital
435 E. Henrietta Road
Rochester, NY 14620
585-760-5440
Email: prisminster@hotmail.com

San Antonio, TX
OASIS
c/o Foley's Furniture Galleries
6161 NW Loop 410
San Antonio, TX 78238
210-647-2546
Fax: 210-647-2432
Email: bschmachtenberger@oasisnet.org

San Diego, CA
OASIS, c/o Robinsons-May
1702 Camino del Rio North
Third Floor
San Diego, CA 92108
619-574-0674
Fax: 619-574-0156
Email: oasissd@yahoo.com

St. Louis, MO
OASIS, c/o Famous-Barr
601 Olive Street
St. Louis, MO 63101
314-539-4555
Fax: 314-539-4559
Email: bsolomon@oasisnet.org

Syracuse, NY
OASIS
Shoppingtown Mall
3649 Erie Blvd. East
Dewitt, NY 13214
315-464-6555
Email: FeiglinL@upstate.edu

Tucson, AZ
OASIS
c/o Robinsons-May
3435 E. Broadway
Tucson, AZ 85716
520-795-3950 ext. 2113
Email: Prindl.GormanOomens@tmcaz.com

Washington, DC
OASIS
c/o Lord & Taylor
5255 Western Avenue NW
Washington, DC 20015
202-362-9600 ext. 560
Email: jsilberman@suburbanhospital.org

Computer Skills Workshop

CyberSeniors.org is dedicated to connecting seniors 50 and older to the computer world. They offer a self-paced, on-line tutorial covering basic computer information. Their Learning Centers present computer classes at low or no-cost. Learning Centers are located in: Alaska, North Dakota, Maine, Massachusetts, New Hampshire, Oregon, Pennsylvania, South Carolina, Texas, Vermont and Virginia with more to come. Contact CyberSeniors.org, One Monument Way, Portland, ME 04101; 888-676-6622; www.cyberseniors.org/artman/publish/.

Computer Courses for Seniors

SeniorNet entitles seniors, 50 or older, to take classes at one of over 240 learning centers, online courses and a subscription to their quarterly newsletter. Contact SeniorNet, 121 Second Street, 7th Floor, San Francisco, CA 94105; 415-495-4990; Fax: 415-495-3999; www.seniornet.org.

Free Online Workshops

AARP Learning online courses are free seminars that can be completed in an hour or two. Titles of courses include *Keep Active: Get Movin' at 50 Plus, How to Get the Most out of Your Managed Care, Navigating Your Way to a Quality Assisted Living Facility* and more.

AARP also offers low cost, in class Driver Safety Program. The 8-hour refresher program is offered throughout the country to help drivers tune-up their driving skills.

Discounts are also available for AARP members to learn computer skills through Gateway. Contact AARP, 601 E Street NW, Washington, DC 20049; 888-OUR-AARP; www.aarp.org/learn.

10,000 College Programs for Seniors All Over the World

If you want to learn and explore close to home or half way around the world, Elderhostel can help. Elderhostel is a nonprofit organization that provides learning adventures for people 55 years of age and older throughout the world. They offer over 10,000 programs a year in more than 90 countries. You can receive a catalog by mail or view the catalog on their web site. Contact Elderhostel, 11 Avenue de Lafayette, Boston, MA 02111-1746; 877-426-8056; www.elderhostel.org.

Lifelong Learning Institutes Affiliated with Elderhostel

Alabama

Auburn University Academy for Lifelong Learners
Auburn University
301 O.D. Smith Hall
Auburn University, AL 36849
334-844-3102
Fax: 334-844-3101
www.auburn.edu/outreach
This program is design to provide a place for retired persons to continue the learning process. The program is administered through the Outreach Program Office.

Institute for Learning in Retirement
University of North Alabama
P.O. Box 5036
Florence, AL 35632
256-765-4862
Fax: 256-765-4872
www.una.edu/conted
The small membership fee entitles you to be part of courses with other active seniors for the pleasure of learning. Courses include: Current Events, Potpourri, Great Books, Queens of Screens, Travel the World, Music Appreciation, Joy of Opera, Introduction to Computers, How to Live Longer and Better and Understanding the Universe.

Odyssey USA
University of South Alabama
2001 Old Bay Front Drive
Mobile, AL 36615-1427
251-431-6405
Fax: 251-431-6408
www.southalabama.edu/casc/odyssey.html
Odyssey USA is a community of mature learners that love learning. The participants design their own curriculum based on their own interests. Odyssey also sponsors monthly luncheon lectures and special events. There is a small fee to join.

The Academy for Lifetime Learning
University of Alabama in Huntsville
Wilson Hall, Room 133
Huntsville, AL 35899-0650
256-824-6959
www.alluah.com
The Academy for Lifetime Learning offers: access to Academy classes at UAH, newsletters, social events, Wednesday Bonus days, access to UAH library and fitness center, free local industrial tours and more for only $15 a year. There is a small additional fee to take Academy classes.

Arizona

Central Arizona Lifelong Learners
Central Arizona College
Superstition Campus
273 Old West Highway
Apache Junction, AZ 85219-5231
800-237-9814
480-288-4023
Fax: 480-288-4022
www.centralaz.edu/call
Members may take unlimited classes for a year for a small fee. Members also receive a newsletter and access to the Central Arizona library and computer center.

.

Gerontology Program
Arizona State University
P.O. Box 872902
Tempe, AZ 85287-2902
480-965-3225
Fax: 480-965-9008
www.age-wise.com
Age-Wise.com is an online resource that provides seniors information regarding issues on aging.

New Adventures in Learning for Seniors
Chandler-Gilbert Community College
c/o Sun Lakes Education Center
25105 So. Alma School Rd.
Sun Lakes, AZ 85248
480-857-5500
www.cgc.maricopa.edu/slec/nails
New Adventures in Learning provides a variety of educational experiences for mature adults for a full year for $50.

New Frontiers for Learning in Retirement
Community Education Department
Mesa Community College
1833 West Southern Avenue
Mesa, AZ 85202
480-461-7497
Fax: 480-461-6215
www.newfrontiers-mesa.org
New Frontiers for Learning in Retirement is a peer-led, self-directed organization that provides classes and social events for mature adults for $60 a year.

Osher Lifelong Learning Institute
Yavapai College
1100 E. Sheldon Street, #6872
Prescott, AZ 86301
928-717-7634
Fax: 928-717-7635
www2.yc.edu/content/olli/

Rio Institute for Senior Education-RISE
Rio Salada Community College
12535 Smokey Drive
Surprise, AZ 85374
480-517-8770
Fax: 480-517-8779
www.rio.maricopa.edu/rise
RISE offers classes, social experiences and a variety of programs to seniors. Classes are free for members. Membership dues are $35 a year.

Seniors' Achievement and Growth through Education-SAGE
University of Arizona - Extended University
888 North Euclid Avenue
P.O. Box 210158
Tucson, AZ 85721
520-626-9039
Fax: 520-621-3269
www.sagesociety.org
SAGE offers seniors stimulating noncredit classes, discussion groups, brown bag lectures, access to the University of Arizona library and social activities. Memberships are $225/year.

Sun City Vistoso Lifelong Learning Institute
1565 E. Rancho Vistoso Boulevard
Oro Valley, AZ 85737
520-825-3711
ebammel@earthlink.net

California

Osher Lifelong Learning Institute
P.O. Box 6050
Irvine, CA 92616
949-824-8316
www.unex.uci.edu/all/index.asp
Osher offers members classes in the fields of science, social science, music, art, literature, history, religion, theater and field studies. Classes are held at the University of California Irvine and at local senior centers. Membership fees are $80/year for unlimited classes.

San Jose State University Osher Lifelong Learning Institute
2160 Lundy Avenue, Suite 250
San Jose, CA 95131-1862
408-519-1286
Fax: 408-519-0128
http://iesweb.sjsu.edu/profdev/osher/index.html
Members can enjoy a variety of programs including courses and brown bag lunches. Memberships are $25/year.

Osher Lifelong Learning Institute
College of Extended Studies
San Diego State University
5250 Campanile Drive, Suite 2503
San Diego, CA 92182

619-594-2863
Fax: 619-594-0147
www.ces.sdsu.edu/osher/
The Osher Lifelong Learning Institute offers university inspired courses taught by emeritus faculty. Classes are for the enjoyment of learning without grades or tests. Membership includes: three courses per semester for three semesters, two-for-one special event tickets, special lecture series, SDSU library access, parking permit and other discounts. Memberships are $35 single, $50 couple for early registration.

ENCORE
Glendale Community College
1500 North Verdugo Road
Glendale, CA 91208
818-243-5196
www.glendale.edu/actc/Lifelong_learning_seminars.htm
Programs are available for seniors who want to keep learning. Classes include: Beginning Sketching, World Religions, Email and Internet, Intro to Computers, Lip Reading and many more.

Learning is For Everyone-LIFE
Mira Costa Community College
One Barnard Drive
Oceanside, CA 92056
760-721-8124
www.miracosta.cc.ca.us/info/commun/life/
LIFE is open to all ages 18 and over but most members are retired. LIFE meetings are held on most Friday afternoons offering discussion groups, guest speakers, study groups and more. Memberships cost $30/year and include parking and access to the library.

Osher Lifelong Learning Institute-OLLI
California State University, Bakersfield
Extended University
9001 Stockdale Highway
Bakersfield, CA 93311-1099
661-664-2441
www.csub.edu/olli/
OLLI offers short, four to five week classes, taught by retired professors and community leaders. Classes are offered fall, winter and spring quarters with more than 20 classes to choose from. Memberships are $45/year.

Modesto Institute for Continued Learning-MICL
Modesto Junior College
Community Education Division
435 College Avenue
Modesto, CA 95350
209-576-6359
www.micl.info
"Learning Never Retires", that's Modesto's retiree-run retirement program motto. A variety of classes are offers in five-week sessions with no homework or tests. In addition to classes, MICL offers field trips and social events at reasonable fees. Memberships are $40 with an additional $10 parking fee.

Omnilore
California State University - Dominguez Hills
P.O. Box 7000-236
Redondo Beach, CA 90277
310-540-6011
www.omnilore.org/
Special lectures are offered each term to members. Discussion groups of 8-16 focus on a chosen subject for eight bi-weekly sessions. Members may choose from several discussions per term. Memberships are $90/year per single and $150/year per couple. Omnilore offers optional activities including luncheons, field trips and social events.

Older Adults Program
City College of San Francisco
106 Bartlett Street
San Francisco, CA 94110
415-550-4384
www.ccsf.edu/Campuses/Mission/oadults.html
The Older Adults Program offers 85 free non-credit classes in art, music, health and exercise, sewing, literature and theater, current events and computers to seniors 55 and older.

Osher Lifelong Learning Institute
Cal Poly Continuing Education
California Polytechnic State University
San Luis Obispo, CA 93407
866-CAL-POLY
805-756-2053
805-756-5933
www.continuing-ed.calpoly.edu/osher.html
Cal Poly Continuing Education's Osher Lifelong Learning Institute offers classes to those 50 and older who are retired or semi-retired. Members have access to a variety of classes and programs. Memberships are $40 for a term, $110 for a year (3 terms), and $1500 for a lifetime.

Osher Lifelong Learning Institute-OLLI
College of Extended Learning
San Francisco State University
425 Market Street, 2nd Floor
San Francisco, CA 94105
415-405-7700 press 5
Fax: 415-405-7760
www.cel.sfsu.edu/olli/
The OLLI program offers people 50 and over innovative educational experiences. Members can be retired, semi-retired or still working. Memberships entitle you to participate in three courses per semester, a weekly newsletter, special presentations, lunchtime discussions and an end of semester celebration. Memberships are $195/semester ($165 for early registration).

Osher Lifelong Learning Institute
University of California, Riverside
1200 University Avenue, Suite 333
Riverside, CA 92507
951-827-7139
www.ucrextension.net/olli/
The University of California, Riverside offers seniors 50 and older, with a variety of courses including: dance, drama, music and others. Members may choose two of five courses offered and may attend lectures and other special events. Memberships are $100/quarter with scholarships available.

Emeritus College Osher Lifelong Learning Institute
Sierra College
5000 Rocklin Road
Rocklin, CA 85677
916-781-7174
Fax: 916-789-2996
www.sierracollege.edu/ed_programs/emeritus/index.html
The Osher Lifelong Learning Institute at Sierra College invites all adults 55 years old and older to participate in their tuition free courses.

Institute for Continued Learning
University of California, San Diego
ICL Office, USDA Extension 0176-AA
La Jolla, CA 92093-0176
858-834-3409
Fax: 858-534-7385
www.icl.ucsd.edu
The Institute for Continued Learning offers its members a variety of activities, member led courses and the option of auditing classes at the University. Members should be 50 years old or older and retired or semi-retired. Memberships are $150/year.

Prime Timers
California State University
Chico Research Foundation
Building D, Room 117
Chico, CA 95929-0792
530-898-6679
http://rce.csuchico.edu/primetimers/
Prime Timers are active seniors 60 and older or retired that want to continue to learn. Memberships are $45/year.

Senior University
California State University, Long Beach
1250 Bellflower Boulevard
Long Beach, CA 90840-5605
562-985-8237
www.csulb.edu/centers/senior-university/
Senior University offers four eight-week sessions yearly to persons 50 years and older. Classes are offered in a wide variety of subjects including art, anthropology, computers, music, math, science, history and more. Memberships are $40/year. There are additional charges for computer classes.

Seniors Learning Unlimited
University of California
Davis Extension
1333 Research Park Drive
Davis, CA 95616
530-752-9695
http://extension.ucdavis.edu/seniorlearning/
Senior Learning Unlimited offers senior-led classes in a variety of subjects including: history, art appreciation, computers, web technology and literature. Members are offered: 10-12 classes per quarter- fall, winter and spring, a free seminar and field trips. Memberships are $25/year plus a small fee per class. Non-members may take courses if space is available with members receiving priority enrollment.

Stockton Institute for Continued Learning
5151 Pacific Avenue
Stockton, CA 95207
209-931-1551
209-464-7895
www.deltacollege.edu/dept/sicl/
The Stockton Institute for Continued Learning is a member-run educational program for older adults in the San Joaquin Delta community. Members can choose from classes that include: bridge, art, computers, Spanish, music, landscaping, travel presentations and tours. Memberships are $25/semester.

The Fromm Institute for Lifelong Learning
University of San Francisco
2130 Fulton Street
San Francisco, CA 94117
415-422-6805
Fax: 415-422-6535
www.usfca.edu/fromm
The Fromm Institute for Lifelong Learning is an educational program for retired persons at the University of San Francisco. About fifty college-level, non-credit courses are offered each year, taught by retired professors. They offer eight-week sessions: fall, winter and spring. A modest membership fee allows members to take up to four classes a session with scholarships available based on need.

The Renaissance Society
6000 J Street, Foley Hall 234
Sacramento, CA 95819-6074
916-278-7834
www.csus.edu/org/rensoc/
The Renaissance Society is a partnership between the Retired Community of Sacramento area and California State University, Sacramento. Seminars are offered on and off-campus with most of them scheduled on Fridays. Membership is open to seniors and includes seminars and a parking permit for Fridays.

Membership is $60/year, for an additional $5 you may receive library privileges for the year.

SAGE (Study, Activity, Growth, Enrichment)
California State University, Northridge
18111 Nordhoff Street
Northridge, CA 91330-8383
818-831-5064
http://exlweb.csun.edu/sage/index.html
SAGE is an organization dedicated to providing a learning environment to retired and semi-retired seniors. Study discussion groups are formed with members researching topics and making presentations on subjects determined by the members. Memberships are $200/year single and $300/year couple.

VISTAS Lifelong Learning, Inc.
P.O. Box 23228
Santa Barbara, CA 93121
805-745-8224
www.vistaslifelonglearning.org/
VISTAS Seminars are held weekdays from 9:30 am until noon, one day a week for six weeks. Seminars are based on one or two assigned readings and discussed during the seminar. Seminar fees are $45 for VISTA members and $75 for non-members. Memberships are $40/year single and $60/year couple.

Seniors With Inquiring Minds-SWIM
Victor Valley College
18422 Bear Valley Road
Victorville, CA 92392
760-240-2729
Seniors With Inquiring Minds is a self-guided educational group that meets on Friday afternoons. They meet to discuss a variety of topics with members preparing and presenting the programs.

L.I.F.E. Society
University of California, Riverside
1200 University Avenue
Riverside, CA 92507-4596
951-827-4102
www.unex.ucr.edu/Life/default.html
L.I.F.E. Society is a self-run educational organization for retirement age adults. Study groups, seminars, lectures and field trips are available to members. Memberships are $110/year.

The University of the Third Age
University of San Diego
Division of continuing Education
5998 Alcala Park
San Diego, CA 92210-2492
619-260-4531
www.sandiego.edu/ce/u3a/
The University of the Third Age promotes lifelong learning for people 55 year of age and older. They offer two three-week programs per year offering speakers and courses in a variety of subjects. Membership is $100/year per person.

Colorado

Colorado Academy of Lifelong Learning
P.O. Box 371318
4101 East Hampden Avenue
Denver, CO 80237
303-770-0786
www.academyll.org/
The Academy offers adults in the Denver area a variety of way to explore and continue learning. Members receive access to all classes although there is a fee per class. Memberships are $30/year or $20/term.

Front Range Forum
Fort Collins Senior Center
1200 Raintree Drive
Fort Collins, CO 80526
970-613-9967
http://fcgov.com/recreation/frf-index.php
Front Range Forum is a membership organization of life-long learners. There are no age restrictions but classes are held during the day on weekdays. Topics change each term including: music, visual arts, literature, philosophy, history and other issues. Membership includes classes, outside speakers and other events. Memberships are $15/year.

VIVA! (Vibrant Intellectually Vigorous Adults)
University College
2211 S. Josephine
Denver, CO 80208
303-871-3090
www.universitycollege.du.edu/program/ppe/viva/index.asp
VIVA! is a member-run educational program that offers three quarters of classes lasting eight weeks each. Memberships are available for adults 55 and older and include classes, a newsletter, summer events and social events. Memberships are $100/term single; $290/year single; and $475/year couple. Membership scholarships are available.

Connecticut

Adventures in Lifelong Learning
Three Rivers Community College
Continuing Education Department
574 New London Turnpike
Norwich, CT 06360-6598
860-885-2608
www.trcc.commnet.edu/Cont_Ed/lifelong.html
Adventures in Lifelong Learning offers an extensive selection of courses. Members can participate in classes and field trips.

Institute For Learning in Retirement, Inc.
Albertus Magnus College
801 Grassy Hill Road
Orange, CT 06477
800-220-0458
www.ilralbertus.org/
The Institute for Learning in Retirement is for retired and semi-retired people who love learning. They offer over 36 courses that cost $10 for the first two classes and $5 for each additional course.

Institute for Learning in Retirement
Sacred Heart University
Jewish Center for Community Services
4200 Park Avenue
Bridgeport, CT 06604
203-372-6567
Fax: 203-374-0770
www.jccs.org/html/adults_seniors.html
The Institute for Learning in Retirement offers classes held in the community. Memberships are $10/yearly and $20 for each class.

Institute for Learning in Retirement
Fairfield Senior Center
100 Mona Terrace
Fairfield, CT 06430
203-256-3166
www.fairfieldct.org/rec-actseniors.htm

Learning in Retirement
Quinebaug Valley Community College
Center for Community & Professional Learning
742 Upper Maple Street
Danielson, CT 06239
860-774-1133
www.qvcc.commnet.edu/cpl/2LIR.htm
Learning in Retirement provides adults 55 and older, intellectual and social activities in retirement. Members can register for a variety of classes. Memberships are $15/year single; $25/year couple and $5 per class.

Learning in Retirement
Sacred University at Stamford
12 Omega Drive
Stamford, CT 06907
203-358-8081
Email: ralangen@aol.com

Lifetime Learners Institute
Norwalk Community College
188 Richards Avenue
Norwalk, CT 06854
West Campus Room W012
203-857-3330
www.lifetimelearners.org
Lifetime Learners is a volunteer organization for people over 50 who love learning. About 40 classes are offered each spring and fall. Members can register for classes and attend Brown Bag Lunch and Learn series. Memberships are $25/year and $15 for each class.

Middlesex Adult Learning Center
Middlesex Community College
100 Training Hill Road
Middletown, CT 06457
203-343-5742
Email: rmcn0408@aol.com

The Taconic Learning Center
P.O. Box 1752
Lakeville, CT 06039
860-435-2922
www.taconiclearningcenter.org/
The Taconic Learning Center offers non-credit college level courses to anyone who loves to learn. Classes are help weekly for two-hours at local locations. Classes include: art, astronomy, writing, poetry, languages, history economic, current events and more. Members may register for classes with no additional charge. Memberships are $60/year single and $120/year family.

The Adult Learning Program
University of Connecticut
85 Lawler Road
West Hartford, CT 06117
860-570-9079
www.uconnalp.org/
The Adult Learning Program offers seminars, special events and field trips. Memberships are $30/term, $70/year.

Delaware

Academy of Lifelong Learning
University of Delaware
115 Arsht Hall
2700 Pennsylvania Avenue
Wilmington, DE 19806
302-573-4417
www.academy.udel.edu/
The Academy of Lifelong Learning is a member-run organization for adults 50 and older to learn and exchange ideas. Members may register for classes and participate in most Academy events. Memberships are $290/year; $170/term. Scholarships are available on a need basis.

Southern Delaware Academy of Lifelong Learning
820A Savannah Road
Lewes, DE 19958
302-645-4111
www.academy.udel.edu/sdall/

The Academy of Lifelong Learning is a member-run organization for adults 50 and older to learn and exchange ideas. Members may register for classes and participate in most Academy events. Memberships are $195/year; $120/half year and scholarships are available on a need basis.

District of Columbia

Institute For Learning in Retirement
4400 Massachusetts Avenue, NW
Washington, DC 20016
202-885-3920
www.american.edu/ilr/
The Institute offers over 40 Study Group Courses each term including: politics, music, art, science, history, and more. Members are retired and semi-retired people interested in lifelong learning. Members can register for three courses per term from over 40 courses. Memberships are $190/term and $350/year.

Florida

The Academy at Florida State University
Pepper Institute on Aging and Public Policy
636 West Call Street
Tallahassee, FL 32306-1121
850-644-3520
www.pepperinstitute.org/academymain.html
The Academy at Florida State is an academic program for mature adults to promote learning. The program consists of two six-week academic sessions offered in the fall and spring. There are three levels of membership: $150 includes lunch lectures, field trips, special lectures, art and book groups, $225 includes all of above plus your choice of two classes per year, and $325 includes all benefits of $150 membership plus unlimited classes of your choice throughout the year.

Brevard ElderLearning
Brevard Community College
1519 Clearlake Road
Cocoa, FL 32922
321-433-7528
www.brevardcc.edu/

Elderhostel at Eckerd College
4200 54th Avenue S.
St. Petersburg, FL 33711
727-864-8444
www.eckerd.edu/seniorcollege
Elderhostel offers a variety of learning programs.
The Academy of Senior Professional is a group of over 300 mainly retired members who are elected on the basis of successful business, professional, academic and governmental careers.

Center for Lifelong Learning
University of West Florida
1170 Martin Luther King J. Boulevard
Fort Walton Beach, FL 32547
850-863-6548
www.uwf-cll.org/
The Center for Lifelong Learning offers more than 60 courses covering a variety of topics. Classes meet one day a week for eight weeks during two semester programs in January and September. Membership is $40 to take up to four classes; additional classes can be taken at $10 each.

Center for Lifelong Learning of International College
2655 Northbrooke Drive
Naples, FL 34119
239-513-1122 ext 133
www.internationalcollege.edu/CRC/
The Center for Lifelong Learning offers courses throughout the year that focus on the interests of the members. Members may take courses and programs at no additional charge. Members may also use the library but do not have borrowing privileges. Memberships are $125/year.

Education Encore-Lifelong Learning
Gulf Coast Community College
5230 West U.S. Highway 98
Panama City, FL 32401
850-872-3823
800-311-3685 ext 3823
http://lll.gulfcoast.edu/encore
Education Encore offers non-credit learning opportunities for seniors 50 and older. Two series of classes are offered, one in the spring and one in the fall. Memberships are $80 for the six-week program at the Bay County campus and $60 for the six-week program at the Gulf/Franklin campus. Scholarships are available on a need basis.

Center for Lifetime Learning
4200 Congress Avenue
Lake Forth, FL 33461
561-868-3556
www.pbcc.edu/LifetimeLearning/index.asp
The Center for Lifetime Learning offers over 130 courses with classes held in the afternoons. Members receive unlimited admission to classes, a yearly catalog of courses, invitations to special events, discounts to theater events, newsletters and a parking permit. Memberships are $155/year. Summer memberships are $60/year for a eight-week program.

Institute for Learning in Retirement
Nova Southeastern University
3301 College Avenue
Ft. Lauderdale, FL 33314
954-262-8471
www.nova.edu/cwis/ilr/
The Institute for Learning in Retirement offers two days a week summer programs and four days a week academic year

programs. Sessions include: philosophy, politics, health issues, science, music, art, literature, current events and more. Members may enjoy unlimited lectures and sessions and may audit two undergraduate Nova Southeastern University classes. Memberships are $300/year single, $550/year couple plus a $25 one-time application fee. One-month trial memberships are available for $100 plus the $25 application fee.

Institute of Retired Professionals
University of Miami
P.O. Box 248276
Coral Gables, FL 33124-5851
305-284-5072
www.education.miami.edu/irp/
The Institute of Retired Professionals provides retired persons with a learning environment. Membership allows seniors to attend study and discussion groups, audit regular University courses (as space allows), attend lunch-time lectures, and participate in social activities. Memberships range from $125/session to $585/semi-annually for a couple.

Learning Institute for Elders Institute
University of Central Florida
Phillips Hall, Room 309B
P.O. Box 161390
Orlando, FL 32816-1390
407-823-5433
http://pegasus.cc.ucf.edu/~life-ucf/
The Learning Institute for Elders Institute is an educational program designed to meet the need of retired people in the Orlando area. Memberships are $75/year.

Learning in Retirement
University of South Florida
Educational Outreach-Continuing Education
4202 East Fowler Avenue, NEC116
Tampa, FL 33620-6758
813-974-2403
866-541-7124
www.outreach.usf.edu/conted/SEN1.html
Learning in Retirement is a member-run educational organization. Members are eligible for early bird study group registration, library privileges, Coffee Exchange programs, and Brown Bag Lunch and Learn Series. Memberships are $30/year.

Learning in Retirement Institute
Charlotte County Foundation, Inc.
639 E. Hargreaves
Punta Gorda, FL 33950
941-637-0077
www.charlottecountyfoundation.org/lir.htm
The Learning in Retirement Institute is an educational organization that offers programs in the areas of the Humanities, the Sciences and Public Interest Topics. Members may enroll in Learning in Retirement Institute classes for $35 a semester.

Leisure Learning Society
University of Western Florida
11000 University Parkway
Pensacola, FL 32514
850-474-3491
http://uwf.edu/survey/cde/leisurelearning/
The Leisure Learning Society offers educational and social opportunities for everyone over 55 year of age. Members are eligible for a variety of classes, Lunch 'N' Learn programs, excursions and special events. Membership is $15/year.

Lifelong Learning Society
Florida Atlantic University
777 Glades Road
P.O. Box 3091
Boca Raton, FL 33431-0991
561-297-3171
www.fau.edu/lls
A variety of performances and lectures are available at two locations. Memberships are $15/year.

Oak Hammock
University of Florida
5100 SW 25th Boulevard
Gainesville, FL 32608
352-548-1000
888-311-6483
www.oakhammock.org/learning/ilr.asp
Oak Hammock is a member-run educational organization dedicated to continued learning in mature adults. The institute organizes coffees, study groups, guest speakers and other special events. Members pay a small fee for the events.

PRIME TIME (Positive Retirement Through Imaginative Education)
Okaloosa-Walton Community College
100 College Boulevard
Niceville, FL 32578
850-729-6085
www.owcc.cc.fl.us/departs/cont_ed/programs/prime_time.cfm
PRIME TIME students receive many benefits including: library privileges, free parking, access to computer labs, free admission to athletic events and tickets to selected productions at The Arts Center. Classes are available in drawing, fishing, Tai Chi, French and many more.

Seminole Adult Learning Institute (SALI)
Seminole Community College
100 Weldon Boulevard
Sanford, FL 32773
407-328-2121
www.scc-fl.edu/communityeducation/#SALI
SALI is a program for adults 50 and older to take a variety of classes and to attend workshops, lectures, special events and travel. There is a fee for classes and some programs.

Senior Academy
University of South Florida Sarasota/Manatee
5700 North Tamiami Trail
Sarasota, FL 34243
941-359-4296
www.sarasota.usf.edu/SeniorAcademy/
Senior Academy is a member-run organization dedicated to retired persons with a love of learning. Study and interest groups are 6-8 week courses offered each quarter. Members also receive access to special events, library and parking privileges, and discounts at campus stores. Memberships range from $75 for a single course to $350 for unlimited classes.

The Glenridge Academy
The Glenridge on Palmer Ranch
7333 Scotland Way
Sarasota, FL 34238
941-552-5300
888-999-GLEN
www.theglenridge.com/academy/academy.asp
The Glenridge Academy provides courses that interest mature adults. Memberships are available for residents of The Glenridge on Palmer Ranch.

Georgia

Columbus Academy of Lifelong Learning-CALL
4225 University Drive
Columbus, GA 31907
706-568-2023
www.colstate.edu/
Lifelong Learning offers CALL classes, field trips, learning lunches, and much more. Members may attend all for free. Memberships are $125/year, $55/quarter.

Center for Lifelong Learning
Emory Briarcliff Campus
1256 Briarcliff Road
Atlanta, GA 30306
404-727-6000
www.cll.emory.edu
The Center for Lifelong Learning is a non-credit adult education organization that provides a variety of experiences for seniors.

Institute for Continuing Learning
Young Harris College
P.O. Box 68
Young Harris, GA 30582
706-379-4311 ext 5194
http://w3.yhc.edu/external/icl/
The Institute for Continuing Learning offers a series of courses every quarter. Classes usually meet two hours a week for eight weeks. Memberships are $20/year, class tuition is typically $15/course.

Learning in Retirement
Georgia College & State University
Campus Box 040
Milledgeville, GA 31061
478-445-1239
www.gcsu.edu/acad_affairs/ce_ps/continue_ed/learning_in_retirement.htm
Learning in Retirement is a member-led program that strives to meet the intellectual, educational, physical and social needs of retirement-age individuals.

Learning in Retirement
Valdosta State University
Valdosta, GA 31698-0993
229-245-6484
www.valdosta.edu/conted/Programs/lir/lirinfo.htm
Learning in Retirement is a member-led organization to support individuals 50 years and older. Members may attend as many LIR classes, meetings and other social activites as they wish. You may also receive a Valdosta State University Library card free of charge. Memberships are $35/term.

Learning in Retirement, Inc.
University of Georgia
P.O. Box 49182
Athens, GA 30604-9182
706-549-7350
http://omega.geron.uga.edu/lir/
Learning in Retirement offers 20 courses each semester that interest older learners. Classes are held during the day meeting once a week for two hours with two to six sessions. Memberships are $35/year, courses cost $6 to $18.

Idaho

New Knowledge Adventures
Idaho State University Continuing Education
ISU Box 8062
Pocatello, ID 83209
208-282-3155
www.isu.edu/conteduc/

Friends For Learning
1770 Science Center Drive
Idaho Falls, ID 84302
208-282-3155
www.isu.edu/conteduc/nka/nka.htm
This member organization offers classes and other learning experience to adults 50 years old and older.

Illinois

The Institute for Learning in Retirement
Continuing Education
Bradley University
1501 W. Bradley Avenue
Peoria, IL 61625
309-677-2523

www.bradley.edu/continue/ilr/ilr.html
The Institute for Learning in Retirement offers mature learners 55 and older many opportunities to learn. Courses are offered in the fall, winter and spring. Memberships are $75/term.

Center for Learning in Retirement
Rock Valley College
3301 North Mulford Road
Rockford, IL 61114
815-921-3930
800-973-7821
www.rockvalleycollege.edu/show.cfm?durki=275
The Center for Learning in Retirement is a member-run organization for retired and semi-retired people who love learning. Members may register for CLR classes, participate in field trips and social events, computer help groups and receive a quarterly newsletter. Memberships are $20/year.

Continuing Center for Lifetime Learning
Danville Area Community College
2000 East Main Street
Danville, IL 61832
217-443-8778
www.dacc.cc.il.us/cce/ccll.html
The Continuing Center for Lifetime Learning provides courses for people 55 years and older. There is a cost for the classes.

Lifelong Learning Institute
Harper College
1200 W. Algonquin Road
Palatine, IL 60067-7398
847-925-6065
www.harpercollege.edu/learning/ce/program/pe/ll.shtml
The Lifelong Learning Institute offers many opportunities for mature adults 55 years and older. Members may participate in noncredit courses, seminars, study groups, field trips, tours and lectures. Memberships are $35/year.

Institute for Continued Learning
Roosevelt University
1400 Roosevelt Boulevard, Room 147
Schaumburg, IL 60173
847-619-7288
www.roosevelt.edu/icl/
The Institute for Continued Learning is a member-run organization providing programs for adults 50 and over. Memberships are $110/year.

Institute for Learning in Retirement
Prairie State College
4821 Southwick Drive
Matteson, IL 60443
708-709-3953
www.matteson.prairiestate.edu/institute.htm
The Institute for Learning in Retirement is a member-run organization dedicated to meeting the educational needs of seniors.

Institute for Learning in Retirement
Rend Lake College
468 N Ken Gray Parkway
Ina, IL 62846
618-437-5321 ext 1367
800-369-5321 ext 1367
www.rlc.edu/comed/ilr/
The Institute for Learning in Retirement is an organization that provides courses and opportunities for seniors. There are no membership fees, but there is a fee for classes.

Learning is ForEver
Western Illinois University
1 University Circle
Macomb, IL 61455-1399
309-298-1864
www.wiu.edu/unews/release.sphp?id=2721
Learning is ForEver offers self-directed study groups to anyone interested in learning with no age requirements. Classes are mainly held during the day in a variety of topics.

Academy of Lifelong Learning
Lincoln Land Community College
5250 Shepherd Road
P.O. Box 19256
Springfield, IL 62794-9256
217-756-2477
800-727-4161 ext 6-2477
www.llcc.cc.il.us/all/
The Academy of Lifelong Learning offers learning opportunities for adults 55 and older. Study groups, workshops and courses, monthly Breakfast Roundtable, field trips, social events are all available for members. Memberships are $15/year.

Lifelong Learning Institute
Parkland College
2400 West Bradley Avenue
Champaign, IL 61821-1899
217-403-1429
www.parkland.edu/schedule/landl/2004/lli.pdf
The Lifelong Learning Institute offers programs designed for adults 55 who are retired or semi-retired. They offer travelogues, computer classes and water aerobics. Memberships are $50/year single, $80/year couple.

Institute for Learning in Retirement
External Programming
College of Liberal Arts & Sciences
Northern Illinois University
DeKalb, IL 60115-2854

www3.niu.edu/ilr/
The Institute for Learning in Retirement is a member-run organization of retirement-age people that love learning. Members participate in study groups, workshops and lectures. Memberships range from $45 to $165 with a one-time application fee.

Lifelong Learning Institute
Waubonsee Community College
Route 47 at Waubonsee Drive
Sugar Grove, IL 60554-9454
630-466-7900 ext 5731
www.wcc.cc.il.us/community/lli.php
The Lifelong Learning Institute is a member-run organization offering mature adults 50 and older an educational environment. Memberships are $20/year.

Institute for Learning in Retirement
Northwestern University School of Continuing Studies
339 E. Chicago Avenue, Room 513
Chicago, IL 60611-3008
312-503-6950
www.scs.northwestern.edu/nuilr/
Members may take up to three study groups per semester. Memberships are $350/half year, $475/year. Financial assistance is available.

Pursuit of Learning in Society (POLIS)
1800 College
Quincy, IL 62301
217-228-5594
www.quincy.edu/community/polis/
POLIS provides college-level experiences to retired and semi-retired adults at a modest cost. Members may also attend special events and use the University's library.

Renaissance Academy
Saint Xavier University
3700 West 103rd Street
Chicago, IL 60655
773-298-3149
www.sxu.edu/about/renaissance_academy.asp
The Renaissance Academy is for retired and semi-retired people who love learning. Classes are peer-facilitated and include topics like philosophy, history, literature, current events, poetry, and computer technology.Memberships range from $45/term to $100/academic year.

Retired Adult Program for Lifelong Learners-RAP
McHenry County College
8900 US Highway 14
Crystal Lake, IL 60012-2738
815-479-7605
www.mchenry.edu/coneducation/RAP.asp
RAP is designed to give adults 55 and older noncredit classes and activities. Memberships are $25/year with a small fee for classes.

Senior Professionals
Illinois State University
Campus Box 8610
Normal, IL 61790-8610
309-438-2818
www.exu.ilstu.edu/seniors/

Southern Illinois Learning in Retirement
Division of Continuing Education
Mail Code 6705
Southern Illinois University
Carbondale, IL 62901
www.dce.siu.edu/community/comm1.htm
The Southern Illinois Learning in Retirement program is an education organization of mature learners 55 year and old. Members are eligible for sponsored courses, monthly newsletters, free parking, library privileges, discount tickets and social activities. Memberships are $25/year.

Indiana

Association of Lifelong Learners
Ball State University
School of Continuing Education & Public Service
Muncie, IN 47306
765-285-2762
www.bsu.edu

Dewey Institute for Lifelong Learning-DILL
Erickson Hall 124
Terre Haute, IN 47809
812-237-8707
http://web.indstate.edu/DILR/
The Dewey Institute for Lifelong Learning is open to all people regardless of age or educational background that want to learn. Members may attend one class per semester and unlimited lectures and special events. Memberships are $30/year.

Wabash Area Lifetime Learning Association-WALLA
Purdue University
222 N Chauncey Street, Room 209
West Lafayette, IN 47906-3006
765-746-2006
800-218-2414
www.wcic.org/WALLA

Iowa

Learning After Fifty
Hawkeye Community College
P.O. Box 8015
Waterloo, IA 50704
319-296-2320 ext. 1248
www.wplwloo.lib.ia.us/learningafterfifty/
The Institute for Learning After Fifty is a member-run organization open to everyone over fifty who loves to learn.

Members may audit regular college courses for $10 if space is available. Members also have access to the library and discounts. Memberships are $15/year.

Lifelong Learning
Western Iowa Tech Community College
4647 Stone Avenue
Sioux City, IA 51106
712-274-8733 ext 1334
www3.witcc.com/lifelong_learning/
Lifelong Learners is primarily geared to the interests of retirement age people but anyone may join. There are a variety of classes for members. Memberships are $5/year.

Loess Hill Learners
Iowa Western Community College
2700 College Road, Box 4-C
Council Bluffs, IA 51502
712-325-3210
Email: jkeasling@iwcc.edu

Iowa City/Johnson County Senior Center
28 S Lin Street
Iowa City, IA 52240
319-365-5220
www.icgov.org/senior/default.asp
The Iowa City/Johnson County Senior Center provides residents of Johnson County who are 50 years of age and older a variety of lifelong learning experiences.

Kansas

Institute of Lifelong Learning
Cowley County Community College
P.O. Box 1147
Arkansas City, KS 67005
620-441-5286
800-593-2222
www.cowley.cc.ks.us/outreach/continue/ILL/ILL.HTML
The Institute of Lifelong Learning provides opportunities to seniors to enrich their love of learning. They offer a variety of classes and opportunities.

Office of Lifelong Learning
Emporia State University
1200 Commercial
Campus Box 4052
Emporia, KS 66801
620-341-5625
www.emporia.edu/lifelong/elder/index.htm
The Elderhostel at Emporia is an educational program for older adults. They offer inexpensive short-term programs. Classes, field trips and presentations are available.

Kentucky

Veritas Society
Bellarmine University
2001 Newburg Road
Louisville, KY 40205
502-452-8374
www.bellarmine.edu/ce/veritas.asp
Veritas is available to Louisville residents who are 54 and older who love to learn. A variety of six-week member initiated programs in the fall and spring. Members may participate in classes, discussions, Lunch and Learn, field trips and social activities. Members also are provided free parking, use of the library and discounts. Memberships are $65/term for three courses and $38 for Lunch and Learn Series.

Louisiana

Lapniappe Studies Unlimited
1888 Pleasant Hall
Baton Rouge, LA 70803
225-578-6763
www.doce.lsu.edu/lagniappe/index.htm
Lapniappe Studies Unlimited offers courses to seniors 50 and older who love to learn. Two six-week sessions are offered each fall and spring and a four week session is offered in the summer. Memberships are $45/year with course fees ranging from $13 to $33.

Maine

Downeast Senior College
University College of Ellsworth
248 State Street, Suite 1
Ellsworth, ME 04605
207-667-3897
800-696-2540
http://maine.edu/~grimmig/dsc.html
Downeast Senior College is a member-led organization for people 55 and older. Members may take courses throughout any Senior College Program in Maine. Memberships are $25/year plus $25 for each course.

Gold Leaf Institute
University of Maine at Farmington
Merrill Hall
Farmington, ME 04938
207-778-7063
www.umf.maine.edu
The Gold Leaf Institute Program offers educational and cultural experiences for citizens who are 50 and older. The members create and administer the courses, excursions and social events.

Osher Lifelong Learning Institute
University of Southern Maine
101 Payson Smith Hall, Portland Campus
96 Falmouth
Portland, ME 04104
207-780-4406

www.usm.maine.edu/~eap/seniorcollege/index.htm
The Osher Lifelong Learning Institute offers Portland-area residents who are 55 years old and older opportunities for continued learning. Members may attend classes, learning experiences and social events for a nominal fee. Members may also use the library and receive discounts for many University sponsored events. Memberships are $25/year.

Penobscot Valley Senior College
5723 Corbett Business Building
Orono, ME 04469-5723
207-521-1947
www.umaine.edu/mainecenteronaging/seniorcollege.htm
The Penobscot Valley Senior College offers seniors 50 years old and older many opportunities to learn. A variety of non-credit courses are offered in the fall and spring. Memberships are $25/year single, $40/year couple.

Senior College
University of Maine at Augusta
46 University Drive
Augusta, ME 04330
207-621-3447
www.uma.maine.edu/SeniorCollege/UMASC_Home.html
University of Maine at Augusta Senior College provides learning experiences for seniors 50 and older and their spouses. Memberships are $25/year and $25 for each course.

Senior College at Lewiston-Auburn Campus
University of Southern Maine
51 Westminster Street
Lewiston, ME 04083
207-753-6510
www.usm.maine.edu/lac/seniorcollege/
Senior College offers a variety of courses to persons 50 and older. Memberships are $25/year.

Senior College at University of Maine Hutchinson Center
80 Belmont Avenue
Belfast, ME 04915
207-338-8000
800-753-9044
www.hutchinsoncenter.umaine.edu/seniorcollege.htm
Senior College is open to seniors who love learning. Memberships are $25/year and $25 for each course.

Maryland

Legacy College for Lifelong Learning
University of Maryland
4321 Hartwick Road, Suite 220
College Park, MD 20742
301-403-4467
www.hhp.umd.edu/AGING/SRU/
Lifelong Learning for You is for seniors 50 and older to continue learning throughout their loves. For a nominal fee, members may participate in social and cultural events as well as University privileges.

Institute for Learning in Retirement
Frederick Community College
7932 Opossumtown Pike
Frederick, MD 21702
301-624-2732
www.frederick.edu/programCourses/ILR/index.cfm?documentid=242
The Institute for Learning in Retirement is a member-run educational organization for Frederick County residents age 55 and older. Courses include: art and music, computers, philosophy, political science and more. Memberships are $20 for a lifetime membership. Nonmembers may take courses but members receive a discount on course fees.

Renaissance Institute
College of Notre Dame
4701 N. Charles Street
Baltimore, MD 21210
410-532-3162
www.ndm.edu/institutes/renaissance/index.cfm
The Renaissance Institute is a member-run educational organization for seniors 50 and older. They offer two 13-week semesters of non-credit courses. Membership includes unlimited courses, lunchtime lectures, privileges at the library, and invitations to Renaissance social activities.

SAGE (Seasoned Adults Growing through Education)
Prince George's Community College
301 Largo Road
Largo, MD 20774-2199
301-322-0990
http://pgweb.pg.cc.md.us/

Evergreen Society, John Hopkins University
6740 Alexander Bell Drive
Columbia, MD 21046-2248
410-309-9531 (Baltimore/Columbia)
301-294-7058 (Montgomery County)
http://evergreen.jhu.edu/
The Hopkins Evergreen Society serves semi-retired and retired educational organization. Classes meet during the day on Tuesday, Wednesday and Thursday.

Massachusetts

Academy of Lifelong Learning of Cape Cod, Inc.
Cape Cod Community College
2240 Iyanough Road
West Barnstable, MA 02668-1599
508-362-2131 ext 4400
www.allcapecod.org/
The Academy is open to all persons 50 and older who love learning. Members may take 2 courses per semester, participate

in social events, and have access to the library, gymnasium and other facilities. Memberships are $75/semester.

Berkshire Institute for Lifetime Learning-B.I.L.L.
Berkshire Community College
1350 West Street
Pittsfield, MA 01201
413-499-4660 ext 456
www.cc.berkshire.org/lifelong/bill.html
B.I.L.L. is a member-run educational organization that offers a variety of experiences.

Osher Lifelong Learning Institute@Brandeis (BOLLI)
MS 085
415 South Street
Waltham. MA 02454
781-736-2992
www.brandeis.edu/programs/bali/
BOLLI offers a variety of courses, seminars, lectures and programs for semi-retired, retired and adult learners. Memberships are $285 for up to two courses, all lunch and learn, use of the library and other BOLLI programs.

Explorers Lifelong Learning Institute of Salem State College
10 Federal Street
Salem, MA 01970
978-744-0804
www.salemstate.edu/explorers/
Explorers offer seniors in the Salem area peer learning to share knowledge. They have two academic terms per year with a variety of other educational experiences. Memberships are $150/year single, $250/family. Full and partial scholarships are available.

Five College Learning in Retirement
Mason Hall
Smith College
Northampton, MA 01063
413-585-3756
www.5clir.org/
Five College Learning in Retirement serves the Pioneer Valley of Massachusetts. Members may participate in seminars, special events and have library privileges. Memberships are $175/year.

Harvard Institute for Learning in Retirement
51 Brattle Street
Cambridge, MA 02138
617-495-4072
www.hilr.harvard.edu/
The Harvard Institute for Learning in Retirement maintains a membership cap of 500 therefore, a limited number of memberships are offered each year. There are no annual membership fees for each semester of enrolment but there is a charge per semester for courses.

Lasell Institute for Learning in Retirement
Lasell Village
120 Seminary Avenue
Newton, MA 02466
617-663-7000
www.lasellvillage.com/
A variety of educational programs and learning opportunities are available.

Learning in Retirement Association
Office of Community Service
University of Massachusetts Lowell
71 Wilder Street, Suite 6
Lowell, MA 01851
978-934-3135
www.uml.edu/Dept/comm_service/LIRA/
The Learning in Retirement Association is a member-run educational organization. Memberships are $100/year.

Life Enrichment Through Studies (LETS)
Gerontology Institute
UMass Boston
100 Morrissey Boulevard
Boston, MA 02125-3393
617-287-7312
www.lets.umb.edu
LETS is for adult learners 50 years and older that are semi-retired or retired. They offer over 50 non-credit educational courses, lectures and social events each year. Each member may take up to three seminars per semester. Memberships are $145/year.

The Middlesex Institute for Lifelong Education for Seniors (MILES)
Middlesex Community College
591 Springs Road
Building 9, Room 220
Bedford, MA 01730
781-280-3663
800-818-3434
http://noncredit.middlesex.mass.edu/miles/
MILES offers people 50 and over lifelong learning opportunities through study groups. Memberships are $150/year, $85/fall session.

Lifelong Learning Institute
Regis College
235 Wellesley Street
Weston, MA 02493
781-768-7000
www.regiscollege.edu/acad/lll/lll.htm
Lifelong Learning offers mature learners short-term daytime courses on a variety of topics.

Norton Institute for Learning in Retirement
EPOCH Assisted Living of Norton
190 Mansfield Avenue
Norton, MA 02766
508-285-3355
Email: gloria.obrien@epochsl.com

Second Half: Lifelong Learning @ 50+
University of Massachusetts Dartmouth
139 South Main Street
Fall River, MA 02721
508-677-4694
www.umassd.edu/secondhalf
The Second Half is a member-based educational organization for seniors 50 and older. Study groups and special events are offered to members. Memberships are $125/semester for full membership including study groups, $15/semester for affiliate memberships which gives access to social events, trips and lectures.

Tufts Institute for Lifelong Learning
039 Carmichael Hall
Tufts University
Medford, MA 02155
617-627-5885
www.tufts.edu/alumni/ed-till.html
The Tufts Institute for Lifelong Learning is for semi-retired and retired alumni and community members, as well as other interested learners. Learners can participate in study groups and distance learning courses.

Worchester Institute for Senior Education (W.I.S.E.)
Assumption College
Center for Continuing Education
500 Salisbury Street
Worchester, MA 01609
508-767-7364
www.assumption.edu/nhtml/gradce/conted/WISE.html
W.I.S.E. is a Learning in Retirement Institute for seniors living in Central Massachusetts that have a love for learning. Members create their own educational programming.
Memberships are $120/year, $70/half-year.

Michigan

Adult Learning Institute
Oakland community College
Orchard Ridge Campus
27055 Orchard Lake Road
Farmington Hills, MI 48334
248-522-3518
www.occ.cc.mi.us/catalog/AboutOCC/purposes.htm#Adult%20Learning
The Adult Learning Institute offers mature learners a member-run educational experience. Study Circles, Speakers' Forums and Special Events are scheduled in the fall and the spring.

Albion Academy for Lifelong Learning
203 S. Superior
Albion, MI 49224
517-629-5574
www.chamber.albionmi.net/aall.html
Albion Academy for Lifelong Learning is for adults 55 and over that love learning. The program includes: classes, discussions and trips to cultural events. Memberships are $20/year single, $30/year couple.

Association of Lifelong Learners
ACC Center Building, Room 108
666 Johnson Street
Alpena, MI 49707
989-358-7335
888-468-6222 ext 7335
www.alpenacc.edu/services/volunteer/all/
The Association of Lifelong Learners is a member-run organization for seniors 50 and older or that are retired. Memberships are $35/year single, $60/year couple.

Calvin Academy for Lifelong Learning
3201 Burton Street, SE
Grand Rapids, MI 49546
616-526-6000
800-688-0122
www.calvin.edu/academic/call/
The Calvin Academy for Lifelong Learning (CALL) is an educational program for retired and semi-retired people over the age of 50. Member benefits include: classes, field trips, library card, newsletter, free parking and an annual luncheon. Memberships are $30/year and $15 for each class.

ELDERWISE
Eastern Michigan University
Senior Health Building
5361 McAuley Drive
P.O. Box 995
Ann Arbor, MI 48106
734-572-2035
www.elderwiseemu.org/
ELDERWISE is a member-run educational organization for adults 50 and older who love learning. ELDERWISE membership benefits include: reduced class rates, some free programs, library privileges, and the ELDERWISE newsletter.

Lifelong Learning
Kellogg Community College
405 Hill Brady Road
Battle Creek, MI 49015
269-965-4134
www.kellogg.cc.mi.us/lifelong/seniors.html
The Lifelong Learning Institute is a member-run educational organization for retirement age seniors who love learning. Classes are offered in the fall, winter and spring in Battle Creek, Hastings and Coldwater. Memberships are $15/year.

Lake Superior Elders
Lake Superior State University
Norris Center
Sault Ste. Marie, MI 49783
906-635-2802
www.lssu.edu/extlearning/elders.php
Lake Superior Elders is a member-run educational organization for semi-retired and retired seniors who love learning. The group meets monthly with mini-courses and field trips held throughout the year. Memberships are $30/year.

Learning in Retirement
2401 Plymouth Road
Ann Arbor, MI 48105-0786
734-998-9351
http://comnet.org/lir/
Learning in Retirement is committed to providing educational experiences for people 55 years old and older. They offer lectures, movies, mini-courses and field trips. Memberships are $15/year with additional costs for lecture programs.

Institute for Learning in Retirement
Office of Continuing Education
Saginaw Valley State University
7400 Bay Road
University Center, MI 48710
989-964-4475
www.svsu.edu/oce/ilr.htm
The Institute for Learning in Retirement offers seniors 50 and over many learning opportunities. Member benefits include: discounted classes, monthly meetings, newsletter subscription,, library privileges and other special events. Memberships are $50/year.

Seniors Active in General Education (SAGE)
Jackson Community College
2111 Emmons Road
Jackson, MI 49203
517-796-8445
www.geocities.com/sagesociety/jackson.html

SOAR (Society of Active Retirees)
Wayne State University
2614 A/AB
5700 Cass Avenue
Detroit, MI 48202
313-577-7589
www.ll.wayne.edu/SOAR/
SOAR offers classes and lecture on a variety of subjects for adults 50 and older. Memberships are $50/term.

Lifelong Learning
The Aquinas Emeritus College
1607 Robinson Road SE
Grand Rapids, MI 49544
616-632-2430
www.aquinas.edu/emeritus/
Emeritus College offers non-credit courses taught by professors and professionals to seniors 50 and older.

Lifelong Learners
Montcalm Community College
2800 College Drive
Sidney, MI 48885-9723
989-328-1260
www.montcalm.cc.mi.us

Minnesota

ElderLearning Institute
University of Minnesota
250 McNamara Alumni Center
200 Oak Street SE
Minneapolis, MN 55455
612-624-7847
www.cce.umn.edu/eli/
The ElderLearning Institute is a volunteer run educational program for seniors. Members may participate in up to two courses per session, educational tours, lectures and social events. Memberships are $195/year.

Learning is ForEver (LIFE)
Rochester Community and Technical College
851-30th Avenue SE
Rochester, MN 55904
507-280-3157
www.rctc.edu/workforce/community/LIFE.htm
www.learningisforever.net
Learning is ForEver is an educational program for adults 55 and older offering a variety of classes and other learning opportunities. Memberships are $25/year with additional fees per class or event.

Michigan State University for Seniors
220 Alumni Foundation Center
Mankato, MN 56001
507-389-2011
www.mnsu.edu/dept/msus/welcome.html
Michigan State University for Seniors sponsors classes for seniors 55 and older in the fall, winter, spring and summer. Memberships are $25/term.

Continuing Education-Learning Club
Winona State University
Adult, Continuing, Education and Extension Office
Somsen Hall, Room 109
Winona, MN 55987
507-457-5080
www.winona.edu/catalog/adultceed.htm
WSU offers seniors 62 years old and older, no-credit classes for a service fee of $15 per credit hour. They also offer a week-long

Elderhostel for residential learning for anyone 55 or over. WSU sponsors the Learning Club, an organization that provides continuing education programs for seniors retired and semi-retired.

University for Seniors
Lifelong Learning Intstitue
251 Darland Administration Building
1049 University Drive
Duluth, MN 55812-3011
218-726-7637
www.d.umn.edu/ce/html/seniors.html
University for Seniors is a member-run educational organization for seniors who love learning. They offer a variety classes, field trips, lectures and social events. Memberships are $75/term.

Mississippi
Creative Learning in Retirement
Hinds Community College Workforce Development Center
P.O. Box 1100
Raymond, MS 39154-1100
601-857-3773
www.hindscc.edu
Creative Learning in Retirement offers seniors classes in a relaxed atmosphere. Classes usually meet for two hours, once a week for five weeks. Activities include: lectures, field trips, two-day seminars, and social events.

Institute for Learning in Retirement
Southwest Mississippi Community College
College Drive-Kenna Hall
Summit, MS 39666
301-276-3889
www.smcc.edu/support/ccenter/ilr.htm
The Institute of Learning in Retirement provides educational and social activities for retired adults fifty years old and older. Members may attend non-credit courses, workshops, seminars and field trips. Memberships are $50/year. Ten hour classes average $15.

Institute for Learning in Retirement
Copiah Lincoln Community College
Hwy 51 South
P.O. Box 649
Wesson, MS 39191
601-643-8705
www.colin.edu/communityservi/ILR/ilr.htm
The Institute for Learning in Retirement provides retired and semi-retired seniors 50 and older, an educational program for lifelong learning. Members may attend classes, social events, lectures, seminars and field trips.

Institute for Learning in Retirement
The University of Southern Mississippi
Center for International and Continuing Education
118 College Drive #5055
Hattiesburg, MS 39406-0001
601-266-4186
www.cice.usm.edu/ce/ilr/
The Institute for Learning in Retirement offers college-level non-credit educational experiences for senior learners 50 years old and older. Members may attend classes, seminars, field trips, luncheon lectures, and social events.

Institute for Learning in Retirement
Mississippi Gulf Coast Community College
2226 Switzer Road
Gulfport, MS 39507
228-897-4360
www.mgccc.edu/LOCcommunity_campus_ILR.htm
The Institute for Learning in Retirement offers adults 50 and over with a variety of educational experiences. Member benefits include: library privileges, the ILR newsletter, access to classes, lectures, field trips and more. Memberships are $50/year.

Lifetime Quest Center
Meridian Community College
910 Hwy 19N
Meridian, MS 39307
601-484-8696
www.mcc.cc.ms.us
Meridian Community College Lifetime Quest Center offers seniors 50 and older enrichment activities.

Missouri
Institute for Mature Learning
900 N. Benton Avenue
Springfield, MO 65802
417-873-6924
www.drury.edu/cgcs/iml/index.cfm
The Institute for Mature Learning offers senior learners 50 and older educational experiences. They offer two or more classes each week. Memberships are $35/year.

Learning in Retirement
Lincoln University
P.O. Box 105166
Jefferson City, MO 65110
Soldiers Hall, Room 7
573-681-6152
www.lincolnu.edu/~gscu/contedu.htm#CE-LIR
Learning in Retirement offers non-credit university level classes for senior citizens. They also offer social activities, field trips and other educational experiences. Memberships are $40/year.

Lifelong Learning Institute
Washington University in St. Louis
Campus Box 1154
7425 Forsyth
St. Louis, MO 63105-2161

314-935-4237
www.lli.wustl.edu/
The Lifelong Learning Institute offers non-credit peer-learning classes to lifelong learners 55 years old or older. They offer study groups in the fall, winter, spring and summer. Each study group meets once a week for two hours for an eight-week term.

SPARK (Senior Peers Actively Renewing Knowledge)
University of Missouri-Kansas City
4825 Troost, Room 214E
Kansas City, MO 64110
816-235-2870
800-735-2966
http://spark.umkc.edu/index2.html
SPARK promotes shared learning in persons 55 years old and older. Membership includes: classes, social events, cultural activities and special events. Memberships are $25/year.

Nebraska
Osher Lifelong Learning Institute
University of Nebraska
1520 R Street
Lincoln, NE 68501-0129
402-472-2841
888-353-1874
www.huskeralum.com/programs/olli/index.htm
Members may register for unlimited regularly scheduled six-week classes. Members may also bring one guest to attend a six-week class at no charge. Memberships are $150/year.

Nevada
EXCELL
University of Nevada, Las Vegas
4505 Maryland Parkway
Las Vegas, NV 89154
702-895-3394
http://edoutreach.unlv.edu/excell/index.html
EXCELL is a Learning in Retirement Program providing a college atmosphere for adult learners who are retired or semi-retired. They offer over twenty study group topics, field trips, lectures and social events. Memberships are $45/semester, $25/summer term.

New Hampshire
Cheshire Academy for Lifelong Learning
Office of Continuing Education
Keene State College
229 Main Street
Keene, NH 03435-2605
www.keene.edu/conted/call.cfm
The Cheshire Academy for Lifelong Learning offers non-credit courses for senior residents of the Moonadnock Region. Eight-week courses are offered in the fall and spring. Membership fees are required.

Institute for Lifelong Learning at Dartmouth-ILEAD
10 Hilton Field Road
Hanover, NH 03755
603-653-0154
www.dartmouth.edu/~ilead/
ILEAD is a non-credit peer-led and taught educational organization for adult learners. ILEAD offers 20 to 30 study groups each term in a variety of topics. Memberships are $50/year with additional fee for courses.

Learning Institute at New England College-LINEC
New England College
NEC Box 75
Henniker, NH 03242
603-428-7524
www.nec.edu/linec/
LINEC offers community adult learners a variety of educational experiences. Members benefits include: library privileges, invitations to special College events, reduced fees for NEC classes, and discounts at the College store. Memberships are $35/year single, $50/year per household.

RISE (Rivier Institute for Senior Education)
Rivier College
420 Main Street
Nashua, NH 03060
603-897-8623
www.rivier.edu/departments/rise/
RISE offers courses that meet during the day once a week for 5 to 10 weeks. Member benefits include: classes, field trips, library and health and fitness center privileges, free parking, and social activities. Memberships are $90/term.

New Jersey
Institute For Learning in Retirement
Bergen Community College
400 Paramus Road, Room B-105
Paramus, NJ 07652-1595
201-447-7156
www.bergen.edu/pages/602.asp
The Institute For Learning in Retirement at Bergen Community College offers adults 55 and older educational opportunities. Member benefits include: classes, library privileges, discount theater tickets, and field trips.

Academy for Lifelong Learning
Ocean County College
College Drive
P.O. Box 2001
Toms River, NJ 08754-2001
732-255-0469
www.ocean.edu/conted/index.htm
The Academy for Lifelong Learning is an educational organization that offers programs for adults 55 and older. Membership benefits include: discounts on courses, field trips,

discounts at the bookstore, library and swimming pool privileges, and the newsletter. Memberships are $10/year.

Lifelong Learning Institute
Caldwell College
Center for Continuing Education
9 Ryerson Avenue
Caldwell, NJ 07006-6195
973-618-3543
www.caldwell.edu/adult-ed/lifelong_index.html
The Lifelong Learning Institute provides non-credit, educational courses for adult learners 50 and older. Member benefits include: free parking, courses, field trips, previews of special events, and social events. Memberships are $10/term.

RU-ALL (Rutgers Academy for Lifelong Learning)
191 College Avenue
New Brunswick, NJ 08901
732-932-7233
http://ruall.rutgers.edu/
RU-ALL offers noncredit classes that meet for 90 minutes once a week for seniors 50 and older. Memberships range from $50 introductory rates to $150 per semester for full privileges.

New Mexico

Encore: The Senior College
Community Learning Center at San Juan College
4601 College Boulevard
Farmington, NM 87402
505-566-3414
www.sanjuancollege.edu/CLearnCenter/
Classes are available for adults 50 and older at a reduced fee.

Renesan Institute for Lifelong Learning
University of New Mexico
1200 Old Pecos Trail
Santa Fe, NM 87505
505-982-9274
http://internet.cybermesa.com/~renesan/
Membership includes: courses, field trips, lectures and social events. Memberships are $20/year with additional fees for lectures.

New York

Academy for Learning in Retirement@ Sarasota Springs
Empire State College
111 West Avenue
Sarasota Springs, NY 12866
518-587-2100 ext 415
www.esc.edu/alr
The Academy for Learning in Retirement is a member-run educational organization offered to semi-retired and retired adults. Membership includes: three courses, lunch and learns and special events. Memberships are $100/term to $190/year.

Adult Learning Institute
Columbia-Greens Community College
4400 Route 23
Hudson, NY 12534
518-828-4181 ext 3431
www.sunycgcc.edu/

The Athenaeum
Rochester Institute of technology
30 Fairwood Drive
Rochester, NY 14623
585-292-8989
www.rit.edu/~athenwww/
The Athenaeum offers courses in a variety of interests to adults 50 and over. Memberships include: courses, social events, travel, lecture series and other activities. Memberships are $250/year with trial memberships available.

Center for Creative Retirement
Southampton College
School of Continuing Studies
239 Montauk Highway
Southampton, NY 11968
631-287-8316
www.southampton.liu.edu/academic/cont_studies/retirement.ht ml
The Center for Creative Retirement offers seniors an opportunity to continue learning. Membership includes: study groups, cultural events, field trips, and social events.

Institute for Learning in Retirement
Farmingdale State University
Memorial Hall, Room 135
Farmingdale, NY 11735
631-420-2160
www.farmingdale.edu/ifs_search.html
The Institute for Learning in Retirement provides lifelong learning experiences for mature learners.

Institute for Retired Professionals
New School University
66 West 12th Street
New York, NY 10011
212-229-5682
www.newschool.edu/centers/irp/

Institute for retired Professionals
Syracuse University
Continuing Education
700 University Avenue
Syracuse, NY 13244-2530
315-443-4846
http://suce.syr.edu/community/irp/

The Institute for Retired Professionals provides educational opportunities for retired adults. Memberships are $25/single, $40/couple.

L.I.F.E. (Learning Is Forever Enriching)
Mount Saint Mary College
Desmond Campus
6 Albany Post Road
Newburgh, NY 12550
845-565-2076
www.msmc.edu
L.I.F.E. is a non-credit program open to adults 55 and older.

Lyceum
School of Education and Human Development
P.O. Box 6000
Binghamton, NY 13902-6000
607-777-2587
http://sehd.binghamton.edu/affprograms/lyceum/
Lyceum offers courses to adults 50 and older. Memberships are $35/year single, $60/year couple with an additional small fee per course. Scholarships are available for membership and class fees based on need.

Learning in Retirement at Iona College
715 North Avenue
New Rochelle, NY 10801
914-633-2675
www.iona.edu/liric/
Learning in Retirement at Iona College is a member-run institute for adults of retirement age. It offers educational courses and social activities to meet a variety of interests. Memberships are $150/year single, $250/year couple.

Lifetime Learning Institute
Bard College
P.O. Box 22
Annandale-on-Hudson, NY 12504-0022
www.bard.edu/institutes/lli/
The Lifetime Learning Institute offers non-credit courses in the fall and spring to all adults. Membership includes: four courses a year, library privileges, Memberships are $125/year.

Mohawk Valley Institute for Learning in Retirement
P.O. Box 3050
Utica, NY 13504-3050
315-792-7192
www.mvilr.sunyit.edu/
The Mohawk Valley Institute for Learning in Retirement Program offers seniors an educational learning environment. Membership includes: two courses per session, social activities, coffee programs and field trips. Memberships are $150/year.

Molloy Institute for Lifelong Learning
Molloy College
1000 Hempstead Avenue
P.O. Box 5002
Rockville Center, NY 11571
516-678-5000 ext 6880
www.molloy.edu/acad_affairs/mill/
The Molloy Institute for Lifelong Learning offers two chapters, one meets on Tuesdays and the other meets on Fridays. Memberships benefits include: audited college level courses, field trips, lectures, luncheons, seminars and social events. Memberships are $290/year single, $550/year couples.

Professionals and Executives in Retirement- PEIR
University of Continuing Education
250 Hofstra University
Hempstead, NY 11549-2500
516-463-5373
www.hofstra.edu/home
PEIR is an educational organization for retired professionals. Courses are developed and presented by PEIR members. Memberships are $400/year single, $730/year couple.

QUEST
The Community for Lifelong Learning in Manhattan
99 Hudson Street
New York, NY 100131
212-925-6625 ext 229
www.questonline.org/
QUEST offers over 40 college-level courses to retired and semi-retired people. Members may take as many classes as they wish at no additional charge. Memberships are $450 for three semesters.

SOAR (Stimulating Opportunities After Retirement)
Office of Continuing Education
Raymond Hall 206
SUNY Potsdam
Potsdam, NY 13676
800-458-1142
315-267-2690
www.potsdam.edu/CONT.ED
SOAR offers educational opportunities for its members, Classes run from one session to eight sessions, in two semesters.

Center for Continuing Adult Learning, Inc.-CCAL
31 Maple Street
P.O. Box 546
Oneonta, NY 13820
607-432-6554
http://external.oneonta.edu/ccal/
CCAL offers a variety of courses and workshops, meeting once or twice a week for four to eight weeks. Memberships include: courses, field trips, and access to many on-campus facilities. Memberships are $100/year.

The Round table
State University of NY-Stony Brook
SBS Building Room S109
Stony Brook, NY 11794-0001
631-632-7063
www.sunysb.edu
The Round Table is a member-run educational organization for semi-retired and retired individuals interested in learning.

North Carolina

Duke Institute for Learning in Retirement
Continuing Studies
Box 90704
Durham, NC 27708
919-684-2703
www.learnmore.duke.edu/DILR
The Duke Institute for Learning in Retirement is an educational organization offering classes to all adults 50 and older. Memberships are $30/year with additional costs for classes.

Encore Center for Lifelong Enrichment
NC State University
225 McKimmon Center, Box 7401
Raleigh, NC 27695
919-515-5782
www.ncsu.edu/encore
The Encore Center for Lifelong Enrichment offers non-credit programs for adults 50 and older. Memberships include courses, study trips, and special events. Adults 65 and older may receive tuition waiver for credit courses. Memberships are $40/year, $30/spring term and $20/summer term. Six week courses are $40.

Lifelong Learning in Mayland Community College
Mayland Community College
P.O. Box 547
Spruce Pine, NC 28777
828-765-7351
www.mayland.cc.nc.us/continuinged/llim

Sandhills Center for Creative Retirement
Sandhills Community College
3395 Airport Road
Pinehurst, NC 28374
919-695-3779
www.sandhills.cc.nc.us/ced/sccr.html
The Sandhills Center for Creative Retirement provides programs, promotes access to services and community resources for seniors. Courses and other programs are designed around the needs of the members.

Ohio

BGSU Firelands ElderCollege
BGSU Firelands
One University Drive
Huron, OH 44839-9719
419-433-5560 ext 20632
800-322-4787
www.firelands.bgsu.edu/offices/oeo/eldercollege
BGSU Firelands ElderCollege is a member-run educational organization offering a wide variety of programs for seniors. In addition to classes, they offer field trips, and social events. Memberships are $25/semester.

ElderCollege
Terra State Community College
2830 Napoleon Road
Fremont, OH 43420
419-334-8400 ext 252
800-826-2431 ext 252
www.terra.edu/learning/eldercollege.asp
ElderCollege offer seniors 50 and older a place to learn and meet people. More than 40 classes and educational programs meet the interests of their members. Memberships are $20/year single, $35/year couple.

Eldervision
Lourdes College
6832 Convent Boulevard
Sylvania, OH 43560
419-824-3707
Email: gburke@lourdes.edu

Institute for Learning in Retirement
University of Cincinnati
P.O. Box 210093
Cincinnati, OH 45221-0093
www.uc.edu/ace/ilr
Institute for Learning in Retirement offers a variety of classes for retired adults. You can search their web site for classes by class, location or class time to find the perfect class for you. Members may take as many classes as they choose. Memberships are $79/quarter, $180/three quarters.

Institute for Learning in Retirement
Bluffton College
Box 1117
280 W. College Avenue
Bluffton, OH 45817-1196
419-358-3346
www.bluffton.edu/ilr
The Institute for Learning in Retirement offers study sessions in a variety of topics including: music, literature, cooking, economics and other topics that interest their members. A membership fee is required.

Institute for Learning in Retirement
The Ohio State University at Lima
4240 Campus Drive
Lima, OH 45804

419-995-8857
www.lima.ohio-state.edu/ced/ilr.htm
The Institute for Learning in Retirement is a member-run educational organization for seniors who love to learn. For a small fee, members can attend study classes and attend social gatherings. Programs are usually held in October and April of each year.

Institute for Learning in Retirement
Clark State Community College
Continuing Education Department
P.O. Box 570
Springfield, OH 45501-0570
937-328-6047
www.clarkstate.edu/noncredit.html
The Institute for Learning in Retirement offers people of retirement age a variety of programs. They provide two terms of nine weeks in the fall and spring. Members may attend as many classes as they wish. Memberships are $85/term, $125/year.

Institute for Learning in Retirement
Kettering Center for Continuing Education
Wright State University
140 East Monument Avenue
Dayton, OH 45402-1267
937-775-1100
http://goto.wright.edu/cpd/ilr/
The Institute for Learning in Retirement offers a variety of stimulating courses for Miami Valley adults. Members may take unlimited classes and free parking is available at all three of their locations. Memberships are $55/term.

Institute For Learning in Retirement
Miami University
Office of Continuing Education
Joyner House
Oxford, OH 45056
513-529-1508
www.units.muohio.edu/continuingeducation/ilr/
The Institute For Learning in Retirement promotes educational opportunities for adults 50 and order who are retired or semi-retired. Membership includes: choice of unlimited ILR classes, parking, field trips, travel opportunities, and special events. Memberships are $50/year.

Osher Lifelong Learning Institute at University of Dayton
300 College Park
Dayton, OH 45469-0800
937-229-2605
http://artssciences.udayton.edu/continuingeducation/UDLLI.asp
The Osher Lifelong Learning Institute at University of Dayton provides educational opportunities for men and women 50 and older. Osher offers a series of seminars led by volunteer moderators.

Sinclair Community College
444 West Third Street
Dayton, OH 45402-1460
937-512-5184
www.sinclair.edu/stservices/rsr/Registration/Seniors/index.cfm
Golden Age Classes: The Sinclair tuition waiver program allows seniors 60 and older to audit any credit course on the main campus on a space available basis. Seniors must pay for lab fees and purchase books and materials.
Senior Academy: The Senior Academy offers short-term, non-credit courses for senior citizens. Course fees are $45 for first class and $15 for each additional course in a quarter.
Senior Adults at Off-Campus Locations: Sinclair offers a number of tuition free, credit courses at several senior centers and nursing homes in Montgomery County.

Center for Lifelong Learning
Lorain Community College
Connections Center
1005 Abe Road North
Elyria, OH 44035-1691
www.lorainccc.edu/noncredit
The Center for Lifelong Learning offers seniors 50 years old and older a variety of courses including: computers, history, astronomy, gardening, genealogy and more. Lorain Community College also offers an adult tuition-free program for seniors 60 years old and older.

Youngstown State University Metro College
100 DeBartolo Place
200 DeBartolo Executive Center
Youngstown, OH 44512
330-965-5800
www.ysu.edu/metro/creative_retirement.htm
College for the Over-Sixty: Seniors that are over sixty and have been Ohio residents for the past 12 months are eligible to enroll in tuition-free regular credit courses on a space available basis. Students are responsible for lab, studio, parking fees and books.
Institute for Learning in Retirement: The Institute for Learning in Retirement offers residents of Mahoning or Shenango Valley who are retired or semi-retired an educational opportunity. Members may take Institute for Learning in Retirement courses that meet once a week for two hours and last six weeks. There is a membership fee.
Creative Retirement Opportunities Work-CROW: This is an intense week-long learning experience for seniors in the area.

Oregon

Chemeketa Center for Learning in Retirement
Chemeketa Community College
Woodburn Campus
120 E Lincoln Street
Woodburn, OR 97071
503-981-8820
www.chemeketa.edu

The Chemeketa Center for Learning in Retirement offers classes to seniors 55 and older who want to continue to learn. Two classes are offered on Mondays and two on Thursdays. Memberships are $30/year.

ENCORE (Exploring New Concepts of Retirement Education)
Clatsop Community College
1653 Jerome Avenue
Astoria, OR 97103
503-338-2408
www.clatsopcc.edu/Programs/encore
ENCORE is a member-run educational organization for retired and semi-retired resident 50 years old and older. Members may enroll in any of the ENCORE classes. Memberships are $50/year.

Institute for Continued Learning
Willamette University
900 State Street
Salem, OR 97301
503-370-6162
www.willamette.edu/cla/icl/
The Institute for Continued Learning offers retired and semi-retired seniors continuing academic studies. Sessions are offered in a variety of subject areas on Tuesdays and Thursdays during the academic year. Members have access to Institute sessions, the university library, free admission to university athletics and free city bus service. Memberships are $100/year.

Learning in Retirement
Continuing Education
127 University of Oregon
Eugene, OR 97403-1277
541-346-0697
800-824-2714
http://lir.uoregon.edu
Learning in Retirement is open to all seniors 55 years old and older who want to continue to learn through retirement. Membership includes: lectures, discussions, field trips, courses and other activities. Those interested may even try a class for free before joining. Memberships are $120/year.

Senior Studies Institute
Portland Community College
P.O. Box 19000
Portland, OR 97280-0990
503-977-4122
www.pcc.edu/pcc/pro/seniorstudies.htm
The Senior Studies Institute offers seniors an educational experience through membership.

Pennsylvania

Academy for Lifelong Learning
Carnegie Mellon University
Hunt Library
4909 Frew Street
Pittsburgh, PA 15213-3890
412-268-7489
www.cmu.edu/all/index.html
The Academy for Lifelong Learning is a member-run educational organization for seniors. Memberships are limited and there is a waiting list for new members. Memberships are $40/year plus $40/semester when taking classes.

Community Academy for Lifelong Learning-CALL
P.O. Box 10661
State College, PA 16805-0661
814-238-2368
http://call.centreconnect.org/
The Community Academy for Lifelong Learning is open to all adults who want to continue learning. Memberships are $40/year. Enrollment fees for classes are $10 per class. Scholarships are available on a need basis.

Institute for Lifelong Learning
Slippery Rock University
165 Elm Street
Slippery Rock, PA 16057
724-738-1604
www.sru.edu/pages/453.asp
The Institute for Lifelong Learning is a member-run educational organization that offers a variety of programs for the retired and semi-retired. Memberships include: unlimited classes, Lunch and Lecture Series, parking, library privileges, field trips and social events. Memberships are $70/half year, $120/year.

Older Adult Learning Center
Office of Continuing Education
East Stroudsburg University
200 Prospect Street
East Stroudsburg, PA 18301
570-422-7810
www3.esu.edu/continuinged/learninginretirement.asp
The Older Adult Learning Center is a member-run educational organization that offers courses to retire aged adults. Memberships are $35/year, tuition fee $25/term.

Alvernia Seniors College
400 Saint Bernardine Street
Reading, PA 19607
610-796-8357
www.alvernia.edu/seniorscollege
The Alvernia Seniors College offers men and women 55 years old and older educational opportunities. Memberships range from $35/year to $1,000.

The Forum
Rosemont Community College
School of Continuing Studies
14500 Montgomery Avenue

Rosemont, PA 19010
610-527-0200 ext 2380
www.rosemont.edu/root/cont_studies/forum.html
The Forum is open to all adults 55 years old and older. The program offers fall and spring courses in six-week sessions.

Lifelong Learning at Neumann College-LINC
Neumann College
Continuing Adult and Professional Studies
One Neumann Drive
Aston, PA 19014-1298
610-558-5551
www.neumann.edu/academics/undergrad/linc.asp
LINC offers courses and workshops in a variety of subjects. Prices vary per course.

Rhode Island
Circle of Scholars
Salve Regina University
100 Ochre Point Avenue
Newport, RI 02840
401-341-2120
www.salve.edu/programs/cos/index.cfm
Circle of Scholars offers adults 50 years old and older a chance to continue learning. Seminars offer a variety of subjects and meet once a week for four to eight weeks. Memberships are $40/year single, $65/year couple. Seminar fees range from $20-$40/seminar.

South Carolina
Academy for Lifelong Learning
University of South Carolina Aiken
Continuing Education Department
471 University Parkway
Aiken, SC 29801
803-641-3288
www.usca.edu/academy/
The Academy for Lifelong Learning is a co-educational program for seniors. Membership includes: courses, lectures, field trips, discussion groups and seminars. Memberships are $50/year, $30/second semester. Short course fees are $15/course, $30/semester, and $50/year.

The Institute for Lifelong Learning
Anderson College
316 Boulevard
Anderson, SC 29621
864-231-2058
www.anderson-college.edu/learning/

Center for Creative Retirement
College of Charleston
160 Calhoun Street
Charleston, SC 29424
843-953-5488
www.cofc.edu/visitors/CCR.html
The Center for Creative Retirement is a member-run educational organization for retired or semi-retired adults. Membership includes: lectures, discussion groups, field trips social events and other activities.

Clemson University Lifelong Learning-CULL
Clemson University
279 Lehotsky Hall
P.O. Box 340735
Clemson, SC 29634-0735
864-656-6912
www.clemson.edu/cull/
The Clemson University Lifelong Learning Program offers classes and activities for active adults. Memberships are $100/semester for up to three classes or $50 for one class.

Furman University Learning in Retirement
Furman University
3300 Poinsett Highway
Greenville, SC 29613
864-294-2997
www.furman.edu/fulir/fulir.htm
The Furman University Learning in Retirement offers a variety of educational experiences for retired adults. Memberships are $275/year, $125/term which entitles you to attend up to four classes per term.

Lifelong Learning Society
Coastal Carolina University
P.O. Box 261954
Conway, SC 29528
843-349-2544
www.coastal.edu/lifelonglearn/
The Lifelong Learning Society offers members workshops and seminars in a variety of topics. Memberships are $35/year.

The Learning Exchange
University of South Carolina Beaufort
801 Carteret Street
Beaufort, SC 29902
843-521-4113
www.sc.edu/beaufort/communitypartnerships/tlx/
The Learning Exchange provides an educational program to all adults who love learning. Memberships are $150/year.

Tennessee
Kingsport Institute for Continued Learning
East Tennessee State University
P.O. Box 70559
Johnson City, TN 37614
423-392-8001
www.etsu.edu/kingsport/kingsport3.htm
The Kingsport Institute for Continued Learning is an educational organization that offers non-credit courses to adults 50 and

older. The classes meet once a week for six weeks during two terms throughout the year.

Oak Ridge Institute for Continued Learning
Roane State Community College
701 Briarcliff Avenue
Oak Ridge, TN 37830
865-481-8222
www.kornet.org/oricl
The Oak Ridge Institute for Continued Learning is open to residents of Oak Ridge and surrounding areas who are interested in learning. Memberships are $90/three terms, $70/winter and summer term, and $40/summer term. There are additional fees for labs, materials and field trips.

Retirement Living at Vanderbilt
Vanderbilt University
P.O. Box 6009, Station B
Nashville, TN 37235
615-343-0553
www.vanderbilt.edu/cngr/rlv/
The Retirement Living at Vanderbilt offers adults educational programs, field trips and a variety of social activities. Memberships are $70/term. Scholarship assistance is available.

Texas
Academy of Learning in Retirement
The University of Texas
801 S. Bowie Street
San Antonia, TX 78205-3296
210-458-2294
www.texancultures.utsa.edu/alir/alir.htm
The Academy of Learning in Retirement is a member-run educational organization open to adults 50 years old and older. Membership includes: unlimited courses, free admission to the Institute Exhibit Floor during ALIR sessions and a discount at the gift shop. Memberships are $90/semester.

Academy for Lifelong Learning
Montgomery College
3200 College Park Drive
Conroe, TX 77384
936-273-7260
www.all-mc.com
The Academy for Lifelong Learning at Montgomery College (AAL@MC) is an educational organization for older adults that provide courses, lectures and other activities. Courses are offered in the fall and spring with additional summer classes offered. Memberships are $35/year.

Academy for Lifelong Learning
North Harris Montgomery Community College
Corporate and Continuing Education
2700 W.W. Thorne Boulevard
Houston, TX 77073
281-618-7133
www.northharriscollege.com/cce/home.cfm?programID=32
The Academy for Lifelong Learning is committed to enhancing the learning experiences for older residents of north Harris County.

Baylor Institute for Learning in Retirement
Division of continuing Education
Baylor University
One Bear Place #97362
Waco, TX 76798
254-710-3550
www.baylor.edu/ce/index.php?id=4257
The Institute for Learning in Retirement offers a variety of learning opportunities for persons of retirement age. Membership includes: BILR courses, discount on continuing education short courses, field trips and social events. Memberships are $60/year singles, $100/year couples. Additional courses are $15 per course.

The Center for Lifelong Learning
The University of Texas at El Paso
Miners' Hall, Room 209
El Paso, TX 79968
915-747-6280
www.utep.edu/cll
The Center for Lifelong Learning is a member-run educational organization for adults 50 year old and older. Memberships include: unlimited CCL course, parking permit, discounts to University events and library privileges. Memberships are $60/semester and an additional one-time $25 membership fee.

Seniors Active in Learning-SAIL
Collin Count Community College
Courtyard Center for Professional and Economic Development
4800 Preston Park Boulevard
Plano, TX 75093
972-985-3788
www.ccccd.edu/SailSite/index.html
SAIL is a member-run educational organization for adults 50 years old and older. They offer classes for the fall and spring sessions with lecture series in the summer and social activities throughout the year. Memberships are $25/year, $50/session per session to enroll in classes.

UTMB's Academy for Lifelong Learning
University of Texas Medical Branch
301 University Boulevard
Galveston, TX 77555-0460
409-747-4657
www.utmb.edu/aging/outreach/ALL/
The Academy for Lifelong Learning offers community members 55 years and older a venue for continued learning. They offer semester-long college level classes that meet for two hours a week for 8 weeks. Tuition is $25/class.

Utah

Elder Quest
Utah Valley State College
MS 132
School of Continuing and Adult Education
800 West University Parkway
Orem, UT 84058
801-863-8398
www.uvsc.edu/conted/lifelong/elderquest/
Elder Quest is an adult peer taught learning organization. They offer classes, field study, travel experiences and social activities. Memberships are $35/year, $10/class.

Vermont

Osher Lifelong learning Institutes
The University of Vermont-Continuing Education
322 South Prospect Street
Burlington, VT 05401
802-656-4220
www.uvm.edu/~learn/osher/
The Osher Lifelong Learning Institute is a member-run educational organization led by community members. Institutes are available at the following locations: Brattleboro, Montpelier, Rutland, Springfield and St. Johnsbury. Memberships are $40/year.

Virginia

Arlington Learning in Retirement Institute
2801 Clarendon Boulevard #306
Arlington, VA 22201
703-228-2144
http://arlingtonlri.gmu.edu/
The Arlington Learning in Retirement Institute offers members college-level courses, lectures, special events and other activities for adults 50 years old and older. Memberships are $55/year, $45/class.

Christopher Wren Association
South Henry Street
P.O. Box 8795
The College of William and Mary
Williamsburg, VA 23187-8795
757-221-1079
www.wm.edu/cwa/
The Christopher Wren Association offers adults in retirement the opportunity to study and learn. Regular memberships are $75/semester that includes one to twelve class units, newsletter, Town and Gown/Brown-bag lunch series and other activities. Associate memberships are $25/semester that includes Town and Gown/Brown-bag lunch series, newsletter and certain special events.

Mary Washington ElderStudy Learning in Retirement
University of Mary Washington
1301 College Avenue
Fredericksburg, VA 22401
540-654-1769
www.jmc.mwc.edu/elder/index.htm
Mary Washington ElderStudy is a member-run educational organization for retired adults who love learning. They offer about forty 2-hour sessions each semester on a variety of topics, led by professionals or college staff. Memberships are $75/year single, $125/year couple.

Institute for Learning in Retirement
Old Dominion University
1881 University Drive
Virginia Beach, VA 23453-8083
757-368-4160
www.lions.odu.edu/org/ilr/
The Institute for Learning in Retirement is an educational member-run organization for adults fifty-five years old and older. Courses are offered throughout the year. Courses include: social issues, science and technology, the arts, history and current events, health topics and many others. Memberships are $15/year single, $25/year couple. Short courses cost an additional $10 per two-hour course.

Jefferson Institute for Lifelong Learning (JILL)
The University of Virginia
104 Midmont Lane
P.O. Box 400764
Charlottesville, VA 22904
434-982-5272
www.jilluva.org/jill_page1.html
The Jefferson Institute for Lifelong Learning offers university-level classes in a wide variety of subjects for 3 to 6 weeks. Membership includes: 12 units of courses per semester, JILL catalog, JILL newsletter and other JILL functions. Memberships are $75/semester.

Life Long Learning Society
Christopher Newport University
1 University Place
Newport News, VA 23606
757-594-7000
http://users.cnu.edu/~lls/
The Life Long Learning Society is a member-run educational organization. Retired adults are encouraged to choose from a variety of activities including: lectures, courses, discussion groups, lunches and field trips. Full memberships are $120/spring and summer session. Scholarships are available for economic hardship.

Lifelong Learning Institute
The James Madison University
MSC 9006
Harrisburg, VA 22807
540-568-2923
www.jmu.edu/socwork/lli/

The Lifelong Learning Institute offers adults 50 years old and older two five-week sessions with a variety of classes. There are also field trips, social events and brown bag lunches. Memberships are $10/year. Courses are typically $35 each.

Lifelong Learning Institute
Northern Virginia Community College-Manassas Campus
6901 Sudley Road
Manassas, VA 20109
703-361-6310
www.lli-manassas.org/
The Lifelong Learning Institute offers adults 50 years and older a member-run educational organization. They offer daytime and evening classes, monthly lectures, special events and many other activities in the fall and spring. Memberships are $100/year.

Lifelong Learning Institute
Brandermill Woods
14311 Brandermill Woods Trail
Midlothian, VA 23112
804-744-0141
800-552-6579
www.brandermillwoods.com/lifelonglearning.htm
The Lifelong Learning Institute serves Chester County senior adults in their retirement years. LLI offers daytime courses, lectures, special events, trips and other activities. Courses are offered during an eight-week term in the fall and spring, and a four-week midwinter and early summer program. Memberships are $150/year.

Lifetime Learning Institute
Northern Virginia Community College
8333 Little River Turnpike
Annandale, VA 22003
703-503-0600
http://groups.msn.com/llinova/mainpage.msnw
The Lifelong Learning Institute is a member-run educational organization for older adults to continue their love of learning. Courses are offered in the fall and the spring. Memberships are $100/year.

Osher Lifelong Learning Institute
George Mason University
4210 Roberts Road
Fairfax, VA 22032
709-503-3384
www.olli.gmu.edu
The Osher Lifelong Learning Institute at George Mason University provides retired residents of Northern Virginia an opportunity for intellectual and cultural experiences. Memberships are $270/year. Scholarships are available on a need basis.

Shenandoah University College for Lifelong Learning
Shenandoah University
1460 University Drive
Winchester, VA 22601
540-665-4643
www.su.edu/cont-ed/programs.asp?programid=1
Lifelong Leaning offers a wide variety of non-credit courses for adults. Memberships include: vouchers for courses, discounts at the university book store, library privileges, social events and many other activities.

Washington

Academy for Lifelong Learning
Western Washington University
MS 5293, 516 High Street
Bellingham, WA 98225
360-650-3308
www.acadweb.wwu.edu/eesp/all_programs.shtml
Academy for Lifelong Learning is a member driven educational organization. They offer courses during the fall, winter, and spring in a variety of subjects. Memberships include: priority registration, discounts on courses, special events, and participation in discussion groups. Memberships are $65/semester.

Creative Retirement Institute
Edmonds Community College
728 134th Street SW, Suite 128
Everett, WA 98204
425-640-1243
http://new.cri.edcc.edu/cri_welcome.html
The Creative Retirement Institute offers members a variety of college-level courses, field trips, and other learning experiences. Memberships include a free course for every $100 you spend on classes, reduced rates for luncheons and library privileges. Memberships are $30/semester.

Quest: An Institute for Learning
Walla Walla Community College
500 Tausick Way
Walla Walla, WA 99362
509-527-4561
www.wwcc.edu/programs/continuing/community.cfm
Quest offers senior adults 50 years old and older opportunities for learning, socializing and other activities. Membership allows you to take Quest classes, attend social events and entitles you to full privileges of a WWCC student. If you are 90 years old or older membership is free! Memberships are $50/year.

West Virginia

Appalachian Lifelong Learning
West Virginia University Center on Aging
P.O. Box 9125
Morgantown, WV 26506-9125
304-293-1793

www.hsc.wvu.edu/coa/all/
The Appalachian Lifelong Learners at WVU is a member-run organization for adults 55 years old or older. Courses are offered in three six-week semesters. Course topics include: social studies, liberal arts, music, literature, gardening, financial planning and Appalachian culture. Memberships include unlimited courses with priority registration. Memberships are $65/year.

Lifelong Learning at Fairmont State College
Fairmont State College
1201 Locust Avenue
Fairmont, WV 26554
304-367-4052
www.fscwv.edu/fsctc/lifelong.shtml
Lifelong Learning at Fairmont State College is an educational and recreational program for adults 55 years old and older. Members may attend multi-week courses, special seminars and field trips. Memberships are $50/year.

Wisconsin

Adventure in Lifelong Learning (ALL)
University of Wisconsin Parkside
900 Wood Road
P.O. Box 2000
Kenosha, WI 53141-2000
262-595-2137
www.uwp.edu/departments/community.partnerships/all/
Adventures in Lifelong Learning offers a variety of educational, creative and social opportunities. Programs are offered on the first and third Mondays from 2-3 p.m. Memberships are $40/year.

Door County Learning in Retirement
Northeast Wisconsin Technical College-Sturgeon Bay
229 N 14th
Sturgeon Bay, WI 54235
920-746-8007
Email: doorcountylir@yahoo.com
The Door County Learning in Retirement Program is a peer driven educational organization for older adults.

Guild for Learning in Retirement
University of Wisconsin Milwaukee
161 West Wisconsin Avenue, Suite 6000
Milwaukee, WI 53203
414-227-3222
http://cfprod.imt.uwm.edu/sce/dci.cfm?id=10
The Guild for Learning in Retirement is a forum for older adults to continue learning. Members can attend short courses, peer-directed special interests groups, day bus tours, lectures and social activities. Memberships are $40/year.

Institute for Learning in Retirement
Nicolet College
P.O. Box 518
Rhinelander, WI 54501
715-365-4512
800-544-3039 ext 4512
www.nicoletcollege.edu/ilr/welcome.htm
The Institute for Learning in Retirement is a member-run educational organization for retired and semi-retired adults of Northwoods. They offer more than 50 programs during the fall and spring semesters. Members may attend all programs, many social events and field trips. Memberships are $35/year.

Learning in Retirement
Wood Hall, Room 470A
Green Bay, WI 54311
920-465-2356
www.uwgb.edu/outreach/lir/
Learning in Retirement is for adults near or in retirement to explore their interests. Courses are peer-led on a variety of topics. Classes usually meet weekly for four to twelve weeks depending on the class. Members may take as many courses as they choose. Memberships are $50/year.

Institute for Learning in Retirement
130 Home Economics Building
University of Wisconsin-Stout
Menomonie, WI 54751
715-232-5230
www.uwstout.edu/chd/ilr
The Institute for Learning in Retirement offers a variety of course for retired adults. Members may take course tuition free. Memberships are $25/year.

Learning in Retirement
University of Wisconsin-La Crosse
1725 State Street
La Crosse, WI 54601
608-785-6506
www.uwlax.edu/conted/html/learning-in-retirement.htm
Learning in Retirement offers retired adults classes in the fall and spring that usually meet two hours, once a week, for three to five weeks. Members may take unlimited classes and participate in field trips, lecture series and social events.

Learning in Retirement
University of Wisconsin-Oshkosh
Division of Continuing Education
800 Algoma Boulevard
Oshkosh, WI 54901-8623
920-424-1129
800-633-1442
www.uwosh.edu/cont_ed/ilr.htm
Learning in Retirement is a member-run educational organization for retired adults. Two semesters of courses are offered with a variety of topics available. Members may take an

unlimited number of courses offered by Learning in Retirement. Memberships are $60/year.

Learning is ForEver (LIFE)
University of Wisconsin-Steven Point
UWSP Extension
2100 Main Street
032 Main Building
Stevens Point, WI 54481
715-346-3838
800-898-9472
www.uwsp.edu/extension/programs/life/index.asp
LIFE is a member-run educational organization for adults to have the opportunity to continue learning. Memberships are $60/year.

PLATO
University of Wisconsin-Madison
905 University Avenue
Madison, WI 53715
609-262-5823
www.dcs.wisc.edu/students/PLATO.htm
PLATO is a learning in retirement organization that offers members a variety of learning experiences. Memberships are $50/year.

Learning in Retirement
Waukesha County Technical College
A-Building, Room A102E
800 Main Street
Pewaukee, WI 53072
262-695-3473
www.wctc.edu/web/activities/lir/lir.htm
Learning in Retirement is an educational organization open to older adults. Courses are usually held once a week for four to six weeks during the daytime. Memberships include: classes at a nominal fee, day trips, special discussion groups and other activities. Memberships are $40/year.

Local Senior Learning Opportunities

Good as Gold
Columbus State Community College
550 E. Spring Street
Columbus, OH 43216
800-621-6407
614-287-2453
http://cscc.edu/docs/Admissions/gold.htm
Good as Gold is a service of Columbus State that offers adults 60 and older the opportunity to enroll in credit courses tuition free, on a space available basis. Good as Gold students must pay a $10 application fee, course lab fees and the cost of books.

Connecticut Tuition Waiver Public Colleges and Universities

Senior citizens 62 and older may take courses and earn degrees tuition-free. This program is available at the institutions listed below. Generally, waivers are available only when there is space at the end of registration. Contact each college or university for additional details. See what colleges and universities in your area have to offer.

University of Connecticut
Main Campus
Storrs, CT 06269
860-486-2000
www.catalog.uconn.edu/fees.htm

Central Connecticut State
1615 Stanley Street
New Britain, CT 06050
860-832-2010
www.ccsu.edu

Eastern Connecticut State
83 Windham Street
Willimantic, CT 06226
860-465-5224
www.ecsu.ctstateu.edu/

Southern Connecticut State
501 Crescent Street
New Haven, CT 06515
203-392-5238
www.southernct.edu

Western Connecticut State
181 White Street
Danbury, CT 06810
203-837-9000
www.wcsu.edu

Asnuntuck Community College
170 Elm Street
Enfield, CT 06082
860 253-3012
www.acc.commnet.edu/

Capital Community College
950 Main Street
Hartford, CT 06103
860-906-5000
www.ccc.commnet.edu/

Gateway Community College
Long Wharf Campus
60 Sargent Drive
New Haven, CT 06511
203-285-2010
www.gwctc.commnet.edu/

Gateway Community College
North Haven Campus
88 Bassett Road
North Haven, CT 06473
203-285-2010
www.gwctc.commnet.edu/

Housatonic Community College
900 Lafayette Blvd.
Bridgeport, CT 06604
203 332-5100
www.hctc.commnet.edu/index2.html

Manchester Community College
Great Path
P.O. Box 1046
Manchester, CT 06045
860-512-3000
www.mcc.commnet.edu

Middlesex Community College
100 Training Hill Road
Middletown, CT 06457
860 343-5800
www.mxctc.commnet.edu

Naugatuck Valley Community College
750 Chase Parkway
Waterbury, CT 06708
203-575-8055
www.nvctc.commnet.edu/

Northwest Community College
Park Place
Winsted, CT 06098
860-738-6300
www.nwctc.commnet.edu/

Norwalk Community College
188 Richards Avenue
Norwalk, CT 06854
860-857-7000
www.nctc.commnet.edu

Quinebaug Valley
742 Upper Maple Street
Danielson, CT 06239
860 774-1130
www.qvctc.commnet.edu/

Three Rivers Community College
Mahan Drive
Norwich, CT 06360
860-866-0177
www.trcc.commnet.edu/

Tunix Community College
271 Scott Swamp Road
Farmington, CT 06032
860-255-3500
http://tunxis.commnet.edu/

Senior Jobs and Job Training

Senior Jobs and Job Training

Keeping your mind and body active keeps the juices flowing through the brain. Often though, it is hard for a senior citizen to find a job, so several agencies have stepped in to provide training and assistance to help seniors upgrade their skills and search for employment. We have listed several agencies that will help you find your dream job, and have included some good starting places for your job search.

$8,000 To Train For A New Job

If you have found yourself on the losing end of a plant closing or mass layoff, apply for money and re-training under the Economic Dislocation and Worker Adjustment Assistance Act. The program is administered by each state, and because of that, the program differs from state to state. Workers can receive classroom, occupational skills, and/or on-the-job training to qualify for jobs in demand. Basic and remedial education, entrepreneurial training, and instruction in literacy or English-as-a-second-language may be provided. For more information, contact your state Department of Labor in the blue pages of your phone book, or contact Employment and Training Administration, U.S. Department of Labor, 200 Constitution Ave., NW, Washington, DC 20210; 877-US-2JOBS; 202-693-3500; www. doleta.gov/programs/.

Free Resume Writing, On-Line Job Search Training and Free Computers

You can go to a local government office or sometimes a local nonprofit organization that is contracted by the federal government to provide the job seeker with free help in resume writing, job interview techniques, or job searching on the internet. They will even let you use free computers to prepare your resume or search the web. To see if there are offices like this near you, contact your state One-Stop Labor Information Center headquarters located in your state capital, or online at www.doleta.gov/usworkforce/onestop/onestopmap.cfm.

Show A Potential Employer How To Get $7,000 To Hire You

Many state governments have programs that offer free money if they hire new employees. Other states will give employers free money to take a new employee and train them in a needed skill, like computers, or in certain occupations like food service. Employers can also get $2,400 from the government for hiring people with disabilities, people who live in certain zip codes, people who received government assistance, ex-felons or even veterans. To find out about programs in your area, contact your state Office of Labor, your state Office of Economic Development and your state Office of Taxation all located in your state capital www.govengine.com.

Money and Help For Divorced Or Widowed Women

Recently divorced women and women in transition sometimes need a helping hand. Women Work! is an organization whose mission is to help women become self-sufficient. This is accomplished by helping them get the education, training and jobs they need to be successful. Women Work! has over 1,000 programs across the country doing just that. To learn what is offered in your neighborhood, contact Women Work! 1625 K St., NW, Suite 300, Washington, DC 20006; 202-467-6346; 800-235-2732; Fax: 202-467-5366; www.womenwork.org .

Free Help For Women

Many states have Women's Commission whose job is to advocate with the state legislatures on the role of women. In fact there are over 270 women's commissions at city, county and state levels. Since the Commissions are a link between the government and the private sector, they may be aware of programs and services available to women. A map is available on the website showing where commissions are located. To learn more contact the National Association of Commissions for Women, 8630 Fenton St., Suite 934, Silver Spring, MD 20910; 301-585-8101; Fax: 301-585-3445; www.nacw.org.

Temp Jobs For Seniors At Dept Of Ag

The U.S. Dept of Agriculture along with the National Older Worker Career Center (NOWCC) are offering full time and part time jobs just to work with the Environmental Protection Agency's SEE Program and the U.S. Department of Agriculture's NCEP project. For information on the jobs available under these programs contact: National Older Worker Career Center, Inc., 3811 North Fairfax Drive, Suite 900, Arlington, VA 22203, 703-558-4200. To learn about available jobs go to www.nowcc.org/applicants/positions/index.html. If you wish to find as local office of NOWCC go to www.nowcc.org/aboutUs/fieldOffices.asp.

12,345 Seniors Over 70 Work For Uncle Sam

It's never too late to get a job in the federal government. There are over 18,000 job openings now. Contact your congressman's or senators' offices for information about working for the federal government at www.congress.org or call the Capitol Hill switchboard at 202-224-3121. Take a look at what federal jobs are available now at www.usajobs.opm.gov/.

Show Your Boss How To Get Money To Train You For A Better Job

Show your boss how to make you become more productive (and more employable when you leave) by tapping into free government money to upgrade your skills. You can learn computer skills, customer service skills, new technologies or even stress management. See what your state offers and let your boss know about it. Contact your state Office of Labor or Department of Economic Development located in your state capital www.govengine.com.

$400/wk When You Are Out of Work

If you have been laid off or downsized from your job through no fault of your own, then help is available to you. Unemployment compensation is the government's first line of defense against the ripple effects of unemployment. By cash payments made directly to laid off workers, the program ensures that at least a significant portion of the necessities of life, such as food, shelter, and clothing, can be met while a search for work takes place. The Federal-State Unemployment Insurance Program provides unemployment benefits to eligible workers who are unemployed through no fault of their own, and meet other eligibility requirements. Check to see if you qualify for any additional benefits above and beyond the Unemployment Insurance Program.

Extended Benefits Program

Extended Benefits are available to workers who have exhausted regular unemployment insurance benefits during periods of high unemployment. The basic Extended Benefits program provides up to 13 additional weeks of benefits when a State is experiencing high unemployment. Some states have a program to pay up to seven (7) additional weeks of Extended Benefits.

Unemployment Compensation for Federal Employees Program

The Unemployment Compensation for Federal Employees program provides benefits for eligible unemployed former civilian This program is operated under the same terms and conditions that apply to regular State Unemployment Insurance (see State Unemployment Insurance). In general, the law of the State in which your last official duty station in Federal civilian service was located will be the State law that determines eligibility for unemployment insurance benefits. There is no payroll deduction from a Federal employee's wages for unemployment insurance protection. Benefits are paid for by the various Federal agencies.

Free Help If You Lose Your Job Because of Increased Imports

As the business world becomes more and more competitive, many US businesses are moving their companies to other parts of the globe. The President signed into law the Trade Adjustment Assistance Reform Act of 2002 (TAA Reform Act), which provides you with assistance if you lose your job because of increased imports. The Trade Adjustment Assistance Reform Act of 2002 can help you learn marketable skills to move you on to new and better job opportunities. Workers may be eligible for up to 130 weeks of on-the-job and classroom training; you can receive 78 weeks of income benefits after your unemployment expires; you can receive $1,250 for job search and relocation expenses; health care benefits may also be available. This program is also available to farmers who have been hurt by imports! For more information contact U.S. Department of Labor, Employment and Training Administration, Division of Trade Adjustment Assistance, 200 Constitution Avenue, NW, Room C-5311, Washington, DC 20210; 202-693-3046; http://www.doleta.gov/tradeact.

Free Job Training

Actually many state Departments of Labor offer a variety of job training programs to help employers train new hires or upgrade the skills of their current workers. Although these programs need to be initiated by the employer with the Labor Department, you can take the initiative and see what they have to offer. Then show your boss how eager you are to learn new skills, at no cost to them!

- Ohio Training Tax Credit Program provides tax credits of up to $100,000 per year to help offset costs of training current workers.
- Pennsylvania offers Customized Job Training grants for specialized job training for existing or new employees; Guaranteed Free Training Program up to $700 per employee; and Critical Job Training Grants for high demand jobs or jobs with a shortage of skilled workers.
- Rhode Island has a Job Creation Grant Fund to offer customized training and an Excellence Through Training Grant Program that provides grants to upgrade and retrain existing employees.
- Arkansas' Business and Industry Training program will provide financial assistance to companies to recruit new workers, will provide customized training before employment, and will pay for more training once you hire the employee. They also offer the Existing Workforce Training Program which will pay for upgrading the skills of your current employees.

Contact your state Department of Labor in your state capitol or go to www.govengine.com to see what special programs your state may offer.

One-Stop Career Shopping

Are you tired of your old job? Do you need help training for a new career? Are you ready for a new exciting job? Career One Stop is a national online career development resource, which provides internet-based access for Americans, needing job search assistance, career guidance, salary data and training and education resources. You can find jobs from entry level to technical to professional to CEO. In addition to the online program, there are also Comprehensive One-Stop Career Centers located throughout the country. Each community has tailored their system to meet the needs of the citizens in their area. The centers may offer computers, career counseling, workshops and many other services. The number of centers is growing everyday. To locate the Career One-Stop Program go to their web site. For additional information and to locate your closest Career One-Stop Center, go to the service locator web site or refer to the appendix of this book for a listing. Contact U.S. Department of Labor, Frances Perkins Building, 200 Constitution Avenue, NW, Washington, DC 20210; 877-US-2JOBS; 202-693-2700; 877-889-5627 TTY; www.doleta.gov/usworkforce/onestop/; Career One-Stop: www.careeronestop.org/; Career One-Stop Center Locator: www.servicelocator.org/nearest_onestop.asp.

Craftsman Can Still Apply Their Trade

The Elder Craftsman offers different programs that allow seniors to use their skills and creativity to build things, which then can be sold on the website. This is for Sacramento area seniors only. Check with your local Senior Center or Area Agency on Aging to see what your city may offer. Contact Elder Craftsman, 1011 2nd Street, Old Sacramento, CA 95814; 916-264-7676; www.eldercraftsman.com/.

A Job, Education and Training For Over 55

Green Thumb provides seniors with job training and assistance finding work. Another part of the program funded by the Department of Labor offers education, job training, and placement in community service jobs. Contact Green Thumb, Experience Works, Inc, 2200 Clarendon Blvd,, Suite 1000, Arlington, VA 22201; 703-522-7272; 866-397-9757; Fax: 703-522-014; http://www.experienceworks.org/.

Clearinghouse of Free Job Help Services

The National Association of Area Agencies on Aging helps link the elderly and their families with different agencies that can help the elderly live happier and make the best of their benefits. For more information contact National Association of Area Agencies on Aging, 1730 Rhode Island Ave., NW, Suite 1200, Washington, DC 20036; 202-872-0888; Fax: 202-872-0057; www.n4a.org/default.cfm. Eldercare Locator can be contacted at 800-677-1116.

Get Free And Low Cost Computer Job Skills

SeniorNet provides services that help the elderly become more familiar with the Internet. It also provides seniors with different technology discounts through the website. There are over 200 Learning Centers across the United States. Contact SeniorNet, 1171 Homestead Road, Suite 280, Santa Clara, CA 95050; 408- 615- 0699; Fax: 408- 615-0928; www.seniornet.org/php/default.php.

55+ Get Jobs With EPA

The Senior Environmental Employment (SEE) Program provides an opportunity for retired and unemployed older Americans age 55 and over to share their expertise with the Environmental Protection Agency. Several national agencies recruit workers for clerical, technical, and professional positions. For more information contact SEE Program, U.S. Environmental Protection Agency, 1200 Pennsylvania Ave., NW, MC3650A, Washington, DC 20460; 202-564-0420; www.epa.gov/epahrist/see/brochure/index.htm.

Starting at 40, Seniors Are Protected In the Workplace

Don't be discriminated against because of your age! The Equal Employment Opportunity Commission protects individuals who are 40 years of age or older from employment discrimination based on age. In 2004 EEOC received 17,837 charges of age discrimination and resolved 15,792 case, recovering $60 million in monetary benefits for charging parties. All for free. For information on the laws and how to file a complaint contact U.S. Equal Employment Opportunity Commission, P.O. Box 7033, Lawrence, KS 66044; 800-669-4000; www.eeoc.gov.

Get Paid 20 Hours a Week To Learn A New Skill

Seniors all across the United States are getting the help and training they need to get better paying jobs through the Senior Community Service Employment Program. SCSEP is a work training program funded through Title V of the Older Americans Act. It provides temporary, paid, community service jobs to low income persons age 55 and older so that they can develop marketable job skills while searching for permanent employment. The program is designed to benefit both individuals and their communities. Participants help to meet community needs by performing necessary services at nonprofit organizations and government agencies, while at the same time receiving on the job training and employment assistance. Program services include an assessment of skills; a program orientation; an Individual Employment Plan that identifies barriers to employment, recommended assignments, training, and services to overcome these barriers; help in setting employment goals; résumé preparation; referrals to employment opportunities; and follow up meetings, reviews and evaluations to determine progress and the next step. Enrollees are placed in temporary jobs at Host Agencies. These jobs are part time, up to 20 hours per week, and pay at least the current minimum wage. During their temporary assignments, enrollees work with the director of their local SCSEP project office to update their resumes and locate permanent employment. The average amount of time spent in a temporary assignment is 9 months. Types of job assignments vary, but can include educational support and assistance, general office and computers, clerical, home health, food service, and building maintenance at government agencies and nonprofit organizations such as day care facilities, schools, libraries and recreational centers.

Clara Feely, a 75 year old mother of 7, grandmother of 14, and great grandmother of 3, heard about the Senior Community Service Employment Program through her local AARP Office in Park Hill, South Carolina. After 25 years employed as a cafeteria worker with the local school district, Clara found herself looking for a new job while possessing few marketable skills. She wanted to try something new, but was hesitant when offered an office assignment because it was so different from her previous job. Clara was placed at the 16th Circuit Juvenile Solicitor's Office in a temporary position to receive training as an office assistant. She also added to her skills by taking a computer course offered by the

SCSEP at a local technical college. The Staff at the Solicitor's Office was so taken with Clara and her job performance; they made funding possible to offer Clara a permanent job in their office. Clara accepted the position and still works there.

After a difficult divorce, Jo Hunt left her old job and life in Missouri and moved to Tulsa, OK to start a new life near her family. She had to move in with her daughter and as a senior was very discouraged about her job prospects. Jo did not have a college degree, but did have some computer skills and a lot of determination. Researching job opportunities and programs for seniors led her to the AARP and their SCSEP Office in Tulsa. Jo completed a Job Readiness Workshop and was placed at a host agency as an office assistant. After a few weeks, she became an Employment Specialist at the SCSEP Project Office. Jo used this time to help others find work while looking for the perfect job for herself. Six months later she was hired by the Tulsa Nursing Center as a payroll clerk making $10.00 an hour. Jo now has her own apartment and is enjoying her new life. Jo says "I took full advantage of this opportunity to start over with a new career. The training has been wonderful, and I enjoy my job very much. The SCSEP staff has been very supportive and really gave me the chance to do something with my life."

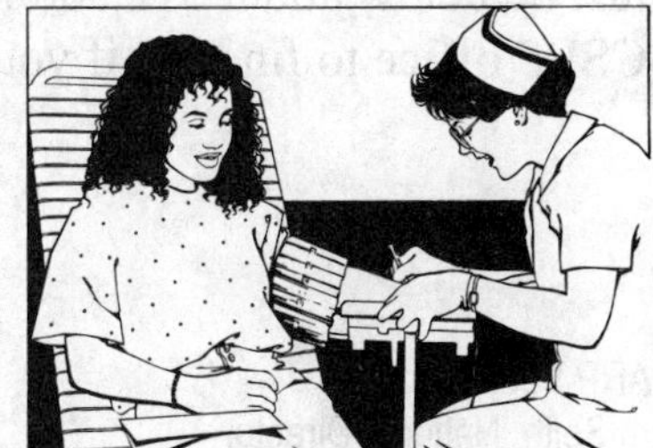

Juanita Erlandsen of Richmond, VA was ready for a career change. After losing her job 4 times in 7 years due to corporate downsizing, she knew it was time to find a new line of work. She took a job as a home health aide, but needed more education and training to earn enough to live on. The Senior Community Service Employment Program at the AARP office got her relevant work experience as an adult day care program assistant and enrolled her in a Certified Nurses Aide (CNA) training program. Juanita completed her training, passed the licensing exam for the State of Virginia and is now working as a full time CNA earning $10.00 per hour.

Richard Hernandez of Spokane, WA was unemployed and had limited marketable job skills when he went to the SCSEP office for help finding a job. Upon completing a skills assessment and Individual Employment Plan, Richard expressed an interest in becoming a truck driver. He was referred to the local WIA, who paid more than $4000 for Richard to attend school to receive the training and certification he needed. One week after completing his training, Richard was traveling the U.S. and earning over $30,000 per year. The SCSEP helped put him back on the road to success.

Sharon Wells of Fort Worth, TX enrolled in SCSEP after her husband passed away. Together, they had owned and operated a successful used car business. Alone, she was unable to keep the business going. Sharon found herself depressed and unemployed, with no income and not even a high school diploma to put on her resume. She entered the SCSEP Program determined to get both her G.E.D. and a full time job with benefits. Sharon attended G.E.D. classes and improved her computer and keyboarding skills while working in her SCSEP training assignments. Sixteen months later, after a lot of hard work and with tons of support from the SCSEP staff, she passed the G.E.D. exam. Sharon now has her G.E.D. Certificate and her dream job with the Tarrant County Sheriff's Department, permanent and full time, plus excellent pay and benefits.

Shedred Bean was forced to retire earlier than planned due to his failing eyesight. Living in poverty and unemployed for three years, Mr. Bean contacted the SCSEP Project Office to get help finding a job to supplement his retirement income. His enthusiasm and desire to work were apparent and he was soon placed in a temporary assignment at the Eureka Rescue Mission. His job included testing electrical donations and light janitorial duties. One month after enrolling in the program, Shedred had an interview at the Northcoast Cleaning Service. Mr. Bean was unable to drive himself due to his eyesight, so his wife drove and accompanied him to the interview. The company ended up hiring both of them as a cleaning team! The Eureka Rescue Mission missed him so much they re-hired him on their own payroll to work part time testing the electrical donations. With the help of SCSEP, Shedred and his wife ended up with three earned incomes to supplement his pension and a much brighter future!

Contact the national grantees and your state contacts listed below. To find your closest SCSEP office you can check the America's Service Locator site at www.servicelocator.org//office_search.asp. Simply type in your zip code and use the drop down menu to choose "Older Worker - SCSEP." Your income must be below about $12,000 for one person but not all income is counted. So it is best to contact the SCSEP office to find out if you are eligible.

SCSEP Contacts
National Grantees

AARP Foundation
Jim Seith, National Director
601 E Street, NW
Washington, DC 20049
202-434-2030
Fax: 202-434-6446
Email: jseith@aarp.org
www.AARP.org/scsep

Asociacion Nacional Pro Personas Mayores (ANPPM)
Dr. Carmela G. Lacayo, President/CEO
234 E. Colorado Boulevard, Suite 300
Pasadena, CA 91101
626-564-1988
Fax: 626-564-2659
Email: support@anppm.org
www.ANPPM.org

Easter Seals, Inc.
Carol A. Salter, National Director SCSEP
230 West Monroe St., Suite 1800
Chicago, IL 60606-4802
800-221-6827
312-551-7132
Fax: 312-726-1494
Email: csalter@easterseals.com
www.easterseals.com/scsep

Experience Works, Inc.
Sally Boofer, Vice President of Operations
2200 Clarendon Blvd., Suite 1000
Arlington, VA 22201
703-522-7272 Ext. 3018
Fax: 703-522-1041
Email: sally_boofer@experienceworks.org
www.ExperienceWorks.org

Mature Services, Inc.
Paul Magnus, Director- Senior Employment Center
415 South Portage Path
Akron, OH 44320
330-762-8666 ext. 164
Fax: 330-762-8644
Email: paul@matureservices.org
www.matureservices.org

National Able Network
Rick Kurtz, Chief Operating Officer
180 Wabash Avenue
Chicago, IL 60601-3600
312-782-3335
Fax: 312-580-0348
Email: rkurtz@nationalable.org
www.nationalable.org

National Asian Pacific Center on Aging (NAPCA)
Polly Chang Colby, National SCSEP Director
1511 Third Avenue, #914
Seattle, WA 98101-1626
206-624-1221 ext. 16

Fax: 206-624-1023
Email: pollyc@napce.org
www.NAPCA.org

National Caucus and Center on Black Aged, Inc. (NCBA)
Karyne Jones, President & CEO
1220 L Street, NW, Suite 800
Washington, DC 20005
202-637-8400
Fax: 206-347-0895
Email: KJones@ncba-aged.org
www.NCBA-Aged.org

National Council on the Aging, Inc. (NCOA)
Donald Davis, Vice-President
Workforce Development Division
300 D Street, SW, Suite 801
Washington, DC 20024
202-479-1200
Fax: 202-479-0735
Email: donald.davis@ncoa.org
www.ncoa.org

National Indian Council on Aging (NICOA)
Frieda Clark, National SCSEP Director
10501 Montgomery Blvd., NE
Suite 210
Albuquerque, NM 87111
505-292-2001
Fax: 505-292-1922
Email: frieda@nicoa.org
www.nicoa.org

National Older Worker Career Center, Inc. (NOWCC)
3811 North Fairfax Dr., Suite 900
Arlington, VA 22203
703-558-4200
www.nowcc.org

Senior Service America, Inc.
Jodie Fine, Deputy Director
8403 Colesville Rd., Suite 1200
Silver Spring, MD 20910
301-578-8900
Fax: 301-587-8947
Email: jfine@ssa-i.org
www.SeniorServiceAmerica.org

SER-Jobs for Progress National, Inc
Rosalina Trevino-Ortega, National SCSEP Director
5215 North O'Conner, Suite 2500
Irving, TX 75039
972-830-6369
Fax: 972-506-7832
Email: rortega@ser-national.org
www.ser-national.org

USDA Forest Service
Bridget Harris, National Program Manager
1400 Independence Ave., SW
Mail Stop 1136
Washington, DC 20250-0003
703-605-4847
Fax: 703-605-5115
Email: bharris02@fs.fed.us
www.fs.fed.us

SCSEP State Contacts

For more information about the Senior Community Service Employment Program in your area, contact one of the state offices below.

Alabama
Michael Malandro, SCSEP Project Director
Alabama Department of Senior Services
770 Washington Ave., Suite 470
RSA Plaza
800-243-5463
334-242-5754
Fax: 334-242-5594
Email: mmalandro@adss.state.al.us
www.ageline.net

Easter Seals Alabama
Pat Smith, VP of Adult Programs
2444 Gordon Smith Drive
Mobile, AL 36617
251-471-1581
Fax: 251-476-4303
http://alabama.easterseals.com

Alaska
Jeff Kemp, SCSEP Program Coordinator
Department of Labor and Workforce Development
Employment Security Division
1111 W. 8th Street, Room 210
Juneau AK 99801
907-465-4872
Fax: 907-465-5945
Email: jeff_kemp@labor.state.ak.us
www.labor.state.ak.us

American Samoa
Fa'aolatia Siatuu, Acting Director
Attention: Taumaude Suiaunoa,
SCSEP Program Manager
Territorial Administration on Aging
Government of American Samoa
Pago Pago, American Samoa 96799
011-684-633-1251
Fax: 011-684-633-2533
Email: taoa@blueskynet.as

Arizona
Henry Blanco, Program Administrator
Attention: David Reyes
Arizona Department of Economic Security
1789 W. Jefferson, 950-A
Phoenix, AZ 85007
602-542-6457
Fax: 602-542-6575
Email: davidreyes@azdes.gov
www.de.state.az.us/aaa/programs/owp/default.asp

AARP/SCSEP Offices
Maria Ramirez-Trillo, SCSEP Project Director
1830 West Colter St., Suite 104
Phoenix, AZ 85015
602-841-0403
Fax: 602-864-0142
Email: scphoenixaz@aol.com

Serving Maricopa County
Easter Seals Arizona, SCSEP Program
Karen Latimer, ATP
Director of Assistive Technology/SCSEP
2075 S. Cottonwood Drive
Tempe, AZ 85282
480-222-4100
Fax: 480-222-4123
www.az.easterseals.com

Experience Works
Clayton Thomas, Regional Director
1481 River Park Drive, Suite 100
Sacramento, CA 95815
800-288-1324
916-641-7700
Fax: 916-646-8118
www.eworkscal.org
Serving Arizona, California, Oregon and Utah

National Indian Council on Aging
Frankie Thompson, Arizona State Director
3625 N. 16th Street, Suite 128
Phoenix, AZ 85016
602-241-1663
Fax: 602-241-1675
Email: Frankie@nicoa.org

Arkansas
Herb Sanderson, Director
Attention: Nadine Grice, Management Project Analyst I
Division of Aging and Adult Services
Arkansas Department of Human Services
700 Main Street, 5th Floor
Donaghey Plaza South Building
Little Rock, AR 72201-4608
501-682-9992
Fax: 501-682-8155
Email: nadine.grice@arkansas.gov
www.arkansas.gov/dhs/aging

Experience Works
Becky Scott, Regional Director
936 Front Street, Slot 4
Cottonport, LA 71327
Toll Free: 888-926-1739
318-876-3954
Fax: 318-876-3927
Email: Becky_Scott@ExperienceWorks.org
Serving Arkansas, Louisiana, Mississippi and Oklahoma

AARP/SCSEP Program Office
Steve Boone, SCSEP Project Director
835 Central Avenue, Suite 100
Hot Springs, AR 71901
501-321-9788
Email: scsboone@aol.com
Serving Clark, Columbia, Garland, Hempstead, Hot Springs, Miller, Montgomery and Nevada Counties

AARP/SCSEP Program Office
Mitzi Johnson, SCSEP Project Director
Westpark Building #1
7101 West 12th Street, Suite #201
Little Rock, AR 72204
501-661-1098
Fax: 501-296-9654
Email: scmjohnson@aol.com
Serving Faulkner, Jefferson, Pulaski, Saline and White Counties.

California
AARP/SCSEP Program Office
Gretchen Campbell, SCSEP Project Director
1125 16th Street, Room 212
Arcata, CA 95521
707-822-7027
Fax: 707-822-7167
Email: scgcampbel@aol.com
Serving Del Norte and Humboldt Counties

AARP/SCSEP Program Office
Thomas Bennetts, SCSEP Project Director
4555 Orange Grove Avenue
Sacramento, CA 95841
916-483-5991
Fax: 916-483-5993
Email: scsacramen@aol.com
Serving Sacramento and Yolo Counties

AARP/SCSEP Program Office
Gretchen Campbell, SCSEP Project Director
2050 West Steele Lane, Suite E-2
Santa Rosa, CA 95403
707-525-9190
Fax: 707-525-0839
Email: scsantaros@aol.com
Serving Marin and Sonoma Counties

AARP/SCSEP Program Office
Linda Herrera, SCSEP Project Director
240 West Caldwell Avenue
Visalia, CA 93277
800-830-2829
559-625-8088
Fax: 559-625-8089
Email: scvisalia@aol.com
Serving Kings and Tulare Counties
Lora Connolly, Interim Director
Attention: Johnna Meyer, SCSEP Policy Manager

California Department of Aging
1600 K Street
Sacramento, CA 95814
916-322-0788
Fax: 916-327-2801
Email: jmeyer@aging.ca.gov
www.aging.ca.gov/html/programs/scsep.html

National Indian Council on Aging
Patricia Woodruff, California State Manager
5997 Brockton Ave., Suite C
Riverside, CA 92506
909-369-8581
Fax: 909-369-8565
Email: patricia@nicoa.org

Experience Works
Clayton Thomas, Regional Director
1481 River Park Drive, Suite 100
Sacramento, CA 95815
800-288-1324
916-641-7700
Fax: 916-646-8118
www.eworkscal.org
Serving Arizona, California, Oregon and Utah

Colorado
Susan Cornejo, Section Manager for Aging and Adult Services
Audrey Krebs, Program Specialist
Colorado Department of Human Services
Aging and Adult Services Division
1575 Sherman Street, 10th Floor
Denver, CO 80203
303-866-2846
Fax: 303-866-2696
Email: audrey.krebs@state.co.us
www.cdhs.state.co.us/ADRS/AAS/index1.html

AARP/SCSEP Program Office
Sandra Wagner, SCSEP Project Director
77 Grant Street, Suite 302
Denver, CO 80203
720-946-2901
Fax: 720-946-2902
Email: scdenver@aol.com
Serving Adams, Arapahoe, Boulder, Denver, Jefferson and Teller Counties

AARP/SCSEP Program Office
Mary Corrow, SCSEP Program Director
2128 East Bijou
Colorado Springs, CO 80909
719-635-3579
Fax: 719-635-3570
Email: mcorrow@aarp.org
Serving El Paso and Freemont Counties

Connecticut
Pamela Giannini, Director
Attention: Dee Ana White
State of Connecticut
Department of Social Services
Elderly Services Division
25 Sigourney St., 10th Floor
Hartford, CT 06106
860-424-5293
Fax: 860-424-5301
Email: dee.white@po.state.ct.us
www.ctelderlyservices.state.ct.us/OWP.htm

Easter Seals, SCSEP
Hugh Caldwell, Director of Program Development
152 Norwich
New London Turnpike
Uncasville, CT 06382
860-848-9264
Fax: 860-848-4462
www.ct.easterseals.com

Experience Works
Sharon Zimmerman, Regional Director

55 Lake Street
Gardner, MA 01440
800-562-2776
Fax: 978-630-1205
Email: Admin_Neng@ExperienceWorks.org
Serving Connecticut, Massachusetts, New Hampshire and New York

Delaware
Allan R. Zaback, Director
Attention: William Abernathy, Management Analyst
Division of Services for Aging & Adults with Physical Disabilities (DSAAPD)
1901 North Dupont Highway
Main Building Annex
New Castle, DE 19720
302-255-9390
800-223-9074
Fax: 302-255-4445
Email: william.abernathy@state.de.us
www.state.de.us/dhss/dsaapd/employment.html

District of Columbia
Gregory P. Irish, Director
Attention: Lillian Huff
Department of Employment Services
609 H Street, NE, Room 543
Washington, DC 20002
202-698-5821
Fax: 202-698-5734
Email: lillian.huff@dc.gov
http://does.ci.washingtondc.us/does/site

Florida
JoAnn Williams, SCSEP State Director
Florida Department of Elder Affairs
4040 Esplanade Way
Tallahassee, FL 32399-7000
850-414-2065
Fax: 850-414-2042
Email: williamsja@elderaffairs.org
http://elderaffairs.state.fl.us/doea/english/senioremp.html

AARP/SCSEP Program Office
Sonia Pasquariello, SCSEP Assistant Project Director
One Stop Career Center
359 Bill France Blvd.
Daytona Beach, FL 32114
386-323-7068
Email: sunnyp413@bellsouth.net
Serving Volusia County

AARP/SCSEP Program Office
Tom Mulligan, SCSEP Project Director
7537 West Oakland Park Blvd.
Lauderhill, FL 33319-4909
954-749-4920/0968
Fax: 954-749-4921
Email: scftlauder@aol.com
Serving Broward County

AARP/SCSEP Program Office
Leon Ruttenberg, SCSEP Project Director
One Stop Career Center
2401 S. 29th Street
Fort Pierce, FL 34981
772-462-6131
Fax: 772-745-2497
Email: lruttenberg@aarp.org
Serving St. Lucie and Martin Counties

AARP/SCSEP Program Office
Howard Basse, SCSEP Project Director
134 East Church Street
Jacksonville, FL 32202
904-353-2301
Fax: 904-353-2302
Email: schbasse@aol.com
Serving Duval County

AARP/SCSEP Program Office
Pam Bettis, SCSEP Project Director
936 East Parker Street
Lakeland, FL 33801-1968
863-683-5627, ext. 121
Fax: 863-682-9691
Email: scseplakeland@aol.com
Serving Polk County

AARP/SCSEP Program Office
Carolyn Brown, SCSEP Project Director
1964 Dairy Road
West Melbourne, FL 32904
321-956-1444
Fax: 321-956-7778
Email: scmelbourn@aol.com
Serving Brevard County

AARP/SCSEP Program Office
Octavio Acosta, SCSEP Project Director
8360 West Flagler Street, #205
Miami, FL 33144
305-476-5925
Fax: 305-476-5269
Email: scdade@aol.com
Serving Miami-Dade County

AARP/SCSEP Program Office
Conrad Ruiz, SCSEP Project Director
8100 Oak Lane, #308

Miami Lakes, FL 33016
305-698-3436
Fax: 305-698-7702
Email: cruiz@aarp.org
Serving Miami-Dade County

AARP/SCSEP Program Office
Barbara Albro, SCSEP Project Director
6014 US 19, Suite 503
New Port Richey, FL 34652
727-848-6649
Fax: 727-849-3169
Email: scbalbro@aol.com
Serving Pasco and Pinellas County

AARP/SCSEP Program Office
Deborah Fadool, SCSEP Project Director
720 W. Colonial Dr., Suite 101
Orlando, FL 32804
407-420-6936
Fax: 407-420-6939
Email: scorlando@bellsouth.net
Serving Orange County

AARP/SCSEP Program Office
Nedra Savoia, SCSEP Project Director
Workforce Alliance Center
1951-D North Military Trail
West Palm Beach, FL 33409
561-616-5200
Fax: 561-616-5229
Email: scpalmbeach@pbcalliance.com
Serving Palm Beach County

AARP/SCSEP Program Office
Bonnie Quigley, SCSEP Project Director
1550A 16th Street
Palm Harbor, FL 34683
727-785-1309
Fax: 727-785-2370
Email: scbquigley@aol.com
Serving Pinellas County

AARP/SCSEP Program Office
Cynthia Reitz, SCSEP Project Director
7800 66th Street North, Suite 202
Pinellas Park, FL 33781
727-547-0534
Fax: 727-544-0340
Email: sckreitz@aol.com
Serving Pinellas County

AARP/SCSEP Program Office
David Leopard, SCSEP Project Director
73 South Palm Avenue, Suite 225
Sarasota, FL 34236
941-366-9039
Fax: 941-906-1287
Email: scsarasota@aol.com
Serving Manatee and Sarasota Counties

AARP/SCSEP Program Office
Carlos Rodriguez, SCSEP Project Office
Workforce One Stop Center
7550 Davee Road Extension
Hollywood, FL 33024
954-967-1010, ext. 141
Email: scsouthbroward@aol.com
Serving South Broward County

AARP/SCSEP Program Office
Marilyn Rams, SCSEP Project Director
South Dade Office Tower
10700 Caribbean Boulevard, #101
Miami, FL 33189
305-378-1944
Fax: 305-256-6044
Email: scsouthdade@aol.com
Serving South Dade County

AARP/SCSEP Program Office
Susan Cooper, SCSEP Project Director
13153 North Dale Mabry Hwy., #125
Tampa, FL 33618
813-962-4600
Fax: 813-962-2039
Email: sctampa@aol.com
Serving Hillsborough County

Experience Works
Madaline Simpson, Regional Director
1079 Atlantic Boulevard, Suite 2
Atlantic Beach, FL 32233-0006
904-241-8188
Fax: 904-241-8523
Email: Madaline_Simpson@ ExperienceWorks.org
Serving Florida and Puerto Rico

Georgia
Maria Greene, Director
Attention: Marti Padgett
Department of Human Resources
Division of Aging Services
2 Peachtree Street
Suite 9-398
Atlanta, GA 30303
404-657-5330
Fax: 404-657-5285
Email: mhpadget@dhr.state.ga.us
www2.state.ga.us/departments/dhr/aging/html

AARP/SCSEP Program Office
Jerome Webb, SCSEP Project Director
Peachtree 25th Building
1718 Peachtree St., NW
Suite 991 South
Atlanta, GA 30309-2495
404-892-4446
Fax: 404-892-4464
Email: scjewbb@aol.com
Serving Cobb, Douglas, Fayette and Fulton Counties

AARP/SCSEP Program Office
Holly Brack, SCSEP Project Director
2754 N. Decatur Road, Suite 115
Decatur, GA 30033
404-292-1330
Fax: 404-292-1331
Email: ScDekalb@aol.com
Serving DeKalb and Fulton Counties

AARP/SCSEP Program Office
Bill Collins, SCSEP Project Director
337 Telfair Street
Augusta, GA 30901-2449
706-722-4700
Fax: 706-722-2270
Email: scbcollins@aol.com
Serving Columbia, McDuffie, Richmond, Wilkes, Burke, Lincoln, Baldwin, Hancock, Warren, Washington and Taliaferro Counties

AARP/SCSEP Program Office
Billy St. Clair, SCSEP Project Director
1214 First Avenue, Suite 204
Columbus, GA 31901
706-322-3083
Fax: 706-327-8818
Email: sccolumbus@aol.com
Serving Muscogee, Dougherty and Harris Counties

AARP/SCSEP Program Office
Conny Stone-Davis, SCSEP Project Director
221 East 34th Street
Savannah, GA 31401
912-234-1681
Fax: 912-234-1682
Email: sccdavis@aol.com
Serving Chatham County

Easter Seals, Middle Georgia
Ken Carswell, SCSEP Operations Manager
602 Kellam Road
Dublin, GA 31040
478-272-0017
www.middlegeorgia.easterseals.com

Experience Works
Billy Wooten, Regional Director
P.O. Box 2768
Richmond Hill, GA 31324
912-756-7708
Fax: 912-756-7739
Email: Candee_Harris@ ExperienceWorks.org
Serving Georgia, North Carolina, South Carolina and Tennessee

Guam

Dorothy G. Gutierrez, Administrator
Department of Labor
Hakubotan Building, 1st Floor
ET Calvo Parkway
Tamuning, Guam 96931
671-647-6526
Fax: 671-647-6527
Email: dotg_52@yahoo.com
www.labor.gov.gu

Hawaii

Elaine Young, Administrator
Attention: Yvonne Chong
Department of Labor & Industrial Relations
Workforce Development Division
830 Punchbowl St., Room 329
Honolulu, HI 96813
808-586-9262
Fax: 808-586-8822
Email: ychong@dlir.state.hi.us
http://dlir.state.hi.us/divisions/wwd/index2.shtml

Idaho

Melinda Adams
Statewide Older Worker Coordinator
Idaho Commission on Aging
3380 Americana Terrace, Suite 120
Boise, ID 83706
208-334-3833
Fax: 208-334-3033
Email: madams@icoa.state.id.us
www.idahoaging.com/programs/ps_olderworker.htm

AARP/ SCSEP Program Office
Tom Booth, SCSEP Program Director
2115 South Vista Avenue, Suite A
Boise, ID 83705
208-429-8077
Fax: 208-429-8084
Email: sctbooth@aol.com

Experience Works
Peggy Auker, Regional Director
1902 Thomes Avenue, Suite 309

Cheyenne, WY 82001
800-584-9161
307-634-7417
Fax: 307-638-4187
Email: Peggy_Auker@ExperienceWorks.org
Serving Idaho, Montana and Wyoming

National Indian Council on Aging
Jolene Herrera, SCSEP Ass.t Director
10501 Montgomery Blvd., NE
Suite 210
Albuquerque, NM 87111
505-292-2001
Fax: 505-292-1922
Email: Jolene@nicoa.org
Serving Idaho, Nevada, New Mexico and Washington

Illinois
Betsy Kramer, Director
Attention: John Geyston, Employment Coordinator
Illinois Department on Aging
421 East Capital Avenue
Springfield, IL 62701-1879
800-252-8966
217-782-5039
Fax: 217-785-1564
Email: john.geystone@aging.state.il.us
www.state.il.us/aging/1athome/employ.htm

AARP/SCSEP Program Office
Karen Lentsch, SCSEP Project Director
1020 South Matthews Street
Peoria, IL 61605
309-674-4172
Fax: 309-674-0510
Email: scpeoria@aol.com
Serving Peoria and Tazewell counties

AARP/SCSEP Program Office
Karen Lentsch, SCSEP Project Director
1104 South Second Street, Suite #1
Springfield, IL 62704
217-544-5776
Fax: 217-544-5740
Email: scspringfieldil@aol.com
Serving Macon and Sagamon counties

AARP/SCSEP Program Office
Robert Clark, SCSEP Project Director
9B West Ferguson Avenue
Wood River, IL 62095
618-254-0195
Fax: 618-254-0197
Email: scwoodrivil@aol.com
Serving Madison and St Clair counties

Easter Seals, Metropolitan Chicago
Ernesto Corvo, SCSEP Program Manager
1116 North Kedzie Ave., Suite 528
Chicago, IL 60651-4178
773-235-0915
Fax: 773-235-1439
www.chicago.easterseals.com

Experience Works
Janice Bramwell, Regional Director
505 S. Ash
Buffalo, MO 65622
800-368-7569
417-345-2797
Fax: 417-345-2998
Email: EWMO@Positech.net
Serving Illinois and Missouri

Indiana
Kristen Schunk, Acting Director
Attention: Virginia Morris
Family and Social Services Administration
Division of Disability, Aging & Rehabilitative Services
Bureau of Aging and In-Home Services
402 West Washington St., Room W454
Indianapolis, IN 46207-7083
317-232-1731
Fax: 317-232-7867
Email: gmorris@fssa.state.in.us
www.in.gov/fssa/elderly/aging/index.html

AARP/SCSEP Program Office
David Granholm, SCSEP Project Director
1100 W. Lloyd Expressway
Evansville, IN 47708
812-422-3910
Email: scevansvillein@aol.com
Serving Perry, Spencer, Wanderburgh and Warrick Counties

AARP/SCSEP Program Office
Ellen Jackson, SCSEP Project Director
603 E. Washington Street
Indianapolis, IN 46204
317-634-6416
Fax: 317-634-6444
Email: scejackson@aol.com
Serving Marion and Hancock Counties

AARP/SCSEP Program Office
Leona Stasko, SCSEP Project Director
6111 Harrison Street
Suite 306
Merrillville, IN 46410
219-980-2723/3275
Fax: 219-908-3297

Email: scmerrillville@netnitco.net
Serving Lake and Porter Counties

AARP/SCSEP Program Office
Floyd Kirby, SCSEP Project Director
PAC Plaza Business Center
Suite B101, 2346 South Lynhurst Drive
Indianapolis, IN 46241
317-244-8116
Fax: 317-244-8117
Email: scwmarion@aol.com
Serving Vigo and Marion Counties

Experience Works
Pam Fox, Regional Director
200 E. Third, Suite 201
Seymour, IN 47274
800-843-0885
Fax: 812-522-7684
Email: Marvin_Jones@ExperienceWorks.org
Serving Indiana and Michigan

Iowa
Mark Haverland, Director
Attention: Phyllis Anderson
State of Iowa, Department of Elder Affairs
200 Tenth St., 3rd floor
Des Moines, IA 50309
515-242-3323
Fax: 515-242-3300
Email: phyllis.anderson@iowa.gov
www.state.ia.us/elderaffairs/living/employment.html

AARP/SCSEP Program Office
Gay-Ellen Fisher, SCSEP Project Director
3311 South West 9th Street
Suite 300
Des Moines, IA 50315-3913
515-287-1555
Fax: 515-287-1787
Email: scdesmoines@aol.com
Serving Adair, Dallas, Madison, Polk and Union Counties

AARP/SCSEP Program Office
Sandy Johnson, Employment Specialist
590 Iowa Street
Des Moines, IA 52001
563-582-0902
Serving Dubuque

AARP/SCSEP Program Office
Gaye-Ellen Fischer, SCSEP Project Director
Iowa Workforce Development Center
310 West Main Street
P.O. Box 717
Ottumwa, IA 52501
641-684-5401 ext. 125
Fax: 641-684-4351 attn. AARP
Email: scottumwaia@aol.com
Serving Jefferson, Keotuk and Mahaska Counties

AARP/SCSEP Program Office
Christi Mason, SCSEP Project Director
223 East 4th Street
Waterloo, IA 50703
319-234-0206
Fax: 319-433-0592
Email: scwaterloo@aol.com
Serving Black Hawk, Clinton, Delaware, Dubuque, Jackson and Linn Counties

Experience Works
Richard Freeman, Regional Director
3720 N. 2nd Avenue
Des Moines, IA 50313
800-782-7519
515-243-2430
Fax: 515-243-1426
Email: Dick_Freeman@ ExperienceWorks.org
Serving Iowa, Nebraska and Wisconsin

Kansas
Toni Wellshear, Older Worker Programs Coordinator
Kansas Department of Commerce
1000 SW Jackson St., Suite 100
Topeka, KS 66612-1354
785-296-1865
Fax: 785-291-3512
Email: twellshear@kansascommerce.com
http://kdoch.state.ks.us/public

National Indian Council on Aging
Ed Littlecook, Middle State Region Manager
205 W. Hartford, Suite 126
Ponca City, OK 74601
580-718-5222
Fax: 580-718-5233
Email: elc@nicoa.org
Serving Kansas, Nebraska and South Dakota

Kentucky
VivEllen Chesser, Coordinator
Kentucky Title V Programs
Division of Aging Services
275 East Main St., 5C-D
Frankfort, KY 40621
502-564-6930
Fax: 502-564-4595
Email: vivellen.chesser@ky.gov
www.chs.ky.gov/Aging/programs/default.htm

AARP/SCSEP Program Office
Hank Ridsdale, SCSEP Program Director
600 West Cedar Street
Louisville, KY 40202-2396
502-584-0309
Fax: 502-584-03-7
Email: schridsdal@aol.com

West Kentucky Easter Seals
Crystal Lukens, SCSEP Project Director
2229 Mildred Street
Paducah, KY 42001
270-444-9687
Fax: 270-444-0655
http://eswky.easterseals.com

Experience Works
Carole Kincaid, Regional Director
1031 Broadway
Beattyville, KY 41311
Toll Free: 877-265-7876
606-464-3675
Fax: 606-464-9514
Email: Carole_Kincaid@ ExperienceWorks.org
Serving Kentucky, Ohio, Virginia and West Virginia

Louisiana
Godfrey P. White, Executive Director
Attention: Rosemary Davis
Office of Elderly Affairs
412 North 4th Street
Baton Rouge, LA 70898-0374
225-342-7030
Fax: 225-342-7133
Email: rkdavis@goea.state.la.us
www.gov.state.la.us/depts/elderly.htm

AARP/SCSEP Program Office
Rodger Scott, SCSEP Project Director
2475 Canal Street, Suite 240
New Orleans, LA 70119
504-822-2671
Fax: 504-822-2672
Email: scrscott1@aol.com
Serving Jefferson, Orleans, Placquemine, St. Bernard, and St. John the Baptist parishes

AARP/SCSEP Program Office
Lynda Harper, SCSEP Project Director
820 Jordan Street, Suite 310
Shreveport, LA 71101-4576
318-221-7611
Fax: 318-221-7612
Email: sclharper@aol.com
Serving Bossier and Caddo counties

Experience Works
Becky Scott, Regional Director
936 Front Street, Slot 4
Cottonport, LA 71327
Toll Free: 888-926-1739
318-876-3954
Fax: 318-876-3927
Email: Becky_Scott@ExperienceWorks.org
Serving Arkansas, Louisiana, Mississippi and Oklahoma

National Indian Council on Aging
Kevin Billiot, Executive Director
Institute for Indian Development
5723 Superior Drive, Suite B-1
Baton Rouge, LA 70816
225-292-2474
Fax: 225-292-2480
Email: itclakb@aol.com

Maine
Christine Gianopoulus, Director
Attention: Jim McGrath
Administrative Services Specialist
Bureau of Elder and Adult Services
Department of Human Services
State of Maine
442 Civic Center Drive
State House Station 11
Augusta, ME 04333
800-262-2232
207-287-9200
Fax: 207-287-9229
Email: james.mcgrath@maine.gov
www.maine.gov/dhs/beas/scsep_main.htm

Maryland
Jean W. Roesser, Secretary
Attention: Karen C. Fields, Project Director
Maryland Department of Aging
301 West Preston St., Suite 1007
Baltimore, MD 21201
800-243-3425
410-767-1100
Fax: 410-333-7943
Email: kcf@ooa.state.md.us
www.mdoa.state.md.us/services/senemp.html

Experience Works
Elizabeth Fry, Regional Director
817 South Market Street
Mechanicsburg, PA 17055-4700
800-854-1578
717-790-0165
Fax: 717-790-0119

Email: PA_Receptionist@ ExperienceWorks.org
Serving Maryland, New Jersey and Pennsylvania

Massachusetts
Ellie Shea Delany, Deputy Assistant Secretary
Attn: Gene Williams, SCSEP Program Manager
Executive Office of Elder Affairs
Commonwealth of Massachusetts
250 Washington
Boston, MA 02108-4619
617-727-7750
Fax: 617-727-9368
Email: gene.willaims@massmail.state.ma.us
www.state.ma.us/elder

Experience Works
Sharon Zimmerman, Regional Director
55 Lake Street
Gardner, MA 01440
800-562-2776
Fax: 978-630-1205
Email: Admin_Neng@ExperienceWorks.org
Serving Connecticut, Massachusetts, New Hampshire and New York

Michigan
Sharon L. Gire, Director
Attention Julia Thomas, Field Rep/SCSEP Program Manager
Michigan Office of Services to the Aging
7109 W. Saginaw Highway, First Floor
Lansing, MI 48917
517-373-0623
Fax: 517-373-4092
Email: thomasju@michigan.gov
www.miseniors.net/MiSeniors+Home

AARP/SCSEP Program Office
1010 North Avenue
Battle Creek, MI 49017
269-968-1200
Fax: 269-968-1167
Serving Barry County

AARP.SCSEP Program Office
Ralph Rausch, SCSEP Project Director
Mercy Center
960 Agard Ave.
Benton Harbor, MI 49022
269-925-3838
Fax: 269-925-8443
Email: scbharbor@aol.com
Serving Berrien, Cass, Kalamazoo and Van Buren counties

AARP/SCSEP Program Office
Sandra Purcell, SCSEP Project Director
2504 Ardmore SE
Grand Rapids, MI 49506-4965
616-942-1181
Fax: 616-942-1192
Email: scspurcell@aol.com
Serving Kent County

AARP/SCSEP Program Office
Joan Hulet, SCSEP Project Director
15100 Northline Road, Room 134
Southgate, MI 48195-2408
724-281-2470
Fax: 734-281-2471
Email: scjhulet@aol.com
Serving Wayne County

Experience Works
Pam Fox, Regional Director
200 E. Third Street, Suite 201
Seymour, IN 47274
800-772-5550
Fax: 812-522-7684
Email: Marvin_Jones@ExperienceWorks.org
Serving Indiana and Michigan

National Indian Council on Aging
Sharon Dukes, Michigan State Manager
19678 Harper Avenue
Grosse Point Woods, MI 48236
313-882-4604
Fax: 313-882-4618
Email: Sharon@nicoa.org

Minnesota
Mr. Charles Robinson, Director
Attention Taryn Galehdari
Minnesota Department of Employment & Economic Development
Workforce Partnership Division
390 N. Robert Street
St. Paul, MN 55101
651-296-3634
Fax: 651-297-4689
Email: taryn.galehdari@state.mn.us
www.deed.state.mn.us/oldwkr

Experience Works
Jean Bennett, Regional Director
120 S. Indiana Avenue
Sioux Falls, SD 57103
800-450-5627
605-332-7991
Fax: 605-332-3602
Email: Jean_Bennett@ExperienceWorks.org
Serving Minnesota, North Dakota and South Dakota

National Indian Council on Aging
Peggy Roy, Project Manager
2380 Wycliff St., Suite 200
St. Paul, MN 55114
651-659-0202
Fax: 651-659-0168
Email: peggy@nicoa.org
Serving Minnesota and Montana

Mississippi
Dr. Marion Dunn Tutor, Director
Attention Henry Griffith
Mississippi Department of Human Services
Division of Aging, Adult Services
750 North State Street
Jackson, MS 39202
800-948-3090
601-359-4929
Fax: 601-359-9664
Email: hgriffith@mdhs.state.ms.us
www.mdhs.state.ms.us/aas_info.html

Experience Works
Becky Scott, Regional Director
936 Front Street, Slot 4
Cottonport, LA 71327
Toll Free: 888-926-1739
318-876-3954
Fax: 318-876-3927
Email: Becky_Scott@ExperienceWorks.org
Serving Arkansas, Louisiana, Mississippi and Oklahoma

Missouri
Virginia Gearhart
Dept. of Health & Senior Services
Division of Senior Services & Regulation
3418 Knipp Drive
Jefferson City, MO 65102
800-235-5503
573-526-3128
Fax: 573-751-8493
Email: gearhg@dhss.mo.gov
www.dhss.mo.gov/SeniorGuide/toc/fa/csep.html

AARP/SCSEP Program Office
Rebecca Olson, SCSEP Project Director
214 W. 39th St.
Kansas City, MO 64106
816-471-1884
Fax: 816-931-1880
Email: scrolson@aol.com
Serving Clay and Jackson Counties

AARP/SCSEP Program Office
1302 Faraon Street
St. Joseph, MO 64501
816-232-0056
Fax: 816-232-0076
Serving St. Joseph

AARP/SCSEP Program Office
Rex Miller, SCSEP Project Director
300 South Grand Boulevard
Union Plaza Suite 220A
St. Louis, MO 63103
314-533-5566
Fax: 314-533-7878
Email: scjford@aol.com
Serving St. Louis County and the city of St. Louis

AARP.SCSEP Program Office
Lisa Bishop, SCSEP Project Director
11681 West Florissant
Seven Hills Plaza
St. Louis, MO 63033
314-830-3600
Fax: 314-830-3674
Email: stlcountyaarp@sbcglobal.net
Serving St. Louis County

AARP/SCSEP Program Office
Sherri Wright, SCSEP Project Director
1704 East Sunshine
Springfield, MO 65804
417-869-0509
Fax: 417-869-0500
Email: scswright@aol.com
Serving Greene County

Experience Works
Janice Bramwell, Regional Director
505 S. Ash
Buffalo, MO 65622
800-368-7569
417-345-2797
Fax: 417-345-2998
Email: EWMO@Positech.net
Serving Illinois and Missouri

Montana
Charlie Rehbein, Bureau Chief
Aging Services Bureau, Senior & Long Term Care Division
Montana Department of Public Health & Human Services
111 North Sanders Street
Helena, MT 59601-4520
406-444-4077
Fax: 406-444-7743
Email: crehbein@state.mt.us
www.dphhs.mt.us/sltc

Experience Works
Peggy Auker, Regional Director
1902 Thomes Avenue, Suite 309
Cheyenne, WY 82001
800-584-9161
307-634-7417
Fax: 307-638-4187
Email: Peggy_Auker@ExperienceWorks.org
Serving Idaho, Montana and Wyoming

National Indian Council on Aging
Peggy Roy, Project Manager
2380 Wycliff St., Suite 200
St. Paul, MN 55114
651-659-0202
Fax: 651-659-0168
Email: peggy@nicoa.org
Serving Minnesota and Montana

Nebraska
Joann Weis, Administrator
Attention: Gary Richards
Division of Aging and Disability Services
Department of Health and Human Services
State Office Building, 5th Floor
301 Centennial Mall South
Lincoln, NE 68508-2529
800-942-7830
402-471-4555
Fax: 402-471-4619
Email: gary.richards@hhss.state.ne.us

AARP/SCSEP Program Office
Kammie Reile-Renter, SCSEP Program Director
825 M Street, Suite 209
Lincoln, NE 68508-2253
402-475-3283
Fax: 402-476-5565
Email: sclincolnne@aol.com
Serving Colfax, Cummings, Dodge, Lancaster, Madison, Platte, Stanton and Wayne Counties.

Experience Works
Richard Freeman, Regional Director
3720 N. 2nd Avenue
Des Moines, IA 50313
800-782-7519
515-243-2430
Fax: 515-243-1426
Email: Dick_Freeman@ ExperienceWorks.org
Serving Iowa, Nebraska and Wisconsin

National Indian Council on Aging
Ed Littlecook, Middle State Region Manager
205 W. Hartford, Suite 126
Ponca City, OK 74601
580-718-5222
Fax: 580-718-5233
Email: elc@nicoa.org
Serving Kansas, Nebraska and South Dakota

Nevada
Carol Sala, Administrator
Attention: Shirley Chantrill, Resource Development Specialist
State of Nevada
Division for Aging Services
Department of Human Resources
850 Elm Street
Elko, NV 89801
775-738-1966
Fax: 775-753-8543
Email: schantrill@aging.state.nv.us
http://aging.state.nv.us/index.htm

AARP/SCSEP Program Office
Jacqueline Phillips, SCSEP Program Director
3230 E. Charleston Blvd., Suite 117
Las Vegas, NV 89101
702-648-3356/3357
Fax: 702-648-3928
Email: scvegas@lvcoxmail.com
Serving Clark, Nye and Lincoln Counties

AARP/SCSEP Program Office
Tom Booth, SCSEP Program Director
244 Claremont St.
Reno, NV 89502
775-323-2243
Fax: 775-323-7368
Email: screnolv@aol.com
Serving Humboldt, Pershing, Lyon, Washoe, Carson, Douglas, and Churchill Counties

National Indian Council on Aging
Jolene Herrera, SCSEP Assistant Director
10501 Montgomery Blvd., NE
Suite 210
Albuquerque, NM 87111
505-292-2001
Fax: 505-292-1922
Email: Jolene@nicoa.org
Serving Idaho, Nevada, New Mexico and Washington

New Hampshire
Ellery Hathorn, Plan Manager
New Hampshire Department of Labor
State Office Park South
Spaulding Building
95 Pleasant Street
Concord, NH 03301

603-271-6172
Fax: 603-271-2668
Email: ehathorn@labor.state.nh.us
http://labor.state.nh.us/default.asp

AARP/SCSEP Program Office
Paula Lehmann, SCSEP Program Director
997 Elm St.
Manchester, NH 03101
800-652-8808
603-623-5627
Fax: 603-623-5277
Email: scnhampshire@aol.com
Serving Belknap, Carroll, Coos, Grafton, Hillsborough and Merrimack Counties

Experience Works
Sharon Zimmerman, Regional Director
55 Lake Street
Gardner, MA 01440
800-562-2776
Fax: 978-630-1205
Email: Admin_Neng@ExperienceWorks.org
Serving Connecticut, Massachusetts, New Hampshire and New York

New Jersey
Tamara Thomas, Deputy Assistant Commissioner
Attention: Deborah Rago, Assistant Director of Programs
Division of One-Stop Programs & Services
New Jersey Department of Labor & Workforce Development
1 John Fitch Plaza, 2nd Floor
Trenton, NJ 08625
Toll free: 877-222-3737
609-984-2477
Fax: 609-396-1685
Email: deborah.rago@dol.state.nj.us
www.state.nj.us/health/senior/federalbenefits/employment.shtml#scsep

Easter Seals New Jersey
Tom Rauen, Director of SCSEP
1 Kimberly Road
East Brunswick, NJ 08816
732-257-6662
Fax: 732-257-3204
www.nj.easterseals.com

Experience Works
Elizabeth Fry, Regional Director
817 South Market Street
Mechanicsburg, PA 17055-4700
800-854-1578
717-790-0165
Fax: 717-790-0119
Email: PA_Receptionist@ ExperienceWorks.org
Serving Maryland, New Jersey and Pennsylvania

New Mexico
Michelle Lujan Grisham, Secretary
Attention: Doug Calderwood
New Mexico Aging & Long-Term Services Department
2550 Cerrillos Road
Santa Fe, NM 87505
800-432-2080
505-476-4799
Fax: 505-476-0346
Email: doug.calderwood@state.nm.us
www.nmaging.state.nm.us/njob.html

AARP/SCSEP Program Office
Art Lopez, SCSEP Program Director
1500 Walter, SE
Albuquerque, NM 87102
505-248-0052
Fax: 505-248-1494
Email: scalopez@aol.com
Serving Bernalillo, Sandoval, Santa Fe and Valencia Counties

National Indian Council on Aging
Jolene Herrera, SCSEP Assistant Director
10501 Montgomery Blvd., NE
Suite 210
Albuquerque, NM 87111
505-292-2001
Fax: 505-292-1922
Email: Jolene@nicoa.org
Serving Idaho, Nevada, New Mexico and Washington

New York
Neal E. Lane, Acting Director
Attention: Polly Windels
State of New York
Office for the Aging, Title V Unit
Empire State Plaza, Agency Building #2
Albany, NY 12223
Toll-Free 800-342-9871 (in state only)
518-474-8736
Fax: 518-486-2225
Email: polly.windels@ofa.state.ny.us
http://aging.state.ny.us/findhelp/employment/scsep.htm

AARP/SCSEP Program Office
Rodolfo Colon, SCSEP Project Director
384 East 149th Street, Suite 604
Bronx, NY 10455
718-585-2500
Fax: 718-292-5613
Email: scbronx@aol.com
Serving Bronx County

AARP/SCSEP Program Office
Joseph Dirac, SCSEP Project Director
235 Main Street, 2nd Floor
Poughkeepsie, NY 12601
866-296-7996-Tollfree
845-485-8030
Fax: 845-485-8031
Email: scjdirac@aol.com
Serving Dutchess, Orange and New York (Manhattan) Counties

Easter Seals, New York
Jim Berry, SCSEP Project Director
Director of Vocational Services
787 Seventh Avenue, 9th Floor
New York, NY 10019
212-786-6080
Fax: 212-786-6085
www.ny.easterseals.com

Experience Works
Sharon Zimmerman, Regional Director
55 Lake Street
Gardner, MA 01440
800-562-2776
Fax: 978-630-1205
Email: Admin_Neng@ExperienceWorks.org
Serving Connecticut, Massachusetts, New Hampshire and New York

North Carolina
Debbie Brantley, Chief
Attention: Marty Martinez, Project Coordinator
Elder Rights Section/Division of Aging
North Carolina Department of Human Resources
693 Palmer Drive, Taylor Building
Raleigh, NC 27699-2101
919-733-8395 ext. 225
Fax: 919-715-0868
Email: marty.martinez@ncmail.net
www.dhhs.state.nc.us/aging/scsep.htm

Experience Works
Billy Wooten, Regional Director
P.O. Box 2768
Richmond Hill, GA 31324
912-756-7708
Fax: 912-756-7739
Email: Candee_Harris@ ExperienceWorks.org
Serving Georgia, North Carolina, South Carolina and Tennessee

North Dakota
Attention: Julie McKenzie
Job Service North Dakota
1000 East Divide Avenue
Bismarck, ND 58501
701-328-2997
Fax: 701-328-4894
Email: jmckenzi@state.nd.us
www.jobsnd.com/seekers/train_senior.html

Experience Works
Jean Bennett, Regional Director
120 S. Indiana Avenue
Sioux Falls, SD 57103
800-450-5627
605-332-7991
Fax: 605-332-3602
Email: Jean_Bennett@ExperienceWorks.org
Serving Minnesota, North Dakota and South Dakota

Northern Mariana Islands
Joseph M. Palacios, Director
Attention: Rhonda Fleming-Nogis, Title V Unit
Department of Community & Cultural Affairs
Office on Aging
Capitol Hill, Building 1341
Saipan, MP 96950
670-233-1320
Fax: 670-233-1327
Email: scsepspn@vzpacifica.net
www.dcca.gov.mp/index.html

Ohio
Joan W. Lawrence, Director
Attention: Kathleen Dorcy
Ohio Department on Aging
50 West Broad Street, 9th Floor
Columbus, OH 43215-3363
614-995-0883
Fax: 614-644-1471
Email: kdorcy@age.state.oh.us
www.goldenbuckeye.com/scsepprov.html

AARP/SCSEP Program Office
John Phillips, SCSEP Project Director
700 Walnut Street, Suite 210
Cincinnati, OH 45202
513-721-0717
Fax: 513-721-6701
Email: scjohnphil@aol.com
Serving Hamilton County

AARP/SCSEP Program Office
Marianne Wills, SCSEP Project Director
4614 Prospect Ave.
Suite 211
Cleveland, OH 44103
216-881-1155
Fax: 216-881-4311

Email: scmills@aol.com
Serving Cuyahoga County

AARP/SCSEP Program Office
Robert Cole, SCSEP Project Director
1393 E. Broad Street, Suite 105
Columbus, OH 43205
614-258-7295
Fax: 614-258-7723
Email: sccolumbusoh@sbcglobal.net
Serving Franklin and Scioto Counties

AARP/SCSEP Program Office
Blanche Babela, SCSEP Project Director
164 North 4th Street
Steubenville, OH 43952
740-282-0928
Fax: 740-282-5809
Email: scbbabela@aol.com
Serving Belmont, Harrison and Jefferson Counties

Experience Works
Carole Kincaid, Regional Director
1031 Broadway
Beattyville, KY 41311
Toll Free: 877-265-7876
606-464-3675
Fax: 606-464-9514
Email: Carole_Kincaid@ ExperienceWorks.org
Serving Kentucky, Ohio, Virginia and West Virginia

Oklahoma
Jon Brock, Executive Director
Attention: C.W. Bennett
Employment Security Division
Will Rogers Building
2401 North Lincoln, Room 408
Oklahoma City, OK 73152
405-557-5328
Fax: 405-557-1478
Email: cw.bennet@oesc.state.ok.us
www.oesc.state.ok.us

AARP/SCSEP Program Office
Michele Dziadik-Willingham, Assistant SCSEP Project Director
6539 E. 31st Street, Suite 6
Tulsa, OK 74145
918-621-4480
Fax: 918-622-2690
Email: sctulsaok@aol.com
Serving Creek and Tulsa Counties

AARP/SCSEP Program Office
Rosemary Isom, SCSEP Project Director
2200 North Classen Blvd., Suite 920
Oklahoma City, OK 73106
405-525-8144
Fax: 405-525-8152
Email: scrisom@aol.com
Serving Oklahoma County

Experience Works
Becky Scott, Regional Director
936 Front Street, Slot 4
Cottonport, LA 71327
Toll Free: 888-926-1739
318-876-3954
Fax: 318-876-3927
Email: Becky_Scott@ExperienceWorks.org
Serving Arkansas, Louisiana, Mississippi and Oklahoma

National Indian Council on Aging
Maudean Harden, Oklahoma State Director
5350 S. Western Avenue, Suite 316
Oklahoma City, OK 73109
405-632-7786
Fax: 405-632-9751
Email: maudean@nicoa.org

Oregon
James Toews, Assistant Director
Attention: Amy Evenson, SCSEP Program Coordinator
Seniors and People with Disabilities
Office of Home & Community Services
500 Summer Street, NE, E-10
Salem, OR 97301-1076
503-945-5734
Fax: 503-373-7902
Email: amy.r.evenson@state.or.us
www.dhs.state.or.us/seniors/employment

AARP/SCSEP Program Office
Ted Costa, SCSEP Project Director
5621 E. Burnside, 2nd Floor
Portland, OR 97215
503-231-8078
Fax: 503-231-0480
Email: scportlandor@aol.com
Serving Multnomah and Clackamas Counties

AARP/SCSEP Program Office
Daisy Rush, SCSEP Project Director
1313 Mill St. SE
Salem, OR 97301
503-363-1572
Fax: 503-362-4734
Email: scsalem@aol.com

Experience Works
Clayton Thomas, Regional Director

1481 River Park Drive, Suite 100
Sacramento, CA 95815
800-288-1324
916-641-7700
Fax: 916-646-8118
www.eworkscal.org
Serving Arizona, California, Oregon and Utah

Pennsylvania
Nora Dowd Eisenhower, Secretary
Attention: Rocco Claroni, Aging Services Specialist
Pennsylvania Department of Aging
555 Walnut Street, 5th Floor
Harrisburg, PA 17101-1919
717-783-6207
Fax: 717-783-6842
Email: rclaroni@state.pa.us
www.aging.state.pa.us

AARP/SCSEP Program Office
Susan Shanahan, SCSEP Project Director
10 East Church Street, #501
Bethlehem, PA 18018
610-865-3002
Fax: 610-865-1017
Email: scsshanaha@aol.com
Serving Lehigh and North Hampton Counties

AARP/SCSEP Program Office
Cathy Kotjarapoglus, SCSEP Project Director
2941 North Front Street, Suite 300
Harrisburg, PA 17110
717-234-5961
Fax: 717-234-3518
Email: scckotjara@aol.com
Serving Dauphin, Cumberland and Lebanon Counties

AARP/SCSEP Program Office
Rebecca Cottle, SCSEP Project Director
425 Sixth Avenue, #1840
Pittsburgh, PA 15219
412-434-6533
Fax: 412-434-6686
Email: scpittsburgh@aol.com
Serving Allegheny County

Experience Works
Elizabeth Fry, Regional Director
817 South Market Street
Mechanicsburg, PA 17055-4700
800-854-1578
717-790-0165
Fax: 717-790-0119
Email: PA_Receptionist@ ExperienceWorks.org
Serving Maryland, New Jersey and Pennsylvania

Puerto Rico
Carmen R. Nazario, Administrator
Attention: Lizbeth Piar
Puerto Rico Department of Family
Administration for Families and Children
Program ROW
Plaza Sevilla Building #58
Hato Rey, PR 00917
787-788-1279
Fax: 787-725-3019
Email: lpiar_adfan@yahoo.com

AARP/SCSEP Program Office
Julia Robles, SCSEP Project Director
Antiguo Hospital de Distrito
Primer Piso, Carretera #129 Km.8
Arecibo a Lares
Arecibo, PR 00612
787-878-1775
Fax: 787-878-1820
Email: scarecibopr@aol.com
Serving Arecibo, Barceloneta, Camry, Hatillo, Manati, Morovis, and Vega Baja Counties

AARP/SCSEP Program Office
Zelma Mendez, SCSEP Project Director
5 Flor Gerena Street North
Humacao, PR 00791
787-852-6972
Fax: 787-852-6865
Email: schumacaopr@aol.com
Serving Caguas, Humacao, Juncos, Maunabo, Naguabo, Patillas and Yabucoa Counties

AARP/SCSEP Program Office
Luz Maldonado, SCSEP Project Director
Santa Maria Shopping Center
471-Calle Ferrocarril, Suite 215
Ponce, PR 00717-1101
787-844-6925
Fax: 787-844-5825
Email: scponcepr@aol.com
Serving Guayama, Lajas, Mayaguez and Ponce Counties

AARP/SCSEP Program Office
Olga Viruet, SCSEP Project Director
Museo de Arte Contemp #306
Ponce de Leon ESQ. R. Todd/Pda 18
San Juan, PR 00907-4011
787-723-4404/4405
Fax: 787-723-4707
Email: scsanjuanpr@aol.com
Serving Carolina, San Juan, Loiza, Vega Alta and Gurabo Counties

Experience Works
Madaline Simpson, Regional Director
1079 Atlantic Boulevard, Suite 2
Atlantic Beach, FL 32233-0006
904-241-8188
Fax: 904-241-8523
Email: Madaline_Simpson@ ExperienceWorks.org
Serving Florida and Puerto Rico

Rhode Island
Corinne Calise Russo, Director
Attention: Marie Strauss, Assistant Administrator
Rhode Island Dept. of Elderly Affairs
John O. Pastore Center
Benjamin Rush Building #55
35 Howard Avenue
Cranston, RI 02920
401-462-0535
Fax: 401-462-0586
Email: mstrauss@dea.state.ri.us

South Carolina
Terri Whirret, Director
Attention: Jennifer Hall, Title V Program Coordinator
Aging Network Services
Office on Aging
Office of the Lieutenant Governor
1801 Main Street
Columbia, SC 29202-8206
803-898-2833
Fax: 803-255-8202
Email: halljen@dhhs.state.sc.us
www.dhhs.sc.us

AARP/SCSEP Program Office
Beaufort County One Stop
914 Boundary Street
Beaufort, SC 29902
843-524-3351
Serving Beaufort County

AARP/SCSEP Program Office
Ron Carson, SCSEP Project Director
301 University Ridge, #5550
Greenville, SC 29601
864-467-3325
Fax: 864-467-3328
Email: scgreenvil@aol.com
Serving Anderson, Cherokee, Greenville, Laurens, Oconee, Pickens and Spartanburg Counties

AARP/SCSEP Program Office
Earnest Chisholm, SCSEP Project Director
103 Franklin Dr.
Florence, SC 29501
843-665-1344
Fax: 843-622-1734
Email: sckallen@aol.com
Serving Chesterfield, Arlington, Dillon, Florence, Georgetown, Horry, Lee, Marion, Marlboro, Sumter and Williamsburg Counties

AARP/SCSEP Program Office
Jasper County One Stop
110 Main Street
Ridgeland, SC 29936
843-726-3750
Serving Jasper County

AARP/SCSEP Program Office
Earnest Chisholm, SCSEP Project Director
204 Johnston Street
Rock Hill, SC 29730
803-817-6537
Fax: 803-817-6549
Email: scschisholm@aol.com
Serving Chester, Lancaster, Union and York Counties

Experience Works
Billy Wooten, Regional Director
P.O. Box 2768
Richmond Hill, GA 31324
912-756-7708
Fax: 912-756-7739
Email: Candee_Harris@ ExperienceWorks.org
Serving Georgia, North Carolina, South Carolina and Tennessee

South Dakota
Lloyd Schipper, Deputy Secretary
Attention: Todd Kolden
South Dakota Department of Labor
420 South Roosevelt Street
Aberdeen, SD 57401-5131
605-626-7652 ext. 4418
Fax: 605-626-2322
Email: todd.kolden@state.sd.us
www.state.sd.us/dol

Experience Works
Jean Bennett, Regional Director
120 S. Indiana Avenue
Sioux Falls, SD 57103
800-450-5627
605-332-7991
Fax: 605-332-3602
Email: Jean_Bennett@ExperienceWorks.org
Serving Minnesota, North Dakota and South Dakota

National Indian Council on Aging
Ed Littlecook, Middle State Region Manager
205 W. Hartford, Suite 126
Ponca City, OK 74601
580-718-5222
Fax: 580-718-5233
Email: elc@nicoa.org
Serving Kansas, Nebraska and South Dakota

Tennessee
James G. Neely, Commissioner
Attention: Paulette Osborne, SCSEP
Employment and Workforce Development Division
Tennessee Department of Labor & Workforce Development
Davy Crockett Tower, 12th Floor
500 Robertson Pkwy.
Nashville, TN 37245
615-741-8777
Fax: 615-741-3003
Email: paulette.osborne@state.tn.us
www.state.tn.us/labor-wfd/seniorcomm.html

Experience Works
Billy Wooten, Regional Director
P.O. Box 2768
Richmond Hill, GA 31324
912-756-7708
Fax: 912-756-7739
Email: Candee_Harris@ ExperienceWorks.org
Serving Georgia, North Carolina, South Carolina and Tennessee

Texas
Larry E. Temple, Executive Director
Attention: Lucretia Dennis Small
Texas Workforce Commission
101 East 15th Street
Austin, TX 78778-0001
512-936-3150
Fax: 512-475-2321
Email: lucretia.dennis-small@twc.state
www.twc.state.tx.us/svcs/scsep/svsep.html

AARP/SCSEP Program Office
Stella Carrier, SCSEP Project Director
304 Pearl, Suite 212
Beaumont, TX 77701
409-839-8045 ext. 283
Fax: 409-833-8142
Email: scbeaumonttx@aol.com
Serving Jefferson, Harden and Orange Counties

AARP/SCSEP Program Office
Eva Trevino Garcia, SCSEP Project Director
1110 South Alamo
San Antonio, TX 78212
210-223-7588
Fax: 210-223-7593
Email: scbexar@aol.com
Serving Bexar and San Antonio Counties

AARP/SCSEP Program Office
Martha Balboa-Crixell, SCSEP Project Director
164 Oak Street, Office A
Brownsville, TX 785-20
956-544-5300
Fax: 956-544-5356
Email: scmcrixell@aol.com
Serving Cameron and Willacy County

AARP/SCSEP Program Office
Juan Vela, SCSEP Project Director
720 Buffalo Street
Corpus, Krista, TX 78401
361-879-0076/0454
Fax: 361-879-0452
Email: sccorpus@aol.com
Serving Nueces and Valverde Counties

AARP/SCSEP Program Office
Virginia Huey-You, SCSEP Project Director
1625 W. Mockingbird, #108
Dallas, TX 75235
214-741-0200
Fax: 214-741-0500
Email: sctxdallas@aol.com
Serving the city of Dallas

AARP/SCSEP Program Office
Sylvester Barron, SCSEP Project Director
8144 Walnut Hill Lane, #380
Dallas, TX 75231
214-346-9221
Fax: 214-346-9388
Email: scdallas2@aol.com
Serving Dallas County

AARP/SCSEP Program Office
Adriana Garza, SCSEP Project Director
El Tule Community Building
703 South 19th Avenue
Edinburg, TX 78539
956-316-2244
Fax: 956-316-2549
Email: scagarza@aol.com
Serving Hidalgo County

AARP/SCSEP Program Office
Richard Sida, SCSEP Project Director
1221 East San Antonio Avenue

El Paso, TX 79901
915-542-1705/4995
Fax: 915-544-2303
Email: scelpasotx@aol.com
Serving El Paso County

AARP/SCSEP Program Office
Ellen Swift, SCSEP Project Director
1000 Circle Drive, Suite 100
Fort Worth, TX 76119
817-536-3600
Fax: 817-536-3601
Email: sceswift@aol.com
Serving Tarrant County

AARP/SCSEP Program Office
Sherri Chapman, SCSEP Project Director
7015 Gulf Freeway, Suite 140
Houston, TX 77087
713-643-3200
Fax: 713-643-3344
Email: scharriscounty@aol.com
Serving Harris County

AARP/SCSEP Program Office
Ocie Green, SCSEP Project Director
170 Heights Boulevard
Houston, TX 77007
713-868-2950
Fax: 713-868-2977
Email: scheights@aol.com
Serving the city of Houston

AARP/SCSEP Program Office
Veronica Kenney, SCSEP Project Director
1405 North Main, #222
San Antonio, TX 78212
210-222-1294
Fax: 210-222-9326
Email: scsacantonio@aol.com
Serving Bexar County and the city of San Antonio

Experience Works
Anthony Billings, Regional Director
801 Washington, Avenue, Suite 100
Waco, TX 76701
254-776-4081
Fax: 254-776-8690
Email: Anthony_Billings@ ExperienceWorks.org

Utah
Robin Arnold-Williams
Attention: Sally Brown
Division of Aging and Adult Services
120 North 200 West
Salt Lake City, UT 84103-1550
801-538-3910
Fax: 801-538-4395
Email: sabrown@utah.gov
www.hsdaas.state.ut.us/ss_employment.htm

Easter Seals Utah
Larry Witherow, SCSEP Program Director
638 East Wilmington Avenue
Salt Lake City, UT 84106
801-486-3778
Fax: 801-486-3123
www.ut.easterseals.com

Experience Works
Clayton Thomas, Regional Director
1481 River Park Drive, Suite 100
Sacramento, CA 95815
800-288-1324
916-641-7700
Fax: 916-646-8118
www.eworkscal.org
Serving Arizona, California, Oregon and Utah

Vermont
Patrick Flood, Commissioner
Attention: Marie Bean
Dept. of Aging & Independent Living
103 South Main Street
Waterbury, VT 05671-2301
802-241-4425
Fax: 802-241-2325
Email: marieb@dad.state.vt.us
www.dad.state.vt.us/dail/guidetoservices/socialfunctions/informationcounselingplacement.htm

Virgin Islands
Cecil R. Benjamin, Commissioner
Attention: Eleuteria Roberts
Virgin Islands Department of Labor
21-31 Hospital Street
Christiansted, VI 00820-4620
340-773-1994
Fax: 340-773-0094
Email: labor@usvi.org
www.usvi.org/labor/index.html

Virginia
Jay W. DeBoer, Commissioner
Attention: Patricia Cummins
Virginia Department for the Aging
1610 Forest Avenue, Suite 100
Richmond, VA 23229
804-662-7256
Fax: 804-662-9354

Email: pat.cummins@vda.virginia.gov
www.aging.state.va.us/index.htm

AARP/SCSEP Program Office
Barbara Zack Murphy, SCSEP Project Director
201 Granby Street #424
Norfolk, VA 23510
757-625-7001
Fax: 757-625-6750
Email: scbmurphy@aol.com
Serving Norfolk, Portsmouth, Virginia Beach, Chesapeake, Hampton, Newport News and Suffolk Counties

AARP/SCSEP Program Office
Carolyn Crighton, SCSEP Project Director
1806 Chantilly Street, #100
Richmond, VA 23230
804-355-3600
Fax: 804-355-3842
Email: scccrichto@aol.com
Serving the City of Richmond and Petersburg, Chesterfield and Henrico Counties

Experience Works
Carole Kincaid, Regional Director
1031 Broadway
Beattyville, KY 41311
Toll Free: 877-265-7876
606-464-3675
Fax: 606-464-9514
Email: Carole_Kincaid@ ExperienceWorks.org
Serving Kentucky, Ohio, Virginia and West Virginia

Washington
Kathy Leitch, Assistant Secretary
Attention: Hank Hibbard
Department of Social & Health Services
Aging & Disability Services Administration
640 Woodland Square Loop SE
Lacey, WA 98504-5600
360-725-2557
Fax: 360-438-8633
Email: hibbaea@dshs.wa.gov
www.aasa.dshs.wa.gov

AARP/SCSEP Program Office
Cara Lee Landes, SCSEP Project Director
655 South Orcas Street
Suite 116
Seattle WA 98108
206-624-6698
Fax: 206-624-6699
Email: scsep047@aol.com
Serving King, Kitsap and Snohomish Counties

AARP/SCSEP Program Office
Steve Reiter, SCSEP Project Director
1801 West Broadway, Suite 110
Spokane, WA 99201-1874
509-325-7712/7483
Fax: 509-325-7729
Email: scsreiter@aol.com
Serving Adams, Chelan, Douglas, Grant, Kittitas, Spokane, Whitman, and Yakima Counties

National Indian Council on Aging
Jolene Herrera, SCSEP Assistant Director
10501 Montgomery Blvd., NE, Suite 210
Albuquerque, NM 87111
505-292-2001
Fax: 505-292-1922
Email: Jolene@nicoa.org
Serving Idaho, Nevada, New Mexico and Washington

West Virginia
William E. Lytton, Deputy Commissioner
Attention: Chuck Conroy Jr., Director
West Virginia Bureau of Senior Services
1900 Kanawha Blvd., East,
Holly Grove, Building 18
Charleston, WV 25305-1060
304-558-3317
Fax: 304-558-0004
Email: cconroy@boss.state.wv.us
www.state.wv.us/seniorservices

AARP/SCSEP Program Office
Blanche Babela, SCSEP Project Director
Work4WV Career Center
887 National Road, Suite 4
Wheeling, WV 26003
Toll Free: 866-956-2669
304-232-6280
Fax: 304-223-8007
Email: scbbabela@aol.com
Serving Brooke, Hancock, Marshall, Ohio and Wetzel Counties

Experience Works
Carole Kincaid, Regional Director
1031 Broadway
Beattyville, KY 41311
Toll Free: 877-265-7876
606-464-3675
Fax: 606-464-9514
Email: Carole_Kincaid@ ExperienceWorks.org
Serving Kentucky, Ohio, Virginia and West Virginia

Wisconsin
Donna McDowell, Director

Attention: Monica Snittler, Senior Employment Program Coordinator
Department of Health & Family Services
Aging and Long Term Care Resources
1 West Wilson Street, Room 450
Madison, WI 53702-0007
608-267-9097
Fax: 608-267-3203
Email: snittma@dhfs.state.wi.us
http://dhfs.wisconsin.gov/aging/Genage/SENCSEP.HTM

Experience Works
Richard Freeman, Regional Director
3720 N. 2nd Avenue
Des Moines, IA 50313
800-782-7519
515-243-2430
Fax: 515-243-1426
Email: Dick_Freeman@ ExperienceWorks.org
Serving Iowa, Nebraska and Wisconsin

National Indian Council on Aging
Jan Belleau, Project Manager
1823 S. Webster Avenue
Green Bay, WI 54301
920-433-0290
Fax: 920-433-0291
Email: jan@nicoa.org

Wyoming
Glenna Campagnaro, Administrator
Attention: Edna Vajda, Program Manager
Business Training & Outreach Division
Wyoming Department of Workforce Services
Herschler Building 2-E, Room 2012
122 West 25th Street
Cheyenne, WY 82002
307-777-8717
Fax: 307-777-5857
Email: evajda@state.wy.us
www.wyomingworkforce.org/programs/scsep/index.asp

Experience Works
Peggy Auker, Regional Director
1902 Thomes Avenue, Suite 309
Cheyenne, WY 82001
800-584-9161
307-634-7417
Fax: 307-638-4187
Email: Peggy_Auker@ExperienceWorks.org
Serving Idaho, Montana and Wyoming

Job Training for Veterans

Veterans have served our country bravely for years. There are 25 million veterans currently alive and of those nearly 75% of them served during a war or official period of hostility. About a quarter of the nation's population – approximately 70 million people – are eligible for Veteran Benefits and Services because they are veterans, family members or survivors of veterans. The Veterans' Affairs office goal is to provide patient care, veterans' benefits and customer satisfaction. They are committed to help veterans get the services they have earned and deserve. If you think you might be eligible for one or more of the Veterans' Benefits take the time to apply. It may just bring you free money and free services.

$2,000 for Taking A Test

You can receive reimbursement of up to $2,000 for some licensing and certification tests. The tests must be approved for the G.I. Bill. The Veterans' Administration will only pay for the costs of the tests and not for other fees connected with obtaining a license or certification. For additional information, contact your regional office or vet center listed on page 330, call 1-800-827-1000, or check their web site at www.gibill.va.gov.

Veterans' Vocational Rehabilitation and Employment Services

The Veterans' Administration's Vocational Rehabilitation and Employment (VR&E) is a national employment resource to provide information about employment and independent living to disabled veterans, vocational counseling to service-members and veterans recently discharged and vocational counseling or special rehabilitation services to dependents of veterans who meet certain requirements.

This program's primary function is to help veterans who have service-connected disabilities to become employed and to maintain suitable employment. Services that you may be eligible for through the VR&E program include:

- Vocational counseling and planning
- Assistance finding and keeping a job, including special employer incentives
- Training such as on-the-job training, non-paid work experiences
- Educational training such as 2- or 4- year degree programs
- Supportive rehabilitation services and additional counseling

Call 800-827-1000, or check their web site at www.va.gov.

Everything You Need to Find and Get a Job as a Veteran

The Veterans' Vocational Rehabilitation and Employment Program offers a variety of employment services as a means to obtain suitable employment for veterans.

- assistance in finding employment
- job seeking skills training,
- on-the-job training and apprenticeships
- job development,
- vocational training,
- 1-year certification programs,
- 2-year diploma programs,
- 2 and 4 year post secondary training programs.

For additional information, contact your regional office or vet center listed on page 330, call 1-800-827-1000, check their web site at www.vba.va.gov/bln/vre/emp_resources.htm. You can also apply online at http://vabenefits.vba.va.gov/vonapp/main.asp.

Get Free Individualized Help

The Independent Living Program (ILP) is designed to be tailored for each individual's needs. A veteran whose service-oriented disability makes employment impossible can receive help. An Independent Living Program will be designed with input from the veteran, medical professionals, family members and other consultants to provide the assistance needed by the veteran. Subsistence allowances are paid each month of enrollment in the ILP. You can receive money for yourself and your dependents. If you believe your service-connected disabilities and overall condition are so serious that employment goals are impossible, you may qualify for the Independent Living Program. For additional information, contact your regional office or vet center listed on page 330, call 1-800-827-1000, or check their web site at www.vba.va.gov/bln/vre/ilp.htm.

Choose a Career For Free

Vocational Rehabilitation and Employment Service provides vocational-educational counseling to veterans and certain dependents. Eligibility for this service is based on having eligibility for a VA Education program such as the Montgomery Bill, Veterans' Education Assistance Program or Dependents Education Assistance. Vocational Rehabilitation and Education can provide a wide range of vocational and educational counseling services to veterans and dependents. These services are designed to help an individual choose a vocational direction and determine the course needed to achieve the chosen goal. Assistance may include interest and aptitude testing; occupational exploration; setting occupational goals; locating the right type of training program and exploring educational or training facilities which might be utilized to achieve an occupational goal. Counseling services are provided to eligible persons at no charge. To provide a full service, the counseling may take more than one session. Request VA Form 28-8832. For additional information, contact your regional office or vet center listed on page 330, call 1-800-827-1000, or check their web site at www.vba.va.gov/bln/vre/vec.htm.

Free Help to Start Your Own Business

The Center for Veterans Enterprise (CVE) is a centralized program to help veterans start-up and succeed in business. Their goal is to support economic empowerment for every veteran entrepreneur and to provide assistance for veterans and service-disabled veterans who are considering business ownership. They provide assistance in management, marketing, financing and even provide a mentoring program. The Center for Veterans Enterprise works in conjunction with the Small Business Administration (SBA) to maximize the benefits for veterans. There are SBA Veterans Business Development Offices in each state. To declare your firm as a veteran owned business, a veteran or group of veterans must have 51% ownership and control of the business. A similar 51% rule is applied to businesses owned by service-disabled veterans. Contact U.S. Department of Veterans Affairs, The Center for Veterans Enterprise (00VE), 810 Vermont Avenue, NW, Washington, D.C. 20420; 202-565-8336; 866-584-2344 Toll free; Fax: 202-565-4255; Email: VACVE@mail.va.gov; www.vetbiz.gov.

Dream It, Find It, Get It

If you are looking for a dream job, you may find it on Job Seekers. Veterans may search online through the database of over one million jobs, post their resume online or set-up an automated job search. Go to http://dva.jobsearch.org/ to begin your search.

Get Paid to Train for a New Career

You may be able to receive living expenses or training allowances for vocational rehabilitation training programs if you are a veteran who is required to take additional education or training to become employable. A subsistence allowance is paid each month during training and is based on the rate of attendance (full-time or part-time), the number of dependents, and the type of training. A full-time veteran training at an Institute of Higher Learning can receive $655 a month for their family of two dependents. For additional information, contact your regional office or vet center listed on page 330, call 1-800-827-1000, or check their web site at www.vba.va.gov/bln/vre/InterSubsistence 100103.htm.

Free Job Outreach Programs

Disabled Veterans' Outreach Program (DVOP) is managed by the Department of Labor and specializes in the development of job and training opportunities for veterans, with special emphasis on veterans with service-related disabilities. DVOP specialists provide direct services to veterans enabling them to be competitive in the labor market. They provide outreach and offer assistance to disabled and other veterans by promoting community and employer support for employment and training opportunities, including apprenticeship and on-the-job training. DVOP specialists are available to those veterans and their employers to help ensure that necessary follow up services are provided to promote job retention. To contact a DVOP specialist, call or visit the nearest State Employment Service (sometimes known as Job Service) agency listed in the State Government section of your phone book. Contact Office of the

Assistant Secretary for Veterans' Employment and Training, U.S. Department of Labor, 200 Constitution Avenue, NW, Room S-1325, Washington, D.C. 20210; 866-4-USA-DOL; 202-693-4700; Fax: 202-693-4754; www.dol.gov/vets/programs/fact/Employment_Services_fs01.htm#LVEP.

Free Job Finding Assistance

If you need help finding a job, Local Veterans' Employment Representatives (LVERs) are available at state job service offices throughout the country. The LVER contact employers to develop job openings for veterans, and monitor job listings from federal contractors to assure that eligible veterans get priority in job referrals. They provide free job counseling, testing, training, referral, and placement services to veterans. LVER works with the Department of Veterans' Affairs to identify and aid veterans who need work-related prosthetic devices, sensory aids, or other special equipment to improve their employability. They also contact community leaders, employers, unions, and training programs and veterans' service organizations to be sure eligible veterans receive the services to which they are entitled. For additional information call or visit the nearest State Employment Service (sometimes known as Job Service) agency listed in the State Government section of your phone book. Contact Office of the Assistant Secretary for Veterans' Employment and Training, U.S. Department of Labor, 200 Constitution Avenue, NW, Room S-1325, Washington, D.C. 20210; 866-4-USA-DOL; 202-693-4700; Fax: 202-693-4754; www.dol.gov/vets/programs/fact/Employment_Services_fs01.htm#LVEP.

Get Your Old Job Back After Military Time With A Raise

When you have finished serving your country, The Uniformed Services Employment and Reemployment Rights Act of 1994 (USERRA) may be a big help in getting your previous job back. The USERRA was signed into law on October 13, 1994. USERRA clarifies and strengthens the Veterans' Reemployment Rights (VRR) Statue. USERRA is intended to minimize the disadvantages to an individual that occur when that person needs to be absent from his or her civilian employment to serve in this country's uniformed service which includes the Armed Forces, the Army National Guard and the Air National Guard. USERRA makes major improvements in protecting service member rights and benefits by clarifying the law and improving enforcement mechanisms. It also provides employees with Department of Labor assistance in processing claims. Specifically, USERRA expands the cumulative length of time that an individual may be absent from work for uniformed services duty and retain reemployment rights. USERRA potentially covers every individual in the country who serves in or has served in the uniformed services and applies to all employers in the public and private sectors, including Federal employers. The law seeks to ensure that those who serve their country can retain their civilian employment and benefit, and can seek employment free from discrimination because of their service. USERRA provides enhanced protection for disabled veterans, requiring employers to make reasonable efforts to accommodate the disability. USERRA is administered by the United States Department of Labor, through the Veterans' Employment and Training Service (VETS). VETS provides assistance to those persons experiencing service connected problems with their civilian employment and provides information about the Act to employers. VETS also assists veterans who have questions regarding Veterans' Preference. For more information, please visit the Veterans' Preference Advisor at www.dol.gov/elaws/vetspref.htm. This USERRA Advisor has been designed to answer questions about the rights and responsibilities for both the employee and employer. For additional information, contact your regional office or vet center listed on page 330, call 1-800-827-1000; call 866-4-USA-DOL; or check their web site at www.dol.gov/elaws/vets/userra/userra.asp.

Unemployment Compensation When Leaving The Military

Ex-service members are eligible for a weekly income for a limited period of time to help meet basic needs while searching for employment. The amount and duration of payments are governed by state laws, which vary considerably. Be sure to bring a copy of military discharge form DD-214 when you are applying. Contact your nearest state employment office listed in the blue pages of your telephone book under State Government.

Free Workshop Before Heading Back to Civilian Life

The Transition Assistance Program (TAP) was established to meet the needs of separating service members during their period of transition into civilian life by offering job-search assistance and related services. The law creating TAP established a partnership between the Departments of Defense, Veterans Affairs, Transportation and the Departments of Labor's Veterans' Employment and Training Service (VETS), to give employment and training information to armed forces members within 180 days of separation or retirement. TAP consists of comprehensive three-day workshops at selected military installations nationwide. Professionally-trained workshop facilitators provide information about job searches, career decision-making, current occupational and labor market conditions, and resume and cover letter preparation and interviewing techniques. Participants also are provided with an evaluation of their employability relative to the job market and receive information on the most current veterans' benefits. Service members leaving the military with a service-connected disability are offered the Disabled Transition Assistance Program (DTAP). DTAP includes the normal three-day TAP workshop plus additional hours of individual instruction to help determine job readiness and address the special needs of disabled veterans. For additional information about U.S. Department of Labor employment and training programs for veterans contact Office of the Assistant Secretary for Veterans' Employment and Training, U.S. Department of Labor, 200 Constitution Avenue, NW; Room S-1316, Washington, D.C. 20210; 202-693-4700; Fax: 202-693-4754; www.dol.gov/vets/programs/fact/TAPFS_02.htm.

Government Contractors That Have to Hire a Vet

When you are looking for a job, you should consider applying at companies that have contracts and subcontracts with the Federal government. Any contractor or subcontractor with a contract of $25,000 or more with the Federal Government must take affirmative action to hire and promote qualified targeted veterans which includes, special disabled veterans, veterans of the Vietnam-era, or recently separated veterans. Contractors and subcontractors with openings for jobs, other than executive or top management positions, positions which are to be filled from within the contractor's organization, and positions lasting 3 days or less, must list them with the nearest State Job Service (also known as State Employment Service) office. Qualified targeted veterans receive priority for referral to Federal contractor job openings listed at those offices. Federal contractors are not required to hire those referred, but must have affirmative action plans. Companies must file an annual VETS-100 report, which shows the number of targeted veterans in their work force by job category, hiring location, and number of new hires. Instructions, information and follow-up assistance is provided at VETS-100 Internet site at http://vets100.cudenver.edu/ or employers may contact the VETS-100 Processing Center at 703-461-2460 or Email at helpdesk@vets100.com. For copies of Affirmative Action Obligations of Contractors and Subcontractors for Disabled Veterans and Veterans of the Vietnam Era, Rules and Regulations, contact Office of Federal Contract Compliance Programs, Employment Standards Administration, 200 Constitution Ave., NW, U.S. Department of Labor, Washington, DC 20210.

e-VETS Resource Advisor to the Rescue

If you are a veteran in need of help preparing to enter the job market, e-VETS may be a just what you need. It includes information on a broad range of topics, such as job search tools and tips, employment openings, career assessment, education and training, and benefits and special services available to veterans. E-VETS was developed by the US Department of Labor to help employees and employers understand their rights and responsibilities under numerous Federal employment laws. There are two sections on e-VETS Resource Advisor, General Services and Personal Profile. If you are a veteran, use both to achieve the best results. Contact Veterans' Employment and Training, U.S. Department of Labor, 200 Constitution Avenue, NW, Room S-1316, Washington, D.C. 20210; 866-4-USA-DOL; 202-693-4700; Fax: 202-693-4754; www.dol.gov/elaws/evets.htm.

Receive a $10,000 Bonus

WOW, a $10,000 bonus to teach school. Troops to Teachers (TTT) was established in 1994 as a Department of Defense program. The National Defense Authorization Act for FY 2000 transferred the responsibility for program oversight and funding to the U.S. Department of Education but continued operation by the Department of Defense. TTT is managed by the Defense Activity for Non-Traditional Education Support (DANTES). The "No Child Left Behind Act of 2001" provides for the continuation of the Troops to Teachers program. Troops to Teacher's primary objective is to help recruit quality teachers for schools that serve low-income families throughout America. TTT helps relieve teacher shortages, especially in math, science, special education and other high-needs subject areas, and assists military personnel in making successful transitions to second careers in teaching. Financial assistance may be provided to eligible individuals as stipends up to $5K to help pay for teacher certification costs or as bonuses of $10K. Stipend and bonus recipients must agree to teach for three years in school locations that meet certain Department of Education criteria. Contact DANTES Troops to Teachers, 6490 Saufley Field Road, Pensacola, FL 32509-5243; 850-452-1320; 800-231-6242; www.Dantes.doded.mil/dantes_web/troopsto teachers/index.htm?Flag=True.

An Umbrella of Protection

The nature of military service can often compromise the ability of service members to fulfill their financial obligations. Congress and the state legislatures have long recognized the need for "umbrella" protective legislation. The Servicemembers Civil Relief Act (SCRA) protects active duty, reservists and members of the National Guard while on active duty. However, some protections extend for a limited time beyond discharge. Additionally, some of the Act's protections extend to the members' dependents. Benefits include:

- Reduced interest rates on mortgage payments
- Reduced interest rates on credit cards
- Protection from eviction if your rent is $1,200 or less
- Delay of all civil court actions

Contact your local unit or installation legal assistance office or http://usmilitary.about.com/od/sscra/ for additional information.

Get a Job Without Any Competition

Get your foot in the door by applying for civil service appointments. The Veterans Readjustment Appointment (VRA) is a special authority by which agencies can employ eligible veterans without competition. VRA appointees are initially hired for a 2-year period. Successful completion of the VRA leads to a permanent civil service appointment. You must have served on active duty for more than 180 days, except if you were released due to a service-connected disability. For additional information, veterans should contact the personnel office at the Federal agency where they wish to work or contact the Office of Personnel Management at 202-606-1800 or online at www.opm.gov/index.htm.

Veterans' Employment and Training Service and Regional Administrators

The Veterans' Employment and Training Service has 10 regional offices, as well as, at least one service office in each state. The regional offices are administered by Regional Administration (RAVET) and the state offices are administered by a Director for Veterans' Employment and Training. These offices can give you information about veterans employment and training programs and reemployment rights for veterans reservists and members of the National Guard.

Veterans Employment and Training Services Offices

Veterans' Employment and Training Service National Office
U.S. Department of Labor
200 Constitution Avenue, NW
Room S-1325
Washington, DC 20210
Asst Secretary, Frederico Juarbe Jr.
Deputy Assistant Secretary, Charles S. Ciccolella
202-693-4754
202-693-4700
www.dol.gov/vets/

Region I
(Connecticut, Maine, Massachusetts, New Hampshire, Rhode Island, Vermont)
Regional Administrator, David Houle
Email: houle-david@dol.gov
Veterans' Employment and Training Service
U.S. Department of Labor
J.F. Kennedy Federal Building
Room E-315
Government Center
Boston, MA 02203
617-565-2080
Fax: 617-565-2082

Region II
(New Jersey, New York, Puerto Rico, Virgin Islands)
Regional Administrator, Vacant
Veterans' Program Specialist, Tim Hays
Email: Hays-Timothy@dol.gov
Veterans' Employment and Training Service
U.S. Department of Labor
201 Varick Street, Room 766
New York, NY 10014
212-337-2211
Fax: 212-337-2634

Region III
(Delaware, District of Columbia, Maryland, Pennsylvania, Virginia, West Virginia)
Regional Administrator, Joseph W. Hortiz. Jr.
Email: Hortiz-Joseph@dol.gov
Veterans' Employment and Training Service
U.S. Department of Labor
The Curtis Center
VETS/770 West
170 S. Independence Mall
Philadelphia, PA 19106-3310
215-861-5390
Fax: 215-861-5389

Region III
Director Patrick D. Harvey
Email: Harvey.patrick@dol.gov
U.S. Department of Labor
Veterans' Employment and Training Service
2699 Park Avenue, Suite 210D
Huntington, WV 25704
304-528-5873
Fax: 304-528-5874

Region IV
(Alabama, Florida, Georgia, Kentucky, Mississippi, North Carolina, South Carolina, Tennessee)
Regional Administrator, William J. Bolls, Jr.
Email: bolls-william@dol.gov
Veterans' Employment and Training Service
U.S. Department of Labor
Sam Nunn Atlanta Federal Center
61 Forsyth Street, SW, Room 6-T85
Atlanta, GA 30303
404-562-2305
Fax: 404-562-2313

Region V
(Illinois, Indiana, Michigan, Minnesota, Ohio, Wisconsin)
Regional Administrator, Ronald G. Bachman
Email: bachman-ronald@dol.gov
Veterans' Employment and Training Service
U.S. Department of Labor
230 South Dearborn, Room 1064
Chicago, IL 60604
312-353-4942
312-353-0970 (ans. machine)
Fax: 312-886-1184

Region V
Heather Higgins
Email: Higgins.heather@dol.gov
U.S. Department of Labor
Veterans' Employment and Training Service
1795 West Main Street, Suite 520
Owosso, MI 48867
989-729-9100
Fax: 989-729-4689

Region VI
(Arkansas, Louisiana, New Mexico, Oklahoma, Texas)
Regional Administrator, Lester L. Williams, Jr.
Email: williams-lester@dol.gov
Veterans' Employment and Training Service
U.S. Department of Labor
525 Griffin Street, Room 858
Dallas, TX 75202
214-767-4987
Fax: 214-767-2734

Region VII
(Iowa, Kansas, Missouri, Nebraska)
Regional Administrator, Lester L. Williams, Jr.
Email: williams-lester@dol.gov
Veterans' Employment and Training Service
U.S. Department of Labor
City Center Square Building
1100 Main Street, Suite 850
Kansas City, MO 64105-2112

Mailing Address:
P.O. Box 59
Jefferson City, MO 65104-0059
816-426-7151
Fax: 816-426-7259

Region VIII
(Colorado, Montana, North Dakota, South Dakota, Utah, Wyoming)
Regional Administrator, Ronald G. Bachman
Email: bachman-ronald@dol.gov
Veterans' Employment and Training Service
U.S. Department of Labor
1999 Broadway, Suite 1730
Denver, CO 80202
303-844-1175
303-844-1176
Fax: 605-844-1179

Region IX
(Arizona, California, Hawaii, Nevada)
Regional Administrator, Rosendo "Alex" Cuevas
Email: cuevas.rosendo@dol.gov
Veterans' Employment and Training Service
U.S. Department of Labor
71 Stevenson Street, Suite 705
San Francisco, CA 94105
415-975-4701
415-975-4700 (ans. machine)
Fax: 415-975-4704

Region X
(Alaska, Idaho, Oregon, Washington)
Regional Administrator, Vacant
Veterans' Program Specialist, Karen Marin
Email: Marin-Karen@dol.gov
Veterans' Employment and Training Service
U.S. Department of Labor
1111 Third Avenue, Suite 800
Seattle, WA 98101-3212
206-553-4831
Fax: 206-553-6853

Veterans' Employment And Reemployment Rights Assistance And Information

Alabama
Director, Thomas M. Karrh
Email: Karrh-Thomas@dol.gov
Veterans' Employment and Training Service
U.S. Department of Labor
649 Monroe Street
Room 2218
Montgomery, AL 36131-6300
334-223-7677, 242-8115
Fax: 334-242-8927

Alaska
Director, Dan Travis
Email: Travis-Dan@dol.gov
Veterans' Employment and Training Service
U.S. Department of Labor
P.O. Box 25509

1111 West 8th Street
Juneau, AK 99802-5509
907-465-2723
Fax: 907-465-5528

Arizona
Director, Michael Espinosa
Email: Espinosa-Michael@dol.gov
Veterans' Employment and Training Service
U.S. Department of Labor
P.O. Box 6123-SC760E
1400 West Washington
Phoenix, AZ 85005
602-379-4961
Fax: 602-542-4103

Arkansas
Director, Billy R. Threlkeld
Email: Threlkeld-Billy@dol.gov
Veterans' Employment and Training Service
U.S. Department of Labor
Baptist Memorial Hospital
#1 Pershing Circle, Room 1208
Little Rock, AR 72114
Mailing address:
P.O. Box 128
Little Rock, AR 72203
501-682-3786
Fax: 501-682-3752

California
Director, Virginia Stickler
Email: stickler.virginia@dol.gov
Veterans' Employment and Training Service
U.S. Department of Labor
800 Capitol Mall, Roorn W1142
P.O. Box 826880
Sacramento, CA 94280-0001
916-654-8178
Fax: 916-654-9469

Assistant Director, Steven L. Bragman
Email: Bragman-Steven@dol.gov
Veterans' Employment and Training Service
U.S. Department of Labor
2550 Mariposa Mall, Room 1080
Fresno, CA 93721-2296
559-445-5193
Fax: 559 445-5023

Assistant Director, Dennis Longyear
Email: longyear.dennis@dol.gov
Veterans' Employment and Training Service
U.S. Department of Labor
363 Civic Drive
Pleasant Hills, CA 94523-1987
925-602-1541
Fax: 925-602-1540

Assistant Director, Kevin D. Nagel
Email: Nagel-Kevin@dol.gov
EDD, Redlands Field Office
814 W. Colton Avenue
Redlands, CA 92374-2930
909-335-6763
Fax: 909-335-8303

Assistant Director, Linda Jacobe
Email: Jacobe-Linda@dol.gov
Veterans' Employment and Training Service
U.S. Department of Labor
320 Campus Lane
Suisun, CA 94583
707-863-3583
Fax: 714-687-0502

Assistant Director, Michael S. Beadle
Email: Beadle-Michael@dol.gov
Veterans' Employment and Training Service
U.S. Department of Labor
914 Broadway
Santa Monica, CA 90401
310-576-6444
Fax: 310-395-6597

Assistant Director, Nancy Ise
Email: Ise-Nancy@dol.gov
Veterans' Employment and Training Service
U.S. Department of Labor
2450 E. Lincoln Avenue
Anaheim, CA 92806-4175
714 687-4845
Fax: 714-518-2391

Assistant Director, Edward J. Scheer
Email: scheer-edward@dol.gov
Veterans' Employment and Training Service
U.S. Department of Labor
8977 Activity Road
San Diego, CA 92126-4427
858-689-6008
Fax: 619-689-6012

Director Vacant
U.S. Department of Labor
Veterans' Employment and Training Service
933 South Glendora Avenue
West Covina, CA 91790
626-960-5106
Fax: 909-593-8913

Colorado
Director, Mark A. McGinty
Email: McGinty-Mark@dol.gov
Veterans' Employment and Training Service
U.S. Department of Labor
1515-Arapahoe St., Tower #2, Suite 400
P.O. Box 46550
Denver, CO 80202
303-844-2151, 844-2152
Fax: 303-620-4257

Connecticut
Director, Louis Kennedy.
Email: kennedy.louis@dol.gov
Veterans' Employment and Training Service
U.S. Department of Labor
Connecticut Dept. of Labor Building
200 Folly Brook Boulevard
Wethersfield, CT 06109
860-263-6490
Fax: 860-263-6498

Delaware
Director, David White
Email: white-david@dol.gov
U.S. Department of Labor
Veterans' Employment and Training Service
4425 North Market Street
Room 108, Annex Building
Wilmington, DE 19809-0828
302-761-8138/9
Fax: 302-761-6621 (temp)

District of Columbia
Director, Stanley K. Williams
Email: Williams-Stanley@dol.gov
Veterans' Employment and Training Service
U.S. Department of Labor
64 New York Avenue, NE, Room 3156
Washington, D.C. 20002
202-671-2179
Fax: 202-671-4103

Florida
Director, Derek W. Taylor
Email: taylor-derek@dol.gov
Mailing address:
Veterans' Employment and Training Service
U.S. Department of Labor
c/o Caldwell Building
107 E. Madison Street, Suite B30
Tallahassee, FL 32399
850-245-7199
Fax: 850-245-7186

Assistant Director, Richard Bate
Email: bate-richard@dol.gov
Mailing address:
Veterans' Employment and Training Service
U.S. Department of Labor
P.O. Box 17747
Jacksonville, FL 32245-7747
Located at:
215 Market Street, Suite 300
Jacksonville, FL 32202-2851
904-798-0060, ext. 2191
Fax: 904-359-6151

Assistant Director, Oscar G. Fuentes
Email: fuentes-oscar@dol.gov
Veterans' Employment and Training Service
U.S. Department of Labor
Ft. Lauderdale Jobs & Benefits Office
P.O. Box 5124
Ft. Lauderdale, Fl, 33310-5124
Located at:
2610 West Oakland Parks Boulevard
Ft. Lauderdale, FL 33311-1347
954-677-5818
Fax: 954-677-5820

Assistant Director, Ronnie L. Carter
Email: carter-ronnie@dol.gov
Veterans' Employment and Training Service
U.S. Department of Labor
P.O. Box 149084
Orlando, FL 32814-9084
Located at:
Workforce Central Florida
1801 Lee Road, Suite 270
Winter Park, FL 32789
407-531-1222, ext. 2005
Fax: 407-741-5394 (call ahead)

Assistant Director, Craig K. Spry
Email: spry-craig@dol.gov
Veterans' Employment and Training Service
U.S. Department of Labor
P.O. Box 12528
St. Petersburg, FL 33713
Located at:
3251 3rd Avenue North, Suite 150
St. Petersburg, FL 33713
727-893-2415
Fax: 727-893-2981

Georgia
Director, Ed Gresham
Email: gresham-ed@dol.gov
Veterans' Employment and Training Service
U.S. Department of Labor

Georgia State Care Building
151 Ellis Street, NE, Suite 203
Atlanta, GA 30303
404-656-3127, -3138
404-331-3893
Fax: 404-657-7403

Director Miguel "Mike" Hernandez
Email: hrnandez.migel@dol.gov
U.S. Department of Labor
Veterans' Employment and Training Service
c/o Middle Georgia Consortium Inc.
124 Osigian Boulevard, Suite A
Warner-Robbins, GA 31095
478-953-4771 ext 311
Fax: 478-953-2509

Hawaii
Director, vacant
Veterans' Employment and Training Service
U.S. Department of Labor
P.O. Box 3680
Honolulu, HI 96811
Located at:
830 Punchbowl Street, Rm. 315
Honolulu, HI 96813
808-522-8216 (ans. service)
Fax: 808-586-9258

Idaho
Director, Vacant
Assistant Director, Pamela "Pam" Langley
Email: Lengley-Pamela@dol.gov
Veterans' Employment and Training Service
U.S. Department of Labor
413 Main Street, Suite 101
Boise, ID 83702
Located at:
317 Main Street, 4th Floor, East Wing
Boise, ID 83735
208-332-3570, ext. 3168
Fax: 208-334-6389, 334-6300

Illinois
Director, Vacant
Veterans' Employment and Training Service
U.S. Department of Labor
33 South State Street, Room 8174-S
Chicago, IL 60605
312-793-3433
Fax: 312-793-4795

Assistant Director, David Lyles
Email: lyles-davidl@dol.gov
Veterans' Employment and Training Service
U.S. Department of Labor
850 E. Madison Street, Floor #3
Springfield, IL 62794-9295
217-524-7769
Fax: 217-785-9715

Assistant Director, James R. Harris
Email: harris-james@dol.gov
Veterans' Employment and Training Service
U.S. Department of Labor
800 Lancer Lane - Suite E-107
Grayslake, IL 60030
847-523-7400, ext. 273
Fax: 847-543-7465

Indiana
Bruce Redman, Director
Director, David "Bruce" Redman
Email: redman-david@dol.gov
Veterans' Employment and Training Service
U.S. Department of Labor
10 North Senate Ave., Room SE 103
Indianapolis, IN 46204
317-232-6804
317-232-6805
Fax: 317-232-4262

Iowa
Director, Anthony J. Smithhart
Email: Smithhart-Anthony@dol.gov
Veterans' Employment and Training Service
U.S. Department of Labor
150 Des Moines Street
Des Moines, IA 50309-5563
515-281-9061
Fax: 515-281-9063

Kansas
Director, Gayle A. Gibson
Email: Gibson-Gayle@dol.gov
Veterans' Employment and Training Service
U.S. Department of Labor
401 Topeka Boulevard
Topeka, KS 66603-3182
785-296-5032
Fax: 785-296-0264

Kentucky
Director, Charles R. "Rick" Netherton
Email: Netherton-Charles@dol.gov
Veterans' Employment and Training Service
U.S. Department of Labor
Department for Employment Services
275 East Main Street, 2nd Floor West - 2WD
Frankfort, KY 40621-2339

502-564-7062
Fax: 502-564-1476

Veterans' Program Specialist, Robert Kuenzli
Email: Kuenzli-Robert@dol.gov
Veterans' Employment and Training Service
U.S. Department of Labor
320 Garrard Street
Covington, KY 41011
859-292-6666 Ext. 253
Fax: 859-292-6708

Louisiana
Director, Lester L. Parmenter
Email: Parmenter-Lester@dol.gov
Veterans' Employment and Training Service
U.S. Department of Labor
Louisiana Department of Labor
Administration Building, Room 184
1001 North 23rd Street
Baton Rouge, Louisiana 70802
Mailing address:
P.O. Box 94094, Room 184
Baton Rouge, LA 70804-9094
225-389-0440
Fax: 225-342-3066

Maine
Director, Jon Guay
Email: Guay-Jon@dol.gov
Veterans' Employment and Training Service
U.S. Department of Labor
P.O. Box 3106
Lewiston, ME 04243
Located at:
5 Mollison Way
Lewiston, ME 04240
207-753-9090
Fax: 207-783-5304

Maryland
Director, Stanley A. Seidel
Email: seidel.stanley@dol.gov
U.S. Department of Labor
Veterans' Employment and Training Service
1100 North Eutaw Street, Room 205
Baltimore, MD 21201
410-767-2110, -2111
Fax: 410-333-5136

Director Larry Mettert
Email: mettert.larry@dol.gov
U.S. Department of Labor
Veterans' Employment and Training Service
67 Thomas Johnson Drive
Frederick, MD 21702
301-694-2185
Fax: 301-694-1916

Massachusetts
Director, Paul Desmond
Email: desmond-paul@dol.gov
Veterans' Employment and Training Service
U.S. Department of Labor
C.F. Hurley Building, 5th Floor
19 Staniford Street
Boston, MA 02114
617-626-6699
Fax: 617-727-2330

Assistant Director, Reginald E. Dupuis
Email: Dupuis-Reginald@dol.gov
Veterans' Employment and Training Service
U.S. Department of Labor
Division of Employment Security
72 School Street
Taunton, MA 02780
508-977-1414
Fax: 617-727-2112

Michigan
Director, Kim Fulton
Email: Fulton-Kim@dol.gov
Veterans' Employment and Training Service
U.S. Department of Labor
Candillac Place
3032 West Grand Blvd., Suite 9-550
Detroit, MI 48202
313-456-3180
Fax: 313-456-3181

Assistant Director, Edgar J. Hekman
Email: hekman-edgar@dol.gov
Veterans' Employment and Training Service
U.S. Department of Labor
Employment Security Commission
Michigan Works Sheldon Complex
121 Franklin SE
Grand Rapids, MI 49507
616-336-4021
Fax: 616-336-4015

Minnesota
Director, Michael Graham
Email: graham-michael@dol.gov
Veterans' Employment and Training Service
U.S. Department of Labor
390 Robert Street North, 1st Floor
St. Paul, MN 55101-1812
651-296-3665
Fax: 651-282-2711

Mississippi
Director, Angelo Terrell
Email: Terrell-Angelo@dol.gov
Veterans' Employment and Training Service
U.S. Department of Labor
P.O. Box 1699
1520 West Capitol Street
Jackson, MS 39215-1699
601-965-4204, 961-7588
Fax: 601-961-7717

Missouri
Director, Mick Jones
Email: Jones-Mickey@dol.gov
Veterans' Employment and Training Service
U.S. Department of Labor
421 East Dunklin Street
Jefferson City, MO 65102-1087
Mailing address:
P.O. Box 59
Jefferson City, MO 65104-0059
573-751-3921
Fax: 573-751-6710

Montana
Director, H. Polly LaTray
Email: Latray-Hazel@dol.gov
Veterans' Employment and Training Service
U.S. Department of Labor
301 South Park #578
Helena, MT 59604
Mailing address:
P.O. Box 1728
Helena, MT 59624
406-841-2005/2006
Fax: 406-841-2007

Nebraska
Director, Richard "Rick" Nelson
Email: Nelson-Richard@dol.gov
Veterans' Employment and Training Service
U.S. Department of Labor
1010 N Street
Lincoln, NE 68508
Mailing address:
P.O. Box 194
Lincoln, NE 68509
402-471-9833
Fax: 402-471-2092

Nevada
Director, Darrol Brown
Email: brown-darrol@dol.gov
Veterans' Employment and Training Service
U.S. Department of Labor
1923 North Carson Street, Room 205
Carson City, NV 89702
775-687-4632
Fax: 775-687-3976

New Hampshire
Director, John Gagne
Email: gagne-john@dol.gov
Veterans' Employment and Training Service
U.S. Department of Labor
55 Pleasant Street
James C. Cleveland Federal Building, Room #3602
Concord, NH 03301
603-225-1424
Fax: 603-225-1545

New Jersey
Director, Alan E. Grohs
Email: grohs-alan@dol.gov
U.S. Department of Labor
Veterans' Employment and Training Service
Labor Building, 11th Floor
P.O. Box 058
Trenton, NJ 08625
609-292-2930
609-989-2305 and 989-2396
Fax: 609-292-9070

Assistant Director, James J. Curcio
Email: curcio-james@dol.gov
U.S. Department of Labor
Veterans' Employment and Training Service
2600 Mt. Ephraim Avenue
Camden, NJ 08104
856-614-3163
Fax: 856-614-3156

New Mexico
Director, Sharon I Mitchell
Email: Mitchell-Sharon@dol.gov
Veterans' Employment and Training Service
U.S. Department of Labor
501 Mountainroad N.E.
Albuquerque, NM 87102
Mailing address:
P.O. Box 25085
Albuquerque, NM 87125-5085
505-346-7502
Fax: 505-242-6179

New York
Director, Frank Merges
Email: merges.frank@dol.gov
U.S. Department of Labor
Veterans' Employment and Training Service
Harriman State Campus

Bldg. 12, Room 518
Albany, NY 12240-0099
518-457-7465, 435-0831
Fax: 518-435-0833

Veterans' Program Specialist, Frank Carey
Email: Carey-Frank@dol.gov
Veterans' Employment and Training Service
U.S. Department of Labor
Leo O'Brien Federal Bldg., Room 819
Albany, NY 12207
518-431-4276
Fax: 518-431-4283
Aux Office: 518-270-5872

Assistant Director, Alice F. Jones
J Email: ones-Alice@dol.gov
212-352-6183 (M-Tu-W-F)
212-227-5213 (Thursday only)
Assistant Director, Daniel A. Friedman
Friedman-Daniel@dol.gov
212-352-6184 (M-F)
Fax: 212-352-6184
212-227-5213 (M-F only)
Veterans' Employment and Training Service
U.S. Department of Labor
345 Hudson Street, Rm. 8209
P.O. Box 668, Mail Stop 8C
New York, NY 10014-0668

Assistant Director, Vacant
U.S. Department of Labor
Veterans' Employment and Training Service
State Office Building, Room 702
207 Genesee Street
Utica, NY 13501
315-793-2323
Fax: 315-793-2303

North Carolina
Director, Steven W. Guess
Email: Guess-Steven@dol.gov
Veterans' Employment and Training Service
U.S. Department of Labor
P.O. Box 27625
Raleigh, NC 27611-7625
Located at:
700 Wade Avenue, Room G-217
Raleigh, NC 27605 – 1154
919-733 -7402
Fax: 919-733-1508

Assistant Director, Thomas E. West
Email: west-tom@dol.gov
Veterans' Employment and Training Service
U.S. Department of Labor
c/o North Carolina Employment
Security Commission
3301 Hwy US 70, S.E.
Newton, NC 28658
828-466-5535
Fax: 828-466-5545

Director Evon Digregorio
Email: digregorio.evon@dol.gov
U.S. Department of Labor
Veterans' Employment and Training Service
c/o North Carolina Employment Security Commission
112 W. Third Street
Washington, NC 27889
252-946-2141
Fax: 252-946-0257

North Dakota
Director, Gerald (Jerry) H. Meske
Email: Gerald-Meske@dol.gov
Veterans' Employment and Training Service
U.S. Department of Labor
P.O. Box 1632
1000 E. Divide Avenue
Bismarck, ND 58501
701-250-4337
701-328-2865
Fax: 701-328-2890

Ohio
Director, Kevin Patterson
Email: patterson.kevin@dol.gov
Veterans' Employment and Training Service
U.S. Department of Labor
145 South Front Street, Room 523
Columbus, OH 43215
614-466-2768/2769
Fax: 614-752-5007

Assistant Director, Kevin Patterson
Email: patterson-kevin@dol.gov
Veterans' Employment and Training Service
U.S. Department of Labor
2026 South Avenue
Youngstown, OH 44502
330-744-5201, ext. 113
Fax: 330-744-0085

Assistant Director, William Forester
Email: forester-william@dol.gov
Veterans' Employment and Training Service
U.S. Department of Labor
P.O. Box 40222
Cleveland, OH 44140-0222

216-787-5164
Fax: 216-787-5213

Assistant Director, John E. Moon
Email: moon-john@dol.gov
Veterans' Employment and Training Service
U.S. Department of Labor
P.O. Box 4506
Sherwood, OH 43556
419-783-3488
Fax: 419-782-4755

Oklahoma
Director, Joe Dyer
Email: dyer.joe@dol.gov
Veterans' Employment and Training Service
U.S. Department of Labor
2401 North Lincoln Blvd., Rm. 304-2
Oklahoma City, OK 73105
Mailing address:
P. O. Box 52003
Oklahoma City, OK 73152-2003
405-231-5088, 557-7189
Fax: 405-557-7123

Oregon
Director, Ron Cannon
Email: Cannon-Ron@dol.gov
Veterans' Employment and Training Service
U.S. Department of Labor
Employment Division Bldg., Rm. 108
875 Union Street, N.E.
Salem, OR 97311-0100
503-947-1490
Fax: 503-947-1492

Assistant Director, Tonja Pardo
Email: pardo-tonja@dol.gov
Veterans' Employment and Training Service
U.S. Department of Labor
1433 Southwest 6th Avenue
Portland, OR 97201
503-731-3478
Fax: 503-229-5829

Pennsylvania
Director, Larry Babitts
Email: babitts-lawrence@dol.gov
U.S. Department of Labor
Veterans' Employment and Training Service
Labor and Industry Bldg., Room 1108
Seventh and Forster Streets
Harrisburg, PA 17121
717-787-5834, 5835
Fax: 717-783-2631

Assistant Director, Dennis M. Ero
Email: Ero-Dennis@dol.gov
Somerset Job Center
218 North Kimberly Ave.
Somerset, PA 15501-4161
814-445-4161, ext. 239

Veterans' Program Specialist, Denise M. Adair
Email: adair-denise@dol.gov
U.S. Department of Labor
Veterans' Employment and Training Service
State Office Building
300 Liberty Avenue, Room 1307
Pittsburgh, PA 15222
412-565-2469
Fax: 412-565-2518

Assistant Director, Wayne E. Faith
Email: faith-wayne@dol.gov
U.S. Department of Labor
Veterans' Employment and Training Service
Job Service Office
135 Franklin Avenue
Scranton, PA 18503
717-963-4735

U.S. Department of Labor
Veterans' Employment and Training Service
Lehigh Valley Career Link
1601 Union Boulevard
Allentown, PA 18109-1509
610-493-1123 ext 455

Director Richard P. Schaffer
Email: schaffer.richard@dol.gov
U.S. Department of Labor
Veterans' Employment and Training Service
701 Crosby Street, Suite B
Chester, PA 19013-6096
610-447-3306
Fax: 610-447-3173

Puerto Rico
Director, Angel Mojica
Email: Mojica-Angel@dol.gov
U.S. Department of Labor
Veterans' Employment and Training Service
Puerto Rico Department of Labor and Human Resources
#198 Calle Guayama
Hato Rey, PR 00917
787-754-5391, 751-0731, 766-6425
Fax: 787-754-2983

Rhode Island
Director, Stephen Durst
Email: durst.stephen@dol.gov

Veterans' Employment and Training Service
U.S. Department of Labor
Oliver Stedman Government Center
4808-Tower Hill Road
Wakefield, RI 02879
401-792-7144
Fax: 401-792-7146

South Carolina
Director, William C. Plowden, Jr.
Email: plowden-william@dol.gov
Veterans' Employment and Training Service
U.S. Department of Labor
P.O. Box 1755
Columbia, SC 29202-1755
Located at:
Lem Harper Building
631 Hampton Street, Suite 141
Columbia, SC 29201
803-765-5195, 253-7649
Fax: 803-253-4153

South Dakota
Director, Earl R. Schultz
Email: Schultz-Earl@dol.gov
Veterans' Employment and Training Service
U.S. Department of Labor
P.O. Box 4730
420 South Roosevelt Street
Aberdeen, SD 57402-4730
605-626-2325
Fax: 605-626-2322

Tennessee
Director, Richard E. Ritchie
Email: Ritchie-Richard@dol.gov
Veterans' Employment and Training Service
U.S. Department of Labor
P.O. Box 280656
Nashville, TN 37228-0656
615-736-7680
Fax: 615-741-4241
615-736-5037

Clarksville Montgomery County Career Center
350 Pageant Lane, Suite 406
Clarksville, TN 37040
931-572-1688
Fax: 931-648-5564

Assistant Director, Jim George Pearson
Email: Pearson-Jim@dol.gov
Veterans' Employment and Training Service
U.S. Department of Labor
1309 Poplar Avenue
Memphis, TN 38104-2006
901-543-7853
Fax: 901-543-7882

Texas
Director, John D. McKinny
Email: McKinny-John@dol.gov
Veterans' Employment and Training Service
U.S. Department of Labor
TwC Building, Room 516-T
1117 Trinity Street
Austin, TX 78701
Mailing address:
P.O. Box 1468
Austin, TX 78767
512-463-2207
512-463-2814
Fax: 512-475-2999

Assistant Director, Alberto Navarro
Email: mailto:walker-randolph@dol.gov
Veterans' Employment and Training Service
U.S. Department of Labor
1550 Foxlake Drive, Suite 360
Houston, TX 77084-4739
281-579-8071, ext. 130
Fax: 281-579-2438

Assistant Director, Vacant
Veterans' Employment and Training Service
U.S. Department of Labor
412 South High Street
Longview, TX 75606
Mailing address:
P.O. Box 2152
Longview, TX 75606-2152
903-758-1783 Ext. 211
Fax: 903-757-7835

Assistant Director, Linda Sundance
Email: sundance.linda@dol.gov
Veterans' Employment and Training Service
U.S. Department of Labor
301 W. 13th Street, Room 407
Ft. Worth, TX 76102-4699
Mailing address:
P.O. Box 591
FT. Worth, TX 76101-0591
817-336-3727, ext. 1101
Fax: 817-335-0731

Director Will Jackson
Email: Jackson.willie@dol.gov
U.S. Department of Labor
Veterans' Employment and Training Service

6723 South Flores
San Antonia, TX 78221-1608
210-582-1739
Fax: 210-932-2484

Utah
Director, Howard "Dale" Brockbank
Email: Brockbank-Howard@dol.gov
Veterans' Employment and Training Service
U.S. Department of Labor
140 East 300 South, Suite 209
Salt Lake City, UT 84111-2333
801-524-5703
Fax: 801-524-3099

Vermont
Director, Richard Gray
Email: gray-richard@dol.gov
Veterans' Employment and Training Service
U.S. Department of Labor
P.O. Box 603
Montpelier, VT 05601
Located at:
Post Office Building
87 State Street, Room 303
Montpelier, VT 05602
802-828-4441
Fax: 802-828-4445

Virginia
Director, Paul Hinkhouse
Email: hinkhouse.paul@dol.gov
U.S. Department of Labor
Veterans' Employment and Training Service
703-East Main Street, Room 118
Richmond, VA 23219
804-786-7270, 7269, 6599
Fax: 804-786-4548

Terry Schaefer
Email: shaefer.terry@dol.gov
U.S. Department of Labor
Veterans' Employment and Training Service
5145 East Virginia Beach Boulevard
Norfolk, VA 23502
757-455-3970

Virgin Islands
Director, Angel Mojica
Email: Mojica-Angel@dol.gov
U.S. Department of Labor
Veterans' Employment and Training Service
Puerto Rico Department of Labor and Human Resources
#198 Calle Guayama
Hato Rey, PR 00917
787-754-5391, 751-0731, 766-6425
Fax: 787-754-2983

Washington
Director, Thomas "Tom" Pearson
Email: Pearson-Thomas@dol.gov
Veterans' Employment and Training Service
U.S. Department of Labor
P.O. Box 165
Olympia, WA 98507-0165
Located at:
605 Woodview Square Loop, SE, 3rd Floor
Lacey, WA 98503-1040
360-438-4600
Fax: 360-438-3160

West Virginia
Director, Charles W. Stores, Jr.
Email: Stores.Charles@dol.gov
U.S. Department of Labor
Veterans' Employment and Training Service
Capitol Complex, Room 204
112 CA Avenue
Charleston, WV 25305-0112
304-558-4001
Fax: 304-344-4591

Wisconsin
Director, Daniel Schmitz
Email: Schmitz.daniel@dol.gov
Veterans' Employment and Training Service
U.S. Department of Labor
P.O. Box 8310
Madison, WI 53708-8310
Located at:
Jeff Building, Room G-201A
201 East Washington Ave.
Madison, WI 53703
608-266-3110
Fax: 608-261-6710

Wyoming
Director, David McNulty
Email: McNulty-David@dol.gov
Veterans' Employment and Training Service
U.S. Department of Labor
P.O. Box 2760
100 West Midwest Avenue
Casper, WY 82602-2760
307-261-5454
307-235-3281
Fax: 307-473-2642

Housing

Money to Purchase, Fix Up or Invest

Each year the government gives out millions of dollars in real estate programs, yet many who qualify don't even apply or know that these programs exist. Remember, information is power. We have attempted to hit all the main programs offered, but many programs and services, like home repair grants and specialized services, are offered on the local level by community action agencies, senior agencies, or local governments. We have included some of these to show you the possibilities, but you will need to contact your local offices to see what is offered in your town.

According to a government report, close to 1 million housing units, available through the U.S. Department of Housing and Urban Development and U.S. Department of Agriculture's Rural Housing Program, are designated for senior citizens (GAO-05-174). Some housing options specifically have supportive services provided, whereas others have teamed with private organizations, such as church or volunteer groups, to provide help and assistance with things like transportation or food. There is even a Neighborhood Networks program that provides resources for establishing computer centers at senior sites. Although no funds are provided, the U.S. Department of Housing and Urban Development does encourage the centers to seek cash grants, in-kind support, and donations from sources for the computers. The U.S. Department of Health and Human Services has a Public Housing Primary Care Program that provides resides with affordable, comprehensive primary and preventive health care through clinics located wither within public housing properties or nearby.

Here are the main sources to contact for identifying money programs for real estate:

1. ***Find Federal Money Programs For Real Estate***
   Anyone selling you information about federal programs on real estate has to get the information from this source. It's printed every six months by the federal government, and is the major source of all federal programs. You can do a free search identifying all the federal real estate programs by going on the web to http://www.cfda.gov. The book is also available in almost every public library and for sale from the U.S. Government Printing Office www.gpo.gov.

2. ***Find State Money Programs For Real Estate***
   Every state has offices that provide financing for buying and fixing up homes and for real estate investing. Call your State Capitol Operator located in your state capital, or go to http://www.govengine.com/ and look for your state housing office for information about all their programs. You can find a listing of State Housing Finance Agencies at the National Council of State Housing Agencies website at www.ncsha.org.

3. ***Find Local Government and Nonprofit Programs For Real Estate***
   Contact your city and county officials as well as national and local nonprofit organizations. Almost every local jurisdiction has money for housing and real estate. Many have money for closing costs,

down payments, repairs and even rental assistance. It will take some effort but it's worth the time. You can also locate your local and county government offices on the web at http://www.govengine.com/localgov/index.html.

4. ***Eldercare Locator***
   The Eldercare Locator is a hotline provided by the U.S. Administration on Aging to assist older people and their families find community services for seniors anywhere in the country. Through the easy-to-use Eldercare Locator Web portal, older people and their families can search any time of day to find the nearest senior information and assistance service. Search the locator by state and zip code and also find links to other Web resources for seniors. Contact Eldercare Locator at 800-677-1116; http://www.n4a.org/locator.cfm.

Main Federal Sources of Housing

Four federal government agencies handle most of the federal government's housing programs. Don't let this limit you, but these are the best places to start:

- U.S. Department of Housing and Urban Development, 451 7th St., SW, Washington, DC 20410; 202-708-1112; www.hud.gov.
- Rural Housing Service, U.S. Department of Agriculture, Room 5037, South Building, 14th St., and Independence Ave., SW, Washington, DC 20250; 202-720-4323; www.rurdev.usda.gov.
- Bureau of Indian Affairs, Office of Tribal Services, MS 4660 MIB, 1849 C St., NW, Washington, DC 20240; 202-308-3667; www.doi.gov/bureau-indian-affairs.html.
- U.S. Department of Veterans Affairs, Washington, DC 20420; 202-273-7355; 800-827-1000; www.va.gov.

Housing Help From HUD

The U.S. Department of Housing and Urban Development is a great place to start if you are looking for senior housing information throughout the country. You can research a variety of assistance and living options that you will be able to afford. They even can help you by letting you talk to a HUD-approved housing counselor, as well as provide information on home modifications, reverse mortgages, finding in-home help and more. On the website you can locate affordable rental housing units specifically designed for the elderly and rural rental assistance. For specific senior help and programs check out their web site at www.hud.gov/groups/seniors.cfm or U.S. Department of Housing and Urban Development, 451 7th Street SW, Washington, DC 20410; 202-708-1112.

Save 70% On Your Rent

Studies show that people with less income pay a higher portion of their salary on housing than people in higher income categories. It is not unusual for lower income renters to pay 70% of their salary in rent. The government has a program called Housing Choice Vouchers (Formerly Section 8 Rental Assistance Program) that offers vouchers and direct payments to landlords. This will, in turn, cut your rent to only 30% of your income. Of course, there are income requirements for this program. For example, in

Arlington County, VA, a one-person household with an income of $30,450 qualifies for the program. Some of the programs have waiting lists, but it could be worth the wait. You can find your Local Public Housing Agency (PHA) by going to the U.S. Housing and Urban Development web site and click on your state for a complete listing. Contact: U.S. Department of Housing and Urban Development, 451 7th Street S.W., Washington, DC 20410; 202-708-1112; www.hud.gov/offices/pih/pha/contacts/index.cfm.

Your Rich Uncle Will Cosign A Loan to Buy or Fix Up a Home

The Rural Housing Service of the U.S. Department of Agriculture offers loan guarantees to lending agencies around the country. A loan-guarantee assures the lending agency that the government will pay for the loan if you can't. This Section 502 Rural Housing Guarantee Loan is targeted primarily to low-income individuals to purchase homes in rural areas. You must have an income level of up to 115% of the median income for the area. Seniors get special deductions when calculating their income eligibility. Funds can be used to build, repair, renovate or relocate a home or to purchase and prepare sites including providing water and sewage. Applicants must be without adequate housing and be able to afford the mortgage payments, including taxes and insurance. Contact your state Rural Housing Agency or the Rural Housing Service National Office, U.S. Department of Agriculture, Room 5037, South Building, 14th Street and Independence Avenue, S.W., Washington, DC 20250; 202-720-4323; www.rurdev.usda.gov/rhs.

$7,500 in Grants to Help Fix Up Your Home

Remember that a loan must be paid back but a grant is free money! The Rural Housing Service of the U.S. Department of Agriculture offers their Section 504 Rural Housing Repair Rehabilitation Program. Loans are available to very low-income rural residents who own and occupy their home in need of repairs. Funds can be used to improve, modernize or improve health and safety conditions. This is a 1% loan of up to $20,000 payable over 20 years. Applicants must be unable to get traditional credit and be below 50% of the area median income. Grants are only available to applicants 62 years old and older. Grants of up to $7,500 are available and the application process is very easy. Contact your state Rural Housing Agency or the Rural Housing Service National Office, U.S. Department of Agriculture, Room 5037, South Building, 14th Street and Independence Avenue, S.W., Washington, DC 20250; 202-720-4323; www.rurdev.usda.gov/rhs.

Grants and Loans When A Natural Disaster Hits

The Rural Housing Service offers seniors 62 and older help when natural disasters hit. The Direct Housing-Natural Disaster Loans and Grants Program meets the needs of qualified rural recipients. Funds must be used to help out very low-income owner occupants to repair or replace damaged property as a direct result of a natural disaster. Contact your State Rural Development Office or Single Family Processing Division, Rural Housing Services, Department of Agriculture, Washington, DC 20250; 202-720-1474; www.rurdev.usda.gov.

$2,700 Per Year for Rent

Rental Assistance is available through the Rural Housing Service Section 521 to seniors if you are unable to pay the basic monthly rent within 30% of adjusted monthly income in Rural Renting Housing. Income eligibility is required, although seniors get special deductions when calculating income eligibility. Contact your state Rural Housing Agency or the Rural Housing Service National Office, U.S.

Department of Agriculture, Room 5037, South Building, 14th Street and Independence Avenue, S.W., Washington, DC 20250; 202-720-4323; www.rurdev.usda.gov/rhs.

$20,000 For a Mobile Home

The VA Guaranteed Manufactured Home Loans are made by private lenders. The VA offers a guarantee to protect the lender against loss if you (the veteran) fail to repay the loan. They will guarantee 40% of the loan amount or the veteran's available entitlement up to $20,000. Eligibility requirements must be met. Contact your local Veterans Affairs Office or U.S. Department of Veterans Affairs, 810 Vermont Avenue, Washington, DC 20420; 800-827-1000; www.homeloans.va.gov/VAP26-71-1.htm.

HUD-man Goes After The Mobile Home Salesman

If your mobile home is not all that was promised, call HUD. The U.S. Department of Housing and Urban Development regulates the construction of mobile homes and investigates complaints about their performance. Contact: Manufactured Housing and Standards, U.S. Department of Housing and Urban Development, 451 7th Street, SW, Washington, DC 20410; 202-708-1112; 800-927-2891; www.hud.gov/offices/hsg/sfh/mhs/mhshome.cfm.

Free Legal Help For Renters and Home Buyers

It's illegal for landlords, realtors, bankers and others to discriminate against you because of your race, religion, sex, family status or handicap. Landlords also have rules to follow in dealing with you as a tenant. If you feel you have been discriminated against or you are having trouble with your landlord you can learn more about your rights. Contact your local state housing office, your state Attorney Generals Office or Office of Fair Housing and Equal Opportunity, Department of Housing and Urban Development, Room 5204, 451 7th Street, SW, Washington, DC 20410-2000; 202-708-1112; 800-669-9777; www.hud.gov/complaints/housediscrim.cfm.

Stay Clear of Deadly Radon Gases

If you have been living in your home for years or you are buying a new home, you need to know if there is radon present. Radon is an odorless gas that is present in nearly one in 15 homes in the U.S. at high levels. This is important because radon is the second leading cause of lung cancer. The EPA can help determine if your home is at risk, how to test for the gas and how to reduce it. There is also a Radon FIX-IT Program operated by the National Safety Council, a nonprofit organization that provides free guidance to consumers who are trying to fix their homes. For information call the National Radon Information Hotline at 800-767-7236 or Radon FIX-IT at 800-644-6999. Contact: U.S. EPA, Office of Radon and Indoor Air, Indoor Environments Division, 1200 Pennsylvania Avenue, NW, Mail Code 6609J, Washington, DC 20460; 202-343-9370; www.epa.gov/radon/.

Extra Money And Help For Your Home When You Don't Know Where to Turn

If you need emergency money to pay a bill, health care, or additional support, the following agencies can be of service and they are likely to have an office near you. Although these are private organizations they do receive a portion of their funds from Uncle Sam. Services and eligibility requirements vary from place to place, so there is no guarantee about what services are provided as many things are decided on a case by case basis. You need to contact the local office to see what they can do to help you in your hour of need.

1) ***Community Action Agencies***: Nearly 1,000 agencies around the country receive funds from the Community Services Block Grant to offer education, counseling, employment training, food packages, vouchers, weatherization and utility assistance, and more. To locate an agency near you, contact National Association of Community Action Agencies, 1100 17th St., NW, Suite 500, Washington, DC 20036; 202-265-7546; www.communityactionpartnership.com.
2) ***Catholic Charities***: Over 14,000 local organizations offer a variety of services including child care, elderly services, emergency shelter, housing assistance, health care, and more. For an office near you, contact Catholic Charities USA, 1731 king St., #200, Alexandria, VA 22314; 703-549-1390; www.catholiccharitiesusa.org.
3) ***Salvation Army***: Families in need can receive a wide range of services including utility assistance, transitional housing, emergency food, and even clothing. For an office near you, contact Salvation Army National Headquarters, 615 Slaters Lane, P.O. Box 269, Alexandria, VA 22313; 703-684-5500; www.salvationarmy.org.

Is Your Drinking Water Safe?

Many Americans are worried about the quality of the water they drink. Often they purchase bottled water or purification devices for drinking water, but is it a wise use of your money? The EPA offers information about your local drinking water system. They also offer publications including: *Water on Tap: What You Need to Know, Is Your Drinking Water Safe?, Home Water Testing* and *Bottled Water Fact Sheet* and more. Contact: Office of Ground Water and Drinking Water, Ariel Rios Building, 1200 Pennsylvania Avenue, NW, Washington, DC 20460-0003; 202-564-3750; 800-426-4791; www.epa.gov/OGWDW.

Volunteers Will Fix Your Home For Free

Many service organizations have begun to organize community service days, where the town is spruced up and volunteers help to rehabilitate homes in need of repair. *Rebuild Together* is a national organization operating in 865 cities throughout the country that bring together volunteers to help rehabilitate the homes of low-income homeowners. The work is done for free with the goal being to provide a safe and secure home for those in need. Contact your city or county government to learn about local programs. Contact: Rebuild Together, 1536 16th Street, NW, Washington, DC 20036; 202-483-9083, 800-4-REHAB9; www.rebuildtogether.org.

Save 10% - 50% on Your Fuel Bill

You may spend a large portion of your monthly expenses on your home's utility bills and most of that energy is wasted. By using a few inexpensive energy efficient measures, you can reduce your energy bills by 10% to 50%. With the publication, Energy Savers: Tips on Saving Energy and Money at Home, you can go step by step through your home to learn energy saving strategies. Topics include insulation/weatherization, water heating, lighting, appliances and more. There is even a major appliance shopping guide that explains the energy labels on appliances and shows how to choose the best one for you. Contact: Energy Efficiency and Renewable Energy, Mail Stop EE-1, Department of Energy, Washington, DC 20585, 202-586-9220, 877-337-3463; www.eere.energy.gov/consumerinfo/energy_savers/.

Keep Your Air Clean
Keep your air clean of asbestos, carbon monoxide, second hand smoke and more toxins. You don't have to hire a high priced consultant to find how to keep the air in your home clean of pollution. The Indoor Air Quality Information Clearinghouse is the expert on all forms of indoor air pollution. They have publications and information on second hand smoke, asbestos, carbon monoxide, air cleaners and more. Contact: Indoor Air Quality Information Clearinghouse, P.O. Box 37133, Washington, DC 20013-7133; 800-438-4318; www.epa.gov/iaq/iaqinfo.html.

1,000 To Get Help With Housing
Over 1,000 local nonprofit offices offer free money and/or help to improve your housing situation. Each local office will offer different programs. The following is a sample of programs that are offered by various offices around the country.

Get a $3 grant for every $1 you save to buy a house
Community Action Partnership http://www.managingmymoney.com/

$10,000 no interest, no payment, forgivable loans for home repairs
CFS Economic Opportunity Corporation http://www.advant.com/cefs/energy.htm

Buy a home with only $1,000
CEFS Economic Opportunity Corporation www.advant.com/cefs/homebuy.htm

$3,000 grant to fix your furnace
CEFS Economic Opportunity Corporation http://www.advant.com/cefs/ihwap.htm

$25,000 no interest, no payment, forgivable loan for home fix-up
CEFS Economic Opportunity Corporation http://www.advant.com/cefs/rehab.htm

$2,000 to pay heating bills
CEFS Economic Opportunity Corporation http://www.advant.com/cefs/liheap.htm

Eviction Prevention
TEAM, Inc Derby, CT http://www.teamcaa.org/housing.htm

$350 for an air conditioner
City of Des Moines, Iowa http://www.ci.des-moines.ia.us/departments/CD/Comm%20Serv/L-I%20Assist%20Programs.htm

$1,000 To Repair Furnace
City of Des Moines, Iowa http://www.ci.des-moines.ia.us/departments/CD/Comm%20Serv/L-I%20Assist%20Programs.htm

To find a community action agency near you go to: http://www.communityactionpartnership.com/about/links/map.asp or contact Community Action Partnership, 1100 17th St NW Suite 500, Washington, DC 20036; 202-265-7546; Fax: 202-265-8850; info@communityactionpartnership.com; www.communityactionpartnership.com.

75% Rebates On a New Heating System

The California Energy Commission offers residences up to 75% of the cost of new heating or air conditioning system if it meets their standards for "emerging renewable technologies," like solar heating and more. The *Emerging Renewables Program* may be able to help you afford a new system. This is for California only. Contact: Emerging Renewables Program, California Energy Commission, 1516 Ninth Street, MS-45; Sacramento, CA 95814; 800-555-7794, 916-654-4058; www.consumerenergycenter.org.

$7,000 For a Bathroom or Kitchen

Money is available to help those in rural areas install basic services to make their homes more inhabitable. Grant funds may be used to connect service lines to residence, pay utility hook-up fees, install plumbing and related fixtures, i.e. a bathroom sink, bathtub or shower, commode, kitchen sink, water heater, outside spigot, or bathroom if lacking. These grants are available to households who own or occupy the dwelling and are available in Arizona, California, New Mexico and Texas. This program is called *Individual Water and Waste Grants.* Contact: Rural Housing Service National Office, U.S. Department of Agriculture, Room 5037, South Building, 14th Street and Independence Avenue, SW, Washington, DC 20250; 202-720-4323; www.rurdev.usda.gov.

$$ To Fix Up Your Home

The Housing Preservation Grants Program provides funds to repair or rehabilitate individual housing owned or occupied by very low and low-income rural persons in towns of less than 20,000. Housing Preservation Grant assistance is available from grantees to assist very low and low-income homeowners to repair and rehabilitate their homes. Contact: Rural Housing Service National Office, U.S.Department of Agriculture, Room 5037, South Building, 14th Street and Independence Avenue, SW, Washington, DC 20250; 202-720-4323; www.rurdev.usda.gov.

Loans to Help Your Country Home After a Disaster

Disasters can strike at any time. The Farm Service Agency provides emergency loans to help recover from production and physical losses due to drought, flooding and other natural disasters. Emergency loan funds may be used to restore or replace essential property, pay all or part of production costs associated with the disaster year, pay essential family living expenses, refinance certain debts and more. Contact: USDA, 1400 Independence Avenue, SW, Washington DC 20250; 202-720-1632; www.fsa.usda.gov.

Money To Build Senior Housing

Section 202 Supportive Housing for the Elderly won't get you money directly but it can help you with your housing. The program's goal is to help nonprofit organizations develop supportive housing for the elderly. This means that if you are 62 or older with very low-income, you may qualify to live in one of these projects. These units must provide supportive services either on-site or provide access to off-site services. Contact: U.S. Department of Housing and Urban Development, 451 7th Street, Washington, DC 20410: 202-708-1112, Fax: 202-708-1455; www.hud.gov/offices/hsg/mfh/progdesc/eld202.cfm.

Help with Home Modifications

Do you have trouble getting around your house? Taking a shower? Cooking in the kitchen? There are many products available for this exact purpose and people who can help you determine your needs. The

National Resource Center on Supportive and Home Modification can help you learn more about all of the assistive products. They offer online courses for a small fee including: *Basics and Beyond, Funding Sources and Financing,* and *How to Get it Done.* You can also browse a listing of online publications, find a contractor in your area or get a home safety checklist. Contact: National Resource Center on Supportive and Home Modification, Andrus Gerontology, University of Southern California, 3715 McClintock Avenue, Los Angeles, CA 90089-0191; 213-740-1364, Fax: 213-740-7069; www.homemods.org.

$50,000 Grants for Disabled Veterans

Qualifying service-connected disabled veterans may receive grants for up to 50 percent of approved costs of building, buying or adapting existing homes or paying to reduce indebtedness on previously owned homes that are being adapted. In certain circumstances, the full grant amount may be applied toward remodeling costs. Contact: Veterans Benefit Administration, 810 Vermont Avenue, NW, Washington, DC 20420; 800-827-1000; www.va.gov.

$10,000 Make Changes to Your Home

The Veterans Administration offers a grant to qualifying disabled veterans. The grant may be used to help acquire a residence already adapted with special features or for making changes to an already owned home. Grants are for actual costs, up to $10,000. Contact: Veterans Benefit Administration, 810 Vermont Avenue, NW, Washington, DC 20420; 800-827-1000; www.va.gov.

Home Modification Tax Benefits

Many people can take advantage of income deductions on their federal tax returns. The costs of the modifications must be treated as a medical deduction when itemizing taxes. This means all modifications must be certified by a physician as being required for health reasons. Your state may have additional tax benefits for home modifications. Contact your state taxation department or the IRS at 800-829-1040 or www.irs.gov.

Medicaid Can Help with Home Modification

Home modifications and repairs improve your safety, improve daily activities and maintain the value of your home if you are a senior citizen. Medicare does not pay for home adaptations but does pay for some durable medical equipment. Medicaid may pay for home modification and medical equipment. Contact: Centers for Medicare & Medicaid Services, 7500 Security Boulevard, Baltimore, MD 21244-1850; 800-MEDICARE; www.medicare.gov.

Low Rent Apartment Search

You can search low rent apartment funded directly by the government which lowers the cost of rent for low-income elderly. You can search by city or county and even by the number of bedrooms. Check it out at www.hud.gov/apps/section8/index.cfm.

Help For Housing Options

The American Association of Homes and Services for the Aging offers tips to help you find home and community based services, assisted living facilities, nursing homes and continuing care retirement communities. You can search their web site to find services by state or zip code. Contact: American

Association of Homes and Services for Aging, 2519 Connecticut Avenue, NW, Washington, DC 20008; 202-783-2242, Fax: 202-783-2255; www2.aahsa.org.

$144 to Keep You Connected

Link-Up America and Lifeline are programs designed to help low-income people afford basic telephone service. Local phone companies are required to provide both services. You must meet income requirements set by your state. Link-up offers a 50% discount, up to $30, to install a phone. You can also defer the rest of the hook-up fee for up to one year with no interest charges. Lifeline offers monthly discounts for local phone charges. If your state offers a matching program, you may receive as much as $12 per month. Contact your local telephone company. If you have trouble applying, contact your state Public Service or Public Utilities Commission by looking in the blue pages of your phone book.

Elder Housing Information

The Administration on Aging helps seniors with a variety of services and opportunities for older Americans. Their Housing section offers information including: assistive technology, house remodeling, housing services, independent living and nursing facilities. If you have question, call the Administration on Aging, Washington, DC 20201; 202-619-0724; www.aoa.gov/eldfam/Housing/Housing.asp.

Elder Cottages

Elder Cottage Housing Opportunities (ECHO), also called "granny flats", may be a wonderful solution for you if you want to be independent but want or need to be closer to family. The Elder Cottage concept enables seniors who are no longer able to maintain a home alone to continue living independently with the family nearby. An ECHO unit is a separate, small manufactured home which is installed at a single family home, usually the senior's child. When the unit is no longer needed is can be removed. Zoning codes may present a problem but you may be able to contact your local zoning commission to get special permission.

Shared Housing

Many seniors are looking for ways to stay in their homes with the high cost of housing. Shared housing may be a viable and affordable alternative. In homesharing, everyone is allowed to use the common areas of the house while maintaining a personal living space. AARP offers a checklist to see if homesharing may be for you. If you decide you want to pursue homesharing, the National Shared Housing Resource Center can provide their members with technical assistance, problem solving strategies, a directory and more for a $20/year membership fee. Contact: AARP, 601 E Street NW, Washington, DC 20049; 888-OUR-AARP; www.aarp.org or National Shared Housing Resource Center, 364 South Railroad Avenue, San Mateo, CA 94401; www.nationalsharedhousing.org.

Certified Aging-in-Place Specialist

A number of national organizations have collaborated to develop the Certified Aging-in-Place Specialist Program (CAPS). The program is designed to help those homeowners that want to make their house a home for a lifetime. CAPS design and build barrier free living environments in conjunction with local building codes. You can search the database for a certified contractor in your area. Contact National

Association of Home Builders, 1201 15th Street, NW, Washington, DC 20005; 202-266-8200, 800-368-5242, Fax: 202-266-8400; www.nahb.org/generic.aspx?sectionID=126&genericContentID=8484.

Rate Your Home

Rate your home for safety, especially designed with seniors in mind. They offer a checklist for bathrooms, kitchens, lighting, floors, storage and safety. You can use the online checklist at www.aarp.org/families/home_design/rate_home/.

Grants to Get Rid of Lead Paint

If you are living in a house or apartment that was built before 1978, you or even your landlord, may be eligible for grant money and other assistance to make sure that you do not suffer the effects of lead poisoning from lead-based paint. Chips or dust from this type of paint can be highly dangerous to humans, especially your grandchildren. The U.S. Department of Housing and Urban Development operates the Lead-Based Paint Hazard Control Program providing grants to state and local departments of housing to help homeowners and apartment owners eliminate the problems associated with lead paint. Contact your state or local department of housing to see if you qualify for free inspections, free guides or even free lead paint removal. To obtain information about the grant program contact, Office of Healthy Homes and Lead Hazard Control, 451 7th Street S.W., Washington, DC 20410; 202-708-1112; www.hud.gov/offices/lead/lhc/index.cfm.

Free Information About Lead in Your Home

Lead is a highly toxic metal that was used in many products that can be found around homes in the U.S. Lead poisoning can lead to health related problems in all humans but especially in children. The EPA works to minimize the amount of lead exposure to protect your family. The Agency's Lead Awareness Program provides information about lead, lead hazards and provides steps to take to protect your home and family. Contact: The National Lead Information Center, 422 South Clinton Avenue, Rochester, NY 14620; 800-424-LEAD; www.epa.gov/lead/nlic.htm.

Find a Nursing Home to Meet Your Needs

Nursing Home Compare provides detailed information about the past performance of every Medicare and Medicaid certified nursing home in the country. Their online data base helps you search by state, city or nursing home name. Go to the Medicare web site and click on "Compare Nursing Homes in Your Area". The web site only provides information for Medicare and Medicaid homes. For information on other nursing homes, contact your state ESRD State Survey Agency. You can find links to your state organization on the Nursing Home Compare website. Contact Centers for Medicare & Medicaid Services, 7500 Security Boulevard, Baltimore, MD 21244-1850; 1-800-MEDICARE; www.medicare.gov.

NeighborWorks America

Created by Congress, NeighborWorks America in conjunction with local NeighborWorks organizations and Neighborhood Housing Services helps to build healthier communities throughout the country. Aging in Place is one program they address by helping seniors stay in their homes or communities as they age. They offer publications on many housing issues including Aging in Place. To find a local NeighborWorks program they offer an online NeighborWorks Lookup which lists member organizations by state. Contact: NeighborWorks America, 1325 G Street, NW, Suite 800, Washington, DC 20005-3100; 202-220-2300, Fax: 202-376-2600; www.nw.org.

Home Loan Guaranty for Veterans

There are millions of veteran's and service personnel eligible for VA home financing. Even though many veterans have already used their loan benefits, it may be possible for them to buy another home with VA financing using remaining or restored loan entitlement. VA loans often are made without any downpayment and frequently offer lower interest rates than ordinarily available through conventional loans. Aside from the veteran's certificate of eligibility and the VA-assigned appraisal, the application process is about the same as any other loan. VA guaranteed loans are made by private lenders, such as banks, savings & loans or mortgage companies. The guaranty means the lender is protected if you or a later owner fails to repay the loan.

There are many benefits to the VA home loans program including:

- Equal opportunity
- No downpayment (unless required by lender or the purchase price is more than the reasonable value of the property)
- Buyer informed of reasonable value
- Negotiable interest rate
- Ability to finance the VA funding fee(plus reduced funding fees with downpayment of at least 5% and exemption for veterans receiving VA compensation)
- No mortgage insurance premiums
- An assumable mortgage
- Right to repay without penalty
- For homes inspected by VA during construction, a warranty from builder and assistance from VA to obtain cooperation of builder
- VA assistance to veteran borrowers in default to temporary financial difficulty

You can find out more about the VA home loan program by checking out the web site at www.homeloans.va.gov. For Loan Eligibility contact one of the following Centers.

- If you live in one of the following states: Alabama, Connecticut, District of Columbia, Delaware, Florida, Georgia, Indiana, Kentucky, Maine, Maryland, Massachusetts, Michigan, Mississippi, New Hampshire, New Jersey, New York, North Carolina, Ohio, Pennsylvania, Puerto Rico, Rhode Island, South Carolina, Tennessee, Vermont, Virginia or West Virginia, send your determination of Eligibility VA Form 26-1880 www.va.gov/vaforms/, along with proof of military service to: Winston-Salem Eligibility Center, P.O. Box 20729, Winston-Salem, NC 27120;888-244-6711; Email: NCELIGIB@vba.va.gov. For overnight delivery- VA Loan Eligibility Center, 251 N. Main Street, Winston-Salem, NC 27155.

- If you live in one of the following states: Alaska, Arizona, Arkansas, California, Colorado, Hawaii, Idaho, Illinois, Iowa, Kansas, Louisiana, Minnesota, Missouri, Montana, Nebraska, Nevada, New Mexico, North Dakota, Oklahoma, Oregon, South Dakota, Texas, Utah, Washington, Wisconsin or Wyoming, send your determination of Eligibility VA Form 26-1880 www.va.gov/vaforms/, along with proof of military service to: Los Angeles Eligibility Center, P.O. Box 240097, Los Angeles, CA 90024; 888-487-1970; Email: vavbalan/lgyeli@vba.va.gov; www.vahomes.org/la/home.htm.

– If you live outside of the United States, you may use either Eligibility Center.

Homeless Vets

On any given day, there are as many as 200,000 veterans that are homeless and as many as 400,000 experience homelessness at some point during the year. The VA offers a variety of special programs specifically for homeless veterans, both men and women. The VA is the only Federal agency that provides hands-on assistance directly to homeless persons. Their program includes:

- outreach to those veterans living on the streets and in shelters that may not seek assistance
- clinical assessment and referral to medical treatment centers for physical and psychiatric disorders
- long-term sheltered transitional assistance
- employment assistance
- supported permanent housing

For information on the many programs and initiatives offered by the VA, contact: Department of Veteran Affairs, 810 Vermont Avenue NW, Washington, DC 20420; 800-827-1000; www1.va.gov/homeless.

Online Publications to Help With Home Modification and Safety

Here is a listing of online publications that can help you decide if you need home modifications and if you do, what kind of home modifications would be best for you. Also listed, are several publications on general safety.

- *Caregiver Adaptations to Reduce Environmental Stress: The Role of Home Modifications*: Help for caregivers that provide services to older adults with at least one limitation of activity. www.homemods.org/folders/cares-project/cares_testimony.shtml

- *C.A.R.E.S. Brochure*: This brochure suggests strategies for minimizing the physical burden associated with caregiving and maximizing the care recipients' independence. www.homemods.org/folders/cares-project/ecs1_resources.pdf

- *C.A.R.E.S. Fact Sheet*: The Center fact sheet provides information on home modifications and assistive devices. The Fact Sheet also is available in Armenian, Chinese, Korean, Spanish and Vietnamese. www.homemods.org/folders/cares-project/cares_factsheets/ecs_cg_fact_sheet.pdf

- *A Balancing Act: Simple Steps to Help Seniors See the Need for Home Modifications*: The article gives helpful hints to caregivers and family members on how to help loved ones recognize the need for home modifications. www.homemods.org/folders/cares-project/balancing_act.htm

- *Bathroom Safety Design*: Helpful suggestions to help prevent falls and accidents in the bathroom. www.homemods.org/folders/ cares-project/Bathroom%20Safety%20Design.pdf

- *Caregivers' Perceptions of the Effectiveness of Home Modifications for Community Living Adults with Dementia*: This study looked at the effectiveness of various home modifications to increase the safety or autonomy of persons with dementia. www.homemods.org/folders/cares-project/calkins.html

- *Eldercare Locator*: A fact sheet listing the services and resources provided by the U.S. Administration on Aging. www.homemods.org/folders/cares-project/aoa_eldercare_fs.pdf

- *Lighting the Way: A Key to Independence*: This is a series of booklets on lighting and how it can affect older adults. www.lrc.rpi.edu/programs/lightHealth/AARP/healthcare/lightingOlderAdults/index.asp

- *Practical Skills Training for Family Caregivers*: This overview provides strategies and techniques to caregivers to help the elderly or chronically ill person at home. www.homemods.org/folders/ cares-project/op_2003_skills_training.pdf

- *Solutions for Living with Alzheimer's: The Caregiver's Guide to Home Modification*: This article provides practical solutions on modifying your home to care for persons with Alzheimer's. www.homemods.org/folders/cares-project/Solutions%20for%20Living%20with%20Alzheimer.pdf

- *Keep Active, Safe at Any Age*: This brochure provides older Americans important tips on remaining safe while enjoying the benefits of exercise. www.cpsc.gov/cpscpub/pubs/grand/aging/703.html

- *Grandparents! Prevent Your Grandchildren from Being Poisoned: Safety Alert!*: Children may look at your bottle of medication as candy. Don't let them become poisoned from the medications that keep you healthy. This article will provide suggestions on how to keep your grandchildren safe. www.cpsc.gov/cpscpub/pubs/5041.html

- *Safety for Older Consumers: Home Safety Checklist*: The booklet offers a home safety checklist geared towards older consumers. www.cpsc.gov/cpscpub/pubs/701.html

- *Fire Safety Checklist for Older Consumer*: Make sure your home is safe with this fire safety checklist. www.cpsc.gov/cpscpub/pubs/702.pdf

- *A Grandparents' Guide For Family Nurturing & Safety*: Practical advice to grandparents for when their grandchildren are visiting including a grandchild safety checklist. www.cpsc.gov/cpscpub/pubs/grand/704.html

- *Older Consumer Safety Checklist*: Falls and fires are two leading causes of unintentional injuries and deaths among adults 65 and older. This publication offers tips on staying safe. www.cpsc.gov/cpscpub/pubs/705.pdf

- *Older Consumer Safety Test*: Take this short quiz to test your knowledge on issues involving fire safety, good health, vision, falls and other information. www.cpsc.gov/cpscpub/pubs/ocquiz/start.html

Living Options Tool

CarePlanner is a free planner to help you and your family choose between different living options. All you have to do is answer some questions about your current situation and you will receive feedback concerning your potential living options. This program is funded by the Centers for Medicare & Medicaid Services. Contact: Clinical Tools, Inc., 431 West Franklin Street, Suite 24, Chapel Hill, NC 27516; 919-960-8118, Fax: 919-960-7745; www.careplanner.org.

Long Term Care Ombudsman
An Ombudsman is an advocate for residents of long term care facilities. They can also provide information on how to find a facility and how to receive quality care. Every state is required to have an Ombudsman Program. To find your state representative go to the website below. Contact: Ombudsman Resource Center, 1828 L Street, NW, Suite 801, Washington, DC 20036; 202-332-2275, Fax: 202-332-2949; www.ltcombudsman.org/.

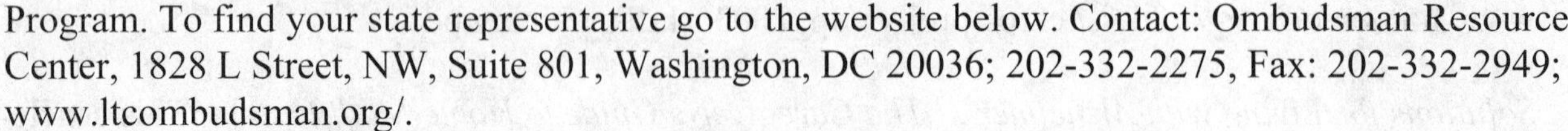

Long Term Care Information and Handling Complaints
If you or someone you love needs long term care you may need some help. Medicare offers articles and advice on choosing, paying for and living in nursing homes or other long term care facility. Check out their web site for a wealth of information, including *Guide to Choosing a Nursing Home* and *Nursing Home Checklist* Contact: Centers for Medicare & Medicaid Services, 7500 Security Boulevard, Baltimore, MD 21244-1850; 1-800-MEDICARE; www.medicare.gov/LongTermCare/Static/Home.asp.

More Information on Nursing Homes
The AARP offers seniors many resources and the subject of nursing homes is no exception. They have information on starting a nursing home search, a "what to look for" checklist, and what to do if a problem occurs. Contact: AARP, 601 E Street NW, Washington, DC 20049; 888-OUR-AARP; www.aarp.org.

$100,000 To Help Buy A Mobile Home and A Mobile Home Lot
Sometimes banks charge a very high interest for a manufactured home and lot, but the U.S. Department of Housing and Urban Development (HUD) offers a loan guarantee program to make it more affordable. This program insures mortgage loans made by private lenders to buyers of manufactured homes and the lots on which to place them. Title I insurance may be used for loans of up to $64,800 for a manufactured home and lot and $16,200 for a lot only. The lot must be appraised by a HUD-approved lender. The dollar limits for combination and lot loans may be increased up to 85 percent in designated high-cost areas. The maximum loan term is 20 years for a single-module home and lot, 25 years for a multiple module home and lot, and 15 years for a lot only. 1,500 homes used this program last year. The budget for this program is $52,000,000. (14.162 Mortgage Insurance-combination and Manufactured Home Lot Loans Title I). For more information contact your local HUD office or check out the program online at www.hud.gov/offices/hsg/sfh/title/ti_home.cfm; or call HUD Customer Service at 800-767-7468 for brochure.

$100,000 Direct Loans To Buy or Fix Up Homes In The Country
Want to buy a home in the country, but don't think you can afford it? Think again. Rural Housing Service provides financing for individuals and families who cannot obtain credit from other sources to purchase homes in rural areas. Applications are received at USDA offices. Funds may be used to purchase suitable existing homes, new site build homes, approved modular units, and new manufactured units from an approved dealer/contractor. Funds may also be used to repair or remodel homes, or to

make the home accessible and usable for persons who are developmentally disabled. Loans may be made for up to 100% of the appraised value of the site and the home. Maximum repayment period is 33 years, or under certain conditions, 38 years. Downpayment is not required if your net assets do not exceed $7,500. Certain fees must be paid and you cannot currently own a home. Applicants for direct loans from RHS must have very low or low incomes. Very low income is defined as below 50 percent of the area median income (AMI); low income is between 50 and 80 percent of AMI; moderate income is 80 to 100 percent of AMI. Form required: *Uniform Residential Loan Application*. Over 17,000 homes were purchased through this program. The budget for the program is $1,076,998,750. (Section 502 Direct Loan Program- 10.410 Very Low to Moderate Income Housing Loans). For more information contact your state, area or local Rural Development office or contact Single Family Housing, Direct Loan Division, U.S. Department of Agriculture, Washington, DC 20250; 202-720-1474; www.rurdev.usda.gov.

Help Finding Local Money

The following organizations can help you find local nonprofit organizations that offer financial assistance with housing in your area. These organizations do not provide money to home owners. What they can do is direct you to organizations in your area that may have funds or know where funds can be found for housing issues.

- ***National Association of Housing and Redevelopment Officials***, 630 Eye St., NW, Washington, DC 20001; 202-289-3500, 877-866-2476, Fax: 202-289-8181; www.nahro.org.
- ***Information Center***, Office of Community Planning and Development, P.O. Box 7189, Gaithersburg, MD 20898; 800-998-9999; Fax: 301-519-5027; www.comcon.org.
- ***Association of Community Organizations for Reform Now (ACORN),*** 88 3rd Avenue, Brooklyn, NY 11217, 1-877-55ACORN; Fax: 718-246-7939; www.acorn.org.
- ***The National Community Action Foundation***, 810 First St., Suite 530, Washington, DC 20002; 202-842-2092; Fax: 202-842-2095: www.ncaf.org/linkcaas.htm.
- ***All your elected representatives***. Your U.S. Congressman and Senator, your State Representative or Senator, your mayor or city councilman. Most of these people have a staff member whose job it is to assist the people they represent, that is, their constituents with issues such as housing. This person should know the local community and how you can best go about finding the services you need. If you cannot find their phone number, your local library can help.
- ***Your local library***. See your reference librarian.

Below is a list of programs available from local organizations that we were able to identify in a recent research project we did on the city of Riverdale, California. This serves as an example of the kinds of programs that can be available in your local area:

1. No-Cost Weatherization for Riverside County
2. Utility Assistance Helps Riverside County Pay the Bills
3. FREE Technical Assistance & Fair Housing Services
4. FREE Legal Assistance on Housing Issues
5. One-Time Move-In and Other Assistance for Southern California
6. More Temporary Assistance for Those in Need
7. Build Your Home & Save Money on the Down Payment!

8. Training, Technical Assistance & Information for Housing Professionals
9. Low-Cost Housing for Families and Seniors throughout California
10. FREE for Seniors: Moving Services Cover Everything!
11. Shared Housing for Qualified People
12. Complimentary Email Updates of Homes For-Sale
13. $25,000 Grants for Community Redevelopment Projects
14. Consulting & Technical Assistance Services for Developers
15. Seniors Get $300 Home Repairs and Loans for Home Rehab
16. Home Improvement Loans for Eastern LA County
17. Down Payment and Other Help for SoCal Homebuyers
18. More Down Payment Options for Eligible Buyers
19. First Mortgages for Homebuyers who Need Extra Help
20. Services to Help You Purchase the Home of Your Dreams
21. Sweat Equity Gets You a New Home
22. More Housing for Persons with AIDS
23. No-Cost Weatherization Services in Southern California
24. Study Program for Community Developers
25. Multi-Family Housing: Financing Helps Make it Affordable!
26. $5.0 Million Financing for Affordable Housing
27. Get Paid to Build an Energy-efficient Home
28. FREE Home Improvements Plus Lower Utility Bills
29. New Windows Pay Off
30. Money Back When You Shop for Your Home!
31. Utility Bills Cut by 20% for Qualified Customers
32. Golden Opportunity to Find a HUD Home!
33. Grants & Loans for Disabled Homebuyers
34. $4,500 Down Payment Assistance for First-Time Homebuyers
35. Emergency Funds Help Pay Winter Energy Bills
36. FREE Energy Analysis Helps Homebuyers Save Money!
37. No Money Down, 100% Financed Home Purchases
38. Flexible Mortgage Program for Hard-to-Qualify Borrowers
39. High Quality Housing AND Technical Assistance for Homebuyers and Renters
40. Affordable Homes for Rent in Southern California
41. Down Payment Rebates up to $5,000
42. Assistance for Tenants and Developers of HUD Housing
43. Mortgage Assistance and Other Services Help Make Homeownership Affordable
44. Loans and Technical Assistance to Help Keep Housing Affordable
45. 90% Financing to Buy, Build or Rehab Multi-Family Housing
46. $1.0 Million to Invest in an Apartment Building
47. Money to Buy, Build or Save Affordable Housing
48. Bank Foundation Provides Affordable Housing Grants to Developers
49. Affordable Housing Investment Opportunity
50. Real Estate Agents Specializing in HUD Housing and Other Government Programs
51. Assistance for Organizations Who Own Farm Worker Housing
52. Sweat Equity for Homes Built in the Country
53. Up to $1.5 Million Loan Fund for Local Nonprofit Community Developers and Municipalities

54. Up to $450,000 Grant Money for Members to Develop Housing
55. $200,000 Available to Economic Developers for Housing Projects
56. Up to $15,000 in Down Payment and/or Closing Costs!
57. Grants Up to $15,000 for Homeownership Opportunities
58. Low-Cost Funding for Community Developers
59. Over $26.5 Million for Nonprofits to Develop Housing
60. FREE Housing Information from Legal Experts
61. More Housing Help for All of California
62. Homebuyers Get 5% of Home Price for Down Payment Costs
63. Long-Term Real Estate Financing
64. Up to $1.0 Million Loans with Interest-Only Payments!
65. $100,000 Pre-Development Loans for Housing Projects
66. $2.3 Million Loans for Housing Development
67. Technical Assistance Helps Housing Projects Succeed
68. Help to Sell Your Land
69. $19.0 Million Available for Working Families to Buy a Home
70. $10.0 Million to Develop Housing in California
71. Up to $15.0 Million for Housing Developers in California
72. Tax Reductions for Affordable Housing Developers
73. Affordable and Special Needs Housing Assistance for Tenants and Developers
74. Loans for First-Time Homebuyers in California
75. Money to Rehabilitate Your California Home!
76. Find a Homebuilder in Your Area
77. Help for Those Looking to Buy a New Home
78. Construction Assistance for Residential Developments
79. Financing Services Helps Developers Get Funding for Rental Housing
80. Make Money; Sell Land for Affordable Housing Development
81. Website Offers Homeownership Information
82. $5,000 Grants for Projects that Benefit the Community
83. FREE Home Repairs for the Elderly & Disabled in Riverside
84. Newly Renovated Housing for Riverside Tenants
85. Information & Referral for Disabled Housing Needs

Reverse Mortgages Give You Cash Now

If you are 62 years old or older and you own your own home, you may want to use a reverse mortgage to get some cash. In the past, the only ways to get cash out of your home was to sell your home or borrow against it. Now, reverse mortgages are available to help seniors tap into the wealth that has built up in their homes. Reverse mortgages don't require you to move or take on extra debt. Reverse Mortgages work like traditional mortgages but in reverse. Instead of making a house payment each month, you receive a payment from your lender. Depending on the type of Reverse Mortgage and the lender, you can take the money in a lump sum, in monthly advances, through line-of-credit, or a combination of the three. Most Reverse Mortgage do not require any repayment of principal, interest or servicing fees, as long as you live in your home. These loans are called rising-debt loans for that reason. The money you receive

usually may be used for any reason. Homeowners must stay current on property taxes, home repairs, and homeowners insurance. Loans are typically repaid when you sell your home or upon your death. The loan can be paid off from the proceeds of the sale of the house or your heirs may keep the house if the loan balance can be paid off using other assets. The amount due will be the lesser of your loan balance or the market value of your property. To qualify for Reverse Mortgages, you must be at least 62 years old and have paid for most of your home mortgage. Income is generally not a factor. The amount you may borrow depends on your age, equity in your home, value of your home and the interest rate.

There are generally three types of Reverse Mortgages:

- Home Equity Conversion Mortgage (HECM)-this is a federally funded program administered by HUD. If you choose HECM, you must agree to free mortgage counseling from an independent government-approved "housing agency".
- Single-Purpose Reverse Mortgage-usually offered by state or local government agencies for a specific reason.
- Proprietary Reverse Mortgage-offered by banks, mortgage companies and other private lenders and backed by the companies that develop them.

Because of the costs and complexity of a Reverse Mortgage, other options should be considered before you obtain a loan. Like any loan, there are fees and pros and cons depending on your individual situation. It is important to learn as much as you can about any program before you sign up. If you want to learn about Reverse Mortgage, contact one of the agencies listed below or check out their web site for a wealth of Reverse Mortgage information. Remember, if you change your mind there is a Federal law to help you. The Federal law provides you a three-day "right of rescission," option to cancel the contract without penalty within three business days (including Saturdays).

- Federal Trade Commission, 600 Pennsylvania Avenue, NW, Washington, DC 20580; 877-FTC-HELP; www.ftc.gov.
- U.S. Department of Housing and Urban Development, 451 7th Street, SW, Washington, DC 20410; 888-466-3487; www.hud.gov/offices/hsg/sfh/hecm/rmtopten.cfm.
- The National Center for Home Equity Conversion, 360 N Robert Street, #403, St. Paul, MN 55101; 651-222-6
- AARP, 601 E Street, NW, Washington, DC 20049; 800-424-3410; www.aarp.org/revmort.
- Fannie Mae, 3900 Wisconsin Avenue, NW, Washington, DC 20016-2892; 202-752-7000; www.fanniemae.com/homebuyers/findamortgage/reverse/index.jhtml.

Armed Forces Retirement Home

The Armed Forces Retirement Home is available for those who meet the service and age requirements of the AFRH. Veterans who have served for more than twenty years and are over the age of sixty, veterans who are unable to provide for themselves due to injuries sustained during service, veterans who are unable to provide for themselves due to injury, disease, or other problem and who served in a war or are earning hostile fire pay, and female veterans who served before the year 1948 are eligible for residence. For more information on the AFRH and how to apply or how to visit one of the two campuses, contact 3700 N. Capitol Street, Washington, DC 20011-8400; 800-422-9988; Fax: 202-730-3492; or 1800 Gulf Beach Drive, Gulfport, MS 39507; 800-332-3527; http://www.afrh.gov/DWP/afrh/afrhhome.htm.

Housing in the Country

The U.S. Rural Housing Service's mission is to improve the quality of life in rural areas. The Rural Housing Service provides loans and grants for housing and community facilities. They offer funding for single family homes, apartments for low-income persons or the elderly and more. For housing information if you live in a rural area, contact your state or national office:

Rural Housing Service National Office
U.S. Department of Agriculture
Room 5037, South Building
14th Street and Independence Avenue, SW
Washington, DC 20250
202-720-4323
www.rurdev.usda.gov/rhs

Alabama
USDA Rural Development Office
Suite 601, Sterling Centre
4121 Carmichael Road
Montgomery, AL 36106-3683
334-279-3400
Fax: 334-279-3403
www.rurdev.usda.gov/al/

Alaska
USDA Rural Development Office
800 W. Evergreen, Suite 201
Palmer, AK 99645
907-761-7705
Fax: 907-761-7783
www.rurdev.usda.gov/ak/

Arizona
USDA Rural Development Office
230 North 1st Avenue
Suite 206
Phoenix, AZ 85003
602-280-8701
Fax: 602-280-8708
www.rurdev.usda.gov/az/

Arkansas
USDA Rural Development Office
700 West Capitol, Room 3416
Little rock, AR 72201-3225
501-301-3200
Fax: 501-301-3278
www.rurdev.usda.gov/ar/

California
USDA Rural Development Office
430 G Street
Agency 4169
Davis, CA 95616-4169
530-792-5800
Fax: 530-792-5848
www.rurdev.usda.gov/ca/

Colorado
USDA Rural Development Office
655 Parfet Street
Room E-100
Lakewood, CO 80215
720-544-2903
Fax: 720-544-2981
www.rurdev.usda.gov/co/

Connecticut
USDA Rural Development Office
451 West Street, Suite 2
Amherst, MA 01002-2999
413-253-4333
Fax: 413-253-4347
www.rurdev.usda.gov/ma/

Delaware
USDA Rural Development Office
1221 College Park Drive
Suite 200
Dover, DE 19904
302-857-3580
Fax: 302-857-3640
www.rurdev.usda.gov/de/

Florida
USDA Rural Development Office
4440 N.W. 25th Place
Gainesville, FL 32606
352-338-3402
Fax: 352-338-3405
www.rurdev.usda.gov/fl/

Georgia
USDA Rural Development Office
Stephens Federal Building
355 East Hancock Avenue
Athens, GA 30601-2768
706-546-2162
Fax: 706-546-2152
www.rurdev.usda.gov/ga/

Hawaii
USDA Rural Development Office
Federal Building, Room 311
154 Waianuenue Avenue
Hilo, HI 96720
808-933-8380
Fax: 808-933-8327
www.rurdev.usda.gov/hi/

Idaho
USDA Rural Development Office
9173 West Barnes Drive, Suite A1
Boise, ID 83709
208-378-5600
Fax: 208-378-5643
www.rurdev.usda.gov/id/

Illinois
USDA Rural Development Office
2118 West Park Court, Suite A
Champaign, IL 61821
217-403-6202
Fax: 217-403-6243
www.rurdev.usda.gov/il/

Indiana
USDA Rural Development Office
5975 Lakeside Boulevard
Indianapolis, IN 46278-1996
317-290-3100
Fax: 317-290-3095
www.rurdev.usda.gov/in/

Iowa
USDA Rural Development Office
210 Walnut Street, Room 873
Des Moines, IA 50309-2196
515-284-4663
Fax: 515-284-4821
www.rurdev.usda.gov/ia/

Kansas
USDA Rural Development Office
1303 SW First American Place
Suite 100
Topeka, KS 66604
785-271-2700
www.rurdev.usda.gov/ks/

Kentucky
USDA Rural Development Office
771 Corporate Drive, Suite 200
Lexington, KY 40503-5477
859-224-7300
Fax: 859-224-7340
www.rurdev.usda.gov/ky/

Louisiana
USDA Rural Development Office
3727 Government Street
Alexandria, LA 71302
318-473-7921
Fax: 318-473-7661
www.rurdev.usda.gov/la/

Maine
USDA Rural Development Office
967 Illinois Avenue, Suite 4
P.O. Box 405
Bangor, ME 04402-0405
207-990-9160
www.rurdev.usda.gov/me/

Maryland
USDA Rural Development Office
1221 College Park Drive, Suite 200
Dover, DE 19904
302-857-3580
Fax: 302-857-3640
www.rurdev.usda.gov/md/

Massachusetts
USDA Rural Development Office
451 West Street, Suite 2
Amherst, MA 01002-2999
413-253-4302
Fax: 413-253-4347
www.rurdev.usda.gov/ma/

Michigan
USDA Rural Development Office
3001 Coolidge, Suite 200
East Lansing, MI 48823
517-324-5190
800-944-8119
www.rurdev.usda.gov/mi/

Minnesota
USDA Rural Development Office
410 Farm Credit Service Building
375 Jackson Street

St. Paul, MN 55101-1853
651-602-7800
Fax: 651-602-7824
www.rurdev.usda.gov/mn/

Mississippi
USDA Rural Development Office
100 West Capitol Street
Suite 831, Federal Building
Jackson, MS 39269
601-965-4316
Fax: 601-965-4088
www.rurdev.usda.gov/ms/

Missouri
USDA Rural Development Office
601 Business Loop 70 West
Parkade Center, Suite 235
Columbia, MO 65203
573-876-0976
Fax: 573-876-0977
www.rurdev.usda.gov/mo/

Montana
USDA Rural Development Office
P.O. Box 850
Bozeman, MT 59771
406-585-2580
Fax: 406-585-2565
www.rurdev.usda.gov/mt/

Nebraska
USDA Rural Development Office
100 Centennial Mall North
Room 152, Federal Building
Lincoln, NE 68508
402-437-5551
Fax: 402-437-5408
www.rurdev.usda.gov/ne/

Nevada
USDA Rural Development Office
1390 S. Curry Street
Carson City, NV 89703
775-887-1222
Fax: 775-885-0841
www.rurdev.usda.gov/nv/

New Hampshire
USDA Rural Development Office
City Center 3rd Floor
89 Main Street
Montprlier, VT 05602
802-828-6080
Fax: 802-828-6018
www.rurdev.usda.gov/vt/

New Jersey
USDA Rural Development Office
5th Floor North, Suite 500
8000 Midlantic Drive
Mt. Laurel, NJ 08054
856-87-7700
Fax: 856-87-7783
www.rurdev.usda.gov/nj/

New Mexico
USDA Rural Development Office
6200 Jefferson NE
Albuquerque, NM 87109
505-761-4950
www.rurdev.usda.gov/nm/

New York
USDA Rural Development Office
441 South Salina Street, Suite 357
Syracuse, NY 13202
315-477-6400
Fax: 315-477-6438
www.rurdev.usda.gov/ny/

North Carolina
USDA Rural Development Office
4405 Bland Road
Raleigh, NC 27609
919-873-2000
Fax: 919-873-2075
www.rurdev.usda.gov/nc/

North Dakota
USDA Rural Development Office
Federal Building, Room 208
220 East Rosser Ave.
P.O. Box 1737
Bismarck, ND 58502
701-530-2037
Fax: 701-530-2108
www.rurdev.usda.gov/nd/

Ohio
USDA Rural Development Office
Federal Building, Room 507
200 North High Street
Columbus, OH 43215
614-255-2500
www.rurdev.usda.gov/oh/

Oklahoma
USDA Rural Development Office
100 USDA, Suite 108
Stillwater, OK 74074
405-742-1000

Fax: 405-742-1005
www.rurdev.usda.gov/ok/

Oregon
USDA Rural Development Office
101 SW Main, Suite 1410
Portland, OR 97204-3222
503-414-3300
Fax: 503-414-3392
www.rurdev.usda.gov/or/

Pennsylvania
USDA Rural Development Office
One Credit Union Place, Suite 330
Harrisburg, PA 17110-2996
717-237-2299
Fax: 717-237-2191
www.rurdev.usda.gov/pa/

Puerto Rico
USDA Rural Development Office
654 Munoz Rivera Avenue, Suite 601
San Juan, PR 00918
787-766-5095
Fax: 787-766-5844
www.rurdev.usda.gov/pr/

Rhode Island
USDA Rural Development Office
451 West Street, Suite 2
Amherst, MA 01002-2999
413-253-4302
Fax: 413-253-4347
www.rurdev.usda.gov/ma/

South Carolina
USDA Rural Development Office
Strom Thurmond Federal Building
1835 Assembly Street, Room 1007
Columbia, SC 29201
803-765-5163
Fax: 803-765-5633
www.rurdev.usda.gov/sc/

South Dakota
USDA Rural Development Office
200 4th Street, SW
Federal Building, Room 210
Huron, SD 57350
605-352-1100
Fax: 605-352-1146
www.rurdev.usda.gov/sd/

Tennessee
USDA Rural Development Office
3322 West End Avenue, Suite 300
Nashville, TN37203
615-783-1300
800-342-3149
Fax: 615-783-1301
www.rurdev.usda.gov/tn/

Texas
USDA Rural Development Office
101 South Main Street, Suite 102
Temple, TX 76501
254-742-9700
Fax: 254-742-9709
www.rurdev.usda.gov/tx/

Utah
USDA Rural Development Office
125 South State Street, Room 4311
Wallace F. Bennett Federal Building
Salt Lake City, UT 84138
801-524-4320
Fax: 801-524-4406
www.rurdev.usda.gov/ut/

Vermont
USDA Rural Development Office
City Center 3rd Floor
89 Main Street
Montpelier, VT 05602
802-828-6080
Fax: 802-828-6018
www.rurdev.usda.gov/vt/

Virginia
USDA Rural Development Office
Culpepper Building, Suite 238
1606 Santa Rosa Road
Richmond, VA 23229
804-287-1553
Fax: 804-287-1718
www.rurdev.usda.gov/va/

Washington
USDA Rural Development Office
1835 Black Lake Boulevard, SW, Suite B
Olympia, WA 98501-5715
360-704-7740
Fax: 360-704-7742
www.rurdev.usda.gov/wa/

West Virginia
USDA Rural Development Office
75 High Street, Suite 320
Morgantown, WV 26505
304-284-4860

Fax: 304-284-4893
www.rurdev.usda.gov/wv/

Wisconsin
USDA Rural Development Office
4949 Kirschling Court
Stevens Point, WI 54481
715-345-7615
Fax: 715-345-7669
www.rurdev.usda.gov/wi/

Wyoming
USDA Rural Development Office
100 E. B Street, Room 1005
Casper, WY 82601
Mailing address:
P.O. Box 11005
Casper, WY 82602-5006
307-233-6700
Fax: 307-233-6727
www.rurdev.usda.gov/wy/

Don't Pay Your Property Tax

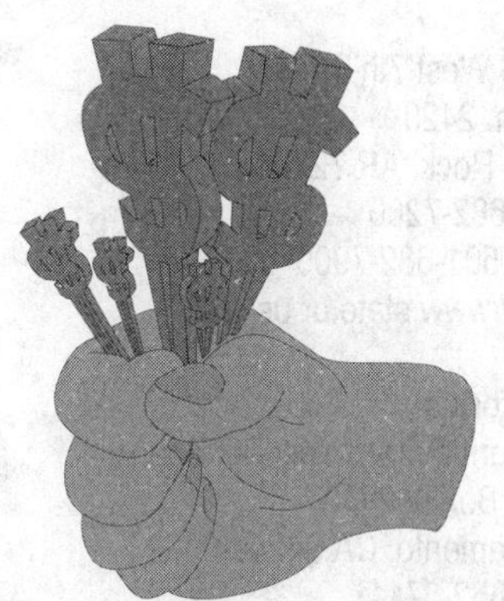

Or pay a reduced amount. Almost all states have some type of property or homestead tax exemption for the elderly and disabled, and often for those with low incomes or veterans. For example, the program in Massachusetts offers a tax credit of $850 for senior homeowners or renters, 65+, with income below $55,000. And they can get a check for $850 even if they owe no taxes. The program varies from state to state, with some states offering a reduced tax rate off a percentage of the home's value. Other states offer a property tax deferral program for the elderly, where the state would pay the homeowner's property taxes. This would be considered a loan, and the equity would be the value of the home. The loan would be repaid when the home was sold or the homeowner dies. Contact your state or county tax office to see what your area offers.

State Tax Agencies

Alabama
Alabama Department of Revenue
50 N. Ripley
Montgomery, AL 36132-7123
334-242-1170
http://www.ador.state.al.us/advalorem/index.html
Alabama Homestead Exemption provides property tax exemption for citizens over 65 years of age on homes less than 160 acres of land. Permanent & totally disabled citizens may also apply for the homestead exemption. Certain income levels also apply.

Alaska
Alaska State Office Building, Amanda Luloff
333 Willoughby Ave., 11th Floor
P.O. Box 110400
Juneau, AK 99811-0400
907-465-2326
Fax: 907-465-3470
http://www.revenue.state.ak.us/ or http://www.pfd.state.ak.us/
Alaska has a Permanent Fund Dividend Program. You must meet certain requirements such as residency to apply. Contact the state office for more information.

Anchorage
Kimberly Rydberg
616 E Street
Anchorage, AK 99501
907-269-0370
Fax: 907-269-0384

Fairbanks
Marjorie Marlow
1005 Cushman Street
Fairbanks, AK 99701
907-451-2820
Fax: 907-451-5142

Arizona
Arizona Department of Revenue
1600 W. Monroe
Phoenix, AZ 85007
602-542-3572
Fax: 602-542-3867
http://www.revenue.state.az.us/
In order to qualify for exemption from property tax in Arizona, you must be totally and permanently disabled, complete with a physician or psychiatrist's certification of disability.

East Phoenix Metro Area
3191 N. Washington
Chandler, AZ 85225

Tucson
400 W. Congress
Tucson, AZ 85701

Arkansas
Office of Excise Tax Administration
Little Rock, AR 72203
P.O. Box 8054
or
1816 West 7th Street
Room 2420
Little Rock, AR 72201
501-682-7200
Fax: 501-682-7900
http://www.state.ar.us/dfa/

California
California Franchise Tax Board
P.O. Box 942840
Sacramento, CA 94240-0002
800-852-5711
http://www.ftb.ca.gov/
California provides a Homeowner Assistance Program that allows a once-a-year payment form the State of California to qualified individuals based on part of the property taxes assessed and paid on their homes. You may be eligible if you are 62 years of age or older, blind, or disabled, and had a limited income. There is also a Renter Assistance Program.

Los Angeles
300 S. Spring Street
Suite 5701
Los Angeles, CA 90013-1265

San Diego
7575 Metropolitan Drive
Suite 201
San Diego, CA 92108-4421

Oakland
1515 Clay Street
Suite 305
Oakland, CA 94612-1431

Santa Ana
600 W. Santa Ana Boulevard
Suite 300
Santa Ana, CA 92701-4532

Sacramento
3221 Power Inn Road
Suite 250
Sacramento, CA 95826-3893

San Francisco
121 Spear Street
Suite 400
San Francisco, CA 94105-1584

Colorado
Division of Property Tax
1313 Sherman St.
Room 419
Denver, CO 80203
303-866-2371
http://www.dola.state.co.us/PropertyTax/
The Colorado Department of Local Affairs, Division of Property Taxation Department administers the Senior Homestead Exemption Program. To qualify residents must be 65 years of age or older, a 10 year owner of the residence and they must currently occupy the residence. Fifty percent of the first $200,00 value of the property is exempt from taxes. The state will pay the exempted property tax.

Connecticut
Department of Policy and Management
450 Capitol Avenue
Hartford, CT 06106-1308
860-418-6200
Fax: 860-418-6487
http://www.ct.gov/drs

Delaware
Patrick Carter, Director
Delaware Division of Revenue
Carvel State Office Building
820 N. French Street
Wilmington, DE 19801
302-577-8200
Fax: 302-577-8202
http://www.state.de.us/revenue/
Delaware grants permission to certain school districts to give property tax credit to senior citizens (65 and older) who live within the school district against the regular school property taxes up to 50%, which can equal up to $500.

Kent County
Thomas Collins building
540 S. Dupont Highway
Dover, DE 19901
302-744-1095
Fax: 302-744-1095

Sussex County
422 N. Dupont Highway
Georgetown, DE 19947

302-856-5358
Fax: 302-856-5697

District of Columbia
Office of Tax and Revenue
941 North Capitol Street, NE
Washington, DC 20002
202-727-4829
Fax: 202-442-6477
http://cfo.dc.gov/otr/site/
The District of Columbia provides for a variety of property tax relief including: homestead deductions. Property tax deferral, senior citizen and low-income exemptions.

Florida
Tax Payer Services
Florida Department of Revenue
1379 Blountstown HWY.
Tallahassee, FL 32304-2716
800-352-3671
850-488-6800
http://www.state.fl.us/dor/property/exemptions.html
Every person who has legal or equitable title to real property in the State of Florida and who resides on the property may be eligible for a homestead exemption. Check to see if you qualify to reduce your property taxes. There are additional exemptions for elderly and disabled homeowners.

Georgia
Georgia Department of Revenue
Taxpayer Services Division
1800 Century Blvd., NE
Atlanta, GA 303415-3205
404-968-0707
http://www.tax.dor.ga.gov/
There are several types of homeowner tax relief. The homestead exemption exempts a portion of the value of the home from property tax. The basic homestead exemption is not age or income dependent and varies from county to county. Other large exemptions are age and income dependent. Contact the office or web site for your specific situation.

Hawaii
Hawaii Department of Taxation
P.O. Box 259
Honolulu, HI 96809-0259
808-587-4242
Fax: 808-587-1488
http://www.state.hi.us/tax/tax.html

Idaho
Idaho State Tax Commission
800 Park Blvd. Plaza IV
Boise, ID 83712
208-334-7736
http://tax.idaho.gov
Idaho provides a "Circuit Breaker" program that gives property tax relief to the elderly, disabled, and veterans with a qualifying income. This program is administered at a local level.

Illinois
Illinois Department of Revenue
Willard Ice Building
101 West Jefferson Street
Springfield, IL 62702
217-782-3627
http://www.ILtax.com
Illinois provides for a number of tax relief provisions. Homeowners 65 year and older with total household income of less that $25,000 may qualify for tax relief. Veterans also may be eligible for property tax exemptions up to $58,000 of the value of the assessed value.

Indiana
Indiana Department of Revenue
Department of Local Government Finance
100 N. Senate Ave, N-1058 (B)
Indianapolis, IN 46204
317-233-3777
Fax: 317-232-8778
http://www.in.gov/dlgf/
Indiana has property tax deductions for the elderly and the disabled; each has different requirements. Indiana also has a homestead credit and standard deduction, which all homeowners are eligible to receive. All of these are filed in the office of the county auditor where the property is located.

Iowa
Iowa Department of Revenue and Finance
Taxpayer Services
P.O. Box 10457
Des Moines, IA 50306-0457
Or
Hoover Building
Taxpayer Services, 4th Floor
1305 E. Walnut
Des Moines, IA 50319
Fax: 800-367-3388 or 515-281-3114
http://www.state.ia.us/tax/index.html
To be eligible for property tax reduction in Iowa residents must meet certain income levels and be 65 years old or totally disabled and 18 years of age or older.

Kansas
Kansas Department of Revenue
Docking State Office Building
915 SW Harrison St., Room 150
Topeka, KS 66612
785-368-8222
Fax: 785-291-3614

http://www.ksrevenue.org/
There are currently no homestead property exemptions in Kansas.

Kentucky
Kentucky Revenue Cabinet
200 Fair Oaks Lane
Frankfort, KY 40620
502-564-4581
Fax: 502-564-3875
http://revenue.ky.gov/
The homestead exemption in Kentucky is for homeowners who are at least 65 years of age or totally disabled.

Louisiana
Louisiana Tax Commission
5420 Corporate Blvd., Suite 107
P.O. Box 66788
Baton Rouge, LA 70896
504-925-7830
Fax: 504-925-7827
http://www.latax.state.la.us/

New Orleans
234 Loyola Avenue, Suite 1000
New Orleans, LA 70112
504-586-5259
Fax: 504-568-5119

Maine
Maine Revenue Services
Property Tax Division
P.O. Box 91006
Augusta, ME 04332
207-287-2013
http://www.state.me.us/revenue/propertytax/homepage.html
Maine provides a property tax or rent refund if you meet residency and income qualifications. They also provide a program for the disabled and elderly.

Maryland
Maryland State Department of Assessments and Taxation
301 W. Preston St.
Baltimore, MD 21201-2395
888-246-5941
http://www.dat.state.md.us/sdatweb/homestead.html
The State of Maryland has developed a program that allows credits against the homeowner or renter's property tax bill if the property taxes exceed a fixed percentage of the person's gross income. In other words, it sets a limit on the amount of property taxes any homeowner must pay based upon his or her income. There are many tax exemptions for the disabled, veterans, elderly, and charitable property. Check with the Maryland State Department of Assessments and Taxation for details on your specific situation.

Massachusetts
Massachusetts Department of Revenue
P.O. Box 7010
Boston, MA 02204
617-887-MDOR or 800-392-6089
http://www.dor.state.ma.us/
The credit for real estate taxes paid for persons Age 65 and Older, also known as the "Circuit Breaker" allows certain senior citizens in Massachusetts to claim a credit on their state income tax returns for the real estate taxes paid on their Massachusetts residential property.

Michigan
Michigan Department of Treasury
Lansing, MI 48922
517-373-3200
517-636-4999
http://www.michigan.gov/treasury/
Michigan has several options for homestead tax reduction. Contact your state and local agencies to determine your level of savings.

Minnesota
Minnesota Property Tax Division
Department of Revenue
Mail Station 3340
St. Paul, MN 55146-3340
651-296-3781
http://www.taxes.state.mn.us/
Refunds on property tax are available for all citizens within a certain income limit, depending on the number of dependents per household. The income limit is increased for senior and disabled homeowners.

Mississippi
Mississippi State Tax Commission-Collective Division
P.O. Box 23338
Jackson, MS 39225-3338
Or
1577 Springridge Rd.
Raymond, MS 39154-9602
601-923-7390
Fax: 601-923-7334
http://www.mstc.state.ms.us/taxareas/property/rules/homeruls.html
Mississippi has two kinds of homestead exemptions: regular and additional. Each program has its own criteria for qualification.

Missouri
Missouri Department of Revenue
Harry S. Truman State Office Building
301 West High Street
Jefferson City, MO 65101
573-751-4450
http://dor.state.mo.us/

Missouri has a property tax exemption for senior and disabled citizens that are determined by income. Check with your tax office or the web site to see if you qualify.

Montana
Montana Department of Revenue
Sam W. Mitchell Blvd.
125 N. Roberts, 3rd floor
Helena, MT 59604
Or
P.O. Box 5805
Helena, MT 59604-5805
406-444-6900
http://www.state.mt.us/revenue/forindividuals/property/relief.asp
Montana has property exemption programs for veterans, disabled persons, the elderly, and low-income families.

Nebraska
Nebraska Department of Revenue
Nebraska State Office Building
301 Centennial Mall South
P.O. Box 94818
Lincoln, NE 68509-4818
402-471-5729
http://www.revenue.state.ne.us/
Nebraska has property exemption for persons over 65, certain disabled individuals and certain disabled veterans and their widows.

Scottsbluff
Panhandle State Office Complex
4500 Avenue 1
Box 1500
Scottsbluff, NE 69363-1500
308-632-1200

North Platte
Craft State Office Building
200 South Silber Street
North Platte, NE 69101-4200
308-535-8250

Grand Island
Tier One Bank Building
1811 West Second Street
Suite 460
Grand Island, NE 68803-5469
308-385-6067

Norfolk
304 North 5th Street
Suite D
Norfolk, NE 68701-4091
402-370-3333

Omaha
Nebraska State Office Building
1313 Franam-on-the-Mall
Omaha, NE 68102-1871
402-595-2065

Nevada
http://aging.state.nv.us
Homesteads are handled on a county level and apply to all taxpayers. Contact Nevada Department on Aging for Senior Citizens Property Tax Assistance Act.

Carson City
Division for Aging Services
3416 Goni Road
Building D, Suite 132
Carson City, NV 89706
775-687-4210
Fax: 775-687-4264

Reno
445 Apple Street, Suite 104
Reno, NV 89502
775-688-2964
Fax: 775-688-2969

Las Vegas
3100 W. Sahara Avenue
Suite 103
Las Vegas, NV 89102
702-486-3572

Elko
850 Elm Street
Elko, NV 89801
775-738-1966
Fax: 775-753-8543

New Hampshire
Department of Revenue Administration
45 Chenell Drive
Concord, NH 03302-0457
603-271-3121
http://www.state.nh.us/revenue/proptery_tax/index.htm
New Hampshire provides property tax exemptions to elderly, disabled, veterans and deaf citizens.

New Jersey
State of New Jersey, Division of Taxation
Information and Publications Branch
PO Box 281
Trenton, NJ 08695-0281
609-292-6400
http://www.state.nj.us/treasury/taxation/

New Jersey has property exemption programs for the disabled, the elderly and low-income families.

New Mexico
New Mexico Taxation and Revenue Department:
1100 S. St. Francis Dr.
P.O. Box 630
Santa Fe, NM 87504-0630
505-476-3092
Fax: 505-827-0782
http://www.state.mn.us/tax/
New Mexico provides a Property Tax Rebate for citizens age 65 and older

New York
Office of Real Property Services
16 Sheridan Avenue
Albany, NY 12210-2714
518-474-2982
Fax: 518-474-9276
http://www.orps.state.ny.us/star/index.cfm
New York States Real Property Tax Credit is available to low-income families and residents 65 years old and older. Most taxpayers receive relief through exemptions to their property assessments for school tax purposes. The exemptions vary depending on the age of the taxpayer, income, and the county where the property is located.

North Carolina
North Carolina Property Tax Division
501 North Wilmington Street
Raleigh, NC 27602
877-308-9103
http://www.dor.state.nc.us/practitioner/property/index.html
North Carolina has property tax exemptions for elderly and disability persons and disabled veterans.

North Dakota
Office of State Tax Commissioner
State Capitol
600 E. Boulevard Avenue
Bismarck, ND 58505-0599
http://www.state.nd.us/taxpt/property/
North Dakota provides property tax credits for homeowners and renters who are disabled.

Ohio
Ohio Department of Taxation
Tax Commissioner's Office
30 E. Broad Street, 22nd Floor
Columbus, OH 43215
888-644-6778
Fax: 614-466-6401
http://www.state.oh.us/tax/
Ohio's Homestead tax relief is granted to qualified elderly and disabled homeowners.

Oklahoma
Oklahoma Tax Commissions
Connors Building Capitol Complex
2501 North Lincoln Boulevard
Oklahoma City, OK 73194
405-521-3160
http://www.oktax.state.ok.us/
Oklahoma offers a homestead exemption for homeowners. A taxpayer who is at least 65 years old, or who is totally disabled, and whose gross household income from all sources does not exceed the current income levels may apply for a homestead exemption that reduces the assessed value of a taxpayer's actual residence.

Oregon
Oregon Department of Revenue
955 Center Street NE
Salem, OR 97301
503-378-4988
800-356-4222
Fax: 503-945-8738
http://www.dor.state.or.us/
Oregon offers property tax deferral programs for disabled and senior citizens age 62 and older. There is also a tax exemption for veterans.

Pennsylvania
Pennsylvania Department of Revenue
Property Tax or Rent Rebate Program
Dept. 280503
Harrisburg, PA 17128-0503
717-787-8201
http://www.revenue.state.pa.us/revenue/cwp/browse.asp
The Property Tax or Rent Rebate Program provides residents 65 years of age or older, widows or widowers 50 years of age or older and the permanently disabled 18 years of age or older meeting income eligibility requirements, rebates of paid property tax or rent.

Rhode Island
Rhode Island Division of Taxation
One Capitol Hill
Providence, RI 02908
401-222-3050
http://www.tax.state.ri.us/

South Carolina
South Carolina Department of Revenue
301 Gervais Street
Post Office Box 125
Columbia, SC 29214
803-898-5480

Fax: 803-898-5822
http://www.sctax.org/
South Carolina provides a homestead exemption to residents who are 65 years of age, who are totally disabled or who are totally blind.

South Dakota
South Dakota Department of Revenue
445 East Capitol Avenue
Pierre, SD 57501
605-773-3311
Fax: 605-773-6729
http://www.state.sd.us/drr2/revenue.html
To receive a property tax refund on your home, you must meet the residence, age or disability and income requirements.

Tennessee
Tennessee Comptroller of the Treasury
Property Tax Relief Program
1600 James K. Polk Building
505 Deaderick Street
Nashville, TN 37243-0278
615-747-8858
http://www.comptroller.state.tn.us/pa/patxr.htm
Tennessee provides tax relief for residents 65 years and older, totally disabled residents and veterans.

Texas
Texas Comptroller of Public Accounts
Lyden B. Johnson State Office building
111 E, 17th Street
Austin, TX 78774
800-252-9121
http://www.cpa.state.tx.us/taxinfo/proptax/proptax.html
Texas provides for several types of exemptions. All residence may receive a homestead exemption for their home's value for school taxes. Additional exemptions are available for disabled, veterans and homeowners 65 and older.

Utah
Utah Tax Commission
210 North 1950 West
Salt Lake City, UT 84134
801-297-2200.
800-662-4335
http://www.tax.utah.gov/
Utah provides abatement and deferral programs for veterans, disabled, and low-income residence age 65 or older.

Vermont
Vermont Department of Taxes
109 State Street
Montpelier, VT 05609-1401
http://www.state.vt.us/tax/index.htm
Vermont provides a School Property Tax adjustment that is based on family income.

Virginia
Virginia Department of Taxation
Office of Customer Services
Post Office Box 1115
Richmond, VA 23218-1115
804-367-8031
Fax: 804-367-2537
http://www.tax.virginia.gov/

Washington
Washington Department of Revenue
Property Tax Division
PO Box 47471
Olympia, WA 98504-7471
360-570-5867
http://dor.wa.gov/content/taxes/property/default.aspx
Any homeowner or mobile homeowner is eligible for property tax exemption if they use their home as their principle residence, have a limited income, and will be age 61 by December 31st or is a disabled person of any age.

West Virginia
West Virginia Property Tax Division
P.O. Box 2389
Charleston, WV 25328-2389
304-558-3333
http://www.state.wv.us/taxdiv/
West Virginia provides a Homestead program for veterans, disabled homeowners and elderly 65 years and older.

Wisconsin
Wisconsin Department of Revenue
2135 Rimrock Road
P.O. Box 8941
Mail Stop 6-94
Madison, WI 53708-8971
608-266-9758
Fax: 608-267-6887
http://www.dor.state.wi.us/

Wyoming
Wyoming Department of Revenue
Herschler Bldg., 2nd Floor West
122 West 25th Street
Cheyenne, WY 82002-0110
307-777-7961
http://revenue.state.wy.us/
Wyoming provides for property tax relief for veterans and other residents.

$2,500 To Pay Your Insulation Bills

Storm windows, insulation and even weather stripping can help reduce your heating and cooling bills. The U.S. Department of Energy offers the Weatherization Assistance Program. Many people are eligible for this program from renters to homeowners, from those who live in single family or multi-family housing to those who live in mobile homes. Preference is given to the elderly and those families with children. You must apply through your state weatherization agency. States allocate dollars to nonprofit agencies for purchasing and installing energy-related repairs. For information on eligibility and where to apply in your state contact your state's office below or the National office at Department of Weatherization, Energy Efficiency and Renewable Energy, Mail Stop EE-1, Department of Energy, Washington, DC 20585; 202-586-9220; www.eere.energy.gov/weatherization/.

Alabama
Department of Economic and Community Affairs
Community Services Division
401 Adams Avenue
P.O. Box 5690
Montgomery, AL 36103-5690
334-242-4909
Fax: 334-242-5099
www.adeca.state.al.us

Alaska
Alaska Housing Finance Corporation
4300 Boniface Parkway
Anchorage, AK 99504
Mailing address:
P.O. Box 101020
Anchorage, AK 99510-1020
907-330-8164
800-478-4636
Fax: 907-338-1747
www.ahfc.state.ak.us

Arizona
Department of Commerce
1700 N. Washington
Suite 600
Phoenix, AZ 85007
602-771-1100
800-528-8421
www.azcommerce.com

Arkansas
Office of Community Services
P.O. Box 1437
Slot S300
Little Rock, AR 72203-1437
501-682-8722
www.arkansas.gov/dhs/dco/ocs/

California
Department of Community Services and Development
P.O. Box 1947
Sacramento, CA 95814
916-341-4200
Fax: 916-341-4203
www.csd.ca.gov/

Colorado
Governor's Office of Energy Management and Conservation
225 E. 16th Avenue, Suite 650
Denver, CO 80203
303-866-2100
800-632-6662
Fax: 303-866-2930
www.state.co.us/oemc/

Connecticut
Department of Social Services
25 Sigourney Street
Hartford, CT 06106-5033
800-842-1508
www.dss.state.ct.us/svcs/energy/

Delaware
Division of State Service Centers
Office of Community Service
1901 North Dupont Highway
New Castle, DE 19720
302-255-9675
Fax: 302-255-4465
www.dhss.delaware.gov/dhss/dssc/

District of Columbia
District of Columbia Energy Office
2000 14th Street, NW
Suite 300 East
Washington, DC 20009
202-673-6700

Fax: 202-673-6725
www.dcenergy.org

Florida
Florida Department of Energy
Department of Community Affairs
2555 Shurmard Oak Boulevard
Tallahassee, FL 32399-2100
850-488-7541
www.floridacommunitydevelopment.org

Georgia
Division of Energy Resources
Georgia Environmental Facilities Authority
100 Peachtree Street, NW
Atlanta, GA 30303-1911
404-962-3000
www.gefa.org/energy_program.html

Hawaii
Office of Community Services
Department of Labor and Industrial Relations
830 Punchbowl Street, Room 420
Honolulu, HI 96813
808-586-8687
http://hawaii.gov/labor/ocs/serviceprograms_index.shtml

Idaho
Department of Health and Welfare
450 West State Street
P.O. Box 83720
Boise, ID 93720-0036
208-334-5500
www.healthandwelfare.idaho.gov

Illinois
Illinois Department of Public Aid
201 South Grand Avenue East
Springfield, IL 62763-1200
800-252-8643
www.dpaillinois.com

Indiana
Family and Social Services Administration
Office of Communication
P.O. Box 7083
Indianapolis, IN 46207-7083
317-233-4454
Fax: 317-233-4693
www.in.gov/fssa/families/housing/wap.html

Iowa
Division of Community Action Agencies
Department of Human Rights
Lucas State Office Building
Des Moines, IA 50319
515-242-5655
www.weatherization.iowa.gov/

Kansas
Weatherization Program
611 S. Kansas Avenue
Suite 300
Topeka, KS 66603-3803
785-296-4990
Fax: 785-296-8985
www.kshousingcorp.org/programs/wap.shtml

Kentucky
Cabinet for Health and Family Services
Department of Community Based Services
275 East Main Street, 3E-I
Frankfort, KY 40621
502-564-7514
http://chfs.ky.gov/dcbs/dfs/Weatherization.html

Louisiana
Housing Finance Agency
Energy Assistance Section
2415 Quail Drive
Baton Rouge, LA 70808
225-763-8700
888-454-2001
Fax: 225-763-8753
www.lhfa.state.la.us/

Maine
Energy and Housing Services
Maine State Housing Authority
353 Water Street
Augusta, ME 04330-4633
207-626-4600
800-452-4668
TTY: 800-452-4603
Fax: 207-626-4678
www.mainehousing.org

Maryland
Department of Housing and Community Development
100 Community Place
Crownsville, MD 21032-2023
410-514-7000
800-758-0119
Fax: 410-541-7291
www.dhcd.state.md.us

Massachusetts
Bureau of Energy Programs
Department of Housing and Community Development
100 Cambridge Street, Suite 300

Boston, MA 02114
617-573-1400
800-632-8175
www.mass.gov/dhch/

Michigan
Department of Human Services
P.O. Box 30037
Grand Tower, Suite 1313
Lansing, MI 48909
517-373-2035
Fax: 517-335-6101
www.michigan.gov/dhs

Minnesota
Energy Division Department of Commerce
85 7th Place East, Suite 500
St. Paul. MN 55101
651-296-5175
800-657-3710 (MN only)
Fax: 651-297-7891
www.commerce.state.mn.us

Mississippi
Departmenr of Human Services
750 North State Street
Jackson, MS 39202
601-359-4500
800-345-6347
Fax: 601-359-4370
www.mdhs.state/ms/us

Missouri
Division of Energy
Department of Natural Resources
P.O. Box 176
Jefferson City, MO 65102
573-751-3443
800-361-4827
Fax: 573-751-6860
www.dnr.state.mo.us

Montana
Department of Public Health and Human Services
P.O. Box 4210
Helena, MT 59604
406-444-5622
www.dphhs.state.mt.us

Nebraska
Nebraska Energy Office
1111 "O" Street
Suite 223
Lincoln, NE 68508
402-471-2867
Fax: 402-471-3064
www.nol.org/home/NEO

Nevada
Housing Division
1802 N. Carson Street
Suite 154
Carson City, NV 89701
775-687-4258
Fax: 775-687-4040
http://nvhousing.state.nv.us/
or
1771 E. Flamingo, Suite 103-B
Las Vegas, NV 89119
702-486-7220
Fax: 702-486-7227

New Hampshire
Office of Energy and Planning
57 Regional Drive, Suite 3
Concord, NH 03301-8519
603-271-2155
Fax: 603-271-2615
www.nh.gov/oep

New Jersey
Department of Community Affairs
P.O. Box 800
101 South Broad Street
Trenton, NJ 08625-0800
609-292-6420
Fax: 609-984-6696
www.state.nj.us/dca

New Mexico
Mortgage Finance Authority
344 Fourth Street, SW
Albuquerque, NM 87102
505-843-6880
800-444-6880 (NM only)
Fax: 505-243-3289
www.housingnm.org

New York
Energy Service Bureau
New York State Division of Housing and Community Renewal
38-40 State Street
Albany, NY 12207
518-402-3728
www.dhcr.state.ny.us

North Carolina
Department of Health and Human Services
Adams Building
2013 Mail Service Center

Raleigh, NC 27699
919-715-5850
Fax: 919-715-5855
www.nh.gov/oep/index.htm

North Dakota
Department of Commerce
Division of Community Services
1600 East Century Avenue, Suite 2
P.O. Box 2057
Bismarck, ND 58503
701-328-5300
Fax: 701-328-5320
www.state.nd.us/dcs/energy

Ohio
Office of Energy Efficiency
Ohio Department of Development
77 South High Street, Floor 26
Columbus, OH 43215-1001
614-466-6797
800-848-1300
www.odod.state.oh.us/cdd/oee/

Oklahoma
Division of Community Affairs and Development
Department of Commerce
900 N. Stiles Avenue
Oklahoma City, OK 73104
408-815-5339
800-879-6552
www.odoc.state.ok.us

Oregon
Housing and Community Services
P.O. Box 14508
Salem, OR 97309-0409
503-986-2000
Fax: 503-986-2020
www.oregon.gov/OHCS

Pennsylvania
Department of Community and Economic Development
400 North Street, 4th Floor
Commonwealth Keystone Building
Harrisburg, PA 17120
717-787-1984
www.inventpa.com

Rhode Island
Central Services Division
State Energy Office
One Capitol Hill
Providence, RI 02908
401-222-3370
Fax: 401-222-1260
www.riseo.state.ri.us

South Carolina
Office of Governor
1205 Pendleton Street
Columbia, SC 29201
803-734-0662
Fax: 803-734-0356
www.govoepp.state.sc.us/oeo.htm

South Dakota
Office of Energy Assistance
Department of Social Services
206 W. Missouri
Pierre, SD 57501
605-773-3165
Fax: 605-773-4855
800-233-8503
www.state.sd.us/social/ENERGY

Tennessee
Tennessee Department of Human Services
400 Deaderick Street, 15th Floor
Nashville, TN 37248-0001
615-313-4766
Fax: 615-741-4165
www.state.tn.us/humanserv/commsrv.htm

Texas
Texas Department of Housing & Community Affairs
Waller Creek Office Building
507 Sabine Street
Austin, TX 78701
Mailing address:
P.O. BOX 13941
Austin, TX 78711-3941
512-475-3800
Fax: 512-475-3935
888-606-8889
www.tdhca.state.tx.us/ea.htm

Utah
Division of Community Development
Utah Office of Energy Services
1594 W. North Temple
Suite 3610
Salt Lake City, UT 84111-6480
801-538-4781
Fax: 801-538-4795
www.energy.utah.gov/

Vermont
Vermont Office of Economic Opportunity
Agency of Human Services

103 South Main Street
Waterbury, VT 05671-1801
802-241-2452
Fax: 802-241-2325
www.ahs.state.vt.us/oeo/

Virginia
Department of Housing and Community Development
501 North Second Street
Richmond, VA 23219-1321
804-371-7000
www.dhcd.virginia.gov

Washington
Department of Community, Trade & Economic Development
Ali Raad Building
128 10th Avenue, SW
P.O. Box 42525
Olympia, WA 98504-2525
360-725-2948
Fax: 360-586-5880
www.cted.wa.gov

West Virginia
Office of Economic Opportunity
950 Kanawha Boulevard, East
Charleston, WV 25301
304-558-8860
Fax: 304-558-4210
www.wvdo.org

Wisconsin
Home energy Plus
P.O. Box 7868
Madison, WI 53707-7868
608-266-3680
Fax: 608-264-6688
866-432-8947
http://homeenergyplus.wi.gov/

Wyoming
Department of Family Services
2300 Capitol Avenue, 3rd Floor
Cheyenne, WY 82002-0490
307-777-7564
Fax: 307-777-7747
http://dfsweb.state.wy.us/

$$ To Pay Your Heating Bill

Even if you are not approved by the U.S. Department of Energy's Weatherization Assistance Program, you might still be eligible for short-term assistance on your utility bill for Low-Income Home Energy Assistance Program (LIHEAP). Funded by the U.S. Department of Health and Human Services, LIHEAP serves low-income families by offering heating and cooling subsides, energy crisis intervention to assist in weather-related and fuel supply shortages and household energy-related emergencies, such as utility shutoffs. The amount of money and eligibility for this program varies from state to state, so you need to contact your state LIHEAP coordinator to learn how to apply. Contact your state listed below or the National office at U.S. Administration for Children and Families, 370 L'Enfant Promenade, SW, Washington, DC 20447; www.acf.hhs.gov/programs/liheap.

Alabama
Department of Economic and Community Affairs
Community Services Division
401 Adams Avenue
P.O. Box 5690
Montgomery, AL 36103-5690
334-242-4909
Fax: 334-242-5099
www.adeca.state.al.us

Alaska
Heating Energy Assistance
Department of Health and Social Services
Division of Public Assistance
400 W. Willoughby Avenue, Room 301
Juneau, AK 99801-1700
907-269-5777
Fax: 907-465-3319
800-470-3058
www.hss.state.ak.us/dpa/programs/hap/

Arizona
Community Services Administration
Department of Economic Security

P.O. Box 6123
Site Code 086z
Phoenix, AZ 85005-6123
602-542-6600
800-3357-4486
www.azdes.gov

Arkansas
Assistance Program
Office of Community Services
Department of Human Services
P.O. Box 1437, Slot 1330
Little Rock, AR 72203-1437
501-682-8726
Fax: 501-682-6736
www.state.ar.us/dhs/dco/ocs/

California
Department of Community Services and Development
P.O. Box 1947
Sacramento, CA 95814
916-341-4200
Fax: 916-341-4203
www.csd.ca.gov/LIHEAP.html

Colorado
Office of Self Sufficiency
Department of Human Services
1575 Sherman Street, 3rd Floor
Denver, CO 80203-1714
303-866-5981
866-432-8435
Fax: 303-866-5098
www.cdhs.state.co.us/oss/FAP/LEAP/

Connecticut
Energy Services Unit
Department of Social Services
25 Sigourney Street, 10th Floor
Hartford, CT 06106
800-842-1508
www.dss.state.ct.us/svcs/energy/

Delaware
Department of Health and Social Services
Division of State Service Centers
1901 N. Dupont Highway
New Castle, DE 19720
302-255-9675
Fax: 302-255-4465
New Castle County: 654-9295
Kent County: 674-1782
Sussex County: 856-6310
www.dhss.delaware.gov/dhss/dssc/liheap.html

District of Columbia
Citizens Energy Resources Division
District of Columbia Energy Office
2000 14th Street NW, 300 East
Washington, DC 20009
202-673-6750
Fax: 202-673-6725
www.dcenergy.org/programs/fuel.htm

Florida
Department of Community Affairs
2555 Shumard Oak Boulevard
Tallahassee, FL 32399-2100
850-488-7541
www.floridacommunitydevelopment.org/liheap/

Georgia
Community Services Section
Division of Family and Children Services
Two Peachtree Street, NW
Suite 18-486
Atlanta, GA 30303
404-657-3780
800-869-1150
http://dfcs.dhr.georgia.gov

Hawaii
Benefit, Employment and Support Services Division
820 Mililani, HI 96813
808-586-5734
Fax: 808-586-5744
Email: pwilliams@dhs.hawaii.gov

Idaho
Department of Health and Welfare
450 W. State Street
Boise, ID 83720-0036
208-3334-5500
www.healthandwelfare.idaho.gov/

Illinois
Illinois Department of Public Aid
201 South Grand Avenue East
Springfield, IL 62763-1200
800-252-8643
www.dpaillinois.com

Indiana
Family and Social Services Administration
P.O. Box 7083
Indianapolis, IN 43207-7083
317-232-7045
800-622-4973
www.in.gov/fssa/families/housing/eas.html

Iowa
Division of Community Action Agencies
Department of Human rights
Lucas State Office Building
Des Moines, IA 50319
515-281-0859
www.state.ia.us/government/dhr/caa/LIHEAP.html

Kansas
Department of Social and Rehabilitation Services
915 S.W. Harrison Street
Topeka, KS 66612
785-296-3959
800-432-0043
Fax: 785-368-2173
www.srskansas.org/ISD/ees/lieap.htm

Kentucky
Department of Health and Family Services
Department for Community Based Services
Division of Policy Development
275 East Main Street, 3W-B
Frankfort, KY 40621
502-564-7536
800-456-3452
Fax: 502-564-0328
http://chfs.ky.gov/dcbs/dfs/LIHEAP.htm

Louisiana
Energy Assistance Department
Housing Finance Agency
2415 Quail Drive
Baton Rouge, LA 70808
225-763-8700
888-454-2001
Fax: 225-763-8753
www.lhfa.state.la.us/

Maine
Energy and Housing Services
Maine State Housing Authority
353 Water Street
Augusta, ME 04330
207-626-4600
800-452-4668
www.mainehousing.org/homerepair.html

Maryland
Department of Humans Resources
311 West Saratoga Street
Baltimore, MD 21202
410-767-7218
800-352-1446
Fax: 410-333-0079
www.dhr.state.md.us/meap/

Massachusetts
Community Services Programs
Department of Housing and Community Development
100 Cambridge Street, Suite 300
Boston, MA 02114-2524
617-573-1400
800-632-8175
www.mass.gov/dhcd/components/cs/Fuel/

Michigan
Department of human Services
P.O. Box 30037
Lansing, MI 48909
517-373-2035
Fax: 517-335-6101
www.michigan.gov/dhs

Minnesota
Energy Division
Department of Commerce
85 7th Place East, Suite 500
St. Paul, MN 55101-2198
651-284-3275
Fax: 651-284-3277
www.state.mn.us/cgi-bin/portal/mn/jsp/home.do?agency=commerce

Mississippi
Division of Community Services
Department of Human Services
750 N. State Street
Jackson, MS 39202
601-359-4500
800-345-6347
Fax: 601-359-4370
www.mdhs.state.ms.us/

Missouri
Department of Social Services
P.O. Box 1527
221 West High Street
Jefferson City, MO 65102-1527
573-751-4815
www.dss.state.mo.us/dfs/liheap.htm

Montana
Department of Public Health and Human Services
P.O. Box 4210
Helena, MT 59604
406-444-5622
www.dphhs.state.mt.us

Nebraska
Department of Health and Human Services
P.O. Box 95044

Lincoln, NE 68509-5044
402-471-2306
www.hhs.state.ne.us/fia/energy.htm

Nevada
Nevada Department of Human Resources
Employment and Support Services
1470 East College Parkway
Carson City, NV 89706
775-684-0500
Fax: 775-684-0646
http://welfare.state.nv.us/ess/eap.htm

New Hampshire
Fuel Assistance Program Manager
Office of Energy and Community Services
57 Regional Drive, Suite 3
Concord, NH 03301-8519
603-271-8317
Fax: 603-271-2615
http://nh.gov/oep/programs/fuelassistance/about.htm

New Jersey
Home Energy Assistance Program
Division of Family Development
P.O. Box 716
Trenton, NJ 08625-0716
609-588-2400
800-510-3102
www.state.nj.us/humanservices/dfd/liheap.html

New Mexico
Human Service Department
2009 S. Pacheco
P.O. Box 2348
Santa Fe, NM 87504-2348
505-827-7775
800-432-6217
Fax: 505-827-6262
www.state.nm.us/hsd/liheap.html

New York
Office of Temporary and Disability Assistance
New York State Department of Family Assistance
40 North Pearl Street
Albany, NY 122423
518-473-0332
800-342-3009
Fax: 518-474-9347
www.otda.state.ny.us/otda/heap/

North Carolina
Division of Social Services
Albemarle Building 8th Floor
325 N. Salisbury St.
Raleigh, NC 27601
919-733-9370
800-662-7030
Fax: 919-733-9386
www.dhhs.state.nc.us/dss/energy/index.htm

North Dakota
Economic Assistance Policy Division
Low Income Home Energy Assistance Program
600 E Boulevard, Dept 325
Bismarck, ND 58505-0250
701-328-2065
800-755-2716
www.state.nd.us/humanservices/services/financialhelp/energyassist.html

Ohio
HEAP
Ohio Department of Development
P.O Box 1240
Columbus, OH 43216
614-752-8808
Fax: 614-728-6832
www.odod.state.oh.us/cdd/ocs/heap.htm

Oklahoma
Division of Community Affairs and Development
P.O. Box 26980
Oklahoma City, OK 73126-0980
405-815-6552
Fax: 405-815-5377
www.okdhs.org/fssd/ProgramInformation.htm#low-income

Oregon
Oregon Housing and Community Services
P.O. Box 14508
Salem, OR 97301-4246
503-986-2094
Fax: 503-986-2006
www.ohcs.oregon.gov/

Pennsylvania
Department of Public Welfare
P.O. Box 2675
Harrisburg, PA 17105
717-772-7906
Fax: 717-772-6451
866-857-7095
www.dpw.state.pa.us/LowInc/HeatAssistance/

Rhode Island
Rhode Island Energy Office
Department of Administration
Division of Central Services
State Energy Office

One Capitol Hill
Providence, RI 02908
401-222-3370
401-222-6920
Fax: 401-222-1260
www.riseo.state.ri.us/programs/liheap.html

South Carolina
Division of Economic Opportunity
1205 Pendleton Street
Columbia, SC 29201
803-734-0662
Fax: 803-734-0356
www.govoepp.state.sc.us

South Dakota
Office of Energy Assistance
Department of Social Services
206 W. Missouri
Pierre, SD 57501
605-773-3766
Fax: 605-773-6657
800-233-8503
www.state.sd.us/social/ENERGY

Tennessee
Tennessee Department of Human Services
400 Deaderick Street, 15th Floor
Nashville, TN 37248-0001
615-313-4766
Fax: 615-741-4165
www.state.tn.us/humanserv/commsrv.htm

Texas
Texas Department of Housing & Community Affairs
Waller Creek Office Building
507 Sabine Street
Austin, TX 78701
Mailing address:
P.O. Box 13941
Austin, TX 78711-3941
512-475-3800
Fax: 512-475-3935
888-606-8889
www.tdhca.state.tx.us/ea.htm

Utah
Division of Community Development
Utah Office of Energy Services
1594 W. North Temple
Suite 3610
Salt Lake City, UT 84111-6480
801-538-4781
Fax: 801-538-4795
www.energy.utah.gov/

Vermont
Office of Home Heating Fuel Assistance
103 South Main Street
Waterbury, VT 05671-1201
802-241-1165
800-479-6151
www.dsw.state.vt.us/Programs_Pages/Fuel/fuel.htm

Virginia
Department of Housing and Community Development
501 North Second Street
Richmond, VA 23219-1321
804-371-7000
www.dhcd.virginia.gov

Washington
Department of Community, Trade & Economic Development
Ali Raad Building
128 10th Avenue, SW
or
P.O. Box 42525
Olympia, WA 98504-2525
360-725-2948
Fax: 360-586-5880
www.cted.wa.gov

West Virginia
Division of Family Assistance
350 Capitol Street, Room B-18
Charleston, WV 25301
304-558-8290
Fax: 304-558-2059
www.wvdhhr.org/bcf/family_assistance/utility.asp

Wisconsin
Home energy Plus
P.O. Box 7868
Madison, WI 53707-7868
608-266-3680
Fax: 608-264-6688
866-432-8947
http://homeenergyplus.wi.gov/

Wyoming
Casper LIHEAP Office
400 East 1st Street, Suite 206
Casper, WY 82601
307-472-4221
800-246-4221
Fax: 307-472-2078
http://dfsweb.wy.us

State Housing Help

The federal government may have many programs, but don't overlook your state. Every state has some type of Housing Finance Authority, as well as other offices, that offers a multitude of programs for renters and home buyers. The range of options are astounding. Many offer assistance for repair, renovation, or handicapped access improvement to homes. In addition, don't forget to contact county and city housing offices to see what may be available in your area.

Below is a list of programs available from state offices that we were able to identify in a recent research project we did on the state of Nebraska. This serves as an example of the kinds of programs that can be available in your state.

1. Up to a $20,000 Loan or a $7,500 Grant for Seniors in Rural Areas
2. Reverse Mortgages for Seniors
3. Tax Exemptions up to $40,000 for Eligible Senior Residents
4. Grants Help Develop Low-Cost Housing Statewide
5. Technical Assistance for Housing & Planning Projects
6. Lease-to-Own a Home of Your Own!
7. Low-Interest Loans for Energy Efficiency
8. Up to $674 in Energy Assistance for Qualified Residents
9. Home Weatherization Saves You Money & It's FREE!
10. Historical Rehabilitation Tax Credit
11. $1,000 Historical Research Grant
12. Historical Preservation Assistance for Local Governments
13. Down Payment & Closing Cost Money for Homebuyers
14. Low-Interest Rates for First-Time Homebuyers
15. Low-Interest Financing for Pre-Made Homes in the Country
16. Tax Credit Help Create Affordable Housing in Nebraska
17. Financing for Multi-Family Properties
18. $20,000 Revolving Loan Fund for Housing Developments
19. Loan Program for Community-Based Projects
20. Agricultural Loan Program
21. Loan Guarantee up to $500,000 for Developers
22. Loan Guarantee for Local, Affordable Housing
23. $10.0 Million in Bond Financing for Community Projects
24. Technical Assistance to Develop Low-Cost Housing
25. Homes For-Sale to Qualified Buyers
26. Housing Options for Working Homebuyers
27. Future Home Improvement Program Offered Statewide
28. $14,999 Worth of Home Modifications for Disabled Owners/Renters
29. Money to Rehabilitate Your Home
30. Housing Fund Offers More Housing Options in Nebraska
31. Community Improvement Program
32. $3.0 Million to Build Rental Houses in the Country

33. State Funding for Income-Affordable Housing
34. Financial Assistance for Homeless Housing & Other Services
35. Housing Opportunities for HIV-Infected People

You can contact your state Housing Finance Agency listed in this section. If you have trouble locating your county and city information, you can go online at www.govengine.com or www.consumer.gov.

Alabama
Alabama Housing Finance Authority
2000 Interstate Park Dr.
Suite 408
Montgomery, AL 36109
Mailing address:
P.O. Box 230909
Montgomery, AL 36123
334-244-9200
800-325-2432
www.ahfa.com

Alaska
Alaska Housing Finance Corporation
4300 Boniface Parkway
Anchorage, AK 99504
Mailing Address
P.O. Box 101020
Anchorage, AK 99510
907-338-6100
800-478-2432
www.ahfc.state.ak.us

Arizona
Arizona Department of Commerce
Office of Housing Development
3800 North Central
Suite 1500
Phoenix, AZ 85012
602-280-1365
www.housingaz.com

Arkansas
Arkansas Development Finance Authority
423 Main St.
Suite 500
Little Rock, AR 72201
501-682-5900
www.state.ar.us/adfa

California
California Housing Finance Agency
1121 L St.
Sacramento, CA 95814
916-322-3991
www.calhfa.ca.gov

Connecticut
Connecticut Housing Finance Authority
999 West St.
Rocky Hill, CT 06067
860-721-9501
www.chfa.org

Delaware
Delaware State Housing Authority
18 The Green
Dover, DE 19901
302-739-4263
www2.state.de.us/dsha

District of Columbia
DC Department of Housing and Community Development
801 North Capitol St., NE
Suite 8000
Washington, DC 20002
202-442-7200
http://dhcd.dc.gov

Florida
Florida Housing Finance Corporation
227 North Bronough St., Suite 5000
Tallahassee, FL 32301
850-488-4197
www.floridahousing.org

Georgia
Georgia Department of Community Affairs
60 Executive Parkway South NE
Atlanta, GA 30329
404-679-4940
www.dca.state.ga.us

Hawaii
Housing and Community Development Corporation of Hawaii
677 Queen St., Suite 300
Honolulu, HI 96813
800-587-0597
www.hcdch.state.hi.us

Idaho
Idaho Housing and Finance Association
565 West Myrtle
P.O. Box 7899

Boise, ID 83707
208-331-4882
www.ihfa.org

Illinois
Illinois Housing Development Authority
401 North Michigan Ave., Suite 900
Chicago, IL 60611
312-836-5200
www.ihda.org

Indiana
Indiana Housing Finance Authority
115 West Washington St.
Suite 1350, South Tower
Indianapolis, IN 46204
317-232-7777
800-872-0371
www.in.gov/ihfa

Iowa
Iowa Finance Authority
100 East Grand, Suite 250
Des Moines, IA 50309
515-242-4990
800-432-7230
www.ifahome.com

Kansas
Kansas Housing Resources Corporation
1000 SW Jackson St.
Suite 100
Topeka, KS 66612
785-296-5865
www.kshousingcorp.org

Kentucky
Kentucky Housing Corporation
1231 Louisville Rd.
Frankfort, KY 40601
502-564-7630
800-633-8896
www.kyhousing.org

Louisiana
Louisiana Housing Finance Agency
2415 Quail Dr.
Baton Rouge, LA 70808
225-763-8700
www.lhfa.state.la.us

Maine
Maine State Housing Authority
353 Water St.
Augusta, ME 04330
270-626-4600
800-452-4668
www.mainehousing.org

Maryland
Maryland Department of Housing and Community Development
100 Community Place
Crownsville, MD 21032
410-514-7000
800-756-0119
www.dhcd.state.md.us

Massachusetts
MassHousing
One Beacon St.
Boston, MA 02108
617-854-1000
www.mhfa.com

Massachusetts Department of Housing and Community Development
One Congress St., 10th Floor
Boston, MA 02114
617-727-7765
www.state.ma.us/dhcd

Michigan
Michigan State Housing Development Authority
735 E. Michigan Ave.
P.O. Box 30044
Lansing, MI 48912
517-373-8370
www.mshda.org

Minnesota
Minnesota Housing Finance Agency
400 Sibley St., Suite 300
St. Paul, MN 55101
651-296-7608
800-657-3769
www.mhfa.state.mn.us

Mississippi
Mississippi Home Corporation
840 River Place
Suite 605
P.O. Box 23369
Jackson, MS 39225
601-718-4642
www.mshc.com

Missouri
Missouri Housing Development Commission
3435 Broadway
Kansas City, MO 64111

816-759-6600
www.mhdc.com

Montana
Montana Board of Housing- Department of Commerce
301 S. Park Ave.
Helena, MT 59601
Mailing Address
P.O. Box 200501
Helena, MT 59620
406-841-2700
http://commerce.state.mt.us/Housing/Hous_Prog_BHB.html

Nebraska
Nebraska Investment Finance Authority
200 Commerce Court
1230 O St.
Lincoln, NE 68508
402-434-3900
800-204-6432
www.nifa.org

Nevada
Nevada Housing Division
1802 North Carson St., Suite 154
Carson City, NV 89701
775-687-4258
800-227-4960
http://nvhousing.state.nv.us

New Hampshire
New Hampshire Financing Authority
P.O. Box 5087
Manchester, NH 03108
603-472-8623
800-640-7239
www.nhhfa.org

New Jersey
New Jersey Housing and Mortgage Finance Agency
647 South Clinton Ave.
P.O. Box 18550
Trenton, NJ 08650
609-278-7400
800-NJ-HOUSE
www.state.nj.us/dca/hmfa

New Mexico
New Mexico Mortgage Finance Authority
344 4th St., SW
Albuquerque, NM 87102
505-843-6880
800-444-6880
www.nmmfa.org

New York
New York State Division of Housing and Community Renewal
Hampton Plaza
38-40 State St.
Albany, NY 12207
518-473-2517
www.dhcr.state.ny.us

New York Housing Finance Agency
641 Lexington Ave.
New York, NY 10022
212-688-4000
www.nyhomes.org

North Carolina
North Carolina Housing Finance Agency
3508 Bush St.
Raleigh, NC 27609
919-877-5700
800-393-0988
www.nchfa.com

North Dakota
North Dakota Housing Finance Agency
1500 E. Capital Ave.
P.O. Box 1535
Bismarck, ND 58502
701-328-8080
800-292-8621
www.ndhfa.org

Ohio
Ohio Housing Finance Agency
57 E. Main St.
Columbus, OH 43215
614-466-7970
www.odod.state.oh.us/ohfa

Oklahoma
Oklahoma Housing Finance Agency
100 N. 63rd St.
Suite 200
P.O. Box 26720
Oklahoma City, OK 73126
405-848-1144
800-256-1489
www.ohfa.org

Oregon
Oregon Housing Agency
P.O. Box 14508
Salem, OR 97309
503-986-2000
www.hcs.state.or.us

Pennsylvania
Pennsylvania Housing Finance Agency
2101 North Front St.
P.O. Box 8029
Harrisburg, PA 17105
717-780-3800
www.phfa.org

Rhode Island
Rhode Island Housing and Mortgage Finance Corporation
44 Washington St.
Providence, RI 02903
401-751-5566
www.rihousing.com

South Carolina
South Carolina State Housing Finance and Development Authority
919 Bluff Rd.
Columbia, SC 29201
803-734-2000
www.sha.state.sc.us

South Dakota
South Dakota Housing Development Authority
221 South Central Ave.
Pierre, SD 57501
605-773-3181
www.sdhda.org

Tennessee
Tennessee Housing Development Agency
404 James Robertson Parkway, Suite 1114
Nashville, TN 37243
615-741-2400
www.state.tn.us/thda

Texas
Texas Department of Housing and Community Affairs
507 Sabine St.
Austin, TX 78701
Mailing Address
P.O. Box 13941
Austin, TX 78711
512-475-3800
www.tdhca.state.tx.us

Utah
Utah Housing Finance Agency
554 South 300 East
Salt Lake City, UT 84111
801-521-6950
800-284-6950 (UT only)
800-344-0452 (outside UT)
www.utahhousingcorp.org

Vermont
Vermont Housing Finance Agency
One Burlington Square
P.O. Box 408
Burlington, VT 05402
802-864-5743
www.vhfa.org

Vermont State Housing Authority
One Prospect St.
Montpelier, VT 05602
802-828-3295
www.vsha.org

Virginia
Virginia Housing Development Authority
601 South Belvidere St.
Richmond, VA 23220
804-782-1986
800-968-7837
www.vhda.com

Washington
Washington State Housing Finance Commission
1000 Second Ave.
Suite 2700
Seattle, WA 98104
206-464-7139
800-767-4663
www.wshfc.org

West Virginia
West Virginia Housing Development Fund
814 Virginia St. East
Charleston, WV 25301
304-345-6475
800-933-9843
www.wvhdf.com

Wisconsin
Wisconsin Housing and Economic Development Authority
201 West Washington, Suite 700
P.O. Box 1728
Madison, WI 53701
608-266-7884
800-334-6873
www.wheda.com

Wyoming
Wyoming Community Development Authority
155 North Beech
Casper, WY 82602
307-265-0603
www.wyomingcda.com

$35,000 From National Nonprofits

There are over 100 national nonprofit organizations that offer financial assistance to home buyers, home owners and even developers. The problem is that there is no one source for identifying all these organizations. But a good place to start is the 2 organizations that keep track of nonprofit organizations:

The Foundation Center
79 Fifth Avenue
New York, NY 10003
212-620-4230
www.fdncenter.org
They have a database of over 75,000 nonprofit organizations that give out grants. This database is accessible on the web for a fee or you can go into one of the Foundation Center libraries around the country and use their database for free. They also publish directories of foundations that give out grant money. You can call their office and they will tell you what libraries in your area have these directories for you to look at for free.

Guidestar
4801 Courthouse Street
Suite 220
Williamsburg, VA 23188
757-229-4631
www.guidestar.org
They have a similar database as The Foundation Center, but do not offer training and classes on other aspects of grantsmanship. Their database seems to have much more information in it about any given foundation. The best part is that you can use the database that will only show partial information on the records, but it is good enough for many applications.

Listed below is a sample of national nonprofits that are available to help with your housing needs

1) **Save up to $2,400 on Housing Costs Each Year**
Sharing housing with other people can reduce the amount of money you spend on housing by as much as $2,400 per year. Contact: Shared Housing Resource Center, Inc., 6344 Greene St., Philadelphia, PA 19144; 215-848-1220

2) **Special Loans to Help Build a Brand New Home**
95% financing for construction of new home; buyer serves as building project manager. Contact: American Home Partners, 20 Realty Drive, Cheshire, CT 06410; 800-343-2884; www.americanhomepartners.net

3) **Homeownership Made Possible for Those with Debt Problems**
Credit Works homeownership program includes mortgage loans, free debt management services and homeownership counseling. Contact: Consumer Credit Counseling Services, Housing Department, 100 Edgewood Avenue, Suite 1800, Atlanta, GA 30303. ATTN: CreditWorks Program; 866-616-3716; www.cccsinc.org; housing@cccsinc.org

4) **Union Members Save Big When Buying Homes**
Money-saving package for Union homebuyers (closing cost cuts, low and no down payment mortgages, free appraisals, counseling). Contact: AFL-CIO Housing Investment Trust, 1717 K Street, NW, Suite 707, Washington, DC 20036; 1-866-HIT-HOME; 202-331-8055, aflcio-hit.com

5) **Foundation Grants and Funding for Housing**
Partners with housing organizations and foundations and provides grants and funding for community and housing projects. To apply for a grant, contact Executive Director, The Allstate Foundation, 2775 Sanders Road, Suite F4, Northbrook, IL 60062-6127; 847-402-5502; www.allstate.com; allfound@allstate.com

6) **$50,000 Grants to Fund Housing Projects**
Grants of up to $50,000 for projects that provide public benefit. Contact: Ludwick Family Foundation, PO Box 1796, Glendora, CA 91740; 626-852-0092; Fax: 626-852-0776; www.ludwick.org; ludwickfndn@ludwick.org

7) **$25,000 Grants for Affordable Housing Construction**
Averaging $5,000 to $25,000 for affordable housing construction and other housing projects.Contact: The Home Depot Foundation, 2455 Paces Ferry Road, Atlanta, GA 30339; (770) 384-3889; Fax: 770-384-3908; www.homedepotfoundation.org/; hd_foundation@homedepot.com

8) **Unable to Qualify for a Mortgage? Now You Can!**
Low-interest mortgages offering no or low down payments for hard-to-qualify homebuyers. Contact: Neighborhood Assistance Corporation of America, 3607 Washington Street, Boston, MA 02130; 888-297-5568; www.naca.com

55 Federal Grants, Loan, And Loan Guarantee Housing Programs

Listed below is a brief description of 55 housing programs available from the federal government. For more information on any of these programs refer to the program number and name as they are described in the government publication called the "Catalog of Federal Domestic Assistance". This book is published every 6 months by the U.S. Government Printing Office www.gpo.gov and is available in most public libraries. It is also available FREE on the web at www.cfda.gov. This web site is probably the best way to view the material. The detailed description of each program in the Catalog of Federal Domestic Assistance will tell you how to apply and where to get the necessary application.

1) **Get a $100,000 Home for $1 plus Fix-Up Money**
Called the "Dollar Home Sales" and referred to as Program #14.313 in the Catalog of Federal Domestic Assistance, this program expands HUD's partnership with local governments in helping to foster housing opportunities for low- to moderate-income families and address specific community needs.

2) **$100,000 to Buy or Fix-Up Houses in Older Areas of a Town**
Called the "Mortgage Insurance – Housing In Older, Declining Areas" and referred to as Program #14.123 in the Catalog of Federal Domestic Assistance, this program helps in the purchase or rehabilitation of housing in older, declining urban areas.

3) $150,000 to Purchase a Condominium
Called the "Mortgage Insurance – Purchase of Condominium Units" and referred to as Program #14.133 in the Catalog of Federal Domestic Assistance, it enables families to purchase units in condominium projects.

4) $300,000 Grant to Help Families Build Part of Their Own Home
Called "Rural Self-Help Housing Technical Assistance" and referenced as Program #10.420 in the Catalog of Federal Domestic Assistance, this program provides Self Help Technical Assistance Grants to provide financial assistance to qualified nonprofit organizations and public bodies that will aid needy very low and low-income individuals and their families to build homes in rural areas by the self help method.

5) Money to Buy, Fix-Up or Refinance a Home
Called "Rehabilitation Mortgage Insurance" and referred to as Program #14.108 in the Catalog of Federal Domestic Assistance, this program helps families repair or improve, purchase and improve, or refinance and improve existing residential structures more than one year old.

6) 50% Discount for Teachers K-12 to Buy a Home
Called the 'Teacher Next Door Initiative" and referred to as Program #14.310 in the Catalog of Federal Domestic Assistance, this program is designed to strengthen America's communities by encouraging public and private school teachers to live in low and moderate income neighborhoods.

7) 50 % Discount for Law Enforcement Officers to Buy a Home
Called "Officer Next Door Sales Program" and referred to as Program #14.198 in the Catalog of Federal Domestic Assistance, this program strengthens America's communities by providing homeownership opportunities to law enforcement officers in HUD- designated revitalization areas, and to improve the quality of life in these neighborhoods by their presence.

8) $100,000 to Buy or Fix-Up Homes in the Country
Called "The Very Income Housing Loans Program" and referred to as Program #10.410 in the Catalog of Federal Domestic Assistance, this program helps very low, low-income, and moderate-income households to obtain modest, decent, safe, and sanitary housing for use as a permanent residence in rural areas.

9) $782,000 to Buy a Ranch or Farm
Called the "Farm Ownership Loans Program" and referred to as Program #10.407 in the Catalog of Federal Domestic Assistance, this program helps eligible farmers, ranchers, and aquaculture operators, including farming cooperatives, corporations, partnerships, and joint operations, through the extension of credit and supervisory assistance, to become owner-operators of not larger than family farms; make efficient use of the land, labor, and other resources; carry on sound and successful farming operations; and enable farm families to have a reasonable standard of living.

10) $200,000 to Buy or Fix-Up Farms and Homes in the Country
Called "The Farm Labor Housing Loans and Grants Program" and referred to as Program #10.405 in the Catalog of Federal Domestic Assistance, this program provides decent, safe, and sanitary low-rent housing and related facilities for domestic farm laborers.

11) Get 4% Interest Rate Reduction Subsidy
Called "The Interest Assistance Program" and referred to as Program #10.437 in the Catalog of Federal Domestic Assistance, this program provides a 4 percent subsidy to farmers and ranchers, who do not qualify for standard commercial credit.

12) Government Mortgages with Smaller Initial Payments
Called the "Section 245 Graduated Payment Mortgage Program" and referred to as Program #14.159 in the Catalog of Federal Domestic Assistance, this program helps early home ownership for households that expect their incomes to rise.

13) Uncle Sam Will Co-Sign an Adjustable Rate Mortgage
Called "The Adjustable Rate Mortgages Program" and referred to as Program #14.175 in the Catalog of Federal Domestic Assistance, this program provides mortgage insurance for an adjustable rate mortgage which offers lenders more assurance of long term profitability than a fixed rate mortgage, while offering consumer protection features.

14) $150,000 to Help Veterans and Unmarried Spouses of Veterans to Buy or Fix-Up a Home
Called "Veterans Housing – Guaranteed and Insured Loans" and referred to as Program #64.114 in the Catalog of Federal Domestic Assistance, this programs assists veterans, certain service personnel, and certain unmarried surviving spouses of veterans, in obtaining credit for the purchase, construction or improvement of homes on more liberal terms than are generally available to non-veterans.

15) $200,000 to Help Buy a Home in an Area Affected By a Base Closing
Called the "Mortgage Insurance – Home – Military Impacted Areas" and referred to as Program #14.165 in the Catalog of Federal Domestic Assistance, this program helps families undertake home ownership in military impacted areas.

16) $48,000 to Buy a Mobile Home
Called the "Manufactured Home Loan Insurance – Financing Purchase of Manufactured Homes as Principal Residences of Borrowers Program" and referred to as Program #14.110 in the Catalog of Federal Domestic Assistance, this program insures lenders against loss on loans.

17) $65,000 to Help Buy a Mobile Home and a Mobile Home Lot
Called the "Mortgage Insurance – Combination and Manufactured Home Lot Loans Program" and referred to as Program #14.162 in the Catalog of Federal Domestic Assistance, this program makes possible reasonable financing for the purchase of a manufactured home and a lot on which to place the home.

18) Money to Buy or Build a Home after a Natural Disaster
Called "Direct Housing – Natural Disaster" and referred to as Program #10.445 in the Catalog of Federal Domestic Assistance, this program assists qualified lower income rural families to meet emergency assistance needs resulting from natural disaster to buy, build, rehabilitate, or improve dwellings in rural areas

19) $300,000 for People who's Homes Were Hurt By a Disaster
Called the "Mortgage Insurance – Home For Disaster Victims Program" and referred to as Program #14.119 in the Catalog of Federal Domestic Assistance, this program helps victims of a major disaster undertake homeownership on a sound basis.

20) Low-Cost Flood Insurance
Called "Flood Insurance" and referred to as Program #97.022 in the Catalog of Federal Domestic Assistance, this program, named the National Flood Insurance program, allows persons to purchase insurance against physical damage to or loss of buildings and/or contents therein caused by floods, mudslide (i.e., mudflow), or flood-related erosion, thereby reducing Federal disaster assistance payments, and to promote wise floodplain management practices in the Nation's flood-prone and mudflow- prone areas.

21) $150,000 to Help Native Americans Buy a Home
Called "Public and Indian Housing – Indian Loan Guarantee" and referenced as Program #14.865 in the Catalog of Federal Domestic Assistance, this program provides homeownership opportunities to Native Americans, Tribes, Indian Housing Authorities including Tribally Designated Housing Entities (TDHEs), and Indian Housing Authorities on Indian land, through a guaranteed mortgage loan program available through private financial institutions.

22) $277,000 to Help Purchase a 1-4 Family Unit
Called 'The Mortgage Insurance –Homes Program" and referred to as Program #14.117 in the Catalog of Federal Domestic Assistance, this program helps people undertake home ownership.

23) $4,000,000 for Your Nonprofit to Help People Buy Homes
Called the "Self Help Ownership Opportunity Program" and referred to as Program #14.247 in the Catalog of Federal Domestic Assistance this program encourages innovative homeownership opportunities through the provision of self-help housing where the homebuyer contributes a significant amount of sweat equity toward the construction of the dwellings

24) Grants to Local Communities to Provide Money to Buy or Fix-Up Homes or to Pay or Rent
Called the "Home Investment Partnership Program" and referred to as Program #14.239 in the Catalog of Federal Domestic Assistance, this program, also known as HOME, expands the supply of affordable housing, particularly rental housing, for low and very low income Americans;

25) $5,000,000 to Build or Fix-Up an Apartment Building
Called "Mortgage Insurance For the Purchase or Refinancing of Existing Multifamily Housing Projects," and referred to as Program #14.155 in the Catalog of Federal Domestic Assistance this program provides money for existing multifamily housing projects, whether conventionally financed or subject to federally insured mortgages at the time of application for mortgage insurance.

26) $2,000,000 to Build or Rehabilitate Condominiums,
Called "Mortgage Insurance for Construction for Substantial Rehabilitation of Condominium Projects" and referred to as Program #14.112 in the Catalog of Federal Domestic Assistance this program enables sponsors to develop condominium projects in which individual units will be sold to home buyers.

27) $1,000,000 to Purchase or Fix-Up Rental Housing in Small Towns
Called the "Rural Rental Housing Loans Programs and referred to as Program #10.415 in the Catalog of Federal Domestic Assistance it provides economically designed and constructed rental and cooperative housing and related facilities suited for rural residents.

28) Reverse Mortgages for Seniors
Called "Reverse Mortgages For Seniors" and referred to as Program #14.183 in the Catalog of Federal Domestic Assistance, this program enables elderly homeowners, 62 years of age or older, to convert equity in their homes to monthly streams of income or, except for Texas, lines of credit.

29) $1,000,000 to Build or Fix-Up Housing for People with Disabilities
Called the "Supportive Housing for Persons With Disabilities Program" and referred to as Program #14.181 in the Catalog of Federal Domestic Assistance this program provides for supportive housing for persons with disabilities Capital advances may be used to construct, rehabilitate or acquire structures to be used as supportive housing for persons with disabilities.

30) Dream of Moving to Paradise? Money to Buy or Fix-Up Houses in the Pacific Islands or the Virgin Islands
Called "Community Development Block Grants/Special Purpose Grants/Insular Areas" and referred to as Program #14.225 in the Catalog of Federal Domestic Assistance, this program provides community development assistance to the Pacific Islands of American Samoa, Guam, the Northern Mariana Islands, and the Virgin Islands in the Caribbean.

31) $10,000 Grant to Fix-Up a Home and Make It Healthier
Called the "Healthy Homes Demonstration Grants" and referred to as Program #14.901 in the Catalog of Federal Domestic Assistance this program is designed to develop, demonstrate, and promote cost-effective, preventive measures to correct multiple safety and health hazards in the home environment that produce serious diseases and injuries in children of low-income families.

32) $27,500 in Grants and Loans to Fix-Up Your Home
Called the "Very Low Income Housing Repair Loans and Grants Programs" and referred to as Program #10.417 in the Catalog of Federal Domestic Assistance it provides loans and grants to very low-income homeowners in rural areas to repair, improve, or modernize their dwellings or to remove health and safety hazards.

33) $60,000 for Renters, Homeowners or Investors to Improve Their Property
Called "Property Improvement Loan Insurance for Improving All existing Structures and Building of New Nonresidential Structures Program" and referred to as Program #14.142 in the Catalog of Federal Domestic Assistance it provides financing of improvements to homes and other existing structures and the building of new nonresidential structures.

34) $3 Billion in Grants to Fix-Up Homes in Cities
Called "Community Development Block Grants/Entitlement Grants" and referred to as Program #14.218 in the Catalog of Federal Domestic Assistance this money can be used to develop viable

urban communities, by providing decent housing and a suitable living environment, and by expanding economic opportunities, principally for persons of low and moderate income.

35) $5 Million in Grants to Fix-Up Homes in Small Towns
Called the "Community Development Block Grants/Small Cities Program" and referred to as Program #14.219 in the Catalog of Federal Domestic Assistance its primary objective is the development of viable urban communities by providing decent housing, a suitable living environment, and expanding economic opportunities, principally for persons of low and moderate income.

36) $570,000,000 for Local Communities to Fix-Up Your House
Called "Community Development Block Grants, Section 108 Loan Guarantees" and referred to as Program #14.248 in the Catalog of Federal Domestic Assistance this program provides communities with a source of financing for economic development, housing rehabilitation, public facilities, and large scale physical development projects.

37) $15,000 Grant for Owners or Developers in Small Towns to Fix-Up Their Home
Called "The Rural Housing Preservation Grants Program" and referred to as Program #10.433 in the Catalog of Federal Domestic Assistance, this program helps very low- and low-income rural residents individual homeowners, rental property owners (single/multi-unit) or by providing the consumer cooperative housing projects (co-ops) the necessary assistance to repair or rehabilitate their dwellings.

38) $2,500 to Make Your Home Energy Efficient
Called the "Weatherization Assistance for Low-Income Persons Program" and referred to as Program #81.042 in the Catalog of Federal Domestic Assistance it provides grants to insulate the dwellings of low-income persons, particularly the elderly, persons with disabilities, families with children, high residential energy users, and households with a high energy burden, in order to conserve needed energy and to aid those persons least able to afford higher utility costs.

39) Money to Build or Renovate Single Room Occupancy Units
Called "Mortgage Insurance for Single Room Occupancy Projects" and referred to as Program #14.184 in the Catalog of Federal Domestic Assistance it provides mortgage insurance for multifamily properties consisting of single-room units.

40) $2,000,000 to Fix-Up Multifamily Units
Called the "Supplemental Loan Insurance Multifamily Rental Housing Program" and referred to as Program #14.151 in the Catalog of Federal Domestic Assistance it can be used to finance repairs, additions and improvements to multifamily projects, group practice facilities, hospitals, or nursing homes already insured by HUD or held by HUD.

41) Money to Fix-Up Apartment Buildings
Called "The Multifamily Assisted Housing Reform and Affordability Act" and referred to as Program #14.197 in the Catalog of Federal Domestic Assistance it provides grants to retain critical affordable housing resources represented by the supply of FHA-insured Section 8 assisted housing

and maintain it in good physical and financial condition while, at the same time, reducing the cost of the ongoing Federal subsidy.

42) Money to Rehabilitate a Trailer Home Park
Called "Mortgage Insurance- Manufactured Home Parks" and referred to as Program #14.127 in the Catalog of Federal Domestic Assistance the program makes it possible to finance the rehabilitation of manufactured home parks.

43) Local Colleges Get Money to Fix-Up Your Home
Called the "Historically Black Colleges and Universities Program" and referred to as Program #14.520 in the Catalog of Federal Domestic Assistance, this program assists Historically Black Colleges and Universities (HBCUs) expand their role and effectiveness in addressing community development needs in their localities, including neighborhood revitalization, housing, and economic development consistent with the purposes of Title I of the Housing and Community Development Act of 1974.

44) Money for Teens to Learn to Fix-Up Houses
Called "Opportunities for Youth/Youthbuild Program" and referred to as Program #14.243 in the Catalog of Federal Domestic Assistance provides funding assistance for a wide range of multi-disciplinary activities and services to assist economically disadvantaged youth.

45) $5,000 to Get Rid of Lead Paint in Your Home
Called the "Lead-based Paint Hazard Control in Privately-Owned Housing Program" and referred to as Program #14.900 in the Catalog of Federal Domestic Assistance it provides grants to identify and control of lead-based paint hazards in privately- owned housing that is owned by or rented to low- or very-low income families.

46) $50,000 to Fix-Up Your Home after a Natural Disaster
Called "Direct Housing-Natural Disaster Loans and Grants" and referred to as Program #10.444 in the Catalog of Federal Domestic Assistance it provides grants to assist very-low income owner-occupants to repair or replace damaged property as a direct result of a natural disaster.

47) More Money to Fix-Up Your Home after a Disaster
Called "Federal Housing Assistance to Individuals and Households" and referred to as Program #97.048 in the Catalog of Federal Domestic Assistance this program provides grants to individuals and households affected by a disaster to enable them to address their disaster-related housing needs.

48) $33,000 for Disabled Veterans to Fix-Up a Home
Called the "Veterans Housing Direct Loans For Certain Disabled Veterans" and referred to as Program #64.118 in the Catalog of Federal Domestic Assistance it provides veterans who are eligible for a Specially Adapted Housing grant with loan directly from the VA in certain circumstances.

49) $48,000 Grant for Veterans to Adapt Their Home for a Disability
Called the "Specially Adapted Housing for Disabled Veterans Programs" and referred to as Program

#64.106 in the Catalog of Federal Domestic Assistance it provides grants to certain severely disabled veterans acquire a home which is suitably adapted to meet the special needs of their disabilities.

50) $55,000 to Fix-Up a Home for Native Americans
Called "Indian Housing Assistance" and referred to as Programs #15.141 in the Catalog of Federal Domestic Assistance and is primarily devoted to providing decent, safe, and sanitary housing through renovations, repairs, or additions to existing homes.

51) More Money for Native Americans to Fix-Up a Home
Called the "Indian Housing Block Grants" and referred to as Program #14.867 in the Catalog of Federal Domestic Assistance, this program provides Federal assistance for Indian tribes in a manner that recognizes the right of tribal self-governance, and for other purposes.

52) Grants to Native American Communities to Fix-Up Homes
Called the "Indian Community Development Block Grant Program" and referred to as Program #14.862 in the Catalog of Federal Domestic Assistance it provides grants to improve the housing stock, provide community facilities, make infrastructure improvements, and expand job opportunities by supporting the economic development of their communities.

53) $4,000,000 to Build or Fix-Up Housing for Seniors
Called the "Supportive Housing for the Elderly Program" and referred to as Program #14.157 in the Catalog of Federal Domestic Assistance it can be used to provide capital advances shall be used to finance the construction or rehabilitation of a structure or portion thereof, or the acquisition of a structure to provide supportive housing for the elderly, which may include the cost of real property acquisition, site improvement, conversion, demolition, relocation and other expenses of supportive housing for the elderly.

54) $450,000 to Make an Apartment Building Assisted Living
Called the "Assisted Living Conversion For Eligible Multifamily Housing Projects" and referred to as Program #14.314 in the Catalog of Federal Domestic Assistance, this program provides financial assistance to private nonprofit owners of eligible developments designed for the elderly with a grant to allow the conversion of some or all of the dwelling units in the project into Assisted Living Facilities (ALF's) serving frail elderly,

55) Funds Help Community Organizations Provide Assistance to Residents
The Community Development Financial Institutions (CDFI) Fund was created to expand the availability of credit, investment capital, and financial services in urban and rural communities throughout the country.

Money To Equip Your Home For A Disability

Any of the sources mentioned in this chapter under the item heading of "Home Fix Up For Seniors In 955 Cities and Towns", "$5,000 Emergency Grant To Fix Up Your Home", "Volunteers Fix Up Senior Homes With Incomes Up To $33,169", "Handyman Services For Free Or Low Cost", "Low and 0% Interest Loans To Fix Up Your House", or "Ramps For Free Or At A Discount" can be used to make your home more handicapped accessible. But there is another service that can help you evaluate your needs as a person with disabilities. They will help you learn about the latest in technology that can improve your life. It can be a specially equipped van, a talking computer, a special kitchen or eating aid or adaptive toys for children. A project funded by the U.S. Department of Education, called Technical Assistance Project has established an office in each state that can provide: information services, equipment loan program, recycling program, funding and loan information. Contact your state Office of Social Services or Vocational Rehabilitation. Contact Rehabilitation Engineering and Assistive Technology Society of North America, (RESNA), 1700 North Moore Street, Suite 1540, Arlington, VA 22209-1903; 703-524-6686; Fax: 703-524-6630; TTY: 703-524-6639; www.resna.org.

$5,000 Emergency Grant To Fix Up Your Home

Cities, counties, townships, and even local nonprofit organizations around the country offer grants to people who need emergency work done on their home or apartment. The income requirements can go up to $42,000 for a couple. To find programs you may qualify for in your area you must search 1) your city or township government, 2) your county government, as well as 3) local nonprofit agencies and local development corporations. Make sure you check with all of the following offices for help in locating appropriate organizations in your area 1) your local library, 2) your local elected officials, 3) your local United Way and 4) all housing agencies in your area. Local government offices can be identified at www.govengine.com and your local United Way can be identified at http://national.unitedway.org/myuw/ . Listed below is a sampling of similar local programs around the country. They should give you an indication of the kind of help that may be available in your area too.

1) **$2,500 Grant For Emergency House Repairs for 62 or older**
   Neighborhood Housing Services of Jamaica, Inc.
   Jamaica, New York
   http://nhsjamaica.org/services/senior-emergency-loans.asp
2) **Free Minor Home Repairs For 62 or older and Income less than $41,000**
   Los Angeles Housing Department
   Los Angeles, CA
   http://losangeles.about.com/gi/dynamic/offsite.htm?site=http%3A%2F%2Fwww.lacity.org%2Flahd%2Fhndywrkr.htm
3) **$5,000 Home Repair Grant For 55+ and 50% Of Median Income**
   First Ward Action Council, Inc.
   Binghamton, NY
   http://www.firstwardaction.org/seniorepair.html
4) **$3,500 Grant For Emergency Repairs for Seniors Making $25,650**
   Sacramento Housing & Redevelopment Agency
   Sacramento, CA
   http://www.shra.org/Content/Housing/HomeRepair/ERP.htm
5) **Roof, Plumbing, Heating-Cooling and other Repairs For Seniors Making $42,200**
   Community Services of Arizona, Inc.
   Chandler, AZ
   http://www.csaz.org/emergency_housing_repairs.html
6) **$2,500 Grant for Emergency Repair For Seniors Making $25,350**
   City of Colorado Springs, Housing Rehabilitation Program, Emergency Repair
   Colorado Springs, CO
   http://www.servingourseniors.org/services.htm

7) **$5,000 Grant To Fix Up 1 to 4 Family Unites of Seniors Making $25,100**
Margert Community Corporation
New York City's Queens County, NY
http://www.margert.org/majorprograms/restore.html

8) **$20,000 Forgivable Loans To Fix Your Roof, Broken Windows, Water Damage, Structural Deficiencies For Seniors Making $46,680**
Housing Program, Emergency Repair Program
Deltona, Florida
http://www.ci.deltona.fl.us/2001/departments/development_services/SHIP_Emergency_Repair.html

9) **$1,500 Grant In Emergency Money For 55+ With $21,700 Income**
Dept of Housing and Business Development
Fontana, CA
http://www.fontanabusiness.org/housing/emr_grt.html

Volunteers Fix Up Senior Homes with Incomes Up To $33,169

A nonprofit organization called Hearts and Hammers has volunteers around the country who perform house repairs for seniors and people with disabilities, They can repair porches, siding and trim, replace windows or doors, provide landscaping, repair or replace exterior, and more. Income requirement can go up to $34,000. George and Laura Bush even contributed to this organization. Contact your local public library to see if there are volunteers in your area. Or contact one or both of the larger groups mentioned below to see if they can identify a group near you. Hearts and Hammers – Twin Cities, Inc., Po. Box 26124, St Louis Park., NM 55426; 952-922-2451; http://www.heartsandhammers.org or Hearts and Hammers, P.O. Box 29747, Dallas, TX 75229; http://www.heartsandhammers-dallas.org/contacts.htm

Handyman Services for Free Or Low Cost

Getting little repairs done around the home is not only difficult for low income seniors, it can be a problem for all seniors. Many communities now have programs run by volunteers or with public or private grant money that provide small repairs for seniors under certain incomes. Other areas offer handy man services at reduced costs from safe providers. To find programs you may qualify for in your area you must search 1) your city or township government, 2) your county government, as well as 3) local nonprofit agencies and local development corporations. Make sure you check with all of the following offices for help in locating appropriate organizations in your area 1) your local library, 2) your local elected officials, 3) your local United Way and 4) all housing agencies in your area. Local government offices can be identified at www.govengine.com and your local United Way can be identified at http://national.unitedway.org/myuw/. You can also contact your local Area Office on Aging by calling 1-800-677-1116 or go to http://www.aoa.gov/eldfam/How_To_Find/Agencies/Agencies.asp Listed below is a sampling of the types of programs that are available around the country. They should give you an indication of the kind of help that may be available in your area too.

1) **Senior Volunteers Do Handyman Chores For Price of Supplies**
Council on Aging Winchester Seniors Association
Winchester, MA
http://www.jenkscenter.org/new_page_9_COA.htm

2) **39 Organizations In NY Get State Money To Fix Up Senior Homes With Incomes Up To $34,000**
Residential Emergency Services To Offer Home Repairs To Elderly (RESTORE)
New York State
http://www.dhcr.state.ny.us/ocd/progs/restore/ocdprgre.htm
3) **$25 First Hour + Cost Of Materials For 60+**
Handyman Services For Tier Township Residents
Willmett, IL
http://www.wilmette.com/health/nurse.asp?nId=7
4) **Minor Repairs, Home Modifications For Low- Income Over 60**
Safety of Seniors Handyman Program
Denver, CO
http://www.voacolorado.org/handyman/
5) **Free Handyman For 62+ and Income Under $41,900**
Handyworker Program Housing Department
Los Angeles, CA
http://www.lacity.org/lahd/hndywrkr.htm

Free Lights and Locks

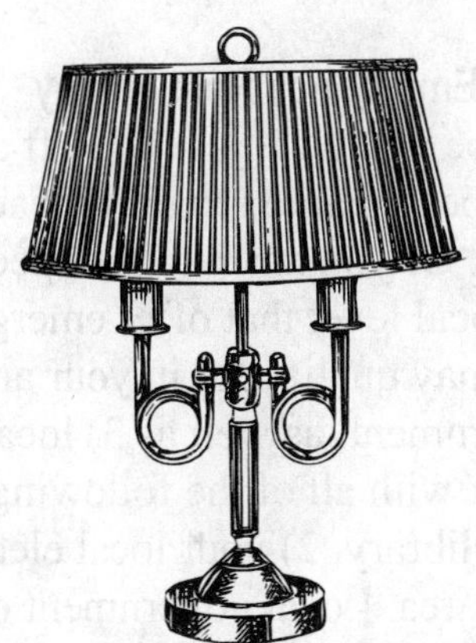

The proper lights and deadbolt locks can provide needed safety for seniors or anyone for that matter. There are many programs that provide these products and their installation for free, or at great discounts. To find programs you may qualify for in your area you must search 1) your city or township government, 2) your county government, as well as 3) local nonprofit agencies and local development corporations. Make sure you check with all of the following offices for help in locating appropriate organizations in your area 1) your local library, 2) your local elected officials, 3) your local United Way and 4) all housing agencies in your area. Local government offices can be identified at www.govengine.com and your local United Way can be identified at http://national.unitedway.org/myuw/. You can also contact your local Area Office on Aging by calling 1-800-677-1116 or go to http://www.aoa.gov/eldfam/How_To_Find/Agencies/Agencies.asp

Listed below is a sampling of the types of programs that are available around the country. They should give you an indication of the kind of help that may be available in your area too.

1) **Free Grab Bars, Nightlights, Door and Window Locks For Seniors Up To $34,900**
Home Secure Program
Los Angeles, CA
http://www.la4seniors.com/home_secure.htm
2) **Locks and Lights For Seniors 60+**
Tulsa Area Agency on Aging
Tulsa, OK
http://www.cityoftulsa.org/resources/septoctcoming+of+age.pdf#search='lights%20and%20locks%20seniors%20program

3) **Volunteers Will Install Locks and Motion Lights in Homes Of Seniors**
RSVP Triad Program, Work with Law Enforcement
La Crosse, WI
http://www.rsvplacrosse.org/voluntr3.html

4) **Installation of Dead Bolt Locks or Locks On Screen Doors or Windows For 60+ With Income Requirements**
Senior Home Repair Service Champaign County
Urbana, IL
http://helpbook.prairienet.org/new/w5157c5t.htm

5) **Free Locks For Over 55 and Income Up To $27,150**
Senior Locks Programs, Portland Police Bureau
Portland. OR
http://www.portlandonline.com/police/index.cfm?c=30679

6) **Free Installation If You Buy The Locks**
Lock Program, City of Euclid Social/Safety Services
Euclid, OH
http://www.socialservices-ccrpc.org/programs/rentassistance.php

$750 Emergency Rent Money

Maybe you were just laid off and haven't found a new job yet. Or that unexpected auto repair bill had to be paid or you wouldn't be able to get to work. Or you have an unexpected health bill that had to be taken care of. There are many programs on the local level that offer emergency rent money when you are facing difficult times. To find programs you may qualify for in your area you must search 1) your city or township government, 2) your county government, as well as 3) local nonprofit agencies and local development corporations. Make sure you check with all of the following offices for help in locating appropriate organizations in your area 1) your local library, 2) your local elected officials, 3) your local United Way and, 4) all housing agencies in your area. Local government offices can be identified at www.govengine.com and your local United Way can be identified at http://national.unitedway.org/myuw/.You can also contact your local Area Office on Aging by calling 1-800-677-1116 or go to
http://www.aoa.gov/eldfam/How_To_Find/Agencies/Agencies.asp
Listed below is a sampling of the types of programs that are available around the country. These are obviously only for these areas, but we wanted you to see what kinds of programs exist.

1) **$750 For One-Time Emergency Need For Seniors With Up To $31,150**
Expanded Rent Assistance Collaboration Program
Seattle, WA
http://cityofseattle.net/humanservices/csd/survivalservices/Erace.htm

2) **4 Emergency Rent Programs In Indianapolis**
Indianapolis Marion County Public Library, Rent Assistance
Indianapolis, IN
http://www.imcpl.org/cgi-bin/irnget.pl?keyword=Rent+assistance

3) **$97,000 Given for Emergency Rent and Utility Assistance**
Cross-Lines Cooperative Council, Inc.
Kansas City, KS
http://www.cross-lines.org/

4) **Emergency Money To Pay Rent Assistance, Security Deposits, Moving Costs, Last Months Rent, and Cleaning Deposits**
Housing Assistance Program, Aging and Disability Services
Portland, OR
http://www.co.multnomah.or.us/ads/
5) **Six Emergency Rent Programs In Houston**
Community and Economic Development Dept. Harris County Texas
Houston, TX
http://www.cedd.hctx.net/HRC_Emergency_Rent_Mortgage.htm
6) **$500 If 15 Days Late Paying Rent Or Mortgage and Income Up To $15,100**
Emergency Assistance Program, Hamilton Country Social Services
Chattanooga, TN
http://www.hamiltontn.gov/Social/ASSIST.HTM

Emergency Money To Pay Utilities

Heating bills are going up and the winter months can create financial havoc with a senior's utility bill payments. There are many programs around the country that help people financially and legally from having their utilities turned off. To find programs you may qualify for in your area you must search 1) your city or township government, 2) your county government, 3) your state government, 4) local nonprofit agencies and local development corporations, 5) as well as your utility company. Make sure you check with all of the following offices for help in locating appropriate organizations in your area 1) your local library, 2) your local elected officials, 3) your local United Way and, 4) all housing agencies in your area. Local government offices can be identified at www.govengine.com and your local United Way can be identified at http://national.unitedway.org/myuw/. You can also contact your local Area Office on Aging by calling 1-800-677-1116 or go to http://www.aoa.gov/eldfam/How_To_Find/Agencies/Agencies.asp
You should also seek out your local community action agency near you to see if they have a program to help you. You can find your local agency at www.communityactionpartnership.com/about/links/map.asp or by contacting Community Action Partnership in Washington, DC at 202-265-7546.

A lot of Local Utility Programs can be identified on the web by going to www.hud.gov then choose your state under the title 'Information by State". Most state pages have a link called "Renting Help Page". Click there even if you are a home owner. Most Rental Help pages have a link called 'Help With Your Utility Bills" which describes programs for both renters and homeowners.

Listed below is a sampling of the types of programs that are available around the country.

1) **$200 For 60 + Who Face Shut Off or No Fuel**
Care and Share, American Red Cross/Niagara Mohawk
Cortland, NY
http://cortland.redcross.org/e-utility.htm

2) **Payments Made To Utility Companies To Avoid Shut Off**
Charlotte Neighborhood Development/Crisis Assistance Ministry
Charlotte, NC
http://www.charmeck.org/Departments/Neighborhood+Dev/Housing+Services/Energy+Assistance.htm
3) **$500 To Pay Utility Bills for Seniors Making $22,453**
Utility Emergency Services Fund
Philadelphia, PA
http://www.uesfacts.org/about.html
4) **Hardship Funds For People Who Fall Through The Cracks**
Pennsylvania Public Utility Commission
PA
http://www.puc.state.pa.us/general/consumer_ed/energy_asst_progs.aspx
5) **Up To $500 in 5 Funds To Stop Utility Cut Offs**
Mid America Assistance Coalition-Managed Utility Funds
Kansas City, MO
http://www.maaclink.org/utility_individual_funds.htm
6) **Money For Seniors Who Don't Qualify For Government Programs**
Share The Warmth Program, Oklahoma Natural Gas
OK
https://www.ong.com/residential/customerprograms-sharewarm.jsp

Local Grants & Discounts To Pay Utility Bills

There is a large collection of hundreds of programs around the county offering money or discounts to help people pay their utility bills. Although most of the grant programs have income limits there are discount programs that have no income limits. To find programs you may qualify for in your area you must search 1) your city or township government, 2) your county government, 3) your state government, 4) local nonprofit agencies and local development corporations, 5) as well as your utility company. Make sure you check with all of the following offices for help in locating appropriate organizations in your area 1) your local library, 2) your local elected officials, 3) your local United Way and, 4) all housing agencies in your area. Local government offices can be identified at www.govengine.com and your local United Way can be identified at http://national.unitedway.org/myuw/. You can also contact your local Area Office on Aging by calling 1-800-677-1116 or go to http://www.aoa.gov/eldfam/How_To_Find/Agencies/Agencies.asp. You should also seek out your local community action agency near you to see if they have a program to help you. You can find your local agency at www.communityactionpartnership.com/about/links/map.asp or by contacting Community Action Partnership in Washington, DC at 202-265-7546

A lot of Local Utility Programs can be identified on the web by going to www.hud.gov then choose your state under the title 'Information by State". Most state pages have a link called "Renting Help Page". Click there even if you are a home owner. Most Rental Help pages have a link called 'Help With Your Utility Bills" which describes programs for both renters and homeowners.
Listed below is a sampling of the types of programs that are available around the country.

1) **Millionaires Over 65 Get 20% Off Gas Bills**
   Assistance Programs, Philadelphia Gas Works
   Philadelphia, PA
   http://www.pgworks.com/new%20site/C0008a.htm
2) **Seniors Making $24,400 Can Get $280 Discount**
   Energy Assistance Program Rate, Sacramento Municipal Utility District
   Sacramento. CA
   http://www.smud.org/residential/bill/eapr.html
3) **50% Discount For Seniors 65+ Making $31,992**
   Utility Discount Program, Mayor's Office for Senior Citizens
   Seattle, WA
   http://www.cityofseattle.net/humanservices/mosc/utility_discount_program.htm
4) **25% Discount On Water, Sewer, And Solid Waste For Seniors Making $19,248**
   Low Income Assistance Program, Tacoma Power
   Tacoma, WA
   http://www.ci.tacoma.wa.us/power/ResidentialServices/low_income_assistance.htm
5) **Pay Only 10% Of Income If Income Less Than $19,245**
   Percentage of Income Payment Plan, Public Utilities Commission of Ohio
   Ohio
   http://www.puco.ohio.gov/PUCO/Consumer/information.cfm?doc_id=93
6) **Pay No More Than 6% On Utilities If Income Under $24,464**
   Universal Service Fund New Jersey Board of Public Utilities
   NJ
   http://www.bpu.state.nj.us/home/USFQA.shtml

Utility Discounts For Medical Devices or In-Home Patients

No matter what your income, you may be eligible for a discount on your utility bill if someone in your home is dependent on a medical device that uses electricity. Or if you need heating and air-conditioning to care for someone with special needs. To find programs you may qualify for in your area you must search 1) your city or township government, 2) your county government, 3) your state government, 4) local nonprofit agencies and local development corporations, 5) as well as your utility company. Make sure you check with all of the following offices for help in locating appropriate organizations in your area 1) your local library, 2) your local elected officials, 3) your local United Way and, 4) all housing agencies in your area. Local government offices can be identified at www.govengine.com and your local United Way can be identified at http://national.unitedway.org/myuw/. You can also contact your local Area Office on Aging by calling 1-800-677-1116 or go to http://www.aoa.gov/eldfam/How_To_Find/Agencies/Agencies.asp. You should also seek out your local community action agency near you to see if they have a program to help you. You can find your local agency at www.communityactionpartnership.com/about/links/map.asp or by contacting Community Action Partnership in Washington, DC at 202-265-7546.

A lot of Local Utility Programs can be identified on the web by going to www.hud.gov then choose your state under the title 'Information by State". Most state pages have a link called "Renting Help Page". Click there even if you are a home owner. Most Rental Help pages have a link called 'Help with Your Utility Bills" which describes programs for both renters and homeowners.
Listed below is a sampling of the types of programs that are available around the country.

1) **30% Rate Discount To Run Medical Equipment Or Care or Paraplegic, Hemiplegic, Quadriplegic or MS Patient**
   Medical Equipment Discount Rate, Sacramento Municipal Utility District
   Sacramento, CA
   http://www.smud.org/residential/services/med_rate.html
2) **Rate Discounts For Life Equipment Or Special Needs**
   Services For Medical Baseline and Life-Support Customers, Pacific Gas and Electric
   California
   http://www.pge.com/res/financial_assistance/medical_baseline_life_support/
3) **Pay No More For Extra Electricity To Run Medical Machines or Heating and Air-conditioning for Patient**
   Medical Baseline Allowance, Utility Consumers' Action Network
   San Diego, CA
   http://www.ucan.org/consumer_info/Elec_Bill/reduce_utility_bill.htm
4) **Get 25% Discount On Utility Bills With No Income Requirement**
   Medical Residential Assistance Programs, Municipal Services Division
   Santa Clara, CA
   http://www.ci.santa-clara.ca.us/pub_utility/pu_help_paying.html

Ramps For Free Or At A Discount

A doorway ramp to make it easier to get into and out of a home make life a lot easier for seniors and those with a disability. The item above entitled "$5,000 Emergency Grant To Fix Up Your Home" can certainly be used to put in a ramp but you should be also be aware that are special programs available just for ramps. To find programs you may qualify for in your area you must search 1) your city or township government, 2) your county government, 3) your state government, 4) local nonprofit agencies and local development corporations. Make sure you check with all of the following offices for help in locating appropriate organizations in your area 1) your local library, 2) your local elected officials, 3) your local United Way and, 4) all housing agencies in your area. Local government offices can be identified at www.govengine.com and your local United Way can be identified at http://national.unitedway.org/myuw/. Listed below is a sampling of similar local programs around the country. You can also contact your local Area Office on Aging by calling 1-800-677-1116 or go to http://www.aoa.gov/eldfam/How_To_Find/Agencies/Agencies.asp. You should also seek out your local community action agency near you to see if they have a program to help you. You can find your local agency at www.communityactionpartnership.com/about/links/map.asp or by contacting Community Action Partnership in Washington, DC at 202-265-7546

1) **Free Ramp For Seniors Making $26,750**
   SeniorWise Home Repair Program
   Des Moines, IA
   http://www.chdcdesmoines.org/programs/participate/eligibility.shtml

2) **Free Loan Ramp and Cost Sharing Installation**
Ramps Program, Serving Our Seniors
Erie County, OH
http://www.servingourseniors.org/services.htm
3) **Volunteers Build Ramps For Income Qualified Seniors**
Seniors Resource Center
Denver, CO
http://www.srcaging.org/volunteer2.html
4) **Grants To Install A Ramp**
Cleveland Department of Aging, Senior Homeowner Assistance Program
Cleveland, OH
http://www.city.cleveland.oh.us/government/departments/aging/agingind.html

Low and 0% Interest Loans To Fix Up Your House

No matter what your income and as long as your improvements will create a more energy efficient home you can save a lot on interest rates and finance charges by using a subsidized energy conservation loan program. These programs are typically available from your state department of energy, a local government office or your utility company. State and local government offices can be found by contacting your state or city operators or www.govengine.com. Your local phone directory and library can help you locate your local utility companies. Be sure to check them all. Here is a sample of the kinds of programs available.

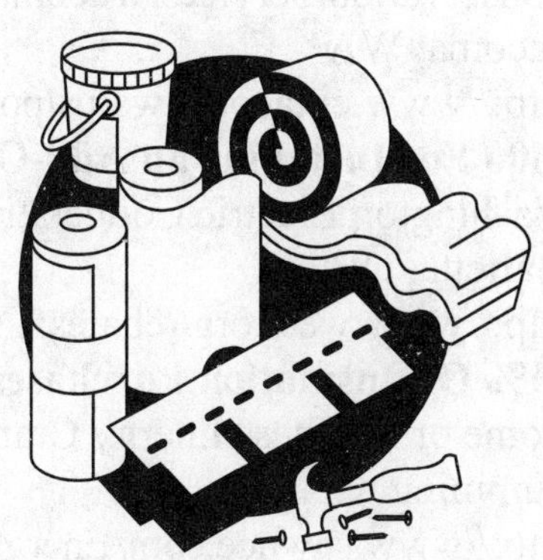

1) **$35,000 Low Interest Loan For Fireplaces, Freezers, Clothes Washers, Etc.**
Dollar and Energy Saving Loans, Nebraska Energy Office
Lincoln, NE
http://www.neo.state.ne.us/loan/improv.htm
2) **$50,000 Low Interest Loan For New Energy Saving Appliances**
Energy Loan Fund, Ohio Department Of Development
Columbus, OH
http://www.odod.state.oh.us/cdd/oee/ELFDS.htm
3) **$20,000 Low Interest Loan To Make Energy Saving Improvements**
NY Energy Smart Loan Program, NY Energy Research & Development Authority
Albany, NY
http://www.nyserda.org/loanfund/
4) **0% Interest Loans For Energy Efficiency Improvements**
Residential Weatherization Program, Tacoma Power
Tacoma, WA
http://www.ci.tacoma.wa.us/power/ResidentialServices/default.htm
5) **$3,000 For New Storm Doors Or Windows**
5% Weatherization Loans, Tideland EMC
Pantego, NC
http://www.tidelandemc.com/p&sincentives.htm

$750 Rebate For Any Income Level

A rebate is another form of free money and it's available for consumers with any income level as long as you buy the product. Utility companies around the country offer such rebates to encourage energy efficient products that will save you on your heating bill and save them from having to generate more services. Your local phone directory and library can help you locate your local utility companies. Be sure to check them all. Here is a sample of the kinds of programs available.

1) **70% on Insulation Purchases Up To $700**
   Home Check, Mid-America Energy Company
   Des Moines, IA
   http://www.midamericanenergy.com/html/energy3g.asp
2) **$20 On A Lamp and $750 On A Heat Pump**
   Conservation Services, Tacoma Power
   Tacoma, WA
   http://www.ci.tacoma.wa.us/power/ResidentialServices/default.htm
3) **$600 For Installing an Add-On Heat Pump**
   Washington Electric Cooperative, Inc
   Marietta, OH
   http://www.weci.org/rebates.html
4) **50% On Insulation Purchases Up to $200**
   Home or Business Energy Grant, Sawnee EMC
   Cumming, GA
   http://www.sawnee.com/Energy/incentives.htm
5) **$150 On A Dish Washer**
   Energy Star Appliances, Minnesota Power
   Duluth, MN
   http://www.mnpower.com/energystar/special_offers/index.htm

$8,000 to Improve Your Home So It Cuts Your Utility Bills

This program is called the "Energy Efficient Mortgages Program" and can be used to make energy-efficient improvements in one to four existing and new homes. The improvements can be included in a borrower's mortgage only if their total cost is less than the total dollar value of the energy that will be saved during their useful life. The cost of the improvements that may be eligible for financing as part of the mortgage is either 5 percent of the property's value (not to exceed $8,000) or $4,000--whichever is greater. The maximum mortgage limit for a single-family home is $160,950, plus the cost of the eligible energy-efficient improvements. (Limits may be lower in some areas of the country.) Contact: U.S. Department of Housing and Urban Development, 451 7th Street SW, Washington, DC 20410; 202-708-1112; http://www.hud.gov/offices/hsg/sfh/eem/energy-r.cfm.

Homebuying and Homeownership Counseling Services

There are hundreds of government funded counseling centers around the country that will give you advice on buying a home, renting, defaults, foreclosures, credit issues and reverse mortgage. To locate offices near you contact: Housing Counseling Agencies, U.S. Department of Housing and Urban Development (HUD), 451 7th St SW, Washington, DC 20410; 1-800-569-4287, http://www.hud.gov/offices/hsg/sfh/hcc/hccprof14.cfm.

In addition to the HUD supported agencies, every area of the country will have their own local nonprofit housing counseling organization. Listed below is sample of the kinds of free and low cost services available in Oklahoma City. To find similar services in your area contact your local library to start your search.

1) **FREE Budgeting Counseling and Money Management Workshop**
Consumer Credit Counseling Service, Oklahoma City, OK 800-364-2227
http://www.cccsok.com/Home.htm
2) **Homebuyer Education for Spanish Speaking Homebuyers**
Latino Community Development Agency, Oklahoma City, OK 405-236-0701
http://www.latinoagencyokc.org/index2.html
3) **Free Housing Counseling**
Community Action Agency of Oklahoma City, Oklahoma City, OK 405-232-0199, ext. 3217; Fax: (405) 232-9074; http://www.caaofokc.org/special%20projects.htm#housing
4) **FREE Homebuyer Education for Everyone**
Contact: Community Action Agency of Oklahoma City, 1900 NW 10th Street, Oklahoma City, OK 405-232-0199, ext. 3217 http://www.caaofokc.org/special%20projects.htm#homebuying
5) **FREE Fair Housing Counseling**
The Metropolitan Fair Housing Council (MFHC) of Greater Oklahoma City, Inc., Oklahoma City, OK 405-232-3247
6) **FREE Housing Counseling for Native Americans**
Chickasaw Nation Division of Housing, Ada, OK 580-421-8856;
http://www.chickasaw.net/alivecity/servlet/NavForward?sid=94&appactive=yes&req=mSitePage_cn2&iReq=mInfo&mi=500:3327181&moi=200:3363618; kay.perry@chickasaw.net
7) **FREE Homebuyer Education in Oklahoma County**
Council of Neighborhoods, Oklahoma City, OK 405-619-9305;
http://www.councilofneighborhoods.org/engine/emw.exe/*qshome=home
8) **Homeowner Workshops Help You Buy a New House!**
Neighborhood Housing Service of Oklahoma City, Inc., Oklahoma City, OK 405-231-4663
9) **Even More FREE Counseling for Homebuyers & Owners**
Oklahoma Housing Finance Agency, Oklahoma City, OK 405-848-1144
http://www.ohfa.org/
10) **Lots of Information for Homebuyers**
Oklahoma Homebuyer Education Association, Oklahoma City, OK 405-524-4124
http://www.homebuyereducation.info/homebuyers.htm
11) **FREE for Native Americans: Homebuyer Education**
Housing Authority of the Apache Tribe, Anadarko, OK 405-247-7305;
http://www.apachehousing.org/
12) **FREE Home Education Seminars**
Countrywide Home Loans, Inc., Oklahoma City, OK 405-842-7751 Greg_Nurse@countrywide.com
13) **Homeownership Counseling for Oklahoma City Residents**
Northeast Homeownership Consortium, Inc., Oklahoma City, OK 405-272-9622
14) **Homeownership Counseling for Native Americans**
Native American Housing Services, Inc., Oklahoma City, OK 405-598-5742

Have Fun For the Rest of Your Life

Free Money For Senior Artists

Artists don't have to be struggling if they know how to use the system. If you cannot find what you need in the programs presented in this chapter you should also investigate the following.

1) ***Federal Government Money Programs For Artists***
   These are the two most important federal agencies that offer money for artists.
   - National Endowment Of the Arts
     Washington, DC
     202-682-5400
     http://arts.endow.gov

   - National Endowment of the Humanities
     Washington, DC
     202-NEH-1121
     www.neh.gov

2) ***More Federal Government Money Programs For Artists***
   You can always stay up to date on programs from the federal government by checking out the Catalog of Federal Domestic Assistance. This book is available at your local public library or the U.S. Government Printing Office (www.gpo.gov). You can also search the contents of this book for free on the web at www.cfda.gov.

3) ***Sell Your Art To The Government***
   There are many government offices which purchase artists freelance work. For help in finding out how to sell your services to the government you can contact one of the 1,000 offices all over the country called Small Business Development Centers. They will help you tackle any business problem you. All their services are free or for very little cost. Contact 800-8-ASK-SBA; www.sba.gov/.

4) ***Find State Money Programs For Artists***
   Every state has money for artists. Look for your state office of the Arts or the state arts commission. You can find them by dialing 411 and asking for your state capitol operator or by going to www.govengine.com.

5) ***Money From Foundations For Artists***
   The following are the major sources of information for finding grants from nonprofit organizations.
   - The Foundation Center
     79 Fifth Avenue

New York, NY 10003
212-620-4230
www.fdncenter.org

They have a database of over 75,000 nonprofit organizations that give out grants. This database is accessible on the web for a fee or you can go into one of the Foundation Center libraries around the country and use their database for free. You can call their office and they will tell you what libraries in your area have these directories. The Foundation Center also gives short courses on topics like "How to Search for Grant Money", or "How to Write a Grant". Don't pay thousands of dollars for courses on these subjects when you can get it from one of the best for a very reasonable price.

- Guidestar
  4801 Courthouse Street
  Suite 220
  Williamsburg, VA 23188
  757-229-4631
  www.guidestar.org

Guidestar has a similar database to The Foundation Center, but do not offer training and classes.

$10,000 To Teach Art To Kids

The Arts in Education program offers grants to strengthen arts education in the school curriculum. The program awards two grants, one to Very Special Arts and the other to the John F. Kennedy Center for the Performing Arts. VSA supports projects for disabled people in the arts and the Kennedy Center provides educational activities that emphasize the importance of the arts in education. Funding is used for educator training and activity development. Contact the U.S. Department of Education, Improvement Programs, 400 Maryland Ave., S.W., Rm. 4W308, FB-6, Washington DC 20202-6140; 202-260-1393; www.ed.gov/programs/artsed/index.html.

$ To Produce A Radio Show

Did you know that Radio One started out as a small business that received venture capital funding? The New Markets Venture Capital Program is a business funding program designed to promote economic development and the creation of job opportunities for individuals living in low-income areas. Recipients use funds to make equity capital investments in smaller enterprises located in low-income geographic areas. Contact the New Markets Venture Capital Program, 409 3rd Street, NW, Suite 6300, Washington, DC 20416; 800-U-ASK-SBA; 202-205-6510; www.sba.gov/INV/venture.html.

$5,000 For A Writers Workshop

Get money to start your own writers' workshop. Through the National Endowment for the Arts' Challenge America program, the Writers' Colony at Dairy Hollow received support for readings and workshops. Find out how your group could be the next to receive support. Contact the National Endowment for the Arts, 1100 Pennsylvania Ave. NW, Washington D.C., 20506; 202-682-5400; www.arts.endow.gov/.

$10,000 For Storytelling

Share the great tradition of storytelling with others. Through the NEA's Challenge America program, the California Indian Storytelling Association will bring together storytellers from four states to meet and share their stories. Contact the National Endowment for the Arts, 1100 Pennsylvania Ave. NW, Washington D.C. 20506; 202-682-5400; www.arts.endow.gov/.

$23,000 For Photo Exhibit
Looking for funding to exhibit your art? Through the National Endowment for the Arts' Challenge America program, the Sixth Street Photography Workshop will produce a photography exhibit entitled *Stories of the City*. How can you be next? Contact the National Endowment for the Arts, 1100 Pennsylvania Ave. NW, Washington D.C. 20506; 202-682-5400; www.arts.endow.gov/.

$7,500 To Play Your Piano
Ever dreamed of playing in a music festival? The National Endowment for the Arts' Challenge America program is offering grant support for the three-day Crestone Music Festival in CO. Contact the National Endowment for the Arts, 1100 Pennsylvania Ave. NW, Washington D.C. 20506; 202-682-5400; www.arts.endow.gov/.

$ To Create A Crafts Website
Are you a skilled crafter who would like to share your talent? The National Endowment for the Arts' Challenge America program is currently providing support to launch a new website. For your chance to share your passion with others, contact the National Endowment for the Arts, 1100 Pennsylvania Ave. NW, Washington D.C. 20506; 202-682-5400; www.arts.endow.gov/.

$ For A Tap Dance Festival
Have a love and a talent for dance? Through the National Endowments for the Arts' Heritage & Preservation grant program, American Tap Dance Foundation is receiving support for the Tap City Festival. Find out how your feet could earn you funding, contact the National Endowment for the Arts, 1100 Pennsylvania Ave. NW, Washington D.C. 20506; 202-682-5400; www.arts.endow.gov.

$15,000 To Teach Writing
Have an idea for teaching writing, art, or music? Through the National Endowment for the Arts' Learning in the Arts program, grant support for the Merging of Cultures project has been awarded. Contact the National Endowment for the Arts, 1100 Pennsylvania Ave. NW, Washington D.C. 20506; 202-682-5400; www.arts.endow.gov.

$20,000 To Write A Novel
Dream of writing the great American novel, but the demands of the real world keep you from picking up a pen? The National Endowment for the Arts' Literature Fellowship program encourages the production of new work by affording writers the time and means to write. Each literature fellow receives a $20,000 award. Contact the National Endowment for the Arts, 1100 Pennsylvania Ave. NW, Washington D.C. 20506; 202-682-5400; www.arts.endow.gov.

STAR

$ To Produce A New Play
Think you might be the next Tom Stoppard or Sam Shepard? The National Endowment for the Arts' Services to Arts Organizations and Artists program is supporting the Continued Life Fund, an initiative that provides production stipends to theaters committed to presenting sequential productions of a new play. Find out how you can get

funding for the world premiere of your play. Contact the National Endowment for the Arts, 1100 Pennsylvania Ave. NW, Washington D.C. 20506; 202-682-5400; www.arts.endow.gov.

$200,000 To Make An Independent Film

Independent films are one of the hottest commodities in the movie world today. The Independent Television Service was established by Congress to fund and present innovative public television programs. ITVS offers an Open Call, which is an open invitation to independent producers to propose single public television programs on any subject. Applicants must be independent producers, who own the copyright of their production, have artistic, budgetary and editorial control of their project, and are not regularly employed by a public or commercial broadcast entity or film studio. Contact the Independent Television Service, 501 York Street, San Francisco, CA 94110; 415-356 8383, ext. 259; www.itvs.org/producers.

$25,000 For Performing Artists To Perform Overseas

Get your artwork the exposure it deserves. The Fund for U.S. Artists at International Festivals and Exhibitions awards grants to performing artists and organizations that have been invited to participate in international festivals. Contact the Cultural Programs Division Staff, Bureau of Educational and Cultural Affairs, U.S. Department of State, SA-44, 301 4th Street, SW, Suite 568, Washington, D.C. 20547; 202-203-7523; http://exchanges.state.gov/education/citizens/culture/.

$50,000 To Produce A Film

Did you know that through the Miller Brewing Company you can make your business dreams come true? Through the Miller Urban Entrepreneurs Business Grant Competition, individuals have received funding for their film company, and other endeavors. Entrepreneurs have the chance to vie for $50,000, $20,000 and $2,500 business grants. A team of national judges select the grant awardees based upon the business plans developed and submitted by individuals age 21-35 years old. Contact Miller urban Entrepreneur Series, c/o Flowers Communications, 542 S. Dearborn, Suite 1150, Chicago, IL 60605; 877-493-4400; www.millerbrewing.com/inthecommunity/urban/businessGrant.asp.

$6,000 To Start A Hip-Hop Magazine

What do a hip-hop magazine, a backpack design company, and a skin care salon have in common? They are all micro businesses funded through the Micro Business Development Corporation. MBD offers economic opportunities and business growth by providing access to variety of resources. MBD is a Colorado nonprofit organization providing micro enterprise support services. This is for Colorado entrepreneurs. Check with your local Economic Development Association to see what your area may offer. Contact the MicroBusiness Development Corporation, 3003 Arapahoe St., Suite 112A, Denver, CO 80205; 303-308-8121; www.microbusiness.org.

$5,000 to Make Comic Books

The Foundation offers financial assistance to fully committed, self-publishing comic book creators and qualified charitable and nonprofit organizations. The purpose is to assist comic book creators with some of the costs in self-publishing their work. Contact Xeric Foundation, 351 Pleasant St., PMB 214, Northampton, MA 01060-3900; 413-585-0671; www.xericfoundation.com.

$500 To Teach Ceramics
Want to put your artistic talents to work, but not sure where to start? Here's the answer you have been looking. Through the Dorchester Bay Economic Development Corporation small business loan, you can get the funds you need to make your business dreams a reality. The program awarded ten small business loans totaling $132,300 in the past year. This is only for businesses in the Dorchester Bay area. Check with your local Economic Development Association to see what your area may offer. Contact Dorchester Bay Economic Development Corporation, 594 Columbia Rd., Dorchester, MA 02125; 617-825-4200; www.dbedc.com.

Free Art Exhibits
Want to learn more about medieval art? Or maybe teach your kids a thing or two about Monet? Through the National Gallery of Art Loan Program, you can get educational material on the Gallery's collections and exhibitions, free of charge. The program is open to individuals, schools, colleges, and libraries across the Nation. Check out the easy-to-use website for ordering your materials. Contact the Department of Education Resources, National Gallery of Art, 2000B South Club Drive, Landover, MD 20785; 202-737-4215; www.nga.gov/resources.

Actors Get $40 to Buy Shoes
The Conrad Cantzen Memorial Shoe Fund offers entertainment professionals up to $40, once in a twelve month period for shoes costing no more than $80. Contact The Actors' Fund of America, 729 Seventh Avenue, 10th Floor, New York, NY 10019; 212-221-7300, ext. 146; Fax: 212-221-7300, ext. 146; www.actorsfund.org/human/social/cantzen.html.

$300,000 to Make a Film
The primary focus of funding is independent documentary film. Grant awards for production typically range from $50,000 to $300,000 and provide partial support for documentary series and individual independent films. Contact John D. and Catherine T. MacArthur Foundation, 140 S. Dearborn St., Ste. 1100, Chicago, IL 60603-5285; 312-726-8000; Fax: 312-920-6258; www.macfound.org.

$ to Educating the Public on Modern Art
This foundation provides grants to individuals, in-kind gifts, internship funds, scholarship funds to educate the public about modern art and modernism and the art of Robert Motherwell. Contact Dedalus Foundation, Inc., 555 West 57th Street, Suite 1222, New York, NY 10019; 212-220-0014; www.motherwellcatalogueraisonne.org.

Grants of $100,000 or More for Songwriters
The funds are provided to preserve and enhance the legacy of Johnny Mercer as well as providing educational programs for music appreciation, assisting in the development of songwriters, and enhance the general appreciation of American popular music. Contact The Johnny Mercer Foundation630 Ninth Avenue, Suite 610, New York, NY 10036; 212-589-5477; www.johnnymercerfoundation.org/.

Music Teachers and Others: Grants, Scholarships and Funds for You!
Over $2.0 million is available through this foundation to provide scholarship aid grants to accredited colleges and universities in the field of music, to increase music education and to popularize the teaching of music as a profession. Grants to individuals limited to providing emergency aid to worthy

music teachers in need. Contact The Presser Foundation, 385 Lancaster Ave., No. 205, Haverford, PA 19041; 610-658-9030.

Grants from $500 up to $56,500 for Art Scholars
Grant awards are available to art scholars so that they can go to Los Angeles to study at the Rifkind Center for German Expressionist Studies. Giving is done primarily to the arts, especially art museums. Contact Robert Gore Rifkind Foundation, 5905 Wilshire Blvd., Los Angeles, CA 90036; 323-857-6165; www.lacma.org/info/resource/rifkind.htm.

$30,000 Grants for Artists
This national giving foundation awards up to $30,000 in an effort to promote artistic development. Grants are given to individuals interested in media and communications and the visual arts. Contact The Penny McCall Foundation, Inc., c/o Jennifer McSweeney Reuss, 170 E. 83rd Street, 2M, New York, NY 10029; Fax: 212-988-9714; pennymccallfnd@aol.com; www.pennymccallfoundation.org.

$2,500 to Dance, Act, or Take Pictures
The Puffin Foundation Ltd. makes grants that encourage emerging artists in the fields of art, music, theater, dance, photography, and literature whose works due to their genre and/or social philosophy might have difficulty being aired. Grants range from $1,000 to $2,500. Contact Puffin Foundation Ltd., 20 East Oakdene Avenue, Teaneck, NJ 07666-4111; www.puffinfoundation.org/.

$10,000 to Develop Your Art
Grants ranging from $4,000 to $10,000 are awarded to artists who have dedicated their lives to developing their art, regardless of their level of commercial success. Artists must have been working in a mature phase of their art for at least 20 years. The Emergency Assistance Program is intended to provide interim financial assistance to qualified artists whose needs are the result of an unforeseen, catastrophic incident, and who lack the resources to meet that situation. Contact: Adolph and Esther Gottlieb Foundation, Inc., 380 West Broadway, New York, NY 10012; 212-226-0581; Fax: 212-226-0584; http://www.gottliebfoundation.org.

Artists Live Rent-FREE for One Month
The Foundation maintains the William Flanagan Memorial Creative Persons Center (better known as "The Barn") in Montauk, on Long Island in New York, as a residence for writers, painters, sculptors and composers. The Center is open from June 1st to October 1st. Residencies are for one month periods of time. The standards for admission are, simply, need and talent. Contact: Edward F. Albee Foundation, 14 Harrison St., New York, NY 10013; 212-226-2020; www.albeefoundation.org.

Grants for Radio & Television Professionals
This foundation provides grants in time of personal or family crisis for radio and television professionals. The foundation provides anonymous financial grants to those who, through no fault of their own, are in acute need due to critical illness, advanced age, death of a spouse, an accident or other serious misfortune. Contact: Broadcasters' Foundation, 7 Lincoln Ave., Greenwich, CT 06830; 203-862-8577; Fax: 203-629-5739; www.broadcastersfoundation.org/index.html.

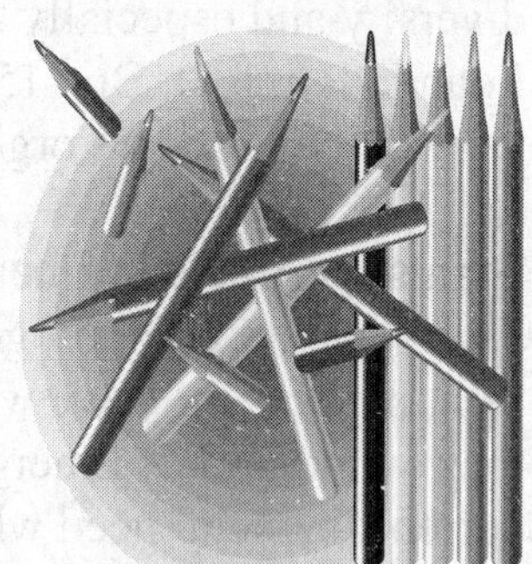

$27,000 in Emergency Aid for Artists
Grants from $500 up to $27,000 are provides for visual artists and their families. Financial aid is available through the Emergency Funding Grant Program to support professional artists and their families in the event of illness, distress, disability, or bereavement. Contact Artists Fellowship, Inc., c/o Salmagundi Club, 47 5th Avenue, New York, NY 10003; 646-230-9833; www.artistsfellowship.com/financial.html.

$2,000 Grants for Pop/Rock Latin Songwriters
The ASCAP Foundation and Heineken USA Incorporated offers grants to Pop/Rock songwriters residing in one of the three greater metropolitan areas of Boston, Chicago and New York; and to Latin songwriters living in Miami or Los Angeles. These $2,000 grant programs are designed to assist up-and-coming Pop/Rock Latin songwriters with career advancement. Contact The ASCAP Foundation Heineken USA, ASCAP Foundation, One Lincoln Plaza, New York, NY 10023-7142; 212-621-6000; www.ascapfoundation.org.

$1,000 for Pianists
The Scholarship Program for Young American Pianists offers $1,000 scholarships awarded on competitive basis to outstanding young American pianists, especially those who demonstrate a special affinity for the interpretation of Chopin's music. Contact The Chopin Foundation, 1440 79th Street Causeway, Suite 117, Miami, FL 33141; 305-868-0624; Fax: 305-868-5150; www.chopin.org.

$5,000 for Composers
The American Music Center provides grants of up to $5000 to composers to help them realize their music in performance, and in some cases, on a recording. Grants are project-based, for a specific work and specific event associated with the work, such as a performance, reading or recording. Contact American Music Center, Anna Smith, Manager of Grantmaking Programs, RE: CAP Application, 30 West 26th Street, Suite 1001, New York, NY 10010-2011; 212-366-5260, ext. 10; www.amc.net/.

Grants for Emerging Playwrights
Provides grants to emerging playwrights. Grants are available directly to an individual through a residency at New Dramatists, Inc. in New York. Playwrights may submit applications independently and do not have to be nominated. Contact Princess Grace Foundation USA, 150 East 58th Street, 25th Floor, New York, NY 10155; 212-317-1470; Fax: 212-317-1473; www.pgfusa.com.

$6,000 for Women Artists
Artist Enrichment program provides grants to feminist artists and arts organizations to be used for artistic development, artist residencies, the exploration of new areas or techniques, and the creation of new art. Art Meets Activism program provides grants to feminist social change artists and arts organizations for projects. This is for Kentucky women artists. Contact Kentucky Foundation for Women, 1215 Heyburn Building, 332 West Broadway, Louisville, KY 40202-2184; 502-562-0045; Fax: 502-561-0420; www.kfw.org/.

Up to $2,000 for Women Musicians or Music Educators
Provides grants to women who are composers, music educators, musicologists, and performers. The mission of the Fund is to seek out women's music projects from women of ethnic, cultural, and racial

diversity and especially the work of lesbians. Contact The PatsyLu Music Fund, Open Meadows Foundation, P.O. Box 150-607, Van Brunt Station, Brooklyn, NY 11215-607; 718-768-2249; www.openmeadows.org/.

Grants for Artists in Financial Need

Two separate grant programs for artists in financial need: 1) Grants for painters, sculptors, and printmakers who have worked at least 20 years on their art, and are in current financial need to support their work; and 2) Emergency grants of up to $10,000 for painters, sculptors, and printmakers who are in current financial need which is the result of a recent emergency occurrence such as a fire, flood or medical emergency. Contact Adolph and Esther Gottlieb Foundation, Inc., Sara Ross, Grants Manager, 380 W. Broadway, New York, NY 10012-5115; 212-226-0581; Fax: 212-226-0584; www.gottliebfoundation.org/.

$20,000 for Contemporary Music Composers

Provides grants through a commissioning program for composers and their orchestras and chamber groups that have a record of excellence in the performance of contemporary music. Contact Koussevitzky Music Foundation, Inc., c/o Brown Raysman LLP, 900 Third Avenue, New York, NY 10022; 212-895-2367; Fax: 212-895-2900; www.koussevitzky.org/; info@koussevitzky.org.

$10,000 to Support Media Projects

This foundation offers funding that supports independent media projects in post- production that address the economy, class issues, poverty, women, war and peace, race, and labor. Contact Center for Alternative Media and Culture, P.O. Box 0832, Radio City Station, New York, NY 10101; 212-977-2096; www.mediarights.org/workshop/prod_workshop/dyn_res_list2.php.

1,000 Grants to Write Fiction

The Arch and Bruce Brown Foundation awards yearly grants to writers in three rotating disciplines: Theatre, Full-length Fiction, and Short Stories. All works submitted must present the gay and lesbian lifestyle in a positive manner and be based on, or inspired by, a historic person, culture, event, or work of art. The Foundation also offers grants to production companies to offset expenses in producing gay-positive theatrical works based on history. Contact Arch and Bruce Brown Foundation, PMB 503, 31855 Date Palm Drive, Suite 3, Cathedral City, CA 92234; www.aabbfoundation.org.

Artists Get $1,500 to Finish Their Media and Film Art Works

Finishing Funds provides artists with grants up to $1,500 to help with the completion of electronic media and film art works which are currently in progress. Eligible forms include a variety of media. Work must be innovative, creative and approach the various media as art forms; all genres are eligible, including experimental, narrative and documentary art works. Individual artists can apply directly to the program and do not need a sponsoring organization. Applicants must be residents of New York State; students are not eligible. Contact Electronic and Film Arts Grants Program, Experimental Television Center, 109 Lower Fairfield Rd., Newark Valley, NY 13811; 607-687-4341; Fax: 607-687-4341; www.experimentaltvcenter.org/.

$1,000 to Fund Events for Independent Media Artists

Presentation Funds provides grants to not-for-profit organizations throughout New York State. The program seeks to encourage events which increase understanding of and appreciation for independent media work in all areas of the State. Events must be open to the public; courses, classes and workshops with limited enrollments are not eligible. The intention of this program is to provide partial assistance; organizations must also provide additional support for the event. Publicly supported educational institutions are not eligible. Contact Electronic and Film Arts Grants Program, Experimental Television Center, 109 Lower Fairfield Rd., Newark Valley, NY 13811; 607-687-4341; Fax: 607-687-4341; www.experimentaltvcenter.org/.

$2,000 Per Project to Strengthen Artistic Activities

The Media Arts Technical Assistance Fund is designed to help nonprofit media arts programs in New York State stabilize, strengthen or restructure their media arts organizational capacity, services and activities. The Fund will provide up to $2,000 per project to organizations which receive support from NYSCA's. Contact Electronic and Film Arts Grants Program, Experimental Television Center, 109 Lower Fairfield Rd., Newark Valley, NY 13811; 607-687-4341; Fax: 607-687-4341; www.experimentaltvcenter.org/.

Grants to Produce Films in New York City & Los Angeles

This Foundation offers grants and other incentives to individuals who produce films or videos in New York City or L.A. The programs are as follows: The Roy W. Dean New York City Film Grant, The Roy W. Dean Los Angeles Video Grant, and The Roy W. Dean Los Angeles Film Grant. Contact From the Heart Productions, Attn: Roy W. Dean Film and Video Grants, 1455 Mandalay Beach Road, Oxnard, CA 93035-2845; 805-984-0098; www.fromtheheartproductions.com/grant.

Writers: Grants up to $1,500

Grants of up to $1,000 are given to U.S. or Canadian poets, fiction writers, and non-fiction writers "whose work addresses women's concerns or speaks for peace and justice from a feminist perspective." Contact Money for Women / Barbara Deming Memorial Fund, P.O. Box 630125, Bronx, NY 10463; www.lgbtfunders.org/lgbtfunders/dstate.htm#Money%20for%20Women.

$50,000 Grant to Film in New Zealand

The New Zealand film grant is for all residents of New Zealand. If you are a resident living abroad, you can enter but you must film in New Zealand. Contact From the Heart Productions, Attn: Roy W. Dean Film Grant, 1455 Mandalay Beach Road. Oxnard, CA 93035-2845; 805-984-0098; www.fromtheheartproductions.com/grant-nz.shtml.

$15,000 to Promote Social Change through Media Production

The Paul Robeson Fund for Independent Media, a program of the New York City-based Funding Exchange, supports media activism and grassroots organizing by funding the pre-production and distribution of social issue film and video and radio projects. The fund is interested in projects that address critical social and political issues. The primary purpose of the fund is to support independent media productions that are not only compelling politically and artistically but will also be used as tools for progressive social change activism and organizing. Contact Funding Exchange, 666 Broadway, Suite 500, New York, NY 10012; 212-529-5300; Fax: 212-982-9272; www.fex.org/grantmaking.shtml#robeson.

$10,000 for Native American Artists

The Kookyangw Fund was created to provide financial support, encouragement, and exposure to emerging Native American graphic and visual artists. The goals of the fund are to increase knowledge, awareness and understanding of Native American arts; to encourage aesthetic expression by promoting the use of high-technology tools by Native American artists; and to enable their participation in the profession. (The Kookyangw Fund is currently NOT accepting applications, check the website for updates.) Contact First Nations Development Institute, 2300 Fall Hill Ave., Ste. 412, Fredericksburg, VA 22401; 540-371-5615; Fax: 540-371-3505; www.firstnations.org.

$5,000 Cash Awards for Women Filmmakers

The Film Finishing Fund offers cash awards to support independent and nonprofit women filmmakers in completing documentary, dramatic, educational, animated, or experimental films or videos which promote equal opportunities for women, enhance media images of women, and influence prevailing attitudes and practices regarding and on behalf of women. Contact Women in Film Foundation, 8857 W. Olympic Blvd., Ste. 201, Beverly Hills, CA 90211; 310-657-5154; www.wif.org/info_page.cfm?id=11.

Grants to Help Publish History of Art Books

The Millard Meiss Publication Grants award grants for the purpose of subsidizing book length scholarly manuscripts in the history of art and related subjects that have been accepted by a publisher on their merits, but cannot be published in the most desirable form without a subsidy. Contact College Art Association, 275 7th Ave., 18th Floor, New York, NY 10001-6708; 212-691-1051; Fax: 212-627-2381; www.collegeart.org/meiss.

Gap Funding for Artists who Have Recently Graduated

The Professional Development Fellowships help MFA, terminal MA and Ph.D. students bridge the gap between graduate study and professional careers. By offering support at this critical juncture in scholars' and artists' careers, the Association makes timely degree completion more viable and employment opportunities more accessible. Each fellow receives support over a period of two years. Contact College Art Association, 275 7th Ave., 18th Floor, New York, NY 10001-6708; 212-691-1051; Fax: 212-627-2381; www.collegeart.org/fellowships.

Emergency Funds for Artists up to $8,000

The Craft Emergency Relief Fund is a nonprofit organization making loans and small grants to professional craft artists experiencing career-threatening illness, accident, fire, theft, or natural disaster. CERF is a small revolving fund with loans ranging from $500 to $8,000 and grants up to $1,000. Services include referrals to craft suppliers who have agreed to offer discounts on materials and equipment to craft artists eligible for CERF funds, and booth fee waivers with certain craft show producers. Contact Craft Emergency Relief Fund, Inc., P.O. Box 838, Montpelier, VT 05601-0838; 802-229-2306; Fax: 802-223-6484; http://craftemergency.org/.

Grants of $1,500 to Aid Artists Worldwide

Aid to Artisans offers practical assistance to artisans world-wide, working in partnerships to foster artistic traditions, cultural vitality and community well-being. Aid to Artisans makes approximately 50 modest grants each year to craft-based associations worldwide. Typically, these grants range from $500 to $1,500 and are used to help these groups purchase much needed equipment and materials to improve or increase their craft production. Contact Aid to Artisans, 331 Wethersfield Avenue, Hartford, CT 06114; 860-947-3344; Fax: 860-947-3350; www.aidtoartisans.org/what/grants.html.

Financial Assistance for Artists Living with HIV/AIDS

Visual AIDS provides direct services to artists living with HIV/AIDS. The Visual AIDS Artist Material Grants are awarded to Visual AIDS active members, who are low income artists in need of financial assistance in obtaining materials for their artwork. Contact Visual AIDS, 526 W. 26th St. # 510, New York, NY 10001; 212-627-9855; Fax: 212-627-9815; www.visualaids.org; visaids@earthlink.net.

$12,000 Grants for Visual Artists

The Grants Program for Individuals in the Visual Arts offers grants of up to $12,000 to visual artists whose work can be viewed advantageously through slides. This program has been suspended until 2007. Contact The Elizabeth Foundation for the Arts, P.O. Box 2670, New York, NY 10108; 212-563-5855; Fax: 212-563-1875; www.efa1.org/; grants@efal.org.

Low-Rent Studios for Artists in New York City

The EFA Studio Center program provides subsidized artists' studios in New York City. This program was established to help visual artists develop their careers and achieve financial self-sufficiency. Contact The Elizabeth Foundation for the Arts, P.O. Box 2670, New York, NY 10036; 212-563-5855; Fax: 212-563-1875; www.efa1.org/; grants@efal.org.

Fellowships for Poets, Writers, and Visual Artists

The center seeks to give talented individuals the opportunity to engage in the process of discovery. There are two kinds of fellowships available through this Foundation: The Visual Arts Fellowship, which is available to artists in any of the visual arts media, however, facilities may limit certain types of work; and the Writing Fellowship, which offers fellowships to fiction and poetry writers of merit. Contact Fine Arts Work Center in Provincetown, Inc., 24 Pearl Street, Provincetown, MA 02657-1504; 508-487-9960; Fax: 508-487-8873; www.fawc.org; info@fawc.org.

$50,000 Grants for Contemporary Art

Grants are awarded annually to outstanding or unusually promising artists and arts organizations that create, present, or support work of an imaginative, contemporary nature. Funding is given in the areas of dance, music, performance art/theater, poetry, and the visual arts. Some additional funding is available to organizations and to individuals through a discretionary grants program for urgent situations related to their work. The foundation biennially awards the John Cage Award for Music by a formal nomination process. Contact Foundation for Contemporary Arts, Inc., 820 Greenwich Street, New York, NY 10014; 212-807-7077; Fax: 212-807-7177; www.foundationforcontemporaryarts.org.

$2,000 for Professional Artists

This Foundation gives primarily to professional artists, 25 years of age or older, working in paint and to arts organizations serving these artists. Individual artists must submit (6) 35mm color slides of the highest quality, representing permanent work in the visual arts. Contact Sam and Adele Golden Foundation for the Arts, 188 Bell Road, New Berlin, NY 13411; 607-847-8158; Fax: 607-847-8158; www.goldenfoundation.org.

Up to $350,000 for Writers

The Literary Program supports the creation of exceptional poetry and prose written originally in the English language and to increase the audience for contemporary literature. The foundation honors writers whose work reflects and changes our understanding of the world. Contact Lannan Foundation. 313 Read St., Santa Fe, NM 87501; 505-986-8160; Fax: 505-986-8195; www.lannan.org.

$22,500 for Dissertations on American Art

The Luce Foundation awards fellowships to doctoral candidates working on dissertations in American art. Funds are used solely to advance completion of the student's dissertation. Contact The Henry Luce Foundation, Inc., 111 W. 50th St., Suite 4601, New York, NY 10020; 212-489-7700; Fax: 212-581-9541; www.hluce.org/4disfm.html.

$1,000 Grants for Sculptors

Grants ranging from $350 up to $1,000 are provided to encourage the creation and appreciation of sculpture throughout the U.S.; one award given annually to a sculptor for outstanding ability as well as commitment to sculpture. Contact National Sculpture Society, Inc., 237 Park Ave., New York, NY 10017; 212-764-5645; Fax: 212-764-5651; www.nationalsculpture.org/.

$30,000 for Working Artists in Need

The Pollock-Krasner Foundation's dual criteria for grants are recognizable artistic merit and demonstrable financial need, whether professional, personal or both. The Foundation encourages applications from artists who have genuine financial needs that are not necessarily catastrophic. Grants are intended for a one-year period of time. The Foundation will consider need on the part of an applicant for all legitimate expenditures relating to his or her professional work and personal living, including medical expenses. The maximum grant amount is $30,000. Contact The Pollock-Krasner Foundation, Inc., 863 Park Ave., New York, NY 10021; 212-517-5400; Fax: 212-288-2836; www.pkf.org/grant.html.

Up to $5,000 for Photographers

The W. Eugene Smith Grant in Humanistic Photography is presented annually to a photographer whose past work and proposed project, as judged by a panel of experts, follows the tradition of W. Eugene Smith's compassionate dedication exhibited during his 45-year career as a photographic essayist. Contact W. Eugene Smith Memorial Fund, Inc., c/o Intl. Ctr. of Photography, 1133 Ave. of the Americas, New York, NY 10036; 212-857-0038 or 212- 857-0000, ext. 138; www.smithfund.org.

$10,000 for Individual Artists

Tanne Awards recognize prior outstanding achievement by individual artists who have demonstrated exceptional talent and creativity but have limited financial resources or have difficulty obtaining funding. The awards are intended to enrich the recipient's artistic life and are unconditional. Grants range from $5,000 up to $10,000. Contact Tanne Foundation, c/o Grants Mgmt. Associates, 77 Summer

Street, Boston, MA 02110; 617-426-7080; www.tannefoundation.org/; mjenney@grantsmanagement.com.

More Money for Artists of All Kinds

The Louis Comfort Tiffany Foundation awards grants in painting, sculpture, printmaking, photography, video and craft media. Emerging American artists and craftspeople are recognized every two years by a series of monetary grants. The awards go to the artists whose work shows promise, but who have not yet received widespread critical or commercial recognition. Contact The Louis Comfort Tiffany Foundation, c/o Artists Space, 38 Greene St., 3rd Fl., New York, NY 10013; http://louiscomforttiffanyfoundation.org/grants_program.html.

$500 Plus Artists Can Live & Work on a Farm

Selected artists from all over the country spend two weeks to one month living and working in excellent facilities located within a short walk from the farm. The Artist-in-Residence facility is primarily available for one artist at a time although two artists working collaboratively may be in residence together. Artists will be given a monthly stipend of $500 to offset the cost of food, travel, supplies or other related needs. (A collaborative team will receive one stipend.) Artists are responsible for their own personal living expenses, travel, supplies, long distance telephone charges and for any other expenses relating to the cost of producing work that may be incurred while in the program. Contact Weir Farm Trust, Inc., 735 Nod Hill Road, Wilton, CT 06897; 203-761-9945; Fax: 203-761-9116; www.nps.gov/wefa; evanswft@optonline.net.

Artists Work Outdoors & Get $500!

The Weir Farm Trust invites professional visual artists to apply to the Visiting Artists Program at Weir Farm National Historic Site. The program will begin in the summer and continue for one year. Housing and studio space are not provided for this program - rather artists use Weir Farm as an "open air" studio. A $500 honorarium to help cover travel expenses or supplies is available. The purpose of the Visiting Artists program, is to give selected artists the opportunity to create a cohesive body of work based on each artist's personal interpretation of Weir Farm. Contact Weir Farm Trust, Inc., 735 Nod Hill Road, Wilton, CT 06897; 203-761-9945; Fax: 203-761-9116; www.nps.gov/wefa; evanswft@optonline.net.

$15,000 for Musical Theatre Artists

The Jonathan Larson Performing Arts Foundation provides financial assistance and encouragement to emerging composers, lyricists and book writers, as well as nonprofit producing companies with a commitment to developing and supporting the work of new musical theatre projects and musical theatre artists. The Foundation is one of the few places that individual creative artists in the performing arts can go to apply for direct financial support. Contact Jonathan Larson Performing Arts Foundation, Inc., c/o Nancy Kassak Diekmann, P.O. Box 672, Prince St. Station, New York, NY 10012; 212-529-0814; Fax: 212-253-7604; www.jlpaf.org/; JLPAF@ jlpaf.org.

$5,000 Scholarships for Design Students and Others

The Worldstudio Foundation provides scholarships to minority and economically disadvantaged students who are studying the design/arts disciplines in colleges and universities in the United States.

Scholarship recipients are selected not only for their ability and their need, but also for their demonstrated commitment to giving back to the larger community through their work. Basic scholarships are awarded in the amount of $1,000, $1,500 and $2,000. One or two awards are also given each year in the amount of between $3,000 and $5,000 at the jury's discretion. These awards are paid directly to your school to be applied toward your tuition. In addition, Honorable Mention prizes are awarded. Contact Worldstudio Foundation, Inc., 164 Fifth Avenue, New York, NY 10010; 212-807-1990, ext. 246; Fax: 212-807-1799; www.worldstudio.org; scholarships@worldstudio.org.

Up to $30,000 for Music Composers

Commissioning Music/USA is available both to consortia and to individual organizations. Organizations may form a consortium to commission one or more composers to write works which the participating groups will perform or present a total of six times. Recognizing that emerging composers may not have access to the resources necessary to put together a consortium, Meet The Composer also accepts applications from individual organizations, which will perform or present the work a total of four times. Individual organizations may only apply on behalf of one composer. Contact Meet The Composer, Inc., 75 Ninth Ave., Ste. 3RC, New York, NY 10011; 212-645-6949; Fax: 212-645-9669; www.meetthecomposer.org; metrevino@meetthecomposer.org.

$5,000 to Compose Music

Meet The Composer has created *Global Connections* to create support for composers to share their work with a global community. *Global Connections* helps ensure that international audiences see and hear the impressive and creative range of work offered by today's living composers. Grants will range from $500 to $5,000. Contact Meet The Composer, Inc., 75 Ninth Ave., Ste. 3RC, New York, NY 10011; 212-645-6949; Fax: 212-645-9669; www.meetthecomposer.org; metrevino@meetthecomposer.org.

Get $100,000 to Join an Orchestra!

A partnership program of the American Symphony Orchestra League and Meet The Composer, *Music Alive* offers support for composer residencies with professional and youth orchestras of all sizes. There are two types of *Music Alive* composer residencies: the Short Term Residencies offer support for residencies of two to eight weeks within one season; the Extended Residencies offer support for multi-year, full-season residencies of up to three years. Funding amounts range from $7,000 to $28,000 for Short Term Residencies, and from $30,000 up to $100,000 per year for Extended Residencies. Contact Meet The Composer, Inc., 75 Ninth Ave., Ste. 3RC, New York, NY 10011; 212-645-6949; Fax: 212-645-9669; www.meetthecomposer.org; metrevino@meetthecomposer.org.

$1,000 to Perform Music

Creative Connections, the founding program of Meet The Composer, awards grants that enable composers to participate actively in performances of their work. Participation may include performing, conducting, speaking with the audience, presenting workshops, giving interviews, and coaching rehearsals. Awards will range from $250 to $1000 per composer and will be based on the amount of the composer's activity related to the proposed event. Contact Meet The Composer, Inc., 75 Ninth Ave., Ste. 3RC, New York, NY 10011; 212-645-6949; Fax: 212-645-9669; www.meetthecomposer.org; metrevino@meetthecomposer.org.

Fellowships, Housing & $1,000 for Visual Artists
The Fellowships in the Visual Arts program is conducted in collaboration with the Corcoran Gallery of Art in Washington, D.C., and provides a six-month residency that is renewable for two years. Each fellow receives round-trip transportation to Miami, FL; housing and studio space in Miami Beach; $1,000 monthly stipend; and funds for supplies. At the end of the residency, the Corcoran Gallery of Art hosts an exhibit and publishes a catalog of the show for distribution to museums, art dealers, curators and galleries. Contact National Foundation for Advancement in the Arts, 444 Brickell Ave., P-14, Miami, FL 33131; 305-377-1140; Fax: 305-377-1149; www.nfaa.org/artprograms/fellow.htm; info@nfaa.org.

$200 to Meet Artists' Expenses
The Astral Career Grants of up to $200 are awarded to meet modest expenses in response to external opportunities requiring timely action by an artist. Grants are only available in the fields of music and dance. The grant does not cover funds for medical care or general living support. Applicants must be U.S. citizens or permanent residents, and cannot be full-time students. Contact National Foundation for Advancement in the Arts, 444 Brickell Ave., P-14, Miami, FL 33131; 305-377-1140; Fax: 305-377-1149; www.nfaa.org/artprograms/astral-app.html; info@nfaa.org.

Up to $250,000 to Make Videos for T.V.
Grant for programs that take creative risks, explore complex issues and express points of view seldom seen on commercial or public television by reflecting voices and visions of underrepresented communities and address the needs of underserved audiences, particularly minorities and children. Grants range from $20,000 up to $250,000. Contact Independent Television Service, 501 York Street, San Francisco, CA 94110; 415-356-8383; Fax: 415-356-8391; www.itvs.org; itvs@itvs.org.

$1,000 + Publication to Write About Museums
The Brooking Paper on Creativity in Museums is a writing competition that awards a $1,000 to an author with notable examples of creativity, innovation, and imagination in museum operations. The winning paper will be published in Museum News. Contact American Association of Museums, 1575 Eye St., N.W., Ste. 400, Washington, DC 20005-1105; 202-289-1818; Fax: 202-289-6578; www.aam-us.org.

Museum Professionals Get $1,000 for Excellence
The Nancy Hanks Memorial Award for Professional Excellence awards a certificate of $1,000 stipend to be used in furtherance of the honoree's professional development with less than ten years in the field. Application for the award must be made by the nominee's director. The presentation takes place during the AAM annual meeting. Contact American Association of Museums, 1575 Eye St., N.W., Ste. 400, Washington, DC 20005-1105; 202-289-1818; Fax: 202-289-6578; www.aam-us.org.

$1,200 per Month Plus Travel Costs for Performers, Artists, Writers, Filmmakers
The Artist Fellowship Program provides residencies of four to eight weeks at the AAS library for creative and performing artists, writers, filmmakers, and journalists to conduct historical research. Recipients receive $1,200/month stipends plus a travel allowance. Successful applicants are those whose work is for the general public rather than for academic or educational audiences. Contact American Antiquarian Society, 185 Salisbury Street, Worcester, MA 01609-1634; 508-755-5221; Fax: 508-753-3311; www.americanantiquarian.org; cfs@mwa.org.

$1,000 per Month to Research & Write on American Culture

Short-Term Fellowships provides support for one to three months' residence in the Society's library at stipends of $1,000 per month. Open to individuals engaged in scholarly research and writing in any area of American history and culture through 1876. Currently there are nine short-term fellowships available. For a complete list of the different programs offered, Contact American Antiquarian Society, 185 Salisbury Street, Worcester, MA 01609-1634; 508-755-5221; Fax: 508-753-3311; www.americanantiquarian.org; cfs@mwa.org.

$3,000 for Published Works in Science by Adults, Children, Journalists, Broadcasters

The Science Writing Award in Physics and Astronomy for articles, booklets, or books intended for children preschool to 15 years of age offers awards for works published between Jan. and Dec. of the previous year. Winning authors receive a $3,000 prize, a Windsor Chair, and a testimonial. Applicants must be physicists, astronomers, or members of AIP or its affiliated societies. Contact American Institute of Physics, Inc., 1 Physics Ellipse, College Park, MD 20740-3843; 301-209-3100; Fax: 301-209-0843; www.aip.org/aip/writing; aipinfo@aip.org.

$5,000 to Write a Book on War

An annual award consisting of $5,000 and a 24k gold-framed citation of achievement honoring the best fiction set in a period when the United States was at war. It recognizes the service of American veterans and military personnel and encourages the writing and publishing of outstanding war-related fiction. Contact American Library Association, 50 E. Huron Street, Chicago, IL 60611-2795; 800-545-2433; Fax: 312-944-0379; www.ala.org; ala@ala.org.

Awards for Anyone to Write a Novel

This foundation offers several award programs, which are for authors or publishers of books for everyone. Non-fiction, fiction, poetry, children's picture books, and young adult literature are subjects included in the awards. For a complete list of the different programs offered, contact ALA directly. Contact American Library Association, 50 E. Huron Street, Chicago, IL 60611-2795; 800-545-2433; Fax: 312-944-0379; www.ala.org; ala@ala.org.

Up to $20,000 to Create Dance Performances

The Dance: Creation to Performance program awards a three-year initiative in amounts of $20,000, $15,000, $10,000 and $5,000 each year. Artists applying for a grant must be a U.S. citizen or permanent resident, have been a permanent resident of California for at least two years at the time of application, and have demonstrated experience in presenting concert choreography, dance/theater, or traditional dance forms to the public. Contact Dance/USA, 1156 15th St., N.W., Ste. 820, Washington, DC 20005-1726; 202-833-1717; Fax: 202-833-2686; www.danceusa.org; asnyder@danceusa.org.

Financial Assistance for Rhythm and Blues Musicians

The foundation provides emergency financial assistance and career recognition awards to artists and practitioners of rhythm and blues music who worked and/or recorded rhythm and blues music in the 1940's, 50's, and 60's. There are two programs providing assistance and recognition: 1) the Doc Pomus

Financial Assistance Grant Program that supports the current and specific financial needs of legendary artists; and 2) the Pioneer Awards Program that recognizes legendary artists whose lifelong contributions have been instrumental in the development of rhythm and blues music. Awards recipients are nominated by foundation trustees, advisory board and artist steering committee, and past Pioneer Award honorees, and are selected by the board of trustees. Contact The Rhythm and Blues Foundation, Inc., 100 S. Broad Street, Suite 620, Philadelphia, PA 19110; 215-568-1080; Fax: 215-568-1026; www.rhythm-n-blues.org/.

Up to $5,000 for Music Students

The organization seeks to promote and raise the standard of music, including history, composition, performances, appreciation and criticism, and to aid and recognize those learning or serving in the field of music. The organization offers a variety of grants and scholarships to universities, colleges and individuals. Individual grants and scholarships range from $500 up to $5,000. Contact Sigma Alpha Iota Philanthropies, Inc., One Tunnel Road, Asheville, NC 28805; 828-251-0606; Fax: 828-251-0644; www.sai-national.org; nh@sai-national.org.

Financial Assistance for Barbershop Quartet Singers

The organization provides music education for members and support for leadership of other chapters. Any individual, quartet, or chorus in the Evergreen District can apply to the trustees to use the Bud Leabo Memorial Fund. Contact Society for the Preservation & Encouragement of Barbershop Quartet Singing in America (also known as SPEBSQSA - Evergreen District), 4241 21st Ave. W., No. 100, Seattle, WA 98199; 206-282-3883; www.evg.org/default.asp; support@evg.org.

$2,500 for Scientific Journal Writing

The objective of the Journal of Bone and Joint Surgery Resident Journal Club Grants is to support journal club activities for orthopaedic residents. Participation in this program is open to existing and new journal clubs. The program will enhance residency training by providing educational information on managing an effective journal club, and will teach residents how to evaluate current scientific literature. Grants of $2,500 per program are available. Contact Orthopaedic Research Education Foundation, 6300 N. River Rd., Ste. 700, Rosemont, IL 60018-4261; 847-698-9980; Fax: 847-698-7806; www.oref.org; wurth@oref.org.

Up to $3,500 for Playwrights

This Foundation awards grants of $1,000 to $3,500 in support of individual playwrights (and other writers and artists). Criteria are merit and need. Contact Ludwig Vogelstein Foundation, Inc., P.O. Box 510, Shelter Island, NY 11964-0510; lvf@earthlink.net.

$40,000 for Emerging Writers

The Whiting Writers Awards are given annually to ten emerging writers in fiction, nonfiction, poetry and plays. The awards of $40,000 each, are based on accomplishment and promise. Candidates are proposed by nominators from across the country. Winners are chosen by a selection committee, a small group of recognized writers, literary scholars, and editors, appointed annually by the Foundation. The Foundation does not accept applications to the Writers' Program. Contact Mrs. Giles Whiting Foundation, 1133 Ave. of the Americas, 22nd Floor, New York, NY 10036-6710; 212-336-2138; www.whitingfoundation.org.

Money for Creative Writers

The foundation supports writers in all disciplines and attempts to highlight the importance of writers in the society as well as their contributions to the worldwide community. This foundation awards to writers in the categories of playwriting, screenplay, original sitcom, original TV drama, novel, short fiction, children's picture book and poetry. Contact The Writers Foundation, Inc., 3936 Semoran Blvd., No. 368, Orlando, FL 32822; 407-679-3777; www.writersfoundation.com; info@writersfoundation.com.

$10,000 for Artists to Travel to Europe or Russia

Project grants enable U.S. artists, curators and presenters to implement projects in Central Europe, Russia and Eurasia with grants ranging from $2,000 to $10,000. Cooperative arts projects resulting in the creation of new work or those that establish a mutually beneficial exchange of ideas and expertise among artists, curators and arts organizations are eligible to apply. Contact CEC ArtsLink, Inc., 435 Hudson Street, 8th Floor, New York, NY 10014; 212-643-1985; www.cecartslink.org.

Up to $9,000 to Write Poetry

This organization offers 12 awards and prizes to professional and student poets. The awards range from $250 up to $9,000 and are as follows: 1) the Writer Magazine/Emily Dickinson Award, which awards $250 in honor of the memory and poetry of Emily Dickinson, for a poem inspired by Dickinson though not necessarily in her style; 2) the Cecil Hemley Memorial Award, which grants $500 for a lyric poem that addresses a philosophical or epistemological concern; 3) the Lyric Poetry Award of $500 for a lyric poem on any subject; 4) the Lucille Medwick Memorial Award, which awards $500 for an original poem in any form on a humanitarian theme; 5) the Alice Fay Di Castagnola Award offering $1,000 for a manuscript-in-progress of poetry or verse-drama; 6) the Louise Louis/Emily F. Bourne Student Poetry Award, which grants $250 for the best unpublished poem by a student in grades 9 through 12 from the United States; 7) the George Bogin Memorial Award of $500 for a selection of four or five poems that use language in an original way to reflect the encounter of the ordinary and the extraordinary and to take a stand against oppression in any of its forms; 8) the Robert H. Winner Memorial Award, which awards $2,500 in acknowledgment of original work being done in mid-career by a poet who has not had substantial recognition, and it is open to poets over forty who have published no more than one book; 9) the Norma Farber First Book Award of 500 for a first book of original poetry written by an American and published in either a hard or soft cover in a standard edition during the calendar year; 10) the William Carlos Williams Award, which offers between $500 and $1,000 for a book of poetry published by a small press, nonprofit, or university press; 11) the Frost Medal, which awards $2,500 for distinguished lifetime service to American poetry; and 12) the Shelley Memorial Award, which awards between $6,000 and $9,000 to a living American poet, selected with reference to his or her genius and need. There may be entry fees associated with each submission. Contact Poetry Society of America, 15 Gramercy Park, New York, NY 10003-1705; 212-254-9628; www.poetrysociety.org/.

Money for Actors to Go to School

The John L. Dales Scholarship Fund helps qualified Guild members and their children reach their educational potential by providing more than a million dollars in scholarships for study at accredited institutions of higher learning. An applicant may receive up to five scholarships. Grants range from

$3,000 to $5,000. Contact The Screen Actors Guild Foundation, 5757 Wilshire Blvd., 7th Floor, Los Angeles, CA 90036; 323-549-6649; Fax: 323-549-6710; www.sagfoundation.org; dlloyd@sag.org.

Grants To Actors to Help Pay for Health Care
The Foundation's Catastrophic Health Fund provides grants to eligible Guild members and their dependents that suffer from catastrophic illness or injury and are unable to afford the Guild Health Plan's Self-Pay Program. The Fund ensures that every eligible Guild member and his or her family can depend on continued health benefits when they need them most. Contact The Screen Actors Guild Foundation, 5757 Wilshire Blvd., 7th Floor, Los Angeles, CA 90036; 323-549-6649; Fax: 323-549-6710; www.sagfoundation.org; msmith@sag.org.

Emergency Assistance for Actors
The Foundation provides funds for the aid, relief and care of needy, sick, indigent and aged Guild members. When assistance is needed, it is given quickly and compassionately, always maintaining strict confidentiality and dignity for each recipient. Contact The Screen Actors Guild Foundation, 5757 Wilshire Blvd., 7th Floor, Los Angeles, CA 90036; 323-549-6649; Fax: 323-549-6710; www.sagfoundation.org; msmith@sag.org.

FREE Rent & Utilities for Artists to Go to New Mexico
The Foundation's purpose is to provide a quiet haven where artists may pursue their creative endeavors without pressure to produce while they are in residence. Artists can live in the fully furnished apartments for a period of up to three months rent-free and utility-free. No spouses, children or pets are permitted to reside at the Foundation during the period of a residence grant. Artists are responsible for purchasing and preparing their own meals, paying their own travel expenses and providing their own working material. Contact: The Helene Wurlitzer Foundation of New Mexico, P.O. Box 1891, Taos, NM 87571; 505-758-2413; Fax: 505-758-2559; hwf@ taosnet.com.

$50,000 to Write a Civil War Book
The Lincoln Prize at Gettysburg College shall be awarded annually for the finest scholarly work in English on the era of the American Civil War. The $50,000 Prize will generally go to a book but in rare instances an important article or essay might be honored. The Prize is intended chiefly to encourage outstanding new scholarship, but a lifetime contribution to the study of Lincoln, or the American Civil War soldier, may qualify for the award. Contact The Lincoln and Soldiers Institute, 233 N. Washington St., Gettysburg, PA 17325; 717-337-6590; www.gettysburg.edu/academics/cwi/lincoln_prize/.

$1,000 Travel Money for Food Writers
The IACP Foundation has a travel grant program for professional food writers whose research requires or will benefit from access to the holdings of specific libraries with significant culinary collections in the U.S. Applicants must demonstrate that they are under contract for a book, magazine or newspaper article. The average stipend is $1,000 but may vary according to the proposal. Contact The International Association of Culinary Professionals Foundation, 304 W. Liberty St., Ste. 201, Louisville, KY 40202-3068; 502-581-9786, ext. 264; Fax: 502-589-3602; www.iacpfoundation.com/.

$20,000 for Pianists And Music Students
The Murray Dranoff Foundation, Inc. provides prizes and awards for pianists and music students who perform chamber music. It sponsors piano competitions and awards prizes for these competitions ranging from $20,000 to $200. Contact The Murray Dranoff Foundation, Inc., 180 N.E. 39th St., Ste. 207, Miami, FL 33137; 305-572-9900; Fax: 305-572-9922; www.dranoff2piano.org.

Help for Actors and Others with AIDS
Broadway Cares/Equity Fights AIDS is a foundation that provides assistance to people living with AIDS/HIV. Projects include providing food, shelter, transportation, emergency financial aid, emotional/practical support systems, and nonreimbursable medical expenses. Contact Broadway Cares/Equity Fights AIDS, 165 W. 46th St., Ste. 1300, New York, NY 10036; 212-840-0770; Fax: 212-840-0551; www.bcefa.org; info@bcefa org.

Emergency Funds for Writers with AIDS
The PEN American Center, Inc. provides financial support to writers and others in the publishing industry through several awards programs and with emergency funds made available to published professional writers and editors for unexpected financial and HIV/AIDS-related crisis situations. In especially urgent cases the PEN Writers Fund can release up to $200 within 24 hours. Contact PEN American Center, Inc., 588 Broadway, Ste. 303, New York, NY 10012; 212-334-1660; Fax: 212-334-2181; www.pen.org; PEN@pen.org.

$10,000 Scholarships for Songwriters and Musicians
BMI Foundation, Inc. encourages the creation, performance and study of music through awards, scholarships, internships, grants, and commissions. Funding includes: the Jazz Composition Prize of $3,000; general grants to music organizations; the John Lennon Scholarship for Songwriters and Composers which consists of one $10,000 scholarship, and two $5,000 scholarships to young songwriters 15-25; and the Peermusic Latin Scholarship, which awards a $5,000 scholarship for the best song or instrumental work in any Latin genre. Contact BMI Foundation, Inc., 320 W. 57th St., New York, NY 10019; 212-830-2520; www.bmifoundation.org.

$10,000 to Promote American Dance
Capezio/Ballet Makers Dance Foundation, Inc. provides funding for dance-related organizations. It offers the Capezio Dance Award, which annually awards $10,000 to an individual, company, or organization that has made a significant contribution to American dance. Contact Capezio/Ballet Makers Dance Foundation, Inc., 1 Campus Rd., Totowa, NJ 07512; 973-595-9000; www.capeziodance.com.

$25,000 for Puppet Theatre
The Jim Henson Foundation provides grants to develop and encourage the creative art of puppetry in the United States. Emphasis is on contemporary puppet theater for adults, with some focus on new works suitable for family audiences. Giving activities include $44,762 for 12 grants to individuals ranging from $25,000 to $358. Contact The Jim Henson Foundation, 627 Broadway, 9th Floor, New York, NY 10012; 212-680-1400; Fax: 212-680-1401; www.hensonfoundation.org; email: info@hensonfoundation.org.

$$ for Needy Professional Musicians
The Musicians Foundation, Inc. helps professional musicians by providing emergency financial assistance in meeting current living, medical and allied expenses. The Foundation does not award scholarships, loans, or composition grants. Contact Musicians Foundation, Inc., 875 6th Ave., Ste. 2303, New York, NY 10001; 212-239-9137; Fax: 212-239-9138; www.musiciansfoundation.org; info@musiciansfoundation.org.

$50,000 to Promote Opera
Opera America, Inc. seeks to promote opera as exciting and accessible to individuals from all walks of life. Awards ranging from $50,000 to $5,000 are available for audience development, repertoire development and artist development. Contact Opera America, Inc., 1156 15th St., Ste. 810, Washington, DC 20005-1704; 202-293-4466; Fax: 202-393-0735; www.operaamerica.org; frontdesk@operaamerica.org.

$25,000 for Education, Arts, and the Environment
The New Earth Foundation provides grants for wide variety of innovative programs related to education, social services, the arts, communication, and the environment. The foundation typically funds programs connected with newer and smaller nonprofit organizations. It may consider programs for children and youth, garden and other such programs if they show that they reach outside the norm in their vision and approach and are innovative and effective. Programs must demonstrate a practical means of planning and implementation. Grants available to individuals working under the umbrella of an established nonprofit organization. Contact New Earth Foundation, 2940 Southwest Drive, Suite 4A, Sedona, AZ 86336; 928-204-1151; www.newearthfoundation.org/neweath/home.cfm; director@newearthfoundation.org.

$1,000 for Puppeteers
The Puppeteers of America Endowment Fund gives to members of Puppeteers of America, Inc. for projects related to their work in puppetry. Contact Len Gerwick, Puppeteers of America Endowment Fund, 184 Hildreth Street, Marlborough, MA 01752; www.puppeteers.org/; len@gerwickpuppets.com.

Money for Classical Music Composers
REC Music Foundation promotes new classical music composers, primarily through the development of new computer tools. Contact REC Music Foundation, c/o Robert E. Crawford, Jr., 61 Crestwood Dr., Clayton, MO 63105; www.recmusic.org/siteindex.html; recrawfo@recmusic.org.

$70,000 for Education and the Arts
The Wallace Foundation provides grants for developing effective educational leaders to improve student learning; providing informal learning opportunities for children and families in communities; and increasing participation in the arts. Contact The Wallace Foundation, 5 Penn Plaza., 7th Floor, New York, NY 10001; 212-251-9700; www.wallacefunds.org; wrdf@wallacefunds.org.

Over $1.0 Million for Film Video, and Media Artists
This foundation provides grants and project funding for independent film and video makers and other media artists who have little likelihood of being supported through traditional funding sources. They

offer several grant categories. Contact them to see if they can help you with your artistic venture. Film Arts Foundation, 145 Ninth Street, San Francisco, CA 94103; 415-552-8760; www.filmarts.org.

Up to $5,000 for Film Production Projects

The Frameline for the Horizons/ Frameline Film & Video Completion Fund provides grants to lesbian, gay, bisexual and transgender film and video makers. Completion funds include post-production for films and videos, including sub-titling and video- to-film transfer. Contact Frameline, 145 Ninth Street, Suite 300, San Francisco, CA 94103-2636; 415-703-8650; Fax: 415-861-1404; www.frameline.org/, info@frameline.org.

Artists Receive Funding to Promote Their Work

The Jerome Foundation makes grants to support the creation and production of new artistic works by emerging artists, and contributes to the professional advancement of those artists. The Jerome Foundation supports programs in dance, literature, media arts, music, theater, performance art, the visual arts, multidisciplinary work and arts criticism. It provides financial assistance to nonprofit arts organizations that support emerging creative artists who are residents of Minnesota and New York City; artists receive direct support from funded programs. Contact The Jerome Foundation, 400 Sibley Street, St. Paul, MN 55101-1928; 800-995-3766; 651-224-9431; Fax: 651-224-3439; www.jeromefdn.org.

$1,400 for Artistic Endeavors

The Artist Trust has provided more than $2.4 million in direct grant support to 1,192 Washington State promising musicians, writers, visual and craft artists, playwrights, choreographers, composers, performers and filmmakers. The GAP Program provides support for artist-generated projects, which can include the development, completion or presentation of new work. GAP awards are open to artists of all disciplines. Contact Artist Trust, 1835 12th Avenue, Seattle, WA 98122-2437; 206-467-8734; Fax: 206-467-9633; www.artisttrust.org.

$20,000 Grants to be Artistic

Creative Capital provides grants to artists in four disciplines: visual arts, film/video arts, performing arts, and emerging art fields. They are looking for innovative and unique projects. Initial grants range from $5000 to $20,000, with grantees eligible for additional funding of more than $20,000 for a number of purposes. Applicants must be a U.S. citizen or permanent resident, at least 25 years old and have 5 years of professional working artist experience. Contact Creative Capital, 65 Bleecker Street, 7th Floor, New York, NY 10012; 212-598-9000, Box 300; http://creative-capital.org/, info@creative-capital.org.

Photography Grants up to $5,000

The Aaron Siskind Foundation provides grants of up to $5,000 to photographers using still-photography based media. Grant awards are based upon quality of work and the promise of future achievement. Funds must be used to support the artist's creative endeavors. Contact Aaron Siskind Foundation, c/o School of Visual Arts, MFA Photography, 209 East 23rd Street, New York, NY 10010; 609-348-5650; www.aaronsiskind.org; info@aaronsiskind.org.

$10,000 to Create and Display Artwork in the U.S.

Provides grants to artists in the amounts ranging from $500 to $10,000 for the production and display of interactive artworks in communities and venues across the United States and around the globe. Targets innovative interactive art: projects designed to be touched, handled, played with, and moved through in a public arena; art that solicits a collaborative response from its audience, even as it encourages collaboration between artists. Contact the Black Rock Arts Foundation, 1900 Third Street, 2nd Floor, San Francisco, CA 94158; 415-626-1248; www.blackrockarts.org, info@blackrockarts.org.

Free Money to Write a Book

Yes, you can make money writing a book. Sometimes you can even make a lot of money. I've made a bundle, and I even got a D in college English. So, if I can do it, there is no reason why you can't.

There are a number of ways you can make money writing a book:

1) You can get a grant from the government or a nonprofit organization
2) You can go directly to publishers
3) You can find a literary agent who will contact publishers for you
4) You can publish the book yourself

What Kind Of Money Is Available

The government money that's available is in the form of a grant. That's money you don't have to pay back, so of course, there's no better money than that. The money you might get from a publisher will usually be in the form of an advance towards future royalties. That means they will give you a certain amount of money when you sign the contract. Sometimes this money will be spread out in payments, some you could receive at the signing and some when you turn in the manuscript. This advance will be deducted from the royalties you earn when the book sells. If the book sells more than what the publisher gave you in the advance, you will receive more money. If the book sells less than the advance figure, the publisher loses.

Using the government or a publisher will usually mean **you get money up front**. Publishing yourself means **you put up your own money**. There is more risk, but it can also mean more reward. I've published about 12 books with New York publishers, but in the last five years I've been publishing myself. And to tell you the truth, I'm a lot happier now.

What You Need To Start

So many people believe that you have to have the entire book completed in order to get anyone interested in your project. Not so. All you usually need to have completed is a chapter or two along with an outline to get someone interested. I believe that it is important not to write the entire book, especially for the commercial market. If your idea is of any value, people are going to give you ideas on how to make it better. More importantly, they will tell you what they want to see in the book in order for them to publish it. And a bigger issue today is that no one has time to read a complete manuscript. They are more likely to review your book if you give them as little to do as possible. Most people want to see the basic concept of a book in progress, and nothing more.

Government Grants To Publish Your Books

This can be the most difficult way to get published mainly because so few books are published this way each year. Approximately 50,000 books are published annually by commercial publishers, while the government only publishes a few hundred titles. However, the odds of getting a grant from the government are probably a lot better than getting money from private sources. You have about a one in eight chance of getting a government grant for your book, which as odds go, isn't bad at all. Many of the government programs have now stopped giving money directly to individuals and only give money to organizations who in turn pass it on to the individuals who have applied for it.

The point is to ignore what I just said, because if you want to change your life you have to try everything, and I mean **everything!** Listed below are the sources of government grants for writers. When you call the organizations listed below, be thorough in your questioning of the person on the other end of the line — have they told you about every program available that might be able to give you some money?

National Endowment for the Arts
1100 Pennsylvania Ave., NW
Washington, DC 20506
202-682-5400
www.nea.gov
Email: webmgr@arts.endow.gov

National Endowment for the Humanities
1100 Pennsylvania Ave., NW
Washington, DC 20506
202-606-8400
800-NEH-1121
www.neh.fed.us
Email: info@neh.gov

Going Directly To Publishers

This seems to be the most obvious method and it works for many people. The world of publishing is very big and there is probably an editor at some publishing house who would be interested in your idea. Life, like so many things, is a numbers game. So the more publishers you call, the more editors you talk with, and the more likely you are to find someone interested in your book idea.

Listed below are the sources that identify publishers in the United States. You can find these sources in most local libraries.

- *Literary Marketplace*, Reed Reference Publishing Co., New Providence, NJ
- *Literary Agents of North America*, The Associates, New York, NY
- *Insider's Guide to Book Editors, Publishers, and Literary Agents*, Prima Publishing, Rocklin, GA
- *Literary Agents: A Writer's Guide*, Adam Begley, Penguin, New York, NY

Publishing Your Own Book

With a successful book, you'll make a lot more money publishing it yourself. What profits a publishing company would have made will end up being yours to keep. But you'll need money up front to publish your own book. How much? That depends on the kind of book.

There are three major issues involved in publishing your own book: printing, distribution and marketing. The most expensive part of it can be printing. There are ways of getting the other two necessities for free, but you need to have books to sell first. The first book is the most expensive to produce. If you print 5,000 to 10,000 copies of a 300 page book you may be able to have them printed for about $2 each. But printing only 300 books can cost you $30 each. If you are going to sell your book for $20, you're in big trouble if you only print 300 copies. But if you print 5000 copies, it's going to cost you $10,000 before you make even one sale. A $10,000 advance from a publisher may start to look a lot better after adding up these numbers.

If you are publishing a self help book, you can consider other alternatives. You can make single copies of books at a local copy store, or your home computer and put it into a three ring binder. You can also charge more for the book in this kind of format. This could work well for books like: How To Fix Your Credit, How To Get Free Legal Advice, How To Travel Cheap, Make Money On The Internet, etc.

Distribution is an important element in anything you produce in this country. Getting your book in bookstores can be a major problem. You can find distributors who will do it for you and charge you a commission for doing so, or you can contact the bookstore chains directly. Either way it's hard, but not impossible. The bigger problem for a self publisher is that bookstores work on consignment. That means if they sell your book, you get the money. If they don't, you get the book back and get no money. And it may take three to six months to find out which of these two events actually occur.

When I first started publishing my own books, I decided that I couldn't afford to be in bookstores. If every bookstore purchased 10 copies of my book, I'd be out of business. If there are 5,000 book stores, that would mean 50,000 books at $2 each. I would have to put up $100,000 to cover printing costs and have no idea if and when I'd get anything back. So I decided on distributing my publications through mail order. If someone sent me the money, I would send them the book.

Nothing happens without successful marketing. You can have production and distribution all figured out but if you don't know how to sell your book, you're sunk. I use talk shows. I was on talk shows when I was writing for New York publishers, so I knew how the system works (you make hundreds of telephone calls and try to convince the producers you have something interesting to say.) But this time when I got on the shows, instead of saying the book was in book stores, I'd say the book was only available by calling 1-800-UNCLE-SAM.

If you want to sell your own book, you'll find the way that works best for you.

Using A Literary Agent

This may be the most productive method for someone trying to get their first book published. Using a middle man, in this case a literary agent, can save you time in finding a publisher. Also, most big publishers would rather deal with an agent who knows the business rather than dealing directly with you. They don't want to spend time explaining contracts and educating you about the process. The agent performs this role for them.

Every literary agent has her area of expertise, collection of publishers, and editors within those companies, whom they are close to and know the kinds of books for which they are looking. So instead of contacting hundreds of publishers and editors directly, you can now concentrate on just dozens of agents. To contact an agent, write a brief letter describing your work, list any prior publications, and include a self-addressed stamped envelope (SASE) to receive a reply. The cost? They will normally ask you for 10% to 15% of what they get for you from the publisher. Some particularly successful agents are in such demand for their time that they charge a flat fee just to read your book outline or sample chapters.

Listed below is a small collection of literary agents around the country who do not charge reading fees. For additional information on literary agents contact: Association of Authors' Representatives (AAR), mailing address: P.O. Box 237201, Ansonia Station, New York, NY 10023; office address: 676 Ninth Ave., #312, New York, NY 10036; Email: aarinc@mindspring.com; www.aar-online.org. The AAR will send you a list of 22 suggested questions to ask, the AAR's *Canon of Ethics*, and a listing of agents who are members for $5, plus postage and handling.

Literary Agents

California

Linda Allen Literary Agency
1949 Green St. #5
San Francisco, CA 94123
415-921-6437
Fax: 415-921-3733
Email: linda@lallenlitagency.com
This agency handles fiction and non-fiction. For non-fiction send a proposal. For fiction, send a synopsis and the first 20-40 pages. Query first with a SASE. No reading fee.

Atchity Editorial/Entertainment International Literary, Inc.
Management and Film Production
9601 Wilshire Blvd., Box 1202
Beverly Hills, CA 90212
323-932-0407
www.aeionline.com
Subjects this agency is most interested in include: fiction; mainstream that can also be made into television or feature films, screenplays (especially true stories with television potential). Non-fiction: entrepreneurial business books, heroic and true stories, general interest, and reference books. Screenplays; heroic true stories, action, thrillers, romance, comedy, or science fiction. Submit query letter and 25 sample pages. Include an SASE.

Castiglia Literary Agency
1155 Camino del Mar, Suite 510
Del Mar, CA 92014
858-755-8761
Fax: 858-755-7063
Email: jaclagency@aol.com
This agency will look at query letters, synopsis, and two chapters but will return unread unsolicited complete manuscripts. They represent fiction and non-fiction. In non-fiction: science, business, finance, health, spiritual, women's issues, biography, and niche books. In fiction: ethnic, mainstream, literary, and some genre.

Sandra Dijkstra Literary Agency
1155 Camino del Mar, Suite 515
Del Mar, CA 92014
Fax: 858-794-2822
858-755-3115
Email: sdla@dijkstraagency.com
This agency requires the first 50 pages with synopsis or outline along with an SASE. They specialize in literary and commercial fiction and non-fiction.

Peter Fleming Agency
P.O. Box 458
Pacific Palisades, CA 90272
310-454-1373
The Agency handles adult non-fiction, specializing in innovative, professional, business, and pro-free market topics. Submit query letter first with an SASE.

The Charlotte Gusay Literary Agency
10532 Blythe, Suite 211
Los Angeles, CA 90064

310-559-0831
Fax: 310-559-2639
Email: gusay1@aol.com (queries only)
www.mediastudio.com/gusay
Both fiction and non-fiction are handled. Prefers commercial, mainstream, quality material (especially books that can be marketed as film material). Projects on children's books are limited. They like material that is innovative, unusual, eclectic, and nonsexist. The agency will consider literary fiction with crossover potential. No unsolicited manuscripts are accepted, submit a succinct and clear query letter with an SASE.

Reece Halsey Agency
8733 Sunset Blvd., Suite 101
Los Angeles, CA 90069
310-652-2409
Fax: 310-652-7595
This agency specializes in literary fiction, writing they feel is exceptional in its field. Submit a query letter with one or two sample chapters and an SASE.

Frederick Hill/ Bonnie Nadell Literary Agency
1842 Union St.
San Francisco, CA 94123
415-921-2910
Fax: 415-921-2802
Submit query first along with an SASE. This agency handles fiction and non-fiction. They do not accept westerns, romance, or science fiction.

Michael Larsen/Elizabeth Pomada Literary Agents
1029 Jones St.
San Francisco, CA 94109-5023
415-673-0939
Email: larsenpoma@aol.com
www.larsen-pomada.com
This agency handles fiction and non-fiction. For fiction, send the first 30 pages and a synopsis and an SASE. For non-fiction, contact the agency.

The Maureen Lasher Agency/ The LA Literary Agency
Attn: Ann Cashman
P.O. Box 46370
Los Angeles, CA 90046
323-654-5288
Fax: 323-654-5388
Email: laliteraryag@aol.com
Send written inquiry, synopsis, 50 pages, and include an SASE. No telephone or fax inquiries are accepted. The agency handles general fiction and non-fiction, and it does not handle science fiction or romance novels.

Julie Popkin, Literary Agent
15340 Albright St., #204
Pacific Palisades, CA 90272
310-459-2834
Fax: 310-459-4128
Email: jpopkin@verizon.net
This agency handles fiction, literary and popular including mysteries; non-fiction, especially social issues. Film rights only for clients whose books are under contract. Queries accepted if by mail with SASE only. No phone or fax inquiries.

The Angela Rinaldi Literary Agency
P.O. Box 7877
Beverly Hills, CA 90212-7877
310-842-7665
Fax: 310-837-8143
Email: amr@RinaldiLiterary.com
The agency is interested in fiction and non-fiction submissions. Prefers non-fiction topics that appeal to a wide audience, such as women's issues, pop culture, current issues, biography, popular reference, business, popular science and books written by academics, doctors, and therapists based on their research. Queries only by mail, no phone or fax. If you are sending a novel, send a synopsis, the first 100 pages, and a chapter outline with an SASE. For non-fiction, send a draft of your proposal which includes an outline and a sample chapter, but a detailed query letter which includes a brief synopsis and outline is acceptable. Include an SASE.

Ken Sherman & Associates
9507 Santa Monica Blvd., Suite 211
Beverly Hills, CA 90210
310-273-8840
Fax: 310-271-2875
Email: ksassociates@earthlink.net
This agency does not accept unsolicited material. All material must come through a referral only from either a client, producer or writer who they already know who has read the material and can vouch for the quality. They handle film television, fiction and non-fiction writers.

Spieler Agency/West
Contact: Victoria Shoemaker
4096 Piedmont Ave.
Oakland, CA 94611
510-985-1422
Fax: 310-985-1323
Email: spielerlit@aol.com
www.spieleragency.com
Literary non-fiction areas include history, social issues, the environment, economics, and business. Literary fiction is also handled. Reports on queries in 2 weeks, reports on manuscripts in 5 weeks. Manuscripts without an SASE or sufficient money to cover postage will not be returned.

Susan Travis Literary Agency
1317 N. San Fernando Blvd., Suite 175
Burbank, CA 91504

818-557-6538
Fax: 818-557-6549
This agency is currently looking for submissions of fiction and non-fiction. Fiction interests include mainstream and literary fiction, romance, mystery, historical, and thrillers. Non-fiction should be for the general trade market, including but not limited to business, health, parenting, cookbooks, and reference. Fiction submissions should be in the form of a query letter with a one page synopsis. You may attach the first 15-20 pages and indicate the page length of your manuscript. Non-fiction submissions should be in the form of a query letter giving a brief overview, the target audience/market, your credentials, and indicate whether you have written a proposal or have completed the entire manuscript. Always include an SASE.

Annette Van Duren Agency
11684 Ventura Blvd., #235
Studio City, CA 91604
818-752-6000
Fax: 818-752-6985
Television and film writers, writer/directors, or writer/producers are represented. No unsolicited manuscripts will be accepted. Submit query with SASE.

Waterside Productions, Inc.
2187 Newcastle Ave., Suite 204
Cardiff, CA 92007-1839
760-632-9190
Fax: 760-632-9295
www.waterside.com
This agency specializes in computer books. Other areas of strength include business, education, health, biography, sports, psychology, spiritual/self-help, how-to, and science book placement. Submit query letter or request the submission guidelines for non-fiction.

West Coast Literary Associates
951 Old Country Rd., #140
Belmond, CA 94002
650-557-0438
Email: wstlit@aol.com
The agency represents authors of book length fiction (literary, mainstream, all genres) and book length non-fiction. Submit a one page synopsis and the first 25 manuscript pages for preliminary review and evaluation. Include an SASE.

Colorado
Jody Rein Books, Inc.
7741 S. Ash Court
Centennial, CO 80122
303-694-4430
Fax: 303-694-0687
Email: jodyrein@jodyreinbooks.com
www.jodyreinbooks.com
This agency sells primarily very commercial non-fiction.
Unsolicited manuscripts are not accepted. Send query letter with SASE.

Connecticut
New England Publishing Associates
P.O. Box 5
Chester, CT 06412-005
860-345-READ
Fax: 860-345-3660
Email: nepa@nepa.com
www.nepa.com
New England Publishing Associates provides editorial guidance, representation, and manuscript development for book projects with a focus on general interest non-fiction for the adult market, particularly reference, science, health, crime, biography, women's issues, current events, history and politics. They do accept unsolicited manuscripts which should include a proposal, outline and sample chapter (guidelines available upon request).

The Shepard Agency
73 Kingswood Dr.
Bethel, CT 06801
203-790-4230
Fax: 203-798-2924
Email: shepardagcy@mindspring.com
http://home.mindspring.com/~shepardagcy
The Sheppard Agency specializes in adult, children, general trade fiction and non-fiction, professional, reference and business titles. Submit query letter first, including an SASE.

District of Columbia
Graybill & English Literary Agency
1875 Connecticut Ave., NW, Suite 712
Washington, DC 20005
202-588-9798
Fax: 202-457-0662
www.graybillandenglish.com
A large part of the firm's work is book, television and movie agentry. Manuscripts are accepted on an exclusive basis only and they try to respond within 6-8 weeks. They want to know if the material has been seen and rejected by any other agents or publishers. Any writer may submit a proposal by sending it to the address above. A SASE is required.

Literary and Creative Artists Agency, Inc.
3543 Albemarie St., N.W.
Washington, DC 20008-4213
202-362-4688
Fax: 202-362-8875
Email: query@lcadc.com (no attachments)
www.lcadc.com
The agency considers general non-fiction by credentialed authors and both literary and commercial fiction. Send query letter with a synopsis or outline, 3 sample chapters, and an author biography, including publication and representation

history. Include SASE. Unsolicited manuscripts are not accepted. If a full manuscript is requested, allow review period of two weeks.

Florida

The Westchester Literary Agency, Inc.
2533 Egret Lake Dr.
West Palm Beach, FL 33413
561-642-2908
Fax: 561-439-2228
Most genres of fiction and non-fiction are acceptable. Preference for fiction is for mainstream/literary but important genres that approach mainstream appeal will be considered. Protocol Sheets for preparing and submitting manuscripts are available at no cost, but an SASE is required.

Georgia

The Knight Agency
577 S. Main St.
Madison, GA 30650
Mailing Address:
P.O. Box 550648
Atlanta, GA 30355
706-752-0096
Email: knightagent@aol.com (queries)
www.knightagency.net
No unsolicited manuscripts are accepted. For fiction send query letter, synopsis or outline (no more than 3 pages), the first three chapters of your completed manuscript, and an SASE. For non-fiction, send the same as for fiction, but add a bibliography and a summary of your qualifications.

Talent Source Agency
1711 Dean Forest Rd., Suite H
Savannah, GA 31408
912-963-0941
Fax: 912-963-0944
www.talentsource.com
Work handled includes feature film, all types, especially character driven dramas, comedies, and children's films. Submit query letter with synopsis and SASE. Allow 4-6 weeks for responses.

Illinois

Browne & Miller Literary Associates
Multimedia Product Development, Inc.
410 South Michigan Ave., Suite 460
Chicago, IL 60605
312-922-3063
Fax: 312-922-1905
Email: mail@browneandmiller.com
www.mpdinc.net
Submit a 1-3 page query letter along with an SASE. No unsolicited materials are accepted. The agency is interested in commercial, overnight sellers in the areas of mainstream fiction and non-fiction. For fiction: mainstream, women's fiction, mystery/suspense, romances and thrillers. For non-fiction: biography, business, current events, gardening, health/medicine, how-to, humor, parenting, pop culture, psychology, reference, science, and true crime.

Maryland

The Sagalyn Literary Agency
7201 Wisconsin Ave., Suite 675
Bethesda, MD 20814
301-718-6440
Fax: 301-718-6444
Email: agency@sagalyn.com
www.sagalyn.com
This agency asks that people who are submitting send a query letter first and be sure to include an SASE. They will only accept submissions through the mail. They handle adult fiction and non-fiction.

Massachusetts

The Doe Coover Agency
P.O. Box 668
Winchester, MA 01890
781-721-6000
Fax: 781-721-6727
No unsolicited manuscripts are accepted. Send query letter and sample manuscript along with an SASE. The agency handles non-fiction and fiction, specializing in literary and commercial fiction, social sciences, journalism, science, biography, and cookbooks.

The Jeff Herman Agency, Inc.
9 South St.
P.O. Box 1522
Stockbridge, MA 01262
413-298-0077
Fax: 413-298-8188
www.jeffherman.com
Subjects handled include all areas of commercial non-fiction, with particular interest shown in business, investigative, spiritual, self-help, history, humor, popular culture, and computers. Submit a query letter and include an SASE.

Alison J. Picard
Literary Agent
P.O. Box 2000
Cotuit, MA 02635
508-477-7192
Fax: 508-477-7192 (call first)
Email: ajpicard@aol.com
This agent represents mainstream and literary fiction, contemporary and historical romances, non-fiction, mysteries and thrillers, juvenile and young adult books. Preferences are toward commercial non-fiction, romances, and mysteries/suspense/thrillers. Submit query letter with SASE.

Helen Rees Literary Agency
376 North St.
Boston, MA 02113-2103
617-227-9014
Fax: 617-227-8762
Email: Helen@reesagency.com
This agency handles business books, literary fiction, biography, women's issues and current political issues. Do not submit short stories, poetry, cookbooks, children's literature, science fiction or sports. Submit query letter with a brief outline and an SASE.

Minnesota
The Lazear Agency
Editorial Board
860 Washington Ave., N, Suite 660
Minneapolis, MN 55401
612-332-8640
Fax: 612-332-4648
Email: info@lazear.com
www.lazear.com
This is a full service agency assisting clients in all phases of the publication process. They handle fiction and non-fiction. Submit a 1-2 page query letter, including a synopsis of the work you would like considered, and any relevant writing experience, such as previously published works along with an SASE. Allow 4-6 weeks for a response.

Sebastian Agency
557 W. Seventh St., Suite 2
St. Paul, MN 55102
651-224-6670
Fax: 651-224-6855
Email: laurie@sebastianagency.com
www.sebastianagency.com
No new fiction authors are being accepted at this time. New clients, mainly on referral, are being accepted in the areas of business, biographies (no family memoirs), consumer reference, health/nutrition, psychology/ self-help, gift/inspirational, popular culture; social issues/current affairs, humor, and sports. Send query explaining project, telling about the author and why you are doing this book. Submit proposal, outline or synopsis and sample chapter with SASE.

New Jersey
Reid Boates Literary Agency
269 Cooks Crossroad
P.O. Box 328
908-730-8523
Fax: 908-730-8931
Pittstown, NJ 08867-0328
Email: boatesliterary@att.net
This agency deals with non-fiction, adult general interest areas such as biography and autobiography, investigative journalism, current affairs, spirituality and personal enrichment, health and self-help. Query first with SASE.

Max Gartenberg, Literary Agent
12 Westminster Dr.
Livingston, NJ 07039-1414
973-994-4457
Fax: 973-994-4457
Email: gartenbook@att.net
This agent handles adult fiction and non-fiction. Unsolicited manuscripts are not accepted. Writers must send a query letter first, enclosing an SASE and receive an explicit invitation to submit material.

March Tenth, Inc.
4 Myrtle St.
Haworth, NJ 07641
201-387-6551
Fax: 201-387-6552
Email: scharon@aol.com
The subjects this agency is most interested in representing are popular culture, music, general non-fiction, biography, and fiction. Submit a query letter describing the project in a concise way, state credentials, and include an SASE.

Puddingstone Literary, Authors' Agents
11 Mabro Dr.
Denville, NJ 07834
973-366-3622
This agency handles general trade and mass market fiction and non-fiction, motion picture scripts and teleplays. Submit query letter first with SASE. If interested, you will be notified to send outline and sample chapters.

New York
Marcia Amsterdam Agency
41 West 82nd St.
New York, NY 10024-5613
212-873-4945
Mostly fiction, mainstream non-fiction, young adult, television and movie scripts are handled by this agency. Submit query letter with an SASE. No unsolicited manuscripts are accepted.

Malaga Baldi Literary Agency
233 W. 99, Suite 19C
New York, NY 10025
212-579-5075
Fax: 212-579-5078
Email: mbaldi@nyc.rr.com
This agency handles cultural history, non-fiction and literary-edgy fiction, no children or young adult. No unsolicited manuscripts or phone calls, submit query letter with an SASE. Allow 10 weeks minimum for response.

Pam Bernstein & Associates Inc.
790 Madison Ave. Suite 310
New York, NY 10021
212-288-1700

Fax: 212-288-3054
Email: pbernassoc@aol.com
A query letter (not a full manuscript) with an SASE is requested as a first step. If interested in further materials, such as sample chapters or an entire manuscript, they will contact the author. They handle fiction and non-fiction.

Georges Borchardt, Inc.
Literary Agency
136 East 57th St.
New York, NY 10022
212-753-5785
Fax: 212-838-6518
Email: georges@gbagency.com
This agency does not consider unsolicited manuscripts, but does consider new writers who come recommended by authors and/or editors whom they know and trust. They handle literary fiction and high quality non-fiction.

Brandt & Hochman Literary Agents, Inc.
1501 Broadway
Suite 2310
New York, NY 10036
212-840-5760
Fax: 212-840-5776
The agency does not accept unsolicited manuscripts, but they will respond to a letter about the author and the work in question. They are a general literary agency, but do not handle poetry or film scripts.

Patricia Breinin Literary Services
212 Inwood Rd.
Scarsdale, NY 10583
914-472-6417
The Service handles quality fiction and non-fiction (no children or young adult books). They prefer to have new clients referred to them by publishers, editors, or authors known to the agent.

Marie Brown Associates
412 W 154 St.
New York, NY 10032
212-939-9725
Fax: 212-939-9728
Email: mbrownlit@aol.com
Unsolicited query letters are accepted, (does not review unsolicited manuscripts), multiple submissions, encourages unpublished/unproduced writers, enclose an SASE for all correspondence. They specialize in commercial fiction, contemporary fiction, erotica, gay/lesbian fiction, juveniles picture books and 6-8 year old and 9-12 year old literary fiction, mainstream fiction, novella, novel length fiction, poetry collections, professional books, quality fiction, self-help, screen plays, short stories, short story collections, trade non-fiction, translations, women's fiction, young adult fiction and non-fiction.

Knox Burger Associates, Ltd.
425 Madison Ave.
New York, NY 10017
212-759-8600
Fax: 212-759-9428
Fiction and non-fiction, excluding romance, fantasy, science fiction, poetry and juvenile are handled by this agency. No phone queries or unsolicited manuscripts are accepted. They will consider and respond to letters of inquiry, provided they are accompanied by an SASE.

Sheree Bykofsky Associates, Inc.
16 W 36th St., 13th Floor.
PMB 107
New York, NY 10018
212-244-4144
Email: shereebee@aol.com
www.shereebee.com
Subjects and categories the agent is most enthusiastic about representing include popular reference, adult non-fiction, and quality fiction. Submit a query letter with an SASE.

Clausen, Mays & Tahan Literary Agency
P.O. Box 1015 Cooper Station
New York, NY 10276-1015
212-714-8181
Fax: 212-714-8282
Email: cmtassist@aol.com
This agency handles mostly non-fiction: memoirs, biography, true stories, medical, health and nutrition, psychology, how-to, financial, women's issues, spirituality, true crime, fashion/beauty, style, and humor. Submit a query letter or proposal, including an SASE.

Don Congdon Associates, inc.
156 Fifth Ave., Suite 625
New York, NY 10010-7002
212-645-1229
Fax: 212-727-2688
Email: dca@doncongdon.com
Submit a query letter with an SASE as a first step. The agency handles fiction and non-fiction.

Richard Curtis Associates, Inc.
Authors' Representatives
171 East 74th St., Suite 2
New York, NY 10021
212-772-7363
Fax: 212-772-7393
Email: rcurtis@curtisagency.com
www.curtisagency.com
Authors are requested to send a query letter with an SASE for a reply. Do not send manuscripts or outlines until or unless requested to do so. The agency handles popular fiction and non-fiction in all fields.

Donadio & Olson Inc.
Literary Representatives
121 West 27th St., Suite 704
New York, NY 10001
212-691-8077
Fax: 212-633-2837
Email: mail@donadio.com
www.donadioandolson.com
No unsolicited manuscripts are accepted. The agency handles fiction and non-fiction. Submit a query letter with an SASE.

Nicholas Ellison, Inc.
55 Fifth Ave.
New York, NY 10003
212-206-6050
Fax: 212-463-8718
www.greenburger.com
No unsolicited manuscripts will be accepted. Submit query first and include sample chapters. Fiction and non-fiction (all subjects) are accepted.

Ann Elmo Agency, Inc.
60 East 42nd St.
New York, NY 10165
212-661-2880/2881
Fax: 212-661-2883
The Ann Elmo Agency handles books, plays, movie and TV rights. No unsolicited manuscripts are accepted. Submit query letter with an SASE.

Farber Literary Agency
14 East 75th St.,
New York, NY 10021
212-861-7075
Fax: 212-861-7076
Email: farberlit@aol.com
The agency handles both fiction and non-fiction, including young adult and children's works. They also handle stage plays. Prospective clients should submit a proposal and approximately three chapters and should include an SASE if the material is to be returned.

Samuel French, Inc.
45 West 25th St.
New York, NY 10010-2751
212-206-8990
Fax: 212-206-1429
Email: samuelfrench@earthlink.net
www.samuelfrench.com
The agency handles stage plays for publication and representation. A variety of subject areas are considered such as comedy, contemporary issues, crime, ethnic, experimental, fantasy, horror, mystery, religious, and thrillers. Submit query or manuscript with an SASE.

Gelfman Schneider Literary Agents, Inc.
250 West 57th St., Suite 2515
New York, NY 10107
212-245-1993
Fax: 212-245-8678
Email: mail@gelfmanschneider.com
This agency does not accept unsolicited manuscripts. Anyone seeking representation should send a query letter detailing the work they have written and mention any previous publishing experience. The agency specializes in literary and mystery novels as well as business and political non-fiction. They do not typically represent science fiction, romance, or children's books.

Richard Henshaw Group
Authors Representatives
127 W. 24th St., 4th Floor
New York, NY 10011
212-414-1172
Fax: 212-414-1182
Email: RHGAGENTS@aol.com
www.richh.addr.com
Areas of specialty are mainstream novels and genre fiction including mystery, thriller, suspense, crime, science fiction, fantasy, horror, historical, young adult and literary. In non-fiction, the group is open to a wide variety of areas including popular reference, business, popular science, parenting, health, humor, popular culture, how-to, celebrity biography, and true crime. Writers of fiction should submit a query letter and the opening 50 pages, along with an SASE. Writers of non-fiction should send a query letter and an SASE. Any writer may send a query letter to the Email address, provided the letter does not exceed one page.

Susan Herner Rights Agency, Inc.
P.O. Box 357
Scarsdale, NY 10576
914-725-8967
Fax: 914-725-8769
Email: shernerагency@optonline.net
The agency handles adult fiction and non-fiction. No unsolicited manuscripts are accepted. Submit query letter with first three chapters along with an SASE.

International Creative Management, Inc.
40 West 57th St.
New York, NY 10019
212-556-5600
Fax: 212-556-5665
www.icmtalent.com
This agency handles film and television rights. Send query letter briefly describing yourself and the project. You may include a two page outline of your work, or enclose the first one or two pages. Also enclose an SASE and allow one or two months for a response.

IMG Literary
825 Seventh Ave., 9th Floor
New York, NY 10019
212-774-6900
Fax: 212-246-1118
www.imgworld.com
IMG represents a wide range of fiction and non-fiction titles. Potential authors must send in a query letter with an SASE before a manuscript will be reviewed.

Janklow & Nesbit Associates
445 Park Ave.
New York, NY 10022
212-421-1700
Fax: 212-980-3671
Email: postmaster@janklow.com
At this time, the agency is only taking work referred to them by authors known to Janklow & Nesbit.

Harvey Klinger, Inc.
301 West 53rd St.
New York, NY 10019
212-581-7068
Fax: 212-315-3823
Email: queries@harveyklinger.com
www.harveyklinger.com
Type of work handled includes broad based commercial fiction and non-fiction. Submit a query letter first and include an SASE. Queries by fax are not accepted.

Trident Media Group
Ellen Levine Literary Agency, Inc.
41 Madison Ave., 36th Floor
New York, NY 10010-1505
212-262-4810
Fax: 212-725-4501
www.tridentmediagroup.com
Submit a query letter with an SASE. This agency handles literary and commercial fiction and non-fiction, and some children's books.

Levine Greenberg Literary Agency
307 Seventh Ave., Suite 1906
New York, NY 10001
212-337-0934
Fax: 212-337-0948
Email: LevineJA@aol.com
www.levinegreenberg.com
For non-fiction books send proposal including contents, summary, and information about the author. For novels, send a 50 page excerpt, plus a synopsis of no more than 10 pages. Enclose an SASE to have material returned. For more complete instructions, request a copy of "The JLC Kit," which contains information about the agency, including services, practices, and book proposals.

The Literary Group International
270 Lafayette St., Suite 1505
New York, NY 10012
212-274-1616
Fax: 212-274-9876
www.theliterarygroup.com
This agency prefers that authors submit a complete novel and for non-fiction projects a thorough proposal is sufficient. All submissions require an SASE. The Literary Group is a full service agency and handles all general trade titles.

Nancy Love Literary Agency
250 East 65th St., Suite 4A
New York, NY 10021
212-980-3499
Fax: 212-308-6405
For novels submit a query letter and synopsis; for non-fiction submit a query letter and proposal. This agency is interested in: fiction - mysteries, thrillers, multi-cultural; non-fiction - current affairs, biography, health, and medicine (including alternative), true crime, psychology, self-help, social issues, women's issues, nature, spiritual and inspirational.

Donald Maass Literary Agency
160 W. 95th St., Suite B
New York, NY 10025
212-866-8200
Fax: 212-866-8181
Email: dmla@mindspring.com
The Donald Maass literary agency specializes in handling commercial novels, with an emphasis on genre fiction; mystery, suspense, science fiction, fantasy, and romance. For initial contact, send a typed, one page query letter, with an SASE for reply.

Manus & Associates Literary Agency, Inc.
445 Park Ave.
New York, NY 10022
212-644-8020
Fax: 212-644-3374
Email: manuslit@manuslit.com
www.manuslit.com
Prospective clients should send a query letter and, if they wish, sample chapters, with an SASE for a reply. Never submit a full manuscript unsolicited. The agency handles both fiction and non-fiction, particularly mystery/thrillers, true crime, and commercial fiction.

Henry Morrison Inc.
P.O. Box 235
Bedford Hills, NY 10507-0235
914-666-3500
Fax: 914-241-7846
This agency represents a large range of books, from international thrillers to general novels, women's fiction, mystery

and science fiction, and the occasional non-fiction book on contemporary subjects. Prospective clients should write a letter outlining in some detail what the book is about and include an SASE.

Fifi Oscard Agency, Ltd.
110 West 40th St., 17th Floor
New York, NY 10018
212-764-1100
Fax: 212-840-5019
Email: agency@fifioscard.com
www.fifioscard.com
This agency covers all areas of fiction and non-fiction. Do not send unsolicited manuscripts. Submit a query letter with an SASE.

The Richard Parks Agency
138 East 16th St., Suite 5-B
New York, NY 10003
212-254-9067
Fax: 212-228-1786
This agency handles general trade fiction and non-fiction. Fiction is read only by referral. Writers of non-fiction book proposals may submit a query letter provided that it is accompanied by an SASE. Unsolicited manuscripts and fax queries are not accepted.

Inkwell Management
521 Fifth Ave., 26th Floor
New York, NY 10175
212-922-3500
Fax: 212-922-0535
Email: contact@ inkwellmanagement.com
www.inkwellmanagement.com
Represents authors in all fields (book publishing, motion pictures, and TV production, etc.). No unsolicited manuscripts are accepted, nor are manuscripts that have previously been submitted to other agencies or simultaneous submissions. A proposal of the manuscript with SASE should be sent first.

Aaron M. Priest Literary Agency
708 Third Ave., 23rd Floor
New York, NY 10017
212-818-0344
Fax: 212-573-9417
Submit query letter and proposal/synopsis along with an SASE. The agency handles mainstream fiction and some non-fiction. Do not submit screenplays, plays, or poetry.

RLR Associates, Ltd.
7 West 51st St.
New York, NY 10019
212-541-8641
Fax: 212-541-6052
www.rlrassociates.net
RLR handles a broad range of fiction and non-fiction. The agency is not taking new children's book clients. Submit query letter first with an SASE.

The Robbins Office, Inc.
405 Park Ave., 9th Floor
New York, NY 10022
212-223-0790
Fax: 212-223-2535
The type of work handled by this agency include general, literary fiction and non-fiction, television and motion picture rights. No unsolicited manuscripts, query first by referral only; submit proposal or outline (non-fiction) or outline and sample chapters (fiction).

Russel & Volkening, Inc.
50 West 29th St., Suite 7E
New York, NY 10001
212-684-6050
Fax: 212-889-3026
Any writer who would like to submit information about a project should do so with a query letter describing the project and information about the author, along with an SASE. This agency handles literary fiction, non-fiction, and children's books.

Victoria Sanders Literary Agency
241 Avenue of the Americas, Suite 11H
New York, NY 10014
212-633-8811
Fax: 212-633-0525
Email: queriesvsa@hotmail.com
www.victoriasanders.com
The agency handles fiction, both literary and commercial, African American, Latino and Asian. Of special interest: women's biography, history, autobiography, psychology, women's studies, gay studies, and politics. Submit query letter first along with an SASE.

Susan Schulman Literary Agency
454 West 44th St.
New York, NY 10036
212-713-1633
Fax: 212-581-8830
Email: schulman@aol.com
www.susanschulmanagency.com
Submit a query letter with an SASE. This agency specializes in non-fiction books by and about women and family issues. Emphasis on popular psychology, self-help, wisdom, spirituality, alternative spirituality and the social sciences, literary memoir, and biography.

Spectrum Literary Agency
320 Central Park W., Suite 1-D
New York, NY 10025
212-362-4323

Fax: 212-362-4562
www.spectrumliteraryagency.com
Submit query letter first with an SASE. The agency handles commercial fiction and non-fiction.

Spieler Agency
154 West 57th St.,13th Floor, Room 135
New York, NY 10019
212-757-4439
Fax: 212-233-2019
www.spieleragency.com
This agency handles non-fiction, most notably in the areas of history, social issues, the environment, economics and business; and literary fiction. Reports on queries in two weeks, reports on manuscripts in five weeks. Manuscripts without an SASE or sufficient money to cover return postage will not be returned.

Weiser & Elwell, Inc.
80 Fifth Ave., Suite 1101
New York, NY 10010
212-260-0860
Fax: 212-675-1381
Email: jelwell8@earthlink.net
Submit query first with outline and sample chapters along with an SASE. The agency specializes in trade and mass market adult fiction and non-fiction books.

Ann Wright Representatives
165 46th St., Suite 1105
New York, NY 10036-2501
212-764-6770
Fax: 212-764-5125
Email: danwrightlit@aol.com
Clients include screen writers, authors, television writers, and playwrights. Novels and movie scripts with themes that have film potential are handled. Writers should send letter with SASE giving information about themselves and their material. If the agency is interested in your work, you will receive a response.

Writers House Inc.
21 West 26th St.
New York, NY 10010
212-685-2400
Fax: 212-685-1781
Writers House is interested in trade books of all types, fiction and non-fiction. Unsolicited manuscripts are accepted, but you must first submit a query letter with an SASE.

Susan Zeckendorf Associates, Inc.
171 West 57th St., Suite 11-B
New York, NY 10019
212-245-2928
Type of material handled includes literary fiction, commercial fiction, thrillers, mysteries, and women's fiction. Non-fiction areas are science, music, biography, self-help, sports, parenting, and psychology. Send a brief query letter with an SASE.

Oregon
Rainmaker Literary Agency
25 NW 23 Place, Suite 6
PMB 460
Portland, OR 97210-5599
503-222-2249
Email: info@rainmakerliterary.com
www.rainmakerliterary.com
First Books will accept unsolicited manuscripts for book length fiction and non-fiction for adults and children. Be sure to include SASE with sufficient postage.

Pennsylvania
Toad Hall, Inc.
R.R. 2, Box 12090
Laceyville, PA 18623
570-869-2942
Fax: 570-869-1031
Email: toadhallco@aol.com
www.laceyville.com/Toad-Hall
Submit a query letter describing yourself and your project. Include a synopsis or a table of contents of not more than three pages, a biography or curriculum vitae, the length of the book, and any pertinent information. They are currently interested in popular non-fiction of all types, and are also interested in New Age, occult, paranormal, UFO's, etc.

Texas
DHS Literary, Inc.
10711 Preston Rd., Suite 100
Dallas, TX 75206
214-363-4422
Fax: 214-363-4423
Email: submissions@dhsliterary.com
www.dhsliterary.com
DHS offers representation to a broad range of fiction and non-fiction literary properties. The agency handles work by published and unpublished writers. It seeks to maintain a diverse mix of projects, including literary and mainstream fiction; category fiction such as mystery, historical, horror and romance; as well as quality commercial non-fiction. Submit query letter with SASE. You may also request a copy of the agency's submission guidelines.

The Fogleman Literary Agency
7515 Greenville Ave., Suite 712
Dallas, TX 75231
214-361-9956
Fax: 214-361-9553
Email: info@fogleman.com
www.fogleman.com

This agency is interested in women's fiction (both category and mainstream, including romance and mysteries), popular business, psychological self-help; non-fiction geared for the women's market; political biography; author biography. Submit query letter or call. If calling, be prepared to give a short synopsis of your book, including what category it falls into, and the word count.

Utah
Executive Excellence
1366 East 1120 South
P.O. Box 50360
Provo, UT 84605-0360
800-304-9782
801-375-4060
Fax: 801-377-5960
www.eep.com
The agency works with authors of non-fiction trade books in the areas of business, management, and personal development/self-help. The agency also offers assisted self-publishing services, including editorial, design, and printing. Please query by phone, fax, or letter first. After initial query, submit outline/proposal with approximately 20-40 pages of sample material.

Washington
The Catalog
Literary Agency & Book Publicity
P.O. Box 2964
Vancouver, WA 98668-2964
360-694-8531
Fax: 360-694-8531
The agency is currently looking for manuscripts in almost all subjects, especially business, health, psychology, money, science, how-to, self help and women's interest. Also considered are text books, professional books, juvenile fiction and non-fiction, and adult mainstream fiction. Query with an outline, sample chapters, and an SASE.

Wales Literary Agency, Inc.
P.O. Box 9428
Seattle, WA 98109-9428
206-284-7114
Fax: 206-322-1033
Email: waleslit@waleslit.com
www.waleslit.com
This agency is particularly interested in works of narrative non-fiction, often called "creative non-fiction" or "literary journalism", especially if the work espouses a progressive cultural or political view, projects a new voice, or, simply shares an important, compelling story. The agency looks for talented story tellers in fiction or non-fiction with a special interest in writers from the northwest, Alaska, the West Coast, and Pacific Rim countries. Send a query letter, including a brief description of the book project, as well as a writing sample from the project. Include an SASE.

Wisconsin
The Lazear Agency
431 Second St., Suite 300
Hudson, WI 54016
Email: jmayo@lazear.com
www.lazear.com
This is a full service agency assisting clients in all phases of the publication process. They handle fiction and non-fiction. Submit a 1-2 page query letter, including a synopsis of the work you would like considered, and any relevant writing experience, such as previously published works along with an SASE. Allow 4-6 weeks for a response.

Writer's Organizations

Writing can be a lonely and isolating profession. Writer's organizations are there to assist you with networking and to provide you with some added inspiration when you most need it. Membership entitles you to a variety of services such as newsletters, job information, workshops, and other types of support services. Associations typically focus on a specific genre (i.e. mystery writing, science writing), and membership fees or dues are usually required. The list that follows provides information on a variety of organizations to get you started on finding your place among fellow writers.

American Medical Writers Association (AMWA)
40 W. Gude Dr., Suite 101
Rockville, MD 20850
301-294-5303
Fax: 301-294-9006
Email: amwa@amwa.org
www.amwa.org
Since 1940, AMWA has served an interdisciplinary membership of medical writers, editors, public relations specialists, audiovisual experts, and other professionals with varied roles in biocommunications. Benefits of membership in AMWA include: professional identification as a communicator; meetings, workshops, and Core Curriculum program; and professional development. The membership fee is $130 for a regular membership and $45 for a student membership.

American Society of Journalists and Authors, Inc. (ASJA)
1501 Broadway, Suite 302

New York, NY 10036
212-997-0947
Fax: 212-937-2315
www.asja.org
ASJA membership is open only to professional freelance writers of non-fiction for general audiences, produced over a substantial period of time. ASJA provides its members with an array of professional supports including: monthly newsletter, membership directory, and an ongoing survey of payment rates. A $25 application fee will be applied to the $100 initiation fee upon acceptance. Annual membership dues are $195.

American Translators Association (ATA)
225 Reinekers Lane, Suite 590
Alexandria, VA 22314
703-683-6100
Fax: 703-683-6122
Email: ata@atanet.org
www.atanet.org
The ATA is the largest professional association of translators and interpreters in the US. Their primary goals include fostering and supporting professional development for translators and interpreters and promoting the translation profession. ATA membership is open to anyone with an interest in translation as a profession or as a scholarly pursuit. Benefits of membership include: networking opportunities, subscription to the ATA Chronicle, job information, and a copy of the ATA Membership Directory. Membership fees are $80 for students, $145 for Associate Member, $180 for Institutional Membership, and $300 for Corporate Membership, and $380 for a joint Individual/Corporation Membership.

The Association of Writers and Writing Programs (AWP)
Tallwood House, Mail Stop 1E3
10808 Kelley Dr.
George Mason University
Fairfax, VA 22030-4444
703-993-4301
Fax: 703-993-4302
Email: services@awpwriter.org
www.awpwriter.org
For 29 years, writers and teachers have joined the AWP for community and support, for information and inspiration, for contacts and new ideas. The $59 annual membership fee ($99 for 2 years) includes six issues of AWP Chronicle, seven issues of AWP Job List, a 33% discount to enter Award Series, and an 18% discount on annual conferences. Student memberships are available for $37.

The Authors Guild, Inc.
31 East 28th St., 10th Floor
New York, NY 10016-7923
212-563-5904
Fax: 212-564-8363
Email: staff@authorsguild.org
www.authorsguild.org
The Authors Guild is the nation's oldest, largest, and most prestigious professional society of published authors. A few benefits of membership include the quarterly Bulletin; symposia and seminars; online services; business advice on problems that arise with publishers, agents, booksellers, or editors, as well as legal and accounting advice. There is no initiation fee. First year dues are $90. After the first year of membership the dues are based on an individual's annual writing income.

The Dramatists Guild, Inc.
1501 Broadway, Suite 701
New York, NY 10036-3909
212-398-9366
Fax: 212-944-0420
Email: membership@dramatistsguild.com
www.dramaguild.com
The Guild works to protect and promote the professional interests and rights of writers of dramatic and musical works. Membership privileges include Dramatists Guild production contracts, business advice, marketing information, royalty collection, publications, free Guild symposia, and access to health and dental insurance programs. Categories of membership and dues are: Active members who have had a theater production, $150; Associate members are all other theater writers, $95; Estate members services are available to the estate of any playwright, composer, book writer, or lyricist, $125; Student members must be currently enrolled in an accredited writing degree program, $35.

Editorial Freelancers Association (EFA)
71 West 23rd St., Suite 1910
New York, NY 10010-4181
866-929-5400 (toll free)
212-929-5400
Fax: 212-929-5439
Email: info@the-efa.org
www.the-efa.org
Any full or part time freelancer may apply for membership. All EFA members receive: bimonthly newsletter, annual membership directory, Business Practices Survey; admission to all meetings and events; reduced tuition for courses; and eligibility for medical, dental, and disability insurance. Annual membership is $125 for resident members living in the greater New York City metropolitan area, and $105 for non-resident members.

Educational Writers Association (EWA)
2122 P St., NW, #201
Washington, DC 20037
202-452-9830
Fax: 202-452-9837
Email: ewa@ewa.org
http://www.ewa.org
Members include over 800 education reporters from

newspapers, television and radio; and education writers and public information offers from organizations, school districts and colleges. Membership brings free copies of all EWA publications, the bimonthly newsletter Education Reporter, useful referral and source information by phone, Email, and through mailings, and study opportunities. Annual membership fees are $65.

Horror Writers Association (HWA)
P.O. Box 50577
Palo Alto, CA 94303
Email: hwa@horror.org
http://www.horror.org
The HWA is devoted to helping writers at every point in their career. Whether you're an aspiring writer or trying to make that first sale, or a seasoned novelist with a dozen books to your name, the HWA has something for you. Benefits include publicity information, agent database, networking, regional chapters, Internet connections, grievance committee and worldwide organizations. Annual dues are $65 for an individual, $110 for a corporation, and $85 for a family membership.

International Association of Crime Writers (IACW)
(North American Branch)
P.O. Box 8674
New York, NY 10116-8674
Phone/Fax: 212-243-8966
Email: info@crimewritersna.org
www.crimewritersna.org
IACW is an organization of professional published writers whose primary goal is to promote communication among writers of all nationalities and to promote crime writing as an influential and significant art form. IACW sponsors a number of conferences and an annual celebration. The North American branch publishes a newsletter, sponsors social events, and has created several anthologies of international crime writing. Membership dues are $60.

Media Communications Association International
2810 Crossroads Drive, Suite 3800
Madison, WI 53718
608-443-2464
Fax: 608-443-2478
Email: info@mca-i.org
www.mca-i.org
MCA-I is the only association dedicated to serving the needs of video professionals in nonbroadcast video production. The association has worked to advance the video profession and to promote the growth and quality of video related media through providing relevant member services. Membership offers you: career advancement, networking, special services, discounts, industry leadership, and periodicals. Annual fee is $160.

The International Women's Writing Guild
Box 810, Gracie Station
New York, NY 10028-0082
212-737-7536
Fax: 212-737-9469
Email: iwwg@iwwg.com
http://www.iwwg.com
The Guild is a worldwide nonprofit organization open to all women, regardless of portfolio, which offers its members services including: annual subscription to NETWORK newsletter, membership listing, list of 35 agents and other writing services, health plans, opportunities to participate in regional and national writing conferences, and various online services. Annual dues are $45.

Mystery Writers of America
17 East 47th St., 6th floor
New York, NY 10017
212-888-8171
Fax: 212-888-8107
Email: mwa@mysterywriters.org
www.mysterywriters.org
This is a nonprofit professional organization of mystery and crime writers in all categories. Benefits of membership include: mystery writing courses, the Edgar Allan Poe Awards Banquet, monthly meetings, local bulletins, the Third Degree, which is published 10 times a year, and the MWA Anthology, which is published annually. There is no initiation fee and dues for all categories of memberships are $95 per year.

National Association of Science Writers (NASW)
P.O. Box 890
Hedgesville, WV 25427
304-754-5077
Fax: 304-754-5076
Email: info@nasw.org
www.nasw.org
The NASW sponsors directly or works closely with regional science writing groups and around the country where members gather for workshops, meetings, and field trips. Members receive the newsletter, ScienceWriters, which provides timely, incisive reports on professional issues. To join, you must show evidence of science writing ability and be sponsored by at least two active NASW members. Membership dues are $25 for Student and $60 for a Regular membership.

The National League of American Pen Women, Inc.
Pen Arts Building
1300 17th St., NW
Washington, DC 20036-1973
202-785-1997
Email: info@americanpenwomen.org
www.americanpenwomen.org
The League offers its members association with creative professional women, workshops, discussion groups and lectures. The Pen Woman, the official publication of The League, is published six times a year and features news,

accomplishments, and works of its members. Membership requires the submission of at least three sample chapters and proof of sale. Authors who are self published (not vanity published) shall submit copies to be evaluated by the Branch.

The National Writers Association
10940 S. Parker Rd., #508
Parker, CO 80134
303-841-0246
Fax: 303-841-2607
www.nationalwriters.com
It doesn't matter if you're a new writer needing to know proper manuscript format, or a professional needing contract suggestions and assistance, the Association offers help with searching out competent and reliable agents, assistance in writing a good synopsis, and professional advice about self publishing. Membership fees are $65 for General member, $85 for Professional member (credits required), and $35 for Student member.

National Writers Union
113 University Place, 6th Floor
New York, NY 10003
212-254-0279
Fax: 212-254-0673
Email: nwu@nwu.org
www.nwu.org
The National Writers Union is an innovative labor union committed to improving the working conditions of freelance writers through the collective strength of its members. The Union welcomes all writers whether you write for money or publication. Dues start at $95 a year and are based on one's annual writing income. The National Writers Union also has a Supporter's Circle open to individuals who are not writers, but advocate on their behalf.

The PEN American Center
568 Broadway, Suite 303
New York, NY 10012-3225
212-334-1660
Fax: 212-334-2181
www.pen.org
PEN American Center, the largest of the 124 centers worldwide that compose International PEN, is a membership association of prominent literary writers and editors. The 2,800 members are poets, playwrights, essayists, editors, and novelists, as well as literary translators and those agents who have made a substantial contribution to the literary community. Among the activities, programs, and services are public literary events, literary awards, outreach projects, and assistance to writers in financial need. Members of American PEN are elected by the Membership Committee. Dues are $75 per year.

Poets and Writers, Inc.
72 Spring St., Suite 301
New York, NY 10012
212-226-3586
Fax: 212-226-3963
www.pw.org
Poets and Writers is a central source of practical information for the Literary community. Their Information Center keeps track of addresses for over 7,000 poets and fiction writers and compiles a Directory of American Poets and Fiction Writers. The Reading/Workshops Program provides matching fees for readings and workshops given by emerging and established writers. The Writers Exchange is a national program that introduces emerging writers to literary communities outside their home state. Poets and Writers is not a membership organization, and therefore, anyone can use their services.

Poetry Society of America (PSA)
15 Grammercy Park
New York, NY 10003
212-254-9628
www.poetrysociety.org
The PSA is the nation's oldest poetry organization reaching more people daily with poetry than any other literary organization. Membership is open to everyone. Members are entitled to: enter all PSA contests, discount admission to PSA readings, workshops, the PSA newsletter, program calendars and invitations to readings and events, discounts on book purchases, and vote in PSA elections. Membership fees are tax deductible and range from $25 Student, $44 Member, and can go as high as $1000.

Romance Writers of America (RWA)
16000 Stuebner Airline Rd.
Spring, TX 77379
832-717-5200
Fax: 832-717-5201
Email: info@rwanational.org
www.rwanational.org
RWA is dedicated to promoting excellence in romantic fiction. General membership is open to all writers actively pursuing a career in romantic fiction. Associate membership is open to all editors, agents, booksellers, and other industry professionals. Membership benefits include workshops; networking opportunities with authors, editors, agents and industry professionals; awards; and RWA publications. There is a $25 processing fee for new applicants and annual dues are $75.

Science-Fiction and Fantasy Writers of America, Inc. (SFWA)
P.O. Box 877
Chestertown, MD 21620
Email: execdir@sfwa.org
www.sfwa.org

The SFWA has brought together the most successful and daring writers of speculative fiction throughout the world, and has grown in numbers and influence and is now recognized as one of the most effective nonprofit writers' organizations in existence. Over 1200 SF/Fantasy writers, artists, editors, and allied professionals are members. The SFWA Bulletin, published quarterly, is subscribed to by many non-members. Beginning writers might be particularly interested in its informative market reports and articles about the business of writing and selling science fiction and fantasy. Dues are collected annually. There is a $10 installation fee for new members. Dues are $50 for Active/Associate/Estate members, $35 for Affiliate members, and $60 for Institutional members.

Society of American Travel Writers
1500 Sunday Dr., Suite 102
Raleigh, NC 27607
919-861-5586
Fax: 919-787-4916
Email: satw@satw.org
www.satw.org
The Society of American Travel Writers is a nonprofit, public service organization dedicated to serving the interest of the traveling public, to promote international understanding and good will, and to further promote unbiased, objective reporting of information on travel topics. Membership in the Society is by invitation. Applicants must be sponsored by two members. The initiation fee for Active members is $200 (yearly dues $130), for Associate members $400 (yearly dues $250). A nonrefundable $50 application fee ($100 for Associates) will be applied toward the initiation fee of accepted members.

Society of Children's Book Writers and Illustrators (SCBWI)
8721 Beverly Blvd.
Los Angeles, CA 90048
323-782-1010
Fax: 323-782-1892
Email: scbwi@scbwi.org
www.scbwi.org
The SCBWI acts as a network for the exchange of knowledge between writers, illustrators, editors, publishers, agents, librarians, educators, bookstore personnel, and others involved with literature for young people. Membership is open to anyone with an active interest in children's literature. Membership dues are $75 per year for new members, and $60 each renewing year.

Society of Professional Journalists (SPJ)
3909 N. Meridian St.
Indianapolis, IN 46208
317-927-8000
Fax: 317-920-4789
www.spj.org
SPJ membership offers many benefits, including: continuing professional education, career services and support, and journalism advocacy. Membership dues range from $36 to $90.

Washington Independent Writers (WIW)
1001 Connecticut Ave., NW, Suite 701
Washington, DC 20026
202-775-5150
Fax: 202-775-5810
Email: info@washwriter.org
www.washwriter.org
WIW's membership includes recognized writers, writers with a growing number of credits and those who are just beginning their careers in the freelance profession. Membership benefits include: WIW's newsletter , the Independent Writer; the Job Bank; access to Small Groups based on areas of mutual interest; and the availability of a group health insurance plan and a legal services program. Dues are: Students/Senior-1yr $95 & 2yr $175; Dual-new members 1yr $220 & 2yr $410; Full and Associate-new members 1yr $135 & 2yr $245. There is a new member initiation fee of $40.

Western Writers of America
209 E. Iowa
Cheyenne, WY 82009
www.westernwriters.org
Western Writers of America (WWA) is an association of professional writers dedicated to preserving and celebrating the heritage of the American West, past and present. For over 40 years, WWA has served both fiction and non-fiction writers recognized for their work in all types of books, periodicals, screenplays, and other media. To be eligible for membership in WWA, you must be published. Annual dues are $75.A subscription to Roundup Magazine is included with membership dues or if you are interested in subscribing to the Roundup Magazine, the cost is six issues a year for $30.

Writers Guild of America-East
555 West 57th St.
New York, NY 10019
212-767-7800
Fax: 212-582-1909
www.wgaeast.org

Writers Guild Of America-West
7000 West 3rd St.
Los Angeles, CA 90048
323-951-4000
Fax: 323-782-4800
www.wga.org
Writers Guild of America is a labor union representing professional writers in motion pictures, television, and radio. Membership can be acquired only through the sale of literary material or employment for writing services in one of these areas. There is an initiation fee of $2,500 for new members, basic dues of $100 paid in quarterly installments of $25, and an

assessment of 1-11/2 on earnings from the sale of material or from employment as a writer in motion pictures, television, or radio. The Guild also provides a registration service for literary material. Writers are advised to register their material before showing it to a producer or agent.

Start or Expand Your Own Business

UNCLE SAM WANTS YOU TO START A BUSINESS or expand your current business. The job of the government is to help create jobs. So, if you start a small business, you are creating a job for yourself. The government will love you for that. And if you start a big business, and create 50 jobs, the government will love you even more. If you start a giant business, the government will love you so much they may create a new law to legally adopt you.

The same is true if you want to improve your business, make it more profitable, or if you want to make your employees more efficient, or sell into new markets. The government needs as many people as possible to start and expand businesses. They need more and more people working and increasing their wages. All this creates prosperity for America and generates more taxes for the government.

The government shows its love for job creators by giving them money. Under the guise of making America stronger, elected officials have created hundreds and even thousands of programs at the federal, state and local level to start and expand businesses. These programs are for big businesses to get bigger, small business to get to the next level or for the solitary dreamers to make their dreams come true.

Because there are literally thousands and thousands of programs available, almost every living person is eligible for something. Every program has different requirements. For some programs you have to have some of your own money in your pocket to be able to get government money. For other programs you don't have to bring any money to the table. And still for other programs, you have to be flat broke and out of work before they give you money to start or expand your business.

Every year over 1 million entrepreneurs get money from the government including many of the rich and famous like:

- Donald Trump
- H. Ross Perot
- Nike Shoes
- Federal Express
- George W. Bush, and
- Dick Cheney

So why don't you use this government money too? It's out there waiting for any citizen, or even a non-citizen (as long as you are here legally). You just have to know where to go.

If you wish to do the research necessary yourself you can follow the outline below of the major sources of getting money and help to start or expand a business or nonprofit organization.

1) ***Find Federal Money Programs for Business***
Look at a book called the *Catalog of Federal Domestic Assistance*. This book is available at your local public library or the U.S. Government Printing Office www.gpo.gov. You can also search the contents of this book for free on the web at www.cfda.gov. In this chapter you will find items which have a five digit number associated with them (such as 10.471). These numbers refer to the *Catalog of Federal Domestic Assistance*.

2) ***Find State Money Programs for Business***
Look for the state office of economic development located in your state capitol. You can find them by dialing 411 and asking for your state capitol operator or by going to the web at www.govengine.com and clicking on your state. Then start looking for web sites on business or economic development. Every state offers a wealth of help and information on starting a business. Some offer job training funds, export assistance, technology resources, tourism promotion, industrial revenue bonds, revolving loan funds, and more. Most have a State Business Resource Guide to assist you in your search.

3) ***Find Local City and County Programs for Business***
Start looking at every local city and county government for programs that help businesses. They all have them. If you don't know where to go you can call 411 and ask for the mayor's office or the office of the county executive. Just tell them you want to start or expand a business and want to know about any and all programs. You can also go to www.govengine.com and under each state there will be a listing of all cities and counties. Click on those of interest and search for economic development or business programs. Remember, you can start a business in any state, city or county and not live there. The people who give out the money just want your business to be there and you can commute.

4) ***Find Money From Nonprofit Organizations for Business***
There are 3 major sources for finding money from these groups:

A. The Association for Enterprise Opportunity in Arlington, VA maintains a database of nonprofit organizations that provide financial assistance to entrepreneurs. Contact them at 703-841-7760 or www.microenterpriseworks.org/nearyou/.

B. The Foundation Center of New York City maintains a database of all foundations that provide money to nonprofit organizations or individuals. Their information is available on the web at http://fdncenter.org or from their participating libraries by contacting 212-620-4230 or 800-424-9836.

C. The Guidestar Company in Williamsburg, VA also maintains a database of foundations and they can be reached at 757-229-4631 or www.guidestar.com. Much of their database is accessible for free on the web.

D. The Aspen Institute's mission is to identify, develop, and disseminate microenterprise program information. To find resources near you contact The Aspen Institute, One Dupont Circle, NW, Suite 700, Washington, DC 20036; 202-736-1071; Fax: 202-467-0790; http://fieldus.org.

5) ***Find Help With Any Part Of Starting Or Expanding A Business***
The government supports over 1,000 offices all over the country called Small Business Development Centers. They will sit down with you and help tackle any problem you may be having with your business like: finding money, filling out forms, taxes, marketing, technical problems, contracting, etc. All their services are free or for very little cost. These Centers do not have money for entrepreneurs, but will know of local money sources available. For a Center near you contact 1-800-8-ASK-SBA or www.sba.gov/sbdc/sbdcnear.html.

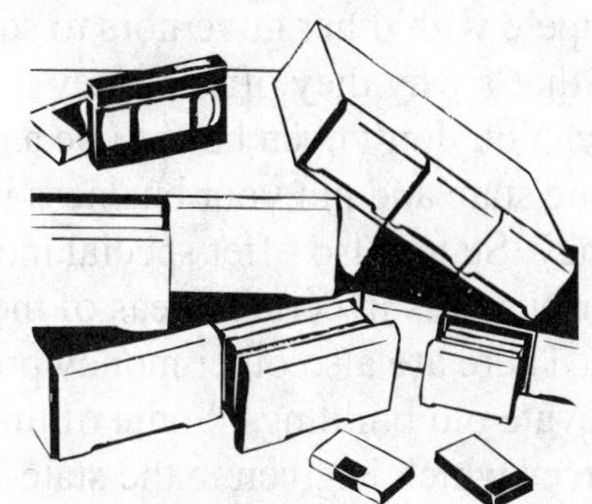

6) ***Fill out 1 to 3 pages for grants up to $50,000***
I keep trying to dispel the myth that all grant applications are big and complicated. Some do have large applications, but they are normally for people going after money as a nonprofit organization. But a majority of grant money for business, housing, education or personal expenses normally require only a few pages of a form to complete. Here are some real sample applications for business facade grants:

- 2-Pages Gets You a $32,500 Grant To Build A Business
  www.ci.toledo.oh.us/images/EconDev/0428ccfacadeapp.pdf
- 1-Page Application Gets A $7,500 Grant For New Landscaping For Your Business
  www.chooserockledge.com/Facade%20%20and%20LandscapeGrant%20Program.pdf
- 2-Pages Gets You a $50,000 Grant For Your Business
  www.downtownbillings.com/dbp/docs/Download/AppsFY05/Facade05.pdf
- 2-Pages Get You A $10,000 Grant To Fix Up Your Business
  www.sumter-sc.com/client_resources/departments/downtown/2005%20facade%20grant%20program.pdf

Don't stop here. Because next year the government is going to give money to over 1 million entrepreneurs and you can be one of them.

$200,000 From Washington To Open Or Expand A Business
You can actually get up to $1,000,000 in grants and or loans to open or expand a business from the U.S. Federal Government alone. There are over 100 different money programs available from offices ranging from the U.S. Small Business Administration to the U.S. Department of Agriculture to the U.S. Department of Commerce. For the best source identifying all federal only government money programs available, look at a government published book called The Catalog of Federal Domestic Assistance published by the U.S. Government Printing Office (www.gpo.gov) or look at it for free on the web at www.cfda.gov. Another good starting place to find anything in the federal government is a free service called the Federal Information Center at 1-800-FED-INFO or www.pueblo.gsa.gov/call.

$150,000 To Open A Business In A Certain Zip Code

In addition to the federal government you also have to contact your state government. Every state has a number of money programs for people to start or expand a business in their state. Governors compete with other governors to see who can create the most jobs, and that's why they offer money for people who create jobs in their state. You don't even have to be a resident of the state. You can live in one state and put your business in a state that offers you more money. States also offer special money for entrepreneurs to put their business in certain areas of the state or in certain areas of a city. There are also other money programs to build buildings or renovate old buildings. Some of this money comes from federal sources which is given to the states and distributed to entrepreneurs in the state. Other money is generated from local taxes. And some states use the winnings from their lottery money to give to entrepreneurs to create or expand businesses. Many states offer programs from more than one agency. So it may take some time to find all the programs in a given state. A good place to start is your State Government Office of Economic Development located in your state capital. You can call 411 and ask for the state capital operator in your state capital or go to www.govengine.com and click on your state and find the office that is listed under business and/or economic development.

$10,000 To Put A New Sign On Your Business

Most local governments have money programs to help businesses in their area. Be sure to check your city, your county or your local development agency. The money for these programs can originate from the federal government, state government or local generated taxes. These programs can be for buildings, equipment, working capital, hiring employees or for local beautification projects like painting the front of your store and putting up a new sign. If you are opening up a business, you can shop around at different cities and counties to see who may have the most money for you. If you don't know who to contact, call the information operator at 411 and ask for the mayor of the city or the head of the county government. The top office is always the best place to start. You can also go to www.govengine.com and click on your state. You will see a list of all the counties and cities in your state along with the relevant web sites.

Let The Government Be Your Biggest Customer

Question: Do you know what is better than a $100,000 government grant?
Answer: A $100,000 government contract. Because with a grant you are most likely to get it once and with a contract you can keep getting it over and over again.
Question: Do you know who buys more of anything than anyone else in the world?
Answer: The government, including federal, state, local and county.

Someone has to sell all those products and services to the government and it might as well be you. You just have to find out who in the government buys your product and figure out the paperwork on how to get paid. But don't worry too much about the work required and the paperwork involved, because there are offices that will help you do all this and they will do it FOR FREE. Find your local, state and federal financed Small Business Development Center office by contacting 800-8-ASK-SBA or www.sba.gov/sbdc/sbdcnear.html. Or you can also contact one of the local free offices financed by the Department Defense's Defense Logistics Agency at 703- 767-1661 or www.dla.mil/db. Tell them you need help selling to the government. But remember one thing. Selling to the government is like going elephant hunting. When you bag one of these babies you have meat for a long time.

Get Free Legal Help, Free Financial Help, Free Marketing Help

Have you ever wished you could call a great lawyer for legal advice and have her do the work for free? Have you ever dreamed about calling a great financial consultant for advice on a money matter and get your answer for free? Have you every worried about how in the world you would pay for a PR agency to promote your store so everyone would know how great you are? Have you ever wished you didn't have to pay to hire a management consultant to show you the secrets of how to double your sales in one year? You can get the answer to all these questions by knowing about the government's best kept secret called the Small Business Development Centers. There are over 1,000 of these offices around the country that will give you all these services and more for free or for very little cost. You don't even have to know how to spell entrepreneur and they will sit down with you and can help with any business problem you have. Don't pay for something when you can get it FOR FREE. Find an office near you by contacting 800-8-ASK-SBA or www.sba.gov/sbdc/sbdcnear.html.

Let The Government Be Your Collection Agency

Do you have a supplier in another state who owes you money and won't pay you back? Well, you don't have to hire an attorney and pay hundreds or even thousands of dollars to get your money. Try calling the attorney general's office in the state of your supplier and complain about how a company in their state mistreated you. Many of these offices will investigate, for free, by contacting the business in question. No matter who is right in the matter the supplier does not want a government office on their back because this government office can put them out of business. The smartest business decision is to just give you the money owed and have the problem go away.

Maybe your credit card company does not treat you right and holds back money you think is due to you. Maybe your health insurance company will not pay a claim you think is covered in your policy. Maybe the package delivery service or airline shipping your product did you wrong. Maybe the radio station running your ads cheated you. All of these problems can be handled more effectively, and FOR FREE, by contacting the government agency that regulates the business with whom you are dealing. All businesses are regulated by some agency. If your customers have a problem with you they can contact the state attorney general's office or the postal inspector if you sent a product by mail. So why hire an attorney who will charge you $200 an hour to get you satisfaction, when you can call a government office who will do the job for free. And don't forget, a business can fight an attorney because the worst they have to lose is that they have to pay what they owe you. But it does not pay a business to fight a government agency, because a government agency has the power to put them out of business.

To find who regulates a specific business call 411 and ask for your state capital operator. Then ask for the office that regulates the profession or organization that hurt you. Or go to www.govengine.com and start by looking for the office of attorney general. You can also try the Consumer Action Website at www.consumeraction.gov/.

Start A Business With No Money and No Products

Who says you have to have an actual store to have a store? And who says that you even have to have any products to have a store. You can start a virtual store on the web. For this you only need pictures of the products and a source to get the products when someone actually buys them from your website. Call a dozen suppliers of the product you are interested in and see if they would go into a 50/50 partnership when sales come in. You can find suppliers for any product from books in the library. Once you learn how to bring in sales, you can get your own store and keep all the money yourself. If you want to start a bookstore you can contact local hospitals, office buildings or other big structures, and make a deal with them to sell products in the lobby for people hanging out all day. And then contact a local bookstore to share the profits with them. Or you can approach a local bookstore and tell them that you will figure out how to sell books to the government and want a 50/50 deal. The bookstore has nothing to lose and you get to have a business with no money or books. And how are you going to learn to sell to the government? The government will teach you for free. Contact your local government sponsored Small Business Development Center and they will teach you. Contact: 800-8-ASK-SBA or www.sba.gov/sbdc/sbdcnear.html.

$150,000 To Hire Certain Employees Or To Open an Employee Day Care Center

The government will give you:

- $8,500 if you hire someone who has a certain income
- $150,000 to open an on site day care center for employees
- $3,000 if you hire someone from a certain zip code
- $44,000 for buying new computers
- $2,500 to hire a teacher during the summer

The money is in the form of tax credits on your federal and/or your state income taxes. If you are paying any taxes then this is truly free money because it is taken right off your tax bill. To find out about every tax credit at your state level contact your state Department of Revenue by calling 411 and asking for the state capital operator, or go to www.govengine.com and click on your state and start looking for the Department of Revenue. For information on all federal tax credits contact Internal Revenue Service, 202-622-5000 or 800-829-1040 (Business Tax Questions) or go to www.irs.ustreas.gov/formspubs/.

Where To Find The Best Customers For Your Business

Or where is the best place to put up a store? Or which surrounding zip codes offer the best potential for increasing sales? Or where can I get a list of all the accountants in my area to tell them about my new product or service? You don't have to hire a high priced marketing consultant to get answers to questions like these. You can tap into the government's rich vein of free marketing data collected by the Bureau of Census and other government agencies. This is where the multibillion dollar companies get their marketing data and it's where the high priced consultants also get it and the resell it to clients at outrageous fees. That is what I used to do when I was a consultant. To get detailed information about data available for your state contact your local Census State Data Center in your state capital by calling your state capital operator at 411 or going to www.census.gov/sdc/www/. You can also get lots of free and low cost marketing help from your local Small Business Development Center. You can find them by contacting 800-8-ASK-SBA or www.sba.gov/sbdc/sbdcnear.html.

Money To Start A Business In A Small Town

The government is so concerned about creating jobs in small towns they gave someone $150,000 to start a winery in the middle of Iowa. See www.rurdev.usda.gov/rd/newsroom/2003/vadglist03-final.pdf. There is a lot of money and help to start a business in a small town. The government is concerned about unemployment in small towns so it has committed a number of loans and grant programs to encourage almost any kind of entrepreneuring venture. Montana gave out a $25,000 grant to help small businesses in rural areas figure out how to get government contracts. See www.rurdev.usda.gov/mt/News/Montana/2004/63004RBEG.htm. So check out the small towns in your area. Who cares if you have to drive an additional hour to work if someone is going to give you $150,000 to start your business? A good place to start to see what kind of money is available is your local U.S. Department of Agriculture Rural Development Office www.rurdev.usda.gov/recd_map.html.

Free Help Writing Business Plans Or Grant Applications

Don't believe it when some professional tries to scare you into thinking how hard it is to write a business plan or fill out a money application. This is the least of your problems plus there is plenty of free help in filling them out when the time comes. The first thing you must do in getting government money is get a copy of the application that you believe may give you the money you need. No one should ever investigate hiring a professional before you even know where you are going to apply for the money. And once you get an application in hand and you think you need help contact your local Small Business Development Center at 800-8-ASK-SBA or www.sba.gov/sbdc/sbdcnear.html. They will help you for free or for next to nothing. You can get help from the best grant writing experts in the country at a nonprofit organization called The Foundation Center. Their materials are available for free in libraries all over the country. You can find out where by contacting them at 212-620-4230 or www.fdncenter.org. By the way, I've seen a lot of applications for government money and many of them were so sloppy and unintelligible that any teacher would have given them a flunking grade, but they still got their money. And some applications are only one page long and you can get up to $150,000 for filling them out. Worrying about filling out an application before you have one in hand, is like buying a prom dress before you are invited to the prom. First things first.

Money To Buy Out Your Boss

A dream come true can be buying out your boss and running the whole business yourself. You probably always thought you could do it better anyway. Government money programs can be used for this too. Your boss may secretly be looking for someone to buy the place so she can go to the beach and finally write that "Great American Novel" that she has always been dreaming of. Start looking for federal money in the Catalog of Federal Domestic Assistance published by the U.S. Government Printing Office (www.gpo.gov) or look at it for free on the web at www.cfda.gov. Then check your State Government Office of Economic Development and tell them what you are trying to do. You can call 411 and ask for the state capital operator in your state capital or go to www.govengine.com and click on your state and find the office that is listed under business and/or economic development

$12 Million To Start A Real Big Business

No matter how much money you need there probably is a program for you. You can also collect large amounts of money by putting together money from a number of programs. The government also offers venture capital through the Small Business Administration's Small Business Investment Companies (SBIC). Over 75,000 entrepreneurs received money from this source to get their dreams off the ground including the big guys like Compaq, Apple, Federal Express and Staples. See how they can help you at

Associate Administrator for Investment, U.S. SBA, 202-205-6510 or www.sba.gov/inv. Many states also have venture capital programs or will help you locate private venture capitalists and state governments can also help you prepare the necessary paperwork. A good place to look for this kind of help is your State Government Office of Economic Development located in your state capital. You can call 411 and ask for the state capital operator in your state capital or go to www.govengine.com and click on your state and find the office that is listed under business and/or economic development

Get A $5,000 Grant With Bad Credit
Maybe you don't need a bunch of money to get your idea off the ground. Maybe all you need is just a few thousand dollars to get your idea to go. Well, there are hundreds of nonprofit organizations that offer small grants and easy loans aimed at people who would never be able to get money from traditional sources. It is difficult to locate all of these groups around the country but two good starting places are (remember these places do not give out money but can help you locate resources): 1) Association for Enterprise Opportunity at 703-841-7760 or www.microenterpriseworks.org/nearyou/ and 2) The Foundation Center at 212-620-4230 or www.fdncenter.org

Free Or Discounted Rent, Office Supplies, Management Services, etc.
The concept of "incubators" offers new entrepreneurs a place to start their business with free use of, or discounts on, everything you need to start and run a business. Some of these "incubators" even help with getting money for your project. It's a great support system for new ventures. To find "incubators" near you contact National Business Incubator Association at 740-593-4331 or www.nbia.org.

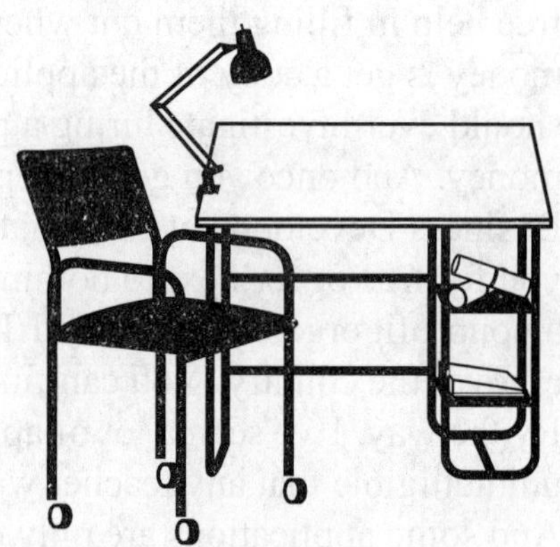

Money For Women and Minorities To Start A Business
Two out of every three businesses are started by women, and women are more successful at starting businesses than men. So the government has set up a number of money programs especially for woman who want to start or grow a business. There are also special programs for minorities and those with disabilities. To find these programs start looking for federal money in The Catalog of Federal Domestic Assistance published by the U.S. Government Printing Office (www.gpo.gov) or look at it for free on the web at www.cfda.gov. Then check your State Government Office of Economic Development and tell them what you are trying to do. You can call 411 and ask for the state capital operator in your state capital or go to www.govengine.com and click on your state and find the office that is listed under business and/or economic development

$50,000 Grant To Train Your Employees
The more employees you have the more money you can get. The government wants your employees to be the best trained in the world so America can compete in a world economy. You can get money to train your employees in almost any skill including computers, customer service or even stress management. Although it is a federal program the money is distributed through local training boards in your state capital. Then check your State Government Office of Economic Development and tell them what you are trying to do. You can call 411 and ask for the state capital operator in your state capital or go to www.govengine.com and click on your state and find the office that is listed under business and/or economic development.

$14,000 To Learn To Operate A Business

If you are out of work, you may be able to get money to live on as well as money to pay for entrepreneur training in order to run your own business. These programs are run with federal money and state money. Each state has different rules and the main idea is that they have money for you to train to get a better job along with money to live on while you are training. And your new job can be starting your own business. These programs are run through your state One-Stop Career Center located in your state capital but will have additional offices all over your state. You can find your local office by calling 411 and asking for the state capital operator in your state capital. Ask for your local 'One –Stop Career Center". Or go to www.servicelocator.org/.

$1,500 a Month To Live On While You Start Your Own Business

There are a number of states, including New York and Iowa that will allow you to collect unemployment money while you try to get your business started. It used to be that you could only receive unemployment compensation if you were actively looking for a job. Now Uncle Sam considers entrepreneuring to be a legitimate job. Contact your state unemployment labor office to see what your local rules are on entrepreneuring.

$10,000 to Take Entrepreneur Training Courses

Each state has established local job-training centers that provide money to job seekers to upgrade their skills and get better jobs. Many of these local centers allow residents to use this money to train to become an entrepreneur. Contact your state's One-Stop Labor Information Center headquarters located in your state capital and they can direct you to a local office. Check them out at www.doleta.gov/usworkforce/onestop/onestopmap.cfm.

$100,000 to Become A Freelancer Working From Your Kitchen Table

My wife got over $100,000 of government money to do consulting right out of our home. My sister got over $350,000 from the government to frame pictures. They are both government freelancers. There are free offices around the country that will help any freelancer get government contracts. The government buys: legal services, web design, aerobic instructors, landscaping, cleaning, and even stand-up comics. Contact the state Office of Economic Development located in your state capital or your local Procurement Assistance Office who can match the product or service you are selling with the appropriate agency, and then help you market your wares effectively. To find the office nearest you, contact Small and Disadvantaged Business Utilization Office, Cameron Station, Room 4B110, Defense Logistics Agency, Alexandria, VA 22304; 703-767-1661; www.dla.mil.

Free Accounting Services for Nonprofits and Small Business

There are a number of organizations around the country that provide free accounting services to help nonprofits, small businesses, and even needy individuals get the accounting help they need. They can help with bookkeeping instruction, system analysis, preparation of 990 forms, preparation for audits and free publications. A minimal one-time cost may be required. To find free accounting help in your area, contact Accountants for the Public Interest, University of Baltimore, Thurnel Business Center, Room 519, 1420 North Charles Street, Baltimore, MD 21201; 410-837-6533; Fax: 410-837-6532. You can also contact your state association of Certified Public Accountants, as many may be able to direct you to a volunteer CPA who would be willing to help.

Get $75,000 in Trees and Bushes

If you are a landscaper/orchardist and had plants damaged or destroyed by natural disaster, you can be reimbursed up to $75,000 for the cost to replant eligible trees, bushes, and vines. Contact the Department of Agriculture, Farm Service Agency, 1400 Independence Ave., S.W., Washington, DC 20250-0506; 202-720-7809; www.fsa.usda.gov/pas/publications/facts/html/tap04.htm.

Get Paid $75,000 to Send Product Samples Overseas

Through the Quality Samples Program, let the government help you transport and market your products overseas, with funding up to $75,000. You can introduce new foreign buyers to your agricultural products with the help of the USDA. Contact the USDA-FAS Marketing Operations Staff, AG Box 1042, 1400 Independence Ave., Washington, DC 20250-1042; 202-720-4327; www.as.usda.gov/mos/programs/qsp.html.

Free Air Transportation to Send Supplies Overseas

Through the Denton Program, you can ship approved cargo weighing 2,000 to 100,000 pounds to approved countries. Contact Information Center, U.S. Agency for International Development, Ronald Reagan Building, Washington, D.C. 20523-1000; www.usaid.gov/our_work/cross-cutting_programs/private_voluntary_cooperation/denton.html.

$7,000 to Work At Home With Your Kids

The United Planning Organization has created a project entitled Childcare Entrepreneurial Expansion Development Initiative that is designed to expand childcare services to provide 24 hour care and to create new businesses through training, certification, and start-up of consumer owned home based child care businesses. Contact the U. S. Department of Health and Human Services, Administration for Children and Families, Office of Community Services, Division of Community Discretionary Programs, 370 L'Enfant Promenade, S.W - 5th Floor West, Washington, D.C. 20447; 202-401-5307; www.acf.hhs.gov/programs/ocs/dcdp/joli/revised/sum2000.htm.

$30 Million to Invest Overseas

The Overseas Private Investment Corporation (OPIC) provides financing for projects sponsored by private U.S. businesses in developing countries and emerging economies throughout the world. OPIC's goal is to provide financing for investments in developing countries in projects that contribute to the economic and social development of the host country while having a positive impact on the U.S. economy. To get more information, contact the Information Officer, Overseas Private Investment Corporation, 100 New York Ave., NW, Washington, DC 20527; 202-336-8799; www.opic.gov/.

$300,000 for a Small Town Business

The New Markets Venture Capital Program is a developmental venture capital program designed to promote economic development and the creation of wealth and job opportunities in low-income geographic areas. Recipients use funds to make equity capital investments in smaller enterprises located in low-income geographic areas. Recipients can also use funds to provide management and technical assistance to smaller enterprises in connection with such investments. Contact the New Markets Venture Capital Program, 409 3rd Street, NW, Suite 6300, Washington, DC 20416; 202-205-6510; www.sba.gov/INV/.

$75,000 for Businesses Hurt By Imports
Through Trade Adjustment Assistance, the Economic Department Administration uses a national network of twelve Trade Adjustment Assistance Centers to help manufacturers and producers affected by increased imports prepare and implement strategies to guide their economic recovery. Contact your local regional EDA office or the U.S. Department of Commerce, Economic Development Administration, 14th Street and Constitution Ave., N.W., Washington, DC 20230; www.eda.gov/.

$10,000 to Start a Cleaning Business
Through the help of the Utah Microenterprise Loan Fund (UMLF), individuals have started up their own cleaning businesses, quilting companies, and even a group home for autistic children. The Micro-Loan is available to start-up and existing businesses, offering up to $10,000. This program is available in Salt Lake, Davis, Summit, Tooele, Utah, Box Elder, Morgan, Wasatch, and Weber counties in Utah only. Contact the Utah Microenterprise Loan Fund, 154 East Ford Avenue, Salt Lake City, UT 84115; 801-746-1180, Fax: 801-746-1181; www.umlf.com.

$10,000 to Start a Business in St. Croix
Find out how you can start a business in the exotic Virgin Islands, or one of 16 qualified States. Loans are made available through the USDA Rural Development Intermediary Relending Program. The aim of business revolving loan funds is to finance business facilities and community development projects in rural areas. Loans from intermediaries to the recipients must be used to establish new businesses, expand existing businesses, create employment opportunities, save jobs or complete community development projects. Contact the USDA, Rural Business-Cooperative Service, 1400 Independence Avenue, SW, Room 5050 South Building, Washington DC 20250; 202-720-1400; www.rurdev.usda.gov/rbs/busp/irp.htm.

$3,000 to Help Your Business Grow
The Utah Microenterprise Loan Fund (UMLF) helps people who cannot qualify for traditional small business loans. The Next Small Step Micro-Loan is available to existing small businesses, and offers up to $3000 in funding to help businesses take the next small step forward in growth. This program is available in Salt Lake County only. Contact the Utah Microenterprise Loan Fund, 154 East Ford Avenue, Salt Lake City, UT 84115; 801-746-1180, Fax: 801-746-1181; www.umlf.com.

$10,000 to Start a Child Care Business
The Child Care Provider Micro-Loan is available to home or center-based child care providers. This loan can help individuals to start or grow their child care business with funding up to $10,000. This program is available in Salt Lake, Davis, Summit, Tooele, Utah, Box Elder, Morgan, Wasatch, and Weber counties only. Contact the Utah Microenterprise Loan Fund, 154 East Ford Avenue, Salt Lake City, UT 84115; 801-746-1180, Fax: 801-746-1181; www.umlf.com.

$20,000 to Open a Market
The Vocational Rehabilitation Micro-Loan of the Utah Microenterprise Loan Fund is available to individuals who have been injured on the job and have an open Workers Compensation claim. This loan can help individuals to start a new business as an avenue to return to the workforce. Funding up to $20,000 is available. This program serves the entire state of Utah only. Contact the Utah Microenterprise

Loan Fund, 154 East Ford Avenue, Salt Lake City, UT 84115; 801-746-1180, Fax: 801-746-1181; www.umlf.com.

$25,000 to Open a Coffee Shop

The Salt Lake City Micro-Loan is available to start-up and existing businesses located inside Salt Lake City limits. Funding is available up to $25,000. Contact the Utah Microenterprise Loan Fund, 154 East Ford Avenue, Salt Lake City, UT 84115; 801-746-1180, Fax: 801-746-1181; www.umlf.com.

$10,000 to Start a Cookie Business

Count Me In offers women access to business loans, consultation, and education, making loans of $500-$10,000 available to women who are trying to obtain their first business loan. The organization provides access to networks that expand contacts, markets, skills, and confidence. Loans can be used for working capital, purchase of inventory or equipment, marketing materials for a sales event, or other uses. Contact Count Me In, 240 Central Park South, Suite 7H, New York, NY 10019; 212-245-1245; www.count-me-in.org.

Money to Start a Small Business in Dorchester, Massachusetts

The Dorchester Bay Economic Development Corporation small business loan program awarded ten small business loans totaling $132,300 in the past year. This is for the Dorchester Bay area only. Contact Dorchester Bay Economic Development Corporation, 594 Columbia Rd., Dorchester, MA 02125; 617-825-4200; www.dbedc.com.

$50,000 to Start a Support Hose Store

The GO TEXAN Partner Program is a dollar-for-dollar matching fund program open to small businesses that are members of GO TEXAN, Texas Department of Agriculture's comprehensive marketing campaign for Texas agricultural products. The program's funding assists with promotional and marketing costs. Contact the GO TEXAN Partner Program, Texas Department of Agriculture, P.O. Box 12847, Austin, TX 78711; 512-463-7731; www.gotexan.org.

$50,000 in Venture Capital for Small Business

The Growth Opportunities Fund (GO Fund) provides financing to small businesses that does not require immediate repayment. Through this funding, it is easier to attract investors, and the GO Fund does not take an ownership stake in the business. This program serves the Ithaca community only. Contact the Alternatives GO Fund, 301 W. State St. Ithaca, NY 14850; 607-273-3582; Email: GoFund@alternatives.org; www.alternatives.org/GoFund.html.

Money and Help to Start Food Businesses

The Food Ventures Project works to create opportunities for new specialty food jobs and businesses in Southeast Ohio only. The program offers market and trend information, access to loan and venture funds, small business and financial planning assistance, food production information and training, links to industry exports, and links to other specialty food businesses within a network of firms. To find out more, contact Appalachian Center for Economic Networks, Inc., Food Ventures, 94 North Columbus Road, Athens, OH 45701; 740-592-3854; www.acenetworks.org/frames/framesabout.htm.

Over $10,000 for Entrepreneurs

This foundation works with partners to encourage entrepreneurship across America and improve the education of children and youth. The foundation focuses its operations and grant making on two areas: entrepreneurship and education. Giving is limited to the U.S., with emphasis on the bi-state Kansas City area (KS/MO) for youth development. Contact Ewing Marion Kauffman Foundation, 4801 Rockhill Road, Kansas City, MO 64110-2046; 816-932-1000; Fax: 816-932-1100; www.kauffman.org; info@kauffman.org.

$90,000 for Entrepreneurs

Through the two-year fellowship program, the Foundation helps passionate social entrepreneurs develop new solutions to some of society's most difficult problems. These social entrepreneurs and their organizations work to close deeply-rooted social, economic and political inequities to ensure equal access and help all individuals reach their potential. Fellowships are awarded to individuals and are $30,000 a year for two years. Fellowships awarded to partnerships are $45,000 (total per project not per individual) for two years. Echoing Green pays the grants in four equal installments over two years. Contact Echoing Green Foundation, 60 East 42nd Street, Suite 520, New York, NY 10165; 212-689-1165; Fax: 212-689-9010; www.echoinggreen.org; Email: info@echoinggreen.org.

$10,000 for Women to Start or Expand a Business

Balance Bar annually awards four grants of $10,000 to creative and dynamic entrepreneurial women who want to implement a new and creative business idea to improve their existing business or organization. Contact Balance Bar Company Contributions Program, 800 Westchester Avenue, Rye Brook, NY 10573; www.balance.com/grants/default.asp. Application address for Balance Grants: c/o Grants Program, Hunter PR, 5th Fl., 41 Madison Ave., New York, NY 10010.

$1,000 for Pharmacists

The Incentive Grants for Practitioner Innovation in Pharmaceutical Care awards up to twenty $1,000 grants each year to practitioners in all practice settings to develop innovative services and to share their experiences with other pharmacists. Applicants must be members of APHA, currently licensed and actively engaged in ambulatory pharmacy practice. Contact American Pharmaceutical Association Foundation (also known as The APHA Foundation), 2215 Constitution Ave., N.W., Washington, DC 20037-2985; 202-429-7565; Fax: 202-429-6300; www.aphafoundation.org; Email: info@aphafoundation.org.

Funding for Harness Racers

The Horsemen's Welfare Trust provides grants to distressed horsemen in the harness racing industry or their families on the basis of need for essential items such as medical care, food, clothing and basic necessities. Contact Horsemen's Welfare Trust, c/o Delaware SOA, 830 Walker Sq., Dover, DE 19904-2748.

Grants to Dairy Farmers Whose Milk is Contaminated Because of Pesticides

This program provides money to dairy farmers and manufacturers of dairy products who are forced to remove their products from commercial markets due to contamination. For more information on the program (10.053 Dairy Indemnity Program) contact the U.S. Department of Agriculture, Farm Service Agency, 1400 Independence Av., SW, Washington, DC 20250-0512; 202-720-7641; www.fsa.usda.gov.

Grants to Producers of Wheat, Corn, Grain Sorghum, Barley, Oats, Upland Cotton and Rice

This program provides financial assistance to farmers in order to ensure a steady supply of food, while maintaining the flexibility necessary to adjust to the condition of the economy while complying with farm conservation and wetland protection requirements. For more information on the program (10.055 Production Flexibility Payments for Contract Commodities) contact Philip W. Stronce, U.S. Department of Agriculture, Farm Service Agency, Economic and Policy Analysis Staff, Stop 0508, 1400 Independence Ave., SW, Washington, DC 20250-0508; 202-720-2711; www.fsa.usda.gov.

Money to Implement Emergency Conservation Programs

This program enables farmers to perform emergency conservation measures to control wind erosion on farmlands, to rehabilitate farmlands damaged by wind erosion, floods, hurricanes or other natural disasters and to carry out emergency water conservation or water enhancing measures during periods of severe drought. For more information on the program (10.054 Emergency Conservation Program) contact the U.S. Department of Agriculture, Farm Service Agency, Stop 0513, 1400 Independence Ave., SW, Washington, DC 20250-0513; 202-720-6221; www.fsa.usda.gov.

Grants to Livestock Producers

This program provides grants to eligible livestock producers who suffered grazing losses due to drought, hot weather, disease, insect infestation, fire, hurricane, flood, earthquake, severe storm or other disasters occurring after January 1, 2000. Benefits are provided to producers who suffered 40% or greater grazing loss for three or more months. For more information on the program (10.066 Livestock Assistance Program) contact the U.S. Department of Agriculture, Farm Service Agency, Production, Emergencies and Compliance Division, Emergency Preparedness and Program Branch, Stop 0517, 1400 Independence Ave., SW, Washington, DC 20250-0517; 202-720-7641; www.fsa.usda.gov.

Loans to Purchase and Construct On-Farm Storage Facilities

The purpose of this program is to support the construction of on-farm grain storage facilities and to help farmers adapt to identify preserved storage and handling requirements for genetically enhanced production. For more information on the program (10.056 Farm Storage Facility Loans) contact the U.S. Department of Agriculture, Farm Service Agency, Director, Price Support Division, 1400 Independence Ave., SW, Washington, DC 20250; 202-720-7935; www.fsa.usda.gov/dafp/psd/FSFL.html.

Grants to Bioenergy Producers

This program provides financial assistance to producers of Bioenergy. The money is to be used to increase purchases of eligible commodities for the purpose of expanding production of Bioenergy, such as ethanol and bio-diesel, and to support new production capacity for Bioenergy. For more information on the program (10.078 Bioenergy Program) contact the U.S. Department of Agriculture, Farm Service Agency, Kansas City Commodity Office, Contract Reconciliation Division, P.O. Box 419205, Stop 8758, Kansas City, MO 64141-6205; 816-926-6525; www.fsa.usda.gov/daco/bio_daco.htm.

Money to Farmers, Ranchers, and Aquaculture Businesses

Loan funds may be used to enlarge, improve, and buy family farms; provide necessary water and water facilities; provide basic soil treatment and land conservation measures; construct, repair, and improve essential buildings needed in the operation of a family farm; construct or repair farm dwellings; or provide facilities to produce fish under controlled conditions. For more information on the program (10.407 Farm Ownership Loans) contact the U.S. Department of Agriculture, Farm Service Agency, Director, Loan Making Division, Ag Box 0522, Washington, DC 20250; 202-720-1632; www.fsa.usda.gov.

Loans to Family Farms That Can't Get Credit

Operating loans obtained through the Interest Assistance Program can be used to finance livestock or farm equipment; to pay annual operating expenses or family living expenses; or to refinance debts under certain conditions. For more information on the program (10.437 Interest Assistance Program) contact the U.S. Department of Agriculture, Farm Service Agency, Director, Loan Making Division, Ag Box 0522, Washington, DC 20250; 202-720-1632; www.fsa.usda.gov.

Grants to Market Food Related Products Overseas

The purpose of this program is to develop, maintain and expand long-term export markets for U.S. agricultural products. Funding from this program may be used for trade servicing, market research and technical assistance to actual or potential foreign purchasers of U.S. commodities. For more information on the program (10.600 Foreign Market Development Cooperation Program) contact the U.S. Department of Agriculture, Foreign Agricultural Service, Deputy Administrator, Commodity and Marketing Programs, 1400 Independence Ave., SW, Washington, DC 20250; 202-720-4761; www.fas.usda.gov/mos/programs/fmd.html.

Grants to Sell Food Related Products Overseas

Program funds may be used for consumer advertising, point of sale demonstrations, public relations, trade servicing activities, participation in trade fairs and exhibits, market research and technical assistance. For more information on the program (10.601 Market Access Program) contact the Deputy Administrator, Commodity and Marketing Programs, Foreign Agricultural Service, U.S. Department of Agriculture, 1400 Independence Ave., SW, Washington, DC 20250; 202-720-4761; www.fas.usda.gov/mos/programs/mapprog.html.

Loans and Grants to Build Housing for Farm Laborers

Funds from this program can be used for construction, repair, or purchase of year-round or seasonal housing; land acquisition and the improvements necessary to build; and developing related support facilities such as central cooking and dining areas, small infirmaries, laundry facilities, day care centers, and other essential equipment and facilities or recreation areas. For more information on the program (10.405 Farm Labor Housing Loans and Grants) contact the Multi-Family Housing Processing Division, Department of Agriculture, 1400 Independence Ave., SW, Washington, DC 20250; 202-720-1604; www.rurdev.usda.gov.

Grants to Nonprofits to Lend Money to New Businesses

The grant funds may be used for learning networks or programs that provide educational or job training instruction; to establish revolving loan funds; or refinancing services and fees. Funds may also be used to develop, construct or purchase land, buildings, plants, equipment, access streets and roads, parking areas, utility extensions, or necessary water supply and waste disposal facilities. Television Demonstration Grants (TDG) may be used for television programming to provide information on agriculture and other topics of importance to farmers and rural residents. All uses must assist a small or emerging private business enterprise except for the TDG Program. For more information on the program (10.769 Rural Business Enterprise Grants) contact Director, Specialty Lenders Division, Rural Business-Cooperative Service, U.S. Department of Agriculture, Washington, DC 20250-3222; 202-720-1400; www.rurdev.usda.gov.

Grants and Loans to Telephone Companies That Then Provide Financing to Small Businesses
The goal of this program is to fund rural economic development and job creation projects through electric and telephone utility companies. For more information on the program (10.854 Rural Economic Development Loans and Grants) contact Director, Specialty Lenders Division, Rural Business-Cooperative Service, U.S. Department of Agriculture, Washington, DC 20250; 202-720-1400; www.rurdev.usda.gov.

Free Plants for Conservation Studies
This program's goal is to develop technology for land management and restoration with plant materials by promoting the use of new and improved plant materials for soil, water, and related resource conservation and environmental improvement programs. For more information on the program (10.905 Plant Materials for Conservation) contact Deputy Chief for Science and Technology, Natural Resources Conservation Service, U. S. Department of Agriculture, P.O. Box 2890, Washington, DC 20013; 202-720-4630; www.nrcs.usda.gov.

Grants to Communities That Provide Money and Help to Small Business Incubators
The EDA provides funding for special projects to support long-term economic development in areas experiencing substantial economic distress. Such projects could include water and sewer system improvements, industrial access roads, industrial and business parks, port facilities, railroad sidings, distance learning facilities, skill training facilities, business incubator facilities, eco-industrial facilities and telecommunications infrastructure improvements needed for business retention and expansion. For more information on the program (11.300 Grants for Public Works and Economic Development) contact David L. McIlwain, Director, Public Works Division, Economic Development Administration, Room H7326, Herbert C. Hoover Building, U.S. Department of Commerce, Washington, DC 20230; 202-482-5265; www.doc.gov/eda.

Grants to Fisherman Hurt by Oil and Gas Drilling on the Outer Continental Shelf
This program compensates U.S. Commercial fishermen for damage/loss of fishing gear and 50% of resulting economic loss due to oil and gas related activities in any area of the Outer Continental Shelf. For more information on the program (11.408 Fishermen's Contingency Fund) contact Michael Grable, Chief, Financial Services Division, National Marine Fisheries Service, 1315 East-West Highway, Silver Spring, MD 20910; 301-713-2396; Fax: 301-713-1306; www.noaa.gov.

Grants to Communities That Help Finance New or Old Businesses Due to Military Base Closings
The goal of this program is to assist state and local areas in the development and/or implementation of strategies designed to address structural economic adjustment problems resulting from sudden and severe economic dislocation such as plant closings, military base closures and defense contract cutbacks, and natural disasters, or from long term economic deterioration in the area's economy. For more information on the program (11.307 Economic Adjustment Assistance) contact David F. Witschi,

Director, Economic Development Administration, Room H7327, Herbert C. Hoover Building, U.S. Department of Commerce, Washington, DC 20230; 202-482-2659; www.doc.gov/eda.

Grants to Develop New Technologies for Your Business

Working in partnership with industry, the Advanced Technology Program provides funding for development of new, high-risk technologies that offer the potential for significant, broad based economic benefits for the entire country. For more information on the program (11.612 Advanced Technology Program) contact Barbara Lambis, Advanced Technology Program, National Institute of Standards and Technology, 100 Bureau Drive, Stop 4700, Gaithersburg, MD 20899-4700; 301-975-4447; Fax: 301-869-1150; Email: Barbara.lambis@nist.gov; www.atp.nist.gov/atp. To receive application kits call ATP customer service staff at 800-ATP-FUND.

Grants to Organizations That Help Minorities Start Their Own Businesses

The Minority Business Development Agency provides funding for Minority Business Development Centers. For a nominal fee, these centers provide a wide range of services from initial consultations, to the identification and resolution of specific business problems. For more information on the program (11.800 Minority Business Development Centers) contact Barbara Curry, Business Development Specialist, Room 5071, Minority Business Development Agency, U.S. Department of Commerce, 14th and Constitution Ave., NW, Washington, DC 20230; 202-482-1940; www.mbda.gov.

Grants to Organizations That Help Native Americans Start Their Own Businesses

This program provides funding for eight Native American Business Development Centers that provide electronic and one-on-one business development service to Native Americans interested in entering, expanding, or improving their efforts in the marketplace. For more information on the program (11.801 Native American Program) contact Barbara Curry, Business Development Specialist, Room 5071, Minority Business Development Agency, U.S. Department of Commerce, 14th and Constitution Ave., NW, Washington, DC 20230; 202-482-1940; www.mbda.gov.

Grants to Help Minority Businesses Enter New Markets

This Program supports minority business development through indirect business assistance programs that identify and develop private markets and capital sources; expand business information and business services through trade associations; promote and support the utilization of Federal, State and local government resources; and assist minorities in entering new and growing markets. For more information on the program (11.803 Minority Business Opportunity Committee) contact the Office of Business Development, Minority Business Development Agency, Department of Commerce, 14th and Constitution Avenue, NW, Washington, DC 20230; 202-482-1940; www.mbda.gov.

Grants to Bus Companies

This program provides technical and financial assistance to rural transportation providers. Funding may be used for operating and administrative expenses, and for the acquisition, construction, and improvement of facilities and equipment. For more information on the program (20.509 Formula Grants for Other Than Urbanized Areas) contact the Federal Transit Administration, Office of Program Management, Office of Capital and Formula Assistance, 400 Seventh Street, SW, Washington, DC 20590; 202-366-2053; www.fta.dot.gov.

Grants to Become a Women-Owned Transportation Related Company

This program provides financial assistance to national, regional, and local initiatives that address public transportation. Projects may include employment training programs; outreach programs to increase minority and women's employment in public transportation activities; research on training and public transportation manpower needs; and training and assistance for minority businesses. For more information on the program (20.511 Human Resources Program) contact Director, Office of Civil Rights, Federal Transit Administration, U.S. Department of Transportation, 400 Seventh Street, SW, Room 9102, Washington, DC 20590; 202-366-4018; www.fta.dot.gov.

Money for Airlines to Fly to Small Towns and Make a Profit

The purpose of this program is to assure that air transportation services are provided to eligible communities. Subsidy payments are made to air carriers providing air services to eligible locations in order to ensure the continuation of service. Subsidies are paid to cover the carrier's prospective operating loss plus an element of profit. For more information on the program (20.901 Payments for Essential Air Services) contact Director, Office of Aviation Analysis, X-50, U.S. Department of Transportation, 400 Seventh Street, SW, Washington, DC 20590; 202-366-1030; www.ost.dot.gov.

Grants to Women-Owned Businesses to Help Get Contracts from the Department of Transportation

This program is designed to help small businesses, socially and economically disadvantaged persons, and businesses owned and operated by women increase their participation in Department of Transportation programs and funded projects. For more information on the program (20.903 Support Mechanisms for Disadvantaged Businesses) contact the Office of Small and Disadvantaged Business Utilization, S-40, Office of the Secretary, 400 Seventh Street, SW, Washington, DC 20590; 800-532-1169; 202-366-1930; www.dot.gov.

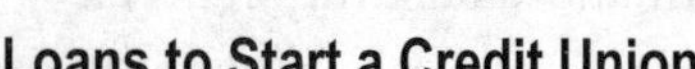

Loans to Start a Credit Union

The Community Development Revolving Loan Program for Credit Unions provides funding to support low-income credit unions' efforts to provide a variety of financial and related services designed to meet the needs of their community. For more information on the program (44.002 Community Development Revolving Loan Program for Credit Unions) contact Mr. Anthony Lacreta, Community Development Revolving Loan Program for Credit Unions, National Credit Union Administration, 1775 Duke Street, Alexandria, VA 22314-3428; 703-518-6610; www.ncua.gov.

Help for Contractors and Others to Get Bonded to Obtain Contracts

Under this program, small contractors unable to obtain a bond are guaranteed surety bonds issued by commercial surety companies. Guarantees are for up to ninety percent of the losses incurred and are paid by participating sureties when conditions are met. For more information on the program (59.016 Bond Guarantees for Surety Companies) contact Associate Administrator, Robert J. Moffitt, Office of Surety Guarantees, Small Business Administration, 409 Third Street, SW, Washington, DC 20416; 202-205-6540; www.sba.gov.

Grants to Local Organizations That Help Veterans Start Their Own Businesses

This program establishes Veteran Business Outreach Centers to provide long term training, counseling, and mentoring to small businesses and potential small businesses owned and operated by eligible U.S. Veterans. For more information on this program (59.044 Veteran's Entrepreneurial Training and

Counseling) contact Reginald Teamer, Office of Veteran Affairs, Small Business Administration, 5th Floor, 409 Third Street, SW, Washington, DC 20416; 202-205-6773; www.sba.gov.

Help for Disabled Veterans to Start New Businesses

This Vocational Rehabilitation Program provides services and assistance to help disabled veterans get and keep a suitable job. The program also provides the needed services and assistance to help individuals achieve the necessary skills to maximize independence in daily living. Veterans who meet certain requirements may receive an initial supply of goods and commodities to start a small business. For more information on the program (64.116 Vocational Rehabilitation for Disabled Veterans) contact the Veterans Benefits Administration, Vocational Rehabilitation and Counseling Service (28), U.S. Department of Veteran Affairs, Washington, DC 20420; 202-273-7419; www.va.gov.

Help for Retired Military to Start a Business

This program provides vocational and counseling to recipients of VA pensions so they may get and keep a suitable job. Veterans who meet certain eligibility requirements may be provided with the goods or commodities to start a small business. For more information on the program (64.123 Vocational Training for Certain Veterans Receiving VA Pension) contact the Veterans Benefits Administration, Vocational Rehabilitation and Counseling Service (28), U.S. Department of Veterans Affairs, Washington, DC 20420; 202-273-7419; www.va.gov.

Money to Invest in Companies Overseas

The Overseas Private Investment Corporation provides financing for investments in developing countries for projects that contribute to the social and economic development of the host country and at the same time have a positive impact on the U.S. economy. OPIC disqualifies projects that may have a negative effect on the environment, U.S. employment, the host country's development, or would violate internationally recognized worker rights. For more information on the program (70.002 Foreign Investment Financing) contact Information Officer, Overseas Private Investment Corporation, 1100 New York Ave., NW, Washington, DC 20527; 202-336-8799; Fax: 202-336-8700; Email: info@opic.gov; www.opic.gov.

Money to Privately Owned Community Drinking Water Utilities for Security Improvements

Large privately owned community drinking water utilities that serve 100,000 or more people are eligible to apply for this funding. The money may be used to conduct a vulnerability assessment, develop or revise an emergency response operating plan, enhance security plans, or a combination of these efforts. For more information on this program (66.477 Vulnerability Assessments and Related Security Improvements as Large Privately Owned Drinking Water Utilities) contact U.S. Environmental Protection Agency, Private Water Utility Security Grant Program, Room 2104A, EPA East Building, 1201 Constitution Avenue, NW, Washington, DC 20004; 800-426-4791; 202-564-3750; www.epa.gov.

Grants for Security Improvements at Drinking Water Utilities

Large publicly owned community drinking water utilities that serve at least 100,000 people are eligible to apply for this funding. Recipients of these grants may use the money to conduct a vulnerability assessment, develop or revise an emergency response operating plan, enhance security measures, or any combination of these efforts. For more information on the program (66.476 Vulnerability Assessments and Related Security Improvements at Large Drinking Water Utilities) contact the U.S. Environmental Protection Agency, Public Water Utility Security Grant Program, 1201 Constitution Ave., NW, Washington, DC 20004; 800-426-4791; www.epa.gov.

Insurance Against Your Business in Another Country Being Hurt by Foreign Politics
To encourage private U.S. investment in developing countries, OPIC provides insurance to protect against the risks of inconvertibility, expropriation and political violence. Insurance is available for contractors and exporters against arbitrary drawings of letters of credit posted as bid, performance or advance payment guaranties; petroleum exploration, development and production; leasing operations; and debt financials, including securities. For more information on this program (70.003 Foreign Investment Insurance) contact the Information Officer, Overseas Private Investment Corporation, 1100 New York Avenue, NW, Washington, DC 20527; 202-336-8799; Fax: 202-336-8700; Email: info@opic.gov; www.opic.gov.

Free Patent Licenses to Develop and Market Energy Saving Inventions
The Department of Energy grants nonexclusive, revocable patent licenses to qualified applicants with plans to develop and/or market one of the more that 1,200 DOE owned U.S. Patents. For more information on the program (81.003 Granting of Patent Licenses) contact Robert J. Marchick, Office of the Assistant General Counsel for Patents, U.S. Department of Energy, Washington, DC 20585; 202-586-2802; www.doe.gov.

Money to Work on an Energy Related Invention
The U.S. Department of Energy's Inventions and Innovation program provides financial and technical support to inventors and businesses to develop energy saving concepts and technologies. Grant recipients are selected through a competitive process. For more information on this program (81.036 Invention and Innovations) contact Lisa Barnett, Office of Industrial Technologies (EE-23), U.S. Department of Energy, Weatherization and Intergovernmental Programs, 1000 Independence Avenue, SW, Washington, DC 20585; 202-586-2212; www.eere.energy.gov/inventions.

Help for Farmers to Control Plant and Animal Diseases
This program's objective is to protect U.S. agriculture from harmful plant and animal diseases and pests. It provides for inspections to detect and evaluate infestations and carries out regulatory actions to prevent the interstate spread of diseases and infestations. For more information on the program (97.003 Agricultural Inspections) contact the Department of Homeland Security, 245 Murray Drive, SW, Washington, DC 20528; 202-282-8000; www.dhs.gov.

Grants for Commercial Fisheries Failing Due to a Natural Disaster
This program provides assistance to fishing vessel owners, operators, and crew, and fish processors that are facing failure due to a fishery resource disaster. For more information on the program (11.477 Fisheries Disaster Relief) contact Alicia Jarboe, Financial Services Division (F/CS2), National Marine Fisheries Service, 1315 East-West Highway, Silver Spring, MD 20910; 301-713-2358; Fax: 301-713-1939; Email: Alicia.jarboe@ noaa.gov; www.fakr.noaa.gov/omi/grants/default.htm for Alaska, or http://caldera.sero.nmfs.gov/grants/programs/disaster.htm for the Southeast.

Grants to Work on Solar Energy Products

The Department of Energy provides funding to conduct research and development efforts in the following energy technologies: distributed energy and electric reliability, solar, hydrogen, biomass, fuel cells and infrastructure, geothermal, wind and hydropower. Grants are also offered to develop and transfer these renewable energy technologies to the scientific and industrial communities, and state and local governments. For more information on the program (81.087 Renewable Energy Research and Development) contact the Office of Energy Efficiency and Renewable Energy (EERE), Mail Stop EE-1, Department of Energy, Washington, DC 28585; 800-DOE-3732; 202-586-9220; www.eere.energy.gov.

Grants to Develop Uses of Fossil Fuels

The focus of the Fossil Energy Research and Development program is to promote the development and use of environmentally and economically advanced technologies for supply, conversion, delivery and utilization of fossil fuels. For more information on the program (81.089 Fossil Energy Research and Development) contact Mary J. Roland, Fossil Energy Program, Mail Stop FE-3, 19901 Germantown Road, Department of Energy, Germantown, MD 20874; 301-903-3514; www.fe.doe.gov.

Grants to Develop Energy Saving Products

This program offers grants to conduct research in the areas of buildings, industry and transportation. Grants are also offered to develop and transfer conservation technology to the non-federal sector. For more information on this program (81.086 Conservation Research and Development) contact the Office of Energy Efficiency and Renewable Energy (EERE), Mail Stop EE-1, Department of Energy, Washington, DC 28585; 800-DOE-3732; 202-586-9220; www.eere.energy.gov.

Grants to Telecommunications Companies to Provide Services to Schools

This program provides grants to telecommunications companies to provide facilities and equipment, educational and instructional programming, and necessary technical assistance to elementary and secondary schools. Priority is given to companies that provide services to schools in underserved areas, individuals excluded from careers in math and science due to discrimination or economic disadvantages, areas with scarce resources, and areas with limited access to courses in math, science, and foreign languages. For more information on this program (84.203 Star Schools) contact Joseph Wilkes, U.S. Department of Education, Office of Innovation and Improvement, Technology in Education Programs, 555 New Jersey Ave., NW, Washington, DC 20208-5645; 202-219-2186; Email: joseph.wilkes@ed.gov; www.ed.gov/offices/OII.

Money to Develop Health and Safety Programs for Construction Workers

The purpose of this program is to develop health and safety programs for construction workers in order to reduce occupational injuries and illnesses. Funds may be used for salaries of personnel employed specifically for the project, consultant fees, supplies and equipment necessary to conduct the project, essential travel expenses, and other project related expenses. For more information on this program (93.955 Health and Safety Programs for Construction Workers) Grant Management Contact: Mildred Garner, Grants Management Branch, Procurement and Grants Office, Centers for Disease Control and Prevention, 2920 Brandywine Road, Atlanta, GA 30341; 770-488-2745 or Program Management Contact: Office of Extramural Programs, National Institute for Occupational Safety and Health, Centers for Disease Control and Prevention, 1600 Clifton Road, Mail Stop E-74, Atlanta, GA 30333; 404-498-2530; www.cdc.gov.

Grants to Improve Emergency Medical Service in Rural Areas

This program makes grants for research and demonstration projects designed to improve the quality and availability of emergency medical services in rural areas. Funds may be used to develop and use new, innovative communications technologies; develop model curricula for training emergency medical services personnel; make training, certification, and continuing education more accessible; develop increased access to pre-hospital care and improve the availability of emergency transportation services; and evaluate the effectiveness of current emergency medical services and systems. For more information on the program (93.952 Improving EMS/Trauma Care in Rural Areas) contact Richard J. Smith III, Chief, Injury/EMS Branch, Maternal and Child Health Bureau, Health Resources and Services Administration, Public Health Service, Department of Health and Human Services, Parklawn Building, Room 18A-38, 5600 Fishers Lane, Rockville, MD 20857; 301-443-0324 or Grants Management Branch, Maternal and Child Health Bureau, Health Resources and Services Administration, Public Health Service, Department of Health and Human Services, Parklawn Building, Room 18-12, 5600 Fishers Lane, Rockville, MD 20857; 301-443-1440; www.mchb.hrsa.gov.

Pension Plan Termination Insurance for Small Businesses

This program encourages the continuation and maintenance of voluntary private pension plans, provides for timely and uninterrupted payment of pension benefits to participants and beneficiaries in plans covered by the PBGC, and maintains premiums at the lowest possible level. For more information on this program (86.001 Pension Plan Termination Insurance) contact the Pension Benefit Guaranty Corporation, 1200 K Street, NW, Washington, DC 20005-4026; 202-326-4000; www.pbgc.gov.

Crop Insurance for Owners or Operators of Farmlands

The Federal Crop Insurance Corporation (FCIC) is a government owned corporation created to provide comprehensive crop insurance nation wide. Catastrophic crop insurance protection (CAT) is fully subsidized except for administrative fees paid by the producer. This coverage compensates the producer for yield losses greater than 50% at a price equal to 55% of maximum price. For more information on the program (10.450 Crop Insurance) contact the Department of Agriculture, Administrator, Risk Management Agency, Ag Box 0801, Washington, DC 20250; 202-690-2803; www.fsa.usda.gov.

Money for Livestock Owners Hurt by a Natural Disaster

This program provides emergency assistance to eligible livestock owners in an area, county or state where an official emergency has been declared due to insect infestation, disease, fire, drought, flood, hailstorm, hurricane, earthquake, hot weather, c old weather, ice, snow, freeze, winter kill, or other natural disaster. For more information on this program (10.452 Disaster Reserve Assistance) contact the Department of Agriculture, Farm Service Agency, Emergency and Noninsured Assistance Program Division, Mail Stop 0526, 1400 Independence Avenue, SW, Washington, DC 20250-0526; 202-720-3168; www.fsa.usda.gov.

Help for Farmers and Ranchers on Indian Lands

This program helps Indian farmers, ranchers and landowners manage and develop their land for farming and grazing. It also provides for noxious weed eradication by means of chemical, mechanical, cultural, and biological control methods. For more information on this program (15.034 Agriculture on Indian Lands) contact Mark Bradford, Office of Trust Responsibilities, Division of Water and Land Resources, Branch of Agriculture and Range, Bureau of Indian Affairs, 1849 C Street, NW, Mail Stop 4513 MIB, Washington, DC 20240; 202-208-3598; www.doi.gov/bia/otrhome.htm or www.doi.gov/bureau-indian-affairs.html.

Money to Indian Tribes for Economic Development

Funds from this program can be used to administer revolving loan and guaranty loan programs to promote economic development on tribal lands. Assistance is provided to American Indian owned businesses in obtaining financing from private sectors. For more information on the program (15.032 Indian Economic Development) contact Woodrow Sneed, Office of Economic Development, Bureau of Indian Affairs, 1849 C Street, NW, Mail Stop 4640, Washington, DC 20240; 202-208-4796; www.doi.gov/bia/ecodev/index.htm or www.doi.gov/bureau-indian-affairs.html.

Grants to Market Food Related Products to Emerging Markets Overseas

The Emerging Markets Program's goal is to promote, enhance, or expand the export of U.S. agricultural commodities in low to middle income counties that are likely to emerge as promising export markets in the near future. U.S. agricultural and agribusiness firms, especially those that need assistance in obtaining or maintaining access to overseas markets, may be eligible for cost-share assistance to implement an Emerging Markets Program. For more information on this program (10.603 Emerging Markets Program) contact the Director, Marketing Operations Staff, Foreign Agricultural Services, Department of Agriculture, Washington, DC 20250; 202-720-4327; www.fas.usda.goc/mos/em-markets/em-markets.html.

Help for Farmers and Ranchers to Conserve Natural Resources

This program provides technical, educational and financial assistance to eligible farmers and ranchers to address soil, water and other natural resource concerns on their lands through the implementation of structural, vegetative, and land management practices. Technical assistance is provided for conservation planning measures. Educational and financial assistance is provided for the implementation of structural, vegetative and land management practices. For more information on the program (10.912 Environmental Quality Incentives Program) contact the Deputy Chief for Natural Resource Conservation Programs, Natural Resources Conservation Service, U.S. Department of Agriculture, P.O. Box 289, Washington, DC 20013; 202-720-1845; Fax: 202-72-4265; www.nrcs.usda.gov.

Money for Great Plains Farmers and Ranchers to Conserve Soil and Water

In order to conserve and develop the Great Plains water and soil resources, technical and financial assistance is provided to farmers and ranchers to plan and implement conservation practices. Cost-share funds are available for many of the soil and water conservation measures necessary to protect and stabilize a farm or ranch against the effects of climate and erosion in the Great Plains area. Land must be located in one of the 556 designated counties in Colorado, Kansas, Montana, Nebraska, New Mexico, Oklahoma, South Dakota, Texas or Wyoming. For more information on the program (10.900 Great

Plains Conservation) contact the Deputy Chief, National Resources Conservation Programs, Natural Resources Conservation Services, Department of Agriculture, P.O. Box 2890, Washington, DC 20013; 202-720-1873; www.nrcs.usda.gov.

Money for Businesses to Reduce High Energy Costs in Rural Communities
This program provides assistance to rural communities with extremely high energy costs. Funds must be used to acquire, construct, extend, upgrade, or otherwise improve the energy generation, transmission, or distribution facilities in these communities. For more information on this program (10.859 Assistance to High Energy Cost-Rural Communities) contact the Administrator, Rural Utilities Service, Department of Agriculture, Washington, DC 20250-1500; 202-720-9540; www.rurdev.usda.gov.

Grants to Agricultural Producers and Rural Small Businesses to Conserve Energy
The Rural Business-Cooperative Service provides direct loans, loan guarantees and grants to farmers, ranchers, and rural small businesses for measures to help reduce the cost and consumption of energy. Funds must be used to purchase renewable energy systems or energy efficiency improvements. For more information on this program (10.775 Renewable Energy Systems and Energy Efficiency Improvements Program) contact Rural Business-Cooperative Services, Department of Agriculture, 1400 Independence Avenue, SW, Washington, DC 20013; 202-720-1400; www.rurdev.usda.gov/rbs.

Money to Enhance Production and Marketing in the Sheep and Goat Industries
The National Sheep Industry Improvement Center provides financial assistance to the U.S. Sheep and Goat Industries to strengthen and enhance the production and marketing of sheep, goats, and their products within the United States. For more information on this program (10.774 National Sheep Industry Improvement Center) contact the National Sheep Industry Improvement Center, U.S. Department of Agriculture, 1400 Independence Avenue, SW, Room 2117, Washington, DC 20250; 202-690-0632; Fax: 202-236-6576; www.rurdev.usda.gov/coops/cssheep.htm.

Grants for Rural Businesses and Communities

Grant funds from this program can be used to improve the economic development of rural areas by providing technical assistance for rural businesses, training for rural entrepreneurs and economic development officials, or planning for business and economic development. For more information on the program (10.773 Rural Business Opportunity Grants) contact the Rural Business-Cooperative Service, U.S. Department of Agriculture, Specialty Lenders Division, Mail Stop 3225, Room 6767, 1400 Independence Avenue, SW, Washington, DC 20250-1521; 202-720-1400; www.rurdev.usda.gov.

Grants to Improve and Extend Public Telecommunications Services in the U.S.
This program's purpose is to assist in the planning, acquisition, installation and modernization of public telecommunication facilities. Grants are given to extend public telecommunications service by the most efficient and economical means; including the use of broadcast and non-broadcast technologies; increasing public telecommunications services and facilities owned and operated by women and minorities; and strengthening the capability of existing public television and radio stations to provide public telecommunications service to the public. For more information on this program (11.550 Public Telecommunications Facilities-Planning and Construction) contact William Cooperman, Director, Public Telecommunications Facilities Program, Office of Telecommunications and Information

Application/ NTIA, Room 4625, Department of Commerce, 1401 Constitution Avenue, NW, Washington, DC 20230; 202-482-5802; www.ntia.doc.gov/ptfp.

Money to Help Bus Operators Comply With "Transportation for Individuals with Disabilities" Requirements
This program provides funding to private operators of over-the-road buses to assist with the costs and training necessary to comply with the Department of Transportation's "Transportation for Individuals with Disabilities" rule. Capital projects eligible for funding include adding wheelchair lifts and other accessibility equipment to new vehicles, and purchasing lifts to retro-fit existing vehicles. Eligible training costs can be included. For more information on this program (20.518 Capital and Training Assistance Program for Over-the Road Bus Accessibility) contact Brenda Younger, Program Coordinator, Federal Transit Administration, Office of Program Management, Office of Resource Management and State Programs, 400 7th Street, SW, Washington, DC 20590; 202-366-2053; www.fta.dot.gov.

Help to Establish and Operate a Credit Union
NCUA staff will explain Federal Credit Union chartering requirements to any group interested in forming a credit union. They also help with the preparation of the charter application, assist newly chartered credit unions begin operation, and will assist credit unions and their members in consumer matters. For more information on the program (44.001 Credit Union Charter, Examination, Supervision, and Insurance) contact the Chairman, NCUA Board, National Credit Union Administration, 1775 Duke Street, Alexandria, VA 22314-3428; 703-518-6300; www.ncua.gov.

Institutional, Collections Management, Public Dimension and Governance Assessments for Museums, Nature Centers, Science and Technology Centers and Botanical Gardens
The Museum Assessment Program (MAP) is funded by the Institute of Museum and Library Services and administered by the American Association of Museums. It is designed to help museums assess their strengths and weaknesses and plan for the future. The program provides non-competitive grants of technical assistance for four types of assessments: Institutional, Collections Management Public Dimension, and Governance. For more information on this program (45.302 Museum Assessment Program) contact Jeannette Thomas, Institute of Museum and Library Services, 1100 Pennsylvania Avenue, NW, Room 510, Washington, DC 20506; 202-606-8339 (Public Affairs) or 202-606-8458 (Jeanette Thomas); Email: imlsinfo@ imls.gov; www.imls.gov.

Grants to Museums, Aquariums, Zoological Parks, and Planetariums for Conservation Programs
The Conservation Assessment Program (CAP) supports a two day site visit by conservation professional to perform the assessment and up to three days to write the report. The general conservation survey or assessment provides an overview of all the museum's collections, as well as its environmental conditions, policies and procedures relating to collections care. For more information on the program (45.304 Conservation Assessment Program) contact Noelle Giguere, Institute of Museum and Library Services, 1100 Pennsylvania Avenue, NW, Room 510, Washington, DC 20506; 202-606-8339 (Public Affairs) or 202-606-8550 (Noelle Giguere); Email: imlsinfo@imls.gov; www.imls.gov.

Grants to Museums, Botanical Gardens, Arboretums, and Nature Centers for Conservation Projects

The IMLS Conservation Project Support program awards matching grants to help museums identify conservation priorities and needs, and perform activities to ensure the safekeeping of their collections. The primary goal of each project must be conservation care and not collection management or maintenance. Conservation Project Support also funds exceptional projects with far reaching effects that benefit multiple institutions. For more information on this program (45.303 Conservation Project Support) contact Steven Shwartzman, Institute of Museum and Library Services, 1100 Pennsylvania Avenue, NW, Room 510, Washington, DC 20506; 202-606-8339 (Public Affairs) or 202-606-4641 (Steven Shwartzman); Email: imlsinfo@imls.gov; www.imls.gov.

Business Development Help for Small Businesses

This program provides assistance to prospective, as well as present, small business persons to improve the skills necessary to manage and operate a business. The assistance includes workshops for prospective small business owners; management counseling including assistance from the Service Corps of Retired Executives (SCORE) and other volunteer groups; management courses, conferences, and seminars; and educational materials to assist in the management of a small business. For more information on this program (59.005 Business Development Assistance to Small Business) contact the Associate Administrator for Business Initiatives, Small Business Administration, 409 3rd Street, SW, Washington, DC 20416; 800-8ASK-SBA; 202-205-6665; www.sba.gov.

Help in Obtaining Federal Contracts for Small Businesses

This program helps small business obtain a "fair" share of contracts and sub-contracts for Federal government supplies and services, and a "fair" share of property sold by the government. Assistance includes: the application of small business set-asides to increase the Federal procurement and disposal requirements awarded to small business; consultations to optimize procurement activities; review and analysis of small firms in order to certify competence as a prime contractor; review of large prime contractors' sub-contracting plans and programs to insure sub-contracting opportunities; consultation and advice for small firms regarding government procurement and property sales matters; assistance in specific contract administration problems; and determination of small business eligibility for SBA's procurement financial programs. For more information on this program (59.009 Procurement Assistance to Small Businesses) contact the Associate Administrator for Government Contracting, Small Business Administration, 409 3rd Street, SW, Washington, DC 20416; 800-8ASK-SBA; 202-205-6460; www.sba.gov.

New Markets Venture Capital for Small Business in Low-Income Geographic Areas

The goal of this program is to promote economic development and job opportunities in low-income geographic areas through developmental venture capital investments in smaller businesses located in such areas. The SBA designates New Markets Venture Capital companies which are eligible to receive guaranteed loans and project grants. The guaranteed loan funds are used to make equity capital investments in smaller businesses located in low-income geographic areas. For more information on the program (59.051 New Markets Venture Capital) contact the Director, New Markets Venture Capital

Program, 409 3rd Street, NW, Suite 6300, Washington, DC 20416; 800-8ASK-SBA; 202-205-6510; Fax: 202-205-6013; www.sba.gov/INV/venture.html.

$500,000 for Small Businesses

The SBA's Small Business Loan Programs provide guaranteed loans to small businesses that are unable to obtain traditional financing, but have shown the ability to repay loans granted. Priority is given to low income business owners, businesses located in high unemployment areas, nonprofit sheltered workshops, small businesses owned or being established by handicapped individuals, and the support of small businesses in the manufacturing, design, marketing, installation or serving of specific energy measures. For more information on this program contact the Director, Policy Procedures Branch, Small Business Administration, 409 Third Street, SW, Washington, DC 20416: 202-205-6570: 800-UASK-SBA; www.sba.gov.

Help to Start or Expand a Micro-enterprise

The PRIME program was created to help the smallest of small businesses, those with fewer than six employees. Under the Program for Investment in Micro-entrepreneurs (PRIME), the SBA provides federal funds to community based organizations that in turn offer training and technical assistance to low-income and very low-income micro-entrepreneurs. For more information on the program (59.050 Micro-Enterprise Development Grants) contact Judy Raskind, Office of Financial Assistance, Small Business Administration, 409 Third Street, SW, Washington, DC 20416; 800-UASK-SBA; 202-205-6497; www.sba.gov/INV.

Free Counseling and Mentoring Services for Potential and Existing Small Businesses

SCORE uses the management experience of retired and active business professionals to counsel and train potential and existing small business owners. SCORE members volunteer their counseling and mentoring services to the public free of charge, though small business training workshops are offered for a low fee. For more information on the (59.026 Service Corps of Retired Executives Association) program contact W. Kenneth Yancey, National SCORE Association Office, Small Business Administration, 409 Third Street, SW, Washington, DC 20025; 800-634-0245; 202-205-6762; www.score.org or www.sba.gov.

Business Development Help for Asian American, African American, Hispanic American, Native American and Asian Pacific American Businesses

This program offers business development assistance to business owners who are both socially and economically disadvantaged. The assistance provided includes: management and technical assistance, access to capital and other forms of financing, business training and counseling, and access to sole source and limited competition Federal Contract opportunities. For more information on the (59.006 8(a) Business Development) program contact the Associate Administrator for 8(a) Business Development, Small Business Administration, 409 Third Street, SW, Washington, DC 20416; 202-205-6421; 800-UASK-SBA; www.sba.gov/8abd.

Grants to Museums for Projects that Sustain Our Cultural Heritage and Support Life Long Learning in the Community

Museums for America Grants support projects and activities that strengthen museums as active resources and centers of community engagement. These grants may be used to fund ongoing museum activities; purchase equipment or services; research and scholarships; upgrading and integration of new technology; improve institutional infrastructure; or to plan new programs or activities. For more information on (45.301 Museums for America Grants) contact Christine Henry, Senior Program Officer, Office of Museum Services, Room 609, Institute of Museum and Library Services, 1100 Pennsylvania Avenue, NW, Washington, DC 20506; 202-606-8687; Fax: 202-606-0010; Email: chenry@imls.gov; www.imls.gov/grants/museum/mus_mfa.htm.

Grants to Nonprofit Museums for Innovations in Public Services and Meeting Community Needs
National Leadership Grants support innovation in providing public service and meeting community needs through the creative use of new technologies; model projects to be replicated though out the field; increased public access to museum collections; and collaborative projects to extend the impact of funding. Museum Online Grants address the technological needs and issues of museums. Museums in the Community Grants support museum and community partnerships that enhance the quality of community life. Professional Practice Grants support projects that improve the professional practices in the museum field. For more information on (45.312 National Leadership Grants for Museums) contact Dan Lukash, Senior Program Officer, Office of Museum Services, Room 609, Institute of Museum and Library Services, 1100 Pennsylvania Avenue, NW, Washington, DC 20506; 202-606-4644; Fax: 202-606-0010; Email: dlukash@imls.gov; www.imls.gov/grants/museum/mus_nlgm.asp.

Grants to Libraries that Serve Native Americans and Native Hawaiians
Grants from the Native Hawaiian Library Services Program can be used to support improvements in library services to Native Hawaiians. Funds may be used to establish or enhance electronic links between libraries; link libraries electronically with social, educational or information services; help libraries access information through electronic networks; encourage libraries in different areas, and different types of libraries to establish consortia and share resources; pay costs for libraries to acquire or share computer systems and telecommunications technologies; and target library and information services to persons having difficulty using a library and to underserved urban and rural communities. For more information on the Native American and Native Hawaiian Library Services Program contact Alison Freese, Senior Program Specialist, Office of Library Services, Room 802, Institute of Museum and Library Services, 1100 Pennsylvania Avenue, NW, Washington, DC 20506; 202-606-5408; Fax: 202-606-1077; Email: afreese@imls.gov; www.imls.gov/grants/library/lib_nhls.asp.

Help for Manufacturers and Producers Hurt by Increased Imports
The EDA provides assistance to manufacturers and producers injured by increased imports. A network of 12 Trade Adjustment Assistance Centers (TAAC) help affected firms complete and submit an eligibility petition to the EDA. Once approved, the TAAC helps the firm to prepare an adjustment proposal that includes an objective analysis of the firm's weaknesses, strengths, and opportunities. After the EDA approves the adjustment plan, the firm can receive cost share assistance from the TAAC. For more information on the Trade Adjustment Assistance Program contact David A. Sampson, Economic Development Administration, Department of Commerce, 1401 Constitution Avenue, NW, Washington, DC 20230; 202-482-5081; www.eda.gov/InvestmentsGrants/Investments.xml.

Help for Marine Suppliers and Owners and Operators of U.S. Shipbuilding and Repair Facilities to Improve Their Competitiveness in International Markets
The Maritime Administration (MARAD) established the National Maritime Resource and Education Center to assist marine suppliers, and the owner/operators of U.S. shipbuilding and repair facilities in

improving their international competitiveness. For more information on the National Maritime Resource and Education Center contact Joseph Byrne, Director, Office of Shipbuilding and Marine Technology, Maritime Administration, U.S. Department of Transportation, 400 7th Street, SW, Washington, DC 20590; 202-366-1931; 800-99-MARAD; Fax: 202-366-7197; www.marad.dot.gov/NMREC/index.html.

Help for Owners and Operators of U.S. Flag Ships to Construct, Reconstruct or Acquire New Vessels
The CCF Program was established to help owners and operators of U.S. Flag vessels accumulate the capital necessary to modernize and expand the U.S. Merchant Marine. The program promotes the construction, reconstruction or acquisition of vessels by deferring Federal Income Taxes on money or property placed into a Capital Construction Fund. For more information on the Capital Construction Fund contact the Office of Ship Financing, Maritime Administration, U.S. Department of Transportation, 400 7th Street, SW, Room 8122, Washington, DC 20950; 202-366-5744; 800-99-MARAD; www.marad.dot.gov/TitleXI/ccf.html.

Help for Exporters of U.S. Dairy Products
The Dairy Export Incentive Program helps exporters of U.S. dairy products meet world prices for certain dairy products and destinations. Through this program, the USDA pays cash bonuses to exporters, allowing them to sell certain U.S. dairy products at prices lower that their acquisition costs. The goal of this program is to develop export markets for dairy products where U.S. products are not competitive due to the presence of subsidized products from other countries. For more information on the Dairy Export Incentive Program contact the Operations Division, Export Credits, Foreign Agricultural Service, USDA, Mail Stop 1035; 1400 Independence Avenue, SW, Washington, DC 20250-1035; 202-720-3224 or 202-720-6211; Fax: 202-720-0938; www.fas.usda.gov/excredits/deip.html.

Cash Bonuses to Exporters of U.S. Agricultural Products

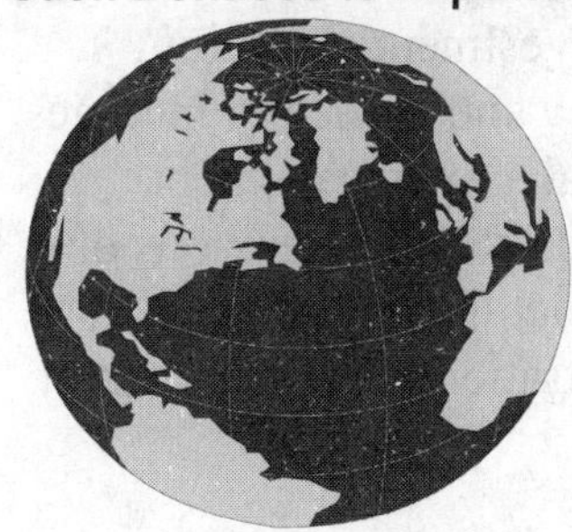

The main objectives of the program are to expand U.S. agricultural exports and to challenge unfair trade practices. The EEP helps products produced by U.S. farmers meet competition from subsidized products from other countries, and especially the European Union. To achieve these objectives, the USDA pays cash bonuses to exporters, allowing them to sell U.S. agricultural products in targeted countries at prices below their cost of acquiring them. For more information on the Export Enhancement Program contact the Operations Division, Export Credits, Foreign Agricultural Service, USDA, Mail Stop 1035; 1400 Independence Avenue, SW, Washington, DC 20250-1035; 202-720-3224 or 202-720-6211; Fax: 202-720-0938; www.fas.usda.gov/excredits/eep.html

Money for Farmers to Incorporate Conservation into their Farming Operations
Agricultural Management Assistance (AMA) provides cost share assistance to agricultural producers to voluntarily incorporate conservation efforts, such as water management, water quality and erosion control, into their farming operations. AMA provides the personnel and resources needed to conduct conservation planning, conservation practice surveys, layout design, installation and certification, quality assurance and assessment of the program. For more information on Agricultural Management Assistance contact David B. Mason, National AMA Program Manager, Natural Resources Conservation Service, USDA, 1400 Independence Avenue, SW, Room 5242-S, Washington, DC 20250; 202-720-1873; Email: dave.mason@usda.gov; www.nrcs.usda.gov/programs/ama.

Money for Farmers and Ranchers to Conserve Soil and Water

The SWCA program helps farmers and ranchers address threats to water, soil and other related natural resources, including grazing land, wetlands and wildlife habitat, by providing cost share and incentive payments. SWCA also helps landowners comply with Federal and state environmental laws, and make cost effective changes to nutrient management, irrigation, grazing management and cropping systems. For more information on the Soil and Water Conservation Assistance, SWCA program contact Walley Turner, National Program Manager, Natural Resources Conservation Service, USDA, 1400 Independence Avenue, SW, Washington, DC 20250; 202-720-1875; Email: walley.turner@usda. gov; www.nrcs.usda.gov/programs/swca.

Grants to Business Partnerships to Provide Technical Skills Training to American Workers

The goal of the H-1B Technical Skills Training Grant Program is to raise the technical skill levels of American workers. Grants are awarded to local Workforce Investment Boards and business partnerships. The grants are to be used for training workers in high technology, information technology and biotechnology skill areas, including software and communications services, telecommunications, systems installation and integration, computers and communication hardware, advanced manufacturing, health care technology, biomedical research and manufacturing, and innovation services. For more information on the H-1B Technical Skills Training Grant Program contact Mindy Feldbaum, Program Officer, U.S. Department of Labor, Employment and Training Administration, Room 4659, 200 Constitution Avenue, NW, Washington, DC 20210; 202-693-3382; Fax: 202-693-2982; Email: Feldbaum.Mindy@dol.gov; www.doleta.gov/h-1b/h-1b_index.cfm.

Loans and Technical Assistance for Small Businesses in New Market Areas

Community Express is a SBA loan program with the National Community Reinvestment Coalition (NCRC). It is offered in pre-designated geographic areas that primarily serve low and moderate incomes and New Market small businesses. The program also includes hands-on technical and management assistance. Loan funds may be used for start-up, working capital, expansion, real estate acquisitions or equipment purchases. For more information on Community Express Loans contact the Office of Financial Assistance, Special Purpose Loan Programs, Small Business Administration, 409 Third Street, SW, Washington, DC 20416; 800-UASK-SBA; 202-205-6490; www.sba.gov/financing/lendinvest/comexpress.html.

Venture Capital to Start Infrastructure Projects in the Baltic Region

This fund provides equity investments in the Baltic, Russia, and NIS for large infrastructure projects including transportation, power, natural resource development and related industries. The AIG Brunswick Millennium Fund is a privately owned, privately managed investment fund supported by the Overseas Private Investment Corporation. For more information on the AIG Brunswick Millennium Fund contact Peter Yu, American International Group, 175 Water Street, 24th Floor, New York, NY 10038 ; 212-458-2156; Fax: 212-458-2153; www.opic.gov/investmentfunds.

Venture Capital to Start a Business in Russia

This program supports equity investments in Russia in natural resource related companies, telecommunications, light manufacturing, and consumer services and products. This fund may also invest in other OPIC covered NIS states. The Russia Partners Fund, A is a privately owned, privately managed investment fund supported by the Overseas Private Investment Corporation. For more information on the Russia Partners Fund, A contact Drew Guff, Managing Director, Siguler, Guff & Company, 630 Fifth Avenue, 16th Floor, New York, NY 10111; 212-332-5108; Fax: 212-332-5120; www.opic.gov/investmentfunds.

Venture Capital to Start a Business in the Ukraine, Russia and Other East European Countries
This fund provides equity investment in consumer products, financial and service industries, and diversified manufacturing in the following target areas: Latvia, Ukraine, Lithuania, Russia, Estonia, Kazakhstan, Moldova, Armenia, Bulgaria, Romania, Belarus, and Georgia. By supplementing the capital of privately owned, privately managed investment funds, OPIC can help profit oriented enterprises in emerging market areas gain access to venture capital, management guidance and financial expertise. For more information on the New Century Capital Partners LP Fund contact George Rohr, Chief Executive Officer, NCH Advisors, 712 Fifth Avenue, 46th Floor, New York, NY 10019-4018; 212-641-3229; Fax: 212-641-3201; www.opic.gov/investmentfunds.

Venture Capital to Start a Telecommunications Business in Southeast Asia
This program funds equity investment in consumer products, financial services and telecommunication in the emerging market areas of Bangladesh, India, Vietnam, Thailand, Indonesia, Korea, Sri Lanka, Laos and the Philippines. By supplementing the capital of privately owned, privately managed investment funds, OPIC can help profit oriented businesses in emerging market areas gain access to venture capital, management guidance, and financial expertise. For more information on the Asia Development Partners LP Fund contact Daniel Mintz, Managing Director, Olympus Capital Holdings, Asia, 153 East 53rd Street, 43rd Floor, New York, NY 10022; 212-292-6531; Fax: 212-292-6570; Email: dmintz@zbi.com; www.opic.gov/investmentfunds.

Venture Capital to Start a Business in South America
This program supports equity investments in South America, with emphasis on Argentina, Brazil, Chile and Peru, for diversified manufacturing, service and financial services. By supplementing the capital of privately owned and managed investment funds, OPIC can help profit oriented enterprises in emerging market areas gain access to venture capital, management guidance and financial expertise. For more information on the South American Private Equity Growth Fund contact Varel D. Freeman, Vice President and Managing Director, Baring Latin American Partners, LLC, 230 Park Avenue, New York, NY 10169; 212-309-1795; Fax: 212-309-1794; www.opic.gov/investmentfunds.

Venture Capital to Start a Business in Southern Africa
This fund provides equity investment in South Africa and regional SADC countries for financial and service industries and diversified manufacturing. By supplementing the capital of privately owned and managed investment funds, OPIC can help profit oriented businesses in emerging market areas gain access to venture capital, management guidance, and financial expertise. For more information on the New Africa Opportunity Fund contact Thomas C. Barry, Chief Executive Officer, Zephyr Management, LP, 320 Park Avenue, New York, NY 10022-6815; 212-508-9410; Fax: 212-508-9494; Email: info@opic.gov; www.opic.gov/investmentfunds.

Venture Capital to Start a Manufacturing or Computer Business in India
This fund supports equity investment in India for basic manufacturing, consumer goods, computer, banking and related industries. By supplementing the capital of privately owned and managed investment funds, OPIC can help profit oriented enterprises in emerging market areas gain access to venture capital, management guidance and financial expertise. For more information on the India Private Equity Fund contact Michele J. Buchignani, Managing Director, CIBC Oppenheimer & Company, Oppenheimer Tower, World Financial Center, New York, NY 10281; 212-667-8190; Fax: 212-667-4468; Email: Michele.buchignani@ us.cibc.com; www.opic.gov/investmentfunds.

Venture Capital to Start a Business in Latin America
This program funds equity investments in Belize, Bolivia, Brazil, Columbia, Ecuador, Peru, Argentina, Venezuela, El Salvador, Costa Rica, Honduras, Guatemala, Uruguay, Panama, Paraguay, Nicaragua and Chile for diversified manufacturing, financial and service industries. By supplementing the capital of privately owned, privately managed investment funds, OPIC can help profit oriented businesses in emerging market areas gain access to venture capital, management guidance and financial expertise. For more information on the Newbridge Andean Partners LP Fund contact Bernard Aronson, ACON Investments, LLC, 1133 Connecticut Avenue, NW, Suite 700, Washington, DC 20036; 202-861-6060 ext. 103; 202-861-6061; Email: infp@opic. gov; www.opic.gov/investmentfunds.

Venture Capital to Start an Environment Related Business in an Emerging Market

This fund provides equity investments in all OPIC eligible countries for environment oriented sectors relating to the development, financing, operating or supplying of infrastructure relating to clean water and energy. By supplementing the capital of privately owned, privately managed investment funds, OPIC can help profit oriented enterprises in emerging market areas gain access to venture capital, management guidance and financial expertise. For more information on Global Environment Emerging Markets Fund I contact H. Jeff Leonard, President, GEF Management, 1225 Eye Street, NW, Suite 900, Washington, DC 20005; 202-789-4500; Fax: 202-789-4508; Email: info@opic.gov; www.opic.gov/investmentfunds.

Venture Capital to Start a Business in Southeast Europe
This program provides equity investments in Albania, Bosnia, Bulgaria, Croatia, Herzegovina, FYR Macedonia, Montenegro, Romania, Slovenia, Turkey, and should they become eligible, Serbia and Kosovo. By supplementing the capital of privately owned, privately managed investment funds, OPIC can help profit oriented businesses in emerging market areas gain access to venture capital, management guidance and financial expertise. For more information on Soros Investment Capital Ltd contact David Matheson, Manager, Soros Private Funds Management, LLC, 888 Seventh Avenue, New York, NY 10106; 212-333-9727; Fax: 212-397-0139; Email: info@opic.gov; www.opic.gov/investmentfunds.

Venture Capital to Start an Agriculture Business in the Baltic Region
This program provides equity investments in the NIS/Baltic region for agriculture, food firms, infrastructure projects, privatizations, and food storage and distribution facilities. By supplementing the capital of privately owned, privately managed investment funds, OPIC can help profit oriented enterprises in emerging market areas gain access to venture capital, management guidance and financial expertise. For more information on Agribusiness Partners International contact Robert Peyton, President, Agribusiness Management Company, c/o America First Companies, 11004 Farnam Street, Omaha, NE

68102; 402-930-3060; Fax: 402-930-3007; Email: bpeyton@am1st.com; www.opic.gov/investmentfunds.

Venture Capital to Start an Environment Related Business in an Emerging Market
This fund provides equity investments in all OPIC eligible countries for environment oriented sectors relating to the development, financing, operating or supplying of infrastructure relating to clean water and energy. By supplementing the capital of privately owned, privately managed investment funds, OPIC can help profit oriented enterprises in emerging market areas gain access to venture capital, management guidance and financial expertise. For more information on the Global Environment Emerging Markets Fund II contact H. Jeff Leonard, President, GEF Management, 1225 Eye Street, NW, Suite 900, Washington, DC 20005; 202-789-4500; Fax: 202-789-4508; Email: info@opic.gov; www.opic.gov/investmentfunds.

Venture Capital to Start a Business in a Sub-Sahara Country
This fund supports equity investments in all sub-Saharan countries, except South Africa, with a focus on telecommunications, natural resources and manufacturing. By supplementing the capital of privately owned, privately managed investment funds, OPIC can help profit oriented businesses in emerging market areas gain access to venture capital, management guidance and financial expertise. For more information on the Modern Africa Growth and Investment Fund contact Steve Cashin, Managing Director, Modern Africa Fund Managers, 1100 Connecticut Avenue, NW, Suite 500, Washington, DC 20036; 202-887-1772; Fax: 202-887-1788; Email: info@opic.gov; www.opic.gov/investmenfunds.

Venture Capital to Start a Business in Central Europe
This fund supports equity investments in basic manufacturing, distribution networks, consumer goods and related services networks. Eligible countries include Central Europe/Baltic Republics, Albania, Bulgaria, Croatia, the Czech Republic, Estonia, Hungary, Latvia, Lithuania, Poland, Romania, Slovakia and Slovenia. By supplementing the capital of privately owned, privately managed investment funds, OPIC can help profit oriented enterprises in emerging market areas gain access to venture capital, management guidance and financial expertise. For more information on the Bancroft Eastern Europe Fund contact Fred Martin, President, Bancroft UK, LTD, 7/11 Kensington, High Street, London W8 5NP; 44-20-736-8334; Fax: 44-20-738-3348; Email: martin@bancroftgroup.com; www.opic.gov/investmentfunds.

Venture Capital to Start a Telecommunications Business in Armenia, Georgia or Azerbaijan
This fund provides equity investments for telecommunications projects in Georgia, Armenia and Azerbaijan. By supplementing the capital of privately owned, privately managed investment funds, OPIC can help profit oriented enterprises in emerging markets gain access to venture capital, management guidance and financial expertise. For more information on the Caucasus Fund contact Irakli Rukhadze, CEO, Caucasus Advisors, Suite 901, 31 Milk Street, Boston, MA 02109; 617-646-4512; Fax: 617-646-4512; Email: info@opic.gov; www.opic.gov/investmentfunds.

Venture Capital to Start a Business in Southeast Asia
This program supports equity investments in financial, construction, high tech, light manufacturing and telecom services in Indonesia, Singapore, Taiwan, Malaysia, Thailand and the Philippines. The Asia Pacific Growth Fund is a privately owned, privately managed investment fund supported by the Overseas Private Investment Corporation. It is designed to promote and facilitate U.S. investment in

emerging markets by working with private capital to make direct equity and equity related investments. For more information on the Asia Pacific Growth Fund contact Ta-Lin Hsu, Chairman, Hambrecht & Quist Asia Pacific, 156 University Avenue, Palo Alto, CA 94104; 650-838-8098; Fax: 650-838-0801; Email: info@opic.gov; www.opic.gov/investmentfunds.

Venture Capital to Start a Business in West Bank/Gaza and Jordan
This program provides equity investments in West Bank/Gaza and Jordan for basic services and manufacturing companies. The West Bank/Gaza & Jordan Fund is a privately owned, privately managed investment fund supported by the Overseas Private Investment Corporation. It promotes and facilitates U.S. investment in emerging markets by working with private capital to make direct equity and equity related investments. For more information on the West Bank/Gaza & Jordan Fund contact Scott Stupay, International Capital Advisors, 6862 Elm Street, Suite 720, McLean, VA 22101; 703-847-0870; Fax: 703-847-3068; Email: info@opic.gov; www.opic.gov/investment funds.

Venture Capital to Start a Business in Central and Eastern Europe
This program supports equity investments in Central and Eastern Europe for sustainable development industries. Eligible countries include Poland, Czech Republic, Slovakia, Romania, Bulgaria, Hungary and Slovenia. Investments are capped at 40% of commitments in any single country. By supplementing the capital of privately owned, privately managed investment funds, OPIC can help profit oriented enterprises in emerging market areas gain access to venture capital, management guidance and financial expertise. For more information on the Emerging Europe Fund contact Jamie Halper, Managing Director, TDA Capital Partners, Inc, 15 Valley Drive , Greenwich, CT 06831; 203-625-4525; Fax: 203-625-4525; Email: jhalper@templeton. com; www.opic.gov/investmentfunds.

Venture Capital for Starting a Business in India
This program supports equity investments in India for information technology, telecommunications and consumer goods. Draper International India Fund is a privately owned, privately managed investment fund supported by the Overseas Private Investment Corporation. It promotes and facilitates U.S. investment in emerging markets by working with private capital to make direct equity and equity related investments. For more information on the Draper International India Fund contact Robin Richard Donohoe, Draper International, 50 California Street, Suite 2925, San Francisco, CA 94111; 415-616-4056; Fax: 415-616-4060; Email: rarichards@draperintl. com; www.opic.gov/investmentfunds.

Venture Capital for Starting a Business in Poland
This program provides equity investments in Poland for consumer goods, manufacturing, distribution networks, merchandising, and related service networks. The Poland Partners LP Fund is a privately owned, privately managed investment fund supported by the Overseas Private Investment Corporation. OPIC promotes and facilitates U.S. investment in emerging markets by working with private capital to make direct equity and equity related investments. For more information on this program (Poland Partners LP Fund) contact Landon Butler, President, Landon Butler & Company, 700 Thirteenth Street, NW, Suite 1150, Washington, DC 20005; 202-737-7360; Fax: 202-737-7604; Email: info@opic.gov; www.opic.gov/investmentfunds.

Venture Capital for Starting a Business in Oman, Jordan and West Bank/Gaza

This program supports equity investments in Oman, Jordan and West Bank/Gaza for basic industries that create intra/inter-regional synergies. By supplementing the capital of privately owned and managed investment funds, OPIC can help profit oriented enterprises in emerging market areas gain access to venture capital, management guidance and financial expertise. For more information on this program (Inter-Arab Investment Fund) contact Dr. Fuad S. Abu Zayyad, Chairman, Inter-Arab Management, Inc, 2468 Embarcadero Way, Palo Alto, CA 94303; 650-917-0390; Fax: 650-856-9864; Email: info@opic.gov; www.opic.gov/investmentfunds.

Venture Capital to Start a Business in Israel

This program supports equity investment in Israel for technology, telecommunications, consumer retail and consumer products. The Israel Growth Fund is a privately owned, privately managed investment fund supported by the Overseas Private Investment Corporation. OPIC promotes and facilitates U.S. investment in emerging markets by working with private capital to make direct equity and equity related investments. For more information on this program (Israel Growth Fund) contact Allan Barkat, General Manager, Apax-Leumi Partners, Inc, Herzliya Business Park, 2 Maskit Street, 6th Floor, P.O. Box 2034, Herliza, Israel 46120; 972-3-696-5992; Fax: 972-9-958-8366; Email: allan@apax.co.il; www.opic.gov/investmentfunds.

Venture Capital for Starting a Mining or Manufacturing Business in Sub-Sahara Africa

This program provides equity investments in Sub-Sahara Africa for mining, manufacturing and financial services. The Africa Growth Fund is a privately owned, privately managed investment fund supported by the Overseas Private Investment Corporation. OPIC promotes and facilitates U.S. investment in emerging markets by working with private capital to make direct equity and equity related investments. For more information on this program (Africa Growth Fund) contact Joe Jandreau, Managing Director, Equator Overseas Services, LTD, 45 Glastonbury Boulevard, Glastonbury, CT 06033; 860-633-9999; Fax: 860-633-6799; Email: info@opic.gov; www.opic.gov/investmentfunds.

Venture Capital to Start a Small Business Overseas

This program supports equity investments for basic manufacturing and service industries sponsored by qualifying U.S. small businesses in any OPIC eligible country. The Allied Small Business Fund is a privately owned, privately managed investment fund supported by the Overseas Private Investment Corporation. OPIC promotes and facilitates U.S. investment in emerging markets by working with private capital to make direct equity and equity related investments. For more information on this program (Allied Small Business Fund) contact Cabell Williams, Allied Capital Corporation, 1919 Pennsylvania Avenue, NW, Washington, DC 20006-3434; 202-973-6319; Fax: 202-659-2053; Email: info@opic.gov; www.opic.gov/investmentfunds.

Fight Suppliers Who Won't Give You Credit

The Federal Trade Commission (FTC) enforces the laws that prohibit creditors and credit bureaus from discriminating against women because of their sex or marital status, and they can send you the free publication, *Equal Credit Opportunity*. This pamphlet explains your credit rights under the law, how to get help in establishing your own credit, and what to do if you feel your credit application has been unfairly denied. Contact the Federal Trade Commission (FTC), 600 Pennsylvania Ave., NW, Washington, DC 20580; 877-FTC-HELP; 202-326-2222; www.ftc.gov/bcp/conline/pubs/credit/ecoa.htm.

28 States Offer Free Consulting To Women Only

Contact your state office of Economic Development located in your state capital. 28 states have set up special offices just for women entrepreneurs. Contact your State Office of Economic Development to see what your state has to offer. If they don't have a "Women Only" office, don't let that stop you. It just means you'll have to share the help available with the men in your state.

Federal Government Set-Asides for Women Entrepreneurs

Many Federal government contracting offices are trying to insure that a certain percentage of their contracts go to women entrepreneurs. Most even have special offices that will help women entrepreneurs sell to their agencies. For help in selling your product or service to the government, contact your State Economic Development Office in your state capital and obtain a copy of Equal Credit Opportunity. It is available from the Government Printing Office or free online. Contact Superintendent of Documents, Government Printing Office, Washington, DC 20402; 866-512-1800; Fax: 202-512-2168; www.onlinewbc.gov/DOCS/procure/sellgov.doc.

15% Set-Aside for Women Entrepreneurs

Not only is the Federal government active in insuring that women get a fair share of government contracts, but many state governments are becoming involved. Some states, like California for example, have passed laws that force their state agencies to give at least 15% of their contracts to women and minority-owned firms. Other states like Illinois, Iowa, Maine, Minnesota, Montana, New Jersey, Oregon, and Washington are among those who are active in insuring that women obtain a fair share of state government contracts. Contact your State Office of Economic Development located in your state capital to see how your business can take advantage of set-asides in your state.

Free Publications For Women Business Owners

If you're interested in finding out more about women in the workforce, including trends and future projections, you might find the following free publications informative:

Characteristics of Self-Employed Women
Developments in Women's Labor Force Participation
Employed Women About as Likely as Men to be Looking for Jobs
Marriage, Children and Women's Employment: What Do We Know
Married Women, Work and Values
Much Variation in Women's Employment Across Metropolitan Areas
'Second-Chance' Strategies for Women Who Drop Out of School
Twenty Facts on Women Workers
Women Business Owners
Women in High-Tech Jobs
Women in Jobs Recessions
Women in Jobs Recoveries
Women at the Millennium
Women's Share of Labor Force to Edge Higher by 2008
Differences in Women's and Men's Earnings by Age
Income and Spending Patterns for Working Women
Women in Managerial, Professional Occupations Earn More Than Others

Women's Earning's: An Overview
Job Absence Rate Higher for Women Than for Men
Women in the Construction Workplace: Providing Equitable Safety and Health Protection
Work Injuries and Illnesses Occurring to Women

These titles can also be accessed online at www.dol.gov/dol/audience/aud-women.htm. Contact the Women's Bureau, Office of the Secretary, U.S. Department of Labor, 200 Constitution Ave., NW, Room S-3311; Washington, DC 20210; 800-827-5355; 202-693-6731.

How to Get Start-Up Capital from Being Pregnant, Sexually Harassed, or From A Bad Shopping Experience

As a business owner, there are times you may come across unscrupulous wholesalers who try to sell you some counterfeit products at cut-rate prices. Instead of risking your business by buying and reselling the bogus products, report the fraud to the U.S. Customs Service. If your complaint, which will be kept completely anonymous, leads to the seizure of counterfeit goods, you could receive a reward of up to $250,000, depending on the size of the case. Contact the U.S. Customs Service, Fraud Division, 1300 Pennsylvania Avenue, NW, Washington, DC 20229; 800-BE-ALERT; www.customs.ustreas.gov.

So you want to start your own business because you've just been fired because you were pregnant, or wouldn't sleep with your boss to get a promotion? Contact the Equal Employment Opportunity Commission (EEOC) and report how you think your former boss discriminated against you. The EEOC will investigate your complaint, and if they think there are grounds for prosecuting your former boss, they'll proceed with the case. If they prove the case, you could end up with enough money in back pay and other remedies to finance your own company. Contact the Equal Employment Opportunity Commission (EEOC), 1801 L St., NW, Washington, DC 20570; 202-663-4900; 800-669-4000; 800-669-3362 (publications); www.eeoc.gov.

Health Insurance for Divorcees Who Start Their Own Business

Under the new law, divorced and separated women and their children can continue to receive the same health insurance coverage they had before they were divorced or separated from their husbands at the group rate. The only difference is that they must pay the premium. This law applies to all private businesses that employ more than 20 people and to federal, state, and local government plans. For more information on this law, contact Women Work, 1625 K St. NW, #300, Washington, DC 20006; 202-467-6346; Fax: 202-467-5366; www.womenwork.org.

Seminars on How Women Can Sell to the Government

If you're not sure how to start doing business with the government, you might consider taking a seminar sponsored by the U.S. Small Business Administration on the procurement process. These seminars will give you a complete overview on what you'll need to know and do to get involved in bidding on and landing government business contracts. For information on when these seminars are scheduled in your area, contact the Office of Women's Business, U.S. Small Business Administration, 409 3rd St., SW, Washington, DC 20416; 202-205-6673; 800-8-ASK-SBA; www.sba.gov/womeninbusiness/wnet.html.

Creative Financing for Women Entrepreneurs

The Women's Business Ownership Office runs seminars on how women can use creative ways to locate financing if they've been turned down for loans by regular banks. For more information about these seminars, contact the Office of Women's Business Ownership, U.S. Small Business Administration, 409 3rd St., SW, Washington, DC 20416; 800-8-ASK-SBA; 202-205-6673; www.sba.gov/womeninbusiness/wnet.html.

Millions Set Aside For Welfare Moms To Start Their Own Businesses

The Job Opportunities for Low Income Individuals (JOLI) program can turn any good idea into a money making powerhouse, and it won't cost you a cent. Under the JOLI program, grants are awarded each year to nonprofit organizations that, in turn, work to create permanent jobs for people who are interested in running their own successful small businesses. As a collaborative partnership, the JOLI projects bring together community support services to lend a hand to those who want to climb that tough ladder of success. For federal information on grants in your area, contact the federal JOLI office at the Department of Health and Human Services, Office of Community Services, 370 L'Enfant Promenade, SW, Fifth Floor, Washington, DC 20447; 202-401-9346, Fax: 202-401-4687; www.acf.hhs.gov/programs/joli/welcome.htm. They have a complete list.

Minority Business Development Centers

The Minority Business Development Agency funds Business Development Centers (MBDC), Native American Business Development Centers (NABDC), Business Resource Centers (BRC) and Minority Business Opportunity Committees (MBOC) nationwide to assist with the start-up, expansion, and acquisition of competitive minority owned firms offering quality goods and services. These centers provide business assistance for bonding, bidding, estimating, financing, procurement, international trade, franchising, acquisitions, mergers, and joint ventures to increase opportunities in domestic and international markets for minority entrepreneurs. The centers provide one-on-one counseling for accounting, administration, business planning, construction, and marketing information. They also identify minority owned firms for contract and subcontract opportunities with federal, state, and local government agencies, and the private sector. The centers identify both private and public sector sources of financing for minority owned firms and assist with the preparation of financial documents and plans for submission to lenders. Contact the national headquarters at Minority Business Development Agency, 14th and Constitution, Washington, DC 20230; 202-482-3917; 888-324-1551; www.mbda.gov; Email: help@mbda.gov.

Free Help and Money for the Disabled

The Federal Government has stepped in and funded programs across the country to help the disabled and handicapped reach their goals by providing them with all kinds of services to get them on their way. The help available ranges from free information services, self help groups, free legal aid, and independent living programs, to free money for education, job training, living expenses, transportation, equipment, and mobility aids. You can even get money to have your home retrofitted to make it more accessible to you, given your specific handicap. And if you're denied any of these programs or services, there are several free sources of legal help that can get you what you're legally entitled to. Your state Vocational Rehabilitation office will evaluate your skills, needs, and goals, and work with you to keep you a productive member of society.

The Office of Disability Employment Policy www.dol.gov/odep knows that people with disabilities have a strong interest in working for themselves. The U.S. Department of Labor has developed a new office call Small Business Self-Employment Service that links to other entrepreneurship sites, provides information on a variety of technical assistance resources, as well as resources for writing business plans, financing, and other issues. Contact: Small Business and Self-Employment Service, Job Accommodation Network, P.O. Box 6080, Morgantown, WV 26506; 800-526-6234; Fax: 304-293-5407; www.jan.wvu.edu/SBSES.

You can also learn about programs and activities in your state for people with disabilities who want to work by checking out www.ssa.gov/work. Also don't forget to check out the federal government's website www.disability.gov that lists all the government programs relating to disabilities.

Banks Friendly To Those In Need

The government supports certain banks and credit unions who help people who have trouble getting loans elsewhere, so they can make their dreams come true. The U.S. Department of Treasury's Community Development Financial Institutions (CDFI) Fund is designed to award money to banks in support of their activities benefiting needy communities across the county. These banks provide a range of financial products and services including: mortgage financing for first-time-home-buyers, financing for needed community facilities, commercial loans and investments to start or expand small businesses and more. To learn what CDFI Fund institutions are near you contact Community Development Financial Institutions Fund, 601 13th St., NW, Suite 200, Washington, DC 20005; 202-622-8662; Fax: 202-622-7754; www.cdfifund.gov.

Money For Americans With Disabilities

The Abilities Fund is a nationwide developer targeted exclusively to advancing entrepreneurial opportunities for Americans with disabilities. They deliver a combination of training, technical assistance services, and advisory supports to individuals with disabilities and the organizations that support them. For more information contact The Abilities Fund, 332 S. Linn St., Suite 15, Iowa City, IA 52240; 866-720-38631 319-338-2521; Fax: 319-338-2528; www.abilitiesfund.org.

Entrepreneurial Loans and Assistance

The goal of the National Community Reinvestment Coalition's CommunityExpress program is to provide financing and technical assistance to entrepreneurs who have been underserved by financial institutions. The SBA guarantees business loans, community-based organizations provide the technical support, and lenders compensate these groups for the cost of support. Eligible small businesses must be located in low-income areas, or owned by women, minorities or veterans. Contact National Community Reinvestment Coalition, 733 15th St., Suite 540, Washington, DC 20005; 202-628-8866; Fax: 202-628-9800; www.ncrc.org.

Help For DC Area Businesses

The Foundation for International Community Assistance (FINCA) works hard to help metropolitan Washington DC entrepreneurs achieve economic and personal success. FINCA offers self-employment loans to business founders through its unique Village Banking program. The program offers market-rate loans and savings products to those who could not otherwise obtain them. Services in the DC area include monthly training classes in entrepreneurship, marketing strategies, and more. Contact FINCA International Inc., 1101 14th St., NW, 11th Floor, Washington, DC 20005; 202-682-1510, www.villagebanking.org.

Loans For Low-Income Entrepreneurs

Very low-income individuals can start their own businesses with the assistance of a loan from the Grameen Foundation USA. This international organization dedicated to stopping poverty administers a microcredit program for poor Americans looking to start a small or home-based commercial business. Contact Grameen Foundation USA, 1029 Vermont Ave., NW, Suite 400, Washington, DC 20005; 202-628-3560; Fax: 202-628-3880; www.gfusa.org.

Money For Environmentalists

Entrepreneurs with a focus on environmental and energy conservation have a source of business funding in the Strategic Environmental Project Pipeline (StEPP) foundation. They specialize in finding loans and grants for renewable energy, energy efficiency or pollution prevention projects to be undertaken by emerging businesses. The program is primarily designed for businesses that have past the start-up stage and are looking to expand. Contact The StEPP Foundation, P.O. Box 468, Golden, CO 80402; 303-277-0932; Fax: 303-384-3636; www.steppfoundation.org.

$8,000 For a Car, School, Business, or Home

Over 500 programs run by nonprofit organizations will give you up to $5 for every $1 you place into a savings account that is used to complete a life goal like education, housing, starting a business, or even transportation. They are called Individual Development Accounts, and they are designed for people with little money to save. To find a program near you contact IDA Network, Corporation for Enterprise Development, 777 N. Capitol St., NE, Suite 800, Washington, DC 20002; 202-408-9788; www.idanetwork.org.

$700 Grant To Start Your Business

Trickle Up provides grants of $700 (in two installments) to people wishing to start a business. Frequently these businesses are based in the home. They provide business training and seed capital to low income individuals who want to become entrepreneurs. Trickle Up works with 250 different coordinating agencies to provide the business training necessary to receive this grant. To see if there is a program near you contact Trickle Up, 104 W. 27th St., 12th Floor, New York, NY 10001; 212-255-9980; 866-246-9980; Fax: 212-255-9974; www.trickleup.org.

Money For Youth Entrepreneurs

Young entrepreneurs can learn skills that can be translated into successful business ventures, better job opportunities, and enhanced real-world skills. They can also meet other entrepreneurs and successful business people, have access to PYEP facilities, and may be eligible for $15,000 in loans to assists the launching of a business. For information on where programs are located contact Prudential Young Entrepreneur Program, 240 Dr. Martin Luther King Jr. Blvd., Newark, NJ 07102; 973-643-4063; www.njit-edc.org/PYEP.htm.

$35,000 Loan For Your Business

The U.S. Small Business Administration's Microloan Program was developed for those times when just a small loan can make the real difference between success and failure. Under this program, loans range for less than $100 to $35,000. The SBA has made these funds This program is currently available in 44 states. To learn which nonprofit organizations in your area offer this program contact U.S. Small Business Administration, 409 3rd St., SW, Suite 8300, Washington, DC 20416; 800-8-ASK-SBA; www.sba.gov.

$1.3 Million To Help Your Business

The Certified Development Company (504) Loan Program is a financing tool for economic development. The 504 Program provides growing businesses with long-term fixed-rate financing for major fixed assets such as land and buildings. Funds can be used for purchasing land, and improvements, including existing buildings, grading, street improvements, utilities, parking lots and landscaping, construction of new facilitates or purchasing long-term machinery and equipment. To learn more about these programs contact U.S. Small Business Administration, 409 rd St., SW, Suite 8300, Washington, DC 20416; 800-8-ASK-SBA; www.sba.gov.

How To Get Money For A Business When You Have Low-Income Or Bad Credit

There are many programs specifically aimed at helping people with low-income or bad credit to start a business. These programs are available because the data show that they work. The Aspen Institute Self-Employment Learning Project studied 405 low-income people who started their own business and found that 53% were able to use their business to get out of being low income. These businesses also had better survival rates than the average business traced by the U. S. Small Business Administration (SBA) See www.microenterpriseworks.org/about/factsheets/factsheet1.pdf, page #6.

There are hundreds, and probably even thousands of national and local programs around the country to help low income people become self employed or start businesses. The list below represents a starting place to find the help you need. To locate additional sources contact your local library or see our publication, "Free Money For Entrepreneurs" www.lesko.com.

400 Organizations That Help Low-Income People Start a Business

Members of the Association for Enterprise Opportunity provide free and low cost assistance and training, as well as financial assistance, to underserved populations who want to start a business including "people with low incomes and welfare recipients".

Association for Enterprise Opportunity
1601 North Kent Street, Suite 1101
Arlington, VA 22209
703-841-7760
Fax: 703-841-7748
aeo@assoceo.org
www.microenterpriseworks.org

Unemployed Can Get Free Money to Live on to Start a Business or Receive Entrepreneur Training

The U.S. Department of Labor has a program where people can use their unemployment money to become an entrepreneur. It is called "Self Employment Assistance Program".

U.S. Department of Labor
Employment and Training Agency
Self-Employment Assistance Program
Frances Perkins Building
200 Constitution Avenue, NW
Washington, DC 20210
877-US-2JOBS
www.workforcesecurity.doleta.gov/unemploy.self.asp

Community Action Agencies Offer Money and Help for Low-Income Entrepreneurs

There are over 1,000 Community Action Agencies across America and 39% of these offices provide help to low-income people who want to start or expand a business. Their programs include "Be Your Own Boss" and "Start a Home Day Care".

Community Action Partnership
1100 17th Street NW, Suite 500
Washington, DC 20036
202-265-7546
Fax: 202-265-8850
info@2005communityactionpartnership.com
www.communityactionpartnership.com

100 Venture Capitalists Looking to Invest in Poor Areas

The Community Development Venture Capital Alliance is an association of over 100 venture capitalists who want to advance the livelihoods of low-income people and the economies of distressed communities through entrepreneurial activity.

Community Development Venture Capital Alliance
330 Seventh Avenue, 19th Floor
New York, NY 10001
212-594-6747
Fax: 212-594-6717
cdvca@cdvca.org
www.cdvca.org

Over 500,000 Businesses are Assisted by Small Business Development Center Programs on an Annual Basis

Start-up and existing businesses can receive referrals to business experts, training in information access techniques, an equity financing course, educational assistance, and more. To find a center near you contact the following:

Association of Small Business Development Centers
8990 Burke Lake Road
Burke, VA 22015
703-764-9850
Fax: 703-764-1234
ann@asbc-us.org
www.asbdc-us.org

U.S. Treasury Provides Money to Low-Income Communities

The Community Development Financial Institutions Fund of the U.S. Department of the Treasury provides business loans and venture capital to people in low-income neighborhoods who would otherwise not have access to funding. To find funding sources near you contact the following:

U.S. Department of the Treasury
Community Development Financial Institutions Fund
601 13th Street, NW
Suite 200, South
Washington, DC 20005
202-622-8662
Fax: 202-611-7754
cdfihelp@cdfi.treas.gov
www.cdfifund.gov

Learn Financial and Money Management Principles

The Centers for Financial Education develops and offers curricula and materials covering a full range of financial management skills including borrowing basics, budgeting, goal setting, credit management, savings, and more.

Centers for Financial Education
2800 San Jacinto, Suite 400
Houston, TX 77004
800-845-5669 or 713-394-3456
Fax: 713-394-9690
tommye.white@moneymanagement.org
www.crediteducation.org

Realize Your Business Dreams and Apply for a Loan Through Count Me In For Women's Economic Independence

Count Me In makes loans of $500 to $10,000 available to women across the country who have nowhere to turn for their first business loan. The Make Mine a Million Business Program offers mentoring and financing to women business owners-a dream team creates the roadmap businesses need to grow from a micro to a million dollar enterprise. First place winners receive loans up to $45,000 from Count Me In, a year of mentoring from a team of business advisors and an OPEN American Express Business charge card. Runners up receive loans up to $20,000.

Count Me In
240 Central Park South, Suite 7H
New York, NY 10019
212-245-1245
info@count-me-in.org
www.count-me-in.org

Low-Income and Disadvantaged Individuals Can Start Businesses and Accumulate Assets

ISED Ventures focuses on helping low-income individuals and disadvantaged communities find, create or access employment, start businesses and acquire assets. Services include microenterprise development, asset accumulation, Job training, life skills, consulting services, research and evaluation services.

Institute for Social and Economic Development
1111 9th Street, Suite 200
Des Moines, IA 50314
515-283-0940
Fax: 515-283-0348
ised@ised.org
www.ised.org

Funding For Low-Income Teen Entrepreneurs

The National Foundation for Teaching Entrepreneurship's BizCamp is a 2-week intensive summer program for youth ages 13-18 who are interested in entrepreneurship. At the end of the camp, students compete for cash awards to fund their businesses.

National Foundation for Teaching Entrepreneurship
120 Wall Street, 29th Floor

New York, NY 10005
212-232-3333 or 800- For-NFTE
Fax: 212-232-2244
www.nfte.com

Financial Assistance for Minority-Owned Businesses

A wide range of programs and services are available including: referrals to corporate buyers of minority suppliers; working capital loans as well as longer-term financing; business consulting services; educational seminars and technical assistance; certification of minority business enterprises; access to the Minority Business Information Center; an advanced management education program; business opportunity fairs and more.

National Minority Supplier Development Council
1040 Avenue of the Americas, 2nd Floor
New York, NY 10018
212-944-2430
Fax: 212-719-9611
www.nmsdcus.org

Money for American Indian Farmers, Ranchers and Youth

This Initiative provides loans to American Indian farmers ranchers and youth and also offers loan counseling, loan preparation and loan closing services. Money is available for farm ownership loans, operating loans, beginning farmer and rancher loans, downpayment farm ownership loans for beginning farmers and loans to socially disadvantaged farmers and ranchers. Also available are loans to rural youth to establish and operate income-producing projects.

National Tribal Development Association
RR1, Box 694
Box Elder, MT 59521
800-963-0015 or 406-395-4095
Fax: 406-395-4096
billianne@indiancreditoutreach.com
www.indiancreditoutreach.com

$60 Million for Economic Empowerment Programs

Over 100 National Urban League Affiliates serve more than 2 million African-Americans and people of all ages and financial levels including securing funding for entrepreneurs and small businesses.

National Urban League, Inc.
120 Wall Street
New York, NY 10005
212-558-5300
Fax: 212-344-5332
info@nul.org
www.nul.org

Financing for Native American Entrepreneurs

This organization offers accessible business programs, services, financing and positive business to business relationships, artists in business program, small business management and counseling to Indian communities.

A Native American Business Network (ONABEN)
11825 SW Greenburg Road, Suite B-3
Tigard, OR 97223
800-854-8289 or 503-968-1500
Fax: 503-968-1548
selena@onaben.org
www.onaben.org

Support for Small Business Activity in Low-Income Communities

Micro-loans and flexible financing is available for real estate and construction, working capital, equipment financing and guarantees.

Structured Employment Economic Development Corporation (Seedco)
915 Broadway, 17th Floor
New York, NY 10010
212-473-0255
Fax: 212-473-0357
info@seedco.org
www.seedco.org

Money to Start or Expand a Business for People Receiving TANF

Program number 93.593, Job Opportunities for Low-Income Individuals, from the U.S. Department of Health and Human Services, offers money and training for people who are receiving Temporary Assistance for Needy Families (TANF).

U.S. Department of Health and Human Services
Temporary Assistance for Needy Families (TANF)
Administration for Children and Families
Office of Family Assistance
370 L'Enfant Promenade, SW
Washington, DC 20447
202-401-9351
www.acf.dhhs.gov

Help For Minorities To Get Government Contracts

The NAACP's Fair Share Program helps minority small businesses get government contracts,

National Association for the Advancement of Colored People (NAACP)
4805 Mt. Hope Drive
Baltimore, MD 21215
877- NAACP-98 or 410-521-4939
www.naacp.org

Contracts for Women Business Owners

Helps women business owners receive more corporate and government contracts.

National Women Business Owners Corporation
1001 W. Jasmine Drive, Suite G
Lake Park, FL 33403
800-675-5066

Fax: 561-881-7364
info@nwboc.org
www.nwboc.org

Venture Capital for Women Business Owners

They offer a venture capital forum that prepares and showcases 20-25 women-led high-growth businesses to local investors along with other assistance educational programs; access to information, experts and investors needed to grow a business for alumni; and a virtual bootcamp.

Springboard Enterprises
2100 Foxhall Road, NW
Washington, DC 20007
202-242-6282
Fax: 202-242-6284
info@springboardenterprises.org
www.springboardenterprises.org

$1,000 For Teen Entrepreneurs

Youth Venture is a national nonprofit organization that empowers young people 12-20 to start their own enterprises by providing them with a variety of resources including up to $1,000 in seed capital.

Youth Venture
1700 North Moore Street, Suite 2000
Arlington, VA 22209
703-527-4126
Fax: 703-527-8383
ssalomon@youthventure.org
www.youthventure.org

$25,000 Non-Credit Based Loans

Credit and business training is available to micro-entrepreneurs, low- and moderate-income and self-employed. Lending methodology is character-based. Unlike traditional lenders, they don't make loans based on credit history or collateral alone. Services are available California, Florida, Georgia, Illinois, Massachusetts, New Mexico, New York, and Texas.

ACCION USA
56 Roland Street, Suite 300
Boston, MA 02129
617-625-7080
Fax: 617-625-7020
info@accionusa.org
www.accionusa.org/default.asp

$15,000 for Women Entrepreneurs

Money is available for women entrepreneurs in under-served urban communities who do not qualify for credit with conventional lenders.

Women's Venture Fund, Inc.
240 West 35 Street, Suite 501
New York, NY 10001

212-563-0499
Fax: 212-868-9116
info@wvf-ny.org
www.wvf-ny.org/whatwedo.asp

There are hundreds more nonprofit organizations like those below who serve only a specific local area

Loans $25,000- $750,000
The SBA•Cisco Systems•San Jose Entrepreneur Center is a collaborative effort providing financing, training, expert consulting, and technology information. Services available for San Jose, East Palo Alto, San Francisco and Oakland.

Entrepreneur Center
84 West Santa Clara Street
San Jose, California 95113-1815
408-494-0210
www.ecenteronline.org/home.htm

Get $25,000+ In 2 Weeks
The New Mexico Community Development Loan Fund is a private, nonprofit organization that provides loans up to $25,000, training and technical assistance to owners of established businesses, individuals who want to start their own business, and Nonprofit Organizations who have trouble accessing traditional loans, such as from a from a bank.

NMCDLF
NM Business Resource Center
700 4th Street, SW
Albuquerque, NM 87102
505-243-3196
Fax: 505-243-8803
nmcdlfgen@aol.com
www.nmcdlf.org/loans.htm

Loans from 5,000 to $1 Million
Small businesses can receive from $5,000 to $1 million in loans for starting-up businesses, business expansion, equipment, and working capital lines of credit, in parts of Arkansas and Mississippi.

Southern Financial Partners
605 Main Street, Suite 203
Arkadelphia, Arkansas 71923,
870-246-9739
www.southernfinancialpartners.org/about/index.html

New Business Loans up to $5000, Existing Business up to $35,000
The Self-Employment Loan Fund, Inc. (SELF) is a nonprofit community based agency who helps persons getting started in business who are not quite ready for traditional business and lending opportunities. SELF provides training, technical assistance, and access to micro-loans up to $5000. Loans, ranging from $3,000 to $35,000, are available to qualified individuals who have operated a business for a minimum of one year and have an updated business plan. Available in Maricopa County, Arizona only.

Self-Employment Loan Fund, Inc.
1601 N. 7th St., Ste. 340
Phoenix, AZ 85006
602-340-8834
Fax: 602-340-8953
www.selfloanfund.org/

Up to $25,000 for New or Existing Business
This program offers simple flexible terms, fixed interest rate loans up to $25,000 to start-ups as well as established businesses. Available in Riverside County, California only.

The Community Investment Corporation
4250 Brockton Avenue, Suite 100
Riverside, California 92501
909-383-0242
pwatson@cicontheweb.com
www.cicontheweb.com/index.htm

Capital From $500.00 up to $50,000.00
Struggling entrepreneurs in Colorado at any stage of business can access support services and up to $50,000 of capital through three complimentary loan programs.

Micro Business Development Corporation
3003 Arapahoe St. - Suite 112A
Denver, Colorado 80205
303-308-8121
Fax: 303-308-8120
www.microbusiness.org/content.asp?CID=9

Up to $250,000 for Small and Medium Native Businesses.
Commercial financing up to $250,000 is available for small and medium Native businesses. The loan program is opened to businesses owned by individuals or organizations belonging to the Abenakis, Algonquin, Huron-Wendat, Micmac, Atikamekw Nations, or to the Native Alliance of Quebec inc., and who reside in the province of Quebec.

The Native Commercial Credit Corporation (NACCC)
265, Place Chef Michel-Laveau, Suite 201
Wendake (Québec) G0A 4V0
418-842-0972 or 1-800-241-0972
418-842-8925
www.socca.qc.ca/english.html

$1,000 to $150,000 for Your Business Needs
Achieve your dream and own your own business with help from the Colorado Enterprise Fund. They offer small business loans up to $150,000 and management assistance to entrepreneurs in Colorado Front Range counties, who are unable to obtain financing from traditional sources.

The Colorado Enterprise Fund
1888 Sherman Street, Ste. 530

Denver, CO 80203
303-860-0242
303-860-0409
www.coloradoenterprisefund.org/index.html

$50,000 Support for Business Owners

Purchase inventory, equipment, and real estate, as well as working capital for your business by applying for a micro-loan or small business loan. The First State Community Loan Fund provides Business support training and loans up to $15,000 to all types of micro entrepreneurs, including caterers, day care centers, seamstresses, screen printers, and computer specialists. It also supports home-based businesses, store front businesses and street vendors. Program is available in the state of Delaware.

First State Community Loan Fund
100 West 10th Street, Suite 1005
Wilmington, DE 19801
800-652-4779
302-656-1272
www.firststateloan.org/index.html

$25,000 to $150,000 Loans for Start-up and Existing Businesses

Loans are available in traditional terms or Lines of Credit and are obtainable in Palm Beach County, Florida.

The Business Loan Fund of the Palm Beaches, Inc.
1016 N. Dixie Hwy,
West Palm Beach, FL 33401
561-838-9027
561-838-9029
www.businessloanfund.org/index.htm

Up to $35,000 for Businesses

A three level loan program is available in southern Florida to take you from start-up to running an established business. Also included with each phase is a business skills training course to enhance your business skills.

Micro-Business USA,
3000 Biscayne Blvd., Ste 102A
Miami, FL 33137
877-722-4505
www.microbusinessusa.org/

$50,000 Business Loans for Minority and Women

Several types of business loans are available in Orange County Florida ranging from the Express Loan of $5000 up to the Bank Program of $50,000.

M/WBE Alliance, Inc.
625 E. Colonial Drive
Orlando, FL 32803
407-428-5860
Fax: 407-428-5869
alliance@allianceflorida.com
www.allianceflorida.com/index.html

Up to $15,000 Available

This program helps the Jewish and general communities in the Chicago area to become established through entrepreneurship. The center offers loans up to $15,000 including some with zero interest, and have available a business and training program.

JVS
216 West Jackson Blvd., Suite 700
Chicago, IL 60606
312-673-3400
Fax: 312-553-5544
jvs@jvschicago.org
www.jvschicago.org/duman/

Business Loans from $500 to $100,000

People in 22 Washington Counties who are thinking about opening a small business, or already operating a small business, can come to create a business plan, research potential markets and marketing ideas, discuss management issues with experienced counselors and business assistance providers, and apply for a small business loan up to $100,000.

CCD
1437 South Jackson
Seattle, WA 98144
206-324-4330
www.seattleccd.com/index.htm

$10,000 for Women Entrepreneurs

Funds are available for women in Wyoming who are unable to get loans through traditional means.

Wyoming Women's Business Center
PO Box 764
Laramie, WY 82073
307-766-3084
Fax: 307-766-3085
www.wyomingwomen.org/index.htm

$60,000 for Texas Entrepreneurs

By delivering both small business financing up to and nationally-acclaimed education, BiGAUSTIN is the single-source solution for entrepreneurs who have limited time and prefer to form a single relationship with one business development partner.

BiGAUSTIN
Business Investment Growth
1150 East11th Street, Suite 350
Austin, TX 78702
512-928-8010
512-926-2997
info@bigaustin.org
www.bigaustin.org/about/

Start Your Own Nonprofit

If you have a nonprofit organization, or you are thinking of starting a nonprofit organization, this is the section for you. It is a collection of programs that are just for nonprofit organizations.

Should you become a nonprofit organization? The real answer is, "It Depends." You may or may not have to become a nonprofit organization. If it is a new venture, I would not worry about the answer to that question until you know for sure where you are going to apply for the money you need. Some sources require you to be a registered nonprofit and some do not. There are programs, listed here and elsewhere, that will give you the money to do your good work as an individual, so you don't have to be a nonprofit. So why go thru all the time, energy and expense to become a nonprofit if you are not positive of where you are going to apply for the money. Don't waste time. Find out exactly where you are going to apply for the money and if they require you to become a nonprofit, then go become one.

Another way around becoming a nonprofit is by working with an existing nonprofit. For example, you want to start a center training unemployed teenagers to become car mechanics, and you found a program that gives out money for this kind of activity, but only to nonprofits. You can contact your local church, community college or any other nonprofit and talk with them about an opportunity of doing the project together. Organizations like this can let you use their name, give you a desk and collect maybe 20% of what you get as an overhead activity.

There is always more than one way to accomplish anything. You just have to search for it.

Start Your Own Nonprofit

You say you're committed to starting your own nonprofit but you're afraid that the paperwork involved makes it much too complicated and time consuming? Contrary to popular belief, you don't have to hire a lawyer and have thousands of dollars in the bank to consider starting your own nonprofit. With as little as $35 and 30 minutes of paperwork that you can complete sitting at your kitchen table, you can be well on your way to raising funds and raising the consciousness of the country.

Try The Easy, Cheap Way - First!

Dan Meeks of Columbus, Ohio had a dream of starting his own nonprofit that could be staffed by Vietnam veterans who would help local kids tackle various personal and community-related problems. He called a lawyer to investigate the costs associated with becoming a nonprofit. He was astounded to hear that it would cost $800, and that it would take several months to complete the lengthy process. Since theirs was a new and fledgling organization, Dan and the other interested participants didn't have that kind of money. Through a friend, Dan heard of a special IRS office that does nothing but assist people in starting nonprofits. They sent Dan the necessary forms and instructions which were easily completed in a few hours, after clarifying a few points over the telephone with the IRS office. A letter soon followed notifying Dan that his organization had qualified as a nonprofit, and the entire process cost him less than $20.00! Within a few months, Dan had raised $5,000 through a fundraiser and donated the money to several other nonprofit organizations, including the local Ronald McDonald House. Success stories like Dan's don't necessarily take lots of time and effort — just the right information.

Tamara Gates is another individual determined to make a difference. She wanted to start a chapter of V-COPS (Veteran-Civilian Observation Patrol) in Cleveland, to tackle the dual problem of a high crime rate coupled with a high number of homeless veterans residing on the city's streets. The V-COPS program offers shelter for homeless veterans in exchange for their services patrolling the streets at night, acting as the eyes and ears of the police. Ms. Gates contacted the special IRS office to find out how to apply for nonprofit status, and was sent the appropriate forms. It took her a little over a week to complete the forms, and several months later she received her confirmation as a nonprofit. Because of the budget for her organization, Ms. Gates was required to pay a fee of several hundred dollars, but it was still much less than the $50,000 that a consultant estimated that she would be required to pay. Thanks to her commitment to forge ahead and get the right information, Ms. Gates can point to the very tangible shelter services that her V-COPS program offers to Cleveland's homeless veterans, in exchange for the valuable services that they provide to the local community.

If you are thinking about establishing a nonprofit, check out this FREE source of valuable information before you decide that the obstacles are too great. Just like Dan and Tamara, you may find yourself pleasantly surprised and able to achieve your goal, without handing over a ton of your hard earned money to someone just to figure it out for you!

Sound impossible? No way!

Yes it can be bureaucratic and there's some red tape you'll have to wade through, but if you are a qualifying type of organization, getting nonprofit status is definitely the way to go, especially if you want to get grants from funding groups. Attaining nonprofit status for yourself as a group or organization may be critical in order to receive those grants that you are hoping will fund you, and it will only cost you a couple hundred dollars! Many grants are only available to nonprofits. So don't wince at the mention of what may sound like an overwhelming and daunting task. Dive in! It may be easier than you think.

First and foremost in establishing or creating a nonprofit is filing for Federal and state nonprofit tax status. Nonprofit status is not available to individuals, only to organizations, so your group must be incorporated or exist as an association or trust. To help you determine if your organization may qualify for tax-exempt status, or to find out what you will need to do in order to qualify, request Publication 557 from the local office of the Internal Revenue Service. This publication takes you step-by-step through the filing process, and contains instructions and checklists to help you provide all of the necessary information required to process your application the first time around. The fee to become exempt can be as low at $150! The IRS has even established a hotline at 877-829-5500 staffed with experts on completing the forms and can help you with any questions you may have. They can't make it any easier for you! You can also check out any questions you may have at http://www.irs.ustreas.gov/charities/index.html.

Most organizations seeking tax-exempt status from the Federal government must use either Form 1023, Application for Recognition of Exemption Under Section 501(c) (3) of the Internal Revenue Code; Form 1024, Application for Recognition of Exemption Under Section 501(a) or for Determination Under Section 120. The forms will ask you to provide the following information:

- A description of the purposes and activities of your organization
- Financial information, and if you have not yet begun operation, a proposed budget, along with a statement of assets and liabilities (if you have any)
- Information on how you intend to finance your activities, through fundraisers, grants, etc.

Another great feature available directly from the IRS is the Tax-Exempt Organization Tax Kit. Basically it's a packet that contains all the necessary forms for filing for exemption status, all informational publications and even forms for filing your tax return, the various versions of Form 990, Return of Organization Exempt from Income Tax. These publications are downloadable, grouped together at the IRS website, within the Tax-Exempt section. They are also available by calling 800-TAX-FORM, toll-free.

Critical when filing for tax-exempt status, obviously, is to have an organization that has a darned good reason for asking for exemption. The IRS has separated the classifications of acceptable organizations into ten groups within which your potential organization may fall, thus possibly qualifying for exemption.

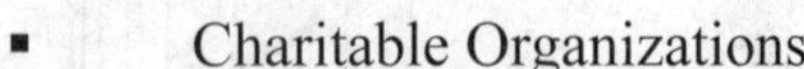

- Charitable Organizations
  - Charitable
  - Religious
  - Educational
  - Scientific
  - Literary
  - Testing for public safety
  - Fostering national or international amateur sports competition
  - Prevention of cruelty to children or animals

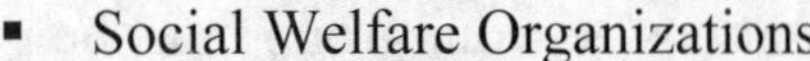

- Social Welfare Organizations
  - Civic Leagues
  - Community Organizations

- Labor and Agricultural Organizations
  - Labor Unions, Councils or Committees
  - Farm Bureaus
  - Agricultural and Horticultural Organizations

- Social Clubs
  - Hobby Clubs
  - Country Clubs

- Business Leagues
  - Trade Associations
  - Chambers of Commerce
  - Real Estate Boards
  - Professional Associations

- Fraternal Societies
  - Lodges and Similar Orders and Associations

- Veteran's Organizations
  - Posts or organizations of past or present members of the Armed Forces of the United States

- Employees' Associations
  - Voluntary employees' benefit associations
  - Local associations of employees

- Political Organizations
  - Campaign committees
  - Political parties
  - Political action committees

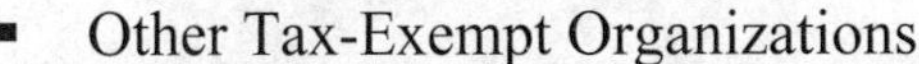

- Other Tax-Exempt Organizations
  - Miscellaneous qualifying organizations

The organization must also have an Employer Identification Number (EIN), be in the process of applying, or apply directly while applying for exemption status. Form SS-4, Application for Employer Identification Number, gives detailed instructions on obtaining an EIN over the phone, online, by fax, or by mail. The form is downloadable from the IRS web site. Once you have your EIN enter it into your application for exemption form. Please note the correct IRS contact information for exempt organizations seeking an EIN.

If you have no legal residence, principal place of business, or principal office or agency in any state, contact:

Internal Revenue Service
Attn: EIN Operation
Philadelphia, PA 19255
215-516-6999
Fax/TIN: 215-516-3990
www.irs.gov/pub/irs-pdf/fss4.pdf

If your principal business, office, agency, or, in the case of an individual, legal residence is located in Connecticut, Delaware, Washington District of Columbia, Florida, Georgia, Maine, Maryland,

Massachusetts, New Hampshire, New Jersey, New York, North Carolina, Ohio, Pennsylvania, Rhode Island, South Carolina, Vermont, Virginia, or West Virginia contact:

Internal Revenue Service
Attn: EIN Operation
Holtsville, NY 11742-9003
800-829-4933
Fax: TIN 631-447-8960

If your principal business, office, agency, or, in the case of an individual, legal residence is located in Illinois, Indiana, Kentucky, or Michigan contact:

Internal Revenue Service
Attn: EIN Operation
Cincinnati, OH 45999
800-829-4933
Fax: TIN 859-669-5760

If your principal business, office, agency, or, in the case of an individual, legal residence is located in Alabama, Alaska, Arizona, Arkansas, California, Colorado, Hawaii, Idaho, Iowa, Kansas, Louisiana, Minnesota, Mississippi, Missouri, Montana, Nebraska, Nevada, New Mexico, North Dakota, Oklahoma, Oregon, Puerto Rico, South Dakota, Tennessee, Texas, Utah, Washington, Wisconsin, or Wyoming contact:

Internal Revenue Service
Attn: EIN Operation
Philadelphia, PA 19255
800-829-4933
Fax: TIN 215-516-3990

Call the business and specialty tax line for assistance applying for an EIN: 800-829-4933

The applications require detailed financial status. If it is a new organization, current financial statements must be provided along with projected budgets for the coming two years. Organizations in existence three years or more also must provide current information as well as detailed info from the last two years. Once you have submitted the necessary forms and fees, and all goes well, a ruling or determination letter should be on its way to you in no time.

To receive help and information directly from the IRS, contact your local office listed in the government pages of your telephone book or contact:

Exempt Organizations Technical Division
Internal Revenue Service
U.S. Department of Treasury
1111 Constitution Ave., NW, Room 6411
Washington, DC 20224
202-283-2300
www.irs.gov

Once you are granted tax-exempt status, you must move on to the task of filing new forms to account for your tax year. And careful, detailed accounting is a must. Filing your organization's Form 990, the IRS nonprofit tax return, requires some rigorous financial reporting. As a nonprofit organization, you must report carefully the following:

- An object revenue & income statement, with particular categories specified (rental revenue),
- A balance sheet, with particular categories specified like cash, accounts receivable, accounts payable (salaries, postage etc.),
- A statement of functional expenses, in which all expenses are allocated to program services, fundraising, or operations,
- A report of expenses segregated by individual program service (educational mailings, a seminar program),
- A support schedule that details the organization's sources of revenue, with particular categories specified (charitable donations, membership fees, investment income).

Never fear! While it may sound confusing and tedious, there is hope! Luckily there is accounting software available to help you with your reporting. Sort of like Turbo Tax for nonprofits, these available software systems, if set up appropriately, can make your IRS reporting pretty easy. Thank goodness!

Although we do not recommend any particular accounting software, a simple Internet search turned up a wealth of software systems. Here is a sampling of what we found:

- NfpAcounting Technologies, 4540 Kearny Villa Road, Suite 221, San Diego, CA 92123; 800-273-1514; Fax: 858-499-8958; www.nfpaccounting.com.
- CYMA Systems, 2330 W. University Dr., Suite 7, Tempe, AZ 85281; 800-292-2962; 480-303-2962; Fax: 480-303-2969; www.cyma.com.
- Araize, 130 Iowa Lane, Suite 102, Cary, NC 27511; 800-745-4037; 919-460-3990; Fax: 919-460-5983; www.araize.com.
- SunGard Bi-Tech, 890 Fortress St., Chico, CA 95973; 866-488-2800; 530-891-5281; Fax: 530-891-5011; www.bitech.com.
- Fund EZ Department Corp., 106 Corporate Park, White Plains, NY 10604; 877-696-0900; Fax: 914-696-0948; www.fundez.com.
- Sage Software, 12301 Research Boulevard, Building IV, Suite 350, Austin, TX 78759; 800-811-0961; www.sagenonprofit.com.

State Registration

As with any filing of a tax application or return, when you send in something to the Federal government, you need to notify your state government as well. Although it is the IRS that gives you the authority to raise money as a tax-exempt organization, your state government will want to know about the proposed activities of your organization. Relevant information that your state will be interested in includes:

- The name and address of registrant
- The purpose of the nonprofit
- Any articles of incorporation
- The names and addresses of any board of directors

In existence is something known as the Unified Registration Statement, (URS) www.multistatefiling.org which serves as a kind of standard form that most of the states in the country accept as the ample documentation to register within said state as a nonprofit organization. The state will also want to know how much of a tax-exempt contribution you expect to attain over the course of a year. Some states have maximum amounts before you must register, while others have no minimum. Some states' fees are based upon the amount of contributions, and some are flat fees. The usual fee for filing this information with most states is minimal, usually from $30.00 to $50.00, with some states requiring no fee, and others going much higher. The state will also require an annual financial report, and most will accept a completed Federal IRS report.

Don't forget that state and Federal laws are not the only ones to which nonprofit organizations are subject. Governments of smaller jurisdictions, such as counties, cities, municipalities, small towns, and really any form of governmental authority, can and do implement laws that may be stricter or at least different than their superior governments. Such an authority may require organizations to register specifically within their jurisdiction, in addition to all other state and Federal registrations. Any soliciting organizations, no matter where they are based, that make charitable solicitations to residents of these jurisdictions, and don't adhere to the local law and its associated regulations, may be subject to legal action by that jurisdiction's governmental authority.

You can call your state capitol operator in your state capitol by calling 411. When you get the operator ask for the office where you can file to become a nonprofit. If they don't know ask for the office of the Secretary of State. You can also search under your state government at www.govengine.com

Your Local Representative's or Senator's Office
or
Your Representative or Senator
U.S. Capitol
Washington, DC 20515
202-224-3121
www.congress.org to find your congressman or senator

Check with their offices and see how they can help you set up your nonprofit or even help get you money.

There are over one hundred thousand organizations, both public and private, that give money to individuals or to nonprofit groups. This section describes a number of these programs, but certainly not all. To look for more programs that give out money for nonprofit organizations contact:

1) ***Money From Foundations For Nonprofits***
The following are the major sources of information for finding grants from nonprofit organizations. Their databases contain information on most of the non-government grant sources.

The Foundation Center
79 Fifth Avenue
New York, NY 10003
212-620-4230

www.fdncenter.org
They have a database of over 75,000 nonprofit organizations that give out grants. This database is accessible on the web for a fee or you can go into one of the Foundation Center libraries around the country and use their database for free. They also publish directories of foundations that give out grant money. You can call their office and they will tell you what libraries in your area have these directories for you to look at for free.

The Foundation Center also gives short courses on topics like "How to Search for Grant Money", or "How to Write a Grant". Don't pay thousands of dollars for courses on these subjects when you can get it from one of the best for a very reasonable price.

Guidestar
4801 Courthouse Street
Suite 220
Williamsburg, VA 23188
757-229-4631
www.guidestar.org
They have a similar database as The Foundation Center, but do not offer training and classes on other aspects of grantsmanship. Their database seems to have much more information in it about any given foundation. The best part is that you can use the database that will only show partial information on the records, but it is good enough for many applications.

2) ***Money From The Government For Nonprofits***
Money is available to nonprofit organizations from all three levels of government, Federal, State, and local.

Money From The Federal Government
All the major money programs in the Federal government are described in a book called the *Catalog of Federal Domestic Assistance*. This book is available at your local public library or the U.S. Government Printing Office (www.gpo.gov). You can also search the contents of this book for free on the web at www.cfda.gov. The government has also recently started a web site devoted to government grants called www.grants.gov. In addition they have a web site http://www.firstgov.gov/Business/Nonprofit.shtml.

Money From State Governments
There is not likely to be a single source of information at the state level for grants for nonprofits from the state government. The best bet seems to be to identify those agencies that may be involved in your area of expertise and to start fishing. For example, if you are interested in training youth, try locating those agencies that are involved with youth like the departments of education, training, and health. If you don't know any likely departments, you can call any department you want and ask them "who deals with youth?" Your state capital operator can help you identify state offices. You can call them in your state capital by calling 411. Or on the web go to www.govengine.com and click on your state. Then start looking for web sites for departments that may be relevant. You can

also get assistance in forming and registering as a nonprofit through your state office of Attorney General or Secretary of State.

Money From City and County Governments
There is not likely a single source for information on nonprofits at the local government level. Contact your city and county offices to see if they can provide you with some direction. Your local chamber of commerce can also be of assistance.

3) ***Free Help In Starting A Nonprofit***
There are over 1,000 Small Business Development Centers around the country that will help you with any problem you may have in starting or expanding a nonprofit organization. They can assist you with becoming a nonprofit, finding money (although they themselves do not offer money), management problems, technical issues and more. To find a Small Business Development Center in your area contact: 1-800-8-ASK-SBA; http://www.sba.gov/sbdc/sbdcnear.html.

4) ***Money For Arts Or Humanities***
The National Endowment for the Arts and the National Endowment for the Humanities are the two main resources for these types of funds offered by the federal government. Money is also handed about by state councils for arts and humanities. You can learn more by checking out the arts site at www.arts.gov and the humanities site at www.neh.fed.us. Both offer a link to state websites for more information.

So, go start saving the world. There are a lot of problems out there to solve and now you know where to get the money to do it.

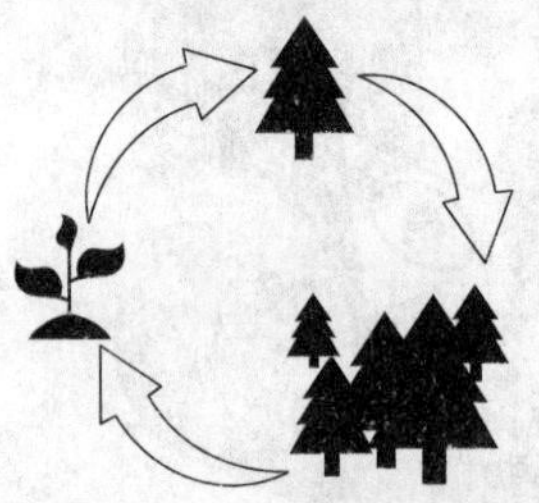

$50,000 to Preserve Ecosystems
Grants are awarded with a primary focus on ecological issues. Agriculture, economic globalization, land resources, and international affairs are some of the topics of interest. This foundation is both national and international in giving. Contact Foundation for Deep Ecology, 1062 Fort Cronkhite, Sausalito, CA 94965; Fax: 415-229-9340; http://www.deepecology.org; info@deepecology.org.

Up to $30,000 to Advocate for Freedom of Choice
Provides grants to grassroots organizations, coalitions and other groups for efforts and projects related to the reproductive and other rights of women. Grants range from $15,000 to $30,000. Grants are given to individual organizations and coalitions implementing grassroots organizing strategies or other collective approaches to improve access to reproductive health services. Contact Ms. Foundation for Women, 120 Wall Street, 33rd Floor, New York, NY 10005; 212-742-2300; Fax: 212-742-1653; http://www.ms.foundation.org/; info@ms.foundation.org.

$7,500 to Plant and Preserve Trees
Provides grants up to $7,500 to community organizations and volunteer groups to tree-planting, tree preservation and other forestry projects in urban areas in California. Contact California ReLeaf / National Tree Trust, 2311 Tustin Avenue, Newport Beach, CA 92660; 949-642-0127; http://www.nationaltreetrust.org/releaf/; ehoskins@nationaltreetrust.org.

Money to Sponsor Women-Based Projects
Makes grants to projects designed and implemented by women and girls that reflect the cultural and ethnic diversity of our society and promote the empowerment of women and girls in any and all facets of society. Contact Open Meadows Foundation, P.O. Box 150-607, Van Brunt Station, Brooklyn, NY 11215-607; 718-768-2249; http://www.openmeadows.org/; openmeadows@igc.org.

Lesbians Get $2,000 for Lesbian-Related Projects
$2,000 grants to fund projects supporting and developed by lesbians age 60 and older. Contact The Edie Windsor Fund for Old Lesbians, Open Meadows Foundation, P.O. Box 150-607, Van Brunt Station, Brooklyn, NY 11215-607; 718-768-2249; http://www.openmeadows.org/; openmeadows@igc.org.

Up to $233,000 to Foster Awareness for a Better World
Grants ranging from $10,000 up to $233,000 are available for those individuals who want to foster awareness of the power of love and forgiveness in the merging global community through research, education and service programs. The institute does not accept unsolicited proposals, but occasionally offers funding opportunities in the form of fellowships, requests for proposals, and awards that are open for application. Contact John E. Fetzer Institute, Inc., (formerly John E. Fetzer Foundation, Inc., 9292 West KL Ave., Kalamazoo, MI 49009-9398; 269-375-2000; Fax: 269-372-2163; http://www.fetzer.org; info@fetzer.org

$20,000 Grants Supporting Women's Human Rights
The Global Fund provides general program and operating support grants to women's organizations and individuals focused on advancing the human rights of women and girls. Grants range from $500 to an annual funding of $20,000. The majority of the funding remains devoted to general grants supporting universal issues such as reproductive health and choice, improved access to media and communications, the advancement of women in positions of elected leadership, the rights of sexual minorities, and the prevention of violence against women and children; however, there are grants that support special projects and initiatives. Funding is on an international basis. Contact Global Fund For Women, 1375 Sutter St., Suite 400, San Francisco, CA 94109; 415-202-7640; Fax: 415-202-8604; www.globalfundforwomen.org; gfw@globalfundforwomen.org.

FREE Computers and Technology Equipment
NCF encourages corporations and individuals to donate surplus and used computers, software, peripherals and related business technology. NCF directs those donations to training and educational organizations. All the organizations are pre-screened and qualified grass-roots partners of NCF. All donated equipment is distributed to these organizations FREE with no charges to the donor or recipients. Contact The Christina Foundation, 500 West Putnam, Greenwich, CT 06830; 203-863-9100; http://www.cristina.org/; ncf@christina.org.

Up to $5,000 for Activism Efforts
Organizing and Advocacy Grants support organizing and activism work that exists to challenge sexism, racism, homophobia, economic injustice, and other forms of oppression. Support is offered to young women between the ages of 15 and 30 and to projects which serve them in the areas of reproductive health and justice, scholarships and grassroots organizing and advocacy. Projects with a budget over

$500,000 are rarely supported. Grants range from $100 to $5,000. Contact Third Wave Foundation, 511 W. 25th Street, Suite 301, New York, NY 10001; 212-675-0700; Fax: 212-255-6653; http://www.thirdwave foundation.org/programs/grants.html; info@thirdwavefoundation.org.

$5,000 to Support Women's Rights
There are of two types: 1) Training access, and education grants which are awarded for projects that benefit, target, and are developed by women between the ages of 15 and 30, with an emphasis on low-income women, women of color and lesbian and bisexual women. Projects with budgets exceeding $500,000 are rarely supported. Grants range from $100 to $5,000; and 2) Emergency grants which fund travel, accommodation, and abortion procedures on an on-going and immediate basis. Also, grants are awarded to organizations that grant money directly and immediately to young women in need of abortions. Contact Third Wave Foundation, 511 W. 25th Street, Suite 301, New York, NY 10001; 212-675-0700; Fax: 212-255-6653; http://www.thirdwavefoundation.org/programs/grants.html; info@thirdwave foundation.org.

Up to $5,000 for Activism Efforts
Third Wave Foundation Scholarship Program is available to all full-time or part-time young women and transgender activists age 30 and under who are enrolled in, or have been accepted to, an accredited university, college, vocational/technical school or community college. The primary criteria to qualify for a Third Wave scholarship is vigorous engagement in activist work and financial need. Students applying for grants should also be involved as activists, artists, or cultural workers working on issues such as racism, homophobia, sexism, or other forms of inequality. Scholarships range in amount from $500 and $5,000 each. Contact Third Wave Foundation, 511 W. 25th Street, Suite 301, New York, NY 10001; 212-675-0700; Fax: 212-255-6653; http://www.thirdwavefoundation.org/programs/grants.html; info@thirdwave foundation.org.

Over $350,000 for Charitable Causes
Autodesk makes charitable contributions to nonprofit organizations involved with arts and culture, education, the environment, health and human services, community development, science and technology, civic affairs, and to disabled people for product donations. Support is given on a national and international basis. Contact Autodesk, Inc. Corporate Giving Program, c/o Community Rels. Department, 111 McInnis Parkway, San Rafael, CA 94903; 415-507-6603; Fax: 415-507-6138; julie.wilder@ autodesk.com. Application address for product donations: Gifts In Kind Intl., 333 N. Fairfax St., Alexandria, VA 22314.

$10,000 Grants for Projects Supporting Worldwide Unity
The Eric Berne Fund for the Future awards grants of up to $10,000 to individuals or organizations, both not-for-profit and for-profit, demonstrating an interest in the evaluation of effectiveness of various applications of transactional analysis theory. Priority is given to those applicants who either are current members of the ITAA or have demonstrated a high level of competency in the theory and practice of TA. Contact Eric Berne Fund of the International Transactional Analysis Association, c/o Rosa Krauscz, 436 14th St., Ste. 1301, Oakland, CA 94612-2710; 510-625-7720; Fax: 510-625-7725; http://www.itaa-net.org; itaa@itaa-net.org.

Grants of $1,500 for Catholic Missions
This Foundation gives primarily to Roman Catholic missionaries selected by the Foundation. Grants range from $50 up to $1,500. Contact Pro Deo Guild, Inc., P.O. Box 304, Hartsdale, NY 10530-0304; http://www.paracleteinc.com/pro_deo_guild.htm.

Financial Assistance for Philanthropy Projects
The Rockefeller Philanthropy Advisors supports organizations and individuals engaged in philanthropy, and administer a donor-advised fund, The Philanthropic Collaborative. Assistance ranges from $5,000 up to $4.0 million. Contact Rockefeller Philanthropy Advisors, Inc. (formerly The Philanthropic Collaborative, Inc.), 437 Madison Ave., 37th Floor, New York, NY 10022; 212-812-4330; Fax: 212-812-4335. West Coast office address: 101 2nd St., 24th Fl., San Francisco, CA 94104; 415-543-0733; Fax: 415-543-0735; http://www.rockpa.org; info@rockpa.org.

$7,500 for Human Rights and Social Justice
This Foundation offers support to individuals and organizations "for the purpose of enabling them to carry on research, teaching, and education in the areas of civil and human rights and social justice." Grants are available up to $7,500 per individual. Contact Petra Foundation Charitable Trust, c/o Law Firm of Hill & Barlow, One International Pl., 21st Floor, Boston, MA 02110-2600; Application address: c/o Muriel Morisey Spence, Chair., Award Comm., P.O. Box 11579, Washington, DC 20008; 202-364-8964.

Grants up to $20,000 for Community Projects
Grants are currently awarded once a year and are mostly in the $10,000 to $20,000 range. Funding is allocated among three categories: 1) Environment; 2) Social; and 3) Jewish/. Whatever the specific area of interest, the foundation encourages projects which are concerned with promoting community, social justice, a healthy environment and a sustainable economy, either by developing alternatives to the status quo or by responsibly modifying existing systems, institutions, conditions, and attitudes which block promising innovation. Contact Max and Anna Levinson Foundation, P.O. Box 6309, Santa Fe, NM 87502-6309; 505-995-8802; Fax: 505-995-8982; http://www.levinsonfoundation.org; info@levinsonfoundation.org.

Grant Funding for Missionaries
The foundation assists projects of national and international scope which have special importance for the mission of the Catholic Prelature of Opus Dei, including capital expansion projects. Contact Woodlawn Foundation, 524 North Ave., Ste. 203, New Rochelle, NY 10801-3410; 914-632-3778; Fax: 914-632-5502.

Up to $5,000 for Essays on Human Rights
The Elie Wiesel Prize in Ethics offers a first prize of $5,000, second prize of $2,500, third prize of $1,500 and two honorable mentions of $500 each to undergraduates who are or will be registered as full-time juniors or seniors at accredited four-year colleges or universities in the U.S and Canada. All entries must be in the formal or informal voice, ranging from 3,000 to 4,000 words, and may take the form of an analysis that is biographical, historical, literary, philosophical, psychological, sociological or

theological. All candidates must be sponsored by a faculty member. The foundation advances the causes of human rights throughout the world by creating forums for the discussion of urgent ethical and moral issues confronting humankind. Contact The Elie Wiesel Foundation for Humanity, 529 5th Ave., Ste. 1802, New York, NY 10017; 212-490-7777; Fax: 212-490-6006; http://www.eliewieselfoundation.org; info@eliewieselfoundation.org.

$90,000 to Pursue Your Career Goals

Each year, the Fannie Mae Foundation selects up to six seasoned professionals as Johnson Fellows. These Fellows design and pursue development plans that can include research, travel, study, self-designed internships, and other activities that enhance their skills and knowledge. The program is a unique opportunity for individuals to identify and pursue personal and professional goals in the affordable housing and community development fields. The Johnson fellowship provides each fellow with a $70,000 grant and a stipend of up to $20,000 for travel and education-related expenses. The nonprofit organization with which each fellow is associated may receive a grant of up to $25,000 for transitional costs related to the temporary absence of the employee or volunteer. Contact Fannie Mae Foundation, Policy and Leadership Development, 4000 Wisconsin Ave. N.W., N. Tower, Ste. 1, Washington, DC 20016-2804; 202-274-8066 or 202-274-8057 or 202-274-8000; Fax: 202-274-8100; http://www.fanniemaefoundation.org; llucs@ fanniemaefoundation.org.

FREE Tuition for Affordable Housing Providers

The Fannie Mae Foundation Fellowship Program is intended to enhance the management and decision-making skills of accomplished leaders experienced in managing housing and community development programs. The State and Local program curriculum focuses on: organizational strategy; political management; policy development; management control and operations; and management of human resources. Fellowship funds cover the cost of the admission deposit, program tuition, and room and board for the session. Applicants must be able to attend the entire three-week session and are responsible for their own transportation and other incidental costs. Contact Fannie Mae Foundation, Policy and Leadership Development, 4000 Wisconsin Ave. N.W., N. Tower, Ste. 1, Washington, DC 20016-2804; 202-274-8066 or 202-274-8057 or 202-274-8000; Fax: 202-274-8100; http://www.fanniemaefoundation.org; llucs@fanniemaefoundation.org.

$1,500 to Provide Medical Services to Those in Need

The Paul S. McCord, D.O. Memorial Scholarship Fund is awarded annually to one student from the 3rd year class at College of Osteopathic Medicine at Midwestern University (CCOM). The recipient must demonstrate a commitment to providing medical services in an underserved and/or disadvantaged area, provide volunteer services beyond those required by his/her college, demonstrate a high degree of care and concern for the underserved, and show leadership qualities in serving the underserved and the disadvantaged. One $1,500 scholarship will be awarded to a student chosen by CCOM. Contact American Osteopathic Foundation (formerly National Osteopathic Foundation), 142 E. Ontario, Ste. 502, Chicago, IL 60611; 312-202-8232 or 800-621-1773, ext. 8232; Fax: 312-202-8216; http://www.aoffoundation.org; vheck@aof-foundation.org.

$70,000 or More for Education, Medicine or Religion
The organization provides educational, medical, and religious support in the U.S. and overseas. Over $70,000 is available for grants to individuals. Contact Voice in the Wilderness, Inc., P.O. Box 210098, Dallas, TX 75211-0098; www.voice-wilderness.com.

$25,000 Plus a One-Year Lease on a New Car
Through the Volvo Heroes USA program, Volvo annually awards $5,000 to ten Volvo or Volvo retailer employees for the charity of their choice who go above and beyond the call of duty to act with conscience, care, and character to help others in need in the areas of safety, quality of life, and environment. Special emphasis is directed towards employees working to benefit many people, improve the natural environment, and help underserved communities. The three top winners receive an additional $20,000 for the charity of their choice and the top winner receives a one-year lease on a Volvo automobile. All U.S. citizens or legal residents of the U.S. of any age, including U.S. citizens living abroad, are eligible to submit nominations for the Volvo for life Awards. Contact Volvo Cars of North America, LLC Corporate Giving Program, 1 Volvo Drive, Rockleigh, NJ 07647-2507; http://www.volvoforlifeawards.com; nominate@volvo4lifeawards.com; info@volvoforlifeawards.com.

$48,000 for Peace and Disarmament
The Ploughshares Fund provides financial support for projects related to preventing the spread of weapons of mass destruction, controlling the sale of conventional weapons, addressing the environmental impact of nuclear weapons production, promoting new approaches to conflict prevention, and building global and regional security. Grant awards to individuals range from a high of $48,000 to a low of $1,500. Contact Ploughshares Fund, Fort Mason Ctr., Bldg. B, Ste. 330, San Francisco, CA 94123; 415-775-2244; Fax: 415-775-4529; http://www.ploughshares.org; email: ploughshares@ploughshares.org.

Money for All Kinds of Charities
The Philanthropic Ventures Foundation's financial support, including scholarships and grants, covers a wide variety of areas, including the arts, economic development, education, environment, and human services. PVF takes the investment approach to charitable giving, seeking outstanding people and opportunities whose impact in the community will be significant and bringing them to the attention of donors. Applications not accepted. Giving primarily in the San Francisco Bay Area, CA, but extends nationally pursuant to donors' recommendations. Foundation grants to individuals range between $215,000 and $15. Contact Philanthropic Ventures Foundation, 1222 Preservation Park Way, Oakland, CA 94612-1201; 510-645-1890; Fax: 510-645-1892; http://www.venturesfoundation.org/index.html; email: info@venturesfoundation.org.

Funding for Helping People
The Lodestar Foundation seeks to initiate or support innovative nonprofit endeavors that are directed towards the betterment of the human condition, whether physically, educationally, emotionally, or spiritually. Primary consideration will be given to those endeavors that: (1) encourage cooperation, collaboration, best practices and efficiency among nonprofits addressing common or related issues or (2) encourage philanthropy, charity, volunteerism or public service. Contact The Lodestar Foundation, 4455 East Camelback Road, Suite 215A, Phoenix, Arizona 85018; 602-956-2699; Fax: 602-840-1543; http://www.lodestarfoundation.org/; email: lsavage@lodestarfoundation.org.

$250,000 to Improve the World's Food Supply
Grants of up to $250,000 are given to individuals for achievement in improving the world food supply. Giving is both national and international. Contact World Food Prize Foundation, 666 Grand Ave., Ste. 1700, Des Moines, IA 50309; 515-245-3783; Fax: 515-245-3785; http://www.worldfoodprize.com; wfp@worldfoodprize.org; jpim@worldfoodprize.org. Application Address: World Food Prize Foundation, 1700 Ruan Ctr., 666 Grand Ave., Des Moines, IA 50309.

$12,000 to Do Good for Others
College graduates may be eligible to receive grants ranging from $7,000 up to $12,000 to pursue meaningful projects which can also benefit others. Awards are usually made on a one-year basis and are not renewed. This is a national award program. Contact Ella Lyman Cabot Trust, Inc., c/o Palmer & Dodge, LLP, 111 Huntington Avenue, 19th Floor, Boston, MA 02199. Application Address Ella Lyman Cabot Trust, Inc. c/o Brooks Thompson, 109 Rockland St., Holliston, MA 01746.

$12,000 For Nonprofits To Develop Housing
The PreDevelopment Program provides community-based nonprofit funds for "soft costs" of specific projects. Funds are available for housing or economic development projects that target low-income people. Maximum award is $12,000. Funds can be used for costs directly related to the planning of the project, including, but not limited to, architecture drawings, site plans, legal costs, engineering costs, market studies, real estate options, and zoning/permit fees. Contact the Ohio Community Development Finance Fund, 17 South High Street, Suite 900, Columbus, OH 43215; 614-221-1114; www.financefund.org/pd.html.

Over $500,000 For Parental Assistance Centers
An average of $513,000 in funding is available to nonprofit organizations to assist them in establishing parental information and resource centers. These grants will enable centers to assist parents in helping their children to meet State and local standards, develop resource materials and provide information about high-quality family involvement programs; plan, implement, and fund activities for parents that coordinate the education of their children with other programs that serve their children and families. Projects generally include a focus on serving parents of low-income, minority, and limited English proficient children enrolled in elementary and secondary schools. Contact the U.S. Department of Education, Parental Options and Information, 400 Maryland Ave., S.W., Rm. 3E209, FB-6, Washington DC 20202-6100; 202-260-2225; www.ed.gov/programs/pirc/index.html.

$500,000 Grants Available To Nonprofits
Through the Challenge Grants program, nonprofits can expand their volunteer efforts with up to $1 million in funding. The program has $2.6 million available, and anticipates offering up to four grants this year alone. Contact the Corporation for National and Community Service Headquarters Address, 1201 New York Avenue, NW, Washington, D.C. 20525; 202-606-5000; http://www.nationalservice.org/news/pr/051304.html.

$100,000 To Mentor Children of Prisoners
Get up to $5 million through the Family and Youth Services Bureau to make a difference in the lives of children. The Mentoring Children of Prisoners program is looking for organizations that are interested in

helping children of incarcerated individuals. Find out how your organization can get involved. Contact Family and Youth Services Bureau, Administration for Children and Families, Department of Health and Human Services, 330 C Street, SW., Washington, DC 20447; 202-205-8102; www.acf.hhs.gov/programs/fysb/. For additional information go to www.nwrel.org/mentoring/children_prisoners.html and http://12.46.245.173/pls/portal30/CATALOG.PROGRAM_TEXT_RPT.SHOW?p_arg_names=prog_nbr&p_arg_values=93.616.

Get $150,000 To Send Donated Supplies Overseas

Get the government to pay for the transporting of donated supplies overseas. Through the Ocean Freight Reimbursement (OFR) Program, Private Voluntary Organizations (PVO) can obtain funding to ship commodities overseas by ocean freight. OFR awards up to $150,000 per year and ships only those commodities and only to those countries approved by USAID. Contact Information Center, U.S. Agency for International Development, Ronald Reagan Building, Washington, D.C. 20523-1000; www.usaid.gov/our_work/cross-cutting_programs/private_volun tary_cooperation/ofr.html.

Free Accounting Services For Nonprofits and Small Business

There are a number of organizations around the country that provide free accounting services to help nonprofits, small businesses, and even needy individuals get the accounting help they need. They can help with bookkeeping instruction, system analysis, preparation of 990 forms, preparation for audits and free publications. A minimal one-time cost may be required. To find free accounting help in your area, contact Accountants for the Public Interest, University of Baltimore, Thurnel Business Center, Room 155, 1420 North Charles Street, Baltimore, MD 21201; 410-837-6533; Fax: 410-837-6532. You can also contact your state association of Certified Public Accountants, as many may be able to direct you to a volunteer CPA who would be willing to help.

Help for Inventors

Patents, Trademarks, and Copyrights

Most inventors realize that it's vitally important to protect their idea by copyrighting it and obtaining the necessary patents and copyrights, but did you know that it's also important to look around for loans and other grants to support your business while working on your invention? If you want an idea to become an actual product, you have to invest an awful lot of your time into its research, and not just on a part time basis. Loans and grants programs for inventors help you do just that. For example, Hawaii offers low cost loans to inventors, as do other states around the country. First, let's talk about getting the necessary information concerning trademark and patent procedures.

Patent and Trademark Office

United States patent and trademark laws are administered by the Patent and Trademark Office (PTO). States also have trade secret statutes, which generally state that if you guard your trade secret with a reasonable amount of care, you will protect your rights associated with that secret. The PTO examines patent and trademark applications, grants protection for qualified inventions, and registers trademarks. It also collects, assembles, and disseminates the technological information patent grants. The PTO maintains a collection of almost 6 million United States patents issued to date, several million foreign patents, and more than 2.2 million trademarks, together with supporting documentation. Here's how to find out what you need to do to patent your idea.

What a Great Idea!

To help you get started with patenting your invention, the Patent and Trademark Offices will send you a free booklet upon request called *General Information Concerning Patents*. There are three legal elements involved in the process of invention: the conception of the idea, diligence in working it out, and reducing it to practice - i.e., getting a finished product that actually works. If you have a great idea you think might work, but you need time to develop it further before it is ready to be patented, what should you do? For answers to general questions on patent examining policies and procedures, contact the Inventors Assistance Center at 800-PTO-9199 or 571-272-1000; TTY: 571-272-9950; Email: usptoinfo@uspto.gov. They will not answer legal questions or opinions. Applications, forms, and part or all of pamphlets are at their website; www.uspto.gov. You can order them online from http://bookstore.gpo.gov. To order them through the mail write to:

Superintendent of Documents
U.S. Government Printing Office
P.O. Box 371954
Pittsburgh, PA 15250-7954
Fax: 202-512-2104
202-512-1800
www.gpoaccess.gov

What is a Patent?
A patent is a grant of a property right to the inventor for an invention. It lasts for 20 years from the date that the application is filed. United States patent grants are effective within the US, its territories and its possessions. By the language of the grant it is "the right to exclude others from making, using, offering for sale, or selling" the invention in the US or "importing" the invention into the US. It is not the right of the inventor to do so himself that is granted. It is personal property and can be sold or mortgaged, bequeathed or transferred and that person then has the same rights as the original grantee.

What Can Be Patented?
A patent can be received for an invention or discovery of any new and useful process, machine, manufacture, or composition of matter, or any new and useful improvement to the original. A design patent is the invention of any new and non-obvious ornamental design for an article of manufacture. Its appearance is protected, not its structural or functional features. A plant patent is the invention or discovery and asexually reproduction of any distinct and new variety of plant. This includes cultivated sports, mutants, hybrids, and newly found seedlings, other than a tuber-propagated plant or a plant found in an uncultivated state. Physical phenomena, abstract ideas, and laws of nature can not be patented. There must be a complete description and not just an idea or suggestion of a subject. It must also do what it claims to do; it must work. If an invention has been described in a publication anywhere in the world, or has been used publicly, or put up for sale, a patent must be applied for before one year passes, or the right to a patent is lost.

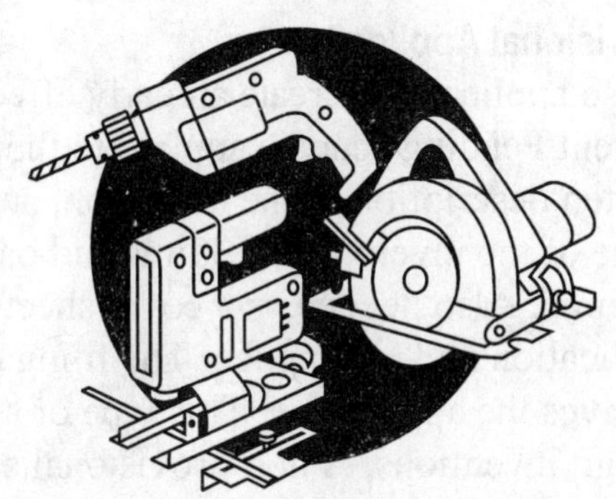

Who May Apply?
There are only a few situations where a person other than the inventor may apply for a patent application.

- a representative if the inventor has died
- a guardian if the inventor is insane
- a joint inventor or a person that has ownership interest if the inventor refuses to apply or can not be found

If two or more persons are the inventors, they may file jointly. However, someone who contributed only financially is not a joint inventor and cannot be included on the application.

Non-Provisional Application
The application must include:

1) a written document consisting of the specifications of the invention, and an oath or declaration
2) a drawing where it is necessary
3) the filing fee.

It must be in English, legible and written on only one side of white paper with a typewriter or its equivalent. The applicant will be notified if all the requirements are not met. The date that the completed application is filed will then become the filing date. Specifications must include a written description of the invention and the method and process of how it was made and is to be used. It must be in clear, concise, and exact terms to allow any skilled person related to the area of the invention to make and use the same discovery. The oath or declaration is a statement made by the inventor that he/she is the original and first inventor of the subject matter, as well as various other statements, made in front of a notary. The filing fee, excluding design and plant inventions, is a basic fee and additional fees. The basic fee covers 20 claims, including not more than 3 in independent form. There is an additional fee for each claim over 20, whether independent or dependent. The filing fees are cut in half for applicants that file a verified statement claiming small entity status; independent inventor, small business or nonprofit. The drawing must show every feature of the invention specified in the claim. Generally, photographs are not accepted. Applications have legal requirements and must be followed precisely.

Provisional Application

These applications create an early effective filing date and the term "Patent Pending" can be applied to the invention. There must be a written description of the invention, any necessary drawings and the name of the inventor(s). Claims and oath or declarations are not required. Also needed, is a cover sheet that states it is a provisional application and a filing fee. The filing date is the date that the PTO receives the application. This type of application can not be filed for design inventions. A non-provisional application must be filed within 12 months or else it will be discarded.

Protect Your Idea for $10

You can file a Disclosure Document with the Patent and Trademark Office, and they will keep it in confidence as evidence of the date of conception of the invention or idea.

Disclosure Document
Commissioner for Patents
Box DD
Washington, DC 20231
Disclosure Office
800-786-9199
www.uspto.gov/web/offices/pac/disdo.html

Send an 8 1/2 x 11" drawing, a copy, signed disclosure, SASE, and a check or money order for $10 to file. Upon request, the above office will also send you a free brochure on Disclosure Documents. This is the best way to keep the idea you are working on completely secret and yet document the date you conceived the idea. You can file the Disclosure Document at any time after the idea is conceived, but the value of it will depend on how much information you put into it - so put as much detail into this statement as you can.

The Purpose of Documenting The Date of Conception

If someone else should try to patent your idea, filing a Disclosure Document shows that you thought of it first, although filing this statement does not legally protect your invention. Documentation of the conception date gives you time to patent your invention, and is invaluable if you need to prove when you thought of your idea if a dispute should arise. (Note that filing a Disclosure Document gives you limited defensive legal protection only if you follow it up with a patent in two years. Unlike a patent, it cannot be used offensively, to stop someone else from patenting the same idea.) When you go to file for a patent, if you and a competitor get into a dispute as to who was the first to invent it, the Patent and Trademark Office (PTO) will hold an Interference Proceeding. If you thought of the idea first, your

Disclosure Document will go a long way towards establishing that you were the first inventor and should therefore receive the patent for it.

Examining the Application

They look to see that the application follows the legal requirements and also that the invention is new, useful and non-obvious and meets all requirements. It is not unusual for some, or all, of the claims to be rejected on the first examination few are accepted as filed The applicant will be notified in writing of any errors found. Then the inventor must request reconsideration, specifically pointing out and addressing any errors found and any amend any claims that to be revised. The second examination will generally be made final. Patents are granted in about every 2 out of 3 applications that are filed.

Patent Electronic Business Center

This is the center where you can do business electronically with the USPTO. In order to check the status of your patent application and also find general patent information, you can access the Patent Application Information Retrieval (PAIR). You will also be able to search for specific patents or applications by their number. The Electronic Filing System (EFS) accepts electronically filed applications, but you must have a digital certification and meet other requirements first. This program is only open to select number of people at this time because it is in the beginning stages of operation. Contact the office to see if you may participate!

Research Resources That Can Help You Turn Your Idea Into Reality

While diligently working out the details of your invention you can use the extensive resources of over 190,000 scientific and technical journals, articles, and books at the Scientific and Technical Information Center in Arlington, VA.

Facilitating public access to the more than 25 million cross-referenced United States patents is the job of PTO's Technology Assessment and Forecast Program (TAF); 703-306-2600. It has a master database which covers all United States patents, and searches are available free. A TAF search will not result in an in-depth patent search. (More on that, and how to find classifications in the *Conducting Your Own Patent Search* section below.) TAF extracts information from its database and makes it available in a variety of formats, including publications, custom patent reports, and statistical reports. The purpose of most of the reports generated by a TAF search is to reveal statistical information.

Copies of the specifications and drawings of all patents are available from PTO. Design patents and trademark copies are $3 each. Plant patents in color are $15 each. To make a request, you must have the patent number. For copies, contact:

Office of Public Records (OPR)
Crystal Gateway 4, Suite 300
Arlington, VA 22202
800-972-6382
571-272-3150
Fax: 703-305-8759
Email: dsd@uspto.gov

Conducting Your Own Patent Search

Before investing too much time and money on patenting your idea, you will want to see if anyone has already patented it. You may conduct the search yourself on the PTO website at http://www.uspto.gov or hire someone to do it for you. If you wish to hire a professional to do your patent search, consult the local yellow pages or again, search the PTO website for a roster of patent attorneys. Even if your search is not as in-depth as that of a patent attorney or a patent agent, you may still find the information that you need. You may also conduct your patent search at the Patent and Trademark Office Search Room.

Patent and Trademark Office (PTO)
Patent and Trademark Search Room
P.O. Box 1451
Alexandria, VA 22313-1450
800-786-9199

For information about the Patent and Trademark Depository Library, contact the office listed below.

Patent and Trademark Depository Library (PTDL)
U.S. Patent and Trademark Office
P.O. Box 1451
Alexandria, VA 22313-1450
800-786-9199

You may also conduct your patent search at any of the 83 Patent Depository Libraries (PDLs) throughout the country. The Patent and Trademark Library Program distributes the information to the 83 PDLs. The information is kept on CD-Rom discs, which are constantly updated, and you can use them to do a patent search. CD-Rom discs have been combined to incorporate CASSIS (Classification and Search Support Information System). CD-Rom discs do not give you online access to the PTO database. Online access is available through APS (Automated Patent Systems), and is presently available to public users of the PTO Search Room and to the 83 Patent Libraries. Each PDL with the online APS has its own rules regarding its use. To use the online APS at the PTO Search Room, it is recommended that you take a class at the Search Room. West, East, and X-Search classes are offered once per month for a cost of $25. Off Schedule 3-hour personal training sessions are available for a fee of $120. Online access costs $40 per connect hour, and the charge for paper used for printouts is an additional $.25 per sheet. Public user Ids are required to access all Public Search Facilities. They are available at the Search Room Reception Desk with a valid government issued photo ID.

If you do not live near a PDL, several CD-Rom discs are available through subscription. You may purchase the Classification disc, which dates back to 1790, for $300; the Bibliography disc, which dates back to 1969, for $300; and the ASIST disc, which contains a roster of patent attorneys, assignees, and other information for $200. You can also conduct your patent search and get a copy of it through commercial database services such as:

MeadData Central, Nexis, Lexis: 1-800-227-4908 or 1-800-422-1337; Fax: 518-487-3584 (bookstore support); www.lexisnexis.com/patentservices. Printouts are billed per page plus shipping. Copies are available via email, mail, fax, or on a CD-Rom. If you intend on doing many searches over time, Nexis Lexis will customize a package for you as a subscriber for approximately $250 per month.

Thompson Scientific, 3501 Market Street, Philadelphia, PA 19104; 1-800-336-4474; 215-386-0100; http://scientific.thomson.com. Patent searches are free, but the printouts range from $3.95 to $29.50 per page plus shipping.

If you are going to do your own patent search at your local Patent Depository Library, begin with the Manual and Index to U.S. Patent Classifications to identify the subject area where the patent is placed. Then use the CD-Rom discs to locate the patent. CD-Rom discs enable you to do a complete search of all registered patents but do not enable you to view the full patent, with all its specific details. Lastly, view the patent, which will be kept on microfilm, cartridge, or paper. What information there is to view varies by library, depending on what they have been able to purchase. If the library you are using does not have the patent you want, you may be able to obtain it through inter-library loan.

Copies of patents can be ordered from the PTO at 571-272-3150; 800-972-6382; for $3 per copy. To obtain a certified copy of a patent, call 571-272-3150 (Patent Search Library at the PTO). The fee is $25 and you must have the patent number. For a certified copy of an abstract of titles, the fee is $25. For a certified copy of patent assignments, with a record of ownership from the beginning until present, call 571-272-3150. The cost is $25, and to request specific assignments you must have the reel and frame number.

Now You Have Got Your Patent

Once a Notice of Allowance stating that your application for patents approved, you have 3 months to pay another filing fee. If not, the application will be deemed abandoned. There are also maintenance fees due at 31/2, 71/2, and 111/2 years after the original grant. After it has expired, anyone may make, use, offer for sale, or sell or import the invention without the patentee's approval. A patent is personal property.

Tips

- Most importantly, do not reveal the details of your invention to anyone! If you need to do so, establish a confidential relationship with them by law or regulation, or a written agreement. Your plans and information you have gathered can be trade secrets and you must protect them.
- Record your discovery in detail as soon as possible and keep a record as you go. Have it witnessed by two reliable persons with a confidentiality agreement.
- Developing a new product is time consuming and expensive. Determine how much of your time, money, and effort you can invest. Know your personal limitations and when to get professional help.
- Twenty percent of patents issued each year are to private inventors. They must be effective business people to also research business concepts.
- Read articles by successful inventors for tips on what it took for them to market their product. Talk to potential customers to see what they would look for in the type of product that you are discovering.
- Remember, if a product similar to yours exists, you can still patent an improvement that is significant.

- Lastly, many times it is not the first try at inventing a product that is successful, it gets better as you go.

What Are Trademarks and Servicemarks?

A trademark is a word, name, symbol or device used in trade with goods to indicate the source of the goods and to set them apart from the goods of others. A servicemark is used to distinguish the source of a service instead of a product. Trademark or mark is generally the term used to refer to both trademarks and servicemarks. They are to keep others from using a confusingly similar mark, but not to keep others from making or selling the same goods or services under a clearly different mark. The Trademark Assistance Center will provide general information about the registration process and will respond to questions concerning the status of a specific trademark application and registration. They are available Monday through Friday from 8:30am to 5pm at 571-272-3150; 800-786-9199; www.uspto.gov/main/trademarks.htm.

Trademarks

Registering a trademark for your product or service is the way to protect the recognition quality of the name you are building. The PTO keeps records on more than 2.2 million trademarks and records. Over 500,000 active trademarks are kept on the floor of the library, while "dead" trademarks are kept on microfilm. Books contain every registered trademark ever issued, starting in 1870. You can visit the Patent and Trademark Office to research a trademark using the US Trademark Search Database at www.uspto.gov/tmdb/index.html. However, it will be replaced by the US Trademark Electronic Search System (TESS) soon. For now, both systems will be running. You can access TESS at http://tess.uspto.gov. You can then conduct your search manually for no charge or use their Trademark Search System (T-Search) for $40 per hour, plus $.25 cents per page.

Assistant Commissioner of Trademarks
Trademark Search Library
P.O. Box 1451
Alexandria, VA 22313-1451

If you can't do it yourself, you can hire someone to do the search for you. For an agent to do this, consult the local yellow pages under "Trademark Agents/Consultants" or "Trademark Attorneys". You can also locate an agent by calling your local bar association for a referral.

To conduct your own search at a Patent Depository Library, use the CD-Rom disc on trademarks. It is available for purchase. The CD-Rom discs deliver patent and trademark information including full-text facsimile images and searchable text records. Images can be found in the *Official Gazette*, which contains most current and pending trademarks. The price for an annual subscription to the *Official Gazette* for trademarks is $980. It is issued every Tuesday and can be ordered from the U.S. Government Printing Office. You can also purchase an image file which contains pending and registered trademarks and corresponding serial or registration numbers through Thomson and Thomson by calling 1-800-692-8833. The information contained in it dates back to April 1, 1987 and is updated by approximately 500 images weekly. However, the PDL you use is likely to have an image of the trademark on microfilm or cartridge, and also have copies of the *Official Gazette*. If not, and you have the registration number, you may obtain a copy of the trademark you want for $3 from the PTO. Contact:

Assistant Commissioner of Trademarks
P.O. Box 1451
Alexandria, VA 22313-1451

There are also several commercial services you can use to conduct trademark searches.

Trademark Scan produced by Thomson and Thomson. It can be purchased by calling 1-800-477-3447 (ask for online services), or accessed directly via Saegis. Trademark Scan is updated three times per week, and includes state and federal trademarks, foreign and domestic. To access Trademark Scan you must already have Dialog or Saegis. Many online options are free. The Internet address is www.thomson-thomson.com.

Online services and database discs for both patents and trademarks are constantly being expanded. For information on an extensive range of existing and projected products, call the PTO Office of Electronic Information at 800-786-9199 and ask for the U.S. Department of Commerce, PTO Office of Information Systems' *Electronic Products Brochure*. For example, there is a Weekly Text File, containing text data of pending and registered trademarks. Information can be called up by using almost any term. It can be purchased from Thomson & Thomson. You can reach Thomson & Thomson at 1-800-477-3447 or online at www.thomson-thomson.com.

How to Register a Trademark

The right of a trademark comes from either the actual use of the mark, or by filing the correct application. There are two types of rights in a mark, the right to register it and the right to use the mark. The right to register is given to the first party that uses a mark in commerce, or who files an application at the PTO. The right to use a mark can be a complicated matter. For example, in the case where two people who do not know each other, start to use the same or similar marks without a registration. A court will have to decide who has the right to use the mark. Trademark rights last indefinitely if the owner continues its use. The registration lasts 10 years with 10-year renewal periods. You can order a free copy of Basic Facts about Trademarks from the U.S. Government Printing Office, or by calling the Trademark Search Library at 800-786-9199.

Types of Applications

The "use" application is for an applicant that already has been using their mark in commerce. The "intent-to-use" application is for those who have a bona fide intention of using the mark in commerce. These offer protection only in the US and its territories. Applications must be filed in the name of the owner of the mark. For automated information about the status of a trademark application and registration, call 571-272-1000.

The Trademark Electronic Center

The Trademark Electronic Application System (TEAS) has step-by-step instructions for filling out forms and also contains information about the USPTO's procedures and practices. It also allows you to fill out the trademark forms, check them to be sure they are complete, and using e-TEAS, submit it on-line. You must be able to attach either a black-and-white GIF or JPG file to apply for a stylized or design mark. If a sample of actual use in commerce is needed, a scanned image or digital photo in GIF or JPG format must be attached. The final requirement is payment with a credit card or from an account already set up with the PTO. One mark can be filed with each application for a fee of $325, except for Class 9 and

Class 25, where there is a $650 fee. E-TEAS will not accept applications from 11pm Saturday to 6am Sunday. Also, if you prefer to send the forms by mail, you can use PrinTEAS to print out your completed forms. You can send check, money order, or make arrangements for payment through a USPTO account. This system can be accessed 24 hours a day, 7 days a week. You can check the status of marks using TARR-Trademark Applications and Registrations Retrieval at http://tarr.uspto.gov.

Symbols

Anyone who claims rights in a mark can use the symbols, TM (trademark) or SM (servicemark) to show that right. However, the registration symbol, an r in a circle ®, can not be used until the mark is registered.

The Right Way to Get a Copyright

Copyrights are filed on intellectual property. A copyright protects your right to control the sale, use of distribution, and royalties from a creation in thought, music, films, art, or books. It is an automatic form of protection for authors of published and unpublished "original works of authorship." The concrete form of expression as opposed to the subject matter is what is protected. Since a copyright is automatic when a work is created, registration is not required for protection. However, there are advantages to registration. If it is registered within 5 years of publication of the work, it establishes prima facie evidence of its validity and can be helpful in case of a court action. Generally the work is protected for the author's life plus 70 years after death.

For more information, contact:

Library of Congress
Copyright Office
101 Independence Avenue SE
Washington, DC 20559-6000
Public Information Office
202-707-3000
Email: copyinfo@loc.gov
www.loc.gov
www.copyright.gov

If you know which copyright application you require, you can call the Forms Hotline, open 7 days per week, 24 hours per day at 202-707-9100. The fee is $30 for each registration. Information on all of the different types of copyrights and their applications can be found at their web site.

The Library of Congress provides information on copyright registration procedures and copyright card catalogs that cover several million works that have been registered since 1870. The Copyright Office will research federal copyrights only for varying fees. Requests must be made in writing and you must specify exactly what information you require. If a work does not show any elements of copyright notice, you can search the Copyright Office's catalogs and records. The records from January 1, 1978, to the present can be searched on the Internet through the Library of Congress Information System (LOCIS). That web site address is www.loc.gov/ copyright/rb.html.

Contact the Copyright Office, Reference and Bibliography, Library of Congress, 101 Independence Ave., SE, Washington, DC 20559; 202-707-6850, Public Information 202-707-3000.

What is Not Protected by Copyright

Works that have not been notated, recorded, or written can not be protected by copyright. Here are some others:

- titles, short phrases, and slogans; familiar symbols or designs; variations of ornamentation, lettering or coloring, listings of ingredients or contents
- concepts, methods, systems, principles, or devices, as opposed to description, explanation, and illustration
- works that are entirely made of information that is common property and do not contain any original authorship

Invention Scams: How They Work

Fake product development companies prey on amateur inventors who may not be as savvy about protecting their idea or invention as experienced inventors might be. Most of the bogus/fake companies use escalating fees. The following is a description of how most of them operate:

- The inventor is invited to call or write for free information.
- The inventor is then offered a free evaluation of his idea.
- Next comes the sales call. The inventor is told he has a very good potential idea and that the company is willing to share the cost of marketing, etc. Actual fact, there is no sharing with these companies. Most times the inventor has to come up with the money (usually several hundred dollars or more) for a patent search and a market analysis. Neither of these are worth anything.

- Then the inventor receives a professional/ impressive looking portfolio which contains no real information at all. All the paper crammed into this portfolio looks topnotch, but it's all computer generated garbage.
- Upon receiving this portfolio, the inventor is lured into signing a contract that commits him to giving the company thousands of dollars to promote/license the product. The company sends some promotional letters to fulfill their obligation, but large manufacturers simply toss them into the trash.

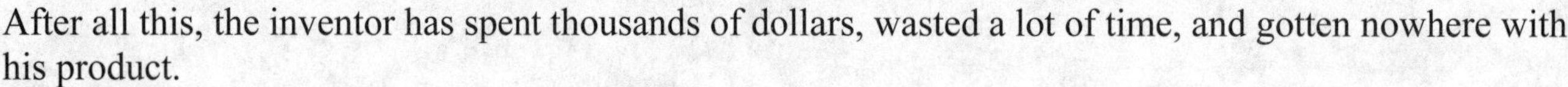

After all this, the inventor has spent thousands of dollars, wasted a lot of time, and gotten nowhere with his product.

How To Avoid Losing a Fortune

According to the experts, the inventor should:

- Beware of the come-ons offered by these unethical companies. Avoid using the invention brokers who advertise on TV late in the evening; in public magazines; those who offer 800 numbers; and those on public transit display signs.
- When upfront money is required, look out. There are very few legitimate consultants who insist on a retainer or hourly fee.
- Don't allow the enthusiasm of your idea to take over your inherent common sense. Talk to your patent attorney and see if he knows anything about this company. Plus, check with inventors associations in the state, and see what they have to say about this particular company.
- Demand to know what percentage of ideas the company accepts. Legitimate brokers might accept 2 ideas out of every 100. The fake companies tend to accept about 99 out of 100.
- Find out their actual success rate. Any corporation/ company that will not give you their success rate (not licensing agreements) is a company to stay away from.
- Get an objective evaluation of your invention from reputable professionals. This will save you plenty of money on a bad idea.

A number of highly recommended programs are listed in the next section.

Free Help for Inventors

If you have a great idea and want to turn it into reality, don't rush out and spend what could be thousands of dollars for a private invention company and a patent attorney. You can get a lot of this help for free or at a fraction of the cost. There is a lot of help out there; university-sponsored programs, not-for-profit groups, state affiliated programs, profit-making companies, etc. Depending on the assistance and the organization, some services are free, others have reasonable fees.

Many of the inventors' organizations hold regular meetings where speakers share their expertise on topics such as licensing, financing and marketing. These groups are a good place for inventors to meet other inventors, patent attorneys, manufacturers, and others with whom they can talk and from whom they can get help. You can also contact one of the following organizations for help.

1. **Small Business Development Center**
   Washington State University
   Parkplace Building
   1200 6th Ave., Suite 1700
   Seattle, WA 98101
   206-553-7328
   Fax: 206-553-7044
   www.wsbdc.org

This service will evaluate your idea for a fee. They also provide counseling services and can assist you with your patent search if you are a business in Washington.

2. **Wisconsin Innovation Service Center/Technology**
   Small Business Development Center
   Melissa Rick, Director
   University of Wisconsin - Whitewater
   402 McCutchan Hall
   Whitewater, WI 53190
   262-472-1365
   Fax: 262-472-1600
   www.sbdc.uww.edu

The only service that is guaranteed is the evaluation. However, efforts are made to match inventors with exceptional high evaluation scores with manufacturers seeking new product ideas. (Do not offer direct invention development or marketing services). WISC charges a $595 flat fee for an evaluation. The goal is to keep research as affordable as possible to the average independent inventor. Most evaluations are completed within 30 - 45 days. Those inventions from specialized fields may require more time. WISC also provides preliminary patent searches via on-line databases to client.

3. **INVENTURE Program**
   Mid Iowa SBDC
   Sherry Shafer
   10861 Douglas Avenue
   Urbandale, IA 50322
   515-331-8954
   www.iowasbdc.org/sbdc/inventure.cfm

INVENTURE is a program of the Drake University Business Development and Research Institute designed to encourage the development of valid ideas through the various steps to becoming marketable items. INVENTURE has no paid staff. The entire panel is made up of volunteers. The administration of the program is handled by existing staff from the Small Business Development Center and the College of Business and Public Administration. They will review items from **any person** regardless of their place of residence. They will review a product idea and check it for market feasibility. INVENTURE may link individuals with business and/or financial partners. INVENTURE screens every product submitted, but will not consider toy/game or food items. Products are evaluated on 33 different criteria, (factors related to legality, safety, business risk, and demand analysis, to market acceptance/ competition). It normally takes up to 6 weeks to receive results of the evaluation. Evaluators are experienced in manufacturing, marketing, accounting, production, finance and investments. INVENTURE acts in a responsible manner to maintain confidence of an idea, but cannot guarantee confidentiality. For assistance with business plans, financial projections, and marketing help, you're encouraged to contact your Small Business Development Center (SBDC).

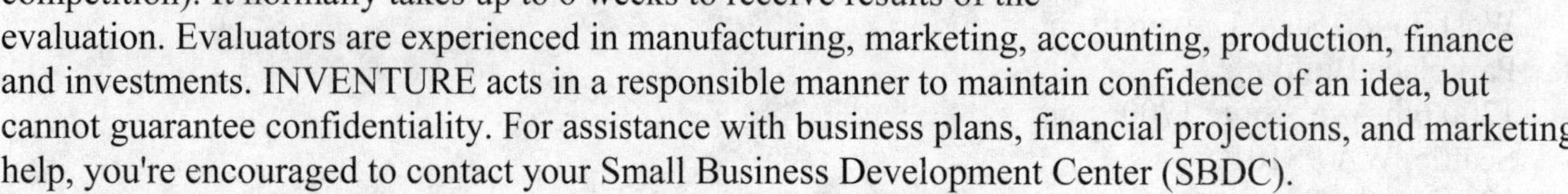

4. **Efficiency and Renewable Energy-Inventions and Innovation**
   Mail Stop EE-1
   U.S. Department of Energy
   Washington, DC 20585
   202-586-9220
   222.eere.energy.gov/inventions

Financial assistance is available at 2 levels: up to $50,000 and up to $250,000 by the Inventions and Innovations program as stated by the Office of Industrial Technologies (OIT) Department of Energy (DOE) for ideas that significantly impact energy savings and future commercial market potential. Successful applicants will find technical guidance and commercialization support in addition to financial assistance. DOE has given financial support to more than 500 inventions with nearly 25% of these reaching the marketplace bringing in nearly $710 million in cumulative sales.

5. **U.S. Environmental Protection Agency**
   Center for Environmental Research Information
   Cincinnati, OH 45268
   513-569-7578
   www.epa.gov

Directory Description: Environmental Protection Agency, Office of Research and Development, 1200 Pennsylvania Ave., NW, Mail Code 8101R, Washington, DC 20460; 202-272-0167.

The Office of Research and Development conducts an Agency wide integrated program of research and development relevant to pollution sources and control, transport and fate processes, health/ecological effects, measurement/monitoring, and risk assessment. The office provides technical reviews, expert consultations, technical assistance, and advice to environmental decision-makers in federal, state, local, and foreign governments.

Office of Research and Development
Is responsible for working with laboratories, program offices, regions to produce information products that summarize research, technical, regulatory enforcement information that will assist non-technical audiences in under-standing environmental issues. Contact Office of Research and Development, U.S. Environmental Protection Agency, 1200 Pennsylvania Ave., NW, Washington, DC 20460; 202-564-6620; Fax: 202-272-0167.

Goals are accomplished through four core programs:

1. **The Research Grants Program:**
   Supports research initiated by individual investigators in areas of interest to the agency.
2. **The Environmental Research Centers Program:**
   Has two components: The Academic Research Center Program (ARC) and the Hazardous Substance Research Centers Program (HSRC).
3. **The Small Business Innovation Research (SBIR) Program:**
   Program supports small businesses for the development of ideas relevant to EPA's mission. Focuses on projects in pollution control development. Also receives 1.5% of the Agency's resources devoted to extramural Superfund research.
4. **The Visiting Scientists Program:**
   Components are an Environmental Science and Engineering Fellows Program and a Resident Research Associateship Program. The Fellows Program supports ten mid-career post-doctoral scientists and engineers at EPA headquarters & regional offices. The Research Associateship Program attracts national and international scientists and engineers at EPA research laboratories for up to 3 years to collaborate with Agency researchers on important environmental issues.

Other programs available are:
Greater Research Opportunities (GRO)
The Agency's Senior Environmental Employment Program (SEE)
The Federal Workforce Training Program
An Experimental Program to Stimulate Competitive Research (EPSCoR).

To learn more, contact Grants Administration, U.S. Environmental Protection Agency, 1200 Pennsylvania Ave., NW, Washington, DC 20460; 202-272-0167. The best way, though, is to search for the word "grant" at the EPA's website, www.epa.gov.

Government Buys Bright Ideas From Inventors: Small Business Innovative Research Programs (SBIR)

The Small Business Innovative Research Program (SBIR) stimulates technological innovation, encourages small science and technology based firms to participate in government funded research, and provides incentives for converting research results into commercial applications. The program is designed to stimulate technological innovation in this country by providing qualified U.S. small business concerns with competitive opportunities to propose innovative concepts to meet the research and development needs of the Federal government. Eleven federal agencies with research and development budgets greater than $100 million are required by law to participate: The Departments of Defense, Health and Human Services, Energy, Agriculture, Commerce, Transportation, and Education; the National Aeronautics and Space Administration; the National Science Foundation; the Nuclear Regulatory Commission; and the Environmental Protection Agency.

Businesses of 500 or fewer employees that are organized for profit are eligible to compete for SBIR funding. Nonprofit organizations and foreign owned firms are not eligible to receive awards, and the research must be carried out in the U.S. All areas of research and development solicit for proposals, and the 2004 awards for SBIR was over $2 billion. There are three phases of the program: Phase I determines whether the research idea, often on high risk advanced concepts, is technically feasible; whether the firm can do high quality research; and whether sufficient progress has been made to justify a larger Phase II effort. This phase is usually funded for 6 months with awards up to $100,000. Phase II is the principal research effort, and is usually limited to a maximum of $750,000 for up to two years. The third phase, which is to pursue potential commercial applications of the research funded under the first two phases, is supported solely by nonfederal funding, usually from third party, venture capital, or large industrial firms. SBIR is one of the most competitive research and development programs in the government today. About one proposal out of ten received is funded in Phase I. Generally, about half of these receive support in Phase II. Solicitations for proposals are released once a year (in a few cases twice a year). To assist the small business community in its SBIR efforts, the U.S. Small Business Administration publishes the Pre-Solicitation Announcement (PSA) in December, March, June, and September of each year. Every issue of the PSA contains pertinent information on the SBIR Program along with details on SBIR solicitations that are about to be released. This publication eliminates the need for small business concerns to track the activities of all of the federal agencies participating in the SBIR Program. In recognition of the difficulties encountered by many small firms in their efforts to locate sources of funding essential to finalization of their innovative products, SBA has developed the Commercialization Matching System. This system contains information on all SBIR awardees, as well as financing sources that have indicated an interest in investing in SBIR innovations. Firms interested in obtaining more information on the SBIR Program or receiving the PSA, should contact the Office of Technology, Small Business Administration, 409 3rd St., SW, MC/6470, Washington, DC 20416, 202-205-6450.

SBIR representatives listed below can answer questions and send you materials about their agency's SBIR plans and funding:

Department of Agriculture
Dr. Charles Cleland, Directory SBIR Program, U.S. Department of Agriculture, Stop 2201, Waterfront Centre, Suite 2312, 1400 Independence Avenue, SW, Washington, DC 20250-2201; 202-401-4002, Fax: 202-401-6070; Email: Ccleland@csrees.usda.gov; www.csrees.usda.gov/fo/fundview.cfm?fonum=1220

Department of Commerce
Dr. Joseph Bishop, Department of Commerce, 1335 East-West Highway, Room 106, Silver Springs, MD 20910, 301-713-3565, Fax: 301-713-4100, Email: Joseph.Bishop@NOAA.GOV; www.ago.noaa.gov/ad/sbirs/sbir.html

Department of Defense
Ivory Fisher, SBIR/STTR Program Manager, Office Under Secretary of Defense, U.S. Department of Defense, 1777 North Kent Street, Rosslyn Plaza North, Suite 9100, Arlington, VA 22209, 866-724-7457, 703-588-8616, Fax: 703-588-7561, Email: fisherij@acq.osd.mil; www.acq.osd.mil/sadbu/sbir/homepg.htm

Department of Education
Lee Eiden, SBIR Program Coordinator, Department of Education, Room 508 D-Capitol Place, 555 New Jersey Avenue, NW Washington DC 20208, 202-219-2004, Fax: 202-219-1407, Email: Lee.Eiden@ed.gov; www.ed.gov/offices/OERI/SBIR

Department of Energy
Dr. Robert E. Berger, SBIR/STTR Program Manager, US Department of Energy, SC-21.2, 1000 Independence Avenue, SW, Washington, DC 20585-1290; 301-903-0569, Fax: 301-903-5488, Email: walter.warnick@science.doe.gov; http://sbir.er.doe.gov/sbir

Department of Health and Human Services
Debbie Ridgely, Director OSDBU, Office of the Secretary, U.S. Department of Health and Human Services, 200 Independence Ave., Room 360G, Washington, DC 20201; 202-690-7235, Fax: 202-260-4872; Email: debbie.ridgely@hhs.gov.

Department of Transportation
Joseph D. Henebury, SBIR Program Director, DTS-22, US Department of Transportation, Volpe Center, 55 Broadway, Kendall Square, Cambridge, MA 02142-1093, 617-494-2051, Fax: 617-494-2370, Email: Henebury@volpe.dot.gov; www.volpe.dot.gov/sbir

Environmental Protection Agency
James Gallup, Office of Research and Development, US Environmental Protection Agency, ORD/NCER (8722F), 1200 Pennsylvania Ave., NW, Washington DC 20460, 202-343-9703, Fax: 202-233-0678, Email: Gallup.James@epa.gov; http://es.epa.gov/ncer/sbir

National Aeronautics and Space Administration
SBIR Program, National Aeronautics Space Administration-HQ, 300 E. St, SW, Washington, DC 20546-0001; 202-358-4652, http://sbir.gsfc.nasa.gov/SBIR/SBIR.html

Small Business Administration
Maurice Swinton, US Small Business Administration, 409 3rd Street, SW, Mail Code:6470, Washington, DC 20416, 202-205-6450, Fax: 202-205-7754, Email: Robert.connolly@sba.gov; www.sba.gov/sbir

Homeland Security
Tim Sharp, Department of Homeland Security, DHS S&T/HSARPA, Washington, DC 20528; 202-254-6105; 800-754-3043; Email: helpdesk@hsarpasbir.com; www.hsarpasbir.com

National Science Foundation
Kesh Narayanan, National Science Foundation, 4201 Wilson Boulevard, Room 550, Arlington, VA 22230; 703-292-7076; Fax: 703-292-9057; Email: knarayan@nsf.gov; www.nsf.gov/eng/sbir

Volunteering: The Most Fun In Life Is Giving

The kids are out of the house, you've saved for your retirement and now what do you do? You may find that you have some extra time on your hands. Volunteering is a fantastic opportunity and may be just what you need to stay young and involved. Seniors not only have the extra time, but also the experiences and expertise to benefit our society in a variety of ways. According to the federal government's Department on Aging, nearly half of all Americans volunteering are seniors, about 23 million. This is a huge number but it is still not enough to fill the needs of our communities. We have put together a list of volunteer opportunities to get you started. Use this list as a starting point to find the perfect volunteer program. Many nonprofits are involved in work that is fascinating. You can get involved by preserving rain forests, recording oral histories of elderly immigrants, helping a young entrepreneur or by teaching low-income children to read. If you check around, you'll be sure to find an organization that piques your interest or passion.

President Bush recognized and met with volunteer Grace McCarthy in 2004. Grace McCarthy is an active 83 year old senior volunteer, who has served over 4000 hours with the Retired and Senior Volunteer Program, an organization that matches seniors' interests with needs in their communities. McCarthy spends an average 20 hours a week in a variety of volunteer activities, including volunteering three days a week performing administrative work at the Upper Peninsula Children's Museum. She also served on the County Citizen Corps council and has completed Community Emergency Response Team (CERT) training. These programs and many others can be found through the USA Freedom Corps. http://www.usafreedomcorps.gov/content/about_usafc/ newsroom/local_vols_dynamic.asp?ID=631

The following letter from Ms. G. shows the positive impact volunteering has had in her life.

> Good morning. I'm Ms. G and I'm a volunteer for the Off Our Rockers Program. My volunteer work consists of helping elementary school children increase their ability to read.
>
> Volunteering has definitely helped me regain some of my positive outlook on life. My husband died at the age of 62 after a courageous 4-year battle with Multiple Systems Atrophy. Since I provided all of his medical care, I didn't get a chance to meet many of my neighbors or become involved in any activities or groups. I also had thyroid surgery, which resulted in my right vocal chord being paralyzed. This left me very self-conscious about speaking. My only stress reducer was exercising at the gym in the evening with my daughter. However, during the day I had little to fill up my time.
>
> That's when Suzanna came to my rescue! My daughter came up with the address for The Senior Source. When I contacted them it was Suzanna who set up a meeting at the

elementary school that was within walking distance of my house! (Yes, now I walk to the school on my volunteer days. The exercise is an added benefit!). I work with the kids on a one-to-one basis and other times with groups that read at different levels. Their goal is to read Chapter books.

The kids are great! At Christmas the class was delighted to present me with an apron that I was delighted to receive. The apron was decorated with their names and drawings. On Valentines Day I received a 6-foot banner that they created with Valentine sayings. I baked heart shaped cookies that they decorated with frosting, writing gels, and sprinkles.

The Off Our Rockers program has made such a difference to me. It gets me "off my rocker" and out of the house. We have so much fun reading the books and the kids constantly amaze me wit their own literary interpretations. We came across a new word, the lady was wearing a "broach" and I asked them-"Who knows what a "broach" is?" they answered in amazement "Why Mrs. G-That's a bug that crawls on the wall!"

Suzanna, thank you for getting me involved in the Off Our Rockers Program.

Here are some great starting places to begin your search:

1) ***Eldercare Locator*** is a public service operated by the Administration on Aging, connecting older Americans with sources of information on senior services. Volunteers of all ages are encouraged to make a difference by volunteering. To meet the needs of older Americans, Area Agency on Aging programs are operated in over 650 local levels. "Area Agency on Aging" is a generic term; specific names of local Agencies may vary. Area programs offer services to help older adults remain in their homes by providing services such as Meals-on-Wheels, homemaker assistance and other independent living needs. The Eldercare Locator web site provides a search engine to find an Agency in your area. Contact Eldercare Locator; 800-677-1116; www.eldercare.gov.

2) ***1-800-VOLUNTEER****.org* is a national website portal providing volunteers with direct connection to local volunteer opportunities that match their interests, skills and common desire to make a difference. *50+ Volunteering Initiatives* is a program that builds expertise and capacity of individuals to develop high-impact and rewarding volunteer opportunities for people over the age of 50. *Season of Service* offers national volunteer days throughout the year that include: Join Hand Day, Make a Difference Day, Martin Luther King Jr. Day, National Family Volunteer Day, and National Volunteer Week. Contact Points of Light Foundation, 1400 I Street, NW, Suite 800, Washington, DC 20005-2208; 800-750-7653; 202-729-8000; www.pointsoflight.org.

3) ***VolunteerMatch*** is a nonprofit organization that offers a variety of online services to support community programs. Volunteers can enter their ZIP code on the web site to locate local volunteer opportunities posted by nonprofit organizations throughout the United States. Contact VolunteerMatch, 385 Grove Street, San Francisco, CA 94102; 415-241-6868; Fax: 415-241-6869; www.volunteermatch.org.

Share Your Business Experience

Just because you have retired from a small business as an owner or manager doesn't mean that you still can't be active in the small business community. SCORE, the Service Corps of Retired Executives needs volunteers to act as part time counselors for individuals who are thinking of going into business or who have already started one and are encountering problems. There are more than 389 SCORE chapters across the country. You can check the web site or call the 800 number to find a chapter near you. Contact SCORE Association, 409 3rd Street, SW, 6th Floor, Washington, DC 20024; 800-634-0245; www.score.org.

The President's Clearinghouse On Volunteer Opportunities

The President created the President's Council on Service and Civic Participation in 2003 to recognize the important contributions Americans are making in our communities through volunteer service. The Council has created the USA Freedom Corps Network where individuals can find service opportunities that match their interests and talents in their hometowns. The web site lists specific information for seniors. Contact USA Freedom Corps, 1600 Pennsylvania Avenue NW, Washington, DC 20500; 877-USA-CORPS; www.freedomcorps.gov.

Keep Our Homeland Safe

Following the events on September 11, 2001, state and local government officials have increased opportunities for citizens to become an integral part of protecting the homeland and supporting the local first responders. Citizen Corps, a part of USA Freedom Corps, was created to help coordinate volunteer activities that will make our communities safer, stronger and better prepared to respond to any emergency situation. Citizen Corps operates four programs: Medical Reserve Corps, USA on Watch, Community Emergency Response Team, and Volunteers in Police Service. Contact Citizen Corps, Department of Homeland Security; www.citizencorps.gov. Click on Programs and Partners to see how you can volunteer.

Help With Hospitals, Shelters, & First Aid

The Medical Reserve Corps establishes teams of local medical and public health professional volunteers to help during times of community need. Retired professionals such as doctors, nurses, emergency medical technicians, pharmacists, nurses' assistants are encouraged to apply. Contact Medical Reserve Corps, Office of the Surgeon General, U.S. Department of Health and Human Services, 5600 Fishers Lane, Room 18-66, Rockville, MD 20857; 301-443-4951; Fax: 301-480-1163; www.medicalreservecorps.gov.

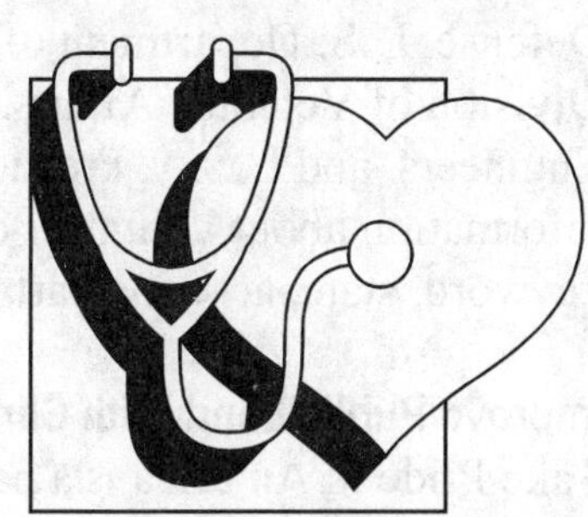

Help Law Enforcement Keep Your Community Safe

USA on Watch is an effort to unite law enforcement, private organizations and individual citizens in an effort to reduce residential crime. All you need to start a program in your area is to gather a few neighbors, have a place to meet and make a call to your local police office. You will then be assigned a crime prevention officer who will attend your first meeting. For additional information check the web site or call your local police station. Contact USA on Watch, National Sheriffs' Association, 1450 Duke Street, Alexandria, VA 22314-3490; 703-836-7827; Fax: 703-683-6541; www.usaonwatch.org.

Help FEMA Prepare For The Next Disaster

The Community Emergency Response Team educates volunteers about disaster preparedness for hazards that may impact their area and trains them in basic disaster response skills. Contact Community Emergency Response Team (CERT), Emergency Management Institute, 16825 South Seton Avenue, Emmitsburg, MD 21727; 301-447-1000; Fax: 301-447-1052; http://training.fema.gov/emiweb/CERT/.

Didn't You Always Want To Be A Policeman?

Volunteers offer their time and skills to local law enforcement agencies. Volunteer's roles may include performing clerical tasks, serving as an extra set of "eyes and ears", assisting with search and rescue activities and writing citations for accessible parking violations. Contact Volunteers in Police Service (VIPS), International Association of Chiefs of Police, 515 N Washington Street, Alexandria, VA 22314; 800-THE-IACP; www.policevolunteer.org.

Volunteer To Travel The World

Volunteers for Prosperity is an initiative of the USA Freedom Corps which gives highly skilled professional Americans opportunities to serve abroad. The program enlists American doctors, nurses, teachers, engineers, economists, computer specialists and others to work on specific development initiatives. These volunteers will serve in the countries of their choice, for however long their project takes. Professional seniors are encouraged to participate. Contact Volunteers for Prosperity, US Agency for International Development, Room 8.06-099 RRB, 1300 Pennsylvania Avenue NW, Washington, DC 20523; 202-712-1010; www.volunteersforprosperity.gov.

Be A Park Ranger In Arizona, A Tour Guide At Alcatraz, A Camp Ground Host At Cape Hatteras, Or Ride Horses In Idaho

Volunteer.Gov/Gov is a partnership among the U.S. Department of Agriculture, U.S. Department of Defense, U.S. Department of the Interior, U.S. Department of Veterans Affairs, State of New York Division of Veterans Affairs, the Corporation for National and Community Service, U.S. Army Corps of Engineers, and U.S.A. Freedom Corps aimed at providing a single, easy-to-use web portal with information about volunteer opportunities. The site allows you to search for volunteer opportunities by keyword, state, activity, partner, and/or date range. Contact www.volunteer.gov/gov.

Improve Public Land With Clint Eastwood

Take Pride in America is a national partnership that recruits, supports and recognizes volunteers who work to improve the special legacy all Americans share – our public lands and waters. The web site will locate state and federal volunteer opportunities in your area. Clint Eastwood serves as the group's national spokesman. Contact Take Pride in America; 202-208-5848; Fax: 202-208-5873; www.takepride.gov .

Live In A National Forest For The Summer!

Live in a national forest for the summer! These volunteer opportunities are available to seniors who have free time in the summer. If you don't have a whole summer you can still help out in the Forest Service. Volunteers can perform a wide variety of tasks. Your talents and skills are matched with your work preference to fulfill the mission of the Forest Service. Contact USDA Forest Service, Mail Stop 1125, 1400 Independence Avenue, SW, Washington, DC 20250-0003; 202-205-1706; www.fs.fed.us.

Have You Always Dreamed Of Being An Archaeologist?

Have you always dreamed of being an archaeologist? If so, Passport in Time (PIT) is the volunteer program for you. PIT is a program of the USDA Forest Service. Volunteers can work on projects including archaeological excavation, rock art restoration, survey, archival research, historic structure restoration, gathering oral histories, or writing interpretive brochures to name a few. Projects vary in length from 2 days to two weeks or longer. Check the web site or contact Passport in Time for current projects. Contact Passport in Time, P.O. Box 31315, Tucson, AZ 85751-1315; 520-722-2716; 800-281-9176; Fax: 520-298-7044; www.passportintime.com.

Be A Cowboy On The Range

The public lands administered by the BLM range from saguaro cactus desert to Douglas fir tundra. Overall, these lands, located primarily in the Western part of the United States, comprise nearly one-eighth of our nation's land area. Volunteers can help protect and restore streams, serve as a campground host, conduct tour groups at visitor centers, plant trees, work in an office or many other opportunities. Contact Bureau of Land Management, Environmental Education and Volunteers Group, 1849 C Street NW, 406 LS, Washington, DC 20240; 202-452-5125; Fax: 202-452-5199; www.blm.gov/volunteer/.

Do You Love Wildlife?

Then volunteering at the Fish and Wildlife Service may be great for you. You may conduct population surveys, lead tours, assist with lab research, work in administration, take photographs or any number of other tasks. Contact U.S. Fish & Wildlife Service, 1849 C Street, NW, Washington, DC 20240; 800-344-WILD; http://volunteers.fws.gov/.

Science Savvy Seniors Needed In The Park

The Volunteers-In-Parks volunteers donated 4.5 million hours of their time to national parks in 2003. Volunteers can help in a variety of ways and must contact each park to find out about available opportunities.

International Volunteers-In-Parks Program offers opportunities to individuals from all over the world. Call 202-354-1807 for information on the International Program.

Natural Resource Laureate Program is a new program that hosts science-based professionals in the national parks. The program matches volunteers possessing proven science backgrounds with parks needing specific natural resource expertise. Contact National Park Service, Volunteers-In-Parks (VIP) Program; 540-788-3274; http://nps.gov/volunteer/; www.nature.nps.gov/partnerships/laureateprogram.htm.

Help Restore The Land

The Bureau of Reclamation offers volunteer opportunities in several geographical areas. Contact Bureau of Reclamation, 1849 C Street, NW, Washington, DC 20240-0001; 202-513-0501; Fax: 202-513-0315; www.usbr.gov.

Peace Corps Makes It Never Too Late To Save The World

Counseling teenagers in Belize, launching an Armenian computer center, promoting HIV/AIDS awareness in Malawi or teaching chemistry in a Ghanaian high school. These are just some of the projects you may be able to volunteer for in the Peace Corp. Peace Corp Volunteers work in the following areas: education, youth outreach and community development; health and HIV/AIDS; agriculture and environment; business development; and information technology. Contact Peace Corps, Paul D. Coverdell Peace Corps Headquarters, 1111 20th Street, NW, Washington, DC 20526; 800-424-8580; www.peacecorp.gov.

Help Seniors Get Getter Medical Care

The Administration on Aging administers the Senior Medicare Patrol project which teaches volunteer retired professionals, such as doctors, nurses, accountants, investigators, law enforcement personnel, attorneys and teachers, to help Medicare and Medicaid beneficiaries to be better health care consumers, help identify and prevent billing errors and potential fraud. Contact Administration on Aging, 330 Independence Ave., SW, Washington, DC 20201; 202-619-0724; Fax: 202-260-1012; www.aoa.gov/smp.

Help Special Needs Children

Family Friends volunteers are men and women over 55 years of age who are interested in working with children who have special needs. They advocate for children who need a helping and loving hand. Family Friends volunteers are recruited from the community at large. There are no income guidelines for either volunteers or families. Volunteers receive extensive training. Contact The National Center for Family Friends, Council on Aging, 300 D Street SW, Suite 801, Washington, DC 20024; 202-479-6672; www.family-friends.org.

Seniors Work One-On-One With School Kids

Experience Corps places a critical mass of older adult volunteers in schools and youth-focused organizations in their communities. Among their many roles, the older adults work one-on-one with young children, create before- and after-school programs, get parents more fully involved in schools, and serve as advocates for children and their needs in the larger community. The program is available in the following cities: Baltimore, Boston, Cleveland, Indianapolis, Kansas City, Minneapolis, New York City, Philadelphia, Port Arthur, TX, Portland, San Francisco, Tucson, and Washington, DC. Contact Experience Corps, 2120 L Street NW, Suite 400, Washington, DC 20037; 202-478-6190; www.experiencecorps.org.

AARP Needs You

You can fill out an interest form online which will help AARP identify volunteer opportunities for you. You can also find out information on the web sites message boards on volunteering.

Grief and Loss Program: AARP uses volunteers to offer one-to-one peer outreach including online support.

Tax-Aide Needs You: Volunteers assist with AARP's free, volunteer-run tax counseling service.

Driver Safety Program: The AARP Driver Safety Program is taught and administered by a nationwide network of AARP-trained volunteers. Volunteer positions include instructors, coordinators, trainers and telephone coordinators. Contact American Association of Retired Persons (AARP), 601 E. Street NW, Washington, DC 20049; 888-OUR-AARP; www.aarp.org.

Do you want to travel to Australia or Brazil?
Amizade encourages intercultural exploration and understanding through service –learning and volunteer programs throughout the world. Seniors are welcomed to participate in either Amizade's short or long-term programs. There is a program contribution for room and board and transportation during the program. In addition, volunteers are responsible for the costs of travel to and from the program site and some other travel costs. Contact Amizade Global Service-Learning and Volunteer Programs, P.O. Box 110107, Pittsburgh, PA 15232; 888-973-4443; 412-441-6655; www.amizade.org.

Business Types Can Travel Overseas For FREE
IESC is an economic development organization that recruits volunteers with technical, managerial and professional backgrounds. These volunteer experts use their knowledge to assist entrepreneurs, businesses, business support organizations, government agencies and non-government agencies. Economy air fare and specified travel related expenses, such as immunizations and visas, are covered. Volunteers receive a per diem set by the U.S. government for meals and housing. In most cases, volunteers stay in quality hotels or they may stay in a client's guest quarters. If an overseas project lasts 28 days or longer, IESC may pay expenses to enable a spouse to accompany a volunteer. Certain restrictions apply and spouses are expected to volunteer locally. Volunteers work in countries of the developing world and in emerging democracies. Contact International Executive Service Corps, 901 15th Street NW, Suite 1010, Washington, DC 20005; 202-326-0280; www.iesc.org

Volunteers Down The Street
The National Retiree Volunteer Coalition forms a partnership between retirees, their former employers and their communities. Contact Volunteers of America, 1660 Duke Street, Alexandria, VA 22314; 800-899-0089; 703-341-5000; www.volunteersofamerica.org .

Help A Local Nonprofit Thrive
Volunteers are successful senior-level executives or professionals who are willing to contribute their time, business experience and expertise to help nonprofit organizations. Contact National Executive Service Corps, 120 Wall Street, 16th Floor, New York, NY 10005; 212-269-1234; www.nesc.org.

Help ½ Million Disaster Victim or One Child Who Needs Blood
The Red Cross depends on volunteers, who make-up about 97% of their total work force, to help with all types of disasters. Contact your local Red Cross organization to volunteer. Contact American Red Cross National Headquarters, 2025 E. Street, NW, Washington, DC 20006; 202-303-4498; www.redcross.org.

Be A Mentor To A Third Grade Child
AARP Big Brothers and Big Sisters volunteers meet one-on-one with their third-grade "Littles" once a week in schools for about an hour to engage in activities that promote learning and academic success. Volunteers often participate in peer sharing following time with their "Littles". Contact Big Brothers Big Sisters National Office, 230 North 13th Street, Philadelphia, PA 19107; 215-567-7000; www.bbbsa.org.

Advocate For The Rights Of Seniors

Are you interested in the government and especially issues having to do with seniors? The Seniors Coalition is a nonprofit, non-partisan organization that represents the concerns of senior citizens at both state and federal levels. This group is for those interested in volunteering for legislative issues. Contact The Seniors Coalition, 4401 Fair Lakes Court, Suite 210, Fairfax, VA 22033; 800-325-9891; 703-631-4211; www.senior.org.

Travel The Globe While You Save It

Global Volunteers offers "volunteer vacations" abroad and USA volunteer programs. Both programs offer volunteers the opportunity to live and work with local people on life-affirming community development projects for one, two or three weeks. Volunteers are responsible for program tuition. Contact Global Volunteers, 375 East Little Canada Road, St. Paul, MN 55117-1628; 651-407-6100; 800-487-1074; www.globalvolunteers.org.

Learn To Toot... Become A Tutor

OASIS is a national nonprofit educational organization designed to enhance the quality of life for mature adults, including volunteer opportunities. Programs are available throughout the country in many communities. Check the web site to see if there is a program in your area.

OASIS Tutoring: If you have one hour a week and enjoy working with young children this program may be for you. You will receive 12 hours of initial training, and continuing support through regular tutor meetings.

Science Across the Generations: This hands-on program emphasizes science, math and technology and is available in ten cities around the country. Contact The OASIS Institute, 7710 Carondelet Avenue, St. Louis, MO 63105; 314-862-2933; Fax: 314-862-2149; www.oasisnet.org.

You Can Talk To The Animals In Hawaii, Idaho, Utah, etc.

America's wild lands are for all Americans, and Wilderness Volunteers help to maintain their beauty. This nonprofit organization offers a variety of trips throughout the US. Volunteers must be physically fit. Trips are ranked by physical activity ratings. The cost for the 6 or 7 day trips is around $240 and covers all the basics. It is the volunteer's responsibility to provide transportation to and from the site. Contact Wilderness Volunteers, P.O. Box 22292, Flagstaff, AZ 86002; 928-556-0038; www.wildernessvlunteers.org.

Teach Economics To Budding Entrepreneurs

Junior Achievement uses hands-on experiences to help young people understand the economics of life in the school setting. Depending on the grade level your volunteer commitment could vary from a single school day to a weekly one hour visit for ten weeks. Volunteers lead classes in understanding the Junior Achievement curriculum. Contact Junior Achievement, One Education Way, Colorado Springs, CO 80906; 719-540-8000; Fax: 719-540-6299; www.ja.org.

Teach Seniors Internet Skills

CyberSeniors.org Learning Centers present computer classes designed to meet the needs of adults 50 and over at low or no cost. The Learning Center are managed and taught by volunteers of all ages. Centers are currently open in Maine, Virginia, Pennsylvania, Vermont, New Hampshire, Massachusetts,

Oregon, South Carolina, and Texas. New Centers are opening across the country, so check the web site to see if a Center is in operation near you. Contact CyberSeniors.org, One Monument Way, Portland, ME 04101; 888-676-6622; www.cyberseniors.org.

Help Build A Home For Others

Do you love to build and work with your hands? Then Habitat may be the place for your volunteer hours. Sites are available throughout the country. You can search online for projects in your area. Contact Habitat for Humanity, 121 Habitat Street, Americus, GA 31709-3498; 229-924-6935; www.habitat.org.

Ring A Bell For Santa

From ringing the bell at Christmas to working with young people in character-building activities, Salvation Army volunteers provide valuable service in every Salvation Army program. You can check online or your local phone book for a location in your area. Contact The Salvation Army National Headquarters, 615 Slaters Lane, P.O. Box 269, Alexandria, VA 22313; www.salvationarmyusa.org.

Fix Computers To Give Away For Free

Volunteers take in donated computer equipment and refurbish, repair and combine them to make useful working systems. The systems are then given away, free of charge, to nonprofit organizations in the Cleveland area only. Contact Computers Assisting People, Inc., 3150 Payne Avenue, Cleveland, OH 44114; 216-781-4131; www.capinc.org.

Help Someone Learn To Read

If you love literature and books, then The Loft is a great place for you to volunteer. Volunteers can work at events, support office staff, or fund raise. This is for the Minneapolis area only. See what your local area may have to offer. Contact The Loft Literacy Center, 1011 Washington Avenue South, Suite 200, Open Book, Minneapolis, MN 55415; 612-215-2575; Fax: 612-215-2576; www.loft.org/volunteer.htm.

Ride The Rapids In The Wilderness

Wilderness Inquiry is for you if you love the outdoors. Wilderness Inquiry is a nonprofit organization that focuses on getting people from all walks of life to experience the outdoors. Wilderness Inquiry has many opportunities for volunteers from office work to assisting with a paddling class. This is for the Minneapolis area only. See what local organizations in your area may have to offer. Contact Wilderness Inquiry, 808 14th Avenue SE, Minneapolis, MN 55414-1516; 800-728-0719; 612-676-9400; Fax: 612-676-9401; www.wildernessinquiry.org.

Honorary Grandparents Get Reduced Rents

Generations of Hope, a nonprofit organization, is an innovative program to help families of foster children through intergenerational neighborhoods. There are approximately 60 older adults living and volunteering in the community. These seniors serve as "honorary grandparents" and are required to volunteer at least six hours a week in exchange for reduced rent of $350 or less per month for a three-bedroom, air-conditioned apartment. This is for the Rantoul, Illinois area only. Check with organizations in your area to see what they may have to offer. Contact Generations of Hope, 1530 Fairway Drive, Rantoul, IL 61866; 217-893-4673; Fax: 217-893-3126; www.generationsofhope.org.

They May Call You Doctor
TMC is a non-profit community hospital with volunteer opportunities for seniors.

Health Care Information Center: Seniors help customers access information in the reference center.
TMC Auxiliary: The TMC Auxiliary provides supplemental services to hospital personnel in almost every aspect of the hospital. This is for the Tucson, Arizona area only. Contact your local hospital to see how you can volunteer. Contact TMC HealthCare, 5301 E. Grant Road, Tucson, AZ 85712; 520-327-5461; www.tmcaz.com.

Give Back Doing Community Social Work
There are many opportunities, in numerous services across Minnesota. They include one-on-one relationships, group work projects, disaster relief, internships, helping provide needed goods and services, serving on advisory boards, fund raising and advocacy work. Descriptions of specific opportunities are listed by geographical area on their web site. This is for Minnesota only. Contact Social Services agencies in your area to see how you can be of assistance. Contact Lutheran Social Service of Minnesota, 2485 Como Avenue, St. Paul, MN 55108; 651-642-5990; 800-582-5260; www.lssmn.org/volunteers.

Fight For Seniors In Long Term Care Facilities
Volunteer Ombudsmen identify, investigate and resolve complaints by or on behalf of facility residents. You complete a certification process and then are assigned to weekly visits to one long-term care facility. Ombudsmen programs can be found throughout the country. Contact The Senior Source Ombudsmen Program, 1215 Skiles Street, Dallas, TX 75204; 214-823-5700; Fax: 214-826-2441; www.theseniorsource.org.

Make The Air Safer For Seniors EPA
The Environmental Protection Agency is committed to all Americans, including seniors. The Aging Initiative's mission is to protect the health of older persons when it comes to environmental hazards. An important part of the Aging Initiative is to encourage volunteerism among older adults in their communities. There are many programs across the country that can make a difference to our environment. Contact: US Environmental Protection Agency, Aging Initiative, 1200 Pennsylvania Avenue NW, Mail Code 1107A, Rom 2512 Ariel Rios North, Washington, DC 20460, 202-564-2188; www.epa.gov/aging/.

Light Up the Day of a Senior Shut-In
Senior Service America is a nonprofit organization that can help you with training if you are a senior. The Senior AIDES Program offers training and educational opportunities. One program in Ohio trains Senior AIDES to talk to senior shut-ins through daily telephone calls. There are many other programs throughout the country. Contact: Senior Service America, 8403 Colesville Road, Suite 1200, Silver Springs, MD 20910; 301-578-8900; www.seniorserviceamerica.org.

Local SeniorCorps Offers Money And Benefits
Senior Corps taps the skills, talents, and experience of more than 500,000 Americans age 55 and older to meet a wide range of community challenges through the following four programs. You can search for volunteer opportunities in your community online at www.joinseniorservice.org. SeniorCorps is part of

The Corporation for National & Community Service which provides opportunities for Americans to serve their communities and country. Contact Corporation for National & Community Service, 1201 New York Avenue, NW, Washington, DC 20525; 202-606-5000; 800-424-8867; www.cns.gov.

***RSVP (Retired and Senior Volunteer Program)**: RSVP is open to people age 55 and over. Grants are available to sponsoring organizations to help train volunteers and for reimbursement of costs incurred during service. Projects recruit seniors to serve from a few hours a month to almost full time; the average commitment is four hours a week. RSVP volunteers serve in a diverse range of nonprofit organizations, public agencies, and faith-based groups. Among other activities, they mentor at-risk youth, organize neighborhood watch programs, test drinking water for contaminants, teach English to immigrants, and lend their business skills to community groups that provide critical social services.

***Foster Grandparent Program (FGP)**: The Foster Grandparent Program is open to people age 60 and over with limited incomes. All applicants undergo a background check and a telephone interview, as well as pre-service and in-service training. Foster Grandparents serve 20 hours a week. For their service, Foster Grandparents receive $2.65 an hour (tax free), reimbursement for transportation, meals during service, annual physical examinations, and accident and liability insurance while on duty. Local nonprofit organizations and public agencies receive grants to sponsor and operate local Foster Grandparent projects. Foster Grandparents serve as mentors, tutors, and caregivers for at-risk children and youth with special needs through a variety of community organizations, including schools, hospitals, drug treatment facilities, correctional institutions, and Head Start and day-care centers.

***Senior Companions (SCP)**: The Senior Companion Program is open to healthy individuals age 60 and over with limited incomes. All applicants undergo a background check and a telephone interview, as well as pre-service and in-service training on such topics as Alzheimer's disease, diabetes, and issues related to mental health. Senior Companions serve 20 hours a week. For their service, Senior Companions receive $2.65 an hour (tax free), reimbursement for transportation, annual physical examinations, meals, and accident and liability insurance during service. Senior Companions serve one-on-one with the frail elderly and other homebound persons who have difficulty completing everyday tasks. They assist with grocery shopping, bill paying, and transportation to medical appointments, and they alert doctors and family members to potential problems. Senior Companions also provide short periods of relief to primary caregivers.

***Ask A Friend**: Ask a Friend is a nationwide campaign developed by Senior Corps, which taps the experience, skills and talents of volunteers over 55 to meet many community challenges. Contact Ask a Friend to find volunteer opportunities in your community. Contact 800-424-8867; www.volunteerfriends.org.

Corporation for National & Community Service State Offices

Alabama
Corporation for National & Community Service
Medical Forum
950 22nd Street, North, Suite 428
Birmingham, AL 35203
205-731-0030
Fax: 205/731-0031
Email: AL@cns.gov

Alaska
Corporation for National & Community Service
Jackson Federal Building
915 Second Avenue
Suite 3190
Seattle, WA 98174-1103
206-220-7736
Fax: 206-553-4415
Email:AK@cns.gov

Arkansas
Corporation for National & Community Service
Federal Building, Room 2506
700 West Capitol Street
Little Rock, AR 72201
501-324-5234
Fax: 501-324-6949
Email:AR@cns.gov

Arizona
Corporation for National & Community Service
522 North Central, Room 205A
Phoenix, AZ 85004-2190
602-379-4825
Fax: 602-379-4030
Email: AZ@cns.gov

California
Corporation for National & Community Service
11150 West Olympic Boulevard, Suite 670
Los Angeles, CA 90036
310-235-7709
Fax: 310-235-7422
Email: CA@cns.gov

Colorado
Corporation for National & Community Service
999 Eighteenth Street
Suite 1440 South
Denver, CO 80202
303-312-7953
Fax: 303-312-7954
Email: CO@cns.gov

Connecticut
Corporation for National & Community Service
280 Trumbull Street
Hartford, CT 06103-3510
860-240-3237
Fax: 860-240-3238
Email: CT@cns.gov

District of Columbia
Corporation for National & Community Service
1201 New York Avenue, N.W., Suite 9215
Washington, DC 20525
202-606-5000, x485
Fax: 202-565-2789
Email: DC@cns.gov

Delaware/Maryland
Corporation for National & Community Service
Fallon Federal Building
31 Hopkins Plaza, Suite 400-B
Baltimore, MD 21201
410-962-4443
Fax: 410/962-3201
Email: MD@cns.gov

Florida
Corporation for National & Community Service
3165 McCrory Street, Suite 115
Orlando, FL 32803-3750
407-648-6117
Fax: 407-648-6116
Email: FL@cns.gov

Georgia
Corporation for National & Community Service
75 Piedmont Avenue, N.E.
Room 902
Atlanta, GA 30303-2587
404-331-4646
Fax: 404-331-2898
Email: GA@cns.gov

Hawaii
Corporation for National & Community Service
300 Ala Moana Boulevard, Room 6213
Honolulu, HI 96850-0001
808-541-2832
Fax: 808/541-3603
Email: HI@cns.gov

Idaho
Corporation for National & Community Service
304 North 8th Street, Room 344

Boise, ID 83702-5835
208-334-1707
Fax: 208-334-1421
Email: ID@cns.gov

Illinois
Corporation for National & Community Service
77 West Jackson Boulevard
Suite 442, Room 457
Chicago, IL 60604-3511
312-353-3622
Fax: 312-353-6496
Email: IL@cns.gov

Indiana
Corporation for National & Community Service
46 East Ohio Street, Room 226
Indianapolis, IN 46204-4317
317-226-6724
Fax: 317-226-5437
Email: IN@cns.gov

Iowa
Corporation for National & Community Service
Federal Building, Room 917
210 Walnut Street
Des Moines, IA 50309-2195
515-284-4816
Fax: 515-284-6640
Email: IA@cns.gov

Kansas
Corporation for National & Community Service
444 S.E. Quincy, Room 260
Topeka, KS 66683-3572
785-295-2540
Fax: 785-295-2596
Email: KS@cns.gov

Kentucky
Corporation for National & Community Service
600 Martin Luther King Place, Room 190
Louisville, KY 40202-2230
502-582-6384
Fax: 502-582-6386
Email: KY@cns.gov

Louisiana
Corporation for National & Community Service
707 Florida Street
Suite 316
Baton Rouge, LA 70801
225-389-0473
Fax: 225-389-0510
Email: LA@cns.gov

Maine/New Hampshire/Vermont
Corporation for National & Community Service
J.C. Cleveland Federal Building
55 Pleasant Street, Room 1501
Concord, NH 03301
603-225-1450
Fax: 603-225-1459
Email: NH@cns.gov

Massachusetts
Corporation for National & Community Service
10 Causeway Street, Room 473
Boston, MA 02222-1038
617-565-7018
Fax: 617/565-7011
Email: MA@cns.gov

Maryland/Delaware
Corporation for National & Community Service
Fallon Federal Building
31 Hopkins Plaza, Suite 400-B
Baltimore, MD 21201
410-962-4443
Fax: 410-962-3201
Email: MD@cns.gov

Michigan
Corporation for National & Community Service
211 West Fort Street, Suite 1408
Detroit, MI 48226-2799
313-226-7848
Fax: 313-226-2557
Email: MI@cns.gov

Minnesota
Corporation for National & Community Service
431 South 7th Street, Room 2480
Minneapolis, MN 55415-1854
612-334-4083
Fax: 612-334-4084
Email: MN@cns.gov

Missouri
Corporation for National & Community Service
801 Walnut Street, Suite 504
Kansas City, MO 64106-2009
816-374-6300
Fax: 816-374-6305
Email: MO@cns.gov

Mississippi
Corporation for National & Community Service
100 West Capitol Street
Room 1005A
Jackson, MS 39269-1092

601-965-5664
Fax: 601-965-4617
Email: MS@cns.gov

Montana
Corporation for National & Community Service
208 North Montana Avenue, Suite 206
Helena, MT 59601-3837
406-449-5404
Fax: 406-449-5412
Email: MT@cns.gov

Nebraska
Corporation for National & Community Service
100 Centennial Mall North, Room 156
Lincoln, NE 68508-3896
402-437-5493
Fax: 402-437-5495
Email: NE@cns.gov

Nevada
Corporation for National & Community Service
400 South Virginia Street, Suite 548
Reno, NV 89501
775-686-5872
Fax: 775-686-5877
Email: NV@cns.gov

New Hampshire/Vermont/Maine
Corporation for National & Community Service
J.C. Cleveland Federal Building
55 Pleasant Street, Suite 1501
Concord, NH 03301
603-226-7780
Fax: 603-225-1459
Email: NH@cns.gov

New Jersey
Corporation for National & Community Service
44 South Clinton, Suite 312
Trenton, NJ 08609-1507
609-989-0474
Fax: 609-989-2304
Email: NJ@cns.gov

New Mexico
Corporation for National & Community Service
120 S. Federal Place, Room 315
Sante Fe, NM 87501-2026
505-988-6577
Fax: 505-988-6661
Email: NM@cns.gov

New York
Corporation for National & Community Service
Leo O'Brien Federal Bldg.
1 Clinton Square, Suite 900
Albany, NY 12207
518-431-4150
Fax: 518-431-4154
Email: NY@cns.gov

North Carolina
Corporation for National & Community Service
Federal Bldg, PO Century Station
300 Fayetteville Street Mall, R. 414
Raleigh, NC 27601
919-856-4731
Fax: 919-856-4738
Email: NC@cns.gov

North Dakota
Corporation for National & Community Service
225 S. Pierre Street, Room 225
Pierre, SD 57501-2452
605-224-5996
Fax: 605-224-9201
Email: SD@cns.gov

Ohio
Corporation for National & Community Service
51 North High Street, Suite 800
Columbus, OH 43215
614-469-7441
Fax: 614-469-2125
Email: OH@cns.gov

Oklahoma
Corporation for National & Community Service
215 Dean A. McGee, Suite 324
Oklahoma City, OK 73102
405-231-5201
Fax: 405-231-4329
Email: OK@cns.gov

Oregon
Corporation for National & Community Service
2010 Lloyd Center
Portland, OR 97232
503-231-2103
Fax: 503-231-2106
Email: OR@cns.gov

Pennsylvania
Corporation for National & Community Service
Robert N.C. Nix Federal Building
900 Market Street, Room 229
P.O. Box 04121
Philadelphia, PA 19107
215-597-2806

Fax: 215-597-2807
Email: PA@cns.gov

Puerto Rico/Virgin Islands
Corporation for National & Community Service
150 Carlos Chardon Avenue, Suite 662
San Juan, PR 00918-1737
787-766-5314
Fax: 787-766-5189
Email: PR@cns.gov

Rhode Island
Corporation for National & Community Service
400 Westminster Street, Room 203
Providence, RI 02903
401-528-5426
Fax: 401-528-5220
Email: RI@cns.gov

South Carolina
Corporation for National & Community Service
1835 Assembly Street, Suite 872
Columbia, SC 29201-2430
803-765-5771
Fax: 803-765-5777
Email: SC@cns.gov

South Dakota/North Dakota
Corporation for National & Community Service
225 S. Pierre Street, Room 225
Pierre, SD 57501-2452
605-224-5996
Fax: 605-224-9201
Email: SD@cns.gov

Tennessee
Corporation for National & Community Service
233 Cumberland Bend Drive
Nashville, TN 37228
615-736-5561
Fax: 615-736-7937
Email: TN@cns.gov

Texas
Corporation for National & Community Service
300 East 8th Street, Suite G-100
Austin, TX 78701-3220
512-916-5671
Fax: 512-916-5806
Email: TX@cns.gov

Utah
Corporation for National & Community Service
125 South State Street, Suite 8416
Salt Lake City, UT 84138
801-524-5411
Fax: 801-524-3599
Email: UT@cns.gov

Virginia
Corporation for National & Community Service
400 North 8th Street, Suite 446
P. O. Box 10066
Richmond, VA 23240-1832
804-771-2197
Fax: 804-771-2157
Email: VA@cns.gov

Vermont/New Hampshire/Maine
Corporation for National & Community Service
J.C. Cleveland Federal Building
55 Pleasant Street, Suite 1501
Concord, NH 03301
603-225-1450
Fax: 603-225-1459
Email: NH@cns.gov

Washington
Corporation for National & Community Service
Jackson Federal Bldg.
915 Second Ave., Suite 3190
Seattle, WA 98174-1103
206-220-7745
Fax: 206-553-4415
Email: WA@cns.gov

West Virginia
Corporation for National & Community Service
10 Hale Street, Suite 203
Charleston, WV 25301-1409
304-347-5246
Fax: 304-347-5464
Email: WV@cns.gov

Wisconsin
Corporation for National & Community Service
310 West Wisconsin Avenue, Room 1240
Milwaukee, WI 53203-2211
414-297-1118
Fax: 414-297-1863
Email: WI@cns.gov

Wyoming
Corporation for National & Community Service
308 West 21st Street, Room 203
Cheyenne, WY 82001-3663
307-772-2385
Fax: 307-772-2389
Email: WY@cns.gov

State Commissions

Most states have a Governor appointed commission for national and community service for state and local programs.

Alabama
Governor's Office of Faith Based and Community Initiatives
Executive Director
RSA Union Building
Suite 134
100 North Union Street
Montgomery, AL 36130-9534
334-242-7110
Fax: 334-242-2885
www.goncs.state.al.us

Alaska
Alaska State Community Service Commission
550 W. 7th Ave., Suite 1770
Anchorage, AK 99501
907-269-4659
Fax: 907-269-5666
www.dced.state.ak.us/ascsc/home.htm

Arizona
Arizona Governor's Commission on Service & Volunteerism
1700 West Washington, Suite 101
Phoenix, AZ 85007-2806
602-542-3489
Fax: 602-542-3423
www.volunteerarizona.org

Arkansas
Arkansas Commission on National and Community Service
700 South Main Street
P.O. Box 1437, Slot S230
Little Rock, AR 72201-4608
501-682-7540
Fax: 501-682-1623
www.state.ar.us/dhs/adov/ns_programs.html

California
California Service Corps
1110 K Street, Suite 210
Sacramento, CA 95814-3905
916-323-7646
Fax: 916-323-3227
www.csc.ca.gov

Colorado
Governor's Commission on Community Service
1059 Alton Way
Building 758, Suite 253
Denver, CO 80230
303-595-1541
Fax: 702-904-9738
www.gcncs.cccs.edu

Connecticut
Connecticut Commission on National and Community Service
Department of Higher Education
61 Woodland Street
Hartford, CT 06105-2326
860-947-1827
Fax: 860-947-1310
www.ctdhe.org/ccncs

District of Columbia
441 4th Street, N.W., Suite 1040S
Washington, DC 20001
202-727-7925
Fax: 202-727-3765
www.cncs.dc.gov

Delaware
Delaware Community Service Commission
Charles Debnam Building
Herman Holloway Campus
1901 North Dupont Highway
New Castle, DE 19720-1100
302-255-9881
Fax: 302-255-4462
Email: elisa.diller@state.de.us

Florida
Volunteer Florida
401 S. Monroe St.
Tallahassee, FL 32399
850-921-5172
Fax: 850-921-5146
www.volunteerflorida.org

Georgia
Commission for Service and Volunteerism
60 Executive Park South, NE
Atlanta, GA 30329-2296
404-327-6844
Fax: 404-327-6848
www.dca.state.ga.us

Hawaii
Commission for National and Community Service
Office of Community Services

2600 Campus Road Room 405
Honolulu, HI 96822-2205
808-956-8145
Fax: 808-956-2950
www.hawaii.edu/americorpshawaii/

Idaho
Serve Idaho
1299 North Orchard Street
Suite 110
Boise, ID 83706-2265
208-658-2000
Fax: 208-327-7470
www.serveidaho.org

Illinois
Commission of volunteerism & Community Service
Illinois Dept of Human Services
623 E. Adams, 1st Floor
Springfield, IL 62701-1614
217-558-2663
Fax: 217-558-2678
www.illinois.gov/volunteer

Indiana
Commission on Community Service and Volunteerism
302 West Washington Street, Room E220
Indianapolis, IN 46204-4701
317-233-4273
Fax: 317-233-5660
www.state.in.us/iccsv

Iowa
Volunteer Iowa
200 East Grand Avenue
Des Moines, IA 50309-1856
515-242-5466
800-308-5987
Fax: 515-242-4809
www.volunteeriowa.org

Kansas
Kanserve
120 SE 10th Avenue
Topeka, KS 66612-1103
785-368-6207
Fax: 785-368-6284
www.kanserve.org

Kentucky
Volunteer Kentucky
275 East Main Street - Mail Stop 3W-C
Frankfort, KY 40621-0001
502-564-7420
800-239-7404
Fax: 502-564-7478
http://volunteerky.ky.gov

Louisiana
Louisiana Serve Commission
263 Third Street, Suite 610-B
Baton Rouge, LA 70801-1306
225-342-2038
Fax: 225-342-0106
www.crt.state.la.us/laserve

Maine
Maine Commission for Community Service
Maine State Planning Office
184 State Street - 38 State House Station
Augusta, ME 04333-0038
207-287-5313
Fax: 207-287-8059
www.state.me.us/spo/mccs/

Maryland
Governor's Office on Service and Volunteerism
300 West Preston Street, Suite 608
Baltimore, MD 21201
410-767-4803
800-321-VOLS
Fax: 410-333-5957
www.gosv.state.md.us

Massachusetts
Massachusetts Service Alliance
100 North Washington Street, 3rd Floor
Boston, MA 02114
617-542-2544 x228
Fax: 617-542-0240
www.msalliance.org

Michigan
Michigan Community Service Commission
1048 Pierpont, Suite #4
Lansing, MI 48913
517-335-4295
Fax: 517-373-4977
www.michigan.gov/mcsc

Minnesota
Serve Minnesota!
431 South 7th Street #2540
Minneapolis, MN 55415
612-333-7740
Fax: 612-333-7758
www.serveminnesota.org

Mississippi
Commission for Volunteer Service

3825 Ridgewood Road, Suite 601
Jackson, MS 39211-6463
601-432-6779
888-353-1793
Fax: 601-432-6790
www.mcvs.org

Missouri
Community Service Commission
Harry S Truman Building, Suite 770
P. O. Box 118
Jefferson City, MO 65102
573-751-7488
877-210-7611
Fax: 573-526-0463
www.movolunteers.org

Montana
Montana Community Services Network
1301 Lockey Avenue, 3rd Floor
P.O. Box 200801
Helena, MT 59620-0801
406-444-5547
Fax: 406-444-4418
http://state.mt.us/mcsn

Nebraska
Volunteer Service Commission
State Capitol, 6th Floor
P.O. Box 98927
Lincoln, NE 68509-8927
800-291-8911
402-471-6225
Fax: 402-471-6286
www.state.ne.us/home/NVSC

Nevada
Commission for National & Community Service
90 North Maine Street #204
Fallon, NV 89406-2956
775-423-1461
888-338-9759
Fax: 775-423-8039
www.americorpsnevada.org

New Hampshire
Volunteer NH!
117 Pleasant Street
Dolloff Building, 4th Floor
Concord, NH 03301-3852
603-271-7200
800-780-8058
Fax: 603-721-7203
www.volunteernh.org

New Jersey
Commission on National & Community Service
225 West State Street
P.O. Box 459
Trenton, NJ 08625-0459
609-633-9627
Fax: 609-777-2939
www.state.nj.us/state/americorps

New Mexico
Commission for Community Volunteerism
3401 Pan American Freeway, NE
Albuquerque, NM 87107-4785
505-841-4837
Fax: 505-841-4839
www.newmexserve.org

New York
Commission on National and Community Service
52 Washington Street
Capital View Office Park
Rensselaer, NY 12144-2796
518-473-8882
Fax: 518-402-3817
www.nyscncs.org

North Carolina
Commission on Volunteerism & Community Service
0312 Mail Service Center
116 West Jones Street
Raleigh, NC 27699-0312
919-715-3470
800-820-4483 (NC only)
Fax: 919-715-8677
www.volunteernc.org

North Dakota
Workforce Development
State Commission on National and Community Service
400 E. Broadway, Suite 50
P.O. Box 2057
Bismarck, ND 58502-2057
701-328-5345
Fax: 701-328-5320
www.ndcommerce.com

Ohio
Ohio Community Service Council
51 North High Street, Suite 800
Columbus, OH 43215
614-728-2916
Fax: 614-728-2921
www.serveohio.org

Oklahoma
Oklahoma Community Service Commission
505 NE 13th Street
Oklahoma City, OK 73104
405-235-7278
Fax: 405-235-7036
www.okamericorps.com

Oregon
Oregon Volunteers!
PSU/CSC 850 ATT
P.O. Box 751
1600 SW Fourth Avenue, Suite 850
Portland, OR 97201-5522
503-725-5903
888-353-4483
Fax: 503-725-8335
www.nwrel.org/ecc/americorps/states/oregon

Pennsylvania
PPennSERVE
1306 Labor and Industry Building
7th and Forster Streets
Harrisburg, PA 17120
717-787-1971
Fax: 717-705-4215
www.dli.state.pa.us/landi/cwp/view.asp?a=143&q=207630

Rhode Island
Service Alliance
143 Prairie Avenue
P.O. Box 72822
Providence, RI 02907
401-331-2298 x15
fax: 401-331-2273
www.riservicealliance.org

South Carolina
Commission on National and Community Service
3710 Landmark Drive, Suite 200
Columbia, SC 29204-4062
803-734-4796
877-349-2258
Fax: 803-734-4825
www.servicesc.org

South Dakota
There is no Commission on Service in South Dakota. You can contact your local Corporation for National and Community Service Office.
225 S. Pierre Street, Room 225
Pierre, SD 57501-2452
605-224-5996
Fax: 605-224-9201
Email: SD@cns.gov

Tennessee
Commission on National and Community Service
312 8th Avenue North, Suite 1200
Nashville, TN 37243-0001
615-532-9416
Fax: 615-532-6950
www.state.tn.us/finance/rds/tcncs.html

Texas
One Star Foundation
1700 North Congress
P.O. Box 13385
Austin, TX 78701-3385
512-463-1814
800-489-2627
Fax: 512-463-1861
www.onestarfoundation.org

Utah
Commission on Volunteers
527 West 400 North, Suite 3
Orem, UT 84057-1916
801-764-0704
Fax: 801-764-9502
http://volunteers.utah.gov

Vermont
Vermont Commission on National and Community Service
109 State Street
Montpelier, VT 05609-4801
802-828-4982
Fax: 802-828-4988
www.state.vt.us/cncs

Virginia
Commission for National and Community Service
7 North Eighth Street, 5th Floor
Richmond, VA 23219
804-726-7064
800-638-3839
Fax: 804-726-7024
www.vaservice.org

Washington
Commission for National and Community Service
P.O. Box 43113
Olympia, WA 98504-3113
360-902-0656
Fax: 360-586-3964
www.ofm.wa.gov/servewa/

West Virginia
Commission for National & Community Service
601 Delaware Avenue
Charleston, WV 25302

304-558-0111
800-WV-HELPS
Fax: 304-558-0101
www.volunteerwv.org

Wisconsin
National and Community Service Board
1 West Wilson Street - Room 456
Madison, WI 53703
Mailing Address:
P.O. Box 8916
Madison, WI 53708
608-261-6716
800-620-8307
Fax: 608-266-9313
www.servewisconsin.org/

Wyoming
Workforce Development
122 W. 25th Street
Herschler Building, 2E
Cheyenne, WY 82002
307-777-8650
Fax: 307-777-5857
www.wyomingworkforce.org/

Travel Opportunities

Now is the time to hit the open road. You are free of the 9-5 grind, and can follow your heart to explore our country or the world! We have attempted to hit the high points to make sure you get the discounts, information, and free travel opportunities that are available to you. Some good starting places include:

1) ***Catalog of Federal Domestic Assistance***: This catalog contains all the money programs the federal government has to offer. You can look at the catalog at your local library or you can look online at www.cfda.gov and search by keyword.
2) ***State Tourism Offices***: Every state has a tourism office that can provide information on sights to see, discounts and coupons available, and more. In addition don't forget to ask about local tourism boards that will have specific information regarding their town and surrounding areas. You can locate both of these by calling information or by going online at www.govengine.com and clicking on a state.
3) ***The U.S. Department of State***: The Bureau of Consular Affairs can help with any question or concern you have about overseas travel and can refer you to particular offices if you need help regarding appropriate shots and immunizations, VISA questions, emergency services, and more. You may contact them at Bureau of Consular Affairs, U.S. Department of State, 2201 C Street NW, Washington, DC 20520; 202-647-5225; http://travel.state.gov/.

Free Research Before You Go Overseas

Going to a country where you've never been before? *Background Notes on the Countries of the World* is a series of short, factual pamphlets with information on the country's land, people, history, government, political conditions, economy, foreign relations, and U.S. Foreign policy. Each pamphlet also includes a factual profile, brief travel notes, a country map, and a reading list. Contact Public Affairs Bureau, U.S. Department of State, 2201 C St., NW, Washington, DC 20520; 202-647-4000; www.state.gov/r/pa/ei/bgn/.

Go Here When You're In Trouble In A Foreign Land

Are you overseas and need medical assistance? What about if you are arrested or someone has died in another country? The Department of State has the Office of Citizens Services that can answer all your questions and direct you to places for further assistance. They have lists of doctors and lawyers located in the various countries that can help you, along with a multitude of other resources to help those in crisis in a foreign land. For more information contact The Office of Citizens Services, U.S. Department of State, Room 4811, 2201 C St., NW, Washington, DC 20520; 202-647-5225; http://travel.state.gov.

Find Out If That Country Is Safe

Before you pack your bags, everyone should check out the latest news on the country or countries they are planning to visit. Consular Information Sheets are available for every country of the world. They include information as to the location of the U.S. Embassy or Consulate in the country, unusual practices, health conditions, currency, crime, and much more. Travel Warnings are issued when the State Department decides based on all relevant information to recommend that Americans avoid travel to a certain country. For more information contact The Office of Citizens Services, U.S. Department of State, Room 4817 NS, 2201 C St., NW, Washington, DC 20520; 202-647-5225; http://travel.state.gov/travel.

Some Nighttime Reading

Know before you go is a good motto to live by when traveling. The Department of State has put together a series of travel publications that provide good tips for travelers to various countries, as well as general information about traveling overseas. These are available for sale at a minimal cost or you can view them for free online. Publications include:

U.S. Consuls Help Americans Abroad
Crisis Abroad
Overseas Citizens Services
Travel Warning on Drugs Abroad
Sending Money Overseas to a U.S. Citizen in an Emergency
Your Trip Abroad
A Safe Trip Abroad
Tips for Older Americans
Tips for Students
Tips for Residing Abroad
Tips for Travelers to Canada
Tips for Travelers to the Caribbean
Tips for Travelers to Central and South America
Tips for Travelers to Mexico
Tips for Business Travelers to Nigeria
Nigerian Advance Fee Fraud
Tips for Travelers to Sub-Saharan Africa
Tips for Travelers to the Middle East and North Africa
Tips for Travelers to the Middle East and North Africa
Tips for Travelers to Russia
Tips for Travelers to China
Tips for Travelers to South Asia
Foreign Entry Requirements
Human Immunodeficient Virus (HIV) Testing Requirements for Entry to Foreign Countries
Medical Information For Americans Traveling Abroad
Teaching English in Korea

To order your copies, contact Superintendent of Documents, P.O.371954, Pittsburgh, PA 15250; 202-512-1800; http:// travel.state.gov/travel/tips/brochures/brochures_1231.html.

Today's Travelers Know About Counterterrorism

Office of Counterterrorism coordinates all U.S. Government efforts to improve counterterrorism cooperation with foreign governments. The coordinator chairs the Interagency Working Group on Counterterrorism and the State Department's terrorism task forces to coordinate responses to major international terrorist incidents that are in progress. The coordinator has primary responsibility for developing, coordinating, and implementing American counterterrorism policy.

The U.S. Counterterrorism Policy is: First, make no concessions to terrorists and strike no deals; second, bring terrorists to justice for their crimes; third, isolate and apply pressure on states that sponsor terrorism to force them to change their behavior; and fourth, bolster the counterterrorism capabilities of those countries that work with the U.S. and require assistance. You can also view their annual publication Patterns of Global Terrorism on their website. For more information contact, Office of the Coordinator for Counterterrorism, Office of Public Affairs, Room 2507, Department of State, 2201 C St., NW, Washington, DC 20520; www.state.gov/s/ct/.

Overseas Security

The Overseas Security Advisory Council (OSAC) was established in 1985 by the U.S. Department of State to foster the exchange of security related information between the U.S. Government and American private sector operating abroad. This has helped the American private sector and colleges and universities protect their investments and their personnel abroad. The OSAC publish a series of publications, including:

Security Guidelines for American Families Living Abroad
Security Guidelines for American Enterprises Abroad
Emergency Planning Guidelines for American Businesses Abroad
Security Awareness Overseas
Guidelines for Protecting U.S. Business Information Overseas
Personal Security Guidelines for the American Business Traveler Overseas
Security Guidelines for Children Living Abroad

For more information contact Overseas Security Advisory Council, Bureau of Diplomatic Security, U.S. Department of State, Washington, DC 20522; 571-345-2223; www.ds-osac.org/.

Help From Dept of Ed To Learn Overseas

U.S. Network for Education Information was created in the fall of 1996 as a national information and referral service to assist American educators, students, and parents with access to reliable information about international education and to provide basic information and referral contacts to resources within U.S. education. The United States Information Service (USIS) administers a worldwide network of overseas Educational Advising Centers (EACs) whose mission is to help persons and organizations in a particular country who are interested in education in the United States. While the main work of these Centers consists in advising local nationals, they can also provide information and assistance to Americans living or working within the areas that they serve. The website has links to study abroad programs, and for teachers interested in teaching overseas. Contact U.S. Network for Education Information, National Library of Education, 400 Maryland Ave., SW, Washington, DC 20202; 800-424-1616; www.ed.gov/about/offices/ list/ous/international/usnei/edlite-index.html.

Free Travel On A Research Ship

Teachers from elementary to college can climb aboard a NOAA research and survey ship to work under the tutelage of knowledgeable scientists and crew. Teachers can gain first hand knowledge to help enrich their classrooms. Teachers may choose from one of 18 ships that conduct a variety of scientific research.

NOAA-Marine Operations Center, Pacific, 1801 Fairview Avenue, E, Seattle, WA 98102-3767; 206-553-2633; www.tas.noaa.gov/.

Take Your Arts and Crafts To Other Countries

Many state arts councils support travel, exhibitions and performances throughout the state, region, or even overseas. Illinois has an Access Program which provides funds to bring art to communities normally deprived of performances. They also have money for Touring Art Groups. Most states have funds to help bring art to rural areas or to groups with minimal access. To see what your state has to offer, contact your state Arts Council in your state capitol. If you have trouble locating it, you can call your state operator at 411, or check online at www.govengine.gov. Nonprofit arts organizations may be able to access travel funds by applying for a National Endowment for the Arts grants. Contact National Endowment for the Arts, 1100 Pennsylvania Ave., NW, Washington, DC 20506; 202-682-5400; http://arts.endow.gov.

Get Paid To Take Your Work Overseas

Get paid to represent America at a conference in India for 2 weeks, or take your jazz group to tour Japan. These programs are part of the activities at the U.S. Department of State's Office of Citizen Exchanges. The Office manages professional, youth and cultural program exchanges. Grants are awarded to American participants or nonprofit organizations, but individuals are encouraged to have foreign co-sponsors. Cultural exchanges show the creativity and dynamism of American society, and the participants in these programs are enriched through the exposure to other cultures. Contact Office of Citizen Exchanges (ECA/PE/C), Bureau of Educational and Cultural Affairs, U.S. Department of State, SA-44, 301 Fourth Street, S.W., Washington, D.C. 20547; 202-453-8181; http:// exchanges.state.gov/education/citizens/.

Show Off Your Art

Get your artwork the exposure it deserves. The Fund for U.S. Artists at International Festivals and Exhibitions awards grants to performing artists and organizations that have been invited to participate in international festivals. The Fund supports the creative and professional development of U.S. artists through the presentation of their work at significant international festivals worldwide. Contact the Cultural Programs Division Staff, Bureau of Educational and Cultural Affairs, U.S. Department of State, SA-44, 301 4th Street, SW, Suite 568, Washington, D.C. 20547; 202-203-7523; http://exchanges.state.gov/ education/citizens/culture/visual_arts.htm.

How To Write Off Your Vacation

There's still time to take advantage of leftover tax laws that favor the well-heeled. The Internal Revenue Service has changed some of the rules regarding business deductions, but there are still ways you can write off parts of your summer vacation as a business expense. Anyone can do it even if you're just an employee. Find out how by calling the IRS at 800-829-1040 and asking for a free copy of Publication 463, Travel, Entertainment, Gift and Car Expenses. You can also check them out online at www.irs.gov.

Eight Week Foreign Tours For Jazz Musicians And Bands

The Jazz Ambassador Program is designed to use the wealth of often undiscovered musical talent in the U.S. to enhance the mission of promoting cross-cultural understanding. Jazz Ambassadors travel to four or five countries for a period of four to eight weeks. In addition to public performances, they may conduct workshops and master classes. Nominations of classical musicians in various categories are sought from music schools, conservatories, colleges and universities throughout the U.S. Contact Cultural Programs Division, Bureau of Educational and Cultural Affairs, U.S. Department of State, SA-44, 301 4th St., SW, Room 568, Washington, DC 20547; 202-203-7523; Fax: 202-619-7525; http://exchanges.state.gov/education/citizens/culture/jazzamb.htm.

You Can Teach Overseas

American-sponsored overseas schools are independent, non-government schools sponsored by Americans or in which American citizens have considerable interest. Although the relationship between our American embassies and the various schools overseas may be close, the schools are private institutions, responsible for hiring their own teachers and staff. Generally, the schools are not joined together under any administrative umbrella; each does its own hiring and establishes its own qualification requirements and application procedures. Although the Department of State does not employ teachers for assignment abroad, they have assembled general information about teaching overseas and a list of organizations that provide teaching opportunities. Contact http://exchanges.state.gov/education.

Thousands Of Government Jobs In Foreign Countries

The Federal government hires personnel to do everything from typing to spying, and there are posts all around the world. Those interested in jobs overseas can contact the Office of Personnel Management to learn current job openings and the skills required. Other government agencies also hire for jobs abroad, and you could contact them directly for information on employment opportunities. Contact Federal Job Information Center, Office of Personnel Management, 1900 E St., NW, Washington, DC 20415; 202-606-1800; http://www.usajobs. opm.gov; or you may contact the Career America Connection at 912-757-3000. Other agencies that hire for overseas employment include:

Agency For International Development
Information Center
Ronald Reagan Building
Washington, DC 20523-1000
202-712-4810
www.usaid.gov

U.S. Customs Service
1300 Pennsylvania Avenue, NW
Washington, DC 20229
202-354-1000
www.customs.treas.gov

Central Intelligence Agency
Office of Public Affairs
Washington, DC 20505
703-482-0623
Fax: 703-482-1739
www.cia.gov

U.S. Department of Commerce
Human Resources Management Office
U.S. and Foreign Commercial Service
1401 Constitution Ave., NW, Room 5001
Washington, DC 20230
202-482-4883
www.commerce.gov

U.S. Department of Agriculture
Foreign Agricultural Service
Personnel Division
1400 Independence Ave., SW
Washington, DC 20250
202-720-HELP
www.fas.usda.gov

Money For Artists, Filmmakers, Playwrights, And Museum Professionals To Go Overseas

The Culture Program supports projects by U.S. nonprofit organizations for exchanges of professionals in the arts and museum fields. Priority is given to institutionally-based projects involving artists in the creation of their particular art forms and projects which will lead to institutional linkages. Two way exchanges are encouraged and cost sharing is required. This exchange program is designed to introduce American and foreign participants to each other's cultural and artistic life and traditions. It also supports international projects in the United States or overseas involving composers, choreographers, filmmakers, playwrights, theater designers, writers and poets, visual artists, museum professionals, and more. Contact Cultural Programs Division, Bureau of Educational and Cultural Affairs, U.S. Department of State, SA-44, 301 4th St., SW, Suite 568, Washington, DC 20547; 202-203-7523; Fax: 202-203-7525; http://exchanges.state.gov/education/citizens/culture/.

Save If You Take The Train Overseas

The train may be the way to travel as you take in all of the sights of Europe. Discounts for seniors are available for some of the ticket combinations. When you purchase your tickets remember to ask if there is a savings for which you are eligible.

Free Rollercoaster Rides

Some of the nation's top amusement parks offer seniors discounts on daily admissions. Six Flags Kentucky Kingdom offers adults 55 and older discount tickets and adults 65 and older FREE admission. Most of the other Six Flag Parks offer senior discounts. These are not the only parks offering senior discounts, so make sure that you ask.

Retired Military Save Big On Vacations in Hawaii and Disney

Military Retirees are eligible for many discounts throughout the world. *Shades of Green Resort* is a military-owned resort within Walt Disney World. *Shades of Green* provides all of the benefits of staying at a Disney Hotel including transportation and a nine-hole golf course. They even offer discounts on tickets to the parks. The Hale Koa Hotel in Honolulu, Hawaii is a resort on 72 tropical acres on the beach at Waikiki. Room rates are determined by pay grade of retired personnel. For information on these and other resorts contact Military Advantage, Inc., 799 Market Street, Suite 700, San Francisco, CA 94103-2045; 415-820-3434; www.military.com/Travel.

Discounted Air Travel For Retired Military Personnel and Their Families

Space Available Flight, sometimes called Space A or military hops, provides retirees and their families a unique travel opportunity. Space A offers eligible passengers the privilege to fill unused seats on DoD-owned or controlled aircraft. Travel has been reduced post 9/11 because access to flight information is not public domain. There are many restrictions which may make discounted flights on commercial airlines more manageable. But, if you have the time and stay flexible you may be able to fly at a great discount. For additional information, contact Military Advantage, Inc., 799 Market Street, Suite 700, San Francisco, CA 94103-2045; 415-820-3434; www.military.com/Travel.

Free Passport and Travel Information

The American Battle Monuments Commission administers, operates and maintains twenty-four permanent American burial grounds on foreign soil. They provide a number of services to the families of these fallen heroes. They offer letters authorizing fee-free passports and travel information for members of the immediate family traveling overseas to visit a grave or memorial. For additional information, contact American Battle Monuments Commission, 2300 Clarendon Boulevard, Suite 500, Arlington, VA 22201; 703-696-6897; www.abmc.gov.

Spend Your Vacation as a Moose Crossing Guard at Old Faithful

The Volunteers-In-Parks volunteers donated 4.5 million hours of their time to national parks in 2003; what a great way to spend your vacation time. If you are interested, you can help in a variety of ways and must contact each park to find out about available opportunities. http://nps.gov/volunteer/. *International Volunteers-In-Parks Program* offers opportunities to individuals from all over the world. Call 202-354-1807 for information on the International Program. *Natural Resource Laureate Program* is a new program that hosts science-based professionals in the national parks. The program matches volunteers possessing proven science backgrounds with parks needing specific natural resource expertise. Call 540-788-3274 or check the web site at www.nature.nps.gov/partnerships/laureateprogram.htm for additional information.

Travel The World

The Peace Corps' objective is to promote world peace and friendship, to help other countries in meeting their needs for trained manpower, and to help promote understanding between the American people and other peoples served by the Peace Corps. Volunteers serve for a period of 2 years, living among the people with whom they work. Volunteers are expected to become a part of the community and to demonstrate, through their voluntary service, that people can be an important impetus for change. Volunteers receive a stipend and health insurance. Contact: Peace Corps, 1111 20th St., NW, Washington, DC 20526; 800-424-8580; Fax: 202-606-9410; www.peacecorps.gov.

Free Cars and Air Fare To Go On Vacation

Not quite as easy as it sounds, but there are companies out there to help people move their cars. Most of the cars need to be driven across the country and in exchange, many car moving companies offer free gas and airline travel home. This is not to say that you can take your family on a minivan vacation across the country. Certain rules and restrictions apply. But I have known many a college kid that has gotten to drive across the U.S. for free. Obviously, you do not get to pick your make and model, and you need to be flexible as to the departure time and destination, but this is one way to see America. Contact local moving companies to see what they have to offer. There is even a website for those interested in having their cars moved at www.movecars.com, and they may be able to provide you with information.

Air courier services operate the same way, but you are required to have a valid passport. Most air freight services don't do enough business to send a plane overseas each day. As a courier, you carry a package checked as baggage to an overseas destination. There have been no incidences of contraband problems, and customs is familiar with this service. You deliver the package to a company representative in the customs section of the airport, and then you are on our own. In exchange, you get to fly to exotic ports for FREE or cheap. Children are not allowed to accompany couriers. Contact companies listed in the air courier section of your phone book, do a web search using the terms "air courier service," or contact Air Courier Association at 800-211-5119; or online at www.aircourier.org.

Learning Vacations For Seniors

Interhostel learning vacations are sponsored by the University of New Hampshire Continuing Education in cooperation with many other institutes of higher education throughout the world. The program is open to adults 50 years and older. The programs include lectures, excursions and other activities to provide an in-depth look at the country. If you love to travel with your grandchildren then check out *Familyhostel*. *Familyhostel* offers programs for children (8-15), parents and grandparents. So get your family together and go make memories. Interhostel/Familyhostel, University of New Hampshire, 6 Garrison Avenue, Durham, NH 03824; 800-733-9753; 603-862-1147; http://www.learn.unh.edu/interhostel/.

Cruise For Less

You can get special perks like free use of a bathrobe while onboard or money off each onboard cabin. AARP members can access a variety of benefits by booking through them. You can also contact the cruise line directly and ask if they offer any benefits or discounts for seniors.

Discounts on Car Rentals

You never should pay full-price for car rentals and there are deals aplenty if you keep your eyes open. AAA and AARP membership will save you a few bucks, as will many other membership programs. Car rental agencies also often offer discounts to senior citizens (check what age they consider "senior"). Many times, if you book your flight and rental car at the same time, you can get a discount rate, plus get miles added to your frequent flier program. All you have to do is ask! The free brochure, *Renting a Car: What Everyone Should Know*, outlines some points to consider and questions to ask when you reserve a rental car. You can learn how to choose a rental car company and understand the terms they use for insurance and charges. For your copy, contact Public Reference, Federal Trade Commission, Washington, DC 20580; 202-326-2222, 877-FTC-HELP; www.ftc.gov.

Travel Tips For Older Americans

What do you do is you lose your passport or have a health emergency? Is it safe to travel to a particular country? What about your medications? *Travel Tips for Older Americans* explains all this and more, and can be viewed for free online at http://travel.state.gov.

Get Out of the House and Into the Woods

If you prefer saving spotted owls and counting woodchucks to playing bridge with the girls, you can be a volunteer with the Forest Service and be a nature hike leader or help with fascinating research. Contact your nearest national forest. For a list of national forests nearest you, contact U.S. Forest Service, U.S. Department of Agriculture, 1400 Independence Avenue, SW, Washington, DC 20250-0003; 202-205-8333; www.fs.fed.us.

Go On A Free Archeological Dig

Have you always dreamed of being an archaeologist? If so, Passport in Time (PIT) is the volunteer program for you. PIT is a program of the USDA Forest Service. Volunteers can work on projects including archaeological excavation, rock art restoration, survey, archival research, historic structure restoration, gathering oral histories, or writing interpretive brochures to name a few. Projects vary in length from 2 days to two weeks or longer. Check the web site or contact Passport in Time for current projects. Passport in Time, P.O. Box 31315, Tucson, AZ 85751-1315; 520-722-2716, 800-281-9176; www.passportintime.com.

Travel and Learn

If you want to learn and explore close to home or half way around the world, Elderhostel can help. Elderhostel is a nonprofit organization that provides learning adventures for people 55 years of age and older throughout the world. They offer over 10,000 programs a year in more than 90 countries. You can receive a catalog by mail or view the catalog on their web site. Elderhostel, 11 Avenue de Lafayette, Boston, MA 02111-1746; 877-426-8056; www.elderhostel.org.

Tons of Travel Options

Are you interested in travel, learning about new photography techniques, golf, tennis or cooking? This web site lists thousands of learning and travel programs. Sponsors list their educational programs on this site, then you can be search in a variety of ways and find just the right program for you! ShawGuides, Inc., P.O. Box 231295, New York, NY 10023; 212-799-6464; www.shawguides.com.

Cheaper Car Rentals

When you travel and you need to rent a car, you may save some money because you are a senior. Payless Car Rentals offers the "Nifty, Fifty" program which offers up to 5% off their rates. Thrifty offers seniors up to 5% on US bookings. It is important to remember to ask, any car rental agency, if they offer discounts for seniors. Contact each rental agency for additional information.

Low Rates and Free Nights at Hotels

Almost all major hotel chains offer discounts 10-30% off the cost of rooms. Some require that you belong to AARP or AAA or other organizations, so it is best to call ahead and ask. Three hotel chains Ramada, Hilton and, and Red Roof inns offer special deals to guests who frequent their hotels. Ramada's TripRewards Program is free to join and you can redeem your points for hotel stays and other prizes (800-367-8747). Hilton Senior HHotels program charges $55 ($40 annual renewal fee), and seniors receive up to $50 off rooms and discounts at hotel restaurants (800-548-8690). Red Roof offers the Redicard for their guests. The program is free to join and members can receive many benefits including: free nights, member only reservations, free USA Today paper during stays and more (800-733-7663).

Discounts on Airline Tickets if You Are a Senior

Most airlines offer discounts to seniors amounting to as much as 10%. What happens though is that some of the airlines' special offers may be exempt from the discount. It is best to see what the lowest available rate is and then inquire about the senior discount. In many instances, the airline only requires that one person meet the age requirements for the discount, so your companion can receive the lower rate as well. Contact the specific airline or check with AARP for discounts currently available.

5-15% Off When You Travel

All car rental chains offer senior discounts, but again AARP or AAA membership may be required. The amount of discount varies from location to location, but usually is 10%. You should call ahead to see if a discount is available. Some chains also require reservations 24 hours in advance. For those that prefer to leave the driving to others, two other discount programs include AMTRAK and Greyhound. AMTRAK offers 15% off any fare available to those 62 and older (800-USA-RAIL). Greyhound bus has a 5%

discount for people 55 and over (800-229-8425). Greyhound offers the Student Advantage Discount Card that can save students 15% on walk-up fares and more. The card costs $20 per year.

Free (Or Cheap) Hunting and Fishing Licenses

Practically every state has a special license rate for seniors. States such as Alabama, Alaska, Delaware, Georgia, Kansas and others do not require that people 65 and older carry fishing and hunting licenses. Other states offer seniors, on average, half off the cost of licenses. These rules change so you will need to contact each state to receive specific details and discounts.

50% Off Camping

Almost all states offer discounts to seniors at state parks. Entrance fees are usually waived for seniors, or states like Illinois offer 50% off camping fees. Eighteen states have no residency requirements to receive the discount, so if you are planning a cross country camping trip, contact the state Parks Department to find out about eligibility criteria. For those wanting to camp in the National Forest, the Golden Age Passport is available to those 62 and over. For $10 you receive free lifetime admission to the parks, plus 50% off camping and many other services. The Passport is available at all National Parks, online at www.nationalparks.orgor by calling 888-GOPARKS.

Travel Tour Companies For Seniors

There are a number of travel tours companies that are dedicated to seniors. Check them out to see what they may have to offer.

- *Senior Women's Travel*: If you are 50 years old or older and you love to travel, check out Senior Women's Travel. They offer a variety of tours including Travel-By-the Book Literary Tours and New York Lifestyle Tours. Contact them at Senior Women's Travel, Mary Ann Zimmerman, 136 E 56th Street, New York, NY 10022; 212-838-4740; www.poshnosh.com.
- *Walking the World*: Adventure travel is not just for the young. If you are 50 or better, Walking the World gets you out of the bus and into the countries you travel. Tours are ranked on degree of strenuous walking required. So get your walking shoes on and see the world. Contact them at Walking the World, P.O. Box 1186, Fort Collins, CO 80522-1186; 800-340-9255; www.walkingtheworld.com.
- *50Plus Expeditions*: 50plus Expeditions offers active, tours that frequently are off-the-beaten-path. For additional information contact 50plus Expeditions, 40 Brisbane Road, Toronto, Ontario M3J2J8, Canada; 866-318-5050; www.50plusexpeditions.com.
- *Eldertreks*: Eldertreks is an adventure travel company dedicated to people 50 years old and older. They offer tours in over 60 countries that focus on adventure, culture and nature. In you are interested, contact them at Eldertracks; 800-741-7956; www.eldertreks.com.
- *Gold Circle Travel* strives to provide mature travelers: value, pacing, choices and new discoveries through their vacation packages. They offer packages throughout the world on land or water. For trip information contact Gold Circle Corporation, 347 Congress Street, Boston, MA 02210; 800-321-2835; www.gct.com.
- *CIE Tours* has been providing tours for 73 years to Britain and Ireland. Seniors will be smiling when they ask for the "55 & Smiling" discount. Selected tours offer $55 off per person for travelers 55 years old and older. For information contact CIE Tour International, Inc., 10 Park Place, Suite 510, P.O. Box 1965, Morristown, NJ 07962-1965; 800-CIE-TOUR, 973-2992-0463; www.cietours.com.

- *Globus Vacations and Cosmos Vacations* are both a part of the AARP Passport Program which gives AARP members travel discounts. You can save $25-100 per person on selected itineraries that are offered. Globus provides options from independent travel to escorted tours throughout the world. For additional information contact Globus, 5301 South Federal Circle, Littleton, CO 80123; 866-755-8581; www.globusjourneys.com, www.cosmosvacations.com.

Save By Exchanging Homes on Your Next Vacation
Seniors Home Exchange is a home exchange program designed exclusively for adults 50 years old and older. You can save hundreds of dollars on hotels and meals by using the home exchange philosophy. You open your home to visitors and in exchange can stay in their home for free. Currently Seniors Home Exchange offers a listing of 1761 homes in over 40 countries. There is a membership fee of $79 for three years or $100 for a lifetime membership. You can check out the listings at www.seniorhomeexchange.com.

Museums for Less
Many museums give discounts to seniors. Here are a few examples of some that are available. The Cleveland Museum of Natural History gives seniors 60 and older a $2 savings. You can save a $1 if you are 55 and older at the Cherokee Heritage Center in Oklahoma. Don't forget that many of the museums in Washington DC are free to all including the Smithsonian. Make sure that you carefully check out the price list or ask if a discount is available.

Pretend You Are Tom Sawyer For A Day
Have you ever dreamed of traveling down the Mississippi for the day? Enjoy the sights and sounds of stepping back in time on a riverboat. The Memphis Queen offers discounts on their Day Cruise and Sightseeing Cruise for seniors with identification. To make a reservation contact Memphis Queen Riverboats, P.O. Box, Memphis, TN 38173-0188; 800-221-6197, 901-527-BOAT; www.memphisquees.com.

Play Softball Around the World
If you are 50 years old or older, love softball and travel this is the place for you! They offer several trips each year that focus on shopping, sightseeing and softball. All skill levels are welcome to play with people from other cultures around the world. You can even bring your non-playing spouse, friend or family member to cheer you on at the games. For additional information contact Senior Softball-USA, 2701 K Street, Suite 101A, Sacramento, CA 95816; 916-326-5303; www.seniorsoftball.com/internationaltours.php.

Hostel All Around The World
Hostelling may be just what you need to afford travel throughout the world. They offer inexpensive overnight accommodations for travelers. Hostels offer dorm-like rooms with separate men and women sections. Some of the hostels even offer couple or family rooms. Most hostels provide kitchens, common rooms and secure storage. HI-USA is a nonprofit organization that offers more than 4,000 hostels in 60 countries. Memberships for seniors 55 years and older are $18 per year, a $10 discount from the adult fee. For additional information contact Hostelling International-USA, National Office, 8401 Colesville Road, Suite 600, Silver Spring, MD 20910; 301-495-1240; www.hiusa.org.

Take the Grandkids with You

Grandtravel is all about family, especially the grandparent/grandchild relationship. They consider school curricula to extend the educational experience for the students. Most trips are scheduled in the summer months when school is out. To get going on this exciting program contact Grandtravel, Abroad, Inc., 1920 N Street, NW, Suite 200, Washington, DC 20036-1601; 800-247-7651; www.grandtrvl.com.

Travel Tips on the Internet

Senior-site.com is dedicated to adults 50 and older. Their travel section has an array of topics to help you organize all of your plans including: security on the road, tour and travel packages, travel bulletins, airline safety and much more. Check out all of these at Seniors-site.com, 5443 Stag Mt. Road, Weed, CA 96094; 530-938-3163; http://seniors-site.com/travel.

Take a Kid to Camp (You Can Stay Too)

Grandkidsandme can bring you and your grandchildren many memories. They offer weekend camps in Wisconsin to enjoy the outdoors together. Camps are designed for grandkids between 4 and 12 years old. Activities include canoeing, hoe-downs, crafts, hiking and many others. To get information contact Grandkidsandme Inc., 1764 Hampshire Avenue, St. Paul MN 55116; 651-695-1988; www.grandkidsandme.com.

Learn to Sail and Save

Have you always dreamed of being the master of your own helm? Learn to sail with the New York Sailing School and save $100 on the course fee if you are over 60 years old. To begin to sail away contact New York Sailing School, 22 Pelham Road, New Rochelle, NY 10801-5753; 914-235-6052; www.nyss.com.

Discounts to Ski (Maybe Even Free)

There are many seniors that are not relaxing in their easy chairs after retirement but rather hitting the slopes for fun. Many of the ski resorts offer discounts to senior citizens. Discounts vary from resort to resort so you have to ask. Some offer free skiing to skiers 70 years old and older. There are even clubs just for older skiers.

- *The Over the Hill Gang* is open to ski-loving seniors 50 and older and their spouses. Memberships range from $50 to $760 depending in the type of membership you desire. Membership benefits range from discounts to special outings. Contact Over the Hill Gang, International, 1820 W. Colorado Avenue, Colorado Springs, CO 80904; 719-389-0022; www.othgi.com.
- *GO50-Global Over 50 Ski Club* offers older skiers 50 and older discounts at many ski resorts in North America. Memberships are $50 a year. Contact them at Global Over 50 Ski Club, P.O. Box 352, South Hadley, MA 01075; 866-TRY-GO50; www.go50.org.
- *70 + Ski Club* was established in 1977 and is still going strong with several hundred members in their 90's. They offer ski trips. Memberships are $10/single and $15/couple per year. Contact President Richard Lambert, 70+ Ski Club, 1633 Albany Street, Schenectady, NY 12304; 518-346-5505; www.skiinghistory.org/70PLUS.html.

World Senior Games Vacation
Every October St. George, Utah hosts the World Senior Games. You can spend some time there competing in a number of events including: biking, bowling, bridge, golf, horseshoes and many more. Participants must be 50 years old or older. When you are not competing, you can take part in social activities and area attractions. Find out more about this program at www.hwsg.com.

If You Still Want a New Bike for Your Birthday
If you still love biking like you did as a kid, Senior Cycling can keep you busy. They offer trips for seniors that are beginners, intermediate or advanced riders. Don't worry, they have a sag wagon if you don't quite make it through the ride. For a complete listing of tours contact Senior Cycling, Inc., 37419 Branch River Road, Loudoun Heights, VA 20132; 540-668-6307; www.seniorcycling.com.

Myrtle Beach Senior Discounts
Senior citizens are welcome at this resort and earn a 10% discount on weekly and monthly rates for condominiums. Guests must be 55 years old and older to qualify for this discount. For information on these sunny vacations, contact Myrtle Beach Resort Vacations Services, P.O. Box 3936, Myrtle Beach, SC 29578; 888-627-3767, 843-238-1559; www.myrtle-beach-resort.com.

Enjoy Wine Country for Less
San Francisco Tours offers a discount to adults 60 years old and older for their Wine Country Tour. The nine hour tour starts across the Golden Gate Bridge through the wine region of Northern California and back across the San Francisco-Oakland Bay Bridge. For additional information contact them by phone or online at 415-899-0060; www.sftour.com.

Free Books on Tape
The National Library Service (NLS) maintains a large collection of books, magazines, journals, and music materials in Braille, large type, and recorded formats for individuals who cannot read or use standard printed materials because of temporary or permanent visual loss or physical limitations. Reading materials and necessary playback equipment for books on record and cassette are distributed through a national network of cooperating libraries. Books in the collection are selected on the basis of their appeal to a wide range of interests. Bestsellers, biographies, fiction, and how-to books are in great demand.

Contact your local library to find out what they have available to you, or you may contact handicapped Readers Reference Section, National Library Service for the Blind and physically Handicapped, Library of Congress, Washington, DC 20542; 202-707-5100; 800-424-8567; www.loc.gov/ nls.

Save As You Step Back in Time
See the bus that Rosa Parks rode to help change history or walk into the Wright Cycle Shop. Enjoy these and many other parts of history at The Henry Ford Museum and Greenfield Village. Seniors 62 years old and older will find discounts for both venues. For additional information or to purchase tickets contact The Henry Ford Museum, 20900 Oakwood Boulevard, Dearborn, MI 48124-4088; 313-271-1620, 313-982-6001; www.hfmgv.org.

Golf Away Your Retirement

If you enjoy spending your time on the green, there are many savings opportunities out there for you. Many public and private golf courses offer senior discounts on green fees. There may be certain restrictions such as days of week or time of day that these discounts apply.

- *Senior Golfers Association of America* is open to ladies and gentleman who love the game of golf. Members must be at least 50 years old and be able to play a round of golf on less than 4 ½ hours. They sponsor a number of tournaments throughout the country so you can travel all over. Contact them at The Senior Golfers Association of America, 3013 Church Street, Myrtle Beach, SC 29577; 843-626-8100; www.seniorgolfersamerica.com.
- *National Senior Golf Association* offers senior citizens discounted travel events to new courses around the world. Golfers of any age are invited to play although awards are only for those 50 years old and older. Annual memberships are $35 per year per family. For additional information on these golf outings contact National Senior Golf Association, 3673 Nottingham Way, Hamilton Square, NJ 08690; 609-631-8145; www.nsgatour.com.

Be Sent Overseas To Represent America

The Office of Citizen Exchanges of the U.S. Department of State offers a variety of exchange programs overseas. The Professional Programs Division demonstrates how Americans deal with the issues of professional interest to foreign participants. Subject areas vary. The Cultural Programs Division serves to highlight the creativity and dynamism of American Society. Programs include professional American artists, musicians, and other specialists. For information contact Office of Citizen Exchanges (ECA/PE/C), Bureau of Educational and Cultural Affairs, U.S. Department of State, SA-44, 301 Fourth St., SW, Washington, DC 20547; 202-619-5348; http://exchanges.state.gov/education/citizens/.

Free Concert or Theater Tickets

Many music and theater groups offer special programs to older adults in the form of discounted tickets, free concerts, transportation, afternoon teas, and/or daytime events. Contact your state arts group, state Department of Aging or local senior citizens groups to see what is available in your area.

Tourism Offices

What is there to do in Alabama? A great deal if you check out their State Tourism Office. Each state's Tourism Office provides information about what there is to see and do while visiting the state. Specific events, historic sites, scenic trails are described, as well as fun stuff for kids and vacation guides. Many offices also provide information on climate and transportation available. In order to encourage more tourism visits some states offer special deals and packages on their sites, and a few even have coupons for specific events or attractions. Before you hit the open road, take advantage of what these state offices have to offer to make the most of your visit.

Alabama
Bureau of Tourism & Travel
P.O. Box 4927
Montgomery, AL 36103-4927
1 334 242-4169
1-800-ALABAMA toll-free in USA
Fax: 1 334 242-4554
http://www.touralabama.org

Alaska
Alaska Tourism Office
P.O. Box 110801
Juneau AK 99811-0801
1-800-862-5275 toll-free in USA
1-907-465-2012
Fax: 1-907-465-3767
http://www.dced.state.ak.us/tourism/

Arizona
Office of Tourism
1110 W. Washington St., Suite 155
Phoenix, AZ 85007
888-520-3433 toll-free in USA and Canada
http://www.arizonaguide.com/

Arkansas
Arkansas Department of Parks and Tourism
One Capitol Mall
Little Rock, AR 72201
1-501-682-7777
1-800-NATURAL toll-free in USA
Fax: 1-501-682-1364
http://www.arkansas.com/

California
California Division of Tourism
P.O. Box 1499
Sacramento, CA 95812
800-GO-CALIF toll-free USA and Canada
http://gocalif.ca.gov/

Colorado
Colorado Tourism Office
1625 Broadway, Suite 1700
Denver, CO 80202
1-303-892-3885
1-800-265-6723 to order Colorado Vacation Guide toll-free in USA
http://www.colorado.com

Connecticut
Connecticut Office of Tourism
Department of Economic and Community Development
505 Hudson Street
Hartford, CT 06106
1-860-270-8080
1-800-CT-BOUND toll-free in USA
http://www.tourism.state.ct.us/

Delaware
Delaware Tourism Office
99 Kings Highway
Dover, DE 19901
1-866-2-VISIT-DE toll-free in USA and Canada
1-302-739-4271
Fax: 1-302-739-5749
http://www.visitdelaware.net/

District of Columbia
DC Committee to Promote Washington
1212 New York Avenue, NW, Suite 200
Washington, DC 20005
1-202-724-5644
1-800-422-8644 toll-free in USA
http://www.washington.org/

Florida
Visit Florida
661 E. Jefferson Street
Tallahassee, FL 32301
1-850-488-5607
1-888-7-FLA-USA toll-free in USA
http://www.flausa.com

Georgia
Georgia Department of Industry Trade & Tourism
285 Peachtree Center Avenue, Suite 1100
Atlanta, Georgia 30303
1-404-656-3590
800-VISIT-GA (800-847-4842) toll-free in USA
http://www.georgia.org/tourism/

Hawaii
Hawaii Visitors and Convention Bureau
2270 Kalakaua Ave., 8th Floor
Honolulu, HI 96815
1-808-923-1811
1-800-464-2924 toll-free in USA
Fax: 1-808-924-0290
http://www.gohawaii.com/

Idaho
Idaho Division of Tourism Development
P.O. Box 83720
Boise, ID 83720-0093
http://www.visitid.org

Illinois
Illinois Bureau of Tourism
100 West Randolph Street, Suite 3-400
Chicago IL 60602
800-2- CONNECT toll-free in USA and Canada
1-312-814-4732
Fax: 1-312-814-6175
http://www.enjoyillinois.com

Indiana
Department of Commerce, Tourism Development Division
1 North Capitol, Suite 700
Indianapolis, IN 46204-2288
1-888-ENJOY-IN toll-free in USA
1-317-232-8860
Fax: 1-317-233-6887
http://www.enjoyindiana.com/

Iowa
Iowa Tourism Office
200 East Grand Avenue

Des Moines, IA 50309
1-515-242-4705
1-888-472-6035 toll-free in USA
Fax: 1-515-242-4718
http://www.traveliowa.com/

Kansas
Kansas Department of Commerce and Housing
Travel & Tourism Development Division
1000 SW Jackson Street, Suite 100
Topeka, KS 66612-1354
1-785-296-2009
Fax: 1-785-296-6988
http://www.travelks.com/

Kentucky
Kentucky Department of Travel
500 Mero Street, Suite 2200
Frankfort, KY 40601
800-225-8747 toll-free in USA
1-502-564-4930
Fax: 1-502-564-5695
http://www.kytourism.com/

Louisiana
Louisiana Office of Tourism
P.O. Box 94291
Baton Rouge LA 70804-9291
1-225-342-8100 reception
800-334-8626 toll-free in USA -- Consumer inquiries
800-227-4386 toll-free in USA -- Travel agents only
Fax: 1-225-342-8390
http://www.louisianatravel.com/

Maine
Maine Office of Tourism
#59 State House Station
Augusta, ME 04333-0059
1-888-624-6345 toll-free in USA
http://www.visitmaine.com

Maryland
Maryland Office of Tourism Development
217 East Redwood Street
Baltimore MD 21202
1-410-767-3400
800-MD-IS-FUN toll-free in USA only
http://www.mdisfun.org/

Massachusetts
Office of Travel and Tourism
10 Park Plaza, Suite 4510
Boston, MA 02116
1-617-973-8500
800-227-MASS 800-227-6277 toll-free in USA and Canada
Fax: 1-617-973-8525
http://www.mass-vacation.com/

Michigan
Travel Michigan
P.O. Box 30226
Lansing MI 48909
1-888-78-GREAT 1-888-784-7328 toll-free USA & Canada
1-800-722-8191 TDD
1-517-373-0670 Business office
Fax: 1-517-373-0059
http://www.michigan.org/

Minnesota
Minnesota Office of Tourism
100 Metro Square
121 Seventh Place East
St. Paul, MN 55101
800-657-3700 toll-free in USA and Canada
1-651-296-5029
Fax: 1-651-296-7095
http://www.exploreminnesota.com/

Mississippi
Mississippi Division of Tourism
Post Office Box 849
Jackson, MS 39205
1-800-WARMEST 927-6378 brochure request line toll-free in USA
1-601-359-3297
Fax: 1-601-359-5757
http://www.visitmississippi.org/

Missouri
Department of Natural Resources, Division of State Parks
P. O. Box 176
Jefferson City, MO 65102
1-573-751-2479
1-800-334-6946 toll-free in USA
1-800-379-2419 TDD toll-free in USA
Fax: 1-573-751-8656
http://www.mostateparks.com

Montana
Travel Montana
1424 Ninth Avenue
P.O. Box 200533
Helena, MT 59620-0533
1-800-VISITMT 1-800-847-4868 toll-free in USA
1-800-548-3390 ext 2 toll-free in USA
1-406-444-2654
http://visitmt.com/

Nebraska
Nebraska Division of Travel & Tourism
P.O. Box 98907

Lincoln, NE 68509-8907
1-800-228-4307 toll-free in USA
Fax: 1-402-471-3026
http://www.visitnebraska.org

Nevada
Nevada Commission on Tourism
401 North Carson
Carson City, NV 89701
1-775-687-4322
800-NEVADA-8 toll-free in USA
Fax: 1-775-687-6779
http://www.travelnevada.com/

New Hampshire
New Hampshire Division of Travel and Tourism Development
PO Box 1856
Concord NH 03302-1856
1-603-271-2665
800-FUN-IN-NH 386-4664 toll-free in USA/Canada
Fax: 1-603-271-6870
http://www.visitnh.gov

New Jersey
New Jersey Commerce & Economic Growth Commission
P.O. Box 820
20 W. State Street
Trenton, NJ 08625
1–609-777-0885
800-VISIT NJ toll-free in USA
Fax: 1-609-633-7418
http://www.state.nj.us/travel/

New Mexico
The New Mexico Department of Tourism
491 Old Santa Fe Trail
P.O. Box 20002
Santa Fe, NM 87501
1-800-SEE-NEWMEX 800-733-6396 toll-free in USA
http://www.newmexico.org/

New York
New York State Division of Tourism
P.O. Box 2603
Albany, NY 12220-0603
1-518-474-4116
1-800-CALL-NYS toll-free in USA and Canada
Fax: 1-518-486-6416
http://www.iloveny.com/

North Carolina
North Carolina Division of Tourism, Film and Sports Development
PO Box 29571
Raleigh, N.C. 27826-0571
1-919-733-8372
800-VISIT-NC toll-free in USA
Fax: 1-919-733-8582
http://www.visitnc.com/

North Dakota
North Dakota Tourism Division
Century Center
1600 E. Century Ave. Suite 2
PO Box 2057
Bismarck, N.D. 58503-2057
800-HELLO ND 800-435-5663 toll-free in USA
1-701-328-2525
Fax: 1-701-328-4878
http://www.ndtourism.com/

Ohio
Ohio Division of Travel and Tourism
Box 1001
Columbus OH 43216-1001
1-614-466-8844
800-BUCKEYE toll-free in USA
800-282-5393 toll-free in Canada
Fax: 1-614-466-6744
http://www.ohiotourism.com/

Oklahoma
Oklahoma Tourism and Recreation Department
15 North Robinson, Room 801
P.O. Box 52002
Oklahoma City OK 73152-2002
1-405-521-2409
800-652-OKLA toll-free in USA and Canada
Fax: 1-405-521-3992
http://www.travelok.com

Oregon
Oregon Tourism Commission
Oregon Economic and Community Development Department
775 Summer Street NE
Salem, OR 97301-1282
1-503-986-0000
800-547-7842 toll-free in USA
Fax: 1-503-986-0001
http://www.traveloregon.com/

Pennsylvania
Tourism, Film and Economic Development Marketing Office
4th Floor, Commonwealth Keystone Building
400 North Street
Harrisburg, PA 17120-0225
1-717-787-5453
1-800-VISIT-PA toll-free in USA
Fax: 1-717-787-0687
http://www.experiencepa.com/experiencepa/home.do

Rhode Island
Economic Development Corporation, Tourism Division
1 West Exchange Street
Providence RI 02903
1-401-222-2601
800-556-2484 toll-free in USA
Fax: 1-401-273-8270
http://www.visitrhodeisland.com/

South Carolina
South Carolina Department of Parks, Recreation and Tourism
1205 Pendleton St.
Columbia, SC 29201-0071
1-803-734-1700
1-800-346-3634 toll-free in USA and Canada
Fax: 1-803-734-0133
http://www.discoversouthcarolina.com

South Dakota
South Dakota Department of Tourism
711 East Wells Avenue
Pierre SD 57501-3369
1-605-773-3301
1-800-S-DAKOTA 1-800-732-5682 toll-free in USA
Fax: 1-605-773-3256
http://www.travelsd.com/

Tennessee
Tennessee Department of Tourist Development
320 Sixth Avenue N.
5th Floor Rachel Jackson Bldg.
Nashville, TN 37243
1-615-741-2159
800-GO2TENN toll-free in USA
Fax: 1-615-741-7225
http://www.tnvacation.com/

Texas
Department of Commerce, Tourism Division
P.O. Box 12728
Austin, TX 78711
1-512-462-9191
800-8888-TEX
http://www.traveltex.com/

Utah
Utah Travel Council
P.O. Box 147420
Salt Lake City, UT 84114-7420
1-801-538-1030
1-800-UTAH-FUN toll-free in USA
http://www.utah.com/

Vermont
Vermont Department of Tourism & Marketing
6 Baldwin St., Drawer 33
Montpelier, VT 05633-1301
1-800-VERMONT (1-800-837-6668) toll-free in USA
1-802-828-0587 travel information
1-802 828-3237 administration
Fax: 1-802-828-3233
http://www.1-800-vermont.com/

Virginia
Virginia Tourism Corporation
901 East Byrd Street
Richmond, VA 23219
1-804-786-4484
800-VISIT-VA 248-4833 toll-free in USA
http://www.virginia.org/

Washington
Centralia-Chehalis Chamber of Commerce
500 NW Chamber of Commerce Way
Chehalis, WA 98532
1-800-525-3323 toll-free in USA
1-360-748-8885
Fax: 1-360-748-8763
http://www.tourism.wa.gov/

West Virginia
West Virginia Division of Tourism
90 MacCorkle Ave. SW
South Charleston WV 25303
1-304-558-2200
1-800-CALL-WVA toll-free in USA
http://www.callwva.com/

Wisconsin
Wisconsin Department of Tourism
201 West Washington Avenue
PO Box 7976
Madison WI 53707-7976
1-608-266-2161
1-800-432-8747 toll-free in USA
http://www.travelwisconsin.com/

Wyoming
Wyoming Business Council, Tourism and Travel Division
Interstate 25 at College Drive
Cheyenne, WY 82002
1-307-777-7777
800-225-5996 toll-free in USA
Fax: 1-307-777-2877
http://www.wyomingtourism.org/

Hunting, Fishing, and The Parks

Every state has specific rules about who is required to have a hunting or fishing license, as well as where these licenses are offered and at what price. The following provides detailed information about what you need to do before you try to land "The Big One." State Parks also have special deals for the senior set, often giving a half-price camping discount and more. Learn what is available in your destination location so you can save some extra money for those souvenirs.

Alabama

Hunting and Fishing
Alabama Department of Conservation and Natural Resources
64 N. Union Street
Montgomery, AL 36130
334-242-3486
http://www.dcnr.state.al.us/licenses
Residents of Alabama who are 64 or older can purchase a lifetime hunting and trapping license or a fishing license for $15.00, the price of a regular annual license. Hunting licenses are required for all residents from age 16 to 65 and non-residents from 16 and older. Residents 64 years or older can purchase a lifetime freshwater fishing license for $9.50, the price of a regular annual license. Licenses can be purchased by phone at 1-888-848-6887 with convenience fee of $3.95 (including shipping) that will be charged in addition to the cost of the license. Licenses can also be purchased online at http://www.alabamainteractive.org/dcnr/licencse/index.cgi.

State Parks
Division of State Parks
Alabama Department of Conservation and Natural Resources
64 North Union Street
Montgomery, AL 36130
1-800-ALA-PARK
http://www.dcnr.state.al.us/parks/state_parks_index_1a.html
Alabama residents 65 years or older can purchase fishing permits for state parks for $17.50 instead of the regular $35.

Alaska

Hunting and Fishing
ADF&G Headquarters
P.O. Box 25526
Juneau, AK 99802-5526
907-465-4100
http://www.adfg.state.ak.us/
Residents of Alaska are not required to purchase a fishing license or a hunting and trapping license, but are required to apply for a ADF&G Permanent Identification Card (PID), which serves as a lifetime hunting, fishing, and trapping license. Applications forms are available by mail from the ADF&G Licensing Section at P.O. Box 25525, Juneau, AK 99802-5525 with the phone number 907-465-2376 or online at www.admin.adfg.state.ak.us/license. A PID card must be in your possession while fishing or hunting and a lost PID can be replaced for free at any ADF&G office.

State Parks
550 W 7th Ave, Suite 1260
Anchorage, AK 99501-3557
907-269-8400
TDD: 907-269-8411
Fax: 907-269-8901
http://www.dnr.state.ak.us/parks/asp/fees.htm
The annual passes that are available are a daily parking pass for $40, a boat launch pass for $75 (or $100 for both together for Alaska residents for a discount of $15) and an annual camping pass for disabled veterans is free. Individual fees are $10-$15 per night for nightly camping, $3-$5 per vehicle for daily parking, $10-$15 per day for boat launches, $5 for sanitary dump station, $5-$8 per bundle where available for firewood, and $3 for guided tours of historic sites. There is a mail-in form for park passes available at http://www.dnr.state.ak.us/parks/asp/passes.htm. The form can also be faxed to 907-269-8901. For more information, call the Anchorage Public Information Center at 907-269-8400.

Arizona

Hunting and Fishing
Phoenix
2221 W. Greenway Rd.
Phoenix, AZ 85023-4399
602-942-3000
http://www.azgfd.com or http://www.gf.state.az.us/
All Arizona residents above the age of fourteen are required to purchase fishing and hunting licenses, the prices of which range from $10 to $750 depending on what type of game will be hunted. Licenses can be purchase by phone at 1-866-462-0433 or, for additional assistance, at 602-942-3000. Licenses can also be purchased online at http://www.sci-nevada.com/webazlic.AZMAINF2.ASP#top. There will be a single $2.00 convenience fee for either the phone or internet service, regardless of the number of licenses purchased.

State Parks
Arizona State Parks

1300 W. Washington
Phoenix, AZ 85007
602-542-4174
All adults must purchase passes to enter any of the state parks. The fee schedule is available at http://www.pr.state.ax.us/feeschedule.html. The daily entrance fee ranges from $2.00 for an individual on a bicycle to $9.00 per vehicle containing one to four adults. Daily oversize parking is $15.00. Nightly camping ranges from $10.00 to $60.00 and seasonal/conditioning camping rates range from $60.00 to $375.00. Annual passes to state parks can be purchased for $45 (day use only) by calling 602-542-4174, at any of the Arizona State Parks offices, or by visiting http://www.pr.state.az.us/mkting/orderpass.pdf, downloading the order form and mailing it in to:

Arizona State Parks
1300 W. Washington
Phoenix, AZ 85007
602-542-4174
http://www.pr.state.az.us/

Arkansas
Hunting and Fishing
2 Natural Resources Drive
Little Rock, AR 72205
800-364-4263
501-223-6300
Residents of Arkansas over the age of 65 can purchase a 65 Plus Lifetime Fishing License for $10.50, which entitles persons 65 years of age or older toe the privileges of the Resident Fisheries Conservation License. In order to retain trout or to fish in certain waters, residents 65 or older must purchase a 65 Plus Lifetime trout permit. Applicants must provide proof of age as well as proof of a three-year or more residence in Arkansas.

The 65 Plus Lifetime Hunting License (PLH) can be purchased for $35.50 and entitles Arkansas residents 65 years of age or older to the privileges of the Resident Sportsman's License. HIP registration is required in order to hunt migratory birds. A state lifetime waterfowl permit is required to hunt waterfowl as well as federal waterfowl stamps in addition to HIP. Proof of a three-year residence and proof of age are required in order to apply.

65 Plus Lifetime Combination License (PLC) can be purchased for $35.50, which entitles Arkansas residents 65 years of age or older to the privileges of the Resident Sportsman's License (hunting) and the Resident Fisheries Conservation License (fishing). In order to hunt migratory gamebirds, HIP registration is required. A 65 Plus Lifetime waterfowl permit and federal waterfowl stamps are required in addition to HIP in order to hunt waterfowl. A lifetime trout permit must be purchased in order to fish in certain waters and proof of age and three-year residency is required to apply for this license.

HIP is the Harvest Information Program, which is a nationwide effort to improve the harvest estimates of small game. Information from HIP will improve the management of migratory birds and will help ensure that decisions on hunting season will be based on sound scientific evidence. Registration for HIP is free and can be obtained by completing a short survey available from license dealers, any Game and Fish Commission office or online at http://www.ark.org/agfc.license/index.php.

Licenses can be purchased at sporting goods stores, hunting and fishing supplies stores, some discount chains and the Little Rock or regional offices of AFGC. Lifetime licenses cannot be purchased by phone or online.

Little Rock Office:
2 Natural Resources Drive
Little Rock, AR 72205
501-223-6300 or toll-free: 1-800-364-4263

Northwest Regional Office
455 Dam Site Road
Eureka Springs, AR 72631
479-253-2506 or toll-free: 1-800-253-2506

East Central Regional Office
1201 North Highway 49
Brinkley, AR 72021
870-734-4851 or toll-free: 1-800-734-4851

North Central Regional Office
Highway 56 North
Calico Rock, AR 72519
870-297-4331 or toll-free: 1-800-297-4331

South Central Regional Office
500 Ben Lane
Camden, AR 71701
870-836-4612 or toll-free: 1-800-836-4612

Fort Smith Regional Office- Fort Chaffee
8000 Taylor Avenue
Fort Smith, AR 72917
479-478-1043 or toll-free: 1-800-478-1043

Southwest Regional Office
7004 Highway 76 E
Perrytown, AR 71801
870-777-5580 or toll-free: 1-877-777-5580

Hot Springs Regional Office
350 Fish Hatchery Road
Hot Springs, AR 71913
501-525-8606 or toll-free: 1-877-525-8606

Northeast Regional Office
2920 McClellan Drive
Jonesboro, AR 72401
870-972-5438 or toll-free: 1-877-972-5438

Southeast Regional Office
771 Jordan Drive
Monticello, AR 71655
870-367-3553 or toll-free: 1-877-467-3559

West Central Regional Office
1266 Lock and Dam Road
Russelville, AR 72802
479-967-7577 or toll-free: 1-877-967-7577
http://www.agfc.state.ar.us/

State Parks
Division of State Parks
Arkansas Department of Parks and Tourism
One Capitol Mall
Little Rock, AR 72201
1-888-287-2757
http://www.arkansasstateparks.com
In all Arkansas state parks, fees for camping range from $5.00 per day to $21.00 per day. Residents of Arkansas who are 65 years of age or older will be admitted to park campgrounds for fifty percent off the regular campsite fee year-round. Annual Museum passes can be purchased for $17.00 for individuals or $28.00 for Family Admission (parents and children through age 18) and allow unlimited visits, including special events, to the Arkansas Post Museum, Hampson Museum, Jacksonport, Mammoth Spring, Parkin, Plantation Agriculture Museum, Powhatan Courthouse, Prairie County Museum, Prairie Grove and Toltec Mounds. There is a $5.00 fee per use and a $5.00 deposit for the use of the following equipment: volleyball set, horseshoe set, tables, badminton set, tennis rackets (including balls), basketball, football, bat and ball, and croquet set. All rented equipment must be returned to the Visitors Center by closing time.

California
Hunting and Fishing
DFG Headquarters
1416 Ninth Street
Sacramento, CA 95814
916-445-0411
Any person who is 65 years of age or older who is receiving Aid to the Aged or is a resident of California and whose total income per month does not exceed $778 for single persons or $1,382 for married persons (combined income), or any person who is an honorably-discharged veteran of the United States Armed forces with a service-connected disability rating of 50% or more is eligible for a reduced-fee fishing license.

For residents of California who are 65 years of age or older, a lifetime license for sport fishing is $365.00 and a lifetime license for hunting is the same price. A lifetime Sportsman's license, which is both hunting and fishing, is $730.00.
An annual fishing license is $32.80 for California residents and the fishing stamps range from $3.00 to $10.50.

An annual hunting license is $32.80 for California residents. Big game hunting licenses range from $5.50 to $500.00. Game bird hunting licenses range from $1.30 to $112.10.
The locations of the California Department of Fish and Game are:

619 Second Street
Eureka, CA 95501
707-445-6493

1234 East Shaw Avenue
Fresno, CA 93710
559-222-3761

4665 Lampson Avenue
Suite C
Los Alamitos, CA 90720
562-342-7100

20 Lower Ragsdale Drive
Suite 100
Monterey, CA 93940
831-649-2870

7329 Silverado Trail
Napa, CA 94599
707-944-5500

1701 Nimbus Road
Rancho Cordova, CA 95670
916-358-2900

601 Locust Street
Redding, CA 96001
530-225-2300

3211 S Street
Sacramento, CA 95816
916-227-2245

4949 Viewridge Avenue
San Diego, CA 92123
858-467-4201

4001 N. Wilson Way
Stockton, CA 94205
209-948-7800

The Rancho Cordova office does not issue commercial fishing licenses and the Stockton office issues only Sport Fishing licenses.

The License and Revenue Branch, which issues commercial and business licenses only, is located at

3211 S Street
Sacramento, CA 95816
916-227-2245
http://www.dfg.ca.gov/

State Parks
Dept. of Parks and Recreation
1416 9th Street
Sacramento, CA 95814
P.O. Box 942896
Sacramento, CA 94296
http://www.parks.ca.gov/

Residents of California who are 62 years of age or older with income limitations that are specified on the application form, receiving Aid to Families with Dependent Children, or are receiving aid for the aged, blind, or disabled can purchase the Golden Bear Pass for $5.00 per year. This pass entitles its bearer and spouse to the use of all the parking facilities in state-operated parks.

Residents of California who are 62 years of age or older may purchase the Limited Use Golden Bear Pass for $10.00 per year, which permits the use of the parking facilities in all of the state-operated parks. It is not valid during the peak season, which is between Memorial Day weekend and Labor Day.

California residents who are 62 or older are eligible for the Senior Citizen Discount, which is a $1.00 discount for vehicle parking and $2.00 discount for family camping in state-operated parks. The discount cannot be used with any other discount or pass program and does not apply to fees that are under $2.00 or that are supplementary fees.
Passes and discounts are not valid at locally operated state park units.

Call 1-800-777-0369 for applications for the Disabled Discount, Disabled Veteran, and Golden Bear Passes. Applications for the Golden Bear Pass must be made in person at most units of California State Parks. All other passes are available at the California State Parks e-store at
http://www.store.parks.ca.gov/park/product.asp?dept_id=201&pf_id=201&mscssid=FSNTABVSA6089PMJRVUCW2KBUUFHE7AB.

Colorado

Hunting and Fishing and State Parks
Colorado residents 64 years of age or older may purchase an annual fishing pass for a discounted rate of $10.25 instead of the normal $30.25. Licenses can be purchased by phone at 1-800-244-5613.

Hunting licenses for Colorado residents range from $5.00 to $30.25. There is no discount for senior citizens. Licenses can be purchased at a licensing agent or over the phone at 1-800-244-5613.

Senior passes to Colorado state parks are available at any Colorado state park or Colorado state park office. Passes cannot be purchased online, due to the age requirements and the necessity for proof of age. The Aspen Leaf pass is an annual vehicle pass that may be purchased for $27 for entrance to any of the state parks. Residents must be 64 years of age or older in order to qualify for the Aspen Leaf pass, or 62 years of age by December 31st, 2003. The offices where the Aspen Leaf pass can be purchased are located at

1313 Sherman Street
Suite 618
Denver, CO 80203
303-866-3437

3745 E. Prospect Road
Suite 2
Fort Collins, CO 80525
970-491-1168

P.O. Box 700
Clifton, CO 81520
970-434-6862

4255 Sinton Road
Colorado Springs, CO 80907
719-227-5250
http://www.dnr.state.co.us/

Connecticut

Hunting and Fishing
Fishing licenses for residents of Connecticut who are 65 years of age or older can be obtained free at any town hall. A lifetime hunting license for Connecticut residents who are 65 years of age is also free and can be obtained from town clerks or their agents.

State Parks
The Department of Environmental Protection,
79 Elm Street,
Hartford, CT 06106-5127.
The Charter Oak Pass is available for free to Connecticut residents who are 65 years of age or older. The Charter Oak

pass is a lifetime pass and is accepted at all daytime use parks. It is not, however, accepted for camping. The Charter Oak Pass can be purchased by mailing in an application to DEP Charter Oak Pass, State Parks Division, 79 Elm Street, Hartford, CT 06106-5127; 860-424-3200, with a legible photocopy of a Connecticut drivers license or other form of identification that is proof of age and residency. Passes can be purchased in person at the following locations:

DEP State Parks Division
79 Elm Street
Hartford, CT 06106-1650
860-424-3200

DEP Eastern District H.Q.
209 Hebron Road
Marlborough, CT 06447-1207
860-295-9523

DEP Western District H.Q.
230 Plymouth Road
Harwinton, CT 06791-2819
860-485-0226

DEP Office of Boating
333 Ferry Road
Old Lyme, CT 06371
860-434-8638

Dinosaur State Park
West Street
Rocky Hill, CT 06067
860-529-5816

Quinebaug Valley Hatchery
Cady Lane
Danielson, CT 06239
860-564-7542

Kellogg Environmental Center
Office of Communications and Education
500 Hawthorne Avenue
Derby, CT 06418-1020
203-734-2513

Fort Griswold Battlefield St. Park
Park Avenue
Groton, CT 06340
860-445-1729

Sherwood Island State Park
Exit 18 off I-95
Westport, CT 06880
203-226-6983

Fort Trumbull State Park
90 Walbach Street
New London, CT 06320-5507
860-444-7591

Sleeping Giant State Park
200 Mt. Carmel Avenue
Hamden, CT 06518-1906
203-789-7498

Harkness Memorial State Park
275 Great Neck Road
Waterford, CT 06385-3823
860-443-5725

Delaware
State Parks
http://www.destateparks.com
Senior citizens who are residents of Delaware and are 62 years of age or older can purchase annual passes for $10, which is half the price of the regular annual pass. Annual passes can be purchased at any of the following state park offices:

New Castle County
Eastern Marine
931 S. Chapel Street
Newark, DE 19713
302-737-6603

Kent County
Boscov's Sporting Goods
3000 Dover Mall
Dover, DE 19901
302-734-9210

DAFB/ Outdoor Rec.
262 Chad St.
Room 208
Dover AFB, DE 19902-7262
302-677-5553 or 302-677-3959
(Military, DE Annuals, DE Sr. Citizen Annuals, & DE Surf Fishing)

Sussex County
A & K Enterprises
201 N. Central Ave.
Laurel, DE 19956
302-875-5513

Bill's Sport Shop
1566 Highway One
Lewes, DE 19958
302-645-7654

Burton Brothers
407 High Street
Seaford, DE 19973
302-629-8595

Cape Henlopen Fishing Center
Hook, Line and Sinker Bait and Tackle
Cape Henlopen Fishing Pier
Lewes, DE 19958
302-644-BAY1

M & H General Store
Rd 1 Box 135B
Milton, DE 19968
302-684-4570

O'Neal Brothers
Rt. 13 & DE Ave.
Laurel, DE 19956
302-875-7588

Rehoboth /Dewey Beach Chamber of Commerce
501 Rehoboth Ave.
Rehoboth, DE 19971
302-227-2233

Taylored Tackle
Rt. 2 Box 115
Seaford, DE 19973
302-629-9017

or online at
https://egov.dnrec.state.de.us/egovpublic/dnrec/disp?doc=shoppingcart&op=catalog&channel=public&CatalogType=ParksAndRecreationPasses.

There is no special discount for seniors for fishing or hunting licenses, but for a resident of Delaware, a fishing license is $8.50 and a hunting license is $12.50. Licenses can be purchased online at
https://egov.dnrec.state.de.us/egovpublic/dnrec/disp?doc=shoppingcart&op=catalog&channel=public&CatalogType=FishAndWildlifePermits&LicenseType=HuntingAndFishing.

Florida

Hunting and State Parks

Florida residents who are 65 years of age or older and are in possession of a Resident Senior Citizen Hunting and Fishing Certificate may take or attempt to take fish or game consistent with state and federal regulations and the rules of the Florida Commission at the time of the taking of the fish or game. The Certificate can be obtained at any county tax collector's office. The Certificate is also accepted in Georgia for freshwater fishing and hunting, but a trout stamp may be required.

There is no senior citizen discount for annual passes to state parks, but individual passes are $40 and family passes are $80. There is half price senior discount for the base camping fee, which is originally $10 to $50, so the senior price is between $5 and $25. The daily entrance fee is $4.00 per carload and $5.00 at some parks. Passes can be purchased online at http://www.floridastateparks.org/annualpass/default.htm or by phone at 352-628-1002 or at any state park office.

Georgia

Hunting and Fishing

Georgia Department of Natural Resources
Commissioner's Office
2 Martin Luther King, Jr. Drive, SE
Suite 1252, East Tower
Atlanta, GA 30334
404-656-3500
http://www.gadnr.org/

Georgia residents who are 65 years of age or older may purchase a lifetime fishing license for $10. A Senior Citizen Discount License may be purchased for $95 by Georgia residents who are 60 years of age or older. Licenses may be purchased online at
https://georgiawildlife.dnr.state.ga.us/service/login1.asp?JumpPage=/service/buyreclicense.asp?Title=Fishing&Title=Fishing or by phone at 1-888-748-6887 (toll free) with a $3.95 processing fee or at Department of Natural Resources, License Unit, 2189 Northlake Parkway, Suite 108, Bldg. 10, Tucker, Georgia 30084. 770-414-3333.

Lifetime hunting licenses are free for Georgia residents who are 65 years of age or older. Licenses can be purchased by phone at 1-888-748-6887 with a $3.95 processing fee. Licenses can also be purchased in person at many sporting goods shops and hardware shops throughout the state or can be sent in to Department of Natural Resources, License Unit, 2189 Northlake Parkway, Suite 108, Bldg. 10, Tucker, GA 30084. Licenses can also be purchased online at
https://georgiawildlife.dnr.state.ga.us/service/login1.asp?JumpPage=/service/buyreclicense.asp?Title=Hunting&Title=Hunting.

State Parks

2 Martin Luther King Jr. Dr., Suite 1352 East
Atlanta, GA 30334
404-656-2770
http://www.gastateparks.org

Residents of Georgia who are 62 years of age or older may purchase an annual pass to state parks for half the regular price. They also receive a twenty percent discount off of individual lodge rooms, campsites, and cottages (Sunday through Thursday, December 1st- March 31st on cottages only). Members of the Friends of Georgia State Parks and Historic Sites can get the Annual ParkPass free. To purchase an annual pass, visit any state park office or call 1-800-864-7275.

Hawaii

State Parks

Kalanimoku Bldg.
Room 130, 1151 Punchbowl St.,
Honolulu, HI 96813
808-587-0400
Fax: 808-587-0390

There is no discounted fee for Hawaii senior citizens for state park entry. Fees range from $5.00 to $55.00. Permits can be purchased at the following locations.

Hawai'I District
P.O. Box 936
75 Aupuni Street, No. 204
Hilo, Hi 96721-0936
808-974-6200
Fax: 808-974-6333

O'ahu District
P.O. Box 621
1151 Punchbowl Street
Honolulu, HI 96809
808-586-0300
Fax: 808-587-0311

Kaua'I District
3060 Eiwa Street
No. 306
Lihu'e, HI 96766-1875
808-274-3444
Fax: 808-274-3448

Maui District
54 South High Street
Wailuku, HI 96793
808-984-8109
Fax: 808-984-8111

Hunting and Fishing

State of Hawaii, Department of Land and Natural Resources
Kalanimoku Bldg.,
1151 Punchbowl St.,
Honolulu, HI 96813
808-587-0400
Fax: 808-587-0390
http://www.hawaii.gov/dlnr/

Hawaii residents who are sixty-five years of age or older may obtain a freshwater fishing license free. Hawaii residents who are sixty-five years of age or older may obtain a hunting license free of charge. The licenses can be purchased online at https://www.ehawaiigov.org/dlnr/fish/exe/fresh_main_page.cgi for the fishing license and http://www.ehawaiigov.org/DLNR/hunting/ for the hunting license. All licenses can be purchased at local convenience stores.

Idaho

Hunting and Fishing

Idaho residents who are sixty-five years of age or older and have been a resident of Idaho for five years or more can purchase a combined hunting and fishing license for a discounted price at $4.50. All licenses can be purchased at any office of the Idaho Department Fish and Game:

Headquarters
600 S. Walnut
PO Box 25
Boise, ID 83707
208-334-3700
Fax: 208-334-2114 or
208-334-2148

Panhandle Region
2750 Kathleen Ave.
Coeur d'Alene, ID 83814
208-769-1414
Fax: 208-769-1418

Clearwater Region
1540 Warner Ave.
Lewiston, ID 83501
208-799-5010
Fax: 208-799-5012

Southwest Region
3101 S. Powerline Rd.
Nampa, ID 83686
208-465-8465
Fax: 208-465-8467

McCall Subregion
555 Deinhard Lane
McCall, ID 83638
208-634-8137
Fax: 208-634-4320

Magic Valley Region
868 E. Main St. / PO Box 428
Jerome, ID 83338
208-324-4359
Fax: 208-324-1160

Southeast Region
1345 Barton Road
Pocatello, ID 83204
208-232-4703
Fax: 208-233-6430

Upper Snake Region
4279 Commerce Circle
Idaho Falls, ID 83401

208-525-7290
Fax: 208-523-7604

Salmon Region
99 Hwy. 93 N.
PO Box 1336
Salmon, ID 83467
208-756-2271
Fax: 208-756-6274
http://www.fishandgame.idaho.gov/

State Parks
There are no discounts for entrance to state parks for seniors.

Indiana
Hunting and Fishing
Department of Natural Resources
402 West Washington Street
Indianapolis, IN 46204
There is no hunting or fishing license discount for senior citizens. For residents of Indiana, hunting and fishing licenses are $14.25 each. They can be purchased online at http://www.ai.org/dnr/fishwild/licensing/, in person at independent agencies, county clerks, and most Department of Natural Resources properties throughout the state. Licenses can also be purchased by mail at

DNR Customer Service Center
402 W. Washington St., Rm. W160
Indianapolis, IN 46204-2739
317-233-4976

State Parks
Residents of Indiana who were born before 1938 can purchase a Golden Hoosier Passport, which serves as an annual pass to state parks and is $12.00, half the price of a regular annual pass.

Iowa
Hunting and Fishing
Iowa Department of Natural Resources
502 E. 9th Street,
Des Moines, IA 50319-0034
http://www.iowadnr.com/license/options.html
There is no discounted price for senior citizens for fishing or hunting licenses. Annual licenses can be purchased online or at any licensed dealer or by calling 1-800-367-1188 for $17.00 and lifetime licenses can be purchased at the same locations for $51.00.

State Parks
There is also no discount to enter state parks. Information can be found by mailing letters to the above address or by emailing kevin.szcodronski@dnr.state.ia.us or visiting http://www.iowadnr.com/parks/index.html.

Kansas
Hunting and Fishing
Kansas Department of Wildlife & Parks
512 SE 25th Ave.
Pratt KS 67124
620-672-5911
http://www.kdwp.state.ks.us/permits/permits.html
There is no senior citizens discount on hunting or fishing permits in the state of Kansas. For residents of Kansas, fishing licenses can be purchased for $19.00, hunting licenses for $19.00 or a combined hunting and fishing license for $37.00. Licenses can be purchased online at https://www.accesskansas.org/cgi-bin/hunt_online/online_sales.cgi?purchase_type=L.

State Parks
All Kansas residents who are 65 years of age or older may purchase a permit to enter any of the state parks for one half the regular price at the time of purchase. Prices range from $3.75 to $23.25. Permits can be purchased at

1020 S. Kansas
Topeka, KS 66612-1327
785-296-2281

or at any of other regional offices or at the office of the state park itself, all of which can be found at http://www.kdwp.state.ks.us/office.html#regoff.

Kentucky
Hunting and Fishing
Kentucky Department of Fish and Wildlife Resources
#1 Game Farm Road
Frankfort, KY 40601
800-858-1549
http://www.kdfwr.state.ky.us/
Residents of Kentucky who are 65 years of age or older must purchase a permit for $5.00 to hunt and fish and must provide both the permit and proof of the reason for the discounted license in order to hunt or fish. Licenses can be purchased at https://fw.ky.gov/license/licsaleintro.asp, by phone at 1-877-KYTAG-01 (877-598-2401) or at any local license agent.

State Parks
http://parks.ky.gov/
Senior citizens (62 years of age or older with identification) may rent lodges in any of the state parks for a discounted rate. For more information on individual park rates, visit http://parks.ky.gov/parkrate.htm.

Louisiana
Hunting and Fishing
http://www.wlf.state.la.us/apps/netgear/index.asp?cn=lawlf&pid=1052
Louisiana residents who reached the age of 60 before June 1st, 2000 are not required to have a license to fish or hunt in Louisiana, but must have proof of age.

State Parks
P.O. Box 44426
Baton Rouge, LA 70804-4426
1-888-677-1400 toll free phone
225-342-8111 in Baton Rouge
http://www.lastateparks.com/
Senior citizens who are 62 years of age or older may enter any Louisiana state park for day use for free.

Maine
Hunting and Fishing
There is no discount for senior citizens in Maine, but for residents, fishing and hunting licenses each cost $22.00 but a combination fishing and hunting license costs $39.00. Licenses can be purchased online at https://www.informe.org/moses/ or from any licensing agent in Maine.

State Parks
Bureau of Parks and Lands
22 State House Station
18 Elkins Lane
Augusta, ME 04333-0022
207-287-3821
Fax: 207- 287-8111
There is no fee for state park entrance for residents of Maine who are 65 years of age or older. Birth certificate or driver's license is required as proof of age. For more information visit http://www.state.me.us/doc/parks/programs/index.html.

Maryland
Hunting and Fishing
Residents of Maryland who are 65 years of age or older can purchase a fishing license at a discounted price of $5.00 that allows them to fish in Maryland's fresh waters and the Chesapeake Bay and its tributaries. The senior discount applies also to residents who are turning 65 in the calendar year in which they wish to purchase the fishing license. Residents of Maryland who are 65 years of age or older or who will be turning 65 during that year are eligible for the discounted price of $5.00 for a hunting license. Licenses can be purchased online at http://www.wildlifelicense. com/md/, at most sporting goods stores and tackle and bait shops as well as at the following service centers located throughout the state.

Annapolis Service Center
580 Taylor Avenue
Annapolis, MD 21401
410-260-3220

Central Service Center
2 Bond Street
Bel Air, MD 21014
410-836-4550

Dundalk Service Center
7701 Wise Avenue
Baltimore, MD 21222
410-284-1654

Eastern Service Center
201 Baptist Street #22
Salisbury, MD 21801
410-543-6700

East Central Service Center
120 Broadway Avenue
Centreville, MD 21617
410-819-4100

Southern Service Center
6904 Hallowing Lane
Prince Frederick, MD 20678
410-535-3382

Western Service Center
3 Pershing Street
Room 103
Cumberland, MD 21502
301-777-2134
http://www.dnr.state.md.us/service/fishinfo.asp

State Parks
Residents of Maryland who are 62 years of age or older can obtain a Golden Age Pass that allows them free entry to state parks that charge a service fee and that also is valid for camping for half price through Thursday. License applications are available at http://www.dnr.state.md.us/outdoors/parkpass.html. Applications must be sent in to

Maryland Department Of Natural Resources
State Forest and Park Service
580 Taylor Avenue, E-3
Annapolis, MD 21401
Attn: Golden Age Pass Application
410-260-8186

Massachusetts
Hunting and Fishing
Residents of Massachusetts who are between the ages of 65 and 69 can purchase fishing licenses at a discounted price of $16.25 and those who are age 70 or over can purchase one for free. Hunting licenses operate under the same prices. Sporting licenses, which covers both hunting and fishing, cost $25.00 for residents between the ages of 65 and 69 and are free for those who are 70 or over. Licenses expire at the end of December of each year. Licenses can be purchased online at http://www.sport.state.ma.us/ or at http://www.mass.gov/massoutdoors. They can also be purchased from various vendors throughout the state, the addresses of which can be found at

http://www.mass.gov/dfwele/dfw/dfwvend.htm. Licenses can also be purchased at the District offices of MassWildlife as follows:

Western Wildlife District
Division of Fisheries and Wildlife
400 Hubbard Avenue
Pittsfield, MA 01201
413-447-9789
Fax: 413-442-0047

Connecticut Valley Wildlife District
Division of Fisheries and Wildlife
East Street
Belchertown, MA 01007
413-323-7632
Fax: 413-323-9623

Central Wildlife District
Division of Fisheries and Wildlife
Temple Street
West Boylston, MA 01583
508-835-3607
Fax: 508-792-7420

Northeast Wildlife District
Division of Fisheries and Wildlife
68 Harris Street
Acton, MA 01720
978-263-4347
Fax: 978-635-0292

Southeast Wildlife District
Division of Fisheries and Wildlife
195 Bournedale Road
Buzzards Bay, MA 02532
508-759-3406
Fax: 508-759-0381

Vehicle passes to Massachusetts state parks cost $35.00 per calendar year for residents, regardless of age. They are good for one calendar year, January 1 to December 31, and can be purchased by phone at 617-626-4969 or at any one of the following offices.

Boston Office
251 Causeway Street, Suite 900
Boston, MA 02114
617-626-4969

Southeastern
Borderland State Park
259 Massapoag Avenue
Easton/Sharon, MA 02356
508-238-6566

Northeastern
817 Lowell Street
Carlisle, MA 01741
617-727-9676
617-727-0197

Central
40 Cold Storage Drive
Amherst, MA
413-545-5993

Clinton Field Office
155 West Boylston St.
Clinton, MA 01510
978-368-0126

Western
740 South Street
Pittsfield, MA 01201
413-442-8928

Michigan

Hunting and Fishing

The following hunting licenses are available at a discounted rate for residents of Michigan who are 65 years of age or older: Firearm Deer hunting ($5.60), Archery Deer ($5.60), Combination Deer ($11.20), Fur Harvester ($5.60), Bear ($5.60) Small Game ($5.60), Fall Turkey ($5.60), and Spring Turkey ($5.60). License vendors can be found throughout the state and the full list can be found online at http://michigan.gov/dnr/0,1607,7-153-10363_14518-34869--,00.html.

Fishing licenses can be purchased for a discounted price of $3.00 by Michigan residents aged 65 years or older for a 24 hour license, $5.60 for a restricted license, which is good for all fish except for trout and salmon, and $10.80 for an All Species license. Licenses can be purchased online at http://www.michigan.gov/dnr.

State Parks

Annual Motor Vehicle permits to state parks in Michigan can be purchased for $6.00 by seniors who are 65 years of age or older and have a vehicle registered in Michigan. Permits are available online at the Michigan Mall at http://mi-mall.michigan.gov/webapp/wcs/stores/servlet/StoreCatalogDisplay?storeId=10101&langId=-1&catalogId=10051 or by phone at 517-373-9900.

Minnesota

Hunting and Fishing

There is no discounted price for fishing or hunting licenses for senior citizens in Minnesota. Fishing licenses cost between $9.50 and $27.00 for the various types available for residents of Minnesota. Hunting licenses cost between $0.00 and $310.00.

Licenses can be purchased online at http://www.wildlifelicense.com/mn/index.html, by phone at 888-665-4236, or in person at various locations throughout the state, the full list of which can be found online at http://www.dnr.state.mn.us/licenses/agents.html.

State Parks
There is also no discount for entrance to state parks. The price for vehicle passes are $25 for annual permit, $7 for a daily permit, $5 for a daily group permit, and $12 for a Minnesota handicapped annual permit, and $18 for a second vehicle permit. Vehicle permits can be purchased in person at any state park or at the Department of Natural Resources headquarters at 500 Lafayette Road, St. Paul Minnesota. Permits can also be purchased by phone at 651-296-6157 in the Twin Cities metro area, or toll free at 888 MINNDNR 646-6367.

Mississippi
Hunting and Fishing
1505 Eastover Drive
Jackson, MS 39211-6374
601-432-2400
http://www.mdwfp.com/
Residents of Mississippi who are 65 years of age or older are exempted from obtaining a fishing or hunting license, but are required to have proof of age, residency, and disability, if that applies, while fishing or hunting.

State Parks
1505 Eastover Drive
Jackson, MS 39211-6374
601-432-2400
http://www.mdwfp.com/
Senior citizens can purchase vehicle passes to any state park in Mississippi for a discounted price of $2, can camp for a discounted price of $11-$12, $50 for boat launch, and $3 for entrance to museums. Vehicle permits can be purchased at 1505 Eastover Drive, Jackson, MS 39211-6374 or by phone at 601-432-2400.

Missouri
Hunting and Fishing
P.O. Box 180 zip 65102
2901 W. Truman Blvd.
Jefferson City, MO 65109
573-751-4115
Fax: 573-751-4467
Residents of Missouri who are 65 years of age or older do not need an annual, lifetime, or daily permit in order to fish in Missouri, but it may be required to purchase a daily fishing tag or a trout permit. Trout tags cost $7.00 and daily permits cost $5.50. Any Missouri resident who is 65 or older may hunt without a permit, but may not trap at all or hunt deer or wild turkey without a permit, and must carry proof of age and residency while hunting. All Missouri residents must purchase a Missouri Migratory Bird Hunting Permit in order to hunt waterfowl, snipe, doves, woodcock, and rails. Fishing and hunting licenses may be purchased online at https://www.wildlifelicense.com/mo/.

State Parks
Missouri State Park System
P.O. Box 176
Jefferson City, MO 65102
1-800-334-6946
http://www.mostateparks.com/
Missouri residents who are 65 or older can camp in any Missouri state park for a discounted price. The basic campsite is $7 and electric campsite is $12, and electric/water campsite is also $12, and a sewer/electric/water campsite is $13. There is a reservation fee of $8.50 in addition to the campsite fee and it is non-refundable and non-transferable. All fees are due at the time the reservation is made and there is a $5 fee to change or cancel a reservation.

Montana
Hunting Fishing and State Parks
Residents of Montana who are 62 or older may fish without a fishing license and hunt upland game birds, excluding turkey, without a hunting license, but must purchase a Conservation License for $6.25 in order to fish or hunt. Licenses are available at Montana FWP (Fish, Wildlife, and Parks) offices. Licenses can be purchased at the following locations

Montana Fish, Wildlife, and Parks
1420 East Sixth Avenue
P.O. Box 200701
Helena, MT 59620-0701
406-444-2535
Fax: 406-444-4952
Email: fwpgen@state.mt.us

FWP Region 1 Headquarters
490 North Meridian Road
Kalispell, MT 59901
406-752-5501
Fax: 406-257-0349
Email: fwprg12@mt.gov

FWP Region 2 Office
3201 Spurgin Road
Missoula, MT 59804
406-542-5500
Fax: 406-542-5529
Email: fwprg22@mt.gov

FWP Region 3 Office
1400 South 19th
Bozeman, MT 59718

406-994-4042
406-994-4043
Fax: 406-994-4090
Email: fwprg3@mt.gov

FWP Region 4 Office
4600 Giant Springs Road
Great Falls, MT 59405
406-454-5940
Fax: 406-761-8477
Email: fwprg42@mt.gov

FWP Region 5 Office
2300 Lake Elmo Drive
Billings, MT 59105
406-237-2940
Fax: 406-248-5026
Email: fwprg52@mt.gov

FWP Region 6 Headquarters
Route 1-4210
Glasgow, MT 59230
406-228-3700
Fax: 406-228-8161
Email: fwprg62@mt.gov

FWP Region 7 Headquarters
Industrial Site West
Miles City, MT 59301
406-234-0900
Fax: 406-234-4368
Email: fwprg72@mt.gov

Licenses can also be purchased from license agents throughout the state, the complete listing of which is available online at http://fwp.state.mt.us/hunting/obtainlicenses/agents.html. Licenses are also available online at https://app.discoveringmontana.com/elicensesales.

Montana residents, starting in 2004, can enter any state park simply by having a valid Montana state license plate, as a $4 fee is included in vehicle registration, which can be waived if the resident is not intending to visit state parks or fishing access sites.
http://fwp.state.mt.us/default.html

Nebraska
Residents of Nebraska who are 70 or older may obtain a fee-exempt fishing permit. This permit is also available to veterans who are 65 or older. A fee-exempt hunting license is also available. Fishing and hunting permits can be purchased online at https://www.greatlodge.com/scripts/ipos/GLNEpermits.cgi. Or, to obtain an application, send an email to busing@ngpc.state.ne.us, including your complete name and regular mail address in the message. Applications can also be obtained by phone at 402-471-0641. Hunting licenses can also be purchased in person at any of the following offices.

Alliance
299 Husker Road
P.O. Box 725
Alliance, NE 69301-0725
308-763-2940

Bassett
524 Panzer Street
P.O. Box 508
Bassett, NE 68714-0508
402-684-2921

Kearney
1617 1st Avenue
Kearney, NE 68847-6057
308-865-5310

Lincoln
2200 North 33rd Street
Lincoln, NE 68503
402-471-0641

Norfolk
2201 N. 13th Street
Norfolk, NE 68701-2267
402-370-3374

North Platte
301 East State Farm Road
North Platte, NE 69101-0430
308-535-8025

Omaha
1212 Bob Gibson Boulevard
Omaha, NE 68108-2020
402-595-2144

Ak-Sar-Ben Aquarium
21502 Hwy 31
Gretna, NE 68028
402-332-3901

State Parks
2200 N. 33rd St.,
Lincoln, NE 68503
402-471-0641
http://www.ngpc.state.ne.us/
There is no discounted price for entrance to Nebraska state parks. Annual entrance permits are $17.00 and daily permits cost $3.00. A $0.35 issuing fee may be required when purchasing a permit. Permits are available online at http://www.outdoornebraska.com or at any Game and Parks office.

Nevada

Hunting and Fishing
1100 Valley Rd.
Reno, NV 89512
775-688-1500
http://www.nevadadivisionofwildlife.org/
Residents of Nevada who are 65 years of age or older may purchase an annual fishing license or an annual hunting license each for a discounted price of $13.00. Combination hunting and fishing licenses are available for the discounted price or $21.00. Applications for licenses are available online at http://www.nevadadivisionofwildlife.org/about/license/pdf/04reslic.pdf. The application forms can be mailed in or licenses can be purchased in person at any of the license agents throughout the state of Nevada. A complete listing of the agents and their locations is available at http://www.nevadadivisionofwildlife.org/about/license/agents.shtm.

State Parks
901 S. Stewart Street,
Suite 5005,
Carson City, NV 89701-5248
Residents of Nevada who are 65 or older and have been a resident of Nevada for 5 consecutive years can purchase for a discounted price of $15.00 an annual pass that allows for unlimited entry to all of Nevada's state parks and use of camping and boat launch facilities for 12 months after the date of purchase. Passes can be purchased at any of the individual state parks. More information is available online at http://parks.nv.gov/.

New Hampshire

Hunting and Fishing
Residents of New Hampshire who are 68 years of age or older and have been a resident of New Hampshire for at least two consecutive years can be issued a permanent fishing license free of charge. Permits are not available online, but can be obtained at any license agent in the state. A valid driver's license or other non-driver's license photo identification is required to obtain a fishing license. Senior residents can also obtain combination fishing and hunting licenses, Muzzleloader, Archery, and Clam and Oyster licenses. Any license type not listed above must be purchased annually, at the regular price. The full listing of license agents in New Hampshire can be found online at http://www.wildlife.state.nh.us/Licensing/agents_table.htm.

State Parks
Residents of New Hampshire who are 65 years of age or older may enter any of the following state parks or historic sites in New Hampshire free of charge: Bear Brook State Park, Clough State Park, Echo Lake Beach, Echo Lake in Franconia Notch State Park, Ellacoya State Park, Forest Lake State Park, Greenfield State Park, Kingston State Beach, Milan Hill State Park, Miller State Park, Mollidgewock State Park, Monadnock State Park, Moose Brook State Park, Odiorne Point State Park, Pawtuckaway State Park, Pillsbury State Park, Rhododendron State Park, Rollins State Park, Rye Harbor State Park, Silver Lake State Park, Sunapee State Park, Umbagog State Park, Wadleigh State Park, Wellington State Beach, Wentworth State Beach, White Lake State Park, Winslow State Park, Daniel Webster Birthplace, Franklin Pierce Homestead, John Wingate Weeks Estate, Robert Frost Farm, Tip-Top House at Mt. Washington State Park, and Wentworth Coolidge Mansion. More information is available online at http://www.nhstateparks.org/.

New Jersey

Hunting and Fishing
Residents of New Jersey who are 65 years of age or older can purchase a firearm hunting license for a discounted price of $15.50, a bow and arrow license for $16.50, a trapping license for $32.50, a deer permit for bow, shotgun, or muzzleloader for $28.00, a turkey season permit for $21.00, a rifle permit for $9.50, a pheasant and quail stamp for $40.00, or a resident waterfowl stamp for $5.00. For New Jersey residents who are between the ages of 65 and 69, a fishing license is available for a discounted price of $12.50. For those who are aged 70 or older proof of age functions as a fishing license. An All Around Sportsman license is available for $72.50 and it covers bow and arrow hunting, fishing, and firearm hunting. Licenses are available online at https://www6.state.nj.us/DEP_Fish/ChildSupportServ?action=R or at any license agent throughout the state. The full list of license agents is available online at http://www.state.nj.us/dep/fgw/agentlst.htm.

State Parks
Entrance fees for New Jersey state parks varies from park to park. For walk-ins, entrance is either free or $2.00 depending on the state park, and for vehicles, the fee ranges from free to $6.00 on weekdays and free to $10.00 on weekends. A full list of fees for each park is available online at http://www.state.nj.us/dep/parksandforests/parks/feeschedule.htm. There is also a State Park Pass that is available for $50 that allows for entrance to any of the state parks for one calendar year. Applying for a State Park pass can also waive the fee for residents of New Jersey who are 62 years of age or older and obtain a $2.00 discount per night in camping fees. The Park Pass application is available online at http://www.state.nj.us/dep/parksandforests/parks/parkform.pdf. Applications are also available by calling the Division of Parks and Forestry at 800-843-6420 or 609-984-0370.

New Mexico

Hunting and Fishing
Residents of New Mexico who are senior citizens may purchase a fishing license for a discounted price of $5.00. Those who are 70 years of age or older may obtain a license for free. A hunting

license is available for a discounted price of $18.00. A general hunting and fishing combination license is also available for the discounted price of $23.00. Licenses are available online at https://www.greatlodge.com/cgi-bin/licenses/customer_options.cgi?st=NM&btype=Licensing&r=0.9173021259262346.

State Parks
P.O. Box 1147,
Santa Fe, NM 87504
888 NMPARKS 667-2757
For entrance to state parks, there is no senior citizen discount. For walk-ins or bicycles, entrance is free of charge. For vehicles, daily entrance is $5.00 and by bus it is $15.00. Camping fees range from $4.00 to $14.00 depending on the type of campsite. Day use annual entrance passes are available for $35.00 and annual camping passes are $100 for residents of New Mexico who are 62 years of age or older. A full list of state park fees is available online at http://www.emnrd.state.nm.us/nmparks/PAGES/fees/fees.htm. Passes can be purchased at any of the state parks or at the division of state park's office in Santa Fe at P.O. Box 1147, Santa Fe, NM 87504 (888) NMPARKS (888-667-2757).

New York
Hunting and Fishing
New York State Department of Environmental Conservation
625 Broadway
Albany, NY 12233
Residents of New York who are 65 years of age or older can purchase a sportsman license for the discounted price of $5.00. This license works as a fishing license as well as a small and big game hunting license. Residents applying for this license must have either previously held a hunting license or must currently hold a Hunters Education certificate. Lifetime resident sportsman licenses are also available for the discounted price of $50 for residents of New York who are 65 years of age or older. A lifetime resident senior fishing license is available, also for the price of $50. Lifetime licenses are only available to those who have been residents of New York for at least one year immediately prior to the purchase of the license and proof of this residency is required at the time of purchase. Licenses may be purchased from any license issuing outlet, such as sporting goods stores, town clerk offices, and some major discount stores throughout the state. Licenses may also be purchased at the New York Department of Environmental Conservation License Sales Office at 625 Broadway, Albany, NY 12233-4790, by phone at 866-933-2257, or by mail to MCI, P.O. Box 36985, Phoenix, AZ 85067-6985. More information is available online at http://www.dec.state.ny.us/index.html.

State Parks
Empire State Plaza
Agency Building 1
Albany NY, 12238
518-474-0456
518-486-1899 TDD
Residents of New York may purchase an Empire Pass, which works as an annual pass to any of New York's State Parks and recreational facilities. Passes are available for $59 and are good from April 1 to March 31 of the following year. The pass pays for itself in eight visits. The Empire Pass can be purchased at any of the state parks or state park regional offices or by writing to Empire Pass, New York State Parks, Albany, NY 12238. Applications are available online at https://www.mybizz.net/www.nysparks.state.ny.us/passport/application.shtml. The application can be submitted online or mailed in. The Empire Pass is not applicable at the following state parks: Prospect Mountain Veteran Memorial Highway, Irondequoit Bay Marine Park, Whiteface Mountain Veteran Memorial Highway, Oak Orchard Marine Park (East), Hearthstone Point Public Campground, Newtown Battlefield, Lake George Islands Public Campground, Jennings Pond, Saranac Locks, Lake Lauderdale State Park, Minnewaska Cross Country Skiing, Lake Superior State Park, or Fahnestock Winter Park. More information on state parks is available at http://nysparks.state.ny.us/.

North Carolina
Hunting and Fishing
Residents of North Carolina can purchase basic annual fishing and hunting licenses for $15.00 each or a trapping license for $25.00. A combination fishing and hunting license is $20.00. Fishing, hunting, and trapping licenses are available for just the county of residence rather than for state-wide use for a discounted price of $10.00. Residents of North Carolina who are 70 years of age or older can purchase a Special Sportsman lifetime license for the discounted price of $10.00. This license is good for state-wide fishing and hunting, hunting for big game, on game lands, for waterfowl (not including a federal duck stamp), and fishing of mountain trout. More information on license fees is available online at http://www.ncwildlife.org/fs_index_03_fishing.htm. Licenses can be purchased online at http://www.ncwildlife.org/fs_index_03_fishing.htm, from a wildlife service agent (the complete listing of which is available online at the website listed above) or by phone at (888) 2HUNTFISH 888-248-6834.

State Parks
512 N. Salisbury Street,
Archdale Building,
7th Floor, Room 732
Raleigh, NC 27699
Residents of North Carolina who are 62 years of age or older may enter any of North Carolina's state parks for a discounted daily fee of $3.00. There are also discounted camping fees, ranging from $9.00 to $20.00 per day. A full list of state park fees is available online at http://ils.unc.edu/parkproject/visit/fees.html.

Noth Dakota

Hunting and Fishing

North Dakota Game and Fish Department
Licensing Division
100 N. Bismarck Expressway
Bismarck, ND 58501-5095
701-328-6335

Residents of North Dakota who are 65 years of age or older may purchase a fishing license for a discounted fee of $3.00. The application is available online at http://www.state.nd.us/gnf/licenses/docs/sfn-6075.pdf and can be mailed in to North Dakota Game and Fish Department, Licensing Division, 100 N. Bismarck Expressway, Bismarck, ND 58501-5095, 701-328-6335. The Resident Fishing, Hunting, and Furbearer Certificate, which is required for all hunters and anglers, is available for $1.00. Hunting licenses vary from $5.00 to $20.00 depending on the type of license, the full listing of which is available on the application at the website listed above. A resident combination license is also available, for $32.00 and can be used for fishing, small game, general game/habitat, and furbearer. Licenses can also be ordered by telephone at 800-406-6409 with a $4 service charge. Licenses can also be purchased online at http://www.discover.com/gnf with no service charge.

State Parks

North Dakota Parks & Recreation Department
1600 E. Century Avenue, Suite 3
Bismarck, ND 58503-0649
Ph. 701-328-5357

The daily entrance fee to state parks in North Dakota is $5, but residents of North Dakota who are 65 years of age or older can purchase an annual pass at a discounted price of $20.00. Camping fees range from $5.00 to $14.00 per night and an annual, daily, or Senior pass is required in addition to the camping fee. A full list of fees is available online at http://www.ndparks.com/Parks/Fees.htm and more information on state parks is available at http://www.ndparks.com/.

Ohio

Hunting and Fishing

Ohio Department of Natural Resources
Division of Wildlife
2045 Morse Rd., Bldg. G
Columbus, OH 43229-6693

Residents of Ohio who are 66 years of age or older, born on or after January 1 1938 and who have resided in Ohio for the six months immediately prior may purchase a fishing license at the discounted price of $10.00. The $10.00 fee includes a $1.00 writing fee. Senior citizens are also able to purchase annual hunting licenses for a discounted price of $10.00, and HIP survey (needed to hunt waterfowl or migratory game birds) for free, Special Deer Permit for $12.00, Urban Deer Permit for $15.00, Spring Turkey Permit for $12.00, Fall Turkey Permit for $12.00, Ohio Wetlands Stamp for $15.00, Federal Migratory Bird Hunting Stamp for $15.00, and Fur-Taker Permit for $15.00. Ohio residents who were born on or before January 1, 1937 may obtain the following licenses for free: Fishing License, Hunting License, HIP survey, Special Deer Permit, Urban Deer Permit, Spring Turkey Permit, Fall Turkey Permit, Ohio Wetlands Stamp, Federal Migratory Bird Hunting Stamp, and Fur-Taker Permit. License applications as well as a full list of license vendors in the state of Ohio are available online at http://www.dnr.state.oh.us/wildlife/License/main.htm.

State Parks

Senior Citizens in Ohio, with a Golden Buckeye card, can get 50% off camping rates from Sunday to Thursday, 10% off camping rates on Friday and Saturday, and 10% off the total rate for getaway rentals, cottages, and lodge rooms on any night at any state park in Ohio. More information on state parks is available online at http://www.dnr.state.oh.us/parks/default.htm.

Oklahoma

Oklahoma Department of Wildlife Conservation
P.O. Box 53465
Oklahoma City, OK 73152

Residents of Oklahoma who are 65 years of age or older are not required to purchase the new Fishing and Hunting Legacy permit. Fishing hunting licenses are available for a discounted price of $6.00 each or for $10.00 when purchased as a combination fishing and hunting license. The application is available is online at http://www.wildlifedepartment.com/seniorapplication.pdf and can be mailed in to Oklahoma Department of Wildlife Conservation at P.O. Box 53465, Oklahoma City, OK 73152.

State Parks

There is no discount for camping in state parks in Oklahoma for seniors. The fees for camping range from $8.00 to $26.00 depending on the type of campsite and the state park. A full list of fees is available online at http://www.touroklahoma.com/campingfees.asp and more information on state parks in Oklahoma is available online at http://www.touroklahoma.com/.

Oregon

Hunting and Fishing

ODFW-Licensing
3406 Cherry Avenue NE
Salem, OR 97303
503-947-6100

Residents of Oregon who are 70 years or older can purchase annual fishing licenses for a discounted price of $12.00 and an annual hunting license for $11.00 and an annual combination hunting and fishing license for $21.50. Hunting license applications are available at http://www.dfw.state.or.us/ODFWhtml/Regulations/2005_huntreg_application.pdf and fishing license applications are available at http://www.dfw.state.or.us/ODFWhtml/Regulations/05fish_mail_order.pdf. Combination licenses are available on either application. Applications should be mailed to ODFW-Licensing, 3406 Cherry Avenue NE, Salem, OR 97303 503-947-6100. License orders may be faxed to 503-947- 6117 or 503-947-6113. Telephone orders will not be accepted.

State Parks
There is no discounted price for entrance to state parks for senior citizens. Entrance fees are $3 daily at parks that charge entrance fees and an annual entrance pass is $25 where applicable. A full listing of fees and which parks charge and which do not is available online at http://www.oregonstateparks.org/rates.php.

Pennsylvania
Hunting and Fishing
Residents of Pennsylvania who are 65 years of age or older may purchase an annual fishing license for a discounted price of $10.00. There is a fee of $1.00 and a replacement fee of $4.25. Fishing license applications are available online at https://www.theoutdoorshop.state.pa.us//fbg/fish_secured/FishLicenses.asp?ShopperID=3468318CDFF746DF91CAAD050AFF5C22. Annual hunting licenses are available for senior citizens for a discounted price of $13.00, a lifetime hunting license for $51.00, or a lifetime combination license for $101.00. A complete list of all the hunting licenses and fees for Pennsylvania is available online at http://www.theoutdoorshop.state.pa.us/FBG/game/GameLicenseInfo.asp?ShopperID=B041FFEADEDB4075B70A5347DE027E61. Licenses are available online at http://www.greatlodge.com/cgi-bin/permits/license_links.cgi?fr=Y&url=PA3&cobrand=.

State Parks
Department of Conservation and Natural Resources
Rachel Carson State Office Building
PO Box 8767
400 Market Street
Harrisburg, PA 17105-8767
1-888-727-2757
There is no discount for senior citizens for entrance to state parks in Pennsylvania. However, residents of Pennsylvania who are 62 years of age or older may get a $3.00 discount off any campsite in any state park with identification that is proof of age. More information on Pennsylvania's state parks is available online at http://www.dcnr.state.pa.us/.

Rhode Island
Hunting and Fishing
http://www.state.ri.us/dem/programs/bpoladm/manserv/hfb/
Residents of Rhode Island who are 65 years of age or older may obtain a hunting, fishing, or combination hunting and fishing license for free. Applications are available online at http://www.state.ri.us/dem/programs/bpoladm/manserv/hfb/fishing/fishing.htm for the fishing license and http://www.state.ri.us/dem/programs/bpoladm/manserv/hfb/hunting/hunting.htm for hunting licenses. Combination licenses can be obtained using either the fishing or hunting license application. Applications can be sent to

Rhode Island Department of Environmental Management
Office of Boat Registration and Licensing
235 Promenade Street
Third Floor, Room 360
Providence, RI 12908-5767
401-222-6647

Licenses can also be obtained in person at any license vendor throughout the state. A full list of vendors is available online at http://www.state.ri.us/dem/programs/bpoladm/manserv/hfb/hunting/pdfs/huntvend.pdf.

State Parks
There are no discounts for senior citizens in Rhode Island state parks. Entrance to state parks is free. Beach parking rates are $4.00 for weekdays and $5.00 for weekends. Season passes to beaches cost $25.00. Camping rates range from $8.00 to $12.00 depending on the type of campsite. A full list of the fees is available online at http://www.state.ri.us/dem/pubs/regs/regs/parksrec/userfees.pdf.

South Carolina
Hunting and Fishing
Residents of South Carolina who are 64 years of age or older may purchase a lifetime combination hunting and fishing license for a discounted price of $9.00. A full listing of all the licenses and fees is available online at http://www.dnr.state.sc.us/etc/rulesregs/pdf/licensefees.pdf. Individual annual hunting, fishing, big game, wildlife management areas, duck stamp, and saltwater fishing license can be obtained for free. Licenses can be obtained online at http://www.dnr.state.sc.us, by phone at 888-434-7472, or at any license sales agent state-wide. License agents can be found at many local sporting goods stores, bait and tackle shops, major retailers, and Department of Natural Resources offices. A license application for those who are 64 and older is available online at http://www.dnr.state.sc.us/licenses/images/Dis-65-LicenseApp.pdf. Applications can be sent in to

South Carolina Department of Natural Resources
License Division
P.O. Box 11710

Columbia, SC 29211
803-734-3838
Fax: 803-734-9377

State Parks
SC Department of Parks, Recreation & Tourism
1205 Pendleton St., Room 200
Columbia SC 29201
803-734-1700
Residents of South Carolina who are 64 years of age or older may purchase a Palmetto Pass, which works as an annual pass to all of South Carolina's state parks, but for $25.00, half the normal $50.00 fee. Licenses can be purchased at any state park or at the Park Service central office in Columbia. More information is available online at http://www.southcarolinaparks.com/stateparks/annualpasses.asp.

South Dakota
Hunting and Fishing
South Dakota Game Fish and Parks
523 East Capitol Avenue
Pierre, SD 57501
605-773-3485
Residents of South Dakota who are 65 years of age or older may purchase annual fishing licenses for a discounted price of $10.00. Combination fishing and small game licenses may be purchased for $49.00. Other hunting license fees range from $10.00 to $505.00 depending on the type of game. A full list of licenses and fees is available online at http://www.sdgfp.info/Wildlife/LicenseFee.htm. Licenses are available with any licensing agent in the state of South Dakota. A full list of license agents and their locations is available online at http://www.sdgfp.info/Wildlife/Agents/Index.htm/. Licenses can also be purchased online at https://www.state.sd.us/applications/gf82/Default.htm.

State Parks
http://www.sdgfp.info/
There is no discount for senior citizens for state park entrance. Annual passes are $20.00 for the first vehicle and $10.00 for a second. Passes can be purchased by mailing a request with check or money order made out for the appropriate amount to:
Game, Fishing, and Parks Licensing Office
412 West Missouri
Pierre, SD 57501
605-773-3391
Entrance passes are also available at any of the state parks. More information on state parks, hunting, and fishing licenses is available online at http://www.sdgfp.info/licenses.htm.

Tennessee
Hunting and Fishing
Residents of Tennessee who turned 65 years of age on or after March 1, 1991 may purchase a discounted license to fish, hunt and trap for $11.00. Residents who turned 65 on or before March 1 1991 may fish, hunt, and trap without a license. The application is available online at http://www.state.tn.us/twra/senior.pdf and must be mailed to:
Tennessee Wildlife Resources Agency
P.O. Box 40747
Nashville, TN37204
Attn: License Division

State Parks
There is no discounted entrance rate for state parks. The entrance fee is $3.00 per vehicle. Multi-visit passes can be purchased for $30.00 Multi-visit passes can be purchased at the state park office or visitor center of participating parks or by mailing the following information:
Name
Full mailing address
License plate of the vehicle that will have the pass
Make of the vehicle that will be assigned the pass
Day time phone number
Check or money order (no cash) in the amount of $30.00 made payable to Tennessee State Parks
This information can be sent to any of the following locations:

MVP
Big Hill Pond State Park
984 John Howell Road
Pocahontas, TN 38061
731-645-7967

MVP
Booker T. Washington State Park
5801 Champion Road
Chattanooga, TN 37416-1614
423-894-4955

MVP
Cedars of Lebanon State Park
328 Cedar Forest Road
Lebanon, TN 37090-7678
615-443-2769

MVP
Cove Lake State Park
110 Cove Lake Lane
Caryville, TN 37714
423-566-9701

MVP
Davy Crockett Birthplace State Park
1245 Davy Crockett Park Road
Limestone, TN 37681-5825
423-257-2167

MVP
Edgar Evins State Park

1630 Edgar Evins Park Road
Silver Point, TN 38582-7917
931-858-2114

MVP
Harrison Bay State Park
8411 Harrison Bay Road
Harrison, TN 37341-9616
423-344-6214

MVP
Hiwassee/Ocoee River State Park
Spring Creek Road
P.O. Box 5
Delano, TN 37325-0255
423-263-0050

MVP
Long Hunter State Park
2910 Hobson Pike
Hermitage, TN 37076
615-885-2422

MVP
Montgomery Bell State Park
1020 Jackson Hill Road
Burns, TN 37029-0039
615-797-9051

MVP
Meeman-Shelby Forest State Park
910 Riddick Road
Millington, TN 38053-5099
901-876-5201

MVP
Nathan Bedford Forrest State Park
1825 Pilot Knob Road
Eva, TN 38333-9801
731-584-6356

MVP
Pinson Mounds State Archaeological Area
460 Ozier Road
Pinson, TN 38366-9626
731-988-5614

MVP
Radnor Lake State Natural Area
1160 Otter Creek Road
Nashville, TN 37220-1700
615-373-3467

MVP
Rock Island State Park

82 Beach Road
Rock Island, TN 38581-4200
931-686-2471

MVP
T.O. Fuller State Park
1500 Mitchell Road
Memphis, TN 38109
901-543-7581

MVP
Old Stone Fort State Park
732 Stone Fort Drive
Manchester, TN 37355-3026
731-723-5073

Texas

Hunting and Fishing

Residents of Texas who were born before September 1, 1930 do not need to purchase a license in order to fish. Any resident of Texas who is 65 years of age or older may purchase a fishing license for a discounted price. The available fishing licenses are Special Resident Freshwater Fishing for $11.00, Special Resident Saltwater Fishing for $16.00, and Special Resident All-Water Fishing for $28.00. Resident of Texas who are 65 years of age or older are also eligible to purchase a hunting license for a discounted price of $6.00. Senior Residents 'Super Combo' License Packages are also available for a discounted price of $30.00 and work as a combination fishing and hunting license. Licenses may be purchased by phone at 800-TX LIC 4 U (800-895-4248) for an administrative fee of $5.00. Licenses are also available in more than 2,000 locations throughout the state at such places as sporting goods stores, gun shops, department stores, discount stores, bait and tackle shops, grocery stores and many others. Licenses are also available online at http://www.tpwd.state.tx.us/licenses/online_sales/.

State Parks

Residents of Texas who are 65 years of age or older may purchase a Texas Parklands Passport with a 50% discount off the original price. The Texas Parklands Passport works as an annual pass to any state park in Texas that collects entrance fees. Both residents and non-residents of Texas who turned 65 before September 1, 1995 are entitled to waived entry fees at those state parks that collect entry fees. The Texas Parklands Passport can be purchased at most state parks or historic sites or through the Customer Contact Center in Austin, Texas at 512-389-8900. More information is available on both licenses and state parks online at http://www.tpwd.state.tx.us/

Utah

Hunting and Fishing

Utah Division of Wildlife Resources
P.O. Box 146301
Salt Lake City, UT 84114-6301

801-538-4700
Fax: 801-538-4745
Residents of Utah who are 65 years of age or older may purchase a fishing license for the discounted price of $21.00. Small game licenses are $17.00. Combination fishing and hunting licenses are available for $34.00. Licenses can be purchase online at https://secure.utah.gov/hflo/hflo. Licenses can also be purchased at any license agent in the state, a full list of which is available online at http://www.wildlife.utah.gov/licenses/agents.html.

State Parks
1-800-200-1160
http://www.utah.com/stateparks/
There are no discounted fees for entrance to state parks. Fees range from $5-$9 for day-use vehicle entrance depending on the park. A detailed list of fees is available online at http://www.stateparks.utah.gov/visiting/2004fee.pdf. Walk-in daily entrance fees range from $3-$5 and annual passes cost $70.00. Annual passes can be purchased at any state park, region office or the state office at1594 West North Temple in Salt Lake City or by calling 801-538-7220.

Vermont
Hunting and Fishing
Residents of Vermont who are 65 years of age or older may purchase a permanents hunting and fishing license for $36.00. Licenses can be purchased in person or by mail to the Waterbury Fish and Wildlife office. A list of licensing agents and their locations is online at http://www.vtfishandwildlife.com/buy_where.cfm. More information is available online at http://www.vtfishandwildlife.com/.

State Parks
Vermont State Parks
103 South Main Street
Waterbury, VT 05671-0601
802-241-3655
Fax: 802-244-1481
There is no discount for senior citizens for state park entry. The daily entry fee per person is $2.50. Season passes are available as individual passes for $25.00 or as vehicle passes for $75.00. More information on state parks is available online at http://vtfpr.anr.state.vt.us/parks/.

Virginia
Hunting and Fishing
4010 West Broad Street
Richmond, VA 23230
804-367-1000
Residents of Virginia who are 65 years of age or older can purchase annual fishing licenses for a discounted price of $1.00. Lifetime licenses can also be purchased for the discounted price of $10.00. Lifetime licenses for both hunting and fishing can be purchased online at http://www.dgif.virginia.gov under 'Forms'. Annual licenses can be purchased from any license agent in the state, a full list of which is available online at http://www.dgif.virginia.gov/hunting/license_agents.html. There is a $0.50 issuance fee if the license is purchased through a license agent. More information on fishing and hunting in Virginia is available online at http://www.dgif.virginia.gov/index.asp.

State Parks
Department of Conservation and Recreation
203 Governor Street, Suite 213
Richmond, VA 23219-2094
804-786-1712
Entrance fees vary from state park to state park. However, there is no senior discount. The following state parks have no entrance fee: Sailor's Creek Battlefield, Staunton Creek Battlefield. Parks that are under construction and have limited services charge $2 for both weekdays and weekends. The following parks charge $2 on weekdays and $3 on weekends: Bear Creek, Belle Isle, Caledon, Chippokes, Douthat, Grayson Highlands, Holliday Lake, Hungry Mother, James River, Natural Tunnel, New River Trail, Occoneechee, Staunton River, Twin Lakes, Wilderness Road, York River. The following parks charge $3 on weekdays and $4 on weekends: Claytor Lake, Fairy Stone, First Landing, Kiptopeke, Lake Anna, Leesylvania, Mason Neck, Pocahontas, Shenandoah River, Sky Meadows, Smith Mountain Lake, Westmoreland. All state parks charge a $2 entrance fee on both weekends and weekdays during the off-season. More information is available online at http://www.dcr.state.va.us/parks/.

Washington
Hunting and Fishing
WDFW Main Office
600 Capitol Way N.
Olympia, WA 98501-1091
360 902-2200
Residents of Washington who are 70 years of age or older can purchase fishing licenses for freshwater and saltwater fishing each for $5.48. Big game hunting licenses can be purchased for a discounted price that varies from $21.90 to $72.27. Small game hunting licenses cost $32.85. Licenses can be purchased online at https://www.greatlodge.com/cgi-bin/licenses/customer_search.cgi?st=WA&btype=Licensing&r=0.19738899360269052. Licenses can also be purchased in person from and license vendor in the state. License vendors' locations can be found online at http://wdfw.wa.gov/lic/vendors/vendors.htm. More information on fishing and hunting is available online at http://wdfw.wa.gov/.

State Parks
Washington State Parks and Recreation Commission
7150 Cleanwater Lane
P.O.Box 42650

Olympia, WA 98504
360-902-8844
888-226-7688
www.parks.wa.gov
Four passes are offered for senior citizens, veterans, and people with disabilities. An Off-Season Senior Citizen Pass is available for $50 for free nightly camping and moorage off season. Senior Citizen Limited Income Pass and the Disability Pass is free and offers free day vehicle parking and 50% off camping. Disabled Veteran Lifetime Pass is free and offers free camping/moorage, day vehicle parking and more.

West Virginia
Hunting and Fishing
State Capitol
Building 3, Room 812
Charleston WV 25305
304-558-2771
Residents of West Virginia who are 65 years of age or older do not need a license to hunt or fish. However, valid photo identification must be on hand while hunting or fishing as proof of age. More information on hunting and fishing is available online at http://www.wvdnr.gov/.

State Parks
State Capitol
Building 3, Room 713
Charleston WV 25305
304-558-2764
Information on state parks is available online at http://www.wvparks.com/. There is no discounted entrance fee for senior citizens.

Wisconsin
Hunting and Fishing
1-877-945-4236
Residents of Wisconsin who are senior citizens can purchase fishing and hunting licenses for discounted prices. Fishing licenses cost $7.00 and small game hunting licenses cost $8.00. Licenses can be purchased online at http://www.wildlifelicense.com/wi/ or at any license sale location, a full list of which is available online at http://dnr.wi.gov/org/caer/cs/licenseagents/.

State Parks
DNR Parks and Recreation
P.O. Box 7921
Madison WI 53707-7921
608-266-2181
Residents of Wisconsin who are 65 years of age or older can purchase entrance stickers to state parks for discounted rates of $10.00 for annual passes or $3.00 for daily or hour-long passes. More information on state parks is available online at http://www.dnr.state.wi.us/org/land/parks/.

Wyoming
Hunting and Fishing
Wyoming Game and Fish
5400 Bishop Boulevard
Cheyenne, WY 82006
307-777-4600
Residents of Wyoming can purchase fishing licenses for $4 for daily licenses and $19 for annual licenses. There is no discount for senior citizens. Hunting licenses cost $7 daily and $19 for an annual license. License applications are available online at http://gf.state.wy.us/wildlife/hunting/2005Applications/index.asp. More information on the specific types of licenses and their fees is available online at http://gf.state.wy.us/fiscal/license/index.asp.

State Parks
2301 Central Avenue
Cheyenne, WY 82002
307-777-6303
Residents of Wyoming can purchase daily passes to state parks for $2.00 or historic sites for $1.00. Annual passes to state parks cost $25.00. Overnight camping permits cost $6.00 and annual camping permits cost $30.00. Passes can be purchased at various locations, a full listing of which is available online at http://wyoparks.state.wy.us/selling%20agents.htm. More information on state parks is available online at http://wyoparks.state.wy.us/index1.htm.

Caregivers

Senior Caregivers

Caregiving may be one of the most important roles you will undertake in your lifetime. Typically it is not an easy role, nor is it one for which most of us are prepared. Like most people, you may have questions about how to cope with your care receiver's illnesses or disability. If you have a job and are juggling several responsibilities or if your family member or friend needs a lot of assistance, you may need help with caregiving, too. Whether you are expecting to become a caregiver or have been thrust into the role overnight, it is useful to know where you can get information and help. More than 50 million people are informal caregivers- providing unpaid help to older persons who live in the community and have a least one limitation on their activities of daily living. These caregivers include spouses, adult children, and other relatives and friends. The economic value of our nation's family and informal caregivers has been estimated at $257 billion annually.

To help give caregivers some relief and assistance, we have compiled a list of good starting places, along with some organizations that offer a variety of programs to provide aid to the caregiver. Remember that you are not alone in this endeavor.

IMPORTANT NOTE:

If you are a caregiver it is very important to you review the other sections of this book. You will be able to find money and help for the person you are caring for including

Money and help to pay the patients expenses
Money and help for housing
Money and help for pay for medications and health care

Some good starting places include:

1) ***Eldercare Locator***
The U.S. Administration on Aging offers this free service to older adult Americans and their caregivers to help them connect with available services. Eldercare Locator links older adults who need assistance with state and local area agencies on aging and community-based organizations. If you need help with any health related problem go to the web site and follow the directions or call a specialist. The web site is available in many different languages. Contact: 800-677-1116, www.eldercare.gov.

2) ***Helpful Health Hotlines***
The National Health Information Center and the National Library of Medicine both offer an online database of health-related organizations operating toll-free telephone services. The databases also include information on services and publications available in Spanish. You can find out whom to call

for almost any health issue. Contact: Health Information Resources Database, Referral Specialist, P.O. Box 1133, Washington, DC 20013-1133; 800-336-4797, 301-565-4167; www.health.gov/NHIC/Pubs/tollfree.htm or http://healthhotlines.nlm.nih.gov/.

3) ***National Institute on Aging***
The National Institute on Aging, is the government's leading effort on aging research. In addition to research information and professional training, NIA disseminates health information to the general public. Contact: National Institute on Aging, Building 31, Room 5C27, 31 Center Drive, MSC 2292, Bethesda, MD 20892; 301-496-1752, 800-222-4225, Fax: 301-496-1072; www.nia.nih.gov.

4) ***SeniorHealth.gov***
The National Institute of Health offers an on-line information web site for older adults. Their goal is to make age-related health information easily accessible to seniors, family members and friends. The web site is senior friendly including large print, short, easy to read segments and simple navigation. There is even a "talking" feature which reads the text. Information is updated regularly. Contact: http://nihseniorhealth.gov/.

5) ***Seniors.gov***
has information on a variety of topics including diet, exercise, and consumer protection. It has links to all federal government web sites with information for seniors. Check them out at www.seniors.gov.

Caregiver Support

Funded through money from the Older Americans Act, the National Family Caregiver Support Program provides services to help meet the needs of caregivers including: information about available services, assistance in gaining access to support services, individual counseling and caregiver training, respite care, and possibly supplemental services. Contact your State Unit on Aging at www.aoa.gov/eldfam/How_To_ Find/Agencies/Agencies.asp or contact Administration on Aging, Washington, DC 20201; 202-619-0724; www.aoa.gov.

Alzheimer's Support

The Alzheimer's Association provides support services for people with Alzheimer's and their families. It also funds research on Alzheimer's and provides information on caregiving. You can learn about safety service and local chapters for support for all family members, as well as education programs, fact sheets on a wide range of topics, clinical trials, and more. Contact Alzheimer's Association, 225 N. Michigan Ave., Fl. 17, Chicago, IL 60601; 800-272-3900; Fax: 202-393-2109; http://www.alz.org/; Email: advocate@alz.org.

Family Relief

The American Health Assistance Foundation provides information on different age-related illnesses. It also supports other research organizations and can provide emergency grants for the elderly and their care givers through the Alzheimer's Family Relief Program. Their toll-free hotline can provide information, support and referrals for caregivers. Contact American Health Assistance Foundation,

22512 Gateway Center Drive, Clarksburg, MD 20871; 800-437-2423; 301-948-3244; Fax: 301-258-9454; http://www.ahaf.org/.

How To Choose Long Term Care

The American Health Care Association is an organization that represents many of the nursing homes and other living centers. They help to sponsor a website www.longtermcareliving.com that explains types of long-term care facilities, how to choose the right one, tips, and information on paying for care. Contact American Health Care Association, 1201 L Street, NW, Washington, DC 20005; 202-842-4444; Fax: 202-842-3860; http://www.ahca.org/.

Red Cross Will Help With Care

The Red Cross offers programs for the elderly dealing with things like crime prevention, fall prevention, and home nurse care instructions. Contact American Red Cross, 2025 E Street, NW, Washington, DC 20006; 202-303-4498; http://www.redcross.org/.

Choosing Assisted Living

Assisted Living Federation of America represents all the providers that work in assisted living homes, nursing homes or other services. ALFA works to improve and advance the care given to the elderly. Through their website you can access the provider database, see a description of types of assisted living facilities, and read a guide to choosing a facility that is right for you or your family member. Contact Assisted Living Federation of America, 11200 Waples Mill Rd, Suite 150, Fairfax, VA 22030-7407; 703-691-8100; Fax: 703-691-8106; http://www.alfa.org/.

Transportation Issues

The Beverly Foundation provides information for caregivers on research they have done to improve elderly life through mobility and transportation. It also works to improve the mobility of the elderly through out their community by conducting research and examining model programs. Research and resources are available on their website. Contact Beverly Foundation, 566 El Dorado St. #100, Pasadena, CA 91101; 626-792-2292; Fax: 626-792-6117; http://www.beverlyfoundation.org/.

Get Training in Caregiving

The Brookdale Center offers programs to train people to become better caregivers. Classes offered for a fee include advocacy and guardianship training, as well as certificate programs for practitioners in the geriatric field. Contact Brookdale Center on Aging of Hunter College, 425 East 25th Street, 13th Floor North, New York, NY 10010-2590; 212-481-3780; Fax: 212-481-3791; http://www.brookdale.org/.

Online Caregiver Info

Elderweb is a research site for the elderly and their caregivers. It offers information on how to better a caregiver's service along with employment opportunities. The website provides links to long-term care information, searchable database of organizations, articles, reports, and more. Contact Elderweb, 1305 Chadwick Drive, Normal, IL 61761; 309-451-3319; http://www.elderweb.com.

You Are Not Alone

The Family Caregiver Alliance provides information for the elderly and their caregivers. They offer a state-by-state resource for caregiver support programs, as well as providing fact sheets, publications, and more. You can download a copy of a *Handbook for Long Distance Caregivers*. The website posts information and also has online discussion groups, education, and training programs. Contact Family Caregiver Alliance, 180 Montgomery Street, Suite 1100, San Francisco, CA 94104; 415-434-3388; www.caregiver.org; Email: info@caregiver.org.

Home Care and Hospice Locator

If you are looking for a home care or hospice agency, the National Association for Home Care can help. They offer an online database with over 20,000 agencies listed. The first step is to read their two publications to get you started, *How to Choose a Home Care Provider* and *All About Hospice: A Consumer's Guide*. The second step is to use the database to locate a home care or hospice agency near you. They also offer a variety of useful consumer information through their online bookstore for a small fee. Contact: National Association for Home Care, 228 7th Street, SE, Washington, DC 20003; 202-547-7424, Fax: 202/547-3540; www.nahc.org.

Help to Care for Loved Ones

The National Family Caregivers Association is dedicated to helping you if you are caring for a chronically ill or disabled family member. They support and educate the more than 50 million Americans who are family care givers all for free. They offer a newsletter, guides, tips, education pages and resources to help you learn all you can about helping your loved one while taking care of yourself too. Contact: National Family Caregivers Association, 10400 Connecticut Avenue, Suite 500, Kensington, MD 20895-3944; 800-896-3650, 301-942-6430, Fax: 301-942-2302; Email: info@thefamilycaregiver.org, www.thefamilycaregiver.org.

Give Yourself A Break: Respite Locator Database

If you are a family caregiver, you sometimes need a break from all of your duties. Respite is a service that can provide temporary help to you in your home or at another site. You can search a respite service by state or by a service that you need on the National Respite Locator database. Contact: National Respite Locator, 800 Eastowne Drive, Suite 105, Chapel Hill, NC 27514; 919-490-5577, Fax: 919-490-4905; www.respitelocator.org.

Get The Help of a Visiting Nurse

Home health care is a large part of the overall health care in the United States today. Many people need professional health care assistance to help care for a family member who is chronically ill or disabled. The Visiting Nurse Associations of America (VNA) is a non-profit national organization committed to home health care. They offer help from choosing an agency to deciding who will pay for the service. You can also search the database to help you find a VNA in your areas. Contact: Visiting Nurse Associations of America, 99 Summer Street, Suite 1700, Boston, MA 02110; 617-737-3200, Fax: 617-737-1144; www.vnaa.org.

Adult Day Care Selection Guide

The National Adult Day Care Services Association is a national advocacy, educational and networking group for the adult day care industry. Their *Guide to Selecting an Adult Day Center* will help you search for the quality day care service you need. The step-by-step guide will help you with everything from determining your needs to trying it out. Contact: National Adult Day Services Association, Inc., 2519 Connecticut Avenue, NW, Washington, DC 20008; 800-558-5301, 703-435-6830, Fax: 703-435-8631; www.nadsa.org.

Support Group Gives Laughs To Caregivers

Caregiving.com understands that care giving can be very tough, so they provide resources that can make you chuckle and stay healthy. They also offer online support groups to help you get through the care giver maze. You can even email a question to one of their experts or get three free months *Caregiving* for free. There are many more care giving programs, so be sure to contact them to see how they can help you. Contact: Caregiving.com, Tad Publishing Co., P.O. Box 224, Park Ridge, IL 60068; 847-823-0639; www.caregiving.com.

Free Sample Magazine Issue

You can try out the *Caregiver's Home Companion* magazine online. In addition, you can subscribe to the *The Caregiver's Hotline* email newsletter. The Caregiver's Home Companion can provide you with tips, resources and information to help you care for your elderly loved one. Contact: The Caregiver's Home Companion, P.O. Box 693, Southport, CT 06890-0693; 203-254-3538, Fax: 203-259-5073; www.caregivershome.com.

Caregivers Empowering Caregivers

Empowering Caregivers is a division of the National Organization For Empowering Caregivers, a non-profit organization. They are dedicated to helping caregivers as much as possible through a variety of programs including: live chats, message boards, a newsletter, and more. Contact: National Organization For Empowering Caregivers, 425 West 23rd Street, Suite 9B, New York, NY 10011; 212-807-1204, Fax: 212-645-5143; www.care-givers.com.

Senior Resources in Wisconsin

Wisconsin's Senior Resources offers a variety of Wisconsin senior directories for a small fee or online for free. Contact: Senior Resources, P.O. Box 285, Germantown, WI 53022; 262-253-0901, Fax: 262-253-0903; www.seniorresourcesonline.com.

Find The Best Info On Caregiving

The National Alliance for Caregiving is a non-profit organization which conducts research, develops national programs and increases public awareness on family caregiving issues. One of their programs, the Family Care Resource Connection, can help you find reviews and ratings on a number of books, websites and other resources. Contact: National Alliance for Caregiving, 4720 Montgomery Lane, 5th Floor, Bethesda, MD 20814; www.caregiving.org.

Learn The Stages Of Caregiving

The National Family Caregivers Association and the National Alliance for Caregiving have collaborated to assist family caregivers. *Caregiving 101* is an online resource for the more than 50 million families in the United States providing family care. The site provides families with a place to begin and a place to return to as their needs change. www.familycaregiving101.org.

Help With Alzheimer's Patients

Caring for someone with Alzheimer's is a difficult and stressful job. In order to provide assistance, the U.S. Administration on Aging (AoA) has announced over $10.5 million in funding for grant projects to develop innovative models of care for persons with Alzheimer's disease and their family caregivers. Starting July 1, 2005, the $10.5 million funding allocation will support new grants to 10 states and continuation grants to 28 states. The program's mission is to expand the availability of diagnostic and support services for persons with Alzheimer's disease, their families, and their caregivers, as well as to improve the responsiveness of the home and community based care system to persons with dementia. The program focuses on serving hard-to-reach and underserved people with Alzheimer's disease or related disorders. For more information contact Alz Demo Project Officer, Administration on Aging, Washington, DC 20201; 202-357-3452; www.aoa.gov/alz.

See If Patient Qualifies For Free Home Health Care and Therapy

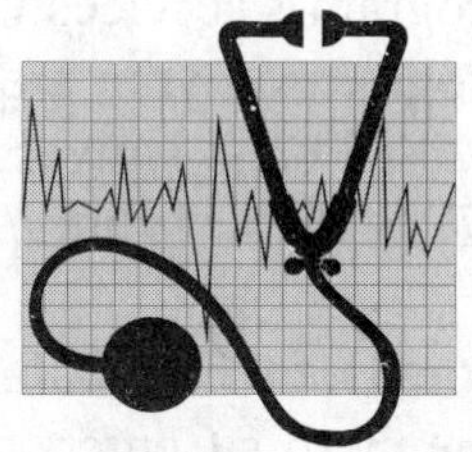

Sometimes home health care, or physical, speech, or occupational therapy is covered by insurance. It is usually only for a limited amount of time. To check eligibility you will need to contact Medicare and/or Medicaid to see what services are covered and what you need to do to apply. There is a free publication titled, "Medicare and Home Health Care" that explains the benefits available. For more information contact Centers for Medicare & Medicaid Services, 7500 Security Boulevard, Baltimore MD 21244-1850; 800-MEDICARE; www.medicare.gov.

Sometimes You May Need Professional Help

Sometimes it is difficult to care for a loved one long-distance or you may need help in organizing care. The National Association of Professional Geriatric Care Managers is group of health care professionals who are trained specifically to help with caring for the elderly. This association can refer you to your state chapter, who in turn can refer you to case managers in your area. You can also find a wealth of information online. For more information contact The National Association of Professional Geriatric Care Managers, 1604 North Country Club Road, Tucson, AZ 85716; 520-881-8008; http://www.caremanager.org.

Before The Frustration Level Raises Check These Services

Need help caring for an elderly family member? Many large service organizations have local offices that provide assistance. Services vary depending upon the needs of the community, but you can find out what your local area may offer. Contact:

- **Catholic Charities USA**, 1731 King St., #200, Alexandria, VA 23314; 703-549-1390; www.catholiccharitiesusa.org.
- **Salvation Army**, 615 Slaters Lane, P.O. Box 269, Alexandria, VA 22313; 703-684-5500; 800-SAL-ARMY; www.salvationarmyusa.org.
- **United Way of America**, 701 N. Fairfax St., Alexandria, VA 22314; 800-411-UWAY; www.unitedway.org.
- Also contact your county **Department of Health and Human Services** or **Social Services** agency to see what they can offer.

Check If Patient is Eligible For Some Major Programs

Not sure who qualifies for what? Spend a few minutes and check out www.benefitscheckup.org. It takes you step by step through the eligibility process and at the end will tell you what benefits you or your loved one may qualify for as well as who you need to contact to learn more. This service is offered by the National Council on the Aging and connects you to all government programs. There is also a special section regarding prescription drug programs. Remember, if the database says you are not eligible for a program there may be some other organization that will provide you with the service or help you need. You have to keep checking other sources.

Local Free Caregiving Volunteers

Faith in Action is a volunteer caregiving program supported by the Robert Wood Johnson Foundation. This program brings together volunteers of all faiths to help local citizens in need of assistance. These volunteers can help with transportation, running errands, visiting homebound, reading, and more. This program's services vary from location to location. You can contact Faith in Action to learn about programs in your area, or you can search for them online. For more information contact Faith in Action, Wake Forest University School of Medicine, Medical Center Boulevard, Winston-Salem, NC 27157; 877-324-8411; http://www.fiavolunteers.org.

More Local Free Caregiving Help

Shepherd's Centers of America is a group of volunteer organizations whose focus is helping older Americans in their communities. Services vary from place to place but may include things such as: health screenings, home health aides, medication and health classes, adult day care, support groups, information and referrals, learning and social classes, and more. To see if there is a location near you, contact Shepherd's Centers of America, One West Armour Boulevard, Suite 201, Kansas City, MO 64111; 800-547-7073; http://www.shepherdcenters.org.

A Clearinghouse of Caregiver Info

Best Caregiver Info is an online service that provides articles, and resources to help family caregivers get the information they need. This site was designed to help employers offer assistance to their employees. The idea was to provide a resource that would offer support services and lessen the stress of the employees, so they could better focus on their jobs. Check them out at www.bestcaregiverinfo.com.

More Sources Of Caregiver Help

This web site is for professional caregivers serving the elderly through community and in-home services. But they provide valuable links to family caregivers to locate information throughout the country, www.aginghelp.com/caregiver.

Free 4-Week Online Course Caring For Aging Parents

If you are over 45, you are one of 108 million "ThirdAgers" in midlife in the U.S. today. ThirdAge.com is an online site dedicated to baby boomers and their lives. They offer a free 4-week online course to help you care for your aging parents. In addition, they offer other resources and guides to help you with your caregiving role. Contact: ThirdAge Inc., 25 Stillman Street, Suite 102, San Francisco, CA 94107-1309; www.thirdage.com/family/caregiving/.

Association For Children of Aging Parents

Children of Aging Parents (CAPS), is a non-profit group helping the nation's caregivers. Their website states "You are not alone!" They are there to help their members either online or through support groups in 13 states. Memberships are $25 for an individual and include a quarterly newsletter. Contact: Children of Aging Parents, P.O. Box 167, Richboro, PA 18954; 800-227-7294; www.caps4caregivers.org.

Alzheimer's Caregiver Guide

If you are caring for or about to care for someone with Alzheimer's disease you are facing many challenges. The National Council on Aging offers an *Alzheimer's Caregivers' Guide* to help you cope with new role. Contact: NCOA Headquarters, 300 D Street, SW, Suite 801, Washington, DC 20024; 202-479-1200, Fax: 202-479-0735; www.ncoa.org/content.cfm?sectionID=109&detail=67.

Senior Safety Checklist

Is your home safe for your aging parents? The U.S. Consumer Product Safety Commission publishes two booklets to help you keep your loved ones safe at home. *Safety for Older Consumers: Home Safety Checklist* and *Fire Safety Checklist for Older Consumers* are the two publications you can view online or order at the following address. Contact: U.S. Consumer Product Safety Commission, Washington, DC 20207-0001; 800-638-2772, 301-424-6521, Fax: 301-431-7107; www.cpsc.gov/cpscpub/pubs/older.html.

"One-Stop Shopping Center for Caregivers"

The Family Caregiver Alliance offers many services to meet consumer needs in a "one-stop" program. They offer fact sheets, a newsletter, support and more for the caregivers of the elderly. Contact: Family Caregiver Alliance, 180 Montgomery Street, Suite 1100, San Francisco, CA 94104; 800-445-8106; www.caregiver.org.

Learn The 3 Steps of Caregiving

Coordinating care can be tough if you are planning for an aging loved one. Getcare.com has a simple online three step self-assessment tool to make your search easier. 1. Assess your care needs, 2. Learn about care options, 3. Search for care providers. Go through these steps and you may find the perfect combination of care options to fit your needs. Contact: Getcare.com, 150 Grand Avenue, Oakland, CA 94612; 510-986-6700, Fax: 510-986-6707; www.getcare.com.

Family Caregiver Support Program Contacts

The National Family Caregiver Support Program develops support systems and a range of services to meet the needs of caregivers. The program calls for all states, in coordination with other organizations to provide five basic services to family caregivers;

1. information
2. assistance in gaining access to supportive services
3. individual counseling, support groups, and caregiver training
4. respite care
5. supplemental services

The following state contact list does not provide these services, but manages the government funds for them. They can, though, refer you to local agencies where you can receive this assistance.

Alabama
Tara Shaver-Jarmon, State Coordinator
Alabama Cares
Alabama Dept. of Senior Services
770 Washington Avenue, Suite 470
Montgomery, AL 36130 -1851
334-353-9636 or 877-4252243
Fax: 334-242-5594
Email: tshaver-jarmon@adss.state.al.us

Alaska
Lisa Morley
Department of Health and Social Services
Division of Senior and Disability Services

PO Box 110680
Juneau, AK 99811-0680
907-465-4798
Email: lisa_morley@admin.state.ak.us

Arizona
Chris Andrews
AZ DES, Aging & Adult Administration
1789 W. Jefferson, 950A
Phoenix, AZ 85007
602-542-4446
Fax: 602-542-65756
Email: candrews@mail.de.state.az.us

Arkansas
Bean Murray
Ar Division Of Aging & Adult Service
P.O. Box 1437-5530
Little Rock, AR 72203-1437
501-682-8511
Fax: 501- 682-8155
Email: bean.murray@mail.state.ar.us

California
Mark Sticklin
California Department of Aging
1600 K Street
Sacramento, CA 95814
916-323-6551
Email: mstickli@aging.ca.gov

Colorado
John Treinen or Susan Cornejo
Division Of Aging And Adult Services
Department of Human Services
1575 Sherman Street
Ground Floor
Denver, CO 80203-1714
303-866-2800
Fax: 303-866-2696
Email: John.Treinen@state.co.us | Susan.Cornejo@state.co.us

Connecticut
Donielle Rooks
Elderly Services Division
Department Of Social Services
25 Sigourney St., 10th Floor
Hartford, CT 06106
860-424-5862
Fax: 860-424-5301
Email: donielle.rooks@po.state.ct.us

Delaware
Leah A. Jones
Div Of Svcs For Aging & Adults W/Physical Disabilities
Dept of Health & Social Services
1901 North DuPont Highway
New Castle, DE 19720
302-577-4791 ext. 48
Fax: 302-577-4793
Email: leahjones@state.de.us

District Of Columbia
Sherlyn Taylor
Office On Aging
One Judiciary Square
441 4th St., N.W., 900 S
Washington, DC 20001
202-724-5622
Fax: 202-724-4979
Email: sherlyn.taylor@dc.gov

Florida
Ron Taylor
Department Of Elder Affairs
Suite 315, 4040 Esplanade Way
Tallahassee, FL 32399
850-414-2000
Fax: 850-414-2004
Email: taylorrs@elderaffairs.org

Georgia
Cliff Burt
Division Of Aging Services
#2 Peachtree St. N.W. 9th Floor
Atlanta, GA 30303
404-657-5336
Fax: 404-657-5285
Email: gcburt@dhr.state.ga.us

Guam
Gerrie Gumataoto
FCSP Project Coordinator
Division of Senior Services
Dept of Public Health & Social Services
Government of Guam
PO BOX 2816
Hagaina, Guam
011 (671) 475-0263
Fax: (671) 477-2930
Email: gtgumat@mail.gov.gu

Hawaii
Region IX
Wes Lum
Hawaii Executive Office on Aging
250 South Hotel Street
Suite 406
Honolulu, HI 96813 - 2831
808-586-7319

Fax: 808-586-0185
Email: wlwlum@mail.health.state.hi.us

Idaho
Deedra L. Hunt, Senior Services Program Specialist
Email: dhunt@icoa.state.id.us
Tina Rice, Senior Services Program Specialist
Email: trice@icoa.state.id.us
ICOA address:
3380 Americana Terrace
Suite 120
P.O. box 83702
Boise, ID 83720-0007
208-334-3833
Fax: 208-334-3033

Illinois
Joseph Lugo
Department On Aging
Division of Older American Services
421 East Capitol Avenue
Springfield, IL 62701
217-785-9017
email: joseph.lugo@aging.state.il.us

Indiana
Ginny Morris
Bur Of Aging/In Home Services
402 W. Washington St.
P.O. Box 7083
Indianapolis, IN 46207-7083
317-232-7109
Fax: 317-232-7867
Email: gmorris@fssa.state.in.us

Iowa
Nicki Stajcar, Consumer Protection Advocate
Department Of Elder Affairs
Clemens Bldg., 3rd Fl.
200 Tenth St.
Des Moines, IA 50309-3609
515-242-3320
Fax: 515-242-3300
Email: nicki.stajcar@dea.state.ia.us

Kansas
Joyce Smith, Community Based Srvs. Dir.
Department On Aging
New England Building
503 South Kansas
Topeka, KS 66603-3404
785-291-3356
Fax: 785-296-0256
Email: joyces@aging.state.ks.us

Kentucky
Phyllis Culp
Office Of Aging Services
275 East Main Street, 5 West
Frankfort, KY 40621
502-564-6930
Fax: 502-564-4595
Email: phyllis.culp@mail.state.ky.us

Louisiana
Mary Tonore
Office Of Elderly Affairs
HCBS
PO Box 80374
412 N 4th St.
Baton Rouge, LA 70898-0374
225-342-9722
Fax: 225-342-7133
Email: mftonore@goea.state.la.us

Maine
Mary Walsh
Bureau Of Elder & Adult Svcs
442 Civic Center Drive
#11 State House Station
Augusta, ME 04333-0011
207-624-5335
Fax: 207-287-9229
Email: mary.walsh@state.me.us

Maryland
Sue Vaeth, Manager
Department Of Aging
State Office Building, Room 1007
301 West Preston Street
Baltimore, MD 21201
410-767-1108
Fax: 410-333-7943
Email: sjv@mail.ooa.state.md.us

Massachusetts
Michael R. Banville, Program Coord.
Exec Office Of Elder Affairs
1 Ashburton Place, 5th floor
Boston, MA 02108
617-727-7477
Fax: 617-727-9368
Email: michael.banville@state.ma.us

Michigan
Bonnie Graham
Office Of Svcs To The Aging
P.O. Box 30676
Lansing, MI 48909-8176
517-373-9360

Fax: 517-373-4092
Email: grahamBon@michigan.gov

Minnesota
Jane Vujovich
Aging & Adult Services Division
444 Lafayette Road
St. Paul, MN 55155-3843
800-882-6262
Fax: 651-297-7855
Email: Jane.Vujovich@state.mn.us

Mississippi
Shirley S. Rainey, Program Coord.
Council On Aging
Div of Aging & Adult Svcs
750 N. State St.
Jackson, MS 39202
601-359-4928
Fax: 601-359-9664
Email: srainey@mdhs.state.ms.us

Missouri
Randy Rodger
Aging Program Specialist
Department Of Health & Senior Services
P.O. Box 1337
615 Howerton Court
Jefferson City, MO 65102-1337
573-526-8561
Fax: 573-751-8493
Email: rrodger@mail.state.mo.us

Montana
Debbie Horton or Charlie Rehbein
Office On Aging
Senior Long Term Care Division
111 Sanders Street
PO Box 4210
Helena, MT 59604
406-444-4077
Fax: 406-444-7743
Email: dhorton@state.mt.us | crehbein@state.mt.us

Nebraska
Janis Price
Division Of Aging Services
Dept of Health & Human Services
P.O. Box 95044
301 Centennial Mall-South
Lincoln, NE 68509
402-471-2307
Fax: 402-471-4619
Email: janice.price@hhss.state.ne.us

Nevada
Mel Phillips
Division For Aging Services
3100 W. Sahara Avenue # 103
Las Vegas, NV 89102
702-486-3545
Fax: 702-486-3572
Email: mphillips@aging.state.nv.us

New Hampshire
Mary Gare-Grizwin
Div. Of Elderly & Adult Svcs
State Office Park South
Brown Building
129 Pleasant St.
Concord, NH 03301-3857
603-271-0541
Fax: 603-271-4643
Email:mgrizwin@dhhs.state.nh.us

New Jersey
Barbara Fuller
Division Of Senior Affairs
Department of Health & Senior Services
P.O. Box 807
Trenton, NJ 08625-0807
609-943-3463
Fax: 609-943-3467
Email: barbara.fuller@doh.state.nj.us

New Mexico
Barbara Owens
State Agency On Aging
1410 San Pedro NE .
Albuquerque, NM 87110
505-255-0971 ext. 104
Fax: 505-255-5602
Email: Barbara.Owens@state.nm.us

New York
Nick Rogone
Office For The Aging
Two Empire State Plaza
Albany, NY 12223-1251
518-474-2428
Fax: 518-474-1398
Email: nick.rogone@ofa.state.ny.us

North Carolina
Christine Urso
Division Of Aging
2101 Mail Service Center
693 Palmer Drive
Raleigh, NC 27699-2101
919-733-3983

Fax: 919-733-0443
Email: chris.urso@ncmail.net

North Dakota
Nancy Shantz, Program Administrator
Aging Services Division
Department of Human Services
600 South 2nd St., Suite 1C
Bismarck, ND 58504
701-328-8911
Fax: 701-328-8989
Email: soshan@state.nd.us

Northern Mariana Islands
Ana Dlg.Flores, Director
CNMI Office on Aging, DC&CA
PO Box 2178
Saipan, MP 96950
011 (671) 734-4361
Fax: 011 (670) 233-1327

Ohio
Richard R. LeBlanc
Department Of Aging
50 West Broad Street - 9th Fl
Columbus, OH 43215-3363
644-466-7967
Fax: 644-466-5741
Email: dleblanc@age.state.oh.us

Oklahoma
Susan Tyler, Programs Manager
Aging Services Division
Department of Human Services
P.O. Box 25352
312 N.E. 28th Street
Oklahoma City, OK 73105
405-522-3076
Fax: 405-521-2086
Email: susan.tyler@okdhs.org

Oregon
Holli Crown
Senior & Disabled Svcs Div
500 Summer St., NE, E10
Salem, OR 97301-1076
503-945-6028
Fax: 503-373-7092
Email:Holli.Crown@state.or.us

Pennsylvania
Daniel McQuire
Department Of Aging
Forum Place
555 Walnut Street, 5th Fl
Harrisburg, PA 17101-1919
717-783-1550
Fax: 717-772-3382
Email: dmcquire@state.pa.us

Puerto Rico
Juanita Aponte, Program Director
Gov's Office for Elderly Affairs
PO Box 50063
Old San Juan Station
San Juan, PR 00902
787-721-7835
Fax: 787-725-2919
Email: no email

Republic Of Palau
Lillian Nakamura, Director
Agency on Aging
PO Box 100
Koror, PW 96940

Rhode Island
Kathleen M. McKeon
Department Of Elderly Affairs
35 Howard Avenue
Benjamin Rush Bldg. 55
Cranston, RI 02920
401-222-2858
Fax: 401-462-0586
Email: Kathy@dea.state.ri.us

South Carolina
Eve Barth
Dept Of Health & Human Services
P.O. Box 8206
1801 Main St.
Columbia, SC 29202-8206
803-898-2855
Fax: 803-898-4513
Email: barthe@dhhs.state.sc.us

South Dakota
Carla Leiferman
Office Of Adult Svcs & Aging
700 Governors Drive
Pierre, SD 57501
605-773-3656
Fax: 605-773-6834
Email: carla.leiferman@state.sd.us

Tennessee
Becky Joslin
Comm On Aging & Disability
Andrew Jackson Bldg.
500 Deaderick Street, 9th Fl.

Nashville, TN 37243-0860
615-741-2056
Fax: 615-741-3303
e-ma1l: becky.joslin@state.tn.us

Texas
Gary Jessee, Director, Office of AAA Support and Operations
Department On Aging
4900 North Lamar, 4th Fl.
Austin, TX 78751-2316
512-438-4245
Fax: 512-438-4245
Email: gary.jessee@tdoa.state.tx.us

Utah
Sonnie Yudell
Div Of Aging & Adult Services
Department of Human Services
Box 45500
120 North - 200 West
Salt Lake City, UT 84145-0500
801-538-3926
Fax: 801-538-4395
Email: syudell@utah.gov

Vermont
Camille George
Department of Aging And Disabilities
103 South Main Street
Waterbury, VT 05671-2301
802-241-2400
Fax: 802-241-2325
Email: mailto:camille@dad.state.vt.us

Virgin Islands
Eva Williams, Administrator
Senior Citizen Affairs
Dept. of Human Services
#19 Estate Diamond Fredericksted
St. Croix, VI 08840
340-778-0708
Fax: 340-692-2062

Virginia
Ellen Nau, Program Coordinator
Department For The Aging
1600 Forest Avenue
Preston Building, Suite 102
Richmond, VA 23229
804-662-9340
Fax: 804-662-9354
Email: enau@vdh.state.va.us

Washington
Hilari Hauptman/Lynn Korte
Aging & Adult Svcs Admin
Dept of Social & Hlth Svcs
P.O. Box 45650
640 Woodland Sq. Lp. SE
Olympia, WA 98504-5600
360-725-2556
Fax: 360-902-7848
Email: haupthp@dshs.wa.gov | kortelm@dshs.wa.gov

West Virginia
Jan Bowen, Director, Older Americans Act Programs
West Virginia Bureau Of Senior Services
1900 Kanawha Blvd, East
Holly Grove-Building 10
Charleston, WV 25305-0160
304-558-3317
Fax: 304-558-5609
Email: jbowen@boss.state.wv.us

Wisconsin
Gail Schwersenska
Bureau of Aging & Ltc Resources
Department of Health and Family Services
One West Wilson St., Room 450
PO Box 7851
Madison, WI 53707-7851
608-266-7803
Fax: 608-267-3203
Email: schwega@dhfs.state.wi.us

Wyoming
Dorothy E. Thomas
WDH, Aging Division
6101 Yellowstone Rd, Room 259B
Cheyenne, WY 82009
307-777-7988 or 1-800-442-2766
Fax: 307-777-5340
Email: dthoma@state.wy.us

Respite Services For Caregivers

Money And Help For Caregivers To Get A Break And Care For Themselves

Millions of Americans provide unpaid assistance each year to elderly family, friends, and neighbors to help them remain in their own homes and communities for as long as possible. Sometimes these caregivers need time off to relax or take care of other responsibilities. Respite care provides the family caregivers with the break they need, and also ensures that their elderly loved one is still receiving the attention that he or she needs. The following types of programs are available to provide these services:

1) organizations that offer grants to pay for commercial respite services
2) organizations that provide these services for free or on a sliding scale fee basis
3) volunteer organizations that provide these services for free
4) organizations that will help you find free and fee based respite services

State Government Programs

Every state receives federal money to provide services to seniors and this includes respite care. Contact your state office on aging by calling the Eldercare Locator 1-800-677-1116 or go to http://www.aoa.gov/eldfam/How_To_Find/Agencies/Agencies.asp . Below is a sample of the kinds of programs offered at state agencies:

$500 For Those Making $50,000 And Caring For A Relative

You are eligible for this money if you are a relative caring for someone in Virginia with a mental or physical impairment for at least 6 month. For an application call Virginia Department of Social Services and ask about the Virginia Caregivers Grant Program at 887-648-2817. Applications are also available on the web between January 1 and May 1 at http://www.dss.virginia.gov/family/as/caregivergrant.html . If you do not live in Virginia contact your state office on aging by going to http://www.aoa.gov/eldfam/How_To_Find/Agencies/Agencies.asp or by calling the Eldercare Hotline at 1-800-677-1666. You can also contact the office of your elected representative at the state or federal level.

Gants For Families Caring for Seniors

These grants are for families caring for a senior in Southeastern Vermont and need money for adult care services, a private caregiver, a short term respite, or in home services. Contact Council on Aging for Southeastern Vermont, 56 Main St., Springfield, VT 05156; 802-885-2655; http://www.vermontel.net/~coasevt/caregiver_respite.html. For programs in other areas of Vermont or other states contact your state office on aging by going to http://www.aoa.gov/eldfam/How_To_Find/Agencies/Agencies.asp or by calling the Eldercare Hotline at 1-800-677-1666. You can also contact the office of your elected representative at the state or federal level.

Grants For Alzheimer Caregivers Making $67,000

If you are a caregiver for an Alzheimer's or memory disorder patient in Vermont you may be eligible for a grant to pay for adult day care or a private caregiver, take a short respite, or pay for housekeeping. Income requirements in some areas of Vermont go up to 300% of the poverty level. At the national rate that's $67,000. Contact Council on Aging for Southeastern Vermont, 56 Main St., Springfield, VT 05156; 802-885-2655; http://www.vermontel.net/~coasevt/caregiver_respite.html. For programs in other areas of Vermont or other states contact your state office on aging by going to http://www.aoa.gov/eldfam/How_To_Find/Agencies/Agencies.asp or by calling the Eldercare Hotline at 1-800-677-1666. You can also contact the office of your elected representative at the state or federal level.

$800 To Mental Retardation Patient Caregivers For Respite Care

Connecticut sends families/caregivers up to this amount to help offset the cost of respite care. Contact Department of Mental Retardation, State of Connecticut, 460 Capitol Ave., Hartford, CT 06106; 860-418-6000; http://www.dmr.state.ct.us/srrespite_grants.htm.
If you do not live in Connecticut contact your state office on aging by going to http://www.aoa.gov/eldfam/How_To_Find/Agencies/Agencies.asp or by calling the Eldercare Hotline at 1-800-677-1666. You can also contact the office of your elected representative at the state or federal level.

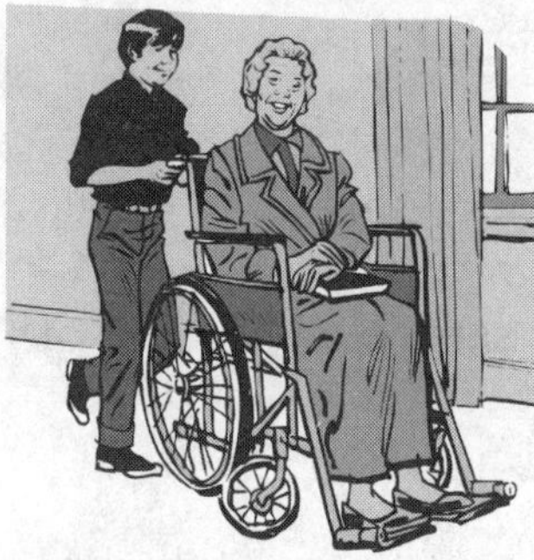

Caregivers To Seniors Making Up To $30,195 (for 2) Get Free Respite Services

For incomes over that amount they are charged on a sliding scale. This income requirement does not count the income of the caregiver. The Program for residents of Massachusetts is part of the Home Care Program for Massachusetts. Contact: 1-800-AGE-INFO or http://www.massresources.org/pages.cfm?contentID=66&pageID=27&Subpages=yes#apply . If you do not live in Massachusetts contact your state office on aging by going to http://www.aoa.gov/eldfam/How_To_Find/Agencies/Agencies.asp or by calling the Eldercare Hotline at 1-800-677-1666. You can also contact the office of your elected representative at the state or federal level.

National Organizations

National nonprofit health and service organizations provide respite grants and other help for caregivers. Below is a sample of the kinds of programs offered from national organizations. One method of finding more national programs is by identifying the patient's illness and contacting the national association that is an advocate for such patients, for example; American Cancer Society.

$750 For Alzheimer's Caregivers

If you are an Alzheimer's patient or caregiver and have less than $10,000 in cash or liquid assets (like savings accounts) you can apply for an emergency grant to help cover health care expenses. If you are denied funding you can apply again after 30 days if your circumstances change. Over 2,250,000 grants have been given out so far. Contact Alzheimer's Family Relief Program, American Health Assistance Foundation, 22512 Gateway Center Drive, Clarksburg, MD 20871; 1-800-437-2423; for an application go to http://www.ahaf.org/afrp/app.htm.

$1,500 For ALS Caregivers To Purchase 40 Hours of Patient Care
ALS (Amyotrophic Lateral Sclerosis also known as "Lou Gehrig's Disease") who have limited income can apply for this money for in-home nursing assistance in the form of a respite program. Contact: Ride for Life, Inc., 18 Grandview Blvd, Miller Place, NY 11764; http://www.rideforlife.com/archives/001268.html.

Free Respite Help From Thousands of Volunteers
A network of over 500 organizations at churches and nonprofits provide respite care, shopping services, transportation, housekeeping, telephone reassurance, and more. Find a local service at : Faith in Action, Wake Forest U School of Medicine, Medical Center Blvd, Winston-Salem, NC 21757; 1-877-324-3284; http://www.fiavolunteers.org/programs/index.cfm.

Local Chapters Of National Organizations

There appears to be many local chapters of national organizations that offer respite programs when their national office does not. Below is a sample of the kinds of programs offered at local chapters of national organizations. One method of finding more national programs is by identifying the patient's illness and contacting the national association that is an advocate for such patients, for example; American Cancer Society.

$2,000 Respite Care for ALS Patients In The Carolinas
Caregivers for ALS (Amyotrophic Lateral Sclerosis) patients can receive up to $2,000 a year for respite care. Contact The ALS Association – Jim "Catfish" Hunter Chapter, 120-101 Penmarc DR, Raleigh, NC 27603; 919-755-9001; http://www.catfishchapter.org/ourchapter/programs.html.

$1,000 Respite Care for ALS Patients In MD, VA, and DC Areas
Caregivers for ALS (Amyotrophic Lateral Sclerosis) patients can receive up to $2,000 a year for respite care. Contact Bobbe & Jerry Marcus Respite Care/Home Care Grant Program, ALS Association, 615 Frederick Ave., 308, Gaithersburg, MD 20877; 301-978-9854; cmaguire@ALSinfo.org; http://www.alsinfo.org/psprogrespite.html.

$1,000 To Help Transport ALS Patients
ALS (Amyotrophic Lateral Sclerosis) patients living in North or South Carolina can apply for up to $1,000 to help defer costs once a patient becomes wheelchair dependent.
Patients can also apply for:

- Augmentative Communication Grant Program
  - To help pay for communication equipment once the patient finds it difficult to speak

Patients can also access:

- Durable Medical Equipment Loan Closet
  - A selection of durable medical equipment that can be borrowed by patients or caregivers

Contact The ALS Association – Jim "Catfish" Hunter Chapter, 120-101 Penmarc DR, Raleigh, NC 27603; 919-755-9001; http://www.catfishchapter.org/ourchapter/programs.html.

$3,600 To MS Patient Caregivers In San Diego Area

If you are a family caregiver for a MS (Multiple Sclerosis) patient you can apply for a grant to help take a much needed break. Contact Multiple Sclerosis Society, Pacific South Coast Chapter, 8840 Complex Dr., Suite 130, San Diego, CA 92123; 1-800-FIGHTMS; msinfo@mspacific.org; http://www.nationalmssociety.org/cas/event/event_detail.asp?e=11943. If you do not live in the San Diego Area contact your local office of the Multiple Sclerosis Society and see if they have a similar program.

$750 For Respite Care For MS Patients In DC Area

The Respite Care program provides funds for short-term home health care for people with MS while the family caregiver takes a break, attends to business, or cares for others. Contact National Multiple Sclerosis Society, National Capital Chapter, 2021 K St, NW, #715, Washington, DC 20006; 202-296-5363; information@msandyou.org; http://www.msandyou.org/. If you do not live in the Washington, DC area contact your local office of the Multiple Sclerosis Society and see if they have a similar program

Local Organizations

Local nonprofit organizations, government offices, and community groups offer the largest number of programs. Listed below is a sampling of the types of programs offered. For help in finding local programs in your area contact:

1) your local area office on aging by calling the Eldercare Locator 1-800-677-1116 or going to http://www.aoa.gov/eldfam/How_To_Find/Agencies/Agencies.asp
2) your local United Way agency by going to http://national.unitedway.org/myuw/ or by calling the information operator and asking for the nearest United Way

Saturday Respite Service for Seniors

Families in Massachusetts can get care relief one Saturday a month from 9am to 3pm. Contact: Adult Day Health Saturday Program, VNA Care Network, 5 Federal St, Danvers, MA 01923; 800-728-1862; http://www.vnacarenetwork.org/news/respite.shtml.

4 Hours A Day For 3 Days Respite Care Plus a $750 Grant

Free respite care is available for caregivers in Colorado to take care of their own lives. There are no income qualifications. This organization also provides a $750 grant to pay for care that is longer that what is provided by their service. Contact; Respite Care Service, Senior Hub, 2360 West 90th Ave, Federal Heights, CO 80260; 303-426-4408; http://www.seniorhub.org/respite.ivnu.

Sliding Scale Fees For Respite Services

A service in Florida says they provide these services because they "don't want the caregiver to wear out before their loved one does." The fee depends upon your income. Contact: Share the Care, 808 W. Central Blvd, Orlando, FL 32805; 407-423-5311; http://www.helpforcaregivers.org/.

Get 8 to 16 Hours of Relief Per Month

Volunteers help those who are caring full time for a person past 60 years of age in Jackson County Oregon. Contact: Rogue Valley Manor Community Services, 1045 Ellendale Drive, Medford, OR 97504; 541-857-7780; http://www.retirement.org/rvmcs/respite.htm.

Help Locating Respite Services

The following organizations will help you locate fee based and free respite services in your area:

1) Eldercare Locator
   1-800-677-1116
   www.eldercare.gov

2) Your Local Area Office On Aging
   www.aoa.gov/eldfam/How_To_Find/Agencies/Agencies.asp

3) Your local United Way
   http://national.unitedway.org/myuw/

4) National Respite Locator Service
   http://www.respitelocator.org/

$750 For ALS Patients To Pay For Legal Assistance

These grants are to be used who ALS patients who are facing critical legal issues, such as dealing with health care providers and insurers, applying for disability benefits, financial matters or protecting an individual's most personal end of life decisions. Contact: Ride for Life, Inc., 18 Grandview Blvd, Miller Place, NY 11764; http://www.rideforlife.com/archives/001269.html.

Get Kidney Dialysis While You Travel

The Sherer Travel-Related Dialysis program gives patients the opportunity to visit friends, family or take vacations. The grant covers 20% of the treatment costs while traveling that is not covered by Medicare or some other source for emergency transient dialysis. American Kidney Fund, 6110 Executive Blvd, Suite 1010, Rockville, MD 20852; 1-800-638-8299; http://www.akfinc.org/pats_sherer.asp.

Disaster Relief For Kidney Dialysis Patients

A Disaster Relief Program is available to help dialysis patients get back on their feet when catastrophic events strike. The program helps patients with medications, food and household items, and pay for other necessities lost because of natural disaster. Contact: American Kidney Fund, 6110 Executive Blvd, Suite 1010, Rockville, MD 20852; 1-800-638-8299; http://www.akfinc.org/pats_disaster.asp.

Funds For Kidney Patients Who May Lose Health Coverage

The Health Insurance Premium Program pays Part B Medicare and Cobra premiums for dialysis patients who lose health insurance coverage and have insufficient income and savings to allow them to continue their coverage. Contact: American Kidney Fund, 6110 Executive Blvd, Suite 1010, Rockville, MD 20852; 301-881-2052; http://www.akfinc.org/pats_hipp.asp.

$500 To Help With Kidney Dialysis Home Treatments

If you need extra money to modify your home for kidney dialysis treatments, like plumbing, electrical, etc., you can apply for the Roundtree Memorial Fund for Home Hemodialysis Patients at American

Kidney Fund, 6110 Executive Blvd, Suite 1010, Rockville, MD 20852; 1-800-638-8299; http://www.akfinc.org/pats_hemodialysis.asp.

Kidney Transplant and Dialysis Patients Apply For Grants For Drugs
Qualify patients who urgently need medications, nutritional products and durable medical supplies can apply to the Pharmacy Grant Program at American Kidney Fund, 6110 Executive Blvd, Suite 1010, Rockville, MD 20852; 1-800-638-8299; http://www.akfinc.org/pats_pharmacy_grant.asp.

Grants To Kidney Patients
Patients who are referred by their physicians and social worker can receive funds for treatment specific expenses such as transportation, over-the-counter medicines, medication co-payments, kidney donor expenses and other expenses such as dentures. Ask for the Individual Grants Program at the American Kidney Fund, 6110 Executive Blvd, Suite 1010, Rockville, MD 20852; 1-800-638-8299; http://www.akfinc.org/pats_individual_grant.asp.

Respite Resources Available From Easter Seals
Easter Seals offers a variety of services for both children and adults with disabilities. They also offer adult day care and in home care, broadening their mission to include older adults with cognitive or social impairments in need of assistance with daily care. Services that are available vary location to location. Contact Easter Seals and they can tell you what services are available in your area. Contact Easter Seals, 230 West Monroe Street, Suite 1800, Chicago, IL 60606; 800-221-6827; http://www.easter-seals.org.

Seniors Caring for Grandchildren

Grandparents raising their grandchildren is not new, but the numbers are startling. According to U.S. Census data 4.5 million children are being raised by their grandparents. That is 6% of the children in the U.S. Over 25% of the grandparents are over the age of 65, and face struggles of their own: living on a fixed income, health issues, and more. Data shows that grandparents raising grandchildren are twice as likely to live in poverty as other households.

In order to better help this population we have included resources and information to benefit grandparents in this endeavor. Some good starting places include:

1) The Federal government has set up a special page for grandparents raising grandchildren at: www.firstgov.gov/Topics/Grandparents.shtml. This webpage includes information on benefits and assistance, health and safety resources, reports and publications, as well as state resources. Check it out to learn more about services available to you and your grandchildren.

2) AARP operates a ***Grandparent Information Center*** that offers booklets, networking, support groups, and more. They also have a wonderful state by state section that includes information and resources specific to your location. You can check them out at AARP Grandparent Information Center, 601 E St., NW, Washington, DC 20049; 888-OUR-AARP; www.aarp.org/families/grandparents/.

3) ***Foundation for Grandparenting*** is a nonprofit organization dedicating to help grandparents improve their relationships with their grandchildren. They have articles, resources, and education programs. For more information contact Foundation for Grandparenting, 108 Farnham Rd., Ojai, CA 93023; www.grandparenting.org.

4) ***Grand Parent Again*** is a website for people who find themselves parenting again after they thought they had finished that phase of their lives. The website offers community support groups, legal information and medical and health information. Check them out at www.grandparentagain.com.

5) ***National Center on Grandparents Raising Grandchildren*** is a nonprofit organization whose mission is to influence public policy, educate professionals, and replicate best practices. They have information on their website that can help those raising their grandchildren. For more information contact national Center on Grandparents Raising Grandchildren, Georgia State University, College of Health and Human Sciences, P.O. Box 3995, Atlanta, GA 30302; 404-651-1049; http://chhs.gsu.edu/nationalcenter/

6) ***Generations United's*** mission is to improve lives through intergenerational strategies, programs, and policies. They have a search function on the website for program sin your area, as well as state and local coalitions. They also have a publications library, state fact sheets, and more. Contact them at Generations United, 1333 H St., NW, Suite 500W, Washington, DC 20005; 202-289-3979; www.gu.org.

7) ***Find All Federal Government Money Programs For Children….***
They are described in a book called the Catalog of Federal Domestic Assistance. This book is available at your local public library or the U.S. Government Printing Office www.gpo.gov. You can also search the contents of this book for free on the web at www.cfda.gov.

8) ***Find All State Money Programs For Children…***
Every state has money programs to help children. Look for your state offices of health, education, or jobs and family services. You can find them by dialing 411 and asking for your state capitol operator or be going to the web at www.govenegine.com and clicking on your state.

9) ***Find Money For Child Care….***
Each state operates a little differently in dealing with child care funds. To learn more about what your state has to offer, you can contact National Child Care Information Center, 243 Church Street, NW, Vienna, VA 22180; 800-616-2242; http://nccic.org. They can direct you to resources in your area to apply for child care funds.

10) ***Find Health Information For Children…***
You can search for health information through the National Health Information Center, P.O. Box 1133, Washington, DC 20013; 800-336-4797; www.health.gov/NHIC.

11) ***Find Helpful Educational Information For Children….***
The U.S. Department of Education has established a helpful website for parents looking for information on how to help their children succeed in school. Check out www.ed.gov to see what they have to offer.

12) ***Find Programs Available Through the Smithsonian***
The Smithsonian offers a wealth of education programs and resources. To learn more about what they offer, check them out on the web at www.si.edu.

13) ***Ask ERIC***
The Education Resources Information Center (ERIC) is sponsored by the U.S. Department of Education and produces a wealth of journals and literature on a wide range of educational topics. ERIC use to sponsor clearinghouses on topics like Math and Science, Elementary and Early Childhood Education, Disabilities and Gifted Education, and more. These have lost their funding, although many of the host organizations are continuing in some form. To learn how to access articles or to be referred to a specific contact go to www.eric.ed.gov or 800-LET-ERIC.

$15,000 to Pay for Child Care

The Child Care and Development Block Grant gives money to states to help families meet their child care needs. Parents may choose from a variety of child care providers, including center-based, family child care and in-home care, care provided by relatives, and even sectarian child care providers. You can even get money to start a day care center! Income qualifications vary from state to state, and each state operates their programs slightly differently. To find out how to take advantage of this program in your state and to learn the eligibility requirements, contact National Child Care Information Center, 243 Church St., NW, Vienna, VA 22180; 800-616-2242; http://nccic.org.

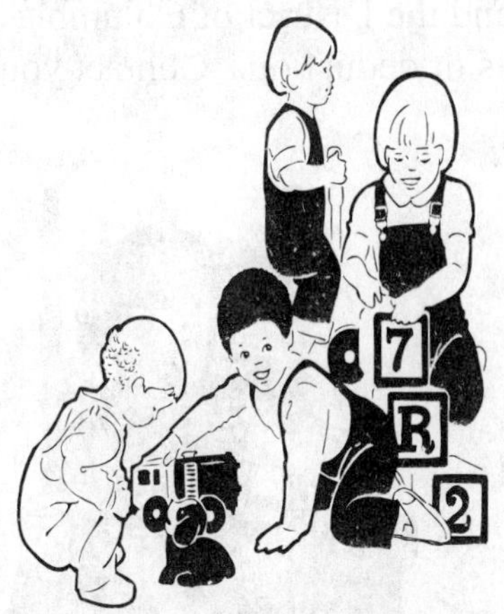

Pay Only $9/wk for Child Care at Local Nonprofits

Local nonprofits around the country get grants from the United Way or other institutions and offer free and sliding scale day care services. The United Way spends about a third of its funds, about $1 billion a year, on programs for children and families.

For example, the Community Partnerships for Children Program in Brockton, MA provides child care for a family of 2 with weekly income of $210 for only $9.00 a week, and families of 4 with income of $1,000 a week can get care for $114 a week per child. There are about 500 local United Way Information and Referral Services around the country that can point you to local groups that can help you solve your child care problems. Look in the phone book for your local United Way agency, or contact United Way of America, 701 N. Fairfax Street, Alexandria, VA 22314-2045; 703-836-7112; www.unitedway.org.

Free Child Care For Teens With Disabilities

48 states provide a subsidy to parents who qualify for childcare for children ages 14 to 19 who are physically and/or mentally incapable of self-care. Each state sets their eligibility requirement and the amount of funds they have available for this type of care. To learn what your state has to offer, contact your state Child Care and Development Block Grant lead agency.

Free Pre-School for Your Child

Head Start is preschool that has a great student teacher ratio and all teachers are certified in early childhood development. It prepares the children with school readiness, and research shows that these children enter kindergarten with the skills necessary to succeed. There are income requirements for acceptance into the program, but the program does allow 10% of the students to have higher incomes. And 10% of the program needs to be offered to kids who have a disability. To learn more about Head Start programs near you, contact your local board of education, the state Department of Social Services, or Administration for Children and Families, U.S. Department of Health and Human Services, Head Start Bureau, 370 L'Enfant Promenade, SW, Washington, DC 20201; 202-737-1030; www.acf.dhhs.gov/programs/hsb.

Money for Your Child Care Center

Child Care Works is a new partnership between the District of Columbia, eight area banks and three community organizations that make training, grants and loans available to licensed neighborhood day care providers to provide slots for 1,000 children. Maryland and Ohio provide special low-interest loans through their Department of Economic Development to fund child care centers. Even the Child Care and Development Block Grant provides money to develop child care centers and before and after school programs. Contact your state Department of Economic Development or your Child Care and Development Block Grant lead agency.

$4,000 To Pay For Child Care

IRS Publication 503, *Child and Dependent Care Expenses*, outlines the rules covering this benefit and describes how to figure the benefit if your employer covers some of the cost. You may claim up to $3,000 for the care of one child (or $6,000 for two or more). For more information, contact the IRS Information Line at 800-829-1040; or www.irs.gov. In addition, 25 states and the District of Columbia offer some type of child care income tax benefit either in the form of credits or deductions. Contact your state Tax Revenue office to see what your state offers.

Free Lunches For Students

The National School Lunch Program (NSLP) is a federally assisted meal program administered by the USDA, operating in public and nonprofit private schools and residential child care institutions. It provides nutritionally balanced, low-cost or free lunches to children each school day. The program was established under the National School Lunch Act, signed by President Harry Truman in 1946. Contact USDA Food and Nutrition Service, 3101 Park Center Drive, Room 914, Alexandria, VA 22302; 703-305-2286; www.fns.usda.gov/cnd/Lunch/.

Rich Kids Pay 2 Cents for Pint of Milk

The Special Milk Program (SMP) provides milk to children in schools and childcare institutions that do not participate in other Federal child nutrition meal service programs. The program reimburses schools for the milk they serve. Schools in the National School Lunch or School Breakfast Programs may also participate in the Special Milk Program to provide milk to children in half-day pre-kindergarten and kindergarten programs where children do not have access to the school meal programs. Contact your local school or the USDA Food and Nutrition Service, 3101 Park Center Drive, Room 914, Alexandria, VA 22302; 703-305-2286; www.fns.usda.gov/cnd/Milk/.

Free Food for Kids in the Summer

The Summer Food Service Program (SFSP) was created to ensure that children in lower-income areas can continue to receive nutritious meals during long school vacations, when they do not have access to school lunch or breakfast. Schools, public agencies, and private nonprofit organizations may sponsor the program. Sponsors provide free meals to a group of children at a central site, such as a school or a community center. Contact USDA Food and Nutrition Service, 3101 Park Center Drive, Room 914, Alexandria, Virginia 22302; 703-305-2286; www.fns.usda.gov/cnd/Summer/.

Get $600 For Each Child

The child tax credit is a credit on your taxes up to $600 for each of your children. This will increase in stages up to $1,000 in 2010. To be able to take this credit you must meet certain requirements. The credit is limited to people with an income below a certain modified adjusted gross income level. The instructions and worksheet needed to figure this credit are included in the 1040 or 1040A tax return packets. If you are claiming an adoption credit, mortgage interest credit, or District of Columbia first time homebuyers credit, you must use Publication 972 from the IRS to figure your child tax credit. You can download that publication and Form 8812, referred to above, from the IRS website at www.irs.gov To receive them by Fax-On-Demand, call 703-368-9694 or call 800-TAX-FORM (829-3676) to have them sent by mail or go to www.irs.gov.

Money To Pay For Your Kid's Bills

The Masonic Angel Fund is a special charity designed for children and sponsored by local Masonic Lodges across the country. Funds can be used to fill a wide variety of children's needs, such as a new winter coat, a pair of glasses or shoes, and can even fund scholarships for music or arts instruction. If professional services are needed, for example a doctor or a dentist, the local Lodge may be able to rely on one of their members to donate their services. Referrals for all these services are done through the school system, which helps build a good relationship between the schools and the Masonic Lodge. Currently the Fund is available in 40 Lodges, but the goal is to have it spread to all the Masonic Lodges. For more information on the Fund contact The Masonic Angel Fund, P.O. Box 1389, Orleans, MA 02653; 508-255-8812; www.masonicangelfoundation.org/goal.htm.

Free Money For Kids To Go To 79 Camps

The Salvation Army is concerned about the happiness of children, so they operate many children's homes and nurseries. In additions there are 239 camps children can attend as well as over 400 clubs. The Salvation Army wants to offer children a healthy alternative, so they can live their lives to the fullest. Contact the Salvation Army Office near you, or Salvation Army National Headquarters, 615 Slaters Lane, P.O. Box 269, Alexandria, VA 22313; 703-684-5500; www.salvationarmyusa.org.

Free Summer Camp For Kids With Parents In Prison

Angle Tree camping serves over 10,000 children each summer in week-long Christian camps. Supported by funds from the local churches and the Prison Fellowship, local children of prisoners are identified and given a week's vacation in the outdoors. In addition, Angel Tree provides gifts at Christmas time to children in need. Contact Angel Tree, P.O. Box 1550, Merrifield, VA 22116; 800-55-ANGEL; www.angeltree.org.

Free Child Safety Seats

There are hospitals that give out free child safety seats as you leave with your new baby, with no questions asked and no income requirements. Local police and fire departments inspect child safety seats to see that they are in proper order and properly installed, and sometimes provide free seats to those whose current equipment is not considered safe. Local organizations, like the Easter Seals Society were part of a federal program that gives out millions of dollars worth of free seats because of a settlement the U.S. Department of Transportation made with General Motors. Other groups will lend you a seat for as little as $5. The state of Minnesota alone has over 225 such programs. To find a program near you, contact your local police or fire department. Or contact your state information operator listed in the Appendix and ask them for your state office for Highway Safety or Traffic Safety. These national organizations may also be able to give you a local source:

- *National SAFEKIDS Campaign*, 1301 Pennsylvania Ave., NW, Suite 1000, Washington, DC 20004; 202-626-0600; fax 202-393-2072; www.safekids.org
- *National Highway Traffic Safety Administration*, U.S. Department of Transportation, 400 Seventh St., SW, Washington, DC 20590; 800-424-9393; www.nhtsa.dot.gov

Free Rides to Pick Up a Sick Child at School

Suppose your child is sick at school and needs you in the middle of the day, but you don't have a way to get there because you go to work most days by some other way than using your car. You can probably get a free ride, taxi, or free rental car from the local *"Guaranteed Ride Home Program."* You can also use the service for most family emergencies if your normal ride falls through, or if you have to work late unexpectedly. Call your local carpool or vanpool service to see if they have a similar program. Most of these programs require that you pre-register, but it is always best to plan ahead for emergencies anyway. If you do a computer search using the terms (including the quotes) "guaranteed ride home program," you will find a listing of many of the programs offered. You can also contact your state Department of Transportation for starting places.

Free or Cheap Legal Help To Get Custody Of Your Grandchild

Grandparents Resource Center helps those in the Denver area to reunify their families, placing children into permanent homes with grandparents. The also provide resources and services to help in raising the children. The Center provides legal assistance when necessary. Some of the programs they offer include: Kinship Care Support, Grandparent Adoption and Child Custody, Grandparent Legal Clinic, Granny's Pantry, Respite Care, and more. Some fees may apply. The website has a library available. For those in the Denver area contact Grandparents Resource Center, P.O. Box 27064, Denver, CO 80227; 303-980-5707; www.grc4usa.org

Resources For Atlanta Grandparents

Project Healthy Grandparents is a program whose goal is to strengthen families headed by grandparents. They offer social work services, health screenings, legal assistance, and support groups. All of these are designed to decrease the stress of raising grandchildren, and improve the lives of the families. For those in the Atlanta area contact Project Healthy Grandparents, Georgia State University, P.O. Box 3984, Atlanta, GA 30302; 404-651-0340; www2.gsu.edu/~wwwalh/index.html.

Grands Place

Grands Place is a online resource for those raising their grandchildren. The information they have available include legal resources, support groups, health issues, guardianship, financial assistance information, and more. They even host a chat room each night. For more information contact 154 Cottage Rd., Enfield, CT 06082; 860-763-5789; www.grandsplace.com.

$5,000 Worth of Free Health Care for Kids

Make up to $38,657 and get free health care for your kids. Almost every state now has a Children's Health Insurance Program (CHIPS), which extends medical coverage to many children who may not be covered. Contact your state Department of Health to see what version of the CHIPS program is offered in your area; or call a new government hotline to help locate free health care for kids at 877-KIDS-NOW; 877-543-7669; www.insurekidsnow.gov.

$5,000 For Teenagers To Start A Business

The U.S. Department of Agriculture has a program that loans money to kids between the ages of 10 and 21, who live in small towns, to start a business. Some states even run entrepreneur camps or special business training programs for kids. Contact your local Farm Service, or the Farm Service Agency, Loan Marketing Division, Ag Box 0522, Washington, DC 20250; 202-720-1632; www.fsa.usda.gov.

$6,000 Worth Of Free Speech Therapy For Pre-Schoolers

You can have your child tested to see if any speech problems are developing and get free speech therapy. It is part of the U.S. Individuals with Disabilities Education Act (IDEA), to make sure that children in need receive special education beginning on their third birthday (in some states it starts at age two). The program is run through your local school district, so check with them first, or your state Department of Education. You can also contact Office of Special Education Programs, U.S. Department of Education, 400 Maryland Avenue, SW, Washington, DC 20202; 202-205-5507; www.ed.gov/about/offices/list/osers/index.html.

$675 Million in Uncollected Child Support

No matter what your income, you can get the most powerful organization in the world, your government, to fight for you to establish paternity; set up a court order for child support; track down a missing parent, collect child support; and get the courts to adjust child support orders. There are a few states that may charge you up to $25. Contact your state Child Support Enforcement Office or contact Office of Child Support Enforcement, U.S. Department of Health and Human Services, 370 L'Enfant Promenade, SW, Washington, DC 20447; 202-401-9383; www.acf.dhhs.gov/programs/cse/.

$2,000 For Day Care While In College

To support low-income parents attending college, the Child Care Access Means Parents In School program supports campus-based child care services. Awards are used to support or establish child care programs for infants and toddlers, as well as before and after school services to the extent necessary to allow students to pursue a postsecondary education. Contact the U.S. Department of Education, OPE, Higher Education Programs, 1990 K Street, NW, 7th Floor, Washington, DC 20006-8510; 202-502-7642; www.ed.gov/programs/campisp/index.html. http://12.46.245.173/pls/portal30/CATALOG.PROGRAM_TEXT_RPT.SHOW?p_arg_names=prog_nbr&p_arg_values=84.335.

$10,000 For Student Science Project

The P3 National Student Design Competition for Sustainability will provide grants to teams of college students to research, develop, and design solutions to sustainability challenges. P3 highlights people, prosperity, and the planet, and challenges from a wide range of categories will be considered. The P3 Award will be given to the winner of a national, intercollegiate design competition among interdisciplinary student teams for their research, development, and design solutions to the scientific and technical challenges of sustainability. Grant awards will average $10,000. Contact the U.S. Environmental Protection Agency, Office of Research and Development, Washington, DC; 202-564-1589; www.epa.gov/ncer, http://es.epa.gov/ncer/P3/.

Money To Help Families

There is a database of over 400 nonprofit and government organizations that was set up to help families who have special needs when they are stuck with a health-related problem. It says it's for kids, but many of the organizations help anyone in need. There are groups that will give out grants like $400 to pay rent, $500 to pay for child care, $800 to spend on camp, or $750 to buy health products. This money is often location specific, so read through carefully. Go to www.bravekids.org and take a look.

Funding to Help Families with Sick Children

The First Hand Foundation provides grants to families with children who have health problems. Grants can be used to pay for expenses associated with clinical procedures and treatment, medical equipment and supplies, and expenses associated with families of seriously ill children who must relocate during treatment. Contact First Hand Foundation, c/o Cerner Corporation, 2800 Rockcreek Parkway, Kansas City, MO 64117; 816-201-1569; Fax: 816-571-1569; www.cerner.com/foundation.

$500 for Young Girls to Promote Health and Fitness

Youth Service America, the cosmetics firm BonneBell and the teen magazine CosmoGirl! offers a Born to Lead Grant program. Grants of $500 are available to young ladies between the ages of 13-25 for service and/or volunteer programs that promote the importance of health and fitness of the community, themselves, and their peers. Contact Born To Lead Grant, Youth Service America, 1101 15th Street, NW Suite 200, Washington, D.C. 20005; 202-296-2992; Fax: 202-296-4030; www.ysa.org/awards/award_grant.cfm; info@ysa.org.

$500 Grants for Community Service Efforts

Youth Service America and AT&T sponsor the AT&T Cares Youth Service Action Fund, which offers fifty annual grants of $500 each to young people (ages 5-25) and organizations to implement service and/or volunteer projects for National Youth Service Day, the largest service event in the world. Contact AT&T Cares Youth Service Action Fund, Youth Service America, 1101 15th Street, NW, Suite 200, Washington, D.C. 20005; 202-296-2992; Fax: 202-296-4030; www.ysa.org/awards/award_grant.cfm; AT&TCARES@YSA.org.

$2,000 for Activism Projects by Young Women

Provides grants of up to $2,000 to young women 19 and under who propose to develop and lead projects that are focused on activism and social change. Contact The Ellen Dougherty Activist Fund, Open Meadows Foundation, P.O. Box 150-607, Van Brunt Station, Brooklyn, NY 11215; 718-768-2249; www.openmeadows.org/; openmeadows@igc.org.

FREE Computers for Children in Need

The Second Byte Foundation provides computers to disadvantaged children. Awards are based in part, on 100-word essay written by the student on why they should receive this opportunity and how they will benefit from the computer. Kids and families receive computers through schools or other organizations that apply for the program. Contact Second Byte Foundation, 2663 Townsgate Road, Westlake Village, CA 91361; 888-263-2983; Fax: 805-495-9935; www.2nd byte.org; info@2ndbyte.org.

$10,000 for Teenagers who Don't Smoke

Lorillard awards grants to students involved with smoking prevention and scholarships to teenagers who choose not to smoke. There are two award programs: TeenH.I.P. Awards, which annually awards 10 $10,000 scholarships to teenagers who choose not to smoke; and TeenH.I.P. Grant Program in which Lorillard annually awards five $10,000 grants to students to create or fund a youth smoking prevention program. Support is given on a national basis. Contact Lorillard Tobacco Company Contributions Program, 72 Green Valley Road, Greensboro, NC 27408; www.lorillard.net. Application address for TeenH.I.P. Grants: Alex Abraham, Weber Shandwick, Inc., c/o TeenH.I.P. Grant Program, 676 N. St. Clair, Ste. 1000, Chicago, IL 60611; teenhip@bsmg.com.

$1,000 for Young Entrepreneurs to Start a Business

Youth Venture provides $1,000 grants to young entrepreneurs to start businesses, clubs, civic-minded organizations, or businesses. Open to those 12 to 20 who want to start a venture that aims at improving their community. Contact Youth Venture, 1700 North Moore Street, Suite 2000, Arlington, VA 22209;

703-527-4126; http://www.youthventure.org; info@youthventure.org; www.youthventure.org/index.php?tg=addon/6/contact.

Up to $15,000 for Youth

Sponsored by The Reader's Digest Foundation, the *National Youth of the Year Program* is designed to promote and recognize service to Club and community, academic performance and contributions to family and spiritual life. Clubs select a Youth of the Year who receives a certificate and medallion then enters state competition. State winners receive a plaque and enter the regional competition. Regional winners receive a $5,000 scholarship and enter a national competition held in Washington, DC. The National Youth of the Year receives an additional $10,000 scholarship and is installed by the President of the United States. Contact Boys & Girls Clubs of America, 1230 W. Peachtree St., N.W., Atlanta, GA 30309-3494; 404-487-5700; www.bgca.org; info@bgca.org.

Education Awards for Qualified Teens and Young Adults

This program, the result of a partnership between Boys & Girls Clubs of America and the Corporation for National Service (AmeriCorps), provides education awards to Club members ages 17 and 18 and Club alumni ages 19-24 who serve their Clubs and communities. CLUB Service recognizes young people's service, helps them access higher education opportunities and encourages them to pursue future careers as Club professionals. Contact Boys & Girls Clubs of America, 1230 W. Peachtree St., N.W., Atlanta, GA 30309-3494; 404-487-5700; www.bgca.org; info@bgca.org.

Money for Special Schooling in the U.S. and Canada

The Foundation provides support for Waldorf education in North America Waldorf Education is a developmentally appropriate, balanced education that integrates the arts and academics for children from preschool through twelfth grade, (Grades 10 through 12 are not yet available in Nelson). Waldorf Education encourages the development of each child's sense of truth, beauty, and goodness – an antidote to violence, alienation, and cynicism. Contact The Michael Foundation, Inc., 518 Kimberton Rd., PMB 320, Phoenixville, PA 19460; Fax: 610-917-0800.

Free Cards, Letters and Photos From the White House

Whether it's about more money for your school or your solution to problems with the environment, all you need to do is send a note to the White House. You will receive a response on official White House stationary that will also include a picture of the President. Or you can simply write and ask for an 8x10 of the President and/or First Lady. Just make sure to include the name and address of where the note or pictures should be sent. If the mail is not quite fast enough for you, then check out the White House website. You can email the President, Vice-President, or First Lady. If you can't make the trip to Washington, you can take a virtual tour of the White House, as well as view pictures and biographies of past presidents. There is even a special White House webpage for kids! Contact The White House, 1600 Pennsylvania Avenue, NW, Washington, DC 20500; www.whitehouse.gov.

Volcano Hotline

Volcanoes can erupt at any time, and are one of the most destructive forces on Earth. You can request several free publications from the U.S. Geological Survey that describe volcanoes and volcanic activity, including: *Volcanoes, Volcanoes of the United States* and *Volcano Information for the General Public.*

These publications are also available online at the address below. With a visit to the website, you can download how to make a paper volcano, and you can be connected with the volcano observatories in Alaska, the Cascade Mountains and Hawaii. Contact U.S. Geological, P.O. Box 25286, Denver, CO 80225; 888-ASK-USGS; http://volcanoes. usgs.gov; www.usgs.gov/education.html.

Money Money Money

You can learn a lot about your money from the Bureau of Engraving and Printing. Some information sheets available include: *Change in $1 From July 1929*, that describes the value of $1, *Engravers and Engraving*, that gives the history of the printed dollar, *Fun Facts About Dollars*, that contains money trivia, and *The Story of Money*. All of these are free and may help when the kids argue for a raise in their allowance. Contact Bureau of Engraving and Printing, U.S. Department of the Treasury, 1500 Pennsylvania Avenue, NW, Washington, DC 20220; 202-622-2000; www.treas.gov.

Free Endangered Species Information

The time that threatened or endangered plants or species have left in this world is limited, but there are steps you can take to help them continue. It is important to teach children about endangered animals, so they can learn how their actions effect wildlife, as well as how to protect these animals from extinction. The U.S. Fish and Wildlife Service has several publications that explain how a plant or animal becomes endangered, and what is being done to protect them. Publications include *Endangered Species* and *Why Save Endangered Species?* Contact Publications Unit, U.S. Fish and Wildlife, National Conservation Training Center, Conservation Library, Rt. 1, Box 166, Shepherdstown, WV 25443; 304-876-7399, Fax: 304-876-7231; www.fws.gov/endangered/index.html.

Earthquake Hotline

The National Earthquake Information Center (NEIC) located approximately 20,000 earthquakes each year, but these are only the most important of the many million earthquakes that are estimated to occur each year. To learn more about epicenters, the Richter scale, and seismology, contact the NEIC, as it is the foremost collector of rapid earthquake information in the world and is responsible for publications and dissemination of earthquake data. You can receive free publications on the severity of earthquakes and safety and survival in an earthquake. Contact the National Earthquake Information Center, U.S. Geological Survey, Box 25046, MS 967, Denver, CO 80225; 303-273-8500; Fax: 303-273-8450; http://neic.cr.usgs.gov.

Why Do Leaves Change Color?

The *Why Leaves Change Color* booklet can be used to learn why leaves change yellow, orange and red each fall. It also contains instructions on how to copy leaves with crayons and how to make leaf prints with a stamp pad. Contact Forest Service, U.S. Department of Agriculture, 12th and Independence Avenue, SW, P.O. Box 96090, Washington, DC 20090-6090; 202-205-8333; www.fs.fed.us

Free Water Safety Coloring Book

Spending a lot of time on your boat this summer? Make sure you follow all the boating safety rules, so your fun-filled summer is accident free. To help educate your kids on water and boating safety without sounding like you are lecturing, contact the Boating Safety Hotline. They have two coloring books for kids called *Water 'N Kids* and *Boats 'N Kids* that explain the basic concepts of water and boat safety. You can even sign up for very inexpensive boating classes. Contact Boating Safety Hotline, Consumer and Regulatory Affairs Branch, (G-NAB-5), Auxiliary, Boating and Consumer Affairs Division, Office of Navigation Safety and Waterways Services, U.S. Coast Guard, 2100 2nd Street, SW, Room 1109, Washington, DC 20593; 800-368-5647; www.uscgboating.org.

Archeology Information

If archeology is your thing, then check out the National Park Service. They have the *Archeology and Ethnography Program* that has developed fascinating materials about our country's past and can help spur on your interests. They have several publications available including *Participate in Archeology* and *Archeology and Education*, and the website includes links to other archeology resources. Contact Publications, Archeology and Ethnography Program (2275), National Park Service, 1849 C Street, NW, Washington, DC 20240; 202-208-6843; www.cr.nps.gov

Help Kids Clean-Up

Let's Reduce and Recycle: Curriculum for Solid Waste Awareness provides lesson plans for grades K-12, and includes activities, skits, bibliographies, and other resources. Other booklets include *A Resource Guide of Solid Waste Educational Materials; School Recycling Programs; Recycle Today!*; and more. Contact RCRA/Superfund Hotline, Office of Solid Waste (5305W), 1200 Pennsylvania Avenue, NW, Washington, DC 20460; 800-424-9346; www.epa.gov/epaoswer/education/teachers.htm.

Free Art Videos

You don't need to leave the comfort of your home or school to view great works of art. The National Gallery of Art's Extension Program is an attempt to develop awareness in the visual arts and make its collections accessible to everyone, no matter how far away the Gallery they may live. The Gallery offers free loans of over 150 videos, slide sets, films, teaching packets, and videodiscs, covering a wide variety of topics and time periods. Contact the Department of Education Resources, Education Division, National Gallery of Art, 2000B South Club Drive, Landover, MD 20785; www.nga.gov.

Learn About Solar Energy

You can learn more about alternative sources of energy through the Energy Efficiency and Renewable Energy Clearinghouse. They have many publications just for kids including: *Learn About Renewable Energy; Solar Heating; Learn About Saving Energy*; and even *Solar Power Science Experiments*. Contact Energy Efficiency and Renewable Energy Clearinghouse, Mail Stop EE-1, Department of Energy, Washington, DC 20585; 202-586-9220; www.eere.energy.gov/kids/.

Learn About Bike Safety

The U.S. Consumer Product Safety Commission has several free publications targeting bicycle use. *Sprocket Man* is a comic book that teachers your child how to ride safely and provides important tips on dealing with traffic and pedestrians. *Ten Smart Routes to Bicycle Safety* gives ten rules everyone should follow while riding. *Kids Speak Out On Bike Helmets* provides facts on bike safety and the importance of wearing a helmet. And *Bicycle Safety: Message to Parents, Teachers and Motorists* is a two page fact sheet urging parents and teachers to teach proper bicycle riding skills and habits to children. Contact the U.S. Consumer Product Safety Commission, Washington, DC 20207; 800-638-2772; 301-504-6816; www.cpsc.gov.

Archeology Vacations

"Passport In Time" helps you open a window to the past by allowing you to join activities such as archeological excavation, site mapping, drafting, laboratory and art work, collecting oral histories, restoration, and much more. Projects vary in length and there is no registration fee. Kids are allowed on many of the projects. Contact Passport In Time Clearinghouse, P.O. Box 31315, Tucson, AZ 85751; 800-281-9176; 520-722-2716; www.passportintime.com.

Help to Care for Your Kids Pet

A household pet needs special care, and no one knows this better than the Center for Veterinary Medicine. For this reason, they have published several fact sheets that help explain to children how to care for pets properly. So, write today. Your dog (cat or even horse) will thank you. Contact Center for Veterinary Medicine, Food and Drug Administration, 7519 Standish Place, HFV-12, Rockville, MD 20855; 240-276-9300; www.fda.gov/cvm.

"Give a Hoot. Don't Pollute"

The *Woodsy Owl Activity Guide* is jam-packed with ideas for classroom activities, list of kid's books, coloring pages, and more! There is a $2 charge for the guide. Contact The Smokey Bear-Woodsy Owl Center of Excellence, 402 SE 11th Street, Grand Rapids, MN 55744; www.fs.fed.us/spf/woodsy/.

"Only You Can Prevent Forest Fires"

Smokey the Bear is 60 years old and he is still teaching kids about forest fires. He now has a web site that gives kids all kinds of free information including: coloring pages, activities books, a story maker, and information on camping. Check out the web site for all kinds of information at www.smokeybear.com.

Help Your Child Learn

ED Pubs offers hundreds of brochures, pamphlets and other information to help your child learn. Titles include: *Put Reading First: Helping Your Child Learn to Read, Helping Your Child Learn History, Helping Your Child Learn Mathematics* and many more. Most titles are free on line or through the mail. Contact ED Pubs, P.O. Box 1398, Jessup, MD 20794-1398; 877-4-ED-PUBS; www.edpubs.org.

Send Your Kids to Outer Space

Space Camp, located in Huntsville, Alabama, offers kids ages 9-18, camp opportunities from weekends to 13 days in length. Full scholarships are available based on financial need, special learning needs or academic achievement for students in fourth through twelfth grades. Scholarships are available only for the specific 6-day programs. Scholarship students may choose from the Space Camp or the Aviation Challenge. Contact the Space Camp Scholarship Office, P.O. Box 070015, Huntsville, AL 35807; 800-63-SPACE; www.spacecamp.com/scholarships/.

Free Reading Information

Reading is Fundamental has something for everyone involved with children: parents, teachers, grandparents or even an older brother or sister. RIF programs throughout the country bring books to children at the greatest risk of failure. The web site offers individuals, as well as organizations a wide variety of information on reading. Parents can access activities, reading lists, motivation ideas and tips and tricks for children of all ages. Do your kids love to put on plays? There is a search that will list drama activities for each specific age group. There are many other searches including: art connections, vocabulary, writing, rainy day activities and home-to-school connections. They also offer brochures and handouts. They can be copied free online or you can contact them for multiple copies. Contact Reading Is Fundamental, 1825 Connecticut Avenue, NW, Suite 400, Washington, DC 20009; 877-RIF-READ; 202-673-0020; www.rif.org.

Get In Shape A Fun Way
The President's Challenge will help motivate all Americans to get fit and stay active. The Challenge offers a whole series of programs designed to help improve anyone's activity level. The Active Lifestyle Program is for those just getting started with daily fitness. You choose an activity from a long list of activities provided and participate in them 60 minutes a day, 5 days a week for children 18 and younger, for a total of six weeks. Track your activity on your personal activity log online and when you are finished you can order Presidential Active Lifestyle Award. The Presidential Champions Program is for those athletes who already active and want a new challenge. You choose an activity from the list and track your activities on the online log. You earn points for each activity you log. Points are based on the amount of energy each activity burns. You can work for the Bronze, Silver or Gold awards and order them when you have attained your goal. Contact The President's Challenge, 501 N. Morton, Suite 104, Bloomington, IN 47404; 800-258-8146; www.presidentschallenge.org.

Make Sure The Kids' Toys Are Safe
Is that toy you just bought safe for your child or has it been recalled? You can check the Consumer Product Safety Commissions *Toy Safety Recall* list. If you have found a toy that you feel isn't safe, you can report the product to the CPSC's hotline or report it online. They also offer a number of publications including: *BB Guns Can Kill, Dangers Associated with Children's Balloons, Strings and Straps on Toy Can Strangle Young Children* and more. Contact U.S. Consumer Product Safety Commission (CPSC), Publication Request, Washington, DC 20207-0001; 800-638-2772; www.cpsc.gov.

Get Your Child Ready For Kindergarten
Getting Your Child Ready for School, Parents as Partners Series is just one of a million bibliographic reports on educational-related resources in the ERIC database. You can download many of these articles at no cost. Contact ERIC Project, c/o Computer Sciences Corporation, 4483-A Forbes Boulevard, Lanham, MD 20706; 800-LET-ERIC; http://eric.ed.gov.

How to Choose and Locate a Child Care Provider
Choosing child care is a very important decision for parents to make. Local Child Care Resources and Referral (CCR&R) organizations can help you. They can make referrals; provide information on state licensing requirements, availability of child care subsidies and other information. You can find your local CCR&R on the web site below. The Child Care Connector is a search engine to research the child care options in your area. They also publish many brochures including: *Finding Help Paying for Child Care, Choosing Quality Child Care for a Child with Special Needs, Matching Your Infant's or Toddler's Style to the Tight Child Care Setting* and more for no charge online or they will send you one in the mail. Contact Child Care Aware, 1319 F Street, NW, Suite 500, Washington, DC 20004; 800-424-2246; www.childcareaware.org.

Take Time Off When You Have A Baby

The Family and Medical Leave Act provides up to 12 weeks of unpaid leave in a 12 month period to take care of a new born baby or the adoption of a new family member. There are some limitations, so you'll need to check with your employer or the U.S. Department of Labor for additional information. Contact U.S. Department of Labor, Frances Perkins Building, 200 Constitution Avenue, NW 20210; 866-4-USWAGE; www.dol.gov/esa/whd/fmla/.

Help Collecting Child Support

The Office of Child Support Enforcement is a great resource for parents dealing with child support issues. They offer a number of publications and offer links to every states Child Support Enforcement Office. Contact the Office of Child Support Enforcement, Administration for Children and Families, 370 L'Enfant Promenade, SW, Washington, DC 20201; 202-401-9383; www.acf.hhs.gov/programs/cse/.

More Child Support Assistance

The Association for Children for Enforcement and Support is a nonprofit organization working to improve child support enforcement. Memberships are available on a sliding scale based on income from$5 to $25 a year. Membership includes: Child Support Collection Guide, child support newsletter, workshops at reduced rates, and additional information. They also have an Absent Parent Locator Service. Contact ACES, P.O. Box 7842, Fredericksburg, VA 22404-7842; 800-738-ACES (2237); www.childsupport-aces.org/.

Legal Assistance

Legal Services Corporation offers civil legal assistance to those in need. The web site has a map of LSC Programs throughout the country. Contact Legal Services Corporation, 3333 K Street, NW, 3rd Floor, Washington, DC 20007-3522; 202-295-1500; www.lsc.gov.

Computer Repair and Training

Tech Corps is a nonprofit organization designed to address the technology needs of the k-12 education group. There are branches in many states where volunteers train teachers and students in computer technology. They also repair and install computers, offer seminars and work with teachers to improve use of computers in the classroom. Contact Tech Corps, P.O. Box 334, Maynard, MA 01754; 978-897-8282; www.techcorps.org.

Free Learning Guide To Ellis Island

What would you bring to America? How would it feel to travel in steerage? What do all the symbols on the Statue of Liberty mean? These and other questions are answered in activity sheets distributed by the National Park Service. In addition, educators can request a two week free loan of "Park In A Pack" which is a kit containing a teacher's guide, several videos, and educational activities dealing with Ellis Island. Contact Statue of Liberty National Monument, Liberty Island, New York, NY 10004; 212-263-3200; www.nps.gov/stli/prod02.htm.

Help Save the Planet

Teach your kids about the environment in a fun way. The U.S. Environmental Protection Agency has coloring books, activity sheets and even a Planet Protector Club for kids. The activities help increase your child's awareness of the Earth and recycling. Contact the U.S. Environmental Protection Agency, Office of Solid Waste, 1200 Pennsylvania, NW, Washington, DC 20460; www.epa.gov/kids.

What is Water?

The U.S. Geological Survey has developed a Water Resources Outreach Program webpage that provides a wealth of information on the Earth's water, water basics and more. They have also developed a series of posters that provide basic knowledge of water resources and cover topics such as wastewater, wetlands, groundwater, water quality and navigation. Contact U.S. Geological Survey Branch Information Services, Box 25286, Denver, CO 80225; 888-ASK-USGS; http://water.usgs.gov/outreach/order.html.

Have Your Kids Do A Family Oral History

The Grand Generation: Interviewing Guide & Questionnaire lists guidelines for collecting folklore and oral history from older tradition-bearers. It includes a general guide to conducting interviews, a list of sample questions, and examples of ways to preserve and present findings. This can be accessed for free at the following web site http://smithsonianeducation.org/migrations/seek1/grand1.html. The Smithsonian Center for Folklore and Cultural Heritage offers the publication, *The Smithsonian Folklore and Oral History Interviewing Guide* with all kinds of suggestions for kids to record their family's oral history. You can view this document at www.folklife.si.edu/resources/pdf/InterviewingGuide.pdf. Contact Smithsonian Institution Center for Folklore and Cultural Heritage, 750 9th Street, NW, Suite 4100, Washington, DC 20560-0953; 202-275-1150.

Create Your Own Family Tree

There is nothing like bringing a family together and showing them they all share the same roots. The Archives maintains ship passenger arrival records dating back to the 1820's, and its staff will even do research for you if you supply some basic information, such as the port of entry, passenger name, and date of arrival. If they find your ancestor, they will send you a notice. The manifests consist of 2-by-3 foot sheets. Listing passengers' age and occupations, and if after 1906 the information will include amount of money, language spoken, even height and weight. If you want to purchase a copy of the page of the manifest, the cost is $1.90 per page with a minimum of $10 for mail order. Contact The National Archives and Records Administration, 8601 Adelphi Road, College Park, MD 20740-6001; 866-272-6272; www.archives.gov.

We The People

We all had to memorize the Preamble of the Constitution during our school years. It might be fun to see the whole text of the Constitution, Bill of Rights, and The Declaration of Independence. You could test you kids' knowledge of each of the documents. The documents can be found at the National Archives & Records Administration website. To view the documents, go to their web site at www.archives.gov/welcome/index.html. You may also contact them at U.S. National Archives & Records Administration, 8601 Adelphi Road, College Park, MD 20740-6001; 866-272-6272.

Bring a Cast-Iron Umbrella

Acid Rain: A Student's First Sourcebook is a great way to teach kids about the environment and what needs to be done to protect it. Designed for grades 4-8, the sourcebook describes the effects of acid rain, solutions, experiments, and activities. The website also has links to other acid rain resources. Contact

Acid Rain Division, Environmental Protection Agency, Ariel Rios Building, 1200 Pennsylvania Avenue, NW, Washington, DC 20460; 202-272-0167; www.epa.gov/Region4/topics/air/acidrain.html.

Become A Disaster Action Kid

Herman the FEMA spokescrab, will help your kids become ready for any disaster. Floods, wildfires, hurricanes, tornadoes, earthquakes, winter storms, even National Security Emergencies are all disasters that can happen that you can prepare for. What can you and your kids do to prepare your family, siblings, and pets before the disaster strikes? Contact the Federal Emergency Management kid's web site for all kinds of informational brochures, fact sheets, posters and more. Contact, FEMA, P.O. Box 2012, Jessup, MD 20794-2012; 800-480-2520; www.fema.gov/kids/.

The Next Thomas Edison

If your kid loves to take things apart and create new things, then he/she has the inventor's spirit. The Patent and Trademark Office has developed a great kids web site. They offer links, puzzles, games and information about obtaining patents. The web site also provides information for parents, teachers and coaches. Contact The United States Patent and Trademark Office, Mail Stop USPTO Contact Center, P.O. Box 1450, Alexandria, VA 22313-1450; 800-786-9199; 703-308-4357; www.uspto.gov/go/kids/.

Bring The Birds To You

Kids love to look at pictures of birds in books. Why not teach them to go outside and look at the real thing? The U.S. Fish & Wildlife Service has a web site for students and educators to learn all about animals. They can view pictures and videos online not just on birds, but many other kinds of animals. For additional information call 800-344-WILD or check out their web site at www.fws.gov/educators.

Free or Low Cost Rocks

Lots of fourth graders across the country study about rocks and minerals. Contact your state geologist located at your state capital. They have informational sheets, brochures, videos, slides, and activities designed to bring rocks alive to kids. Some states even have field trips for teachers and kids to learn more about the rocks and minerals in their region. Many states, like Ohio, offer free rock samples to give kids that hands-on experience at rock and mineral identification and classification.

Free Information On Outer Space

Want to help your child build a solar system? *Solar System Puzzle Kit* is an activity where kids are asked to assemble an eight-cube paper puzzle, and when solved, they can create a miniature solar system. Information on rockets, the moon, all of the planets, current Space Shuttle information, space exploration and more is available through NASA's incredible educational resources system for educators, parents and students. You can download hundreds of publications, chat with experts, and look at the latest pictures form space. Each state has an Educators Resource Center that can provide you with information as well. Contact NASA, Education Division, Washington, DC 20546; www.nasa.gov.

International Studies

What is the leading export from Ireland? How many people live in Ethiopia? The federal government has two websites that can provide enough information for a two page country report, and it doesn't even involve going to the library! Check out http://lcweb2.loc.gov/frd/cs/cshome.html#about and www.state.gov/r/pa/ei/bgn/.

What To Read

Sometimes choosing a book is difficult, and sometimes kids need a little encouragement to keep reading. The Sylvan Learning Foundation has a website where you can plug in your child's reading level, type of books the child finds interesting, and the computer will do a search for you for free. You will be able to print a list of books, including grade level and subject focus, to take with you to the library. Your kids can take quizzes on books they read, as well as earn points and prizes. To sign up, check out Sylvan Learning Foundation at www.bookadventure.com.

Free Help For Parenting Kids

KidsPeace has parenting brochures including: *24 Ways You Can Prevent Child Abuse, 7 Standards for Effective Parenting, 15 Ways to Help Your Kid Through Crisis, What Every Preteen Really Wants You To Know, Grief Packet, Street Drug Information,* and *Join the Fight: Help Kids Eat Right*. To receive your free information, print out the form on the KidsPeace website, or view online. KidsPeace Fulfillment Department, 4125 Independence Drive, Suite #4, Schnecksville, PA 18078; www.kidspeace.org.

$5,000 to Help Low and Moderate Income Families Adopt a Child

The Gift of Adoption Fund provides adoption funding, grants, and financial assistance to low and moderate-income families seeking to adopt, and who could not otherwise afford adoption without assistance. Applicants are evaluated based on their income, assets, liabilities, earning potential and other financial resource opportunities. Average grants to individual families range from $2,000 to $5,000. Contact Gift of Adoption Fund, 101 E. Pier St., 1st Fl., Port Washington, WI 53074; 262-268-1386, 877-905-ADOP (2367); Fax: 262-268-1387.

Private Voucher Clearinghouse

CFA Children First America) serves as a national clearinghouse for privately funded voucher programs that provide everything from support services to new programs on videotapes for K-12 grades. These private tuition grants and tax funded options give low-income families the power to choose the K-12 school that will best accomplish their needs. The website has a list of the U.S. programs. Just click on the area of the program that is located near or in your hometown. The website also gives you a history about school choice legislation, school choice research, and some testimonies on how you can make a difference in the program. Contact the Children First America, P.O. Box 29928, Austin, TX 78755; 512-345-1083; www.childrenfirstamerica.org

$1,700 Washington Scholarship Fund, Inc.

The Washington School Fund provides financial assistance for children to attend either private or parochial schools in the Washington, D.C. area for grades K through 12th. The maximum amount received per child is $7,500 for low-income students. Contact the Washington Scholarship Fund, Inc., 1133 15th Street, NW, Suite 580, Washington, DC 20005; 202-293-5560; Fax: 202-293-7893; www.washingtonscholarshipfund.org.

$1,400 For Elementary Students In New York City

The School Choice Scholarships Foundation provides funds to cover the annual tuition costs up to $1,400 maximum per child and it is guaranteed for at least three years. Scholarships are only for elementary school children who are currently enrolled in a New York City's public schools, and meet the income levels requirements. Students are selected by a lottery drawing with priority given to children who attend the lowest performing schools. Contact the Children's Scholarship Fund, 8 West 38th Street, 9th Floor, New York, NY 10018; 215-515-7137; Fax: 212-750-2840; www.scholarshipfund.org/nyc.

Dentist Offers Scholarships for Elementary School Children

For several years Dr. Albert Landucci has sponsored awards and scholarships to the less fortunate. Scholarships are based on academic excellence, community service, volunteering, science and mathematics excellence and dental assisting. Scholarships are offered in the San Mateo Elementary School District and all the high schools in San Mateo For more information about the awards, scholarships and to see if your school is in the district, visit Dr. Landucci's website. Contact: Albert O. J. Landucci, D.D.S, 2720 Edison Street, San Mateo, CA 94403-2495; 650-574-4444; 650-574-4441; www.drlanducci.com.

Free Private Schools For Kids of Color

A Better Chance's mission is work with minority students from the 6th grade through eleventh to open opportunity doors that otherwise would not be open without a helping hand. There are several programs that include helping students receive financial aid for attending private local schools, boarding schools, or summer programs to help prepare for college. Contact A Better Chance, 240 West 35th Street, 9th Floor, New York, NY 10001-2506; 646-346-1310; Fax: 646-562-7865; www.abetterchance.org.

Tuition Assistance for Black Students

The Black Student Fund has provided financial assistance and support services to African American students and their families in the Washington, DC area for over 34 years. All financial assistance is based on a sliding scale. Contact the Black Student Fund, 3636 16th Street, NW, 4th Floor, Washington, DC 20010; 202-387-1414; www.blackstudentfund.org; Email: mail@blackstudentfund.org.

Money For Future Writers

For those future award-winning writers, Amelia Magazine awards $200 for a high school student's first publication. First publications can be a previously unpublished poem, a nonfiction essay or a short story. Deadline for the contest is May 15. Write or call for further information. Amelia Student Award, Amelia Magazine, 329 East Street, Bakersfield, CA 93304; 805-323-4064.

$2,000 For Children In Arizona

Arizona children in K-12, with incomes up to $29,693 can receive up to $2,000 per child per school year with a minimum three-year commitment to qualified children. Contact the Arizona Scholarship Fund, P.O. Box 2576, Mesa, AZ 85214; 480-497-4564; Fax: 480-497-4737; www.azscholarships.org; Email: ChamBria@Azscholarships.org; or Arizona Scholarship Fund, P.O. Box 31354, Tucson, AZ 85751-1354; 502-271-6857; or Arizona Scholarship Fund, P.O. Box 293, Flagstaff, AZ 86002; 928-286-0233; Email: Sandy@AZscholarships.org.

Education Loans Up To $20,000 For Grades K Thru 12

As with college loans, there are many financial institutions that provide loans for families to send their children to private or parochial schools at the elementary and secondary school levels. Listed below are some of the organizations that are providing these types of loans. Be sure to be aware that you can always contact your state banking commissioner by calling your state capitol operator.

1) The Education Resources Institute (TERI)
   P.O. Box 848108
   Boston, MA 02117
   800-255-TERI
   www.teri.org

2) First Marblehead Corporation
   The Prudential Tower
   800 Boylston Street, 34th Floor
   Boston, MA 02199-8157
   617-638-2231
   http://gateloan.com

3) FACTS SCHOLAR Loan Program
   P.O. Box 67037
   Lincoln, NE 68506
   800-624-7092
   402-466-1063
   Fax: 402-466-1136
   www.factsmgt.com

$25,000 for an Audio Essay

The 57-year-old contest is open to 9th through 12th graders. Students should submit a 3-5 minute essay based on a patriotic theme established by VFW. Contact your school counselor or principal to apply, or contact the VFW listed and they will tell you where your local chapter is located. First place national winners receive a $25,000 savings bond. Contact VFW Voice of Democracy Essay Contest, Veterans of Foreign Wars of the United States, VFW Building, 406 West 34th Street, Kansas City, MO 64111; 816-986-1117; www.vfw.org, info@vfw.org.

Money For Young Writers

Contestants receive a cash award for writing a short story that promotes brotherhood and is 4,000 words maximum. The money can be used for anything. Contact Aim Magazine Short Story Contest, P.O. Box 1174, Maywood, IL 60153; 708-344-4414; www.aimmagazine.org.

$10,000 for Artists

Any high school students that need help with furthering their education can enter the VFW Ladies Auxiliary National Patriotic Creative Art Competition. Students should submit their entry through the VFW Ladies Auxiliary Local Chapter first. Finalists from the local chapters are selected for the grand prize competition. First place grand prize winners receive $10,000, and an all expense paid trip to the VFW Ladies Auxiliary Conference for Community Service in Washington, DC. Second place winners receive $5,000, and 3rd place winners receive $2,500. Contact VFW Ladies Auxiliary National Patriotic

Creative Art Competition, Ladies Auxiliary to the VFW National Headquarters, 406 West 34th Street, Kansas City, MO 64111; 816-561-8655; Fax: 816-931-4753; www.ladiesauxvfw.com.

$1,500 For Young Science Types

Each year General Learning Communication with Dupont sponsors a science essay contest for children in grades 7-12. First place winners of each division receive $1,500, and an expense paid trip to Space Center Houston with their parents. This trip includes airfare, hotel and an allowance. Four finalists receive a $500 prize and honorable mentions receive $50. The deadline for the contest is January 23. Write or visit the website to obtain the entry application and mail first class in a 9x12 envelope. Contact Dupont Science Challenge, Science Essay Awards Program, c/o General Learning Communications, 900 Skokie Blvd, Suite 200, Northbrook, IL 60062; 847-205-3000; Fax: 847-564-8197; www.glcomm.com/dupont.

$150 For Young Artists

American Automobile Association (AAA) awards prizes up to $150 for children in K to 12th grade and $5,000 for college students in their School Traffic Safety Program. In the K-12 division, children submit posters. In the senior high division, students can submit essays, brochures, and even creative videos. Contact your local AAA office and ask for the School Traffic Safety Division; www.aaa.com.

$40,000 Scholarships For Kids From K to 8th Grade

There are 40 programs nationwide and each serves local families. The scholarships averaged $1,100 for children from K through 8th grade to attend private schools. Check the web site for the local offices throughout the country. Contact the Children's Scholarship Fund, 8 West 38th St. 9th Floor, New York, N Y 10018; 212-515-7100; www.scholarshipfund.org.

$10,000 For Young Inventors

Craftsman sponsors a program where students either invent or modify a tool independently. Two winners from grades 2-5 and 6-8 will receive a $10,000 savings bond. Ten finalists, five from each grade will receive a $5,000 savings bond. The teachers of these winners and their schools will receive prizes from Sears. Every contestant will receive a gift and certificate of appreciation. Contact Craftsman/NSTA Young Inventors Awards Program, National Science Teachers Association, 1840 Wilson Boulevard, Arlington, VA 22201; 888-494-4994; www.nsta.org/programs/craftsman, younginventors@nsta.org.

$1,000 For Writing About Technology

Students in K-12 from the U.S. and Canada can use their imagination and creative writing and illustrating skills to compose a ten page or less essay to indicate what technology would be like 20 years from now. There are four categories for students to participate: grades K-3, grades 4-6, grades 7-9 and grades 10-12. Final first place winners receive a $10,000 savings bond, second place winners receive a $5,000 savings bond, and teachers receive Toshiba prizes. Contact Toshiba/ NSTA Explora Vision Awards Program, 1840 Wilson Boulevard, Arlington, VA 22201; 800-EXPLORE9; www.exploravision.org, exploravision@nsta.org.

$1,000 a Year for 3 Years In Kentucky

School Choice Scholarships Inc. (SCSI) in Jefferson County, Kentucky awards its kids with 100 new partial-scholarships per year in addition to the 325 scholarships awarded just last year! If your Jefferson

County child is in K-6 and your family meets the Federal School Lunch regulations, you can be awarded 50%-60% of all tuition (up to $2000) for THREE YEARS! SCSI is willing to make a three-year commitment to making sure your child can enjoy the freedom of school choice! Contact SCSI, P.O. Box 221546, Louisville, KY 40252-1546; 502-254-7274; www.schoolchoiceky.com.

$1,450 For Families In Texas

The Childrens Educational Opportunity Foundation is a private scholarship program that will pay one-half of a child's tuition at any private school or out-of-district public school in Harris County (up to $1450). If your Harris County, TX family meets the Federal School Lunch Program requirements, your child enrolled in 1st to 8th grade may apply. This year, the Foundation hopes to award 550 students with the ability to practice school choice! Contact The Childrens Educational Opportunity Foundation, 109 North Post Oak Lane, Suite 350, Houston, TX 77024; 713-722-8555; Fax: 713- 722-7442; www.houstonceo.org.

$1,200 in Arizona

Arizona School Choice Trust (coupled with the Childrens Scholarship Fund) will grant 25%-75% towards your child's choice of educational institution (up to $3000). If you live in Arizona, meet the Federal School Lunch Program guidelines, and your child is in a grade from K-12, you are eligible to apply! The Arizona School Choice Trust has awarded more than 500 four-year awards and through tax-deductible donations adds more students to the program each year. To ensure your child's success in the program, ASCT requires that while enrolled, your student must maintain a 90% attendance rate. Contact Arizona School Choice Trust, Inc., 1951 W. Camelback Rd., Suite 445, Phoenix, AZ 85015; 602-454-1360; Fax: 602-995-1449; www.asct.org.

Over $5 Million More For Texas Children

The Today Foundation of Dallas, Texas joins with the Children's Education Fund and the Children's Scholarship Fund (CSF) to be able to grant Dallas students in grades K-8 with help to attend their schools of choice. The assistance pays half of the tuition (up to $1500) to any Dallas area school parent. Contact Children's Education Fund, P.O. Box 225748, Dallas, TX 75222-5748; 972-298-1811; Fax: 972-296-6369; www.TodayFoundation.org, today@todayfoundation.org.

Up to $1,800 in Michigan

The Education Freedom Fund provides low-income Michigan families with school choice for their K-8 students by providing tuition assistance through scholarships. Scholarships are need-based to families that qualify for the federal government's free or reduced lunch program. Maximum annual scholarships are $1000 annually. Parents must pay a minimum of $500 tuition. Education Freedom Fund, P.O. Box 230078, Grand Rapids, MI 49523-0078; 800-866-8141; www.educationfreedomfund.org.

Free Classes For Kids With A.D.D.

The nonprofit organization, *Children and Adults with Attention Deficit Disorder (CHADD),* identifies a number of federal laws that require the government to provide children with this disorder special educational services. It is only recently that these children became eligible for such services, so many eligible children may not be receiving what they deserve. To learn more about these free educational services, or to find out more and how to treat a child with ADD, contact: CHADD, 8181 Professional Place, Suite 150, Landover, MD 20785; 800-233-4050, 301-306-7070, Fax: 301-306-7090; www.chadd.org.

Gifts From Uncle Sam

Gifts From Uncle Sam

Sometimes shopping for just the right gift can be difficult. You may be trying to stay within your budget, so a couple of free gifts can't hurt. We have compiled a list of interesting gifts for seniors or the grandkids that you can get for free or cheap simply by making a call or going online. Happy Shopping!

Fly A Flag Over U.S. Capitol In Your Friend's Birthday

If you are at a loss as to what to give someone, then what about purchasing an American flag? These flags are flown over the Capitol and cost between $13.25 to $22.55 plus shipping and handling depending on the size of the flag. The flags also come with certificate, listing the name of the person for whom the flag was flown and the date. You can request a specific day, such as a birthday, anniversary or even the day someone was discharged from the military. The flags are available for purchase through your representatives in the House and Senate. The program has become so popular that the government has set up a web site to provide information on ordering a flag, www.capitolflags.gov/ or contact your representatives at www.senate.gov, www.house.gov. You can also check your local phone book for the numbers to your Representative or Senator, call the Capitol Hill Switchboard at 202-224-3121.

White House Commemorative Certificate For All Vets

You can help commemorate the honor of a deceased veteran by requesting a *Presidential Memorial Certificate*, an engraved paper certificate expressing the nation's recognition of the veteran's service. The veteran's name is inscribed and the certificate is signed by the current President. Eligible recipients include next of kin, loved ones and friends. More than one certificate may be issued. To apply you must submit copies of the veteran's discharge and death certificate. You can request the Presidential Memorial Certificate by mail or in person at any regional office. Contact: Presidential Memorial Certificate (41A1C), Department of Veteran Affairs, 5109 Russell Road, Quantico, VA 22134-3903; 202-565-4964; www.cem.va.gov/pmc.htm.

Get A Copy Of The Census Form That Grandma Filled Out

Your grandma's Census records can provide a wealth of information. Census data starts in 1790 and can get you started on your family tree. From 1850 to 1930, details are provided for all individuals in each household, such as:

- names of family members
- their ages at a certain point in time
- their state or country of birth
- their parent's birthplaces
- year of immigration
- street address
- marriage status and years of marriage
- occupation(s)
- value of their home and personal belongings

- the crops that they grew

The data is available on microfilm. For information on how to access this information contact National Archives and Records Administration, 8601 Adelphi Rd., College Park, MD 20740; 866-272-6272; www.archives.gov The following website at the Census Bureau also provides some basic search facts www.census.gov/prod/2000pubs/cff-2.pdf

Aerial Photographs of Your Neighborhood

Get a picture of your neighborhood or favorite U.S. vacation spot, like the Grand Canyon, from the National Aerial Photography Program. Taken from 20,000 feet and covering a 5.5 square mile area, these photographs provide an incredible perspective of our world. You can search by zip code or city and state. Photographs are available in black and white and color infrared. To purchase a photograph contact: Customer Services, U.S. Geological Survey, EROS Data Center, 47914 252nd St., Sioux Falls, SD 57198-0001; 605-594-6151; 800-252-GLIS; TDD: 605-594-6933; Fax: 605-594-6589; Email: custserv@usgs.gov; http://edcwww.usgs.gov/photofinder.

White House Birthday Cards For Friends 80+ or Married For 5 Years

The White House Greeting Office will send a 50th Anniversary card or an 80th birthday card to your special someone from the President of the United States. What a way to show that you care enough to send the very best! You must send your request at least 6 to 8 weeks prior to the event with the recipient's name or names, their return address, and the occasion for the card. In the case of a wedding or birth send your request in after the event. Send your request to: The White House Greeting Office, 1600 Pennsylvania Ave., NW, Washington, DC 20502-0039; Fax: 202-395-1232; www.whitehouse.gov/greeting.

Girl Scouts Gold Awards or Boy Eagle Scouts Get White House Honors

And they will also honor those having Bar/Bat Mitzvahs with a greeting card signed by the President. You must send your request at least 6 to 8 weeks prior to the event with the recipient's name or names, their return address, and the occasion for the card. In the case of a wedding or birth send your request in after the event. Send your request to: The White House Greeting Office, 1600 Pennsylvania Ave., NW, Washington, DC 20502-0039; Fax: 202-395-1232; www.whitehouse.gov/greeting.

Your Friend's New Baby Can Get a Greeting Signed By The President

IT is probably a machine that does the actual signing but what a surprise when your friends get a letter postmarked from the White House congratulating them on their new baby. They'll think you are a big shot Washington lobbyist. You must send your request with the recipient's name or names, their return address, and the occasion for the card. In the case of a birth send your request in after the event. Send your request to: The White House Greeting Office, 1600 Pennsylvania Ave., NW, Washington, DC 20502-0039; Fax: 202-395-1232; www.whitehouse.gov/greeting

Firewood for $5

That is all is costs to get a cord of wood for your local National Forest or Bureau of Land Management area. You need to contact your nearest office to determine if they currently allow firewood cutting and to obtain a permit to gather the wood. The forests generally only allow gathering of wood in specific areas. For more information contact your local office or you can contact USDA Forest Service, 1400 Independence Ave., SW, Washington, DC 20250; 202-205-8333; www.fs.fed.us or Bureau of Land

Management, Office of Public Affairs, 1849 C St., Room 406 LS, Washington, DC 20240; 202-452-5125; www.blm.gov

How To Beat A Speeding Ticket

Even the most elaborate of modern technology isn't 100% perfect all of the time. The report *Police Traffic Radar* (publication DOT HS-805-254), published in 1980, is still accurate and shows that all police radar tracking devices are not accurate all of the time. Such evidence can be helpful in the defense of your case. The laboratory also has information regarding alcohol breath testing devices, including *Breath Alcohol Sampling Simulator for Qualification Testing of Breath Alcohol Measurement Devices (publication NBS 480-41).* Both publications are free and are available online or by contacting the Office of Law Enforcement Standards, National Institute of Standards and Technology, 100 Bureau Dr., Building 225, Room A-323, Gaithersburg, MD 20899; 301-975-2757; Fax: 301-948-0978; www.eeel.nist.gov/oles/oles_reports_publications.html

Free Videos About Great Artists

The National Gallery of Art in Washington, D.C. lends more than 150 teaching packets, videos, videodiscs, CD-Roms, DVDs, and Slide sets about great art and artists. You can also tour the gallery by visiting its Web site: www.nga.gov/education. Order forms can be found at www.nga.gov/education/classroom/loanfinder. Send orders to : Department of Education Resources, Extension Programs, National Gallery of Art, 2000B South Club Drive, Landover, MD 20785; Fax: 202-842-6937; Email: EdResources@nga.gov.

Free Online Cookbooks For A Healthy Heart

Keep the Beat: Heart Healthy Recipes proves that food that is good for your heart can also taste great. The National Institute of Health publishes this recipes book with over 100 pages of heart healthy, great tasting recipes that you and your family will love. Recipes include: appetizers, soups, desserts, main dishes, dressings, side dishes, beverages and more. You can download all of these recipes for free at www.nhlbi.nih.gov/health/public/heart/other/ktb_recipebk/index.htm or order a printed copy for $4.00 by calling 301-592-8573, faxing 240-629-3246 or by mail to NHLBI Health Information Center, P.O. Box 30105, Bethesda, MD 20824-0105.

90 Free Recipes For Your Heat

Stay Young at Heart offers heart healthy recipes including: carrot-raisin bread, barbeque chicken, heart-healthy pumpkin pie and more. Each recipe lists total fat, saturated fat, cholesterol, sodium and calories per serving. You can access over 90 recipes online at www.nhlbi.nih.gov/health/public/heart/other/syah/index.htm or order 12 recipe cards for $.50 by calling 301-592-8573, faxing 240-629-3246 or by mail to NHLBI Health Information Center, P.O. Box 30105, Bethesda, MD 20824-0105.

Latino Recipes Book

Do you love traditional Latino foods? You can learn to cook some favorites in a heart healthy way. *Delicious Heart Healthy Latino Recipes* is a bilingual cookbook that contains 23 taste tested recipes that reduce fat, saturated fat, cholesterol and sodium. You can access all of the recipes online at www.nhlbi.nih.gov/health/public/heart/other/sp_recip.pdf or order the 56 page cookbook for $3.00 by calling 301-592-8573, faxing 240-629-3246 or by mail to NHLBI Health Information Center, P.O. Box 30105, Bethesda, MD 20824-0105.

Picture Of Dad's Navy Ship

If you or someone you know has ever served in the U.S. Navy or Coast Guard you can get a great gift! Naval artist George Bieda has drawn detailed prints of nearly every U.S. Navy or Coast Guard ship or aircraft. You can even have the artist customize the aircraft drawings with squadron markings and insignia. Prices range from $36 to $105 depending on print size, framing and U.S. Naval Institute membership. There is an additional charge for shipping and handling. Contact: U.S. Naval Institute, 291 Wood Road, Annapolis, MD 21402; 800-233-8764, 410-268-6110, Fax: 410-269-7940; www.usni.org/webstore/shopdisplaysubcat.asp?id=31&cat=Ship%2FAircraft+Profile+Drawings.

Naval History Gift Subscription

Naval History is an extensive naval and maritime history magazine. Anyone interested in naval history would find this magazine fascinating. Bi-monthly issue offers photography, fine art, historical discoveries, essays, interviews, and book reviews. Give the history enthusiast in your life a gift subscription. Your gift will be announced with a personalized gift card. Subscriptions are $20 for Naval Institute members and $27 for non-members. Contact: U.S. Naval Institute, 291 Wood Road, Annapolis, MD 21402; 800-233-8764, 410-268-6110, Fax: 410-269-7940; www.usni.org/accounts/NHWizard/navalhistory.htm.

Exercise Videos For Seniors

Exercise is important to everyone and you are never too old to get moving. The National Institute on Aging offers an exercise video and free exercise guide with valuable information about how exercise and proper nutrition can be crucial in all stages of life but especially as we age. The video shows how to start a program and keep it going through stretching, balancing and strength-training exercises. The presentation can be purchased on video or DVD for $7 and the guide is free. You can order both by contacting NIAIC, Dept W, P.O. Box 8057, Gaithersburg, MD 20898-8057; www.niapublications.org/exercisebook/exercisebookanddvd.asp.

Create Your Family Tree

Tracing your family history has been made much easier with the creation of the American Immigration Family History Center at Ellis Island. Once you get to the website at www.ellisisland.org all you need to do is register by creating a user name and password, then you can conduct searches of Passenger Arrival Records. By simply entering in a last name, you will find all the names from ship passenger logs that match. The passenger's name, country of origin, age, and date of arrival are shown to help you create your family tree. If desired, you can purchase copies of the original ship manifest, ship photographs, and passenger record certificates online. It couldn't be easier! For more information check out their website at www.ellisisland.org or contact The Statue of Liberty-Ellis Island Foundation Inc., Attn: History Center, 292 Madison Ave., New York, NY 10017-7769; 212-561-4588; Email: historycenter@ellisisland.org.

A Great Gift For Ex-Navy Types

For those who spent their military years on a ship or in service to the navy, pictures are available to help you remember those exciting times. The U.S. Naval Institute has over 450,000 photographs chronicling the Navy's ships, battles, and major events. Ship name, hull number, and year of service are helpful in searching for prints. If you request a photo of a ship, make sure to ask for a free two-page history of the vessel to be included with the picture. To purchase a print contact U.S. Naval Institute, 291 Wood Rd., Annapolis, MD 21402; 800-233-8764; Email: customer@usni.org; www.usni.org/webstore/webstore.html.

Free Coloring and Activity Books For Kids

Teach your kids about the environment in a fun way. The U.S. Environmental Protection Agency has several coloring and activity books to help you increase your child's awareness of the Earth and recycling. Titles include: Happy Earth Day, Thirstin's Wacky Water Adventure, and Save Our Species, as well as others. Copies are available online or from the National Center for Environmental Publication and Information, P.O. Box 42419, Cincinnati, OH 452420419; 800-490-9198; 513-489-8190; Fax: 513-489-8695; Email: ncepimal@one.net; www.epa.gov/kids.

Find A Lost Loved One Without A Private Investigator

The Social Security Administration will be glad to forward an unsealed letter that is accompanied with a letter explaining your request, (the request must be for humanitarian reasons.) You need to supply the name and social security number of the recipient, or the person's date and place of birth. Send to Office of Public Inquiries, Social Security Administration, Windsor Park Building, 6401 Security Blvd., Baltimore, MD 21235; 410-965-2736.

The County Board of Elections (also called the Registrar of Voters) has public information from voter registration forms. You can look here to find someone as well. They can do a search to find out if a voter is registered in their district. They may be able to verify the person's full name, date of birth, current address, and political party.

The State Department of Motor Vehicles in most states can help your search with public information from driver's license and car registration forms. You will need to provide them with the person's full name, date of birth, and maybe the person's driver's license number. You also may need to put your request in writing, and there might be a fee for this service. Your State's Department of Motor Vehicles is in your state's capitol.

Give Yourself A Gift: Missing Money Can Don't Know About

Well, actually it is your money that you or someone in your family lost and it is just sitting there waiting to be claimed. According to reports, there may be over $8 billion dollars in abandoned money. This money could be old forgotten utility deposits, bank accounts, insurance payments, stock dividends, utility deposits, or even the contents of a safe deposit box. In 45 minutes one of our researchers found $2,000. All you need to do is contact the National Association of Unclaimed Property Administrators, c/o National Association of State Treasurers, P.O. Box 11910, Lexington, KY, 40578-1910; 859-244-8150; Fax: 859-244-8053; Email: naupa@csg.org; www.unclaimed.org and start searching. Wouldn't that make a nice present?

Free Termpapers

There is a wealth of information and a mess of money to help people change careers or just get ahead by taking some college courses. It is also a great way to meet new minds and make more money. Congressional Research Service reports are **FREE** from the office of your state Representative or

Senator. Ask for Financial Aid for Students: Info Pack, IP042; Guides to Financial Aid for Students: A Checklist, 89-98L; Internships and Fellowships: Info Pack IP0631; College Cost and Student Financial Aid: Selected References, 89-117L. If you cannot find your Congressman or Senator locally, call the Capitol Hill Switchboard at 202-224-3121.

Get the Time In Nanoseconds

Set your watch with the clock of the world. The Observatory's Master Clock is the source for all standard time in the U.S., and is accurate to the 30 trillionths of a second. Contact: Time Service Department, U.S. Naval Observatory, 3450 Massachusetts Ave., NW, Washington, DC 20392-5420; 202-762-1401 and 202-762-1069(Washington, DC) or 719-567-6742 (Colorado Springs, CO); http://tycho.usno.navy.mil.

Give Uncle Sam The Gift To Being Debt Free

Break your cookie jar, cash in all the change and send a personal check to the government's special account for paying off the debt...IT'S TAX DEDUCTIBLE. Plus, you will receive a special thank-you note from Uncle Sam. Remember to make a notation in the memo section of your check stating that it is a gift to reduce debt held by the public. Make checks payable to: Bureau of Public Debt, Department G, P.O. Box 2188, Parkersburg, WV 26106-2188. For more information call: 304-480-7137; www.publicdebt.treas.gov/opd/opd.htm.

Give Free Canoeing Lessons

Don't get lost up-a-creek without a paddle. The Army Corps of Engineers can teach you the proper way to handle a canoe or tie a line. They even have maps and brochures on great canoeing spots all over the country. So paddle over or contact: U.S. Army Corps of Engineers, 441 G Street, NW, Washington, DC, 20314; 202-761-1228; www.usace.army.mil/recreation.

Free Posters for Your Room

Rock stars and sports athletes help spread the word about staying healthy by avoiding drugs, alcohol, and smoking. Several organizations offer free posters to help with the message, including posters of Troy Aikman, the U.S. Women's Soccer Team and even Jackie Chan. Contact: SAMHSA's National Clearinghouse for Alcohol and Drug Information, P.O. Box 2345, Rockville, MD 20847-2345; 800-729-6686; Fax: 301-468-6433; On the website, click on publications then posters.www.health.org; or Centers for Disease Control and Prevention, Office on Smoking and Health, Mail Stop K-50, 4770 Buford Hwy., NE, Atlanta, GA 30341; 800-CDC-1311; www.cdc.gov/tobacco/celebs.htm.

Give Free Boating Safety Lessons

If sun bathing is boring, how about spending some time out on the water? Many boating safety courses are offered for all types of recreational boaters of all ages. Qualified volunteer organizations, such as the U.S. Coast Guard Auxiliary, U.S. Power Squadron, and others sponsor many courses, and many state boating agencies also provide classes. For more information contact U.S Coast Guard, 7323 Telegraph Rd., Arlington, VA 22310; 800-368-5647; Email: uscginfoline@gcrm.com; www.uscgboating.org/safety/courses.htm.

Pet Information

The Center for Veterinary Medicine has many Information for Consumer fliers that address frequently asked questions by consumers. Topics include: protecting pets in a disaster, the care and nurturing of cats, dog ownership-a long term commitment, rabbits as pets, using animals in product testing, selecting nutritious pet foods, and how pet turtles may be harmful to your health. These fliers and more are available online at their website or by contacting the Center for Veterinary Medicine, Food and Drug Administration, 7519 Standish Place, HFV-12, Rockville, MD 20855; 240-276-9300; Fax: 240-276-9115; 888-info-FDA; www.fda.gov/cvm/consumer.html.

Copyright Your Song

Think you have the next big hit? Before you share it with anyone, protect your rights. You can do it simply by filing a form and paying a small fee to the Copyright Office at the Library of Congress. This is the place where you can also copyright your poetry, photographs, games, visual arts, books, and even recipes. For more information contact: Library of Congress, Copyright Office, 101 Independence Ave., SE, Washington, DC 20559-6000; 202-707-3000; www.copyright.gov.

Babe Ruth Hits A Homer

Shots like that were captured on film for the world to see. The National Archives has become home to treasures on motion pictures, video, and sound. You can hear famous speeches, interviews with freed slaves, and more. There are over 200 files for motion picture/video holdings such as Atom bomb, Civil Rights, Pearl Harbor, and Wildlife. There are over 250 files for sound holdings such as D-Day, Fireside Chats, and Watergate Hearings. You can take classes on how to search, or you can hire a researcher to compile topics of interest for you. To learn more contact National Archives and Records Administration, 8601 Adelphi Road, College Park, MD 20740-6001; 866-272-6272; 301-837-3520; http://www.archives.gov/research/formats/film-sound-video.html.

Save Your Life

If you need an ashtray, you need to kick the cigarette habit. If you have tried before, try again. Nicotine patches, biofeedback, exercise...Uncle Sam has tons of information on the methods that work best. Contact: Office of Smoking and Health; Tobacco Information and Prevention Publications ; CDC/Mailstop K-50; 4770 Buford Highway, NE; Atlanta, GA 30341-3717; 770-488-5705; 800-CDC-1311; www.cdc.gov/tobacco or Cancer Information Service; National Cancer Institute; Building 31, Room 10A-18; 9000 Rockville Pike; Bethesda, MD 20892; 1-800-4-CANCER.; Cancer Quit line: 877-44U-QUIT; http://cis.nci.nih.gov.

Save Your Life, Lose Weight

Look better, feel better, have energy to spare...The only thing you might need is more time off. Diets are a dime a dozen, but the government has the facts on which systems work and which don't. For information about losing weight and maintaining a healthy weight contact: Center for Food Safety and Applied Nutrition;5100 Paint Branch Parkway, College Park, MD 20740-3835; 888-INFO-FDA or 888-SAFEFOOD; www.cfsan.fda.gov/~dms/wh-wght.html; or President's Council on Physical Fitness and Sports; Department W; 200 Independence Ave., SW, Room 738-H, Washington, DC 20201; 202-690-9000; Fax: 202-690-5211; www.fitness.gov; Weight-Control Information Network, 1 WIN Way, Bethesda, MD 20892–3665; 877-946-4627; Fax: 202-828-1028 Email: win@info.niddk.nih.gov; http://win.niddk.nih.gov/.

Steal A Home From A Crook
Imagine getting first shot at properties owned by failed savings and loan corporations, sleazebag outfits that speculated with old people's pensions, then went crying to Uncle Sam when the money went bye-bye. The Federal Deposit Insurance Corporation (FDIC) has set up a hotline for a listing of properties for sale from failed savings and loans. Contact the FDIC, 1910 Pacific Ave., Dallas, TX 75201; 800-568-9161 or 888-206-4662; Email: assetinfo@fdic.gov; www.fdic.gov/buying/index.html.

Free Learning Guide to Ellis Island
What was it like to travel by ship to America? What would you bring with you? What happened once you arrived at Ellis Island? What do the symbols on the Statue of Liberty stand for? These questions and many more are answered in free activity sheets available from the National Park Service at the information center, online at www.nps.gov/stli/activity/index.html, or by contacting The Statue of Liberty National Monument, Liberty Island, New York, NY 10004, Attn: Superintendent; 212-363-7620.

Interested in Volcanoes?
You can learn all there is to know about volcanoes on the U.S. Geological Survey website. You can find out about the type, effect, and location of volcano hazards, historical eruptions in the U.S., the current volcano activity in the U.S., how to prepare for volcanic emergencies, get directions on how to build a volcano, or read their weekly report of worldwide volcanic activity. For more information contact: U.S. Geological Survey, P.O. Box 25286, Denver, CO 80225; 888-ASK-USGS; http://volcanoes.usgs.gov.

Endangered Species
The current endangered species list includes almost 1300 plants, fish, birds, mammals and other species that are in danger of becoming extinct. The Division of Endangered Species' website has lots of information on endangered species, and lists of threatened and endangered plants and animals that need our help. Their publication "What Can We Do to Help Save Endangered Species" includes everyday actions that we can all take to help save our endangered animals and plants. For more information contact U.S. Fish and Wildlife Service, Division of Endangered Species, 4401 N. Fairfax Dr., Room 420, Arlington, VA 22203; 703-358-2171; www.fws.gov/endangered.

Why Do Leaves Change Color?
The U.S. Forest Service can answer this and any other question you may have about our forests and grasslands. For more information contact: Forest Service, U.S. Department of Agriculture, 1400 Independence Aves., SW, P.O. Box 96090, Washington, DC 20090; 202-205-8333; Fall Color Hotline: 800-354-4595; www.fs.fed.us.

Explore the Past
The National Park Service's Cultural Resources Program has many publications for those interested in our cultural heritage. Materials cover a range of topics including history, archaeology, historic preservation, and collections management. Publications are available in print or online. Most are free; others are available for a small fee. For more information contact: National Center for Cultural resources, National Park Service, 1849 C St., NW, Washington, DC 20240; 202-354-2100; Fax: 202-371-6485; Email: DCA@nps.gov; www.cr.nps.gov/linkpubs.htm.

Sell Photos Of Elvis With President Richard Nixon

The National Archives and Records Administration has many historical documents on their web site in the online exhibit hall. For example, you can see a picture of the first meeting between Elvis and President Nixon, and also a letter written from the King (Elvis) to President Nixon. You might also wish to look over the Declaration of Independence, the Constitution of the United States, or the Bill of Rights. You can view all the documents and many more by going to the National Archives and Records Administration's web site at: www.nara.gov.

Get Baseball Card From Ty Cobb

The Library of Congress has a vast list of photos, articles, sound bites, and much more from history all at your fingertips. You can go to their web site and find a baseball card from the 1913 New York Giants team. How about a 1910 card of Ty Cobb along with his stats? American Memory is the Library of Congress' collection of the history of the culture of the United States. These images can be printed on your printer for free, or you can order on-line for an 8 X 10 color print to be made and sent to you for $30.00. Just view the collection at http://memory.loc.gov. To order prints (the information is available at the website) contact Library of Congress, Photoduplicatioan Service, 101 Independence Ave., SE, Washington, DC 20540-4570; 202-707-5640; Fax: 202-707-1771; Email: photoduplication@loc.gov; www.loc.gov/preserv/pds. The Library of Congress also has a Walk up Counter located at the Adams Building, 2nd St. and Independence Ave., SE; Room LA 129.

Video Of The News Of The Day When Grandma Was Born

Newsreels were popular before movies, and many have been donated to various libraries to preserve these historical records. The National Archives can help you locate the resource you will need to locate a copy. There is a fee involved that varies by the different sources. For more information you can contact the various Newsreel archives listed at the website below: http://www.archives.gov/research/order/film-sources-contact-list.html.

Free Speakers

You have experts living all around you, and many are more than willing to come give talks on various topics to your group or organization. Want a Top Gun pilot to come talk? Contact your nearest military base or armory and submit your request. You can also check online at www.defenselink.mil to see what the U.S. Department of Defense has to offer. You can also have a local artist come and explain Picasso to you (or actually any art subject). Contact your nearest art museum, arts council or your state arts council. These can be found by calling 411 or by going online to www.govengine.gov. A master gardener can come help your group with their roses. Contact your nearest arboretum, botanical garden or gardening organization. These can be found by calling 411 or by going online to www.govengine.gov.

$50 Bags of Money For $3

Or better yet $10,000 worth for only $45! No it is not too good to be true. For the first time online the Bureau of Engraving and Printing is offering a 5lb bag of Shredded U.S. Currency. This bag contains a minimum of $10,000 worth of Shredded U.S. currency notes and costs only $45. The smaller sized shredded money bags are only available in the gift shop of the Bureau. For more information contact Bureau of Engraving and Printing, Mail Order Sales, Room 515M, 14th & C Streets, SW, Washington, DC 20228; 800-456-3408; http://www.moneyfactory.gov/store/section.cfm/73/435.

Get A Piece of the U.S. Capitol For Your Desk

Well maybe just a replica ornament. The U.S. Capitol Historical Society sells a wide rage of products from books, puzzles, coloring books, and activity guides to ornaments, statues and more. This is a great gift for any U.S. history buff. Prices start at $5 and up. For more information check out their website or contact them at U.S. Capitol Historical Society, 200 Maryland Ave., NE, Washington, DC 20002; 202-543-8919- 800-887-9318; www.uschs.org.

A Photo Of The Pres

If Bush is YOUR President, you can write or fax a request for a photo to be sent to you. You can also get a photo of Mrs. Bush, Vice-President Cheney, or Mrs. Cheney. Be specific in your letter and Make sure you clearly state where the photo is to be sent, including your name and address (you would be amazed at how many people forget that piece of information). Send or fax your request to: Correspondence Office, The White House, 1600 Pennsylvania Ave., NW, Washington, DC 20500; Fax: 202-456-2461; www.whitehouse.gov.

When Your Money Blows Up In The Microwave

Never fear- don't throw the money away. The Office of Currency Standards of the Bureau of Engraving and Printing redeems partially destroyed or badly damaged currency as a free public service. Every year the U.S. Treasury handles approximately 30,000 claims and redeems mutilated currency valued at over $30 million. The Office of Currency Standards, located in the Bureau of Engraving and Printing, uses experts to examine mutilated currency and will approve the issuance of a Treasury check for the value of the currency determined to be redeemable. To learn more contact Chief, Office of Currency Standards, Bureau of Engraving and Printing, Currency Residue Request, 14th & C Streets, S.W., Room - 344A, Washington, DC 20228; 866-575-2361; http://www.moneyfactory.gov/section.cfm/8.

State Aging Office Programs

State Aging Office Programs

Every state offers special services to their seniors. Whether it is transportation, food, prescription drug discounts, or more, there should be something for everyone. If you have a disability with an assessed need and you live in Delaware you can receive up to $25,000/lifetime in assistive devices to help you function more independently. Arkansas and many other states offer seniors a free newsletter with articles that interest seniors. Georgia will even send a Mobile Day Care to you. Their staff travels to rural parts of Georgia to provide day care services so caregivers can get respite. Services vary from state to state, and even from area to area within the state. Check out our lists below, but don't think for one minute that the lists are completely inclusive of all services. We tried to hit the highlights to give you of idea of what may be available. Remember that you need to contact your local Area Agency on Aging. These offices are located throughout the state and are where the services are dispensed. Almost all states have an information and referral line to help you in locating needed services. Remember that help is out there; you just need to know who to ask. If you have trouble locating the correct office, contact:

National Association of Area Agencies on Aging
1730 Rhode Island Ave., NW, Suite 1200
Washington, DC 20036
www.n4a.org
Eldercare Locator: 800-677-1116

Alabama

Alabama Dept. of Senior Services
770 Washington Avenue
RSA Plaza, Suite 470
Montgomery, AL. 36130
334-242-5743
800-AGELINE (800-243-5463)
Fax: 334-242-5594
www.adss.state.al.us/

- ElderConnect-This statewide program is a database of organizations that provide services for older adults, their caregivers and families.
- At Your Service-This weekly statewide Alabama Public Television program is targeted to seniors 50 years old and older proving information to maximize their lives.
- Nursing Facility Transition Program-Provides assistance to Medicaid-eligible persons with dementia.
- Cash and Counseling Grant-A three year program where certain adults who receive Medicaid have the opportunity to direct their own personal care.
- Medicare Outreach & Education-Outreach to inform seniors of community services available to them.
- Eat Better, Move More-Nutrition services include Meals on Wheels, nutrition screening, education and counseling. An eight-week program to encourage walking as daily exercise.
- PACE (People with Arthritis Can Exercise)-Exercise program designed for people with arthritis. Classes held at senior centers throughout the state.
- Alabama SenioRX-Prescription assistance for senior citizens with chronic medical conditions.
- Congregate & Home-Delivered Meals-Nutritious meals delivered to senior centers and homes.

- Medicaid Waiver for the Elderly & Disabled-Services to the elderly whose needs may otherwise require them to live in an assisted living facility. Their goal is to allow seniors to live as long as possible in their own homes.
- Alabama Cares- Alabama Care is the state's version of the National Family Caregivers Support Program providing training and resources to caregivers.
- Alzheimer's Caregivers Education & Support-Statewide training, education and community-based services for people with Alzheimer's and their caregivers.
- SHIP: State Health Insurance Assistance Program-Provides information about Medicare, Medicare Advantage Plans, Medigap, Medicaid and Long-Term Care Insurance.
- Medi$mart Medicare Patrol-Medi$mart trains retired professionals to become experts for Medicare and Medicaid clients.
- Legal Assistance-Statewide non-fee program of legal professionals helping senior citizens with personal legal problems.
- Long-Term Care Ombudsman-Advocates on behalf of residents of nursing homes and assisted-living facilities.
- Senior Centers-Senior Centers offer a variety of programs for senior citizens.
- Senior Employment-Job training and placement for low-income seniors.
- Volunteerism

Alaska
Alaska Commission on Aging
Alaska Department of Health & Social Services
P.O. Box 110693
Juneau, AK 99811-0693
907-465-4879
800-478-6065
Fax: 907-465-1398
www.alaskaaging.org/

- Congregate Meals-Federally funded Elderly Nutrition Program provides at least one hot meal a day to seniors in several communities.
- Home-Delivered Meals-Program for homebound seniors unable to access the Congregate Meals program.
- Transportation-Assisted rides for seniors in need of wheelchair accessible vehicles to get to health care appointments, employment and other personal business.
- Outreach-Outreach to inform seniors of community services available to them.
- Information and Assistance-Information regarding services provided by senior centers and other community resources.
- Homemaker and Chore Services-Home assistance for seniors needing help including: light housekeeping, shopping, meal preparation, assisting with financial and paperwork, hauling, chopping, shoveling, yard work, and minor home repair.
- Disease Prevention and Health Promotion Services-Health assessments and screenings by licensed health care workers. Nutrition education for groups and individuals. Information gathering events such as health fairs and conferences.
- Legal Services-Free legal advice and representation to seniors with economic need and 60 years old and older.
- Senior Voice-A statewide monthly newspaper publication providing information and education to seniors.
- Volunteer Services-Volunteer opportunities throughout the state focusing on seniors including: Foster Grandparents, Senior Companions and the Retired Senior Volunteers Program.
- Medicaid Long-Term Care Waiver
- Caregiver Support-Services include: information, access to support services, counseling, training, respite care and supplemental services.
- Office of Public Advocacy-This program provides guardianship and conservatorship to incapacitated seniors without family and friends or the money to hire someone privately.
- In-Home Respite-Respite care provides assistance so the primary caregiver has temporary relief from caring for their loved one with Alzheimer's.
- Adult Day Care-There are eleven Adult Day Care Programs throughout Alaska. Most programs operate for at least five hours a day, three days per week. The programs provide structured therapeutic activities for their clients.
- Care Coordination-A Care Coordinator's job is to connect you with the support services that you need.
- Alzheimer's Support and Education-This program can help identify people with Alzheimer's disease, educate caregivers, individual consultations and support groups.
- Pioneers' Homes-There are six Pioneers' Homes providing over 600 licensed beds in assisted living homes, specializing in care for Alaskans affected by Alzheimer's disease and related illnesses.
- Senior Residential Care
- Senior Employment Services- Low-income seniors 55 years old and older are placed in jobs. In addition they provide job counseling and coaching services.

- Long-Term Care Ombudsman-This office is an advocate to improve life of Alaskans age 60 and older living in long-term care. 800-730-6393
- Personal Care Attendant-This program assists frail seniors to continue to live in their own homes instead of being placed in long-term care institutions. The program helps with daily living tasks including: bathing, dressing, grooming, shopping, and housekeeping.
- Adult Protective Services-The goal is the prevention of abuse to vulnerable adults. Hotline: 800-478-9996
- Information Helpline-Information about senior programs, guardianship, conservatorship, general relief, trust accounts, and legal services throughout the state. Available weekdays 8:00 am to 4:30 pm. Statewide: 800-478-6065, Anchorage: 269-3666.
- Insurance Helpline-Information about Medicare, Medigap Insurance, Social Security, long-term care insurance and Medicaid. Available weekdays 9:00am to 4:00 pm. Statewide: 800-478-6065, Anchorage: 269-3680.

Arizona
Department of Economic Security
Aging and Adult Administration
1789 West Jefferson Street - #950A
Phoenix, AZ 85007
602-542-4446
Fax: 602-542-6575
www.de.state.az.us/aaa/default.asp

- Adult Protective Services-This office accepts and evaluates reports of abuse and neglect and offers appropriate services.
- Central Intake Unit-This is a 24-hour, toll-free hotline to report adult abuse and neglect. 877-SOS-ADULT (877-767-2385) TDD: 877-815-8390.
- Long-Term Care Ombudsman-Fields complaints and provides investigation and resolution of complaints relating to the health, safety, welfare and rights of older adults who are living in long-term care facilities across Arizona. 602-542-4446
- Congregate Meals-This program offers nutritious meals for older adults in senior centers across Arizona.
- Senior Centers-Senior Centers offer a variety of programs for senior citizens.
- State Health Insurance Assistance Program-This program assists Arizona's Medicare beneficiaries in understanding the healthcare benefits they may be entitled. Hotline: 800-432-4040
- Home Delivered Meals-Think "Meals-on-Wheels". This program provides nutritious meals delivered right to your doorstep.
- Home Nursing-Skilled nursing services are available at home for people who need help with taking medications, changing dressings and other skilled nursing care.
- Personal Care-Personal care provides help with essential personal physical needs such as bathing and grooming.
- Respite-If you are caring for a loved one, respite can relieve you of your duties for a short time.
- Transportation-Many communities offer door-to-door service that accommodates wheelchairs, walkers and other devices. Transportation may be for doctor's visits, medical services and other activities. Some communities even offer escort and shopping assistance.
- Adult Day Care-Some communities offer adult day care which provide social and some rehabilitative activities.
- Home Repair and Adaptation-If you need home repair help, this program offers limited home improvement services to older adults who meet income guidelines. Activities include: roofing, ramps, insulation and minor repairs.
- Information and Referral-These numbers can connect you with the services that you need that are available in your community. Phoenix: 602-263-8856; Tucson: 502-323-1303; In Apache, Coconino, Gila, La Paz, Maricopa (outside Phoenix), Mohave, Navajo, Pinal, Yavapai and Yuma Counties: 800-352-3792; In Cochise, Graham, Greenlee, Pima (outside Phoenix), and Santa Cruz Counties: 800-362-33474.
- Legal Assistance-This program is available to seniors who are unable to manage their own affairs. They advise and counsel older persons and their families in dealing with business and financial concerns.
- Senior Community Service Employment Program-Low-income persons age 55 and older can work for as assigned non-profit or public agency for 20 hours per week at minimum wage. 602-542-4446
- Employer Incentive Program-This program provides employers the opportunity to hire senior workers at no cost to them for a set amount of time, with the agreement that the company will hire the senior after that time.
- Foster Grandparent Program-Limited income seniors' age 60 years old and older are given the opportunity to work with children with exceptional needs. 602-542-6365
- Alzheimer's Caregivers Are Really Extraordinary Program (CARE)-The CARE program offers education, outreach and direct services to low-income minority seniors with dementia and their caregivers. They offer five services: adult day care, home health aid, personal care, respite care, and transportation.

Arkansas
Arkansas Dept of Human Services
P.O. Box 1437, Slot S-530
1417 Donaghey Plaza South
Little Rock, AR 72203-1437
501-682-2441
Fax: 501-682-8155
www.state.ar.us/dhs/aging/

- Arkansas Aging Network-Join for this free online newsletter.
- Adult Day Care-This is a group program that provides care for functionally impaired seniors outside of their own home. Programs are available in many parts of the state and include meals, transportation and recreation activities.
- Adult Protective Services-Working to keep seniors safe from neglect and abuse. Hotline: 800-482-8049
- Alternative-This is a Medicaid Waiver program that can provide home and community-based services to a limited number of adults with physical disabilities.
- Assisted Living Choices-Services are available 24 hours a day to help with living choices. www.arkansas.gov/dhhs/aging/assistedlivingchoices.html
- AR GetCare-This web site is a database of statewide services available to older adults in Arkansas. www.argetcare.com
- Chore Service-This program can help you with the everyday chores of life. Clients must be unable to perform these tasks alone and include: errands, meal preparation, cleaning, yard work and other household tasks.
- Medicaid Service-This program provides heavy cleaning and or yard work. It is only available on an extreme individual basis and not for routine chores.
- Client Representation-Seniors can have their needs assessed and then be connected with services to meet those needs. Client Representation can include: outreach, referral for legal assistance, help determining public benefits, helping filling out paper work, and other information and assistance.
- Employment Services-If you are over 55 years old and would like to work, this program may be able to help. It provides counseling, assessment, training and placement in employment. There may be financial eligibility requirements.
- Health Promotion-This office can provide an array of services including: health information, education programs, health screenings, stress management, nutritional counseling, quit smoking programs and physical fitness programs.
- Homemaker Services-This program offers basic home management and upkeep including: errands, laundry, meal planning and preparation, and other simple household tasks. Clients must be in need and without a support system.
- Independent Choices-This special Medicaid project lets you direct your own home care by providing monthly allowance instead of "Personal Care Services". Contact: www.independentchoices.com, 888-682-0044.
- Information and Assistance-This service is for all older adults and their families. It provides current information about services and links you to the agencies to meet your individual needs.
- Legal Assistance-Legal advice and representation by a lawyer or rights counseling by a non-lawyer are two services offered to seniors with social or economic need.
- Material Aid-In case of an emergency, this program can provide basic goods or payments of bills.
- Congregate Meals-Hot and nutritious meals are provided through area senior centers to clients 60 years old and older.
- Home Delivered Meals-Hot and nutritious meals delivered to your door step if you are homebound and unable to prepare meals on your own. Clients must be 60 years old or older and live in an area where meals can be delivered.
- Ombudsman Services-Statewide advocacy program for the residents living in residential facilities and their families.
- Outreach Services-This program identifies seniors who may be in need of services, especially in rural areas and with the greatest economic need. It strives to inform this group and their caregivers of the availability of services.
- Personal Care Services-This service targets clients with medical requirements who need help in order to remain in their homes. Services include: bathing, dressing, grooming assistance, medications, food preparation, transportation and other household tasks.
- Repair/Modification/Maintenance-Provides home repairs and modifications necessary for maintaining a safe and healthy home for seniors. Clients must be frail, own their own home and have significant social and economic need to qualify.
- Respite-Caregivers need a break now and then and this program provides that temporary relief. Care may be provided at your home or at a facility.
- Socialization-There are many opportunities for social interaction at senior centers throughout Arkansas. They reduce social isolation and provide physical and mental stimulation.
- Supervised Living-Provision of 24-hour care in a group living facility.
- Telephone Reassurance-This program checks in on clients who live alone full time, temporarily or are homebound. They will call at a set time to check on you and if you don't answer they will send assistance.

- Transportation-Clients are transported to medical appointments, shopping, and other errands. Escort service may also be included.
- Arkansas Medicaid Programs-The following programs are available to qualifying Medicaid clients. ElderChoice provides in-home services to seniors 65 years old and older who meet financial requirements. Contact Department of Human Services for additional information.
- Adult Day Care-Care and supervision is provided outside of the client's home from 2-24 hours and may include meals, transportation and activities.
- Adult Day Health Care-Clients who are functionally impaired and are unable to live completely independent can participate in this program. The program provides rehabilitative, therapeutic and supportive health services.
- Adult Foster Care-Foster care provides family living to seniors who are functionally impaired. The home provides services such as bathing, grooming and other assistance. The client pays for room and board.
- Chore-Heavy cleaning and yard work are provided in extreme cases when if left undone would make the home uninhabitable.
- Home Delivered Meals-One hot and nutritious meal is delivered to homebound seniors or seniors unable to prepare their own food.
- Homemaker-Basic home tasks including: menus planning, errands, laundry, shopping, meal preparation, and household chores.
- Medicaid Service Definition-Medicaid clients may receive assistance with transportation to medical appointments and this may include ambulance services.
- Personal Emergency Response System-Help at your fingertips. This program provides in-home 24-hour two-way verbal and electronic communication. This ensures seniors with quick contact to emergency personnel.
- Respite-If you are or have a formal primary caregiver you can receive temporary relief for the caregiver through this program.
- Alternative for Persons with Physical Disabilities-This program provides attendant care and environmental modification services to seniors who meet certain requirements.
- Targeted Case Management-Medicaid clients 60 years old and older may receive assistance in coordinating multiple services and resources.
- Personal Care-Medicaid clients who need help with at least two daily living tasks may be eligible for this program.
- Home Health-Medicaid clients may receive part-time or intermittent care by a registered nurse, practical nurse, student nurse or home health aide to help delay the need for inpatient care.
- Hospice-Terminally ill Medicaid patients may be eligible for hospice care.
- Transportation-Medicaid clients may be eligible for transportation to and from medical appointments.

California
Department of Aging
1300 National Drive, Suite 200
Sacramento, CA 95834
916-419-7500
800-510-2020
Fax: 916-928-2268
www.aging.state.ca.us/

- Adult Day Health Care-Community-based day care program that provides health, therapeutic and social interactions for seniors that are at risk of being placed in a nursing home situation. There are over 300 sites throughout California. 916-445-4600
- Alzheimer's Day Care Resource Center Program-This day care for seniors with dementia provides physical and psychosocial support to persons with moderate to severe levels. They also provide respite care, training and support for families.
- Brown Bag Program-This program distributes surplus and donated fruits, nuts, vegetables and other foods to low-income seniors 60 years old and older.
- Long-Term Care Ombudsman Program-The Ombudsman staff investigate and resolve complaints made by or on behalf of residents of long-term care facilities.
- Foster Grandparent Program-This volunteer program connects seniors with children with special needs.
- Health Insurance Counseling and Advocacy Program (HICAP)-If you need counseling on Medicare, managed care and other health insurance issues HICAP can help. They provide community education programs and individualized one-on-one counseling sessions.
- Information & Assistance-The Information & Assistance staff fields calls of seniors looking for assistance. They link the client to specific services and then follow-up to make sure services were received. They give up-to-date senior services information.
- Legal Assistance-There are 39 Senior Legal Service Projects throughout California. They can counsel seniors in many aspects of law including: housing, consumer fraud, elder abuse, Social Security, Supplemental Security Income, Medicare, Medi-Cal, age discrimination, nursing homes, protective services and other issues.
- Linkage-This comprehensive case management program offers seniors who are at risk of being institutionalized the opportunity to remain in their homes by determining clients' needs and finding services to meet those needs.

- Multipurpose Senior Services Program (MSSP)-MSSP provides social and health care management for frail seniors in California who wish to remain in their communities instead of being placed in a nursing home facility.
- Congregate Meals-Hot and nutritious meals are served to qualifying seniors 60 years old and older at group sites.
- Home Delivered Meals-Hot and nutritious meals are delivered to homebound qualifying seniors 60 years old and older.
- Respite Program-This program provides temporary respite to caregivers caring for frail seniors with functional impairments.
- Senior Companion Program-Senior Companions matches low-income senior volunteers with frail older adults. Volunteers must be 60 years old and older and willing to work 15 to 40 hours per week. After placement volunteers receive a tax-exempt stipend, a free meal each day of service, reimbursement for transportation, supplemental accident, personal liability and excess auto insurance coverage, and an annual physical.
- Elder Abuse Prevention
- Friendly Visitor/Telephone Reassurance-Volunteers check on seniors by visiting or calling daily at a set time. If the senior does not answer help is sent to the home.

Colorado
Division of Aging and Adult Services
Department of Human Services
1575 Sherman Street, 10th Floor
Denver, CO 80203
303-866-2800
Fax: 303-866-2696
www.cdhs.state.co.us/ADRS/AAS/index1.html

- BenefitsCheckUp-A free confidential database to help seniors connect to government programs to help them pay for the things they need to live. http://ssl3.benefitscheckup.org/index.cfm?link=coloradoasu
- Aid to the Needy Disabled-Assistance to residents of Colorado 18 years old or older who have been disabled which prevents them from working for six months or longer.
- Aid to the Blind-Assistance to residents of Colorado 18 years old and older with a blindness condition.
- Old Age Pension Basic Grant and Health and Medical Care Fund-Basic retirement income and health care coverage for low-income seniors 60 years old and older. Must meet eligibility requirements.
- Colorado Supplement Program-Supplemental payment to seniors eligible for federal Supplemental Security Income who don't receive full SSI benefits. Must meet eligibility requirements.
- Burial Assistance-Burial Assistance pays for funeral and burial costs to seniors who receive public assistance.
- Long-Term Care Cases Management Services
- Adult Protection Program-The program provides assistance to seniors who are victims of abuse or neglect.
- Long-Term Care Ombudsman Services for Older Persons-Ombudsman staff identifies, investigates and resolves complaints filed by or on behalf of residents of residential nursing facilities.
- Legal Services-Seniors can receive legal services dealing with a variety of legal issues.
- Coalition for Elder Rights and Adult Protection-This program provides education, training and public awareness to help eliminate the abuse, exploitation and neglect of seniors.
- Senior Community Services Employment Program-Low-income seniors 55 years old and older are placed in jobs. In addition they provide job counseling and coaching services.
- Congregate Nutrition Services Program- Hot and nutritious meals are served to qualifying seniors 60 years old and older at group sites.
- In-Home Nutrition Services Program- Hot and nutritious meals are delivered to homebound qualifying seniors 60 years old and older.
- Transportation Services Program-Transportation is provided to eligible seniors 60 years old and older for medical appointments, grocery shopping and other errands.
- In-Home Services-This program provides seniors 60 years old and older who need assistance with everyday activities because of functional impairments a variety of services.
- Home Maintenance & Repair-Basic home repairs and maintenance for qualifying seniors.
- Health Education-Education to seniors on a variety of health issues.
- Information & Referral-The staff will connect seniors with the services that they need.
- Adult Day Care-Care and supervision is provided outside of the client's home from 2-24 hours and may include meals, transportation and activities.
- Interpreting Services
- Respite Care- If you are or have a formal primary caregiver you can receive temporary relief for the caregiver through this program.

- Employment Assistance- Low-income seniors 55 years old and older are placed in jobs. In addition they provide job counseling and coaching services.
- Counseling & Assessment
- Outreach-Outreach to inform seniors of community services available to them.
- Visitors/Telephone Reassurance- Volunteers check on seniors by visiting or calling daily at a set time. If the senior does not answer help is sent to the home.
- Recreation-A variety of recreational activities are available through community resources.

Connecticut

Department of Social Services
Elderly Services Division
25 Sigourney Street, 10th floor
Hartford, CT 06106
860-424-5274
800-994-9422
Fax: 860-424-5301
www.ctelderlyservices.state.ct.us/

- CHOICES-CHOICES is a one-stop information program for seniors 60 years old and older living in Connecticut.
- ConnPACE-ConnPACE helps eligible seniors afford the costs of most prescription medicines. Contact: www.connpace.com, 800-423-5026.
- The Connecticut Partnership for Long-Term Care-This joint effort between the State of Connecticut and private insurance companies provides seniors with unbiased information on long-term care, the ability to purchase long-term insurance and a way to receive needed care without depleting assets. Contact: www.opm.state.ct.us/pdpd4/ltc/home.htm, 860-418-6318.
- Senior Community Service Employment Program (SCSEP)-This program offers training and employment opportunities to seniors that want to stay in the workforce. Seniors must have limited income and be 55 years old or older.
- Retired & Senior Volunteer Program (RSVP)-Seniors 55 years old and older that would like to share their knowledge and skills with others may volunteer through this program.
- Friendly Visitor-This outreach program sends trained visitors to homebound senior's residents to check on them and help to improve the quality of life of the homebound elder.
- Friendly Shoppers-Volunteers help homebound seniors with basic errands such as the grocery store, pharmacy, bank, barber or beauty salon.
- Humanities Programs For Older Adults (HPOA)-This program offers learning opportunities to older adults by sponsoring cultural programs including book and film discussion groups.
- Protective Services for the Elderly-This program works to protect seniors 60 years old and older from abuse, neglect and exploitation.
- Conservator of Person and Estate-This program can be used for frail seniors 60 years old and older to have an appointee of the court supervise the personal affairs of that frail individual. 860-424-5241
- Elderly Nutrition Program-Eligible seniors 60 years old and older may participate in congregate or homebound meals. There are over 200 Senior Community Cafés to access the nutrition program.
- Long-Term Ombudsman Program- Ombudsman staff identifies, investigate and resolve complaints filed by or on behalf of residents of residential nursing facilities.
- Grandparents as Parents Support Program (GAPS)-This program encourages and promotes services for grandparents raising their grandchildren.
- Respite Care-This program offers assistance for caregivers by providing information, support and the development of a respite plan.
- Home Share Program-There are three Home Share options for seniors living in Connecticut. The Department of Social Services will help connect individuals for Home Sharing. One person in each match must be at least 60 years old.

Delaware

Delaware Division of Services for Aging and
Adults with Physical Disabilities
1901 N. Dupont Hwy. 2nd Fl. Annex
New Castle, DE 19720
302-255-9390
800-223-9074
Fax: 302-255-4445
www.dhss.delaware.gov/dhss/dsaapd/index.html

- Adult Day Services-Adult Day Care facilities are located throughout the state. They provide activities and assistance for seniors with physical and/or mental impairments.
- Adult Foster Care-Foster Care is home living for seniors who need some supervision and can no longer live alone.
- Adult Life Skills-The program assists seniors with disabilities who want to learn life skills to live more independently.
- Adult Protective Services- This program works to protect physically or mentally impaired seniors from abuse, neglect and exploitation.
- Alzheimer's Day Treatment-This program provides medical, recreational and personal care services for seniors with Alzheimer's or other dementia diseases in a day care setting.
- Assisted Living-This housing option provides services for seniors in residence. Services include: personal care and light medical or nursing care.
- Assistive Devices-This program allows seniors with disabilities to buy or rent assistive devices with available funds. Devices may include but are not limited to large grip kitchen utensils, seats for the shower or bath, wheelchairs or specialized computers. There is a lifetime cap of $25,000.
- Attendant Services-Attendant Services provides personal care and support to seniors with physical disabilities. Tasks include; dressing, bathing, grooming, mobility assistance, transportation, meal planning and preparation and health maintenance activities.
- Case Management-A caseworker can help seniors and caregivers get connected with the services they need.
- Congregate Meals-Hot and nutritious meals are served in a group setting at senior centers throughout the state. Nutrition counseling and education is also available.
- Delaware Money Management Program-This money management program offers help to low-income seniors with physical disabilities with budgeting, bill paying and other financial matters.
- Delaware Passport to Independence-This program identifies, informs and assists nursing home residents who wish to move to a community-based setting.
- Eldercare in the Workplace-This program assists both employers and employees by proving information on eldercare and help with eldercare issues.
- Emergency Response System-This electronic button allows high risk seniors to receive help in an emergency situation.
- Hispanic Outreach-This outreach program is targeted to helping Hispanic adults 60 years old and older.
- Home Delivered Meals- Hot and nutritious meals are delivered to homebound qualifying seniors 60 years old and older. Some seniors also receive cold, bagged meals to eat later in the day.
- Home Modification-Home modifications are available for qualifying physically disabled seniors to make their home more livable. There is a $10,000 lifetime cap.
- Housekeeping-In-home light housekeeping is available to frail seniors with physical disabilities. Housekeeping services include: shopping assistance, meal preparation, light housekeeping, and laundry.
- Information & Assistance-Anyone who is a senior or involved in a senior's life, may contact this program to receive free information and be linked with appropriate programs and services.
- Joining Generations-This statewide intergenerational program strives to bring the elderly and youth together. They offer the Family Circles program that supports grandparents raising their grandchildren.
- Legal Services-Legal Services assists with legal issues such as powers of attorney, living wills, consumer issues, housing matters and medical concerns.
- Long Term Care Ombudsman Program-The Ombudsman program investigates and resolves complaints and concerns made by residents of long term care facilities.
- Medicaid Waiver for the Elderly-An alternative to nursing homes, the Waiver program provides services to keep seniors in their homes. Services include: adult day care, emergency response system, orthotics, personal care, prosthetics, respite and more.
- Medical Transportation-The Transportation program provides transportation to health care appointments for seniors 60 years old and older who live in New Castle County but outside the city limits and have no other means of transportation.
- Personal Care-This program provides assistance to frail elderly citizens 60 years old and older that meet medical criteria. Services include: bathing, grooming, meal preparation, menu planning, shopping, light housekeeping and more.
- Respite Care-Respite provides temporary relief to caregivers who care for seniors 60 years old and older. Respite can be in your home, temporary placement in a long-term facility, foster care or other settings.
- Senior Community Service Employment Program-Jobs are available to eligible seniors 55 years old and older. Seniors also receive training.

District of Columbia
District of Columbia Office on Aging
441 4th Street NW Suite 900 S
Washington, DC 20001
202-724-5622

Fax: 202-724-4979
http://dcoa.dc.gov/dcoa/site/

- Never Too Old To Learn-Learning Centers are located throughout the state to help functionally illiterate older adults learn basic math, reading, writing and life skills. A lunch is provided.
- Older Adults Service and Information System (OASIS)-The OASIS creates wonderful opportunities for adults 55 years old and older offering programs in the arts. Humanities, health, wellness, travel and volunteer service. 202-362-9600 ext. 560
- SeniorWorks II-Part-time volunteer assignments are available to seniors in public and private agencies. A small stipend is provided to defray transportation costs.
- Older Workers Employment and Training Program-This program offers employment and training to adults 55 years old and older in the D.C. area. Services include: workshops, on-the-job training, job development, placement and classroom skills training.
- McMasters Program-This McDonalds' sponsored program offers older adults work assistance to promote confidence, self-esteem, and job opportunities.
- AL-C*A*R*E Alzheimer's Disease Program-Home-care services for older adults with Alzheimer's or other dementia disease. Services include home health aide, social worker and nurse practitioner visits and education for the family. 202-638-2382
- BODYWISE-BODYWISE classes are for seniors and consist of water exercise, walking, and stretch class which includes a health education component. 202-274-6651
- Congress Heights Senior Wellness Center-The center offers a variety of programs that promote health and disease prevention for seniors 60 years old and older in the D.C. area. 202-563-7225
- Alzheimer's Weekend Socialization and Respite Program-This program offers families site-based respite care on Saturdays. 202-635-1900
- Heavy Housekeeping Services-Heavy Housekeeping services are provided to frail, mentally impaired seniors that have trouble keeping their homes clean and have been denied homemaker services because of unsanitary living quarters. The goal is to make the home habitable so that homemaker services can be initiated. 202-289-1510 ext 180
- Home Care Partners-This program offers frail or ill seniors with homemakers who can perform daily activities. Duties include meal preparation, light housekeeping, bathing, grooming, grocery shopping and help with exercises. They also offer 24-hour emergency services for seniors at risk of being institutionalized. 202-638-2382
- SOME, Inc (So Others Might Eat)-Trained volunteers help homebound seniors in Ward 7 shop, run errands and be an overall advocate for the senior. 202-581-8000
- UPO Project KEEN Respite Program-Day-care respite for caregivers of persons with Alzheimer's or other dementia disease. 202-279-5820
- Washington Seniors Wellness Center-The Wellness Center offers a variety of activities for seniors including classes in nutrition, exercise, health, creative arts, peer leading training smoking cessation, reflexology and more. 202-581-9355
- Health Insurance Counseling-George Washington University National Law Center's Health Insurance Counseling Project offers free health insurance education, information and counseling services to seniors living in D.C. 202-739-0668
- Dwelling Place-Emergency shelter is available to seniors who are abused, neglected or exploited. This 24-hour emergency shelter provides medical, dental, psychotherapy, and family counseling. Housing is limited to no more than 90 days. 202-583-7602
- DC Housing Authority-This agency manages and subsidizes public housing for low-income, elderly D.C. residents. 202-535-1500
- Christian Communities Group Homes Board, Inc.-They offer two group homes where residents share living expenses. They also provide personal supervision and help with daily tasks. 202-635-9384
- Independent Living Skills Programs-This program assists seniors to live independently by teaching them to use assistive devices to remain in their homes.
- Notary Public Service-The D.C. Office on Aging provides notary service to older residents and other acting on their behalf. 202-724-5622
- Self Help Office (SHO)-You can receive free help to legal questions, writing consumer complaints, contacting an attorney and other legal matters if you are D.C resident 60 years old and older.
- Home Delivered Meals- Hot and nutritious meals are delivered to homebound qualifying seniors. This service is also available on weekends.
- Meals with Friends- Hot and nutritious meals are served in a group setting.
- Nutrition Counseling-Individual counseling is available to seniors at nutritional risk because of their history, medication use or chronic illness.
- Nutrition Education-Education programs which promote better health and nutrition in a group or individual setting.
- Lead Agency Nutrition Program-Provides seniors with nutritious meals and access to other services such as transportation, counseling, recreation, assessment and socialization.
- Senior Lunch Program-Many centers throughout D.C. serve well balanced congregate meals to the elderly or they can arrange for delivery to homebound clients. 202-724-5626

- United Planning Organization-Congregate meals and other services are provided on weekends. 202-610-5857
- Needs Assessment-Seniors can receive a needs assessment that address their social, psychological and physical health. A "Plan of Care" is produced that contains information about the individuals' abilities and services needed.
- Washington Center for Aging Services-This 262-bed, long-term care facility is for Medicaid and Medicare clients. 202-541-6200
- Outreach-The DC aging Office offers the Senior Service Network highlighting the programs available to senior citizens.
- DC Parks and Recreational Project SCORE-Project SCORE offers recreational and cultural activities for seniors including transportation for groups of 10 or more. SCORE is located at 13 senior centers. 202-282-0748
- Senior Companion/Respite Care Program-Relief for caregivers who take care of frail or ill seniors. The service is provided through a telephone request system only. 202-274-6697
- Center Care Day Treatment Center-This Medicaid-certified facility is for seniors who require non-residential care during the day. 202-541-6150
- The Downtown Cluster's Geriatric Day Care Center-Social and emotional support is available to seniors to increase physical independence in a day care center. 202-347-7527
- IONA Day Health Center Program-This Medicaid-certified day care center that helps mentally and physically impaired seniors to improve their quality of life. 202-895-0238
- Genevieve N. Johnson Senior Day Care Program-The Center offer support to seniors to help adjust to the aging process. 202-723-8537
- Call 'N' Ride Transportation Program-Discounted door-to-door taxi service to citizens 60 years old and older. The discount is based on a sliding scale. 202-635-3970
- Washington Metropolitan Area Transit Authority-Discounts are available to seniors who ride the transit system.
- The Washington Elderly Handicapped Transportation Services-If you are a senior and you are unable to access traditional transportation arrangements can be made to get you where you need to go. Qualifying errands include medical appointments, dialysis, appointments to public benefit agencies, banking and more. 202-635-8866

Florida

Department of Elder Affairs
Building B - Suite 152
4040 Esplanade Way
Tallahassee, FL 32399-7000
850-414-2000
800-963-5337
Fax: 850-414-2004
http://elderaffairs.state.fl.us/

- Adult Care Food Program-This program funds eligible facilities for the cost of meals served to the elderly.
- Alzheimer's Disease Initiative (ADI)-Respite care, training and education are provided to Alzheimer patients and their caregivers.
- Chore/Homemaker Services-Eligible seniors can receive chore/homemaker services to help them stay independent and in their homes as long as possible. Services include: housekeeping, laundry, clothing repair, minor home repairs, assistance with bill paying, meal preparation, and shopping assistance.
- Community Care for the Elderly (CCE)-Case management services are provided to frail seniors living independently in their homes. Service may include adult day care, home health care, counseling, home repair, medical therapeutic care, home nursing and emergency alert response.
- Companion/Escort Services-Companionship services can help alleviate the isolation many seniors experience. Companions help with a wide range of everyday tasks.
- Comprehensive Assessment Review and Evaluation for Long-Term Care Services (CARES)-This pre-admission assessment can help determine level of care need for the elderly.
- Congregate Meals- Hot and nutritious meals are served in a group setting.
- Consumer Directed Care (CDC)-Clients are given decision making power over their service dollars to use as wisely as possible to purchase services for their specific needs.
- Elder Helpline-A free statewide toll-free telephone number for information and referral assistance in the state of Florida. 800-963-5337
- Elder Update Newspaper-This free bi-monthly newspaper features topics of interest to Florida senior citizens. To subscribe call the Helpline 800-963-5337 and give them your name and address.
- Emergency Home Energy Assistance for the Elderly (EHEAEP)-Vendor payments are available to low-income residents that are 60 years old and older when there is an emergency.
- Health and Wellness Promotion-This program includes the following activities: medication management education, osteoporosis education and screening, diabetes education and screening and mobile health education and screening.

State Aging Office Programs

- Home Care for the Elderly (HCE)-This program provides subsidy payments to caregivers to help keep low-income elders in their own homes. To be eligible the senior must be at risk of being placed in a nursing home.
- Intergenerational Connections-This program brings different generations together for a variety of activities.
- Legal Assistance-Legal assistance for Florida resident seniors.
- The Long-Term Care Community Diversion Project-A Medicaid waiver program to help the elderly remain in their homes.
- Long-Term Care Nursing Home Diversion Program-This program is for disabled elders who are Medicare and Medicaid eligible. It coordinates the client's regular care with long-term care.
- Long-Term Care Ombudsman Council-The council receives, investigates and resolves complaints by or on the behalf or residents of long-term care facilities.
- Meals on Wheels- Hot and nutritious meals are delivered to homebound qualifying seniors.
- Medicaid Waivers-Medicaid funds are used to keep frail elderly out of nursing homes.
- Respite for Elders Living in Everyday Families (RELIEF)-In-home respite for homebound elders so the caregiver can leave for brief periods of time.
- Senior Community Service Employment Program (SCSEP)-Low-income seniors age 55 and older can receive up to 20 hours of employment in a community service assignment, job training, related educational programs and the opportunity for placement in an unsubsidized job.
- Senior Companion Program-This volunteer program provides rides to medical appointments, shopping assistance, meal preparation, companionship and respite care to the elderly at risk of being institutionalized.
- Serving Health Insurance Needs of Elders (SHINE)-Free insurance counseling and information about Medicare and health insurance coverage.
- Sunshine for Seniors-This program provides counselors for the elderly to inform them of eligibility criteria established by pharmaceutical companies and other drugs covered by certain programs.

Georgia
Division of Aging Services
2 Peachtree Street N.E., Suite 9385
Atlanta, GA 30303-3142
404-657-5258
Fax: 404-657-5285
http://aging.dhr.georgia.gov

- Adult Protective Services-This office handles reports of abuse, neglect or exploitation of the elderly who are not residents of nursing homes. 888-774-0152 or 404-657-5250
- Homemaker Services-Services are available to eligible seniors who wish to stay in their homes. Trained homemakers assist with everyday needs including personal care, some housework and meal preparation.
- Visit and Telephone Reassurance-Daily phone calls to homebound seniors to help reduce isolation and ensure health and safety of the elderly person.
- Chore and Maintenance Services
- Mobile Day Care-Staff and material travel throughout Georgia and especially to rural areas to give caregivers responsible for persons with dementia time away.
- Home Modification
- Personal Care-This program provides assistance to frail elderly senior citizens that meet certain criteria. Services include: bathing, grooming, meal preparation, menu planning, shopping, light housekeeping and more.
- Emergency Response System-Emergency response equipment for at-risk seniors who live alone.
- Congregate Meals- Hot and nutritious meals are served in a group setting.
- Home Delivered Meals- Hot and nutritious meals are delivered to homebound qualifying seniors.
- Adult Day Care- Supervised care in a group setting and may include social interaction, recreation, training, counseling and meals.
- Alzheimer's Services-Out-of-home care and in-home respite to assist clients and their families.
- Transportation-Transportation access to and from nutrition centers and other vital appointments.
- Information and Assistance- Anyone who is a senior or involved in a senior's life, may contact this program to receive free information and be linked with appropriate programs and services.
- Elder Abuse & Prevention-Services to identify prevent and treat elder abuse, neglect and exploitation.
- Ombudsman-Assists residents of long-term care facilities.
- Elderly Legal Assistance Program-Georgia residents 60 years old and older can receive legal representation, information and education in civil legal issues.
- GeorgiaCares-GeorgiaCares educates seniors on the procedures in applying for low-cost prescription drug assistance programs.

- SAVA Program-This program acts as a liaison between victims, social service agencies and the court system for adults 60 years old and older who have been abused, neglected or exploited. 888-774-0152 or 404-657-5250
- Senior Community Service Employment Program (SCSEP)-Provides training and part-time employment and assistance to low-income seniors.

Hawaii
Executive Office on Aging
No 1 Capitol District
250 South Hotel St., Suite 406
Honolulu, HI 96813-2831
808-586-0100
Fax: 808-586-0185
www4.hawaii.gov/eoa/

- Hawaii Family Caregiver's Network-This network brings family caregivers together with information.
- Responsiveness, Encouragement, Assistance through Counseling and Help (REACH)-REACH offers assistance and awareness of elder abuse.
- Personal Assistance-Provides personal assistance to seniors 60 years old and older including: bathing, grooming, eating, walking and other daily activities.
- Homemaker-This program provides assistance to seniors who are unable to perform one or more of the following activities: preparing meals, shopping for personal items, managing money, using the telephone or doing light housework.
- Chore-This program provides assistance to seniors who are unable to perform one or more of the following activities: heavy housework, yard work or sidewalk maintenance.
- Home Delivered Meals- Hot and nutritious meals are delivered to homebound qualifying seniors.
- Adult Day Care-Supervised care in a group setting and may include social interaction, recreation, training, counseling and meals.
- Assisted Transportation-Door-to-door transportation to frail seniors who have trouble using regular vehicles. Escort services may also be available.
- Case Management-Case managers help families assess needs, develop care plans, implement care plans, provide service linkage, monitoring and proving follow-up and reassessment.
- Congregate Meals- Hot and nutritious meals are served in a group setting.
- Nutrition Counseling-Individualized advice to seniors at risk because of history, medications or chronic illness.
- Legal Assistance-Legal advice, counseling and representation by an attorney for eligible seniors or persons acting on their behalf.
- Nutrition Education-Provides nutrition, physical fitness and health information to groups and individuals.
- Information and Assistance-Information on all of the services and agencies available to seniors in Hawaii.
- Outreach-Identifying potential senior clients and encouraging them to use existing benefits.
- Escort-A person is available to accompany seniors to and from a destination to protect and assist them. Transportation is not included.
- Hospice Volunteer Training and Services-Care for terminally ill seniors and their families by creating a caring home environment.
- Health Promotion, Health Maintenance and Wellness Program-The goal of these programs are to help seniors maintain their independence by providing health screenings, monitor chronic illness and follow-up.
- Friendly Visiting-Planned regular visits to the homes of adults 60 years old and older at home or institutionalized to reduce the feelings of isolation.
- Telephone Reassurance-Regularly scheduled telephone calls to homebound adults to help ensure their safety.
- Education and Training-Workshops and seminars either formally or informally to seniors to acquire knowledge to make their lives better.
- Multipurpose Senior Center-Senior Centers offer a variety of programs for adults 60 years old and older.

Idaho
Idaho Commission on Aging
P.O. Box 83720
Boise, ID 83720-0007
208-334-3833
877-471-2777
Fax: 208-334-3033
www.idahoaging.com/abouticoa/index.htm

State Aging Office Programs

- Family Caregiver Support Program-Assistance, information, respite, support and services for families and friends who help care for frail loved ones.
- Ombudsman- Fields complaints and provides investigation and resolution of complaints relating to the health, safety, welfare and rights of older adults who are living in long-term care facilities.
- Legal Assistance-Access to legal advice and counseling or representation by an attorney for eligible senior citizens.
- Adult Protection Services-Investigates reports of abuse, neglect or exploitation of older adults and works to protect them.
- Information and Assistance-This program is a telephone and "walk-in" service to seniors and their families to access available programs and services throughout the state.
- Outreach-This program identifies seniors in the community who may be in need of services or other benefits.
- Transportation-Assistance for seniors who have no other way to run their errands such as senior meal programs, medical appointments and other necessary appointments.
- Adult Day Care-Adult day care provides personal care and a variety of other support services to in need seniors.
- Case Management-Case managers provide assistance to frail seniors who require available services. The goal is to reduce the risk of institutionalization for people that need some intervention.
- Home Delivered Meals-Hot, cold or frozen meals are delivered to home-bound seniors.
- Homemaker-Provides assistance with laundry, meal preparation and other day-to-day essential activities to frail seniors.
- Chore-Assistance to frail seniors who need assistance including: minor home repair, snow shoveling, trash removal, minor plumbing and other typical chores.
- Respite-Time away for full-time caregivers of homebound adults.
- Nutrition Education and Counseling-Individual and group presentations about age-related health and nutrition.
- Senior Community Services Employment Program-This program provides training and support to low-income seniors 55 and old and older in obtaining employment.
- Home Modification- Accessibility modification and minor repairs including: handrails, ramps, door locks, electrical fixtures, and appliances.
- Telephone Reassurance- Regularly scheduled telephone calls to homebound adults to help ensure their safety.
- Shopping Assistance-Volunteers assist frail eligible seniors purchase food, clothing or other necessary items or they may shop for homebound seniors.
- Health Promotion-Senior Centers provide a variety of opportunities including fitness courses and health screenings.
- Friendly Visiting- Planned regular visits to the homes of seniors who live at home or are institutionalized to reduce the feelings of isolation.
- "Stand By You" Program-This program offers free services to persons with Alzheimer's disease and their families.

Illinois
Department on Aging
421 East Capitol Avenue, #100
Springfield, IL 62701-1789
217-785-3356
800-252-8966
Fax: 217-785-4477
www.state.il.us/aging/

- Case Management-Case managers coordinate a variety of support services and make referrals to meet the needs of each client.
- Homemaker-Homemakers provide basic chores including: cleaning, laundry, shopping, errands and meal planning and preparation to eligible frail seniors.
- Adult Day Care-There are over 80 adult day service centers throughout the state. They provide a variety of services to older adults who are unable to stay at home during the day.
- Senior Companion-This program matches frail seniors that can not be left alone with low-income senior volunteers who provide companionship. This program is only available in certain parts of the state.
- Choices for Care-Case managers can meet with you and your family to show you your possible options for home care and long-term care.
- Senior Centers-There are approximately 180 senior centers throughout the state. They provide a variety of services including: meals, transportation, counseling, legal assistance and health screenings.
- Illinois Family Caregiver Support Program-There are over 150 Caregiver Resource Centers throughout the state. They provide a variety of services to caregivers including: information, assistance, respite, counseling, support groups, training, education and emergency support services,
- Congregate Meals- Hot and nutritious meals are served in a group setting.

- Home Delivered Meals- Hot and nutritious meals are delivered to homebound qualifying seniors.
- Information & Assistance- This office provides up-to-date information on available resources and referrals.
- Transportation- Assistance for seniors who have no other way to run their errands such as senior meal programs, medical appointments and other necessary appointments.
- Outreach-One-on-one counseling between seniors and staff to help the older person become informed about services.
- Senior Community Services Employment Program-This program provides training and support to low-income seniors 55 and old and older in obtaining employment.
- Elder Abuse and Neglect-Staff responds to reported cases of elder abuse, neglect and/or exploitation of seniors.
- Long-Term Care Ombudsman- Fields complaints and provides investigation and resolution of complaints relating to the health, safety, welfare and rights of older adults who are living in long-term care facilities.
- Legal Assistance-Over 8,600 Illinois seniors received legal assistance in 2003. They provide help with civil legal matters such as elder abuse and neglect, financial exploitation, consumer fraud, simple estate planning, advance directives, nursing home residents' rights and government benefit programs.
- Senior HelpLine-The Illinois Senior HelpLine receives 235 calls a day helping seniors find services they need. 800-252-8966
- Elder Abuse Hotline-They will take calls pertaining to elder abuse nights, weekends and holidays. 800-279-0400.
- Grandparents Raising Grandchildren-This support program provides education, training, information and referrals to grandparents raising their grandchildren.
- Gatekeeper Program-Customer service employees from major utility, newspaper and pharmacies are trained to be aware of elders who may need assistance.
- Health Awareness Programs-Public awareness programs about elder issues.
- Money Management Program-Financial services program that helps low-income seniors who have trouble managing personal financial tasks such as: paying bills, budgeting, banking, creditors, medical forms and other issues.
- Senior Publications-Illinois publishes an aging newsletter, Network Newsletter which is available at their web site. They also produce a variety of brochures.
- Illinois Cares Rx-Assistance for low-income seniors to help cover the costs of prescription medicines.

Indiana

Bur of Aging/In Home Services
402 W. Washington St.
P.O. Box 7083
Indianapolis, IN 46207-7083
317-232-7020
Fax: 317-232-7867
www.state.in.us/fssa/elderly/index.html

- Pre-Admission Screening Program-This screening process provides assessments to identify the needs of seniors entering or who are thinking about entering a nursing care facility.
- CHOICE-Community and Home Options to Institutionalized Care for the Elderly (CHOICE) provides services to eligible elders who need assistance.
- Home Health Aide-Assistance at home for frail seniors.
- Case Management-Case managers coordinate a variety of support services and make referrals to meet the needs of each client.
- Homemaker-Provides assistance with laundry, meal preparation and other day-to-day essential activities to frail seniors.
- Adaptive Aids and Devices-Access to adaptive aid that improve quality of life for frail seniors.
- Home Delivered Meals-Hot and nutritious meals are delivered to homebound qualifying seniors.
- Neighborhood Lunch Program-Hot and nutritious meals are served in a group setting.
- Adult Day Care-Adult day care provides personal care and a variety of other support services to in need seniors.
- Respite-Time away for full-time caregivers of homebound adults.
- Home Repair/Maintenance-Assistance to eligible frail seniors who have trouble with simple home repairs and maintenance.
- Transportation Services-Assistance for seniors who have no other way to run their errands such as senior meal programs, medical appointments and other necessary appointments.
- Family Caregiver Support-Support to caregivers caring for a loved one aged 60 and older.
- Grandparents Raising Grandchildren-Support to grandparents raising their grandchildren.
- Long-Term Care Ombudsman- Fields complaints and provides investigation and resolution of complaints relating to the health, safety, welfare and rights of older adults who are living in long-term care facilities.
- Senior Community Service Employment Program- Senior Employment offers economically disadvantaged seniors 55 years old and older employment training.

- Information & Assistance-Provides up-to-date information on available resources and referrals.
- Home Modification-Home modification for eligible frail seniors to keep their independence including installing lifts, widening doorways, building wheelchair ramps and roll-in showers and installing bars in the bathroom.
- Senior Companion Services-This program matches frail seniors that can not be left alone with low-income senior volunteers who provide companionship.
- Personal Emergency Response Service- Emergency response equipment for at-risk seniors who live alone.

Iowa
Iowa Department of Elder Affairs
Clemens Building, 3rd Floor
200 Tenth Street
Des Moines, IA 50309-3609
515-242-3333
Fax: 515-242-3300
www.state.ia.us/elderaffairs/

- Senior Internship Program (SIP)-This work-training program is for low-income adults 55 years old and older gain skills to ultimately transition to permanent employment.
- Older Worker Employment Partnership-Connecting older workers with employment.
- Resident Advocate Committee (RAC) Program-Volunteers that are advocates of residents of long-term nursing facilities.
- Senior Health Insurance Information Program-This program provides assistance to seniors who need help with medical bills, insurance claims and insurance questions.
- You Can! Steps to Healthier Aging-This program provides group classes on nutrition and physical activity through area agencies.
- Case Management Program for the Frail Elderly (CMPFE)-CMPFE is designed to postpone the institutionalization of frail older adults.
- Iowa Family Caregiver-A variety of information, services and programs are available to full-time caregivers of frail adults. www.iowafamilycaregiver.org
- The Rural Alzheimer's Demonstration Grant-This project provides services to victims of Alzheimer's disease and their families.
- Legal Assistance-Legal assistance and referral for adults 60 years old and older.
- Elder Abuse Prevention-Educational programs to prevent the abuse, neglect and exploitation of the elderly.
- Long-Term Ombudsman-Fields complaints and provides investigation and resolution of complaints relating to the health, safety, welfare and rights of older adults who are living in long-term care facilities.
- Senior Centers- Senior Centers offer a variety of programs for adults 60 years old and older.
- Adult Day Care- Adult day care provides personal care and a variety of other support services to in need seniors.
- Chore Services- Assistance to frail seniors who need assistance including: minor home repair, snow shoveling, trash removal, minor plumbing and other typical chores.
- Respite- Time away for full-time caregivers of homebound adults.
- Congregate Meals- Hot and nutritious meals are served in a group setting.
- Home Delivered Meals- Hot and nutritious meals are delivered to homebound qualifying seniors.
- Homemaker Services- Provides assistance with laundry, meal preparation and other day-to-day essential activities to frail seniors.
- Transportation- Assistance for seniors who have no other way to run their errands such as senior meal programs, medical appointments and other necessary appointments.
- Home Modification-Accessibility modification and minor repairs including: handrails, ramps, door locks, electrical fixtures, and appliances.
- Telephone Reassurance-Regularly scheduled telephone calls to homebound adults to help ensure their safety.

Kansas
Department on Aging
New England Building
503 South Kansas
Topeka, KS 66603-3404
785-296-4986
800-432-3535
Fax: 785-296-0256
www.agingkansas.org/

- Alzheimer's and Related Disorders Help Line-Information, referrals, assistance and education regarding Alzheimer's is available by calling the Help Line at 800-432-3535.

- Client Assessment, Referral and Evaluation Program (CARE)-This assessment program evaluates seniors before admitting them to nursing care home facilities.
- Elder Rights Protection-This program administers three areas: Prevention of Elder Abuse, Neglect & Exploitation, State Elder Rights and the Legal Assistance Development Program.
- Family Caregiver Support Program- Support to caregivers caring for their elderly loved ones.
- Home & Community Based Services for the Frail Elderly-This program offer seniors an option of community based services instead of being admitted into a nursing care facility.
- Legal Assistance-Advice and representation by a legal provider is available to socially and economically needy adults.
- Long-Term Care Program-Long-term nursing care facility care for Medicaid-eligible seniors who require 24 hours a-day supervision.
- Senior Care Act Program-This is a coordinating program for Kansans 60 years old and older.
- Health Care Attendant 1-Assistance for eligible frail seniors 65 year old and older with housekeeping tasks including: cleaning, level one meal preparation and laundry.
- Health Care Attendant 2- Assistance for eligible frail seniors 65 year old and older with everyday tasks including: level two dressing, bathing and eating.
- Personal Emergency-Personal electronic devices that can be worn and when pushed it signals emergency help.
- Respite Care-Temporary time-away for full-time caregivers that includes supervision and limited physical assistance.
- Adult Day Care-Group day care away from home to adults that can not be left alone.
- Sleep Cycle Support-Assistance in the home during sleeping hours and may include toileting, help getting in and out of bed and reminding to take medications.
- Wellness Monitoring-Health assessment, education, counseling and monitoring of treatment programs.
- Minor Home Repair-Provides a variety of services to residents 60 years old and older that fixes issues of safety and access in the home.
- Home Delivered Meals-Hot meals delivered to homebound seniors 60 years old and older.
- Congregate Meals- Hot and nutritious meals are served in a group setting.
- Information & Assistance-This office provides up-to-date information on available resources and referrals.
- Active Aging Newspaper-A monthly newspaper for seniors in Butler, Harvey and Sedgwick Counties.
- Kansas Support Services for Elders (KSSE)-KSSE is a financial counseling service for adults 60 years old.
- Good Grief-This support group is available for widowed adults in Butler County.
- Transportation-Assistance for seniors who have no other way to run their errands such as senior meal programs, medical appointments and other necessary appointments.

Kentucky
Office of Aging Services
Cabinet for Families and Children
Commonwealth of Kentucky
275 East Main Street
Frankfort, KY 40621
502-564-6930
Fax: 502-564-4595
http://chfs.ky.gov/dhss/das/

- Adult Day Health Care-A medically supervised program open to eligible frail seniors who need some assistance in a non-resident facility.
- Adult Day Care-Group day care away from home to adults that can not be left alone.
- Alzheimer's Respite-Time away for caregivers of Alzheimer's patients.
- Case Management-Case managers provide assistance to frail seniors who require available services. The goal is to reduce the risk of institutionalization for people that need some intervention.
- Chores- Assistance to frail seniors who need assistance including: minor home repair, snow shoveling, trash removal, minor plumbing and other typical chores.
- Escort- A person is available to accompany seniors to and from a destination to protect and assist them.
- Friendly Visits- Planned regular visits to the homes of adults at home or that are institutionalized to help reduce the feelings of isolation.
- Health Promotion
- Home Health Aide-Assistance at home for frail seniors.
- Homemaker- Provides assistance with laundry, meal preparation and other day-to-day essential activities to frail seniors.
- Home Repair- Provides a variety of services to senior residents that repairs issues of safety and access in the home.

State Aging Office Programs

- Information & Referral- This office provides up-to-date information on available resources and referrals.
- Respite- Temporary time-away for full-time caregivers that includes supervision and limited physical assistance.
- Legal Assistance- Advice and representation by a legal provider is available to socially and economically needy adults.
- Home Delivered Meals- Hot meals delivered to homebound seniors.
- Congregate Meals- Hot and nutritious meals are served in a group setting.
- Long-Term Ombudsman-Fields complaints and provides investigation and resolution of complaints relating to the health, safety, welfare and rights of older adults who are living in long-term care facilities.
- Outreach- This program identifies seniors in the community who may be in need of services or other benefits.
- Personal Care-Help for eligible seniors with everyday tasks.
- Telephone Reassurance- Regularly scheduled telephone calls to homebound adults to help ensure their safety.
- Senior Community Service Employment Program- Senior Employment offers economically disadvantaged seniors 55 years old and older employment training.
- Transportation- Assistance for seniors who have no other way to run their errands such as senior meal programs, medical appointments and other necessary appointments.

Louisiana
Governor's Office of Elderly Affairs
P.O. Box 61
Baton Rouge, LA 70821-0061
225-342-7100
Fax: 225-342-7133
www.louisiana.gov/elderlyaffairs/

- Adult Day Care-Group day care away from home to adults that can not be left alone.
- Adult Day Health
- Assisted Transportation-Transportation to and from necessary errands to seniors that can't use regular transportation. Escort service may also be included.
- Case Management-Coordinating assistance to older adults and their caregivers.
- Chore-Assistance is provided to eligible seniors that can't complete the following daily activities: heavy housework, yard work, or sidewalk maintenance.
- Congregate Meals-Hot and nutritious meals are served in a group setting.
- Elderly Protective Services-This office responds to reports of abuse, neglect and exploitation of adults 60 years old and older. 800-259-4990
- Long-Term Care Ombudsman-This office investigates and resolves complaints by and in the behalf of residents of long-term care facilities.
- Home Delivered Meals-Hot meals delivered to homebound seniors.
- Homemaker-Assistance is provided to seniors who are unable to perform one or more of the following activities: preparing meals, shopping for personal items, managing money, using the telephone or doing light house work.
- Information and Assistance-This office provides up-to-date information on available resources and referrals.
- Legal Assistance-Assistance for seniors in securing rights and entitlements including: education, advice and representation.
- Senior Community Service Employment Program-Senior Employment offers economically disadvantaged seniors 55 years old and older employment training.
- Nutrition Counseling-Advice and guidance to seniors at nutritional risk because of history, medications and chronic illness.
- Nutrition Education-This program provides current information on nutrition, physical fitness and health individually or in a group setting.
- Senior Rx-Links eligible seniors 60 years old and older with prescriptions assistance programs.
- Outreach- This program identifies seniors in the community who may be in need of services or other benefits.
- Personal Care- Assistance is provided to seniors who are unable to perform one or more of the following activities: eating, dressing, bathing, toileting, getting in and out of bed or walking.
- Transportation-Provides transportation from one place to another for eligible seniors.
- Counseling-Professional counseling in groups or individually.
- Crime Prevention Services
- Home Repair/Modifications-Accessibility modification and minor repairs including: handrails, ramps, door locks, electrical fixtures, and appliances.
- Material Aid-Access to assistive devices including: walkers, fans, wheelchairs, commodities and personal hygiene items.
- Medical Alert-This program provides eligible seniors with Emergency Response System devices.

- Medication Management-Screening and education to avoid incorrect medications and adverse drug interactions.
- Placement Services-Assistance to families with proper placement.
- Recreation-Fun activities in groups or individually that promote social interaction and well-being.
- Telephoning-Regularly scheduled telephone calls to homebound adults to help ensure their safety.
- Utility Assistance-This program determines utility needs and provides financial assistance.
- Visiting-In-home visits to seniors to provide companionship, comfort, encouragement and safety.
- Wellness-A variety of activities designed to improve seniors quality of life through physical fitness and health screenings.
- Respite-Temporary time-away for full-time caregivers that includes supervision and limited physical assistance.

Maine
Office of Elder Services
11 State House Station
442 Civic Center Drive
Augusta, ME 04333
207-287-9200
800-262-2232
Fax: 207-287-9229
www.state.me.us/dhs/beas

- Adult Day Services-Provides social and health services to meet seniors needs. Services may include: meals, activities, information and referral, assistance with personal care and health monitoring.
- Adult Protective Services-This office responds to reports of abuse, neglect and exploitation of seniors.
- Alzheimer's Care and Support-Support for people with Alzheimer's and other dementia disease and their families including diagnosis, evaluation, adult day services, and respite.
- Transportation-Buses, vans or individual drivers can help you get from here to there.
- Community Dining Sites-There are over 100 sites throughout the State where seniors can get a hot and nutritious mid-day meal.
- Home Delivered Meal-Hot meals delivered to homebound seniors.
- Senior Community Service Employment Program-Senior Employment offers economically disadvantaged seniors 55 years old and older employment training.
- Employment Services-Career Centers throughout Maine help senior workers get into the job market.
- State Health Insurance Assistance Program-One-on-one counseling and assistance to Medicare clients and their families.
- Community Options Program-This program helps seniors who have questions about available services in the community.
- Guardianship and Conservatorship-The Maine Office of Elder Services may serve as public guardian and conservator for incapacitated adults.
- Health Screening and Care-Area Agencies on Aging offer health clinics which may test for blood pressure, diabetes, eye problems and hearing troubles.
- Home Care
- Hospice Services-Hospice provides support to people with a terminal illness and their families. 800-438-5963 or 207-626-0651
- Home Repair-Some Area Agencies on Aging provide minor home repairs for eligible seniors.
- Information and Referral-This office provides up-to-date information on available resources and referrals.
- Adaptive Equipment Loan Program
- Personal Care-Assistance is provided to seniors who are unable to perform one or more of the following activities: eating, dressing, bathing, toileting, getting in and out of bed or walking.
- Legal Service-Free legal services are available to eligible seniors 60 year old and older. 207-623-1797 or 800-750-5353
- Long-Term Ombudsman-Fields complaints and provides investigation and resolution of complaints relating to the health, safety, welfare and rights of older adults who are living in long-term care facilities.
- Low Cost Drug for the Elderly and Disable Program-This program can help you pay for your prescription drugs if you are 62 years old or older and meet income requirements.

Maryland
Maryland Department of Aging
State Office Building, Room 1007
301 West Preston Street
Baltimore, MD 21201-2374
410-767-1100
800-243-3425

Fax: 410-333-7943
www.mdoa.state.md.us

- Health Promotion and Disease Prevention-Services are available to seniors 60 years old and older including: mental and physical health risk assessment, counseling and referral, fitness activities and wellness education.
- Long-Term Ombudsman-Fields complaints and provides investigation and resolution of complaints relating to the health, safety, welfare and rights of older adults who are living in long-term care facilities.
- Home Delivered Meals-Hot meals delivered to homebound seniors.
- Congregate Meals-Hot and nutritious meals are served in a group setting.
- Project SAFE (Stop Adult Financial Exploitation)-This education project helps to inform older citizens of Maryland how to avoid financial exploitation.
- Public Guardianship-The Maryland Office of Aging may serve as public guardian for incapacitated adults 65 years old and older.
- Senior Care System-Case management and funds for services are provided for seniors 65 years old and older who are at risk of being institutionalized.
- Senior Centers-There are 112 senior centers throughout Maryland that provide opportunities for seniors to exercise, socialize, participate in health screening and more.
- Senior Center Plus-These sites offer structures activities to frail or cognitively impaired seniors. Meals and snacks are served to participants in a community dining area.
- Senior Employment Program-Senior Employment offers economically disadvantaged seniors 55 years old and older employment training.
- Senior Health Insurance Assistance Program- One-on-one counseling and assistance to Medicare clients and their families.
- Information and Assistance-This office provides up-to-date information on available resources and referrals.
- Legal Assistance-Assistance for seniors in securing rights and entitlements including: education, advice and representation.
- Medicaid Adult Day Care-This structured group program provides health, social and support services to functionally disabled seniors.
- Home Modification-Accessibility modification and minor repairs including: handrails, ramps, door locks, electrical fixtures, and appliances.
- Personal Care-Assistance is provided to seniors who are unable to perform one or more of the following activities: eating, dressing, bathing, toileting, getting in and out of bed or walking.
- Respite-Temporary time-away for full-time caregivers that includes supervision and limited physical assistance.
- Assisted Living Services
- Personal Emergency Response System-Personal electronic devices that can be worn and when pushed it signals emergency help.
- Dietician and Nutrition Services-Education for improving seniors eating habits.
- Assistive Devices-Devices that can enhance seniors' quality of life.

Massachusetts
Exec Office of Elder Affairs
1 Ashburton Place, 5th floor
Boston, MA 02108
617-727-7750
800-AGE-INFO
Fax: 617-727-6944
www.800ageinfo.com/

- Prescription Advantage-This prescription drug insurance plan is available to Massachusetts seniors 65 years old and older.
- Homemaker-Assistance is provided to seniors who are unable to perform one or more of the following activities: preparing meals, shopping for personal items, managing money, using the telephone or doing light house work.
- Personal Care-Assistance is provided to seniors who are unable to perform one or more of the following activities: eating, dressing, bathing, toileting, getting in and out of bed or walking.
- Adult Day Care-These services provide social and health services to meet seniors needs. Services may include: meals, activities, information and referral, assistance with personal care and health monitoring.
- Home Delivered Meals-Hot meals delivered to homebound seniors.
- Congregate Meals-Hot and nutritious meals are served in a group setting.
- Transportation- Provides transportation from one place to another for eligible seniors.
- Adult Day Health
- Personal Emergency Response System-Personal electronic devices that can be worn and when pushed it signals emergency help.
- Wanderer Locator-This program helps find a loved one who has wandered off.

- Adaptive Equipment/Housing-Devices that can enhance seniors' quality of life.
- Emergency Shelter-This program provides essential needs during emergencies.
- Chore-Assistance is provided to eligible seniors that can't complete the following daily activities: heavy housework, yard work, or sidewalk maintenance.
- Respite-Temporary time-away for full-time caregivers that includes supervision and limited physical assistance.
- Companion-This program matches frail seniors that can not be left alone with low-income senior volunteers who provide companionship.
- Medication Dispensing-Assistance with taking medication for eligible seniors.
- Serving the Health Information Needs of Elders (SHINE)-Provides health insurance counseling services to the elderly.
- Family Caregiver Support Program-Provides information about care giving, available services and local resources.
- Legal Assistance-Assistance for seniors in securing rights and entitlements including: education, advice and representation.
- Long-Term Ombudsman-Fields complaints and provides investigation and resolution of complaints relating to the health, safety, welfare and rights of older adults who are living in long-term care facilities.

Michigan
Office of Services to the Aging
PO Box 30676
7109 West Saginaw, First Floor
Lansing, MI 48909-8176
517-373-8230
Fax: 517-373-4092
www.miseniors.net/

- Assist Transportation/Escort Service-Transportation is provided to any Michigan resident 60 years old and older to go to doctor appointments, the grocery, meal sites, shopping and other errands.
- Benefits Counseling-Coordinated information and assistance pertaining to public benefits.
- Case Management-This program coordinates a client's care from assessment to obtaining services to help the senior remain in their home.
- Information and Referral-This office provides up-to-date information on available resources and referrals.
- Outreach-This program identifies and contacts isolated seniors with social and economic need and helps them gain access to services.
- Caregiver Support Group-Provides information about care giving, available services and local resources.
- Adult Foster Care-A facility for elderly disabled or mentally ill who require supervision but not continuous nursing care.
- Personal Emergency Response System-Personal electronic devices that can be worn and when pushed it signals emergency help.
- Chore-Chore services are non-regular household maintenance that increases the safety of the seniors' residence. Chores may include: washing walls, pest control, leaf raking, snow removal, repairing furniture, replacing faucets, installing safety equipment and more.
- Congregate Meals-Hot and nutritious meals are served in a group setting.
- Home Delivered Meals-Hot meals delivered to homebound seniors.
- Nutrition Counseling-Education for improving seniors eating habits.
- Home Health Aide-Home health aides perform health related activities prescribed for by a physician. These may include: daily living tasks, changing dressings, blood pressure monitoring, and other health related services.
- Home Repair-Permanent repairs to an elderly persons home to extend the life of the home or address safety issues. Home repair services include: roofing, replacement of windows and doors, heating system, electrical, plumbing, weatherization, foundation, floors and stairs.
- Homemaker-Assistance to eligible seniors in maintaining their homes. Services include: laundry, meal planning and preparation, shopping, light housekeeping, and client observation.
- Respite-Temporary time-away for full-time caregivers that includes supervision and limited physical assistance.
- MO Choice Waiver Program-Eligible seniors can receive Medicaid-covered expenses in their homes instead of in a nursing home.
- Personal Care-Assistance is provided to seniors who are unable to perform one or more of the following activities: eating, dressing, bathing, toileting, getting in and out of bed or walking.
- Telephone Reassurance- Daily phone calls to homebound seniors to help reduce isolation and ensure health and safety of the elderly person.
- Legal Assistance-Assistance for seniors in securing rights and entitlements including: education, advice and representation.
- Ombudsman-Fields complaints and provides investigation and resolution of complaints relating to the health, safety, welfare and rights of older adults who are living in long-term care facilities.

- Pension Counseling
- Senior Community Services Employment Program-Senior Employment offers economically disadvantaged seniors 55 years old and older employment training.
- Adult Day Care-These services provide social and health services to meet seniors needs. Services may include: meals, activities, information and referral, assistance with personal care and health monitoring.
- MiCAFE-This federally funded program is available in Cass and Genesee Counties and provides low-income seniors with assistance.
- Michigan's Elder Prescription Insurance Coverage-This program helps eligible seniors 65 years old and older afford their prescription medications.
- Disease Prevention/Health Promotion-These programs provide information and support to help Michigan seniors avoid illness and improve quality of life.
- Foster Grandparent-Low-income seniors are matched with children who need personal attention. The seniors work 20 hours per week and receive a tax-free stipend which does not affect the benefits they are receiving.

Minnesota
Minnesota Board on Aging
444 Lafayette Road
St. Paul, MN 55155-3843
651-296-2770
800-333-2433
TTY: 800-627-3529
Fax: 651-297-7855
www.mnaging.org

- Senior Surf Days-Classes for seniors on using the internet and email.
- Minnesotaheip.info- This online information assistance program can help seniors and their families find available services in their community www.minnesotahelp.info.
- Adult Foster Care-Foster care provides family living to seniors who are functionally impaired. The home provides services such as bathing, grooming and other assistance. The client pays for room and board.
- Adult Day Care-These services provide social and health services to meet seniors needs. Services may include: meals, activities, information and referral, assistance with personal care and health monitoring.
- Chores-Chore services are non-regular household maintenance that increases the safety of the seniors' residence. Chores may include: washing walls, pest control, leaf raking, snow removal, repairing furniture, replacing faucets, installing safety equipment and more.
- Homecare-Regular in-home assistance for eligible seniors.
- Home Modification-Accessibility modification and minor repairs including: handrails, ramps, door locks, electrical fixtures, and appliances.
- Home Delivered Meals-Hot meals delivered to homebound seniors.
- Congregate Meals-Hot and nutritious meals are served in a group setting.
- Personal Care-Assistance is provided to seniors who are unable to perform one or more of the following activities: eating, dressing, bathing, toileting, getting in and out of bed or walking.
- Transportation-Assisted rides for seniors to get to health care appointments, employment and other personal business.
- Indian Elder Desk-Assistance to Indian Elders with a variety of programs. 800-882-6262
- Grandparents Raising Grandchildren-This program encourages and promotes services for grandparents raising their grandchildren.
- Legal Assistance-Assistance for seniors in securing rights and entitlements including: education, advice and representation.
- Long-Tern Care Consultation-A social worker can meet with you and your family to help you make decisions about long-term care.
- Health Insurance Consultation-Free insurance consultation and referrals.
- Elder Abuse-This office responds to reports of abuse, neglect and exploitation of seniors.
- Ombudsman-Fields complaints and provides investigation and resolution of complaints relating to the health, safety, welfare and rights of older adults who are living in long-term care facilities.
- Personal Care-Assistance is provided to seniors who are unable to perform one or more of the following activities: eating, dressing, bathing, toileting, getting in and out of bed or walking.
- Respite-Temporary time-away for full-time caregivers that includes supervision and limited physical assistance.
- Caregiving Education and Training-Information and referrals for caregivers.
- Rx Connect-This program can help you find the right drug patient assistance program to meet your needs.
- Senior Community Services Employment Program-Senior Employment offers economically disadvantaged seniors 55 years old and older employment training.

Mississippi
Division of Aging and Adult Services
750 N. State Street
Jackson, MS 39202
601-359-4929
800-948-3090
Fax: 601-359-9664
www.mdhs.state.ms.us/aas.html

- Transportation-Assisted rides for seniors to get to health care appointments, employment and other personal business.
- Outreach-This program identifies seniors in the community who may be in need of services or other benefits.
- Information and Referral-This office provides up-to-date information on available resources and referrals.
- Home Delivered Meals-Hot meals delivered to homebound seniors.
- Congregate Meals-Hot and nutritious meals are served in a group setting.
- Legal Assistance-Assistance for seniors in securing rights and entitlements including: education, advice and representation.
- Mississippi Insurance Counseling and Assistance Program (MICAP)-A counseling program designed to answer elder's questions about health insurance.
- Senior Community Services Employment Program-Senior Employment offers economically disadvantaged seniors 55 years old and older employment training.
- Case Management-This program coordinates a client's care from assessment to obtaining services to help the senior remain in their home.
- Homemakers-Assistance to eligible seniors in maintaining their homes. Services include: laundry, meal planning and preparation, shopping, light housekeeping, and client observation.
- Adult Day Care-These services provide social and health services to meet seniors needs. Services may include: meals, activities, information and referral, assistance with personal care and health monitoring.
- Ombudsman Program-Fields complaints and provides investigation and resolution of complaints relating to the health, safety, welfare and rights of older adults who are living in long-term care facilities.
- Homestead Exemption-Home tax exemptions for seniors.
- Recreation-A variety of activities for seniors to become involved to keep them young at heart.
- Respite-Temporary time-away for full-time caregivers that includes supervision and limited physical assistance.
- Caregiver Assistance-Information to caregivers on available services and referrals.

Missouri
Department of Health & Senior Services
P.O. Box 570
615 Howerton Court
Jefferson City, MO 65102-0570
573-751-6062
800-735-2466 TDD
Fax: 573-751-8687
www.health.state.mo.us

- Ombudsman for Long-Term Care-Fields complaints and provides investigation and resolution of complaints relating to the health, safety, welfare and rights of older adults who are living in long-term care facilities. 573-526-0727 or 800-309-3282
- Elder Abuse and Neglect Hotline- 800-392-0210
- Legal Services-Assistance for seniors in securing rights and entitlements including: education, advice and representation.
- Home Delivered Meals-Hot meals delivered to homebound seniors.
- Congregate Meals-Hot and nutritious meals are served in a group setting.
- Homemaker-This program provides assistance to eligible seniors having trouble with one or more of the following activities: meal planning and preparation, shopping, light housework, money management, and using the telephone.
- Chore-Help for eligible seniors that may find it difficult to the following chores: sidewalk maintenance, heavy housework, and yard work.
- Personal Care-A personal assistance to help eligible seniors with everyday tasks including: eating, bathing, dressing, toileting and moving in and out of bed.
- Respite-Temporary time-away for full-time caregivers that includes supervision and limited physical assistance.
- Disease Prevention/Health Promotion-Programs on health related issues.
- Transportation-Rides for eligible seniors to get to health care appointments, employment and other personal business.

State Aging Office Programs

- Assisted Transportation-Assistance including escort service to eligible seniors that can not use regular transportation.
- Information and Assistance-This office provides up-to-date information on available resources and referrals.
- Outreach-This program identifies seniors in the community who may be in need of services or other benefits.
- Case Management-This program coordinates a client's care from assessment to obtaining services to help the senior remain in their home.
- Tax Counseling-Counseling for eligible seniors.
- Senior Community Services Employment Program-Senior Employment offers economically disadvantaged seniors 55 years old and older employment training.
- Friendly Visiting-Planned regular visits to the homes of adults 60 years old and older at home or institutionalized to reduce the feelings of isolation.
- Gatekeeper-Customer service employees from major utility, newspaper and pharmacies are trained to be aware of elders who may need assistance.
- Recreation-A variety of activities for seniors to become involved to keep them young at heart.
- Minor Home Repair-Assistance to eligible frail seniors who have trouble with simple home repairs and maintenance.
- Adult Day Care-These services provide social and health services to meet seniors needs. Services may include: meals, activities, information and referral, assistance with personal care and health monitoring.
- Nutrition Counseling-Individual counseling is available to seniors at nutritional risk because of their history, medication use or chronic illness.
- Family Caregiver Support-Assistance, information, respite, support and services for families and friends who help care for frail loved ones.

Montana

Senior and Long Term Care Division
111 Sanders, Room 210
Helena, MT 59620
406-444-4077
800-332-2272
Fax: 406-444-7743
www.dphhs.state.mt.us/sltc

- Adult Day Care-These services provide social and health services to meet seniors needs.
  Services may include: meals, activities, information and referral, assistance with personal care and health monitoring
- Adult Foster Care-Foster care provides family living to seniors who are functionally impaired. The home provides services such as bathing, grooming and other assistance. The client pays for room and board.
- Personal Care Homes-This is an assisted living program.
- Home Health Aides-Assistance at home for frail seniors.
- Homemaker-This program provides assistance to eligible seniors having trouble with one or more of the following activities: meal planning and preparation, shopping, light housework, money management, and using the telephone.
- Home Modifications-Accessibility modification and minor repairs including: handrails, ramps, door locks, electrical fixtures, and appliances.
- Hospice Services- Terminally ill patients may be eligible for hospice care.
- Meals on Wheels-Hot meals delivered to homebound seniors.
- Medicaid Waiver-This program is designed to help eligible seniors stay in their own homes and communities.
- Medical Equipment Loan/Purchase-There are several options for eligible seniors who need medical equipment such as wheelchairs.
- Personal Care Attendant-Personal care attendants help clients with everyday personal activities including: bathing, eating, moving in and out of bed, toileting, dressing, hair and skin care and dispensing medications.
- Respite Care-Temporary time-away for full-time caregivers that includes supervision and limited physical assistance.
- Shopping Assistance
- Case Management-This program coordinates a client's care from assessment to obtaining services to help the senior remain in their home.
- Chemical Dependency Counseling
- Adult Protective Services-This office accepts and evaluates reports of abuse and neglect and offers appropriate services.
- Transportation Services-Rides for eligible seniors to get to health care appointments, employment and other personal business.
- Long-Term Ombudsman-Fields complaints and provides investigation and resolution of complaints relating to the health, safety, welfare and rights of older adults who are living in long-term care facilities
- Legal Services-Assistance for seniors in securing rights and entitlements including: education, advice and representation.
- Aging Horizons-This is a television show that deals with the issues of the aging. The show airs several times per week.

Nebraska
Division of Aging Services
Dept of Health & Human Services
P.O. Box 95044
301 Centennial Mall-South
Lincoln, NE 68509
402-471-4623
800-942-7830 (NE only)
Fax: 402-471-4619
www.hhs.state.ne.us/ags/agsindex.htm

- Adult Protective Services-This office accepts and evaluates reports of abuse and neglect and offers appropriate services.
- Adult Family Homes-These are certified homes to help adults remain in their communities by providing minimum supervision and assistance. 800-358-8802
- Case Management-This program coordinates a client's care from assessment to obtaining services to help the senior remain in their home.
- Senior Community Services Employment Program-Senior Employment offers economically disadvantaged seniors 55 years old and older employment training.
- Legal Services-Assistance for seniors in securing rights and entitlements including: education, advice and representation.
- Congregate Meals-Hot and nutritious meals are served in a group setting.
- Home Delivered Meals-Hot meals delivered to homebound seniors.
- Senior Health Insurance Information Program (SHIP)-One-on-one counseling with elderly residents of Nebraska to provide them with insurance information.
- Long-Term Ombudsman-Fields complaints and provides investigation and resolution of complaints relating to the health, safety, welfare and rights of older adults who are living in long-term care facilities
- Respite-Temporary time-away for full-time caregivers that includes supervision and limited physical assistance.
- Power of Attorney, Guardianship and Conservatorship- The Division of Aging Services may serve as public guardian and conservator for incapacitated adults.
- Durable Medical Equipment-This program provides home care equipment not covered by Medicare to eligible seniors.
- Emergency Pharmacy Assistance-This is an emergency program for eligible seniors who need help obtaining medications they would otherwise not be able to afford.
- Handyman Program-This low-cost program provides minor home repairs and safety modifications to seniors 60 years old and older in Douglas, Sarpy, Dodge, Cass and Washington counties.
- Personal Care Services-Short-term personal care for eligible frail seniors not eligible for Medicare services. Services may include bathing, grooming and other personal activities.
- Homemaker-This program provides assistance to eligible seniors having trouble with one or more of the following activities: meal planning and preparation, shopping, light housework, money management, and using the telephone.
- Information and Assistance-This office provides up-to-date information on available resources and referrals. 402-444-6444
- Nutritional Education-Programs that stress the importance of nutrition for seniors.
- Adult Day Care-These services provide social and health services to meet seniors needs. Services may include: meals, activities, information and referral, assistance with personal care and health monitoring
- Breakfast Clubs-The Eastern Nebraska Office on Aging offers a Breakfast Club serves as an information source for residents 60 years old and older.
- Gatekeeper Program-Customer service employees from major utility, newspaper and pharmacies are trained to be aware of elders who may need assistance.

Nevada
Division for Aging Services
Department of Human Resources
3100 West Sahara Avenue, Suite 103
Las Vegas, NV 89102
702-486-3545
Fax: 702-486-3572
http://aging.state.nv.us/

- RxHelp4NV-RxHelp4NV is a service for seniors who have trouble paying for prescription medications. They will help you find appropriate patient assistance programs.

- State Health Insurance Assistance Program (SHIP)-SHIP provides information, counseling and assistance to Medicare clients.
- Community Home Based Initiatives Program (CHIP)-This program provides non-medical services to eligible seniors to help them maintain their independence by staying in their own homes.
- Homemaker-This program provides assistance to eligible seniors having trouble with one or more of the following activities: meal planning and preparation, shopping, light housework, money management, and using the telephone.
- Nevada Elders on the Net (NEON)-NEON provides seniors with access to senior information through the internet by providing computers at community centers throughout the state.
- Advocate for Elders-Advocacy and assistance to eligible frail seniors who are 60 years old or older living in isolation or in institutionalized facilities.
- Long-Term Ombudsman Program-Fields complaints and provides investigation and resolution of complaints relating to the health, safety, welfare and rights of older adults who are living in long-term care facilities.
- Senior Ride Program-The program offers discounted taxi service to seniors living in Clark County.
- Senior Citizens Property Tax Assistance-This is a refund program on a portion of property taxes paid by eligible senior citizens on their residence.
- Legal Services-Assistance for seniors in securing rights and entitlements including: education, advice and representation.
- Alzheimer's Support Group-Support for caregivers of Alzheimer's patience.
- Health Screenings-Senior sites provide routine health screenings such as blood pressure.
- Congregate Meals-Hot and nutritious meals are served in a group setting.
- Home Delivered Meals-Hot meals delivered to homebound seniors.
- Senior Community Services Employment Program-Senior Employment offers economically disadvantaged seniors 55 years old and older employment training.
- Nevada Care Connection-This is a comprehensive information and referral program for seniors.
- Case Management-Case managers coordinate a variety of support services and make referrals to meet the needs of each client.
- In-Home Attendant Care-Assistance with daily living activities such as bathing, dressing, getting in and out of bed, toileting, eating and meal preparation.
- Homemaker Service-This program offers basic home management and upkeep including: errands, laundry, meal planning and preparation, and other simple household tasks.
- Adult Companion Service-Volunteers provide companion support, task assistance and companionship to adults with exceptional need.
- Adult Day Care-These services provide social and health services to meet seniors needs. Services may include: meals, activities, information and referral, assistance with personal care and health monitoring
- Respite-Temporary supervised care for seniors to give their caregiver a period of relief from caregiving duties.
- Personal Emergency Response System-Help at your fingertips. This program provides in-home 24-hour two-way verbal and electronic communication. This ensures seniors with quick contact to emergency personnel.
- Chore Service-Assistance to frail seniors who need assistance including: minor home repair, snow shoveling, trash removal, minor plumbing and other typical chores.
- Nutrition Therapy-Assessment, education and counseling to seniors improve their eating habits.
- Protective Services-This office accepts and evaluates reports of abuse and neglect and offers appropriate services to seniors 60 years old and older.

New Hampshire
Division of Elderly and Adult Services
State Office Park South
129 Pleasant Street, Brown Bldg. #1
Concord, NH 03301-3857
603-271-4680
800-351-1888
Fax: 603-271-4643
www.dhhs.state.nh.us/DHHS/BEAS/default.htm

- Adult Protection-This office accepts and evaluates reports of abuse and neglect and offers appropriate services to seniors 60 years old and older.
- Long-Term Ombudsman- Fields complaints and provides investigation and resolution of complaints relating to the health, safety, welfare and rights of older adults who are living in long-term care facilities. 800-442-5640 or 603-271-4375
- Personal Care-Short-term personal care for eligible frail seniors not eligible for Medicare services. Services may include bathing, grooming and other personal activities.

- Homemaker Services-This program offers basic home management and upkeep including: errands, laundry, meal planning and preparation, and other simple household tasks.
- Adult Day Care-These services provide social and health services to meet seniors needs. Services may include: meals, activities, information and referral, assistance with personal care and health monitoring
- Case Management-Case managers coordinate a variety of support services and make referrals to meet the needs of each client.
- Transportation-Rides for eligible seniors to get to health care appointments, employment and other personal business.
- Information and Assistance-This office provides up-to-date information on available resources and referrals.
- Respite-Temporary supervised care for seniors to give their caregiver a period of relief from caregiving duties.
- Home Delivered Meals-Hot meals delivered to homebound seniors.
- Congregate Meals-Hot and nutritious meals are served in a group setting.
- In-Home Care-Non-medical and medical services for eligible seniors.

New Jersey
Division of Senior Affairs
Department of Health & Senior Services
P.O. Box 360
Trenton, NJ 08625-08360
609-943-3345
Fax: 609-943-3343
www.state.nj.us/health/senior/sraffair.htm

- Public Awareness, Information, Assistance and Outreach-This office can help elders locate appropriate services and resources. 800-792-8820
- State Health Insurance Assistance Program (SHIP)-Free help to New Jersey Medicare clients who need help with their insurance.
- Adult Day Health Services-A medically supervised program open to eligible frail seniors who need some assistance in a non-resident facility.
- Case Management-Case managers coordinate a variety of support services and make referrals to meet the needs of each client.
- Homemaker-This program offers basic home management and upkeep including: errands, laundry, meal planning and preparation, and other simple household tasks.
- Transportation-Rides for eligible seniors to get to health care appointments, employment and other personal business.
- Respite Care-Temporary supervised care for seniors to give their caregiver a period of relief from caregiving duties.
- Adult Day Care-These services provide social and health services to meet seniors needs. Services may include: meals, activities, information and referral, assistance with personal care and health monitoring
- Prescription Drug Assistance-Assistance to eligible seniors that may not otherwise be able to afford their prescription drugs.
- Home Modifications-Accessibility modification and minor repairs including: handrails, ramps, door locks, electrical fixtures, and appliances
- Personal Emergency Response System-Help at your fingertips. This program provides in-home 24-hour two-way verbal and electronic communication. This ensures seniors with quick contact to emergency personnel.
- Home Delivered Meals-Hot meals delivered to homebound seniors.
- Caregiver Training-Help for caregivers of the frail elderly.
- Chore Service-Assistance to frail seniors who need assistance including: minor home repair, snow shoveling, trash removal, minor plumbing and other typical chores.
- Adult Family Care-This community program allows up to three frail elderly to receive room, board and other health services in the home of another person. The cost is determined by an individual's income, assets and expenses.
- Alzheimer's Adult Day Services Program-This program partially funds adult day care services for Alzheimer patients. 609-943-3475
- Congregate Housing Services Program-These supportive services provide disabled seniors with the option of residing in selected subsidized housing facilities. 609-943-4060
- Adult Protective Services-This office accepts and evaluates reports of abuse and neglect and offers appropriate services to seniors.
- Health Insurance Counseling-Counseling for eligible adults with their insurance questions.
- Money Management-Confidential assistance with money management issues including: paying bills, check writing, banking, and other financial matters.
- Friendly Visitor-This outreach program sends trained visitors to homebound senior's residents to check on them and help to improve the quality of life of the homebound elder.
- Hospice-Hospice services are provided to terminally ill patients and their families.
- Telephone Reassurance-This program checks in on clients who live alone full time, temporarily or are homebound. They will cali at a set time to check on you and if you don't answer they will send assistance.

New Mexico
New Mexico Aging and Long-Term Services
Toney Anaya Building
2550 Cerrillos Road
Santa Fe, NM 87505
505-476-4799
866-451-2901 (toll free)
800-432-2080 (resource center)
Fax: 505-827-7649
www.nmaging.state.nm.us/

- Health Care Directives-Make your own health related decisions by writing and signing a health care directive that states your wishes on health issues.
- Legal Services-Assistance for seniors in securing rights and entitlements including: education, advice and representation.
- Senior Community Services Employment Program-Senior Employment offers economically disadvantaged seniors 55 years old and older employment training.
- Benefits Counseling Program-One-on-one counseling on possible available benefits for seniors.
- Long-Term Ombudsman-Fields complaints and provides investigation and resolution of complaints relating to the health, safety, welfare and rights of older adults who are living in long-term care facilities.
- Senior Companion-Volunteers provide assistance and friendship to seniors who may need help with daily activities.
- Foster Grandparent-Seniors are matched with children with special needs.
- Share Your Care-This program offers respite and free caregiver support programs to families in Albuquerque and Rio Rancho.
- Homemakers-Homemakers provide assistance to eligible elderly including: light housekeeping, cooking, bathing, toileting and other personal care.
- Senior Centers-Senior Centers offer a variety of programs for senior citizens.
- Home Repair Services-Basic repairs to the elderly that want to stay in their homes. Services include: building ramps, replacing showerheads, adding grab bars, plumbing, yard work, and other basic tasks.
- Adult Day Care-These services provide social and health services to meet seniors needs. Services may include: meals, activities, information and referral, assistance with personal care and health monitoring
- Home Health Providers-Providers offer physical therapy, skilled nursing care and personal activities.
- Respite Care-Temporary supervised care for seniors to give their caregiver a period of relief from caregiving duties.
- Hospice Programs-Hospice services are provided to terminally ill patients and their families.
- Elder Abuse Hotline-Assistance if you suspect elder abuse. 800-797-3260
- Home Delivered Meals-Hot meals delivered to homebound seniors.
- Congregate Meals-Hot and nutritious meals are served in a group setting.

New York
Office for the Aging
Two Empire State Plaza
Albany, NY 12223-1251
518-474-7012
800-342-9871
Fax: 518-474-1398
www.aging.state.ny.us/index.htm

- Health Insurance Information, Counseling and Assistance Program (HIICAP)-HIICAP counselors can answer seniors questions about Medicare, managed care, medigap and other long-term insurance programs.
- Elderly Pharmaceutical Insurance Coverage (EPIC)-This program helps eligible seniors cope with the high costs of prescriptions that are otherwise not eligible for Medicaid.
- Long-Term Care Ombudsman-Fields complaints and provides investigation and resolution of complaints relating to the health, safety, welfare and rights of older adults who are living in long-term care facilities.
- Legal Assistance-Assistance for seniors in securing rights and entitlements including: education, advice and representation.
- Elder Abuse Prevention
- Emergency Assistance for Adults (EAA)-Emergency funds to clients receiving SSI.
- Senior Citizen Property Tax Exemption-Many communities throughout the state offer property tax exemptions to reduce the elderly tax burden.

- Adult Day Care-These services provide social and health services to meet seniors needs. Services may include: meals, activities, information and referral, assistance with personal care and health monitoring.
- Expanded In-Home Services for the Elderly Program (EISEP)-EISEP assists eligible seniors with daily tasks including: dressing, bathing, shopping and cooking.
- Home Care Services-This service offers services to seniors with temporary or chronic needs who have difficulties performing day-to-day tasks. Tasks may include: nursing care, shopping, meal preparation, and grooming.
- Hospice Services-Hospice services are provided to terminally ill patients and their families. 518-446-1483
- Grandparents Raising Grandchildren with Developmental Disabilities-This program offers guidance and support to grandparents who have the responsibility of raising their developmentally disabled grandchildren.
- Foster Grandparent Program-Seniors are matched with children with special needs.
- Respite Services-Temporary supervised care for seniors to give their caregiver a period of relief from caregiving duties.
- Senior Centers-Senior Centers offer a variety of programs for senior citizens.
- Telephone Reassurance-This program checks in on clients who live alone full time, temporarily or are homebound. They will call at a set time to check on you and if you don't answer they will send assistance.
- Home Repair-Basic repairs to the elderly that want to stay in their homes. Services include: building ramps, replacing showerheads, adding grab bars, plumbing, yard work, and other basic tasks.
- Recreation-A variety of recreational activities are available through community resources.
- Nutrition Counseling-Individual counseling is available to seniors at nutritional risk because of their history, medication use or chronic illness.
- Transportation-Rides for eligible seniors to get to health care appointments, employment and other personal business.
- Congregate Housing- These supportive services provide disabled seniors with the option of residing in selected subsidized housing facilities
- Senior Community Services Employment Program-Senior Employment offers economically disadvantaged seniors 55 years old and older employment training.
- Congregate Meals-Hot and nutritious meals are served in a group setting.
- Home Delivered Meals-Hot meals delivered to homebound seniors.

North Carolina
Department of Health and Human Services
Division of Aging
2101 Mail Service Center
Raleigh, NC 27699-2101
919-733-3983
Fax: 919-733-0443
www.dhhs.state.nc.us/aging/home.htm

- Case Management-Case managers coordinate a variety of support services and make referrals to meet the needs of each client.
- Adult Care Home-Adult care homes provide 24-hour supervised care for eligible seniors.
- Adult Care Home Assistance-Cash Supplement to assist low-income seniors living in adult care homes pay for their care.
- Health Screenings-Health screening provide tests, screenings and referral to promote early detection.
- Home Health-Eligible seniors may receive health care prescribed by a physician and may include: skilled nursing care, physical, occupational or speech therapy, medical social services and nutrition counseling.
- In-Home Aide-Aides assist eligible functionally impaired seniors and their families with home management and personal care.
- Medication Management
- Respite-Temporary supervised care for seniors to give their caregiver a period of relief from caregiving duties.
- Adult Day Care-These services provide social and health services to meet seniors needs. Services may include: meals, activities, information and referral, assistance with personal care and health monitoring.
- Adult Protective Services-This office accepts and evaluates reports of abuse and neglect and offers appropriate services.
- Congregate Nutrition-Hot and nutritious meals are served in a group setting.
- Guardianship Services-The local human service agency appoints a guardian to serve in the best interest of their client.
- Health Support Services-This program helps individuals and families recognize the health needs of the elderly then choose and obtain appropriate services.
- Housing and Home Improvement-Assistance for older adults obtain and keep adequate housing. Services include: housing options, financing options, providing labor and materials for minor repairs and identifying code violations.
- Information and Assistance-Information regarding services provided by senior centers and other community resources.

- Mental Health Counseling-This service provides consultation, evaluation and outpatient treatment for eligible seniors who experience mental health troubles.
- Senior Centers-Senior Centers offer a variety of programs for senior citizens.
- Home Delivered Meals-Hot meals delivered to homebound seniors.
- Adult Day Care Health- Clients who are functionally impaired and are unable to live completely independent can participate in this program. The program provides rehabilitative, therapeutic and supportive health services.
- General Transportation-Transportation to and from community resources and other necessary destinations.
- Medical Transportation-Transportation to and from medical appointments, nutrition sites and other designated destinations for senior citizens to continue their necessary daily activities.
- At-Risk Case Management Services-Case managers assist adults who are at-risk or show evidence of abuse, neglect or exploitation gain the services they need.
- Family Caregiver Support-Services include: information, access to support services, counseling, training, respite care and supplemental services.
- Legal Assistance-Assistance for seniors in securing rights and entitlements including: education, advice and representation.
- Senior Companion-This program offers part-time volunteer work for low-income seniors 60 years old and old. They provide companion support, task assistance and companionship to adults with exceptional need.

North Dakota
Department of Human Services
Aging Services Division
600 E Boulevard Avenue, Dept 325
Bismarck, ND 58505-0250
701-328-4601
800-451-8693
TTY 701-328-3480
Fax: 701-328-4061
www.state.nd.us/humanservices/services/adultsaging/

- Caregiver Information and Assistance-Information regarding caregiver services provided by senior centers and other community resources.
- Respite-Temporary supervised care for seniors to give their caregiver a period of relief from caregiving duties.
- Adult Family Foster Care-Supervised 24-hour care in a family living environment.
- Case Management-Case managers coordinate a variety of support services and make referrals to meet the needs of each client.
- Chore Service-Assistance to frail seniors who need assistance including: minor home repair, snow shoveling, trash removal, minor plumbing and other typical chores.
- Environmental Modifications-Accessibility modification and minor repairs including: handrails, ramps, door locks, electrical fixtures, and appliances
- Family Home Care-Reimbursement for eligible family caregivers who reside with the client 24-hours a day.
- Homemaker-This program offers basic home management and upkeep including: errands, laundry, meal planning and preparation, and other simple household tasks.
- Personal Care-Short-term personal care for eligible frail seniors not eligible for Medicare services. Services may include bathing, grooming and other personal activities.
- Expanded Service Payments for the Elderly and Disabled Program (Ex-SPED)- Payments for in-home and community based services to help keep seniors out of long-term facilities.
- Emergency Response System-Provides telephone emergency response service.
- Specialized Equipment-Equipment to improve the quality of life of eligible seniors.
- Training Family Members-This program trains non-paid family members to help improve their skills as primary caregiver to an elderly relative.
- Supported Employment Services-Training and employment services to disabled seniors.
- Congregate Meals-Hot and nutritious meals are served in a group setting.
- Escort Shopping Assistance-Personal assistance to eligible seniors who may struggle with cognitive or physical difficulties.
- Health Maintenance-Health monitoring and screening services to promote early detection.
- Home Delivered Meals-Hot meals delivered to homebound seniors.
- Legal Assistance-Assistance for seniors in securing rights and entitlements including: education, advice and representation.
- Outreach-This program identifies seniors in the community who may be in need of services or other benefits.
- Transportation-Transportation to and from community resources and other necessary destinations.

- Senior Companion Services-Volunteers provide companion support, task assistance and companionship to adults with exceptional need.
- Information and Assistance-Information regarding services provided by senior centers and other community resources.
- Long-Term Care Ombudsman Program Fields complaints and provides investigation and resolution of complaints relating to the health, safety, welfare and rights of older adults who are living in long-term care facilities.
- Vulnerable Adult Protective Services-This office accepts and evaluates reports of abuse and neglect and offers appropriate services.

Ohio
Ohio Department of Aging
50 West Broad Street - 9th Floor
Columbus, OH 43215-3363
614-466-5500
Fax: 614-466-5741
www.goldenbuckeye.com/

- Senior Centers-There are 450 full and part-time centers that provide a variety of services to seniors 60 years old and older.
- News and Information-The Ohio Department on Aging e-mails the latest news and information right to your computer.
- Golden Buckeye Card-The Golden Buckeye Card is a free discount card to 18,000 businesses throughout Ohio for seniors 60 years old and older.
- Adult Protective Services-This office accepts and evaluates reports of abuse and neglect and offers appropriate services to seniors.
- Ombudsman-Fields complaints and provides investigation and resolution of complaints relating to the health, safety, welfare and rights of older adults who are living in long-term care facilities.
- Long-Term Care Consumer Guide-This interactive site provides information and customer reviews of long-term facilities.
- Ohio Senior Health Insurance Information Program (OSHIP)-OSHIP provides seniors with insurance information on Medicare, Medicaid, HMO's or private health insurance.
- Home Maintenance & Repairs-Basic repairs to the elderly that want to stay in their homes. Services include: building ramps, replacing showerheads, adding grab bars, plumbing, yard work, and other basic tasks.
- Home Accessibility Modifications-Accessibility modification and minor repairs including: handrails, ramps, door locks, electrical fixtures, and appliances.
- Homestead Property Tax Credit-A tax credit for low-income homeowners 60 years old and older.
- Legal Services-Assistance for seniors in securing rights and entitlements including: education, advice and representation.
- Passport-This program offers eligible seniors 60 years old and older assistance to allow them to stay in their homes as long as possible.
- Emergency Response System-Provides telephone emergency response service.
- Chore Service-Assistance to frail seniors who need assistance including: minor home repair, snow shoveling, trash removal, minor plumbing and other typical chores.
- Home Delivered Meals-Hot meals delivered to homebound seniors.
- Adult Day Care-These services provide social and health services to meet seniors needs. Services may include: meals, activities, information and referral, assistance with personal care and health monitoring.
- Homemaker-This program offers basic home management and upkeep including: errands, laundry, meal planning and preparation, and other simple household tasks.
- Home Medical Equipment and Supplies-Equipment to improve the quality of life of eligible seniors.
- Independent Living Assistance-Short-term personal care for eligible frail seniors.
- Nutrition Consultation-Individual counseling is available to seniors at nutritional risk because of their history, medication use or chronic illness.
- Medical Transportation-Transportation to and from medical appointments, nutrition sites and other designated destinations for senior citizens to continue their necessary daily activities.
- Disease Prevention-These programs provide information and support to help Ohio seniors avoid illness and improve quality of life.
- Senior Community Services Employment Program-Senior Employment offers economically disadvantaged seniors 55 years old and older employment training.
- Senior Companion-Volunteers provide companion support, task assistance and companionship to adults with exceptional need.
- Foster Grandparent-Seniors are matched with children with special needs.

Oklahoma
Aging Services Division
Department of Human Services

2401 NW. 23rd Street, Suite 40
Oklahoma City, OK 73107-2422
405-521-2281
800-211-2116
Fax: 405-521-2086
www.okdhs.org/aging/

- Information & Assistance-Information regarding services provided by senior centers and other community resources.
- Legal Services-Assistance for seniors in securing rights and entitlements including: education, advice and representation.
- Nutrition & Linkage-Individual counseling is available to seniors at nutritional risk because of their history, medication use or chronic illness.
- Transportation-Transportation to and from community resources and other necessary destinations.
- Outreach-This program identifies seniors in the community who may be in need of services or other benefits.
- Ombudsman-Fields complaints and provides investigation and resolution of complaints relating to the health, safety, welfare and rights of older adults who are living in long-term care facilities.
- Caregiver Support-Services include: information, access to support services, counseling, training, respite care and supplemental services.
- Respite-Temporary supervised care for seniors to give their caregiver a period of relief from caregiving duties.
- Adult Day Services-This community-based program individualizes care for functionally impaired seniors providing health, social and service programs.
- Congregate Meals-Hot and nutritious meals are served in a group setting.
- Home Delivered Meals-Hot meals delivered to homebound seniors.
- Health Promotion-Programs and information to provide current and accurate information to seniors about health care issues.
- Nutrition Education-Individual counseling is available to seniors at nutritional risk because of their history, medication use or chronic illness.
- In-Home Assistance-Short-term personal care for eligible frail seniors.

Oregon
Oregon Department of Human Services
Seniors and People with Disabilities
500 Summer St., NE, E02
Salem, OR 97301-1073
503-945-5811
800-282-8096
Fax: 503-373-7823
http://egov.oregon.gov/DHS/spwpd/index.shtml

- Adult Protective Services-This office accepts and evaluates reports of abuse and neglect and offers appropriate services to seniors.
- Health Promotion- Programs and information to provide current and accurate information to seniors about health care issues.
- Case Management- Case managers coordinate a variety of support services and make referrals to meet the needs of each client.
- In-Home Services-Services may include: meal preparation, housekeeping, laundry, personal care, companionship, and adult day care.
- Adult Foster Home- Foster care provides family living to seniors who are functionally impaired. The home provides services such as bathing, grooming and other assistance. The client pays for room and board.
- Gatekeeper Program- Customer service employees from major utility, newspaper and pharmacies are trained to be aware of elders who may need assistance.
- Good Neighbor Program-Volunteers provide minor home repairs and yard work for low-income seniors.
- Health Equipment Loan- There are several options for eligible seniors who need medical equipment such as wheelchairs.
- Client-Employed Provider Program-This program serves Medicaid clients to help them hire their own assistants.
- Home Safety Check Up-Trained volunteer Home Safety Inspectors visit senior's homes to help them evaluate the safety of their homes for accident, fire and crime issues. New smoke detectors are installed at no cost.
- Information and Referral- Information regarding services provided by senior centers and other community resources.
- Senior Companion Program-Volunteers provide companion support, task assistance and companionship to adults with exceptional need.
- Respite Care- Temporary supervised care for seniors to give their caregiver a period of relief from caregiving duties.
- Congregate Meals-Hot and nutritious meals are served in a group setting.
- Home Delivered Meals-Hot meals delivered to homebound seniors.

- Senior Community Services Employment Program-Senior Employment offers economically disadvantaged seniors 55 years old and older employment training.
- Senior Prescription Drug Assistance Program (SPDAP)-SPDAP allows members of the program to purchase prescriptions from participating pharmacies at the State Medicaid rate.
- Legal Services- Assistance for seniors in securing rights and entitlements including: education, advice and representation.

Pennsylvania
Department of Aging
555 Walnut Street, 5th Floor
Harrisburg, PA 17101-1919
717-783-1550
Fax: 717-783-6842
www.aging.state.pa.us/

- Information and Referral- Information regarding services provided by senior centers and other community resources.
- Adult Protective Services-This office accepts and evaluates reports of abuse and neglect and offers appropriate services to seniors.
- Ombudsman-Fields complaints and provides investigation and resolution of complaints relating to the health, safety, welfare and rights of older adults who are living in long-term care facilities.
- Congregate Meals-Hot and nutritious meals are served in a group setting.
- Home Delivered Meals-Hot meals delivered to homebound seniors.
- Senior Community Services Employment Program-Senior Employment offers economically disadvantaged seniors 55 years old and older employment training.
- Alzheimer's Disease Assistance-This program assists families dealing with a loved one affected by Alzheimer's.
- 60+ Aging Waiver Program-Frail Pennsylvanians can receive services to help them live independently in their own homes and communities.
- Adult Day Services- These services provide social and health services to meet senior's needs. Services may include: meals, activities, information and referral, assistance with personal care and health monitoring.
- Attendant Care Program-In-home personal care services to help disabled persons perform everyday tasks.
- Bridge Program
- Respite- Temporary supervised care for seniors to give their caregiver a period of relief from caregiving duties.
- Transportation- Transportation to and from community resources and other necessary destinations.
- Companion Services- Volunteers provide companion support, task assistance and companionship to adults with exceptional need.
- Personal Emergency Response System- Emergency response equipment for at-risk seniors who live alone.
- Home Modification- Accessibility modification and minor repairs including: handrails, ramps, door locks, electrical fixtures, and appliances.
- Caregiver Support- Services include: information, access to support services, counseling, training, respite care and supplemental services.
- Nutrition Education- Education programs which promote better health and nutrition in a group or individual setting.
- OPTIONS Program
- Legal Assistance- Assistance for seniors in securing rights and entitlements including: education, advice and representation.
- Pharmaceutical Assistance Contract for the Elderly (PACE)-This program covers eligible seniors 65 years old and older. Prescription coverage for most medications.
- Protective Services- This office accepts and evaluates reports of abuse and neglect and offers appropriate services to seniors.
- Prime Time Health Program-This program promotes health and disease prevention for older adults.
- Cheaper Dog Licenses-Seniors 65 years old and older receive discounts on their dog licenses.
- Senior Centers- There are 650 full and part-time centers that provide a variety of services to seniors 60 years old and older.
- Free Transit-Seniors 65 years old and older can ride the transit for free during off-peak hours and all day Saturday.
- Foster Grandparent Program- This volunteer program connects seniors with children with special needs.

Rhode Island
Department of Elderly Affairs
John O. Pastore Center
Benjamin Rush Bldg., #55
35 Howard Ave.
Cranston, RI 02920
401-462-0500

Fax: 401-462-3000
www.dea.state.ri.us/

- Adult Day Care- These services provide social and health services to meet seniors needs. Services may include: meals, activities, information and referral, assistance with personal care and health monitoring.
- Assisted Living-Homes that combine housing and social services. Residents must be fairly independent.
- Home/Community Care-Helps seniors who need some assistance but wish to stay in their homes.
- Case Management- Case managers coordinate a variety of support services and make referrals to meet the needs of each client.
- Respite- Temporary supervised care for seniors to give their caregiver a period of relief from caregiving duties.
- Senior Companion- Volunteers provide companion support, task assistance and companionship to adults with exceptional need.
- Community Elder Information Specialists-Specialist to assist families with care eligibility and questions.
- Heating Assistance-Help with heating costs to eligible seniors.
- MicroMax-This computer assessment program is available through senior centers and can find state and federal programs that you may be eligible for.
- Ocean State Senior Dining-Hot lunches are provided to seniors 60 years old and older at more than 70 locations throughout Rhode Island.
- Rhode Island Pharmaceutical Assistance to the Elderly (RIPAE)-Subsidies for eligible seniors to help them pay for medications.
- Senior Community Services Employment Program-Senior Employment offers economically disadvantaged seniors 55 years old and older employment training.
- Transportation- Transportation to and from community resources and other necessary destinations.
- Elder Abuse Unit- This office accepts and evaluates reports of abuse and neglect and offers appropriate services to seniors.
- Commission for the Safety and Care of Elderly-Works to make sure seniors live in a safe environment.
- Legal Services- Assistance for seniors in securing rights and entitlements including: education, advice and representation.
- Long-Term Care Ombudsman- Fields complaints and provides investigation and resolution of complaints relating to the health, safety, welfare and rights of older adults who are living in long-term care facilities.

South Carolina
Lieutenant Governor's Office on Aging
1301 Gervais Street, Suite 200
Columbia, SC 29201
803-734-9900
Fax: 803-734-9886
www.aging.sc.gov

- Alzheimer Resource Coordination Center (ARCC)-This program throughout South Carolina coordinates information, referral and caregiver support services.
- Senior Community Services Employment Program-Senior Employment offers economically disadvantaged seniors 55 years old and older employment training.
- Home Tax Exemption-Seniors 65 years and older are exempt from paying property taxes on the first $50,000 of the value of their home.
- Income Tax Credit-$15,000 deduction for tax payers 65 years old and older.
- Hunting and Fishing Licenses-Free hunting and fishing licenses to seniors 65 years old and older.
- Free Eye Care-Free eye exam to eligible seniors. Call: 800-222-EYES (3937).
- Free Tuition-Free tuition to state universities, colleges and technical schools for seniors 60 years old and older if space is available.
- Insurance Counseling- Counseling for eligible adults with their insurance questions.
- Information, Referral and Assistance- Information regarding services provided by senior centers and other community resources.
- Ombudsman Services- Fields complaints and provides investigation and resolution of complaints relating to the health, safety, welfare and rights of older adults who are living in long-term care facilities.
- Congregate Meals- Hot and nutritious meals are served in a group setting.
- Home Delivered Meals- Hot meals delivered to homebound seniors.
- Home Care- This service offers services to seniors with temporary or chronic needs who have difficulties performing day-to-day tasks.
- Health Promotion- These programs provide information and support to help seniors avoid illness and improve quality of life.
- Transportation- Transportation to and from community resources and other necessary destinations.

South Dakota
Office of Adult Services and Aging
700 Governors Drive

Pierre, SD 57501-2291
605-773-3656
866-854-5465
Fax: 605-773-6834
www.state.sd.us/social/ASA/index.htm

- Adult Day Care- These services provide social and health services to meet senior's needs. Services may include: meals, activities, information and referral, assistance with personal care and health monitoring.
- Adult Foster Care- Foster care provides family living to seniors who are functionally impaired.
- Adult Protective Services- This office accepts and evaluates reports of abuse and neglect and offers appropriate services to seniors.
- Assisted Living- This housing option provides services for seniors in residence
- Assistive Devices- Access to assistive devices including: walkers, fans, wheelchairs, commodities and personal hygiene items.
- Caregiver Program- Services include: information, access to support services, counseling, training, respite care and supplemental services.
- Case Management- Case managers coordinate a variety of support services and make referrals to meet the needs of each client.
- Chore Maintenance- Assistance to frail seniors who need assistance including: minor home repair, snow shoveling, trash removal, minor plumbing and other typical chores.
- Homemaker Services- This program offers basic home management and upkeep including: errands, laundry, meal planning and preparation, and other simple household tasks.
- Information and Referral- Information regarding services provided by senior centers and other community resources.
- Legal Services- Assistance for seniors in securing rights and entitlements including: education, advice and representation.
- Nursing Facility Care-Nursing home care for seniors unable to be cared for at home.
- Nursing Services-Nursing services in the homes of eligible seniors who can not get to a clinic because of limited mobility.
- Ombudsman- Fields complaints and provides investigation and resolution of complaints relating to the health, safety, welfare and rights of older adults who are living in long-term care facilities.
- Personal Care- A personal assistance to help eligible seniors with everyday tasks including: eating, bathing, dressing, toileting and moving in and out of bed.
- Respite- Temporary supervised care for seniors to give their caregiver a period of relief from caregiving duties.
- Rx Access-Prescription assistance for eligible seniors.
- Senior Health Information and Insurance Education (SHINE)-Free and confidential information on Medicare and private insurance.
- Senior Meals- Hot and nutritious meals are served in a group setting.
- Transportation-Transportation may be provided to eligible seniors in buses, vans or other equipped vehicles.

Tennessee
Commission on Aging and Disability
Andrew Jackson Building. 8th floor,
500 Deaderick Street,
Nashville, Tennessee 37243-0860
615-741-2056
Fax: 615-741-330
www.state.tn.us/comaging/

- Caregiver Support- Services include: information, access to support services, counseling, training, respite care and supplemental services.
- Elder Abuse-888-277-8366
- Senior Community Service Employment Program- Senior Employment offers economically disadvantaged seniors 55 years old and older employment training.
- Case Management- Case managers coordinate a variety of support services and make referrals to meet the needs of each client.
- Homemaker Services- This program offers basic home management and upkeep including: errands, laundry, meal planning and preparation, and other simple household tasks.
- Personal Care Services-Assistance for eligible seniors with daily activities including: bathing, grooming, toileting, dressing and moving around.
- Minor Home Modification- Accessibility modification and minor repairs including: handrails, ramps, door locks, electrical fixtures, and appliances.
- Personal Emergency Response System- Emergency response equipment for at-risk seniors who live alone.
- Home Delivered Meals- Hot meals delivered to homebound seniors.
- Respite Care- Temporary supervised care for seniors to give their caregiver a period of relief from caregiving duties.

- Information and Referral- Information regarding services provided by senior centers and other community resources.
- Long-Term Care Ombudsman- Fields complaints and provides investigation and resolution of complaints relating to the health, safety, welfare and rights of older adults who are living in long-term care facilities.
- Nutrition Screening-Nutrition screening and counseling.
- Nutrition Education- Education programs which promote better health and nutrition in a group or individual setting.
- Congregate Meals- Hot and nutritious meals are served in a group setting.
- Public Guardianship- The Tennessee Commission Aging may serve as public guardian for incapacitated adults.
- Senior Centers- Senior Centers offer a variety of programs for senior citizens in 134 centers across the state.
- State Health Insurance Program (SHIP)-SHIP helps to educate seniors about Medicare and other health insurance issues. Contact: 877-801-0044.

Texas
Department of Aging and Disability Services
701 West 51st Street
Austin, TX 78751
512-438-3011
www.dads.state.tx.us/

- Benefits Counseling-A counselor can meet with you and help you find the benefits you are entitled to.
- Care Coordinator-Coordinator assesses the needs of seniors 60 years old and older and connects them with local and state resources.
- Caregiver Support- Services include: information, access to support services, counseling, training, respite care and supplemental services.
- Information, Referral & Assistance- Information regarding services provided by senior centers and other community resources.
- Legal Assistance- Assistance for seniors in securing rights and entitlements including: education, advice and representation.
- Home Delivered Meals- Hot meals delivered to homebound seniors.
- Congregate Meals- Hot and nutritious meals are served in a group setting.
- Ombudsman- Fields complaints and provides investigation and resolution of complaints relating to the health, safety, welfare and rights of older adults who are living in long-term care facilities.
- Transportation- Transportation to and from community resources and other necessary destinations.
- Senior Centers- Senior Centers offer a variety of programs for senior citizens throughout Texas.
- Case Management- Case managers coordinate a variety of support services and make referrals to meet the needs of each client.
- Escort Services- Escort services can help alleviate the isolation many seniors experience. Companions help with a wide range of everyday tasks.
- Health Screenings-A variety of health screenings to reduce diseases for the elderly.
- Homemaker Services- This program offers basic home management and upkeep including: errands, laundry, meal planning and preparation, and other simple household tasks.
- Telephone Reassurance- This program checks in on clients who live alone full time, temporarily or are homebound. They will call at a set time to check on you and if you don't answer they will send assistance.
- Legal Services- Assistance for seniors in securing rights and entitlements including: education, advice and representation.
- Outreach- This program identifies seniors in the community who may be in need of services or other benefits.
- Alzheimer's Support Services-Support, training and education for families in supporting family members with Alzheimer's.
- Foster Grandparent Program- This volunteer program connects seniors with children with special needs.
- Companion Program- Volunteers provide companion support, task assistance and companionship to adults with exceptional need.
- Home Repair Modification Services-Repairs and modifications for eligible seniors 60 years old and older.

Utah
Division of Aging & Adult Services
120 North 200 West, Room 325
Salt Lake City, UT 84103
801-538-3910
877-424-4640
Fax: 801-538-4395
www.kued.org/manyfaces/resources_age.html

- Senior Community Service Employment Program- Senior Employment offers economically disadvantaged seniors 55 years old and older employment training.
- Information and Assistance- Information regarding services provided by senior centers and other community resources.
- Case Management- Case managers coordinate a variety of support services and make referrals to meet the needs of each client.
- Homemaker Services- This program offers basic home management and upkeep including: errands, laundry, meal planning and preparation, and other simple household tasks.
- Chore Services- Assistance to frail seniors who need assistance including: minor home repair, snow shoveling, trash removal, minor plumbing and other typical chores.
- Supportive Maintenance-Assistance for eligible seniors with personal care needs.
- Adult Day Care- These services provide social and health services to meet senior's needs. Services may include: meals, activities, information and referral, assistance with personal care and health monitoring.
- Personal Emergency Response System- Emergency response equipment for at-risk seniors who live alone.
- Respite Care- Temporary supervised care for seniors to give their caregiver a period of relief from caregiving duties.
- Senior Companion- Volunteers provide companion support, task assistance and companionship to adults with exceptional need.
- Personal Care Services- Assistance for eligible seniors with daily activities including: bathing, grooming, toileting, dressing and moving around.
- Non-Medical Transportation- Transportation to and from community resources and other necessary destinations.
- Home Delivered Meals- Hot meals delivered to homebound seniors.
- Legal Services- Assistance for seniors in securing rights and entitlements including: education, advice and representation.
- Nutrition Education- Education programs which promote better health and nutrition in a group or individual setting.
- Foster Grandparent Program- This volunteer program connects seniors with children with special needs.
- Long-Term Ombudsman- Fields complaints and provides investigation and resolution of complaints relating to the health, safety, welfare and rights of older adults who are living in long-term care facilities.
- Adult Protective Services- This office accepts and evaluates reports of abuse and neglect and offers appropriate services to seniors.
- Caregiver Support- Services include: information, access to support services, counseling, training, respite care and supplemental services.

Vermont
Department of Disabilities, Aging & Independent Living
Waterbury Complex
103 South Main Street
Waterbury, VT 05671
802-241-2400
800-642-5119
Fax: 802-241-2325
www.dad.state.vt.us/

- Adult Day Services- These services provide social and health services to meet senior's needs. Services may include: meals, activities, information and referral, assistance with personal care and health monitoring.
- Respite Care- Temporary supervised care for seniors to give their caregiver a period of relief from caregiving duties.
- Case Management- Case managers coordinate a variety of support services and make referrals to meet the needs of each client.
- Foster Grandparents- This volunteer program connects seniors with children with special needs.
- Companion-Eligible seniors 60 years old and older can volunteer to be a companion for homebound seniors. Volunteers are paid a stipend, transportation is covered, and the stipend does not affect benefits.
- Senior Community Service Employment Program- Senior Employment offers economically disadvantaged seniors 55 years old and older employment training.
- Attendant Services Program-This program supports eligible seniors who need assistance with daily activities to remain in their homes.
- Personal Care Services- Assistance for eligible seniors with daily activities including: bathing, grooming, toileting, dressing and moving around.
- Home Modifications- Accessibility modification and minor repairs including: handrails, ramps, door locks, electrical fixtures, and appliances for up to $750 per year.
- Senior Center Meals- Hot and nutritious meals are served in a group setting at 100 centers throughout the state.
- Home Delivered Meals- Hot meals delivered to homebound seniors.
- SERVE New England-Eligible participants who perform two hours of volunteer service may receive discounts on groceries.
- Commodity Supplemental Food Program-This program is available to income eligible seniors 60 years old and older.
- Personal Emergency Response System- Emergency response equipment for at-risk seniors who live alone.

- Homemaker Services- This program offers basic home management and upkeep including: errands, laundry, meal planning and preparation, and other simple household tasks.
- Legal Assistance- Assistance for seniors in securing rights and entitlements including: education, advice and representation.
- Information and Assistance- Information regarding services provided by senior centers and other community resources.
- Prescription Assistance-Eligible senior Vermonters may receive assistance in paying for their prescriptions. Call: 800-250-8427.
- Long-Term Ombudsman- Fields complaints and provides investigation and resolution of complaints relating to the health, safety, welfare and rights of older adults who are living in long-term care facilities.

Virginia
Virginia Department for the Aging
1610 Forest Avenue, Suite 100
Richmond, VA 23229
804-662-9333
800-552-3402
Fax: 804-662-9354
www.aging.state.va.us/

- Adult Day Healthcare Centers-Center that provide some health care resources for eligible seniors.
- Home Delivered Meals- Hot meals delivered to homebound seniors.
- Home Safety & Repair-Basic home repairs for eligible seniors.
- Case Management- Case managers coordinate a variety of support services and make referrals to meet the needs of each client.
- Cool-Aid-Cool-Aid provides fans and air conditioners to seniors whose health may be affected due to the hot weather.
- Senior Centers- Senior Centers offer a variety of programs for senior citizens.
- Health Insurance Counseling-Free one-on-one counseling and claims help to seniors and their families.
- Ombudsman- Fields complaints and provides investigation and resolution of complaints relating to the health, safety, welfare and rights of older adults who are living in long-term care facilities.
- Congregate Meals- Hot and nutritious meals are served in a group setting.
- Legal Assistance- Assistance for seniors in securing rights and entitlements including: education, advice and representation.
- Homemaker Services- This program offers basic home management and upkeep including: errands, laundry, meal planning and preparation, and other simple household tasks.
- Telephone Reassurance- This program checks in on clients who live alone full time, temporarily or are homebound. They will call at a set time to check on you and if you don't answer they will send assistance.
- Transportation- Transportation to and from community resources and other necessary destinations.
- Information & Referral- Information regarding services provided by senior centers and other community resources.
- Caregiver Support- Services include: information, access to support services, counseling, training, respite care and supplemental services.
- Money Management-This in-home financial service assists seniors 60 years old and older with tasks such as check writing, bill paying, banking and other basic financial management.
- Senior Community Service Employment Program- Senior Employment offers economically disadvantaged seniors 55 years old and older employment training.
- Protect and Respect Program-This program matches seniors with children 6-12 years old.
- Foster Grandparent Program- This volunteer program connects seniors with children with special needs.

Washington
Aging and Disability Services Administration
Department of Social & Health Services
P.O. Box 45050
Olympia, WA 98504-5050
360-725-2310
In-state only: 800-422-3263
Fax: 360-438-8633
www.aasa.dshs.wa.gov/

- Adult Day Care- These services provide social and health services to meet senior's needs. Services may include: meals, activities, information and referral, assistance with personal care and health monitoring.
- Adult Protective Services- This office accepts and evaluates reports of abuse and neglect and offers appropriate services to seniors. Contact: 866-363-4276

- Case Management- Case managers coordinate a variety of support services and make referrals to meet the needs of each client.
- Environmental Modifications- Accessibility modification and minor repairs including: handrails, ramps, door locks, electrical fixtures, and appliances.
- Health Screening
- Home Health-In-home health care prescribed by a physician to eligible seniors.
- Home Health Aide-In-home aide provided by a Certified Nursing Assistant to eligible seniors.
- Hospice- Terminally ill patients may be eligible for hospice care.
- Information and Assistance- Information regarding services provided by senior centers and other community resources.
- Minor Household Repairs- Basic home repairs for eligible seniors.
- Personal Care- Assistance for eligible seniors with daily activities including: bathing, grooming, toileting, dressing and moving around.
- Personal Emergency Response System- Emergency response equipment for at-risk seniors who live alone.
- Respite Care- Temporary supervised care for seniors to give their caregiver a period of relief from caregiving duties.
- Senior Centers- Senior Centers offer a variety of programs for senior citizens throughout Washington.
- Home Delivered Meals- Hot meals delivered to homebound seniors.
- Congregate Meals- Hot and nutritious meals are served in a group setting.
- Special Medical Equipment-Assistance in obtaining needed assistive medical devices for eligible seniors.
- Transportation- Transportation to and from community resources and other necessary destinations.
- Long-Term Care Ombudsman- Fields complaints and provides investigation and resolution of complaints relating to the health, safety, welfare and rights of older adults who are living in long-term care facilities. Contact: 800-562-6028
- Caregiver Support- Services include: information, access to support services, counseling, training, respite care and supplemental services.
- Legal Services- Assistance for seniors in securing rights and entitlements including: education, advice and representation.
- Senior Community Service Employment Program- Senior Employment offers economically disadvantaged seniors 55 years old and older employment training.
- Disease Prevention/Foot care-This program offers disease prevention by providing routine foot care to eligible seniors.

West Virginia
West Virginia Bureau of Senior Services
Holly Grove - Building 10
1900 Kanawha Boulevard East
Charleston, WV 25305-0160
304-558-3317
Fax: 304-558-0004
www.state.wv.us/seniorservices/

- Golden Mountaineer Discount Card-Discounts to seniors of West Virginia who are 60 years old and older for businesses throughout the state.
- Legal Services- Assistance for seniors in securing rights and entitlements including: education, advice and representation.
- Long-Term Ombudsman- Fields complaints and provides investigation and resolution of complaints relating to the health, safety, welfare and rights of older adults who are living in long-term care facilities.
- Senior Community Service Employment Program- Senior Employment offers economically disadvantaged seniors 55 years old and older employment training.
- State Health Insurance Program (SHIP)-SHIP helps to educate seniors about Medicare and other health insurance issues.
- Community Care Services-This program serves eligible senior clients and includes: bathing, chores, grooming, housekeeping and other necessities of life.
- Transportation- Transportation to and from community resources and other necessary destinations.
- Congregate Meals- Hot and nutritious meals are served in a group setting.
- Homemaker Services- This program offers basic home management and upkeep including: errands, laundry, meal planning and preparation, and other simple household tasks.
- Adult Day Care- These services provide social and health services to meet senior's needs. Services may include: meals, activities, information and referral, assistance with personal care and health monitoring.
- Respite- Temporary supervised care for seniors to give their caregiver a period of relief from caregiving duties.
- Health Screenings
- Home Delivered Meals- Hot meals delivered to homebound seniors.
- Nutrition Education- Education programs which promote better health and nutrition in a group or individual setting.
- Home Repair-Basic home repairs for eligible seniors.

- Telephoning- This program checks in on clients who live alone full time, temporarily or are homebound. They will call at a set time to check on you and if you don't answer they will send assistance.
- Personal Care- Assistance for eligible seniors with daily activities including: bathing, grooming, toileting, dressing and moving around.
- Chore Services- Assistance to frail seniors who need assistance including: minor home repair, snow shoveling, trash removal, minor plumbing and other typical chores.
- Legal Assistance- Assistance for seniors in securing rights and entitlements including: education, advice and representation.
- Outreach- This program identifies seniors in the community who may be in need of services or other benefits.
- Caregiver Support- Services include: information, access to support services, counseling, training, respite care and supplemental services.
- Annual Senior Conference-The conference offers a variety of workshops including: nutrition, Medicare, exercise, tourism, health care and more.

Wisconsin
Bureau of Aging and Long Term Care Resources
Department of Health and Family Services
1 West Wilson Street
Madison, WI 53707-7850
608-266-0554
Fax: 608-266-7376
www.dhfs.state.wi.us/Aging/

- Adult Protective Services- This office accepts and evaluates reports of abuse and neglect and offers appropriate services to seniors.
- Adult Day Care- These services provide social and health services to meet senior's needs. Services may include: meals, activities, information and referral, assistance with personal care and health monitoring.
- Telecare- This program checks in on clients who live alone full time, temporarily or are homebound. They will call at a set time to check on you and if you don't answer they will send assistance.
- Loan Closet-This program loans assistive devices to eligible seniors.
- Wisconsin Partnership Program (WPP)-This is an integrated health and long-term care program assisting eligible frail seniors and improving their lives.
- Alzheimer's Disease and Dementia Resources-Education, training and support for caregivers of Alzheimer's patients.
- Eat With a Group- Hot and nutritious meals are served in a group setting.
- Meal at Home- Hot meals delivered to homebound seniors.
- Caregiver Support- Services include: information, access to support services, counseling, training, respite care and supplemental services.
- Home Care Services- This program offers basic home management and upkeep including: errands, laundry, meal planning and preparation, and other simple household tasks.
- Respite Services- Temporary supervised care for seniors to give their caregiver a period of relief from caregiving duties.
- Nutritional Counseling-Individual counseling is available to eligible seniors at nutritional risk because of their history, medication use, or chronic illness.
- Information & Assistance- Information regarding services provided by senior centers and other community resources.
- Legal Services- Assistance for seniors in securing rights and entitlements including: education, advice and representation.
- Case Management- Case managers coordinate a variety of support services and make referrals to meet the needs of each client.
- Foster Grandparents- This volunteer program connects seniors with children with special needs.
- Long-Term Care Ombudsman- Fields complaints and provides investigation and resolution of complaints relating to the health, safety, welfare and rights of older adults who are living in long-term care facilities.
- Senior Community Service Employment Program- Senior Employment offers economically disadvantaged seniors 55 years old and older employment training.
- State Health Insurance Assistance Program- One-on-one counseling with elderly residents of Wisconsin to provide them with insurance information.
- Transportation- Transportation to and from community resources and other necessary destinations.

Wyoming
Department of Health
6101 Yellow Stone Road, #259B
Cheyenne, WY 82002
307-777-7986

800-442-2766
Fax: 307-777-5340
http://wdhfs.state.wy.us/aging/index.htm

- Transportation- Transportation to and from community resources and other necessary destinations.
- Outreach- This program identifies seniors in the community who may be in need of services or other benefits.
- Shopping Assistance-Help with shopping for eligible frail seniors.
- Nutrition Education- Education programs which promote better health and nutrition in a group or individual setting.
- Chore Services- Assistance to frail seniors who need assistance including: minor home repair, snow shoveling, trash removal, minor plumbing and other typical chores.
- Hospice- Terminally ill Medicaid patients may be eligible for hospice care.
- Congregate Meals- Hot and nutritious meals are served in a group setting.
- Home Delivered Meals- Hot meals delivered to homebound seniors.
- Case Management- Case managers coordinate a variety of support services and make referrals to meet the needs of each client.
- Personal Care- Assistance for eligible seniors with daily activities including: bathing, grooming, toileting, dressing and moving around.
- Homemaker Services- This program offers basic home management and upkeep including: errands, laundry, meal planning and preparation, and other simple household tasks.
- Respite Care- Temporary supervised care for seniors to give their caregiver a period of relief from caregiving duties.
- Personal Emergency Response System- Emergency response equipment for at-risk seniors who live alone.
- Adult Day Care- These services provide social and health services to meet senior's needs. Services may include: meals, activities, information and referral, assistance with personal care and health monitoring.
- Mental Wellness-Presentations that address a number of elderly topics including: Growing Wiser, Mental Wellness for Everyone, Depression and more.
- Routine Health Screening-Basic screenings to detect diseases at early stages.
- Long-Term Ombudsman- Fields complaints and provides investigation and resolution of complaints relating to the health, safety, welfare and rights of older adults who are living in long-term care facilities.
- Legal Assistance- Assistance for seniors in securing rights and entitlements including: education, advice and representation.

Index

Index

B

E

F

G

H

I

J

K

L

M

P

T

W

Y

NOTES

NOTES